IISS

THE MILITARY BALANCE 2018

published by

Routledge
Taylor & Francis Group

for

The International Institute for Strategic Studies
ARUNDEL HOUSE | 6 TEMPLE PLACE | LONDON | WC2R 2PG | UK

THE **MILITARY BALANCE** 2018

The International Institute for Strategic Studies
ARUNDEL HOUSE | 6 TEMPLE PLACE | LONDON | WC2R 2PG | UK

DIRECTOR-GENERAL AND CHIEF EXECUTIVE **Dr John Chipman**
DIRECTOR FOR DEFENCE AND MILITARY ANALYSIS **Dr Bastian Giegerich**
EDITOR **James Hackett**
ASSOCIATE EDITOR **Nicholas Payne**

MILITARY AEROSPACE **Douglas Barrie**
LAND WARFARE **Brigadier (Retd) Benjamin Barry**
MILITARY FORCES AND EQUIPMENT **Henry Boyd**
NAVAL FORCES AND MARITIME SECURITY **Nick Childs**
DEFENCE ECONOMICS **Dr Lucie Béraud-Sudreau**
RESEARCH ANALYSTS **Joseph Dempsey, Monty d'Inverno, Yvonni-Stefania Efstathiou, Amanda Lapo, Meia Nouwens, Michael Tong, Tom Waldwyn**

EDITORIAL **Thomas Adamson-Green, Alice Aveson, Jill Lally, Chris Raggett, Gaynor Roberts, Sam Stocker, Carolyn West**
DESIGN, PRODUCTION, INFORMATION GRAPHICS **John Buck, Kelly Verity**
CARTOGRAPHY **John Buck, Kelly Verity**
RESEARCH SUPPORT **Harriet Ellis, Katrina Marina, Robert Mitchell, Josephine Niehoff, James Shinnie, Laurence Taylor**

This publication has been prepared by the Director-General and Chief Executive of the Institute and his Staff, who accept full responsibility for its contents. The views expressed herein do not, and indeed cannot, represent a consensus of views among the worldwide membership of the Institute as a whole.

FIRST PUBLISHED February 2018

© The International Institute for Strategic Studies 2018
All rights reserved. No part of this publication may be reproduced, stored, transmitted, or disseminated, in any form, or by any means, without prior written permission from Taylor & Francis, to whom all requests to reproduce copyright material should be directed, in writing.

ISBN 978-1-85743-955-7
ISSN 0459-7222

Cover images: FRONT: *Sukhoi* Su-57 combat aircraft (Sergei Bobylev \ TASS via Getty); South Korea fires its *Hyonmu* II ballistic missile (South Korea Defense Ministry via NUR); Iraqi commandos (Laurent Van der Stockt, Le Monde/Getty); HMS *Queen Elizabeth* sails into Portsmouth (Dan Rosenbaum/UK MoD); Royal Marines exercise *Joint Viking*, 2017 (Royal Navy). BACK: Russian submarines fire *Kalibr* cruise missiles (Vadim Savitsky \ TASS via Getty); Ukrainian independence-day parade 2017 (Baris Oral/Anadolu/Getty); NATO paratroopers (Dimitar Dilkoff/AFP/Getty); Venezuelan independence-day parade 2017 (Carlos Becerra/Anadolu/Getty).

The Military Balance (ISSN 0459-7222) is published annually by Routledge Journals, an imprint of Taylor & Francis, 4 Park Square, Milton Park, Abingdon, Oxfordshire OX14 4RN, UK.

A subscription to the institution print edition, ISSN 0459-7222, includes free access for any number of concurrent users across a local area network to the online edition, ISSN 1479-9022.

All subscriptions are payable in advance and all rates include postage. Journals are sent by air to the USA, Canada, Mexico, India, Japan and Australasia. Subscriptions are entered on an annual basis, i.e. January to December. Payment may be made by sterling cheque, dollar cheque, international money order, National Giro, or credit card (Amex, Visa, Mastercard).

Please send subscription orders to: USA/Canada: Taylor & Francis Inc., Journals Department, 530 Walnut Street, Suite 850, Philadelphia, PA 19106, USA. UK/Europe/Rest of World: Routledge Journals, T&F Customer Services, T&F Informa UK Ltd., Sheepen Place, Colchester, Essex, CO3 3LP, UK. Email: subscriptions@tandf.co.uk

Contents

Indexes of Tables, Figures and Maps 4
Editor's Introduction 5

Part One **Capabilities, Trends and Economics**

Chapter 1 Defence and military analysis 7
Chinese and Russian air-launched weapons 7; Big data, artificial intelligence and defence 10; Russia: strategic-force modernisation 14

Chapter 2 Comparative defence statistics 19
Defence budgets and expenditure 19; Armed unmanned aerial vehicles: production and procurement 21; Key defence statistics 22; China: People's Liberation Army main battle tanks 24; China: air-to-air missile progress 25; Selected Chinese and Asia-Pacific regional naval shipbuilding since 2000 26

Chapter 3 North America 27
United States: defence policy and economics 27;
Canada: defence policy and economics 39;
Armed forces data section 43;
Arms procurements and deliveries 62

Chapter 4 Europe 65
Regional defence policy and economics 65;
France: defence policy 74;
Norway: defence policy and economics 75;
UK: defence policy and economics 80;
Armed forces data section 82;
Arms procurements and deliveries 166

Chapter 5 Russia and Eurasia 169
Russia: defence policy and economics 169;
Ukraine: defence policy 179;
Armed forces data section 181;
Arms procurements and deliveries 216

Chapter 6 Asia 219
Regional defence policy and economics 219;
China: defence policy and economics 225;
Taiwan: defence policy and economics 235;
Armed forces data section 240;
Arms procurements and deliveries 312

Chapter 7 Middle East and North Africa 315
Regional defence policy and economics 315;
Qatar: defence policy and economics 321;
Armed forces data section 325;
Arms procurements and deliveries 372

Chapter 8 Latin America and the Caribbean 375
Regional defence policy and economics 375;
Venezuela: defence policy and economics 380;
Armed forces data section 383;
Arms procurements and deliveries 427

Chapter 9 Sub-Saharan Africa 429
Regional defence policy and economics 429;
Djibouti: defence policy 434;
Sudan: defence policy and economics 435;
Uganda: defence policy and economics 440;
Armed forces data section 445;
Arms procurements and deliveries 497

Chapter 10 Country comparisons and defence data 499
Selected training activity 2016 and 2017 500-1;
International comparisons of defence expenditure and military personnel 502

Part Two **Reference**

Explanatory Notes 509
Principal land definitions 513; Principal naval definitions 514; Principal aviation definitions 515
List of abbreviations for data sections 517
Index of country/territory abbreviations 519
Index of countries and territories 520

Index of TABLES

1 US Army Armored Brigade Combat Team deployments, 2014–18..30
2 US National Defense Budget Function and other selected budgets 1997, 2007–18 36
3 US FY2018 defence-budget request: top 15 equipment programmes by value...62
4 US fixed-wing tactical-aircraft deliveries, 2010–November 2017 63
5 Selected US MRAP donations, 2013–November 2017.................63
6 Selected German bilateral military cooperation from 2014 67
7 European armoured vehicles: selected fleet acquisitions 167
8 Russian defence expenditure as % of GDP..................................... 175
9 Russian procurement of new weapons 2011–16 and goals of the State Armament Programme 2011–20 (approximate) 178
10 9K720 *Iskander*-M/-K (SS-26 *Stone*/SSC-7): brigade-set deliveries to Russia... 216
11 Russia: principal surface- and sub-surface-combatant commissioning, 2012–17 217
12 Asia: ongoing submarine procurements... 313
13 Japan FY2018 defence-budget request: top 10 equipment-procurement programmes by value.. 313
14 Qatar: selected ongoing defence contracts.................................... 373
15 Qatar: selected defence-equipment procurements: pending contract signature... 373
16 North Africa: selected naval deliveries since 2011 374
17 North Africa: selected future naval deliveries................................ 374
18 Brazil: defence spending, 2010–18 (US$bn)................................... 379
19 Patrol vessels in Latin America: selected completed and ongoing contracts.. 428
20 Transport helicopters in Latin America: selected completed and ongoing contracts.. 428
21 International comparisons of defence expenditure and military personnel.. 502
22 List of abbreviations for data sections 517
23 Index of country/territory abbreviations 519
24 Index of countries and territories 520

Index of FIGURES

North America
1 US *Virginia*-class nuclear-powered guided-missile submarine: design evolution..34
2 US defence expenditure as % of GDP...35
3 US National Defense Budget Function: year-on-year changes, 1977–2017...37
4 Canada: Sikorsky CH-148 *Cyclone* multi-role helicopter.....................64

Europe
5 Europe defence spending by country and sub-region 2017................70
6 Europe regional defence expenditure as % of GDP..............................72
7 Europe: selected ongoing or completed procurement priorities in 2017... 166
8 NATO Europe: ageing mine-countermeasures (MCM) vessels and current replacement programmes............................... 167
9 Submarine programmes: ThyssenKrupp Marine Systems/Fincantieri Type-212A.. 168

Russia and Eurasia
10 Russia: estimated total military expenditure as % of GDP............... 176
11 Russian Air Force: tactical-aircraft deliveries, 2010–16 217
12 Russia: Sukhoi Su-57 (T-50).. 218

Asia
13 Asia defence spending by country and sub-region............................ 222
14 Asia regional defence expenditure as % of GDP............................... 224
15 Asia: selected ongoing or completed procurement priorities in 2017... 312
16 Australia: AWD Alliance *Hobart*-class Air Warfare Destroyer........... 314

Middle East and North Africa
17 North Africa defence expenditure 2017: sub-regional breakdown... 318
18 Saudi Arabia defence expenditure as % of GDP............................... 320
19 Middle East and North Africa: selected ongoing or completed procurement priorities in 2017..................................... 372

Latin America and the Caribbean
20 Latin America and the Caribbean defence spending by country and sub-region... 377
21 Latin America and the Caribbean regional defence expenditure as % of GDP.. 379
22 Latin America and the Caribbean: selected ongoing or completed procurement priorities in 2017..................................... 427

Sub-Saharan Africa
23 Sub-Saharan Africa regional defence expenditure as % of GDP.... 431
24 Botswana: defence-budget breakdown, 2010–17 433
25 South Africa: defence spending in (constant 2010) US$ and as share of GDP.. 434
26 Sub-Saharan Africa: selected ongoing or completed procurement priorities in 2017... 497
27 Ukraine: defence exports to sub-Saharan Africa, 1996–2016 498

Index of MAPS

Map 1 Europe regional defence spending...71
Map 2 Norway: key military bases...75
Map 3 Russia: army units near Ukraine's border 172
Map 4 Russia and Eurasia regional defence spending 176
Map 5 Asia regional defence spending... 223
Map 6 China: the People's Liberation Army reorganises 228
Map 7 Syria: foreign military influence and reported operating locations, September 2017... 317
Map 8 Middle East and North Africa regional defence spending 319
Map 9 Latin America and the Caribbean regional defence spending.. 378
Map 10 Venezuela: principal military bases and defence industries 381
Map 11 Sub-Saharan Africa regional defence spending 432
Map 12 Sudan: military facilities and areas of principal security concern.. 436
Map 13 Uganda: military facilities 442
Map 14 Selected exercises: Europe 2016... 500
Map 15 Selected exercises: Europe 2017... 501
Map 16 Selected exercises: Russia and Eurasia 2016 500
Map 17 Selected exercises: Russia and Eurasia 2017 501

Editor's Introduction
Western technology edge erodes further

Defence policymakers worldwide remain challenged by a complex and fractured security environment, marked by increased uncertainty in relations between states and the proliferation of advanced military capabilities. Attacks in 2017 highlighted the continuing threat from transnational terrorists. Persistent conflicts and insecurity in parts of Africa meant that the continent still demanded the deployment of significant combat forces by African and external powers. In the Middle East, the war against ISIS, the civil war in Syria, the destructive conflict in Yemen and Iran's destabilising activities dominated the regional security environment. In Europe, low-level conflict persisted in eastern Ukraine, with Russia reinforcing its military posture across the border and its military capabilities preoccupying European NATO states. In Asia, North Korea tested its first intercontinental ballistic missile. Pyongyang's provocations may be an immediate threat, but there was also an increasingly pervasive concern over China's military programmes and activities. In 2017 Beijing introduced yet more advanced military systems, and deployed elements of its armed forces further afield.

Defence spending

Though much talk in early 2017 was of possible retrenchment, the United States has so far doubled-down on its commitment to European defence. Funding for the European Deterrence Initiative has risen, and the US is deploying – and looking to sell – more equipment to Europe. So, in July 2018, when President Donald Trump arrives in Brussels for the NATO Summit, the US, having increased its own effort, will be looking for additional signs that European leaders are boosting their own defence funding. In early 2017, NATO states redoubled their commitment to boost spending. IISS figures show that the rising trend observed in Europe since 2014–15 has continued; real-terms annual growth in defence spending reached 3.6% in 2017. Some of this may have resulted from US exhortations, but mostly it stemmed from changing threat perceptions among European states.

Indeed, in 2017, Europe was the fastest-growing region when it came to real-terms defence spending. Taken together, northern and central European states increased defence spending in real terms by 4.8% in 2017. However, more NATO states claiming that they will reach the target of spending 2% of GDP on defence is not necessarily the best outcome, and there could more usefully be greater focus on output in terms of combat capability instead of financial targets.

Although the overall balance of global military spending continues to shift towards Asia, the growth in Asian defence spending slowed in 2017, reflecting factors including reduced economic growth in some states. In turn, this indicated that the upwards trend in regional spending of recent years may have owed as much to strong economic growth as it did to changing threat perceptions. China's defence spending, however, has continued to rise. After years of double-digit growth, China's increases have since 2016 been aligned with GDP growth at 6–7%. However, the downturn in spending by some of the top defence-spending states, including Russia and Saudi Arabia, meant that in real terms, global defence spending effectively stagnated in 2017.

China

There has been no slackening in the pace of China's military modernisation. Its progress in defence aerospace remains remarkable. Indeed, China looks on track to field before 2020 its first front-line unit equipped with the Chengdu J-20 low-observable combat aircraft. If so, the US could soon lose its monopoly on operational stealthy combat aircraft. China also continues to develop an array of advanced guided-weapons projects. The IISS now assesses that the latest in China's expanding missile line-up – the PL-15 extended range AAM – could enter service as soon as 2018. This weapon appears to be equipped with an active electronically scanned array radar, indicating that China has joined the few nations able to integrate this capability on an AAM.

These are all part of the air force's goal of being able to challenge any opponent in the air domain. For the past three decades, the ability to operate uncontested in the air has been a key advantage for the US and its allies. This can no longer be assumed. China is pursuing similar ambitions at sea. The launch of the first Type-055 cruiser presages the Chinese navy closing another gap in its developing blue-water capabilities. More broadly, the PLA's suite of increasingly capable military systems points to the growing development of land-, air- and sea-based anti-access/area-denial capabilities to complement its growing power-projection capacity. But using these capabilities to best effect requires that China makes similar progress in improved training, doctrine and tactics.

China's progress in military research and development meant it had already become the single most important external influence on the trajectory of US defence developments. Not only has China's defence industry maintained its relentless development tempo, it has also continued to pursue advanced technologies, including extremely high-performance computing and quantum communications. China's emerging weapons developments and broader defence-technological progress are designed to further its transition from 'catching up' with the West, to becoming a global defence innovator: in some areas of defence technology, China has already achieved its goal. China's willingness to export military equipment – including advanced missiles and armed UAVs – means that Western defence planners will have to take account of a more complex and contested future threat environment.

Russia

Russia remains the principal security concern for states in eastern and northern Europe. Moscow has continued to deploy advanced military equipment, including S-400 air-defence systems and 500km-range *Iskander* ballistic missiles, in the Western Military District. Though Russia's armed forces continue to introduce new equipment, the heralded generational shift in military materiel is taking place more slowly than first anticipated. Russia is experiencing further funding and industrial shortcomings and will likely further slow or delay the delivery of some systems in its 2018–27 State Armament Programme. While advanced systems such as the Su-57 combat aircraft and the T-14 main battle tank will eventually see service, their numbers will likely be fewer than initially thought. This problem is even more pronounced for Russia's navy, but Moscow is seeking to offset the impact of its sclerotic large surface-ship construction by continuing to distribute high-precision weapons systems to smaller, more varied vessel classes.

Continuing allegations of Russian interference in Western electoral processes again indicate that Moscow views its modernising armed forces as just one aspect of the capabilities it can employ to realise strategic goals. Cyber capability should now be seen as a key aspect of some states' coercive power, giving them the chance to wage covert digital campaigns. This might be an adjunct to military power, or employed in its place, in order to accomplish traditional objectives. This has driven some European states to re-examine their industrial, political, social and economic vulnerabilities, influence operations and information warfare, as well as more traditional areas of military power.

Europe

One aspect of the response to this has been greater cooperation between the EU and NATO over so-called 'hybrid' threats. Russia's activities have also spurred some European states to enhance their military inventories. Russia's rocket artillery, and its combat-aviation and precision-missile systems, are generating greater attention on air and missile defence in Europe, notably in the east and north. Some states are eyeing *Patriot* and other ground-based air-defence systems, boosting armoured vehicle fleets, rebuilding fixed-wing combat airpower and developing air-launched stand-off strike power. It seems as if, finally, some European states are looking to rebuild a credible conventional deterrent capability.

Improving the quality of their military systems is one answer; so too is enabling mobility, so that military capabilities can be rapidly brought to bear. Serious thought is now being given to how to make this easier at the bureaucratic level. Discussions in late 2017 examined how to ease the movement of military materiel across Europe. These moves were given impetus by stronger US pressure on European states to do more for their own defence. Without this effort, the Trump administration claimed, Washington might 'moderate' its support for Europe.

These concerns led some in Europe to question the degree to which they could rely on external assistance. Also, EU member states in 2017 finally took steps towards permanent structured defence cooperation, and the European Commission established a European Defence Fund. Both developments have the potential to deliver financial benefits by reducing duplication in defence spending.

Challenges to the West

Increasingly fast, precise and technologically sophisticated military systems are being developed by non-Western countries, particularly China and Russia, and militarily useful technologies are increasingly accessible at relatively low cost. In response, Western states will look to 'leap-ahead' technologies to maintain an edge. This will require greater agility, and greater acceptance of development risks by governments and the defence and technology sectors. Success is by no means assured. The growing democratisation of technology will make it harder still.

The integration of accelerating technical developments into defence organisations could offer transformative capabilities. New information-processing technologies will improve military systems. Indeed, the speed and scope of some modern sensor systems already surpass human processing capability. Greater use will likely be made of artificial intelligence and machine learning, as states look to develop automated decision-making to augment human capacities, boost weapons capabilities and gain early advantage, including through the use of economic and political levers and cyber-enabled information and influence tools.

For all the transformative potential of these technologies, continuities in conflict will persist – certainly in terms of the nature of war fighting. These would be recognisable to the founders of the IISS in 1958, who had just 13 years before emerged from the Second World War. Other aspects of today's military-security environment would also be familiar, including tensions over nuclear weapons. Persistent allegations that Russia has deployed ground-launched cruise missiles and discussions over nuclear weapons on the Korean Peninsula raise the spectre that states could again conceive of theatre nuclear weapons as military complements to increasingly modernised strategic nuclear systems.

Using new technical processing capabilities to augment military systems will compress response times, and may drive more automation in defences in order to minimise an adversary's first-strike advantage. This increases the risk of miscalculation in response and may drive other nations to seek such technologies. This is worrisome in the strategic-weapons arena, which relies on a degree of transparency and shared situational awareness. Combined, these developments should place a premium on more measured and smarter diplomacy, improved military-to-military ties and emphasis on confidence- and security-building measures. Furthermore, at a time when bonds forged during the Cold War are under continued stress, they should mean that states sharpen their focus on the benefits to be gained from alliances or other cooperative relationships.

Chapter One
Chinese and Russian air-launched weapons: a test for Western air dominance

Since the end of the Cold War, the air domain has been one of assured superiority for the United States and its allies. This dominance, however, rests on weapons and technologies that China and Russia are increasingly attaining as part of a broader effort to counter US capabilities, and to deny US and allied forces unimpeded control of the air.

These two nations – emerging and resurgent air powers, respectively – are developing their own 'fifth-generation' combat aircraft with the requisite low-observable characteristics. In parallel, they are pursuing air-launched weapons to complement these projects, and at the same time are recapitalising their weapons inventories with missiles that will enhance their ability to contest control of the air. Some of these weapons are now appearing on the export market.

In 2015–16, Beijing brought into service the PL-10 imaging infrared air-to-air missile (AAM). In 2018, it may well introduce the PL-15. These missiles markedly improve the combat air capability of its air forces. Meanwhile, Russia has brought into service two upgraded versions of existing weapons, along with a new long-range AAM, and this pace of development may continue. Indeed, Moscow is looking to further exploit a range of advanced technologies that are appropriate to guided weapons. This trend is, if anything, more pronounced in Beijing. For example, China has already started to use active electronically scanned array radars for missile applications. It is also developing dual-mode guidance seekers; working on increasing the average speed of weapons; boosting the manoeuvrability of its missiles; and, at the same time, improving on-board processing in order to enhance missile performance. Although Russia is also working on some of these areas, China's efforts are better resourced.

Presently, air combat is increasingly enabled by accelerating technology developments in communications and on-board processing power that enable faster and more coordinated activity between dispersed platforms. As such, and as part of the modernisation of its air-combat capabilities, China is also seeking the ability to create and exploit friendly digital networks, while developing the tactics, techniques and procedures to degrade an opponent's networked environment. With regard to air-to-air systems, this will likely include off-board targeting at extended launch ranges, where another platform (i.e. not the aircraft carrying the missile) would identify and provide the target location and in-flight updates to the missile.

Chinese progress

The extent of Chinese progress in the air-to-air guided-weapons arena was apparent with the introduction of the PL-10 AAM. This weapon provided a marked improvement in performance over the previous generation of short-range missiles operated by the People's Liberation Army Air Force (PLAAF), and its development has placed China among the handful of nations with a defence-industrial base capable of producing such a weapon. The PL-10 uses aerodynamic and thrust-vector control, but the PLAAF will require an advanced helmet-mounted cueing system in order to exploit the manoeuvrability the weapon offers. During 2018, a missile designated PL-15 may also begin to enter front-line service. The PL-15 is an extended-range active radar-guided AAM and, when in service, would be the most capable AAM in the PLAAF inventory. Significantly, in late 2015, it was identified as a weapon of concern by General Hawk Carlisle, then head of the United States Air Force (USAF) Air Combat Command.

However, the PL-10 and the PL-15 are not the only systems with which the US and its allies are having to come to terms. China is also developing a very-long-range AAM intended to be used to attack high-value targets such as tanker, airborne early-warning, and intelligence, surveillance and reconnaissance (ISR) aircraft. Furthermore, Beijing appears to be pursuing two or more configurations of rocket-ramjet AAMs.

By the early to mid-2020s, China will clearly have a broader – and far more capable – range of air-to-air weapons to complement the combat aircraft that are now in development. These will likely force the US and its regional allies to re-examine not only their tactics, techniques and procedures, but also the direction of their own combat-aerospace development programmes.

Russian resurgence

Meanwhile, Russia has also begun to recapitalise its air-to-air-weapons inventory, after funding cuts forced a two-decades-long lull in procurement activity. For example, some 30 years after it was first test fired, the air force has now introduced a version of the Vympel R-77 (AA-12A *Adder*) medium-range active radar-guided missile into service. The R-77 entered production in the 1990s to meet export orders, with the export variant publicly called the RVV-AE. However, only test rounds of the baseline version were procured by the Russian Air Force. It took until 2015 for the air force to introduce into service a variant of the R-77 – the improved and upgraded R-77-1 (AA-12B). This was first deployed operationally in late 2015, when Su-35S aircraft operating from Khmeimim air base in Syria were shown carrying the weapon.

Along with the R-77-1, the air force has also begun to take delivery of an improved version of the short-range R-73 (AA-11 *Archer*) – the R-74M (AA-11B) likely entered the front-line inventory around the same time as the R-77-1. The R-74M has a greater maximum range than the R-74 and is fitted with an improved seeker. Also noteworthy was the introduction into service of the R-37M (AA-13 *Axehead*) active radar-guided long-range AAM in 2015–16. This missile is the primary armament of the MiG-31BM *Foxhound* interceptor. This weapon can also trace its design origins to the late 1980s.

At least some of the renewed stimulus in Russian guided-weapons development has been provided by China, partly as a potential customer and partly as an increasingly credible export rival. The R-37M is being offered as a candidate weapon for the Sukhoi Su-35 *Flanker*, which China has already purchased, and the missile may be part of the aircraft's weapons package. Meanwhile, China's PL-10 AAM is already being offered for export, as is the active radar-guided medium-range PL-12. The high-agility imaging infrared PL-10 is significantly more capable than Russia's R-74/R-74M, while the baseline PL-12 appears to have a better performance than that of the R-77 (AA-12A).

The PL-12 programme – which started in the late 1980s – benefited greatly from Russian technology. The original version of the missile uses a radar seeker designed by the Russian firm Agat, with several other components also provided by Moscow. Without Russian support, the PL-12 programme would, in all likelihood, have taken considerably longer and produced an inferior weapon. Today, however, Beijing is no longer reliant on Russian missile-technology assistance; it is now at least Moscow's equal, and, perhaps in some areas, it is now in the lead.

Going electronic

China appears to be one of the few nations to have used an active electronically scanned array (AESA) radar on an AAM, rather than a traditional mechanically scanned planar array. The PL-15 has been widely reported as using an AESA. Meanwhile, Japan's AAM-4B AAM is also fitted with an AESA seeker, while there is speculation that the US AIM-120D variant of the AIM-120 Advanced Medium-Range Air-to-Air Missile also uses an AESA rather than a mechanically scanned seeker.

AESA technology is increasingly being used as the primary sensor for combat aircraft, with mechanically scanned array radars replaced by either fixed or moveable electronically scanned arrays. These offer a number of advantages, including better detection performance in terms of range and against low-observable targets, greater resistance to countermeasures, a reduced probability of intercept and improved reliability. However, the high cost of introducing these systems (the transmit–receive modules that are the building blocks of AESA technology are comparatively expensive to produce) has, until now, acted as a brake on their introduction, particularly on single-use weapons such as missiles.

Several performance factors have likely contributed to these countries' decisions to overcome the cost barriers relating to AESA technology on AAMs. In the case of China, where weapons research and acquisition is less constrained by funding restrictions, these factors likely included these systems' improved performance against low-observable targets and greater resistance to countermeasures on target aircraft, such as radio-frequency jammers.

The inherent flexibility of AESA technology, in terms of its frequency agility, makes these seekers more difficult to counter by jamming. In contrast, traditional radar countermeasures involve identifying the frequency on which the threat system is operating, and then generating a jamming signal on the same frequency.

Efforts are also under way in Russia to develop AESA seekers for air-to-air applications, including the Izdeliye (Article) 180/K-77M, a development of the R-77, and a new design known as Izdeliye-270. However, some Russian seeker designers remain unconvinced of the value of moving from a mechanically scanned system to electronically scanned arrays. There have also been indications that the Russian microelectronics sector has struggled to produce transmit–receive modules to the required reliability and cost targets.

Long- and very-long-range engagement

In the late 1980s, Soviet guided-weapons designers were considering the development of long-range AAMs to be used against high-value airborne platforms, such as tanker and ISR aircraft, which traditionally remain far behind the forward edge of any air battle. The Novator KS-172 design, for instance, was intended to be used at ranges of up to 300 kilometres. However, it languished with little or no state support throughout the 1990s and beyond, before losing out in a 2009 competition with the Vympel Izdeliye-810 long-range missile. The latter is based to some extent on the long-range R-37M but it has an airframe modified for carriage in internal weapons bays, including on the fifth-generation Sukhoi Su-57 combat aircraft (the prototype is known as the Sukhoi T-50).

It is apparent that China has also decided to pursue a long-range AAM capability, quite possibly tracking Russian developments. Images of a large, long-range missile being carried by a PLAAF Shenyang J-16 combat aircraft appeared on the internet in late 2016. The weapon is estimated to be about six metres long; by comparison, the R-37M is just over four metres long. The design only had four control surfaces at the tail, with no mid-body wing, suggesting a missile design not intended for high manoeuvrability. The missile is well into development. Along with an estimated maximum range of greater than 400km, it probably also uses dual-mode guidance. The images appeared to show that as well as an active radar seeker, the weapon was also fitted with an infrared adjunct seeker. The use of dual-mode guidance would make the missile more resistant to countermeasures, and improve aim-point selection.

In a very-long-range engagement scenario, off-board sensors – those on the launch aircraft – would provide initial targeting information and mid-course updates during the missile's flight. A lofted trajectory would also be used, potentially at altitudes in excess of 30,000 metres, in order to minimise airframe drag. Given the considerable diameter of the missile's body, the radome could accommodate a large antenna, with this providing a detection range of perhaps 40–50km or more against a target with a large radar cross-section, such as a tanker or airborne early-warning aircraft. The infrared or imaging infrared adjunct seeker could be used for terminal aim-point selection to try to ensure maximum damage or as an alternative primary seeker were the missile's radar seeker to be jammed.

A challenging future environment

China's very-long-range weapon will, when it begins to enter service in the next few years, provide the PLAAF with the ability to threaten high-value air targets at extended ranges. This will likely influence how potential opponents consider their own future operations. Coupling the J-16's operational radius with a 400km-range AAM would, for instance, be a forcing factor for an opponent's planning of its tanker-refuelling tracks or large-platform ISR missions. It is perhaps no coincidence that the USAF is increasingly interested in a low-observable tanker-aircraft design. Yet more concerning from a US perspective is the fact that this development is only one aspect of the PLAAF's effort to recapitalise its AAM inventory with more capable systems, including the PL-10, PL-15 and the rocket-ramjet-powered AAMs that offer far greater engagement options. These developments are themselves nested within a combat-aircraft upgrade and re-equipment programme.

China's progress will also continue to spur missile-technology developments in Russia, while collaboration between the two countries, at least at the subsystems level, remains a possibility; indeed, Russian industrialists have suggested that this is already taking place. With the PL-10 and the PL-12 already on offer for export, and the possibility that further upgrades might appear on the export market, Western air forces will have to take account of a more complicated future threat environment. However, although technology might be a central element of air power, it needs to be used appropriately if best advantage is to be gained. The PLAAF is moving towards more demanding and realistic training scenarios, but these developments will need to continue – and the lessons fully integrated into doctrine, training and tactics – if it is to take full advantage of the weapon systems now entering its inventory.

Big data, artificial intelligence and defence

Big-data analysis, machine learning and artificial intelligence (AI) are points along a continuum that will progressively remove human beings from complex decision-making. The automation of inductive 'reasoning' and empirical modelling allows for improved pattern recognition of all sorts, ranging from identifying similar targets to predicting correlated behaviour. Currently, however, these largely involve algorithmic models operating on extremely large data sets rather than genuine cognition or abstract decision-making capabilities that would resemble human intelligence. Although the current position on this technological continuum may be debatable, these technologies are starting to have a transformative effect on defence capability. As in every other aspect of modern economies and societies, automated algorithms are being leveraged to collect, compile, structure, process, analyse, transmit and act upon increasingly large data sets. In the military context, the opportunities for remote-sensing, situational-awareness, battlefield-manoeuvre and other AI applications seem promising. It remains unclear, however, whether these new technical capabilities will ultimately shift the balance in favour of offensive or defensive actions.

Military applications

On 11 May 2017, Dan Coats, the director of US National Intelligence, delivered testimony to the US Congress on his annual Worldwide Threat Assessment. In the publicly released document, he said that 'Artificial intelligence (AI) is advancing computational capabilities that benefit the economy, yet those advances also enable new military capabilities for our adversaries'. At the same time, the US Department of Defense (DoD) is working on such systems. Project Maven, for instance, also known as the Algorithmic Warfare Cross-Functional Team (AWCFT), is designed to accelerate the integration of big data, machine learning and AI into US military capabilities. While the initial focus of AWCFT is on computer-vision algorithms for object detection and classification, it will consolidate all existing algorithm-based-technology initiatives associated with US defence intelligence. The overall objective is to reduce the 'human-factors burden', increase actionable intelligence and enhance military decision-making.

Other armed forces appear equally interested in the potential of AI and are inclined towards similar potential uses. In 2017, the UK's Defence Science and Technology Laboratory launched a challenge that included developing an automated system to identify and classify vehicles from satellite imagery. Meanwhile, NATO's Science and Technology Organization has scheduled a 'specialists' meeting' in France on big data and AI for military decision-making at the end of May 2018, and the UN has announced that it is opening a new office in The Hague to monitor the development of AI and robotics.

Beyond Europe, China is applying facial-recognition algorithms to the domestic video footage collected by closed-circuit television cameras in order, it says, to boost public safety. It is also placing more emphasis on big data and AI for air-force operations. Beijing's state council has set a target output of RMB1 trillion (US$147.1 billion) for Chinese AI industries by the year 2030, asserting that 'breakthroughs should be made in basic theories of AI, such as big data intelligence, multimedia aware computing, human–machine hybrid intelligence, swarm intelligence and automated decision-making'. In 2017, the Russian news agency TASS reported that the Kalashnikov Group has developed an AI-controlled combat module that can independently identify and engage targets, and that radio-electronic technologies firm KRET was working on unmanned systems with swarming and independent decision-making capabilities. Those are but a few of the initiatives under way; the full range of military applications for AI is certainly expansive.

From tactical to operational

Even though technological innovation has not yet replicated human reasoning in independent machines, AI portends significant changes at all levels of military doctrine and practice. The UK's Royal Navy, for example, is pursuing Project Nelson to exploit and enable developments in AI across the 'whole naval enterprise'. AI systems will be introduced to provide 'cognitive support to operators and users', playing a part in mitigating data overload in today's complex sensor- and data-rich operational environment. Military services also emphasise the relevance of these new capabilities to enabling functions, such as logistics, as much as to their use in front-line combat roles; they are about the future, but also about helping today, UK officials have said.

But immediate gains from AI are also being realised in the tactical realm. Command, control, communications, computers, intelligence, surveillance and reconnaissance (C4ISR) are reaching new heights of efficiency that enable data collection and processing at unprecedented scale and speed. When the pattern-recognition algorithms being developed in China, Russia, the UK, the US and elsewhere are coupled with precise weapons systems, they will further increase the tactical advantage of unmanned aerial vehicles (UAVs) and other remotely operated platforms. According to the DoD, however, the 'deep learning' software being integrated into those systems is meant to complement, not replace, the human operator. Instead, it serves to reduce the required reaction time and augments the effectiveness of munitions packages.

For purely computational tasks, big-data analysis and machine learning can now supersede human capabilities. For example, one June 2016 report stated that a US company had developed an AI system (called 'ALPHA') that prevailed in combat simulations against an air-force veteran. In an interview, ALPHA's developer explained that it can process enormous amounts of sensor data and uses mathematical modelling to determine tactical responses. However, it utilises an approach called 'fuzzy logic' (akin to industrial control-system applications that act on sensor inputs), rather than a neural-networking approach, which would seek to emulate the human brain. As such, today's tactical advantage stems from much greater data-processing capabilities, rather than 'smart' machines per se.

Through its 'capability technology' research agenda, the European Defence Agency (EDA) is also exploring big data in defence modelling and simulation environments. In addition to enhancing combat efficiency, research and development (R&D) in military AI applications will create new adaptive methodologies for training personnel (such as fighter pilots). Furthermore, massive processing capabilities available for C4ISR information will almost certainly engender new operational opportunities. China's defence sector has made breakthroughs in UAV 'swarming' technology, including a demonstration of 1,000 EHang UAVs flying in formation at the Guangzhou air show in February 2017. Potential scenarios could include competing UAV swarms trying to impede each other's C4ISR network, while simultaneously engaging kinetic targets.

As the European Council on Foreign Relations said, 'AI will be part of the future of warfare, initially through autonomous weapons that can find and engage targets independently and operate in swarms'. The shift to coordinated networks of smaller, unmanned platforms will pose operational challenges for the large, centralised weapons systems that dominated twentieth-century warfare. This will also have implications for military doctrine, defence procurement and combatant commanders – especially as the reduced human and financial cost per unit of such UAVs renders them more expendable in combat scenarios.

More AI applications for weapons systems of tactical and/or operational significance in the land, sea, air and space domains can be readily envisioned, but the biggest impact of machine learning may be on military decision-making itself. In 2017, the Innovate UK initiative announced £6 million (US$7.7m) in Ministry of Defence funding for 'new technologies, processes and ways of operating that improve the ability of defence staff to analyse and exploit data in decision-making'. Machine learning will soon be employed not only to process sensor data and engage military assets, but also in an attempt to 'outwit' human opponents. Indeed, predictive analytics for adversary behaviour is a key objective of operational AI in the long term.

Strategic advantage

US Chairman of the Joint Chiefs of Staff General Joseph Dunford stated in early 2017 that 'information operations, space and cyber capabilities and ballistic missile technology have accelerated the speed of war, making conflict today faster and more complex than at any point in history'. Nations have less time to marshal their resources in response to security challenges than in the past, Dunford said. Because of this, and in order to stay ahead of the accelerating speed of war, automated decision-making will increasingly be relied upon by military forces. That is particularly true regarding strategic C4ISR assets and nuclear-deterrent capabilities, whose disruption or destruction could pose an existential threat. Smarter offensive weapons will drive an 'arms race' for more automation in defences in order to minimise any first-strike advantage. Yet the strategic balance surrounding nuclear security relies on, and clearly encourages, some degree of transparency and common situational awareness. Substantially raising uncertainty in the nuclear arena could threaten instability and have a mutually deleterious effect.

Meanwhile, integrating capacities, such as AI, that greatly enhance the capability of conventional systems could risk undermining the measures of transparency and predictability around military-platform capability that underpin confidence and security-building measures and treaty regimes. It could also fundamentally alter threat perceptions around the deployment of ostensibly traditional systems by adversaries. Additionally, in conventional military conflict or in peacetime, AI could be utilised to intentionally distort information resources or destabilise the existing state of affairs.

Russia's President Vladimir Putin said that AI raises both 'colossal opportunities and threats that are difficult to predict now'. Although he was speaking in a non-military context, his claim holds true in the military realm too. It is too early to judge whether AI is predominantly an offensive or defensive tool. In fact, the strategic balance may simply tip in favour of the party with the superior military AI algorithms, since they could enhance nearly every type of weapon system. Or essentially, as Putin further stated, whoever leads in developing AI will become dominant.

The real strategic impact of AI will concern its ability to impair or delay decision-making by military and political leaders. As in the operational realm, human processes will be targeted because they remain susceptible to manipulation by AI in a big-data environment. Recent elections have shown that automated efforts can influence social-media perceptions and even temporarily create competing 'factual' accounts. There is an inherent conservativism to modern military theory, which seeks to avoid potentially catastrophic conflicts; reduced levels of confidence in the accuracy of information would delay defensive decision-making, potentially to the benefit of the aggressor.

Ethical considerations

The ethical question of whether or not lethal autonomous-weapons systems (LAWS) should be permitted to make life and death decisions received much media attention during 2017. In August, over 100 prominent science and technology leaders joined Stephen Hawking, Elon Musk and others who had already warned the United Nations two years earlier about the risks of so-called 'killer robots'. Nonetheless, several countries continue to develop LAWS that would be capable of completely independent operation if desired. For his part, the vice-chairman of the Joint Chiefs of Staff, US Air Force General Paul Selva, has argued that humans should be kept in the decision-making loop. As of 2015, the UK's foreign office did not support an explicit prohibition on the use of LAWS, because it felt international humanitarian law (IHL) provided sufficient regulation. The UK armed forces, however, only operate weapons systems that are subject to human oversight and control.

There is a clear distinction between applying IHL or specific rules of engagement to LAWS in the field and 'hard wiring' those ethical limitations into the systems themselves. In that respect, the military considerations are analogous to the current debates regarding how to programme driverless cars to respond in worst-case scenarios – including choosing between different potentially fatal options. Except in the defence sector, it is presumed that the AI guidelines would be set by national military authorities and not by private companies.

2018 and beyond

A July 2017 study conducted on behalf of the US Intelligence Advanced Research Projects Activity highlighted that advances in AI are occurring much faster than originally anticipated. The report also placed AI on a par with aircraft and nuclear weapons as a transformative national-security technology. Accordingly, it will likely warrant new strategic thought to reveal its full implications and create doctrinal models. As such, AI will need its counterparts to Billy Mitchell and Giulio Douhet, or Thomas Schelling and Herman Kahn.

China's Next Generation Artificial Intelligence Development Plan may be the beginning of that process. Released in July 2017, it lays out a holistic national strategy for R&D, economic development and national security pertaining to AI. This includes strengthening integration between the military and civilian sectors, reflective of the fact that AI is a dual-use technology whose fundamental principles have applicability well beyond the military domain.

Indeed, this makes both constraining its development and regulating its proliferation nearly impossible. With Chinese, European, Russian and US leaders all publicly declaring that AI represents the future of national power, there will undoubtedly be large-scale investment and concomitant advances in military AI applications around the world.

Algorithmic warfare will change battlefield armaments, tactics and operations. Effective missile defences enabled by swarming interceptors would also affect the existing strategic dynamic relating to nuclear weapons. But if recent experience with cyber operations is any indicator, then the most potent militarily relevant applications of AI technology may, in the near term, be to manipulate civilian infrastructures for coercive objectives and to conduct influence operations during peacetime. From 2018 onwards, there will likely be further automated social-media campaigns and machine-learning tools employed to detect and/or interdict them. Indeed, by 2020, one may see complex AI-based perception-management operations – perhaps even falsifying or spoofing sensor data – to introduce strategic uncertainty into an adversary's decision-making processes.

Big-data analysis and machine-learning algorithms are already available and vastly expand information-processing capabilities; the defence sector is certain to capitalise on those innovations. Moreover, military applications will go far beyond improvements to specific weapons systems, and qualitative changes to tactics and operations will mandate revisions in strategic doctrine. Automated decision-making will play an increased role at every level of the command-and-control process, from swarming miniature UAVs to the national command authority. Genuine AI in the scientific sense (i.e. truly independent logic systems that can indistinguishably mirror human thought processes and in turn create their own machine-learning algorithms) may still be years away, but it is not too early to begin establishing normative limits for LAWS through IHL and military rules of engagement, in anticipation of this eventuality. Some technologists consider that these decisions will need to be addressed much sooner than we think.

Russia: strategic-force modernisation

Nuclear weapons have long played a fundamental role in Russia's national-security strategy. Moscow sees them as an essential aspect of strategic deterrence – which also comprises conventional and non-military capabilities – enabling it to maintain strategic stability and prevent military conflict. This suggests that Russia does not consider its nuclear capability in narrowly military terms, but rather relies on this to position itself as one of the guarantors of a stable international system.

This does not mean, however, that nuclear weapons do not have a military role. Russia's military doctrine, last updated in 2014, states that the country reserves the right to use its nuclear capability in response to the use of nuclear weapons – or other weapons of mass destruction – against Russia or its allies, and in circumstances where aggression with conventional weapons would put at risk the very existence of the state. While this language indicates that the range of conditions for the use of Russia's nuclear weapons is relatively constrained, it is nuanced enough to allow Moscow to suggest that it can resort to nuclear weapons in a number of scenarios. While the Russian political and military leadership clearly understands the catastrophic consequences of a large-scale nuclear exchange, Moscow appears to be maintaining a degree of ambiguity about its intentions and capabilities that makes it very difficult to completely rule out the possibility of a limited use of nuclear weapons in some eventualities. Indeed, in its military exercises, Russia has practised scenarios that involve the use of such weapons.

Defence industry

Given the role that nuclear weapons play in its national-security strategy, it is unsurprising that Russia devotes substantial resources to the maintenance and modernisation of its nuclear forces. During the financially lean years of the 1990s, Russia focused on maintaining the core components of its strategic arsenal, preserving key defence-industrial enterprises, and consolidating development and production in Russia (although the maintenance of some legacy systems continued with the support of defence enterprises in Ukraine).

These efforts allowed Russia to bring together key elements of the Soviet-era military-industrial infrastructure, and to preserve a significant number of military research and design institutions involved in the development of advanced military systems. In this period, Moscow also developed a broad outline of its nuclear-modernisation programme that helped it maintain its strategic forces with the limited financial resources that were available. As more funds became available in the 2000s, the modernisation effort was intensified and subsequently expanded to include a number of new programmes. To a large extent, this expansion was driven by the defence industry, although the factors that helped justify the modernisation effort included the need to maintain numerical parity with the United States and to counter US missile-defence developments.

Today, key enterprises involved in the development and production of Russia's strategic systems include the Moscow Institute of Thermal Technology, which leads the development of land- and sea-based solid-propellant ballistic missiles (RS-12M2 *Topol*-M (SS-27 mod 1), RS-24 *Yars* (SS-27 mod 2) and *Bulava*), and the Votkinsk Machine Building Plant, which produces the missiles. The Makeyev State Rocket Center is the lead developer of liquid-fuel missiles, including modifications of the R-29RM *Sineva* (SS-N-23 *Skiff*) submarine-launched ballistic missile (SLBM) and the new silo-based *Sarmat*. These missiles are produced at the Krasnoyarsk Machine Building Plant. The Tupolev Design Bureau is the main contractor for work on the current range of strategic bombers. Upgrades to old bombers are carried out at several plants, but it is planned that new aircraft production will be concentrated at the Gorbunov Aviation Plant in Kazan.

Analysts have questioned the demographic profile of the workforce within Russia's defence industries, and the need to make the industry an attractive career option for young engineers. While defence enterprises might be seen as a reliable career path in a period of broader economic difficulty, these industries now have to compete for talent. This was reflected in the pay rises noted in recent years. And although Russia's strategic-defence enterprises appear to have preserved some of their expertise, problems remain, for example, in transferring the necessary skill sets and experience to the younger generation of engineers.

Meanwhile, the *Bulava* missile programme encountered some difficulties at the development and serial-production stages; development of the *Sarmat* missile is now several years behind schedule; and the industry still has to demonstrate that it can resume the production of strategic bombers. However, while economic challenges may be holding at risk some elements of Russia's broader military-modernisation drive, and while time frames might slip, the intention is likely to complete the strategic-modernisation programmes currently under way.

Strategic forces
Land-based systems
Land-based intercontinental ballistic missiles (ICBMs) constitute the main pillar of the Russian strategic nuclear triad. Russia is carrying out an active ICBM modernisation programme, which has accelerated in recent years. The missile system at the centre of this modernisation is the single-warhead *Topol*-M (SS-27 mod 1), which was deployed in 1997–2009, when Russia was constrained from deploying a multiple-warhead version of that missile by the Strategic Arms Reduction Treaty (START). When START expired in 2009, Russia switched to deployment of the RS-24 *Yars* (SS-27 mod 2), which is a version of the *Topol*-M (probably somewhat upgraded) that uses multiple independently-targetable re-entry vehicles (MIRVs). Both of these missiles are deployed in silos as well as on road-mobile launchers. As of early 2017, Russia was estimated to have 78 single-warhead *Topol*-M missiles and 96 multiple-warhead *Yars* ICBMs. The deployment of *Yars* missiles is expected to continue as part of the modernisation process.

The relatively new *Topol*-M and *Yars* missiles carry about half of all the ICBM warheads in Russia's inventory. The other half are deployed with the older ICBMs that were introduced in the early 1980s. One of these missiles, the UR-100NUTTH (SS-19 mod 3), is in the process of being withdrawn from active service.

The other, the heavy R-36M2 (SS-18 *Satan* mod 5), is currently deployed with two missile divisions. With each missile carrying ten warheads, 46 ICBMs of this type account for 460 deployed warheads. These missiles are expected to stay in service until about 2020. After that they will be replaced by *Sarmat*, a new silo-based liquid-fuel ICBM that is currently under development. *Sarmat*, however, is not necessarily an adequate replacement for its heavy predecessor, as its characteristics are closer to those of the UR-100NUTTH (SS-19); this stems, analysts maintain, from the fact that the R-36M2 was built in Ukraine and that as a consequence *Sarmat* is, in effect, the heaviest missile that Russia can currently produce. With a launch weight of about half that of the R-36M2, *Sarmat* is likely to have smaller throw-weight and might carry fewer than ten warheads.

Although most *Sarmat* missiles are expected to carry nuclear warheads, it also appears to be the launcher of choice for Russia's developmental hypersonic glide vehicle (HGV), which is often referred to as Project 4202 or Yu-71. The Yu-71 vehicle is currently undergoing flight tests, which may lead to an initial deployment in the 2020s. The boost-glide HGV will not necessarily be nuclear-armed.

Although the deployment of a MIRVed, silo-based ICBM is often considered a politically destabilising move, Russia appears to believe that *Sarmat* is essential for countering US missile defences. Its calculation is that even if only a small number of these missiles can survive an attack, they could provide an adequate retaliatory response. The hypersonic vehicle also appears to have the penetration of missile defences as its primary mission.

In addition to the two main ICBM development programmes – *Yars* and *Sarmat* – Russia is working to revive the idea of building a rail-mobile ICBM. Even though the project, known as *Barguzin*, was not included in the earlier State Armament Programme, development is under way and the first missile ejection test took place in November 2016.

Another missile under development, known as the RS-26 *Rubezh*, is nominally considered an ICBM, since it demonstrated a range of more than 5,500km in one of its flight tests. *Rubezh*, however, is believed to be an intermediate-range missile that is based on the first two stages of *Yars*. Russia completed flight tests of the missile in 2014 and initially planned to begin deployment in 2015 to missile units near Irkutsk and at Edrovo/Vypolzovo. However, the deployment was postponed and is not expected to begin until at least mid-2018. It is possible that it will be deployed with missile divisions that operate the *Yars* ICBM, perhaps reflecting the judgement that *Rubezh* may comprise two *Yars* stages; if this is the case, co-deploying two different missiles would make more sense as there may be commonalities in terms of training, maintenance and logistics support.

Maritime systems
In 2014 the Russian Navy received the third Project 955 *Borey*-class ballistic-missile submarine. This delivery was part of Moscow's strategic fleet modernisation programme, which calls for the construction of eight submarines of this class. The fourth submarine, which is expected to join the fleet in 2019 – and subsequent boats that are currently at various stages of construction – appears to be an upgraded design, called Project 955A *Borey*-A. Each submarine carries 16 *Bulava* solid-propellant SLBMs, with up to six warheads on each missile. This construction programme is now expected to be completed in 2021.

In the meantime, Russia continues to maintain and operate ballistic-missile submarines of Project 667BDR (*Delta* III) and Project 667BDRM (*Delta* IV) types. These submarines were built in the 1970s and 1980s and are kept in service by regular overhauls and repairs. Both classes carry liquid-fuel SLBMs. The three *Delta*-III submarines that are currently in service rely on the supply of R-29R (SS-N-18) missiles that were built in the 1980s. To equip submarines of the *Delta*-IV class, Russia has relaunched a production line for R-29RMU2 *Sineva* (SS-N-23) SLBMs and developed an upgraded version of that missile, known as the R-29RMU2.1 *Layner*. This latter missile, accepted for service in 2014, is said to be capable of carrying up to ten warheads, although it is perhaps deployed with only four, like *Sineva*.

It seems likely that *Delta*-III submarines will be withdrawn from service when they are replaced by the new Project 955 *Borey*, although *Delta*-IV-class boats will probably remain in service for some time after 2025. However, the plans for future submarine construction are not clear. Most likely, Russia will continue the Project 955 line along with the development of a new submarine with a solid-propellant missile. Given *Bulava*'s patchy test record, it is possible that the missile will be new as well. At the same time, some reports suggest that Russia may be developing a new liquid-fuel SLBM, which would require a different development line; while industry may favour this option, the navy is believed to be more cautious. However, no decision about the direction of the SLBM programme is understood to have been taken at the time of writing.

Strategic aviation
Until recently, Russia's strategic fleet included 16 Tu-160 *Blackjack* and over 50 Tu-95MS *Bear* bombers. These aircraft were originally built as strategic-weapons platforms, with the Kh-55 (AS-15) nuclear-capable air-launched cruise missile (ALCM) as their principal armament. The recent overhaul and modernisation of the Tu-160 fleet has given these aircraft the capability to use conventional weapons as well. Both aircraft can carry the Kh-555 ALCM, which is a conventional version of the Kh-55. They can also carry the new conventional Kh-101 ALCM, and its nuclear version, which is known as Kh-102. The capability of the Tu-160 and Tu-95MS to use conventional ALCMs (Kh-555 as well as Kh-101) was first demonstrated in 2015, when these aircraft were used to attack targets in Syria.

Modernisation plans for Russia's strategic aviation currently include two main projects: the development of a new long-range bomber, known as PAK-DA, and revived production of the Tu-160; these newly produced versions are designated Tu-160M2. PAK-DA, meanwhile, is reported to be a subsonic flying-wing aircraft, although there is only scant information on the project. In order to allow its bombers to conduct stand-off operations, Russia is reportedly working on a new ALCM, known as Kh-BD, with a range that will be considerably greater than that reported for the Kh-101/-102. PAK-DA may conduct its first flight in the 2020s. Once in service, it will replace the old Tu-95MS bombers, although the air force has not yet indicated how many new bombers it would like to procure. The first Tu-160M2 is also expected to be ready in 2019, with serial production starting in 2021, and the air force is considering an order of up to 50 of the aircraft.

Early warning and missile defence
In addition to modernising all elements of its strategic triad, Russia is upgrading its early-warning system and working on the upgrade of its strategic-missile defences. The country's network of early-warning radars has undergone a complete overhaul with the construction of a series of new-generation

radars, known as *Voronezh*-M, *Voronezh*-DM and *Voronezh*-SM. The construction of the first of these began in 2005 and it became operational a few years afterwards. In 2017 Russia announced that it had complete radar coverage of all approaches to its territory.

In 2015, it launched the first *Tundra* satellite, part of a new space-based early-warning system, known as EKS. This was followed by a second launch in mid-2017. These satellites are deployed on highly elliptical orbits and can provide partial coverage of potential ballistic-missile launch areas. When complete, the system will include as many as ten satellites on highly elliptical orbits, as well as geostationary satellites. The current plans call for ten new early-warning satellite launches by 2020. However, it is a new system, so Moscow might be waiting to see how the first satellites function, while there are also likely issues relating to manufacturing capacity, to say nothing of the challenge in launching eight more satellites before 2020.

Russia is also modernising the missile-defence system deployed around Moscow. The new system, sometimes referred to as A-235 or *Samolyot*-M, appears to be a modest upgrade of the current A-135 system, which includes the *Don*-2N battle-management radar and 68 short-range 53T6 *Amur* (SH-8 *Gazelle*) interceptors. The system is known to be nuclear, although it is possible that Russia might look to deploy a successor without nuclear warheads. In 2017 Russia conducted a test of what appeared to be a modified 53T6 interceptor, although it is not known whether this test was part of the A-235 development programme.

Another significant project is the development of what has been claimed to be an anti-satellite system, known as *Nudol*. Russia has been conducting tests of the launcher since 2014, and this programme may also be part of the A-235 missile-defence project.

Non-strategic nuclear weapons

Russia maintains a substantial non-strategic nuclear force that includes a variety of delivery systems. These include bombers, short-range ballistic and cruise missiles used by ground forces, air-defence systems, cruise missiles and torpedoes used by the navy, and weapons operated by naval-aviation and coastal-defence forces. It is estimated that Russia's current active arsenal includes about 2,000 nuclear warheads assigned to non-strategic delivery systems. According to official statements, all Russia's non-strategic nuclear weapons are kept in centralised storage facilities. However, Russia has never clarified which facilities this definition covers. Currently, Russia maintains at least 12 national-level storage sites and an estimated 35 base-level facilities that can be used to store and maintain nuclear weapons for extended periods of time. With the exception of ICBMs and SLBMs (and possibly some cruise missiles), nuclear weapons are not deployed on their delivery vehicles and are stored at some distance from operational bases.

The development and deployment of new nuclear-capable delivery systems is clearly under way, although most of the new systems are designed to be dual-capable. One major project in this area is the development of the *Iskander*-M system, which includes a short-range ballistic missile and a short-range cruise missile. The system is widely believed to be nuclear-capable and has apparently been used in some exercises to simulate nuclear strikes. Russia will soon complete the deployment of *Iskander*-M in all 12 army and navy missile brigades, where they are replacing older *Tochka*-U missiles.

Another important programme is the development of a family of long-range cruise missiles that can be deployed on submarines, surface ships and potentially on land-based launchers. This family includes the long-range missile known as the 3M14, a land-attack cruise missile (LACM) that is part of the *Kalibr* weapon system. Starting in 2015, Russia repeatedly demonstrated the capability of this missile in attacks against targets in Syria. *Kalibr* missiles were launched from surface ships deployed in the Caspian Sea as well as from submarines deployed in the Mediterranean Sea. Russia has announced a plan to deploy *Kalibr* missiles on a range of surface ships and submarines. The first multipurpose submarine of the Project 885 *Yasen*-class, *Severodvinsk*, has demonstrated the capability to launch *Kalibr* missiles as part of its test regime. Older types of submarine are being modified to carry these missiles in their torpedo compartments; *Yasen*, in contrast, is believed to have a mix of vertical-launch tubes and missile-capable torpedo tubes.

The *Kalibr* missile may be at the centre of the allegations of non-compliance with the Intermediate-Range Nuclear Forces (INF) Treaty levelled against Russia by Washington in 2014. According to Washington, Russia has tested, produced and begun to deploy a ground-launched cruise missile (GLCM) with a range between 500km and 5,500km, in violation of its obligations under the INF Treaty, which Moscow denies. Although the US has not disclosed details of the alleged violation, it is possible that Russia did adapt the submarine-launched LACM to a wheeled ground launcher and therefore may have developed a GLCM that is very similar to *Kalibr*. If that is the case, this deployment constitutes a violation of the INF Treaty; so far, diplomatic attempts to resolve the issue have been unsuccessful.

Chapter Two
Comparative defence statistics

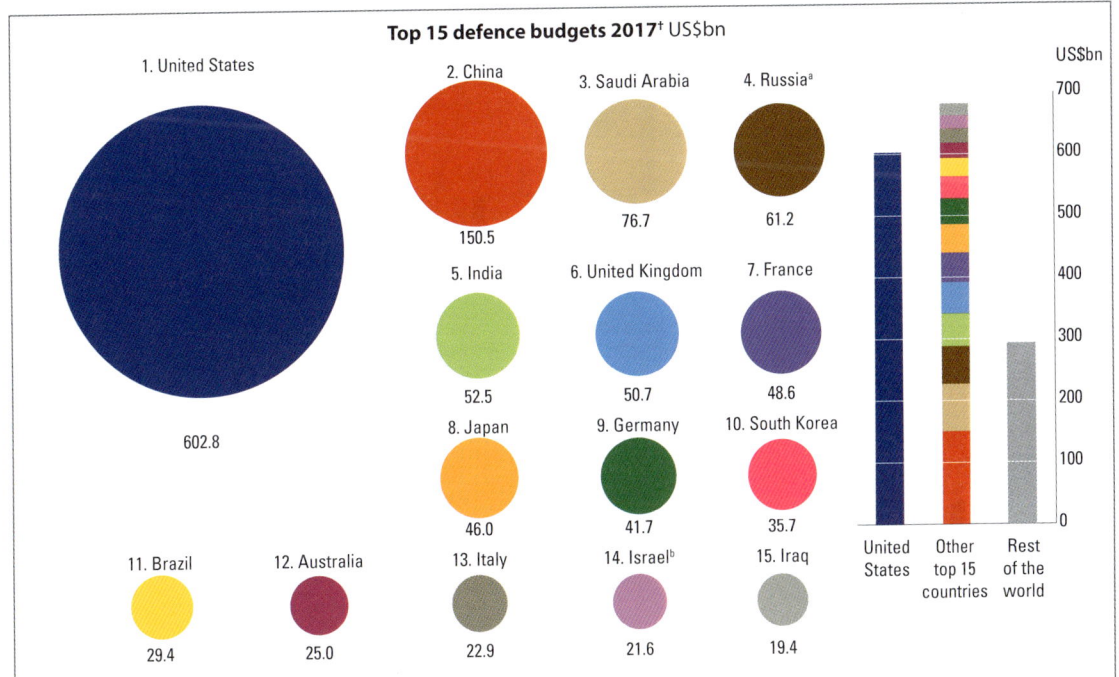

Top 15 defence budgets 2017[†] US$bn

1. United States — 602.8
2. China — 150.5
3. Saudi Arabia — 76.7
4. Russia[a] — 61.2
5. India — 52.5
6. United Kingdom — 50.7
7. France — 48.6
8. Japan — 46.0
9. Germany — 41.7
10. South Korea — 35.7
11. Brazil — 29.4
12. Australia — 25.0
13. Italy — 22.9
14. Israel[b] — 21.6
15. Iraq — 19.4

Bar chart: United States | Other top 15 countries | Rest of the world (US$bn, 0–700)

[a] Under NATO defence-spending definition; [b] Includes US Foreign Military Assistance

Note: US dollar totals are calculated using average market exchange rates for 2017, derived using IMF data. The relative position of countries will vary not only as a result of actual adjustments in defence-spending levels, but also due to exchange-rate fluctuations between domestic currencies and the US dollar. The use of average exchange rates reduces these fluctuations, but the effects of such movements can be significant in a number of cases.

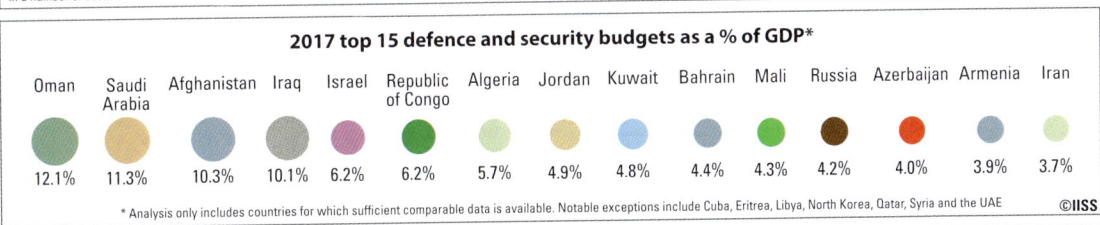

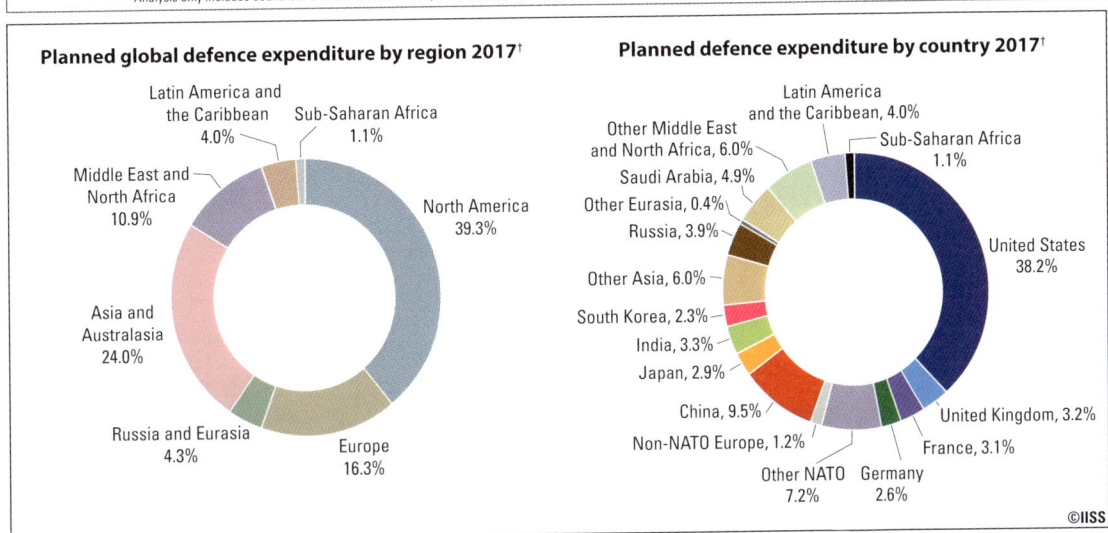

© IISS

2017 top 15 defence and security budgets as a % of GDP*

Oman	Saudi Arabia	Afghanistan	Iraq	Israel	Republic of Congo	Algeria	Jordan	Kuwait	Bahrain	Mali	Russia	Azerbaijan	Armenia	Iran
12.1%	11.3%	10.3%	10.1%	6.2%	6.2%	5.7%	4.9%	4.8%	4.4%	4.3%	4.2%	4.0%	3.9%	3.7%

* Analysis only includes countries for which sufficient comparable data is available. Notable exceptions include Cuba, Eritrea, Libya, North Korea, Qatar, Syria and the UAE

© IISS

Planned global defence expenditure by region 2017[†]

- North America 39.3%
- Asia and Australasia 24.0%
- Europe 16.3%
- Middle East and North Africa 10.9%
- Russia and Eurasia 4.3%
- Latin America and the Caribbean 4.0%
- Sub-Saharan Africa 1.1%

Planned defence expenditure by country 2017[†]

- United States 38.2%
- China 9.5%
- Other NATO 7.2%
- Other Middle East and North Africa 6.0%
- Other Asia 6.0%
- Saudi Arabia 4.9%
- Latin America and the Caribbean 4.0%
- Russia 3.9%
- India 3.3%
- United Kingdom 3.2%
- France 3.1%
- Japan 2.9%
- Germany 2.6%
- South Korea 2.3%
- Non-NATO Europe 1.2%
- Sub-Saharan Africa 1.1%
- Other Eurasia 0.4%

© IISS

[†] At current prices and exchange rates

Real global defence-spending changes by region 2015–17

*Excludes states for which sufficient data is unavailable (Kyrgyzstan, Tajikistan, Turkmenistan, Uzbekistan)
**Excludes states for which sufficient data is unavailable

Selected European defence research and development (R&D) budgets in 2017 and planned European Union defence R&D spending

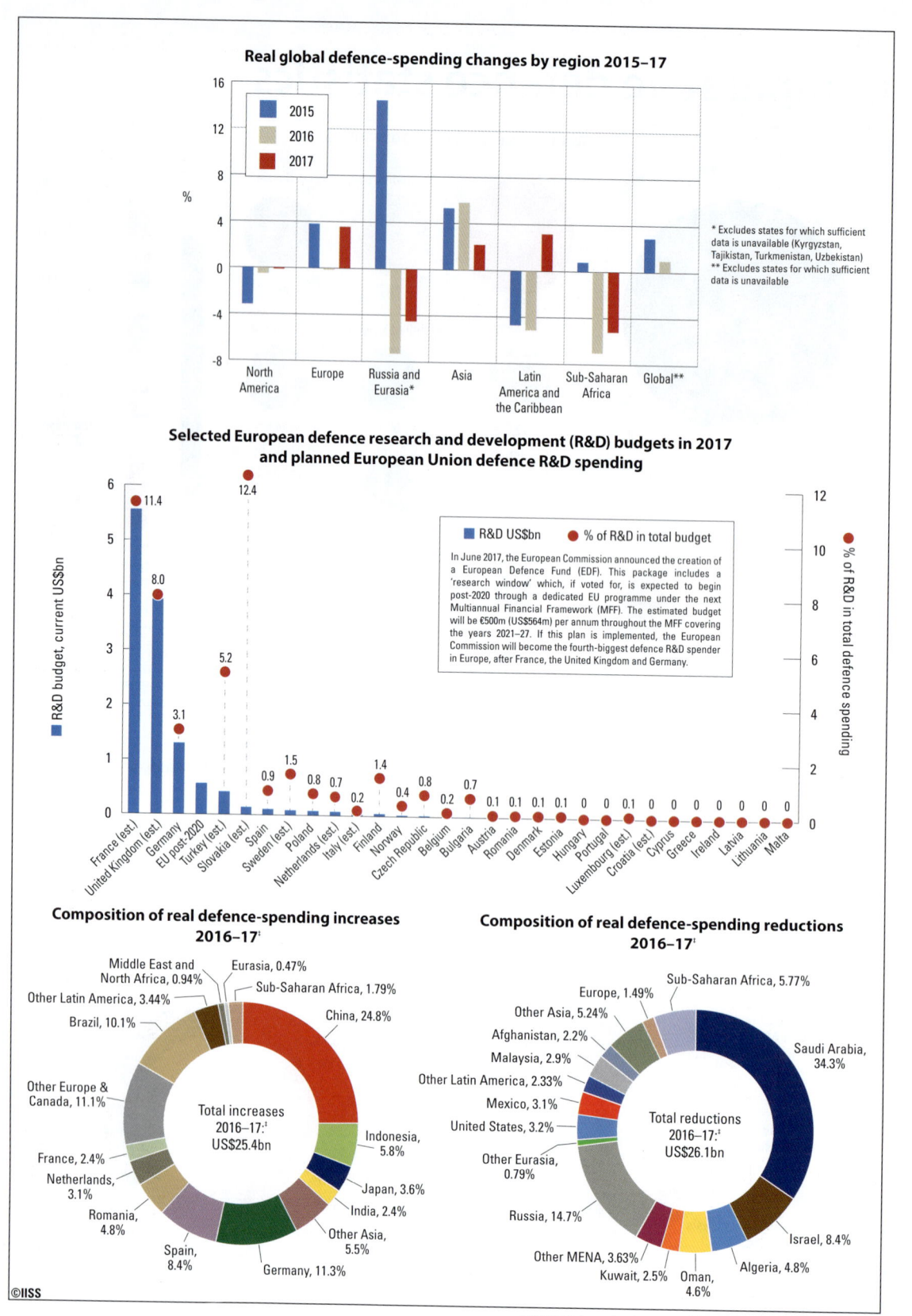

In June 2017, the European Commission announced the creation of a European Defence Fund (EDF). This package includes a 'research window' which, if voted for, is expected to begin post-2020 through a dedicated EU programme under the next Multiannual Financial Framework (MFF). The estimated budget will be €500m (US$564m) per annum throughout the MFF covering the years 2021–27. If this plan is implemented, the European Commission will become the fourth-biggest defence R&D spender in Europe, after France, the United Kingdom and Germany.

Composition of real defence-spending increases 2016–17‡

Total increases 2016–17:‡ US$25.4bn

- China, 24.8%
- Indonesia, 5.8%
- Japan, 3.6%
- India, 2.4%
- Other Asia, 5.5%
- Germany, 11.3%
- Spain, 8.4%
- Romania, 4.8%
- Netherlands, 3.1%
- France, 2.4%
- Other Europe & Canada, 11.1%
- Brazil, 10.1%
- Other Latin America, 3.44%
- Middle East and North Africa, 0.94%
- Eurasia, 0.47%
- Sub-Saharan Africa, 1.79%

Composition of real defence-spending reductions 2016–17‡

Total reductions 2016–17:‡ US$26.1bn

- Saudi Arabia, 34.3%
- Israel, 8.4%
- Algeria, 4.8%
- Oman, 4.6%
- Kuwait, 2.5%
- Other MENA, 3.63%
- Russia, 14.7%
- Other Eurasia, 0.79%
- United States, 3.2%
- Mexico, 3.1%
- Other Latin America, 2.33%
- Malaysia, 2.9%
- Afghanistan, 2.2%
- Other Asia, 5.24%
- Europe, 1.49%
- Sub-Saharan Africa, 5.77%

† At current prices and exchange rates. ‡ At constant 2010 prices and exchange rates.

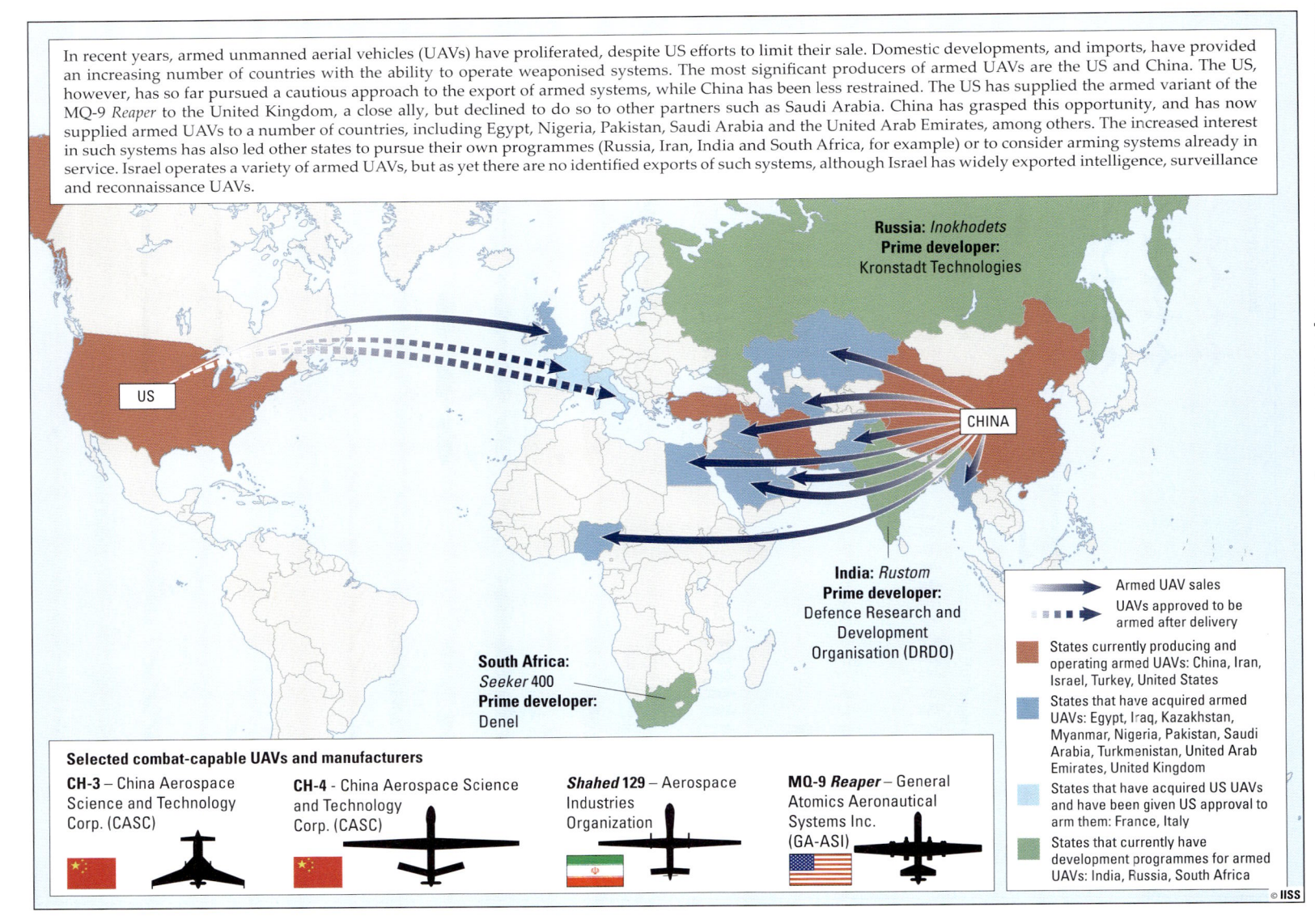

Comparative defence statistics

Armed unmanned aerial vehicles: production and procurement

In recent years, armed unmanned aerial vehicles (UAVs) have proliferated, despite US efforts to limit their sale. Domestic developments, and imports, have provided an increasing number of countries with the ability to operate weaponised systems. The most significant producers of armed UAVs are the US and China. The US, however, has so far pursued a cautious approach to the export of armed systems, while China has been less restrained. The US has supplied the armed variant of the MQ-9 *Reaper* to the United Kingdom, a close ally, but declined to do so to other partners such as Saudi Arabia. China has grasped this opportunity, and has now supplied armed UAVs to a number of countries, including Egypt, Nigeria, Pakistan, Saudi Arabia and the United Arab Emirates, among others. The increased interest in such systems has also led other states to pursue their own programmes (Russia, Iran, India and South Africa, for example) or to consider arming systems already in service. Israel operates a variety of armed UAVs, but as yet there are no identified exports of such systems, although Israel has widely exported intelligence, surveillance and reconnaissance UAVs.

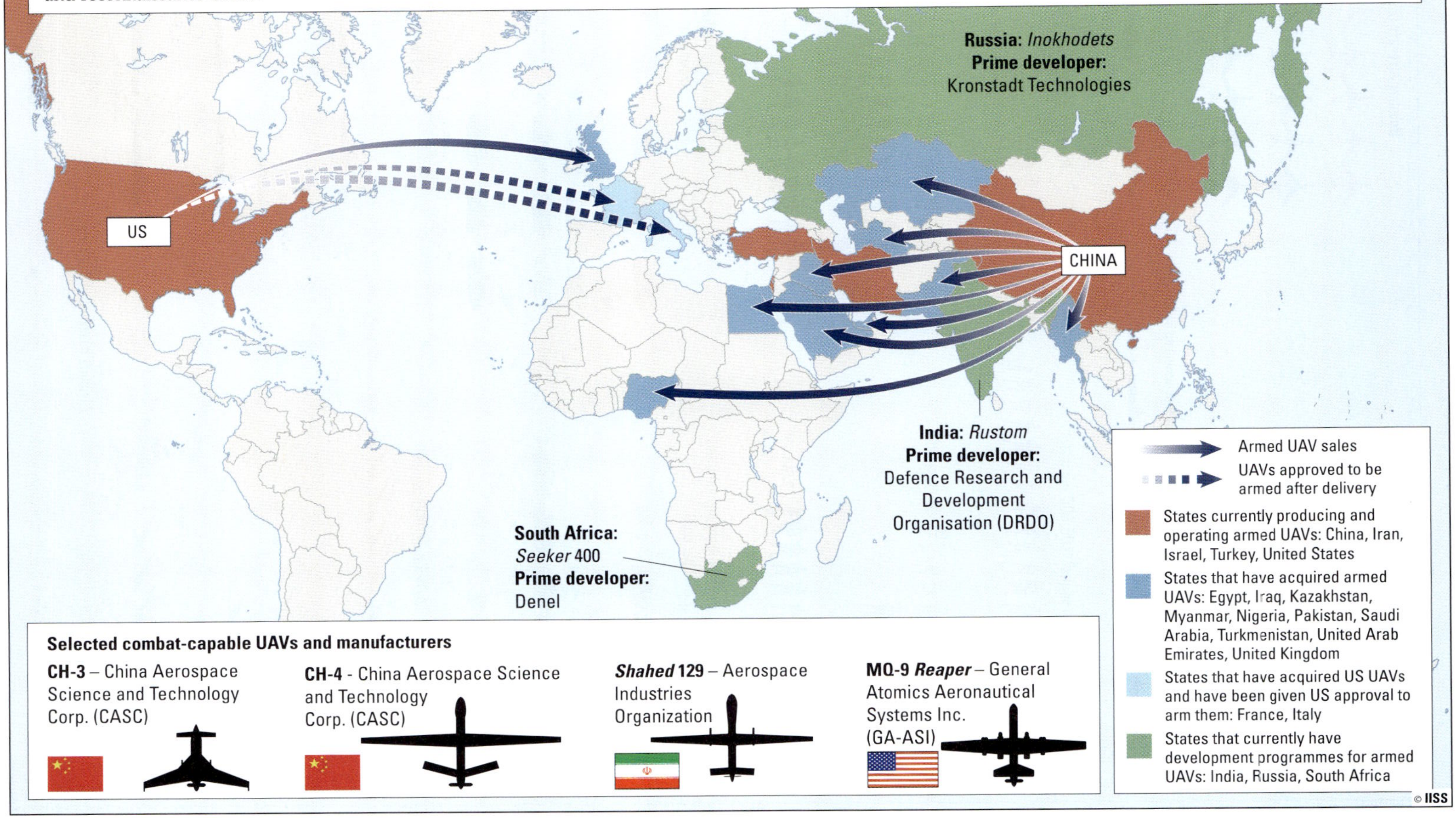

Legend:
- Armed UAV sales
- UAVs approved to be armed after delivery
- States currently producing and operating armed UAVs: China, Iran, Israel, Turkey, United States
- States that have acquired armed UAVs: Egypt, Iraq, Kazakhstan, Myanmar, Nigeria, Pakistan, Saudi Arabia, Turkmenistan, United Arab Emirates, United Kingdom
- States that have acquired US UAVs and have been given US approval to arm them: France, Italy
- States that currently have development programmes for armed UAVs: India, Russia, South Africa

Russia: *Inokhodets*
Prime developer: Kronstadt Technologies

India: *Rustom*
Prime developer: Defence Research and Development Organisation (DRDO)

South Africa: *Seeker 400*
Prime developer: Denel

Selected combat-capable UAVs and manufacturers

CH-3 – China Aerospace Science and Technology Corp. (CASC)

CH-4 – China Aerospace Science and Technology Corp. (CASC)

Shahed 129 – Aerospace Industries Organization

MQ-9 *Reaper* – General Atomics Aeronautical Systems Inc. (GA-ASI)

Key defence statistics

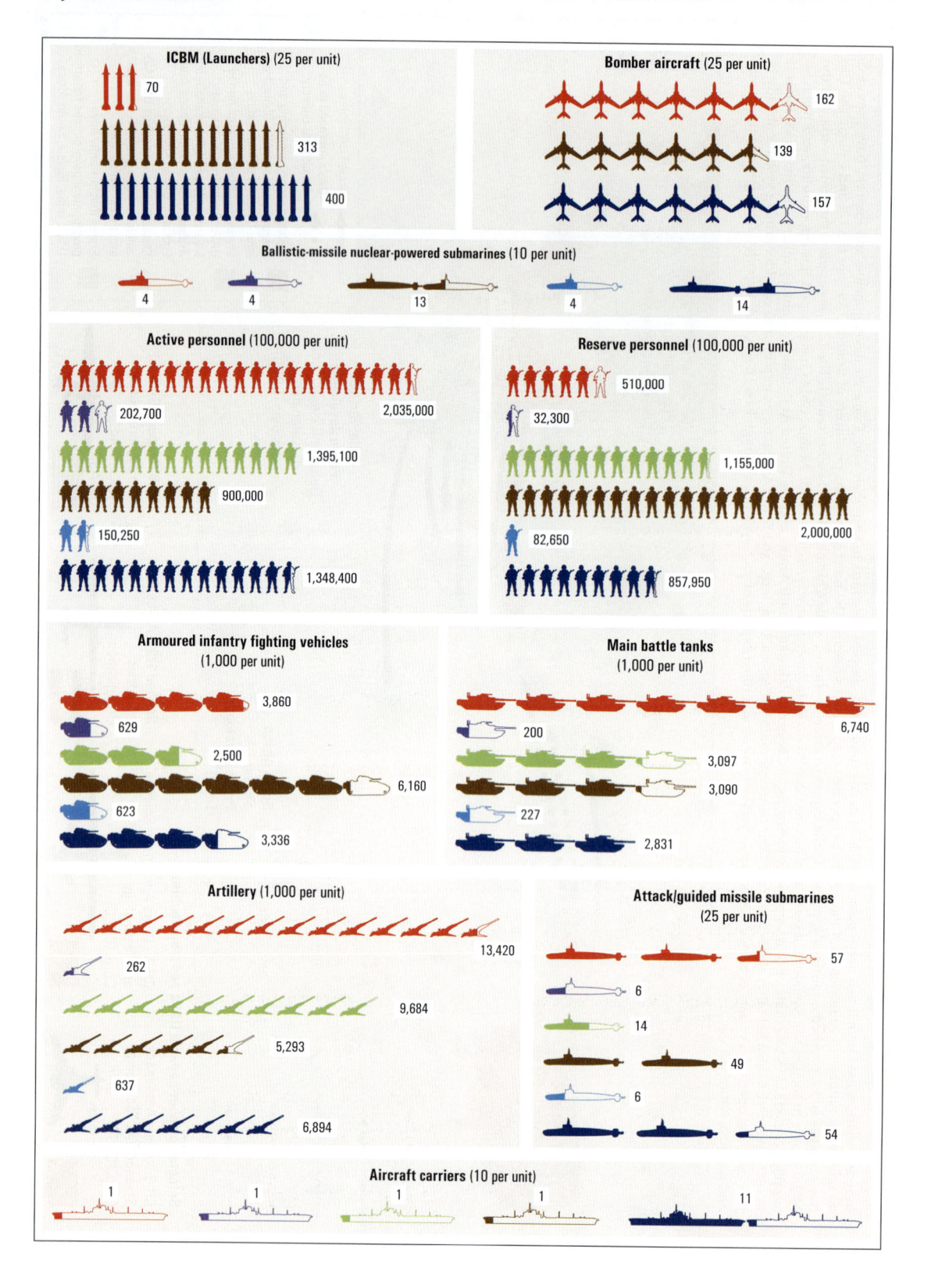

ICBM (Launchers) (25 per unit)
- 70
- 313
- 400

Bomber aircraft (25 per unit)
- 162
- 139
- 157

Ballistic-missile nuclear-powered submarines (10 per unit)
- 4
- 4
- 13
- 4
- 14

Active personnel (100,000 per unit)
- 202,700
- 2,035,000
- 1,395,100
- 900,000
- 150,250
- 1,348,400

Reserve personnel (100,000 per unit)
- 510,000
- 32,300
- 1,155,000
- 2,000,000
- 82,650
- 857,950

Armoured infantry fighting vehicles (1,000 per unit)
- 3,860
- 629
- 2,500
- 6,160
- 623
- 3,336

Main battle tanks (1,000 per unit)
- 6,740
- 200
- 3,097
- 3,090
- 227
- 2,831

Artillery (1,000 per unit)
- 13,420
- 262
- 9,684
- 5,293
- 637
- 6,894

Attack/guided missile submarines (25 per unit)
- 57
- 6
- 14
- 49
- 6
- 54

Aircraft carriers (10 per unit)
- 1
- 1
- 1
- 1
- 11

Comparative defence statistics

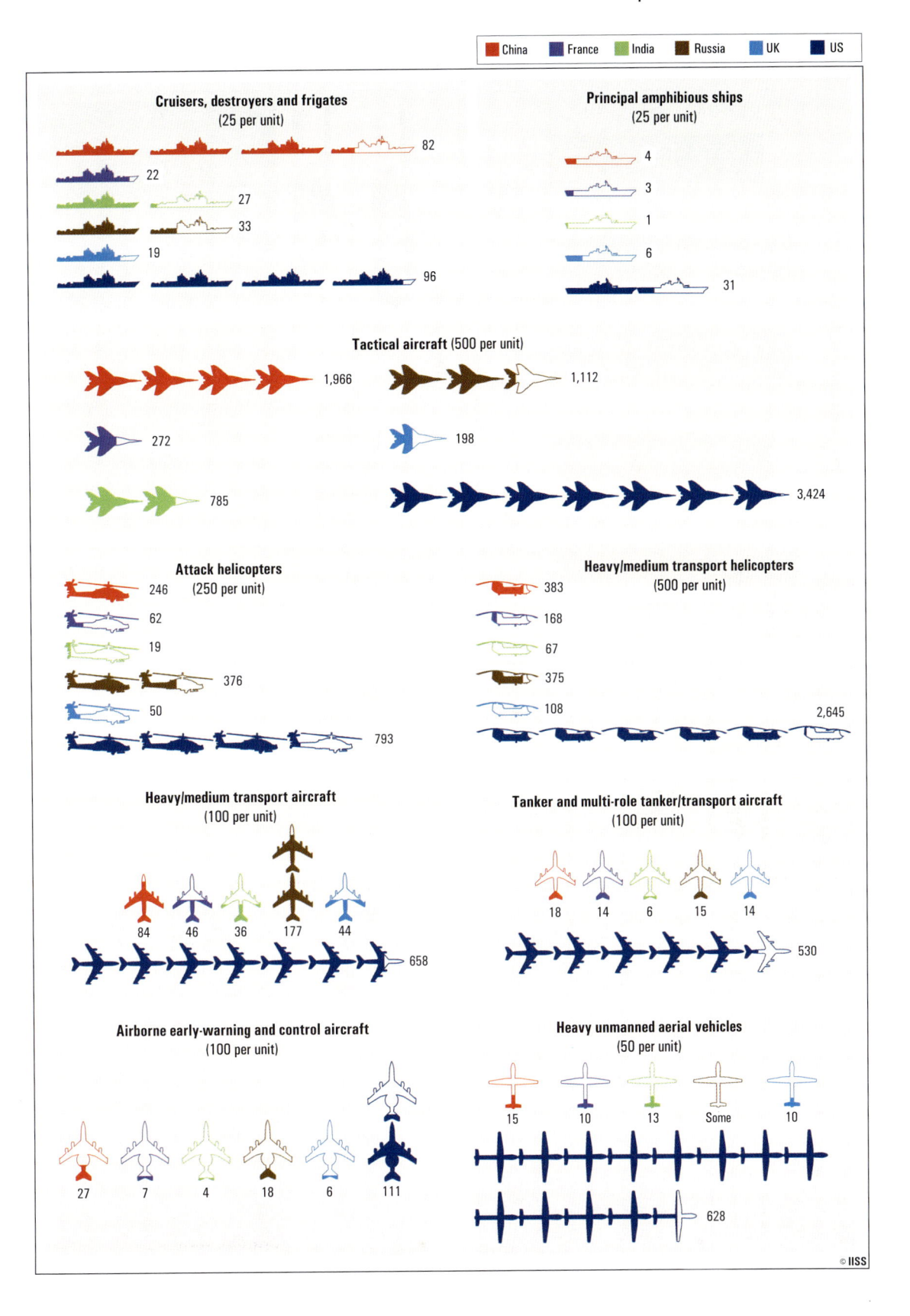

Legend: China | France | India | Russia | UK | US

Cruisers, destroyers and frigates
(25 per unit)

- China: 82
- France: 22
- India: 27
- Russia: 33
- UK: 19
- US: 96

Principal amphibious ships
(25 per unit)

- China: 4
- France: 3
- India: 1
- UK: 6
- US: 31

Tactical aircraft (500 per unit)

- China: 1,966
- Russia: 1,112
- France: 272
- UK: 198
- India: 785
- US: 3,424

Attack helicopters
(250 per unit)

- China: 246
- France: 62
- India: 19
- Russia: 376
- UK: 50
- US: 793

Heavy/medium transport helicopters
(500 per unit)

- China: 383
- France: 168
- India: 67
- Russia: 375
- UK: 108
- US: 2,645

Heavy/medium transport aircraft
(100 per unit)

- China: 84
- France: 46
- India: 36
- Russia: 177
- UK: 44
- US: 658

Tanker and multi-role tanker/transport aircraft
(100 per unit)

- China: 18
- France: 14
- India: 6
- Russia: 15
- UK: 14
- US: 530

Airborne early-warning and control aircraft
(100 per unit)

- China: 27
- France: 7
- India: 4
- Russia: 18
- UK: 6
- US: 111

Heavy unmanned aerial vehicles
(50 per unit)

- China: 15
- France: 10
- India: 13
- Russia: Some
- UK: 10
- US: 628

© IISS

China: People's Liberation Army main battle tanks

PLA main battle tank fleet, 1997–2017

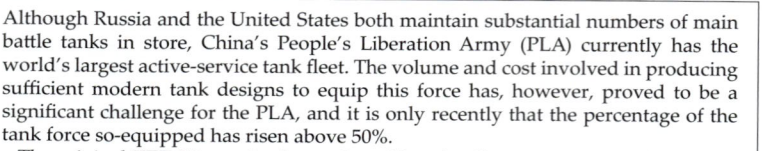

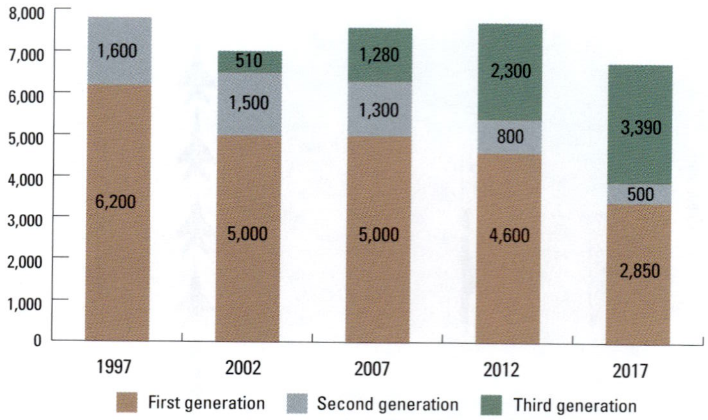

Year	First generation	Second generation	Third generation
1997	6,200	1,600	–
2002	5,000	1,500	510
2007	5,000	1,300	1,280
2012	4,600	800	2,300
2017	2,850	500	3,390

For the purposes of this analysis, generational status of each design is as below.

First generation

ZTZ-59/ZTZ-59-II/ZTZ-59D
- License built T-54 design
- In production 1958–78
- Upgraded versions developed in the 1980s
- 100mm smoothbore main gun (105mm rifled in 59-II and 59D)
- 36 tonnes combat weight
- Steel armour (reactive 59D only)
- Computer fire-control (59D only)

Second generation

ZTZ-79
- In production 1978–80s
- 105mm rifled main gun
- 37 tonnes combat weight
- Steel armour

ZTZ-88A/ZTZ-88B
- In production 1988–90s
- 105mm rifled main gun
- 38 tonnes combat weight
- Steel armour
- Stabilised sights

Third generation

ZTZ-96/ZTZ-96A
- In production 1997–2005
- 125mm smoothbore main gun
- 42+ tonnes combat weight
- Steel/composite armour (reactive 96A)
- Stabilised sights
- Reportedly being upgraded to ZTZ-96B standard from 2017

ZTZ-99/ZTZ-99A
- Currently in production
- 125mm smoothbore main gun
- 50+ tonnes combat weight
- Steel/composite/reactive armour
- Stabilised sights
- Computer fire-control system
- Active-protection system (99A)

Although Russia and the United States both maintain substantial numbers of main battle tanks in store, China's People's Liberation Army (PLA) currently has the world's largest active-service tank fleet. The volume and cost involved in producing sufficient modern tank designs to equip this force has, however, proved to be a significant challenge for the PLA, and it is only recently that the percentage of the tank force so-equipped has risen above 50%.

The original ZTZ-59 remains in service with a significant proportion of the PLA, despite being effectively obsolete, even in its upgraded forms. Early indigenous Chinese tank designs, such as the ZTZ-79 and ZTZ-88, had limited production runs and are now only in the inventory of a small number of units in northern and western China. The reorganisation of PLA manoeuvre units into combined-arms brigades in 2017 may result in these second-generation designs being removed from service altogether as the overall size of the PLA's tank fleet shrinks again.

The latest ZTZ-99A appears to have been produced in relatively small numbers, and issued to strategic-reserve units near Beijing, possibly because of its relatively high cost. The majority of China's third-generation tanks are still versions of the late 1990s ZTZ-96 design. The PLA's new 'light' tank, believed to have entered production with the ZTQ-15 designation, weighs almost as much as a ZTZ-59, but may nonetheless help fill the requirement for modern armour in southern China, where the terrain is not suitable for heavier modern designs such as the ZTZ-99.

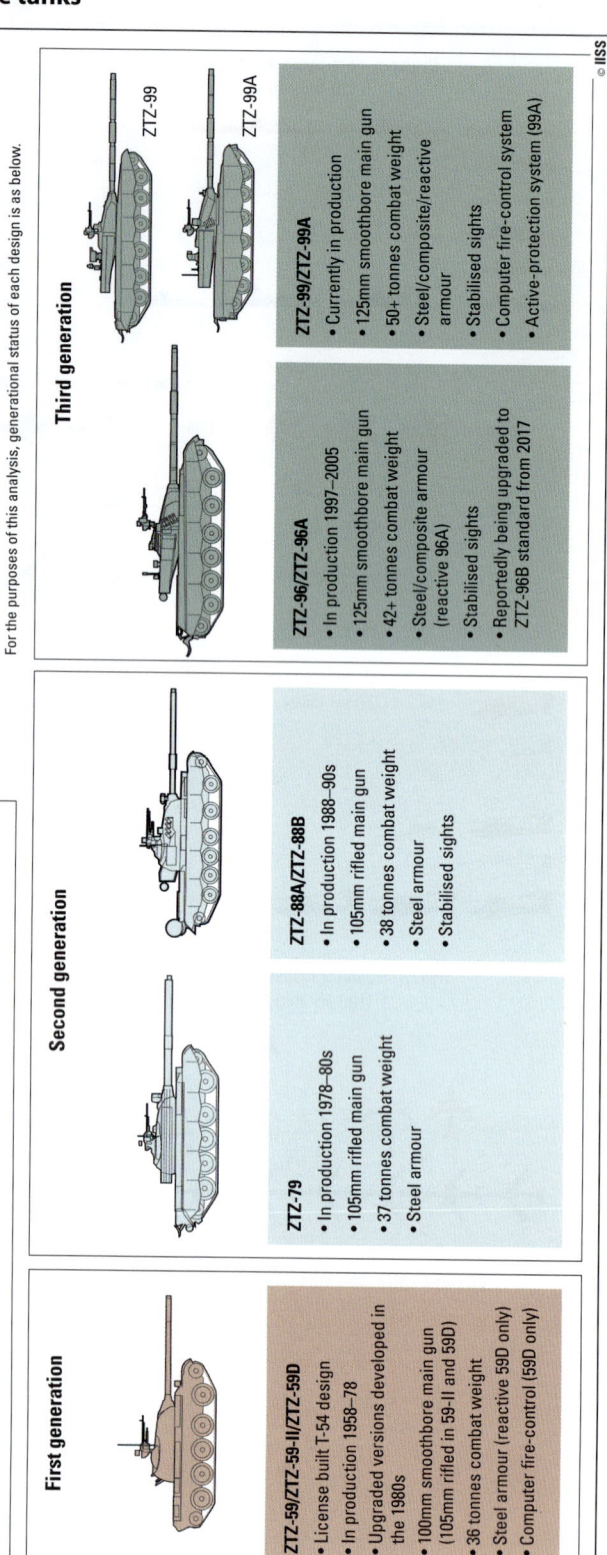

Comparative defence statistics

China: air-to-air missile progress

In 2015, the People's Liberation Army Air Force (PLAAF) introduced the PL-10 imaging infrared-guided short-range air-to-air missile (AAM) into service. It could be followed in 2018 by the PL-15 extended-range active radar-guided missile. Furthermore China may have at least three other medium and very-long-range AAMs in various stages of development. China is in the midst of a near-unprecedented scale and pace of development that will improve considerably its air-to-air weapons inventory, and provide the defence industry with increasingly credible products for the export market. The PL-10 was advertised for export very shortly after its entry into service with the PLAAF.

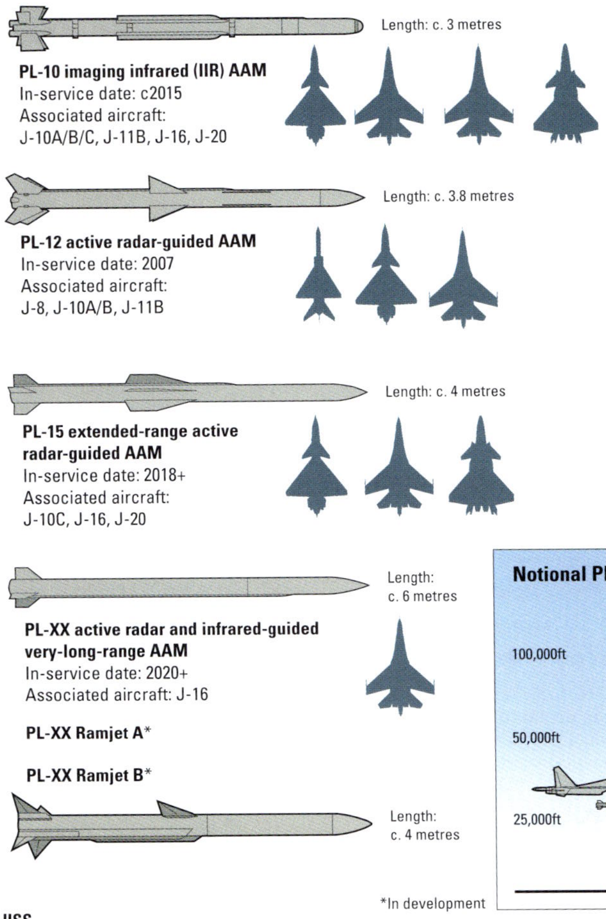

Maximum notional engagement ranges

PL-XX very-long-range AAM
- 400km+
- Large, non-manoeuvring targets

PL-15 and PL-XX ramjet-powered active-radar AAMs
- 150km
- All targets

PL-12 active-radar AAM
- 70km
- All targets

PL-10 IIR AAM
- 30km
- All targets

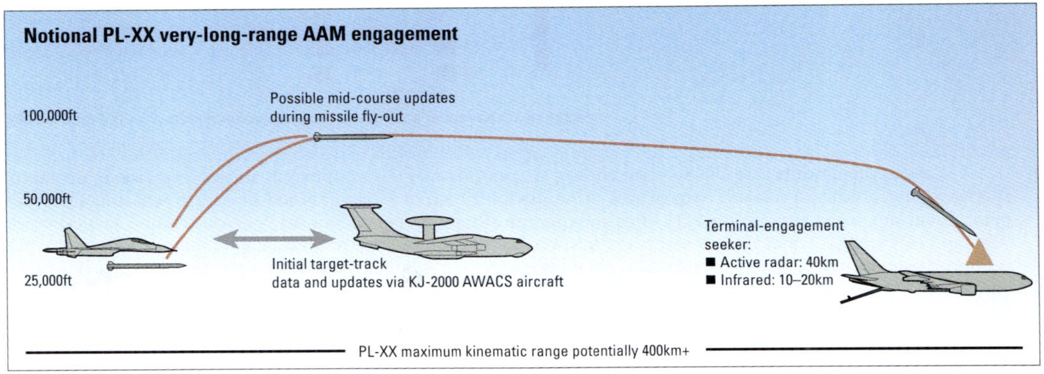

Notional PL-XX very-long-range AAM engagement

Terminal-engagement seeker:
- Active radar: 40km
- Infrared: 10–20km

Possible mid-course updates during missile fly-out

Initial target-track data and updates via KJ-2000 AWACS aircraft

100,000ft
50,000ft
25,000ft

PL-XX maximum kinematic range potentially 400km+

PL-10 imaging infrared (IIR) AAM
In-service date: c2015
Associated aircraft:
J-10A/B/C, J-11B, J-16, J-20
Length: c. 3 metres

PL-12 active radar-guided AAM
In-service date: 2007
Associated aircraft:
J-8, J-10A/B, J-11B
Length: c. 3.8 metres

PL-15 extended-range active radar-guided AAM
In-service date: 2018+
Associated aircraft:
J-10C, J-16, J-20
Length: c. 4 metres

PL-XX active radar and infrared-guided very-long-range AAM
In-service date: 2020+
Associated aircraft: J-16
Length: c. 6 metres

PL-XX Ramjet A*
PL-XX Ramjet B*
Length: c. 4 metres

*In development

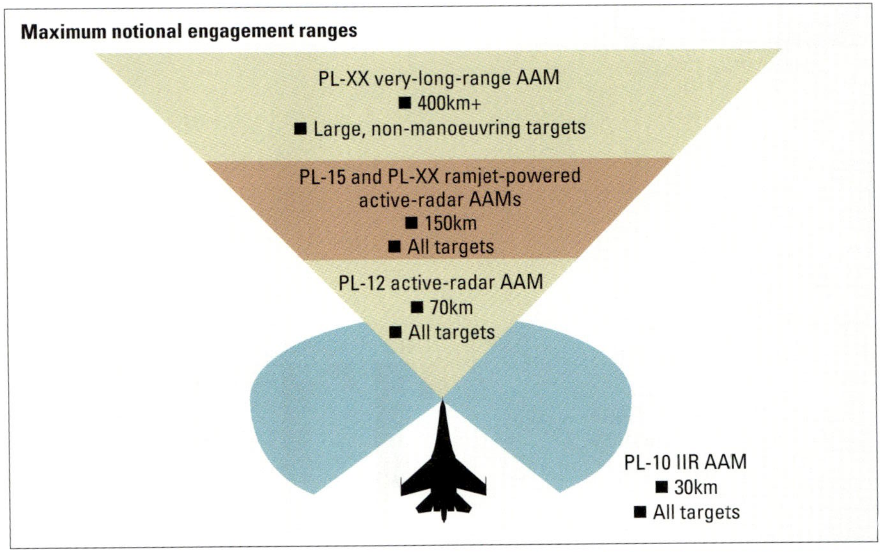

© IISS

Selected Chinese and Asia-Pacific regional naval shipbuilding since 2000

China's naval-shipbuilding output since 2000 has been remarkable both for its scale and breadth, with an industrial base centred on seven major shipyards. For some time, it has been engaged in considerable series production of large and small surface combatants. In the sub-surface arena, the production of a total of 38 new units, including ballistic-missile submarines, is also significant. In terms of submarine, destroyer, frigate and corvette production, China has either exceeded or nearly matched the collective outputs of the next three principal regional navies, whose own naval programmes have themselves been significant by global standards. China has also produced nine new under-way-replenishment vessels and it has launched its first home-built aircraft carrier and first modern cruiser, filling two major capability gaps. Over the time period, the United States has built more carriers (3), nuclear-attack submarines (14), destroyers (33) and large amphibious ships (15) than China, but not as many small surface combatants. There is still uncertainty over how robust Chinese warship designs are relative to their competitors, as well as their systems integration and weapons performance. The critical issue now is China's ability to sustain this level of output and address weaknesses, such as in submarine design and amphibious capacity.

China

No.	Shipyard	Type	Launched (2000–Aug 2017)
①	Bohai Shipbuilding Heavy Industry	SSBN / SSN	4 / 6
②	Dalian Shipbuilding Industry Company	CV / DD	1 / 5
③	Dalian Liaoning Shipyard	FS	9
④	Jiangnan Shipyard	SSK / C / DD	4 / 1 / 18
⑤	Hudong-Zhonghua Shipbuilding	FF / FS / LPD / AORH	14 / 12 / 5 / 2
⑥	Wuchang Shipbuilding Industry Group	SSK / FS	24 / 9
⑦	Huangpu Wenchong Shipbuilding	FF / AOEH / AORH	17 / 13 / 1 / 6

SSBN = 4   CV = 1   FF = 31   AOEH = 1
SSN = 6   C = 1   FS = 43   AORH = 8
SSK = 28   DD = 23 LPD = 5

Japan

Country	Type	Launched (2000–Aug 2017)
Japan	SSK	16
	CV	4
	C	2
	DD	12
	LHD	2
	AOE	2

Korea, Republic of

Country	Type	Launched (2000–Aug 2017)
Korea, Republic of	SSK	9
	C	3
	DD	6
	FF	10
	FS	17
	LPD	4
	AOEH	1

India

Country	Type	Launched (2000–Aug 2017)
India	SSBN	1
	SSK	2
	CV	1
	DD	8
	FF	10
	FS	1
	AORH	2

Approximate full load displacement (tonnes) of selected launched naval vessels (Japan, South Korea, India, US, China) by periods: 2000–02, 2003–05, 2006–08, 2009–11, 2012–14, 2015–17.

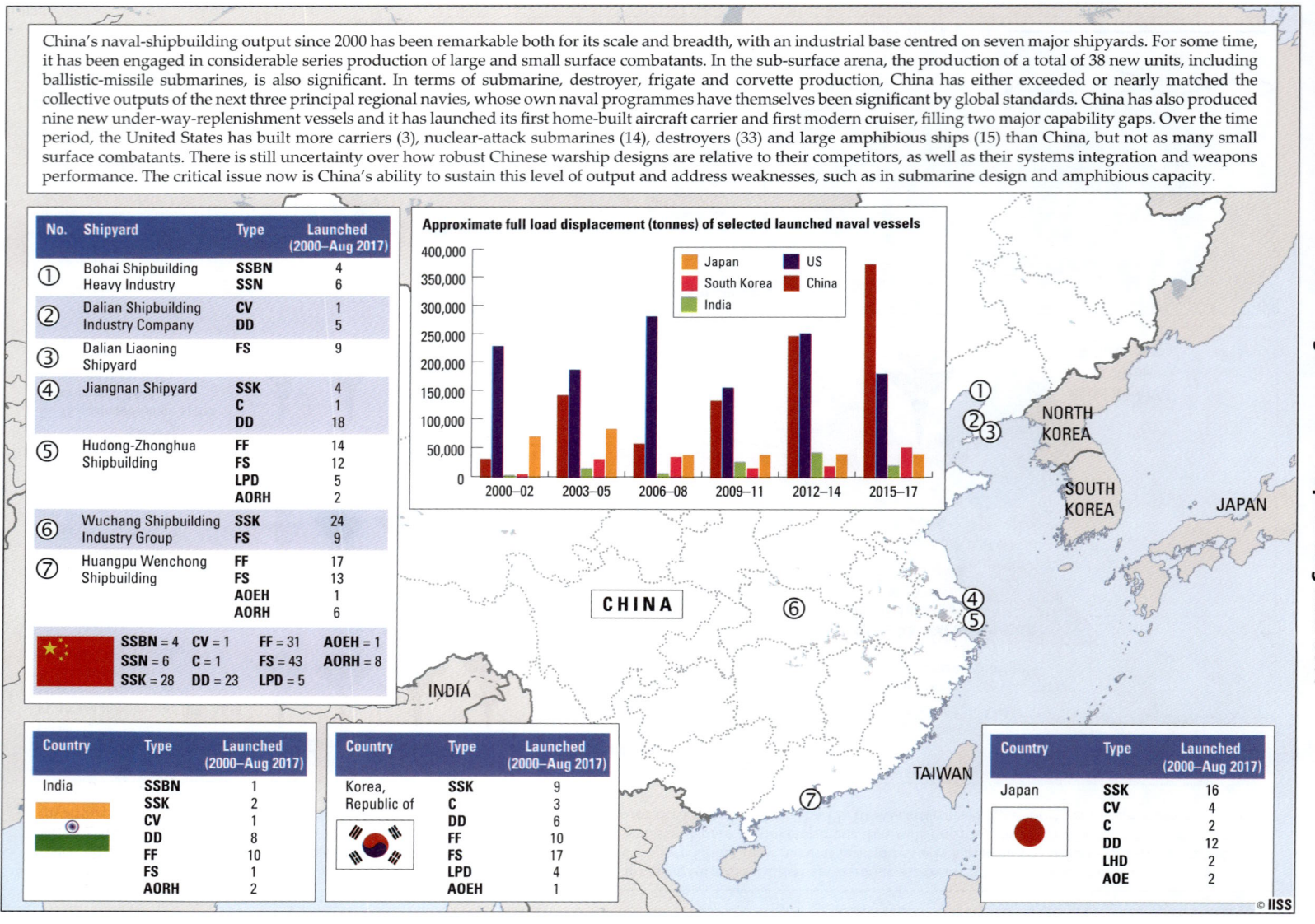

Chapter Three
North America

UNITED STATES

On 20 January 2017, Donald Trump became the 45th President of the United States. The administration quickly moved to take action on the issues Trump had emphasised in his campaign, including tackling perceived disparities over burden-sharing within the transatlantic alliance. In the campaign, Trump had questioned the relevance of NATO. During a May 2017 speech in Brussels, the president returned to the theme, chiding the Alliance's European members for not spending enough on defence. Meanwhile, issues including ongoing investigations into ties with Russia during the 2016 presidential campaign, White House staff turnover, and delays in naming senior and mid-level national-security officials all played a part in a troubled start for the administration.

That said, some coherence in national-security policy had begun to emerge by late August. In addition to Secretary of Defense James Mattis and Secretary of State Rex Tillerson, the shuffling of key players (Lt.-Gen. H.R. McMaster for Michael Flynn as National Security Advisor; John F. Kelly for Reince Priebus as White House Chief of Staff) provided for experienced advice regarding national-security priorities and introduced greater process into the administration's national-security decision-making. Nonetheless, the president's proclivity to comment on policy matters on social media, at times contradicting existing policy (such as on the issue of transgender service members), played a part in unsettling his own appointees, not to mention allies and partners. In addition, key positions in the departments of defense and state (and elsewhere) were only slowly being filled, with the result that career civil servants, and military officers in the case of the Department of Defense (DoD), still occupied many of these posts.

Although debates within the administration persist regarding what should be expected of the United States' allies, Trump has moderated his criticism and increasingly adopted policies similar to those of past administrations. The European Reassurance Initiative continues, with a funding increase under the Fiscal Year (FY) 2018 budget, and in June 2017 Trump delivered a speech in Warsaw assuring Poland of US support. A key milestone came on 21 August 2017, when the president announced his decision to send additional troops to Afghanistan, although their role in the country is expected to be less expansive than in the past: 'We are not nation building again', said Trump, 'we are killing terrorists'.

Afghanistan is only one of the security challenges facing the US, its allies and partners. As Mattis noted in his testimony before the Senate Armed Services Committee in June 2017, these fall into four main areas: 'filling in the holes from trade-offs made during 16 years of war ... the worsening security environment, contested operations in multiple domains, and the rapid pace of technological change'. Mattis also stressed that it is a 'more volatile security environment than any I have experienced during my four decades of military service'.

China and Russia

It has become increasingly apparent that the period of uncontested US strategic primacy is over. In its early days in office, the Obama administration sought cooperation with China and a 'reset' with Russia. But by the time Obama left office, policymakers were openly talking about an era characterised by great-power competition. Indeed, for the first time in decades, in China and Russia Washington faces states that can contest the employment of US military power in their respective regions. Moreover, both China and Russia are active beyond their home territories.

China's military modernisation has been proceeding for some time, while its growing reach has also been increasingly apparent, most notably in the activation of its first military base abroad, in Djibouti in 2017, and growing numbers of naval patrols. In some areas, China's defence-technology developments are seen as the 'pacing threat' for US defence planners. At the same time, Russia's military modernisation continues, albeit with relatively fewer resources. Overall, Russia intends to generate more usable military forces held at higher states of readiness, and there is particular focus on modernising its strategic, ground and air forces, and its electronic-warfare and precision-strike capabilities, including those from maritime platforms. Perhaps most worryingly for the US, Beijing and Moscow do not appear averse to cooperation (see p. 9). Russia's arms sales to China continue, and the countries' navies held joint exercises in September 2017.

US policymakers developing the new National Defense Strategy and conducting the Nuclear Posture Review find themselves increasingly thinking about the requirements of deterring China and Russia with both conventional and nuclear capabilities. The DoD is also considering the requirements of military competition, short of the use of force. Defence planners must increasingly think about the requirements of a conflict with China or Russia. Though still unlikely, it is perhaps a less remote prospect than it appeared several years ago.

Multiple concurrent challenges

Aside from growing competition with China and Russia, the US faces a range of other demands. Chairman of the Joint Chiefs of Staff General Joseph Dunford, reinforcing Mattis's statements in his own testimony before Congress, explained that China and Russia were two of the five challenges facing the DoD; also on the list were 'Iran, North Korea, and Violent Extremist Organisations [VEOs]'. These issues 'most clearly represent the challenges facing the US military. They serve as a benchmark for our global posture, the size of the force, capability development, and risk management.'

A belligerent North Korea, intent on further developing intercontinental ballistic missiles and nuclear-weapons capability; a still-revolutionary Iranian regime pursuing regional hegemony and destabilising its neighbours; an unstable Afghanistan; and the spread of extremist ideologies in Europe, Africa and Asia would individually place significant demands on the DoD. Their concurrence, however, combined with challenges from China and Russia, have placed significant strain on resources. Confronting these multiple challenges is becoming increasingly difficult, given the growing capability of potential adversaries, as well as the effects of the Budget Control Act (BCA) of 2011 (see p. 38). These issues are exacerbated by the fact that, for many years, the US defence budget has operated on the basis of 'continuing resolutions', which make long-term investment difficult and increase costs. Consequently, Dunford stressed that, 'as a result of sustained operational tempo and budget instability, today the military is challenged to meet operational requirements and sustain investment in capabilities required to preserve – or in some cases restore – our competitive advantage'. He continued by saying that the US military 'requires a balanced inventory of advanced capabilities and sufficient capacity to act decisively across the range of military operations'. Furthermore, the US could not 'choose between a force that can address ... Violent Extremist Organisations, and one that can deter and defeat state actors with a full range of capabilities'.

The war against extremist organisations has accelerated during the Trump administration, most notably against the Islamic State, otherwise known as ISIS or ISIL. During their operations against ISIS, Iraq's security forces benefited from military advisers and capabilities from the US and other nations – most notably air, artillery and intelligence. US forces remain engaged in training operations in Iraq.

At the same time, the Trump administration is extremely wary of Iran and came into office vowing to overturn the Obama administration's deal, which aims to keep Tehran from obtaining a nuclear weapon. Countering Iran was one of the objectives of the president's trip to Saudi Arabia in May 2017, while he also hailed the total of US$110 billion in arms deals with Riyadh, although this included previously approved sales agreed under the Obama administration (see p. 320). Meanwhile, although US forces remain in Syria, tackling ISIS and training members of the Syrian Democratic Forces, US policy towards the Assad regime is no longer an unequivocal 'Assad must go'.

Perhaps the most vexing near-term challenge facing US policymakers, however, is North Korea. The prospect of a nuclear-armed North Korea, with the ability to hit the US mainland, looms large and the Kim regime is no longer just a regional threat. Escalating rhetoric from the White House and Pyongyang caused increasing concern but was accompanied by more measured responses. In a joint press conference with US ambassador to the UN Nikki Haley on 15 September, McMaster called for international support for new United Nations sanctions to curb North Korea's provocations and nuclear ambitions. He stressed that, although Washington prefers a diplomatic solution to end North Korea's nuclear capabilities, the US possesses military options.

Finally, in August 2017, Trump directed the elevation of US Cyber Command to a unified combatant command, reflecting the growing importance of defensive and offensive cyber activities in military operations, as well as the requirements in the FY2017 National Defense Authorization Act. The new command will, like other combatant commands, report directly to the secretary of defense and be better positioned to advocate for investments and resources. The remaining question is when Cyber Command will be separated from the National Security Agency (NSA). Congress has dictated that the separation can only take place when the secretary of defense certifies that Cyber Command is ready to operate independently. A key argument for this separation was voiced by Eric Rosenbach, chief of staff to former secretary of defense Ashton Carter, who remarked that the separation would enable Cyber Command to generate its own capabilities and 'gain independence from NSA so that it's a true warfighting command and not an organisation subservient to the intelligence community'. At the time of writing, Admiral Michael Rogers remained in charge of both organisations.

Alliance relationships

Alliance relationships have been central to post-Second World War US national-security strategy. However, recent years have seen growing criticism of allies' lack of willingness to more fully contribute to their own security in an increasingly dangerous security environment. The degree of burden-sharing by Washington's European NATO allies has been central to this discourse, but criticism has not been limited to Europe. President Barack Obama voiced frustration over this issue during the latter years of his term, while Trump's statements during the 2016 presidential campaign and his early months in office sharpened these criticisms. As he argued in his inaugural visit to Europe in May 2017 (referencing NATO's account of states meeting the target to spend 2% of GDP on defence), '23 of the 28 member nations are still not paying what they should be paying and what they're supposed to be paying for their defense'.

The health of Washington's alliance relationships varied in the initial months of the Trump administration. Accounts of a tense telephone call between Trump and Australian Prime Minister Malcolm Turnbull briefly cast a pall over an important defence relationship in the Asia-Pacific, in contrast to the close relationship with Japanese Prime Minister Shinzo Abe. In both cases, however, the high degree of institutionalisation in the alliances, and the large measure of shared interests and values, argued for continuity.

Both Australia and Japan were already increasing their defence expenditures before Trump assumed office, as were some European NATO members, in response to the growing threat from Russia, revelations of deep deficiencies among NATO armed forces and previous encouragement from the US. Nonetheless, many of Washington's allies face real long-term constraints on their defence capacity due to limited economic growth.

Readiness issues

Readiness continues to be a concern for all the US military services. The high tempo of global operations in recent years – with ongoing deployments to Afghanistan and Iraq; counter-terrorism operations; humanitarian and disaster-relief missions; heightened deployments to South Korea; and increased activity to reassure allies, partners and friends in the face of greater competition with China and Russia – has resulted in a dilemma, according to former army vice chief of staff General Dan Allyn, whereby the services are 'consuming readiness as fast as we build it'. The two separate accidents involving the destroyers USS *Fitzgerald* and USS *John S. McCain*, which left 17 sailors dead, were stark evidence of these stresses on the armed forces.

Mattis emphasised the problem in remarks to the Senate Armed Services Committee:

> Worn equipment and constrained supplies have forced our personnel to work overtime while deployed or preparing to deploy. That too has placed an added burden on the men and women who serve and on their families. This further degrades readiness in a negative spiral, for those not in the fight are at a standstill, unable to train as their equipment is sent forward to cover shortfalls or returned for extensive rework.

Readiness challenges are also exacerbated by budget uncertainty and funding reliant on the passage of continuing resolutions. There is some relief in the FY2017 budget, with modest increases in funding and end-strength in all the services (see pp. 35–9). A broader question posed by the funding challenges and the diverse range of current and emerging security problems revolves around what kind of armed forces, postured against which threats, are required.

Table 1 US Army Armored Brigade Combat Team deployments, 2014–18

Division	Bde	2014	2015	2016	2017	2018
1st Armored	2nd	Army Evaluation Task Force			KWT	
	3rd			KWT		KWT
1st Cavalry	1st	EUR*		ROK		EUR
	2nd		ROK		ROK	
	3rd				KWT	
1st Infantry	1st	KWT			ROK	ROK
	2nd			KWT		EUR
2nd Infantry	1st	ROK		Inactivated		
3rd Infantry	1st		EUR*	EUR*	EUR	ROK
	2nd			Infantry Brigade Combat Team		
4th Infantry	2nd	KWT		Inactivated		
	3rd		KWT		EUR	

*Only part of the brigade deployed on these occasions
EUR – Europe, KWT – Kuwait, ROK – South Korea

After a protracted focus on counter-insurgency and stabilisation operations, much investment in the past decade has been in training, organising, equipping and sustaining these missions. Furthermore, a generation of US military officers has been immersed in wars against insurgents and terrorists and have not been trained to fight competent, well-armed state actors. At the same time, much of the equipment in many of the services is either ageing or inadequate for future challenges, such as against peer adversaries (for example, the army's mine-resistant anti-ambush protected (MRAP) vehicles).

In addition, much of the current US force structure dates back to the military build-up initiated during the Cold War. The outlook is perhaps most positive for aviation, with the air force fielding the F-35A *Lightning* II and development of the B-21 *Raider* bomber proceeding. That said, as Air Force Secretary Heather Wilson noted: 'While we continue to extend the life of old aircraft, materials suffer fatigue and maintaining old equipment is time consuming and expensive.' The navy's most recent Force Structure Assessment calls for a fleet of 355 ships by 2030, which will require sustained effort and resources to achieve. Meanwhile, key ground-combat systems are all modernised versions of designs from the 1980s or earlier. Indeed, a constant refrain from US military leaders is that US dominance in all of the domains (land, air, sea, space and cyber) is now contested and, in some areas, overmatched.

Finally, the armed forces are based mainly in the continental US. In Eastern Europe, there is only one rotational armoured brigade combat team (BCT) to provide deterrence against possible Russian aggression and reassurance to allies. The ability to reinforce or deploy in times of crisis is increasingly problematic, given Russian anti-access/area-denial capabilities. Therefore, a debate has begun about whether or not more US forces should be forward-deployed to Europe to provide constant capabilities and deterrence.

Modernisation challenges

The US needs to redress current readiness shortfalls while modernising an ageing force. This feat would be challenging even without the financial constraints noted above. As a result, the US and, increasingly, its allies are placing greater emphasis on military innovation and high-leverage capabilities. The 'third offset strategy', which had been championed by former deputy defence secretary Robert Work, seeks to sustain the United States' advantage through the pursuit of new technology and military doctrine. Indeed, innovation is all the more important in an era in which the US margin of superiority is narrowing. The DoD is increasing its investment in new space capabilities; advanced sensors, communications and munitions for power projection in contested environments; missile defence and cyber capabilities. The department is also investing in new technologies such as unmanned undersea vehicles, advanced sea mines, high-speed strike weapons, advanced aeronautics, autonomous systems, electromagnetic railguns and high-energy lasers. Some of these technologies could have a profound effect, although many of them have yet to prove themselves in an operational setting and are unlikely to be deployed before the 2020s, at the earliest.

US Army

The US Army has arguably been the service most affected by the past 16 years of war. Understandably, the wars in Afghanistan and Iraq were the focus of army training, equipping and organising. These demands remain, albeit on a smaller scale than during the troop surges in Iraq and Afghanistan. Nevertheless, they create a constant requirement for BCTs and headquarters units. In their testimony before the Senate Armed Services Committee in May 2017, Acting Secretary of the Army Robert Speer and Army Chief of Staff Mark Milley described the scale of the Army's commitments: 'Today, the United States Army assigns or allocates over 187,000 Soldiers to meet combatant commanders' needs.'

Indeed, maintaining army readiness in the face of recurring deployments, budget uncertainty and decreasing end-strength has been a challenge for several years. Declining end-strength (the army reduced by 100,000 soldiers and 15 BCTs during the Obama administration), continuing resolutions and the constraints of the BCA 2011 have required the army 'to pay short-term bills at the expense of long-term commitments'. As a consequence, the two army leaders stressed that the service has underfunded modernisation efforts, resulting in 'an Army potentially outgunned, outranged, and outdated on a future battlefield with near-peer competitors'. Other senior army officers echoed this assessment, adding that the 'continued failure to fund modernization will leave the US with a 20th century Army to handle the geostrategic environment of the 21st century'.

However, the army's end-strength picture has improved in the FY2017 National Defense Authorization Act (NDAA), with an increase in personnel numbers to 1,018,000 (476,000 active; 343,000 National Guard; 199,000 reserve), up from a planned 980,000. As with everything else in the NDAA, these numbers are contingent on avoiding sequestration cuts. If those are enacted in FY2018 and beyond, the army's end-strength will drop to 920,000.

At the same time, the army's first priority is to restore readiness for combat with near-peer competitors. To this end, unit rotations to the National Training Center, and home-station training, are now better resourced. The army also began an Associated Units Pilot Programme that is teaming active, national-guard and reserve-army-aviation units in order to enhance training.

Meanwhile, the mission to support train-and-advise missions in Afghanistan and Iraq continues. To better meet this ongoing demand, the army is creating six Security Force Assistance Brigades (SFABs) and establishing a training school for these at the Maneuver Center of Excellence at Fort Benning, Georgia. These units are smaller than normal BCTs, and are mainly composed of officers and senior non-commissioned officers. As well as providing the army with units focused on training and advising, the SFABs make a cadre available that can be expanded in the event that the army needs to grow rapidly.

The army is also investing in Europe. It has accelerated the growth of pre-positioned stocks to provide equipment for a division headquarters, two armoured BCTs, one field-artillery brigade and support units. One armoured BCT is now always deployed to Europe, increasing the total to three, including a *Stryker* BCT in Germany and an airborne-infantry BCT in Italy. Additionally, the *Stryker* BCT's vehicles are being enhanced with 30mm cannons and *Javelin* anti-tank missiles. However, despite this renewed emphasis on Europe, a recent after-action review following a deployment of the Italy-based 173rd Airborne BCT into Eastern Europe revealed significant problems.

Equipment modernisation is also one of the army's biggest challenges. It still relies for its principal combat capabilities on upgraded versions of the 'Big 5' systems procured in the 1980s: the *Abrams* main battle tank, the *Bradley* infantry fighting vehicle (IFV), the *Apache* attack helicopter and *Black Hawk* medium transport helicopter, and the *Patriot* surface-to-air missile system. Investments in the past decade have focused on counter-insurgency and counter-terrorism operations, and resulted in large purchases of MRAPs, more medevac *Black Hawk*s and more personal-protection equipment for soldiers. The army has identified gaps in ten areas, realised through a new Strategic Portfolio Analysis Review (SPAR), that must be closed to regain the overmatch required to deter and defeat near-peer adversaries: air and missile defence; long-range fires; munitions; BCT mobility, lethality and protection; air and ground active protection systems; assured position, navigation and timing; electronic warfare; offensive and defensive cyber; assured communications; and vertical lift.

These modernisation priorities compete with readiness and manpower. Indeed, readiness is the army's first priority and accounts for 24% of its budget, while the FY2017 president's budget allocates nearly 60% to manpower. This leaves only 16% of funding available to close significant capability gaps. Consequently, the army has opted to equip for the near term and restore readiness at the expense of preparing for the future. It has increased its investment in science and technology, but much of the modernisation funding is directed at improving the *Abrams* tank, the *Bradley* IFV, the *Stryker* armoured vehicle, the *Paladin* howitzer, the guided multiple-launch rocket system and the existing aviation fleet. New programmes will only begin if needed to address extremely high-risk capability gaps.

Accordingly, the army is attempting to accelerate efforts in the ten capability areas identified by SPAR. It has also slowed the procurement of new systems in order to keep existing production lines open in the event of increased funding. However, in the absence of additional resources, the army's combat-vehicle modernisation strategy faces a 30-year initial-fielding timeline. Aviation modernisation is a good example of these trade-offs in practice. In its January 2016 report, the National Commission on the Future of the Army recommended retaining 24 *Apache* attack-helicopter units, but to meet this target the army is slowing *Black Hawk* modernisation. The timeline for *Apache* modernisation has also lengthened from FY2026 to FY2028, and for *Black Hawk*s from FY2028 to FY2030.

Meanwhile, the army established the Rapid Capabilities Office in 2016 to address critical mid-term capability gaps. This office works with selected industry partners to acquire equipment and services quickly and at less cost in areas such as positioning, navigation and timing; electronic warfare; counter-electronic warfare; automation; and cyber. To support its programmes, the army requested a base budget of US$137.2bn for FY2018, an increase of 5.3% compared to the FY2017 request of US$130.3bn.

In February 2017, the army and Marine Corps jointly published the 'Multi-Domain Battle: Combined Arms for the 21st Century' white paper. This paper 'describes an approach for ground combat operations against a sophisticated peer enemy threat in the 2025–2040 timeframe'. It forms the basis for much of the war-gaming and concept-development work undertaken by the US Army Training and Doctrine Command, based on the assessment that 'US ground combat forces, operating as part of ... joint, interorganizational, and multinational teams, are currently not sufficiently trained, organized, equipped, nor postured to deter or defeat highly capable peer enemies to win in future war'. Importantly, unlike after Vietnam when the army focused almost exclusively on NATO, it is now focused on providing forces and capabilities across the range of military operations, as shown by its creation of SFABs. However, the central challenge for the army – as well as the other services – is how to meet increased demands within existing resource constraints.

US Air Force

Although the United States Air Force (USAF) remains the world's most capable air arm, able to conduct operations at global reach, it continues to be affected by significant challenges. It retains too many ageing aircraft in its inventory and does not have enough air and ground crew to operate and maintain them, nor does it have enough guided munitions to meet inventory needs.

The USAF has been involved in sustained combat operations since 2001, and during 2016 and 2017 undertook the majority of the air missions against ISIS in Iraq and Syria. However, the continuing tempo of operations impacts the service life of the aircraft, and sometimes the personnel, being employed. Indeed, repeated operational deployment is inevitably a factor in the decision by some personnel to leave the armed forces. Nearly US$1bn per annum is reportedly being spent by the air force to retain personnel, including incentive pay and bonuses. As of mid-2017, the air force was said to be 3,000 personnel below strength in terms of aircraft-maintenance staff, and around 1,200 short of tactical-combat-aircraft pilots.

Although the air force is buying the F-35A *Lightning* II at a lower annual rate than it would like, the type is now at least in the inventory. The USAF deployed the aircraft to Europe for the first time in April 2017, with eight aircraft landing at RAF Lakenheath in the United Kingdom; two F-35As were then flown on a training mission to Amari air base in Estonia. However, managing its legacy fighter fleets to eke out as much remaining service life as possible is still an issue for the air force. In April 2017 the USAF signed off on a service-life-extension programme for the F-16 *Fighting Falcon,* increasing its service life from 8,000 to 12,000 hours. This would, notionally at least, allow the aircraft to remain in the inventory until 2048. Planned production rates for the F-35 mean the air force will likely not receive the last of the 1,763 aircraft it wants to order until after 2040. At the same time, a decision was pending on which bidder would win the air force's T-X competition for an advanced jet fighter-trainer to replace the T-38 *Talon.*

Having awarded the B-21 bomber programme to Northrop Grumman in late 2015, the air force picked Lockheed Martin and Raytheon for the competitive design and development phase of a key complementary weapon: the Long-Range Standoff (LRSO) cruise missile. The two companies were each awarded US$900 million design-maturation and risk-reduction contracts lasting 54 months. The LRSO is intended to replace the AGM-86B nuclear-armed air-launched cruise missile, and is planned to enter the inventory in the late 2020s; but, as of the fourth quarter of 2017, there was scant information on the design options the two winning companies would pursue. The AGM-86B is a subsonic design, but it remained unclear whether a very-low-observable subsonic option for the LRSO was preferred, or whether a high-speed version was still being explored.

US Navy and US Coast Guard

A series of collisions and a grounding over a period of months in 2017 involving major US Navy surface combatants in the western Pacific fuelled concerns that the high tempo of operations was adversely affecting the navy's effectiveness and training. Seventeen US sailors died in two of the incidents, and two ballistic-missile-defence-equipped *Arleigh Burke*-class destroyers were severely damaged, taking them out of service for a considerable period of time. In response, the chief of naval operations launched a number of investigations, including into whether systemic failings were contributory factors. He also announced a brief global stand-down to take stock.

To underscore the sense of overstretch, there was a further gap in aircraft-carrier presence in the Gulf at the end of 2016 and into the early weeks of 2017. In congressional testimony in April, the Pacific Command commander noted that he receives only about half the number of submarines he requests.

Meanwhile, the debate over the future size of the navy has changed significantly. The Trump administration came to office on the back of a campaign for a 350-ship fleet, while in December 2016 the navy released its own new target of 355 ships, up from the previous target of 308 (and the current level of some 279). This new goal is clearly driven by the navy's desire to restore its ability to maintain its global presence in the face of increased competition from countries such as China and Russia. The plan included an additional aircraft carrier, 16 further large surface combatants and, perhaps most significantly, a further 18 attack submarines.

Yet doubts have been expressed as to whether the navy can fund, build or even crew such a force, and the FY2018 navy budget request made little provision for extra shipbuilding. The navy leadership, however, continued to press the case for restoring the readiness of the existing fleet and also for rapidly augmenting the force with additional construction over the next seven years, as well as possibly retaining older ships in service for longer.

At the same time, the growing Littoral Combat Ship (LCS) force was reorganised, with new crewing arrangements, to improve forward-deployment operations. LCS plans for 2018 include two simultaneous deployments in Singapore and, for the first time, one in Bahrain. However, the navy signalled how its thinking on its future small surface combatant had further evolved from the troubled LCS programme. In July it issued a request for information to industry for a more capable guided-missile frigate, dubbed FFG(X), with plans for a first production order in 2020, with the competition potentially open to foreign designs.

As a further sign of the navy's response to the challenge of a more contested maritime environment, it enshrined its concept of 'distributed lethality', to spread more offensive capabilities throughout the fleet, in a new surface-force strategy entitled 'Back to Sea Control'. But efforts to procure a new over-the-horizon anti-ship missile for its future LCS/frigate force appeared to have been hampered when most potential bidders withdrew from the competition.

Despite these challenges, the US Navy still demonstrated that it retains a unique ability to mount operations on a global scale. In April, two destroyers launched 59 *Tomahawk* cruise missiles at a Syrian air base following a suspected chemical attack by the regime against a rebel-held town. And, in May, after what appeared to be a pause, it resumed freedom-of-navigation operations in the South China Sea.

Furthermore, in August, the navy re-designated the Expeditionary Mobile Base support ship, USNS *Lewis B. Puller*, which was formerly operated by the Military Sealift Command. The vessel deployed to the US 5th Fleet's area of responsibility. Now the USS *Lewis B. Puller*, the vessel has replaced the USS *Ponce* in the Gulf, and the navy intends to operate the vessel flexibly, particularly in mine-countermeasures and special-operations missions. The USS *Ponce* decommissioned in 2017, but the USS *Lewis B. Puller* will not inherit its Laser Weapons System.

Figure 1 US *Virginia*-class nuclear-powered guided-missile submarine: design evolution

The design evolution of the *Virginia*-class submarine reflects the United States' requirement to provide an increasingly flexible strike capability, as well as the need to keep platforms in service for longer. Originally designed to replace the *Los Angeles* class, 14 have been commissioned with procurement budgeted for a further 12. The US requirement to sustain 48 attack submarines (and a recent aspiration to raise this to 66) forecasts additional production into the 2040s. This projected lifecycle requires platform evolution, with the ability to integrate emerging technologies and adapt to new operational requirements. Enabled by modern manufacturing techniques, each 'block' incorporates improvements in construction and maintenance cycles. This design evolution also reflects the need for a multi-mission platform capable beyond the traditional anti-submarine-warfare and anti-surface-warfare roles. This includes improved capacity for special-forces insertion and the future operation of unmanned underwater vehicles (UUVs) and unmanned aerial vehicles (UAVs). The design also reaffirms the ongoing importance of conventional land-attack capability. Dedicated vertical-launch-system (VLS) tubes have been included from the outset, enabling increased land-attack cruise-missile (LACM) capacity, without compromising torpedo-tube availability. The US Navy has led development of such VLS capabilities to enable land-attack from the sea. VLS now features in the latest Russian *Yasen* and possibly the Chinese Type-93A *Shang* II attack submarines, and is projected to feature in the South Korean KSS-III. The VLS design in later *Virginia* blocks provides greater payload flexibility and the capacity to respond to projected future requirements.

Filling the SSGN gap

In 2003–08, the US converted four *Ohio*-class ballistic-missile submarines into guided-missile (SSGN) submarines. Their *Trident* missiles were replaced with the VLS capacity for 154 conventional *Tomahawk* LACMs. However, all four are planned to decommission in 2026–28, resulting in the loss of approximately 60% of the US submarine fleet's VLS capacity. The *Virginia* class has been identified as a solution to this, as plans to insert a '*Virginia* Payload Module' (VPM) into the second Block-V would reduce this to only a 37% fall in capacity. The procurement of 20 vessels fitted with VPMs would in effect renew this capacity within the subsequent decade.

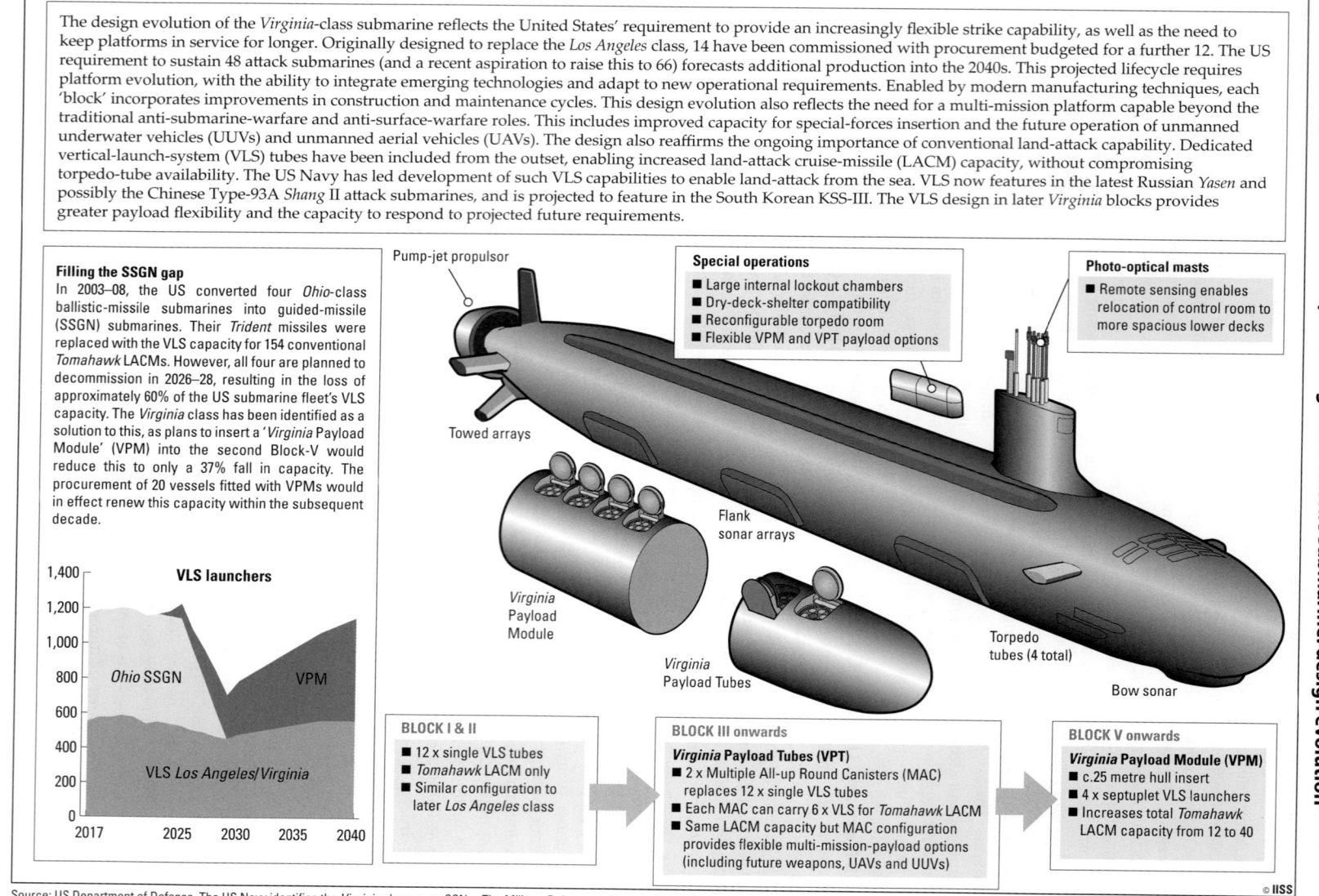

Photo-optical masts
- Remote sensing enables relocation of control room to more spacious lower decks

Special operations
- Large internal lockout chambers
- Dry-deck-shelter compatibility
- Reconfigurable torpedo room
- Flexible VPM and VPT payload options

BLOCK I & II
- 12 x single VLS tubes
- *Tomahawk* LACM only
- Similar configuration to later *Los Angeles* class

BLOCK III onwards
Virginia Payload Tubes (VPT)
- 2 x Multiple All-up Round Canisters (MAC) replaces 12 x single VLS tubes
- Each MAC can carry 6 x VLS for *Tomahawk* LACM
- Same LACM capacity but MAC configuration provides flexible multi-mission-payload options (including future weapons, UAVs and UUVs)

BLOCK V onwards
Virginia Payload Module (VPM)
- 4 x septuplet VLS launchers
- 0.25 metre hull insert
- Increases total *Tomahawk* LACM capacity from 12 to 40

Labels: Bow sonar; Torpedo tubes (4 total); Flank sonar arrays; *Virginia* Payload Tubes; *Virginia* Payload Module; Towed arrays; Pump-jet propulsor

VLS launchers (chart, 2017–2040): *Ohio* SSGN; VPM; VLS *Los Angeles*/*Virginia*; scale 0–1,400

Source: US Department of Defense. The US Navy identifies the *Virginia* class as an SSN – *The Military Balance* applies the SSGN classification due to the presence of dedicated launch tubes for guided missiles.

© IISS

Meanwhile, the US Coast Guard (USCG) faces a growing task list. It commissioned the sixth of its new National Security Cutters, USCGC *Munro*, in April, is seeking to recruit an extra 5,000 personnel over five years, and has also begun design work for three new heavy and three medium icebreakers; the hope is that the first icebreaker can be delivered in 2023. These vessels are needed to replace the one (elderly) heavy and one medium icebreaker currently in service, which represent a significant shortfall in capability. The USCG commandant said that the icebreaker programme could be expanded, and the ships even armed, in response to increased tensions. He also issued a new plea for US ratification of the UN Convention on the Law of the Sea to support US continental-shelf claims in the Arctic.

DEFENCE ECONOMICS

FY2018 Defence Budget Request

The president's Fiscal Year (FY) 2018 budget (PB2018) requested a total of US$677.1 billion for national defence, including US$603bn in base discretionary funding for national defence, US$9.7bn in mandatory spending and an additional US$64.6bn in discretionary supplemental funding for ongoing war-related spending in the Overseas Contingency Operations (OCO) accounts. If Congress were to appropriate funding at this requested level, estimated FY2018 national-defence outlays would total US$652.57bn. The divergence between this total and the total request is due to lags between the appropriation, obligation and actual outlay of funds.

The Department of Defence (DoD) would receive US$639bn, or 95.7% of the total discretionary funding requested in FY2018, while US$21.5bn would go to the Department of Energy for nuclear-weapons-related work and the remaining US$8.3bn would go to defence-related efforts at the Federal Bureau of Investigation and other agencies. (Discretionary spending is funded via annual appropriations acts, while mandatory funding is authorised by prior statutory authority and is thereby appropriated automatically.) The DoD's requested US$639bn in discretionary funding includes US$574.5bn in the base defence budget and US$64.6bn in OCO funding. The total FY2018 request includes US$166bn for the army, US$183bn for the air force (which by tradition includes the DoD's classified spending), US$180bn for the navy and US$110bn for defence-wide spending.

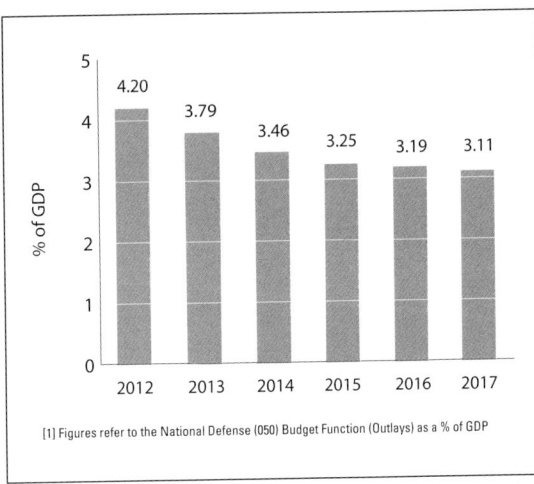

Figure 2 **US defence expenditure** as % of GDP[1]

[1] Figures refer to the National Defense (050) Budget Function (Outlays) as a % of GDP

Year	% of GDP
2012	4.20
2013	3.79
2014	3.46
2015	3.25
2016	3.19
2017	3.11

According to Secretary of Defense James Mattis, the first priority of the FY2018 budget is to 'restore the readiness of the current force', while the second is to increase 'capacity and lethality'. Consequently, the FY2018 defence budget includes large increases on the Obama administration's FY2017 request for operation and maintenance funding (US$21.3bn, or 8.5%), procurement (US$11.9bn, or 10.7%), and research, development, test and evaluation (RDT&E) (US$11.9bn, or 16.3%). However, Congress actually appropriated funding for the DoD at a higher level than the Obama administration's FY2017 request. Most notably, Congress funded an additional US$12bn for procurement, an increase of approximately 10% on the FY2017 request.

Indeed, compared to the actual FY2017 funding levels, the PB2018 request would increase funding levels more modestly, growing funding for military personnel by 5%, to US$146bn, for operation and maintenance by 6.5%, to US$271bn, and for RDT&E by 11.3%, to US$84.9bn. The FY2018 request for US$125bn for procurement is an increase of just US$819 million compared to the FY2017 congressional appropriation. Meanwhile, the FY2018 budget shifts additional funding into munitions, parts and spares, and modifications to current aircraft, when compared to the FY2018 plan in the FY2017 budget. The US$639bn in total discretionary funding (including both base and OCO funding) requested for the DoD for FY2018 is an increase of 7% on the total of US$597.2bn appropriated for FY2017.

Additional force-structure growth and procurement spending are expected in the FY2019 defence-budget request, following the planned

36 THE MILITARY BALANCE 2018

Table 2 **US National Defense Budget Function[1] and other selected budgets[2] 1997, 2007–18**

US$ in billions, current year dollars FY	National Defense Budget Function BA		Atomic Energy Defense Activities BA	Other Defense Activities BA	Total National Defense BA		Department of Homeland Security BA	Department of Veterans Affairs BA	Total Federal Government Outlays	Total Federal Budget Surplus/ Deficit
	BA	Outlay	BA	BA	BA	Outlay	BA	BA		
1997	257.9	258.3	11.3	1.1	270.4	270.5	13.2	39.9	1,601.1	-21.9
2007	603.0	528.5	17.2	5.7	625.8	551.3	39.7	79.5	2,728.7	-160.7
2008	674.7	594.6	16.6	4.9	696.2	616.1	50.6	88.4	2,982.5	-458.6
2009	667.5	636.7	23.0	7.1	697.6	661.0	46.0	96.9	3,517.7	-1,412.7
2010	695.6	666.7	18.2	7.3	721.2	693.5	45.4	124.3	3,457.1	-1,294.4
2011	691.5	678.1	18.5	7.0	717.0	705.6	41.6	122.8	3,603.1	-1,299.6
2012	655.4	650.9	18.3	7.7	681.4	677.9	45.9	124.0	3,536.9	-1,087.0
2013	585.2	607.8	17.5	7.4	610.2	633.4	61.9	136.0	3,454.6	-679.5
2014	595.7	577.9	18.4	8.2	622.3	603.5	44.1	165.7	3,506.1	-484.6
2015	570.9	562.5	19.0	8.5	598.4	589.7	45.3	160.5	3,688.4	-438.5
2016	595.7	565.4	20.1	8.3	624.1	593.4	46.0	163.3	3,852.6	-584.7
2017 est *	626.2	573.0	20.1	8.8	655.1	602.8	51.0	176.6	4,062.2	-602.5
2018 est	646.9	621.7	21.8	8.4	677.1	652.6	49.4	183.1	4,094.5	-440.2

Notes

* Includes March request for additional appropriations
FY = Fiscal Year (1 October–30 September)

[1] The National Defense Budget Function subsumes funding for the DoD, the Department of Energy Atomic Energy Defense Activities and some smaller support agencies (including Federal Emergency Management and Selective Service System). It does not include funding for International Security Assistance (under International Affairs), the Veterans Administration, the US Coast Guard (Department of Homeland Security), nor for the National Aeronautics and Space Administration (NASA). Funding for civil projects administered by the DoD is excluded from the figures cited here.

[2] Early in each calendar year, the US government presents its defence budget to Congress for the next fiscal year, which begins on 1 October. The government also presents its Future Years Defense Program (FYDP), which covers the next fiscal year plus the following five. Until approved by Congress, the budget is called the Budget Request; after approval, it becomes the Budget Authority (BA).

completion of the National Defense Strategy and Nuclear Posture Review in late 2017. Anticipating the FY2019 defence budget, the FY2018 budget functions partially as a one-year placeholder, as it lacks the FY2019–FY2022 budgetary years that comprise the Future Years Defense Program.

The FY2018 defence budget also includes US$64.6bn in OCO funds. In a point of continuity with the Obama administration, the funding requested for each military operation aligns very closely with the amounts requested in FY2017. The FY2018 budget requests US$45.9bn for *Operation Freedom's Sentinel* in Afghanistan to support a force level of 8,448 US troops, including US$4.9bn to train and equip Afghan security forces and US$1.3bn to support NATO-led coalition forces. The Obama administration requested a total of US$46.2bn for this operation in FY2017, including an additional US$3.4bn requested in November 2017 to retain 8,400 US troops in Afghanistan instead of the planned drawdown to 5,500. President Donald Trump's announcement in July that the US will increase its force level in Afghanistan will likely require a similar level of additional funding. The FY2018 budget also requests US$13bn for *Operation Inherent Resolve* in Iraq and Syria, including supporting 5,675 US troops in Iraq and US$1.3bn to train and equip Iraqi forces, as well as US$500m for vetted Syrian opposition forces. The European Reassurance Initiative would receive US$4.8bn, a US$1.4bn increase from the US$3.4bn requested in FY2017, which would be directed to an increased US forward presence and the pre-positioning of an army division's worth of equipment.

Trump campaigned on a promise to make the US armed forces 'so big, so powerful, so strong, that nobody – absolutely nobody – is gonna mess with us' and the administration has characterised the FY2018 defence-budget request as a 'historic' increase, citing the US$603bn requested in base discretionary national-defence funding as a US$52bn, or 9.4%, increase on the Obama administration's request for US$551bn in FY2017, and as a US$54bn, or 10%, increase above the US$549bn limit on national-defence spending for FY2018 set by the amended Budget Control Act of 2011.

However, the FY2018 request is a more modest US$18.5bn, or 3%, increase over the planned US$584.5bn in base discretionary national-defence spending in FY2018 that appeared in the FY2017

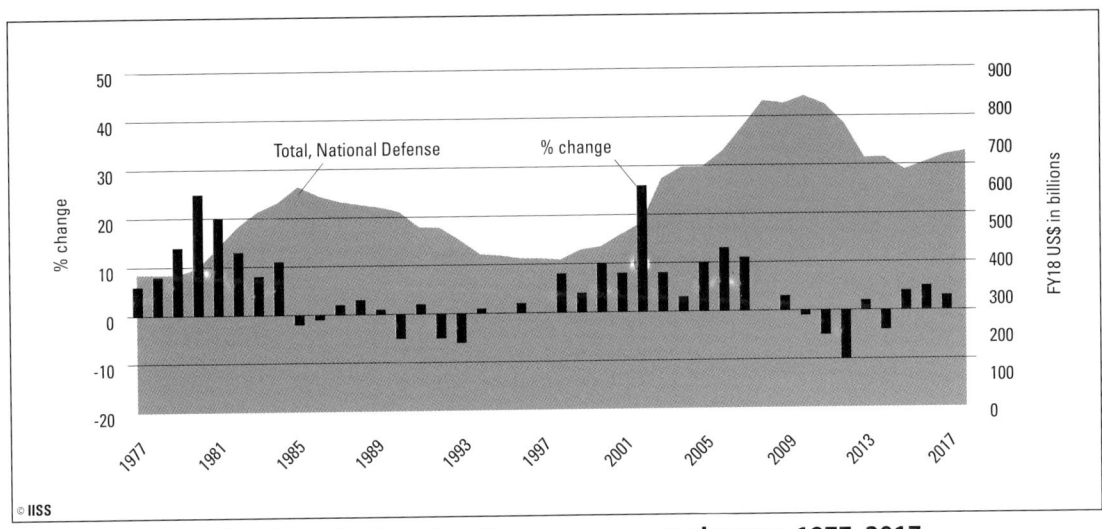

Figure 3 **US National Defense Budget Function: year-on-year changes, 1977–2017**

budget request for that year. Year-on-year increases in discretionary national-defence spending of 10% or more have occurred ten times since FY1978, predominantly during the FY1979–FY1985 Carter–Reagan Cold War build-up and the FY2001–FY2011 growth in national-defence spending relating to the wars in Afghanistan and Iraq.

The Trump administration's proposal for a total of US$667bn in discretionary national-defence spending has been criticised by legislators, including Congressman Mac Thornberry and Senator John McCain, Republican chairmen of the House and Senate armed services committees respectively, as inadequate for US national-security needs in a changing international security order. Congressional frustration has manifested itself in higher than requested troop levels and defence spending in versions of the FY2018 authorisations and appropriations bills. The Congress and Senate passed a National Defense Authorization Act in November 2017, authorising appropriations up to US$700bn. However, the BCA would need to be lifted for it to go through.

Meanwhile, the FY2018 State Department request for a total of US$5.1bn in Foreign Military Financing (FMF) maintains the prior year's request levels for Israel (US$3.1bn), Egypt (US$1.3bn) and Jordan (US$350m), but reduces funding for Pakistan (US$261m to US$100m). For other countries, the FY2018 FMF request includes an unallocated pool of US$200m in direct FMF assistance, a reduction of US$593m, and instead encourages countries to apply for FMF loans. This is a sharp break in FMF policy from the Obama administration, which in FY2017 requested a total of US$703m in FMF for individual countries and regions, in addition to the funding for Egypt, Israel, Jordan and Pakistan mentioned above.

Continued budget turmoil

As it has every year since FY2010, the DoD began FY2017 on 1 October (2016) under a series of continuing resolutions, extending FY2016 funding levels into FY2017 with a slight adjustment for inflation. The first continuing resolution, from 1 October to 9 December 2016, postponed a debate about national-security and domestic funding until after the congressional and presidential elections in November 2016. The second resolution, running from 9 December 2016 through to 28 April 2017, allowed the incoming Trump administration to influence FY2017 defence-funding levels. In March 2017, the Trump administration submitted a request for an additional US$30bn in FY2017, deemed a 'readiness supplemental'. This additional request included US$13.5bn in procurement funding, US$8.2bn in operations and maintenance, US$2bn for RDT&E and US$1bn for military personnel, and brought the total FY2017 DoD request to US$619bn, including US$589bn in base-budget funding and US$69.7bn in OCO funding. After a third short continuing resolution, Congress passed the FY2017 appropriations bill for the DoD on 5 May 2017, 216 days into the fiscal year, ending the longest stretch of budgetary uncertainty ever faced by the DoD. The final FY2017 appropriations level totalled US$597bn for the DoD, complied with the congressional budget-deal levels and included US$15.4bn of the requested US$30bn in additional appropriations to 'restore readiness'.

The differences of opinion between and among Republicans and Democrats in Congress over the appropriate balance between defence and non-defence spending, the level of OCO funding and proper military-force structure remain unresolved. Despite widespread hopes for the swift passage of a FY2018 defence-appropriations bill, and the explicit pleas of Mattis and Chairman of the Joint Chiefs of Staff General James Dunford, the federal government and DoD once again started the fiscal year under a continuing resolution, which continues the FY2017 funding levels through to 8 December 2017. Under this 'strict' continuing resolution, the DoD is prohibited from starting any new programmes or adjusting any production rates, resulting in the misalignment of billions of dollars between the FY2017 budget levels and the FY2018 request.

Despite a broad consensus among national-security policymakers for greater national defence spending, it remains limited through to FY2021 by the caps imposed on both national-defence and non-defence discretionary government spending by the Budget Control Act of 2011. Although Congress has amended the caps for each year by US$9bn–US$27bn in any one year, at the time of writing there was no deal to raise or eliminate them for FY2018 or beyond. Past deals have typically covered two fiscal years, and raised the caps equally for defence and non-defence spending, parity the Democrats have said they will insist upon for the FY2018 budget negotiations. The average amount of so-called 'sequester relief', US$18.8bn, is one-third of the US$54bn requested in the FY2018 budget. OCO funding is not subject to these spending caps, but resistance from Republican fiscal conservatives and Democrats seeking equivalent spending increases for non-defence programmes will limit the amount of defence funding that can be funnelled through OCO. Increasing the Budget Control Act caps requires either the agreement of eight Democrat senators, or the effective elimination of the legislative filibuster, one of the last sacred cows of Senate procedure. Appropriations above the cap levels without amending the caps themselves would trigger a sequester, whereby funding for all defence activities is automatically reduced by an even proportion in order to bring total spending to the cap level. Despite the uncertain prospects for the elimination of the Budget Control Act caps and the magnitude and potential duration of a defence build-up, US defence spending appears to be past the nadir that followed the drawdowns from the wars in Afghanistan and Iraq.

Balancing readiness, capacity and high-end capabilities

Readiness has been a consistent motif in debates over the US defence budget and force structure over the past few years. Many senior Pentagon and congressional officials have described a 'readiness crisis', while Mattis testified before the Senate Armed Services Committee that he was 'shocked' at the erosion of readiness since the FY2013 sequester. However, improving readiness has become somewhat of a catch-all term for remedying training and maintenance shortfalls and increasing troop end-strength and ship and aircraft numbers in order to alleviate the strain on the force, as well as to support current levels of operational demand, invest in high-end capabilities and modernise the force against the prospect of a near-peer adversary.

The March 2017 supplemental request and the FY2018 budget request focused on 'restoring readiness', adding funding for high-end army training and pairing army training with partnership exercises with allies abroad, greater capacity for ship- and aviation depot maintenance, adding to air-force pilot and maintenance-personnel numbers, and increasing funding for installation maintenance and repairs.

Growing the capacity of the armed forces has been a major focus of the congressional defence committees. Congress rejected the FY2017 plan to reduce the army to 450,000 active-duty soldiers, instead adding 16,000; increasing the Marine Corps by 3,000, to 185,000; the air force by 4,000, to 321,000; and the reserve forces by 9,800 to a total of 813,200. If implemented, the administration's FY2018 request would grow the air force's and navy's active-duty forces by an additional 4,000 service members each, while both the House and Senate would add additional soldiers for the army. Congress has been similarly proactive in adding procurement funding (US$12.2bn was added to the US$112.2bn FY2017 procurement request) in order to bolster the armed forces' near-term force structure, particularly for ships and aircraft, and upgrading the army's ground-combat vehicles. However, substantial increases to force structure require large, long-term investments. Increasing the size of the navy to 355 ships, as called for in the December 2016 Force Structure Assessment, will require substantial new funds. Estimates for 340- and 350-ship fleets range between US$23.6bn and US$26.6bn annually in shipbuilding funds, depending on the fleet composition, well above the annual cost of US$19.7bn in the FY2017 shipbuilding plan for a 308-ship fleet.

The FY2018 budget channels additional RDT&E investment towards high-end, innovative capabilities to meet the new challenges of great-power competition with China and Russia; continuing 'Third Offset' investments in high-speed-strike and directed-energy weapons; leap-ahead improvements in turbine engines; electronic warfare and improved capacity to counter anti-access/area-denial capabilities. The budget also requests an additional US$2.2bn for classified programmes, for a total of US$22.4bn, or 28% of all RDT&E funding, continuing a steady growth in classified RDT&E funding since FY2015. In addition, it adds funding to spur innovation, requesting US$345m and US$631m for transitioning to using new technologies and advanced innovation programmes respectively, and increases funding for the Strategic Capabilities Office from US$902m to US$1.2bn.

However, the bulk of RDT&E funding is allocated to programmes currently in development or to improvements to extant systems. The longer-term strategic and budgetary challenge will be to incorporate new capabilities into the force in sufficient quantities. For example, the air force has revised upwards its quantity estimate for the new low-observable bomber currently in development, the B-21 *Raider*, from 80–100 to at least 100. These anticipated investments in new high-end capabilities will add to the procurement 'bow wave' of existing systems being acquired, principally the F-35 *Lightning II*, the *Virginia*-class attack submarine, the *Arleigh Burke*-class guided-missile destroyer, the KC-46A *Pegasus* refuelling tanker, the F/A-18E/F *Hornet* combat aircraft and *Ford*-class aircraft carriers – the largest procurement programmes across the next five years.

CANADA

Canada released its defence-policy review in June 2017. This was immediately preceded by a major speech by Chrystia Freeland, the foreign-affairs minister, in which she signalled a somewhat more robust security posture, with a renewed emphasis on hard power. She also hinted at a slightly looser relationship with the United States, relying less on the US security umbrella. For Canada, 'doing our fair share is clearly necessary', she said, and 'Canadian diplomacy and development sometimes require the backing of hard power'. However, having this capacity, Freeland continued, 'requires substantial investment'.

In the North American context, this will amount to a limited adjustment, given the intimacy of the US–Canada defence relationship. Likewise, while the defence-policy review refocused priorities in some key areas, with a renewed emphasis on deterrence and NATO commitments, for example, there was also a strong emphasis on continuity, not least in re-committing to some long-standing procurements.

Under the defence-policy review, the government set benchmarks for the scale and type of military operations to which Canada could commit in the future. Beyond its direct national and NATO commitments, these include: two sustained deployments of 500–1,500 personnel, including one as lead nation; one time-limited (six to nine months) deployment of similar scale; two smaller sustained deployments of 100–500 personnel; two small time-limited deployments of similar scale; a disaster-assistance mission; and a non-combat evacuation operation.

While the scale of even the larger missions envisaged is relatively modest, the overall ambition for Canada's commitment to peace and stability missions appears considerable. For comparison, the previous review in 2008 spoke more vaguely of a commitment to lead and/or conduct a major international operation for an extended period, and to deploy forces in response to crises elsewhere in the world for shorter periods. At the time, Canada was maintaining some 2,500 personnel on a sustained basis in Afghanistan.

It is a measure of the difficulties and delays that have surrounded Canada's long-term procurement plans that several of these projects now carry the description 'interim', in order to cover capability gaps. Plans for an interim purchase of fighters to fill an air-force capability gap appeared to be thrown into disarray by a dispute between Boeing and Ottawa, after the US firm pursued a legal complaint against Canadian firm Bombardier. The Canadian government had seemed close to an agreement with Boeing to buy 18 F/A-18E/F *Super Hornet*s to supplement the air force's ageing CF-18 *Hornet*s. Lockheed Martin has officially offered the F-35 *Lightning II* as an alternative interim fighter. However,

Defence review

The new Liberal government came into office promising a defence-policy review to take account of the requirement to reassess Canadian defence and security in a post-Afghanistan environment. The review, entitled 'Strong. Secure. Engaged', was published on 7 June, somewhat later than originally planned. The last such review, entitled 'Canada First', was produced in 2008 by the previous Conservative administration.

Both the 2008 and 2017 reviews promised a stable, long-term programme to develop the Canadian armed forces. However, past governments have been criticised for shortfalls in funding that have blighted procurement programmes.

The underlying theme of the review was that the global security outlook has not only altered but deteriorated. The review called for a growth in regular-forces personnel to 71,500, and an increase in reserves by 1,500. It also called for growth in critical capability areas, including space, cyber, intelligence and targeting. In addition, it highlighted transnational threats from violent extremism, climate change and increased international interest in the Arctic, with a consequent requirement for all of the services to improve their ability to operate in the High North. The review also stated that Canada must balance traditional relationships with a need to engage with emerging partners, particularly in the Asia–Pacific region.

Many of the programme commitments have an air of continuity about them because they have been long-standing and subject to long delays and controversy. However, some have been significantly modified and new programmes added.

For the navy, the review firmed up the commitment to what it called a 'full complement' of 15 new Canadian Surface Combatants to replace the recently retired destroyers and current frigates on a one-for-one basis. It stated that these are 'fully funded'. There will also be two new Joint Support Ships and 'five to six' Arctic Offshore Patrol Ships. And there was a commitment to upgrade lightweight torpedoes for surface ships, helicopters and maritime-patrol aircraft.

The review identified a requirement for 88 advanced fighters for the air force, up from the 65 proposed by the previous government, to replace the current ageing CF-18 *Hornet*s, with the intention to procure a force of interim fighters. As well as modernising the CP-140 *Aurora* maritime-reconnaissance aircraft, a new generation of multi-mission aircraft would be acquired in the 2030s. The review also spoke of acquiring space capabilities to improve situational awareness and communications, including throughout Canada's Arctic region.

For the army, the plan is to acquire ground-based air-defence systems and replace a family of armoured combat-support vehicles. Special-operations forces will be increased by 605 personnel, while new airborne intelligence, surveillance and reconnaissance systems will also be acquired.

The review outlined a significant and ambitious programme, some of it meant to make up for time lost through previous delays, but also a rebalancing of focus in key areas. It is a demanding programme, not least in its pledge to improve performance in the procurement process.

the prospects for this and indeed the F-35's chances of fulfilling Canada's ultimate requirement for 88 new combat aircraft remain uncertain.

The C$670 million (US$516m) Project Resolve for an interim supply ship for the navy, based on a converted merchant-ship hull, MV *Asterix*, is due to see the vessel delivered by the end of 2017. The navy has been relying at various times on help from the Chilean and Spanish navies for under-way replenishment since the withdrawal of HMCS *Protecteur* and HMCS *Preserver*. The new purpose-built Joint Support Ships (formerly known as the *Queenston* class, but now renamed the *Protecteur* class and based on the German Navy's *Berlin* class) are scheduled for delivery in 2021 and 2022.

Meanwhile, the navy's surface fleet has been operating at reduced levels following the withdrawal of all the ageing *Iroquois*-class destroyers. Canada's 12 *Halifax*-class frigates started a modernisation and life-extension programme in 2010. The last of these vessels to enter the programme, HMCS *Toronto*, completed its refit in November 2016 and was due to return to operational service only in early 2018. While the defence-policy review made a firm commitment to 15 new Canadian Surface Combatants (the previous commitment had been 'up to 15'), a succession of slippages in the bidding deadline for the contract pushed back completion of the selection process from late 2017 into 2018. However, the plan is still for construction to begin 'in the early 2020s'.

A new focus of concern over future naval capability centres on the long-term plans for Canada's submarine force. Under the latest proposals, the intention is to continue to operate and, in the mid-2020s, to modernise the current four *Victoria*-class boats, to keep them effective until the mid-2030s. Some doubt the viability of this plan, given their age and chequered history. Nevertheless, the renewed strategic focus on the North Atlantic and particularly the Greenland–Iceland–United Kingdom gap (for which the then-*Upholder*-class boats were originally designed for the UK Royal Navy as very quiet, deep-water platforms) make them valuable assets for both Canada and NATO, despite concerns over their operational availability.

International commitments and engagements

Canada has been the recipient of some criticism, not least from Washington, over its defence-spending record, hence the emphasis on an increased commitment in the new review. Nonetheless, Canada makes a significant contribution to the Alliance as one of the four framework nations of NATO's Enhanced Forward Presence in the Baltic states. Canada leads the multinational battlegroup in Latvia, deploying approximately 450 army personnel, alongside contributions from Albania, Italy, Poland, Slovenia and Spain. In addition, Canada temporarily deployed an artillery battery of 100 personnel and four M777 howitzers to Latvia for exercises in 2017.

From August 2017, Canada also undertook a new rotational deployment as part of NATO's air-policing mission, with four CF-18s and 135 air-force personnel based in Romania for four months, while the navy contributes a frigate to one of NATO's standing maritime groups. The government also announced that it would extend its military-training and capacity-building mission in Ukraine, begun in 2014, until the end of March 2019.

The government also extended *Operation Impact*, Canada's contribution to the campaign against the Islamic State, also known as ISIS or ISIL, until March 2019. It changed significantly in character in February 2016 after the Liberal administration enacted its pledge to end Canadian airstrikes and pull out its force of CF-18s, and has become a support and training mission. That said, Canadian personnel – including special forces – have been engaged in firefights on the ground, which indicates a greater combat element than the official characterisation would suggest.

In addition, Canada has extended until the end of April 2021 its commitment to periodically provide forces to the coalition maritime-security mission in and around the Red Sea, the Gulf of Aden, the Gulf of Oman and the Indian Ocean. Under *Operation Artemis*, the Canadian commitment is for up to 375 personnel, a *Halifax*-class frigate once every two years and a CP-140 *Aurora* aircraft once per year.

At the 2017 IISS Shangri La Dialogue, Minister of National Defence Harjit Singh Sajjan also underscored the country's commitment to defence engagement in the Asia–Pacific. This included the twin deployment to the Indo-Asia–Pacific region of the frigates HMCS *Winnipeg* and HMCS *Ottawa* as *Operation Poseidon Cutlass 17*, which lasted nearly six months. Despite the challenges facing the navy in terms of sustained deployments, it also carried out a presence-and-engagement mission to West Africa involving two *Kingston*-class coastal-defence vessels – the first Canadian warship presence in the region for ten years.

Defence economics

Canada has faced criticism for appearing down the league table of NATO defence spenders, at just above 1% of GDP. The new government insists that it is committed to raising defence spending. Even so, the budget is still projected to reach only 1.4% of GDP by 2024–25, still significantly below the NATO minimum target of 2% (and that only because of an adjustment allowing the inclusion of defence spending from other departments, in consultation with NATO).

The new defence review stated that the Department of National Defence budget, excluding the Department of Veterans Affairs, would rise over the next ten years from C$17.1 billion (US$13.2bn) in 2016–17 to C$24bn (US$18.6bn) by 2026–27 on an accrual basis. In cash terms, the rise would be from C$18.9bn (US$14.5bn) to C$32.7bn (US$25.2bn), or an increase of 70%, according to the government, and some C$9.5bn (US$7.3bn) above the total budget increase planned by 2027–28, under pre-review proposals. However, cash spending is then expected to fall substantially as major projects are completed.

More significant perhaps than the overall budget forecast is the anticipated significant increase in capital or procurement spending as a percentage of the budget. This was put at 10.84% in 2016–17 and was set for a significant rise to 19.42% in 2017–18, and then to increase further to 32.17% in 2024–25. That level would significantly exceed the NATO target of 20% of defence spending being on major equipment.

If this materialises, it would represent a major change compared to previous procurement commitments, but whether the defence budget and industrial base is ready to absorb something like a trebling in the proportion of defence resources devoted to capital programmes in less than a decade is another matter. Significantly, the defence-policy review spoke of introducing reforms to streamline the procurement process, with the aim of reducing departmental approval times by 50%.

The main procurement questions continue to revolve around the centrepiece air-force and naval recapitalisation programmes. The current government rowed back on the previous administration's plans to buy 65 F-35As to replace the air force's existing CF-18s. Instead, it has pledged to hold an open competition for new fighters, a requirement now put at 88 aircraft, although Canada has remained part of the F-35 production consortium.

Meanwhile, the full implications that the trade dispute with Boeing may have on the planned interim purchase of 18 *Super Hornet*s appeared uncertain. Although the US State Department approved the potential sale in September, the deal was essentially stalled by the dispute. The Canadian government stated in November 2016 that the age of the existing fleet meant that it was unable to meet its North American Aerospace Defense Command commitment for mission-ready aircraft.

Meanwhile, in November 2016, the government announced that it had selected the Airbus C295W to fulfil its future fixed-wing search-and-rescue requirement under a C$2.4bn (US$1.8bn) contract.

The continuing deferrals of the bidding deadline for the navy's future Canadian Surface Combatant came against the backdrop of a new and significantly higher cost estimate for the programme. The budget was announced at C$26.2bn (US$20.2bn) in 2008. However, in June 2017, the parliamentary budget office estimated that it had risen, in 2008 dollars adjusted for inflation, to C$61.82bn (US$47.6bn), 2.4 times higher than the original target (and equivalent to C$40bn (US$30.8bn) in 2017 dollars), although it also acknowledged that its estimates included a 20% margin of error and depended on the final size and specification of the ships.

Among other naval programmes, the Quebec-based shipyard Chantier Davie, responsible for delivering the interim replenishment ship, has also submitted a proposal to meet Canada's future icebreaker requirement based on the conversion of two classes of commercial icebreaker.

Canada CAN

Canadian Dollar $		2016	2017	2018
GDP	C$	2.03tr	2.13tr	
	US$	1.53tr	1.64tr	
per capita	US$	42,224	44,773	
Growth	%	1.5	3	
Inflation	%	1.4	1.6	
Def exp [a]	C$	24.1bn	27.6bn	
	US$	18.2bn	21.2bn	
Def bdgt [b]	C$	21.4bn	22.1bn	
	US$	16.2bn	17.0bn	
US$1= C$		1.33	1.30	

[a] NATO definition
[b] Department of National Defence and Veterans Affairs

Population   35,623,680

Age	0–14	15–19	20–24	25–29	30–64	65 plus
Male	7.9%	2.8%	3.3%	3.4%	23.8%	8.3%
Female	7.5%	2.6%	3.1%	3.3%	23.5%	10.3%

Capabilities

The government has sought to emphasise its commitments to NATO and North American defence, and also its enhanced support and training role in the coalition against ISIS following Canada's withdrawal from combat air operations. A major defence-policy review published in June 2017 promised to increase regular and reserve forces. It also pledged to finally deliver on a range of delayed procurements aimed at making the services more suitable to future operations, with particular enhancements to cyber and intelligence capabilities. The review raised the target for a new-generation fighter to 88 aircraft, but a trade dispute with Boeing appeared to stall an interim buy of the F/A-18E/F *Super Hornet*. Spending cuts in recent years have particularly affected the procurement schedules of major programmes, sustainment, readiness and the maintenance of forces, but the navy moved to fill the gap in afloat-tanker support with the expected delivery of an interim auxiliary (a converted container ship) in 2018, pending the arrival of the new *Protecteur* class in 2021. Repeated delays in the procurement process for the new surface combatant, however, raised doubts about the schedule for that programme. Canada's leadership of a NATO battlegroup in Latvia, as part of NATO's Enhanced Forward Presence, to which it contributed 450 troops, underscored a continuing capability to deploy medium-sized formations. Canada is also sustaining a frigate deployment to NATO maritime forces in Europe. The deployment of two frigates to the Asia-Pacific region displayed an increased desire to maintain influence there. (See pp. 39–42.)

ACTIVE 63,000 (Army 34,800 Navy 8,300 Air Force 19,900) Paramilitary 4,500

RESERVE 30,000 (Army 23,450 Navy 4,600 Air 1,950)

ORGANISATIONS BY SERVICE

Space
EQUIPMENT BY TYPE
SATELLITES • SPACE SURVEILLANCE 1 *Sapphire*

Army 34,800
FORCES BY ROLE
MANOEUVRE
Mechanised
1 (1st) mech bde gp (1 armd regt, 2 mech inf bn, 1 lt inf bn, 1 arty regt, 1 cbt engr regt, 1 log bn)
2 (2nd & 5th) mech bde gp (1 armd recce regt, 2 mech inf bn, 1 lt inf bn, 1 arty regt, 1 cbt engr regt, 1 log bn)
COMBAT SUPPORT
1 engr regt
3 MP pl
AIR DEFENCE
1 SAM regt
EQUIPMENT BY TYPE
ARMOURED FIGHTING VEHICLES
MBT 82: 42 *Leopard* 2A4 (trg role); 20 *Leopard* 2A4M (being upgraded); 20 *Leopard* 2A6M (61 *Leopard* 1C2 in store)
RECCE ε120 LAV-25 *Coyote*
IFV 635: 226 LAV-III *Kodiak* (incl 33 RWS); 409 LAV 6.0;
APC 443
 APC (T) 268: 235 M113; 33 M577 (CP)
 APC (W) 175 LAV *Bison* (incl 10 EW, 32 amb, 32 repair, 64 recovery)
AUV 245: 7 *Cougar*; 238 TAPV
ENGINEERING & MAINTENANCE VEHICLES
AEV 8: 5 *Buffalo*; 3 *Leopard* 2 AEV
ARV 13: 2 BPz-3 *Büffel*; 11 *Leopard* 2 ARV
ANTI-TANK/ANTI-INFRASTRUCTURE
RCL 84mm 1,075 *Carl Gustav*
ARTILLERY 287
TOWED 163 **105mm** 126: 98 C3 (M101); 28 LG1 MkII; **155mm** 37 M777
MOR 124: **81mm** 100; **SP 81mm** 24 LAV *Bison*
UNMANNED AERIAL VEHICLES • ISR • Light *Skylark*
AIR DEFENCE • SAM • Point-defence *Starburst*

Reserve Organisations 23,450

Canadian Rangers 5,000 Reservists
Provide a limited military presence in Canada's northern, coastal and isolated areas. Sovereignty, public-safety and surveillance roles
FORCES BY ROLE
MANOEUVRE
Other
5 (patrol) ranger gp (187 patrols)

Army Reserves 18,450 Reservists
Most units have only coy-sized establishments
FORCES BY ROLE
COMMAND
10 bde gp HQ

MANOEUVRE
Reconnaissance
18 recce regt (sqn)
Light
51 inf regt (coy)
COMBAT SUPPORT
16 fd arty regt (bty)
3 indep fd arty bty
10 cbt engr regt (coy)
1 EW regt (sqn)
4 int coy
10 sigs regt (coy)
COMBAT SERVICE SUPPORT
10 log bn (coy)
3 MP coy

Royal Canadian Navy 8,300; 4,600 reserve (12,900 total)

EQUIPMENT BY TYPE
SUBMARINES • SSK 4:
4 *Victoria* (ex-UK *Upholder*) with 6 single 533mm TT with Mk48 *Sea Arrow* HWT (3 currently non-operational)
PRINCIPAL SURFACE COMBATANTS • FRIGATES • FFGHM 12:
12 *Halifax* with 2 quad lnchr with RGM-84 Block II *Harpoon* AShM, 2 octuple Mk48 VLS with RIM-7P *Sea Sparrow* SAM/RIM-162 ESSM SAM, 2 twin 324mm ASTT with Mk46 LWT, 1 *Phalanx* CIWS, 1 57mm gun (capacity 1 SH-3 (CH-124) *Sea King* ASW hel) (rolling modernisation programme until 2017)
MINE WARFARE • MINE COUNTERMEASURES • MCO 12 *Kingston*
LOGISTICS AND SUPPORT 10
AGOR 1 *Quest*
AX 9: AXL 8 *Orca*; AXS 1 *Oriole*

Reserves 4,600 reservists
24 units tasked with crewing 10 of the 12 MCOs, harbour defence & naval control of shipping

Royal Canadian Air Force (RCAF) 19,900
FORCES BY ROLE
FIGHTER/GROUND ATTACK
4 sqn with F/A-18A/B *Hornet* (CF-18AM/BM)
ANTI-SUBMARINE WARFARE
2 sqn with SH-3 *Sea King* (CH-124)
MARITIME PATROL
2 sqn with P-3 *Orion* (CP-140 *Aurora*)
SEARCH & RESCUE/TRANSPORT
4 sqn with AW101 *Merlin* (CH-149 *Cormorant*); C-130E/H/H-30/J-30 (CC-130) *Hercules*
1 sqn with DHC-5 (CC-115) *Buffalo*
TANKER/TRANSPORT
1 sqn with A310/A310 MRTT (CC-150/CC-150T)
1 sqn with KC-130H
TRANSPORT
1 sqn with C-17A (CC-177) *Globemaster*
1 sqn with CL-600 (CC-144B)
1 (utl) sqn with DHC-6 (CC-138) *Twin Otter*

TRAINING
1 sqn with F/A-18A/B *Hornet* (CF-18AM/BM)
1 sqn with P-3 *Orion* (CP-140 *Aurora*)
1 sqn with SH-3 *Sea King* (CH-124)
TRANSPORT HELICOPTER
5 sqn with Bell 412 (CH-146 *Griffon*)
3 (cbt spt) sqn with Bell 412 (CH-146 *Griffon*)
1 (Spec Ops) sqn with Bell 412 (CH-146 *Griffon* – OPCON Canadian Special Operations Command)
1 sqn with CH-47F (CH-147F) *Chinook*

EQUIPMENT BY TYPE
AIRCRAFT 95 combat capable
FGA 77: 59 F/A-18A (CF-18AM) *Hornet*; 18 F/A-18B (CF-18BM) *Hornet*
ASW 18 P-3 *Orion* (CP-140M *Aurora*)
TKR/TPT 7: 2 A310 MRTT (CC-150T); 5 KC-130H
TPT 59: **Heavy** 5 C-17A (CC-177) *Globemaster* III; **Medium** 35: 10 C-130E (CC-130) *Hercules*; 6 C-130H (CC-130) *Hercules*; 2 C-130H-30 (CC-130) *Hercules*; 17 C-130J-30 (CC-130) *Hercules*; **Light** 10: 6 DHC-5 (CC-115) *Buffalo*; 4 DHC-6 (CC-138) *Twin Otter*; **PAX** 9: 3 A310 (CC-150 *Polaris*); 6 CL-600 (CC-144B/C)
TRG 4 DHC-8 (CT-142)
HELICOPTERS
ASW 37: 26 SH-3 (CH-124) *Sea King*; 11 CH-148 *Cyclone*
MRH 68 Bell 412 (CH-146 *Griffon*)
TPT 29: **Heavy** 15 CH-47F (CH-147F) *Chinook*; **Medium** 14 AW101 *Merlin* (CH-149 *Cormorant*)
RADARS 53
AD RADAR • NORTH WARNING SYSTEM 47: 11 AN/FPS-117 (range 200nm); 36 AN/FPS-124 (range 80nm)
STRATEGIC 6: 4 Coastal; 2 Transportable
AIR-LAUNCHED MISSILES
ASM AGM-65 *Maverick*
AAM • IR AIM-9L *Sidewinder*; SARH AIM-7M *Sparrow*
ARH AIM-120C AMRAAM
BOMBS
Laser-guided: GBU-10/GBU-12/GBU-16 *Paveway* II; GBU-24 *Paveway* III

NATO Flight Training Canada
EQUIPMENT BY TYPE
AIRCRAFT
TRG 45: 26 T-6A *Texan* II (CT-156 *Harvard* II); 19 *Hawk* 115 (CT-155) (advanced wpns/tactics trg)

Contracted Flying Services – Southport
EQUIPMENT BY TYPE
AIRCRAFT
TPT • **Light** 7 Beech C90B *King Air*
TRG 11 G-120A
HELICOPTERS
MRH 9 Bell 412 (CH-146)
TPT • **Light** 7 Bell 206 *Jet Ranger* (CH-139)

Canadian Special Operations Forces Command 1,500
FORCES BY ROLE
SPECIAL FORCES
1 SF regt (Canadian Special Operations Regiment)
1 SF unit (JTF 2)

COMBAT SERVICE SUPPORT
1 CBRN unit (Canadian Joint Incident Response Unit – CJIRU)
TRANSPORT HELICOPTER
1 (spec ops) sqn, with Bell 412 (CH-146 *Griffon* – from the RCAF)
EQUIPMENT BY TYPE
NBC VEHICLES 4 LAV *Bison* NBC
HELICOPTERS • MRH 10 Bell 412 (CH-146 *Griffon*)

Canadian Forces Joint Operational Support Group
FORCES BY ROLE
COMBAT SUPPORT
1 engr spt coy
1 (close protection) MP coy
1 (joint) sigs regt
COMBAT SERVICE SUPPORT
1 (spt) log unit
1 (movement) log unit

Paramilitary 4,500

Canadian Coast Guard 4,500
Incl Department of Fisheries and Oceans; all platforms are designated as non-combatant
EQUIPMENT BY TYPE
PATROL AND COASTAL COMBATANTS 67
  PSOH 1 *Leonard J Cowley*
  PSO 1 *Sir Wilfred Grenfell* (with hel landing platform)
  PCO 13: 2 *Cape Roger*; 1 *Gordon Reid*; 9 *Hero*; 1 *Tanu*
  PCC 1 *Harp*
  PB 51: 1 *Post*; 1 *Quebecois*; 1 *Vakta*; 10 Type-300A; 36 Type-300B; 1 *S. Dudka*; 1 *Simmonds* (on loan from RCMP)
AMPHIBIOUS • LANDING CRAFT • UCAC 4 Type-400
LOGISTICS AND SUPPORT 43
  ABU 7
  AG 4
  AGB 15
  AGOR 9 (coastal and offshore fishery vessels)
  AGOS 8
HELICOPTERS • TPT 37: **Medium** 1 S-61; **Light** 36: 3 Bell 206L *Long Ranger*; 4 Bell 212; 15 Bell 429; 14 Bo-105

Royal Canadian Mounted Police
In addition to the below, the RCMP also operates more than 370 small boats under 10 tonnes
EQUIPMENT BY TYPE
PATROL AND COASTAL COMBATANTS • PB 3: 1 *Inkster*; 2 *Nadon*

Cyber
In June 2017, Canada's defence-policy review said that Canada 'will develop the capability to conduct active cyber operations focused on external threats to Canada in the context of government-authorized military missions'. This was because a 'purely defensive' cyber posture was 'no longer sufficient'. In November 2017, the first transferees were stood up in the new 'cyber operator' role; civilian recruitment will start in 2018 and reservist recruitment in 2019. Canada published a cyber-security strategy in October 2010 and an action plan on implementation in 2013. The Canadian Forces Network Operation Centre is the 'national operational cyber defence unit' permanently assigned to support Canadian forces' operations. The armed forces' Information Management Group (IMG) is responsible for electronic warfare and network defence. The Canadian Force Information Operations Group, under the IMG, commands the Canadian Forces Information Operations Group Headquarters; the Canadian Forces Electronic Warfare Centre; the Canadian Forces Network Operation Centre, which is the 'national operational cyber defence unit' permanently assigned to support Canadian Forces operations; and other units.

DEPLOYMENT

ALBANIA
OSCE • Albania 1

BOSNIA-HERZEGOVINA
OSCE • Bosnia and Herzegovina 3

CARIBBEAN
Operation Caribbe 1 MCO

CYPRUS
UN • UNFICYP (*Operation Snowgoose*) 1

DEMOCRATIC REPUBLIC OF THE CONGO
UN • MONUSCO (*Operation Crocodile*) 8

EGYPT
MFO (*Operation Calumet*) 70; 1 MP team

IRAQ
Operation Inherent Resolve (*Impact*) 280; 1 SF trg gp; 1 med unit; 1 hel flt with 4 Bell 412 (CH-146 *Griffon*) hel

KUWAIT
Operation Inherent Resolve (*Impact*) 1 P-3 *Orion* (CP-140M); 1 A310 MRTT (C-150T); 1 C-130J-30 *Hercules* (CC-130J)

LATVIA
NATO • Enhanced Forward Presence (*Operation Reassurance*) 450; 1 mech inf bn HQ; 1 mech inf coy(+)

MEDITERRANEAN SEA
NATO • SNMG 1: 1 FFGHM

MIDDLE EAST
UN • UNTSO (*Operation Jade*) 4 obs

PACIFIC OCEAN
Operation Caribbe 1 MCO

ROMANIA
NATO • Air Policing 135; 4 F/A-18A *Hornet* (CF-18)

SERBIA
NATO • KFOR • *Joint Enterprise* (Operation Kobold) 6
OSCE • Kosovo 5

SOUTH SUDAN
UN • UNMISS (*Operation Soprano*) 5; 5 obs

UKRAINE
Operation Unifier 200
OSCE • Ukraine 22

UNITED STATES
Operation Renaissance 1 C-17A *Globemaster* III (C-177A)

FOREIGN FORCES

United Kingdom 370; 1 trg unit; 1 hel flt with SA341 *Gazelle*
United States 150

United States US

United States Dollar $		2016	2017	2018
GDP	US$	18.6tr	19.4tr	
per capita	US$	57,607	59,495	
Growth	%	1.5	2.2	
Inflation	%	1.3	2.1	
Def exp [a]	US$	664bn	683bn	
Def bdgt [b]	US$	593bn	603bn	653bn

[a] NATO definition

[b] National Defense Budget Function (50) Outlays. Includes DoD funding, as well as funds for nuclear-weapons-related activities undertaken by the Department of Energy. Excludes some military retirement and healthcare costs

Population 326,625,791

Age	0–14	15–19	20–24	25–29	30–64	65 plus
Male	9.5%	3.3%	3.5%	3.6%	22.2%	6.9%
Female	9.1%	3.2%	3.3%	3.5%	22.8%	8.7%

Capabilities

The US remains the world's most capable military power. Its forces are well trained and uniquely designed for power projection and intervention on a global scale across the full spectrum of operations. However, the arrival of a new administration has led to a recalibration of key strategic directions. The Pentagon has been working on a new national-defence strategy that is likely to address the US global role in an era of diminishing Western technological advantage. A new Nuclear Posture Review seems likely to retain the triad, but could adjust aspects of the very ambitious and costly nuclear-modernisation programme. The previous administration's plans for a 'rebalance' to the Asia-Pacific have continued, against the backdrop of increased tensions over North Korea. US forces have shown their power-projection capabilities on a number of occasions. A ballistic-missile-defence review was also under way. However, the Pentagon remains concerned with continuing global instability in the form of transnational, hybrid and regional insurgencies; China's military modernisation; increasing Russian assertiveness; and tackling ISIS in Iraq and Syria. In August, the US increased its commitment of combat forces in Afghanistan as part of a renewed strategy. Congress backed a US$700bn National Defense Authorisation Act, but funding for this remained uncertain. Readiness remains a major concern, with senior Pentagon officials warning of continuing significant shortfalls in terms of being ready to engage in high-intensity combat against a peer competitor. The fatal collisions suffered by the US Navy in the western Pacific underscored those concerns. Readiness, retention and equipment recapitalisation are also priorities for the army. As of the first half of 2017, senior military officials were concerned that against a peer or near-peer competitor, the army could soon risk being 'outgunned, outranged and outdated' unless key modernisation programmes are adequately funded. President Trump has also initiated a defence-industrial-base study to identify key vulnerabilities. At the same time, while the administration's first defence-budget request continued the focus on innovation to sustain technological advantage – a theme of the previous government – there remained less clarity on its view towards the 'Third Offset'. The US continues active development of its defensive and offensive cyber capabilities. (See pp. 27–39.)

ACTIVE 1,348,400 (Army 476,250 Navy 323,950 Air Force 322,800 US Marine Corps 184,400 US Coast Guard 41,000)

RESERVE 857,950 (Army 537,900 Navy 100,550 Air Force 174,450 Marine Corps Reserve 38,700 US Coast Guard 6,350)

ORGANISATIONS BY SERVICE

US Strategic Command
HQ at Offutt AFB (NE). Five missions: US nuclear deterrent; missile defence; global strike; info ops; ISR

US Navy
EQUIPMENT BY TYPE
SUBMARINES • STRATEGIC • SSBN 14 *Ohio* SSBN with up to 24 UGM-133A *Trident* D-5/D-5LE nuclear SLBM, 4 single 533mm TT with Mk48 *Sea Arrow* HWT

US Air Force • Global Strike Command
FORCES BY ROLE
MISSILE
  9 sqn with LGM-30G *Minuteman* III
BOMBER
  6 sqn (incl 1 AFRC) with B-52H *Stratofortress* (+1 AFRC sqn personnel only)
  2 sqn with B-2A *Spirit* (+1 ANG sqn personnel only)
EQUIPMENT BY TYPE
SURFACE-TO-SURFACE MISSILE LAUNCHERS
  ICBM • **Nuclear** 400 LGM-30G *Minuteman* III (1 Mk12A or Mk21 re-entry veh per missile)
AIRCRAFT
  BBR 90: 20 B-2A *Spirit*; 70 B-52H *Stratofortress*
AIR-LAUNCHED MISSILES
  ALCM • **Nuclear** AGM-86B

Strategic Defenses – Early Warning

North American Aerospace Defense Command (NORAD) – a combined US–CAN org

EQUIPMENT BY TYPE
RADAR
  NORTH WARNING SYSTEM 50: 14 AN/FPS-117 (range 200nm); 36 AN/FPS-124 (range 80nm)
  SOLID STATE PHASED ARRAY RADAR SYSTEM (SSPARS) 5: 2 AN/FPS-123 Early Warning Radar located at Cape Cod AFS (MA) and Clear AFS (AK); 3 AN/FPS-132 Upgraded Early Warning Radar located at Beale AFB (CA), Thule (GL) and Fylingdales Moor (UK)
  SPACETRACK SYSTEM 10: 1 AN/FPS-85 Spacetrack Radar at Eglin AFB (FL); 6 contributing radars at Cavalier AFS (ND), Clear (AK), Thule (GL), Fylingdales Moor (UK), Beale AFB (CA) and Cape Cod (MA); 3 Spacetrack Optical Trackers located at Socorro (NM), Maui (HI), Diego Garcia (BIOT)
  PERIMETER ACQUISITION RADAR ATTACK CHARACTERISATION SYSTEM (PARCS) 1 AN/FPQ-16 at Cavalier AFS (ND)
  DETECTION AND TRACKING RADARS 5 located at Kwajalein Atoll, Ascension Island, Australia, Kaena Point (HI), MIT Lincoln Laboratory (MA)
  GROUND BASED ELECTRO OPTICAL DEEP SPACE SURVEILLANCE SYSTEM (GEODSS) Socorro (NM), Maui (HI), Diego Garcia (BIOT)
STRATEGIC DEFENCES – MISSILE DEFENCES
  SEA-BASED: *Aegis* engagement cruisers and destroyers
  LAND-BASED: 40 ground-based interceptors at Fort Greely (AK); 4 ground-based interceptors at Vandenburg AFB (CA)

Space

EQUIPMENT BY TYPE
SATELLITES 134
  COMMUNICATIONS 42: 3 AEHF; 6 DSCS-III; 2 *Milstar*-I; 3 *Milstar*-II; 5 MUOS; 1 PAN-1 (P360); 5 SDS-III; 2 SDS-IV; 6 UFO; 9 WGS SV2
  NAVIGATION/POSITIONING/TIMING 31: 12 NAVSTAR Block IIF; 19 NAVSTAR Block IIR/IIRM
  METEOROLOGY/OCEANOGRAPHY 6 DMSP-5
  ISR 15: 4 FIA *Radar*; 5 *Evolved Enhanced/Improved Crystal* (visible and infrared imagery); 2 *Lacrosse* (*Onyx* radar imaging satellite); 1 NRO L-76; 1 ORS-1; 1 *TacSat*-4; 1 *TacSat*-6
  ELINT/SIGINT 27: 2 *Mentor* (advanced *Orion*); 3 Advanced *Mentor*; 4 *Mercury*; 1 NRO L-67; 1 *Trumpet*; 4 Improved *Trumpet*; 12 SBWASS (Space Based Wide Area Surveillance System; Naval Ocean Surveillance System)
  SPACE SURVEILLANCE 6: 4 GSSAP; 1 SBSS (Space Based Surveillance System); 1 ORS-5
  EARLY WARNING 7: 4 DSP; 3 SBIRS *Geo*-1

US Army 476,250

FORCES BY ROLE
Sqn are generally bn sized and tp are generally coy sized
COMMAND
  3 (I, III & XVIII AB) corps HQ
  1 (2nd) inf div HQ

SPECIAL FORCES
(see USSOCOM)
MANOEUVRE
  Armoured
    1 (1st) armd div (2 (2nd & 3rd ABCT) armd bde (1 armd recce sqn, 2 armd bn, 1 armd inf bn, 1 SP arty bn, 1 cbt engr bn, 1 CSS bn); 1 (1st SBCT) mech bde (1 armd recce sqn, 3 mech inf bn, 1 arty bn, 1 cbt engr bn, 1 CSS bn); 1 MRL bde HQ; 1 log bde; 1 (hy cbt avn) hel bde)
    1 (1st) cav div (3 (1st–3rd ABCT) armd bde (1 armd recce sqn, 2 armd bn, 1 armd inf bn, 1 SP arty bn, 1 cbt engr bn, 1 CSS bn); 1 MRL bde (1 MRL bn); 1 log bde; 1 (hy cbt avn) hel bde)
    1 (1st) inf div (2 (1st & 2nd ABCT) armd bde (1 armd recce sqn, 2 armd bn, 1 armd inf bn, 1 SP arty bn, 1 cbt engr bn, 1 CSS bn); 1 log bde; 1 (cbt avn) hel bde)
    1 (3rd) inf div (2 (1st & 2nd ABCT) armd bde (1 armd recce sqn, 2 armd bn, 1 armd inf bn, 1 SP arty bn, 1 cbt engr bn, 1 CSS bn); 1 lt inf bn; 1 MRL bde HQ; 1 log bde; 1 (cbt avn) hel bde)
  Mechanised
    1 (4th) inf div (1 (3rd ABCT) armd bde (1 armd recce sqn, 2 armd bn, 1 armd inf bn, 1 SP arty bn, 1 cbt engr bn, 1 CSS bn); 1 (1st SBCT) mech bde (1 armd recce sqn, 3 mech inf bn, 1 arty bn, 1 cbt engr bn, 1 CSS bn); 1 (2nd IBCT) lt inf bde (1 recce sqn, 3 inf bn, 1 arty bn, 1 cbt engr bn, 1 CSS bn); 1 MRL bde HQ; 1 log bde; 1 (hy cbt avn) hel bde)
    1 (7th) inf div (2 (1st & 2nd SBCT, 2nd ID) mech bde (1 armd recce sqn, 3 mech inf bn, 1 arty bn, 1 cbt engr bn, 1 CSS bn))
    1 (1st SBCT, 25th ID) mech bde (1 armd recce sqn, 3 mech inf bn, 1 arty bn, 1 cbt engr bn, 1 CSS bn)
    2 (2nd & 3rd CR) mech bde (1 armd recce sqn, 3 mech sqn, 1 arty sqn, 1 cbt engr sqn, 1 CSS sqn)
  Light
    1 (10th Mtn) inf div (3 (1st–3rd IBCT) lt inf bde (1 recce sqn, 3 inf bn, 1 arty bn, 1 cbt engr bn, 1 CSS bn); 1 log bde; 1 (cbt avn) hel bde)
    1 (25th) inf div (2 (2 & 3rd IBCT) inf bde (1 recce sqn, 2 inf bn, 1 arty bn, 1 cbt engr bn, 1 CSS bn); 1 log bde; 1 (cbt avn) hel bde)
    1 (Sy Force Assist) inf bde(-)
  Air Manoeuvre
    1 (82nd) AB div (3 (1st–3rd AB BCT) AB bde (1 recce bn, 3 para bn, 1 arty bn, 1 cbt engr bn, 1 CSS bn); 1 (cbt avn) hel bde; 1 log bde)
    1 (101st) air aslt div (3 (1st–3rd AB BCT) AB bde (1 recce bn, 3 para bn, 1 arty bn, 1 cbt engr bn, 1 CSS bn); 1 (cbt avn) hel bde; 1 log bde)
    1 (173rd AB BCT) AB bde (1 recce bn, 2 para bn, 1 arty bn, 1 cbt engr bn, 1 CSS bn)
    1 (4th AB BCT, 25th ID) AB bde (1 recce bn, 2 para bn, 1 arty bn, 1 cbt engr bn, 1 CSS bn)
  Other
    1 (11th ACR) trg armd cav regt (OPFOR) (2 armd cav sqn, 1 CSS bn)
COMBAT SUPPORT
  3 MRL bde (2 MRL bn)
  1 MRL bde (4 MRL bn)

4 engr bde
2 EOD gp (2 EOD bn)
10 int bde
2 int gp
4 MP bde
1 NBC bde
3 (strat) sigs bde
4 (tac) sigs bde
COMBAT SERVICE SUPPORT
2 log bde
3 med bde
1 tpt bde
HELICOPTER
2 (cbt avn) hel bde
1 (cbt avn) hel bde HQ
AIR DEFENCE
5 SAM bde

Reserve Organisations

Army National Guard 343,600 reservists
Normally dual-funded by DoD and states. Civil-emergency responses can be mobilised by state governors. Federal government can mobilise ARNG for major domestic emergencies and for overseas operations
FORCES BY ROLE
COMMAND
8 div HQ
SPECIAL FORCES
(see USSOCOM)
MANOEUVRE
Reconnaissance
1 armd recce sqn
Armoured
3 (ABCT) armd bde (1 armd recce sqn, 2 armd bn, 1 armd inf bn, 1 SP arty bn, 1 cbt engr bn, 1 CSS bn)
1 (ABCT) armd bde (1 armd recce sqn, 2 armd bn, 1 SP arty bn, 1 cbt engr bn, 1 CSS bn)
1 (ABCT) armd bde (1 armd recce sqn, 2 armd bn, 1 SP arty bn, 1 cbt spt bn, 1 CSS bn)
1 armd bn
Mechanised
2 (SBCT) mech bde (1 armd recce sqn, 3 mech inf bn, 1 arty bn, 1 cbt engr bn, 1 CSS bn)
Light
7 (IBCT) lt inf bde (1 recce sqn, 3 inf bn, 1 arty bn, 1 cbt engr bn, 1 CSS bn)
1 (IBCT) lt inf bde (2 recce sqn, 2 inf bn, 1 arty bn, 1 cbt spt bn, 1 CSS bn)
8 (IBCT) lt inf bde (1 recce sqn, 2 inf bn, 1 arty bn, 1 cbt engr bn, 1 CSS bn)
4 (IBCT) lt inf bde (1 recce sqn, 2 inf bn, 1 arty bn, 1 cbt spt bn, 1 CSS bn)
8 lt inf bn
Air Manoeuvre
1 AB bn
COMBAT SUPPORT
8 arty bde
1 SP arty bn
8 engr bde
1 EOD regt
3 int bde
3 MP bde
1 NBC bde
2 (tac) sigs bde
18 (Mnv Enh) cbt spt bde
COMBAT SERVICE SUPPORT
10 log bde
17 (regional) log spt gp
HELICOPTER
8 (cbt avn) hel bde
5 (theatre avn) hel bde
AIR DEFENCE
3 SAM bde

Army Reserve 194,300 reservists
Reserve under full command of US Army. Does not have state-emergency liability of Army National Guard
FORCES BY ROLE
SPECIAL FORCES
(see USSOCOM)
COMBAT SUPPORT
4 engr bde
4 MP bde
2 NBC bde
2 sigs bde
3 (Mnv Enh) cbt spt bde
COMBAT SERVICE SUPPORT
9 log bde
11 med bde
HELICOPTER
1 (theatre avn) hel bde

Army Stand-by Reserve 700 reservists
Trained individuals for mobilisation

EQUIPMENT BY TYPE
ARMOURED FIGHTING VEHICLES
MBT 2,384: 775 M1A1 SA *Abrams*; 1,609 M1A2 SEPv2 *Abrams* (ε3,500 more M1A1/A2 *Abrams* in store)
ASLT 134 M1128 *Stryker* MGS
RECCE 1,745: ε1,200 M3A2/A3 *Bradley*; 545 M1127 *Stryker* RV (ε800 more M3 *Bradley* in store)
IFV 2,834: ε2,500 M2A2/A3 *Bradley*; 334 M7A3/SA BFIST (OP) (ε2,000 more M2 *Bradley* in store)
APC 10,746
  APC (T) ε5,000 M113A2/A3 (ε8,000 more in store)
  APC (W) 2,812: 1,972 M1126 *Stryker* ICV; 348 M1130 *Stryker* CV (CP); 188 M1131 *Stryker* FSV (OP); 304 M1133 *Stryker* MEV (Amb)
  PPV 2,934: 2,633 *MaxxPro Dash*; 301 *MaxxPro* LWB (Amb)
  AUV 9,016: 2,900 M1117 ASV; 465 M1200 *Armored Knight* (OP); 5,651 M-ATV
ENGINEERING & MAINTENANCE VEHICLES
AEV 531: 113 M1 ABV; 250 M9 ACE; 168 M1132 *Stryker* ESV
ARV 1,110+: 360 M88A1; 750 M88A2 (ε1,000 more M88A1 in store); some M578
VLB 60: 20 REBS; 40 *Wolverine* HAB
MW 3+: *Aardvark* JSFU Mk4; 3+ *Hydrema* 910 MCV-2; M58/M59 MICLIC; M139; *Rhino*
NBC VEHICLES 234 M1135 *Stryker* NBCRV

ANTI-TANK/ANTI-INFRASTRUCTURE • MSL
SP 1,133: 133 M1134 *Stryker* ATGM; ε1,000 M1167 HMMWV TOW
MANPATS FGM-148 *Javelin*
ARTILLERY 5,393
SP **155mm** 947: 900 M109A6; 47 M109A7 (ε500 more M109A6 in store)
TOWED 1,339: **105mm** 821 M119A2/3; **155mm** 518 M777A2
MRL **227mm** 600: 375 M142 HIMARS; 225 M270A1 MLRS
MOR 2,507: **81mm** 990 M252; **120mm** 1,076 M120/M1064A3; **SP 120mm** 441 M1129 *Stryker* MC
SURFACE-TO-SURFACE MISSILE LAUNCHERS
SRBM • **Conventional** MGM-140A/B ATACMS; MGM-168 ATACMS (All launched from M270A1 MLRS or M142 HIMARS MRLs)
RADAR • **LAND** 209+: 98 AN/TPQ-36 *Firefinder* (arty); 56 AN/TPQ-37 *Firefinder* (arty); 55 AN/TPQ-53 (arty); AN/MLQ-40 *Prophet*; AN/MLQ-44 *Prophet Enhanced*
AMPHIBIOUS 116
PRINCIPAL AMPHIBIOUS SHIPS 8
LSL 8 *Frank Besson* (capacity 15 *Abrams* MBT)
LANDING CRAFT 70
LCU 34 LCU-2000
LCM 36 LCM 8 (capacity either 1 MBT or 200 troops)
AIRCRAFT
ISR 19: 14 RC-12X *Guardrail*; 5 RC-12 *Guardrail* (trg)
ELINT 8: 5 EO-5C ARL-M (COMINT/ELINT); 2 EO-5B ARL-C (COMINT); 1 TO-5C (trg)
TPT 156: **Light** 152: 113 Beech A200 *King Air* (C-12 *Huron*); 28 Cessna 560 *Citation* (UC-35A/B); 11 SA-227 *Metro* (C-26B/E); **PAX** 4: 1 Gulfstream IV (C-20F); 2 Gulfstream V (C-37A); 1 Gulfstream G550 (C-37B)
TRG 4 T-6D *Texan* II
HELICOPTERS
ATK 603: 400 AH-64D *Apache*; 203 AH-64E *Apache*
SAR 244: 19 HH-60L *Black Hawk*; 225 HH-60M *Black Hawk* (medevac)
TPT 2,807: **Heavy** 450: 60 CH-47D *Chinook*; 390 CH-47F *Chinook*; **Medium** 1,896: 300 UH-60A *Black Hawk*; 975 UH-60L *Black Hawk*; 621 UH-60M *Black Hawk*; **Light** 461: 396 UH-72A *Lakota*; 65 UH-1H/V *Iroquois*
TRG 86 TH-67 *Creek*
UNMANNED AERIAL VEHICLES 361
CISR • **Heavy** 125 MQ-1C *Gray Eagle*
ISR • **Medium** 236 RQ-7B *Shadow*
AIR DEFENCE • SAM 1,183+
Long-range 480 MIM-104D/E/F *Patriot* PAC-2 GEM/PAC-2 GEM-T/PAC-3/PAC-3 MSE
Short-range NASAMS
Point-defence 703+: FIM-92 *Stinger*; 703 M1097 *Avenger*
MISSILE DEFENCE • **Long-range** 42 THAAD
AIR-LAUNCHED MISSILES
ASM AGM-114 *Hellfire*

US Navy 323,950

Comprises 2 Fleet Areas, Atlantic and Pacific. 5 Fleets: 3rd – Pacific; 4th – Caribbean, Central and South America; 5th – Indian Ocean, Persian Gulf, Red Sea; 6th – Mediterranean; 7th – W. Pacific; plus Military Sealift Command (MSC); Naval Reserve Force (NRF). For Naval Special Warfare Command, see US Special Operations Command

EQUIPMENT BY TYPE
SUBMARINES 68
STRATEGIC • SSBN 14 *Ohio* opcon US STRATCOM with up to 24 UGM-133A *Trident* D-5/D-5LE nuclear SLBM, 4 single 533mm TT with Mk48 *Sea Arrow* HWT
TACTICAL 54
SSGN 47:
4 *Ohio* (mod) with total of 154 *Tomahawk* LACM, 4 single 533mm TT with Mk48 *Sea Arrow* HWT
7 *Los Angeles* with 1 12-cell VLS with *Tomahawk* LACM, 4 single 533mm TT with Mk48 *Sea Arrow* HWT
22 *Los Angeles* (Imp) with 1 12-cell VLS with *Tomahawk* LACM, 4 single 533mm TT with Mk48 *Sea Arrow* HWT
10 *Virginia* Flight I/II with 1 12-cell VLS with *Tomahawk* LACM, 4 single 533mm TT with Mk48 ADCAP mod 6 HWT
4 *Virginia* Flight III with 2 6-cell VLS with *Tomahawk* LACM, 4 single 533mm TT with Mk48 ADCAP mod 6 HWT
SSN 7:
4 *Los Angeles* with 4 single 533mm TT with Mk48 *Sea Arrow* HWT
3 *Seawolf* with 8 single 660mm TT with up to 45 *Tomahawk* LACM/Mk48 *Sea Arrow* HWT
PRINCIPAL SURFACE COMBATANTS 107
AIRCRAFT CARRIERS • CVN 11
1 *Gerald R. Ford* with 2 octuple Mk29 mod 5 GMLS with RIM-162D ESSM SAM, 2 Mk49 mod 3 GMLS with RIM-116 SAM, 2 *Phalanx* Mk15 CIWS (typical capacity 75+ F/A-18E/F *Super Hornet* FGA ac, F-35C *Lightning* II FGA ac (IOC planned 08/2018), E-2D *Hawkeye* AEW&C ac, EA-18G *Growler* EW ac, MH-60R *Seahawk* ASW hel, MH-60S *Knighthawk* MRH hel)
10 *Nimitz* with 2–3 octuple Mk29 lnchr with RIM-7M/P *Sea Sparrow* SAM, 2 Mk49 GMLS with RIM-116 SAM, 2 *Phalanx* Mk15 CIWS (typical capacity 55 F/A-18 *Hornet* FGA ac; 4 EA-18G *Growler* EW ac; 4 E-2C/D *Hawkeye* AEW ac; 6 H-60 *Seahawk* hel)
CRUISERS • CGHM 23:
22 *Ticonderoga* with *Aegis* Baseline 5/6/8/9 C2, 2 quad lnchr with RGM-84 *Harpoon* AShM, 2 61-cell Mk41 VLS with SM-2ER SAM/SM-3 SAM/SM-6 SAM/*Tomahawk* LACM, 2 triple 324mm ASTT with Mk46 LWT, 2 *Phalanx* Block 1B CIWS, 2 127mm guns (capacity 2 SH-60B *Seahawk* ASW hel)
1 *Zumwalt* with 20 4-cell Mk57 VLS with RIM-162 ESSM SAM/SM-2ER SAM/ASROC ASW/*Tomahawk* LACM, 2 155mm guns (capacity 2 MH-60R *Seahawk* ASW hel or 1 MH-60R *Seahawk* ASW hel and 3 *Fire Scout* UAV)
DESTROYERS 64
DDGHM 36 *Arleigh Burke* Flight IIA with *Aegis* Baseline 6/7 C2, 1 29-cell Mk41 VLS with ASROC ASW/SM-2ER SAM/SM-3 SAM/SM-6 SAM/*Tomahawk* LACM, 1 61-cell Mk41 VLS with ASROC ASW/SM-2ER SAM/SM-3 SAM/SM-6 SAM/*Tomahawk* LACM, 2 triple 324mm ASTT with Mk46 LWT, 2 *Phalanx* Block

1B CIWS, 1 127mm gun (capacity 2 SH-60B *Seahawk* ASW hel)

DDGM 28 *Arleigh Burke* Flight I/II with *Aegis* Baseline 5/9 C2, 2 quad lnchr with RGM-84 *Harpoon* AShM, 1 32-cell Mk41 VLS with ASROC ASW/SM-2ER SAM/SM-3 SAM/SM-6 SAM/*Tomahawk* LACM, 1 64-cell Mk41 VLS with ASROC ASW/SM-2 ER SAM/*Tomahawk* LACM, 2 Mk49 GMLS with RIM-116 RAM SAM, 2 triple 324mm ASTT with Mk46 LWT, 2 *Phalanx* Block 1B CIWS, 1 127mm gun, 1 hel landing platform (of which two suffered major damage in collisions)

FRIGATES • FFHM 9:

4 *Freedom* with 1 21-cell Mk49 lnchr with RIM-116 SAM, 1 57mm gun (capacity 2 MH-60R/S *Seahawk* hel or 1 MH-60 with 3 MQ-8 *Fire Scout* UAV)

5 *Independence* with 1 11-cell SeaRAM lnchr with RIM-116 SAM, 1 57mm gun (capacity 1 MH-60R/S *Seahawk* hel and 3 MQ-8 *Fire Scout* UAV) (1 fitted with 2 twin lnchr with RGM-84D Block 1C *Harpoon* AShM for trials)

PATROL AND COASTAL COMBATANTS 57

PCFG 10 *Cyclone* with 1 quad Mk 208 lnchr with BGM-176B *Griffin B* SSM

PCF 3 *Cyclone*

PBF 2 Mk VI

PBR 42

MINE WARFARE • MINE COUNTERMEASURES 11

MCO 11 *Avenger* with 1 SLQ-48 MCM system, 1 SQQ-32(V)3 Sonar (mine hunting)

COMMAND SHIPS • LCC 2 *Blue Ridge* with 2 *Phalanx* Mk15 CIWS (capacity 3 LCPL; 2 LCVP; 700 troops; 1 med hel) (of which 1 vessel partially crewed by Military Sealift Command personnel)

AMPHIBIOUS

PRINCIPAL AMPHIBIOUS SHIPS 31

LHA 1 *America* with 2 octuple Mk29 GMLS with RIM-162D ESSM SAM; 2 Mk49 GMLS with RIM-116 RAM SAM, 2 *Phalanx* Mk15 CIWS (capacity 6 F-35B *Lightning* II FGA ac; 12 MV-22B *Osprey* tpt ac; 4 CH-53E *Sea Stallion* hel; 7 AH-1Z *Viper*/UH-1Y *Iroquois* hel; 2 MH-60 hel)

LHD 8 *Wasp* with 2 octuple Mk29 GMLS with RIM-7M/RIM-7P *Sea Sparrow* SAM, 2 Mk49 GMLS with RIM-116 RAM SAM, 2 *Phalanx* Mk15 CIWS (capacity: 6 AV-8B *Harrier* II FGA ac; 4 CH-53E *Sea Stallion* hel; 6 MV-22B *Osprey* tpt ac; 4 AH-1W/Z hel; 3 UH-1Y hel; 3 LCAC(L); 60 tanks; 1,687 troops)

LPD 10 *San Antonio* with 2 21-cell Mk49 GMLS with RIM-116 SAM (capacity 2 CH-53E *Sea Stallion* hel or 2 MV-22 *Osprey*; 2 LCAC(L); 14 AAAV; 720 troops)

LSD 12:

4 *Harpers Ferry* with 2 Mk 49 GMLS with RIM-116 SAM, 2 *Phalanx* Mk15 CIWS, 1 hel landing platform (capacity 2 LCAC(L); 40 tanks; 500 troops)

8 *Whidbey Island* with 2 Mk49 GMLS with RIM-116 SAM, 2 *Phalanx* Mk15 CIWS, 1 hel landing platform (capacity 4 LCAC(L); 40 tanks; 500 troops)

LANDING CRAFT 245

LCU 32 LCU-1600 (capacity either 2 M1 *Abrams* MBT or 350 troops)

LCP 108: 75 LCPL; 33 Utility Boat

LCM 25: 10 LCM-6; 15 LCM-8

LCAC 80 LCAC(L) (capacity either 1 MBT or 60 troops (undergoing upgrade programme))

LOGISTICS AND SUPPORT 14

AFDL 1 *Dynamic*

AGOR 5 (all leased out): 1 *Ocean*; 3 *Thomas G. Thompson*; 1 *Kilo Moana*

ARD 2

AX 1 *Prevail*

ESB 1 *Lewis B. Puller* (capacity 4 MH-53/MH-60 hel)

SSA 2 (for testing)

SSAN 1 (for propulsion plant training)

UUV 1 *Cutthroat* (for testing)

Naval Reserve Forces 100,550

Selected Reserve 57,800

Individual Ready Reserve 42,750

Naval Inactive Fleet

Notice for reactivation: 60–90 days minimum (still on naval vessel register)

EQUIPMENT BY TYPE

AMPHIBIOUS 8

LHA 3 *Tarawa*

LPD 5 *Austin*

LOGISTICS AND SUPPORT • AOE 1 *Supply*

Military Sealift Command (MSC)

Fleet Oiler (PM1)

EQUIPMENT BY TYPE

LOGISTICS AND SUPPORT 15

AOR 15 *Henry J. Kaiser* with 1 hel landing platform

Special Mission (PM2)

EQUIPMENT BY TYPE

LOGISTICS AND SUPPORT 24

AGM 3: 1 *Howard O. Lorenzen*; 1 *Invincible* (commercial operator); 1 Sea-based X-band Radar

AGOR 6 *Pathfinder*

AGOS 5: 1 *Impeccable* (commercial operator); 4 *Victorious*

AGS 1 *Waters*

AS 9 (long-term chartered, of which 1 *C-Champion*, 1 *C-Commando*, 1 *Malama*, 1 *Dolores Chouest*, 1 *Dominator*, 4 *Arrowhead*)

Prepositioning (PM3)

EQUIPMENT BY TYPE

LOGISTICS AND SUPPORT 28

AG 2: 1 *V Adm K.R. Wheeler*; 1 *Fast Tempo*

AK 4: 2 *LTC John U.D. Page*; 1 *Maj. Bernard F. Fisher*; 1 *CPT David I. Lyon*

AKEH 2 *Lewis and Clark*

AKR 10: 2 *Bob Hope*; 1 *Stockham*; 7 *Watson*

AKRH 5 *2nd Lt John P. Bobo*

AP 3: 2 *Guam*; 1 *Westpac Express*

ESD 2 *Montford Point*

Service Support (PM4)
EQUIPMENT BY TYPE
LOGISTICS AND SUPPORT 10
  ARS 2 *Safeguard*
  AH 2 *Mercy* with 1 hel landing platform
  AS 2 *Emory S Land*
  ATF 4 *Powhatan*

Sealift (PM5)
(At a minimum of 4 days' readiness)
EQUIPMENT BY TYPE
LOGISTICS AND SUPPORT 23
  AOT 6 (long-term chartered, of which 1 *Empire State*; 1 *Galveston*; 1 *Lawrence H. Gianella*; 1 *Maersk Peary*; 1 SLNC *Pax*; 1 SLNC *Goodwill*)
  AK 7: 1 *Ocean Crescent*; 3 *Sgt Matej Kocak*; 1 *1st Lt Harry L. Martin*; 1 *LCpl Roy M. Wheat*; 1 *Sea Eagle* (long-term chartered)
  AKR 10: 5 *Bob Hope*; 2 *Gordon*; 2 *Shughart*; 1 *Watson*

Fleet Ordnance and Dry Cargo (PM6)
EQUIPMENT BY TYPE
LOGISTICS AND SUPPORT 14
  AOE 2 *Supply*
  AKEH 12 *Lewis and Clark*

Afloat Staging Command Support (PM7)
EQUIPMENT BY TYPE
LOGISTICS AND SUPPORT 1
  ARC 1 *Zeus*

Expeditionary Fast Transport (PM8)
EQUIPMENT BY TYPE
LOGISTICS AND SUPPORT 8
  EPF 8 *Spearhead*

US Maritime Administration (MARAD)

National Defense Reserve Fleet
EQUIPMENT BY TYPE
LOGISTICS AND SUPPORT 20
  AGOS 2 *General Rudder*
  AGM 2: 1 *Pacific Collector*; 1 *Pacific Tracker*
  AK 7: 2 *Cape Ann* (breakbulk); 1 *Cape Chalmers* (breakbulk); 2 *Cape Farewell*; 1 *Cape Nome* (breakbulk); 1 *Del Monte* (breakbulk)
  AOT 3 *Paul Buck*
  AP 4: 1 *Empire State VI*; 1 *Golden Bear*; 1 *Kennedy*; 1 *State of Maine*
  AX 2: 1 *Freedom Star*; 1 *Kings Pointer*

Ready Reserve Force
Ships at readiness up to a maximum of 30 days
EQUIPMENT BY TYPE
LOGISTICS AND SUPPORT 46
  ACS 6: 2 *Flickertail State*; 1 *Gopher State*; 3 *Keystone State*
  AK 4: 2 *Wright* (breakbulk); 2 *Cape May* (heavy lift)
  AKR 35: 1 *Adm W.M. Callaghan*; 4 *Algol*; 4 *Cape Capella*; 1 *Cape Decision*; 4 *Cape Ducato*; 1 *Cape Edmont*; 1 *Cape Henry*; 2 *Cape Hudson*; 2 *Cape Knox*; 4 *Cape Island*; 1 *Cape Orlando*; 1 *Cape Race*; 1 *Cape Trinity*; 2 *Cape Trinity*; 2 *Cape Victory*; 2 *Cape Washington*
  AOT 1 *Petersburg*

Augmentation Force
COMBAT SERVICE SUPPORT
  1 (active) log bn (Navy Cargo Handling)
  6 (reserve) log bn (Navy Cargo Handling)

Naval Aviation 98,600
10 air wg. Average air wing comprises 8 sqns: 4 with F/A-18; 1 with MH-60R; 1 with EA-18G; 1 with E-2C/D; 1 with MH-60S

FORCES BY ROLE
FIGHTER/GROUND ATTACK
  4 sqn with F/A-18C *Hornet*
  19 sqn with F/A-18E *Super Hornet*
  11 sqn with F/A-18F *Super Hornet*
ANTI-SUBMARINE WARFARE
  11 sqn with MH-60R *Seahawk*
  1 ASW/CSAR sqn with HH-60H *Seahawk*
  3 ASW/ISR sqn with MH-60R *Seahawk*; MQ-8B *Fire Scout*
ELINT
  1 sqn with EP-3E *Aries* II
ELINT/ELECTRONIC WARFARE
  13 sqn with EA-18G *Growler*
MARITIME PATROL
  4 sqn with P-3C *Orion*
  7 sqn with P-8A *Poseidon*
  1 sqn (forming) with P-8A *Poseidon*
AIRBORNE EARLY WARNING & CONTROL
  6 sqn with E-2C *Hawkeye*
  3 sqn with E-2D *Hawkeye*
COMMAND & CONTROL
  2 sqn with E-6B *Mercury*
MINE COUNTERMEASURES
  2 sqn with MH-53E *Sea Dragon*
TRANSPORT
  2 sqn with C-2A *Greyhound*
TRAINING
  1 (FRS) sqn with EA-18G *Growler*
  1 (FRS) sqn with C-2A *Greyhound*; E-2C/D *Hawkeye*; TE-2C *Hawkeye*
  1 sqn with E-6B *Mercury*
  2 (FRS) sqn with F/A-18A/A+/B/C/D *Hornet*; F/A-18E/F *Super Hornet*
  2 (FRS) sqn with F-35C *Lightning* II
  1 (FRS) sqn with MH-53 *Sea Dragon*
  2 (FRS) sqn with MH-60S *Knight Hawk*; HH-60H *Seahawk*
  2 (FRS) sqn with MH-60R *Seahawk*
  1 sqn with P-3C *Orion*
  1 (FRS) sqn with P-3C *Orion*; P-8A *Poseidon*
  6 sqn with T-6A/B *Texan* II
  2 sqn with T-44C *Pegasus*
  5 sqn with T-45C *Goshawk*
  3 hel sqn with TH-57B/C *Sea Ranger*
  1 (FRS) UAV sqn with MQ-8B *Fire Scout*; MQ-8C *Fire Scout*

TRANSPORT HELICOPTER
14 sqn with MH-60S *Knight Hawk*
1 tpt hel/ISR sqn with MH-60S *Knight Hawk*; MQ-8B *Fire Scout*
ISR UAV
1 sqn with MQ-4C *Triton*
EQUIPMENT BY TYPE
AIRCRAFT 987 combat capable
  FGA 736: 22 F-35C *Lightning* II; 10 F-16A *Fighting Falcon*; 4 F-16B *Fighting Falcon*; 10 F/A-18A/A+ *Hornet*; 9 F/A-18B *Hornet*; 90 F/A-18C *Hornet*; 30 F/A-18D *Hornet*; 290 F/A-18E *Super Hornet*; 271 F/A-18F *Super Hornet*
  ASW 120: 65 P-3C *Orion*; 55 P-8A *Poseidon*
  EW 131 EA-18G *Growler*
  ELINT 9 EP-3E *Aries* II
  AEW&C 80: 50 E-2C *Hawkeye*; 30 E-2D *Hawkeye*
  C2 16 E-6B *Mercury*
  TKR 3: 1 KC-130R *Hercules*; 1 KC-130T *Hercules*; 1 KC-130J *Hercules*
  TPT • Light 61: 4 Beech A200 *King Air* (C-12C *Huron*); 6 Beech A200 *King Air* (UC-12F *Huron*); 8 Beech A200 *King Air* (UC-12M *Huron*); 34 C-2A *Greyhound*; 2 DHC-2 *Beaver* (U-6A); 7 SA-227-BC *Metro* III (C-26D)
  TRG 582: 44 T-6A *Texan* II; 232 T-6B *Texan* II; 7 T-38C *Talon*; 55 T-44C *Pegasus*; 242 T-45C *Goshawk*; 2 TE-2C *Hawkeye*
HELICOPTERS
  ASW 225 MH-60R *Seahawk*
  MRH 271 MH-60S *Knight Hawk* (Multi Mission Support)
  MCM 28 MH-53E *Sea Dragon*
  ISR 3 OH-58C *Kiowa*
  CSAR 11 HH-60H *Seahawk*
  TPT 13: **Heavy** 2 CH-53E *Sea Stallion*; **Medium** 3 UH-60L *Black Hawk*; **Light** 8: 5 UH-72A *Lakota*; 2 UH-1N *Iroquois*; 1 UH-1Y *Venom*
  TRG 119: 43 TH-57B *Sea Ranger*; 76 TH-57C *Sea Ranger*
UNMANNED AERIAL VEHICLES • ISR 91
  Heavy 41: 1 MQ-4C *Triton*; 20 MQ-8B *Fire Scout*; 16 MQ-8C *Fire Scout*; 4 RQ-4A *Global Hawk* (under evaluation and trials); **Medium** 35 RQ-2B *Pioneer*; **Light** 15 RQ-21A *Blackjack*
AIR-LAUNCHED MISSILES
  AAM • IR AIM-9M *Sidewinder*; **IIR** AIM-9X *Sidewinder* II; **SARH** AIM-7 *Sparrow*; **ARH** AIM-120C-5/C-7/D AMRAAM
  ASM AGM-65F *Maverick*; AGM-114B/K/M *Hellfire*
  AShM AGM-84D *Harpoon*; AGM-119A *Penguin* 3
  ARM AGM-88B/C/E HARM/AARGM
  ALCM • Conventional AGM-84E/H/K SLAM/SLAM-ER
BOMBS
  Laser-guided: GBU-10/12/16 *Paveway* II; GBU-24 *Paveway* III
  INS/GPS guided: GBU-31/32/38 JDAM; Enhanced *Paveway* II; GBU-54 Laser JDAM; AGM-154A/C/C-1 JSOW

Naval Aviation Reserve

FORCES BY ROLE
FIGHTER/GROUND ATTACK
  1 sqn with F/A-18A+ *Hornet*

ANTI-SUBMARINE WARFARE
  1 sqn with MH-60R *Seahawk*
ELECTRONIC WARFARE
  1 sqn with EA-18G *Growler*
MARITIME PATROL
  2 sqn with P-3C *Orion*
TRANSPORT
  5 log spt sqn with B-737-700 (C-40A *Clipper*)
  2 log spt sqn with Gulfstream III/IV (C-20D/G); Gulfstream V/G550 (C-37A/B)
  4 sqn with C-130T *Hercules*
  1 sqn with KC-130T *Hercules*
TRAINING
  2 (aggressor) sqn with F-5F/N *Tiger* II
  1 (aggressor) sqn with F/A-18A *Hornet*
TRANSPORT HELICOPTER
  2 sqn with HH-60H *Seahawk*
EQUIPMENT BY TYPE
AIRCRAFT 77 combat capable
  FTR 31: 2 F-5F *Tiger* II; 29 F-5N *Tiger* II
  FGA 29 F/A-18A+ *Hornet*
  ASW 12 P-3C *Orion*
  EW 5 EA-18G *Growler*
  TKR 5 KC-130T *Hercules*
  TPT 41: **Medium** 18 C-130T *Hercules*; **PAX** 23: 15 B-737-700 (C-40A *Clipper*); 1 Gulfstream III (C-20D); 3 Gulfstream IV (C-20G); 1 Gulfstream V (C-37A); 3 Gulfstream G550 (C-37B)
HELICOPTERS
  ASW 7 MH-60R *Seahawk*
  MCM 7 MH-53E *Sea Dragon*
  CSAR 16 HH-60H *Seahawk*

US Marine Corps 184,400

3 Marine Expeditionary Forces (MEF), 3 Marine Expeditionary Brigades (MEB), 7 Marine Expeditionary Units (MEU) drawn from 3 div. An MEU usually consists of a battalion landing team (1 SF coy, 1 lt armd recce coy, 1 recce pl, 1 armd pl, 1 amph aslt pl, 1 inf bn, 1 arty bty, 1 cbt engr pl), an aviation combat element (1 medium-lift sqn with attached atk hel, FGA ac and AD assets) and a composite log bn, with a combined total of about 2,200 personnel. Composition varies with mission requirements

FORCES BY ROLE
SPECIAL FORCES
  (see USSOCOM)
MANOEUVRE
  Reconnaissance
  3 (MEF) recce coy
  Amphibious
  1 (1st) mne div (2 armd recce bn, 1 recce bn, 1 tk bn, 2 mne regt (4 mne bn), 1 mne regt (3 mne bn), 1 amph aslt bn, 1 arty regt (3 arty bn, 1 MRL bn), 1 cbt engr bn, 1 EW bn, 1 int bn, 1 sigs bn)
  1 (2nd) mne div (1 armd recce bn, 1 recce bn, 1 tk bn, 3 mne regt (3 mne bn), 1 amph aslt bn, 1 arty regt (2 arty bn), 1 cbt engr bn, 1 EW bn, 1 int bn, 1 sigs bn)
  1 (3rd) mne div (1 recce bn, 1 inf regt (3 inf bn), 1 arty regt (2 arty bn), 1 cbt spt bn (1 armd recce coy, 1 amph aslt coy, 1 cbt engr coy), 1 EW bn, 1 int bn, 1 sigs bn)

COMBAT SERVICE SUPPORT
3 log gp
EQUIPMENT BY TYPE
ARMOURED FIGHTING VEHICLES
  MBT 447 M1A1 *Abrams*
  IFV 502 LAV-25
  APC • APC (W) 207 LAV variants (66 CP; 127 log; 14 EW)
  AAV 1,200 AAV-7A1 (all roles)
  AUV 2,429: 1,725 *Cougar*; 704 M-ATV
ENGINEERING & MAINTENANCE VEHICLES
  AEV 42 M1 ABV
  ARV 185: 60 AAVRA1; 45 LAV-R; 80 M88A1/2
  MW 38 *Buffalo*
  VLB 6 Joint Aslt Bridge
ANTI-TANK/ANTI-INFRASTRUCTURE • MSL
  SP 106 LAV-AT
  MANPATS FGM-148 *Javelin*; FGM-172B SRAW-MPV; TOW
ARTILLERY 1,501
  TOWED 812: **105mm**: 331 M101A1; **155mm** 481 M777A2
  MRL 227mm 40 M142 HIMARS
  MOR 649: **81mm** 535 M252; **SP 81mm** 65 LAV-M; **120mm** 49 EFSS
RADAR • LAND 23 AN/TPQ-36 *Firefinder* (arty)
UNMANNED AERIAL VEHCILES
  ISR • Light 100 BQM-147 *Exdrone*
AIR DEFENCE • SAM • Point-defence FIM-92 *Stinger*

Marine Corps Aviation 34,700

3 active Marine Aircraft Wings (MAW) and 1 MCR MAW
Flying hours   365 hrs/yr on tpt ac; 248 hrs/yr on ac; 277 hrs/yr on hel

FORCES BY ROLE
FIGHTER
  1 sqn with F/A-18A++ *Hornet*
  6 sqn with F/A-18C *Hornet*
  4 sqn with F/A-18D *Hornet*
FIGHTER/GROUND ATTACK
  5 sqn with AV-8B *Harrier* II
  2 sqn with F-35B *Lightning* II
ELECTRONIC WARFARE
  2 sqn with EA-6B *Prowler*
COMBAT SEARCH & RESCUE/TRANSPORT
  1 sqn with Beech A200/B200 *King Air* (UC-12F/M *Huron*); Beech 350 *King Air* (UC-12W *Huron*); Cessna 560 *Citation Ultra/Encore* (UC-35C/D); DC-9 *Skytrain* (C-9B *Nightingale*); Gulfstream IV (C-20G); HH-1N *Iroquois*
TANKER
  3 sqn with KC-130J *Hercules*
TRANSPORT
  14 sqn with MV-22B *Osprey*
  2 sqn (forming) with MV-22B *Osprey*
TRAINING
  1 sqn with AV-8B *Harrier* II; TAV-8B *Harrier*
  1 sqn with F/A-18B/C/D *Hornet*
  1 sqn with F-35B *Lightning* II
  1 sqn with MV-22B *Osprey*
  1 hel sqn with AH-1W *Cobra*; AH-1Z *Viper*; HH-1N *Iroquois*; UH-1Y *Venom*
  1 hel sqn with CH-53E *Sea Stallion*
ATTACK HELICOPTER
  3 sqn with AH-1W *Cobra*; UH-1Y *Venom*
  4 sqn with AH-1Z *Viper*; UH-1Y *Venom*
TRANSPORT HELICOPTER
  8 sqn with CH-53E *Sea Stallion*
  1 (VIP) sqn with MV-22B *Osprey*; VH-3D *Sea King*; VH-60N *Presidential Hawk*
ISR UAV
  2 sqn with RQ-21A *Blackjack*
  1 sqn with RQ-7B *Shadow*
AIR DEFENCE
  2 bn with M1097 *Avenger*; FIM-92 *Stinger* (can provide additional heavy-calibre support weapons)

EQUIPMENT BY TYPE
AIRCRAFT 455 combat capable
  FGA 437: 50 F-35B *Lightning* II; 6 F-35C *Lightning* II; 45 F/A-18A++ *Hornet*; 7 F/A-18B *Hornet*; 107 F/A-18C *Hornet*; 92 F/A-18D *Hornet*; 114 AV-8B *Harrier* II; 16 TAV-8B *Harrier*
  EW 18 EA-6B *Prowler**
  TKR 45 KC-130J *Hercules*
  TPT 20: **Light** 17: 5 Beech A200/B200 *King Air* (UC-12F/M *Huron*); 5 Beech 350 *King Air* (C-12W *Huron*); 7 Cessna 560 *Citation Ultra/Encore* (UC-35C/D); **PAX** 3: 2 DC-9 *Skytrain* (C-9B *Nightingale*); 1 Gulfstream IV (C-20G)
  TRG 3 T-34C *Turbo Mentor*
TILTROTOR • TPT 277 MV-22B *Osprey*
HELICOPTERS
  ATK 153: 77 AH-1W *Cobra*; 76 AH-1Z *Viper*
  SAR 4 HH-1N *Iroquois*
  TPT 280: **Heavy** 139 CH-53E *Sea Stallion*; **Medium** 19: 8 VH-60N *Presidential Hawk* (VIP tpt); 11 VH-3D *Sea King* (VIP tpt); **Light** 122 UH-1Y *Venom*
UNMANNED AERIAL VEHICLES
  ISR 60: **Medium** 20 RQ-7B *Shadow*; **Light** 40 RQ-21A *Blackjack*
AIR DEFENCE
  SAM • Point-defence FIM-92 *Stinger*; M1097 *Avenger*
AIR-LAUNCHED MISSILES
  AAM • IR AIM-9M *Sidewinder*; **IIR** AIM-9X *Sidewinder* II; **SARH** AIM-7P *Sparrow*; **ARH** AIM-120C AMRAAM
  ASM AGM-65E/F IR *Maverick*; AGM-114 *Hellfire*; AGM-176 *Griffin*
  AShM AGM-84D *Harpoon*
  ARM AGM-88 HARM
  LACM AGM-84E/H/K SLAM/SLAM-ER
BOMBS
  Laser-guided GBU-10/12/16 *Paveway* II
  INS/GPS guided GBU-31 JDAM; AGM-154A/C/C-1 JSOW

Reserve Organisations

Marine Corps Reserve 38,700
FORCES BY ROLE
MANOEUVRE
  Reconnaissance
  2 MEF recce coy

Amphibious
1 (4th) mne div (1 armd recce bn, 1 recce bn, 2 mne regt (3 mne bn), 1 amph aslt bn, 1 arty regt (2 arty bn, 1 MRL bn), 1 cbt engr bn, 1 int bn, 1 sigs bn)
COMBAT SERVICE SUPPORT
1 log gp

Marine Corps Aviation Reserve 12,000 reservists
FORCES BY ROLE
FIGHTER
1 sqn with F/A-18A++ *Hornet*
TANKER
2 sqn with KC-130J/T *Hercules*
TRANSPORT
2 sqn with MV-22B *Osprey*
TRAINING
1 sqn with F-5F/N *Tiger* II
ATTACK HELICOPTER
2 sqn with AH-1W *Cobra*; UH-1Y *Venom*
TRANSPORT HELICOPTER
1 sqn with CH-53E *Sea Stallion*
ISR UAV
1 sqn with RQ-7B *Shadow*
EQUIPMENT BY TYPE
AIRCRAFT 23 combat capable
 FTR 12: 1 F-5F *Tiger* II; 11 F-5N *Tiger* II
 FGA 11 F/A-18A++ *Hornet*
 TKR 20: 7 KC-130J *Hercules*; 13 KC-130T *Hercules*
 TPT • **Light** 7: 2 Beech 350 *King Air* (UC-12W *Huron*); 5 Cessna 560 *Citation Ultra/Encore* (UC-35C/D)
TILTROTOR • **TPT** 12 MV-22B *Osprey*
HELICOPTERS
 ATK 37 AH-1W *Cobra*
 TPT 32: **Heavy** 6 CH-53E *Sea Stallion*; **Light** 26 UH-1Y *Venom*
UNMANNED AERIAL VEHICLES
 ISR • **Medium** 8 RQ-7B *Shadow*

Marine Stand-by Reserve 700 reservists
Trained individuals available for mobilisation

US Coast Guard 41,000 (military) 8,500 (civilian)
9 districts (4 Pacific, 5 Atlantic)
EQUIPMENT BY TYPE
PATROL AND COASTAL COMBATANTS 158
 PSOH 24: 1 *Alex Haley*; 13 *Famous*; 4 *Hamilton*; 6 *Legend*
 PCO 38: 14 *Reliance* (with 1 hel landing platform); 24 *Sentinel* (Damen 4708)
 PCC 23 *Island*
 PBI 73 *Marine Protector*
LOGISTICS AND SUPPORT 79
 ABU 52: 16 *Juniper*; 4 WLI; 14 *Keeper*; 18 WLR
 AG 13: 1 *Cosmos*; 4 *Pamlico*; 8 *Anvil*
 AGB 13: 9 *Bay*; 1 *Mackinaw*; 1 *Healy*; 2 *Polar* (of which one in reserve)
 AXS 1 *Eagle*

US Coast Guard Aviation
EQUIPMENT BY TYPE
AIRCRAFT
 SAR 20: 11 HC-130H *Hercules*; 9 HC-130J *Hercules*

 TPT 34: **Medium** 14 C-27J *Spartan*; **Light** 18 CN235-200 (HC-144A – MP role); **PAX** 2 Gulfstream V (C-37A)
HELICOPTERS
 SAR 154: 52 MH-60T *Jayhawk*; 102 AS366G1 (MH-65C/D) *Dauphin* II

US Air Force (USAF) 322,800
Flying hours Ftr 160, bbr 260, tkr 300, airlift 340

Almost the entire USAF (plus active force ANG and AFR) is divided into 10 Aerospace Expeditionary Forces (AEF), each on call for 120 days every 20 months. At least 2 of the 10 AEFs are on call at any one time, each with 10,000–15,000 personnel, 90 multi-role ftr and bbr ac, 31 intra-theatre refuelling aircraft and 13 aircraft for ISR and EW missions

Global Strike Command (GSC)
2 active air forces (8th & 20th); 8 wg
FORCES BY ROLE
SURFACE-TO-SURFACE MISSILE
 9 ICBM sqn with LGM-30G *Minuteman* III
BOMBER
 4 sqn with B-1B *Lancer*
 2 sqn with B-2A *Spirit*
 5 sqn (incl 1 trg) with B-52H *Stratofortress*
COMMAND & CONTROL
 1 sqn with E-4B
TRANSPORT HELICOPTER
 3 sqn with UH-1N *Iroquois*

Air Combat Command (ACC)
2 active air forces (9th & 12th); 12 wg. ACC numbered air forces provide the air component to CENTCOM, SOUTHCOM and NORTHCOM
FORCES BY ROLE
FIGHTER
 3 sqn with F-22A *Raptor*
FIGHTER/GROUND ATTACK
 4 sqn with F-15E *Strike Eagle*
 4 sqn with F-16C/D *Fighting Falcon* (+6 sqn personnel only)
 1 sqn with F-35A *Lightning* II
 1 sqn with F-35A *Lightning* II (forming)
GROUND ATTACK
 3 sqn with A-10C *Thunderbolt* II (+1 sqn personnel only)
ELECTRONIC WARFARE
 1 sqn with EA-18G *Growler* (personnel only – USN aircraft)
 2 sqn with EC-130H *Compass Call*
ISR
 2 sqn with E-8C J-STARS (personnel only)
 5 sqn with OC-135/RC-135/WC-135
 2 sqn with U-2S
AIRBORNE EARLY WARNING & CONTROL
 5 sqn with E-3B/C/G *Sentry*
COMBAT SEARCH & RESCUE
 2 sqn with HC-130J *Combat King* II
 2 sqn with HH-60G *Pave Hawk*

TRAINING
  1 sqn with A-10C *Thunderbolt* II
  1 sqn with E-3B/C *Sentry*
  2 sqn with F-15E *Strike Eagle*
  1 sqn with F-22A *Raptor*
  1 sqn with RQ-4A *Global Hawk*; TU-2S
  2 UAV sqn with MQ-1B *Predator*
  3 UAV sqn with MQ-9A *Reaper*
COMBAT/ISR UAV
  4 sqn with MQ-1B *Predator*
  1 sqn with MQ-1B *Predator*/MQ-9A *Reaper*
  2 sqn with MQ-9A *Reaper*
  2 sqn with RQ-170 *Sentinel*
ISR UAV
  2 sqn with EQ-4B/RQ-4B *Global Hawk*

Pacific Air Forces (PACAF)

Provides the air component of PACOM, and commands air units based in Alaska, Hawaii, Japan and South Korea. 3 active air forces (5th, 7th, & 11th); 8 wg

FORCES BY ROLE
FIGHTER
  2 sqn with F-15C/D *Eagle*
  2 sqn with F-22A *Raptor* (+1 sqn personnel only)
FIGHTER/GROUND ATTACK
  5 sqn with F-16C/D *Fighting Falcon*
GROUND ATTACK
  1 sqn with A-10C *Thunderbolt* II
AIRBORNE EARLY WARNING & CONTROL
  2 sqn with E-3B/C *Sentry*
COMBAT SEARCH & RESCUE
  1 sqn with HH-60G *Pave Hawk*
TANKER
  1 sqn with KC-135R (+1 sqn personnel only)
TRANSPORT
  1 sqn with B-737-200 (C-40B); Gulfstream V (C-37A)
  2 sqn with C-17A *Globemaster*
  1 sqn with C-130J-30 *Hercules*
  1 sqn with Beech 1900C (C-12J); UH-1N *Huey*
TRAINING
  1 (aggressor) sqn with F-16C/D *Fighting Falcon*

United States Air Forces Europe (USAFE)

Provides the air component to both EUCOM and AFRICOM. 1 active air force (3rd); 5 wg

FORCES BY ROLE
FIGHTER
  1 sqn with F-15C/D *Eagle*
FIGHTER/GROUND ATTACK
  2 sqn with F-15E *Strike Eagle*
  3 sqn with F-16C/D *Fighting Falcon*
COMBAT SEARCH & RESCUE
  1 sqn with HH-60G *Pave Hawk*
TANKER
  1 sqn with KC-135R *Stratotanker*
TRANSPORT
  1 sqn with C-130J-30 *Hercules*
  2 sqn with Gulfstream V (C-37A); Learjet 35A (C-21A); B-737-700 (C-40B)

Air Mobility Command (AMC)

Provides strategic and tactical airlift, air-to-air refuelling and aeromedical evacuation. 1 active air force (18th); 12 wg and 1 gp

FORCES BY ROLE
TANKER
  4 sqn with KC-10A *Extender*
  9 sqn with KC-135R/T *Stratotanker* (+2 sqn with personnel only)
TRANSPORT
  1 VIP sqn with B-737-200 (C-40B); B-757-200 (C-32A)
  1 VIP sqn with Gulfstream V (C-37A)
  1 VIP sqn with VC-25 *Air Force One*
  2 sqn with C-5M *Super Galaxy*
  8 sqn with C-17A *Globemaster* III (+1 sqn personnel only)
  1 sqn with C-130H *Hercules* (+1 sqn personnel only)
  5 sqn with C-130J-30 *Hercules* (+1 sqn personnel only)
  1 sqn with Gulfstream V (C-37A)
  2 sqn with Learjet 35A (C-21A)

Air Education and Training Command

1 active air force (2nd), 10 active air wg and 1 gp

FORCES BY ROLE
TRAINING
  1 sqn with C-17A *Globemaster* III
  1 sqn with C-130J-30 *Hercules*
  4 sqn with F-16C/D *Fighting Falcon*
  4 sqn with F-35A *Lightning* II
  1 sqn with KC-46A *Pegasus* (forming)
  1 sqn with KC-135R *Stratotanker*
  5 (flying trg) sqn with T-1A *Jayhawk*
  10 (flying trg) sqn with T-6A *Texan* II
  10 (flying trg) sqn with T-38C *Talon*
  1 UAV sqn with MQ-1B *Predator*

EQUIPMENT BY TYPE
SURFACE-TO-SURFACE MISSILE LAUNCHERS
  ICBM • **Nuclear** 400 LGM-30G *Minuteman* III (1 Mk12A or Mk21 re-entry veh per missile)
AIRCRAFT 1,478 combat capable
  BBR 139: 61 B-1B *Lancer*; 20 B-2A *Spirit*; 58 B-52H *Stratofortress*
  FTR 265: 96 F-15C *Eagle*; 10 F-15D *Eagle*; 159 F-22A *Raptor*
  FGA 903: 211 F-15E *Strike Eagle*; 456 F-16C *Fighting Falcon*; 114 F-16D *Fighting Falcon*; 122 F-35A *Lightning* II
  ATK 141 A-10C *Thunderbolt* II
  EW 14 EC-130H *Compass Call*
  ISR 41: 2 E-9A; 4 E-11A; 2 OC-135B *Open Skies*; 27 U-2S; 4 TU-2S; 2 WC-135 *Constant Phoenix*
  ELINT 22: 8 RC-135V *Rivet Joint*; 9 RC-135W *Rivet Joint*; 3 RC-135S *Cobra Ball*; 2 RC-135U *Combat Sent*
  AEW&C 31: 18 E-3B *Sentry*; 6 E-3C *Sentry*; 7 E-3G *Sentry*
  C2 4 E-4B
  TKR 156: 126 KC-135R *Stratotanker*; 30 KC-135T *Stratotanker*
  TKR/TPT 59 KC-10A *Extender*
  CSAR 15 HC-130J *Combat King* II
  TPT 332: **Heavy** 197: 35 C-5M *Super Galaxy*; 162 C-17A *Globemaster* III; **Medium** 87 C-130J/J-30 *Hercules*; **Light** 21:

4 Beech 1900C (C-12J); 17 Learjet 35A (C-21A); **PAX** 22: 4 B-737-700 (C-40B); 4 B-757-200 (C-32A); 12 Gulfstream V (C-37A); 2 VC-25A *Air Force One*
TRG 1,129: 178 T-1A *Jayhawk*; 445 T-6A *Texan* II; 506 T-38A/C *Talon*

HELICOPTERS
  CSAR 75 HH-60G *Pave Hawk*
  TPT • Light 62 UH-1N *Huey*

UNMANNED AERIAL VEHICLES 350
  CISR • Heavy 310: 110 MQ-1B *Predator* (being withdrawn); 200 MQ-9A *Reaper*
  ISR • Heavy 42: 3 EQ-4B; 29 RQ-4B *Global Hawk*; ε10 RQ-170 *Sentinel*

AIR DEFENCE • SAM • Point-defence FIM-92 *Stinger*

AIR-LAUNCHED MISSILES
  AAM • IR AIM-9 *Sidewinder*; **IIR** AIM-9X *Sidewinder* II; **SARH** AIM-7M *Sparrow*; **ARH** AIM-120C/D AMRAAM
  ASM AGM-65D/G *Maverick*; AGM-130A; AGM-176 *Griffin*
  ALCM • Nuclear AGM-86B (ALCM); **Conventional** AGM-86C (CALCM); AGM-86D (penetrator); AGM-158 JASSM; AGM-158B JASSM-ER
  ARM AGM-88A/B HARM
  EW MALD/MALD-J

BOMBS
  Laser-guided GBU 10/12/16 *Paveway* II, GBU-24 *Paveway* III
  INS/GPS guided GBU 31/32/38 JDAM; GBU-54 Laser JDAM; GBU-15 (with BLU-109 penetrating warhead or Mk84); GBU-39B Small Diameter Bomb (250lb); GBU-43B MOAB; GBU-57A/B MOP; Enhanced *Paveway* III

Reserve Organisations

Air National Guard 105,650 reservists
FORCES BY ROLE
BOMBER
  1 sqn with B-2A *Spirit* (personnel only)
FIGHTER
  5 sqn with F-15C/D *Eagle*
  1 sqn with F-22A *Raptor* (+1 sqn personnel only)
FIGHTER/GROUND ATTACK
  11 sqn with F-16C/D *Fighting Falcon*
GROUND ATTACK
  4 sqn with A-10C *Thunderbolt* II
ISR
  1 sqn with E-8C J-STARS
COMBAT SEARCH & RESCUE
  1 sqn with HC-130P/N *Combat King*
  1 sqn with HC-130J *Combat King* II (forming)
  1 sqn with MC-130P *Combat Shadow*
  3 sqn with HH-60G *Pave Hawk*
TANKER
  17 sqn with KC-135R *Stratotanker* (+1 sqn personnel only)
  3 sqn with KC-135T *Stratotanker*
TRANSPORT
  1 sqn with B-737-700 (C-40C)
  5 sqn with C-17A *Globemaster* (+2 sqn personnel only)
  13 sqn with C-130H *Hercules*
  1 sqn with C-130H/LC-130H *Hercules*
  2 sqn with C-130J-30 *Hercules*
  1 sqn with Learjet 35A (C-21A)
  1 sqn with WC-130H *Hercules*
TRAINING
  1 sqn with C-130H *Hercules*
  1 sqn with F-15C/D *Eagle*
  4 sqn with F-16C/D *Fighting Falcon*
  1 sqn with MQ-9A *Reaper*
COMBAT/ISR UAV
  1 sqn with MQ-1B *Predator*
  10 sqn with MQ-9A *Reaper*

EQUIPMENT BY TYPE
AIRCRAFT 473 combat capable
  FTR 157: 127 F-15C *Eagle*; 10 F-15D *Eagle*; 20 F-22A *Raptor*
  FGA 354: 309 F-16C *Fighting Falcon*; 45 F-16D *Fighting Falcon*
  ATK 86 A-10C *Thunderbolt* II
  ISR 16 E-8C J-STARS
  ELINT 11 RC-26B *Metroliner*
  CSAR 6: 2 HC-130N *Combat King*; 3 HC-130P *Combat King*; 1 HC-130J *Combat King* II
  TKR 172: 148 KC-135R *Stratotanker*; 24 KC-135T *Stratotanker*
  TPT 213: **Heavy** 42 C-17A *Globemaster* III; **Medium** 166: 124 C-130H *Hercules*; 20 C-130J/J-30 *Hercules*; 10 LC-130H *Hercules*; 4 MC-130P *Combat Shadow*; 8 WC-130H *Hercules*; **Light** 2 Learjet 35A (C-21A); **PAX** 3 B-737-700 (C-40C)

HELICOPTERS • CSAR 18 HH-60G *Pave Hawk*
UNMANNED AERIAL VEHICLES • CISR • Heavy 70: 35 MQ-1B *Predator*; 35 MQ-9A *Reaper*

Air Force Reserve Command 68,800 reservists
FORCES BY ROLE
BOMBER
  1 sqn with B-52H *Stratofortress* (personnel only)
FIGHTER
  2 sqn with F-22A *Raptor* (personnel only)
FIGHTER/GROUND ATTACK
  2 sqn with F-16C/D *Fighting Falcon* (+1 sqn personnel only)
  1 sqn with F-35A *Lightning* II (personnel only)
GROUND ATTACK
  1 sqn with A-10C *Thunderbolt* II (+2 sqn personnel only)
ISR
  1 (Weather Recce) sqn with WC-130J *Hercules*
AIRBORNE EARLY WARNING & CONTROL
  1 sqn with E-3B/C *Sentry* (personnel only)
COMBAT SEARCH & RESCUE
  1 sqn with HC-130N *Combat King*
  2 sqn with HH-60G *Pave Hawk*
TANKER
  4 sqn with KC-10A *Extender* (personnel only)
  7 sqn with KC-135R *Stratotanker* (+2 sqn personnel only)
TRANSPORT
  1 (VIP) sqn with B-737-700 (C-40C)
  2 sqn with C-5M *Super Galaxy* (+1 sqn personnel only)

2 sqn with C-17A *Globemaster* (+9 sqn personnel only)
7 sqn with C-130H *Hercules*
1 sqn with C-130J-30 *Hercules*
1 (Aerial Spray) sqn with C-130H *Hercules*
TRAINING
1 (aggressor) sqn with A-10C *Thunderbolt* II; F-15C/E *Eagle*; F-16 *Fighting Falcon*; F-22A *Raptor* (personnel only)
1 sqn with A-10C *Thuinderbolt* II
1 sqn with B-52H *Stratofortress*
1 sqn with C-5M *Super Galaxy*
1 sqn with F-16C/D *Fighting Falcon*
5 (flying training) sqn with T-1A *Jayhawk*; T-6A *Texan* II; T-38C *Talon* (personnel only)
COMBAT/ISR UAV
2 sqn with MQ-1B *Predator*/MQ-9A *Reaper* (personnel only)
ISR UAV
1 sqn with RQ-4B *Global Hawk* (personnel only)
EQUIPMENT BY TYPE
AIRCRAFT 126 combat capable
BBR 18 B-52H *Stratofortress*
FGA 53: 49 F-16C *Fighting Falcon*; 4 F-16D *Fighting Falcon*
ATK 55 A-10C *Thunderbolt* II
ISR 10 WC-130J *Hercules* (Weather Recce)
CSAR 6 HC-130N *Combat King*
TKR 70 KC-135R *Stratotanker*
TPT 86: **Heavy** 24: 6 C-5M *Super Galaxy*; 18 C-17A *Globemaster* III; **Medium** 58: 48 C-130H *Hercules*; 10 C-130J-30 *Hercules*; **PAX** 4 B-737-700 (C-40C)
HELICOPTERS • **CSAR** 16 HH-60G *Pave Hawk*

Civil Reserve Air Fleet
Commercial ac numbers fluctuate
AIRCRAFT • **TPT** 517 international (391 long-range and 126 short-range); 36 national

Air Force Stand-by Reserve 16,858 reservists
Trained individuals for mobilisation

US Special Operations Command (USSOCOM) 63,150; 6,550 (civilian)
Commands all active, reserve and National Guard Special Operations Forces (SOF) of all services based in CONUS

Joint Special Operations Command
Reported to comprise elite US SOF, including Special Forces Operations Detachment Delta ('Delta Force'), SEAL Team 6 and integral USAF support

US Army Special Operations Command 34,100
FORCES BY ROLE
SPECIAL FORCES
5 SF gp (4 SF bn, 1 spt bn)
1 ranger regt (3 ranger bn; 1 cbt spt bn)
COMBAT SUPPORT
1 civil affairs bde (5 civil affairs bn)

1 psyops gp (3 psyops bn)
1 psyops gp (4 psyops bn)
COMBAT SERVICE SUPPORT
1 (sustainment) log bde (1 sigs bn)
HELICOPTER
1 (160th SOAR) hel regt (4 hel bn)
EQUIPMENT BY TYPE
ARMOURED FIGHTING VEHICLES
APC • **APC (W)** 12 *Pandur*
AUV 640 M-ATV
HELICOPTERS
MRH 50 AH-6M/MH-6M *Little Bird*
TPT 130: **Heavy** 68 MH-47G *Chinook*; **Medium** 62 MH-60L/M *Black Hawk*
UAV
CISR • **Heavy** 12 MQ-1C *Gray Eagle*
ISR • **Light** 29: 15 XPV-1 *Tern*; 14 XPV-2 *Mako*
TPT • **Heavy** 28 CQ-10 *Snowgoose*

Reserve Organisations

Army National Guard
FORCES BY ROLE
SPECIAL FORCES
2 SF gp (3 SF bn)

Army Reserve
FORCES BY ROLE
COMBAT SUPPORT
2 psyops gp
4 civil affairs comd HQ
8 civil affairs bde HQ
32 civil affairs bn (coy)

US Navy Special Warfare Command 9,850
FORCES BY ROLE
SPECIAL FORCES
8 SEAL team (total: 48 SF pl)
2 SEAL Delivery Vehicle team

Reserve Organisations

Naval Reserve Force
FORCES BY ROLE
SPECIAL FORCES
8 SEAL det
10 Naval Special Warfare det
2 Special Boat sqn
2 Special Boat unit
1 SEAL Delivery Vehicle det

US Marine Special Operations Command (MARSOC) 3,000
FORCES BY ROLE
SPECIAL FORCES
1 SF regt (3 SF bn)
COMBAT SUPPORT
1 int bn
COMBAT SERVICE SUPPORT
1 spt gp

Air Force Special Operations Command (AFSOC) 16,200

FORCES BY ROLE
GROUND ATTACK
  1 sqn with AC-130U *Spectre*
  2 sqn with AC-130W *Stinger* II
TRANSPORT
  3 sqn with CV-22B *Osprey*
  1 sqn with DHC-8; Do-328 (C-146A)
  2 sqn with MC-130H *Combat Talon*
  3 sqn with MC-130J *Commando* II
  3 sqn with PC-12 (U-28A)
TRAINING
  1 sqn with M-28 *Skytruck* (C-145A)
  1 sqn with CV-22A/B *Osprey*
  1 sqn with HC-130J *Combat King* II; MC-130J *Commando* II
  1 sqn with Bell 205 (TH-1H *Iroquois*)
  1 sqn with HH-60G *Pave Hawk*; UH-1N *Huey*
COMBAT/ISR UAV
  2 sqn with MQ-9 *Reaper*
EQUIPMENT BY TYPE
AIRCRAFT 27 combat capable
  ATK 27: 2 AC-130J *Ghostrider*; 13 AC-130U *Spectre*; 12 AC-130W *Stinger* II
  CSAR 3 HC-130J *Combat King* II
  TPT 97: **Medium** 49: 14 MC-130H *Combat Talon* II; 35 MC-130J *Commando* II; **Light** 48: 9 Do-328 (C-146A); 4 M-28 *Skytruck* (C-145A); 35 PC-12 (U-28A)
TILT-ROTOR 49 CV-22A/B *Osprey*
HELICOPTERS
  CSAR 3 HH-60G *Pave Hawk*
  TPT • Light 34: 24 Bell 205 (TH-1H *Iroquois*); 10 UH-1N *Huey*
UNMANNED AERIAL VEHICLES • CISR • Heavy 30 MQ-9 *Reaper*

Reserve Organisations

Air National Guard
FORCES BY ROLE
ELECTRONIC WARFARE
  1 sqn with C-130J *Hercules*/EC-130J *Commando Solo*
ISR
  1 sqn with Beech 350ER *King Air* (MC-12W *Liberty*)
TRANSPORT
  1 flt with B-737-200 (C-32B)
EQUIPMENT BY TYPE
AIRCRAFT
  EW 3 EC-130J *Commando Solo*
  ISR 13 Beech 350ER *King Air* (MC-12W *Liberty*)
  TPT 5: **Medium** 3 C-130J *Hercules*; **PAX** 2 B-757-200 (C-32B)

Air Force Reserve
FORCES BY ROLE
TRAINING
  1 sqn with AC-130U *Spectre* (personnel only)
  1 sqn with M-28 *Skytruck* (C-145A) (personnel only)
COMBAT/ISR UAV
  1 sqn with MQ-9 *Reaper* (personnel only)

Cyber

The Department of Defense (DoD) Cyber Strategy, released in 2015, named cyber as the primary strategic threat to the US, 'placing it above terrorism' for the first time since 9/11. The US has well-developed cyber capabilities, and there are military-cyber elements within each service branch, under US Cyber Command. Cyber Command was elevated to a unified combatant command in August 2017, and the secretary of defense directed a review into the possibility of splitting Cyber Command from the NSA. Cyber Command requested a budget of US$647m for FY2018, representing a 16% increase on the previous year. Its Cyber Mission Force (CMF) of 133 teams reached IOC in October 2016 and is expected to reach FOC in 2018. The US Air Force plans to merge offensive and defensive cyber operations into a full-spectrum cyber capability called the Cyber Operations Squadron by 2026. The US Army released a field manual for cyber and electronic warfare (EW) in April 2017, and announced in May that it would develop a department-wide EW strategy. High-level DoD cyber exercises include the defence-focused *Cyber Flag* and *Cyber Guard* series, which involve broader actors from across government and includes critical-national-infrastructure scenarios. DARPA's Plan X programme has been funding research on cyber warfare since 2013 and, according to the army, 'gives commanders a way to see and respond to key cyber terrain in the same way they react to actions on the physical battlefield, and enables synchronizing cyber effects with key related war-fighting functions such as intelligence, signal, information operations and electronic warfare'. In March 2017, the Defense Science Board reported that to improve cyber deterrence the DoD should conduct tailored cyber-deterrence campaigns, boost the cyber resilience of select military systems to improve second-strike capabilities and improve attribution capabilities across government. In October 2012, then-president Barack Obama signed Presidential Policy Directive 20 (PPD-20), the purpose of which was to establish clear standards for US federal agencies in confronting threats in cyberspace. This document was made public in the Snowden leaks. It is notable for the distinction it draws between defensive and offensive cyber operations. According to PPD-20, the US 'shall identify potential targets of national importance where [offensive cyber-effects operations] can offer a favorable balance of effectiveness and risk as compared with other instruments of national power, establish and maintain [offensive cyber-effects operations] capabilities integrated as appropriate with other US offensive capabilities, and execute those capabilities in a manner consistent with the provisions of this directive'. PPD-20 states that presidential approval is required for any cyber operations with 'significant consequences'. In April 2017, government officials announced that offensive cyber capabilities had been employed against ISIS.

DEPLOYMENT

AFGHANISTAN
NATO • *Operation Resolute Support* 7,000; 1 div HQ; 1 div HQ (fwd); 1 spec ops bn; 2 AB bde; 1 EOD bn; 1 cbt avn

bde; 1 FGA sqn with F-16C *Fighting Falcon*; 1 ISR gp with MC-12W
US Central Command • *Operation Freedom's Sentinel* 8,000

EQUIPMENT BY TYPE
F-16C *Fighting Falcon*; RC-12X *Guardrail*; EC-130H *Compass Call*; MC-12W *Liberty*; C-130 *Hercules*; AH-64 *Apache*; CH-47 *Chinook*; UH-60 *Black Hawk*; HH-60 *Pave Hawk*; RQ-7B *Shadow*; MQ-1 *Predator*; MQ-9 *Reaper*

ARABIAN SEA
US Central Command • Navy • 5th Fleet: 1 SSGN
Combined Maritime Forces • TF 53: 1 AE; 2 AKE; 1 AOH; 3 AO

ARUBA
US Southern Command • 1 Forward Operating Location

ASCENSION ISLAND
US Strategic Command • 1 detection and tracking radar at Ascension Auxiliary Air Field

ATLANTIC OCEAN
US Northern Command • US Navy: 6 SSBN; 22 SSGN; 6 CVN; 8 CGHM; 14 DDGHM; 10 DDGM; 2 FFHM; 3 PCFG; 4 LHD; 4 LPD; 6 LSD

AUSTRALIA
US Pacific Command • 1,250; 1 SEWS at Pine Gap; 1 comms facility at Pine Gap; 1 SIGINT stn at Pine Gap
US Strategic Command • 1 detection and tracking radar at Naval Communication Station Harold E Holt

BAHRAIN
US Central Command • 5,000; 1 HQ (5th Fleet); 2 AD bty with MIM-104E/F *Patriot* PAC-2/3

BELGIUM
US European Command • 900

BOSNIA-HERZEGOVINA
OSCE • Bosnia and Herzegovina 6

BRITISH INDIAN OCEAN TERRITORY
US Strategic Command • 300; 1 Spacetrack Optical Tracker at Diego Garcia; 1 ground-based electro optical deep space surveillance system (*GEODSS*) at Diego Garcia
US Pacific Command • 1 MPS sqn (MPS-2 with equipment for one MEB) at Diego Garcia with 2 AKRH; 3 AKR; 1 AKEH; 1 ESD; 1 naval air base at Diego Garcia, 1 support facility at Diego Garcia

BULGARIA
US European Command • 300; 2 armd/armd inf coy; M1 *Abrams*; M2 *Bradley*

CAMEROON
US Africa Command • 300; MQ-1C *Gray Eagle*

CANADA
US Northern Command • 150

CENTRAL AFRICAN REPUBLIC
UN • MINUSCA 8

COLOMBIA
US Southern Command • 50

CUBA
US Southern Command • 950 (JTF-GTMO) at Guantánamo Bay

CURACAO
US Southern Command • 1 Forward Operating Location

DEMOCRATIC REPUBLIC OF THE CONGO
UN • MONUSCO 3

DJIBOUTI
US Africa Command • 4,700; 1 tpt sqn with C-130H/J-30 *Hercules*; 1 spec ops sqn with MC-130H/J; PC-12 (U-28A); 1 CSAR sqn with HH-60G *Pave Hawk*; 1 CISR UAV sqn with MQ-9A *Reaper*; 1 naval air base

EGYPT
MFO 410; elm 1 ARNG inf bn; 1 ARNG spt bn

EL SALVADOR
US Southern Command • 1 Forward Operating Location (Military, DEA, USCG and Customs personnel)

GERMANY
US Africa Command • 1 HQ at Stuttgart
US European Command • 37,450; 1 Combined Service HQ (EUCOM) at Stuttgart–Vaihingen

US Army 23,000

FORCES BY ROLE
1 HQ (US Army Europe (USAREUR)) at Heidelberg; 1 div HQ (fwd); 1 SF gp; 1 armd recce bn; 2 armd bn; 1 mech bde(-); 1 arty bn; 1 (cbt avn) hel bde(-); 1 (cbt avn) hel bde HQ; 1 int bde; 1 MP bde; 1 sigs bde; 1 spt bde; 1 (APS) armd bde eqpt set

EQUIPMENT BY TYPE
M1 *Abrams*; M2/M3 *Bradley*; *Stryker*, M109; M777; AH-64D/E *Apache*; CH-47F *Chinook*; UH-60L/M *Black Hawk*; HH-60M *Black Hawk*

US Navy 1,000
USAF 12,300

FORCES BY ROLE
1 HQ (US Air Force Europe (USAFE)) at Ramstein AB; 1 HQ (3rd Air Force) at Ramstein AB; 1 ftr wg at Spangdahlem AB with 1 ftr sqn with 24 F-16C/D *Fighting Falcon*; 1 tpt wg at Ramstein AB with 14 C-130J-30 *Hercules*; 2 Gulfstream V (C-37A); 5 Learjet 35A (C-21A); 1 B-737-700 (C-40B)

USMC 1,150

GREECE
US European Command • 400; 1 naval base at Makri; 1 naval base at Soudha Bay; 1 air base at Iraklion

GREENLAND (DNK)
US Strategic Command • 160; 1 AN/FPS-132 Upgraded Early Warning Radar and 1 Spacetrack Radar at Thule

GUAM
US Pacific Command • 6,000; 3 SSGN; 1 MPS sqn (MPS-3 with equipment for one MEB) with 2 AKRH; 4 AKR; 1 ESD; 1 AKEH; 1 bbr sqn with 6 B-1B *Lancer*; 1 tkr sqn with 12 KC-135R *Stratotanker*; 1 tpt hel sqn with MH-60S; 1 SAM bty with THAAD; 1 air base; 1 naval base

HONDURAS
US Southern Command • 380; 1 avn bn with CH-47F *Chinook*; UH-60 *Black Hawk*

HUNGARY
US European Command • 100; 1 armd recce tp; M3 *Bradley*

IRAQ
US Central Command • *Operation Inherent Resolve* 9,000; 1 armd div HQ; 2 inf coy; 1 mne coy; 1 SP arty bty with 4 M109A6; 1 fd arty bty with 4 M777A2; 1 MRL bty with 4 M142 HIMARS; 1 EOD pl; 1 atk hel sqn with AH-64D *Apache*

ISRAEL
US Strategic Command • 1 AN/TPY-2 X-band radar at Mount Keren

ITALY
US European Command • 12,050
  US Army 4,400; 1 AB IBCT(-)
  US Navy 3,600; 1 HQ (US Navy Europe (USNAVEUR)) at Naples; 1 HQ (6th Fleet) at Gaeta; 1 MP sqn with 4 P-8A *Poseidon* at Sigonella
  USAF 3,850; 1 ftr wg with 2 ftr sqn with 21 F-16C/D *Fighting Falcon* at Aviano
  USMC 200

JAPAN
US Pacific Command • 39,950
  US Army 2,900; 1 corps HQ (fwd); 1 SF gp; 1 avn bn; 1 SAM bn
  US Navy 11,700; 1 HQ (7th Fleet) at Yokosuka; 1 base at Sasebo; 1 base at Yokosuka
  ### FORCES BY ROLE
  3 FGA sqn at Atsugi with 10 F/A-18E *Super Hornet*; 1 FGA sqn at Atsugi with 10 F/A-18F *Super Hornet*; 1 EW sqn at Atsugi with 5 EA-18G *Growler*; 1 AEW&C sqn at Atsugi with 5 E-2D *Hawkeye*; 2 ASW hel sqn at Atsugi with 12 MH-60R; 1 tpt hel sqn with 12 MH-60S
  ### EQUIPMENT BY TYPE
  1 CVN; 3 CGHM; 2 DDGHM; 7 DDGM (2 non-op); 1 LCC; 4 MCO; 1 LHD; 1 LPD; 2 LSD
  USAF 11,450
  ### FORCES BY ROLE
  1 HQ (5th Air Force) at Okinawa – Kadena AB; 1 ftr wg at Misawa AB with (2 ftr sqn with 22 F-16C/D *Fighting Falcon*); 1 wg at Okinawa – Kadena AB with (2 ftr sqn with 27 F-15C/D *Eagle*; 1 FGA sqn with 12 F-35A *Lightning* II; 1 tkr sqn with 15 KC-135R *Stratotanker*; 1 AEW&C sqn with 2 E-3B/C *Sentry*; 1 CSAR sqn with 10 HH-60G *Pave Hawk*); 1 tpt wg at Yokota AB with 10 C-130H *Hercules*; 3 Beech 1900C (C-12J); 1 Spec Ops gp at Okinawa – Kadena AB with (1 sqn with 5 MC-130H *Combat Talon*; 1 sqn with 5 MC-130J *Commando* II); 1 ISR sqn with RC-135 *Rivet Joint*; 1 ISR UAV flt with 5 RQ-4A *Global Hawk*
  USMC 13,600
  ### FORCES BY ROLE
  1 mne div; 1 mne regt HQ; 1 arty regt HQ; 1 recce bn; 1 mne bn; 1 amph aslt bn; 1 arty bn; 1 FGA sqn with 12 F/A-18C *Hornet*; 1 FGA sqn with 12 F/A-18D *Hornet*; 1 FGA sqn with 12 F-35B *Lightning* II; 1 tkr sqn with 12 KC-130J *Hercules*; 2 tpt sqn with 12 MV-22B *Osprey*

US Strategic Command • 1 AN/TPY-2 X-band radar at Shariki; 1 AN/TPY-2 X-Band radar at Kyogamisaki

JORDAN
US Central Command • *Operation Inherent Resolve* 2,500: 1 FGA sqn with 12 F-15E *Strike Eagle*; 1 AD bty with MIM-104E/F *Patriot* PAC-2/3; 6 MQ-1B *Predator*; 2 MQ-9A *Reaper*

KOREA, REPUBLIC OF
US Pacific Command • 28,500
  US Army 19,200
  ### FORCES BY ROLE
  1 HQ (8th Army) at Seoul; 1 div HQ (2nd Inf) located at Tongduchon; 1 armd bde; 1 (cbt avn) hel bde; 1 MRL bde; 1 AD bde; 1 SAM bty with THAAD
  ### EQUIPMENT BY TYPE
  M1 *Abrams*; M2/M3 *Bradley*; M109; M270 MLRS; AH-64 *Apache*; OH-58D *Kiowa Warrior*; CH-47 *Chinook*; UH-60 *Black Hawk*; MIM-104 *Patriot*/FIM-92A *Avenger*; 1 (APS) armd bde eqpt set
  US Navy 250
  USAF 8,800
  ### FORCES BY ROLE
  1 (AF) HQ (7th Air Force) at Osan AB; 1 ftr wg at Osan AB with (1 ftr sqn with 20 F-16C/D *Fighting Falcon*; 1 atk sqn with 24 A-10C *Thunderbolt* II); 1 ftr wg at Kunsan AB with (2 ftr sqn with 20 F-16C/D *Fighting Falcon*); 1 ISR sqn at Osan AB with U-2S
  USMC 250

KUWAIT
US Central Command • 14,300; 1 armd bde; 1 ARNG (cbt avn) hel bde; 1 spt bde; 1 UAV sqn with MQ-9A *Reaper*; 4 AD bty with MIM-104E/F *Patriot* PAC-2/3; 1 (APS) armd bde set; 1 (APS) inf bde set

LATVIA
US European Command • 60; 1 tpt hel flt; 5 UH-60M *Black Hawk*

LIBERIA
UN • UNMIL 2

LIBYA
UN • UNSMIL 1 obs

LITHUANIA
NATO • Baltic Air Policing 4 F-15C *Eagle*

MALI
UN • MINUSMA 26

MARSHALL ISLANDS
US Strategic Command • 1 detection and tracking radar at Kwajalein Atoll

MEDITERRANEAN SEA
US European Command • US Navy • 6th Fleet: 1 CGHM; 4 DDGM; 1 LHD; 1 LPD; 1 LCC

MIDDLE EAST
UN • UNTSO 2 obs

MOLDOVA
OSCE • Moldova 3

NETHERLANDS
US European Command • 410

NIGER
US Africa Command • 800

NORWAY
US European Command • 330; 1 (USMC) MEU eqpt set; 1 (APS) SP 155mm arty bn set

PACIFIC OCEAN
US Pacific Command • US Navy • 3rd Fleet: 8 SSBN; 22 SSGN; 7 SSN; 4 CVN; 10 CGHM; 20 DDGHM; 8 DDGM; 7 FFHM; 3 MCO; 3 LHD; 4 LPD; 3 LSD

PERSIAN GULF
US Central Command • Navy • 5th Fleet: 1 CGHM; 1 LHA; 1 LPD; 1 LSD; 10 PCFG; 6 (Coast Guard) PCC
Combined Maritime Forces • CTF-152: 4 MCO; 1 ESB

PHILIPPINES
US Pacific Command • 100

POLAND
NATO • Enhanced Forward Presence 850; 1 mech bn
US European Command • 2,100; 1 armd bde HQ; 1 armd cav sqn(-); 1 SP arty bn; M1 *Abrams*; M3 *Bradley*; M109; 1 atk hel flt with 4 AH-64E *Apache*; 1 tpt hel flt with 4 UH-60 *Black Hawk*

PORTUGAL
US European Command • 200; 1 spt facility at Lajes

QATAR
US Central Command • 8,000: 1 bbr sqn with 6 B-52H *Stratofortress*; 1 ISR sqn with 4 RC-135 *Rivet Joint*; 1 ISR sqn with 4 E-8C JSTARS; 1 tkr sqn with 24 KC-135R/T *Straotanker*; 1 tpt sqn with 4 C-17A *Globemaster*; 4 C-130H/J-30 *Hercules*; 2 AD bty with MIM-104E/F *Patriot* PAC-2/3
US Strategic Command • 1 AN/TPY-2 X-band radar

ROMANIA
US European Command • 1,000; 1 armd inf bn HQ; 1 armd/armd inf coy; M1 *Abrams*; M2 *Bradley*; 1 tpt hel flt with UH-60L *Black Hawk*

SAUDI ARABIA
US Central Command • 500

SERBIA
NATO • KFOR • *Joint Enterprise* 675; elm 1 ARNG inf bde HQ; 1 ARNG inf bn; 1 hel flt with UH-60
OSCE • Kosovo 5

SINGAPORE
US Pacific Command • 220; 1 log spt sqn; 1 spt facility

SOMALIA
US Africa Command • 500

SOUTH SUDAN
UN • UNMISS 7

SPAIN
US European Command • 3,200; 1 air base at Morón; 1 naval base at Rota

SYRIA
US Central Command • *Operation Inherent Resolve* 1,700+; 1 ranger unit; 1 arty bty with M777A2; 1 MRL bty with M142 HIMARS

THAILAND
US Pacific Command • 300

TURKEY
US European Command • 2,700; 1 atk sqn with 12 A-10C *Thunderbolt* II; 1 tkr sqn with 14 KC-135; 1 CISR UAV sqn with MQ-1B *Predator* UAV; 1 ELINT flt with EP-3E *Aries* II; 1 air base at Incirlik; 1 support facility at Ankara; 1 support facility at Izmir
US Strategic Command • 1 AN/TPY-2 X-band radar at Kürecik

UKRAINE
310 (trg mission)
OSCE • Ukraine 68

UNITED ARAB EMIRATES
US Central Command • 5,000: 1 ftr sqn with 6 F-22A *Raptor*; 1 ISR sqn with 4 U-2; 1 AEW&C sqn with 4 E-3 *Sentry*; 1 tkr sqn with 12 KC-10A; 1 ISR UAV sqn with RQ-4 *Global Hawk*; 2 AD bty with MIM-104E/F *Patriot* PAC-2/3

UNITED KINGDOM
US European Command • 8,300
  FORCES BY ROLE
  1 ftr wg at RAF Lakenheath with 1 ftr sqn with 24 F-15C/D *Eagle*, 2 ftr sqn with 23 F-15E *Strike Eagle*; 1 ISR sqn at RAF Mildenhall with OC-135/RC-135; 1 tkr wg at RAF Mildenhall with 15 KC-135R/T *Stratotanker*; 1 CSAR sqn with 8 HH-60G *Pave Hawk*; 1 Spec Ops gp at RAF Mildenhall with (1 sqn with 8 CV-22B *Osprey*; 1 sqn with 8 MC-130J *Commando* II)
US Strategic Command • 1 AN/FPS-132 Upgraded Early Warning Radar and 1 Spacetrack Radar at Fylingdales Moor

FOREIGN FORCES

Canada *Operation Renaissance* 1 C-17A *Globemaster* III (C-177A)
Germany Air Force: trg units with 40 T-38 *Talon*; 69 T-6A *Texan* II; 24 *Tornado* IDS; • Missile trg at Fort Bliss (TX)
Netherlands 1 hel trg sqn with AH-64D *Apache*; CH-47D *Chinook*
Singapore Air Force: trg units with F-16C/D; 12 F-15SG; AH-64D *Apache*; 6+ CH-47D *Chinook* hel

Arms procurements and deliveries – North America

Selected events in 2017

- United Technologies agreed the purchase of avionics firm Rockwell Collins for US$30 billion. The new venture will be known as Collins Aerospace Systems.

- Boeing and Northrop Grumman each received a US$328 million contract for the Technology Maturation and Risk Reduction phase of the US Air Force's Ground Based Strategic Deterrent (GBSD) programme to replace the *Minuteman* III ICBM.

- Lockheed Martin and Boeing were each awarded a US$900m contract to begin design and development of options for a new Long-Range Standoff (LRSO) missile to replace the US Air Force's AGM-86B air-launched cruise missile.

- The US Navy issued a request for information for its FFG(X) requirement. The navy currently has a requirement for 20 vessels and plans to award a production contract in 2020.

- Boeing and Lockheed Martin withdrew from the US Navy's Over-the-Horizon Weapon System (OTH-WS) competition, leaving the Kongsberg and Raytheon partnership as the only industrial team currently involved.

- The B-21 *Raider* bomber project completed its preliminary design review.

- Northrop Grumman agreed the purchase of aerospace and defence company Orbital ATK for US$9.2bn.

- The US Army took delivery of the first of six M1A2 SEPv3 *Abrams* main battle tank (MBT) prototypes from General Dynamics Land Systems (GDLS). It is planned that all M1A2 SEPv2 MBTs will be upgraded to this standard. GDLS was also awarded a contract to produce seven SEPv4 prototypes. The SEPv4 standard is planned to enter service in 2025.

Table 3 **US FY2018 defence-budget request: top 15 equipment programmes by value**

Equipment	Type	Quantity	Value	Service	Prime contractor
F-35A *Lightning* II	FGA ac	46	US$5.32bn	US Air Force	Lockheed Martin
Virginia class	SSGN	2	US$5.22bn	US Navy	General Dynamics Electric Boat/ Newport News Shipbuilding
Gerald R. Ford class	CVN	1	US$4.48bn	US Navy	Newport News Shipbuilding
Arleigh Burke class	DDGHM	2	US$3.64bn	US Navy	General Dynamics Bath Iron Works/Ingalls Shipbuilding
F-35B *Lightning* II	FGA ac	20	US$2.81bn	USMC	Lockheed Martin
KC-46A *Pegasus*	Tkr ac	15	US$2.54bn	US Air Force	Boeing
B-21 *Raider*	Bbr	R&D	US$2bn	US Air Force	Northrop Grumman
P-8A *Poseidon*	ASW ac	7	US$1.38bn	US Navy	Boeing
F/A-18E/F *Super Hornet*	FGA ac	14	US$1.25bn	US Navy	Boeing
UGM-133A *Trident* II	SLBM	SLEP	US$1.14bn	US Navy	Lockheed Martin
UH-60M *Black Hawk*	Med tpt hel	48	US$1.02bn	US Army	Sikorsky
AH-64E *Apache* Remanufactured	Atk hel	50	US$935m	US Army	Boeing
F-35C *Lightning* II	FGA ac	4	US$845m	USMC/USN	Lockheed Martin
Columbia class	SSBN	LLI	US$842m	US Navy	General Dynamics Electric Boat
E-2D *Hawkeye*	AEW&C ac	5	US$835m	US Navy	Northrop Grumman

Table 4 **US fixed-wing tactical-aircraft deliveries, 2010–November 2017**

Country	Equipment	2010	2011	2012	2013	2014	2015	2016	Nov 2017
Australia	EA-18G								12
Australia	F-35A					2			
Egypt	F-16C/D			7	20				
Indonesia	F-16C/D					5	4	5	4
Iraq	F-16C/D						4	10	7
Israel	F-35I							2	7
Italy	F-35A							6	2
Japan	F-35A							1	3
Korea	F-15K	2	2	3					
Morocco	F-16C/D	3	13	6					
Netherlands	F-35A			1	1				
Norway	F-35A						2	2	6
Pakistan	F-16C/D	14	14	1					
Saudi Arabia	F-15SA							4	19
Singapore	F-15SG	4		2				8	
Turkey	F-16C/D		3	11					
United Arab Emirates	F-16E/F	3	3	1					
United Kingdom	F-35B			2	1			5	5
Total = 242		26	35	34	22	7	10	43	65

Table 5 **Selected US MRAP donations, 2013–September 2017**

Country	Equipment	Type	Quantity accepted	Delivered as of Sep 2017	Year(s) of deliveries
Afghanistan	MaxxPro ARV	ARV	20	20	2015
	MaxxPro M1224	PPV	200	200	2015
Albania	MaxxPro PLUS	PPV	3	3	2017
Burundi	Cougar CAT 1 A1	AUV	10	10	2014
Croatia	MaxxPro PLUS	PPV	32	32	2014–15
	M-ATV	AUV	162	162	2014
	RG-33/L HAGA/HAGA CAT II	PPV	110	109	2014–(ongoing)
Egypt	Caiman CAT I	PPV	400	92	2016–(ongoing)
	MaxxPro ARV	ARV	12	12	2016
	RG-33 CAT II	PPV	260	260	2016
Iraq	Caiman	PPV	267	267	2014–15
Jordan	Cougar CAT II	AUV	15	15	2013
Nigeria	Caiman PLUS	PPV	6	6	2015
	Caiman	PPV	10	10	2015
	MaxxPro AMBULANCE	PPV	2	2	2015
	MaxxPro PLUS	PPV	6	6	2015
Pakistan	MaxxPro	PPV	275	225	2015–(ongoing)
Poland	M-ATV	AUV	45	45	2014
Slovenia	Cougar CAT II	PPV	8	7	2015
Uganda	RG-33L CAT II	PPV	10	10	2014
Uzbekistan	MaxxPro ARV	ARV	20	20	2015
	MaxxPro PLUS CAT I	PPV	50	46	2015
	Cougar CAT I A1/A2	PPV	50	50	2015
	M-ATV UIK2	AUV	159	159	2015
	RG-33L Cat II	PPV	50	50	2015

Figure 4 Canada: Sikorsky CH-148 *Cyclone* multi-role helicopter

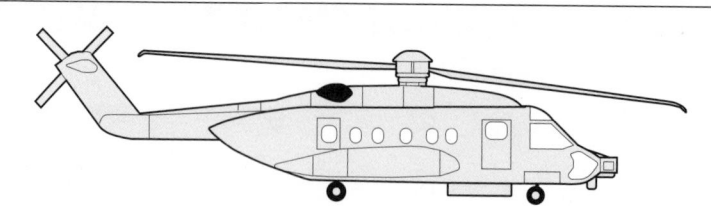

Efforts to replace Canada's CH-124 *Sea King* naval helicopters began in the mid-1980s. The aircraft is still in service 30 years later. A 1992 contract for 50 EH-101 *Merlin* helicopters was cancelled in 1993 by the incoming Liberal government due to cost concerns. A request for proposal for a new type was not issued until 1996, operational requirements were not finalised until 1999 and a production contract for the multi-role CH-148 *Cyclone* was not signed until 2004. As of late 2017, the last of the *Sea Kings* was not due to retire until December 2018.

A 2010 audit report found that the Canadian government underestimated the developmental nature of the *Cyclone*, with a misapprehension that the purchase was almost off-the-shelf. This, as well as early problems including industrial action at the Sikorsky facility in the United States, meant that successive deadlines were missed and renegotiated. Factors including cost overruns now mean that the cost of a *Cyclone* is over US$100 million – more than twice as much as Sikorsky's other anti-submarine-warfare helicopter, the MH-60R *Seahawk*.

Timeline

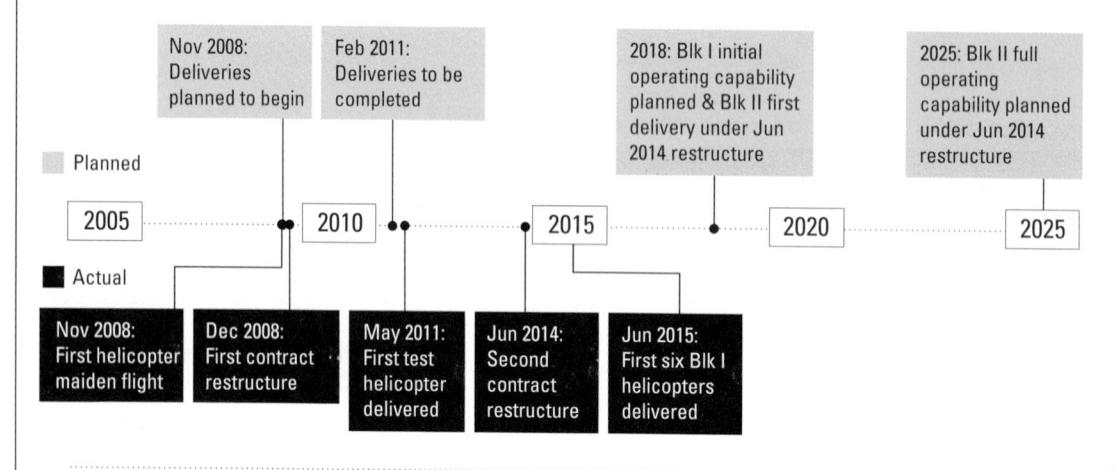

Planned:
- Nov 2008: Deliveries planned to begin
- Feb 2011: Deliveries to be completed
- 2018: Blk I initial operating capability planned & Blk II first delivery under Jun 2014 restructure
- 2025: Blk II full operating capability planned under Jun 2014 restructure

Actual:
- Nov 2008: First helicopter maiden flight
- Dec 2008: First contract restructure
- May 2011: First test helicopter delivered
- Jun 2014: Second contract restructure
- Jun 2015: First six Blk I helicopters delivered

Programme costs (US$)

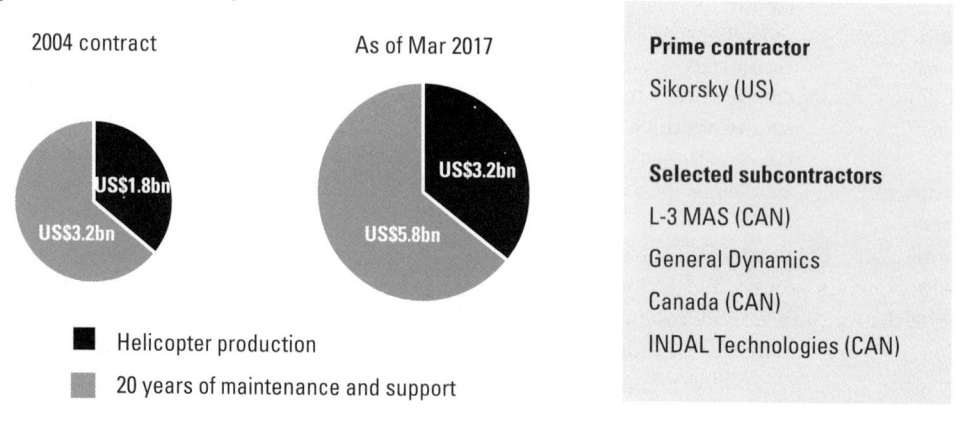

2004 contract:
- US$1.8bn
- US$3.2bn

As of Mar 2017:
- US$3.2bn
- US$5.8bn

■ Helicopter production
■ 20 years of maintenance and support

Prime contractor
Sikorsky (US)

Selected subcontractors
L-3 MAS (CAN)
General Dynamics Canada (CAN)
INDAL Technologies (CAN)

© IISS

Chapter Four
Europe

Throughout 2017, a diverse threat environment and political uncertainty about the cohesiveness of NATO and the European Union continued to put pressure on European governments to strengthen their defence capabilities. In response to this, national governments have launched a series of collaborative initiatives and have adjusted their force postures and strategy. At the same time, many of these governments are augmenting defence budgets that have slowly begun to recover from the extended period of cuts in the last decade.

Public-opinion polling across all EU member states published in December 2016 by the European Commission revealed that alongside unemployment and social inequality, migration and terrorism were seen as the main challenges to Europe. A series of terrorist attacks in Belgium, France, Germany, Spain, Sweden, Turkey and the United Kingdom strained law-enforcement agencies and the armed forces. In some countries, troops were deployed to assist civilian authorities with homeland-security tasks, such as patrolling and presence missions. The attacks also raised questions about the preparedness of civil-emergency authorities to deal with multiple events in a short time frame. Migration to Europe via several Mediterranean routes continued, although it did not reach the levels recorded in 2015. European countries continued to deploy coastguard and naval assets in response, and some (including Austria, Bulgaria and Hungary) contemplated deploying ground troops to help secure their land borders. As a result of this blending of internal and external security tasks, the requirement for closer coordination between civilian and military actors emerged as a more comprehensive challenge for domestic security than was anticipated.

Meanwhile, the challenge posed by an assertive Russia continued to animate defence discussions in many EU and NATO member states. A series of exercises around and including *Zapad 2017* served to demonstrate a more balanced and rounded Russian military capability, including progress in command and control, and the integration of increasingly advanced technology. Turkey's unclear course following the failed July 2016 coup attempt, particularly its deteriorating relations with several other European states (not least Germany) and renewed interest in a closer relationship with Russia, exacerbated the uncertainty. By the end of 2017, there was still little clarity on how the UK's exit from the EU would affect security and defence. With 'Brexit' due to take effect in March 2019, government officials across EU member states were keen to ensure that it would not negatively affect security and defence cooperation: threat assessments across the continent consistently stressed the need for cooperation to tackle contemporary challenges and risks.

The inauguration of Donald Trump as president of the United States left many European leaders uncertain about the durability of the transatlantic bond underpinning European security. Initially vague about NATO's collective-defence guarantee (enshrined in Article 5 of the North Atlantic Treaty), President Trump appeared to make US commitment contingent on increased European defence spending, notably chiding other leaders on this topic when he opened NATO's new headquarters in May 2017. Nonetheless, Trump used a speech in Warsaw on 6 July to declare that the US stood 'firmly behind Article 5', both in terms of words and actions. Indeed, in its FY2018 budget, the US Department of Defense increased the funding allocated to its European Reassurance Initiative, and continued rotational troop deployments in NATO's eastern member states. Even so, Trump's rhetoric gave NATO members pause for thought.

Following a meeting of NATO heads of state and government in Brussels, German Chancellor Angela Merkel had concluded on 28 May, with reference to the new US administration and Brexit, that 'the times in which we could completely rely on others are, to a certain extent, over' and that 'we Europeans truly have to take our fate into our own hands'. While her comments were expressed during an election rally and were therefore mostly intended for domestic consumption, they resonated throughout the Alliance, indicating that cohesion remained fragile, despite efforts to galvanise NATO into tackling the challenges posed by a deteriorating security environment on its eastern and southern flanks.

Merkel's comments also fed into a growing sense of the need to strengthen the security and defence dimension of the EU in the face of adaptation pressures, including the evolving external threat picture and the internal perception that European cooperation had run out of steam. Following the Brexit referendum and several closely fought election campaigns in which eurosceptic candidates posed serious challenges to more mainstream parties, several leaders – including those of the French, German and Italian governments – identified security and defence as a policy area in which closer European collaboration could be seen as benefiting European citizens. Indeed, a reflection paper on the future of Europe released by the European Commission in June 2017 argued that 'enhancing European security is a must. Member states will be in the driving seat, defining and implementing the level of ambition, with the support of the EU institutions. Looking to the future, they must now decide the path they want to take and speed they want to go at to protect Europe's citizens.' On 19 June, in the foreword to an implementation report on the EU Global Strategy, High Representative of the Union for Foreign Affairs and Security Policy and Vice-President of the European Commission Federica Mogherini argued that, in security and defence, 'more has been achieved in the last ten months than in the last ten years'.

Defence collaboration in the EU

Recent initiatives to strengthen the EU's security and defence dimension have worked towards three principal goals: developing practical proposals to encourage and enable member states to cooperate; building EU-level institutions; and making EU funding available for defence purposes.

Some of the proposals – such as that for the European Tactical Airlift Centre (ETAC), inaugurated in the Spanish city of Zaragoza on 8 June 2017 – have been implemented without gaining much public attention. ETAC permanently established a programme that was initiated by the European

Internationalisation of the German armed forces

The Bundeswehr has long been involved in bilateral and multilateral cooperation. The Franco-German Brigade is the best-known example. Created in 1989, it brings together French and German army units under a joint command. A French unit had been based in Germany, but this was disbanded in 2014 following French army restructuring. However, Germany's 291st Light Infantry Battalion continues to be stationed in France, while the brigade also has a binational logistics battalion.

In 1995 Germany and the Netherlands set up the 1st German–Dutch Corps. More recently, a flurry of cooperation initiatives involving the Czech Republic, the Netherlands and Romania have underlined the fact that the German armed forces are systematically strengthening existing links, or creating new ties, with European partners for the purposes of capability development and to generate formations for operations.

Other European nations are considering similar arrangements with Germany. Indeed, plans for cooperation with Poland were already well developed before a new Polish government, elected in October 2015, decided to slow the projects.

The intellectual basis for these more recent initiatives, even though they have not all been directly inspired by it, is the Framework Nations Concept (FNC), a German proposal agreed on by NATO member states at the Alliance's 2014 summit. Since then, Germany, Italy and the United Kingdom have organised collaborative initiatives under the FNC banner, although these efforts differ in focus. The German approach has been, firstly, to try to organise clusters of countries around capability-development goals and, since 2015, to provide large formations for NATO operations. At the time of writing, 16 European NATO nations, plus non-NATO members Austria and Finland, had joined in one format or another.

After the 2016 German defence white paper, and in light of the deteriorating security situation in Europe, systematic cooperation with European partners has turned into a core planning assumption for the German armed forces as they try to regenerate capabilities relevant to core NATO collective-defence tasks. While some observers assume that Berlin is pursuing a federalist European agenda, it would be more accurate to characterise the use of multiple binational- and multilateral-cooperation formats as a pragmatic approach to help Germany and other participating countries meet relevant NATO obligations.

Media discourse on Germany's initiatives often uses the term 'integration' to describe the subordination of one nation's unit to the command structures of another. It is more accurate to describe this practice as an 'association' or 'affiliation' of units, even though cooperation of this kind creates mutual dependency. While all states

Defence Agency (EDA) in 2011 to design and plan advanced tactical-airlift-training activities. The centre is jointly owned by 11 nations and training will be carried out in multiple locations. Although small in terms of personnel numbers, and focused on a narrow field of activity, ETAC is a good example of the use of pooled resources to address interoperability challenges; indeed, the model could be expanded to other training areas.

More wide-ranging proposals have the potential to drive future collaboration. One was the plan to activate Permanent Structured Cooperation (PESCO) in defence by the end of 2017. PESCO featured in the 2009 Lisbon Treaty, but thereafter lay dormant. The concept envisages a group of EU member states pursuing far-reaching defence cooperation within the EU framework. The principal reason why PESCO has lain dormant is a failure to determine how to be inclusive and effective at the same time. Critics maintained that if the criteria governing access to PESCO were too demanding, it would exclude some member states and thereby create divisions within the EU. Yet if the criteria were not demanding enough, any resulting collaboration would likely be ineffective. Nonetheless, on 22 June, the European Council agreed to launch PESCO and, in November, member states notified the council and the high representative of their intention to participate. Other challenges presented by the effort include how to structure defence cooperation with EU member states that do not participate in PESCO, and how to bureaucratically enable multiple projects to proceed in parallel under the overall PESCO structure.

Another idea that stemmed from the EU Global Strategy was the Coordinated Annual Review on Defence (CARD). The ultimate aim of this initiative is to improve the harmonisation of defence planning by establishing a voluntary exchange of information on national defence plans and contributions to the EDA's Capability Development Plan (CDP). The EDA would then analyse the information submitted and prepare a report for a 'steering board' consisting of national

preserve their legal national sovereignty over the units involved, their political autonomy in deployment decisions will likely be somewhat restricted in situations where partners disagree on the wisdom of a particular operation. Nonetheless, over time, and as long as the political will exists, international cooperation like this should improve inter-operability and, to a degree, help harmonise military requirements.

Table 6 **Selected German bilateral military cooperation from 2014**

Partner	Service	Action implemented/planned	Year	Aim
Netherlands	Army	• Association of Dutch Airmobile Brigade to German Rapid Response Forces Division	2014	• Interoperability • Preserving capability through Dutch access to German main battle tanks

		• Association of Dutch 43rd Mechanised Brigade to German 1st Armoured Division
		  ○ Association of German 414th Armoured Battalion to Dutch 43rd Mechanised Brigade
		    • Integration of one Dutch company, using German equipment, into German 414th Armoured Battalion
			2016	

	Navy	• Association of German Seebataillon to Dutch Navy • Provision of German access to Dutch *Karel Doorman* Joint Support Ships	2018	• Development of amphibious capability • Pooled use of resources • Interoperability through joint training and development of operating procedures

	Air Force	• Project Apollo
		  ○ Association of German Surface to Air Missile Group 61 to Dutch Ground-Based Air Defence Command
		  ○ Development of operating procedures, creation of binational Air and Missile Defence Academy
		  ○ Development of binational short-range air-defence task force
		  ○ Assessment of potential for joint procurement
		  ○ Creation of binational command and control capability
			2018
			
			Ongoing
			
			Ongoing
			
			Ongoing
			Ongoing
				• Ability to provide operational air- and missile-defence task force
				• Harmonisation of requirements to enable future synergies in acquisition

Czech Republic	Army	• Association of Czech 4th Rapid Deployment Brigade with German 10th Armoured Division	Ongoing	• Interoperability • Training and exercise opportunities
Romania	Army	• Association of Romanian 81st Mechanised Brigade with German Rapid Response Forces Division	Ongoing	• Interoperability • Training and exercise opportunities

ministers of defence. The exercise is designed to highlight opportunities for collaboration and sharpen member states' focus on capability areas included in the CDP. The CARD concept is to be tested from the end of 2017 to 2019. The potential benefits of CARD could be bolstered by the EDA's plan to launch a 'Cooperative Financial Mechanism'. Member states endorsed this idea, in principle, in May, with a view to establishing it in 2018. Participating member states would contribute to a fund that they could then use to pay for research and development (R&D) or collaborative acquisition projects. The EDA would release funds based on decisions by a steering board, while the mechanism would provide loans to governments that would otherwise struggle to join this kind of cooperative effort. It would therefore make a small contribution towards aligning member states' disparate procurement and spending cycles.

A more significant change is that Commission funding can now be used to finance European defence. The first steps in this process began with small research projects in 2015 and 2016. These paved the way for the Preparatory Action on Defence Research (PADR), which consists of €90 million (US$102m) spread over three years (2017–19) for defence R&D. The third step will be to implement the European Defence Fund (EDF).

The EDF contains three distinct mechanisms. The first is the 'research window', under which the EU will 'offer direct funding (grants) for research in innovative defence products and technologies'. The PADR sets the scene for this. Full funding is expected to begin after 2020, through a dedicated EU programme under the next Multiannual Financial Framework (MFF) – the financial framework regulating the EU budget. The estimated research budget will be €500m (US$564m) annually throughout the 2021–27 MFF. However, only defence R&D projects involving at least three member states will be eligible for funding.

Meanwhile, a 'capability window' will support the joint development and acquisition of defence capabilities. Contributions will mainly come from member states, but the Commission will co-finance some development costs through the European Defence Industrial Development Programme. The capability window will initially run from 2019 to 2020, have a budget of €500m (US$564m) over the two years and accept only projects involving at least three companies from at least two member states. EU funds could cover all the costs of projects in development, but only up to 20% for prototypes.

Lastly, the EDF's 'financial toolbox' includes various mechanisms to help member states overcome differences in the timing of their budget and procurement processes, and to facilitate access to finance for small- and medium-sized enterprises. From a political standpoint, these measures have come to symbolise the Commission's determination to step up its role in defence. If rolled out as planned, they would position the Commission as an increasingly important player in Europe's defence-industrial landscape.

The generation of EU-level institutions has proved more contentious. A Military Planning and Conduct Capability (MPCC) was finally approved in June 2017, one month after it had been vetoed by the UK. The MPCC, which sits within the EU Military Staff (EUMS) and works under the direction of the EUMS director general, will assume strategic-level command of the EU's non-executive military missions, such as the training missions in the Central African Republic, Mali and Somalia. It has a staff of 25, who will also liaise with their counterparts in the Civilian Planning and Conduct Capability. At the time of writing, the ultimate effect of these initiatives remained uncertain, but it was clear that many ideas about closer European defence cooperation, long discussed in governments and think tanks, were being put into practice at an accelerating pace.

NATO: settling into new realities

NATO's southern and eastern flanks are increasingly seen as persistent sources of instability and conflict. At its 2014 and 2016 summit meetings in Wales and Warsaw (see *The Military Balance* 2017, pp. 65–8), the Alliance began to drive a fresh round of adaptation to these changing external circumstances. There has been a renewed focus on collective defence as the Alliance's core mission, and a particular focus on measures to increase capabilities in NATO's Eastern European member states by way of forward presence, improved rapid-reaction capabilities and reinvestment in the ability to conduct rapid reinforcement missions within a contested environment. Significant capability challenges remain, particularly in relation to integrated air and missile defence and interoperability. In November, NATO announced an adapted command structure, including a command for the Atlantic and a command to 'improve the movement of military forces across Europe'. NATO decided on 25 May 2017 to formally join the coalition fighting the Islamic State, also known as ISIS or ISIL, in Iraq and Syria. Giving the organisation a seat at the table was intended to improve information sharing and facilitate the provision of extra flight hours for AWACS surveillance aircraft and air-to-air refuelling assets.

After 2014, NATO enlargement and the Alliance's *Resolute Support* mission in Afghanistan had drawn reduced attention, in comparison to previous years. However, Montenegro officially became the 29th NATO member state on 5 June 2017, when the accession instrument was deposited with the US Department of State. While the move was of little military significance, it sent an important political message that NATO's door, in principle, remained open amid calls to rethink the wisdom of continued enlargement. Meanwhile, *Resolute Support*, NATO's mission to train, advise and assist the Afghan security forces, faced persistent challenges. In the first half of 2017, there was increasing evidence that the Taliban insurgency was gaining ground; this led to NATO's decision on 29 June to reinforce the operation, particularly aircrew and special-forces training. Media reports at the time suggested NATO wanted member states to contribute 2,000–3,000 additional troops to the mission. On a visit to Afghanistan on 27–28 September 2017, NATO Secretary-General

NATO–EU relations

Since establishing a 'strategic partnership' arrangement in 2002, the European Union and NATO have tried to give this cooperation practical meaning. However, the EU's decision to grant EU membership to Cyprus in 2004, and Turkey's resulting decision to effectively block formal exchanges between the two organisations, put the brakes on a relationship that all major stakeholders consider, at least in principle, to be one that should be characterised by complementarity and mutual benefit.

The deteriorating security environment in Europe, particularly the 'hybrid' challenges perceived in the south and east, has provided a new impulse for cooperation. Governments are responding to the perception that tackling modern challenges requires a broad spectrum of civilian–military instruments and that electorates are seeking effectiveness and efficiency from national defence budgets. Against this backdrop, NATO and the EU adopted a Joint Declaration at the Alliance's 2016 Warsaw Summit. The declaration focused on seven areas: hybrid threats; cyber security and defence; security and defence capacity-building in partner countries; enabling defence-industrial research activities; coordinating maritime operations and maritime situational awareness; coordinating exercises; and coherent and complementary defence-capability development. In December 2016, a catalogue of 42 action items spanning the seven priority areas was presented to the staffs of both organisations to take forward from 2017.

A progress report published on 14 June 2017, and endorsed by the NATO and EU councils, suggests that 'cooperation between the two organisations is now becoming the established norm, a daily practice, fully corresponding to the new level of ambition' promoted by the 2016 Joint Declaration. It is premature to speak of a substantive breakthrough, but practical and meaningful progress has been made since the declaration was signed in Poland. For example, the EU and NATO are working on a joint intelligence assessment on aspects of hybrid challenges, and have encouraged interaction between their respective analysis cells. In addition, both the EU's External Action Service and the NATO Secretariat have been involved in the new Helsinki-based European Centre of Excellence for Countering Hybrid Threats, even though neither is a formal member of the centre. Meanwhile, the organisations' respective cyber-emergency-response teams have begun to develop a relationship, and are sharing cyber-security concepts. NATO and the EU are also actively looking to coordinate some of their hybrid-scenario-response exercises under the Parallel and Coordinated Exercises initiative.

Security and defence capacity-building has been a priority for both organisations, although in the past these activities have not been well coordinated and some operations have even revealed a degree of residual institutional competition. In the capacity-building arena, NATO and the EU decided to pursue three pilot projects in Bosnia-Herzegovina, Moldova and Tunisia to test mechanisms for closer coordination; part of the planning for these mechanisms involves the allocation of EU funding to NATO programmes.

Overall, cooperation between NATO and the EU has proceeded pragmatically since mid-2016. While the structures enabling interaction between the two have grown stronger, in many cases they are still informal because the Cyprus question has not yet been resolved. Furthermore, the EU, which has a wider range of tools available for conflict prevention and crisis management than does NATO, is still struggling with internal coherence and capacity. If the trajectory observed in 2017 persists, NATO–EU collaboration will soon come up against political limitations that only member states, not Brussels-based institutions, can overcome.

Jens Stoltenberg stated, 'NATO doesn't quit when the going gets tough'. In November he indicated that troop numbers would rise from 13,000 to 16,000, and that NATO's financial support for Afghanistan's national-security forces was secure until 2020.

US pressure on European allies to spend more on defence intensified after President Trump took office. During the presidential campaign, Trump had expressed his frustration at what he considered to be inadequate efforts by European governments to spend at least 2% of their GDP on defence – the target that NATO members agreed in 2014 to meet by 2024. During the NATO meeting of heads of state and government on 25 May 2017, the first attended by Trump, all members of the Alliance agreed to develop and submit to NATO annual national plans detailing the measures they were taking to meet NATO obligations on spending, troop contributions and capabilities. This decision was meant to signal to the US that NATO was a serious organisation worth investing in. Secretary-General Stoltenberg said that 'the annual national plans will help us keep up the momentum, to invest more and better in our defence'. Trump noted that 'we should recognize that with these chronic underpayments and growing threats, even 2 percent of GDP is insufficient to close the gaps in modernizing, readiness, and the size of forces. We have to make up for the many years lost. Two percent is the bare minimum for confronting today's very real and very vicious threats.' While many NATO member states have indeed begun to increase their defence spending, this seems to be motivated more by changing threat perceptions than US pressure. Nonetheless, the need to explain each nation's NATO commitments more clearly to electorates will be felt across Europe.

DEFENCE ECONOMICS

A favourable economic context

The macroeconomic situation continues to improve across Europe. In the euro area, 2017 was the fifth consecutive year of growth. In general, the continent's economic indicators improved, with a continued fall in unemployment and an increase in private consumption. These trends were enabled not only by the European Central Bank's low-interest-rate policies, which favoured credit growth, but also by increasing (though still relatively low) oil prices. The European Commission forecast growth of 1.9% for EU member states in 2017 and 2018. Central and

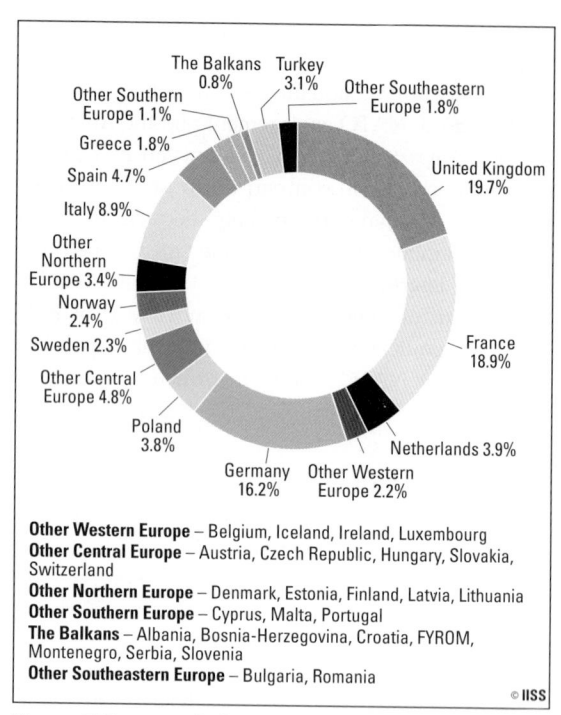

Figure 5 **Europe defence spending by country and sub-region, 2017**

Eastern European states experienced particularly strong growth in 2017, as seen in rates of 5.5% in Romania, 3.8% in Poland and 3.8% in Latvia. Some Southern European economies also performed well, with a return to growth in Greece (1.8%) and another year of strong growth in Spain (3.1%), albeit with Italy experiencing the slowest rate this year in the eurozone (1.5%). However, the long-term consequences of the financial crisis are still felt in many countries. Emergency expenditure and fiscal-stimulus packages, adopted in response to the crisis from 2008 onwards, have generated a legacy of high debt levels and fiscal imbalances. This legacy has prevented governments from significantly raising public expenditure. However, the picture is not uniform. In Northern and Central Europe, the ratio of debt to GDP is lower than in Western and Southern Europe. For instance, Latvia's and Lithuania's debt represents around 40% of their GDP, similar to Denmark and Sweden. In contrast, the level of debt-to-GDP is around 100% in Belgium, France and Spain, and even higher in Italy (133%) and Portugal (129%).

Defence spending: the upturn continues

In 2017 European defence spending increased by 3.6% in real terms (in constant 2010 US$). This is

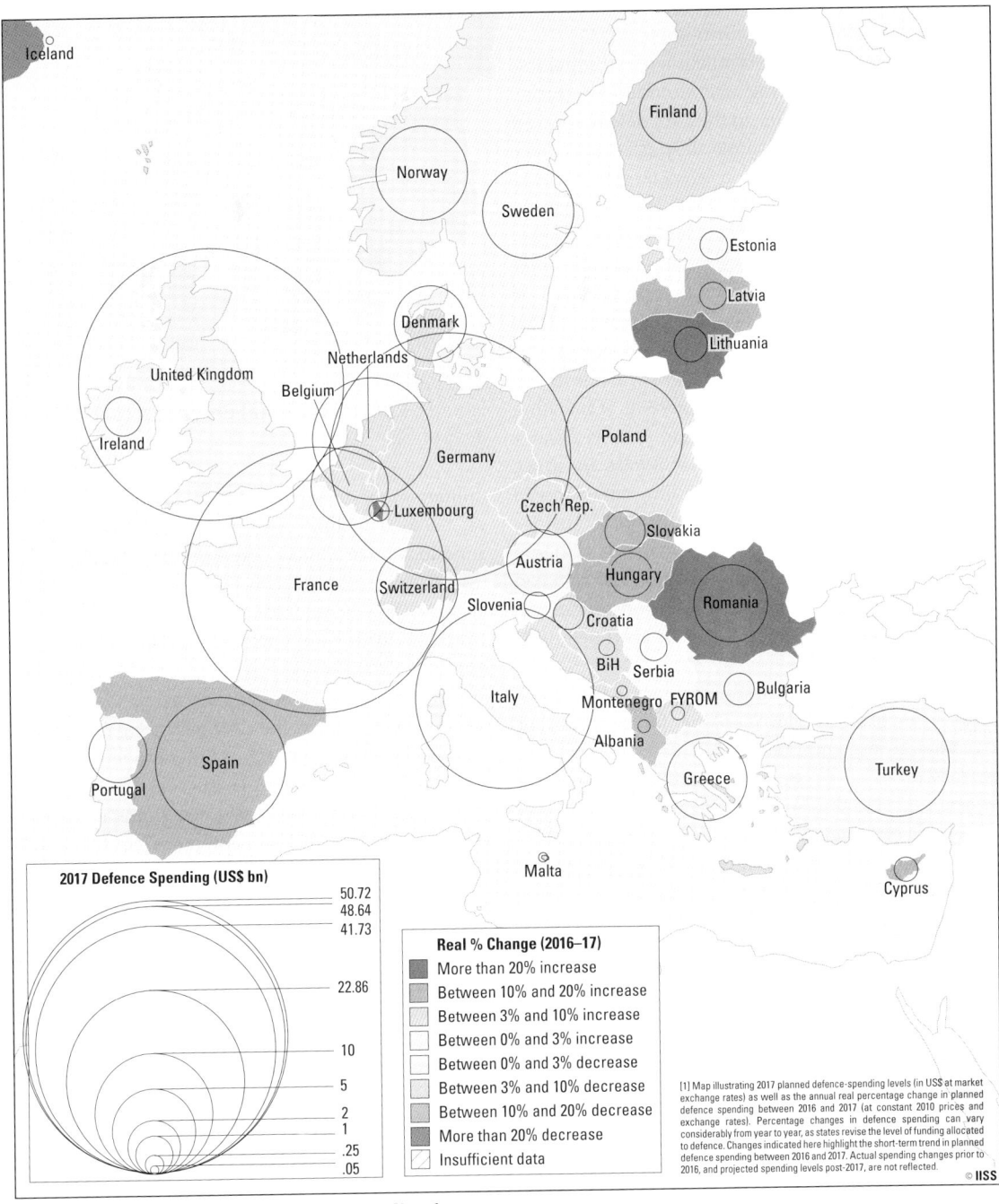

Map 1 **Europe regional defence spending**[1]

Sub-regional groupings referred to in defence economics text: Central Europe (Austria, Czech Republic, Germany, Hungary, Poland, Slovakia and Switzerland), Northern Europe (Denmark, Estonia, Finland, Latvia, Lithuania, Norway and Sweden), Southern Europe (Cyprus, Greece, Italy, Malta, Portugal and Spain), Southeastern Europe (Bulgaria, Romania and Turkey), the Balkans (Albania, Bosnia-Herzegovina, Croatia, FYROM, Montenegro, Serbia and Slovenia) and Western Europe (Belgium, France, Iceland, Ireland, Luxembourg, the Netherlands and the United Kingdom).

a sustained trend, observed since 2015, and driven by economic improvements and changing threat perceptions. Real-terms defence spending increased particularly in Germany (6.9%), Poland (3.2%), Romania (41.2%) and in Baltic countries. Nonetheless, while defence spending is rising across the continent, there are sub-regional variations. Western states aiming to play a global security role are attempting to maintain these levels, despite budgetary constraints. In Central and Eastern

Europe, increased budgets are allowing states to redefine their European security roles.

In France, the new government led by Emmanuel Macron, elected in spring 2017, announced during the summer that it would cut the 2017 defence budget by €850 million (US$959m), despite expectations to the contrary. This decision was taken in order to support the EU's goal to limit public deficits to under 3% of GDP. The announced cuts will primarily affect equipment programmes, likely delaying deliveries, as well as ongoing projects such as modernisation of the *Mirage* 2000D combat aircraft. However, in the wake of this announcement, the government declared that the defence budget would grow in 2018, by €1.8 billion (US$2bn), with the objective of reaching NATO's 2% of GDP target in 2025 (one year later than the target date agreed on in Wales in 2014). Within a context of budget restraint, some media reports assert that Macron may be ready to reconsider the extent of French military engagements at home and abroad, to allow for a closer alignment between means and ambitions. Public-security considerations, however, would likely loom large in any such decision.

The UK finds itself in a similar situation as France, with an increase in total spending, but an apparent overstretch in commitments. UK defence spending increased from £38.8bn (US$52.6bn) in 2016 to £39.7bn (US$50.7bn) in 2017. This meant a nominal growth of 2.3% but, given exchange-rate fluctuations in 2017, a fall of 3.5% in current US dollars. In real terms, this still represented an increase of 0.5%. While the government announced a £178bn (US$228bn) equipment strategy for 2016–26, including £82bn (US$105bn) for new equipment, doubts were raised throughout 2017 about the feasibility of these plans. Both the National Audit Office and the House of Commons Public Accounts Committee cautioned that the cost of the Defence Equipment Plan had been underestimated. The main causes identified were the lack of detailed plans for savings; the fall in sterling, which has increased the cost of purchasing equipment from the United States; and the fact that £10bn (US$13bn) of headroom funds have already been allocated. The risk is that should new emergency requirements arise, the Ministry of Defence will have little flexibility to acquire any significant new capabilities from within its budget.

While the UK and France struggle to maintain capabilities to match their global ambitions, increased spending elsewhere in Europe is enabling

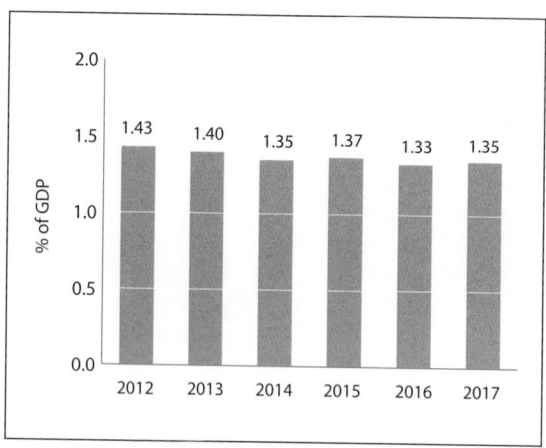

Figure 6 **Europe regional defence expenditure** as % of GDP

military modernisation. In its financial plan for 2017–21, released in June 2017, the German government announced that military expenditure would increase from €37bn (US$41.7bn) in 2017 to €42.4bn (US$50bn) in 2021. This would mean that defence spending would reach 1.16% of GDP by 2021, according to IMF forecasts. To meet the NATO 2% goal by that date, however, the budget would need to rise to more than €70bn (US$79bn). For the time being, the extra funds are expected to support the broader modernisation of the German armed forces. To this end, the Bundestag approved a series of defence programmes in June 2017, in advance of the September elections. This included the modernisation of 104 *Leopard* 2 main battle tanks (MBTs) and the acquisition of five K-130 frigates. There was also some focus on procurements relevant to multinational cooperation, such as the life-extension programme for NATO's AWACS fleet; and Germany's share of the European Defence Agency's (EDA) Multinational Multi-Role Tanker Transport Fleet programme, which, the EDA announced, would expand its projected fleet from two aircraft to seven. (The aircraft will be NATO-owned and will operate as pooled assets.) In June, Germany and Norway joined the Netherlands and Luxembourg in the project.

Although European states are primarily boosting spending due to their own threat perceptions, US pressure has also had an effect. The Romanian government increased its budget, from RON11.2bn (US$2.8bn) in 2016 to RON16.3bn (US$4bn) in 2017, a nominal rise of 46%. This allows Romania to meet the NATO target in 2017, with defence spending of 2.03% of GDP. The Romanian government plans to increase spending to RON20.3bn (US$5bn) by 2020. This shift comes with an increased focus on equipment procurement. In 2017 capital expenses took up 48.2% of the total defence budget. Besides meeting NATO targets, Romania has sent other signals to NATO, and Washington in particular. For instance, the government aims to purchase 36 F-16 combat aircraft from the US, having previously acquired 12 second-hand F-16s from Portugal. Current plans also involve the acquisition of the *Patriot* air-defence system from Raytheon and the High Mobility Artillery Rocket System (HIMARS) from Lockheed Martin.

Procurement trends: modernisation under way

It is estimated that around US$42bn, or around 19% of total EU member state defence spending (US$225bn), was allocated to procurement in 2016, including R&D.

Procurement notably increased in Eastern and Northern Europe, following Russia's annexation of Crimea in 2014. Countries in these regions are trying to reduce their dependence on legacy Russian equipment in favour of Western materiel. For instance, Bulgaria, Poland and Slovakia still operate Russian-built MiG-29 *Fulcrum* combat aircraft, while Croatia and Romania still operate MiG-21 *Fishbed*s. Poland is considering the procurement of F-35 or F-16 combat aircraft, and Romania favours the F-16, while Bulgaria is going to issue another tender for its combat-aircraft requirement. Meanwhile, Croatia's combat-aircraft tender was sent to Greece, Israel and the US for F-16s, South Korea for the FA-50 and Sweden for the *Gripen*. Air defence is also being addressed. Poland is buying the *Patriot* system, while the Baltic states, constrained by relatively small budgets, are reportedly considering the joint procurement of an air-defence capability.

As Central and Northern European countries look to modernise their arsenals by swapping out their Russian systems, Western and Southern European countries are adding new capabilities. Armed unmanned aerial vehicles (UAVs) are a case in point. The UK has operated US-built weapons-capable UAVs since 2007, with its MQ-9A *Reaper*s. In late 2016, the British government announced that these systems would be replaced by the *Protector* MQ-9 variant, which would be capable of carrying MBDA's *Brimstone* 2 missiles and Raytheon's *Paveway* IV guided bombs. In 2015 the US authorised Italy to arm its MQ-9 *Reaper*s with *Hellfire* missiles, although it remains unclear whether this has been carried out. Other European countries are following suit. The German defence ministry intends to lease *Heron* TP UAVs from Israel; these could be armed, although the decision to do so was postponed in June 2017. *Brimstone* is a potential candidate weapon. Meanwhile, summer 2017 saw the French defence ministry announce that its *Reaper*s would be armed in the short term – potentially with *Hellfire* or *Brimstone* missiles.

Industry: manoeuvres in the naval sector

Europe's shipbuilding sector showed divergent trends in 2017. France and Italy, for instance, are eyeing consolidation. In 2016 South Korea's STX Offshore and Shipbuilding filed for bankruptcy. This company owned a 66.6% share in STX Europe, which itself owned French shipbuilding firm STX France/Chantiers de l'Atlantique, located in Saint-Nazaire. The yard in Saint-Nazaire built the *Mistral*-class amphibious assault ships and is the only facility in France capable of building aircraft carriers. After the bankruptcy, the only candidate to take over the French shipyard was Italy's Fincantieri. With the French state retaining 33.4% of the shares in STX France/Chantiers de l'Atlantique, the French and Italian governments agreed in April 2017 to an ownership structure. However, the new French government initially refused to accept this arrangement, announcing in July that it would temporarily nationalise STX France to forestall potential job losses. In late September 2017, Paris and Rome reached a new deal on the joint ownership of STX France, announcing a road map for June 2018 to discuss a future alliance between Naval Group and Fincantieri that could provide a focal point for further efforts to consolidate Europe's fragmented shipbuilding industry.

Meanwhile, the UK government sought to stimulate competition in order to sustain several domestic naval shipyards, in contrast to its previous strategy of consolidation, which had left BAE Systems as a near-monopoly supplier in the UK. The thrust of the UK's National Shipbuilding Strategy, released in September 2017, was to encourage different private UK shipyards to bid to build the new Type-31e frigate (perhaps in distributed blocks, which would be assembled in a single location). Similarly, Germany ordered five Type-K130 frigates from a consortium of domestic shipyards (comprising Lürssen Werft & Co. KG, ThyssenKrupp Marine Systems and German Naval Yards Kiel) – although it did so for legal rather than economic reasons. This focus on competition in

Germany and the UK would seem to indicate that naval shipbuilding in Europe will resist consolidation in the near term, despite recent efforts in this direction in France and Italy.

FRANCE

After winning the May presidential election, and with his new political party La République en Marche victorious in the June parliamentary election, there was international interest not only in Emmanuel Macron's defence views but also the degree to which they would form part of his ambitious reform agenda. However, one of the administration's first moves was to cut €850 million (US$959m) from the 2017 budget, thereby delaying some equipment programmes, in order to try to comply with EU budget rules (see p. 72). General Pierre de Villiers, then chief of defence staff, voiced his opposition to the plan, arguing that French forces were overstretched in view of their operational commitments. Following a dispute with the administration that spilled into the public domain, de Villiers resigned. In July, he was replaced by General François Lecointre, former chief of the prime minister's military cabinet.

Nonetheless, at the same time as reducing the 2017 budget, Macron has also said that he wants France to reach, by 2025, the NATO target to spend 2% of GDP on defence; this would take the budget to more than €53 billion (US$63bn). Moreover, he announced a defence-budget increase of €1.6bn (US$1.8bn) between 2018 and 2022. However, to reach this target by 2025, defence spending would then have to increase by at least €3.5bn (US$3.9bn) each year between 2022 and 2025 (following the 2022 presidential elections). Many observers believe such sharp increases are unlikely to occur.

Integral to the budget debate is not simply the cost of operations and equipment, but also the cost of modernising France's sea- and air-launched nuclear weapons and related delivery systems. It is estimated that the cost of this process will increase from €3.9bn (US$4.4bn) in 2017 to €6bn (US$6.8bn) per year in 2020–25, but decrease thereafter – with these outlays likely to come at the expense of conventional procurements.

The capability of the new generation of French nuclear-powered ballistic-missile submarines is crucial for the navy (submarine construction is supposed to begin in 2019), but so too is the capability of future versions of the M51 submarine-launched missile. The new M51.2 should be delivered in 2020, and the M51.3 in 2025, while research into the M51.4 is due to start in 2022. For the air component, a mid-life upgrade of the current ASMPA missile, called ASMPA-R, is planned for 2022; it is understood that a decision will be made in 2018 about a successor weapon. This successor programme is currently designated ASN4G, and is planned for delivery in 2035. The design is likely to involve a choice between a hypersonic platform and one incorporating stealthy features. While it is expected that the significant outlays associated with this modernisation will come at the expense of conventional capabilities, at the time of writing no decisions on this had been announced.

Compounding these issues is the question of overstretch, which has been gradually acknowledged by political leaders. In early September 2017, the chief of defence staff declared in Toulon at the 'Defence Summer University' that the French armed forces have been used at '130% of their capabilities and now need time to regenerate'. Several ongoing operations – principally, the domestic *Sentinelle* operation, as well as combat missions in Mali and those against the Islamic State, otherwise known as ISIS or ISIL, have added to France's already extensive deployments. *Sentinelle*, which began after the *Charlie Hebdo* attacks in 2015, has mobilised over 10,000 troops in France on surveillance and protection duties designed to prevent terrorist attacks. As the operation has been criticised by defence specialists (and many in the armed forces) for draining resources, it was announced that operational commitments would change at the end of 2017. The two other major operations are *Barkhane* in the Sahel and *Chammal*, France's contribution to the anti-ISIS coalition – which involve around 4,000 personnel and 1,200 personnel respectively.

Immediately after his election, Macron commissioned a strategic defence review. Completed in early October 2017, this was a shorter and less ambitious process than the 2008 and 2013 white books. It maintained many of the key themes in these reports, and also stressed that challenges in cyberspace and from disruptive technologies meant that France had to maintain the capability for independent opposed-entry operations. In addition, it emphasised France's commitment to NATO but also expressed support for EU security tools and the EU's Common Security and Defence Policy.

In a major speech on the EU in September, Macron laid out his European credentials, making reference to a 'European autonomous capacity for action, complementary to NATO', which should be in place 'by the beginning of the next decade'. He went on to call for a joint intervention capability, a common defence fund and a common doctrine, with moves towards the creation of a 'shared strategic culture'. Macron has also called for closer cooperation between France and Germany in the military sphere, announcing with German Chancellor Angela Merkel in July that the two countries would explore the potential development of a new combat aircraft. It was also announced that both countries would reinforce other areas of defence cooperation, including a possible European maritime-patrol aircraft, a medium-altitude long-endurance unmanned aerial vehicle and a joint C-130J transport-aircraft unit from 2021.

NORWAY

Norway's armed forces are undergoing a period of significant readjustment in order to deal with a new security environment in which the country has to balance its response to a resurgent Russia while also maintaining its active international engagement. A long-term defence plan, approved by parliament in November 2016, highlighted the need to procure new and more advanced capabilities; improve combat readiness, logistics support and force protection; and strengthen host-nation support to sustain NATO forces. Defence funding is being increased, and it is planned that around 25% of the budget will be allocated to investments, but, without a further significant increase in defence funding, the budget will not reach NATO's 2% defence-spending pledge by 2024. Nonetheless, Norway's armed forces are on a new course, with the balance of military striking power – and the core of Norway's deterrent capacity – shifting to the air and maritime domains.

Security policy

Russia's assertive security and military policies, and the ongoing modernisation of its conventional and nuclear forces, combine to make it more capable of power projection. In Europe's High North, Russia's military posture underscores the asymmetrical character of the Norwegian–Russian relationship. Russia's military-modernisation process has improved readiness (which would reduce warning times for its opponents in any military contingency), while the country also has the capability to carry out covert and cyber operations. In a worst-case scenario, the concern is that Russia could seek a fait accompli before NATO

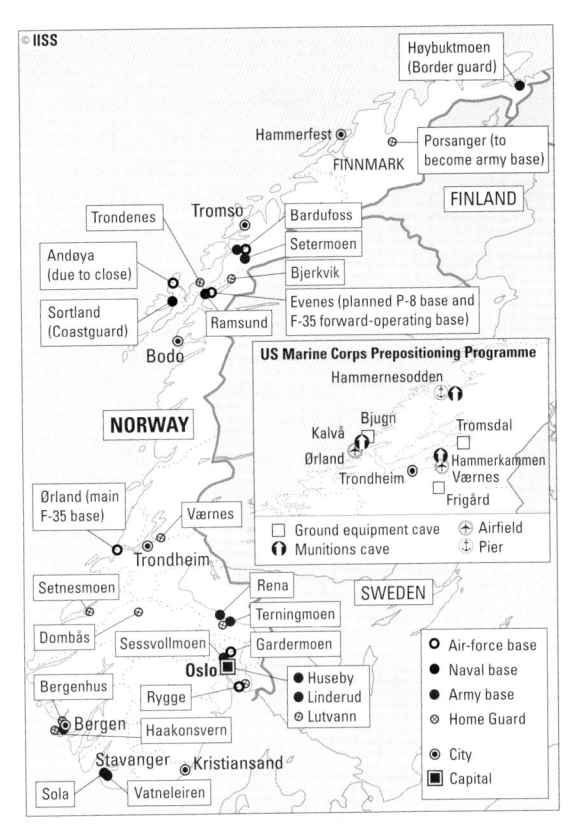

Map 2 **Norway: key military bases**

allies decide to engage or reinforcements arrive, supported by anti-access capabilities that effectively act as a strategic challenge to transatlantic defence. These capabilities hold at risk NATO's ability to rapidly reinforce its eastern and northern allies, and potentially imperil the link between North America and Europe. One aspect that troubles Norwegian defence officials relates to Russia's strategies to protect its nuclear-powered ballistic-missile submarines. In a major conflict, Russia might attempt to defend its strategic submarines in an Arctic 'bastion' by establishing sea control in northern waters and sea denial down to the Greenland–Iceland–United Kingdom gap. Norway's defence planners, including its defence minister, have expressed concern that 'Russia is revitalising the bastion-defence concept'. Another capability challenge relates to the advanced weapons being introduced into Russian service, including precision-guided systems such as the S-400 (SA-21 *Growler*) air-defence system, the *Iskander* (SS-26 *Stone*) short-range ballistic-missile system and the *Kalibr* (SS-N-30) and Kh-101 cruise missiles. All of these systems are being deployed across Russia's military districts, and some of them have been used on operations.

Nonetheless, stability and cooperation remain key objectives for both Norway and Russia in the north; Norway's policy towards Russia combines deterrence and defence with reassurance and collaboration. For instance, in peacetime, Norway does not allow large Alliance exercises in its northernmost county, Finnmark, and there are limits on NATO air operations from Norwegian bases close to the Russian border. In March 2014, Norway suspended most of its bilateral military cooperation with Russia, but, within the limits set by these sanctions, the two countries continue to work together in areas such as coastguard and border-guard activities, search and rescue, and efforts to uphold the Incidents at Sea Agreement. Furthermore, growing tension between Russia and the West has not led to a breakdown of the direct line between Norwegian Joint Headquarters and Russia's Northern Fleet.

NATO

NATO remains the cornerstone of Norwegian security and defence policy. Over the past ten years, however, Norwegian officials have argued that the Alliance has focused too narrowly on international crisis-management operations.

Norway's launch of the Core Area Initiative in 2008 marked a return to traditional thinking. This underlined the importance of collective defence and a better balancing of core functions in the Euro-Atlantic area with out-of-area operations. Since then, Norway has worked systematically to rebuild the credibility of Article 5 in two principal ways. The first is by stressing the need to reform NATO's command structure; prepare for high-end operations; more closely bind together NATO headquarters and national and multinational headquarters; and increase the Alliance's regional focus. Secondly, when preparing for NATO's 2016 Warsaw Summit, Norway – in cooperation with France, Iceland and the UK – launched new proposals aimed at strengthening NATO's posture and activities in the North Atlantic. From Norway's perspective, NATO needs to reintroduce one joint headquarters with primary responsibility for the area. (Allied Command Atlantic, commonly known as SACLANT, was replaced in 2003 by Allied Command Transformation.) Norway also feels that more extensive training and Article 5 exercises are required. In October–November 2018, Norway will host the next iteration of NATO's *Trident Juncture* exercise, the largest exercise in Norway since *Strong Resolve* in 2002. It will involve around 35,000 participants from up to 30 countries and will offer the opportunity to test plans for reinforcements and Oslo's 'total defence' concept, as part of joint and combined operations with allies and partners.

While NATO remains important to Norway, cooperation in smaller groups and strategic partnerships with selected countries is gaining momentum. Partnership with the United States is still the 'alliance within the Alliance' for Oslo, despite uneasiness with US policy under President Donald Trump. Bilateral military cooperation is being expanded in a number of fields. Intelligence and surveillance is one key component of this relationship, based on US technological and financial support for a number of signals-intelligence activities run by the Norwegian Intelligence Service. Another important component is the pre-positioned materiel for the US Marine Corps in central Norway (Marine Corps Prepositioning Program–Norway). In any conflict in Northern Europe, these assets would support a Marine Air-Ground Task Force and, if need be, facilitate the subsequent arrival of an expeditionary brigade. In addition to the US, Germany, the Netherlands, the UK, and potentially France and Poland are identified as strategic partners.

Nordic defence cooperation is also growing in significance, with NORDEFCO, established in 2009, an institutional framework for many activities in this area. The project was initially driven by the prospect of financial savings through common equipment procurement, based mostly on Swedish systems. Now, however, there are more dynamic developments in operations. A web of agreements and arrangements between Nordic countries and with major Western states are combining incrementally to prepare them to operate together in a crisis, should respective governments decide to do so.

Defence policy and military strategy

The long-term defence plan for 2017–20, entitled 'Capable and Sustainable', prioritises readiness, availability and sustainability, as well as investments in core or strategic capabilities. Three main categories are particularly significant:

Detection and identification
Significant resources are being spent on improving intelligence and surveillance. These include major improvements to the Norwegian Intelligence Service,

including the modernisation of ground-based listening stations and the procurement of a new and more capable *Marjata* IV intelligence-collection vessel for operations in the Barents Sea. Moreover, five new P-8A *Poseidon* maritime-patrol aircraft will replace Norway's ageing P-3C *Orion*s. Meanwhile, to enhance protection against digital threats, the government is considering establishing a 'digital border defence', designed to improve the Norwegian Intelligence Service's ability to monitor cable-routed signals passing Norway's border. There will be substantial procurement, maintenance and operational costs for all these systems.

Strike capability

Norway will soon invest heavily in combat platforms with the mobility and firepower to influence the strategic decisions of potential aggressors. These include up to 52 F-35A *Lightning* II combat aircraft, with a weapons suite that includes the Joint Strike Missile, developed by Norwegian defence manufacturer Kongsberg. Norway's F-35s are planned to reach initial operational capability in 2019 and full operational capability in 2025. Furthermore, four new submarines built in Germany will, in 2026–30, replace the navy's six *Ula*-class submarines.

Enhancing defensive capability

The NASAMS II air-defence system will be upgraded and equipped with new short- and medium-range missiles. Norway also plans to enhance NASAMS II by introducing longer-range missiles in 2024–28. They will be concentrated around the two air bases at Ørland and Evenes, in order to protect Norwegian forces 'and the areas that will serve as potential staging areas for allied reinforcements', according to the long-term defence-plan document. The concept of intertwined national and allied defence efforts in the High North is strongly emphasised in the plan.

These capabilities amount to a fundamental change in Norway's military capabilities, whereby maritime and air-striking power are set to become central to Norway's force structure and at the core of its deterrent. This marks a significant shift from the Cold War, when Norway relied on a number of army brigades, supported by sea and air power, whose main mission was to fight defensively in northern Norway until reinforced by allies. This de facto conceptual change has, however, been the subject of less debate than the size of the land forces.

The armed forces

The overall peacetime strength of Norway's armed forces, including conscripts, is approximately 24,000 personnel. In addition, the Home Guard consists of approximately 38,000 high-readiness trained reserves. A key priority in the years to come is to improve combat readiness, logistics support and force protection, and to incorporate new and more advanced capabilities. At the same time, the defence effort is dependent on revitalising the total defence concept, which encompasses mutual support and cooperation between the armed forces and civilian authorities in situations ranging from peace to war; *Trident Juncture 2018* will be a litmus test of this complex structure.

The chief of defence has full command over the armed forces, while the chief of the joint headquarters maintains operational command. The role of the service-branch chiefs changed in 2017. While they had earlier been responsible for force generation and were referred to as 'inspector generals', they have now gained additional responsibility for operational leadership at the tactical level and become chiefs of the service branches.

Recently, three significant reforms have affected Norway's personnel and competency structures. Firstly, universal conscription was introduced in 2015, making military service compulsory for women as well as men. (In 2017 more than 25% of the conscript intake was female.) Secondly, a new personnel structure was introduced in 2016, supplementing the existing category of 'officers' with an 'other ranks' category. This reform brought the Norwegian armed forces in line with most other NATO countries; commissioned officers will comprise 30% of overall personnel numbers. Thirdly, a reform of defence-education structures was launched in 2017, driven by the need to reduce annual costs by approximately NOK500 million (US$59.3m) and streamline military education according to military requirements. As a consequence, the current six colleges and the officer-training system will be merged into one organisational structure, encompassing both the military's higher academic education and its vocational education.

Army

The army's principal capability rests in its three manoeuvre battalions, with associated combat support and combat service support, which form part of Brigade North; two battalions are in the north of the country, and one in the south. The force structure also includes His Majesty the King's Guard (a light infantry battalion) and one light infantry battalion, which patrols Norway's border with Russia.

The army is facing major challenges, notably due to ageing equipment and insufficient readiness and availability. In November 2016, the defence minister initiated a Land Forces Study that was intended to provide an in-depth review of the mission, concept and structure of the land forces, within the fiscal framework set by the long-term plan. Recommendations based on the study were presented to parliament in October 2017. The mission and conceptual framework of the army have been clarified. Professional units will continue with high staffing levels, while conscription and reserves will be better utilised, with longer military service for the most demanding roles. The plans include modernising and procuring new CV90 armoured personnel carriers, establishing a ground-based air-defence capability in Brigade North and procuring a new artillery system. Instead of fully upgrading the *Leopard* 2A4 main battle tanks (MBTs), Norway plans to procure new MBTs from 2025, either in the form of a newer version of the *Leopard* or a new-generation tank that might be lighter and more mobile. The new security challenges have led to a renewed focus on presence in Finnmark. A cavalry battalion will be formed at Porsanger. This comes in addition to the earlier decision to strengthen the Border Guard with a new ranger company. Also, the Home Guard in the area will be strengthened and co-located with the army under a unified Land Forces Command Finnmark.

Navy

The navy is modernising, and intends to build a fleet around fewer, more capable platforms. These include five modern *Fridtjof Nansen* destroyers, which entered service between 2006 and 2011; a new logistics-support vessel (with replenishment-at-sea capability), which is planned to be delivered in 2018; the acquisition of four new submarines to replace the *Ula*-class boats (for which the German-designed Type 212NG was selected in 2017); and three new seagoing coastguard vessels to replace the *Nordkapp* class. Due to high costs, the acquisitions will be combined with cuts in other areas. The six modern *Skjold*-class missile-armed fast patrol boats, the last of which entered service in 2013, are planned to be phased out around 2025, when the navy's F-35As will be operational. Also, Norway plans to reduce the number of mine-countermeasures vessels in its navy from six to four, a shift that likely heralds the gradual transfer of this capability to autonomous systems deployed from support vessels.

Meanwhile, the acquisition of 14 NH90 maritime helicopters will significantly boost naval capability, but this has proven to be one of the most difficult procurements since the turn of the century, with significant supplier delays. The first eight helicopters have been delivered – the last are due in 2018–19 – and all of them are expected to reach full operational capability by 2022 or soon after.

In recent years, much of the navy has been operating at a high tempo, which has proven challenging. The new long-term defence plan outlines measures to increase the responsiveness and endurance of Norway's maritime forces. This includes increasing the number of total frigate crews from three and a half to five, which will allow for the continuous operation of a minimum of four vessels, in contrast to the original plan to operate three.

Air force

The acquisition of up to 52 F-35A combat aircraft will shape the future of the air force. With accompanying reforms to the base and support structure, the new aircraft will serve as the catalyst for adjusting the entire air-force structure. The first aircraft arrived in Norway in November 2017. The main base for the F-35s will be Ørland Air Station in central Norway, while a forward operating base will be established at Evenes Air Station in the north, with aircraft assigned to NATO's Quick Reaction Alert role. By concentrating activity in fewer bases with enhanced protection, and improving the skills of aircrews and ground crews, more resources will become available for operational activity. Yet the concentration strategy has proven controversial, especially in relation to the prospective closure of Andøya Air Station in the north, which is currently home to Norway's maritime-patrol aircraft. Norway plans to co-locate the new P-8As with combat aircraft at Evenes.

Other capabilities

The Home Guard forms the core of Norway's territorial-defence structure. Its main tasks are to secure important infrastructure and other areas, support the main combat services and allied forces, and assist civilian authorities in civil emergencies. Parliament decided in 2017 to reduce the number of personnel in the Home Guard from approximately 45,000 to 38,000 – with 3,000 held at very high readiness – and to disband the Naval Home Guard. Home Guard districts and units will see more varied levels of ambition, and there will be an increase in its presence and operational capability in the north. As the Special Operation Forces remain important in national contingencies and in contributions to international operations, there are few changes envisaged for these formations.

The government is also restructuring and modernising cyber and other information and communications technology (ICT) entities in the defence sector. The armed forces are increasingly reliant on ICT, particularly the ability to maintain freedom of action in the cyber domain. Most ICT entities will be unified within the framework of Norwegian Cyber Defence.

DEFENCE ECONOMICS

Revenues from petroleum continue to form a substantial part of the Norwegian economy, but growth in these revenues is expected to slow. Norwegian petroleum production peaked in the middle of the last decade, and the fall in oil prices has affected revenues. In 2014–16, the government's net cash flow from the petroleum sector fell by more than 60%. In addition, an ageing population will likely increase government spending on pensions and health services, which could further strain public finances.

At the same time, the continued supply of petroleum revenues will still contribute to an increase in the Government Pension Fund Global. As the figures stand, the fund's growth will provide a basis to increase the government's budgets (in a normal economic situation) by between NOK3billion (US$400m) and NOK4bn (US$500m) per year in the next 10–15 years – a significant contribution, albeit much less than in the previous 15 years, when the fund increased revenues by an average of NOK12bn (US$1.4bn) per year, when measured in fixed 2017 kroner.

However, Norway's long-term defence plan rests on a substantial increase in funding. In total, the government recommends additional funding over the coming 20 years of approximately NOK180bn (US$21.3bn), and as a part of this, a gradual increase over the first four years to NOK7.8bn (US$900m) by 2020. Approximately 25% of the defence budget will be allocated to investments, in order to finance the modernisation plans, while more resources will be allocated to alleviate shortfalls in maintenance and to improve readiness, availability and sustainability. The air force will see significantly higher growth than the other armed services because of the heavy investment in aircraft and combat bases. However, despite the increase in defence spending, the budget will remain below 1.55% of GDP in 2017, so substantial additional funding will be necessary by 2024 to meet NATO's 2% defence-spending pledge.

In addition to increased funding, the long-term plan foresees internal efficiency savings, estimated at NOK1.8bn (US$200m) by the end of 2020. This will allow funding to be reallocated to other high-priority areas within the defence sector.

Defence industry

Despite having a relatively small defence-industrial base, Norway's defence industry possesses a number of very advanced technologies and capabilities, producing several leading products and systems in the international market. The industry has a total annual turnover of around NOK12bn (US$1.4bn), and more than 70% of its revenue is generated from customers outside Norway.

The main capabilities are in the following areas:
- Missiles (*Naval Strike Missile* and *Joint Strike Missile*)
- Ground-based air defence
- Rocket motors
- Remote-weapon stations
- Advanced ammunition and shoulder-launched weapons
- Personal reconnaissance systems (nano-UAVs)
- Underwater systems
- Command, control and communication systems
- Secure information systems, including cryptographic equipment
- Soldier systems

Kongsberg is Norway's main supplier of defence and aerospace-related systems. The Norwegian state owns a 50.001% share in the company, which in turn owns a 49.9% stake in Finland's leading defence supplier, Patria Oyj. Kongsberg's product and system portfolio comprises various command-and-control systems for land-, air- and sea-based defence; maritime and land-based surveillance systems for civilian, military and other public installations; and several types of tactical radio and other communications systems, predominantly developed and delivered for land-based defence. It also produces the *Penguin* anti-ship missile and the new *Naval Strike Missile*. One of Kongsberg's major export successes is the *Protector* remote-weapon station. The firm also makes advanced composites and other engineering products for the aircraft and helicopter market.

Nammo is an international aerospace and defence company headquartered in Norway, and the second largest of Norway's defence firms. The group is owned on a 50/50 basis by the Norwegian government and Patria Oyj. Nammo operates from more than 30 sites and offices in 14 countries. It manufactures ammunition and rocket engines for both military and civilian customers, as well as shoulder-launched munitions systems; military and sports ammunition; rocket motors for military and aerospace applications; and demilitarisation services.

UNITED KINGDOM

In Europe, the United Kingdom is equalled only by France in its ability to project credible combat power but, while its forces remain relatively well balanced, many key capabilities are close to critical mass – 'the minimum threshold of operational effectiveness', according to the UK House of Commons Defence Committee. Indeed, plans to field an improved 'Joint Force 2025' face considerable challenges in delivery, not least in terms of affordability, and in sustaining or increasing personnel numbers. Due to these factors, the 'national security capability review', announced by the government after the June 2017 election, may result in further reductions in military capability.

Nonetheless, UK forces continue to be deployed on global operations, playing a major role in the US-led campaign against the Islamic State, also known as ISIS or ISIL, and modestly increasing their presence in Afghanistan. As part of NATO's Enhanced Forward Presence, a battalion-strength UK force led a multinational battlegroup deployed to Estonia, which incorporated a French company. In addition, the UK-led Joint Expeditionary Force was broadened beyond NATO member states to include Sweden and Finland.

An increase in domestic terrorist attacks saw special forces deployed to assist counter-terrorism police. Troops were rapidly mobilised to assist police on two occasions – although in both instances they were quickly demobilised. The scale of destruction in the Caribbean wrought by Hurricane Irma was unanticipated, even though some disaster-relief capabilities had been pre-positioned on a logistics ship in the Caribbean. British force levels in the region were rapidly increased to some 2,000 troops, with the deployment of helicopters, engineers and marines by air – along with the helicopter carrier HMS *Ocean*, on what was likely its final mission.

Armed services

Army reorganisation continued in 2017, with the Specialised Infantry Group (the new dedicated capability-building formation) achieving initial operational capability. The army's existing signal brigades are to be grouped into a single formation along with the intelligence, surveillance and reconnaissance brigade, and 77 Brigade, in order to better conduct 'information manoeuvre'. It was announced that MBDA's Common Anti-air Modular Missile would be bought to replace *Rapier* in the ground-based air-defence role, but the requirement for a new mechanised infantry vehicle remained unfulfilled.

HMS *Queen Elizabeth*, the first of two new aircraft carriers, began sea trials, while work progressed on readying the other, HMS *Prince of Wales*. The government announced a new national shipbuilding strategy, which included the construction of eight Type-26 anti-submarine frigates and five lighter Type-31e general-purpose frigates, cost-capped at £250 million (US$320m) each and optimised for export. Meanwhile, plans were announced to test a laser weapon, *Dragonfire*, on a warship.

The Royal Air Force (RAF) marks the centenary of its foundation in 2018. In 2017, it remained heavily committed to the campaign against ISIS, and to national and NATO air policing, while delivery of A400M *Atlas* transport aircraft continued. RAF *Typhoon* squadrons should begin to receive the *Meteor* rocket-ramjet-powered air-to-air missile in 2018. This missile will provide considerably greater performance than the AIM-120C AMRAAM presently fielded on the aircraft. The first of the UK's F-35B *Lightning* II combat aircraft are due to embark on the *Queen Elizabeth* in 2018, and the first P-8A *Poseidon* maritime-patrol aircraft will be delivered in 2019.

Defence economics

The UK increased defence spending from £38.8billion (US$52.6bn) in 2016 to £39.7bn (US$50.7bn) in 2017. This meant a nominal 2.3% increase, but given the fall in exchange rates in 2017, in current US dollars this meant a fall of 3.5% in dollar purchasing power, although in real terms (constant 2010 US dollars), this still meant a 0.5% increase in the budget. However, since the UK economy was projected to achieve growth of 1.7% in 2017, according to the IMF, this meant that the country's ratio of defence spending to GDP was 1.98% that year. Moreover, reports by the National Audit Office and the House of Commons Public Accounts Committee pointed towards a major shortfall in funding for the Defence Equipment Plan, partly resulting from the fall in the value of the pound.

The armed forces continued to be undermanned by more than 5%, with deficiencies of 5.9% in the army, 5.4% in the RAF and 2.7% in the Royal Navy (RN), particularly in the warfare, submarine, medical, logistics and engineering trades. While the Ministry of Defence has ambitious plans to improve recruitment and retention, these focus on the long term and these shortages call into doubt the plans to sustain the size of the RAF and RN.

Overall, there were multiple indications that the defence budget was coming under increased pressure, especially in relation to funding for personnel and future equipment. The government announced that the national security capability review would 'include [an] examination of the policy and plans which support implementation of the national security strategy, and help to ensure that the UK's investment in national security capabilities is as joined-up, effective and efficient as possible, to address current national security challenges'. Given that the 2017 terrorist attacks highlighted pressure on police numbers and counter-terrorism capabilities, many analysts expect that the review will examine further reductions in armed-forces capability and personnel. While the government announced ambitious plans to sustain and increase defence cooperation with Europe after leaving the EU, any economic shock resulting from Brexit would put public spending, and therefore the defence budget, under further pressure.

Albania ALB

Albanian Lek		2016	2017	2018
GDP	lek	1.47tr	1.56tr	
	US$	11.9bn	13.0bn	
per capita	US$	4,126	4,520	
Growth	%	3.4	3.7	
Inflation	%	1.3	2.1	
Def exp [a]	lek	16.3bn	19.4bn	
	US$	131m	162m	
Def bdgt [b]	lek	14.2bn	13.0bn	13.5bn
	US$	114m	109m	
FMA (US)	US$	3.4m	2.4m	0m
US$1=lek		124.12	119.64	

[a] NATO definition
[b] Excludes military pensions

Population 3,047,987

Ethnic groups: Albanian 82.6%; Greek 0.9%; Romani 0.3%; Macedonian 0.2%; other or unspecified 15.7%

Age	0–14	15–19	20–24	25–29	30–64	65 plus
Male	9.5%	4.2%	4.9%	4.8%	20.5%	5.6%
Female	8.5%	3.8%	4.6%	4.6%	22.5%	6.3%

Capabilities

Principal missions for Albania's armed forces include territorial defence, internal-security and disaster-relief tasks, and small-scale peacekeeping or training deployments. Limited defence modernisation is proceeding under the Long-Term Development Plan 2016–25. In late 2017, naval forces ended a year of operations with NATO's Standing Maritime Group Two in the Aegean Sea. Tirana deployed a further two infantry contingents to Afghanistan and contributed EOD engineers to the NATO Enhanced Forward Presence Battlegroup in Latvia in 2017. Most of the country's Soviet-era equipment has been sold, and its military capability remains limited. The small air brigade has only a rotary-wing capability, while the naval element has only littoral capabilities. The procurement of new equipment has been limited to small numbers of helicopters. However, in 2017, Albania received HMMWVs from the United States as part of a US$12 million assistance package.

ACTIVE 8,000 (Land Force 3,000 Naval Force 650 Air Force 550 Other 3,800) **Paramilitary 500**

ORGANISATIONS BY SERVICE

Land Force 3,000
FORCES BY ROLE
SPECIAL FORCES
 1 SF bn
 1 cdo bn
MANOEUVRE
 Light
  3 lt inf bn

COMBAT SUPPORT
 1 mor bty
 1 NBC coy
EQUIPMENT BY TYPE
ARTILLERY • MOR 93: **82mm** 81; **120mm** 12

Naval Force 650
EQUIPMENT BY TYPE
PATROL AND COASTAL COMBATANTS • PBF 5 *Archangel*

Coast Guard
EQUIPMENT BY TYPE
PATROL AND COASTAL COMBATANTS 22
 PB 9: 4 *Iluria* (Damen Stan Patrol 4207); 3 Mk3 *Sea Spectre*; 2 (other)
 PBR 13: 4 Type-227; 1 Type-246; 1 Type-303; 7 Type-2010

Air Force 550
Flying hours at least 10–15 hrs/yr
EQUIPMENT BY TYPE
HELICOPTERS
 TPT 26: **Medium** 4 AS532AL *Cougar*; **Light** 22: 1 AW109; 5 Bell 205 (AB-205); 7 Bell 206C (AB-206C); 8 Bo-105; 1 H145

Regional Support Brigade 700
FORCES BY ROLE
COMBAT SUPPORT
 1 cbt spt bde (1 engr bn, 1 (rescue) engr bn, 1 CIMIC det)

Military Police
FORCES BY ROLE
COMBAT SUPPORT
 1 MP bn
EQUIPMENT BY TYPE
ARMOURED FIGHTING VEHICLES
 AUV IVECO LMV

Logistics Brigade 1,200
FORCES BY ROLE
COMBAT SERVICE SUPPORT
 1 log bde (1 tpt bn, 2 log bn)

DEPLOYMENT

AFGHANISTAN
NATO • *Operation Resolute Support* 83

BOSNIA-HERZEGOVINA
EU • EUFOR • *Operation Althea* 1

LATVIA
NATO • Enhanced Forward Presence 18; 1 EOD pl

MALI
EU • EUTM Mali 4

MEDITERRANEAN SEA
NATO • SNMG 2: 1 PB

SERBIA
NATO • KFOR 28
OSCE • Kosovo 3

UKRAINE
OSCE • Ukraine 3

FOREIGN FORCES
Armenia OSCE 1
Austria OSCE 1
Bosnia-Herzegovina OSCE 1
Canada OSCE 1
Germany OSCE 2
Hungary OSCE 1
Ireland OSCE 1
Italy OSCE 1
Macedonia (FYROM) OSCE 2
Moldova OSCE 1
Montenegro OSCE 1
Serbia OSCE 2
Spain OSCE 1
United Kingdom OSCE 3

Austria AUT

Euro €		2016	2017	2018
GDP	€	349bn	363bn	
	US$	387bn	409bn	
per capita	US$	44,233	46,436	
Growth	%	1.5	2.3	
Inflation	%	1.0	1.6	
Def bdgt [a]	€	2.61bn	2.65bn	2.62bn
	US$	2.89bn	2.99bn	
US$1=€		0.90	0.89	

[a] Includes military pensions

Population   8,754,413

Age	0–14	15–19	20–24	25–29	30–64	65 plus
Male	7.2%	2.6%	3.1%	3.3%	24.4%	8.4%
Female	6.8%	2.5%	3.0%	3.3%	24.6%	10.9%

Capabilities

Defence-policy objectives are based on the 2013 National Security Strategy, the 2014 Defence Strategy and the 2015 Military Strategy. They include the provision of military capability to maintain Austria's sovereignty and territorial integrity, and enable military assistance to the civil authorities and participation in crisis-management missions abroad. The level of ambition for crisis-response operations is to be able to deploy and sustain a minimum (on average) of 1,100 troops. In February 2016, Austria completed a review of its armed forces reform programme (ÖBH 2018). The review showed that core capability indicators had fallen significantly. But the number of soldiers deployed to international missions remained the same, increasing strain on the force. The review pointed to a security environment where migration flows, international terrorism and international military crisis-management operations threatened to overwhelm defence capacity. The initial plan called for materiel and personnel reductions. However, the review argued that personnel cuts should stop and that investment be directed towards better training and more exercises, command and control, and ISR. A new defence plan (Landesverteidigung 21.1) includes structural changes to the defence ministry, as well as at the operational and tactical command-and-control level, from 2017. As a result, Austria plans to boost its rapid-response capability and to stand up three new Jäger battalions. In addition, army brigades will specialise according to roles, such as rapid response, mechanised (heavy), air-mobile (light) and mountain warfare. Initial steps were taken in 2017. In July, Austria announced it would phase out its *Typhoon* aircraft between 2020 and 2023, which would trigger a replacement procurement.

ACTIVE 22,400 (Land Forces 12,200 Air 2,800 Support 7,400)
Conscript liability 6 months recruit trg, 30 days reservist refresher trg for volunteers; 120–150 days additional for officers, NCOs and specialists. Authorised maximum wartime strength of 55,000

RESERVE 152,200 (Joint structured 25,500; Joint unstructured 126,700)
Some 7,500 reservists a year undergo refresher trg in tranches

ORGANISATIONS BY SERVICE

Land Forces 12,200
FORCES BY ROLE
MANOEUVRE
  Armoured
  1 (4th) armd inf bde (1 recce/SP arty bn, 1 tk bn, 2 armd inf bn, 1 spt bn)
  Mechanised
  1 (7th) mech inf bde (1 recce/SP arty bn, 2 mech inf bn, 1 cbt engr bn, 1 spt bn)
  Light
  1 (Rapid Deployment) inf comd (1 recce bn, 2 inf bn, 1 cbt engr bn, 1 MP bn, 1 CBRN bn, 1 spt bn)
  1 mtn inf comd (1 mtn inf bn, 1 cbt engr bn)
  6 (regional) inf bn
EQUIPMENT BY TYPE
ARMOURED FIGHTING VEHICLES
  MBT 56 *Leopard* 2A4
  AIFV 112 *Ulan*
  APC • APC (W) 78 *Pandur*
  AUV 157: 29 *Dingo* 2; 128 IVECO LMV
ENGINEERING & MAINTENANCE VEHICLES
  ARV 30: 20 4KH7FA-SB; 10 M88A1
  MW 6 AID2000 *Trailer*
NBC VEHICLES 12 *Dingo* 2 AC NBC

ANTI-TANK/ANTI-INFRASTRUCTURE
MSL • **MANPATS** *Bill* 2 (PAL 2000)
ARTILLERY 120
SP 155mm 30 M109A5ÖE
MOR 120mm 90 sGrW 86 (10 more in store)

Air Force 2,800

The Air Force is part of Joint Forces Comd and consists of 2 bde; Air Support Comd and Airspace Surveillance Comd

Flying hours 160 hrs/yr on hel/tpt ac; 110 hrs/yr on ftr

FORCES BY ROLE
FIGHTER
  2 sqn with *Typhoon*
ISR
  1 sqn with PC-6B *Turbo Porter*
TRANSPORT
  1 sqn with C-130K *Hercules*
TRAINING
  1 trg sqn with Saab 105Oe*
  1 trg sqn with PC-7 *Turbo Trainer*
TRANSPORT HELICOPTER
  2 sqn with Bell 212 (AB-212)
  1 sqn with OH-58B *Kiowa*
  1 sqn with S-70A *Black Hawk*
  2 sqn with SA316/SA319 *Alouette* III
AIR DEFENCE
  2 bn
  1 radar bn
EQUIPMENT BY TYPE
AIRCRAFT 33 combat capable
  FTR 15 Eurofighter *Typhoon* Tranche 1
  TPT 11: **Medium** 3 C-130K *Hercules*; **Light** 8 PC-6B *Turbo Porter*
  TRG 30: 12 PC-7 *Turbo Trainer*; 18 Saab 105Oe*
HELICOPTERS
  MRH 24 SA316/SA319 *Alouette* III
  ISR 10 OH-58B *Kiowa*
  TPT 32: **Medium** 9 S-70A *Black Hawk*; **Light** 23 Bell 212 (AB-212)
AIR DEFENCE
  SAM • **Point-defence** *Mistral*
  GUNS 35mm 24 Z-FlAK system (6 more in store)
AIR-LAUNCHED MISSILES • **AAM** • **IIR** IRIS-T

Special Operations Forces

FORCES BY ROLE
SPECIAL FORCES
  2 SF gp
  1 SF gp (reserve)

Support 7,400

Support forces comprise Joint Services Support Command and several agencies, academies and schools

Cyber

The Austrian approach to cyber security encompasses both military and civilian assets. The 2013 National Cyber Security Strategy was developed in conjunction with the Austrian National Security Strategy. A Cyber Security Steering Group coordinates on a government level. An Austrian cyber-security law, based on the EU NIS Directive, will establish structured international coordinating mechanisms. Operational-level coordination structures include the Computer Security Incident Response Capability (Federal Chancellery), the Cyber Security Centre (Ministry of the Interior) and the Cyber Defence Centre (Ministry of Defence). These structures reached IOC at the end of 2015 and FOC was planned for the end of 2017. The defence ministry's primary goal is to ensure national defence in cyberspace, as well as securing ministry and military ICT. A new Communication Information Systems & Cyber Defence (CIS&CD) Command was effective from 1 January 2017.

DEPLOYMENT

AFGHANISTAN
NATO • *Operation Resolute Support* 9

ALBANIA
OSCE • Albania 2

BOSNIA-HERZEGOVINA
EU • EUFOR • *Operation Althea* 191; 1 inf bn HQ

CENTRAL AFRICAN REPUBLIC
EU • EUTM RCA 3

CYPRUS
UN • UNFICYP 4

LEBANON
UN • UNIFIL 183; 1 log bn

MALI
EU • EUTM Mali 12
UN • MINUSMA 3

MIDDLE EAST
UN • UNTSO 4 obs

SERBIA
NATO • KFOR 440; 1 recce coy; 2 mech inf coy; 1 log coy

UKRAINE
OSCE • Ukraine 14

WESTERN SAHARA
UN • MINURSO 5 obs

Belgium BEL

Euro €		2016	2017	2018
GDP	€	422bn	436bn	
	US$	467bn	492bn	
per capita	US$	41,248	43,243	
Growth	%	1.2	1.6	
Inflation	%	1.8	2.2	
Def exp [a]	€	3.90bn	3.97bn	
	US$	4.32bn	4.47bn	
Def bdgt [b]	€	3.49bn	3.77bn	3.81bn
	US$	3.86bn	4.25bn	
US$1=€		0.90	0.89	

[a] NATO definition
[b] Includes military pensions

Population 11,491,346

Age	0–14	15–19	20–24	25–29	30–64	65 plus
Male	8.8%	2.8%	3.0%	3.3%	23.3%	8.1%
Female	8.4%	2.7%	2.9%	3.2%	23.1%	10.5%

Capabilities

In July 2016, the Belgian government published its strategic vision for defence, indicating the general direction for Belgian defence policy until 2030. Brussels intends first of all to stabilise Belgium's defence effort and then to provide for growth after 2020. The plan envisages a reduced personnel component of around 25,000. However, a large number of impending service retirements means that a gradual increase in recruitment is planned after 2017 as part of the overall move towards this number. The government is also keen to ensure that this reduction does not compromise operational capability, and so is investing in short-term requirements related to aircraft readiness, personal equipment and land-forces vehicles. Overall policy priorities remain unchanged, with defence policy based on multilateral solidarity with NATO, the EU and the UN; attacks in 2016 have again highlighted the threat from terrorism and have impelled closer counter-terror cooperation with France. Belgium is working with the Netherlands to consider the replacement of both countries' *Karel Doorman* (M)-class frigates. As part of the defence plan, the government envisages launching five investment projects in the short term: fighter aircraft, frigates, mine countermeasures, UAVs and land-combat vehicles. This includes plans for new light reconnaissance vehicles and upgrades to *Pandur* armoured personnel carriers. The navy has benefited from the acquisition of two new patrol and coastal combatants, while the air force is due to receive F-16 aircraft updates, as well as the long-awaited A400M. Belgium continues to pursue high readiness levels and deployable niche capabilities. Large numbers of Belgian troops were deployed for domestic-security operations following terrorist attacks in 2016, although Belgium maintains overseas deployments on EU and UN missions, as well as in the Middle East on missions targeting ISIS.

ACTIVE 28,800 (Army 10,350 Navy 1,350 Air 5,850 Medical Service 1,400 Joint Service 9,850)

RESERVE 5,000

ORGANISATIONS BY SERVICE

Land Component 10,350
FORCES BY ROLE
SPECIAL FORCES
  1 (lt) spec ops bde (1 SF gp, 1 cdo bn, 1 para bn)
MANOEUVRE
  Reconnaissance
  1 ISR bn (2 ISR coy, 1 surv coy)
  Mechanised
  1 (med) bde (4 mech bn; 1 lt inf bn)
COMBAT SUPPORT
  1 arty bn (1 arty bty, 1 mor bty)
  2 engr bn (1 cbt engr coy, 1 lt engr coy, 1 construction coy)
  1 EOD unit
  1 CBRN coy
  1 MP coy
  3 CIS sigs gp
COMBAT SERVICE SUPPORT
  3 log bn
EQUIPMENT BY TYPE
ARMOURED FIGHTING VEHICLES
  ASLT 18 *Piranha* III-C DF90
  IFV 19 *Piranha* III-C DF30
  APC • APC (W) 120: 36 *Pandur*; 64 *Piranha* III-C; 14 *Piranha* III-PC (CP); 6 *Piranha* III-C (amb)
  AUV 644: 208 *Dingo* 2 (inc 52 CP); 436 IVECO LMV
ENGINEERING & MAINTENANCE VEHICLES
  AEV 8 *Piranha* III-C
  ARV 13: 4 *Pandur*; 9 *Piranha* III-C
  VLB 4 *Leguan*
ANTI-TANK/ANTI-INFRASTRUCTURE
  MSL • MANPATS *Spike*-MR
ARTILLERY 105
  TOWED 105mm 14 LG1 MkII
  MOR 50: 81mm 18; 120mm 32

Naval Component 1,350
EQUIPMENT BY TYPE
PRINCIPAL SURFACE COMBATANTS 2
  FRIGATES • FFGHM 2 *Leopold* I (ex-NLD *Karel Doorman*) with 2 quad lnchr with *Harpoon* AShM, 1 16-cell Mk48 VLS with RIM-7P *Sea Sparrow* SAM, 4 single Mk32 324mm ASTT with Mk46 LWT, 1 *Goalkeeper* CIWS, 1 76mm gun (capacity 1 med hel)
PATROL AND COASTAL COMBATANTS
  PCC 2 *Castor*
MINE WARFARE • MINE COUNTERMEASURES
  MHC 6 *Flower* (*Tripartite*)
LOGISTICS AND SUPPORT 3
  AGFH 1 *Godetia* (log spt/comd) (capacity 1 *Alouette* III)
  AGOR 1 *Belgica*
  AXS 1 *Zenobe Gramme*

Naval Aviation

(part of the Air Component)

EQUIPMENT BY TYPE
HELICOPTERS
ASW 4 NH90 NFH
MRH 3 SA316B *Alouette* III

Air Component 5,850

Flying hours 165 hrs/yr on cbt ac. 300 hrs/yr on tpt ac. 150 hrs/yr on hel; 250 hrs/yr on ERJ

FORCES BY ROLE
FIGHTER/GROUND ATTACK/ISR
4 sqn with F-16AM/BM *Fighting Falcon*
SEARCH & RESCUE
1 sqn with *Sea King* Mk48
TRANSPORT
1 sqn with A321; ERJ-135 LR; ERJ-145 LR; *Falcon* 900B
1 sqn with C-130H *Hercules*
TRAINING
1 OCU sqn with F-16AM/BM *Fighting Falcon*
1 sqn with SF-260D/M
1 BEL/FRA unit with *Alpha Jet**
1 OCU unit with AW109
TRANSPORT HELICOPTER
2 sqn with AW109 (ISR)
ISR UAV
1 sqn with RQ-5A *Hunter* (B-*Hunter*)
EQUIPMENT BY TYPE
AIRCRAFT 88 combat capable
 FTR 59: 49 F-16AM *Fighting Falcon*; 10 F-16BM *Fighting Falcon*
 TPT 17: **Medium** 11 C-130H *Hercules*; **Light** 4: 2 ERJ-135 LR; 2 ERJ-145 LR; **PAX** 2: 1 A321; 1 *Falcon* 900B
 TRG 61: 29 *Alpha Jet**; 9 SF-260D; 23 SF-260M
HELICOPTERS
 ASW 4 NH90 NFH opcon Navy
 MRH 3 SA316B *Alouette* III opcon Navy
 SAR 3 *Sea King* Mk48 (to be replaced by NH90 NFH)
 TPT 17: **Medium** 4 NH90 TTH; **Light** 13 AW109 (ISR) (7 more in store)
UNMANNED AERIAL VEHICLES
 ISR • **Heavy** 12 RQ-5A *Hunter* (B-*Hunter*) (1 more in store)
AIR-LAUNCHED MISSILES
 AAM • **IR** AIM-9M *Sidewinder*; **IRR** AIM-9X *Sidewinder* II; **ARH** AIM-120B AMRAAM
BOMBS
 Laser-guided: GBU-10/GBU-12 *Paveway* II; GBU-24 *Paveway* III
 INS/GPS guided: GBU-31 JDAM; GBU-38 JDAM; GBU-54 Laser JDAM (dual-mode)

Cyber

A national Cyber Security Strategy was released in 2012. The defence ministry released a Cyber Security Strategy for Defence in 2014, outlining three pillars of its cyber-security capability: Cyber Defence, Cyber Intelligence and Cyber Counter-Offensive, with 'full operational capacity' by 2020. A 'Strategic Vision for Defence' covering the period from 2016–30 was published in June 2016. The armed forces' cyber capability falls under the military intelligence service, including defensive and offensive cyber operations. As of mid-2016, the armed forces do not have an offensive cyber capability. Military cyber personnel are based in the Cyber Security Operations Centre.

DEPLOYMENT

AFGHANISTAN
NATO • *Operation Resolute Support* 60

CENTRAL AFRICAN REPUBLIC
EU • EUTM RCA 9

DEMOCRATIC REPUBLIC OF THE CONGO
UN • MONUSCO 2

ESTONIA
NATO • Baltic Air Policing 4 F-16AM *Fighting Falcon*

FRANCE
NATO • Air Component 28 *Alpha Jet* located at Cazaux/Tours

IRAQ
Operation Inherent Resolve (*Valiant Phoenix*) 30

JORDAN
Operation Inherent Resolve (*Desert Falcon*) 110; 4 F-16AM *Fighting Falcon*

LEBANON
UN • UNIFIL 1

LITHUANIA
NATO • Enhanced Forward Presence 100; 1 tpt coy

MALI
EU • EUTM Mali 171
UN • MINUSMA 23

MIDDLE EAST
UN • UNTSO 2 obs

NORTH SEA
NATO • SNMCMG 1: 1 MHC

UKRAINE
OSCE • Ukraine 4

FOREIGN FORCES

United States US European Command: 900

Bosnia-Herzegovina BIH

Convertible Mark		2016	2017	2018
GDP	mark	29.3bn	30.8bn	
	US$	16.6bn	17.5bn	
per capita	US$	4,298	4,540	
Growth	%	2.0	2.5	
Inflation	%	-1.1	1.8	
Def bdgt	mark	291m	286m	
	US$	165m	162m	
FMA (US)	US$	4m	4m	0m
US$1=mark		1.77	1.76	

Population 3,856,181

Ethnic groups: Bosniac 50.1%; Serb 30.7%; Croat 15.4%; other or unspecified 3.7%

Age	0–14	15–19	20–24	25–29	30–64	65 plus
Male	6.9%	2.8%	3.1%	3.7%	26.5%	5.7%
Female	6.4%	2.7%	2.9%	3.5%	27.0%	8.8%

Capabilities

In mid-2017, Bosnia-Herzegovina adopted a 'defence review, development and modernisation plan' for the period 2017–27. The document calls for a reduction in personnel and the restructuring of the Tactical Support Brigade. According to the review, the procurement of armoured vehicles and helicopters is envisaged. The reforms reportedly constitute part of the country's effort to join NATO. Bosnia's aspiration to join NATO's membership action plan remains delayed because of an unresolved defence-property issue, including defence-ministry barracks and buildings. However, an August 2017 constitutional court decision reportedly may help Bosnia move forward in its aspiration. Bosnia contributes to NATO peacekeeping missions, most notably in Afghanistan.

ACTIVE 10,500 (Armed Forces 10,500)

ORGANISATIONS BY SERVICE

Armed Forces 10,500
1 ops comd; 1 spt comd
FORCES BY ROLE
MANOEUVRE
　Light
　　3 inf bde (1 recce coy, 3 inf bn, 1 arty bn)
COMBAT SUPPORT
　1 cbt spt bde (1 tk bn, 1 engr bn, 1 EOD bn, 1 int bn, 1 MP bn, 1 CBRN coy, 1 sigs bn)
COMBAT SERVICE SUPPORT
　1 log comd (5 log bn)
EQUIPMENT BY TYPE
ARMOURED FIGHTING VEHICLES
　MBT 45 M60A3
　APC • APC (T) 20 M113A2
ENGINEERING & MAINTENANCE VEHICLES
　VLB MTU
　MW *Bozena*
ANTI-TANK/ANTI-INFRASTRUCTURE • MSL
　SP 60: 8 9P122 *Malyutka*; 9 9P133 *Malyutka*; 32 BOV-1; 11 M-92
　MANPATS 9K11 *Malyutka* (AT-3 *Sagger*); 9K111 *Fagot* (AT-4 *Spigot*); 9K115 *Metis* (AT-7 *Saxhorn*); HJ-8; *Milan*
ARTILLERY 224
　TOWED 122mm 100 D-30
　MRL 122mm 24 APRA-40
　MOR 120mm 100 M-75

Air Force and Air Defence Brigade 800
FORCES BY ROLE
HELICOPTER
　1 sqn with Bell 205; Mi-8MTV *Hip*; Mi-17 *Hip* H
　1 sqn with Mi-8 *Hip*; SA-342H/L *Gazelle* (HN-42/45M)
AIR DEFENCE
　1 AD bn
EQUIPMENT BY TYPE
AIRCRAFT
　FGA (7 J-22 *Orao* in store)
　ATK (6 J-1 (J-21) *Jastreb*; 3 TJ-1(NJ-21) *Jastreb* all in store)
　ISR (2 RJ-1 (IJ-21) *Jastreb*‡ in store)
　TRG (1 G-4 *Super Galeb* (N-62)‡ in store)
HELICOPTERS
　MRH 13: 4 Mi-8MTV *Hip*; 1 Mi-17 *Hip* H; 1 SA-341H *Gazelle* (HN-42); 7 SA-342L *Gazelle* (HN-45M)
　TPT 21: **Medium** 8 Mi-8 *Hip* **Light** 13 Bell 205 (UH-1H *Iroquois*)
　TRG 1 Mi-34 *Hermit*
AIR DEFENCE
　SAM
　　Short-range 20 2K12 *Kub* (SA-6 *Gainful*)
　　Point-defence 7+: 6 9K31 *Strela*-1 (SA-9 *Gaskin*); 9K34 *Strela*-3 (SA-14 *Gremlin*); 1 9K35M3 *Strela*-10M3 (SA-13 *Gopher*); 9K310 (SA-16 *Gimlet*)
　GUNS 764
　　SP 169: **20mm** 9 BOV-3 SPAAG; **30mm** 154: 38 M53; 116 M-53/59; **57mm** 6 ZSU-57-2
　　TOWED 595: **20mm** 468: 32 M55A2, 4 M38, 1 M55 A2B1, 293 M55A3/A4, 138 M75; **23mm** 38: 29 ZU-23, 9 GSh-23; **30mm** 33 M-53; **37mm** 7 Type-55; **40mm** 49: 31 L60, 16 L70, 2 M-12

DEPLOYMENT

AFGHANISTAN
NATO • *Operation Resolute Support* 55

ALBANIA
OSCE • Albania 1

ARMENIA/AZERBAIJAN
OSCE • Minsk Conference 1

DEMOCRATIC REPUBLIC OF THE CONGO
UN • MONUSCO 5 obs

MALI
UN • MINUSMA 2

SERBIA
OSCE • Kosovo 8

UKRAINE
OSCE • Ukraine 37

FOREIGN FORCES

Part of EUFOR – *Operation Althea* unless otherwise stated

Albania 1
Austria 191; 1 inf bn HQ
Azerbaijan OSCE 1
Bulgaria 10
Canada OSCE 3
Chile 15
Czech Republic 2 • OSCE 1
Finland 4
Greece 1
Hungary 165; 1 inf coy
Ireland 5 • OSCE 1
Italy 4 • OSCE 6
Macedonia (FYORM) 3 • OSCE 1
Netherlands OSCE 1
Poland 39
Romania 39
Russia OSCE 2
Serbia OSCE 1
Slovakia 41
Slovenia 14
Spain 2 • OSCE 1
Switzerland 21
Turkey 199; 1 inf coy
United Kingdom 4; • OSCE 7
United States OSCE 5

Bulgaria BLG

Bulgarian Lev L		2016	2017	2018
GDP	L	92.6bn	97.0bn	
	US$	52.4bn	56.0bn	
per capita	US$	7,377	7,924	
Growth	%	3.4	3.6	
Inflation	%	-1.3	1.1	
Def exp [a]	L	1.19bn	1.51bn	
	US$	671m	870m	
Def bdgt [b]	L	1.19bn	1.17bn	
	US$	671m	676m	
FMA (US)	US$	5m	5m	0m
US$1=L		1.77	1.73	

[a] NATO definition
[b] Excludes military pensions

Population 7,101,510

Age	0–14	15–19	20–24	25–29	30–64	65 plus
Male	7.5%	2.6%	2.6%	3.3%	25.2%	7.8%
Female	7.1%	2.2%	2.4%	3.1%	25.0%	11.5%

Capabilities

Despite long-term plans for reform, Bulgaria's armed forces still rely heavily on Soviet-era equipment. In 2015, a development plan was adopted for the period until 2020. The emphasis in training is on those units intended for international operations and those with certain readiness levels declared to NATO and the EU. There are as-yet-unapproved plans for new or second-hand multi-role combat aircraft to replace the ageing MiG-29 fleet. Questions have reportedly been raised over the airworthiness of older aircraft. Under NATO's assurance measures, allied aircraft were deployed to patrol Bulgarian airspace in 2017 under the Enhanced Air Policing programme. Sofia aims to also acquire naval patrol boats and armoured vehicles, and modernise its warships. In 2017, Bulgaria launched a tender for the purchase of two corvettes, in an attempt to boost its capabilities in the Black Sea. Payments for its military-modernisation projects, when approved, are expected to be deferred, perhaps up to 2029, in an attempt to lessen budget impact. Bulgaria hosted the *Saber Guardian 2017* multinational exercise and reaffirmed its commitment to Afghanistan, Kosovo and the EUFOR mission in Bosnia-Herzegovina, sending additional personnel.

ACTIVE 31,300 (Army 15,300 Navy 3,450 Air 6,700 Central Staff 5,850)

RESERVE 3,000 (Joint 3,000)

ORGANISATIONS BY SERVICE

Army 16,300

FORCES BY ROLE
MANOEUVRE
Reconnaissance
1 recce bn
Mechanised
2 mech bde (4 mech inf bn, 1 SP arty bn, 1 cbt engr bn, 1 log bn, 1 SAM bn)
Light
1 mtn inf regt
COMBAT SUPPORT
1 arty regt (1 fd arty bn, 1 MRL bn)
1 engr regt (1 cbt engr bn, 1 ptn br bn, 1 engr spt bn)
1 NBC bn
COMBAT SERVICE SUPPORT
1 log regt
EQUIPMENT BY TYPE
ARMOURED FIGHTING VEHICLES
MBT 90 T-72
IFV 160: 90 BMP-1; 70 BMP-23
APC 120
    APC (T) 100 MT-LB
    APC (W) 20 BTR-60
AUV 17 M1117 ASV
ENGINEERING & MAINTENANCE VEHICLES
AEV MT-LB
ARV T-54/T-55; MTP-1; MT-LB
VLB BLG67; TMM
NBC VEHICLES Maritza NBC
ANTI-TANK/ANTI-INFRASTRUCTURE
MSL
    SP 24 9P148 Konkurs (AT-5 Spandrel)
    MANPATS 9K111 Fagot (AT-4 Spigot); 9K111-1 Konkurs (AT-5 Spandrel); (9K11 Malyutka (AT-3 Sagger) in store)
GUNS 126: 85mm (150 D-44 in store); 100mm 126 MT-12
ARTILLERY 311
SP 122mm 48 2S1
TOWED 152mm 24 D-20
MRL 122mm 24 BM-21
MOR 120mm 215 2S11 SP Tundzha
RADARS • LAND GS-13 Long Eye (veh); SNAR-1 Long Trough (arty); SNAR-10 Big Fred (veh, arty); SNAR-2/-6 Pork Trough (arty); Small Fred/Small Yawn (veh, arty)
AIR DEFENCE
SAM • Point-defence 9K32 Strela (SA-7 Grail)‡; 24 9K33 Osa (SA-8 Gecko)
GUNS 400
    SP 23mm ZSU-23-4
    TOWED 23mm ZU-23; 57mm S-60; 100mm KS-19

Navy 3,450
EQUIPMENT BY TYPE
PRINCIPAL SURFACE COMBATANTS • FRIGATES • 4
FFM 3 Drazki (ex-BEL Wielingen) with 1 octuple Mk29 GMLS with RIM-7P Sea Sparrow SAM, 2 single 533mm ASTT with L5 HWT, 1 sextuple 375mm MLE 54 Creusot-Loire A/S mor, 1 100mm gun (Fitted for but not with 2 twin lnchr with MM38 Exocet AShM)
FF 1 Smeli (ex-FSU Koni) with 2 RBU 6000 Smerch 2 A/S mor, 2 twin 76mm guns

PATROL AND COASTAL COMBATANTS 3
PCFG 1 Mulnaya† (ex-FSU Tarantul II) with 2 twin lnchr with P-15M Termit-M (SS-N-2C Styx) AShM, 2 AK630M CIWS, 1 76mm gun
PCT 2 Reshitelni (ex-FSU Pauk I) with 4 single 406mm TT, 2 RBU 1200 A/S mor, 1 76mm gun
MINE COUNTERMEASURES 6
MHC 1 Tsibar (Tripartite – ex-BEL Flower)
MSC 3 Briz (ex-FSU Sonya)
MSI 2 Olya (ex-FSU)
AMPHIBIOUS 1
LCU 1 Vydra
LOGISTICS AND SUPPORT 8: 2 **AGS**; 2 **AOL**; 1 **ARS**; 2 **ATF**; 1 **AX**

Naval Aviation
EQUIPMENT BY TYPE
HELICOPTERS • ASW 2 AS565MB Panther

Air Force 6,700
Flying hours   30–40 hrs/yr
FORCES BY ROLE
FIGHTER/ISR
1 sqn with MiG-29A/UB Fulcrum
TRANSPORT
1 sqn with An-30 Clank; C-27J Spartan; L-410UVP-E; PC-12M
TRAINING
1 sqn with L-39ZA Albatros*
1 sqn with PC-9M
ATTACK HELICOPTER
1 sqn with Mi-24D/V Hind D/E
TRANSPORT HELICOPTER
1 sqn with AS532AL Cougar; Bell 206 Jet Ranger; Mi-17 Hip H
EQUIPMENT BY TYPE
AIRCRAFT 22 combat capable
FTR 16: 12 MiG-29A Fulcrum; 4 MiG-29UB Fulcrum (Some MiG-21bis Fishbed/MiG-21UM Mongol B in store)
ISR 1 An-30 Clank
TPT 7: **Medium** 3 C-27J Spartan; **Light** 4: 1 An-2T Colt; 2 L-410UVP-E; 1 PC-12M
TRG 12: 6 L-39ZA Albatros*; 6 PC-9M (basic)
HELICOPTERS
ATK 6 Mi-24D/V Hind D/E
MRH 6 Mi-17 Hip H
TPT 18: **Medium** 12 AS532AL Cougar; **Light** 6 Bell 206 Jet Ranger
UNMANNED AERIAL VEHICLES • EW Yastreb-2S
AIR DEFENCE
SAM
    Long-range S-200 (SA-5 Gammon); S-300 (SA-10 Grumble)
    Medium-range S-75 Dvina (SA-2 Guideline)
    Short-range S-125 Pechora (SA-3 Goa); 2K12 Kub (SA-6 Gainful)
AIR-LAUNCHED MISSILES
AAM • IR R-3 (AA-2 Atoll)‡ R-73 (AA-11 Archer) SARH R-27R (AA-10 Alamo A)
ASM Kh-29 (AS-14 Kedge); Kh-25 (AS-10 Karen)

Special Forces

FORCES BY ROLE
SPECIAL FORCES
1 spec ops bde (1 SF bn, 1 para bn)

DEPLOYMENT

AFGHANISTAN
NATO • *Operation Resolute Support* 160

BLACK SEA
NATO • SNMCMG 2: 1 MSC

BOSNIA-HERZEGOVINA
EU • EUFOR • *Operation Althea* 10

MALI
EU • EUTM Mali 5

MEDITERRANEAN SEA
NATO • SNMG 2: 1 FFM

SERBIA
NATO • KFOR 20
OSCE • Kosovo 1

UKRAINE
OSCE • Ukraine 35

FOREIGN FORCES

Italy NATO Air Policing 4 Eurofighter *Typhoon*

Croatia CRO

Croatian Kuna k		2016	2017	2018
GDP	k	345bn	357bn	
	US$	50.7bn	53.5bn	
per capita	US$	12,165	12,863	
Growth	%	3.0	2.9	
Inflation	%	-1.1	1.1	
Def exp [a]	k	4.24bn	4.55bn	
	US$	623m	682m	
Def bdgt	k	4.02bn	4.39bn	4.58bn
	US$	591m	657m	
FMA (US)	US$	1m	1m	0m
US$1=k		6.80	6.68	

[a] NATO definition

Population 4,292,095

Ethnic groups: Croatian 90.4%; Serbian 4.3%; Bosniac 0.7%; Italian 0.4%; Hungarian 0.3%; other or unspecified 3.9%

Age	0–14	15–19	20–24	25–29	30–64	65 plus
Male	7.3%	2.7%	3.0%	3.1%	24.3%	7.7%
Female	6.9%	2.6%	2.9%	3.0%	24.8%	11.6%

Capabilities

In 2017, Croatia adopted a new National Security Strategy and a Bill on its Homeland Security System. It also announced its intention to increase the military budget. Principal tasks for the armed forces include defending national sovereignty and territorial integrity and tackling terrorism. Croatia joined NATO in 2009 having reformed its armed forces to create a small professional force, with a focus on international peacekeeping duties. Zagreb aims to continue modernising the armed forces, but economic challenges have caused delays, including the replacement of ageing Soviet-era equipment. Modernisation objectives include an inshore patrol vessel, a prototype of which was launched in June 2017. There are also plans to eventually replace the MiG-21 fleet; the defence ministry aims to finish evaluating related acquisition proposals by early 2018. Exports of defence equipment, including small arms, have risen in recent years. Croatia regularly takes part in NATO exercises, and in late 2017 deployed an army contingent to Poland to join the US-led NATO battlegroup there.

ACTIVE 15,650 (Army 11,250 Navy 1,300 Air 1,250 Joint 1,850) **Paramilitary 3,000**
Conscript liability Voluntary conscription, 8 weeks

ORGANISATIONS BY SERVICE

Joint 1,850 (General Staff)
FORCES BY ROLE
SPECIAL FORCES
1 SF bn

Army 11,250
FORCES BY ROLE
MANOEUVRE
  Armoured
  1 armd bde (1 tk bn, 1 armd bn, 2 armd inf bn, 1 SP arty bn, 1 ADA bn, 1 cbt engr bn)
  Light
  1 mot inf bde (2 mech inf bn, 2 mot inf bn, 1 fd arty bn, 1 ADA bn, 1 cbt engr bn)
  Other
  1 inf trg regt
COMBAT SUPPORT
  1 arty/MRL regt
  1 AT regt
  1 engr regt
  1 int bn
  1 MP regt
  1 NBC bn
  1 sigs regt
COMBAT SERVICE SUPPORT
  1 log regt
AIR DEFENCE
  1 ADA regt
EQUIPMENT BY TYPE
ARMOURED FIGHTING VEHICLES
  MBT 75 M-84
  IFV 102 M-80
  APC 222
    APC (T) 15 BTR-50
    APC (W) 150: 1 BOV-VP; 23 LOV OP; 126 *Patria* AMV (incl variants)
    PPV 57: 37 *Maxxpro*; 20 RG-33 HAGA (amb)

AUV 151+: 4 *Cougar* HE; IVECO LMV; 147 M-ATV
ENGINEERING & MAINTENANCE VEHICLES
    ARV M84A1; WZT-3
    VLB 3 MT-55A
    MW *Bozena*; 1 *Rhino*
ANTI-TANK/ANTI-INFRASTRUCTURE • MSL
    SP 28 POLO BOV 83
    MANPATS 9K11 *Malyutka* (AT-3 *Sagger*); 9K111 *Fagot* (AT-4 *Spigot*); 9K111-1 *Konkurs* (AT-5 *Spandrel*); 9K115 *Metis* (AT-7 *Saxhorn*); *Milan* (reported)
ARTILLERY 217
    SP 10: **122mm** 8 2S1; **155mm** 2 PzH 2000 (4 more being modified for delivery)
    TOWED 64: **122mm** 27 D-30; **130mm** 19 M-46H1; **155mm** 18 M1H1
    MRL 39: **122mm** 37: 6 M91 *Vulkan*; 31 BM-21 *Grad*; **128mm** 2 LOV RAK M91 R24
    MOR 104: **82mm** 29 LMB M96; **120mm** 75: 70 M-75; 5 UBM 52
AIR DEFENCE
    SAM • Point 9 *Strela*-10
    GUNS 96
        SP 20mm 39 BOV-3 SP
        TOWED 20mm 57 M55A4

Navy 1,300

Navy HQ at Split
EQUIPMENT BY TYPE
PATROL AND COASTAL COMBATANTS 5
    PCFG 1 *Končar* with 2 twin lnchr with RBS-15B Mk I AShM, 1 AK630 CIWS, 1 57mm gun
    PCG 4:
        2 *Kralj* with 4 single lnchr with RBS-15B Mk I AShM, 1 AK630 CIWS, 1 57mm gun (with minelaying capability)
        2 *Vukovar* (ex-FIN *Helsinki*) with 4 single lnchr with RBS-15B Mk I AShM, 1 57mm gun
MINE WARFARE • MINE COUNTERMEASURES •
MHI 1 *Korcula*
AMPHIBIOUS • LANDING CRAFT 5:
    LCT 2 *Cetina* (with minelaying capability)
    LCVP 3: 2 Type-21; 1 Type-22
LOGISTICS AND SUPPORT • AKL 1
COASTAL DEFENCE • AShM 3 RBS-15K

Marines

FORCES BY ROLE
MANOEUVRE
    Amphibious
        2 indep mne coy

Coast Guard

FORCES BY ROLE
Two divisions, headquartered in Split (1st div) and Pula (2nd div)
EQUIPMENT BY TYPE
PATROL AND COASTAL COMBATANTS • PB 4 *Mirna*
LOGISTICS AND SUPPORT
    AKL 1 PT-71
    AX 2

Air Force and Air Defence 1,250

Flying hours 50 hrs/yr
FORCES BY ROLE
FIGHTER/GROUND ATTACK
    1 (mixed) sqn with MiG-21bis/UMD *Fishbed*
TRANSPORT
    1 sqn with An-32 *Cline*
TRAINING
    1 sqn with PC-9M; Z-242L
    1 hel sqn with Bell 206B *Jet Ranger* II
TRANSPORT HELICOPTER
    2 sqn with Mi-8MTV *Hip* H; Mi-8T *Hip* C; Mi-171Sh
EQUIPMENT BY TYPE
AIRCRAFT 11 combat capable
    FGA 11: 8 MiG-21bis *Fishbed*; 3 MiG-21UMD *Fishbed*
    TPT • Light 2 An-32 *Cline*
    TRG 25: 20 PC-9M; 5 Z-242L
HELICOPTERS
    MRH 27: 11 Mi-8MTV *Hip* H; 16 OH-58D *Kiowa Warrior*
    TPT 21: **Medium** 13: 3 Mi-8T *Hip* C; 10 Mi-171Sh; **Light** 8 Bell 206B *Jet Ranger* II
UNMANNED AERIAL VEHICLES
    ISR • Medium *Hermes* 450
AIR DEFENCE • SAM
    Long-range S-300 (SA-10 *Grumble*)
    Point-defence 9K31 *Strela*-1 (SA-9 *Gaskin*); 9K34 *Strela*-3 (SA-14 *Gremlin*); 9K310 *Igla*-1 (SA-16 *Gimlet*)
RADAR • AIR 11: 5 FPS-117; 3 S-600; 3 PRV-11
AIR-LAUNCHED MISSILES
    AAM • IR R-3S (AA-2 *Atoll*)‡; R-60; R-60MK (AA-8 *Aphid*)
    ASM AGM-114 *Hellfire*

Special Forces Command

FORCES BY ROLE
SPECIAL FORCES
    2 SF gp
EQUIPMENT BY TYPE
ARMOURED FIGHTING VEHICLES
    APC • PPV 5 *Maxxpro*
    AUV 15 M-ATV

Paramilitary 3,000

Police 3,000 armed

DEPLOYMENT

AFGHANISTAN
NATO • *Operation Resolute Support* 94

INDIA/PAKISTAN
UN • UNMOGIP 9 obs

LEBANON
UN • UNIFIL 1

POLAND
NATO • Enhanced Forward Presence 78; 1 MRL bty with BM-21 *Grad*

SERBIA
NATO • KFOR 33; 1 hel unit with Mi-8 *Hip*
OSCE • Kosovo 1

UKRAINE
OSCE • Ukraine 10

WESTERN SAHARA
UN • MINURSO 7 obs

Cyprus CYP

Euro €		2016	2017	2018
GDP	€	17.9bn	18.7bn	
	US$	19.8bn	21.1bn	
per capita	US$	23,352	24,741	
Growth	%	2.8	3.4	
Inflation	%	-1.2	0.8	
Def bdgt	€	302m	352m	352m
	US$	335m	397m	
US$1=€		0.90	0.89	

Population 1,221,549

Age	0–14	15–19	20–24	25–29	30–64	65 plus
Male	8.0%	3.1%	4.4%	4.8%	25.5%	5.2%
Female	7.6%	2.7%	3.6%	4.0%	24.2%	6.9%

Capabilities

Although Cyprus' National Guard contains air, land, sea and special-forces units, it is predominantly a land force. Its main objective is to deter any possible Turkish incursion, and to provide enough opposition until military support can be provided by Greece, its primary ally. The air wing has a small number of rotary- and fixed-wing utility platforms, including attack helicopters, while the maritime wing is essentially a coastal-defence and constabulary force. In 2017, Cyprus displayed its *Buk* M1-2 medium-range SAM systems, which have boosted its air-defence capability. Having reduced conscript liability in 2016, Nicosia began recruiting additional contract-service personnel, as part of the effort to modernise and professionalise its forces. Cyprus exercised with several international partners in 2017. Expeditionary deployments have been limited, with some officers joining EU and UN missions.

ACTIVE 15,000 (National Guard 15,000)
Paramilitary 750
Conscript liability 14 months

RESERVE 50,000 (National Guard 50,000)
Reserve service to age 50 (officers dependent on rank; military doctors to age 60)

ORGANISATIONS BY SERVICE

National Guard 15,000 (incl conscripts)
FORCES BY ROLE
SPECIAL FORCES
 1 comd (regt) (1 SF bn)
MANOEUVRE
 Armoured
 1 lt armd bde (2 armd bn, 1 armd inf bn)
 Mechanised
 1 (1st) mech inf div (1 armd recce bn, 2 mech inf bn)
 1 (2nd) mech inf div (1 armd recce bn, 2 armd bn, 2 mech inf bn)
 Light
 3 (4th, 7th & 8th) lt inf bde (2 lt inf regt)
COMBAT SUPPORT
 1 arty comd (8 arty bn)
COMBAT SERVICE SUPPORT
 1 (3rd) spt bde
EQUIPMENT BY TYPE
ARMOURED FIGHTING VEHICLES
 MBT 134: 82 T-80U; 52 AMX-30B2
 RECCE 69 EE-9 *Cascavel*
 IFV 43 BMP-3
 APC 294
  APC (T) 168 *Leonidas*
  APC (W) 126 VAB (incl variants)
ENGINEERING & MAINTENANCE VEHICLES
 ARV 3: 2 AMX-30D; 1 BREM-1
ANTI-TANK/ANTI-INFRASTRUCTURE
 MSL
  SP 33: 15 EE-3 *Jararaca* with *Milan*; 18 VAB with HOT
  MANPATS *Milan*
 RCL 106mm 144 M40A1
 GUNS • TOWED 100mm 20 M-1944
ARTILLERY 432
 SP 155mm 24: 12 Mk F3; 12 *Zuzana*
 TOWED 84: 105mm 72 M-56; 155mm 12 TR-F-1
 MRL 22: 122mm 4 BM-21; 128mm 18 M-63 *Plamen*
 MOR 302: 81mm 170 E-44 (70+ M1/M9 in store); 107mm 20 M2/M30; 120mm 112 RT61
AIR DEFENCE
 SAM
  Medium-range 4 9K37M1 *Buk* M1-2 (SA-11 *Gadfly*)
  Short-range 18: 12 *Aspide*; 6 9K322 *Tor* (SA-15 *Gauntlet*)
  Point-defence *Mistral*
 GUNS • TOWED 60: 20mm 36 M-55; 35mm 24 GDF-003 (with *Skyguard*)

Maritime Wing
FORCES BY ROLE
COMBAT SUPPORT
 1 (coastal defence) AShM bty with MM40 *Exocet* AShM
EQUIPMENT BY TYPE
PATROL AND COASTAL COMBATANTS 4
 PBF 4: 2 Rodman 55; 2 *Vittoria*
COASTAL DEFENCE • AShM 3 MM40 *Exocet*

Air Wing
EQUIPMENT BY TYPE
AIRCRAFT
 TPT • Light 1 BN-2B *Islander*
 TRG 1 PC-9
HELICOPTERS
 ATK 11 Mi-35P *Hind*

MRH 7: 3 AW139 (SAR); 4 SA342L1 *Gazelle* (with HOT for anti-armour role)
TPT • **Light** 2 Bell 206L3 *Long Ranger*

Paramilitary 750+

Armed Police 500+
FORCES BY ROLE
MANOEUVRE
Other
1 (rapid-reaction) paramilitary unit
EQUIPMENT BY TYPE
ARMOURED FIGHTING VEHICLES
APC • **APC (W)** 2 VAB VTT
HELICOPTERS • **MRH** 4: 2 AW139; 2 Bell 412SP

Maritime Police 250
EQUIPMENT BY TYPE
PATROL AND COASTAL COMBATANTS 10
PBF 5: 2 *Poseidon*; 1 *Shaldag*; 2 *Vittoria*
PB 5 SAB-12

DEPLOYMENT

LEBANON
UN • UNIFIL 2

FOREIGN FORCES

Argentina UNFICYP 277; 2 inf coy; 1 hel flt
Austria UNFICYP 4
Bangladesh UNFICYP 1
Brazil UNFICYP 1
Canada UNFICYP 1
Chile UNFICYP 14
Greece Army: 950; ε200 (officers/NCO seconded to Greek-Cypriot National Guard)
Hungary UNFICYP 77; 1 inf pl
Paraguay UNFICYP 14
Serbia UNFICYP 47; elm 1 inf coy
Slovakia UNFICYP 169; elm 1 inf coy; 1 engr pl
Ukraine UNFICYP 2
United Kingdom 2,260; 2 inf bn; 1 hel sqn with 4 Bell 412 *Twin Huey* • Operation Inherent Resolve (*Shader*) 500: 1 FGA sqn with 6 *Tornado* GR4; 6 *Typhoon* FGR4; 1 *Sentinel* R1; 1 E-3D *Sentry*; 1 A330 MRTT *Voyager* KC3; 2 C-130J *Hercules* • UNFICYP 277: 1 inf coy

TERRITORY WHERE THE GOVERNMENT DOES NOT EXERCISE EFFECTIVE CONTROL

Data here represents the de facto situation on the northern section of the island. This does not imply international recognition as a sovereign state.

Capabilities

ACTIVE 3,500 (Army 3,500) **Paramilitary 150**
Conscript liability 15 months

RESERVE 26,000 (first line 11,000; second line 10,000; third line 5,000)
Reserve liability to age 50

ORGANISATIONS BY SERVICE

Army ε3,500
FORCES BY ROLE
MANOEUVRE
Light
7 inf bn
EQUIPMENT BY TYPE
ANTI-TANK/ANTI-INFRASTRUCTURE
MSL • **MANPATS** *Milan*
RCL • **106mm** 36
ARTILLERY • **MOR** • **120mm** 73

Paramilitary

Armed Police ε150
FORCES BY ROLE
SPECIAL FORCES
1 (police) SF unit

Coast Guard
PATROL AND COASTAL COMBATANTS 6
PCC 5: 2 SG45/SG46; 1 *Rauf Denktash*; 2 US Mk 5
PB 1

FOREIGN FORCES

TURKEY
Army ε36,500
FORCES BY ROLE
1 corps HQ, 1 armd bde, 2 mech inf div, 1 avn comd
EQUIPMENT BY TYPE
ARMOURED FIGHTING VEHICLES
MBT 348: 8 M48A2 (trg); 340 M48A5T1/2
APC • **APC (T)** 627: 361 AAPC (incl variants); 266 M113 (incl variants)
ANTI-TANK/ANTI-INFRASTRUCTURE
MSL • **MANPATS** *Milan*; TOW
RCL **106mm** 192 M40A1
ARTILLERY 648
SP 155mm 90 M44T
TOWED 102: **105mm** 72 M101A1; **155mm** 18 M114A2; **203mm** 12 M115
MRL 122mm 6 T-122
MOR 450: **81mm** 175; **107mm** 148 M30; **120mm** 127 HY-12
PATROL AND COASTAL COMBATANTS 1 **PB**
AIRCRAFT • **TPT** • **Light** 3 Cessna 185 (U-17)
HELICOPTERS • **TPT** 4 **Medium** 1 AS532UL *Cougar* **Light** 3 Bell 205 (UH-1H *Iroquois*)
AIR DEFENCE • **GUNS** • **TOWED 20mm** Rh 202; **35mm** 16 GDF-003; **40mm** 48 M1

Czech Republic CZE

Czech Koruna Kc		2016	2017	2018
GDP	Kc	4.77tr	4.99tr	
	US$	195bn	210bn	
per capita	US$	18,508	19,818	
Growth	%	2.6	3.5	
Inflation	%	0.7	2.3	
Def exp [a]	Kc	45.6bn	52.5bn	
	US$	1.87bn	2.20bn	
Def bdgt [b]	Kc	47.8bn	52.5bn	58,9bn
	US$	1.96bn	2.21bn	
FMA (US)	US$	0.5m	0m	0m
US$1=Kc		24.44	23.82	

[a] NATO definition
[b] Includes military pensions

Population 10,674,723

Age	0–14	15–19	20–24	25–29	30–64	65 plus
Male	7.8%	2.3%	2.7%	3.4%	25.2%	7.9%
Female	7.4%	2.1%	2.5%	3.2%	24.5%	11.1%

Capabilities

The Czech national-security strategy published in 2015 confirms that NATO is central to national security and asserts that stability and security in Europe have deteriorated. A direct military attack was deemed unlikely, but aggression against NATO or EU member states could not be ruled out. The Czech defence strategy, published in March 2017, confirms the overall assessment, pointing to Russian assertiveness, an arc of instability to the south and southeast of Europe, and information warfare, including cyber attacks, as drivers in the government's analysis. According to the Concept of the Czech Armed Forces 2025, adopted in December 2015, armed-forces restructuring will proceed in two phases, with recruitment and equipment procurement the focus to 2020, shifting to the modernisation of existing equipment and infrastructure in 2020–25. The long-term defence-planning guidelines for 2030, published in 2015, support an increase in active personnel to 27,000 (confirmed in the 2017 defence strategy). With defence spending on an upward trajectory since 2015, the government is trying to use these additional resources to replace legacy equipment in order to both modernise the armed forces and reduce dependence on Russia for spares and services. Recruitment is also a priority. Some units are severely under strength, achieving just 60% of their nominal strength. The government adopted an Active Reserve Law in 2016, and an increase in reserve strength is planned. In February 2017, the Czech Republic signed a letter of intent with Germany to affiliate the 4th Czech Rapid Deployment Brigade with the 10th German Armoured Division under NATO's Framework Nations Concept. Training and exercise activities are set to follow, with the aim of improving interoperability and supporting the provision of large formations for follow-on forces in NATO operations.

ACTIVE 23,200 (Army 12,250 Air 5,850 Other 3,650)

ORGANISATIONS BY SERVICE

Army 12,250
FORCES BY ROLE
MANOEUVRE
  Reconnaissance
  1 ISR/EW regt (1 recce bn, 1 EW bn)
  Armoured
  1 (7th) mech bde (1 tk bn, 2 armd inf bn, 1 mot inf bn)
  Mechanised
  1 (4th) rapid reaction bde (2 mech inf bn, 1 mot inf bn, 1 AB bn)
COMBAT SUPPORT
  1 (13th) arty regt (2 arty bn)
  1 engr regt (3 engr bn, 1 EOD bn)
  1 CBRN regt (2 CBRN bn)
COMBAT SERVICE SUPPORT
  1 log regt (2 log bn, 1 maint bn)

Active Reserve
FORCES BY ROLE
COMMAND
  14 (territorial defence) comd
MANOEUVRE
  Armoured
  1 armd coy
  Light
  14 inf coy (1 per territorial comd) (3 inf pl, 1 cbt spt pl, 1 log pl)
EQUIPMENT BY TYPE
ARMOURED FIGHTING VEHICLES
  MBT 30 T-72M4CZ (93 T-72 in store)
  RECCE (34 BPzV *Svatava* in store)
  IFV 222: 120 BMP-2; 102 *Pandur* II (inc variants); (98 BMP-1; 65 BMP-2 all in store)
  APC
    APC (T) (17 OT-90 in store)
    APC (W) (3 OT-64 in store)
  AUV 21 *Dingo* 2; IVECO LMV
ENGINEERING & MAINTENANCE VEHICLES
  ARV 10 VPV-ARV (12 more in store)
  VLB 3 MT-55A (3 more in store)
  MW UOS-155 *Belarty*
ANTI-TANK/ANTI-INFRASTRUCTURE
  MSL • MANPATS 9K111-1 *Konkurs* (AT-5 *Spandrel*); *Spike*-LR
ARTILLERY 96
  SP 152mm 48 M-77 *Dana* (38 more in store)
  MOR 120mm 48: 40 M-1982; 8 SPM-85; (45 M-1982 in store)
RADAR • LAND 3 ARTHUR

Air Force 5,850

Principal task is to secure Czech airspace. This mission is fulfilled within NATO Integrated Extended Air Defence System (NATINADS) and, if necessary, by means of the

Czech national reinforced air-defence system. The air force also provides CAS for army SAR, and performs a tpt role
Flying hours   120 hrs/yr cbt ac; 150 for tpt ac

FORCES BY ROLE
FIGHTER/GROUND ATTACK
  1 sqn with Gripen C/D
  1 sqn with L-159 ALCA; L-159T
TRANSPORT
  2 sqn with A319CJ; C295M; CL-601 Challenger; L-410 Turbolet; Yak-40 Codling
TRAINING
  1 sqn with L-39ZA Albatros*; L-159 ALCA; L-159T
ATTACK HELICOPTER
  1 sqn with Mi-24/Mi-35 Hind
TRANSPORT HELICOPTER
  1 sqn with Mi-17 Hip H; Mi-171Sh
  1 sqn with Mi-8 Hip; Mi-17 Hip H; PZL W-3A Sokol
AIR DEFENCE
  1 (25th) SAM regt (2 AD gp)

EQUIPMENT BY TYPE
AIRCRAFT 44 combat capable
  FGA 14: 12 Gripen C; 2 Gripen D
  ATK 21: 16 L-159 ALCA; 5 L-159T
  TPT 15: **Light** 12: 4 C295M; 6 L-410 Turbolet; 2 Yak-40 Codling; **PAX** 3: 2 A319CJ; 1 CL-601 Challenger
  TRG 9 L-39ZA Albatros*
HELICOPTERS
  ATK 17: 7 Mi-24 Hind D; 10 Mi-35 Hind E
  MRH 5 Mi-17 Hip H
  TPT • Medium 30: 4 Mi-8 Hip; 16 Mi-171Sh; 10 PZL W3A Sokol
AIR DEFENCE • SAM
  Point-defence 9K35 Strela-10 (SA-13 Gopher); 9K32 Strela-2‡ (SA-7 Grail) (available for trg RBS-70 gunners); RBS-70
AIR-LAUNCHED MISSILES
  AAM • IR AIM-9M Sidewinder; **ARH** AIM-120C-5 AMRAAM
BOMBS
  Laser-guided: GBU Paveway

Other Forces
FORCES BY ROLE
SPECIAL FORCES
  1 SF gp
MANOEUVRE
  Other
  1 (presidential) gd bde (2 bn)
  1 (honour guard) gd bn (2 coy)
COMBAT SUPPORT
  1 int gp
  1 (central) MP comd
  3 (regional) MP comd
  1 (protection service) MP comd

Cyber
In 2011, the National Security Authority (NSA) was established as the country's leading cyber-security body. The National Cyber Security Centre, government CERT (as part of the NSA) and the Cyber Security Council were subsequently established. The Cyber Security Act entered into force in January 2015. A new National Cyber Security Strategy and an Action Plan for 2015–20 were published. The former states that the country will look 'to increase national capacities for active cyber defence and cyber attack countermeasures'. The National Cyber and Information Security Agency was established on 1 August 2017 as the central body of state administration for cyber security, including the protection of classified information in the area of information and communications systems and cryptographic protection, which was previously the responsibility of the NSA. The defence ministry is developing its own cyber-defence capabilities according to specific tasks based on NATO or EU documents and the requirements of the National Action Plan. The defence-ministry security director also leads on cyber security.

DEPLOYMENT
AFGHANISTAN
NATO • Operation Resolute Support 267
BOSNIA-HERZEGOVINA
EU • EUFOR • Operation Althea 2
OSCE • Bosnia-Herzegovina 1
DEMOCRATIC REPUBLIC OF THE CONGO
UN • MONUSCO 3 obs
EGYPT
MFO 18; 1 C295M
IRAQ
Operation Inherent Resolve 30
MALI
EU • EUTM Mali 41
UN • MINUSMA 1
SERBIA
NATO • KFOR 9
OSCE • Kosovo 1
UN • UNMIK 2 obs
SYRIA/ISRAEL
UN • UNDOF 2
UKRAINE
OSCE • Ukraine 15

Denmark DNK

Danish Krone kr		2016	2017	2018
GDP	kr	2.06tr	2.14tr	
	US$	307bn	324bn	
per capita	US$	53,745	56,335	
Growth	%	1.7	1.9	
Inflation	%	0.3	1	
Def exp [a]	kr	24.2bn	25.2bn	
	US$	3.59bn	3.81bn	
Def bdgt [b]	kr	23.7bn	25.2bn	24.8bn
	US$	3.51bn	3.81bn	
US$1=kr		6.73	6.61	

[a] NATO definition
[b] Includes military pensions

Population 5,605,948

Age	0–14	15–19	20–24	25–29	30–64	65 plus
Male	8.4%	3.3%	3.4%	3.2%	22.3%	8.6%
Female	8.0%	3.1%	3.3%	3.1%	22.6%	10.6%

Capabilities

Danish military capabilities remain compact but effective despite pressures on spending and deployments. In October 2017, the government presented a new draft defence agreement covering the period 2018–23. It envisages an increase in defence spending to deal with a deteriorating security environment. In particular, it is intended to strengthen deterrence, cyber defence and Denmark's role in international operations, as well as the armed forces' ability to support civilian authorities in national-security tasks. Specifically, Denmark plans to set up a heavy brigade by 2024 with enhanced capabilities, including ground-based air defence, and to establish a light infantry battalion to take on patrol and guard missions in support of the police. In addition, a situation centre to help respond to cyber attacks is planned. Improved ties to NATO, NORDEFCO and other regional neighbours reflect an increasing trend in this area. Denmark has contributed to the NATO Baltic Air Policing mission. A defence agreement, aimed at deterring Russia, was signed in April 2015 between Denmark, Finland, Iceland, Norway and Sweden. Procurement of the F-35A Joint Strike Fighter as a replacement for the country's ageing F-16AM/BM fleet was confirmed in June 2016, with airframe numbers reduced to 27 for cost reasons. Industrial support from Terma, Denmark's largest defence company, may have been important to the decision; some key F-35 sub-components and composites are produced by the firm. The MH-60R *Seahawk* is replacing the ageing *Lynx* helicopter fleet operating on Danish naval vessels.

ACTIVE 16,100 (Army 8,200 Navy 2,000 Air 2,700 Joint 3,200)
Conscript liability 4–12 months, most voluntary

RESERVES 45,700 (Army 34,300 Navy 5,300 Air Force 4,750 Service Corps 1,350)

ORGANISATIONS BY SERVICE

Army 8,200

Div and bde HQ are responsible for trg only; if necessary, can be transformed into operational formations

FORCES BY ROLE
COMMAND
  1 div HQ
  2 bde HQ
MANOEUVRE
  Reconnaissance
  1 recce bn
  1 ISR bn
  Armoured
  1 tk bn
  Mechanised
  3 mech inf bn
  2 mech inf bn(-)
COMBAT SUPPORT
  1 SP arty bn
  1 cbt engr bn
  1 construction bn
  1 EOD bn
  1 MP bn
  1 sigs regt (1 sigs bn, 1 EW coy)
COMBAT SERVICE SUPPORT
  1 log regt (1 spt bn, 1 log bn, 1 maint bn, 1 med bn)
EQUIPMENT BY TYPE
ARMOURED FIGHTING VEHICLES
  MBT 34 *Leopard* 2A5 (23 more in store)
  IFV 44 CV9030 Mk II
  APC 314
    APC (T) 235 M113 (incl variants); (196 more in store awaiting disposal)
    APC (W) 79 *Piranha* III (incl variants)
  AUV 84 *Eagle* IV
ENGINEERING & MAINTENANCE VEHICLES
  ARV 10 *Bergepanzer* 2
  VLB 6 *Biber*
  MW 14 910-MCV-2
ANTI-TANK/ANTI-INFRASTRUCTURE
  RCL 84mm 186 *Carl Gustav*
ARTILLERY 24
  SP 155mm 12 M109
  MOR • TOWED 120mm 12 Soltam K6B1
RADAR • LAND ARTHUR
AIR DEFENCE • SAM • Point-defence FIM-92 *Stinger*

Navy 2,000

EQUIPMENT BY TYPE
PRINCIPAL SURFACE COMBATANTS 3
  DESTROYERS • DDGHM 3 *Iver Huitfeldt* with 4 quad lnchr with RGM-84 *Harpoon* Block II AShM, 1 32-cell Mk41 VLS with RIM-162 ESSM SAM, 2 12-cell Mk56 VLS with RIM-162 SAM, 2 twin 324mm TT with MU90 LWT, 1 *Millennium* CIWS, 2 76mm guns (capacity 1 med hel)
PATROL AND COASTAL COMBATANTS 13
  PSOH 4 *Thetis* 1 76mm gun (capacity 1 *Super Lynx* Mk90B)

PSO 2 *Knud Rasmussen* with 1 76mm gun, 1 hel landing platform
PCC 7: 1 *Agdlek*; 6 *Diana*
MINE WARFARE • MINE COUNTERMEASURES 6
MCI 4 MSF MK-I
MSD 2 *Holm*
LOGISTICS AND SUPPORT 13
ABU 2 (primarily used for MARPOL duties)
AE 1 *Sleipner*
AG 2 *Absalon* (flexible support ships) with 4 quad lnchr with RGM-84 Block 2 *Harpoon* 2 AShM, 3 12-cell Mk 56 VLS with RIM-162B *Sea Sparrow* SAM, 2 twin 324mm TT with MU90 LWT, 2 *Millennium* CIWS, 1 127mm gun (capacity 2 AW101 *Merlin*; 2 LCP, 7 MBT or 40 vehicles; 130 troops)
AGS 2 *Holm*
AKL 2 *Seatruck*
AXL 2 *Holm*
AXS 2 *Svanen*

Air Force 2,700

Flying hours 165 hrs/yr

Tactical Air Command
FORCES BY ROLE
FIGHTER/GROUND ATTACK
  2 sqn with F-16AM/BM *Fighting Falcon*
ANTI-SUBMARINE WARFARE
  1 sqn with *Super Lynx* Mk90B
SEARCH & RESCUE/TRANSPORT HELICOPTER
  1 sqn with AW101 *Merlin*
  1 sqn with AS550 *Fennec* (ISR)
TRANSPORT
  1 sqn with C-130J-30 *Hercules*; CL-604 *Challenger* (MP/VIP)
TRAINING
  1 unit with MFI-17 *Supporter* (T-17)
EQUIPMENT BY TYPE
AIRCRAFT 44 combat capable
  FTR 44: 34 F-16AM *Fighting Falcon*; 10 F-16BM *Fighting Falcon* (30 operational)
  TPT 8: **Medium** 4 C-130J-30 *Hercules*; **PAX** 4 CL-604 *Challenger* (MP/VIP)
  TRG 27 MFI-17 *Supporter* (T-17)
HELICOPTERS
  ASW 9: 6 *Super Lynx* Mk90B; 3 MH-60R *Seahawk*
  MRH 8 AS550 *Fennec* (ISR) (4 more non-operational)
  TPT • Medium 13 AW101 *Merlin* (8 SAR; 5 Tpt)
AIR-LAUNCHED MISSILES
  AAM • IR AIM-9L *Sidewinder*; **IIR** AIM-9X *Sidewinder* II; **ARH** AIM-120 AMRAAM
  ASM AGM-65 *Maverick*
BOMBS
  Laser-guided EGBU-12/GBU-24 *Paveway* II/III
  INS/GPS guided GBU-31 JDAM

Control and Air Defence Group
1 Control and Reporting Centre, 1 Mobile Control and Reporting Centre. 4 Radar sites

Special Operations Command
FORCES BY ROLE
SPECIAL FORCES
  1 SF unit
  1 diving unit

Reserves

Home Guard (Army) 34,300 reservists (to age 50)
FORCES BY ROLE
MANOEUVRE
  Light
  2 regt cbt gp (3 mot inf bn, 1 arty bn)
  5 (local) def region (up to 2 mot inf bn)

Home Guard (Navy) 4,500 reservists (to age 50)
EQUIPMENT BY TYPE
PATROL AND COASTAL COMBATANTS 30
  PB 30: 17 MHV800; 1 MHV850; 12 MHV900

Home Guard (Air Force) 4,750 reservists (to age 50)

Home Guard (Service Corps) 1,350 reservists

Cyber

A National Strategy for Cyber and Information Security was released in December 2014. A Centre for Cyber Security (CFCS) was established in 2012 within the defence-intelligence service. The CFCS is Denmark's national ICT security authority with three primary responsibilities: contribute to protecting Denmark against cyber threats; assist in securing a solid and robust ICT critical infrastructure in Denmark; and warn of, protect against and counter cyber attacks. In addition to existing cyber-defence capabilities, Denmark is in the process of establishing a capacity that can execute defensive and offensive military operations in cyberspace.

DEPLOYMENT

AFGHANISTAN
NATO • *Operation Resolute Support* 100

IRAQ
Operation Inherent Resolve 190; 1 SF gp; 1 trg team

KUWAIT
Operation Inherent Resolve 20

MALI
UN • MINUSMA 64; 1 avn unit

MEDITERRANEAN SEA
NATO • SNMG 1: 1 DDGHM; 1 AG

MIDDLE EAST
UN • UNTSO 12 obs

SERBIA
NATO • KFOR 35

SEYCHELLES
Combined Maritime Forces • CTF-150: 1 CL-604

SOUTH SUDAN
UN • UNMISS 9

UKRAINE
OSCE • Ukraine 4

UNITED ARAB EMIRATES
Operation Inherent Resolve 20

Estonia EST

Euro €		2016	2017	2018
GDP	€	21.1bn	22.8bn	
	US$	23.3bn	25.7bn	
per capita	US$	17,786	19,618	
Growth	%	2.1	4.0	
Inflation	%	0.8	3.8	
Def exp [a]	€	450m	478m	
	US$	497m	539m	
Def bdgt [b]	€	451m	481m	528m
	US$	498m	543m	
FMA (US)	US$	1.75m	1.6m	0m
US$1=€		0.90	0.89	

[a] NATO definition
[b] Includes military pensions

Population 1,251,581

Ethnic groups: Estonian 70%; Russian 25%; Ukranian 1.7%; Belarusian 1%; other or unspecified 2.3%

Age	0–14	15–19	20–24	25–29	30–64	65 plus
Male	8.3%	2.2%	2.4%	3.6%	23.4%	6.7%
Female	7.9%	2.1%	2.2%	3.3%	24.6%	13.1%

Capabilities

Estonian security policy is predicated on the goals of ensuring sovereignty and territorial integrity. These aims have been thrown into sharper focus since Russia's 2014 annexation of Crimea and Moscow's continuing support for rebel forces in eastern Ukraine. In June 2017, the government approved the 2017–26 National Defence Development Plan (NDPP), succeeding the 2013–22 plan. The latest document reflects the worsening security environment in the Baltic region, and identifies the need for additional armoured mobility and armoured firepower, as well as increasing stocks of munitions. The army began to take delivery of Dutch army-surplus CV90 AIFVs in late 2016. Increasing the number of annual conscripts to 4,000, along with growing the total number of active personnel, are also part of the new NDPP. Given the small size and limited capabilities of the armed forces, however, the country is reliant on NATO membership as a security guarantor. A 1,000-strong NATO battlegroup based in Estonia became operational in mid-2017 as part of the Alliance's Enhanced Forward Presence. In November 2017, Estonia once again hosted NATO's Cyber Coalition exercise. The country's Amari air base also hosts a Baltic Air Policing combat-aircraft detachment drawn on a voluntary rotational basis from NATO states. Estonia is a member of the UK-led multinational Joint Expeditionary Force.

ACTIVE 6,600 (Army 5,700 Navy 400 Air 500)
Defence League 15,800

Conscript liability 8 months, officers and some specialists 11 months (Conscripts cannot be deployed)

RESERVE 12,000 (Joint 12,000)

ORGANISATIONS BY SERVICE

Army 2,500; 3,200 conscript (total 5,700)

4 def region. All units except one inf bn are reserve based

FORCES BY ROLE
MANOEUVRE
 Light
 1 (1st) bde (1 recce coy, 3 inf bn, 1 arty bn, 1 AD bn, 1 cbt engr bn, 1 spt bn)
 1 (2nd) inf bde (1 inf bn, 1 spt bn)
COMBAT SUPPORT
 1 sigs bn
COMBAT SERVICE SUPPORT
 1 log bn

Defence League 15,800

15 Districts

EQUIPMENT BY TYPE
ARMOURED FIGHTING VEHICLES
 IFV 14 CV9035 (incl 2 CP)
 APC 158
  APC (W) 151: 56 XA-180 *Sisu*; 80 XA-188 *Sisu*; 15 BTR-80
  PPV 7 *Mamba*
ENGINEERING & MAINTENANCE VEHICLES
 AEV 1 *Leopard* 1 AEV
ANTI-TANK/ANTI-INFRASTRUCTURE
 MSL • MANPATS FGM-148 *Javelin*; Milan
 RCL 160+; **106mm**: 30 M40A1; **84mm** *Carl Gustav*; **90mm** 130 PV-1110
ARTILLERY 376
 TOWED 66: **122mm** 42 D-30 (H 63); **155mm** 24 FH-70
 MOR 310: **81mm** 131: 41 B455; 10 NM 95; 80 M252; **120mm** 179: 14 2B11; 165 M/41D
AIR DEFENCE • **SAM** • Point-defence *Mistral*

Navy 300; 100 conscript (total 400)

EQUIPMENT BY TYPE
MINE WARFARE • **MINE COUNTERMEASURES** 4
 MCCS 1 *Tasuja* (ex-DNK *Lindormen*)
 MHC 3 *Admiral Cowan* (ex-UK *Sandown*)

Air Force 500

Flying hours 120 hrs/yr

FORCES BY ROLE
TRANSPORT
 1 sqn with An-2 *Colt*

TRANSPORT HELICOPTER
1 sqn with R-44 *Raven* II

EQUIPMENT BY TYPE
AIRCRAFT • TPT • Light 2 An-2 *Colt*
HELICOPTERS • TPT • Light 4 R-44 *Raven* II

Special Operations Forces

FORCES BY ROLE
SPECIAL FORCES
1 spec ops bn

Paramilitary

Border Guard

The Estonian Border Guard is subordinate to the Ministry of the Interior. Air support is provided by the Estonian Border Guard Aviation Corps.

EQUIPMENT BY TYPE
PATROL AND COASTAL COMBATANTS 12
  PCO 2: 1 *Kati*; 1 *Kindral Kurvits*
  PCC 1 *Kou* (FIN *Silma*)
  PB 9: 1 *Pikker*; 1 *Valve*; 8 (other)
AMPHIBIOUS • LANDING CRAFT • LCU 3
LOGISTICS & SUPPORT • AGF 1 *Balsam*
AIRCRAFT • TPT • Light 2 L-410
HELICOPTERS • MRH 3 AW139

Cyber

Estonia adopted a national Cyber Security Strategy in 2008 and in 2009 added a Cyber Security Council to the government's Security Committee, which supports strategic-level inter-agency cooperation. Tallinn hosts the NATO Cooperative Cyber Security Centre of Excellence and the NATO *Locked Shields* cyber exercise takes place annually in Estonia, as has the *Cyber Coalition* exercise since 2013. A Cyber Security Strategy for 2014–17 advocates greater integration of capability, saying that specialists from the armed forces and the Estonian Defence League will be integral in developing military cyber-defence capabilities. The Estonian Defence League Act explicitly integrates its (voluntary) Cyber Defence Unit into the national defence system.

DEPLOYMENT

AFGHANISTAN
NATO • *Operation Resolute Support* 6

IRAQ
Operation Inherent Resolve 7

LEBANON
UN • UNIFIL 38

MALI
EU • EUTM Mali 4
UN • MINUSMA 10

MIDDLE EAST
UN • UNTSO 3 obs

MOLDOVA
OSCE • Moldova 1

NORTH SEA
NATO • SNMCMG 1: 1 MHC

SERBIA
NATO • KFOR 2

UKRAINE
OSCE • Ukraine 5

FOREIGN FORCES

All NATO Enhanced Forward Presence unless stated
Belgium NATO Baltic Air Policing 4 F-16AM *Fighting Falcon*
France 300; 1 armd inf coy(+)
United Kingdom 800; 1 armd inf bn HQ; 1 armd inf coy (+); 1 engr sqn

Finland FIN

Euro €		2016	2017	2018
GDP	€	216bn	223bn	
	US$	239bn	251bn	
per capita	US$	43,482	45,693	
Growth	%	1.9	2.8	
Inflation	%	0.4	0.8	
Def bdgt [a]	€	2.80bn	2.83bn	2.87bn
	US$	3.10bn	3.19bn	
US$1=€		0.90	0.89	

[a] Excludes military pensions

Population   5,518,371

Age	0–14	15–19	20–24	25–29	30–64	65 plus
Male	8.4%	2.8%	3.1%	3.2%	22.6%	9.2%
Female	8.0%	2.6%	2.9%	3.1%	22.2%	11.9%

Capabilities

Finland's armed forces are primarily focused on territorial defence. The conflict in eastern Ukraine has sharpened the focus on defence matters, as have incursions into Baltic states' airspace by Russian aircraft. The country's February 2017 Defence Report argues that changes in the security environment have increased the demands on the armed forces. A period of defence-budget decreases was reversed in 2016, but the 2017 report stresses that financial constraints are forcing trade-offs between long-term procurement plans and operational readiness. In October 2015, the air force launched the HX Fighter Programme to replace Finland's F/A-18s with a new combat aircraft. The government sent a request for proposals (RFP) regarding weapons and equipment to seven nations in October 2017, and will issue a request for quotations (RFQ) in spring 2018. The RFQ for the aircraft will also be issued in spring 2018, with the replacement aircraft to be selected around 2021. The programme will likely need additional funding beyond the current budget. The government has also suggested that budget cuts may result in fewer aircraft being procured than originally planned, whilst the 2018 RFP is expected to reflect the need for them to work alongside unmanned systems. Under Finland's Squadron 2020 programme, which is budgeted at €1.2 billion, the navy will replace four patrol boats and two minelayers with corvette-sized vessels capable of operating in shallow water and very cold weather. Construction is scheduled to begin in 2019 and run until 2024, and will be undertaken by local firms, with weapons and sensors procured internationally. Finland's principal multilateral defence relationships include the EU, NATO, NORDEFCO and the Northern Group, as well as strong bilateral cooperation, with Sweden and the US in particular. In February 2017, Finland signed a cyber-defence agreement with NATO. The February 2017 defence report announced that the wartime strength of the Finnish armed forces, after full mobilisation and including Border Guard units, would rise to 280,000 troops.

ACTIVE 21,500 (Army 15,300 Navy 3,500 Air 2,700)
Paramilitary 2,700
Conscript liability 5.5–8.5–11.5 months

RESERVE 216,000 (Army 170,000 Navy 20,000 Air 26,000) **Paramilitary 11,500**
18,000 reservists a year do refresher training: total obligation 80 days (150 for NCOs, 200 for officers) between conscript service and age 50 (NCOs and officers to age 60)

ORGANISATIONS BY SERVICE

Army 5,000; 10,300 conscript (total 15,300)
FORCES BY ROLE
Finland's army maintains a mobilisation strength of about 285,000. In support of this requirement, two conscription cycles, each for about 13,500 conscripts, take place each year. After conscript training, reservist commitment is to the age of 60. Reservists are usually assigned to units within their local geographical area. All service appointments or deployments outside Finnish borders are voluntary for all members of the armed services. All brigades are reserve based

Reserve Organisations 170,000
FORCES BY ROLE
SPECIAL FORCES
  1 SF bn
MANOEUVRE
  Armoured
  2 armd BG (regt)
  Mechanised
  2 (Karelia & Pori Jaeger) mech bde
  Light
  3 (Jaeger) bde
  6 lt inf bde
COMBAT SUPPORT
  1 arty bde
  1 AD regt
  7 engr regt
  3 sigs bn

COMBAT SERVICE SUPPORT
  Some log unit
HELICOPTER
  1 hel bn
EQUIPMENT BY TYPE
ARMOURED FIGHTING VEHICLES
  MBT 160: 100 *Leopard* 2A4; 60 *Leopard* 2A6
  IFV 196: 94 BMP-2; 102 CV90
  APC 613
    APC (T) 142: 40 MT-LBu; 102 MT-LBV
    APC (W) 471: 260 XA-180/185 *Sisu*; 101 XA-202 *Sisu* (CP); 48 XA-203 *Sisu*; 62 AMV (XA-360)
ENGINEERING & MAINTENANCE VEHICLES
  AEV 6 *Leopard* 2R CEV
  ARV 27: 15 MTP-LB; 12 VT-55A
  VLB 27: 12 BLG-60M2; 6 *Leopard* 2S; 9 SISU *Leguan*
  MW *Aardvark* Mk 2; KMT T-55; RA-140 DS
ANTI-TANK/ANTI-INFRASTRUCTURE
  MSL • MANPATS *Spike*-MR; *Spike*-LR
ARTILLERY 681
  SP 122mm 36 2S1 *Gvozdika* (PsH 74)
  TOWED 324: **122mm** 234 D-30 (H 63); **130mm** 36 M-46 (K 54); **155mm** 54 K 83/GH-52 (K 98)
  MRL 56: **122mm** 34 RM-70; **227mm** 22 M270 MLRS
  MOR 279+: **81mm** Krh/71; **120mm** 261 Krh/92; **SP 120mm** 18 XA-361 AMOS
HELICOPTERS
  MRH 7: 5 Hughes 500D; 2 Hughes 500E
  TPT • Medium 20 NH90 TTH
UNMANNED AERIAL VEHICLES
  ISR • Medium 11 ADS-95 *Ranger*
AIR DEFENCE
  SAM
    Short-range 44: 20 *Crotale* NG (ITO 90); 24 NASAMS II FIN (ITO 12)
    Point-defence 16+: 16 ASRAD (ITO 05); FIM-92 *Stinger* (ITO 15); RBS 70 (ITO 05/05M)
  GUNS 400+: **23mm** ItK 95/ZU-23-2 (ItK 61); **35mm** ItK 88; **SP 35mm** *Leopard* 2 ITK *Marksman*

Navy 1,600; 1,900 conscript (total 3,500)
FORCES BY ROLE
Naval Command HQ located at Turku; with two subordinate Naval Commands (Gulf of Finland and Archipelago Sea); 1 Naval bde; 3 spt elm (Naval Materiel Cmd, Naval Academy, Naval Research Institute)

EQUIPMENT BY TYPE
PATROL AND COASTAL COMBATANTS 20
  PCGM 4 *Hamina* with 4 RBS-15SF3 (MTO-85M) AShM, 1 octuple VLS with *Umkhonto*-IR (ITO2004) SAM, 1 57mm gun
  PBF 12 *Jehu* (U-700) (capacity 24 troops)
  PBG 4 *Rauma* with 6 RBS-15SF3 (MTO-85M) AShM
MINE WARFARE 15
  MINE COUNTERMEASURES 10
    MCC 3 *Katanpää*
    MSI 7: 4 *Kiiski*; 3 *Kuha*

MINELAYERS • ML 5:
  2 *Hameenmaa* with 1 octuple VLS with *Umkhonto*-IR (ITO2004) SAM, 2 RBU 1200 A/S mor, up to 100–120 mines, 1 57mm gun
  3 *Pansio* with 50 mines
AMPHIBIOUS • LANDING CRAFT 51
  LCM 1 *Kampela*
  LCP 50
LOGISTICS AND SUPPORT 7
  AG 3: 1 *Louhi*; 2 *Hylje*
  AX 4: 3 *Fabian Wrede*; 1 *Lokki*

Coastal Defence

FORCES BY ROLE
MANOEUVRE
  Amphibious
    1 mne bde
  COMBAT SUPPORT
    1 cbt spt bde (1 AShM bty)
EQUIPMENT BY TYPE
COASTAL DEFENCE
  AShM 4 RBS-15K AShM
  ARTY • 130mm 30 K-53tk (static)
ANTI-TANK/ANTI-INFRASTRUCTURE
  MSL • MANPATS *Spike* (used in AShM role)

Air Force 1,950; 750 conscript (total 2,700)

3 Air Comds: Satakunta (West), Karelia (East), Lapland (North)

Flying hours   90–140 hrs/yr

FORCES BY ROLE
FIGHTER/GROUND ATTACK
  3 sqn with F/A-18C/D *Hornet*
ISR
  1 (survey) sqn with Learjet 35A
TRANSPORT
  1 flt with C295M
  4 (liaison) flt with PC-12NG
TRAINING
  1 sqn with *Hawk* Mk50/51A/66* (air-defence and ground-attack trg)
  1 unit with L-70 *Vinka*
EQUIPMENT BY TYPE
AIRCRAFT 109 combat capable
  FGA 62: 55 F/A-18C *Hornet*; 7 F/A-18D *Hornet*
  MP 1 F-27-400M
  ELINT 1 C295M
  TPT • Light 10: 2 C295M; 3 Learjet 35A (survey; ECM trg; tgt-tow); 5 PC-12NG
  TRG 76: 1 G-115EA; 31 *Hawk* Mk50/51A*; 16 *Hawk* Mk66*; 28 L-70 *Vinka*
AIR-LAUNCHED MISSILES • AAM • IR AIM-9 *Sidewinder*; **IIR** AIM-9X *Sidewinder*; **ARH** AIM-120C AMRAAM
BOMBS
  INS/GPS-guided GBU-31 JDAM; AGM-154C JSOW

Paramilitary

Border Guard 2,700

Ministry of Interior. 4 Border Guard Districts and 2 Coast Guard Districts

FORCES BY ROLE
MARITIME PATROL
  1 sqn with Do-228 (maritime surv); AS332 *Super Puma*; Bell 412 (AB-412) *Twin Huey*; Bell 412EP (AB-412EP) *Twin Huey*; AW119KE *Koala*
EQUIPMENT BY TYPE
PATROL AND COASTAL COMBATANTS 45
  PSO 1 *Turva* with 1 hel landing platform
  PCC 3: 2 *Tursas*; 1 *Merikarhu*
  PB 41
AMPHIBIOUS • LANDING CRAFT • UCAC 6
AIRCRAFT • TPT • Light 2 Do-228
HELICOPTERS
  MRH 5: 3 Bell 412 (AB-412) *Twin Huey*; 2 Bell 412EP (AB-412EP) *Twin Huey*
  TPT 9: **Medium** 5 AS332 *Super Puma*; **Light** 4 AW119KE *Koala*

Reserve 11,500 reservists on mobilisation

Cyber

Finland published a national cyber-security strategy in 2013. A national implementation programme for this was published in 2014 and updated in 2017. The Implementation Programme for 2017–20 addresses the development of cyber security encompassing the state, business and the individual. An updated version of the Security Strategy for Society document was due to be published in autumn 2017. In accordance with the strategy, the Finnish Defence Forces will create a comprehensive cyber-defence capacity. Meanwhile, the defence forces published a Cyber Defence Concept in 2016 and created an internal implementation plan, in order to generate the required capabilities. The national strategy and the defence forces internal concept encompass intelligence as well as offensive and defensive cyber capabilities. FOC is planned by 2020. The cyber division is organised under the defence forces' C5 Agency. The European Centre of Excellence for Countering Hybrid Threats was established in Helsinki on 11 April 2017.

DEPLOYMENT

AFGHANISTAN
NATO • *Operation Resolute Support* 37

BOSNIA-HERZEGOVINA
EU • EUFOR • *Operation Althea* 4

IRAQ
Operation Inherent Resolve 100; 1 trg team

LEBANON
UN • UNIFIL 301; elm 1 inf bn

MALI
EU • EUTM Mali 1
UN • MINUSMA 6

MIDDLE EAST
UN • UNTSO 19 obs

SERBIA
NATO • KFOR 19

SOMALIA
EU • EUTM Somalia 7

SYRIA/ISRAEL
UN • UNDOF 2

UKRAINE
OSCE • Ukraine 17

France FRA

Euro €		2016	2017	2018
GDP	€	2.23tr	2.28tr	
	US$	2.47tr	2.57tr	
per capita	US$	38,178	39,673	
Growth	%	1.2	1.6	
Inflation	%	0.3	1.2	
Def exp [a]	€	40.0bn	40.9bn	
	US$	44.2bn	46.1bn	
Def bdgt [b]	€	42.3bn	43.1bn	45.0bn
	US$	46.8bn	48.6bn	
US$1=€		0.90	0.89	

[a] NATO definition
[b] Includes pensions

Population 67,106,161

Age	0–14	15–19	20–24	25–29	30–64	65 plus
Male	9.5%	3.1%	2.9%	3.0%	22.0%	8.4%
Female	9.1%	2.9%	2.8%	2.9%	22.2%	11.1%

Capabilities

France continues to play a leading military role in the EU, NATO and the UN, and maintains a full-spectrum war-fighting capability. The armed forces are focused on external deployments in sub-Saharan Africa and the Middle East, and the domestic deployment on *Opération Sentinelle*. A Strategic Review, released in late 2017, did not question these commitments, although *Sentinelle* will likely be revised following criticism over its effect. The high tempo of deployments has increased the stress on equipment. There are also concerns about equipment availability. Allies and external contractors are relied on for some military air transport, raising the costs of transporting equipment to operations. France has a sophisticated defence industry, with most procurement undertaken domestically. However, President Macron has called for increased European defence cooperation. France and Germany announced that they were exploring the potential development of a new combat aircraft, and there are ongoing negotiations with Italy for a rapprochement between the two countries' main shipbuilding groups. The government has pledged to meet NATO's 2% of GDP defence-spending target in 2025 and raised the defence budget by €1.8 billion in 2018, including funds earmarked for further equipment purchases. France's deployments abroad have demonstrated its ability to support expeditionary forces independently; however, the more recent focus on domestic security has reduced training and limited the ability to deploy additional troops overseas. Nevertheless, in April 2017 France deployed personnel to Estonia as part of NATO's Enhanced Forward Presence. Troops remain deployed to Djibouti and on EU anti-piracy operations in the Indian Ocean, while personnel and equipment remain active in the campaign against ISIS. (See pp. 74–5.)

ACTIVE 202,700 (Army 112,500 Navy 35,550 Air 41,150, Other Staffs 13,500) **Paramilitary 103,400**

RESERVE 32,300 (Army 18,750 Navy 5,200 Air 4,800 Other Staffs 3,550) **Paramilitary 40,000**

ORGANISATIONS BY SERVICE

Strategic Nuclear Forces

Navy 2,200
EQUIPMENT BY TYPE
SUBMARINES • STRATEGIC • SSBN 4
1 *Le Triomphant* with 16 M45 SLBM with 6 TN-75 nuclear warheads, 4 single 533mm TT with F17 Mod 2 HWT/SM-39 *Exocet* AShM (in refit until 2018/19)
3 *Le Triomphant* with 16 M51 SLBM with 6 TN-75 nuclear warheads, 4 single 533mm TT with F17 Mod 2 HWT/SM-39 *Exocet* AShM
AIRCRAFT • FGA 20 *Rafale* M F3 with ASMP-A msl

Air Force 1,800

Air Strategic Forces Command
FORCES BY ROLE
STRIKE
1 sqn with *Mirage* 2000N with ASMPA msl
1 sqn with *Rafale* B with ASMPA msl
TANKER
1 sqn with C-135FR; KC-135 *Stratotanker*
EQUIPMENT BY TYPE
AIRCRAFT 43 combat capable
FGA 43: 23 *Mirage* 2000N; 20 *Rafale* B
TKR/TPT 11 C-135FR
TKR 3 KC-135 *Stratotanker*

Paramilitary

Gendarmerie 40

Space
EQUIPMENT BY TYPE
SATELLITES 9
COMMUNICATIONS 3: 2 *Syracuse*-3 (designed to integrate with UK *Skynet* & ITA *Sicral*); 1 *Athena-Fidus* (also used by ITA)
ISR 4: 2 *Helios* (2A/2B); 2 *Pleiades*
EARLY WARNING 2 *Spirale*

Army 112,500

Regt and BG normally bn size

FORCES BY ROLE
COMMAND
  1 corps HQ (CRR-FR)
  2 div HQ
MANOEUVRE
  Reconnaissance
  1 recce regt
  Armoured
  1 (2nd) armd bde (2 tk regt, 3 armd inf regt, 1 SP arty regt, 1 engr regt)
  1 (7th) armd bde (1 tk regt, 1 armd BG, 3 armd inf regt, 1 SP arty regt, 1 engr regt)
  1 armd BG (UAE)
  Mechanised
  1 (6th) lt armd bde (2 armd cav regt, 1 armd inf regt, 1 mech inf regt, 1 mech inf regt(-), 1 SP arty regt, 1 engr regt)
  1 (FRA/GER) mech bde (1 armd cav regt, 1 mech inf regt)
  1 mech regt (Djibouti)
  Light
  1 (27th) mtn bde (1 armd cav regt, 3 mech inf regt, 1 arty regt, 1 engr regt)
  3 inf regt (French Guiana & French West Indies)
  1 inf regt (New Caledonia)
  1 inf bn (Côte d'Ivoire)
  1 inf coy (Mayotte)
  Air Manoeuvre
  1 (11th) AB bde (1 armd cav regt, 4 para regt, 1 arty regt, 1 engr regt, 1 spt regt)
  1 AB regt (La Réunion)
  1 AB bn (Gabon)
  Amphibious
  1 (9th) amph bde (2 armd cav regt, 1 armd inf regt, 2 mech inf regt, 1 SP arty regt, 1 engr regt)
  Other
  4 SMA regt (French Guiana, French West Indies & Indian Ocean)
  3 SMA coy (French Polynesia, Indian Ocean & New Caledonia)
COMBAT SUPPORT
  1 MRL regt
  2 engr regt
  2 EW regt
  1 int bn
  1 CBRN regt
  5 sigs regt
COMBAT SERVICE SUPPORT
  5 tpt regt
  1 log regt
  1 med regt
  3 trg regt
HELICOPTER
  1 (4th) hel bde (3 hel regt)
ISR UAV
  1 UAV regt
AIR DEFENCE
  1 SAM regt

Special Operation Forces 2,200

FORCES BY ROLE
SPECIAL FORCES
  2 SF regt
HELICOPTER
  1 hel regt

Reserves 18,750 reservists

Reservists form 79 UIR (Reserve Intervention Units) of about 75 to 152 troops, for 'Proterre' – combined land projection forces bn, and 23 USR (Reserve Specialised Units) of about 160 troops, in specialised regt

EQUIPMENT BY TYPE
ARMOURED FIGHTING VEHICLES
  MBT 200 *Leclerc*
  ASLT 248 AMX-10RC
  RECCE 1,542: 80 ERC-90F4 *Sagaie*; 1,462 VBL/VB2L
  IFV 629: 519 VBCI VCI; 110 VBCI VCP (CP)
  APC 2,342
    APC (T) 53 BvS-10
    APC (W) 2,289: 2,200 VAB; 89 VAB VOA (OP)
  AUV 16 *Aravis*
ENGINEERING & MAINTENANCE VEHICLES
  AEV 54 AMX-30EBG
  ARV 48+: 30 AMX-30D; 18 *Leclerc* DNG; VAB-EHC
  VLB 67: 39 EFA; 18 PTA; 10 SPRAT
  MW 24+: AMX-30B/B2; 4 *Buffalo*; 20 *Minotaur*
NBC VEHICLES 40 VAB NRBC
ANTI-TANK/ANTI-INFRASTRUCTURE • MSL
  SP 295: 110 VAB *Milan*; 185 VAB *Eryx*
  MANPATS FGM-148 *Javelin*; *Milan*
ARTILLERY 262+
  SP 155mm 109: 32 AU-F-1; 77 CAESAR
  TOWED 155mm 12 TR-F-1
  MRL 227mm 13 M270 MLRS
  MOR 128+: **81mm** LLR 81mm; **120mm** 128 RT-F-1
RADAR • LAND 66: 10 *Cobra*; 56 RASIT/RATAC
AIRCRAFT • TPT • Light 13: 5 PC-6B *Turbo Porter*; 5 TBM-700; 3 TBM-700B
HELICOPTERS
  ATK 62: 39 *Tiger* HAP; 23 *Tiger* HAD
  MRH 117: 18 AS555UN *Fennec*; 99 SA341F/342M *Gazelle* (all variants)
  TPT 160: **Heavy** 8 H225M *Caracal* (CSAR); **Medium** 117: 26 AS532UL *Cougar*; 23 NH90 TTH; 68 SA330 *Puma*; **Light** 35 H120 *Colibri* (leased)
UNMANNED AERIAL VEHICLES
  ISR • Medium 25 SDTI (*Sperwer*)
AIR DEFENCE • SAM • Point-defence *Mistral*

Navy 35,500

EQUIPMENT BY TYPE
SUBMARINES 10
  STRATEGIC • SSBN 4:
    1 *Le Triomphant* opcon Strategic Nuclear Forces with 16 M45 SLBM with 6 TN-75 nuclear warheads, 4 single 533mm TT with F17 Mod 2 HWT/SM39 *Exocet* AShM (currently undergoing modernisation programme to install M51 SLBM; expected completion 2018/19)

3 *Le Triomphant* opcon Strategic Nuclear Forces with 16 M51 SLBM with 6 TN-75 nuclear warheads, 4 single 533mm TT with F17 Mod 2 HWT/SM39 *Exocet* AShM

TACTICAL • SSN 6:

6 *Rubis* with 4 single 533mm TT with F17 Mod 2 HWT/SM39 *Exocet* AShM

PRINCIPAL SURFACE COMBATANTS 23

AIRCRAFT CARRIERS 1

CVN 1 *Charles de Gaulle* with 4 octuple VLS with *Aster* 15 SAM, 2 sextuple *Sadral* lnchr with *Mistral* SAM (capacity 35–40 *Rafale* M/E-2C *Hawkeye*/AS365 *Dauphin*) (In refit until late 2018)

DESTROYERS • DDGHM 11:

2 *Cassard* with 2 quad lnchr with MM40 *Exocet* Block 2 AShM, 1 Mk13 GMLS with SM-1MR SAM, 2 sextuple *Sadral* lnchr with *Mistral* SAM, 2 single 533mm ASTT with L5 Mod 4 HWT, 1 100mm gun (capacity 1 AS565SA *Panther* ASW hel)

2 *Forbin* with 2 quad lnchr with MM40 *Exocet* Block 3 AShM, 4 8-cell *Sylver* A50 VLS with *Aster* 30 SAM, 2 8-cell *Sylver* A50 VLS with *Aster* 15 SAM, 2 twin 324mm ASTT with MU90, 2 76mm gun (capacity 1 NH90 TTH hel)

1 *Georges Leygues* with 2 quad lnchr with MM40 *Exocet* AShM, 1 octuple lnchr with *Crotale* SAM, , 2 sextuple *Sadral* lnchr with *Mistral* SAM, 2 single 533mm ASTT with L5 HWT, 1 100mm gun (capacity 2 *Lynx* hel)

3 *Georges Leygues* (mod) with 2 quad lnchr with MM40 *Exocet* AShM, 1 octuple lnchr with *Crotale* SAM, 2 twin *Simbad* lnchr with *Mistral* SAM, 2 single 324mm ASTT with MU90 LWT, 1 100mm gun (capacity 2 *Lynx* hel)

3 *Aquitaine* with 2 8-cell *Sylver* A70 VLS with MdCN (SCALP Naval) LACM, 2 quad lnchr with MM40 *Exocet* Block 3 AShM, 2 8-cell *Sylver* A43 VLS with *Aster* 15 SAM, 2 twin B515 324mm ASTT with MU90 LWT, 1 76mm gun (capacity 1 NH90 NFH hel)

FRIGATES • FFGHM 11:

6 *Floreal* with 2 single lnchr with MM38 *Exocet* AShM, 1 twin *Simbad* lnchr with *Mistral* SAM, 1 100mm gun (capacity 1 AS565SA *Panther* hel)

5 *La Fayette* with 2 quad lnchr with MM40 *Exocet* Block 3 AShM, 1 octuple lnchr with *Crotale* SAM (space for fitting 2 octuple VLS lnchr for *Aster* 15/30), 1 100mm gun (capacity 1 AS565SA *Panther*/SA321 *Super Frelon* hel)

PATROL AND COASTAL COMBATANTS 23

FSM 9 *D'Estienne d'Orves* with 1 twin *Simbad* lnchr with *Mistral* SAM, 4 single ASTT, 1 100mm gun

PSO 3 *d'Entrecasteaux* with 1 hel landing platform

PCC 6: 3 *L'Audacieuse* (all deployed in the Pacific or Caribbean); 3 *Flamant*

PCO 5: 1 *La Confiance*, 1 *Lapérouse*; 1 *Le Malin*; 1 *Fulmar*; 1 *L'Adroit* (*Gowind*)

MINE WARFARE • MINE COUNTERMEASURES 18

MCD 4 *Vulcain*

MHC 3 *Antarès*

MHO 11 *Éridan*

AMPHIBIOUS

PRINCIPAL AMPHIBIOUS SHIPS 3

LHD 3 *Mistral* with 2 twin *Simbad* lnchr with *Mistral* SAM (capacity up to 16 NH90/SA330 *Puma*/AS532 *Cougar*/*Tiger* hel; 2 LCAC or 4 LCM; 13 MBTs; 50 AFVs; 450 troops)

LANDING CRAFT 38

LCT 4 EDA-R

LCM 9 CTM

LCVP 25

LOGISTICS AND SUPPORT 33

ABU 1 *Telenn Mor*

AG 3 *Chamois*

AGE 2: 1 *Corraline*; 1 *Lapérouse* (used as trials ships for mines and divers)

AGI 1 *Dupuy de Lome*

AGM 1 *Monge*

AGOR 2: 1 *Pourquoi pas?* (used 150 days per year by Ministry of Defence; operated by Ministry of Research and Education otherwise); 1 *Beautemps-beaupré*

AGS 3 *Lapérouse*

AORH 3 *Durance* with 1-3 twin *Simbad* lnchr with *Mistral* SAM (capacity 1 SA319 *Alouette* III/AS365 *Dauphin*/*Lynx*)

ATF 3: 2 *Malabar*; 1 *Revi*

AXL 10: 8 *Léopard*; 2 *Glycine*

AXS 4: 2 *La Belle Poule*; 2 other

Naval Aviation 6,500

Flying hours 180–220 hrs/yr on strike/FGA ac

FORCES BY ROLE

STRIKE/FIGHTER/GROUND ATTACK

2 sqn with *Rafale* M F3

1 sqn (forming) with *Rafale* M F3

ANTI-SURFACE WARFARE

1 sqn with AS565SA *Panther*

ANTI-SUBMARINE WARFARE

2 sqn (forming) with NH90 NFH

1 sqn with *Lynx* Mk4

MARITIME PATROL

2 sqn with *Atlantique* 2

1 sqn with *Falcon* 20H *Gardian*

1 sqn with *Falcon* 50MI

AIRBORNE EARLY WARNING & CONTROL

1 sqn with E-2C *Hawkeye*

SEARCH & RESCUE

1 sqn with AS365N/F *Dauphin* 2

TRAINING

1 sqn with EMB 121 *Xingu*

1 unit with SA319B *Alouette* III

1 unit with *Falcon* 10MER

1 unit with CAP 10M

EQUIPMENT BY TYPE

AIRCRAFT 54 combat capable

FGA 42 *Rafale* M F3

ASW 12 *Atlantique* 2 (10 more in store)

AEW&C 3 E-2C *Hawkeye*

SAR 4 *Falcon* 50MS

TPT 26: **Light** 11 EMB-121 *Xingu*; **PAX** 15: 6 *Falcon* 10MER; 5 *Falcon* 20H *Gardian*; 4 *Falcon* 50MI

TRG 7 CAP 10M

HELICOPTERS
ASW 34: 16 *Lynx* Mk4; 18 NH90 NFH
MRH 45: 9 AS365N/F/SP *Dauphin* 2; 2 AS365N3; 16 AS565SA *Panther*; 18 SA319B *Alouette* III
AIR-LAUNCHED MISSILES
AAM • IR R-550 *Magic* 2; **IIR** *Mica* IR; **ARH** *Mica* RF
ASM AASM; AS-30L
AShM AM39 *Exocet*
LACM ASMP-A
BOMBS
Laser-guided: GBU-12 *Paveway* II

Marines 2,000

Commando Units 550
FORCES BY ROLE
MANOEUVRE
  Reconnaissance
  1 recce gp
  Amphibious
  2 aslt gp
  1 atk swimmer gp
  1 raiding gp
COMBAT SUPPORT
  1 cbt spt gp
COMBAT SERVICE SUPPORT
  1 spt gp

Fusiliers-Marin 1,450
FORCES BY ROLE
MANOEUVRE
  Other
  2 sy gp
  7 sy coy

Reserves 5,200 reservists

Air Force 41,150

Flying hours 180 hrs/yr

FORCES BY ROLE
STRIKE
  1 sqn with *Mirage* 2000N with ASMPA msl
  1 sqn with *Rafale* B with ASMPA msl
SPACE
  1 (satellite obs) sqn
FIGHTER
  1 sqn with *Mirage* 2000-5
  1 sqn with *Mirage* 2000B/C
FIGHTER/GROUND ATTACK
  3 sqn with *Mirage* 2000D
  1 (composite) sqn with *Mirage* 2000-5/D (Djibouti)
  2 sqn with *Rafale* B/C
  1 sqn with *Rafale* B/C (UAE)
ELECTRONIC WARFARE
  1 flt with C-160G *Gabriel* (ESM)
AIRBORNE EARLY WARNING & CONTROL
  1 (Surveillance & Control) sqn with E-3F *Sentry*
SEARCH & RESCUE/TRANSPORT
  4 sqn with C-160R *Transall*; CN235M; SA330 *Puma*; AS555 *Fennec* (Djibouti, French Guiana, Gabon, Indian Ocean & New Caledonia)
TANKER
  1 sqn with C-135FR; KC-135 *Stratotanker*
TANKER/TRANSPORT
  2 sqn with C-160R *Transall*
TRANSPORT
  1 sqn with A310-300; A330; A340-200 (on lease)
  1 sqn with A400M
  2 sqn with C-130H/H-30 *Hercules*; C-160R *Transall*
  2 sqn with CN235M
  1 sqn with EMB-121
  1 sqn with *Falcon* 7X (VIP); *Falcon* 900 (VIP); *Falcon* 2000
  3 flt with TBM-700A
  1 (mixed) gp with AS532 *Cougar*; C-160 *Transall*; DHC-6-300 *Twin Otter*
TRAINING
  1 OCU sqn with *Mirage* 2000D
  1 OCU sqn with *Rafale* B/C F3
  1 OCU sqn with SA330 *Puma*; AS555 *Fennec*
  1 OCU unit with C-160 *Transall*
  1 (aggressor) sqn with *Alpha Jet**
  4 sqn with *Alpha Jet**
  3 sqn with Grob G120A-F; TB-30 *Epsilon*
  1 OEU with *Mirage* 2000, *Rafale*, *Alpha Jet**
TRANSPORT HELICOPTER
  2 sqn with AS555 *Fennec*
  2 sqn with AS332C/L *Super Puma*; SA330 *Puma*; H225M
ISR UAV
  1 sqn with *Harfang*; MQ-9A *Reaper*
AIR DEFENCE
  3 sqn with *Crotale* NG; SAMP/T
  1 sqn with SAMP/T

EQUIPMENT BY TYPE
SATELLITES see Space
AIRCRAFT 294 combat capable
  FTR 41: 35 *Mirage* 2000-5/2000C; 6 *Mirage* 2000B
  FGA 189: 67 *Mirage* 2000D; 22 *Mirage* 2000N; 52 *Rafale* B; 48 *Rafale* C
  ELINT 2 C-160G *Gabriel* (ESM)
  AEW&C 4 E-3F *Sentry*
  TKR 3 KC-135 *Stratotanker*
  TKR/TPT 11 C-135FR
  TPT 128: **Heavy** 11 A400M; **Medium** 35: 5 C-130H *Hercules*; 9 C-130H-30 *Hercules*; 21 C-160R *Transall*; **Light** 70: 19 CN235M-100; 8 CN235M-300; 5 DHC-6-300 *Twin Otter*; 23 EMB-121 *Xingu*; 15 TBM-700; **PAX** 12: 3 A310-300; 1 A330; 2 A340-200 (on lease); 2 *Falcon* 7X; 2 *Falcon* 900 (VIP); 2 *Falcon* 2000
  TRG 107: 64 *Alpha Jet**; 18 Grob G120A-F; 25 TB-30 *Epsilon* (incl many in storage)
HELICOPTERS
  MRH 37 AS555 *Fennec*
  TPT 43: **Heavy** 11 H225M *Caracal*; **Medium** 32: 3 AS332C *Super Puma*; 4 AS332L *Super Puma*; 3 AS532UL *Cougar* (tpt/VIP); 22 SA330B *Puma*
UNMANNED AERIAL VEHICLES
  CISR • Heavy 6 MQ-9A *Reaper* (unarmed)
  ISR • Heavy 4 *Harfang*
AIR DEFENCE
  SAM
    Long-range 9 SAMP/T; **Short-range** 12 *Crotale* NG
  GUNS 20mm Cerbere 76T2

AIR-LAUNCHED MISSILES
AAM • **IR** R-550 *Magic* 2; **IIR** *Mica* IR; **ARH** *Mica* RF
ASM AASM; AS-30L; *Apache*
LACM ASMP-A; SCALP EG
BOMBS
Laser-guided: GBU-12 *Paveway* II

Security and Intervention Brigade
FORCES BY ROLE
SPECIAL FORCES
3 SF gp
MANOEUVRE
Other
24 protection units
30 (fire fighting and rescue) unit

Reserves 4,800 reservists

Paramilitary 103,400

Gendarmerie 103,400; 40,000 reservists
EQUIPMENT BY TYPE
ARMOURED FIGHTING VEHICLES
ASLT 28 VBC-90
APC • APC (W) 153 VXB-170 (VBRG-170)
ARTILLERY • MOR 81mm some
PATROL AND COASTAL COMBATANTS 38
PB 38: 2 *Athos*; 4 *Géranium*; 24 VCSM; 8 VSMP
HELICOPTERS • TPT • Light 60: 25 AS350BA *Ecureuil*; 20 H135; 15 H145

Customs (Direction Générale des Douanes et Droits Indirects)
EQUIPMENT BY TYPE
PATROL AND COASTAL COMBATANTS 20
PCO 3: 2 *Jacques Oudart Fourmentin*; 1 *Jean-François Deniau*
PB 17: 7 *Plascoa* 2100; 7 *Haize Hegoa*; 1 *Rafale*; 1 *Vent d'Amont*; 1 *La Rance*

Coast Guard (Direction des Affaires Maritimes)
EQUIPMENT BY TYPE
PATROL AND COASTAL COMBATANTS 25
PCO 1 *Themis*
PCC 1 *Iris*
PB 23: 4 *Callisto*; 19 others
LOGISTICS AND SUPPORT • AG 7

Cyber

In mid-December 2016, the French defence ministry published a new cyber-security doctrine based on a concept of active defence, whereby a newly formed military-cyber corps is authorised to pre-emptively identify, trace and track potential attackers, neutralise such attacks on a pre-emptive basis and retaliate against attacks on the basis of an escalation model that also allows for kinetic responses. Cyber defence is formally designated an art of war and is to be taught to France's entire officer corps. The military-cyber corps, staffed largely by the foreign-intelligence service, will report directly to the chief of general staff. The doctrine acknowledges the presence of a Tailored Access Unit, which has in fact been in existence for over 30 years and is deployed overseas to provide covert coverage of specific targets. The military-cyber corps personnel level is scheduled to rise to 2,600, supplemented by a reserve force, which itself is scheduled to rise to 4,400.

DEPLOYMENT

ARABIAN SEA
Combined Maritime Forces • CTF-150: 1 DDGHM

BURKINA FASO
Operation Barkhane 250; 1 SF gp

CENTRAL AFRICAN REPUBLIC
EU • EUTM RCA 53
UN • MINUSCA 91; 1 UAV unit

CHAD
Operation Barkhane 1,500; 1 mech inf BG; 1 FGA det with 2 *Mirage* 2000D; 2 *Mirage* 2000N; 1 tpt det with 1 C-130H; 4 CN235M

CÔTE D'IVOIRE
950; 1 (Marine) inf bn

DEMOCRATIC REPUBLIC OF THE CONGO
UN • MONUSCO 2

DJIBOUTI
1,450; 1 (Marine) combined arms regt with (2 recce sqn, 2 inf coy, 1 arty bty, 1 engr coy); 1 hel det with 2 SA330 *Puma*; 1 SA342 *Gazelle*; 1 LCM; 1 FGA sqn with 4 *Mirage* 2000-5/D; 1 SAR/tpt sqn with 1 C-160 *Transall*; 2 SA330 *Puma*

EGYPT
MFO 1

ESTONIA
NATO • Enhanced Forward Presence 300; 1 armd inf coy(+)

FRENCH GUIANA
2,100: 1 (Foreign Legion) inf regt; 1 (Marine) inf regt; 1 SMA regt; 2 PCC; 1 tpt sqn with 3 CN235M; 5 SA330 *Puma*; 4 AS555 *Fennec*; 3 gendarmerie coy; 1 AS350BA *Ecureuil*

FRENCH POLYNESIA
900: (incl Centre d'Expérimentation du Pacifique); 1 SMA coy; 1 naval HQ at Papeete; 1 FFGHM; 1 PSO; 1 PCO; 1 AFS; 3 *Falcon* 200 *Gardian*; 1 SAR/tpt sqn with 2 CN235M

FRENCH WEST INDIES
1,000; 1 (Marine) inf regt; 2 SMA regt; 2 FFGHM; 1 LST; 1 naval base at Fort de France (Martinique); 4 gendarmerie coy; 2 AS350BA *Ecureuil*

GABON
350; 1 AB bn

GERMANY
2,000 (incl elm Eurocorps and FRA/GER bde); 1 (FRA/GER) mech bde (1 armd cav regt, 1 mech inf regt)

GULF OF GUINEA
Operation Corymbe 1 LHD; 1 FSM

INDIAN OCEAN

1,600 (incl La Réunion and TAAF); 1 (Marine) para regt; 1 (Foreign Legion) inf coy; 1 SMA regt ; 1 SMA coy; 2 FFGHM; 1 PCO; 1 LCM; 1 naval HQ at Port-des-Galets (La Réunion); 1 naval base at Dzaoudzi (Mayotte); 1 SAR/tpt sqn with 2 CN235M; 5 gendarmerie coy; 1 SA319 *Alouette* III

IRAQ

Operation Inherent Resolve (*Chammal*) 500; 1 SF gp; 1 trg unit; 1 SP arty bty with 4 CAESAR

JORDAN

Operation Inherent Resolve (*Chammal*) 8 *Rafale* F3; 1 *Atlantique* 2

LEBANON

UN • UNIFIL 661; 1 mech inf bn(-); 1 maint coy; VBL; VBCI; VAB; *Mistral*

MALI

Operation Barkhane 1,750; 1 mech inf BG; 1 log bn; 1 hel unit with 4 *Tiger*; 3 NH90 TTH; 6 SA330 *Puma*; 4 SA342 *Gazelle*
EU • EUTM Mali 13
UN • MINUSMA 21

MEDITERRANEAN SEA

Operation Inherent Resolve (*Chammal*) 1 FFGHM
EU • EU NAVFOR MED: 1 FSM

NEW CALEDONIA

1,450; 1 (Marine) mech inf regt; 1 SMA coy; 6 ERC-90F1 *Lynx*; 1 FFGHM; 1 PSO; 2 PCC; 1 base with 2 *Falcon* 200 *Gardian* at Nouméa; 1 tpt unit with 2 CN235 MPA; 3 SA330 *Puma*; 4 gendarmerie coy; 2 AS350BA *Ecureuil*

NIGER

Operation Barkhane 500; 1 FGA det with 2 *Mirage* 2000C; 2 *Mirage* 2000D; 1 tkr/tpt det with 1 C-135FR; 1 C-160 *Transall*; 1 UAV det with 5 MQ-9A *Reaper*

SENEGAL

350; 1 *Falcon* 50MI

SOMALIA

EU • EUTM Somalia 1

SYRIA

Operation Inherent Resolve (*Chammal*) 1 SF unit

UKRAINE

OSCE • Ukraine 14

UNITED ARAB EMIRATES

650: 1 armd BG (1 tk coy, 1 arty bty); *Leclerc*; CAESAR; • *Operation Inherent Resolve* (*Chammal*); 1 FGA sqn with 6 *Rafale* F3; 1 C-135FR

WESTERN SAHARA

UN • MINURSO 2 obs

FOREIGN FORCES

Belgium 28 *Alpha Jet* trg ac located at Cazaux/Tours
Germany 400 (GER elm Eurocorps)
Singapore 200; 1 trg sqn with 12 M-346 *Master*

Germany GER

Euro €		2016	2017	2018
GDP	€	3.14tr	3.24tr	
	US$	3.48tr	3.65tr	
per capita	US$	42,177	44,184	
Growth	%	1.9	2.1	
Inflation	%	0.4	1.6	
Def exp [a]	€	37.6bn	39.5bn	
	US$	41.6bn	44.6bn	
Def bdgt [b]	€	34.3bn	37.0bn	38.5bn
	US$	37.9bn	41.7bn	
US$1=€		0.90	0.89	

[a] NATO definition
[b] Includes military pensions

Population 80,594,017

Age	0–14	15–19	20–24	25–29	30–64	65 plus
Male	6.6%	2.5%	2.7%	3.1%	24.5%	9.7%
Female	6.2%	2.4%	2.6%	3.0%	24.3%	12.4%

Capabilities

The 2016 white paper on security policy and the future of the armed forces commits Germany to a leadership role in European defence. It also emphasises the importance of NATO and the need for the armed forces to be able to contribute to collective-defence tasks. Compared to previous strategy documents, the white paper acknowledges the return of inter-state armed conflict and describes Russia as a challenge to European security rather than a partner. Germany's Cyber Command achieved initial operating capability in April 2017. The initial aim is to centralise responsibility for cyber, information technology, military intelligence and electronic warfare, geographic-information services and some communications tasks in one command. In this process, Germany is expected to strengthen its capacity for Computer Network Operations. Continuing the recent trend, current government budget planning foresees annual defence-budget growth from 2017 to 2021. Budget parameters are reviewed annually by the cabinet and rolling five-year budget plans are agreed on that basis. Available additional funding is likely to mostly benefit the army. Once agreed goals are implemented, for example to increase equipment levels for operational units from 70% to 100%, additional modernisation steps would require yet more funding. The defence ministry has also announced the objective of increasing authorised active force numbers to 198,000 by 2024. Given that the Bundeswehr is already struggling with recruitment and retention after conscription was suspended in 2011, the ministry is due to recommend recruitment goals with a seven-year time horizon and a shift towards a more flexible approach to generating the authorised personnel strength. The German armed forces are struggling to improve their readiness levels in light of increasing demands on NATO's eastern flank. As several reports to parliament have outlined, the budget cuts of previous years have led to a shortage of spare parts and maintenance problems. Guidelines for the future Bundeswehr capability profile, initially expected for summer 2017, were yet to be released as of November.

ACTIVE 178,600 (Army 60,900 Navy 16,300 Air 28,300 Joint Support Service 28,200 Joint Medical Service 19,900 Cyber 12,200; Other 12,800) Paramilitary 500

Conscript liability Voluntary conscription only. Voluntary conscripts can serve up to 23 months

RESERVE 27,900 (Army 6,350 Navy 1,150 Air 3,450 Joint Support Service 12,400 Joint Medical Service 3,100 Other 1,450)

ORGANISATIONS BY SERVICE

Space
EQUIPMENT BY TYPE
SATELLITES 7
  COMMUNICATIONS 2 COMSATBw (1 & 2)
  ISR 5 SAR-*Lupe*

Army 60,900
FORCES BY ROLE
COMMAND
  elm 2 (1 GNC & MNC NE) corps HQ
MANOEUVRE
  Armoured
  1 (1st) armd div (1 (9th) armd bde (1 armd recce bn, 1 tk bn, 2 armd inf bn, 1 lt inf bn, 1 cbt engr bn, 1 spt bn); 1 (21st) armd bde (1 armd recce bn, 1 tk bn, 1 armd inf bn, 1 mech inf bn, 1 cbt engr bn, 1 spt bn); 1 (41st) mech inf bde (1 armd recce bn, 2 armd inf bn, 1 lt inf bn, 1 cbt engr bn, 1 sigs bn, 1 spt bn); 1 tk bn (for NLD 43rd Bde); 1 SP arty bn; 1 sigs bn)
  1 (10th) armd div (1 (12th) armd bde (1 armd recce bn, 1 tk bn, 2 armd inf bn, 1 cbt engr bn, 1 spt bn); 1 (37th) mech inf bde (1 armd recce bn, 1 tk bn, 1 armd inf bn, 1 mech inf bn, 1 engr bn, 1 spt bn); 1 (23rd) mtn inf bde (1 recce bn, 3 mtn inf bn, 1 cbt engr bn, 1 spt bn); 1 SP arty bn; 1 SP arty trg bn; 2 mech inf bn (GER/FRA bde); 1 arty bn (GER/FRA bde); 1 cbt engr coy (GER/FRA bde); 1 spt bn (GER/FRA bde))
  Air Manoeuvre
  1 (rapid reaction) AB div (1 SOF bde (2 SOF bn); 1 AB bde (2 recce coy, 2 para regt, 2 cbt engr coy); 1 atk hel regt; 2 tpt hel regt; 1 sigs coy)
EQUIPMENT BY TYPE
ARMOURED FIGHTING VEHICLES
  MBT 236: 217 *Leopard* 2A5/A6; 19 *Leopard* 2A7
  RECCE 182: 166 *Fennek* (incl 14 engr recce, 14 fires spt); 16 *Wiesel*
  IFV 590: 357 *Marder* 1A3/A4/A5; 160 *Puma*; 73 *Wiesel* 1 Mk20 (with 20mm gun)
  APC 1,046
    APC (T) 316: 194 Bv-206D/S; 122 M113 (inc variants)
    APC (W) 730: 199 *Boxer* (inc CP and trg variants); 531 TPz-1 *Fuchs* (inc variants)
  AUV 424: 202 *Dingo* 2; 222 *Eagle* IV/V

ENGINEERING & MAINTENANCE VEHICLES
  AEV 42 *Dachs*
  ARV 97: 56 ARV *Leopard* 1; 41 BPz-3 *Büffel*
  VLB 47: 22 *Biber*; 25 M3
  MW 15 *Keiler*
NBC VEHICLES 8 TPz-1 *Fuchs* NBC
ANTI-TANK/ANTI-INFRASTRUCTURE • MSL
  SP 102 *Wiesel* with TOW
  MANPATS *Milan*; *Spike-LR* (MELLS)
ARTILLERY 214
  SP 155mm 101 PzH 2000
  MRL 227mm 20 M270 MLRS
  MOR 120mm 93 *Tampella*
RADARS • LAND 82: 9 *Cobra*; 61 RASIT (veh, arty); 12 RATAC (veh, arty)
HELICOPTERS
  ATK 50 *Tiger*
  TPT 110: **Medium** 55 NH90; **Light** 55: 41 Bell 205 (UH-1D *Iroquois*); 14 H135
UNMANNED AERIAL VEHICLES
  ISR 128: **Medium** 44 KZO; **Light** 84 LUNA

Navy 16,300
EQUIPMENT BY TYPE
SUBMARINES • TACTICAL • SSK 6:
  6 Type-212A with 6 single 533mm TT with 12 A4 *Seehecht* DM2 HWT
PRINCIPAL SURFACE COMBATANTS 14
  DESTROYERS • DDGHM 7:
    4 *Brandenburg* with 2 twin lnchr with MM38 *Exocet* AShM, 1 16-cell Mk41 VLS with RIM-7M/P, 2 Mk49 GMLS with RIM-116 RAM SAM, 2 twin 324mm ASTT with Mk46 LWT, 1 76mm gun (capacity 2 *Sea Lynx* Mk88A hel)
    3 *Sachsen* with 2 quad Mk141 lnchr with RGM-84F *Harpoon* AShM, 1 32-cell Mk41 VLS with SM-2MR/RIM-162B ESSM SAM, 2 21-cell Mk49 GMLS with RIM-116 RAM SAM, 2 triple Mk32 324mm ASTT with MU90 LWT, 1 76mm gun (capacity; 2 *Sea Lynx* Mk88A hel)
  FRIGATES 7
    FFGHM 2 *Bremen* with 2 quad Mk141 lnchr with RGM-84A/C *Harpoon* AShM, 1 octuple Mk29 GMLS with RIM-7M/P *Sea Sparrow* SAM, 2 Mk49 GMLS with RIM-116 RAM SAM, 2 twin 324mm ASTT with Mk46 LWT, 1 76mm gun (capacity 2 *Sea Lynx* Mk88A hel)
    FFGM 5 *Braunschweig* (K130) with 2 twin lnchr with RBS-15 AShM, 2 Mk49 GMLS each with RIM-116 RAM SAM, 1 76mm gun, 1 hel landing platform
MINE WARFARE • MINE COUNTERMEASURES 26
  MHO 12: 10 *Frankenthal* (2 used as diving support); 2 *Kulmbach*
  MSO 2 *Ensdorf*
  MSD 12 *Seehund*
AMPHIBIOUS • LCU 1 Type-520
LOGISTICS AND SUPPORT 22
  AFSH 3 *Berlin* (Type-702) (capacity 2 *Sea King* Mk41 hel; 2 RAMs)

AG 4: 2 *Schwedeneck* (Type-748); 2 *Stollergrund* (Type-745)
AGI 3 *Oste* (Type-423)
AGOR 1 *Planet* (Type-751)
AOR 6 *Elbe* (Type-404) with 1 hel landing platform (2 specified for PFM support; 1 specified for SSK support; 3 specified for MHC/MSC support)
AOT 2 *Rhön* (Type-704)
APB 2: 1 *Knurrhahn*; 1 *Ohre*
AXS 1 *Gorch Fock*

Naval Aviation 2,000
EQUIPMENT BY TYPE
AIRCRAFT 8 combat capable
  ASW 8 AP-3C *Orion*
  TPT • Light 2 Do-228 (pollution control)
HELICOPTERS
  ASW 22 *Lynx* Mk88A
  SAR 21 *Sea King* Mk41

Naval Special Forces Command
FORCES BY ROLE
SPECIAL FORCES
  1 SF coy

Sea Battalion
FORCES BY ROLE
MANOEUVRE
  Amphibious
    1 mne bn

Air Force 28,300
Flying hours 140 hrs/yr (plus 40 hrs high-fidelity simulator)

FORCES BY ROLE
FIGHTER
  3 wg (2 sqn with Eurofighter *Typhoon*)
FIGHTER/GROUND ATTACK
  1 wg (2 sqn with *Tornado* IDS)
  1 wg (2 sqn with Eurofighter *Typhoon* (multi-role))
ISR
  1 wg (1 ISR sqn with *Tornado* ECR/IDS; 2 UAV sqn with *Heron*)
TANKER/TRANSPORT
  1 (special air mission) wg (3 sqn with A310 MRTT; A319; A340; AS532U2 *Cougar* II; *Global* 5000)
TRANSPORT
  2 wg (total: 3 sqn with C-160D *Transall*)
  1 wg (1 sqn (forming) with A400M *Atlas*)
TRAINING
  1 sqn located at Holloman AFB (US) with *Tornado* IDS
  1 unit (ENJJPT) located at Sheppard AFB (US) with T-6 *Texan* II; T-38A
  1 hel unit located at Fassberg
TRANSPORT HELICOPTER
  1 tpt hel wg (3 sqn with CH-53G/GA/GE/GS *Stallion*; 1 sqn with H145M)
AIR DEFENCE
  1 wg (3 SAM gp) with MIM-104C/F *Patriot* PAC-2/3
  1 AD gp with ASRAD *Ozelot*; C-RAM *Mantis* and trg unit

1 AD trg unit located at Fort Bliss (US) with MIM-104C/F *Patriot* PAC-2/3
3 (tac air ctrl) radar gp

Air Force Regiment
FORCES BY ROLE
MANOEUVRE
  Other
    1 sy regt
EQUIPMENT BY TYPE
AIRCRAFT 211 combat capable
  FTR 123 Eurofighter *Typhoon*
  ATK 68 *Tornado* IDS
  ATK/EW 20 *Tornado* ECR*
  TKR/TPT 4 A310 MRTT
  TPT 55: **Heavy** 13 A400M; **Medium** 33 C-160D *Transall*;
  PAX 9: 1 A310; 2 A340 (VIP); 2 A319; 4 *Global* 5000
  TRG 109: 69 T-6A *Texan* II, 40 T-38A
HELICOPTERS
  MRH 15 H145M
  TPT 73: **Heavy** 70 CH-53G/GA/GS/GE *Stallion*; **Medium** 3 AS532U2 *Cougar* II (VIP)
UNMANNED AERIAL VEHICLES • ISR • Heavy 8 *Heron* 1
AIR DEFENCE
  SAM
    Long-range 30 MIM-104C/F *Patriot* PAC-2/PAC-3
    Point-defence 10 ASRAD *Ozelot* (with FIM-92 *Stinger*)
  GUNS 35mm 12 C-RAM *Mantis*
AIR-LAUNCHED MISSILES
  AAM • IR AIM-9L/Li *Sidewinder*; **IIR** IRIS-T; **ARH** AIM-120B AMRAAM
  LACM *Taurus* KEPD 350
  ARM AGM-88B HARM
BOMBS
  Laser-guided GBU-24 *Paveway* III, GBU-54 JDAM

Joint Support Service 28,200
FORCES BY ROLE
COMBAT SUPPORT
  3 MP regt
  2 NBC bn
COMBAT SERVICE SUPPORT
  6 log bn
  1 spt regt
EQUIPMENT BY TYPE
ARMOURED FIGHTING VEHICLES
  APC • APC (W) 74 TPz-1 *Fuchs* (inc variants)
  AUV 362: 168 *Dingo* 2; 194 *Eagle* IV/V
ENGINEERING & MAINTENANCE VEHICLES
  AEV 6 *Dachs*
  ARV 30 BPz-3 *Büffel*
NBC VEHICLES 34 TPz-1 *Fuchs* A6/A7/A8 NBC

Joint Medical Services 19,900
FORCES BY ROLE
COMBAT SERVICE SUPPORT
  4 med regt

EQUIPMENT BY TYPE
ARMOURED FIGHTING VEHICLES
APC • **APC (W)** 79: 57 *Boxer* (amb); 22 TPz-1 *Fuchs* (amb)
AUV 21 *Eagle* IV/V (amb)

Cyber & Information Command 12,200
FORCES BY ROLE
COMBAT SUPPORT
4 EW bn
6 sigs bn

Paramilitary

Coast Guard 500
EQUIPMENT BY TYPE
PATROL AND COASTAL COMBATANTS 9
PCO 4: 3 *Bad Bramstedt*; 1 *Bredstedt*
PB 5 *Prignitz*

Cyber

Germany issued a Cyber Security Strategy in February 2011. The National Cyber Security Council, an inter-ministerial body at state-secretary level, analyses cyber-related issues. A National Cyber Response Centre was set up at the Federal Office for Information Security on 1 April 2011. In 2016, Germany boosted its cyber capabilities by implementing far-reaching reforms. A new Directorate-General Cyber/IT (CIT) was created within the Federal Ministry of Defence, with two divisions for Cyber/IT Governance and IT Services/Information Security. The Director-General serves as Chief Information Officer and point of contact for other federal ministries and agencies. The Directorate-General's tasks include advancing technical cyber/IT capabilities, and guiding cyber policies. A Cyber and Information Space Command (KdoCIR) led by a Chief of Staff for Cyber and Information Space (InspCIR) was launched in April 2017. The overall aim of these reforms is to assign current capabilities to defined responsibilities, protect Bundeswehr and national cyber and IT infrastructure, and improve capabilities in order to better respond to cyber attacks. Germany's defence minister stated in April 2017 that the armed forces could respond with offensive cyber operations if its networks are attacked.

DEPLOYMENT

AFGHANISTAN
NATO • *Operation Resolute Support* 980; 1 bde HQ; 1 recce bn; 1 UAV flt with 3 *Heron* 1 UAV
UN • UNAMA 1 obs

ALBANIA
OSCE • Albania 2

ALBANIA
OSCE • Minsk Conference 1

DJIBOUTI
EU • *Operation Atalanta* 1 AP-3C *Orion*

FRANCE
400 (incl GER elm Eurocorps)

IRAQ
145 (trg spt)

JORDAN
Operation Inherent Resolve 284; 4 *Tornado* ECR; 1 A310 MRTT

LEBANON
UN • UNIFIL 122; 1 FFGM

LITHUANIA
NATO • Enhanced Forward Presence 450; 1 armd inf bn HQ; 1 armd inf coy(+)

MALI
EU • EUTM Mali 83
UN • MINUSMA 610; 1 obs; 1 int coy; 1 hel bn

MEDITERRANEAN SEA
EU • EU NAVFOR MED: 1 DDGHM
NATO • SNMG 1: 1 AOT
NATO • SNMG 2: 1 FFGHM

NORTH SEA
NATO • SNMCMG 1: 1 MHO

POLAND
67 (GER elm MNC-NE)

SERBIA
NATO • KFOR 650
OSCE • Kosovo 4

SOMALIA
EU • EUTM Somalia 7

SOUTH SUDAN
UN • UNMISS 5; 11 obs

SUDAN
UN • UNAMID 8

UKRAINE
OSCE • Ukraine 27

UNITED STATES
Trg units with 40 T-38 *Talon*; 69 T-6A *Texan* II at Goodyear AFB (AZ)/Sheppard AFB (TX); 1 trg sqn with 14 *Tornado* IDS at Holloman AFB (NM); NAS Pensacola (FL); Fort Rucker (AL); Missile trg at Fort Bliss (TX)

WESTERN SAHARA
UN • MINURSO 5 obs

FOREIGN FORCES

France 2,000; 1 (FRA/GER) mech bde (1 armd cav regt, 1 mech inf regt)
United Kingdom 3,750; 1 armd bde(-) (1 tk regt, 1 armd inf bn); 1 SP arty regt; 1 cbt engr regt; 1 maint regt; 1 med regt
United States
US Africa Command: **Army**; 1 HQ at Stuttgart
US European Command: 37,450; 1 combined service HQ (EUCOM) at Stuttgart-Vaihingen
  Army 23,000; 1 HQ (US Army Europe (USAREUR) at Heidelberg; 1 div HQ (fwd); 1 SF gp; 1 armd recce bn; 2

armd bn; 1 mech bde(-); 1 arty bn; 1 (cbt avn) hel bde(-); 1 (cbt avn) hel bde HQ; 1 int bde; 1 MP bde; 1 sigs bde; 1 spt bde; 1 (APS) armd bde eqpt set; M1 *Abrams*; M2/M3 *Bradley*; *Stryker*; M109; M119A2; M777; AH-64D/E *Apache*; CH-47F *Chinook*; UH-60L/M *Black Hawk*; HH-60M *Black Hawk*

Navy 1,000

USAF 12,300; 1 HQ (US Airforce Europe (USAFE)) at Ramstein AB; 1 HQ (3rd Air Force) at Ramstein AB; 1 ftr wg at Spangdahlem AB with 1 ftr sqn with 24 F-16CJ *Fighting Falcon*; 1 airlift wg at Ramstein AB with 14 C-130J-30 *Hercules*; 2 Gulfstream V (C-37A); 5 Learjet 35A (C-21A); 1 B-737-700 (C-40B)

USMC 1,150

Greece GRC

Euro €		2016	2017	2018
GDP	€	176bn	181bn	
	US$	195bn	204bn	
per capita	US$	18,049	18,945	
Growth	%	0.0	1.8	
Inflation	%	0.0	1.2	
Def exp [a]	€	4.19bn	4.21bn	
	US$	4.64bn	4.75bn	
Def bdgt [b]	€	4.16bn	4.19bn	4.11bn
	US$	4.60bn	4.73bn	
US$1=€		0.90	0.89	

[a] NATO definition
[b] Includes military pensions

Population 10,768,477

Age	0–14	15–19	20–24	25–29	30–64	65 plus
Male	7.1%	2.4%	2.5%	2.7%	24.9%	9.2%
Female	6.7%	2.3%	2.4%	2.7%	25.3%	11.8%

Capabilities

Principal tasks for Greece's armed forces include ensuring territorial integrity and supporting Cyprus in the event of conflict. The armed forces have traditionally been well funded. The general staff is aiming to produce more flexible, agile and mobile forces at the tactical and operational levels. In 2017, there was growing cooperation with Egypt and Israel, including joint exercises, as well as continued tensions with Turkey over airspace violations. Despite challenging fiscal circumstances, Greece is modernising and upgrading its stored P-3B *Orion* aircraft in order to strengthen its maritime-patrol and anti-submarine-warfare capability, as well as enhancing surveillance capacity in the eastern Mediterranean. Greece is also bolstering its rotary-wing transport capability and in late 2017 the US approved the upgrade of Greece's F-16 fleet. Development of the local defence-industrial base is a priority, in order to preserve local maintenance capabilities and improve equipment readiness. Greece trains widely with NATO allies and other partners.

ACTIVE 141,350 (Army 93,500 Navy 16,250 Air 20,000 Joint 11,600) **Paramilitary 4,000**

Conscript liability Up to 9 months in all services

RESERVE 220,500 (Army 181,500 Navy 5,000 Air 34,000)

ORGANISATIONS BY SERVICE

Army 48,500; 45,000 conscripts (total 93,500)

Units are manned at 3 different levels – Cat A 85% fully ready, Cat B 60% ready in 24 hours, Cat C 20% ready in 48 hours (requiring reserve mobilisation). 3 military regions

FORCES BY ROLE
COMMAND
  2 corps HQ (incl NDC-GR)
  1 armd div HQ
  3 mech inf div HQ
  1 inf div HQ
SPECIAL FORCES
  1 SF comd
  1 cdo/para bde
MANOEUVRE
  Reconnaissance
  4 recce bn
  Armoured
  4 armd bde (2 armd bn, 1 mech inf bn, 1 SP arty bn)
  Mechanised
  9 mech inf bde (1 armd bn, 2 mech bn, 1 SP arty bn)
  Light
  1 inf bde (1 armd bn, 3 inf regt, 1 arty regt)
  Air Manoeuvre
  1 air mob bde
  1 air aslt bde
  Amphibious
  1 mne bde
COMBAT SUPPORT
  1 arty regt (1 arty bn, 2 MRL bn)
  3 AD bn (2 with I-*Hawk*, 1 with *Tor* M1)
  3 engr regt
  2 engr bn
  1 EW regt
  10 sigs bn
COMBAT SERVICE SUPPORT
  1 log corps HQ
  1 log div (3 log bde)
HELICOPTER
  1 hel bde (1 hel regt with (2 atk hel bn), 2 tpt hel bn, 4 hel bn)
EQUIPMENT BY TYPE
ARMOURED FIGHTING VEHICLES
  MBT 1,341: 170 *Leopard* 2A6HEL; 183 *Leopard* 2A4; 513 *Leopard* 1A4/5; 100 M60A1/A3; 375 M48A5
  RECCE 242 VBL
  IFV 398 BMP-1
  APC 2,418
    APC (T) 2,407: 86 *Leonidas* Mk1/2; 2,108 M113A1/A2; 213 M577 (CP)
    PPV 11 *Maxxpro*

ENGINEERING & MAINTENANCE VEHICLES
  ARV 261: 12 *Büffel*; 43 *Leopard 1*; 94 M88A1; 112 M578
  VLB 12+: 12 *Leopard 1*; *Leguan*
  MW *Giant Viper*
ANTI-TANK/ANTI-INFRASTRUCTURE
  MSL
    SP 600: 196 HMMWV with 9K135 *Kornet-E* (AT-14 *Spriggan*); 42 HMMWV with *Milan*; 362 M901
    MANPATS 9K111 *Fagot* (AT-4 *Spigot*); *Milan*; TOW
  RCL 84mm *Carl Gustav*; **90mm** EM-67; **SP 106mm** 581 M40A1
ARTILLERY 3,607
  SP 587: **155mm** 442: 418 M109A1B/A2/A3GEA1/A5; 24 PzH 2000; **203mm** 145 M110A2
  TOWED 553: **105mm** 347: 329 M101; 18 M-56; **155mm** 206 M114
  MRL 147: **122mm** 111 RM-70; **227mm** 36 M270 MLRS
  MOR 2,320: **81mm** 1,700; **107mm** 620 M30 (incl 231 SP)
SURFACE-TO-SURFACE MISSILE LAUNCHERS
  SRBM • Conventional MGM-140A ATACMS (launched from M270 MLRS)
RADAR • LAND 76: 3 ARTHUR; 5 AN/TPQ-36 *Firefinder* (arty, mor); 8 AN/TPQ-37(V)3; 40 BOR-A; 20 MARGOT
AIRCRAFT • TPT • Light 18: 1 Beech 200 *King Air* (C-12C) 2 Beech 200 *King Air* (C-12R/AP *Huron*); 15 Cessna 185 (U-17A/B)
HELICOPTERS
  ATK 28: 19 AH-64A *Apache*; 9 AH-64D *Apache*
  TPT 140: **Heavy** 21: 15 CH-47D *Chinook*; 6 CH-47SD *Chinook*; **Medium** 13 NH90 TTH; **Light** 106: 92 Bell 205 (UH-1H *Iroquois*); 14 Bell 206 (AB-206) *Jet Ranger*
UNMANNED AERIAL VEHICLES
  ISR • Medium 4 *Sperwer*
AIR DEFENCE
  SAM 155
    Medium-range 42 MIM-23B *I-Hawk*
    Short-range 21 9K331 *Tor-M1* (SA-15 *Gauntlet*)
    Point-range 92+: 38 9K33 *Osa-M* (SA-8B *Gecko*); 54 ASRAD HMMWV; FIM-92 *Stinger*
  GUNS • TOWED 727: **20mm** 204 Rh 202; **23mm** 523 ZU-23-2

National Guard 33,000 reservists
Internal security role
FORCES BY ROLE
MANOEUVRE
  Light
    1 inf div
  Air Manoeuvre
    1 para regt
COMBAT SUPPORT
  8 arty bn
  4 AD bn
COMBAT SUPPORT
  1 hel bn

Navy 14,200; 2,050 conscript (total 16,250)
EQUIPMENT BY TYPE
SUBMARINES • TACTICAL • SSK 11:
  3 *Poseidon* (GER Type-209/1200) with 8 single 533mm TT with SUT HWT
  1 *Poseidon* (GER Type-209/1200) (modernised with AIP technology) with 8 single 533mm TT with SUT HWT
  3 *Glavkos* (GER Type-209/1100) with 8 single 533mm TT with UGM-84C *Harpoon* AShM/SUT HWT
  4 *Papanikolis* (GER Type-214) with 8 single 533mm TT with UGM-84C *Harpoon* AShM/SUT HWT
PRINCIPAL SURFACE COMBATANTS 13
  FRIGATES • FFGHM 13:
    4 *Elli* Batch I (ex-NLD *Kortenaer* Batch 2) with 2 quad Mk141 lnchr with RGM-84A/C *Harpoon* AShM, 1 octuple Mk29 GMLS with RIM-7M/P *Sea Sparrow* SAM, 2 twin 324mm ASTT with Mk46 LWT, 1 *Phalanx* CIWS, 1 76mm gun (capacity 2 Bell 212 (AB-212) hel or 1 S-70B *Seahawk* hel)
    2 *Elli* Batch II (ex-NLD *Kortenaer* Batch 2) with 2 quad Mk141 lnchr with RGM-84A/C *Harpoon* AShM, 1 octuple Mk29 GMLS with RIM-7M/P *Sea Sparrow* SAM, 2 twin 324mm ASTT with Mk46 LWT, 2 *Phalanx* CIWS, 2 76mm gun (capacity 2 Bell 212 (AB-212) hel or 1 S-70B *Seahawk* hel)
    3 *Elli* Batch III (ex-NLD *Kortenaer* Batch 2) with 2 quad Mk141 lnchr with RGM-84A/C *Harpoon* AShM, 1 octuple Mk29 lnchr with RIM-7M/P *Sea Sparrow* SAM, 2 twin 324mm ASTT with Mk46 LWT, 1 *Phalanx* CIWS, 1 76mm gun (capacity 2 Bell 212 (AB-212) hel)
    4 *Hydra* (GER MEKO 200) with 2 quad lnchr with RGM-84G *Harpoon* AShM, 1 16-cell Mk48 Mod 5 VLS with RIM-162 ESSM SAM, 2 triple 324mm ASTT each with Mk46 LWT, 2 *Phalanx* CIWS, 1 127mm gun (capacity 1 S-70B *Seahawk* ASW hel)
PATROL AND COASTAL COMBATANTS 33
  CORVETTES • FSGM 5 *Roussen* (*Super Vita*) with 2 quad lnchr with MM40 *Exocet* Block 2 AShM, 1 21-cell Mk49 GMLS with RIM-116 RAM SAM, 1 76mm gun
  PCFG 12:
    2 *Kavaloudis* (FRA *La Combattante* IIIB) with 6 single lnchr with RB 12 *Penguin* AShM, 2 single 533mm TT with SST-4 HWT, 2 76mm gun
    3 *Kavaloudis* (FRA *La Combattante* IIIB) with 2 twin lnchr with RGM-84C *Harpoon* AShM, 2 single 533mm TT with SST-4 HWT, 2 76mm gun
    2 *Laskos* (FRA *La Combattante* III) with 4 MM38 *Exocet* AShM, 2 single 533mm TT with SST-4 HWT, 2 76mm gun
    2 *Laskos* (FRA *La Combattante* III) with 2 twin lnchr with RGM-84C *Harpoon* AShM, 2 single 533mm TT with SST-4 HWT, 2 76mm gun
    1 *Votsis* (ex-GER *Tiger*) with 2 twin Mk-141 lnchr with RGM-84C *Harpoon* AShM, 1 76mm gun
    2 *Votsis* (ex-GER *Tiger*) with 2 twin MM38 *Exocet* AShM, 1 76mm gun
  PCO 8:
    2 *Armatolos* (DNK *Osprey*) with 1 76mm gun
    2 *Kasos* with 1 76mm gun
    4 *Machitis* with 1 76mm gun
  PB 8: 4 *Andromeda* (NOR *Nasty*); 2 *Stamou*; 2 *Tolmi*
MINE COUNTERMEASURES 4
  MHO 4: 2 *Evropi* (ex-UK *Hunt*); 2 *Evniki* (ex-US *Osprey*)

AMPHIBIOUS
LANDING SHIPS • LST 5:
  5 *Chios* (capacity 4 LCVP; 300 troops) with 1 76mm gun, 1 hel landing platform
LANDING CRAFT 15
  LCU 5
  LCA 7
  LCAC 3 *Kefallinia* (*Zubr*) with 2 AK630 CIWS (capacity either 3 MBT or 10 APC (T); 230 troops)
LOGISTICS AND SUPPORT 25
  ABU 2
  AG 2 *Pandora*
  AGOR 1 *Naftilos*
  AGS 2: 1 *Stravon*; 1 *Pytheas*
  AOR 2 *Axios* (ex-GER *Luneburg*)
  AORH 1 *Prometheus* (ITA *Etna*) with 1 *Phalanx* CIWS
  AOT 4 *Ouranos*
  AWT 6 *Kerkini*
  AXS 5

Coastal Defence
EQUIPMENT BY TYPE
COASTAL DEFENCE • AShM 2 MM40 *Exocet*

Naval Aviation
FORCES BY ROLE
ANTI-SUBMARINE WARFARE
  1 div with S-70B *Seahawk*; Bell 212 (AB-212) ASW
EQUIPMENT BY TYPE
AIRCRAFT • ASW (5 P-3B *Orion* in store undergoing modernisation)
HELICOPTERS
  ASW 18: 7 Bell 212 (AB-212) ASW; 11 S-70B *Seahawk*
AIR-LAUNCHED MISSILES
  ASM AGM-114 *Hellfire*
  AShM AGM-119 *Penguin*

Air Force 18,000; 2,000 conscripts (total 20,000)

Tactical Air Force
FORCES BY ROLE
FIGHTER/GROUND ATTACK
  3 sqn with F-16CG/DG Block 30/50 *Fighting Falcon*
  3 sqn with F-16CG/DG Block 52+ *Fighting Falcon*
  2 sqn with F-16C/D Block 52+ ADV *Fighting Falcon*
  1 sqn with *Mirage* 2000-5EG/BG Mk2
  1 sqn with *Mirage* 2000EG/BG
  1 sqn with F-4E *Phantom* II
AIRBORNE EARLY WARNING
  1 sqn with EMB-145H *Erieye*
EQUIPMENT BY TYPE
AIRCRAFT 218 combat capable
  FGA 218: 20 F-4E *Phantom* II; 70 F-16CG/DG Block 30/50 *Fighting Falcon*; 55 F-16CG/DG Block 52+; 30 F-16 C/D Block 52+ ADV *Fighting Falcon*; 20 *Mirage* 2000-5EG Mk2; 5 *Mirage* 2000-5BG Mk2; 16 *Mirage* 2000EG; 2 *Mirage* 2000BG
  AEW 4 EMB-145AEW (EMB-145H) *Erieye*
AIR-LAUNCHED MISSILES
  AAM • IR AIM-9L/P *Sidewinder*; R-550 *Magic* 2;
  IIR IRIS-T; *Mica* IR; **ARH** AIM-120B/C AMRAAM; *Mica* RF
  ASM AGM-65A/B/G *Maverick*
  LACM SCALP EG
  AShM AM39 *Exocet*
  ARM AGM-88 HARM
BOMBS
  Electro-optical guided: GBU-8B HOBOS
  Laser-guided: GBU-10/12/16 *Paveway* II; GBU-24 *Paveway* III; GBU-50 *Enhanced Paveway* II
  INS/GPS-guided GBU-31 JDAM; AGM-154C JSOW

Air Defence
FORCES BY ROLE
AIR DEFENCE
  6 sqn/bty with MIM-104A/B/D *Patriot*/*Patriot* PAC-1 SOJC/*Patriot* PAC-2 GEM
  2 sqn/bty with S-300PMU-1 (SA-10C *Grumble*)
  12 bty with *Skyguard*/RIM-7 *Sparrow*/guns; *Crotale* NG/GR; *Tor*-M1 (SA-15 *Gauntlet*)
EQUIPMENT BY TYPE
AIR DEFENCE
  SAM
    Long-range 48: 36 MIM-104A/B/D *Patriot*/*Patriot* PAC-1 SOJC/PAC-2 GEM; 12 S-300PMU-1 (SA-10C *Grumble*)
    Short-range 13+: 9 *Crotale* NG/GR; 4 9K331 *Tor*-M1 (SA-15 *Gauntlet*); some *Skyguard*/*Sparrow*
  GUNS 35+ 35mm

Air Support Command
FORCES BY ROLE
SEARCH & RESCUE/TRANSPORT HELICOPTER
  1 sqn with AS332C *Super Puma* (SAR/CSAR)
  1 sqn with AW109; Bell 205A (AB-205A) (SAR); Bell 212 (AB-212 - VIP, tpt)
TRANSPORT
  1 sqn with C-27J *Spartan*
  1 sqn with C-130B/H *Hercules*
  1 sqn with EMB-135BJ *Legacy*; ERJ-135LR; Gulfstream V
EQUIPMENT BY TYPE
AIRCRAFT
  TPT 26: **Medium** 23: 8 C-27J *Spartan*; 5 C-130B *Hercules*; 10 C-130H *Hercules*; **Light** 2: 1 EMB-135BJ *Legacy*; 1 ERJ-135LR; **PAX** 1 Gulfstream V
HELICOPTERS
  TPT 31: **Medium** 12 AS332C *Super Puma*; **Light** 19: 12 Bell 205A (AB-205A) (SAR); 4 Bell 212 (AB-212) (VIP, Tpt); 3 AW109

Air Training Command
FORCES BY ROLE
TRAINING
  2 sqn with T-2C/E *Buckeye*
  2 sqn with T-6A/B *Texan* II
  1 sqn with T-41D
EQUIPMENT BY TYPE
AIRCRAFT • TRG 93: 30 T-2C/E *Buckeye*; 20 T-6A *Texan* II; 25 T-6B *Texan* II; 18 T-41D

Paramilitary

Coast Guard and Customs 4,000
EQUIPMENT BY TYPE
PATROL AND COASTAL COMBATANTS 124:
    PCC 3
    PCO 1 *Gavdos* (Damen 5009)
    PBF 54
    PB 66
AIRCRAFT • **TPT** • **Light** 4: 2 Cessna 172RG *Cutlass*; 2 TB-20 *Trinidad*
HELICOPTERS
    SAR: 3 AS365N3

Cyber

A new Joint Cyber Command in the Hellenic National Defence General Staff was established in 2014, replacing the existing Cyber Defence Directorate. The National Policy on Cyber Defence is under development and expected to be complete by the end of 2016.

DEPLOYMENT

AFGHANISTAN
NATO • Operation Resolute Support 4

BOSNIA-HERZEGOVINA
EU • EUFOR • Operation Althea 1

CYPRUS
Army 950 (ELDYK army); ε200 (officers/NCO seconded to Greek-Cypriot National Guard) (total 1,150);
1 mech bde (1 armd bn, 2 mech inf bn, 1 arty bn); 61 M48A5 MOLF MBT; 80 *Leonidas* APC; 12 M114 arty; 6 M110A2 arty

LEBANON
UN • UNIFIL 49; 1 PCFG

MALI
EU • EUTM Mali 2

MEDITERRANEAN SEA
EU • EUNAVFOR MED 1 SSK
NATO • SNMG 2: 1 FSGM; 2 PCO

SERBIA
NATO • KFOR 112; 1 inf coy
OSCE • Kosovo 1

UKRAINE
OSCE • Ukraine 22

FOREIGN FORCES

United States US European Command: 400; 1 naval base at Makri; 1 naval base at Soudha Bay; 1 air base at Iraklion

Hungary HUN

Hungarian Forint f		2016	2017	2018
GDP	f	35.0tr	36.9tr	
	US$	124bn	132bn	
per capita	US$	12,652	13,460	
Growth	%	2.0	3.2	
Inflation	%	0.4	2.5	
Def exp [a]	f	363bn	389bn	
	US$	1.29bn	1.39bn	
Def bdgt [b]	f	299bn	354bn	427bn
	US$	1.06bn	1.26bn	
US$1=f		281.44	279.63	

[a] NATO definition
[b] Excludes military pensions

Population 9,850,845

Age	0–14	15–19	20–24	25–29	30–64	65 plus
Male	7.6%	2.7%	3.0%	3.2%	24.0%	7.2%
Female	7.1%	2.5%	2.8%	3.1%	24.9%	11.9%

Capabilities

A National Security Strategy (NSS) and National Military Strategy (NMS) were published in 2012. Territorial defence and the ability to participate in NATO and other international operations are central tenets of the NMS, including the medium-term aim of having forces capable of taking part in high-intensity operations. A review of the NSS has been under way since 2016. Hungary coordinates policy with the Czech Republic, Poland and Slovakia in the so-called Visegrád 4 (V4) format, including on defence. The V4 EU Battlegroup is scheduled to be on standby for the second time in the second half of 2019. Increasing migration pressure has directly affected Hungary, and its armed forces have been involved in internal border-control operations, assisting national police forces. The government aims to gradually increase defence spending to reach NATO's 2% of GDP benchmark by 2026, to coincide with the completion of the Zrínyi 2026 national-defence and armed-forces modernisation plan announced in December 2016. The defence-modernisation programme aims to reorganise reserve forces on a territorial basis with units in each district. Announced equipment-modernisation priorities focus on individual soldier equipment and fixed- and rotary-wing aircraft. In 2017, the defence ministry established the Military Augmentation Preparation and Training Command (MAPTC) to improve recruitment, training and military education. The NCO Academy and Ludovika Academy will be subordinated to the MAPTC. The defence ministry has also set up an inter-ministerial defence-industry working group to boost domestic capacity in the small-arms sector. Hungary hosts the NATO Centre of Excellence for Military Medicine.

ACTIVE 27,800 (Army 10,450 Air 5,750 Joint 11,600)
Paramilitary 12,000

RESERVE 44,000 (Army 35,200 Air 8,800)

ORGANISATIONS BY SERVICE

Hungary's armed forces have reorganised into a joint force

Land Component 10,450 (incl riverine element)

FORCES BY ROLE
SPECIAL FORCES
  1 SF regt
MANOEUVRE
  Mechanised
  1 (5th) mech inf bde (1 armd recce bn; 3 mech inf bn, 1 cbt engr coy, 1 sigs coy, 1 log bn)
  1 (25th) mech inf bde (1 tk bn; 2 mech inf bn, 1 arty bn, 1 AT bn, 1 log bn)
COMBAT SUPPORT
  1 engr regt
  1 EOD/rvn regt
  1 CBRN bn
  1 sigs regt
COMBAT SERVICE SUPPORT
  1 log regt
EQUIPMENT BY TYPE
ARMOURED FIGHTING VEHICLES
  MBT 30 T-72
  IFV 120 BTR-80A
  APC • APC (W) 260 BTR-80
ENGINEERING & MAINTENANCE VEHICLES
  AEV BAT-2
  ARV BMP-1 VPV; T-54/T-55; VT-55A
  VLB BLG-60; MTU; TMM
NBC VEHICLES 24+: 24 K90 CBRN Recce; PSZH-IV CBRN Recce
ANTI-TANK/ANTI-INFRASTRUCTURE
  MSL • MANPATS 9K111 *Fagot* (AT-4 *Spigot*); 9K111-1 *Konkurs* (AT-5 *Spandrel*)
ARTILLERY 67
  TOWED 152mm 17 D-20
  MOR 82mm 50
PATROL AND COASTAL COMBATANTS • PBR 2
MINE COUNTERMEASURES • MSR 4 *Nestin*

Air Component 5,750

Flying hours   50 hrs/yr

FORCES BY ROLE
FIGHTER/GROUND ATTACK
  1 sqn with *Gripen* C/D
TRANSPORT
  1 sqn with An-26 *Curl*
TRAINING
  1 sqn with Z-143LSi; Z-242L
ATTACK HELICOPTER
  1 sqn with Mi-24 *Hind*
TRANSPORT HELICOPTER
  1 sqn with Mi-8 *Hip*; Mi-17 *Hip* H
AIR DEFENCE
  1 SAM regt (9 bty with *Mistral*; 3 bty with 2K12 *Kub* (SA-6 *Gainful*))
  1 radar regt

EQUIPMENT BY TYPE
AIRCRAFT 14 combat capable
  FGA 14: 12 *Gripen* C; 2 *Gripen* D
  TPT • Light 4 An-26 *Curl*
  TRG 4: 2 Z-143LSi; 2 Z-242L
HELICOPTERS
  ATK 11: 3 Mi-24D *Hind* D; 6 Mi-24V *Hind* E; 2 Mi-24P *Hind* F
  MRH 7 Mi-17 *Hip* H
  TPT • Medium 13 Mi-8 *Hip*
AIR DEFENCE
  SAM • Point-defence 16 2K12 *Kub* (SA-6 *Gainful*); *Mistral*
RADAR 29: 3 RAT-31DL; 6 P-18; 6 SZT-68UM; 14 P-37
AIR-LAUNCHED MISSILES
  AAM • IR AIM-9 *Sidewinder* SARH R-27 (AA-10 *Alamo* A); ARH AIM-120C AMRAAM
  ASM AGM-65 *Maverick*; 3M11 *Falanga* (AT-2 *Swatter*); 9K114 *Shturm*-V (AT-6 *Spiral*)
BOMBS • Laser-guided *Paveway* II

Paramilitary 12,000

Border Guards 12,000 (to reduce)

Ministry of Interior

FORCES BY ROLE
MANOEUVRE
  Other
  1 (Budapest) paramilitary district (7 rapid reaction coy)
  11 (regt/district) paramilitary regt
EQUIPMENT BY TYPE
ARMOURED FIGHTING VEHICLES
  APC • APC (W) 68 BTR-80

Cyber

The National Cyber Security Strategy, coordinating cyber security at the governmental level, is led by the prime minister's office. There is also a National Cyber Defence Forum and a Hungarian Cyber Defence Management Authority within the National Security Authority. In 2013, the defence ministry developed a Military Cyber Defence concept. A Computer Incident Response Capability (MilCIRC) and Military Computer Emergency Response Team (MilCERT) have also been established. In 2015, the ministry launched a modernisation programme as a part of Ministerial Program (2015–19), including military CIS and CIS security/cyber-defence technical modernisation. In 2016, a Defence Sectorial Cyber Defence Centre (CDC) for security management, vulnerability assessment and incident handling in the defence sector was established within the Military National Security Service. IOC is planned for 2018.

DEPLOYMENT

AFGHANISTAN
NATO • *Operation Resolute Support* 110

ALBANIA
OSCE • Albania 1

BOSNIA-HERZEGOVINA
EU • *Operation Althea* 165; 1 inf coy

CENTRAL AFRICAN REPUBLIC
UN • MINUSCA 2; 2 obs

CYPRUS
UN • UNFICYP 77; 1 inf pl

IRAQ
Operation Inherent Resolve 140

LEBANON
UN • UNIFIL 4

MALI
EU • EUTM Mali 3

MOLDOVA
OSCE • Moldova 1

SERBIA
NATO • KFOR 373; 1 inf coy (KTM)
OSCE • Kosovo 1

SOMALIA
EU • EUTM Somalia 4

UKRAINE
OSCE • Ukraine 30

WESTERN SAHARA
UN • MINURSO 7 obs

FOREIGN FORCES
United States US European Command: 100; 1 armd recce tp; M3 *Bradley*

Iceland ISL

Icelandic Krona Kr		2016	2017	2018
GDP	Kr	2.42tr	2.62tr	
	US$	20.0bn	24.8bn	
per capita	US$	59,629	73,092	
Growth	%	7.2	5.5	
Inflation	%	1.7	1.8	
Sy bdgt [a]	Kr	5.53bn	3.94bn	4.27bn
	US$	46m	37m	
US$1=Kr		120.81	105.50	

[a] Coast Guard budget

Population 339,747

Age	0–14	15–19	20–24	25–29	30–64	65 plus
Male	10.4%	3.3%	3.6%	3.7%	22.4%	6.8%
Female	10.0%	3.2%	3.4%	3.5%	22.1%	7.7%

Capabilities
Iceland is a NATO member but maintains only a coastguard service. In 2016, the country established a National Security Council to implement and monitor security policy. Iceland hosts NATO and regional partners for exercises, transits and naval task groups, as well as the Icelandic Air Policing mission. Increased Russian air and naval activities in the Atlantic and close to NATO airspace have led to complaints from Iceland that aircraft could threaten civil flights. In late 2016, the US Navy began operating P-8 *Poseidon* maritime-patrol aircraft from Keflavik air base, and was reportedly upgrading hangars and other infrastructure at the site to enable regular, rotational patrols.

ACTIVE NIL Paramilitary 250

ORGANISATIONS BY SERVICE

Paramilitary

Iceland Coast Guard 250
EQUIPMENT BY TYPE
PATROL AND COASTAL COMBATANTS 3
  PSOH: 2 *Aegir*
  PSO 1 *Thor*
LOGISTICS AND SUPPORT • AGS 1 *Baldur*
AIRCRAFT • TPT • Light 1 DHC-8-300 (MP)
HELICOPTERS
  TPT • Medium 2 AS332L1 *Super Puma*

FOREIGN FORCES
Iceland Air Policing: Aircraft and personnel from various NATO members on a rotating basis

Ireland IRL

Euro €		2016	2017	2018
GDP	€	275bn	289bn	
	US$	304bn	326bn	
per capita	US$	64,782	68,604	
Growth	%	5.1	4.1	
Inflation	%	-0.2	0.4	
Def bdgt [a]	€	898m	921m	946m
	US$	994m	1.04bn	
US$1=€		0.90	0.89	

[a] Includes military pensions and capital expenditure

Population 5,011,102

Age	0–14	15–19	20–24	25–29	30–64	65 plus
Male	11.0%	3.1%	2.9%	3.1%	23.8%	6.0%
Female	10.5%	3.0%	2.8%	3.1%	23.6%	7.0%

Capabilities
The armed forces' core missions remain defending the state against armed aggression, although a 2015 white paper broadened the scope of the national-security risk assessment beyond traditional military and paramilitary threats. It listed as priority threats inter- and intra-state conflict, cyber attacks, terrorism, emergencies and natural disasters, as well as espionage and transnational organised crime. October 2017 saw a major domestic military operation to manage the consequences of Hurricane

Ophelia. Ireland continues to contribute to multinational operations, principally UNDOF on the Golan Heights. After the white paper, Dublin identified 88 projects to be completed over a ten-year period. Key priorities after 2017 include a mid-life upgrade for the army's *Piranha* armoured personnel carriers and the replacement of the existing maritime-patrol aircraft. The army maintains substantial EOD capabilities.

ACTIVE 9,100 (Army 7,300 Navy 1,100 Air 700)

RESERVE 2,480 (Army 2,250 Navy 200 Air 30)

ORGANISATIONS BY SERVICE

Army 7,300
FORCES BY ROLE
SPECIAL FORCES
  1 ranger coy
MANOEUVRE
  Reconnaissance
    1 armd recce sqn
  Mechanised
    1 mech inf coy
  Light
    1 inf bde (1 cav recce sqn, 4 inf bn, 1 arty regt (3 fd arty bty, 1 AD bty), 1 fd engr coy, 1 sigs coy, 1 MP coy, 1 tpt coy)
    1 inf bde (1 cav recce sqn, 3 inf bn, 1 arty regt (3 fd arty bty, 1 AD bty), 1 fd engr coy, 1 sigs coy, 1 MP coy, l tpt coy)
EQUIPMENT BY TYPE
ARMOURED FIGHTING VEHICLES
  RECCE 6 *Piranha* IIIH 30mm
  APC 99
    APC (W) 74: 56 *Piranha* III; 18 *Piranha* IIIH
    PPV 25 RG-32M
ANTI-TANK/ANTI-INFRASTURCTURE
  MSL • MANPATS FGM-148 *Javelin*
  RCL 84mm *Carl Gustav*
ARTILLERY 299
  TOWED • 105mm 24: 18 L118 Light Gun; 6 L119 Light Gun
  MOR 275: 81mm 180; 120mm 95
AIR DEFENCE
  SAM • Point-defence RBS-70
  GUNS • TOWED 40mm 32 L/70 each with 8 *Flycatcher*

Reserves 2,400 reservists
FORCES BY ROLE
MANOEUVRE
  Reconnaissance
    1 (integrated) armd recce sqn
    2 (integrated) cav sqn
  Mechanised
    1 (integrated) mech inf coy
  Light
    14 (integrated) inf coy
COMBAT SUPPORT
  4 (integrated) arty bty
  2 engr gp
  2 MP coy
  3 sigs coy

COMBAT SERVICE SUPPORT
  2 med det
  2 tpt coy

Naval Service 1,100
EQUIPMENT BY TYPE
PATROL AND COASTAL COMBATANTS 8
  PSOH 1 *Eithne* with 1 57mm gun
  PSO 5: 2 *Roisin* with 1 76mm gun; 3 *Samuel Beckett* with 1 76mm gun
  PCO 2 *Orla* (ex-UK *Peacock*) with 1 76mm gun
LOGISTICS AND SUPPORT 2
  AXS 2

Air Corps 700
2 ops wg; 2 spt wg; 1 trg wg; 1 comms and info sqn
EQUIPMENT BY TYPE
AIRCRAFT
  MP 2 CN235 MPA
  TPT • Light 6: 5 Cessna FR-172H; 1 Learjet 45 (VIP)
  TRG 8 PC-9M
HELICOPTERS:
  MRH 6 AW139
  TPT • Light 2 H135 (incl trg/medevac)

Cyber
The Department of Communications, Energy and Natural Resources has lead responsibilities relating to cyber security, and established a National Cyber Security Centre (NCSC) to assist in identifying and protecting Ireland from cyber attacks. The department has produced a Cyber Security Strategy 2015–17, which says that 'the Defence Forces maintains a capability in the area of cyber security for the purpose of protecting its own networks and users'.

DEPLOYMENT

ALBANIA
OSCE • Albania 1

BOSNIA-HERZEGOVINA
EU • EUFOR • *Operation Althea* 5
OSCE • Bosnia and Herzegovina 1

DEMOCRATIC REPUBLIC OF THE CONGO
UN • MONUSCO 4

LEBANON
UN • UNIFIL 374; elm 1 mech inf bn

MALI
EU • EUTM Mali 20

MIDDLE EAST
UN • UNTSO 12 obs

SERBIA
NATO • KFOR 12
OSCE • Kosovo 1

SYRIA/ISRAEL
UN • UNDOF 136; 1 inf coy

UKRAINE
OSCE • Ukraine 12

WESTERN SAHARA
UN • MINURSO 2 obs

Italy ITA

Euro €		2016	2017	2018
GDP	€	1.67tr	1.70tr	
	US$	1.85tr	1.92tr	
per capita	US$	30,507	31,619	
Growth	%	0.9	1.5	
Inflation	%	-0.1	1.4	
Def exp [a]	€	20.2bn	20.8bn	
	US$	22.4bn	23.4bn	
Def bdgt [b]	€	20.0bn	20.3bn	20.1bn
	US$	22.1bn	22.9bn	
US$1=€		0.90	0.89	

[a] NATO definition
[b] Includes military pensions

Population 62,137,802

Age	0–14	15–19	20–24	25–29	30–64	65 plus
Male	7.0%	2.4%	2.5%	2.7%	24.4%	9.3%
Female	6.7%	2.3%	2.5%	2.8%	25.3%	12.3%

Capabilities

In 2017, a defence plan covering 2017–19 and a new defence white paper were released. These outlined the goal of reducing personnel from 190,000 to 150,000 by 2024, with an aspiration for more joint activity between the services. The paper detailed capability-enhancement programmes including upgrades to main battle tanks, systems to counter UAV operations and electronic warfare. Extra funds are to be allocated to continue the lease of the *King Air* SIGINT aircraft, which has been involved in surveillance operations along the Italian and Libyan coasts. The expected retirement of much of the naval fleet over the next ten years has triggered a long-term replacement plan and, according to the white paper, funds have been allocated for the continuation of the FREMM frigate programme. Italy has an advanced defence industry. Leonardo is headquartered there, and the country hosts Europe's F-35 final assembly and check-out facility at Cameri, which is also a European hub for F-35 maintenance. The air force was due to take delivery of its first F-35B by the end of 2017. Italy continues to support NATO operations in Afghanistan and Italian forces contribute to *Operation Inherent Resolve* in Iraq. Maritime deployments have been aimed at countering terrorism and human trafficking, as well as search and rescue in the Mediterranean. Italy is the lead nation in the EUNAVFOR–MED force, which is headquartered in Rome, and the Italian coastguard has been training its Libyan counterpart. The country takes part in NATO exercises and air-policing missions, and in early 2017 deployed to Latvia as part of NATO's Enhanced Forward Presence.

ACTIVE 174,500 (Army 102,200 Navy 30,400 Air 41,900) **Paramilitary 182,350**

RESERVES 18,300 (Army 13,400 Navy 4,900)

ORGANISATIONS BY SERVICE

Space
EQUIPMENT BY TYPE
SATELLITES 9
  COMMUNICATIONS 4: 1 *Athena-Fidus* (also used by FRA); 3 *Sicral*
  ISR 5: 4 *Cosmo* (*Skymed*); 1 OPSAT-3000

Army 102,200
Regt are bn sized
FORCES BY ROLE
COMMAND
  1 (NRDC-ITA) corps HQ (1 spt bde, 1 sigs regt, 1 spt regt)
MANOEUVRE
  Mechanised
  1 (*Friuli*) div (1 (*Ariete*) armd bde (1 cav regt, 2 tk regt, 1 mech inf regt, 1 SP arty regt, 1 cbt engr regt, 1 log regt); 1 (*Pozzuolo del Friuli*) cav bde (1 cav regt, 1 amph regt, 1 arty regt, 1 cbt engr regt, 1 log regt); 1 (*Folgore*) AB bde (1 cav regt, 3 para regt, 1 arty regt, 1 cbt engr regt, 1 log regt); 1 (*Friuli*) air mob bde (1 air mob regt, 1 log regt, 2 avn regt))
  1 (*Acqui*) div (1 (*Pinerolo*) mech bde (3 mech inf regt, 1 SP arty regt, 1 cbt engr regt); 1 (*Granatieri*) mech bde (1 cav regt, 1 mech inf regt); 1 (*Garibaldi Bersaglieri*) mech bde (1 cav regt, 1 tk regt, 2 mech inf regt, 1 SP arty regt, 1 cbt engr regt); 1 (*Aosta*) mech bde (1 cav regt, 3 mech inf regt, 1 SP arty regt, 1 cbt engr regt); 1 (*Sassari*) lt mech bde (3 mech inf regt, 1 cbt engr regt))
  Mountain
  1 (*Tridentina*) mtn div (2 mtn bde (1 cav regt, 3 mtn inf regt, 1 arty regt, 1 mtn cbt engr regt, 1 spt bn, 1 log regt))
COMBAT SUPPORT
  1 arty comd (3 arty regt, 1 NBC regt)
  1 AD comd (2 SAM regt, 1 ADA regt)
  1 engr comd (2 engr regt, 1 ptn br regt, 1 CIMIC regt)
  1 EW/sigs comd (1 EW/ISR bde (1 EW regt, 1 int regt, 1 STA regt); 1 sigs bde with (7 sigs regt))
COMBAT SERVICE SUPPORT
  1 log comd (2 log regt, 1 med unit)
HELICOPTER
  1 hel bde (3 hel regt)
EQUIPMENT BY TYPE
ARMOURED FIGHTING VEHICLES
  MBT 160 C1 *Ariete*
  ASLT 259 B1 *Centauro*
  IFV 428: 200 VCC-80 *Dardo*; 208 VBM 8×8 *Freccia* (incl 36 with *Spike*-LR); 20 VBM 8×8 *Freccia* (CP)
  APC 890
    APC (T) 361: 246 Bv-206; 115 M113 (incl variants)
    APC (W) 529 *Puma*
  AUV 10 *Cougar*; IVECO LMV
  AAV 15: 14 AAVP-7; 1 AAVC-7

ENGINEERING & MAINTENANCE VEHICLES
  AEV 40 *Leopard 1*; M113
  ARV 138: 137 *Leopard 1*; 1 AAVR-7
  VLB 64 *Biber*
  MW 9: 6 *Buffalo*; 3 *Miniflail*
NBC VEHICLES 14 VAB NRBC
ANTI-TANK/ANTI-INFRASTRUCTURE
  MSL • MANPATS *Spike*; *Milan*
  RCL **80mm** *Folgore*
ARTILLERY 992
  SP 155mm 192: 124 M109L; 68 PzH 2000
  TOWED 155mm 163 FH-70
  MRL 227mm 21 MLRS
  MOR 616: **81mm** 270: 212 Brandt; 58 Expal **120mm** 325: 183 Brandt; 142 RT-61 (RT-F1) **SP 120mm** 21 VBM 8×8 *Freccia*
  AIRCRAFT • TPT • **Light** 6: 3 Do-228 (ACTL-1); 3 P-180 *Avanti*
HELICOPTERS
  ATK 43 AW129CBT *Mangusta*
  MRH 15 Bell 412 (AB-412) *Twin Huey*
  TPT 131: **Heavy** 19: 5 CH-47C *Chinook*; 14 CH-47F *Chinook*; **Medium** 31 NH90 TTH; **Light** 81: 6 AW109; 34 Bell 205 (AB-205); 26 Bell 206 *Jet Ranger* (AB-206); 15 Bell 212 (AB-212)
AIR DEFENCE
  SAM
    Long-range 16 SAMP/T
    Short-range 32 *Skyguard/Aspide*
    Point-range FIM-92 *Stinger*
  GUNS • **SP 25mm** 64 SIDAM
AIR-LAUNCHED MISSILES
  ASM *Spike*-ER

Navy 30,400
EQUIPMENT BY TYPE
SUBMARINES • TACTICAL • SSK 8:
  4 *Pelosi* (imp *Sauro*, 3rd and 4th series) with 6 single 533mm TT with Type-A-184 HWT
  4 *Salvatore Todaro* (Type-212A) with 6 single 533mm TT with Type-A-184 Mod 3 HWT/DM2A4 HWT
PRINCIPAL SURFACE COMBATANTS 20
  AIRCRAFT CARRIERS • CVS 2:
    1 *Cavour* with 4 octuple VLS with *Aster* 15 SAM, 2 76mm guns (capacity mixed air group of 20 AV-8B *Harrier* II; AW101 *Merlin*; NH90; Bell 212)
    1 *G. Garibaldi* with 2 octuple *Albatros* lnchr with *Aspide* SAM, 2 triple 324mm ASTT with Mk46 LWT (capacity mixed air group of 18 AV-8B *Harrier* II; AW101 *Merlin*; NH90; Bell 212)
  DESTROYERS • DDGHM 10:
    2 *Andrea Doria* with 2 quad lnchr with *Otomat* Mk2A AShM, 1 48-cell VLS with *Aster* 15/*Aster* 30 SAM, 2 single 324mm ASTT with MU90 LWT, 3 76mm guns (capacity 1 AW101 *Merlin*/NH90 hel)
    2 *Luigi Durand de la Penne* (ex-*Animoso*) with 2 quad lnchr with *Otomat* Mk 2A AShM/*Milas* A/S, 1 Mk13 GMLS with SM-1MR SAM, 1 octuple *Albatros* lnchr with *Aspide* SAM, 2 triple 324mm ASTT with Mk46 LWT, 1 127mm gun, 3 76mm guns (capacity 1 NH90 or 2 Bell 212 (AB-212) hel)
    2 *Bergamini* (GP) with 2 quad lnchr with *Otomat* Mk2A AShM, 1 16-cell VLS with *Aster* 15/*Aster* 30 SAM, 2 triple 324mm ASTT with MU90 LWT, 1 127mm gun, 1 76mm gun (capacity 2 AW101/NH90 hel)
    4 *Bergamini* (ASW) with 2 quad lnchr with *Otomat* Mk2A AShM, 1 16-cell VLS with *Aster* 15/*Aster* 30 SAM, 2 triple 324mm ASTT with MU90 LWT, 2 76mm gun (capacity 2 AW101/NH90 hel)
  FRIGATES • FFGHM 8:
    2 *Artigliere* with 8 single lnchr with *Otomat* Mk 2 AShM, 1 octuple *Albatros* lnchr with *Aspide* SAM, 1 127mm gun (capacity 1 Bell 212 (AB-212) hel)
    6 *Maestrale* with 4 single lnchr with *Otomat* Mk2 AShM, 1 octuple *Albatros* lnchr with *Aspide* SAM, 2 triple 324mm ASTT with Mk46 LWT, 1 127mm gun (capacity 1 NH90 or 2 Bell 212 (AB-212) hel)
PATROL AND COASTAL COMBATANTS 16
  CORVETTES 2
    FS 2 *Minerva* 1 76mm gun
  PSOH 10:
    4 *Cassiopea* with 1 76mm gun (capacity 1 Bell 212 (AB-212) hel)
    4 *Comandante Cigala Fuligosi* with 1 76mm gun (capacity 1 Bell 212 (AB-212)/NH90 hel)
    2 *Comandante Cigala Fuligosi* (capacity 1 Bell 212 (AB-212) or NH90 hel)
  PB 4 *Esploratore*
MINE WARFARE • MINE COUNTERMEASURES 10
  MHO 10: 8 *Gaeta*; 2 *Lerici*
AMPHIBIOUS
  PRINCIPAL AMPHIBIOUS SHIPS 3
    LHD 3:
      2 *San Giorgio* with 1 76mm gun (capacity 3-4 AW101/NH90/Bell 212; 3 LCM 2 LCVP; 30 trucks; 36 APC (T); 350 troops)
      1 *San Giusto* with 1 76mm gun (capacity 2 AW101 *Merlin*/ NH90/Bell 212; 3 LCM 2 LCVP; 30 trucks; 36 APC (T); 350 troops)
  LANDING CRAFT 24: 15 **LCVP**; 9 **LCM**
LOGISTICS AND SUPPORT 63
  ABU 5 *Ponza*
  AFD 9
  AGE 3: 1 *Leonardo* (coastal); 1 *Raffaele Rosseti*; 1 *Vincenzo Martellota*
  AGI 1 *Elettra*
  AGOR 1 *Alliance*
  AGS 3: 1 *Ammiraglio Magnaghi* with 1 hel landing platform; 2 *Aretusa* (coastal)
  AKSL 6 *Gorgona*
  AORH 3: 1 *Etna* with 1 76mm gun (capacity 1 AW101/NH90/Bell 212 hel); 2 *Stromboli* with 1 76mm gun (capacity 1 AW101/NH90 hel)
  AOT 7 *Depoli*
  ARSH 1 *Anteo* (capacity 1 Bell 212 (AB-212) hel)
  ATS 6 *Ciclope*
  AWT 7: 1 *Bormida*; 2 *Simeto*; 4 *Panarea*
  AXL 3 *Aragosta*
  AXS 8: 1 *Amerigo Vespucci*; 1 *Palinuro*; 1 *Italia*; 5 *Caroly*

Naval Aviation 2,200
FORCES BY ROLE
FIGHTER/GROUND ATTACK
  1 sqn with AV-8B *Harrier* II; TAV-8B *Harrier* II
ANTI-SUBMARINE WARFARE/TRANSPORT
  5 sqn with AW101 ASW *Merlin*; Bell 212 ASW (AB-212AS); Bell 212 (AB-212); NH90 NFH
MARITIME PATROL
  1 flt with P-180
AIRBORNE EARLY WANRING & CONTROL
  1 flt with AW101 AEW *Merlin*
EQUIPMENT BY TYPE
AIRCRAFT 16 combat capable
  FGA 16: 14 AV-8B *Harrier* II; 2 TAV-8B *Harrier* II
  MP 3 P-180
HELICOPTERS
  ASW 39: 10 AW101 ASW *Merlin*; 12 Bell 212 ASW; 17 NH90 NFH
  AEW 4 AW101 AEW *Merlin*
  TPT 15: **Medium** 9: 8 AW101 *Merlin*; 1 NH-90 MITT; **Light** 6 Bell 212 (AB-212)
AIR-LAUNCHED MISSILES
  AAM • **IR** AIM-9L *Sidewinder*; **ARH** AIM-120 AMRAAM
  ASM AGM-65 *Maverick*
  AShM *Marte* Mk 2/S

Marines 3,000
FORCES BY ROLE
MANOEUVRE
  Amphibious
  1 mne regt (1 SF coy, 1 mne bn, 1 cbt spt bn, 1 log bn)
  1 (boarding) mne regt (2 mne bn)
  1 landing craft gp
  Other
  1 sy regt (3 sy bn)
EQUIPMENT BY TYPE
ARMOURED FIGHTING VEHICLES
  APC (T) 24 VCC-1
  AAV 18: 15 AAVP-7; 3 AAVC-7
ENGINEERING & MAINTENANCE VEHICLES
  ARV 2: 1 AAV-7RAI; 1 AAVR-7
ANTI-TANK/ANTI-INFRASTRUCTURE
  MSL • MANPATS *Milan*; *Spike*
ARTILLERY
  MOR 23: **81mm** 13 Brandt; **120mm** 10 Brandt
AIR DEFENCE • SAM • Point-defence FIM-92 *Stinger*

Air Force 41,900
FORCES BY ROLE
FIGHTER
  4 sqn with Eurofighter *Typhoon*
FIGHTER/GROUND ATTACK
  1 sqn with AMX *Ghibli*
  1 (SEAD/EW) sqn with *Tornado* ECR
  2 sqn with *Tornado* IDS
FIGHTER/GROUND ATTACK/ISR
  1 sqn with AMX *Ghibli*
MARITIME PATROL
  1 sqn (opcon Navy) with ATR-72MP (P-72A)
TANKER/TRANSPORT
  1 sqn with KC-767A
COMBAT SEARCH & RESCUE
  1 sqn with AB-212 ICO
SEARCH & RESCUE
  1 wg with AW139 (HH-139A); Bell 212 (HH-212); HH-3F *Pelican*
TRANSPORT
  2 (VIP) sqn with A319CJ; AW139 (VH-139A); *Falcon* 50; *Falcon* 900 *Easy*; *Falcon* 900EX; SH-3D *Sea King*
  2 sqn with C-130J/C-130J-30/KC-130J *Hercules*
  1 sqn with C-27J *Spartan*
  1 (calibration) sqn with P-180 *Avanti*
TRAINING
  1 OCU sqn with Eurofighter *Typhoon*
  1 sqn with MB-339PAN (aerobatic team)
  1 sqn with MD-500D/E (NH-500D/E)
  1 OCU sqn with *Tornado*
  1 OCU sqn with AMX-T *Ghibli*
  1 sqn with MB-339A
  1 sqn with MB-339CD*
  1 sqn with SF-260EA, 3 P2006T (T-2006A)
ISR UAV
  1 sqn with MQ-9A *Reaper*; RQ-1B *Predator*
AIR DEFENCE
  2 bty with *Spada*
EQUIPMENT BY TYPE
AIRCRAFT 260 combat capable
  FTR 86 Eurofighter *Typhoon*
  FGA 78: 63 AMX *Ghibli*; 8 AMX-T *Ghibli*; 7 F-35A *Lightning* II (in test)
  ATK 53 *Tornado* IDS
  ATK/EW 15 *Tornado* ECR*
  MP 2 ATR-72MP (P-72A)
  SIGINT 1 Beech 350 *King Air*
  AEW&C 1 Gulfstream G550 CAEW
  TKR/TPT 6: 4 KC-767A; 2 KC-130J *Hercules*
  TPT 66: **Medium** 31: 9 C-130J *Hercules*; 10 C-130J-30 *Hercules*; 12 C-27J *Spartan*; **Light** 25: 15 P-180 *Avanti*; 10 S-208 (liaison); **PAX** 11: 1 A340-541; 3 A319CJ; 2 *Falcon* 50 (VIP); 2 *Falcon* 900 *Easy*; 3 *Falcon* 900EX (VIP)
  TRG 103: 3 M-346; 21 MB-339A; 28 MB-339CD*; 21 MB-339PAN (aerobatics); 30 SF-260EA
HELICOPTERS
  MRH 58: 10 AW139 (HH-139A/VH-139A); 2 MD-500D (NH-500D); 46 MD-500E (NH-500E)
  CSAR 4 AW101 (HH-101A)
  SAR 12 HH-3F *Pelican*
  TPT 31: **Medium** 2 SH-3D *Sea King* (liaison/VIP); **Light** 29 Bell 212 (HH-212)/AB-212 ICO
UNMANNED AERIAL VEHICLES • ISR • Heavy 14: 9 MQ-9A *Reaper*; 5 RQ-1B *Predator*
AIR DEFENCE • SAM • Short SPADA
AIR-LAUNCHED MISSILES
  AAM • IR AIM-9L *Sidewinder*; **IIR** IRIS-T; **ARH** AIM-120B AMRAAM
  ARM AGM-88 HARM
  LACM SCALP EG/*Storm Shadow*
BOMBS
  Laser-guided/GPS: Enhanced *Paveway* II; Enhanced *Paveway* III

Joint Special Forces Command (COFS)

Army
FORCES BY ROLE
SPECIAL FORCES
  1 SF regt (9th *Assalto paracadutisti*)
  1 STA regt
  1 ranger regt (4th *Alpini paracadutisti*)
COMBAT SUPPORT
  1 psyops regt
TRANSPORT HELICOPTER
  1 spec ops hel regt

Navy (COMSUBIN)
FORCES BY ROLE
SPECIAL FORCES
  1 SF gp (GOI)
  1 diving gp (GOS)

Air Force
FORCES BY ROLE
SPECIAL FORCES
  1 wg (sqn) (17th *Stormo Incursori*)

Paramilitary

Carabinieri
FORCES BY ROLE
SPECIAL FORCES
  1 spec ops gp (GIS)

Paramilitary 182,350

Carabinieri 103,750
The Carabinieri are organisationally under the MoD. They are a separate service in the Italian Armed Forces as well as a police force with judicial competence

Mobile and Specialised Branch
FORCES BY ROLE
MANOEUVRE
  Other
    1 (mobile) paramilitary div (1 bde (1st) with (1 horsed cav regt, 11 mobile bn); 1 bde (2nd) with (1 (1st) AB regt, 2 (7th & 13th) mobile regt))
HELICOPTER
  1 hel gp
EQUIPMENT BY TYPE
ARMOURED FIGHTING VEHICLES
  APC • APC (T) 3 VCC-2
PATROL AND COASTAL COMBATANTS • PB 69
AIRCRAFT • TPT • **Light:** 1 P-180 *Avanti*
HELICOPTERS
  MRH 24 Bell 412 (AB-412)
  TPT • **Light** 19 AW109

Customs 68,100
(Servizio Navale Guardia Di Finanza)
EQUIPMENT BY TYPE
PATROL AND COASTAL COMBATANTS 179
  PCF 1 *Antonio Zara*
  PBF 146: 19 *Bigliani*; 24 *Corrubia*; 9 *Mazzei*; 62 V-2000; 32 V-5000/V-6000
  PB 32: 24 *Buratti*; 8 *Meatini*
LOGISTICS AND SUPPORT • AX 1 *Giorgio Cini*

Coast Guard 10,500
(Guardia Costiera – Capitanerie Di Porto)
EQUIPMENT BY TYPE
PATROL AND COASTAL COMBATANTS 332
  PCO 3: 2 *Dattilo*; 1 *Gregoretti*
  PCC 32: 3 *Diciotti*; 1 *Saettia*; 22 200-class; 6 400-class
  PB 297: 21 300-class; 3 454-class; 72 500-class; 12 600-class; 47 700-class; 94 800-class; 48 2000-class
AIRCRAFT • MP 6: 3 ATR-42 MP *Surveyor*, 1 P-180GC; 2 PL-166-DL3
HELICOPTERS • MRH 11: 7 AW139; 4 Bell 412SP (AB-412SP *Griffin*)

Cyber
Overall responsibility for cyber security rests with the presidency of the Council of Ministers and the Inter-Ministerial Situation and Planning Group, which includes, among others, representatives from the defence, interior and foreign-affairs ministries. A Joint Integrated Concept on Computer Network Operations was approved in 2009 and, in 2014, a Joint Interagency Concept on Cyberwarfare. The National Strategic Framework for Cyberspace Security, released in 2013, says that the defence ministry 'plans, executes and sustains Computer Network Operations (CNO) in the cyber domain in order to prevent, localize and defend (actively and in-depth), oppose and neutralise all threats and/or hostile actions in the cyber domain'.

DEPLOYMENT

AFGHANISTAN
NATO • *Operation Resolute Support* 1,037; 1 mtn inf bde HQ; 1 mtn inf regt(-); 1 hel regt(-); AW129 *Mangusta*; CH-47; NH90

ALBANIA
OSCE • Albania 1

BLACK SEA
NATO • SNMCMG 2: 1 MHO

BOSNIA-HERZEGOVINA
EU • EUFOR • *Operation Althea* 4
OSCE • Bosnia and Herzegovina 6

BULGARIA
NATO • Air Policing 4 Eurofighter *Typhoon*

DJIBOUTI
90

EGYPT
MFO 75; 3 PB

GULF OF ADEN & INDIAN OCEAN
EU • *Operation Atalanta* 1 DDGHM

INDIAN/PAKISTAN
UN • UNMOGIP 2 obs

IRAQ
Operation Inherent Resolve (Prima Parthica) 1,220; 1 inf regt; 1 trg unit; 1 hel sqn with 4 AW129 *Mangusta*; 4 NH90

KUWAIT
Operation Inherent Resolve (Prima Parthica) 280; 4 AMX; 2 MQ-9A *Reaper*; 1 KC-767A

LATVIA
NATO • Enhanced Forward Presence 160; 1 mech inf coy

LEBANON
UN • UNIFIL 1,077; 1 AB bde HQ; 1 mech inf bn; 1 engr coy; 1 sigs coy; 1 hel bn

LIBYA
Operation Ippocrate 300; 1 inf coy; 1 log unit; 1 fd hospital
UN • UNSMIL 2 obs

MALI
EU • EUTM Mali 9
UN • MINUSMA 1

MEDITERRANEAN SEA
EU • EU NAVFOR MED: 1 FFGHM

SERBIA
NATO • KFOR 551; 1 inf BG HQ; 1 Carabinieri unit
OSCE • Kosovo 11

SOMALIA
EU • EUTM Somalia 112

TURKEY
NATO • *Operation Active Fence*: 1 SAM bty with SAMP/T

UKRAINE
OSCE • Ukraine 19

UNITED ARAB EMIRATES
120; 1 tpt flt with 2 C-130J *Hercules*

FOREIGN FORCES

United States US European Command: 12,050
Army 4,400; 1 AB IBCT(-)
Navy 3,600; 1 HQ (US Navy Europe (USNAVEUR)) at Naples; 1 HQ (6th Fleet) at Gaeta; 1 ASW Sqn with 4 P-8A *Poseidon* at Sigonella
USAF 3,850; 1 ftr wg with 2 ftr sqn with 21 F-16C/D *Fighting Falcon* at Aviano
USMC 200

Latvia LVA

Euro €		2016	2017	2018
GDP	€	25.0bn	26.8bn	
	US$	27.7bn	30.2bn	
per capita	US$	14,063	15,403	
Growth	%	2.0	3.8	
Inflation	%	0.1	3.0	
Def exp [a]	€	360m	448m	
	US$	398m	506m	
Def bdgt [b]	€	368m	450m	570m
	US$	407m	507m	
FMA (US)	US$	1.75m	1.5m	0m
US$1= €		0.90	0.89	

[a] NATO definition
[b] Includes military pensions

Population 1,944,643

Ethnic groups: Latvian 62%; Russian 27%; Belarusian 3%; Polish 2.2%

Age	0–14	15–19	20–24	25–29	30–64	65 plus
Male	7.8%	2.2%	2.6%	3.7%	23.3%	6.4%
Female	7.4%	2.1%	2.4%	3.5%	25.3%	13.1%

Capabilities

Latvia's National Security Concept was revised in 2015, amid growing concerns over regional security. As with the other Baltic states, central to Latvia's security policy is membership of NATO. Like these countries and Poland, it also hosts a NATO battlegroup. The battlegroup, part of NATO's Enhanced Forward Presence, deployed in June 2017 and was certified as fully operational two months later. Latvia is on course to meet the NATO target of spending 2% of GDP on defence in 2018. This was part of the country's 2018–20 medium-term budget framework, adopted by the government in October 2017. The defence ministry intends to improve combat readiness as well as the equipment inventory. It is acquiring second-hand M109 self-propelled artillery pieces from Austria and has selected the *Stinger* man-portable air-defence system. Latvian forces have deployed on a range of NATO operations and exercises, and EU civilian and military missions.

ACTIVE 5,310 (Army 1,250 Navy 550 Air 310 Joint Staff 2,600 National Guard 600)

RESERVE 7,850 (National Guard 7,850)

ORGANISATIONS BY SERVICE

Joint 2,600
FORCES BY ROLE
SPECIAL FORCES
 1 SF unit
COMBAT SUPPORT
 1 MP bn

Army 1,250
FORCES BY ROLE
MANOEUVRE
  Light
    1 inf bde (2 inf bn, 1 cbt spt bn HQ, 1 CSS bn HQ)

National Guard 600; 7,850 part-time (8,450 total)
FORCES BY ROLE
MANOEUVRE
  Light
    11 inf bn
COMBAT SUPPORT
  1 arty bn
  1 AD bn
  1 engr bn
  1 NBC bn
COMBAT SERVICE SUPPORT
  3 spt bn
EQUIPMENT BY TYPE
ARMOURED FIGHTING VEHICLES
  MBT 3 T-55 (trg)
  RECCE 47+ FV107 *Scimitar* (incl variants)
ANTI-TANK/ANTI-INFRASTRUCTURE
  MANPATS *Spike*-LR
  RCL 84mm *Carl Gustav*; 90mm 130 Pvpj 1110
ARTILLERY 80
  SP 155mm 4 M109A5ÖE
  TOWED 100mm 23 K-53
  MOR 53: 81mm 28 L16; 120mm 25 M120

Navy 550 (incl Coast Guard)
Naval Forces Flotilla separated into an MCM squadron and a patrol-boat squadron. LVA, EST and LTU have set up a joint naval unit, BALTRON, with bases at Liepaja, Riga, Ventspils (LVA), Tallinn (EST), Klaipeda (LTU). Each nation contributes 1–2 MCMVs.
EQUIPMENT BY TYPE
PATROL AND COASTAL COMBATANTS 5
  PB 5 *Skrunda* (GER *Swath*)
MINE WARFARE • MINE COUNTERMEASURES 6
  MHO 5 *Imanta* (ex-NLD *Alkmaar/Tripartite*)
  MCCS 1 *Vidar* (ex-NOR)
LOGISTICS AND SUPPORT 1
  AXL 1 *Varonis* (comd and spt ship, ex-NLD)

Coast Guard
Under command of the Latvian Naval Forces
EQUIPMENT BY TYPE
PATROL AND COASTAL COMBATANTS
  PB 6: 1 *Astra*; 5 KBV 236 (ex-SWE)

Air Force 310
Main tasks are airspace control and defence, maritime and land SAR and air transportation
FORCES BY ROLE
TRANSPORT
  1 (mixed) tpt sqn with An-2 *Colt*; Mi-17 *Hip* H; PZL Mi-2 *Hoplite*
AIR DEFENCE
  1 AD bn
  1 radar sqn (radar/air ctrl)
AIRCRAFT • TPT • Light 4 An-2 *Colt*
HELICOPTERS
  MRH 4 Mi-17 *Hip* H
  TPT • Light 2 PZL Mi-2 *Hoplite*
AIR DEFENCE
  SAM • Point-defence RBS-70
  GUNS • TOWED 40mm 24 L/70

Paramilitary

State Border Guard
EQUIPMENT BY TYPE
PATROL AND COASTAL COMBATANTS
  PB 3: 1 *Valpas* (ex-FIN); 1 *Lokki* (ex-FIN); 1 *Randa*

Cyber
The Cyber Security Strategy of Latvia was published in 2014. Latvia established a military CERT unit in early 2016. The unit cooperates closely with the national CERT, participates in international exercises and increases cyber-defence capabilities. A Cyber Defence Unit has been operational in the National Guard since 2014. Its main role is to ensure the formation of reserve cyber-defence capabilities, which could be used for both civil and military tasks.

DEPLOYMENT

AFGHANISTAN
NATO • *Operation Resolute Support* 22

IRAQ
Operation Inherent Resolve 6

MALI
EU • EUTM Mali 3
UN • MINUSMA 2

NORTH SEA
NATO • SNMCMG 1: 1 MCCS

UKRAINE
OSCE • Ukraine 4

FOREIGN FORCES
All NATO Enhanced Forward Presence unless stated
Albania 18; 1 EOD pl
Canada 450; 1 mech inf bn HQ; 1 mech inf coy(+)
Italy 160; 1 mech inf coy
Poland 160; 1 tk coy
Slovenia 50; 1 CBRN pl(+)
Spain 300; 1 armd inf coy(+)
United States *Operation Atlantic Resolve*: 1 tpt hel flt; 5 UH-60M *Black Hawk*

Lithuania LTU

Euro €		2016	2017	2018
GDP	€	38.6bn	41.4bn	
	US$	42.8bn	46.7bn	
per capita	US$	14,893	16,443	
Growth	%	2.3	3.5	
Inflation	%	0.7	3.5	
Def exp [a]	€	575m	724m	
	US$	636m	816m	
Def bdgt [b]	€	575m	723m	873m
	US$	637m	816m	
FMA (US)	US$	1.75m	1.5m	0m
US$1=€		0.90	0.89	

[a] NATO definition
[b] Includes military pensions

Population 2,823,859

Ethnic groups: Lithuanian 84.2%; Polish 6.6%; Russian 5.8%; Belarusian 1.2%

Age	0–14	15–19	20–24	25–29	30–64	65 plus
Male	7.7%	2.7%	3.0%	3.4%	22.6%	6.7%
Female	7.3%	2.6%	2.8%	3.2%	25.0%	13.0%

Capabilities

In January 2017, Lithuania adopted a new National Security Strategy (NSS) intended to reflect the worsening regional security environment. The NSS identified the main security threat as 'posed by aggressive actions of the Russian Federation'. Sovereignty, territorial integrity and democratic constitutional order are the key tenets of the NSS. Given Lithuania's size and the scale of its armed forces, conventional deterrence and territorial defence are predicated on NATO membership. Lithuania, along with the two other Baltic states and Poland, now hosts a multinational NATO battlegroup as part of the Alliance's Enhanced Forward Presence. The country intends to spend a minimum of 2% of GDP on defence by 2018, with further increases to follow. Improved combat readiness and the exploration of 'universal military service' were also included in the strategy. The country is purchasing the NASAMS medium-range surface-to-air missile system to improve its ground-based air defences. Like the other Baltic states, it is reliant on NATO's air-policing deployment for a combat-aircraft capacity.

ACTIVE 18,350 (Army 11,650 Navy 700 Air 1,100 Other 4,900) **Paramilitary 11,300**

Conscript liability 9 months

RESERVE 6,700 (Army 6,700)

ORGANISATIONS BY SERVICE

Army 6,800; 4,850 active reserves (total 11,650)

FORCES BY ROLE
MANOEUVRE
Mechanised
  1 (1st) mech bde (1 recce coy, 4 mech inf bn, 1 arty bn)
Light
  1 (2nd) mot inf bde (2 mot inf bn, 1 arty bn)
COMBAT SUPPORT
  1 engr bn
COMBAT SERVICE SUPPORT
  1 trg regt

EQUIPMENT BY TYPE
ARMOURED FIGHTING VEHICLES
  APC • APC (T) 238: 234 M113A1; 4 M577 (CP)
ENGINEERING & MAINTENANCE VEHICLES
  AEV 8 MT-LB
  ARV 6: 2 BPz-2; 4 M113
ANTI-TANK/ANTI-INFRASTRUCTURE
  MSL
    SP 10 M1025A2 HMMWV with FGM-148 *Javelin*
    MANPATS FGM-148 *Javelin*
  RCL 84mm *Carl Gustav*
ARTILLERY 52
  SP 4 PzH 2000
  TOWED 105mm 18 M101
  MOR 120mm 30: 5 2B11; 10 M/41D; 15 M113 with Tampella
AIR DEFENCE • SAM • Point-defence GROM

Reserves

National Defence Voluntary Forces 4,850 active reservists

FORCES BY ROLE
MANOEUVRE
Other
  6 (territorial) def unit

Navy 680

LVA, EST and LTU established a joint naval unit, BALTRON, with bases at Liepaja, Riga, Ventpils (LVA), Tallinn (EST), Klaipeda (LTU).

EQUIPMENT BY TYPE
PATROL AND COASTAL COMBATANTS 4
  PCC 4 *Zemaitis* (ex-DNK *Flyvefisken*) with 1 76mm gun
MINE WARFARE • MINE COUNTERMEASURES 4
  MHC 3: 1 *Sūduvis* (ex-GER *Lindau*); 2 *Skulvis* (ex-UK *Hunt*)
  MCCS 1 *Jotvingis* (ex-NOR *Vidar*)
LOGISTICS AND SUPPORT • AAR 1 *Šakiai*

Air Force 1,100

Flying hours 120 hrs/yr

FORCES BY ROLE
AIR DEFENCE
  1 AD bn

EQUIPMENT BY TYPE
AIRCRAFT
  TPT 5: **Medium** 3 C-27J *Spartan*; **Light** 2 L-410 *Turbolet*
  TRG 1 L-39ZA *Albatros*

HELICOPTERS
MRH 3 AS365M3 *Dauphin* (SAR)
TPT • Medium 3 Mi-8 *Hip* (tpt/SAR)
AIR DEFENCE • SAM • Point-defence FIM-92 *Stinger*; RBS-70

Special Operation Force
FORCES BY ROLE
SPECIAL FORCES
1 SF gp (1 CT unit; 1 Jaeger bn, 1 cbt diver unit)

Logistics Support Command 1,400
FORCES BY ROLE
COMBAT SERVICE SUPPORT
1 log bn

Training and Doctrine Command 900
FORCES BY ROLE
COMBAT SERVICE SUPPORT
1 trg regt

Other Units 1,900
FORCES BY ROLE
COMBAT SUPPORT
1 MP bn

Paramilitary 11,300

Riflemen Union 7,800

State Border Guard Service 3,500
Ministry of Interior
EQUIPMENT BY TYPE
PATROL AND COASTAL COMBATANTS • PB 3: 1 *Lokki* (ex-FIN); 1 KBV 041 (ex-SWE); 1 KBV 101 (ex-SWE)
AMPHIBIOUS • LANDING CRAFT • UCAC 2 *Christina* (*Griffon* 2000)
AIRCRAFT • TPT • Light 1 Cessna 172RG
HELICOPTERS • TPT • Light 5: 1 BK-117 (SAR); 2 H120 *Colibri*; 2 H135

Cyber
A law on cyber security was adopted in December 2014. The Ministry of Defence (MoD) is the leading national authority on cyber-security policy formulation and implementation. The National Cyber Security Centre (NCSC) under the MoD supports other national entities in their cyber-security activities by performing a wide range of functions, such as setting standards and regulations, performing network monitoring and penetration testing, tasking national entities to improve their cyber-security measures, assisting in cyber-incident detection and consequence management. A national cyber-incident management plan was approved by the government in January 2016; organisational and technical cyber-security requirements for critical information infrastructure and state-information resources were approved by the government in April 2016; and a cyber-incident management plan for critical information infrastructure was approved in July 2016. The 2016 Military Strategy says that the armed forces will focus on ensuring the reliability of command-and-control systems and investing in cyber-defence capabilities. The 2017 National Security Strategy states that Lithuania will continue to develop the NCSC.

DEPLOYMENT

AFGHANISTAN
NATO • *Operation Resolute Support* 29

CENTRAL AFRICAN REPUBLIC
EU • EUTM RCA 1

MALI
EU • EUTM Mali 2
UN • MINUSMA 5; 1 obs

SERBIA
NATO • KFOR 1

UKRAINE
OSCE • Ukraine 3
JMTG-U 16

FOREIGN FORCES
All NATO Enhanced Forward Presence unless stated
Belgium 100; 1 tpt coy
Germany 450; 1 armd inf bn HQ; 1 armd inf coy(+)
Netherlands 250; 1 armd inf coy
Norway 200; 1 armd coy
United States NATO Baltic Air Policing 4 F-15C *Eagle*

Luxembourg LUX

Euro €		2016	2017	2018
GDP	€	54.2bn	57.3bn	
	US$	60.0bn	63.5bn	
per capita	US$	104,095	107,708	
Growth	%	4.2	3.9	
Inflation	%	0.0	1.2	
Def exp [a]	€	213m	256m	
	US$	236m	284m	
Def bdgt	€	213m	265m	331m
	US$	235m	294m	
US$1=€		0.90	0.90	

[a] NATO definition

Population 594,130

Age	0–14	15–19	20–24	25–29	30–64	65 plus
Male	8.6%	3.0%	3.3%	3.6%	25.1%	6.7%
Female	8.1%	2.9%	3.1%	3.5%	23.9%	8.3%

Capabilities

Luxembourg maintains limited military capabilities in order to participate in European collective security and crisis management. It has contributed troops to the multinational battlegroup in Lithuania as part of NATO's

Enhanced Forward Presence. It is also part of the European Multi-Role Tanker Transport Fleet programme, part funding one A330 MRTT. Delivery of an A400M medium strategic-transport aircraft is expected in 2018–19. Personnel are embedded within European military headquarters and take part in the EU training mission in Mali. Luxembourg contributes a contractor-operated maritime-patrol aircraft to the EU counter-human-trafficking operation in the Mediterranean. The Belgian and Dutch air forces are responsible for policing Luxembourg's airspace.

ACTIVE 900 (Army 900) Paramilitary 600

ORGANISATIONS BY SERVICE

Army 900
FORCES BY ROLE
MANOEUVRE
  Reconnaissance
  2 recce coy (1 to Eurocorps/BEL div, 1 to NATO pool of deployable forces)
EQUIPMENT BY TYPE
ARMOURED FIGHTING VEHICLES
  AUV 48 *Dingo 2*
ANTI-TANK/ANTI-INFRASTRUCTURE
  MSL • MANPATS TOW
ARTILLERY • MOR 81mm 6

Paramilitary 600

  Gendarmerie 600

DEPLOYMENT

AFGHANISTAN
NATO • *Operation Resolute Support* 1

LITHUANIA
NATO • Enhanced Forward Presence 22; 1 tpt pl

MALI
EU • EUTM Mali 2

MEDITERRANEAN SEA
EU • EUNAVFOR MED 2 *Merlin* IIIC (leased)

SERBIA
NATO • KFOR 23

Macedonia, Former Yugoslav Republic FYROM

Macedonian Denar d		2016	2017	2018
GDP	d	607bn	634bn	
	US$	10.9bn	11.4bn	
per capita	US$	5,264	5,500	
Growth	%	2.4	2.5	
Inflation	%	-0.2	0.3	
Def bdgt	d	5.90bn	6.24bn	
	US$	106m	112m	
FMA (US)	US$	3.6m	3.6m	0m
US$1=d		55.66	55.523	

Population 2,103,721

Ethnic groups: Macedonian 64.2%; Albanian 25.2%; Turkish 3.9%; Romani 2.7%; Serbian 1.8%; Bosniac 0.9%

Age	0–14	15–19	20–24	25–29	30–64	65 plus
Male	8.9%	3.3%	3.6%	3.8%	24.5%	5.8%
Female	8.3%	3.1%	3.4%	3.6%	24.2%	7.7%

Capabilities

The small army-focused joint force has modest maritime and air wings, and the forces rely on ageing Soviet-era equipment. A 2014–23 modernisation plan is intended to reform the armed forces and update equipment to NATO standards, but to date progress has been limited. NATO's Membership Action Plan was joined in 1999 and in 2017 the country became part of the NATO Program for the Advancement of Defence Education. FYR Macedonia continues to deploy personnel to *Operation Resolute Support* in Afghanistan. The country hosts the Balkan Medical Task Force Headquarters and has been chosen to host SEEBRIG headquarters in 2020–26. Exercises regularly take place with regional states and the US.

ACTIVE 8,000 (Army 8,000) Paramilitary 7,600

RESERVE 4,850

ORGANISATIONS BY SERVICE

Army 8,000
FORCES BY ROLE
SPECIAL FORCES
  1 SF regt (1 SF bn, 1 Ranger bn)
MANOEUVRE
  Mechanised
  1 mech inf bde (1 tk bn, 4 mech inf bn, 1 arty bn, 1 engr bn, 1 NBC coy)
COMBAT SUPPORT
  1 MP bn
  1 sigs bn
COMBAT SERVICE SUPPORT
  1 log bde (3 log bn)

Reserves
FORCES BY ROLE
MANOEUVRE Light
1 inf bde
EQUIPMENT BY TYPE
ARMOURED FIGHTING VEHICLES
MBT 31 T-72A
RECCE 10 BRDM-2
IFV 11: 10 BMP-2; 1 BMP-2K (CP)
APC 202
APC (T) 47: 9 *Leonidas*; 28 M113; 10 MT-LB
APC (W) 155: 57 BTR-70; 12 BTR-80; 2 *Cobra*; 84 TM-170 *Hermelin*
ANTI-TANK/ANTI-INFRASTRUCTURE
MSL • MANPATS *Milan*
RCL 57mm; 82mm M60A
ARTILLERY 126
TOWED 70: 105mm 14 M-56; 122mm 56 M-30 M-1938
MRL 17: 122mm 6 BM-21; 128mm 11
MOR 39: 120mm 39

Marine Wing
EQUIPMENT BY TYPE
PATROL AND COASTAL COMBATANTS • PB 2 *Botica*

Aviation Brigade
FORCES BY ROLE
TRAINING
1 flt with Z-242; Bell 205 (UH-1H *Iroquois*)
ATTACK HELICOPTER
1 sqn with Mi-24K *Hind* G2; Mi-24V *Hind* E
TRANSPORT HELICOPTER
1 sqn with Mi-8MTV *Hip*; Mi-17 *Hip* H
AIR DEFENCE
1 AD bn
EQUIPMENT BY TYPE
AIRCRAFT
TPT • Light 1 An-2 *Colt*
TRG 5 Z-242
HELICOPTERS
ATK 4 Mi-24V *Hind* E (10: 2 Mi-24K *Hind* G2; 8 Mi-24V *Hind* E in store)
MRH 6: 4 Mi-8MTV *Hip*; 2 Mi-17 *Hip* H
TPT • Light 2 Bell 205 (UH-1H *Iroquois*)
AIR DEFENCE
SAM • Point-defence 8 9K35 *Strela*-10 (SA-13 *Gopher*); 9K310 *Igla*-1 (SA-16 *Gimlet*)
GUNS 40mm 36 L20

Paramilitary

Police 7,600 (some 5,000 armed)
incl 2 SF units
EQUIPMENT BY TYPE
ARMOURED FIGHTING VEHICLES
APC
APC (T) M113
APC (W) BTR-80; TM-170 *Heimlin*
AUV *Ze'ev*

HELICOPTERS
MRH 1 Bell 412EP *Twin Huey*
TPT • Light 2: 1 Bell 206B (AB-206B) *Jet Ranger* II; 1 Bell 212 (AB-212)

DEPLOYMENT

ALBANIA
OSCE • Albania 2

BOSNIA-HERZEGOVINA
EU • EUFOR • *Operation Althea* 3
OSCE • Bosnia and Herzegovina 1

SERBIA
OSCE • Kosovo 14

UKRAINE
OSCE • Ukraine 24

Malta MLT

Euro €		2016	2017	2018
GDP	€	9.94bn	10.7bn	
	US$	11.0bn	12.0bn	
per capita	US$	25,329	27,567	
Growth	%	5.5	5.1	
Inflation	%	0.9	1.3	
Def bdgt [a]	€	52m	57m	
	US$	58m	64m	
US$1= €		0.90	0.89	

[a] Excludes military pensions

Population 416,338

Age	0–14	15–19	20–24	25–29	30–64	65 plus
Male	7.7%	2.7%	3.2%	3.5%	23.9%	8.8%
Female	7.3%	2.6%	3.0%	3.3%	23.2%	10.7%

Capabilities

The armed forces consist of a limited number of army personnel supported by small naval and air units. Principal roles are external security, civil-emergency support and support to the police in certain areas. Defence-spending growth has been modest; however, the European Internal Security Fund is funding some modernisation. With the addition of a third *King Air* maritime-patrol aircraft, Malta can now reportedly ensure a continuous presence in its airspace. The country participates in various European training missions as well as the EUNAVFOR–MED mission. The government has announced a modest increase in personnel and intends to increase reservist numbers.

ACTIVE 1,950 (Armed Forces 1,950)

RESERVE 180 (Emergency Volunteer Reserve Force 120 Individual Reserve 60)

ORGANISATIONS BY SERVICE

Armed Forces of Malta 1,950
FORCES BY ROLE
SPECIAL FORCES
1 SF unit
MANOEUVRE
 Light
  1 (1st) inf regt (3 inf coy, 1 cbt spt coy)
COMBAT SUPPORT
 1 (3rd) cbt spt regt (1 cbt engr sqn, 1 EOD sqn, 1 maint sqn)
COMBAT SERVICE SUPPORT
 1 (4th) CSS regt (1 CIS coy, 1 sy coy)

Maritime Squadron
Organised into 5 divisions: offshore patrol; inshore patrol; rapid deployment and training; marine engineering; and logistics
EQUIPMENT BY TYPE
PATROL AND COASTAL COMBATANTS 8
 PCO 1 *Emer*
 PCC 1 *Diciotti*
 PB 6: 4 Austal 21m; 2 *Marine Protector*
LOGISTICS AND SUPPORT 2
 AAR 2 *Cantieri Vittoria*

Air Wing
1 base party. 1 flt ops div; 1 maint div; 1 integrated log div; 1 rescue section
EQUIPMENT BY TYPE
AIRCRAFT
 TPT • Light 5: 3 Beech 200 *King Air* (maritime patrol); 2 BN-2B *Islander*
 TRG 3 *Bulldog* T MK1
HELICOPTERS
 MRH 6: 3 AW139 (SAR); 3 SA316B *Alouette* III

Montenegro MNE

Euro €		2016	2017	2018
GDP	€	3.77bn	3.97bn	
	US$	4.18bn	4.41bn	
per capita	US$	6,707	7,071	
Growth	%	2.5	3.0	
Inflation	%	-0.3	2.1	
Def exp [a]	€	56m	66m	
	US$	62m	73m	
Def bdgt [b]	€	62m	66m	
	US$	68m	74m	
FMA (US)	US$	1m	1m	0m
US$1=€		0.90	0.90	

[a] NATO definition
[b] Includes military pensions

Population 642,550

Ethnic groups: Montenegrian 45% Serbian 28.7% Bosniac 8.6% Albanian 4.9% Croatian 1%

Age	0–14	15–19	20–24	25–29	30–64	65 plus
Male	7.5%	2.0%	2.3%	3.5%	28.4%	6.1%
Female	7.6%	2.6%	2.7%	3.3%	24.9%	9.0%

Capabilities

Montenegro joined NATO in 2017. The country's armed forces are small and primarily organised around the army, with few air and naval assets. The force is supported by a significant paramilitary organisation. Capability remains focused on internal security and limited support to international peacekeeping. Montenegrin forces have deployed to Afghanistan with NATO, affording them valuable experience. Reform and professionalisation of the armed forces has been slow, with only a limited portion of the defence budget spent on modernisation. Podgorica intends to replace its ageing Soviet-era equipment and procurement priorities include light and medium helicopters and light armoured vehicles. NATO's latest Trust Fund Project in Montenegro opened in February 2017 and is expected to support the demilitarisation of more than 400 tonnes of surplus ammunition. The country's defence industry has sold large numbers of surplus small arms and anti-tank weapons abroad. In 2017, Podgorica signed a defence bilateral cooperation plan with Poland, France and Slovenia as well as a memorandum of understanding with the UK. Montenegro has deepened ties with NATO partners and neighbours, including Croatia, Germany, Serbia, Slovenia and the US, through extensive exercises.

ACTIVE 1,950 (Army 875 Navy 350 Air Force 225 Other 500) **Paramilitary 10,100**

ORGANISATIONS BY SERVICE

Army 875

FORCES BY ROLE
MANOEUVRE
  Reconnaissance
  1 recce coy
  Light
  1 mot inf bn
COMBAT SUPPORT
  1 MP coy
EQUIPMENT BY TYPE
ARMOURED FIGHTING VEHICLES
  APC • **APC (W)** 8 BOV-VP M-86
ANTI-TANK/ANTI-INFRASTRUCTURE
  SP 9 BOV-1
  MSL • **MANPATS** 9K111 *Fagot* (AT-4 *Spigot*); 9K111-1 *Konkurs* (AT-5 *Spandrel*)
ARTILLERY 135
  TOWED 122mm 12 D-30
  MRL 128mm 18 M-63/M-94 *Plamen*
  MOR 105: **82mm** 73; **120mm** 32

Navy 350

1 Naval Cmd HQ with 4 operational naval units (patrol boat; coastal surveillance; maritime detachment; and SAR) with additional sigs, log and trg units with a separate coastguard element. Some listed units are in the process of decommissioning

EQUIPMENT BY TYPE
PATROL AND COASTAL COMBATANTS 5
  PSO 1 *Kotor* with 1 twin 76mm gun (1 further vessel in reserve)
  PCFG 2 *Rade Končar*† (of which 1 in refit) with 2 single lnchr with P-15 *Termit* (SS-N-2B *Styx*) AShM (missiles disarmed)
  PB 2 *Mirna* (Type-140) (Police units)
LOGISTICS AND SUPPORT 1
  AXS 1 *Jadran*†

Air Force 225

Golubovci (Podgorica) air base under army command
FORCES BY ROLE
TRAINING
  1 (mixed) sqn with G-4 *Super Galeb*; Utva-75 (none operational)
TRANSPORT HELICOPTER
  1 sqn with SA341/SA342L *Gazelle*
EQUIPMENT BY TYPE
  AIRCRAFT • **TRG** (4 G-4 *Super Galeb* non-operational; 4 Utva-75 non-operational)
HELICOPTERS
  MRH 13 SA341/SA342L (HN-45M) *Gazelle*

Paramilitary ε10,100

Montenegrin Ministry of Interior Personnel ε6,000

Special Police Units ε4,100

DEPLOYMENT

AFGHANISTAN
NATO • *Operation Resolute Support* 18
ALBANIA
OSCE • Albania 1
MALI
EU • EUTM Mali 1
SERBIA
OSCE • Kosovo 1
UKRAINE
OSCE • Ukraine 2
WESTERN SAHARA
UN • MINURSO 2 obs

Multinational Organisations

Capabilities

The following represent shared capabilities held by contributors collectively rather than as part of national inventories.

ORGANISATIONS BY SERVICE

NATO AEW&C Force

Based at Geilenkirchen (GER). 12 original participating countries (BEL, CAN, DNK, GER, GRC, ITA, NLD, NOR, PRT, TUR, USA) have been subsequently joined by 5 more (CZE, ESP, HUN, POL, ROM).
FORCES BY ROLE
AIRBORNE EARLY WARNING & CONTROL
  1 sqn with B-757 (trg); E-3A *Sentry* (NATO standard)
EQUIPMENT BY TYPE
AIRCRAFT
  AEW&C 16 E-3A *Sentry* (NATO standard)
  TPT • **PAX** 1 B-757 (trg)

Strategic Airlift Capability

Heavy Airlift Wing based at Papa air base (HUN). 12 participating countries (BLG, EST, FIN, HUN, LTU, NLD, NOR, POL, ROM, SVN, SWE, USA)
EQUIPMENT BY TYPE
  AIRCRAFT • **TPT** • **Heavy** 3 C-17A *Globemaster* III

Strategic Airlift Interim Solution

Intended to provide strategic-airlift capacity pending the delivery of A400M aircraft by leasing An-124s. 14 participating countries (BEL, CZE, FIN, FRA, GER, GRC, HUN, LUX, NOR, POL, SVK, SVN, SWE, UK)
EQUIPMENT BY TYPE
  AIRCRAFT • **TPT** • **Heavy** 2 An-124-100 (4 more available on 6–9 days' notice)

Netherlands NLD

Euro €		2016	2017	2018
GDP	€	703bn	731bn	
	US$	778bn	824bn	
per capita	US$	45,658	48,272	
Growth	%	2.2	3.1	
Inflation	%	0.1	1.3	
Def exp [a]	€	8.23bn	8.69bn	
	US$	9.11bn	9.80bn	
Def bdgt [b]	€	8.24bn	8.96bn	9.20bn
	US$	9.12bn	10.1bn	
US$1=€		0.90	0.89	

[a] NATO definition
[b] Includes military pensions

Population 17,084,719

Age	0–14	15–19	20–24	25–29	30–64	65 plus
Male	8.4%	3.1%	3.1%	3.2%	23.2%	8.5%
Female	8.0%	2.9%	3.0%	3.2%	23.2%	10.2%

Capabilities

Dutch defence documents reflect concern over the security situation in Europe's east and south. Defence tasks include securing the integrity of Dutch territory and society; international stability and security in Europe's periphery; and security of supply routes, both physical and technological. Dutch forces are well trained and fully professional, but improving readiness is a key concern and priority will be given to those formations needed for deployments, including rapid-reaction units. Improvements are planned to enabling capabilities such as intelligence, including MALE UAVs, command and control, and strategic transport. The Netherlands makes significant contributions to NATO and EU military operations and its forces have become more integrated with their NATO allies, particularly Belgium and Germany. There are air-policing agreements with France, Belgium and Luxembourg. Elements of the army are increasingly cooperating with the Bundeswehr, and its 43rd mechanised brigade and airmobile brigade are associated with host German divisions. Defence-budget cuts have been arrested and increased allocations will allow for the consolidation of rapid-reaction and expeditionary capabilities. The Netherlands is part of the EDA's MMF project, which is acquiring seven A330 tankers for NATO use. There is a small defence industry. DutchAero, a subsidiary of KMWE, agreed with Pratt and Whitney in January 2016 to manufacture engine components for the F-35, while the country also worked with Germany on the *Fennek* and *Boxer* armoured vehicles. The army continues to replace a proportion of its tracked armoured vehicles with wheeled platforms.

ACTIVE 35,410 (Army 18,860 Navy 8,500 Air 8,050)
Military Constabulary 5,900

RESERVE 4,500 (Army 4,000 Navy 80 Air 420)
Military Constabulary 160
Reserve liability to age 35 for soldiers/sailors, 40 for NCOs, 45 for officers

ORGANISATIONS BY SERVICE

Army 18,860
FORCES BY ROLE
COMMAND
  elm 1 (1 GNC) corps HQ
SPECIAL FORCES
  4 SF coy
MANOEUVRE Reconnaissance
  1 ISR bn (2 armd recce sqn, 1 EW coy, 2 int sqn, 1 UAV bty)
Mechanised
  1 (43rd) mech bde (1 armd recce sqn, 2 armd inf bn, 1 engr bn, 1 maint coy, 1 med coy)
  1 (13th) lt mech bde (1 recce sqn, 2 lt mech inf bn, 1 engr bn, 1 maint coy, 1 med coy)
Air Manoeuvre
  1 (11th) air mob bde (3 air mob inf bn, 1 engr coy, 1 med coy, 1 supply coy, 1 maint coy)
COMBAT SUPPORT
  1 SP arty bn (3 SP arty bty)
  1 AD comd (1 AD sqn; 1 AD bty)
  1 CIMIC bn
  1 engr bn
  2 EOD coy 1 (CIS) sigs bn 1 CBRN coy
COMBAT SERVICE SUPPORT
  1 med bn
  5 fd hospital
  3 maint coy
  2 tpt bn

Reserves 2,700 reservists
National Command
Cadre bde and corps tps completed by call-up of reservists (incl Territorial Comd)
FORCES BY ROLE
MANOEUVRE
  Light
    3 inf bn (could be mobilised for territorial def)
EQUIPMENT BY TYPE
ARMOURED FIGHTING VEHICLES
  RECCE 196 *Fennek*
  IFV 170 CV9035N
  APC • APC (W) 143 *Boxer* (8 driver trg; 52 amb; 60 CP; 23 log)
  AUV 60 *Bushmaster* IMV
ENGINEERING & MAINTENANCE VEHICLES
  AEV 60: 50 *Boxer*; 10 *Kodiak*
  ARV 25 BPz-3 *Büffel*
  VLB 13 *Leopard* 1
  MW *Bozena*
NBC VEHICLES 6 TPz-1 *Fuchs* NBC
ANTI-TANK/ANTI-INFRASTRUCTURE • MSL
  SP 40 *Fennek* MRAT
  MANPATS *Spike*-MR (*Gil*)

ARTILLERY 119:
  SP 155mm 18 PzH 2000
  MOR 101: **81mm** 83 L16/M1; **120mm** 18 Brandt
RADAR • LAND 6+: 6 AN/TPQ-36 *Firefinder* (arty, mor); WALS; 10 *Squire*
AIR DEFENCE • SAM
  Long-range 20 MIM-104D/F *Patriot* PAC-2 GEM/PAC-3 (TMD capable)
  Short-range 6 NASAMS II
  Point-defence 18+: FIM-92 *Stinger*; 18 *Fennek* with FIM-92 *Stinger*

Navy 8,500 (incl Marines)

EQUIPMENT BY TYPE
SUBMARINES • TACTICAL • SSK 4:
  4 *Walrus* with 4 single 533mm TT with Mk48 *Sea Arrow* HWT
PRINCIPAL SURFACE COMBATANTS 6
  DESTROYERS • DDGHM 4:
    3 *De Zeven Provinciën* with 2 quad Mk141 lnchr with RGM-84F *Harpoon* AShM, 1 40-cell Mk41 VLS with SM-2MR/ESSM SAM, 2 twin 324mm ASTT with Mk46 LWT, 1 *Goalkeeper* CIWS, 1 127mm gun (capacity 1 NH90 hel)
    1 *Zeven Provinciën* with 2 quad Mk141 lnchr with RGM-84F *Harpoon* AShM, 1 40-cell Mk41 VLS with SM-2MR/ESSM SAM, 2 twin 324mm ASTT with Mk46 LWT, 2 *Goalkeeper* CIWS, 1 127mm gun (capacity 1 NH90 hel)
  FRIGATES • FFGHM 2:
    2 *Karel Doorman* with 2 quad Mk141 lnchr with RGM-84A/C *Harpoon* AShM, 1 16-cell Mk48 VLS with RIM-7P *Sea Sparrow* SAM, 2 twin 324mm ASTT with Mk46 LWT, 1 *Goalkeeper* CIWS, 1 76mm gun (capacity 1 NH90 hel)
PATROL AND COASTAL COMBATANTS
  PSOH 4 *Holland* with 1 76mm gun (capacity 1 NH90 hel)
MINE WARFARE • MINE COUNTERMEASURES
  MHO 6 *Alkmaar* (*Tripartite*)
AMPHIBIOUS
  PRINCIPAL AMPHIBIOUS SHIPS • LPD 2:
    1 *Rotterdam* with 2 *Goalkeeper* CIWS (capacity 6 NH90/ AS532 *Cougar* hel; either 6 LCVP or 2 LCU and 3 LCVP; either 170 APC or 33 MBT; 538 troops)
    1 *Johan de Witt* with 2 *Goalkeeper* CIWS (capacity 6 NH90 hel or 4 AS532 *Cougar* hel; either 6 LCVP or 2 LCU and 3 LCVP; either 170 APC or 33 MBT; 700 troops)
  LANDING CRAFT 17
    LCU 5 Mk9
    LCVP 12 Mk5
LOGISTICS AND SUPPORT 8
  AFSH 1 *Karel Doorman* with 2 *Goalkeeper* CIWS (capacity 6 NH90/AS532 *Cougar* or 2 CH-47F *Chinook* hel; 2 LCVP)
  AGS 2 *Snellius*
  AK 1 *Pelikaan*
  AOT 1 *Patria*
  AS 1 *Mercuur*
  AXL 1 *Van Kingsbergen*
  AXS 1 *Urania*

Marines 2,650

FORCES BY ROLE
SPECIAL FORCES
  1 SF gp (1 SF sqn, 1 CT sqn)
MANOEUVRE
  Amphibious
  2 mne bn
  1 amph aslt gp
COMBAT SERVICE SUPPORT
  1 spt gp (coy)
EQUIPMENT BY TYPE
ARMOURED FIGHTING VEHICLES
  APC • APC (T) 160: 87 Bv-206D; 73 BvS-10 *Viking*
ENGINEERING & MAINTENANCE VEHICLES
  ARV 4 BvS-10; 4 *Leopard* 1
  MED 4 BvS-10
ANTI-TANK/ANTI-INFRASTRUCTURE
  MSL • MANPATS *Spike*-MR (*Gil*)
ARTILLERY • MOR 81mm 12 L16/M1
AIR DEFENCE • SAM • Point-defence FIM-92 *Stinger*

Air Force 8,050

Flying hours 180 hrs/yr

FORCES BY ROLE
FIGHTER/GROUND ATTACK
  3 sqn with F-16AM/BM *Fighting Falcon*
ANTI-SUBMARINE WARFARE/SEARCH & RESCUE
  1 sqn with NH90 NFH
TANKER/TRANSPORT
  1 sqn with C-130H/H-30 *Hercules*
  1 sqn with KDC-10; Gulfstream IV
TRAINING
  1 OEU sqn with F-35A *Lightning* II
  1 sqn with PC-7 *Turbo Trainer*
  1 hel sqn with AH-64D *Apache*; CH-47D *Chinook* (based at Fort Hood, TX)
ATTACK HELICOPTER
  1 sqn with AH-64D *Apache*
TRANSPORT HELICOPTER
  1 sqn with AS532U2 *Cougar* II
  1 sqn with CH-47D/F *Chinook*
EQUIPMENT BY TYPE
AIRCRAFT 63 combat capable
  FTR 61 F-16AM/BM *Fighting Falcon*
  FGA 2 F-35A *Lightning* II (in test)
  TKR 2 KDC-10
  TPT 5: **Medium** 4: 2 C-130H *Hercules*; 2 C-130H-30 *Hercules*; **PAX** 1 Gulfstream IV
  TRG 13 PC-7 *Turbo Trainer*
HELICOPTERS
  ATK 28 AH-64D *Apache*
  ASW 12 NH90 NFH
  TPT 33: **Heavy** 17: 11 CH-47D *Chinook*; 6 CH-47F *Chinook*; **Medium** 8 AS532U2 *Cougar* II, 8 NH90 TTH
AIR-LAUNCHED MISSILES
  AAM • IR AIM-9L/M *Sidewinder*; **IIR** AIM-9X *Sidewinder* II; **ARH** AIM-120B AMRAAM
  ASM AGM-114K *Hellfire*; AGM-65D/G *Maverick*

BOMBS
Laser-guided GBU-10/GBU-12 *Paveway* II; GBU-24 *Paveway* III (all supported by LANTIRN)
INS/GPS guided GBU-39 Small Diameter Bomb

Paramilitary

Royal Military Constabulary 5,900
Subordinate to the Ministry of Defence, but performs most of its work under the authority of other ministries
FORCES BY ROLE
MANOEUVRE
  Other
  5 paramilitary district (total: 28 paramilitary unit)
EQUIPMENT BY TYPE
ARMOURED FIGHTING VEHICLES
  APC • **APC (W)** 24 YPR-KMar

Cyber

The Defence Cyber Strategy was updated in early 2015. A Defence Cyber Command (DCC) was launched in September 2014 and became operational in early 2017. The DCC is situated in the army, but comprises personnel from all the armed services. An announcement from the Ministry of Defence in November 2016 stated the DCC had an offensive and defensive mandate, though it had not yet performed any offensive operations. According to the defence ministry, 'the armed forces can attack, manipulate and disable the digital systems of opponents. Potential opponents might be other states, terrorist or other organisations, or hackers.' A Joint SIGINT Cyber Unit was stood up in 2014 under the General Intelligence and Security Service and the Dutch Military Intelligence and Security Service. A defence cyber doctrine is under development.

DEPLOYMENT

AFGHANISTAN
NATO • *Operation Resolute Support* 100

BOSNIA-HERZEGOVINA
OSCE • Bosnia and Herzegovina 1

CARIBBEAN
1 AFSH

GULF OF ADEN & INDIAN OCEAN
EU • *Operation Atalanta* 1 LPD

IRAQ
Operation Inherent Resolve 150; 3 trg unit

JORDAN
Operation Inherent Resolve 35

LEBANON
UN • UNIFIL 1

LITHUANIA
NATO • Enhanced Forward Presence 250; 1 armd inf coy

MALI
EU • EUTM Mali 1
UN • MINUSMA 258; 1 SF coy

MIDDLE EAST
UN • UNTSO 13 obs

NORTH SEA
NATO • SNMCMG 1: 1 MHO

SERBIA
OSCE • Kosovo 1

SOMALIA
EU • EUTM Somalia 11

SOUTH SUDAN
UN • UNMISS 6

SYRIA/ISRAEL
UN • UNDOF 2

UKRAINE
OSCE • Ukraine 4

UNITED STATES
1 hel trg sqn with AH-64D *Apache*; CH-47D *Chinook* based at Fort Hood (TX)

FOREIGN FORCES
United States US European Command: 410

Norway NOR

Norwegian Kroner kr		2016	2017	2018
GDP	kr	3.11tr	3.31tr	
	US$	371bn	392bn	
per capita	US$	70,553	73,615	
Growth	%	1.1	1.4	
Inflation	%	3.6	2.1	
Def exp [a]	kr	50.9bn	54.3bn	
	US$	6.06bn	6.44bn	
Def bdgt [b]	kr	50.4bn	51.2bn	55.0bn
	US$	6.0bn	6.08bn	
US$1=kr		8.40	8.43	

[a] NATO definition
[b] Includes military pensions

Population 5,320,045

Age	0–14	15–19	20–24	25–29	30–64	65 plus
Male	9.2%	3.1%	3.4%	3.6%	23.4%	7.7%
Female	8.8%	2.9%	3.2%	3.5%	22.2%	9.0%

Capabilities

Norway sustains small but well-equipped and highly trained armed forces. Territorial defence is at the heart of security policy. In June 2016, Norway published its Long Term Defence Plan, which stated that further adjustments to the armed forces were needed to address evolving security challenges at home and abroad. In October 2017, the defence ministry announced a NOK3 billion increase in defence spending and indicated that there would be a raft of measures to strengthen Norwegian capability in the High North, including a new Arctic Ranger company. Equipment recapitalisation is ongoing. Norway's first F-15A arrived in late 2017 and the government earlier announced that it would procure four submarines as part of a strategic partnership with Germany. The partnership also includes an agreement to cooperate on missiles. In March 2017, Norway ordered five P-8A *Poseidon* slated for delivery between 2022 and 2023. Large procurement items, such as the F-35A, the submarines and the P-8s, will stretch budgetary resources. According to the defence ministry, the F-35 alone will take up 35% of all procurement spending between 2017 and 2025. At any one time, around one-third of the country's troops are conscripts. In January 2015, Norwegian conscription became gender neutral. Around one-third of conscripts in the 2016 intake were female, with expectations that this will rise. A US Marine Corps contingent has been deployed to Vaernes, on a rotational basis, since January 2017. (See pp. 75–81.)

ACTIVE 23,950 (Army 9,350 Navy 4,300 Air 3,600 Central Support 6,150 Home Guard 550)

Conscript liability 18 months maximum. Conscripts first serve 12 months from 19–21, and then up to 4–5 refresher training periods until age 35, 44, 55 or 60 depending on rank and function. Active numbers include conscripts on initial service. Conscription was extended to women in 2015

RESERVE 38,590 (Army 270 Navy 320 Home Guard 38,000)

Readiness varies from a few hours to several days

ORGANISATIONS BY SERVICE

Army 4,350; 5,000 conscript (total 9,350)

The armoured infantry brigade – Brigade North – trains new personnel of all categories and provides units for international operations. At any time around one-third of the brigade will be trained and ready to conduct operations. The brigade includes one high-readiness armoured battalion (Telemark Battalion) with combat support and combat service support units on high readiness

FORCES BY ROLE
MANOEUVRE
  Reconnaissance
  1 (GSV) bn (1 (border) recce coy, 1 ranger coy, 1 spt coy, 1 trg coy)
  Armoured
  1 armd inf bde (1 ISR bn, 2 armd bn, 1 lt inf bn, 1 arty bn, 1 engr bn, 1 MP coy, 1 CIS bn, 1 spt bn, 1 med bn)
  Light
  1 lt inf bn (His Majesty The King's Guards)
EQUIPMENT BY TYPE
ARMOURED FIGHTING VEHICLES
  MBT 36 *Leopard* 2A4 (16 more in store)
  RECCE 21 CV9030
  IFV 89: 74 CV9030N; 15 CV9030N (CP)
  APC 390
    APC (T) 315 M113 (incl variants)
    APC (W) 75 XA-186 *Sisu*/XA-200 *Sisu*
  AUV 20+: 20 *Dingo* 2; IVECO LMV
ENGINEERING & MAINTENANCE VEHICLES
  AEV 28: 22 *Alvis*; 6 CV90 STING
  ARV 9+: 3 M88A1; M578; 6 *Leopard* 1
  VLB 35: 26 *Leguan*; 9 *Leopard* 1
  MW 9 910 MCV-2
NBC VEHICLES 6 TPz-1 *Fuchs* NBC
ANTI-TANK/ANTI-INFRASTRUCTURE
  MANPATS FGM-148 *Javelin*
  RCL 84mm *Carl Gustav*
ARTILLERY 212
  SP 155mm 18 M109A3GN
  MOR 194: **81mm** 150 L16; **SP 81mm** 20: 8 CV9030; 12 M125A2; **SP 107mm** 24 M106A1
RADAR • LAND 12 ARTHUR

Navy 2,300; 2,000 conscripts (total 4,300)

Joint Command – Norwegian National Joint Headquarters. The Royal Norwegian Navy is organised into four elements under the command of the chief of staff of the Navy: the naval units (*Kysteskadren*), the schools (*Sjoforsvarets Skoler*), the naval bases and the coastguard (*Kystvakten*)

FORCES BY ROLE
MANOEUVRE
  Reconnaissance
  1 ISR coy (Coastal Rangers)
COMBAT SUPPORT
  1 EOD pl
EQUIPMENT BY TYPE
SUBMARINES • TACTICAL • SSK 6 *Ula* with 8 single 533mm TT with A3 *Seal* DM2 HWT
PRINCIPAL SURFACE COMBATANTS 5
  DESTROYERS • DDGHM 5 *Fridtjof Nansen* with Aegis C2 (mod), 2 quad lnchr with NSM AShM, 1 8-cell Mk41 VLS with ESSM SAM, 2 twin 324mm ASTT with *Sting Ray* LWT, 1 76mm gun (capacity 1 NH90 hel)
PATROL AND COASTAL COMBATANTS 23:
  PSO 1 *Harstad*
  PCFG 6 *Skjold* with 8 single lnchr with NSM AShM, 1 76mm gun
  PBF 16 S90N (capacity 20 troops)
MINE WARFARE • MINE COUNTERMEASURES 6:
  MSC 3 *Alta* with 1 twin *Simbad* lnchr with *Mistral* SAM
  MHC 3 *Oksoy* with 1 twin *Simbad* lnchr with *Mistral* SAM
LOGISTICS AND SUPPORT 7
  AGI 1 *Marjata* IV
  AGS 2: 1 *HU Sverdrup* II; 1 *Marjata* III with 1 hel landing platform
  ATS 1 *Valkyrien*
  AX 2 *Kvarven*
  AXL 1 *Reine*

Coast Guard

EQUIPMENT BY TYPE
PATROL AND COASTAL COMBATANTS 14
  PSOH 3 *Nordkapp* with 1 57mm gun (capacity 1 med tpt hel)

PSO 4: 3 *Barentshav*; 1 *Svalbard* with 1 57mm gun, 1 hel landing platform
  PCC 5 *Nornen*
  PCO 2: 1 *Aalesund*; 1 *Reine*

Air Force 2,600 ; 1,000 conscript (total 3,600)

Joint Command – Norwegian National HQ

Flying hours   180 hrs/yr

FORCES BY ROLE
FIGHTER/GROUND ATTACK
  2 sqn with F-16AM/BM *Fighting Falcon*
MARITIME PATROL
  1 sqn with P-3C *Orion*; P-3N *Orion* (pilot trg)
ELECTRONIC WARFARE
  1 sqn with *Falcon* 20C (EW, Flight Inspection Service)
SEARCH & RESCUE
  1 sqn with *Sea King* Mk43B
TRANSPORT
  1 sqn with C-130J-30 *Hercules*
TRAINING
  1 sqn with MFI-15 *Safari*
TRANSPORT HELICOPTER
  2 sqn with Bell 412SP *Twin Huey*
  1 sqn with NH90 (forming)
AIR DEFENCE
  1 bn with NASAMS II
EQUIPMENT BY TYPE
AIRCRAFT 73 combat capable
  FTR 67: 47 F-16AM *Fighting Falcon*; 10 F-16BM *Fighting Falcon*; 10 F-35A *Lightning* II (in test)
  ASW 6: 4 P-3C *Orion*; 2 P-3N *Orion* (pilot trg)
  EW 2 *Falcon* 20C
  TPT • Medium 4 C-130J-30 *Hercules*
  TRG 16 MFI-15 *Safari*
HELICOPTERS
  ASW 8 NH90 NFH
  SAR 12 *Sea King* Mk43B
  MRH 18: 6 Bell 412HP; 12 Bell 412SP
AIR DEFENCE
  SAM • Short-range NASAMS II
AIR-LAUNCHED MISSILES
  AAM • IR AIM-9L *Sidewinder*; **IIR** AIM-9X *Sidewinder* II; IRIS-T; **ARH** AIM-120B AMRAAM; AIM-120C AMRAAM
BOMBS
  Laser-guided EGBU-12 *Paveway* II
  INS/GPS guided JDAM

Special Operations Command (NORSOCOM)

FORCES BY ROLE
SPECIAL FORCES
  1 (armed forces) SF comd (2 SF gp)
  1 (navy) SF comd (1 SF gp)

Central Support, Administration and Command 5,550; 600 conscripts (total 6,150)

Central Support, Administration and Command includes military personnel in all joint elements and they are responsible for logistics and CIS in support of all forces in Norway and abroad

Home Guard 600 (45,000 reserves)

The Home Guard is a separate organisation, but closely cooperates with all services. The Home Guard can be mobilised on very short notice for local security operations

Land Home Guard 41,150 with reserves

11 Home Guard Districts with mobile Rapid Reaction Forces (3,000 troops in total) as well as reinforcements and follow-on forces (38,150 troops in total)

Naval Home Guard 1,900 with reserves

Consisting of Rapid Reaction Forces (500 troops), and 17 'Naval Home Guard Areas'. A number of civilian vessels can be requisitioned as required

EQUIPMENT BY TYPE
PATROL AND COASTAL COMBATANTS • PB 11: 4 *Harek*; 2 *Gyda*; 5 *Alusafe* 1290

Air Home Guard 1,450 with reserves

Provides force protection and security detachments for air bases

Cyber

The defence ministry is responsible for defending military networks and national coordination in armed conflict. The 2012 Cyber Security Strategy for Norway contained cross-governmental guidelines for cyber defence. Norwegian Armed Forces Cyber Defence supports the armed forces with establishing, operating and protecting networks. It is responsible for defending military networks against cyber attack. It also supports the Norwegian Armed Forces at home and abroad with the establishment, operation, development and protection of communications systems, and is responsible for defending military networks against cyber attacks as well as developing network-based defence.

DEPLOYMENT

AFGHANISTAN
NATO • Operation Resolute Support 50
EGYPT
MFO 3
IRAQ
Operation Inherent Resolve 60; 1 trg unit
JORDAN
Operation Inherent Resolve 60
LITHUANIA
NATO • Enhanced Forward Presence 200; 1 armd coy
MALI
UN • MINUSMA 16
MEDITERRANEAN SEA
NATO • SNMG 1: 1 DDGHM
MIDDLE EAST
UN • UNTSO 13 obs

NORTH SEA
NATO • SNMCMG 1: 1 MSC

SERBIA
NATO • KFOR 2
OSCE • Kosovo 1

SOUTH SUDAN
UN • UNMISS 15

UKRAINE
OSCE • Ukraine 17

FOREIGN FORCES

United States US European Command: 330; 1 (USMC) MEU eqpt set; 1 (APS) 155mm SP Arty bn eqpt set

Poland POL

Polish Zloty z		2016	2017	2018
GDP	z	1.85tr	1.95tr	
	US$	469bn	510bn	
per capita	US$	12,361	13,429	
Growth	%	2.6	3.8	
Inflation	%	-0.6	1.9	
Def exp [a]	z	37.1bn	39.2bn	
	US$	9.40bn	10.2bn	
Def bdgt [b]	z	35.9bn	37.7bn	41.1bn
	US$	9.10bn	9.84bn	
FMA (US)	US$	9m	3.5m	0m
US$1=z		3.94	3.83	

[a] NATO definition
[b] Includes military pensions

Population   38,476,269

Age	0–14	15–19	20–24	25–29	30–64	65 plus
Male	7.6%	2.5%	3.0%	3.5%	25.2%	6.7%
Female	7.2%	2.4%	2.8%	3.4%	25.7%	10.2%

Capabilities

Territorial defence and NATO membership are two central pillars of Poland's defence policy. A classified Strategic Defence Review was undertaken by the new government following the October 2015 elections. A summary of this was released in May 2017 as 'The Defence Concept of the Republic of Poland'. The primary focus of the public document, covering the period 2017–32, is to prepare Poland's armed forces to provide a deterrent against Russian aggression. Russia is characterised as a direct threat to Poland and to a stable international order in general. The defence concept defines the ambition to restore divisions as tactical combat units, rather than administrative units. Poland is moving once again to a service command structure, assisted by a support inspectorate. Reforms of the defence-acquisition system are planned but a national armaments strategy is yet to be released. While observers expected a new Technical Modernization Programme (TMP) for 2017–26 to be released at the end of 2016, Poland has instead opted to revise plans for 2017–22 within the framework of the TMP 2013–22. In part, these revisions reflect delays caused by financial constraints, inefficiencies in the acquisition process and evolving requirements. Warsaw continues plans to strengthen its domestic defence-industrial base. Technology transfer and international partnering are seen as mechanisms to develop domestic industry, most of which is now consolidated in the government-owned holding company PGZ. Defence spending is planned to reach 2.5% of GDP by 2030. Poland intends to build up its own A2/AD capacity and in its 2017 Defence Concept expressed an interest in pursuing research in emerging technologies. Warsaw has also established a fund to bolster the defence-modernisation ambitions of neighbours under the Regional Security Assistance Programme. Recruitment for the first six brigades of a Territorial Defence Force is under way with the first volunteers completing basic training in May 2017. The full force is due to be established by 2019.

ACTIVE 105,000 (Army 61,200 Navy 7,400 Air Force 18,700 Special Forces 3,400 Territorial 800 Joint 13,500) Paramilitary 73,400

ORGANISATIONS BY SERVICE

Army 61,200
FORCES BY ROLE
COMMAND
  elm 1 (MNC NE) corps HQ
MANOEUVRE
  Reconnaissance
  3 recce regt
  Armoured
  1 (11th) armd cav div (2 armd bde, 1 mech bde, 1 arty regt)
  Mechanised
  1 (12th) div (2 mech bde, 1 (coastal) mech bde, 1 arty regt)
  1 (16th) div (2 armd bde, 2 mech bde, 1 arty regt)
  1 (21st) mech bde (1 armd bn, 3 mech bn, 1 arty bn, 1 AD bn, 1 engr bn)
  Air Manoeuvre
  1 (6th) air aslt bde (3 air aslt bn)
  1 (25th) air cav bde (3 air cav bn, 2 tpt hel bn, 1 (casevac) med unit)
COMBAT SUPPORT
  2 engr regt
  1 ptn br regt
  2 chem regt
HELICOPTER
  1 (1st) hel bde (2 atk hel sqn with Mi-24D/V *Hind* D/E, 1 CSAR sqn with Mi-24V *Hind* E; PZL W-3PL *Gluszec*; 2 ISR hel sqn with Mi-2URP; 2 hel sqn with Mi-2)
AIR DEFENCE
  3 AD regt
EQUIPMENT BY TYPE
ARMOURED FIGHTING VEHICLES
  MBT 937: 142 *Leopard* 2A4; 105 *Leopard* 2A5; 232 PT-91 *Twardy*; 458 T-72/T-72M1D/T-72M1

RECCE 407: 282 BRDM-2; 38 BWR; 87 WD R-5
IFV 1,636: 1,277 BMP-1; 359 *Rosomak* IFV
APC 249
  APC (W) 219: 211 *Rosomak* APC; 8 RAK (CP)
  PPV 30 *Maxxpro*
  AUV 85: 40 *Cougar* (on loan from US); 45 M-ATV
ENGINEERING & MAINTENANCE VEHICLES
  AEV 17+: IWT; MT-LB; 17 *Rosomak* WRT
  ARV 56: 15 BPz-2; 15 MT-LB; 26 WZT-3M
  VLB 62: 4 *Biber*; 48 BLG67M2; 10 MS-20 *Daglezja*
  MW 18: 14 *Bozena*; 4 *Kalina* SUM
ANTI-TANK/ANTI-INFRASTRUCTURE
  MSL • MANPATS 9K11 *Malyutka* (AT-3 *Sagger*); 9K111 *Fagot* (AT-4 *Spigot*); *Spike*-LR
ARTILLERY 807
  SP 427: **122mm** 292 2S1 *Gvozdika*; **152mm** 111 M-77 *Dana*; **155mm** 24 *Krab*
  MRL **122mm** 180: 75 BM-21; 30 RM-70; 75 WR-40 *Langusta*
  MOR 200: **98mm** 89 M-98; **120mm** 95 M120; **SP 120mm** 16 RAK-A
RADAR • LAND 3 LIWIEC (veh, arty)
HELICOPTERS
  ATK 28 Mi-24D/V *Hind* D/E
  MRH 64: 7 Mi-8MT *Hip*; 3 Mi-17 *Hip* H; 1 Mi-17AE *Hip* (aeromedical); 5 Mi-17-1V *Hip*; 16 PZL Mi-2URP *Hoplite*; 24 PZL W-3W/WA *Sokol*; 8 PZL W-3PL *Gluszec* (CSAR)
  TPT 34: **Medium** 9: 7 Mi-8T *Hip*; 2 PZL W-3AE *Sokol* (aeromedical); **Light** 25 PZL Mi-2 *Hoplite*
AIR DEFENCE
  SAM
    Short-range 20 2K12 *Kub* (SA-6 *Gainful*)
    Point-defence 64+: 9K32 *Strela*-2‡ (SA-7 *Grail*); 64 9K33 *Osa*-AK (SA-8 *Gecko*); GROM
  GUNS 352
    SP **23mm** 28: 8 ZSU-23-4; 20 ZSU-23-4MP *Biala*
    TOWED **23mm** 324; 252 ZU-23-2; 72 ZUR-23-2KG/PG

Navy 7,400
EQUIPMENT BY TYPE
SUBMARINES • TACTICAL 5
  SSK 5:
    4 *Sokol* (ex-NOR Type-207) with 8 single 533mm TT
    1 *Orzel* (ex-FSU *Kilo*) with 6 single 533mm TT each with 53-65 HWT (currently non-operational; has been in refit since 2014; damaged by fire in 2017)
PRINCIPAL SURFACE COMBATANTS 2
  FRIGATES • FFGHM 2 *Pulaski* (ex-US *Oliver Hazard Perry*) with 1 Mk13 GMLS with RGM-84D/F *Harpoon* AShM/SM-1MR SAM, 2 triple 324mm ASTT with MU90 LWT, 1 *Phalanx* Block 1B CIWS, 1 76mm gun (capacity 2 SH-2G *Super Seasprite* ASW hel) (1 vessel used as training ship)
PATROL AND COASTAL COMBATANTS 4
  CORVETTES • FSM 1 *Kaszub* with 2 quad lnchr with 9K32 *Strela*-2 (SA-N-5 *Grail*) SAM, 2 twin 533mm ASTT with SET-53 HWT, 2 RBU 6000 *Smerch* 2 A/S mor, 1 76mm gun
  PCFGM 3:
    3 *Orkan* (ex-GDR *Sassnitz*) with 1 quad lnchr with RBS-15 Mk3 AShM, 1 quad lnchr (manual aiming) with *Strela*-2 (SA-N-5 *Grail*) SAM, 1 AK630 CIWS, 1 76mm gun
MINE WARFARE • MINE COUNTERMEASURES 21
  MCCS 1 *Kontradmirał Xawery Czernicki*
  MHO 3 *Krogulec*
  MSI 17: 1 *Gopło*; 12 *Gardno*; 4 *Mamry*
AMPHIBIOUS 8
  LANDING SHIPS • LSM 5 *Lublin* (capacity 9 tanks; 135 troops)
  LANDING CRAFT • LCU 3 *Deba* (capacity 50 troops)
LOGISTICS AND SUPPORT 21
  AGI 2 *Moma*
  AGS 9: 2 *Heweliusz*; 4 *Wildcat* 40; 3 (coastal)
  AORL 1 *Baltyk*
  AOL 1 *Moskit*
  ARS 4: 2 *Piast*; 2 *Zbyszko*
  ATF 2
  AX 1 *Wodnik* with 1 twin AK230 CIWS
  AXS 1 *Iskra*
COASTAL DEFENCE • AShM 6+: 6 NSM; MM40 *Exocet*
AIR DEFENCE • SAM
  Short-range *Crotale* NG/GR

Naval Aviation 1,300
FORCES BY ROLE
ANTI SUBMARINE WARFARE/SEARCH & RESCUE
  1 sqn with Mi-14PL *Haze* A; Mi-14PL/R *Haze* C
  1 sqn with PZL W-3RM *Anakonda*; SH-2G *Super Seasprite*
MARITIME PATROL
  1 sqn with An-28RM; An-28E
TRANSPORT
  1 sqn with An-28TD; M-28B TD *Bryza*
  1 sqn with An-28TD; M-28B; Mi-17 *Hip* H; PZL Mi-2 *Hoplite*; PZL W-3T; 1 PZL W-3A
EQUIPMENT BY TYPE
AIRCRAFT
  MP 10: 8 An-28RM *Bryza*; 2 An-28E *Bryza*
  TPT • **Light** 4: 2 An-28TD *Bryza*; 2 M-28B TD *Bryza*
HELICOPTERS ASW 11: 7 Mi-14PL *Haze*; 4 SH-2G *Super Seasprite*
  MRH 1 Mi-17 *Hip* H
  SAR 8: 2 Mi-14PL/R *Haze* C; 4 PZL W-3RM *Anakonda*; 2 PZL W-3WA RM *Anakonda*
  TPT • **Light** 7: 4 PZL Mi-2 *Hoplite*; 1 PZL W-3A; 2 PZL-W-3T

Air Force 18,700
Flying hours   160–200 hrs/yr
FORCES BY ROLE
FIGHTER
  2 sqn with MiG-29A/UB *Fulcrum*
FIGHTER/GROUND ATTACK
  3 sqn with F-16C/D Block 52+ *Fighting Falcon*
FIGHTER/GROUND ATTACK/ISR
  2 sqn with Su-22M-4 *Fitter*
SEARCH AND RESCUE
  1 sqn with Mi-2; PZL W-3 *Sokol*
TRANSPORT
  1 sqn with C-130E; PZL M-28 *Bryza*
  1 sqn with C-295M; PZL M-28 *Bryza*

TRAINING
  1 sqn with PZL-130 *Orlik*
  1 sqn with TS-11 *Iskra*
  1 hel sqn with SW-4 *Puszczyk*
TRANSPORT HELICOPTER
  1 (Spec Ops) sqn with Mi-17 *Hip* H
  1 (VIP) sqn with Mi-8; W-3WA *Sokol*
AIR DEFENCE
  1 bde with S-125 *Neva* SC (SA-3 *Goa*); S-200C *Vega* (SA-5 *Gammon*)

EQUIPMENT BY TYPE
AIRCRAFT 99 combat capable
  FTR 33: 26 MiG-29A *Fulcrum*; 7 MiG-29UB *Fulcrum*
  FGA 66: 36 F-16C Block 52+ *Fighting Falcon*; 12 F-16D Block 52+ *Fighting Falcon*; 12 Su-22M-4 *Fitter*; 6 Su-22UM3K *Fitter*
  TPT 45: **Medium** 5 C-130E *Hercules*; **Light** 39: 16 C-295M; 23 M-28 *Bryza* TD; **PAX** 1 Gulfstream G550
  TRG 62: 2 M-346; 28 PZL-130 *Orlik*; 32 TS-11 *Iskra*
HELICOPTERS
  MRH 8 Mi-17 *Hip* H
  TPT 69: **Medium** 29: 9 Mi-8 *Hip*; 10 PZL W-3 *Sokol*; 10 PZL W-3WA *Sokol* (VIP); **Light** 40: 16 PZL Mi-2 *Hoplite*; 24 SW-4 *Puszczyk* (trg)
AIR DEFENCE • SAM
  Long-range 1 S-200C *Vega* (SA-5 *Gammon*)
  Short-range 17 S-125 *Neva* SC (SA-3 *Goa*)
AIR-LAUNCHED MISSILES
  AAM • IR R-60 (AA-8 *Aphid*); R-73 (AA-11 *Archer*); AIM-9 *Sidewinder*; R-27T (AA-10B *Alamo*); IIR AIM-9X *Sidwinder* II; ARH AIM-120C AMRAAM
  ASM AGM-65J/G *Maverick*; Kh-25 (AS-10 *Karen*); Kh-29 (AS-14 *Kedge*)
  LACM **Conventional** AGM-158 JASSM

Special Forces 3,400
FORCES BY ROLE
SPECIAL FORCES
  3 SF units (GROM, FORMOZA & cdo)
COMBAT SUPPORT/
  1 cbt spt unit (AGAT)
COMBAT SERVICE SUPPORT
  1 spt unit (NIL)

Territorial Defence Forces 800
FORCES BY ROLE
MANOEUVRE
  Light
    1 (1st) sy bde (2 sy bn)
    2 (2nd & 3rd) sy bde (1 sy bn)

Paramilitary 73,400

Border Guards 14,300
Ministry of Interior

Maritime Border Guard 3,700
EQUIPMENT BY TYPE
PATROL AND COASTAL COMBATANTS 18
  PCC 2 *Kaper*
  PBF 6: 2 *Straznik*; 4 IC16M
  PB 10: 2 *Wisloka*; 2 *Baltic* 24; 1 Project MI-6
AMPHIBIOUS • LANDING CRAFT • UCAC 2 *Griffon* 2000TDX

Prevention Units (Police) 59,100
Anti-terrorist Operations Bureau n.k.
Ministry of Interior

Cyber
The National Security Bureau issued a cyber-security doctrine in January 2015. The doctrine specifies significant tasks needed in order to build national cyber-security capability. It was reported that the document noted the need to pursue 'active cyber defence, including offensive actions in cyberspace, and maintaining readiness for cyberwar'. A draft version of a cyber-security strategy for 2018–22 emerged, noting the requirement for tools to enable military activities in cyberspace. The defence minister said in October 2017 that the defence ministry was to create 'cyberspace forces', numbering around 1,000.

DEPLOYMENT

AFGHANISTAN
NATO • *Operation Resolute Support* 220
UN • UNAMA 1 obs

ARMENIA/AZERBAIJAN
OSCE • Minsk Conference 1

BOSNIA-HERZEGOVINA
EU • EUFOR • *Operation Althea* 39

CENTRAL AFRICAN REPUBLIC
EU • EUTM RCA 1

DEMOCRATIC REPUBLIC OF THE CONGO
UN • MONUSCO 2 obs

IRAQ
Operation Inherent Resolve 60

KUWAIT
Operation Inherent Resolve 4 F-16C *Fighting Falcon*

LATVIA
NATO • Enhanced Forward Presence 160; 1 tk coy

SERBIA
NATO • KFOR 240; 1 inf coy
UN • UNMIK 1 obs

SOUTH SUDAN
UN • UNMISS 1 obs

UKRAINE
OSCE • Ukraine 35

WESTERN SAHARA
UN • MINURSO 1 obs

FOREIGN FORCES

All NATO Enhanced Forward Presence unless stated
Croatia 78; 1 MRL bty with BM-21 *Grad*
Germany MNC-NE corps HQ: 67
Romania 120; 1 ADA bty; 1 MP coy
United Kingdom 150; 1 recce sqn
United States: 850; 1 mech bn • *Operation Atlantic Resolve* 2,100; 1 armd bde HQ; 1 armd cav sqn(-); 1 SP arty bn; M1 *Abrams*; M3 *Bradley*; M109; 1 atk hel flt with AH-64E *Apache*; 1 tpt hel flt with 4 UH-60 *Black Hawk*

Portugal PRT

Euro €		2016	2017	2018
GDP	€	185bn	194bn	
	US$	205bn	212bn	
per capita	US$	19,821	20,575	
Growth	%	1.4	2.5	
Inflation	%	0.6	1.6	
Def exp [a]	€	2.36bn	2.51bn	
	US$	2.62bn	2.74bn	
Def bdgt	€	2.21bn	2.24bn	2.18bn
	US$	2.44bn	2.44bn	
US$1=€		0.90	0.92	

[a] NATO definition

Population 10,839,514

Age	0–14	15–19	20–24	25–29	30–64	65 plus
Male	8.0%	3.0%	3.0%	3.2%	23.8%	7.9%
Female	7.4%	2.7%	2.6%	2.8%	24.2%	11.5%

Capabilities

Principal roles for the armed forces include NATO, EU and UN operations, homeland defence and maritime security. Portugal's military-planning law for 2015–26 set key milestones for platform-acquisition and modernisation programmes. The plan envisages a reduction in army strength and the recalibration of the forces into 'immediate reaction forces', 'permanent forces for the defence of national sovereignty' and modular forces. Investment plans support Portugal's ambition to field rapid-reaction and maritime-surveillance capabilities for territorial defence and multinational operations. Army-upgrade plans include enhancing the electronic-warfare capacity, while in 2017, air defence was bolstered by government approval for the acquisition of the SHORAD missile system via the NATO Support and Procurement Agency. The navy intends to modernise its frigates and submarines and to acquire patrol vessels and a logistic-support vessel. The air force plans to modernise its remaining F-16s and its P-3C *Orion* maritime-patrol aircraft, replace its *Alouette* III helicopters and continue acquiring precision-guided munitions. In June 2017, Portugal began negotiations with Brazil's Embraer for the purchase of KC-390 tanker/transport aircraft, with a planned initial operating capability in 2021.

ACTIVE 30,500 (Army 16,500 Navy 8,000 Air 6,000)
Paramilitary 44,000

RESERVE 211,950 (Army 210,000 Navy 1,250, Air Force 700)
Reserve obligation to age 35

ORGANISATIONS BY SERVICE

Army 16,500
5 territorial comd (2 mil region, 1 mil district, 2 mil zone)
FORCES BY ROLE
SPECIAL FORCES
  1 SF bn
MANOEUVRE
  Reconnaissance
  1 ISR bn
  Mechanised
  1 mech bde (1 cav tp, 1 tk regt, 2 mech inf bn, 1 arty bn, 1 AD bty, 1 engr coy, 1 sigs coy, 1 spt bn)
  1 (intervention) bde (1 cav tp, 1 recce regt, 2 mech inf bn, 1 arty bn, 1 AD bty, 1 engr coy, 1 sigs coy, 1 spt bn)
  Air Manoeuvre
  1 (rapid reaction) bde (1 cav tp, 1 cdo bn, 2 para bn, 1 arty bn, 1 AD bty, 1 engr coy, 1 sigs coy, 1 spt bn)
  Other
  1 (Azores) inf gp (2 inf bn, 1 AD bty)
  1 (Madeira) inf gp (1 inf bn, 1 AD bty)
COMBAT SUPPORT
  1 STA bty
  1 engr bn
  1 EOD unit
  1 ptn br coy
  1 EW coy
  2 MP coy
  1 CBRN coy
  1 psyops unit
  1 CIMIC coy (joint)
  1 sigs bn
COMBAT SERVICE SUPPORT
  1 construction coy
  1 maint coy
  1 log coy
  1 tpt coy
  1 med unit
AIR DEFENCE
  1 AD bn

Reserves 210,000
FORCES BY ROLE
MANOEUVRE
  Light
  3 (territorial) def bde (on mobilisation)
EQUIPMENT BY TYPE
ARMOURED FIGHTING VEHICLES
  MBT 58: 37 *Leopard* 2A6; 21 M60A3 TTS
  RECCE 48: 14 V-150 *Chaimite*; 34 VBL
  IFV 22 *Pandur* II MK 30mm
  APC 416
    APC (T) 255: 173 M113A1; 33 M113A2; 49 M577A2 (CP)

APC (W) 165: 21 V-200 *Chaimite*; 144 *Pandur* II (all variants)
ENGINEERING & MAINTENANCE VEHICLES
AEV M728
ARV 13: 6 M88A1, 7 *Pandur*
VLB M48
ANTI-TANK/ANTI-INFRASTRUCTURE
MSL
SP 20: 16 M113 with TOW; 4 M901 with TOW
MANPATS *Milan*; TOW
RCL 236: **84mm** 162 *Carl Gustav*; **90mm** 29 M67; **106mm** 45 M40A1
ARTILLERY 323
SP 155mm 24: 6 M109A2; 18 M109A5
TOWED 65: **105mm** 41: 17 L119 Light Gun; 21 M101A1; 3 Model 56 pack howitzer; **155mm** 24 M114A1
MOR 234: **81mm** 143; **SP 81mm** 12: 2 M125A1; 10 M125A2; **107mm** 11 M30; **SP 107mm** 18: 3 M106A1; 15 M106A2; **120mm** 50 Tampella
AIR DEFENCE
SAM • Point-defence 24+: 5 M48A2 *Chaparral*; 19 M48A3 *Chaparral*; FIM-92 *Stinger*
GUNS • TOWED **20mm** 24 Rh 202

Navy 8,000 (incl 1,250 Marines)
EQUIPMENT BY TYPE
SUBMARINES • TACTICAL • SSK 2 *Tridente* (GER Type-214) with 8 533mm TT with *Black Shark* HWT
PRINCIPAL SURFACE COMBATANTS 5
FRIGATES • FFGHM 5:
2 *Bartolomeu Dias* (ex-NLD *Karel Doorman*) with 2 quad Mk141 lnchr with RGM-84C *Harpoon* AShM, 1 16-cell Mk48 VLS with RIM-7M *Sea Sparrow* SAM, 2 Mk32 twin 324mm ASTT with Mk46 LWT, 1 *Goalkeeper* CIWS, 1 76mm gun (capacity: 1 *Lynx* Mk95 (*Super Lynx*) hel)
3 *Vasco Da Gama* with 2 quad Mk141 lnchr with RGM-84C *Harpoon* AShM, 1 octuple Mk 29 GMLS with RIM-7M *Sea Sparrow* SAM, 2 Mk32 triple 324mm ASTT with Mk46 LWT, 1 *Phalanx* Block 1B CIWS, 1 100mm gun (capacity 2 *Lynx* Mk95 (*Super Lynx*) hel)
PATROL AND COASTAL COMBATANTS 20
CORVETTES • FS 3:
1 *Baptista de Andrade* with 1 100mm gun, 1 hel landing platform
2 *Joao Coutinho* with 1 twin 76mm gun, 1 hel landing platform
PSO 2 *Viana do Castelo* with 1 hel landing platform
PCC 3: 2 *Cacine*; 1 *Tejo* (ex-DNK *Flyvisken*)
PBR 12: 2 *Albatroz*; 5 *Argos*; 4 *Centauro*; 1 *Rio Minho*
LOGISTICS AND SUPPORT 11
AGS 4: 2 *D Carlos* I (ex-US *Stalwart*); 2 *Andromeda*
AORL 1 *Bérrio* (ex-UK *Rover*) with 1 hel landing platform (for medium hel)
AXS 6: 1 *Sagres*; 1 *Creoula*; 1 *Polar*; 2 *Belatrix*; 1 *Zarco*

Marines 1,250
FORCES BY ROLE
SPECIAL FORCES
1 SF det
MANOEUVRE
Light
2 lt inf bn
COMBAT SUPPORT
1 mor coy
1 MP det
EQUIPMENT BY TYPE
ARTILLERY • MOR **120mm** 30

Naval Aviation
EQUIPMENT BY TYPE
HELICOPTERS • ASW 5 *Lynx* Mk95 (*Super Lynx*)

Air Force 6,000
Flying hours 180 hrs/yr on F-16 *Fighting Falcon*
FORCES BY ROLE
FIGHTER/GROUND ATTACK
2 sqn with F-16AM/BM *Fighting Falcon*
MARITIME PATROL
1 sqn with P-3C *Orion*
ISR/TRANSPORT
1 sqn with C295M
COMBAT SEARCH & RESCUE
1 sqn with with AW101 *Merlin*
TRANSPORT
1 sqn with C-130H/C-130H-30 *Hercules*
1 sqn with *Falcon* 50
TRAINING
1 sqn with *Alpha Jet**
1 sqn with SA316 *Alouette* III
1 sqn with TB-30 *Epsilon*
EQUIPMENT BY TYPE
AIRCRAFT 41 combat capable
FTR 30: 26 F-16AM *Fighting Falcon*; 4 F-16BM *Fighting Falcon*
ASW 5 P-3C *Orion*
ISR: 7: 5 C295M (maritime surveillance), 2 C295M (photo recce)
TPT 13: **Medium** 5: 2 C-130H *Hercules*; 3 C-130H-30 *Hercules* (tpt/SAR); **Light** 5 C295M; **PAX** 3 *Falcon* 50 (tpt/VIP)
TRG 22: 6 *Alpha Jet**; 16 TB-30 *Epsilon*
HELICOPTERS
MRH 6 SA316 *Alouette* III (trg, utl)
TPT • **Medium** 12 AW101 *Merlin* (6 SAR, 4 CSAR, 2 fishery protection)
AIR-LAUNCHED MISSILES
AAM • IR AIM-9L/I *Sidewinder*; ARH AIM-120C AMRAAM
ASM AGM-65A *Maverick*
AShM AGM-84A *Harpoon*
BOMBS
Laser-guided/GPS GBU-49 *Enhanced Paveway* II
INS/GPS guided GBU-31 JDAM

Paramilitary 44,000

National Republican Guard 22,400
EQUIPMENT BY TYPE
PATROL AND COASTAL COMBATANTS 32

PBF 12
PB 20
HELICOPTERS • MRH 7 SA315 *Lama*

Public Security Police 21,600

Cyber

The 2013 Cyber Defence Policy Guidance established a national cyber-defence structure. Portugal released a National Cyberspace Security Strategy in 2015, which called for the country to develop a cyber-defence capacity and consolidate the role of the National Centre for Cyber Security. The strategic-military aspects of cyber defence are the responsibility of the Council of the Chiefs of Staff. A Center for Cyber Defence, under the Directorate of Communications and Information Systems of the General Staff, reached FOC in 2017. Cyber-defence units within the three branches of the armed forces are responsible for responding to cyber attacks.

DEPLOYMENT

AFGHANISTAN
NATO • Operation Resolute Support 10
UN • UNAMA 2 obs

CENTRAL AFRICAN REPUBLIC
EU • EUTM RCA 11
UN • MINUSCA 150; 1 cdo coy

IRAQ
Operation Inherent Resolve 31

MALI
EU • EUTM Mali 11
UN • MINUSMA 2

MEDITERRANEAN SEA
EU • EUNAVFOR MED 1 SSK
NATO • SNMG 1: 1 FFGHM

SERBIA
NATO • KFOR 15
OSCE • Kosovo 1

SOMALIA
EU • EUTM Somalia 4

UKRAINE
OSCE • Ukraine 3

FOREIGN FORCES

United States US European Command: 200; 1 spt facility at Lajes

Romania ROM

New Lei		2016	2017	2018
GDP	lei	761bn	828bn	
	US$	188bn	205bn	
per capita	US$	9,493	10,372	
Growth	%	4.8	5.5	
Inflation	%	-1.6	1.1	
Def exp [a]	lei	10.7bn	16.3bn	
	US$	2.65bn	4.04bn	
Def bdgt [b]	lei	11.2bn	16.3bn	
	US$	2.76bn	4.04bn	
FMA (US)	US$	4.4m	4.4m	0m
US$1=lei		4.06	4.04	

[a] NATO definition
[b] Includes military pensions

Population   21,529,967

Age	0–14	15–19	20–24	25–29	30–64	65 plus
Male	7.4%	2.7%	2.8%	3.6%	25.6%	6.6%
Female	7.0%	2.5%	2.6%	3.5%	26.0%	9.8%

Capabilities

Romania intends to modernise its forces, with ageing Soviet-era equipment seen as a factor limiting its military capability. According to a government strategy approved in August 2017, Romania is to replace its MiG-21 fleet by 2020 and acquire new combat helicopters. The country is additionally seeking to procure corvettes, armoured vehicles and rocket artillery; the plan is to acquire US-manufactured High Mobility Artillery Rocket Systems. Acquisition of the *Patriot* air-defence system was approved by the US State Department, and Romania signed a LoA with the US Army in November. The financing of ongoing projects and meeting critical procurement requirements are key components of the 2017–26 defence plan. The Supreme Defence Council pledged to spend 2% of GDP on defence. In 2017, Canada and the UK, in rotation, deployed forces to Romania as part of a NATO Air Policing Mission. The *Aegis* Ashore ballistic-missile-defence system was activated at the US Naval Support Facility Deveselu. It is expected to become fully operational in 2018. Romania's armed forces have traditionally been structured around territorial defence and support to NATO, contributing to missions in Afghanistan and Iraq during the last decade.

ACTIVE 69,300 (Army 36,000 Navy 6,500 Air 10,300 Joint 16,500) **Paramilitary 79,900**

RESERVE 50,000 (Joint 50,000)

ORGANISATIONS BY SERVICE

Army 36,000

Readiness is reported as 70–90% for NATO-designated forces (1 div HQ, 1 mech bde, 1 inf bde & 1 mtn inf bde) and 40–70% for other forces

FORCES BY ROLE
COMMAND
2 div HQ (2nd & 4th)
elm 1 div HQ (MND-SE)
SPECIAL FORCES
1 SF bde (2 SF bn, 1 para bn, 1 log bn)
MANOEUVRE
Reconnaissance
1 recce bde
2 recce regt
Mechanised
5 mech bde (1 tk bn, 2 mech inf bn, 1 arty bn, 1 AD bn, 1 log bn)
Light
1 (MNB-SE) inf bde (3 inf bn, 1 arty bn, 1 AD bn, 1 log bn)
2 mtn inf bde (3 mtn inf bn, 1 arty bn, 1 AD bn, 1 log bn)
COMBAT SUPPORT
1 MRL bde (3 MRL bn, 1 STA bn, 1 log bn)
2 arty regt
1 engr bde (4 engr bn, 1 ptn br bn, 1 log bn)
2 engr bn
3 sigs bn
1 CIMIC bn
1 MP bn
3 CBRN bn
COMBAT SERVICE SUPPORT
4 spt bn
AIR DEFENCE
3 AD regt

EQUIPMENT BY TYPE
ARMOURED FIGHTING VEHICLES
  MBT 460: 260 T-55; 42 TR-580; 104 TR-85; 54 TR-85 M1
  IFV 124: 23 MLI-84; 101 MLI-84 JDER
  APC 1,253
    APC (T) 76 MLVM
    APC (W) 643: 69 B33 TAB *Zimbru*; 31 *Piranha* III; 390 TAB-71; 153 TAB-77
    TYPE VARIANTS 474 APC
    PPV 60 *Maxxpro*
    AUV 377 TABC-79
ENGINEERING & MAINTENANCE VEHICLES
  ARV 3 BPz-2
ANTI-TANK/ANTI-INFRASTRUCTURE
  MSL • SP 134: 12 9P122 *Malyutka* (AT-3 *Sagger*); 74 9P133 *Malyutka* (AT-3 *Sagger*); 48 9P148 *Konkurs* (AT-5 *Spandrel*)
  GUNS
    SP 100mm 23 SU-100
    TOWED 100mm 222 M-1977
  ARTILLERY 927
    SP 122mm 24: 6 2S1; 18 Model 89
    TOWED 449: **122mm** 98 (M-30) M-1938 (A-19); **152mm** 351: 247 M-1981; 104 M-1985
    MRL 122mm 188: 134 APR-40; 54 LAROM
    MOR 120mm 266 M-1982
  RADARS • LAND 9 SNAR-10 *Big Fred*
AIR DEFENCE
  SAM • Short-range 32 2K12 *Kub* (SA-6 *Gainful*)
  GUNS 60
    SP 35mm 36 *Gepard*
    TOWED 35mm 24 GDF-203

Navy 6,600
EQUIPMENT BY TYPE
PRINCIPAL SURFACE COMBATANTS 3
  DESTROYERS 3
    DDGH 1 *Marasesti* with 4 twin lnchr with P-15M *Termit-M* (SS-N-2C *Styx*) AShM, 2 triple 533mm ASTT with 53–65 HWT, 2 RBU 6000 *Smerch* 2 A/S mor, 2 twin 76mm guns (capacity 2 SA-316 (IAR-316) *Alouette* III hel)
    DDH 2 *Regele Ferdinand* (ex-UK Type-22), with 2 triple 324mm TT, 1 76mm gun (capacity 1 SA330 (IAR-330) *Puma*)
PATROL AND COASTAL COMBATANTS 24
  CORVETTES 4
    FSH 2 *Tetal* II with 2 twin 533mm ASTT, 2 RBU 6000 *Smerch* 2 A/S mor, 2 AK630 CIWS, 1 76mm gun (capacity 1 SA316 (IAR-316) *Alouette* III hel)
    FS 2 *Tetal* I with 2 twin 533mm ASTT with 53-65E HWT, 2 RBU 2500 *Smerch* 1 A/S mor, 2 twin 76mm guns
  PCFG 3 *Zborul* with 2 twin lnchr with P-15M *Termit*-M (SS-N-2C *Styx*) AShM, 2 AK630 CIWS, 1 76mm gun
  PCFT 3 *Naluca* with 4 single 533mm ASTT
  PCR 8:
    5 *Brutar* II with 2 BM-21 MRL, 1 100mm gun
    3 *Kogalniceanu* with 2 BM-21 MRL, 2 100mm guns
  PBR 6 VD141 (ex-MSR now used for river patrol)
MINE WARFARE 11
  MINE COUNTERMEASURES 10
    MSO 4 *Musca* with 2 RBU 1200 A/S mor, 2 AK230 CIWS
    MSR 6 VD141
  MINELAYERS • ML 1 *Corsar* with up to 100 mines, 2 RBU 1200 A/S mor, 1 57mm gun
LOGISTICS AND SUPPORT 8
  AE 2 *Constanta* with 2 RBU 1200 A/S mor, 2 twin 57mm guns
  AGOR 1 *Corsar*
  AGS 2: 1 *Emil Racovita*; 1 *Catuneanu*
  AOL 1 *Tulcea*
  ATF 1 *Grozavu*
  AXS 1 *Mircea*

Naval Infantry
FORCES BY ROLE
MANOEUVRE
  Light
  1 naval inf bn
EQUIPMENT BY TYPE
ARMOURED FIGHTING VEHICLES
  AUV 14: 11 ABC-79M; 3 TABC-79M

Air Force 10,300
Flying hours 120 hrs/yr

FORCES BY ROLE
FIGHTER
  2 sqn with MiG-21 *Lancer* C
FIGHTER GROUND ATTACK
  1 sqn (forming) with with F-16AM/BM *Fighting Falcon*

GROUND ATTACK
1 sqn with IAR-99 *Soim*
TRANSPORT
1 sqn with An-30 *Clank*; C-27J *Spartan*
1 sqn with C-130B/H *Hercules*
TRAINING
1 sqn with IAR-99 *Soim**
1 sqn with SA316B *Alouette* III (IAR-316B); Yak-52 (Iak-52)
TRANSPORT HELICOPTER
2 (multi-role) sqn with IAR-330 SOCAT *Puma*
3 sqn with SA330 *Puma* (IAR-330)
AIR DEFENCE
1 AD bde
COMBAT SERVICE SUPPORT
1 engr spt regt
EQUIPMENT BY TYPE
AIRCRAFT 55 combat capable
  FTR 9: 7 F-16AM *Fighting Falcon*; 2 F-16BM *Fighting Falcon*
  FGA 25: 6 MiG-21 *Lancer* B; 19 MiG-21 *Lancer* C
  ISR 2 An-30 *Clank*
  TPT • Medium 12: 7 C-27J *Spartan*; 4 C-130B *Hercules*; 1 C-130H *Hercules*
  TRG 33: 10 IAR-99*; 11 IAR-99C *Soim**; 12 Yak-52 (Iak-52)
HELICOPTERS
  MRH 30: 22 IAR-330 SOCAT *Puma*; 8 SA316B *Alouette* III (IAR-316B)
  TPT • Medium 36: 21 SA330L *Puma* (IAR-330L); 15 SA330M *Puma* (IAR-330M)
AIR DEFENCE • SAM • Medium-range 14: 6 S-75M3 *Volkhov* (SA-2 *Guideline*); 8 MIM-23 *Hawk* PIP III
AIR-LAUNCHED MISSILES
  AAM • IR AIM-9M *Sidewinder*; R-73 (AA-11 *Archer*); R-550 *Magic* 2; *Python* 3 **ARH** AIM-120C AMRAAM
  ASM *Spike*-ER
BOMBS
  Laser-guided GBU-12 *Paveway*
  INS/GPS guided GBU-38 JDAM

Paramilitary 79,900

Border Guards 22,900 (incl conscripts)
Ministry of Interior
EQUIPMENT BY TYPE
PATROL AND COASTAL COMBATANTS 14
  PCO 1 *Stefan cel Mare* (Damen Stan OPV 950)
  PBF 1 *Bigliani*
  PB 12: 4 *Neustadt*; 3 *Mai*; 5 SNR-17

Gendarmerie ε57,000
Ministry of Interior

Cyber
Romania's 2013 and 2015 cyber-security strategies define the conceptual framework, aim, objectives, priorities and courses of action for providing cyber security at the national level. Romania's 2016 Military Strategy said the country needed to develop the legal framework to conduct operations in cyberspace. The defence ministry contains a military CERT (CERTMIL) and a Cyber Defence Command is expected to be established within the military command structure by 2018. Romania is the lead nation for the NATO Trust Fund established to develop Ukraine's cyber defences.

DEPLOYMENT

AFGHANISTAN
NATO • *Operation Resolute Support* 683; 1 inf bn
UN • UNAMA 4 obs

BOSNIA-HERZEGOVINA
EU • EUFOR • *Operation Althea* 39

CENTRAL AFRICAN REPUBLIC
EU • EUTM RCA 9

DEMOCRATIC REPUBLIC OF THE CONGO
UN • MONUSCO 17 obs

INDIA/PAKISTAN
UN • UNMOGIP 2 obs

IRAQ
Operation Inherent Resolve 50

MALI
EU • EUTM Mali 1
UN • MINUSMA 1

POLAND
NATO • Enhanced Forward Presence 120; 1 ADA bty; 1 MP coy

SERBIA
NATO • KFOR 61
UN • UNMIK 1 obs

SOMALIA
EU • EUTM Somalia 4

SOUTH SUDAN
UN • UNMISS 2; 4 obs

UKRAINE
OSCE • Ukraine 32

FOREIGN FORCES
Canada NATO Air Policing: 135; 4 F/A-18A *Hornet* (CF-18)
United States US European Command: 1,000; 1 armd inf bn HQ; 1 armd/armd inf coy; M1 *Abrams*; M2 *Bradley*; 1 tpt hel flt with 5 UH-60L *Black Hawk*

Serbia SER

Serbian Dinar d		2016	2017	2018
GDP	d	4.20tr	4.43tr	
	US$	37.7bn	39.4bn	
per capita	US$	5,348	5,600	
Growth	%	2.8	3.0	
Inflation	%	1.1	3.4	
Def bdgt	d	55.8bn	58.9bn	
	US$	501m	523m	
FMA (US)	US$	1.8m	1.8m	0m
US$1=d		111.28	112.62	

Population 7,111,024

Ethnic groups: Serbian 83.3%; Hungarian 3.35%; Romani 2.05%; Bosniac 2.02%; Croatian 0.8%

Age	0–14	15–19	20–24	25–29	30–64	65 plus
Male	7.5%	2.7%	3.1%	3.3%	24.6%	7.6%
Female	7.0%	2.6%	2.9%	3.1%	24.9%	10.8%

Capabilities

Principal missions for Serbia's armed forces include territorial defence, internal security and limited support to peacekeeping missions. The forces have reduced in size over the last decade. Plans to acquire Western military equipment have reportedly changed in favour of acquiring Russian hardware. In 2017, Serbia received six disassembled Russian MiG-29 fighters (currently non-operational). As part of a military-technical agreement between Russia and Serbia, Belgrade is expected to also receive a donation of T-72 main battle tanks and BRDM-2 reconnaissance vehicles. Serbia is also seeking to acquire S-300, improving in this way its air-defence capability. In 2017, Serbia joined the HELBROC Balkan battlegroup, led by Greece. The armed forces reportedly saw a 10% salary increase and additional recruitment of professional soldiers. The prime minister announced an intention to invest in the domestic defence industry, particularly to develop new factories and overhaul existing plants. Local production mainly focuses on missile and artillery systems, and small arms and ammunition. In 2017, Serbia took part in regional military exercises with its Balkan neighbours, the UK and the US, as well as with Belarus and Russia.

ACTIVE 28,150 (Army 13,250 Air Force and Air Defence 5,100 Training Command 3,000 Guards 1,600 Other MoD 5,200) **Paramilitary 3,700**
Conscript liability 6 months (voluntary)

RESERVE 50,150

ORGANISATIONS BY SERVICE

Army 13,250
FORCES BY ROLE
SPECIAL FORCES
 1 SF bde (1 CT bn, 1 cdo bn, 1 para bn, 1 log bn)

MANOEUVRE
 Mechanised
 1 (1st) bde (1 tk bn, 2 mech inf bn, 1 inf bn, 1 SP arty bn, 1 MRL bn, 1 AD bn, 1 engr bn, 1 log bn)
 3 (2nd, 3rd & 4th) bde (1 tk bn, 2 mech inf bn, 2 inf bn, 1 SP arty bn, 1 MRL bn, 1 AD bn, 1 engr bn, 1 log bn)
COMBAT SUPPORT
 1 (mixed) arty bde (4 arty bn, 1 MRL bn, 1 spt bn)
 2 ptn bridging bn
 1 NBC bn
 1 sigs bn
 2 MP bn

Reserve Organisations
FORCES BY ROLE
MANOEUVRE
 Light
 8 (territorial) inf bde

EQUIPMENT BY TYPE
ARMOURED FIGHTING VEHICLES
 MBT 212: 199 M-84; 13 T-72
 RECCE 46 BRDM-2
 IFV 335: 323 M-80; 12 *Lazar*-3
 APC 71
  APC(T) 32 MT-LB (CP)
  APC (W) 39 BOV-VP M-86; some *Lazar*-3
ENGINEERING & MAINTENANCE VEHICLES
 AEV IWT
 ARV M84A1; T-54/T-55
 VLB MT-55; TMM
ANTI-TANK/ANTI-INFRASTRUCTURE
 MSL
  SP 48 BOV-1 (M-83) with 9K11 *Malyutka* (AT-3 *Sagger*)
  MANPATS 9K11 *Malyutka* (AT-3 *Sagger*); 9K111 *Fagot* (AT-4 *Spigot*)
 RCL 90mm 6 M-79
ARTILLERY 443
 SP 67+: **122mm** 67 2S1 *Gvozdika*; **155mm** B-52 NORA
 TOWED 132: **122mm** 78 D-30; **130mm** 18 M-46; **152mm** 36 M-84 NORA-A
 MRL 81: **128mm** 78: 18 M-63 *Plamen*; 60 M-77 *Organj*; **262mm** 3 M-87 *Orkan*
 MOR 163: **82mm** 106 M-69; **120mm** 57 M-74/M-75
AIR DEFENCE
 SAM
  Short-range 77 2K12 *Kub* (SA-6 *Gainful*);
  Point-defence 17+: 12 9K31M *Strela*-1M (SA-9 *Gaskin*); 5 9K35M *Strela*-10M; 9K32M *Strela*-2M (SA-7 *Grail*)‡; *Šilo* (SA-16 *Gimlet*)
 GUNS • TOWED 40mm 36 Bofors L/70

River Flotilla
The Serbian–Montenegrin navy was transferred to Montenegro upon independence in 2006, but the Danube flotilla remained in Serbian control. The flotilla is subordinate to the Land Forces

EQUIPMENT BY TYPE
PATROL AND COASTAL COMBATANTS 5
 PBR 5: 3 Type-20; 2 others

MINE WARFARE • MINE COUNTERMEASURES 4
  MSI 4 *Nestin* with 1 quad lnchr with *Strela* 2M (SA-N-5 *Grail*) SAM
AMPHIBOUS • LANDING CRAFT • LCU 5 Type-22
LOGISTICS AND SUPPORT 2
  AGF 1 *Kozara*
  AOL 1

Air Force and Air Defence 5,100

Flying hours: Ftr – 40 hrs/yr
FORCES BY ROLE
FIGHTER
  1 sqn with MiG-21bis *Fishbed*; MiG-29 *Fulcrum*
FIGHTER/GROUND ATTACK
  1 sqn with G-4 *Super Galeb**; J-22 *Orao*
ISR
  2 flt with IJ-22 *Orao* 1*; MiG-21R *Fishbed* H*
TRANSPORT
  1 sqn with An-2; An-26; Do-28; Yak-40 (Jak-40); 1 PA-34 *Seneca* V
TRAINING
  1 sqn with G-4 *Super Galeb** (adv trg/light atk); SA341/342 *Gazelle*; Utva-75 (basic trg)
ATTACK HELICOPTER
  1 sqn with SA341H/342L *Gazelle*; (HN-42/45); Mi-24 *Hind*
TRANSPORT HELICOPTER
  2 sqn with Mi-8 *Hip*; Mi-17 *Hip* H; Mi-17V-5 *Hip*
AIR DEFENCE
  1 bde (5 bn (2 msl, 3 SP msl) with S-125 *Neva* (SA-3 *Goa*); 2K12 *Kub* (SA-6 *Gainful*); 9K32 *Strela*-2 (SA-7 *Grail*); 9K310 *Igla*-1 (SA-16 *Gimlet*))
  2 radar bn (for early warning and reporting)
COMBAT SUPPORT
  1 sigs bn
COMBAT SERVICE SUPPORT
  1 maint bn
EQUIPMENT BY TYPE
AIRCRAFT 65 combat capable
  FTR 13+ : 2+ MiG-21bis *Fishbed*; 2+ MiG-21UM *Mongol* B; 4 MiG-29 *Fulcrum*; 3 MiG-29UB *Fulcrum*; 2 MiG-29S *Fulcrum* C
  FGA 17 J-22 *Orao* 1
  ISR 12: 10 IJ-22R *Orao* 1*; 2 MiG-21R *Fishbed* H*
  TPT • Light 10: 1 An-2 *Colt*; 4 An-26 *Curl*; 2 Do-28 *Skyservant*; 2 Yak-40 (Jak-40); 1 PA-34 *Seneca* V
  TRG 44: 23 G-4 *Super Galeb**; 11 Utva-75; 10 *Lasta* 95
HELICOPTERS
  ATK 2 Mi-24 *Hind*
  MRH 52: 1 Mi-17 *Hip* H; 2 Mi-17V-5 *Hip*; 2 SA341H *Gazelle* (HI-42); 34 SA341H *Gazelle* (HN-42)/SA342L *Gazelle* (HN-45); 13 SA341H *Gazelle* (HO-42)/SA342L1 *Gazelle* (HO-45)
  TPT • Medium 8 Mi-8T *Hip* (HT-40)
AIR DEFENCE
  SAM
    Short-range 15: 6 S-125 *Pechora* (SA-3 *Goa*); 9 2K12 *Kub* (SA-6 *Gainful*)
    Point-defence 9K32 *Strela*-2 (SA-7 *Grail*)‡; 9K310 *Igla*-1 (SA-16 *Gimlet*)
  GUNS • TOWED 40mm 24 *Bofors* L/70
AIR-LAUNCHED MISSILES
  AAM • IR R-60 (AA-8 *Aphid*)
  ASM AGM-65 *Maverick*; A-77 *Thunder*

Guards 1,600
FORCES BY ROLE
MANOEUVRE
  Other
  1 (ceremonial) gd bde (1 gd bn, 1 MP bn, 1 spt bn)

Paramilitary 3,700

Gendarmerie 3,700
EQUIPMENT BY TYPE
ARMOURED FIGHTING VEHICLES
  APC • APC (W) 12+: some *Lazar*-3; 12 BOV-VP M-86
  AUV BOV M-16 *Milos*

DEPLOYMENT

ALBANIA
OSCE • Albania 2

BOSNIA-HERZEGOVINA
OSCE • Bosnia and Herzegovina 1

CENTRAL AFRICAN REPUBLIC
EU • EUTM RCA 7
UN • MINUSCA 69; 1 med coy

CYPRUS
UN • UNFICYP 47; 1 inf pl

DEMOCRATIC REPUBLIC OF THE CONGO
UN • MONUSCO 8

LEBANON
UN • UNIFIL 174; 1 mech inf coy

LIBERIA
UN • UNMIL 1 obs

MALI
EU • EUTM Mali 3

MIDDLE EAST
UN • UNTSO 1 obs

SOMALIA
EU • EUTM Somalia 6

UKRAINE
OSCE • Ukraine 10

TERRITORY WHERE THE GOVERNMENT DOES NOT EXERCISE EFFECTIVE CONTROL

Data here represents the de facto situation in Kosovo. This does not imply international recognition as a sovereign state. In February 2008, Kosovo declared itself independent. Serbia remains opposed to this, and while Kosovo has not been admitted to the United Nations, a number of states have recognised Kosovo's self-declared status.

Kosovo Security Force 2,500; reserves 800

The Kosovo Security Force (KSF) was formed in January 2009 as a non-military organisation with responsibility for crisis response, civil protection and EOD. In 2017, a proposal by Kosovan leaders to establish an army was opposed by Russia, Serbia, the US and NATO. The force is armed with small arms and light vehicles only. A July 2010 law created a reserve force. In 2017, a KSF contingent participated in the joint exercise KFOR 23 at the Joint Multinational Readiness Center in Germany.

FOREIGN FORCES

All under Kosovo Force (KFOR) command unless otherwise specified
Albania 28 • OSCE 3
Armenia 35
Austria 440; 2 mech inf coy
Bosnia-Herzegovina OSCE 8
Bulgaria 20 • OSCE 1
Canada 6 • OSCE 5
Croatia 33; 1 hel flt with Mi-8 • OSCE 1
Czech Republic 9 • OSCE 1 • UNMIK 2 obs
Denmark 35
Estonia 2
Finland 19
Georgia OSCE 1
Germany 650 • OSCE 4
Greece 112; 1 inf coy • OSCE 1
Hungary 373; 1 inf coy (KTM) • OSCE 1
Ireland 12 • OSCE 1
Italy 551; 1 inf BG HQ; 1 Carabinieri unit • OSCE 11
Kyrgyzstan OSCE 2
Lithuania 1
Luxembourg 23
Macedonia (FYROM) OSCE 14
Moldova 41 • OSCE 1 • UNMIK 1 obs
Montenegro OSCE 1
Netherlands OSCE 1
Norway 2 • OSCE 1
Poland 240; 1 inf coy • UNMIK 1 obs
Portugal 15 • OSCE 1
Romania 61 • UNMIK 1 obs
Russia OSCE 1
Slovenia 252; 1 mot inf coy; 1 MP unit; 1 hel unit
Spain OSCE 1
Sweden 3 • OSCE 3
Switzerland 234; 1 inf coy; 1 engr pl; 1 hel flt with AS332 • OSCE 1
Tajikistan OSCE 1
Turkey 307; 1 inf coy • UNMIK 1 obs
Ukraine 40 • OSCE 1 • UNMIK 2 obs
United Kingdom 29 • OSCE 7
United States 675; elm 1 ARNG inf bde HQ; 1 inf bn; 1 hel flt with UH-60 • OSCE 5

Slovakia SVK

Euro €		2016	2017	2018
GDP	€	81.0bn	84.3bn	
	US$	89.5bn	95.0bn	
per capita	US$	16,499	17,491	
Growth	%	3.3	3.3	
Inflation	%	-0.5	1.2	
Def exp [a]	€	907m	1.0bn	
	US$	1.00bn	1.13bn	
Def bdgt	€	881m	990m	1.07bn
	US$	974m	1.12bn	
US$1=€		0.90	0.89	

[a] NATO definition

Population 5,445,829

Age	0–14	15–19	20–24	25–29	30–64	65 plus
Male	7.8%	2.6%	3.0%	3.6%	25.5%	6.0%
Female	7.4%	2.5%	2.8%	3.5%	25.8%	9.4%

Capabilities

Slovakia released a defence white paper in September 2016, setting out its security priorities and a plan to increase defence capabilities. In 2017, the government approved a new defence strategy, a new military strategy and a Long-Term Defence Development Plan, which envisages spending rising to 1.6% of GDP by 2020 and 2% of GDP by 2024. Bratislava is planning to replace its small fighter and rotary-wing transport fleets, though financial constraints will make the outright replacement of the fighter fleet challenging. Slovakia announced in January 2017 that it was considering several offers for the purchase or lease of aircraft, including the *Gripen*-E. The *Gripen* is used by the Czech Republic, with whom the Slovak government signed a Joint Sky agreement to facilitate air policing and closer integration of air-defence capabilities. This was ratified by the Czech and Slovak parliaments in summer 2017. There are also ambitions to replace land equipment and improve the overall technology level in the armed forces. The government stated in May 2017 that it would seek to acquire a large number of 4x4 and 8x8 vehicles, and in November it was announced that Patria would develop a prototype based on the AMVXP 8x8 chassis for the programme. Also in May, and after amending the law on conscription, Slovakia implemented its Active Reserves pilot project, in order to help address shortfalls in specialist capacities, including in engineering.

ACTIVE 15,850 (Army 6,250 Air 3,950 Central Staff 2,550 Support and Training 3,100)
Conscript liability 6 months

ORGANISATIONS BY SERVICE

Central Staff 2,550
FORCES BY ROLE
SPECIAL FORCES
  1 (5th) spec ops bn

Army 6,250
FORCES BY ROLE
MANOEUVRE
Armoured
1 (2nd) armd bde (1 recce bn, 1 tk bn, 1 armd inf bn, 1 mot inf bn, 1 mixed SP arty bn)
Mechanised
1 (1st) mech bde (3 armd inf bn, 1 MRL bn, 1 engr bn, 1 NBC bn)
COMBAT SUPPORT
1 MP bn
COMBAT SERVICE SUPPORT
1 spt bde (2 log bn, 1 maint bn, 1 spt bn)
EQUIPMENT BY TYPE
ARMOURED FIGHTING VEHICLES
MBT 30 T-72M
IFV 239: 148 BMP-1; 91 BMP-2
APC 101+
　APC (T) 72 OT-90
　APC (W) 22: 7 OT-64; 15 Tatrapan (6×6)
　PPV 7+ RG-32M
AUV IVECO LMV
ENGINEERING & MAINTENANCE VEHICLES
ARV MT-55; VT-55A; VT-72B; WPT-TOPAS
VLB AM-50; MT-55A
MW Bozena; UOS-155 Belarty
ANTI-TANK/ANTI-INFRASTRUCTURE
SP 9S428 with *Malyutka* (AT-3 *Sagger*) on BMP-1; 9P135 *Fagot* (AT-4 *Spigot*) on BMP-2; 9P148 *Konkurs* (AT-5 *Spandrel*) on BRDM-2
MANPATS 9K11 *Malyutka* (AT-3 *Sagger*); 9K111-1 *Konkurs* (AT-5 *Spandrel*)
RCL 84mm *Carl Gustav*
ARTILLERY 68
SP 19: **152mm** 3 M-77 *Dana*; **155mm** 16 M-2000 *Zuzana*
TOWED 122mm 19 D-30
MRL 30: **122mm** 4 RM-70; **122/227mm** 26 RM-70/85 MODULAR
RADAR • LAND SNAR-10 *Big Fred* (veh, arty)
AIR DEFENCE • SAM
Point-defence 48+: 48 9K35 *Strela-10* (SA-13 *Gopher*); 9K32 *Strela-2* (SA-7 *Grail*); 9K310 *Igla-1* (SA-16 *Gimlet*)

Air Force 3,950
Flying hours 90 hrs/yr for MiG-29 pilots (NATO Integrated AD System); 90 hrs/yr for Mi-8/17 crews (reserved for EU & NATO)

FORCES BY ROLE
FIGHTER
1 sqn with MiG-29AS/UBS *Fulcrum*
TRANSPORT
1 flt with C-27J *Spartan*
1 flt with L-410FG/T/UVP *Turbolet*
TRANSPORT HELICOPTER
1 sqn with Mi-8 *Hip*; Mi-17 *Hip* H
1 sqn with PZL MI-2 *Hoplite*
TRAINING
1 sqn with L-39CM/ZA/ZAM *Albatros*

AIR DEFENCE
1 bde with 2K12 *Kub* (SA-6 *Gainful*); 9K32 *Strela-2* (SA-7 *Grail*); S-300 (SA-10 *Grumble*)
EQUIPMENT BY TYPE
AIRCRAFT 25 combat capable
FTR 12: 10 MiG-29AS *Fulcrum*; 2 MiG-29UBS *Fulcrum*;
TPT 9: **Medium** 1 C-27J *Spartan*; **Light** 8: 2 L-410FG *Turbolet*; 2 L-410T *Turbolet*; 4 L-410UVP *Turbolet*
TRG 13: 6 L-39CM *Albatros**; 5 L-39ZA *Albatros**; 2 L-39ZAM *Albatros**
HELICOPTERS
ATK (15: 5 Mi-24D *Hind* D; 10 Mi-24V *Hind* E all in store)
MRH 13 Mi-17 *Hip* H
TPT 9: **Medium** 3: 1 Mi-8 *Hip*; 2 UH-60M *Black Hawk*
Light 6 PZL MI-2 *Hoplite*
AIR DEFENCE • SAM
Long-range S-300PS (SA-10B *Grumble*)
Short-range 2K12 *Kub* (SA-6 *Gainful*)
Point-defence 9K32 *Strela-2* (SA-7 *Grail*)‡
AIR-LAUNCHED MISSILES
AAM • IR R-60 (AA-8 *Aphid*); R-73 (AA-11 *Archer*)
SARH R-27R (AA-10A *Alamo*)
ASM S5K/S5KO (57mm rockets); S8KP/S8KOM (80mm rockets)

DEPLOYMENT

AFGHANISTAN
NATO • *Operation Resolute Support* 40

BOSNIA-HERZEGOVINA
EU • EUFOR • *Operation Althea* 41

CYPRUS
UN • UNFICYP 169; 1 inf coy(-); 1 engr pl

MIDDLE EAST
UN • UNTSO 2 obs

UKRAINE
OSCE • Ukraine 10

Slovenia SVN

Euro €		2016	2017	2018
GDP	€	40.4bn	42.6bn	
	US$	44.7bn	48.1bn	
per capita	US$	21,668	23,277	
Growth	%	3.1	4.0	
Inflation	%	-0.1	1.6	
Def exp [a]	€	406m	426m	
	US$	449m	480m	
Def bdgt [b]	€	403m	420m	
	US$	446m	474m	
US$1=€		0.90	0.89	

[a] NATO definition
[b] Includes military pensions

Population 1,972,126

Ethnic groups: Slovenian 83% Serbian 2% Croatian 1.8% Bosniac 1% Other or unspecified 12.2%

Age	0–14	15–19	20–24	25–29	30–64	65 plus
Male	6.9%	2.3%	2.5%	3.0%	26.0%	8.0%
Female	6.5%	2.2%	2.4%	2.9%	25.9%	11.5%

Capabilities

Territorial defence and the ability to take part in peace-support operations are central to Slovenia's defence strategy. The defence ministry completed a Strategic Defence Review in December 2016. Its core conclusion was that the goals of the last review, conducted in 2009, had been missed and that capability development had stalled at a time when Europe's security environment had deteriorated. Underfunding and a bureaucratic failure to implement the agreed policy guidelines were singled out as key reasons for this assessment. The ministry also plans to review the current military doctrine. Slovenia has launched several invitations to tender in order to sell off obsolete equipment to raise funds for defence modernisation. However, given continuing resource challenges, significant modernisation steps seem unlikely during the current Medium-Term Defence Programme, which runs until 2020. The main development goal to 2023 has been defined as the formation and equipping of two battalion-sized battle groups. Recruitment and retention continues to be a challenge and it is questionable whether the planned target size of 10,000 active personnel for 2018 can be met. Slovenia acts as the framework nation for the NATO Mountain Warfare Centre of Excellence. Its small air wing is not equipped to provide air policing; Italy and Hungary currently partner in providing this capability. The country has contributed regularly to NATO and EU operations.

ACTIVE 7,250 (Army 7,250) **Paramilitary 5,950**

RESERVE 1,500 (Army 1,500) **Paramilitary 260**

ORGANISATIONS BY SERVICE

Army 7,250
FORCES BY ROLE
Regt are bn sized
SPECIAL FORCES
  1 SF unit (1 spec ops coy, 1 CSS coy)
MANOEUVRE
  Mechanised
  1 (1st) mech inf bde (1 mech inf regt, 1 mtn inf regt, 1 cbt spt bn (1 ISR coy, 1 arty bty, 1 engr coy, 1 MP coy, 1 CBRN coy, 1 sigs coy, 1 SAM bty))
  1 (72nd) mech inf bde (2 mech inf regt, 1 cbt spt bn (1 ISR coy, 1 arty bty, 1 engr coy, 1 MP coy, 1 CBRN coy, 1 sigs coy, 1 SAM bty))
COMBAT SUPPORT
  1 EW coy
COMBAT SERVICE SUPPORT
  1 log bde (1 log regt, 1 maint regt (1 tk coy), 1 med regt)

Reserves
FORCES BY ROLE
MANOEUVRE
  Mountain
  2 inf regt (territorial – 1 allocated to each inf bde)
EQUIPMENT BY TYPE
ARMOURED FIGHTING VEHICLES
  MBT 14 M-84 (trg role) (32 more in store)
  APC • APC (W) 115: 85 *Pandur* 6×6 (*Valuk*); 30 Patria 8×8 (*Svarun*)
ENGINEERING & MAINTENANCE VEHICLES
  ARV VT-55A
  VLB MTU
NBC VEHICLES 10 *Cobra* CBRN
ANTI-TANK/ANTI-INFRASTRUCTURE
  MSL • MANPATS *Spike* MR/LR
ARTILLERY 68
  TOWED • 155mm 18 TN-90
  MOR 120mm 50 MN-9/M-74
AIR DEFENCE • SAM • Point-defence 9K338 *Igla*-S (SA-24 *Grinch*)

Army Maritime Element 130
FORCES BY ROLE
SPECIAL FORCES
  1 SF unit
EQUIPMENT BY TYPE
PATROL AND COASTAL COMBATANTS 2
  PCC 1 *Triglav* III (RUS *Svetlyak*)
  PBF 1 *Super Dvora* MkII

Air Element 610
FORCES BY ROLE
TRANSPORT
  1 sqn with *Falcon* 2000EX; L-410 *Turbolet*; PC-6B *Turbo Porter*;
TRAINING
  1 unit with Bell 206 *Jet Ranger* (AB-206); PC-9M*; Z-143L; Z-242L

TRANSPORT HELICOPTER
1 sqn with AS532AL *Cougar*; Bell 412 *Twin Huey*
COMBAT SERVICE SUPPORT
1 maint sqn
EQUIPMENT BY TYPE
AIRCRAFT 9 combat capable
  TPT 4: Light 3: 1 L-410 *Turbolet*; 2 PC-6B *Turbo Porter*
  PAX 1 *Falcon* 2000EX
  TRG 19: 9 PC-9M*; 2 Z-143L; 8 Z-242L
HELICOPTERS
  MRH 8: 5 Bell 412EP *Twin Huey*; 2 Bell 412HP *Twin Huey*; 1 Bell 412SP *Twin Huey* (some armed)
  TPT 8: **Medium** 4 AS532AL *Cougar*; **Light** 4 Bell 206 *Jet Ranger* (AB-206)

Paramilitary 5,950

Police 5,950; 260 reservists
Ministry of Interior (civilian; limited elements could be prequalified to cooperate in military defence with the armed forces during state of emergency or war)
PATROL AND COASTAL COMBATANTS • PBF 1 *Ladse*
HELICOPTERS
  MRH 1 Bell 412 *Twin Huey*,
  TPT • Light 5: 1 AW109; 2 Bell 206 (AB-206) *Jet Ranger*; 1 Bell 212 (AB-212); 1 H135

Cyber
A National Cyber Security Strategy was endorsed in February 2016 by the government

DEPLOYMENT

AFGHANISTAN
NATO • Operation Resolute Support 7

BOSNIA-HERZEGOVINA
EU • EUFOR • Operation Althea 14

IRAQ
Operation Inherent Resolve 6

LATVIA
NATO • Enhanced Forward Presence 50; 1 CBRN pl(+)

LEBANON
UN • UNIFIL 15

MALI
EU • EUTM Mali 4

MIDDLE EAST
UN • UNTSO 3 obs

SERBIA
NATO • KFOR 252; 1 mot inf coy; 1 MP unit; 1 hel unit

UKRAINE
OSCE • Ukraine 2

Spain ESP

Euro €		2016	2017	2018
GDP	€	1.11tr	1.16tr	
	US$	1.23tr	1.31tr	
per capita	US$	26,565	28,212	
Growth	%	3.2	3.1	
Inflation	%	-0.2	2	
Def exp [a]	€	9.01bn	10.7bn	
	US$	9.97bn	12.1bn	
Def bdgt [b]	€	9.01bn	10.7bn	
	US$	9.97bn	12.1bn	
US$1=€		0.90	0.89	

[a] NATO definition
[b] Includes military pensions

Population 48,958,159

Age	0–14	15–19	20–24	25–29	30–64	65 plus
Male	7.9%	2.5%	2.5%	2.9%	26.0%	7.7%
Female	7.5%	2.3%	2.3%	2.6%	25.6%	10.3%

Capabilities

The Spanish Army began a comprehensive force-structure review in 2016, which resulted in a reorganisation into multipurpose brigades with heavy, medium and light capabilities, optimised for deployable operations and with a greater emphasis on mechanised formations and special-operations forces. Local defence industry manufactures across all domains and exports globally. However, the S-80 submarine programme, undertaken by Navantia, is significantly behind schedule. Having originally declined to take part in the project, Spain has reportedly expressed interest in acquiring the F-35 to replace its ageing naval-aviation AV-8s. Spain has also announced that it will participate in funding the European MALE 2020 unmanned-aerial-vehicle project, although it has also signed a contract for MQ-9 MALE UAVs. The country's equipment and logistic-support capability appears to be sufficient to meet its national commitments and contribution to NATO operations and exercises. Spain hosts one of NATO's two Combined Air Operations Centres, and the country's Joint Special Operations Command will provide the Special Operations Component Command for the NATO Response Force in 2018. Spain retains a small contingent in Kabul as part of the NATO HQ.

ACTIVE 121,200 (Army 70,950 Navy 20,050 Air 19,250 Joint 10,950) **Paramilitary 76,750**

RESERVE 15,450 (Army 8,800 Navy 2,750 Air 2,750 Other 1,150)

ORGANISATIONS BY SERVICE

Space
EQUIPMENT BY TYPE
SATELLITES • COMMUNICATIONS 2: 1 *Spainsat*; 1 *Xtar-Eur*

Army 70,950

The Land Forces High Readiness HQ Spain provides one NATO Rapid Deployment Corps HQ (NRDC-ESP)

FORCES BY ROLE
COMMAND
1 corps HQ (CGTAD/NRDC-ESP) (1 int regt, 1 MP bn)
2 div HQ

SPECIAL FORCES
1 comd (4 spec ops bn, 1 int coy, 1 sigs coy, 1 log bn)

MANOEUVRE
Reconnaissance
1 armd cav regt (2 armd recce bn)
Mechanised
3 (10th, 11th & 12th) mech bde (1 armd regt (1 armd recce bn, 1 tk bn), 1 mech inf regt (1 armd inf bn, 1 mech inf bn), 1 lt inf bn, 1 SP arty bn, 1 AT coy, 1 AD coy, 1 engr bn, 1 int coy, 1 NBC coy, 1 sigs coy, 1 log bn)
1 (1st) mech bde (1 armd regt (1 armd recce bn, 1 tk bn), 1 mech inf regt (1 armd inf bn, 1 mech inf bn), 1 mtn inf bn, 1 SP arty bn, 1 AT coy, 1 AD coy, 1 engr bn, 1 int coy, 1 NBC coy, 1 sigs coy, 1 log bn)
2 (2nd/La Legion & 7th) lt mech bde (1 armd recce bn, 1 mech inf regt (2 mech inf bn), 1 lt inf bn, 1 fd arty bn, 1 AT coy, 1 AD coy, 1 engr bn, 1 int coy, 1 NBC coy, 1 sigs coy, 1 log bn)
Air Manoeuvre
1 (6th) bde (1 recce bn, 3 para bn, 1 fd arty bn, 1 AT coy, 1 AD coy, 1 engr bn, 1 int coy, 1 NBC coy, 1 sigs coy, 1 log bn)
Other
1 (Canary Islands) comd (1 lt inf bde (3 lt inf regt, 1 fd arty regt, 1 AT coy, 1 engr bn, 1 int coy, 1 NBC coy, 1 sigs coy, 1 log bn); 1 spt hel bn; 1 AD regt)
1 (Balearic Islands) comd (1 inf regt)
2 (Ceuta and Melilla) comd (1 recce regt, 2 inf bn, 1 arty regt, 1 engr bn, 1 sigs coy, 1 log bn)

COMBAT SUPPORT
1 arty comd (1 arty regt; 1 MRL regt; 1 coastal arty regt)
1 engr comd (2 engr regt, 1 bridging regt)
1 EW/sigs bde (1 EW regt, 3 sigs regt)
1 EW regt
1 NBC regt
1 railway regt
1 sigs regt
1 CIMIC bn

COMBAT SERVICE SUPPORT
1 log bde (5 log regt)
1 med bde (1 log unit, 2 med regt, 1 fd hospital unit)

HELICOPTER
1 hel comd (1 atk hel bn, 2 spt hel bn, 1 tpt hel bn, 1 sigs bn, 1 log unit (1 spt coy, 1 supply coy))

AIR DEFENCE
1 AD comd (3 SAM regt, 1 sigs unit)

EQUIPMENT BY TYPE
ARMOURED FIGHTING VEHICLES
MBT 331: 108 *Leopard* 2A4; 223 *Leopard* 2A5E
RECCE 271: 84 B1 *Centauro*; 187 VEC-M1
IFV 227: 206 *Pizarro*; 21 *Pizarro* (CP)
APC 875
    APC (T) 453 M113 (incl variants)
    APC (W) 312 BMR-600/BMR-600M1
PPV 110 RG-31
AUV IVECO LMV

ENGINEERING & MAINTENANCE VEHICLES
AEV 34 CZ-10/25E
ARV 72: 16 *Leopard* REC; 1 AMX-30; 3 BMR REC; 4 *Centauro* REC; 14 *Maxxpro* MRV; 12 M113; 22 M47
VLB 16: 1 M47; 15 M60
MW 6 *Husky* 2G

ANTI-TANK/ANTI-INFRASTRUCTURE
MSL • MANPATS *Spike*-LR; TOW

ARTILLERY 1,556
SP 155mm 96 M109A5
TOWED 281: **105mm** 217: 56 L118 Light Gun; 161 Model 56 pack howitzer; **155mm** 64 SBT 155/52 SIAC
MOR 1,179: **81mm** 777; **120mm** 402

RADAR • LAND 6: 4 ARTHUR; 2 AN/TPQ-36 *Firefinder*
COASTAL DEFENCE • ARTY 155mm 19 SBT 155/52 APU SBT V07

HELICOPTERS
ATK 17: 6 *Tiger* HAP-E; 11 *Tiger* HAD-E
MRH 17 Bo-105 HOT†
TPT 84: **Heavy** 17 CH-47D *Chinook* (HT-17D); **Medium** 40: 16 AS332B *Super Puma* (HU-21); 12 AS532UL *Cougar*; 6 AS532AL *Cougar*; 6 NH90 TTH; **Light** 27: 6 Bell 205 (HU-10B *Iroquois*); 5 Bell 212 (HU.18); 16 H135 (HE.26/HU.26)

UAV • ISR • Medium 6: 2 *Searcher* MkII-J (PASI); 4 *Searcher* MkIII (PASI)

AIR DEFENCE
SAM
  Long-range 18 MIM-104C *Patriot* PAC-2
  Medium-range 38 MIM-23B I-*Hawk* Phase III
  Short-range 21: 8 NASAMS; 13 *Skyguard/Aspide*
  Point-defence *Mistral*
GUNS • TOWED 35mm 67: 19 GDF-005; 48 GDF-007

Navy 20,050 (incl Naval Aviation and Marines)

EQUIPMENT BY TYPE
SUBMARINES • TACTICAL • SSK 3:
3 *Galerna* with 4 single 533mm TT with F17 Mod 2/L5 HWT

PRINCIPAL SURFACE COMBATANTS 11
DESTROYERS • DDGHM 5:
5 *Alvaro de Bazan* with *Aegis* Baseline 5 C2, 2 quad Mk141 lnchr with RGM-84F *Harpoon* AShM, 1 48-cell Mk41 VLS with SM-2MR/RIM-162B *Sea Sparrow* SAM, 2 twin 324mm ASTT with Mk46 LWT, 1 127mm gun (capacity 1 SH-60B *Seahawk* ASW hel)

FRIGATES • FFGHM 6:
6 *Santa Maria* with 1 Mk13 GMLS with RGM-84C *Harpoon* AShM/SM-1MR SAM, 2 Mk32 triple 324mm ASTT with Mk46 LWT, 1 *Meroka* mod 2 CIWS, 1 76mm gun (capacity 2 SH-60B *Seahawk* ASW hel)

AMPHIBIOUS
PRINCIPAL AMPHIBIOUS SHIPS 3:
  LHD 1 *Juan Carlos* I (capacity 18 hel or 10 AV-8B FGA ac; 4 LCM-1E; 42 APC; 46 MBT; 900 troops)
  LPD 2 *Galicia* (capacity 6 Bell 212 or 4 SH-3D *Sea King* hel; 4 LCM or 2 LCM & 8 AAV; 130 APC or 33 MBT; 540 troops)

LANDING CRAFT 14
  LCM 14 LCM 1E
LOGISTICS AND SUPPORT 2
  AORH 2: 1 *Patino* (capacity 3 Bell 212 or 2 SH-3D *Sea King* hel); 1 *Cantabria* (capacity 3 Bell 212 or 2 SH-3D *Sea King* hel)

Maritime Action Force
EQUIPMENT BY TYPE
PATROL AND COASTAL COMBATANTS 23
  PSOH 4 *Meteoro* (*Buques de Accion Maritima*) with 1 76mm gun
  PSO 7:
    3 *Alboran* each with 1 hel landing platform
    4 *Descubierta* with 1 76mm gun
  PCO 4 *Serviola* with 1 76mm gun
  PCC 3 *Anaga* with 1 76mm gun
  PB 4: 2 *P-101*; 2 *Toralla*
  PBR 1 *Cabo Fradera*
MINE WARFARE • MINE COUNTERMEASURES 6
  MHO 6 *Segura*
LOGISTICS AND SUPPORT 29
  AGI 1 *Alerta*
  AGOR 2 (with ice-strengthened hull, for polar research duties in Antarctica)
  AGS 3: 2 *Malaspina*; 1 *Castor*
  AK 2: 1 *Martin Posadillo* with 1 hel landing platform; 1 *El Camino Español*
  AP 1 *Contramaestre Casado* with 1 hel landing platform
  ASR 1 *Neptuno*
  ATF 3: 1 *Mar Caribe*; 1 *Mahon*; 1 *La Grana*
  AXL 8: 4 *Contramaestre*; 4 *Guardiamarina*
  AXS 8

Naval Aviation 850

Flying hours 150 hrs/yr on AV-8B *Harrier* II FGA ac; 200 hrs/yr on hel

FORCES BY ROLE
FIGHTER/GROUND ATTACK
  1 sqn with AV-8B *Harrier* II Plus
ANTI-SUBMARINE WARFARE
  1 sqn with SH-60B/F *Seahawk*
TRANSPORT
  1 (liaison) sqn with Cessna 550 *Citation* II; Cessna 650 *Citation* VII
TRAINING
  1 sqn with Hughes 500MD8
  1 flt with TAV-8B *Harrier*
TRANSPORT HELICOPTER
  1 sqn with Bell 212 (HU-18)
  1 sqn with SH-3D *Sea King*
EQUIPMENT BY TYPE
AIRCRAFT 13 combat capable
  FGA 13: 8 AV-8B *Harrier* II Plus; 4 AV-8B *Harrier* II (upgraded to II Plus standard); 1 TAV-8B *Harrier* (on lease from USMC)
  TPT • Light 4: 3 Cessna 550 *Citation* II; 1 Cessna 650 *Citation* VII
HELICOPTERS
  ASW 21: 7 SH-3D *Sea King* (tpt); 12 SH-60B *Seahawk*; 2 SH-60F *Seahawk*
  MRH 9 Hughes 500MD
  TPT • Light 7 Bell 212 (HA-18)
AIR-LAUNCHED MISSILES
  AAM • IR AIM-9L *Sidewinder*; **ARH** AIM-120 AMRAAM
  ASM AGM-65G *Maverick*
  AShM AGM-119 *Penguin*

Marines 5,800

FORCES BY ROLE
SPECIAL FORCES
  1 spec ops bn
MANOEUVRE
  Amphibious
  1 mne bde (1 recce unit, 1 mech inf bn, 2 inf bn, 1 arty bn, 1 log bn)
  Other
  1 sy bde (5 mne garrison gp)
EQUIPMENT BY TYPE
ARMOURED FIGHTING VEHICLES
  MBT 4 M60A3TTS
  APC • APC (W) 34: 32 *Piranha* IIIC; 1 *Piranha* IIIC (amb); 1 *Piranha* IIIC EW (EW)
  AAV 18: 16 AAV-7A1/AAVP-7A1; 2 AAVC-7A1 (CP)
ENGINEERING & MAINTENANCE VEHICLES
  AEV 4 *Piranha* IIIC
  ARV 2: 1 AAVR-7A1; 1 *Piranha* IIIC
ARTILLERY 30
  SP 155mm 6 M109A2
  TOWED 105mm 24 Model 56 pack howitzer
ANTI-TANK/ANTI-INFRASTRUCTURE
  MSL • MANPATS *Spike*-LR; TOW-2
AIR DEFENCE • SAM • Point-defence *Mistral*

Air Force 19,250

The Spanish Air Force is organised in 3 commands – General Air Command, Combat Air Command and Canary Islands Air Command

Flying hours 120 hrs/yr on hel/tpt ac; 180 hrs/yr on FGA/ftr

FORCES BY ROLE
FIGHTER
  2 sqn with Eurofighter *Typhoon*
FIGHTER/GROUND ATTACK
  5 sqn with F/A-18A/B MLU *Hornet* (EF-18A/B MLU)
MARITIME PATROL
  1 sqn with P-3A/M *Orion*
ISR
  1 sqn with Beech C90 *King Air*
  1 sqn with Cessna 550 *Citation* V; CN235 (TR-19A)
ELECTRONIC WARFARE
  1 sqn with C-212 *Aviocar*; *Falcon* 20D
SEARCH & RESCUE
  1 sqn with AS332B/B1 *Super Puma*; CN235 VIGMA
  1 sqn with AS332B *Super Puma*; CN235 VIGMA
  1 sqn with C-212 *Aviocar*; CN235 VIGMA
TANKER/TRANSPORT
  1 sqn with KC-130H *Hercules*
TRANSPORT
  1 VIP sqn with A310; *Falcon* 900
  1 sqn with C-130H/H-30 *Hercules*

1 sqn with C-212 *Aviocar*
2 sqn with C295
1 sqn with CN235
TRAINING
1 OCU sqn with Eurofighter *Typhoon*
1 OCU sqn with F/A-18A/B (EF-18A/B MLU) *Hornet*
1 sqn with Beech F33C *Bonanza*
2 sqn with C-101 *Aviojet*
1 sqn with C-212 *Aviocar*
1 sqn with T-35 *Pillan* (E-26)
2 (LIFT) sqn with F-5B *Freedom Fighter*
1 hel sqn with H120 *Colibri*
1 hel sqn with S-76C
TRANSPORT HELICOPTER
1 sqn with AS332M1 *Super Puma*; AS532UL *Cougar* (VIP)
EQUIPMENT BY TYPE
AIRCRAFT 168 combat capable
  FTR 80: 61 Eurofighter *Typhoon*; 19 F-5B *Freedom Fighter*
  FGA 85: 20 F/A-18A *Hornet* (EF-18A); 53 EF-18A MLU; 12 EF-18B MLU
  ASW 3 P-3M *Orion*
  MP 8 CN235 VIGMA
  ISR 2 CN235 (TR-19A)
  EW 3: 1 C-212 *Aviocar* (TM.12D); 2 *Falcon* 20D
  TKR 5 KC-130H *Hercules*
  TPT 75: **Heavy** 1 A400M; **Medium** 7: 6 C-130H *Hercules*; 1 C-130H-30 *Hercules*; **Light** 59: 3 Beech C90 *King Air*; 22 Beech F33C *Bonanza*; 10 C-212 *Aviocar* (incl 9 trg); 13 C295; 8 CN235; 3 Cessna 550 *Citation* V (ISR); **PAX** 8: 2 A310; 1 B-707; 5 *Falcon* 900 (VIP)
  TRG 102: 65 C-101 *Aviojet*; 37 T-35 *Pillan* (E-26)
HELICOPTERS
  TPT 37: **Medium** 15: 9 AS332B/B1 *Super Puma*; 4 AS332M1 *Super Puma*; 2 AS532UL *Cougar* (VIP); **Light** 22: 14 H120 *Colibri*; 8 S-76C
AIR DEFENCE • SAM
  Short-range Skyguard/Aspide
  Point-defence Mistral
AIR-LAUNCHED MISSILES
  AAM • IR AIM-9L/JULI *Sidewinder*; **IIR** IRIS-T; **SARH** AIM-7P *Sparrow*; **ARH** AIM-120B/C AMRAAM
  ARM AGM-88B HARM
  ASM AGM-65G *Maverick*
  AShM AGM-84D *Harpoon*
  LACM Taurus KEPD 350
BOMBS
  Laser-guided: GBU-10/12/16 *Paveway* II; GBU-24 *Paveway* III; EGBU-16 *Paveway* II; BPG-2000

Emergencies Military Unit (UME)
FORCES BY ROLE
COMMAND
  1 div HQ
MANOEUVRE
  Other
  5 Emergency Intervention bn
  1 Emergency Support and Intervention regt
COMBAT SUPPORT
  1 sigs bn
HELICOPTER
  1 hel bn opcon Army

Paramilitary 89,050

Guardia Civil 89,050
17 regions, 54 Rural Comds
FORCES BY ROLE
SPECIAL FORCES
  8 (rural) gp
MANOEUVRE
  Other
  15 (traffic) sy gp
  1 (Special) sy bn
EQUIPMENT BY TYPE
PATROL AND COASTAL COMBATANTS 64
  PSO 1 with 1 hel landing platform
  PCC 2
  PBF 34
  PB 27
  AIRCRAFT • TPT • Light 2 CN235-300
HELICOPTERS
  MRH 20: 2 AS653N3 *Dauphin*; 18 Bo-105ATH
  TPT • Light 21: 8 BK-117; 13 H135

Cyber
A Joint Cyber Command was set up in 2013. In 2014, short/medium-term goals included achieving FOC on 'CNDefense, CNExploitation, and CNAttack'. Spain's intelligence CERT (CCN–CERT) coordinates CERT activities.

DEPLOYMENT

AFGHANISTAN
NATO • *Operation Resolute Support* 16

BOSNIA-HERZEGOVINA
EU • EUFOR • *Operation Althea* 2
OSCE • Bosnia and Herzegovina 2

CENTRAL AFRICAN REPUBLIC
EU • EUTM RCA 30

DJIBOUTI
EU • *Operation Atalanta* 1 P-3M *Orion*

GULF OF ADEN & INDIAN OCEAN
EU • *Operation Atalanta* 1 PSOH

IRAQ
Operation Inherent Resolve 400; 2 trg unit

LATVIA
NATO • Enhanced Forward Presence 300; 1 armd inf coy(+)

LEBANON
UN • UNIFIL 628; 1 lt inf bde HQ; 1 mech inf bn(-); 1 engr coy; 1 sigs coy

MALI
EU • EUTM Mali 127
UN • MINUSMA 1

MEDITERRANEAN SEA
NATO • SNMG 1: 1 FFGHM
EU • EU NAVFOR MED: 1 AORH; 1 CN235

SERBIA
OSCE • Kosovo 1

SOMALIA
EU • EUTM Somalia 16

TURKEY
NATO • *Operation Active Fence* 149; 1 SAM bty with MIM-104C *Patriot* PAC-2

UKRAINE
OSCE • Ukraine 13

FOREIGN FORCES
United States US European Command: 3,200; 1 air base at Morón; 1 naval base at Rota

Sweden SWE

Swedish Krona Skr		2016	2017	2018
GDP	Skr	4.38tr	4.61tr	
	US$	511bn	542bn	
per capita	US$	51,125	53,248	
Growth	%	3.2	3.1	
Inflation	%	1.1	1.6	
Def bdgt	Skr	49.1bn	50.7bn	53.8bn
	US$	5.74bn	5.96bn	
US$1=Skr		8.56	8.51	

[a] Excludes military pensions and peacekeeping expenditure

Population 9,960,487

Age	0–14	15–19	20–24	25–29	30–64	65 plus
Male	9.0%	2.7%	3.2%	3.6%	22.2%	9.4%
Female	8.5%	2.5%	3.0%	3.5%	21.7%	10.9%

Capabilities

Sweden's armed forces remain configured for territorial defence. In June 2015, a defence bill for 2016–20 was adopted, which set out the aims of strengthening operational capabilities and deepening multilateral and bilateral defence relationships. Increased cooperation with neighbours and NATO has been a prevalent theme for the last few years. In June 2016, Sweden signed a statement of intent with the US and a Programme of Defence Cooperation with the UK. Concerns over readiness levels have led to greater cooperation with NATO and NORDEFCO partners, as well as further deliberation over Swedish membership of the Alliance. Under the auspices of NORDEFCO, Sweden is expanding its defence cooperation with Finland. In response to security concerns, the government announced an increase in planned defence spending, and confirmed in August 2017 that spending would be put on an upward trajectory at least until 2020. Readiness, exercises and training, as well as cyber defence, are spending priorities.

Sweden intends to establish a Gotland Regiment by 2018, stationed on the island. Readiness challenges in the air force triggered a discussion about extending the service life of its JAS-39C *Gripen* Cs beyond their intended 2026 retirement date, not least since the air force was slated to receive a lower number of JAS-39Es than requested. Plans to replace the C-130H *Hercules* fleet from 2021 have been superseded by a mid-life upgrade to extend service life to about 2030. In September 2017, Sweden conducted *Aurora 2017*, its largest exercise in two decades. Amid recruitment challenges, Sweden announced in March 2017 that it would reinstate conscription from January 2018. The armed-forces chief stated that the change in the post-Cold War landscape will mean the downgrading of international missions in order to prioritise domestic readiness.

ACTIVE 29,750 (Army 6,850 Navy 2,100 Air 2,700 Other 18,100) **Paramilitary 750 Voluntary Auxiliary Organisations 21,200**

ORGANISATIONS BY SERVICE

Army 6,850
The army has been transformed to provide brigade-sized task forces depending on the operational requirement

FORCES BY ROLE
COMMAND
  2 bde HQ
MANOEUVRE
  Reconnaissance
  1 recce bn
  Armoured
  3 armd coy
  Mechanised
  5 mech bn
  Light
  1 mot inf bn
  1 lt inf bn
  Air Manoeuvre
  1 AB bn
  Other
  1 sy bn
COMBAT SUPPORT
  2 arty bn
  2 engr bn
  2 MP coy
  1 CBRN coy
COMBAT SERVICE SUPPORT
  1 tpt coy
AIR DEFENCE
  2 AD bn

Reserves
FORCES BY ROLE
MANOEUVRE
  Other
  40 Home Guard bn

EQUIPMENT BY TYPE
ARMOURED FIGHTING VEHICLES
  MBT 129: 9 *Leopard* 2A4 (Strv-121); 120 *Leopard* 2A5 (Strv 122)
  IFV 354 CV9040 (Strf 9040)
  APC 1,106
    APC (T) 431: 281 Pbv 302; 150 BvS10 MkII
    APC (W) 315: 34 XA-180 *Sisu* (Patgb 180); 20 XA-202 *Sisu* (Patgb 202); 148 XA-203 *Sisu* (Patgb 203); 113 Patria AMV (XA-360/Patgb 360)
    PPV 360 RG-32M
ENGINEERING & MAINTENANCE VEHICLES
  AEV 6 *Kodiak*
  ARV 40: 14 Bgbv 120; 26 CV90
  MW 33+: *Aardvark* Mk2; 33 Area Clearing System
ANTI-TANK/ANTI-INFRASTRUCTURE
  MSL • MANPATS RB-55
  RCL 84mm *Carl Gustav*
ARTILLERY 304
  SP 155mm 8 *Archer*
  MOR 296; 81mm 212 M/86; 120mm 84 M/41D
  RADAR • LAND ARTHUR (arty)
AIR DEFENCE
  SAM
    Medium-range MIM-23B *Hawk* (RBS-97)
    Point-defence RBS-70
  GUNS • SP 40mm 30 Strv 90LV

Navy 1,250; 850 Amphibious (total 2,100)
EQUIPMENT BY TYPE
SUBMARINE • TACTICAL • SSK 5:
  3 *Gotland* (AIP fitted) with 2 single 400mm TT with Tp432/Tp 451, 4 single 533mm TT with Tp613/Tp62
  2 *Sodermanland* (AIP fitted) with 6 single 533mm TT with Tp432/Tp451/Tp613/Tp62
PATROL AND COASTAL COMBATANTS 147
  CORVETTES • FSG 5 *Visby* with 8 RBS-15 AShM, 4 single 400mm ASTT with Tp45 LWT, 1 57mm gun, 1 hel landing platform
  PCGT 4:
    2 *Göteborg* with 4 twin lnchr with RBS-15 Mk2 AShM, 4 single 400mm ASTT with Tp431 LWT, 4 Saab 601 A/S mor, 1 57mm gun
    2 *Stockholm* with 4 twin lnchr with RBS-15 Mk2 AShM, 4 Saab 601 mortars, 4 single 400mm ASTT with Tp431 LWT, 1 57mm gun (in refit)
  PBF 129 Combat Boat 90E/H/HS (capacity 20 troops)
  PB 9 *Tapper*
MINE WARFARE • MINE COUNTERMEASURES 7
  MCC 5 *Koster*
  MCD 2 *Spårö* (*Styrsö* mod)
AMPHIBIOUS • LANDING CRAFT 11
  LCVP 8 *Trossbat*
  LCAC 3 *Griffon* 8100TD
LOGISTICS AND SUPPORT 17
  AG 2: 1 *Carlskrona* with 2 57mm gun, 1 hel landing platform (former ML); 1 *Trosso* (spt ship for corvettes and patrol vessels but can also be used as HQ ship)
  AGF 2 *Ledningsbåt* 2000
  AGI 1 *Orion*
  AGS 2 (Government Maritime Forces)
  AKL 1 *Loke*
  ARS 2: 1 *Belos* III; 1 *Furusund* (former ML)
  AX 5 *Altair*
  AXS 2: 1 *Falken*; 1 *Gladan*

Amphibious 850
FORCES BY ROLE
MANOEUVRE
  Amphibious
    1 amph bn
EQUIPMENT BY TYPE
  ARTILLERY • MOR 81mm 12 M/86
  COASTAL DEFENCE • AShM 8 RBS-17 *Hellfire*

Air Force 2,700
Flying hours 100–150 hrs/yr
FORCES BY ROLE
FIGHTER/GROUND ATTACK/ISR
  6 sqn with JAS 39C/D *Gripen*
TRANSPORT/ISR/AEW&C
  1 sqn with C-130H *Hercules* (Tp-84); KC-130H *Hercules* (Tp-84); Gulfstream IV SRA-4 (S-102B); S-100B/D *Argus*
TRAINING
  1 unit with Sk-60
AIR DEFENCE
  1 (fighter control and air surv) bn
EQUIPMENT BY TYPE
AIRCRAFT 97 combat capable
  FGA 97 JAS 39C/D *Gripen*
  ELINT 2 Gulfstream IV SRA-4 (S-102B)
  AEW&C 3: 1 S-100B *Argus*; 2 S-100D *Argus*
  TKR 1 KC-130H *Hercules* (Tp-84)
  TPT 8: **Medium** 5 C-130H *Hercules* (Tp-84); **Light** 2 Saab 340 (OS-100A/Tp-100C); PAX 1 Gulfstream 550 (Tp-102D)
  TRG 67 Sk-60W
UNMANNED AERIAL VEHICLES
  ISR • Medium 8 RQ-7 *Shadow* (AUV 3 *Örnen*)
AIR-LAUNCHED MISSILES
  ASM AGM-65 *Maverick* (RB-75)
  AShM RB-15F
  AAM • IR AIM-9L *Sidewinder* (RB-74); IIR IRIS-T (RB-98); ARH AIM-120B AMRAAM (RB-99); *Meteor* (entering service)
BOMBS
  Laser-Guided GBU-12 *Paveway* II
  INS/GPS guided GBU-39 Small Diameter Bomb

Armed Forces Hel Wing
FORCES BY ROLE
TRANSPORT HELICOPTER
  3 sqn with AW109 (Hkp 15A); AW109M (Hkp-15B); NH90 (Hkp-14) (SAR/ASW); UH-60M *Black Hawk* (Hkp-16)
EQUIPMENT BY TYPE
HELICOPTERS
  ASW 5 NH90 ASW
  TPT 48: **Medium** 28: 15 UH-60M *Black Hawk* (Hkp-16); 13 NH90 TTH (Hkp-14); **Light** 20: 12 AW109 (Hkp-15A); 8 AW109M (Hkp-15B)

Special Forces

FORCES BY ROLE
SPECIAL FORCES
 1 spec ops gp
COMBAT SUPPORT
 1 cbt spt gp

Other 18,100

Includes staff, logistics and intelligence personnel

FORCES BY ROLE
COMBAT SUPPORT
 1 EW bn
 1 psyops unit
COMBAT SERVICE SUPPORT
 2 log bn
 1 maint bn
 4 med coy
 1 tpt coy

Paramilitary 750

Coast Guard 750

EQUIPMENT BY TYPE
PATROL AND COASTAL COMBATANTS 25
 PSO 3 *Poseidon* (Damen Multipurpose Vessel 8116)
 PCO 1 KBV-181 (fishery protection)
 PCC 6: 2 KBV-201; 4 *Sipe*
 PB 15: 10 KBV-301; 5 KBV-312
AMPHIBIOUS • LANDING CRAFT • UCAC 2: 1 *Griffon* 2000TDX (KBV-592); 1 *Griffon* 2450TD

Air Arm

EQUIPMENT BY TYPE
AIRCRAFT • TPT • Light 3 DHC-8Q-300

Cyber

Sweden has a national CERT, is involved in informal CERT communities and is a member of the European Government CERTs group. The Swedish Civil Contingencies Agency, which reports to the defence ministry, is in charge of supporting and coordinating security nationwide. The 2016–20 defence bill states that 'cyber defence capabilities are an important part of the Swedish Defence. […] This also requires the ability to carry out active operations in the cyber domain.' A new national cyber-security strategy in June 2017 outlined six priority areas for national cyber security, and noted that 'an advanced cyber defence must be in place that includes enhanced military capability to respond to and handle an attack by an advanced opponent in cyberspace'.

DEPLOYMENT

AFGHANISTAN
NATO • *Operation Resolute Support* 25

CENTRAL AFRICAN REPUBLIC
EU • EUTM RCA 9

DEMOCRATIC REPUBLIC OF THE CONGO
UN • MONUSCO 2 obs

INDIA/PAKISTAN
UN • UNMOGIP 6 obs

IRAQ
Operation Inherent Resolve 70

KOREA, REPUBLIC OF
NNSC • 5 obs

MALI
EU • EUTM Mali 3
UN • MINUSMA 212; 1 int coy

MIDDLE EAST
UN • UNTSO 7 obs

MOLDOVA
OSCE • Moldova 1

SERBIA
NATO • KFOR 3
OSCE • Kosovo 3

SOMALIA
EU • EUTM Somalia 4

SOUTH SUDAN
UN • UNMISS 2 obs

UKRAINE
OSCE • Ukraine 10

WESTERN SAHARA
UN • MINURSO 4 obs

Switzerland CHE

Swiss Franc fr		2016	2017	2018
GDP	fr	659bn	667bn	
	US$	669bn	681bn	
per capita	US$	80,346	80,837	
Growth	%	1.4	1.0	
Inflation	%	-0.4	0.5	
Def bdgt [a]	fr	4.59bn	4.74bn	4.87bn
	US$	4.65bn	4.83bn	
US$1=fr		0.99	0.98	

[a] Includes military pensions

Population 8,236,303

Age	0–14	15–19	20–24	25–29	30–64	65 plus
Male	7.8%	2.7%	2.9%	3.2%	24.7%	8.0%
Female	7.4%	2.5%	2.8%	3.2%	24.6%	10.2%

Capabilities

The armed forces are overwhelmingly conscript-based and are geared for territorial defence and limited participation in international peace-support operations. Under the 2017 Military Doctrine, which followed the 2016 Security Policy Report, Switzerland judged as remote a direct military threat but said that potential threats included espionage, cyber attack, influence operations and sabotage, as well as the actions of non-state groups. The Swiss government has begun to reduce the size of its armed forces, reflecting the assessment that in the militia-based system not all personnel would realistically be available for active service in times of conflict. However, the smaller force is supposed to benefit from additional equipment. This armed-forces development plan was approved in March 2016 and emphasises improvements in readiness, training and equipment; implementation is due in 2018–21. Switzerland's approach to readiness is shifting to a more flexible model, in which different units would be called up for active service gradually and on different timelines. Plans to replace combat aircraft and ground-based air-defence (GBAD) capability progressed in late 2017 with the announcement that CHF8 billion would be invested in airspace protection. Bids for new combat aircraft will be requested in early 2018, and a decision is expected around 2020, following a possible referendum. GBAD procurement will proceed in parallel. In the meantime, the government decided in 2017 to fund a service-life-extension programme enabling the country's F/A-18 *Hornet* jets to remain in service until about 2030. The defence budget is planned to increase by 1.4% per year in order to fund these new airspace-protection programmes.

ACTIVE 20,950 (Joint 20,950)

Conscript liability Recruit trg of 18, 21 or 25 weeks (depending on military branch) at age 19–20, followed by 7, 6 or 5 refresher trg courses (3 weeks each) over a 10-year period between ages 20 and 30

RESERVE 144,270 (Army 93,100 Air 22,870 Armed Forces Logistic Organisation 13,700 Command Support Organisation 14,600)

Civil Defence 74,000 (55,000 Reserve)

ORGANISATIONS BY SERVICE

Joint 3,350 active; 17,600 conscript (20,950 total)

Land Forces (Army) 93,100 on mobilisation

4 Territorial Regions. With the exception of military security all units are non-active

FORCES BY ROLE
COMMAND
 4 regional comd (2 engr bn, 1 sigs bn)
MANOEUVRE
 Armoured
  1 (1st) bde (1 recce bn, 2 armd bn, 2 armd inf bn, 1 sp arty bn, 2 engr bn, 1 sigs bn)
  1 (11th) bde (1 recce bn, 2 armd bn, 2 armd inf bn, 1 inf bn, 2 SP arty bn, 1 engr bn, 1 sigs bn)
 Light
  1 (2nd) inf bde (1 recce bn, 4 inf bn, 2 SP arty bn, 1 engr bn, 1 sigs bn)
  1 (5th) inf bde (1 recce bn, 3 inf bn, 2 SP arty bn, 1 engr bn, 1 sigs bn)
  1 (7th) reserve inf bde (3 recce bn, 3 inf bn, 2 mtn inf bn, 1 sigs bn)
  1 (9th) mtn inf bde (5 mtn inf bn, 1 SP Arty bn, 1 sigs bn)
  1 (12th) mtn inf bde (2 inf bn, 3 mtn inf bn, 1 (fortress) arty bn, 1 sigs bn)
  1 (10th) reserve mtn inf bde (1 recce bn, 2 armd bn, 3 inf bn, 2 mtn inf bn, 2 SP arty bn, 2 sigs bn)
 Other
  1 sy bde
COMBAT SERVICE SUPPORT
 1 armd/arty trg unit
 1 inf trg unit
 1 engr rescue trg unit
 1 log trg unit

EQUIPMENT BY TYPE
ARMOURED FIGHTING VEHICLES
 MBT 134 *Leopard* 2 (Pz-87 *Leo*)
 IFV 186: 154 CV9030; 32 CV9030 CP
 APC 914
  APC (T) 238 M113A2 (incl variants)
  APC (W) 676: 346 *Piranha* II; 330 *Piranha* I/II/IIIC (CP)
 AUV 441 *Eagle* II
ENGINEERING & MAINTENANCE VEHICLES
 AEV 12 *Kodiak*
 ARV 25 *Büffel*
 MW 46: 26 Area Clearing System; 20 M113A2
NBC VEHICLES 12 *Piranha* IIIC CBRN
ANTI-TANK/ANTI-INFRASTRUCTURE
 MSL • **SP** 106 *Piranha* I TOW-2
ARTILLERY 433
 SP 155mm 133 M109
 MOR • **81mm** 300 Mw-72
PATROL AND COASTAL COMBATANTS • **PBR** 11 *Aquarius*
AIR DEFENCE • **SAM** • **Point-defence** FIM-92 *Stinger*

Air Force 22,870 (incl air defence units and military airfield guard units)

Flying hours 200–250 hrs/yr

FORCES BY ROLE
FIGHTER
 3 sqn with F-5E/F *Tiger* II
 3 sqn with F/A-18C/D *Hornet*
TRANSPORT
 1 sqn with Beech 350 *King Air*; DHC-6 *Twin Otter*; PC-6 *Turbo Porter*; PC-12
 1 VIP Flt with Beech 1900D; Cessna 560XL *Citation*; *Falcon* 900EX
TRAINING
 1 sqn with PC-7CH *Turbo Trainer*; PC-21
 1 sqn with PC-9 (tgt towing)
 1 OCU Sqn with F-5E/F *Tiger* II
TRANSPORT HELICOPTER
 6 sqn with AS332M *Super Puma*; AS532UL *Cougar*; H135M
ISR UAV
 1 sqn with ADS 95 *Ranger*

EQUIPMENT BY TYPE
AIRCRAFT 85 combat capable
 FTR 54: 42 F-5E *Tiger* II; 12 F-5F *Tiger* II

FGA 31: 25 F/A-18C *Hornet*; 6 F/A-18D *Hornet*
TPT 22: **Light** 21: 1 Beech 350 *King Air*; 1 Beech 1900D; 1 Cessna 560XL *Citation*; 1 DHC-6 *Twin Otter*; 15 PC-6 *Turbo Porter*; 1 PC-6 (owned by armasuisse, civil registration); 1 PC-12 (owned by armasuisse, civil registration); **PAX** 1 *Falcon* 900EX
TRG 44: 28 PC-7CH *Turbo Trainer*; 8 PC-9; 8 PC-21
HELICOPTERS
MRH 20 H135M
TPT • **Medium** 25: 14 AS332M *Super Puma*; 11 AS532UL *Cougar*
UNMANNED AERIAL VEHICLES
ISR • **Medium** 16 ADS 95 *Ranger* (4 systems)
AIR-LAUNCHED MISSILES • **AAM** • **IR** AIM-9P *Sidewinder*; **IIR** AIM-9X *Sidewinder* II; **ARH** AIM-120B/C-7 AMRAAM

Ground Based Air Defence (GBAD)
GBAD assets can be used to form AD clusters to be deployed independently as task forces within Swiss territory
EQUIPMENT BY TYPE
AIR DEFENCE
SAM • **Point** *Rapier*; FIM-92 *Stinger*
GUNS 35mm Some
RADARS • **AD RADARS** *Skyguard*

Armed Forces Logistic Organisation 13,700 on mobilisation
FORCES BY ROLE
COMBAT SERVICE SUPPORT
1 log bde

Command Support Organisation 14,600 on mobilisation
FORCES BY ROLE
COMBAT SERVICE SUPPORT
1 spt bde

Civil Defence 74,000 (55,000 Reserve)
(not part of armed forces)

Cyber
Five major Swiss government organisations maintain an overview of elements of cyber threats and responses: the Federal Intelligence Service; the Military Intelligence Service; the Command Support Organisation; Information Security and Facility Protection; and the Federal Office for Civil Protection. A National Cyber Defence Strategy was published in 2012. As cyber protection is decentralised, the Federal Department of Finance is in charge of implementing the strategy until 2017.

DEPLOYMENT

BOSNIA-HERZEGOVINA
EU • EUFOR • *Operation Althea* 21

DEMOCRATIC REPUBLIC OF THE CONGO
UN • MONUSCO 3

INDIA/PAKISTAN
UN • UNMOGIP 3 obs

KOREA, REPUBLIC OF
NNSC • 5 officers

MALI
UN • MINUSMA 6

MIDDLE EAST
UN • UNTSO 12 obs

SERBIA
NATO • KFOR 234 (military volunteers); 1 inf coy; 1 engr pl; 1 hel flt with AS332M *Super Puma*
OSCE • Kosovo 1

SOUTH SUDAN
UN • UNMISS 2

UKRAINE
OSCE • Ukraine 11

WESTERN SAHARA
UN • MINURSO 2 obs

Turkey TUR

New Turkish Lira L		2016	2017	2018
GDP	L	2.61tr	3.03tr	
	US$	863bn	841bn	
per capita	US$	10,817	10,434	
Growth	%	3.2	5.1	
Inflation	%	7.8	10.9	
Def exp [a]	L	38.1bn	44.2bn	
	US$	12.6bn	12.3bn	
Def bdgt [b]	L	26.2bn	28.8bn	40.5bn
	US$	8.66bn	7.98bn	
US$1=L		3.02	3.60	

[a] NATO definition
[b] Includes funding for Undersecretariat of Defence Industries. Excludes military procurement allocations

Population 80,845,215

Age	0–14	15–19	20–24	25–29	30–64	65 plus
Male	12.6%	4.2%	4.0%	4.0%	22.2%	3.4%
Female	12.1%	4.0%	3.8%	3.9%	21.8%	4.2%

Capabilities

According to government officials, terrorism is designated as Turkey's main security threat. The armed forces are capable and aim to provide a highly mobile force able to fight across the spectrum of conflict. In 2017, Turkey published its 'Strategic Paper 2017–21', which outlined an aspiration to improve local input into national-defence programmes, and develop indigenous platforms across all domains. Following the failed attempt at a military coup in July 2016, Ankara dismissed large numbers of officers from its armed forces, and the loss of experienced personnel will likely have had some impact on both operational effectiveness and training levels. The armed forces remain engaged in ground operations in northern Iraq, as well as in airstrikes against the Kurdistan Workers' Party (PKK) and the People's Protection Units (YPG) in both northern Iraq and Syria. In 2017, Turkey opened a base in Mogadishu to train Somali forces. Turkey has also dispatched personnel to Qatar. To bolster its air-defence capability, Ankara signed a contract with Russia for S-400 surface-to-air missile systems. However, the extent (if any) to which Turkey can integrate the S-400 with Western air-defence systems and NATO air defences remains open to question.

ACTIVE 355,200 (Army 260,200 Navy 45,600 Air 50,000) Paramilitary 156,800
Conscript liability 15 months. Active figure reducing

RESERVE 378,700 (Army 258,700 Navy 55,000 Air 65,000)
Reserve service to age 41 for all services

ORGANISATIONS BY SERVICE

Space
EQUIPMENT BY TYPE
SATELLITES • **ISR** 2 Gokturk-1/2

Army ε260,200 (including conscripts)
FORCES BY ROLE
COMMAND
  4 army HQ
  9 corps HQ
SPECIAL FORCES
  4 cdo bde
  1 mtn cdo bde
  1 cdo regt
MANOEUVRE
  Armoured
  1 (52nd) armd div (2 armd bde, 1 mech bde)
  7 armd bde
  Mechanised
  2 (28th & 29th) mech div
  14 mech inf bde
  Light
  1 (23rd) mot inf div (3 mot inf regt)
  11 mot inf bde
COMBAT SUPPORT
  2 arty bde
  1 trg arty bde
  6 arty regt
  2 engr regt
AVIATION
  4 avn regt
  4 avn bn
EQUIPMENT BY TYPE
ARMOURED FIGHTING VEHICLES
  MBT 2,485: 321 Leopard 2A4; 170 Leopard 1A4; 227 Leopard 1A3; 250 M60A1; 500 M60A3; 167 M60T; 850 M48A5 T1/T2 (2,000 more in store)
  RECCE ε250 Akrep

IFV 645 ACV AIFV
APC 4,138
  APC (T) 3,636: 823 ACV AAPC; 2,813 M113/M113A1/M113A2
  APC (W) 152+: 70+ Cobra; 82 Cobra II
  PPV 350+: 50+ Edjer Yaclin 4×4; 300+ Kirpi
ENGINEERING & MAINTENANCE VEHICLES
  AEV 12+: 12 M48; M113A2T2
  ARV 150: 12 Leopard 1; 105 M48T5; 33 M88A1
  VLB 52 Mobile Floating Assault Bridge
  MW Husky 2G; Tamkar
ANTI-TANK/ANTI-INFRASTRUCTURE
  MSL
    SP 365 ACV TOW
    MANPATS 9K135 Kornet-E (AT-14 Spriggan); Cobra; Eryx; Milan
  RCL 3,869: **57mm** 923 M18; **75mm** 617; **106mm** 2,329 M40A1
ARTILLERY 7,795+
  SP 1,076: **105mm** 391: 26 M108T; 365 M52T; **155mm** 430: ε150 M44T1; ε280 T-155 Firtina (K9 Thunder); **175mm** 36 M107; **203mm** 219 M110A2
  TOWED 760+: **105mm** 75+ M101A1; **155mm** 523: 517 M114A1/M114A2; 6 Panter; **203mm** 162 M115
  MRL 146+: **107mm** 48; **122mm** ε36 T-122; **227mm** 12 M270 MLRS; **302mm** 50+ TR-300 Kasirga (WS-1)
  MOR 5,813+
    SP 1,443+: **81mm**; **107mm** 1,264 M106; **120mm** 179
    TOWED 4,370: **81mm** 3,792; **120mm** 578
SURFACE-TO-SURFACE MISSILE LAUNCHERS
  SRBM • **Conventional** MGM-140A ATACMS (launched from M270 MLRS); J-600T Yildrim (B-611/CH-SS-9 mod 1)
RADAR • **LAND** AN/TPQ-36 Firefinder; 2 Cobra
AIRCRAFT
  ISR 5 Beech 350 King Air
  TPT • **Light** 8: 5 Beech 200 King Air; 3 Cessna 421
  TRG 49: 45 Cessna T182; 4 T-42A Cochise
HELICOPTERS
  ATK 64: 18 AH-1P Cobra; 12 AH-1S Cobra; 5 AH-1W Cobra; 4 TAH-1P Cobra; 9 T129A; 16 T129B
  MRH 28 Hughes 300C
  TPT 224+: **Heavy** 6 CH-47F Chinook; **Medium** 77+: 29 AS532UL Cougar; 48+ S-70A Black Hawk; **Light** 141: 12 Bell 204B (AB-204B); ε45 Bell 205 (UH-1H Iroquois); 64 Bell 205A (AB-205A); 20 Bell 206 Jet Ranger
UNMANNED AERIAL VEHICLES
  CISR • **Medium** 26 Bayraktar TB2
  ISR • **Heavy** Falcon 600/Firebee; **Medium** CL-89; Gnat; **Light** Harpy
AIR DEFENCE
  SAM • **Point-defence** 148+: 70 Altigan PMADS octuple Stinger lnchr, 78 Zipkin PMADS quad Stinger lnchr; FIM-43 Redeye (being withdrawn); FIM-92 Stinger
  GUNS 1,664
    SP 40mm 262 M42A1
    TOWED 1,402: **20mm** 439 GAI-D01; **35mm** 120 GDF-001/GDF-003; **40mm** 843: 803 L/60/L/70; 40 T-1
AIR-LAUNCHED MISSILES
  ASM Mizrak-U (UMTAS)
BOMBS
  Laser-guided MAM-L; MAM-C

Navy ε45,000 (including conscripts)
EQUIPMENT BY TYPE
SUBMARINES • TACTICAL • SSK 12:
  4 *Atilay* (GER Type-209/1200) with 8 single 533mm ASTT with SST-4 HWT
  8 *Preveze/Gür* (GER Type-209/1400) with 8 single 533mm ASTT with UGM-84 *Harpoon* AShM/*Tigerfish* Mk2 HWT/DM2A4 HWT
PRINCIPAL SURFACE COMBATANTS 18
  FRIGATES • FFGHM 18:
    2 *Barbaros* (mod GER MEKO 200 F244 & F245) with 2 quad Mk141 lnchr with RGM-84C *Harpoon* AShM, 1 octuple Mk29 lnchr with *Aspide* SAM, 2 Mk32 triple 324mm ASTT with Mk46 LWT, 3 *Sea Zenith* CIWS, 1 127mm gun (capacity 1 Bell 212 (AB-212) hel)
    2 *Barbaros* (mod GER MEKO 200 F246 & F247) with 2 quad Mk141 lnchr with RGM-84C *Harpoon* AShM, 1 8-cell Mk41 VLS with *Aspide* SAM, 2 Mk32 triple 324mm ASTT with Mk46 LWT, 3 *Sea Zenith* CIWS, 1 127mm gun (capacity 1 Bell 212 (AB-212) hel)
    3 *Gabya* (ex-US *Oliver Hazard Perry* class) with 1 Mk13 GMLS with RGM-84C *Harpoon* AShM/SM-1MR SAM, 1 8-cell Mk41 VLS with RIM-162 SAM, 2 Mk32 triple 324mm ASTT with Mk46 LWT, 1 *Phalanx* Block 1B CIWS, 1 76mm gun (capacity 1 S-70B *Seahawk* ASW hel)
    5 *Gabya* (ex-US *Oliver Hazard Perry* class) with 1 Mk13 GMLS with RGM-84C *Harpoon* AShM/SM-1MR SAM, 2 Mk32 triple 324mm ASTT with Mk46 LWT, 1 *Phalanx* Block 1B CIWS, 1 76mm gun (capacity 1 S-70B *Seahawk* ASW hel)
    4 *Yavuz* (GER MEKO 200TN) with 2 quad Mk141 lnchr with RGM-84C *Harpoon* AShM, 1 octuple Mk29 GMLS with *Aspide* SAM, 2 Mk32 triple 324mm ASTT with Mk46 LWT, 3 *Sea Zenith* CIWS, 1 127mm gun (capacity 1 Bell 212 (AB-212) hel)
    2 *Ada* with 2 quad lnchr with RCM-84C *Harpoon* AShM, 1 Mk49 21-cell lnchr with RIM-116 SAM, 2 Mk32 twin 324mm ASTT with Mk46 LWT, 1 76mm gun (capacity 1 S-70B *Seahawk* hel)
PATROL AND COASTAL COMBATANTS 53:
  CORVETTES • FSGM 6:
    6 *Burak* (ex-FRA *d'Estienne d'Orves*) with 2 single lnchr with MM38 *Exocet* AShM, 4 single 324mm ASTT with Mk46 LWT, 1 Mk54 A/S mor, 1 100mm gun
  PCFG 19:
    4 *Dogan* (GER Lurssen-57) with 2 quad lnchr with RGM-84A/C *Harpoon* AShM, 1 76mm gun
    9 *Kilic* with 2 quad Mk 141 lnchr with RGM-84C *Harpoon* AShM, 1 76mm gun
    4 *Rüzgar* (GER Lurssen-57) with 2 quad lnchr with RGM-84A/C *Harpoon* AShM, 1 76mm gun
    2 *Yildiz* with 2 quad lnchr with RGM-84A/C *Harpoon* AShM, 1 76mm gun
  PCC 15 *Tuzla*
  PBFG 2 *Kartal* (GER *Jaguar*) with 4 single lnchr with RB 12 *Penguin* AShM, 2 single 533mm TT
MINE WARFARE • MINE COUNTERMEASURES 15:
  MHO 11: 5 *Engin* (FRA *Circe*); 6 *Aydin*
  MSC 4 *Seydi* (US *Adjutant*)

AMPHIBIOUS
  LANDING SHIPS • LST 5:
    1 *Bayraktar* with 1 hel landing platform (capacity 20 MBT; 250 troops)
    1 *Ertugrul* (ex-US *Terrebonne Parish*) with 3 76mm guns (capacity 18 tanks; 400 troops) (with 1 hel landing platform)
    1 *Osman Gazi* with 1 *Phalanx* CIWS (capacity 4 LCVP; 17 tanks; 980 troops) (with 1 hel landing platform)
    2 *Sarucabey* with 1 *Phalanx* CIWS (capacity 11 tanks; 600 troops) (with 1 hel landing platform)
  LANDING CRAFT 30
    LCT 21: 2 C-120/130; 11 C-140; 8 C-151
    LCM 9: 1 C-310; 8 C-320
LOGISTICS AND SUPPORT 34
  ABU 2: 1 AG5; 1 AG6 with 1 76mm gun
  AGS 2: 1 *Cesme* (ex-US *Silas Bent*); 1 *Cubuklu*
  AOR 2 *Akar* with 1 twin 76mm gun, 1 *Phalanx* CIWS, 1 hel landing platform
  AOT 2 *Burak*
  AOL 1 *Gurcan*
  AP 1 *Iskenderun*
  ASR 2: 1 *Alemdar* with 1 hel landing platform; 1 *Isin* II
  ATF 9: 1 *Akbas*; 1 *Degirmendere*; 1 *Gazal*; 1 *Inebolu*; 5 *Onder*
  AWT 3 *Sogut*
  AXL 8
  AX 2 *Pasa* (ex-GER *Rhein*)

Marines 3,000
FORCES BY ROLE
MANOEUVRE
  Amphibious
    1 mne bde (3 mne bn; 1 arty bn)

Naval Aviation
FORCES BY ROLE
ANTI-SUBMARINE WARFARE
  2 sqn with Bell 212 ASW (AB-212 ASW); S-70B *Seahawk*
  1 sqn with ATR-72-600; CN235M-100; TB-20 *Trinidad*
EQUIPMENT BY TYPE
AIRCRAFT
  MP 6 CN235M-100
  TPT • Light 7: 2 ATR-72-600; 5 TB-20 *Trinidad*
HELICOPTERS
  ASW 29: 11 Bell 212 ASW (AB-212 ASW); 18 S-70B *Seahawk*

Air Force ε50,000
2 tac air forces (divided between east and west)
Flying hours 180 hrs/yr
FORCES BY ROLE
FIGHTER/GROUND ATTACK
  1 sqn with F-4E *Phantom* 2020
  8 sqn with F-16C/D *Fighting Falcon*
ISR
  1 sqn with F-16C/D *Fighting Falcon*
  1 unit with *King Air* 350
AIRBORNE EARLY WARNING & CONTROL
  1 sqn (forming) with B-737 AEW&C

EW
  1 unit with CN235M EW
SEARCH & RESCUE
  1 sqn with AS532AL/UL *Cougar*
TANKER
  1 sqn with KC-135R *Stratotanker*
TRANSPORT
  1 sqn with A400M; C-160D *Transall*
  1 sqn with C-130B/E/H *Hercules*
  1 (VIP) sqn with Cessna 550 *Citation* II (UC-35); Cessna 650 *Citation* VII; CN235M; Gulfstream 550
  3 sqn with CN235M
  10 (liaison) flt with Bell 205 (UH-1H *Iroquois*); CN235M
TRAINING
  1 sqn with F-16C/D *Fighting Falcon*
  1 sqn with F-5A/B *Freedom Fighter*; NF-5A/B *Freedom Fighter*
  1 sqn with SF-260D
  1 sqn with KT-1T
  1 sqn with T-38A/M *Talon*
  1 sqn with T-41D *Mescalero*
AIR DEFENCE
  4 sqn with MIM-14 *Nike Hercules*
  2 sqn with *Rapier*
  8 (firing) unit with MIM-23 *Hawk*
MANOEUVRE
  Air Manoeuvre
    1 AB bde
EQUIPMENT BY TYPE
  AIRCRAFT 333 combat capable
    FTR 53: 18 F-5A *Freedom Fighter*; 8 F-5B *Freedom Fighter*; 17 NF-5A *Freedom Fighter*; 10 NF-5B *Freedom Fighter* (48 F-5s being upgraded as LIFT)
    FGA 280: 20 F-4E *Phantom 2020*; 27 F-16C *Fighting Falcon* Block 30; 162 F-16C *Fighting Falcon* Block 50; 14 F-16C *Fighting Falcon* Block 50+; 8 F-16D Block 30 *Fighting Falcon*; 33 F-16D *Fighting Falcon* Block 50; 16 F-16D *Fighting Falcon* Block 50+
    ISR 5 Beech 350 *King Air*
    EW 2+ CN235M EW
    AEW&C 4 B-737 AEW&C
    TKR 7 KC-135R *Stratotanker*
    TPT 87: **Heavy** 5 A400M; **Medium** 31: 6 C-130B *Hercules*; 12 C-130E *Hercules*; 1 C-130H *Hercules*; 12 C-160D *Transall*; **Light** 50: 2 Cessna 550 *Citation* II (UC-35 - VIP); 2 Cessna 650 *Citation* VII; 46 CN235M; **PAX** 1 Gulfstream 550
    TRG 169: 34 SF-260D; 70 T-38A/M *Talon*; 25 T-41D *Mescalero*; 40 KT-1T
  HELICOPTERS
    TPT 35: **Medium** 20: 6 AS532AL *Cougar* (CSAR); 14 AS532UL *Cougar* (SAR); **Light** 15 Bell 205 (UH-1H *Iroquois*)
  UNMANNED AERIAL VEHICLES 27+
    CISR • **Heavy** some ANKA-S
    ISR 27+: **Heavy** 9+: some ANKA; 9 *Heron*; **Medium** 18 *Gnat* 750
  AIR DEFENCE
    SAM
      Long-range MIM-14 *Nike Hercules*
      Medium-range MIM-23 *Hawk*
      Point-defence *Rapier*

AIR-LAUNCHED MISSILES
  AAM • **IR** AIM-9S *Sidewinder*; *Shafrir* 2(‡); **IIR** AIM-9X *Sidewinder* II; **SARH** AIM-7E *Sparrow*; **ARH** AIM-120A/B AMRAAM
  ARM AGM-88A HARM
  ASM AGM-65A/G *Maverick*; *Popeye* I
  LACM Coventional AGM-84K SLAM-ER
BOMBS
  Electro-optical guided GBU-8B HOBOS (GBU-15)
  INS/GPS guided AGM-154A JSOW; AGM-154C JSOW
  Laser-guided MAM-C; MAM-L; *Paveway* I; *Paveway* II

Paramilitary 156,800

Gendarmerie 152,100

Ministry of Interior; Ministry of Defence in war
FORCES BY ROLE
SPECIAL FORCES
  1 cdo bde
MANOEUVRE
  Other
    1 (border) paramilitary div
    2 paramilitary bde
EQUIPMENT BY TYPE
ARMOURED FIGHTING VEHICLES
  RECCE *Akrep*
  APC • **APC (W)** 560: 535 BTR-60/BTR-80; 25 *Condor*
AIRCRAFT
  ISR Some O-1E *Bird Dog*
  TPT • **Light** 2 Do-28D
HELICOPTERS
  MRH 19 Mi-17 *Hip* H
  TPT 35: **Medium** 12 S-70A *Black Hawk*; **Light** 23: 8 Bell 204B (AB-204B); 6 Bell 205A (AB-205A); 8 Bell 206A (AB-206A) *Jet Ranger*; 1 Bell 212 (AB-212)
UNMANNED AERIAL VEHICLES
  CISR • **Medium** 6 *Bayraktar* TB2

Coast Guard 4,700

EQUIPMENT BY TYPE
PATROL AND COASTAL COMBATANTS 104
  PSOH 4 *Dost* with 1 76mm gun
  PBF 60
  PB 40
AIRCRAFT • **MP** 3 CN235 MPA
HELICOPTERS • **MRH** 8 Bell 412EP (AB-412EP – SAR)

DEPLOYMENT

AFGHANISTAN
NATO • *Operation Resolute Support* 659; 1 mot inf bn(-)

ARABIAN SEA & GULF OF ADEN
Combined Maritime Forces • CTF-151: 1 FFGHM

BLACK SEA
NATO • SNMCMG 2: 1 MHO

BOSNIA-HERZEGOVINA
EU • EUFOR • *Operation Althea* 199; 1 inf coy

CYPRUS (NORTHERN)
ε43,000; 1 army corps HQ; 1 armd bde; 2 mech inf div; 1 avn comd; 8 M48A2 (trg;) 340 M48A5T1/T2; 361 AAPC (incl variants); 266 M113 (incl variants); 72 M101A1; 18 M114A2; 12 M115; 90 M44T; 6 T-122; 175 81mm mor; 148 M30; 127 HY-12; 66 *Milan*; 48 TOW; 192 M40A1; Rh 202; 16 GDF-003; 48 M1; 3 Cessna 185 (U-17); 1 AS532UL *Cougar*; 3 UH-1H *Iroquois*; 1 PB

IRAQ
Army: 2,000; 1 armd BG

LEBANON
UN • UNIFIL 49; 1 PCFG

MEDITERRANEAN SEA
NATO • SNMG 2: 1 FFGHM

QATAR
Army: 200 (trg team); 1 mech inf coy; 1 arty unit; 12+ ACV AIFV/AAPC; 2 T-155 *Firtina*

SERBIA
NATO • KFOR 307; 1 inf coy
UN • UNMIK 1 obs

SOMALIA
UN • UNSOM 1 obs

SYRIA
500+; 1 SF coy; 1 armd coy(+); 1 arty unit

UKRAINE
OSCE • Ukraine 11

FOREIGN FORCES
Italy *Active Fence*: 1 bty with SAMP/T
Saudi Arabia *Inherent Resolve*: 6 F-15S *Eagle*
Spain *Active Fence*: 149; 1 bty with MIM-104C *Patriot* PAC-2
United States US European Command: 2,700; 1 atk sqn with 12 A-10C *Thunderbolt* II; 1 tkr sqn with 14 KC-135; 1 CISR sqn with MQ-1B *Predator* UAV; 1 ELINT flt with EP-3E *Aries* II; 1 spt facility at Izmir; 1 spt facility at Ankara; 1 air base at Incirlik • US Strategic Command: 1 AN/TPY-2 X-band radar at Kürecik

United Kingdom UK

British Pound £		2016	2017	2018
GDP	£	1.94tr	2.01tr	
	US$	2.63tr	2.57tr	
per capita	US$	40,050	38,847	
Growth	%	1.8	1.7	
Inflation	%	0.7	2.6	
Def exp [a]	£	42.2bn	43.0bn	
	US$	57.2bn	55.0bn	
Def bdgt [b]	£	38.8bn	ε39.7bn	
	US$	52.6bn	ε50.7bn	
US$1=£		0.74	0.78	

[a] NATO definition
[b] Includes total departmental expenditure limits; costs of military operations; and external income earned by the MoD

Population 64,769,452

Age	0–14	15–19	20–24	25–29	30–64	65 plus
Male	9.0%	2.8%	3.2%	3.5%	23.1%	8.1%
Female	8.5%	2.7%	3.1%	3.4%	22.5%	9.9%

Capabilities

In Europe, the UK is equalled only by France in its ability to project credible expeditionary combat power. Its forces are relatively well balanced, but many key capabilities are close to critical mass. The defence budget is under pressure because of the fall in the value of the pound, the cost growth of some major programmes and the difficulty of achieving savings targets. Plans to field an improved 'Future Force 2025' by 2025 face considerable challenges in delivery. A 'national security capability review', ongoing in late 2017, will likely result in further changes to defence-capability plans. The defence ministry's current top policy priorities are contributing to the counter-ISIS coalition in the Middle East and being on standby to assist the police and security services to counter domestic terrorism. Force-modernisation continues, but it will be some time before the forces have a credible full-spectrum combat capability against a peer competitor such as Russia. The UK continues to invest in special-forces, counter-terrorist and cyber capabilities. The army is rebuilding its ability to field a full division of three combat brigades. HMS *Queen Elizabeth*, the new aircraft carrier, began sea trials, while the navy announced it would test a laser weapon on a warship. There has been much investment in strategic airlift. Current lift capacity is sufficient to deploy and sustain small- and medium-scale contingents. Expeditionary logistic capability meets policy requirements, but peacetime logistic support within the UK is dependent on contractors. The sophisticated domestic defence industry cannot meet all of the UK's defence-industrial and logistics requirements. The UK maintains forces in Afghanistan, Iraq and Nigeria and in 2017 rapidly deployed a joint force for hurricane relief in the Caribbean. The UK leads a multinational battlegroup deployed to Estonia as part of NATO's Enhanced Forward Presence, and deploys combat aircraft for NATO air policing. (See pp. 80–81.)

ACTIVE 150,250 (Army 85,000 Navy 32,350 Air 32,900)

RESERVE 82,650 (Regular Reserve 43,600 (Army 29,450, Navy 6,550, Air 7,600); Volunteer Reserve 37,000 (Army 30,500, Navy 3,650, Air 2,850); Sponsored Reserve 2,050)

Includes both trained and those currently under training within the Regular Forces, excluding university cadet units

ORGANISATIONS BY SERVICE

Strategic Forces 1,000

Royal Navy
EQUIPMENT BY TYPE
SUBMARINES • STRATEGIC • SSBN 4:
  4 *Vanguard* with 1 16-cell VLS with UGM-133A *Trident* II D-5/D-5LE nuclear SLBM, 4 533mm TT with *Spearfish* HWT (each boat will not deploy with more than 40 warheads, but each missile could carry up to 12 MIRV; some *Trident* D-5 capable of being configured for sub-strategic role)
MSL • SLBM • Nuclear 48 UGM-133A *Trident* II D-5 (fewer than 160 declared operational warheads)

Royal Air Force
EQUIPMENT BY TYPE
RADAR • STRATEGIC 1 Ballistic Missile Early Warning System (BMEWS) at Fylingdales Moor

Space
EQUIPMENT BY TYPE
SATELLITES • COMMUNICATIONS 8: 1 NATO-4B; 3 *Skynet*-4; 4 *Skynet*-5

Army 82,050; 2,950 Gurkhas (total 85,000)
Regt normally bn size. Many cbt spt and CSS regt and bn have reservist sub-units
FORCES BY ROLE
COMMAND
  1 (ARRC) corps HQ
MANOEUVRE
  Armoured
  1 (3rd) armd div (2 (12th & 20th) armd inf bde (1 armd recce regt, 1 tk regt, 2 armd inf bn, 1 mech inf bn); 1 (1st) armd inf bde (1 armd recce regt, 1 tk regt, 2 armd inf bn); 1 log bde (6 log regt; 4 maint regt; 3 med regt))
  Light
  1 (1st) lt inf div (1 (4th) inf bde (1 recce regt, 1 lt mech inf bn; 2 lt inf bn); 1 (7th) inf bde (1 recce regt, 3 lt mech inf bn; 2 lt inf bn); 1 (11th) inf bde (1 lt mech inf bn; 1 lt inf bn; 1 (Gurkha) lt inf bn); 1 (51st) inf bde (1 recce regt, 2 lt mech inf bn; 1 lt inf bn); 2 (38th & 160th) inf bde (1 lt inf bn); 1 log bde (2 log regt; 2 maint bn; 2 med regt))
  2 lt inf bn (London)
  1 (Gurkha) lt inf bn (Brunei)
  1 (Spec Inf Gp) inf bde(-) (2 inf bn(-))
  Air Manoeuvre
  1 (16th) air aslt bde (1 recce pl, 2 para bn, 1 fd arty regt, 1 cbt engr regt, 1 log regt, 1 med regt)
COMBAT SUPPORT
  1 arty bde (3 SP arty regt, 2 fd arty regt)
  2 AD regt
  1 engr bde (5 cbt engr regt, 2 EOD regt, 1 (MWD) EOD search regt, 1 engr regt, 1 (air spt) engr regt, 1 log regt)
  1 (geographic) engr regt
  1 ISR bde (1 STA regt, 1 EW regt, 3 int bn, 1 ISR UAV regt)
  1 MP bde (3 MP regt)
  1 sigs bde (7 sigs regt)
  1 sigs bde (2 sigs regt; 1 (ARRC) sigs bn)
  1 (77th) info ops bde (3 info ops gp, 1 spt gp, 1 engr spt/log gp)
COMBAT SERVICE SUPPORT
  1 engr spt gp
  1 log bde (2 log regt)
  1 med bde (3 fd hospital)

Reserves

Army Reserve 30,500 reservists
The Army Reserve (AR) generates individuals, sub-units and some full units. The majority of units are subordinate to regular formation headquarters and paired with one or more regular units
FORCES BY ROLE
MANOEUVRE
  Reconnaissance
  3 recce regt
  Armoured
  1 armd regt
  Light
  15 lt inf bn
  Air Manoeuvre
  1 para bn
COMBAT SUPPORT
  3 arty regt
  1 STA regt
  1 MRL regt
  3 engr regt
  4 int bn
  4 sigs regt
COMBAT SERVICE SUPPORT
  11 log regt
  6 maint regt
  4 med regt
  10 fd hospital
AIR DEFENCE
  1 AD regt
EQUIPMENT BY TYPE
ARMOURED FIGHTING VEHICLES
  MBT 227 *Challenger* 2
  RECCE 613: 197 *Jackal*; 110 *Jackal* 2; 130 *Jackal* 2A; 145 FV107 *Scimitar*; 31 *Scimitar* Mk2

IFV 623: 466 FV510 *Warrior*; 88 FV511 *Warrior* (CP); 51 FV514 *Warrior* (OP); 18 FV515 *Warrior* (CP)
APC 1,291
   APC (T) 895 *Bulldog* Mk3
   PPV 396 *Mastiff* (6×6)
AUV 1,238: 399 *Foxhound*; 252 FV103 *Spartan* (incl variants); 23 *Spartan* Mk2 (incl variants); 396 *Panther* CLV; 168 *Ridgback*
ENGINEERING & MAINTENANCE VEHICLES
AEV 92: 60 *Terrier*; 32 *Trojan*
ARV 259: 80 *Challenger* ARRV; 28 FV106 *Samson*; 5 *Samson* Mk2; 105 FV512 *Warrior*; 41 FV513 *Warrior*
MW 64 *Aardvark*
VLB 70: 37 M3; 33 *Titan*
NBC VEHICLES 8 TPz-1 *Fuchs* NBC
ANTI-TANK/ANTI-INFRASTRUCTURE • MSL
   SP *Exactor* (*Spike* NLOS)
   MANPATS FGM-148 *Javelin*
ARTILLERY 598
   SP 155mm 89 AS90
   TOWED 105mm 114 L118 Light Gun
   MRL 227mm 35 M270B1 MLRS
   MOR 81mm 360 L16A1
RADAR • LAND 150: 6 *Giraffe* AMB; 5 *Mamba*; 139 MSTAR
AMPHIBIOUS • LCU 3 Ramped Craft Logistic
AIR DEFENCE • SAM
   Point-defence 74: 60 FV4333 *Stormer* with *Starstreak*; 14 *Rapier* FSC; *Starstreak* (LML)

Joint Helicopter Command

Tri-service joint organisation including Royal Navy, Army and RAF units

Army

FORCES BY ROLE
ISR
   1 regt (1 sqn with BN-2 *Defender/Islander*; 1 sqn with SA341B *Gazelle* AH1)
ATTACK HELICOPTER
   1 regt (2 sqn with AH-64D *Apache*; 1 trg sqn with AH-64D *Apache*)
   1 regt (2 sqn with AH-64D *Apache*)
HELICOPTER
   1 regt (2 sqn with AW159 *Wildcat* AH1)
   1 (spec ops) sqn with *Lynx* AH9A
   1 (spec ops) sqn with AS365N3; SA341B *Gazelle* AH1
   1 flt with Bell 212 (Brunei)
   1 flt with SA341B *Gazelle* AH1 (Canada)
TRAINING
   1 hel regt (1 sqn with AH-64D *Apache*; 1 sqn with AS350B *Ecureuil*; 1 sqn with Bell 212; *Lynx* AH9A; SA341B *Gazelle* AH1)
ISR UAV
   1 ISR UAV regt
COMBAT SERVICE SUPPORT
   1 maint regt

Army Reserve

FORCES BY ROLE
HELICOPTER
   1 hel regt (4 sqn personnel only)

Royal Navy

FORCES BY ROLE
ATTACK HELICOPTER
   1 lt sqn with AW159 *Wildcat* AH1
TRANSPORT HELICOPTER
   2 sqn with AW101 *Merlin* HC3/3A/3i

Royal Air Force

FORCES BY ROLE
TRANSPORT HELICOPTER
   3 sqn with CH-47D/SD/F *Chinook* HC3/4/4A/6
   2 sqn with SA330 *Puma* HC2
TRAINING
   1 OCU sqn with CH-47D/SD/F *Chinook* HC3/4/4A/6; SA330 *Puma* HC2
EQUIPMENT BY TYPE
AIRCRAFT • TPT • Light 12: 9 BN-2T-4S *Defender*; 3 BN-2 *Islander* AL1
HELICOPTERS
   ATK 50 AH-64D *Apache*
   MRH 81: 5 AS365N3; 34 AW159 *Wildcat* AH1; 8 *Lynx* AH9A; 34 SA341B *Gazelle* AH1
   TPT 122: **Heavy** 60: 38 CH-47D *Chinook* HC4/4A; 7 CH-47SD *Chinook* HC3; 1 CH-47SD *Chinook* HC5; 14 CH-47F *Chinook* HC6; **Medium** 48: 25 AW101 *Merlin* HC3/3A/3i; 23 SA330 *Puma* HC2; **Light** 14: 9 AS350B *Ecureuil*; 5 Bell 212
UNMANNED AERIAL VEHICLES • ISR • Medium 8 *Watchkeeper* (21+ more in store)

Royal Navy 32,350

EQUIPMENT BY TYPE
SUBMARINES 10
   STRATEGIC • SSBN 4:
      4 *Vanguard*, opcon Strategic Forces with 1 16-cell VLS with UGM-133A *Trident* II D-5/D-5LE nuclear SLBM, 4 single 533mm TT with *Spearfish* HWT (each boat will not deploy with more than 40 warheads, but each missile could carry up to 12 MIRV; some *Trident* D-5 capable of being configured for sub-strategic role)
   TACTICAL • SSN 6:
      3 *Trafalgar* with 5 single 533mm TT with *Tomahawk* LACM/*Spearfish* HWT
      3 *Astute* with 6 single 533mm TT with *Tomahawk* LACM/*Spearfish* HWT
PRINCIPAL SURFACE COMBATANTS 19
   DESTROYERS 6
      DDGHM 3 *Daring* (Type-45) with 2 quad lnchr with RGM-84C *Harpoon*, 1 48-cell VLS with *Sea Viper* SAM, 2 *Phalanx* Block 1B CIWS, 1 114mm gun (capacity 1 AW159 *Wildcat*/AW101 *Merlin* hel)
      DDHM 3 *Daring* (Type-45) with 1 48-cell VLS with *Sea Viper* SAM, 2 *Phalanx* Block 1B CIWS, 1 114mm gun (capacity 1 AW159 *Wildcat*/AW101 *Merlin* hel)
   FRIGATES • FFGHM 13:
      9 *Norfolk* (Type-23) with 2 quad Mk141 lnchr with RGM-84C *Harpoon* AShM, 1 32-cell VLS with *Sea Wolf* SAM, 2 twin 324mm ASTT with *Sting Ray* LWT,

1 114mm gun (capacity either 2 AW159 *Wildcat* or 1 AW101 *Merlin* hel)

4 *Norfolk* (Type-23) with 2 quad Mk141 lnchr with RGM-84C *Harpoon* AShM, 1 32-cell VLS with *Sea Ceptor* SAM, 2 twin 324mm ASTT with *Sting Ray* LWT, 1 114mm gun (capacity either 2 AW159 *Wildcat* or 1 AW101 *Merlin* hel)

PATROL AND COASTAL COMBATANTS 21
  PSO 3: 2 *River*; 1 *River* (mod) with 1 hel landing platform
  PBI 18: 16 *Archer* (trg); 2 *Scimitar*
MINE WARFARE • MINE COUNTERMEASURES 14
  MCO 6 *Hunt* (incl 4 mod *Hunt*)
  MHC 8 *Sandown* (1 decommissioned and used in trg role)
AMPHIBIOUS
  PRINCIPAL AMPHIBIOUS SHIPS 3
    LPD 2 *Albion* with 2 *Phalanx* Block 1B CIWS (capacity 2 med hel; 4 LCU or 2 LCAC; 4 LCVP; 6 MBT; 300 troops) (of which 1 at extended readiness)
    LPH 1 *Ocean* with 3 *Phalanx* Block 1B CIWS (capacity 18 hel; 4 LCVP; 800 troops)
LOGISTICS AND SUPPORT 4
  AGB 1 *Protector* with 1 hel landing platform
  AGS 3: 1 *Scott*; 2 *Echo* (all with 1 hel landing platform)

Royal Fleet Auxiliary

Support and miscellaneous vessels are mostly manned and maintained by the Royal Fleet Auxiliary (RFA), a civilian fleet owned by the UK MoD, which has approximately 1,900 personnel with type comd under CINCFLEET
  AMPHIBIOUS • PRINCIPAL AMPHIBIOUS SHIPS 3
    LSD 3 *Bay* (capacity 4 LCU; 2 LCVP; 24 CR2 *Challenger* 2 MBT; 350 troops)
  LOGISTICS AND SUPPORT 12
    AORH 4: 2 *Wave*; 1 *Fort Victoria* with 2 *Phalanx* CIWS; 1 *Tide* (capacity 1 AW159 *Wildcat*/AW101 *Merlin* hel)
    AORL 1 *Rover* with 1 hel landing platform
    AFSH 2 *Fort Rosalie*
    AG 1 *Argus* (aviation trg ship with secondary role as primarily casualty-receiving ship)
    AKR 4 *Point* (not RFA manned)

Naval Aviation (Fleet Air Arm) 4,650

FORCES BY ROLE
ANTI-SUBMARINE WARFARE
  4 sqn with AW101 ASW *Merlin* HM2
  2 sqn with AW159 *Wildcat* HMA2
AIRBORNE EARLY WARNING
  1 sqn with *Sea King* AEW7
TRAINING
  1 sqn with Beech 350ER *King Air*
  1 sqn with G-115
  1 sqn with *Hawk* T1
EQUIPMENT BY TYPE
AIRCRAFT 12 combat capable
  TPT • Light 4 Beech 350ER *King Air* (*Avenger*)
  TRG 17: 5 G-115; 12 *Hawk* T1*
HELICOPTERS
  ASW 58: 28 AW159 *Wildcat* HMA2; 30 AW101 ASW *Merlin* HM2
  AEW 7 *Sea King* AEW7

Royal Marines 6,600

FORCES BY ROLE
MANOEUVRE
  Amphibious
  1 (3rd Cdo) mne bde (3 mne bn; 1 amph aslt sqn; 1 (army) arty regt; 1 (army) engr regt; 1 ISR gp (1 EW sqn; 1 cbt spt sqn; 1 sigs sqn; 1 log sqn), 1 log regt)
  2 landing craft sqn opcon Royal Navy
  Other
  1 (Fleet Protection) sy gp
EQUIPMENT BY TYPE
ARMOURED FIGHTING VEHICLES
  APC (T) 99 BvS-10 Mk2 *Viking*
ANTI-TANK/ANTI-INFRASTUCTURE
  MSL • MANPATS FGM-148 *Javelin*
ARTILLERY 39
  TOWED 105mm 12 L118 Light Gun
  MOR 81mm 27 L16A1
PATROL AND COASTAL COMBATANTS • PB 2 *Island*
AMPHIBIOUS • LANDING CRAFT 30
  LCU 10 LCU Mk10 (capacity 4 *Viking* APC or 120 troops)
  LCVP 16 LCVP Mk5B (capacity 35 troops)
  UCAC 4 *Griffon* 2400TD
AIR DEFENCE • SAM • Point-defence *Starstreak*

Royal Air Force 32,900

Flying hours 210 hrs/yr on fast jets; 290 on tpt ac; 240 on hels

FORCES BY ROLE
FIGHTER
  2 sqn with *Typhoon* FGR4/T3
FIGHTER/GROUND ATTACK
  3 sqn with *Typhoon* FGR4/T3
  1 sqn with F-35B *Lightning* II (forming)
GROUND ATTACK
  3 sqn with *Tornado* GR4/4A
ISR
  1 sqn with *Sentinel* R1
  1 sqn with *Shadow* R1
ELINT
  1 sqn with RC-135W *Rivet Joint*
AIRBORNE EARLY WARNING & CONTROL
  1 sqn with E-3D *Sentry*
SEARCH & RESCUE
  1 sqn with Bell 412EP *Griffin* HAR-2
TANKER/TRANSPORT
  2 sqn with A330 MRTT *Voyager* KC2/3
TRANSPORT
  1 (comms) sqn with AW109E/SP; BAe-146; BN-2A *Islander* CC2
  1 sqn with A400M *Atlas*
  1 sqn with C-17A *Globemaster*
  3 sqn with C-130J/J-30 *Hercules*
TRAINING
  1 OCU sqn with *Typhoon*
  1 OCU sqn with E-3D *Sentry*; *Sentinel* R1
  1 sqn with Beech 200 *King Air*
  1 sqn with EMB-312 *Tucano* T1
  2 sqn with *Hawk* T1/1A/1W
  1 sqn with *Hawk* T2
  3 sqn with *Tutor*

COMBAT/ISR UAV
  2 sqn with MQ-9A *Reaper*
EQUIPMENT BY TYPE
AIRCRAFT 258 combat capable
  FGA 152: 13 F-35B *Lightning* II (in test); 139 *Typhoon* FGR4/T3
  ATK 46 *Tornado* GR4/GR4A
  ISR 9: 4 *Sentinel* R1; 5 *Shadow* R1
  ELINT 3 RC-135W *Rivet Joint*
  AEW&C 6 E-3D *Sentry*
  TKR/TPT 14 A330 MRTT *Voyager* KC2/3
  TPT 58: **Heavy** 24: 16 A400M *Atlas*; 8 C-17A *Globemaster*; **Medium** 20: 6 C-130J *Hercules*; 14 C-130J-30 *Hercules*; **Light** 10: 5 Beech 200 *King Air* (on lease); 2 Beech 200GT *King Air* (on lease); 3 BN-2A *Islander* CC2; **PAX** 4 BAe-146 CC2/C3
  TRG 200: 39 EMB-312 *Tucano* T1 (39 more in store); 101 G-115E *Tutor*; 28 *Hawk* T2*; 32 *Hawk* T1/1A/1W* (ε46 more in store)
HELICOPTERS
  MRH 5: 1 AW139; 4 Bell 412EP *Griffin* HAR-2
  TPT • Light 3: 2 AW109E; 1 AW109SP
UNMANNED AERIAL VEHICLES • CISR • Heavy 10 MQ-9A *Reaper*
AIR-LAUNCHED MISSILES
  AAM • IR AIM-9L/L(I) *Sidewinder*; **IIR** ASRAAM; **ARH** AIM-120C-5 AMRAAM
  ASM AGM-114 *Hellfire*; *Brimstone*; *Dual-Mode Brimstone*; *Brimstone* II
  ALCM *Storm Shadow*
BOMBS
  Laser/GPS-guided GBU-10 *Paveway* II; GBU-24 *Paveway* III; Enhanced *Paveway* II/III; *Paveway* IV

Royal Air Force Regiment
FORCES BY ROLE
MANOEUVRE
  Other
    6 sy sqn
COMBAT SUPPORT
  2 CBRN sqn

Tri-Service Defence Helicopter School
FORCES BY ROLE
TRAINING
  1 hel sqn with Bell 412EP *Griffin* HT1
  2 hel sqn with AS350B *Ecureuil*
EQUIPMENT BY TYPE
HELICOPTERS
  MRH 11 Bell 412EP *Griffin* HT1
  TPT • Light 27: 25 AS350B *Ecureuil*; 2 AW109E

Volunteer Reserve Air Forces
(Royal Auxiliary Air Force/RAF Reserve)
MANOEUVRE
  Other
    5 sy sqn
COMBAT SUPPORT
  2 int sqn
COMBAT SERVICE SUPPORT
  1 med sqn
  1 (air movements) sqn
  1 (HQ augmentation) sqn
  1 (C-130 Reserve Aircrew) flt

UK Special Forces
Includes Royal Navy, Army and RAF units
FORCES BY ROLE
SPECIAL FORCES
  1 (SAS) SF regt
  1 (SBS) SF regt
  1 (Special Reconnaissance) SF regt
  1 SF BG (based on 1 para bn)
AVIATION
  1 wg (includes assets drawn from 3 Army hel sqn, 1 RAF tpt sqn and 1 RAF hel sqn)
COMBAT SUPPORT
  1 sigs regt

Reserve
FORCES BY ROLE
SPECIAL FORCES
  2 (SAS) SF regt

Cyber
The National Cyber Security Centre plays a central role in coordinating the UK's cyber policy and works with ministries and agencies to implement cyber-security programmes. The Defence Cyber Operations Group was set up in 2011 to place 'cyber at the heart of defence operations, doctrine and training'. This group was transferred to Joint Forces Command on the formation's establishment in April 2012. A Joint Forces Cyber Group was set up in 2013, including a Joint Cyber Reserve, providing support to two Joint Cyber Units and other information-assurance units across the defence establishment. Increased concern about the potential of information operations in and through the cyber domain was central to the 2015 creation of 77 Bde. The 2015 SDSR designated cyber a tier-one risk and stated that the UK would respond to a cyber attack in the same way as it would an equivalent conventional attack. In October 2016, the UK acknowledged publicly the use of offensive cyber capabilities against ISIS. The 2016 National Cyber Security Strategy outlined £1.9 billion in cyber-security investments in the period up to 2021. In April 2016, it was announced that a Cyber Security Operations Centre would be established under the MoD and tasked with protecting the MoD's cyberspace. A Defence Cyber School was scheduled to open in January 2018, bringing service cyber training together in one organisation.

DEPLOYMENT

AFGHANISTAN
NATO • *Operation Resolute Support* 500; 1 inf bn(-)

ALBANIA
OSCE • Albania 3

ARABIAN SEA & GULF OF ADEN
1 FFGHM

ARMENIA/AZERBAIJAN
OSCE • Minsk Conference 1

ASCENSION ISLAND
20

ATLANTIC (NORTH)/CARIBBEAN
Operation Ruman 1 LSD

ATLANTIC (SOUTH)
1 AORL

BAHRAIN
80; 1 naval base

BELIZE
20

BLACK SEA
NATO • SNMCMG 2: 1 MHC; 1 AGS

BOSNIA-HERZEGOVINA
EU • EUFOR • *Operation Althea* 4
OSCE • Bosnia and Herzegovina 3

BRITISH INDIAN OCEAN TERRITORY
40; 1 navy/marine det

BRUNEI
1,000; 1 (Gurkha) lt inf bn; 1 jungle trg centre; 1 hel flt with 3 Bell 212

CANADA
370; 1 trg unit; 1 hel flt with SA341 *Gazelle* AH1

CYPRUS
2,260; 2 inf bn; 1 SAR sqn with 4 Bell 412 *Griffin* HAR-2; 1 radar (on det)
Operation Shader 500: 1 FGA sqn with 6 *Tornado* GR4; 6 *Typhoon* FGR4; 1 *Sentinel* R1; 1 E-3D *Sentry*; 1 A330 MRTT *Voyager* KC3; 2 C-130J *Hercules*
UN • UNFICYP 277; 1 inf coy

DEMOCRATIC REPUBLIC OF THE CONGO
UN • MONUSCO 6

EGYPT
MFO 2

ESTONIA
NATO • Enhanced Forward Presence 800; 1 armd inf bn HQ; 1 armd inf coy(+); 1 engr sqn

FALKLAND ISLANDS
1,000: 1 inf coy(+); 1 sigs unit; 1 AD det with *Rapier*; 1 PSO; 1 ftr flt with 4 *Typhoon* FGR4; 1 tkr/tpt flt with C-130J *Hercules*

GERMANY
3,750; 1 armd inf bde(-) (1 tk regt, 1 armd inf bn); 1 SP arty regt; 1 cbt engr regt; 1 maint regt; 1 med regt

GIBRALTAR
570 (incl Royal Gibraltar regt); 2 PB

IRAQ
Operation Shader 600; 2 inf bn(-); 1 engr sqn(-)

KENYA
250; 1 trg unit

KUWAIT
30 (trg team)
Operation Shader MQ-9A *Reaper*

LIBYA
UN • UNSMIL 1 obs

MALI
EU • EUTM Mali 8
UN • MINUSMA 2

MEDITERRANEAN SEA
NATO • SNMG 2: 1 LPH

MOLDOVA
OSCE • Moldova 1

NEPAL
60 (Gurkha trg org)

NIGERIA
300 (trg teams)

OMAN
90; 1 hel flt with AW101 ASW *Merlin* HM2; AW159 *Wildcat* HMA2

PERSIAN GULF
Operation Kipion 2 MCO; 2 MHC; 1 LSD

POLAND
NATO • Enhanced Forward Presence 150; 1 recce sqn

SERBIA
NATO • KFOR 29
OSCE • Kosovo 7

SOMALIA
EU • EUTM Somalia 4
UN • UNSOM 4 obs
UN • UNSOS 41

SOUTH SUDAN
UN • UNMISS 373; 1 engr coy; 1 fd hospital

UKRAINE
OSCE • Ukraine 51
Operation Orbital 100 (trg team)

UNITED ARAB EMIRATES
1 tpt/tkr flt with C-17A *Globemaster*; C-130J *Hercules*; A330 MRTT *Voyager*

FOREIGN FORCES

United States
US European Command: 8,300; 1 ftr wg at RAF Lakenheath (1 ftr sqn with 24 F-15C/D *Eagle*, 2 ftr sqn with 23 F-15E *Strike Eagle*); 1 ISR sqn at RAF Mildenhall with OC-135/RC-135; 1 tkr wg at RAF Mildenhall with 15 KC-135R/T *Stratotanker*; 1 CSAR sqn at RAF Lakenheath with 8 HH-60G *Pave Hawk*: 1 Spec Ops gp at RAF Mildenhall (1 sqn with 8 CV-22B *Osprey*; 1 sqn with 8 MC-130J *Commando* II) • US Strategic Command: 1 AN/FPS-132 Upgraded Early Warning Radar and 1 *Spacetrack* radar at Fylingdales Moor

Arms procurements and deliveries – Europe

Selected events in 2017

- France and Germany announced that they are exploring the potential development of a new combat aircraft to be produced after *Rafale* and the *Typhoon*.

- Norway selected ThyssenKrupp Marine Systems (TKMS) and its improved Type-212A design for its future submarine requirement. The new design will be known as Type-212NG (Norway-Germany/Next Generation). The agreement will see both countries purchase the same submarine design, which will be delivered in 2020–30. Norway plans to purchase four boats and Germany two. A production contract is expected in 2019.

- BAE Systems was awarded a US$4.83 billion contract for the United Kingdom's first three Type-26 frigates. The first is planned to enter service in the mid-2020s.

- Naval Group, formerly called DCNS, was awarded a US$4.28bn contract for the first five *Frégates de Taille Intermédiaire* frigates for the French Navy. The first vessel is planned to enter service in 2025.

- France temporarily nationalised STX France after Italian company Fincantieri was on the verge of acquiring Korean company STX Offshore and Shipbuilding's majority share. France and Italy are now negotiating the future of the company.

- France and the UK agreed a three-year concept phase with MBDA for a new generation of cruise missiles. Both countries plan to ultimately replace *Exocet*, *Harpoon*, SCALP and *Storm Shadow*. The current ambition is for the project to result in an operational system by the end of the 2020s.

- Turkey rejected Otokar's initial bid for *Altay* tank series production and issued a tender for the deal. Turkish tractor firm TÜMOSAN had its contract to develop a powerpack for *Altay* cancelled after Austrian partner AVL withdrew due to the Turkish government's crackdown after the coup attempt. It is now unclear what propulsion system a series-production *Altay* would use.

- The Turkish Air Force's ANKA-S UAV carried out its first operational weapons firings. Ten of these are to be supplied by TAI by the end of 2018.

- Belgium issued a request for proposals for its fighter competition. Thirty-four new aircraft are planned to reach initial operating capability in 2025 and full operating capability in 2030. A decision is expected in 2018.

Figure 7 **Europe: selected ongoing or completed procurement priorities in 2017**

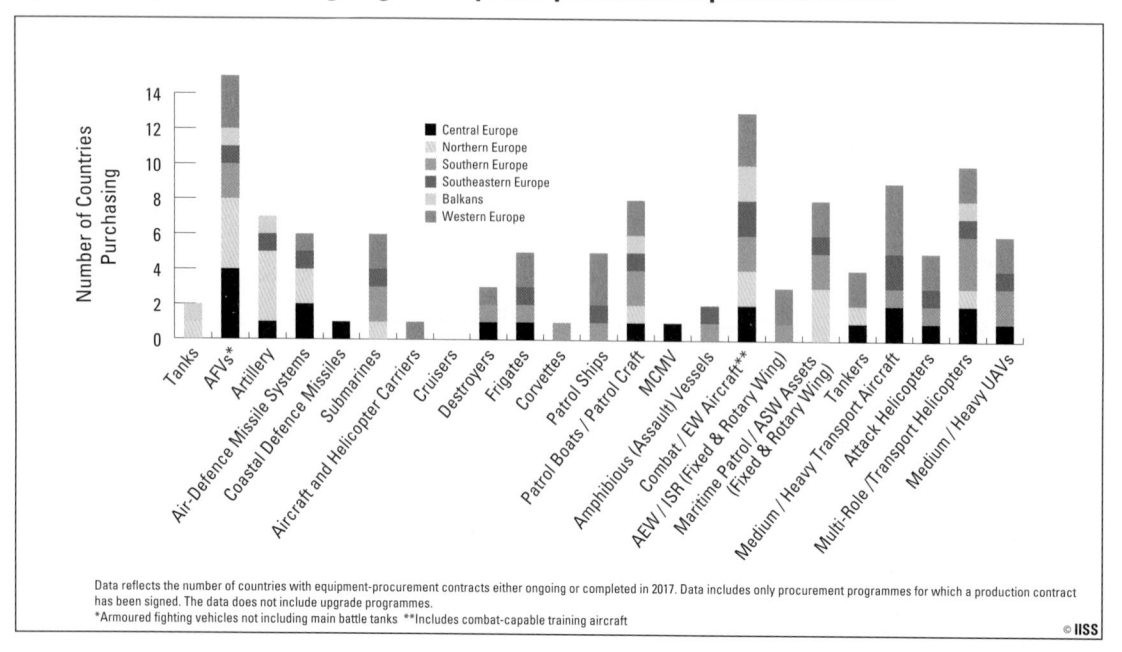

Data reflects the number of countries with equipment-procurement contracts either ongoing or completed in 2017. Data includes only procurement programmes for which a production contract has been signed. The data does not include upgrade programmes.
*Armoured fighting vehicles not including main battle tanks **Includes combat-capable training aircraft

© IISS

Table 7 European armoured vehicles: selected fleet acquisitions*

Country	Equipment	Type	Quantity	Company	Replacing	Date of order
Austria	*Pandur* II	APC (W)	34	(AUT) GDLS – Steyr	–	2016
Denmark	*Piranha* 5	APC (W)	309	(CHE) GDLS – MOWAG	M113	2015
Estonia	CV9035	IFV	44	(NLD) Govt surplus	–	2014
Finland	*Leopard* 2A6	MBT	100	(NLD) Govt surplus	*Leopard* 2A4	2014
France	*Jaguar*	Recce	20	(FRA) Nexter (FRA) Renault Trucks Defense (FRA) Thales	ERC-90F4 *Sagaie*	2017
	Griffon	APC (W)	319		AMX10RC; VAB	2017
Germany	*Puma*	IFV	350	(GER) Rheinmetall (GER) KMW	*Marder* 1	2004
Latvia	CVR (T) family	APC (T)	123	(UK) Govt surplus	–	2014
Lithuania	*Boxer*	IFV	88	(GER/NLD) ARTEC	M113	2016
Netherlands	*Boxer*	APC (W)	200	(GER/NLD) ARTEC	M577; YPR-765	2000
Poland	*Rosomak*	IFV & APC (W)	877	(POL) Rosomak	BMP-1; BRDM-2	2003
Spain	*Pizarro*	IFV	119	(ESP) GDLS – SBS	M113	2004
Turkey	*Cobra* II	APC (W)	n.k.	(TUR) Otokar	–	2015
	ZAHA	AAV	27	(TUR) FNSS	–	2017
UK	*Ajax* family	Recce	589	(UK) General Dynamics UK	CVR (T)	2014

*Not including upgrade contracts

Figure 8 NATO Europe: ageing mine-countermeasures (MCM) vessels and current replacement programmes

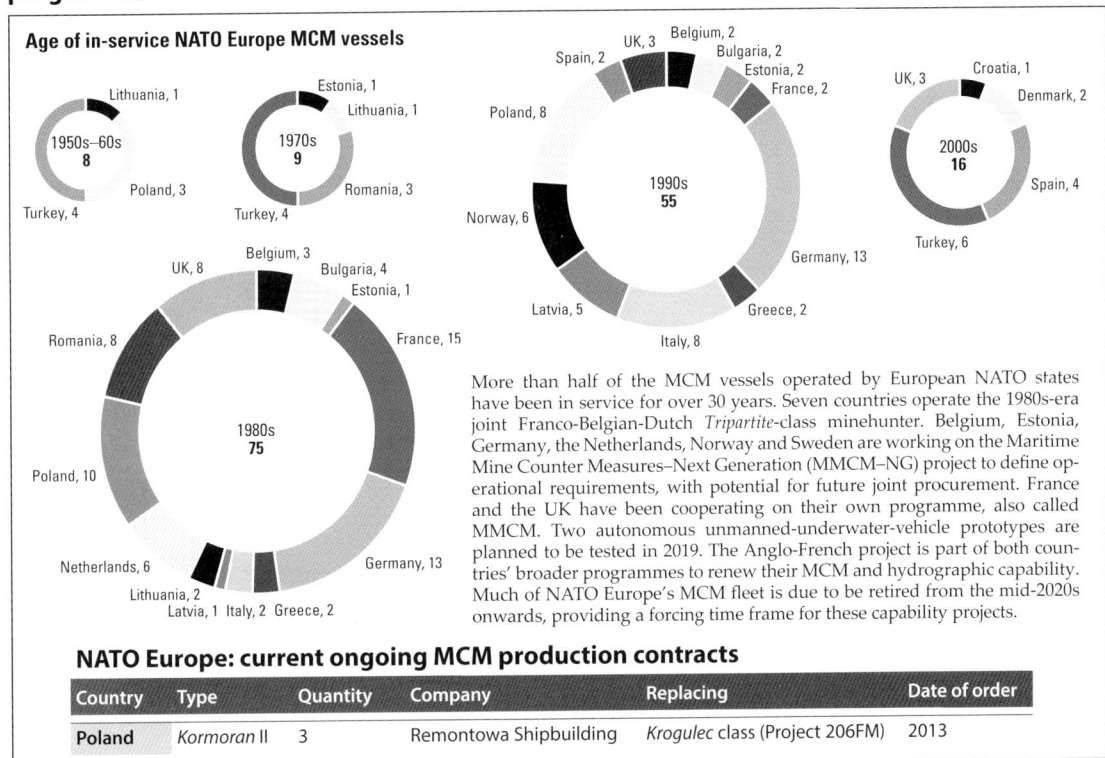

Age of in-service NATO Europe MCM vessels

1950s–60s: 8 (Lithuania, 1; Turkey, 4; Poland, 3)

1970s: 9 (Estonia, 1; Lithuania, 1; Romania, 3; Turkey, 4)

1980s: 75 (UK, 8; Belgium, 3; Bulgaria, 4; Estonia, 1; France, 15; Germany, 13; Italy, 2; Greece, 2; Latvia, 1; Lithuania, 2; Netherlands, 6; Poland, 10; Romania, 8)

1990s: 55 (UK, 3; Belgium, 2; Bulgaria, 2; Estonia, 2; France, 2; Germany, 13; Greece, 2; Italy, 8; Latvia, 5; Norway, 6; Poland, 8; Spain, 2)

2000s: 16 (UK, 3; Croatia, 1; Denmark, 2; Spain, 4; Turkey, 6)

More than half of the MCM vessels operated by European NATO states have been in service for over 30 years. Seven countries operate the 1980s-era joint Franco-Belgian-Dutch *Tripartite*-class minehunter. Belgium, Estonia, Germany, the Netherlands, Norway and Sweden are working on the Maritime Mine Counter Measures–Next Generation (MMCM–NG) project to define operational requirements, with potential for future joint procurement. France and the UK have been cooperating on their own programme, also called MMCM. Two autonomous unmanned-underwater-vehicle prototypes are planned to be tested in 2019. The Anglo-French project is part of both countries' broader programmes to renew their MCM and hydrographic capability. Much of NATO Europe's MCM fleet is due to be retired from the mid-2020s onwards, providing a forcing time frame for these capability projects.

NATO Europe: current ongoing MCM production contracts

Country	Type	Quantity	Company	Replacing	Date of order
Poland	*Kormoran* II	3	Remontowa Shipbuilding	*Krogulec* class (Project 206FM)	2013

168 THE MILITARY BALANCE 2018

Figure 9 **Submarine programmes: ThyssenKrupp Marine Systems/Fincantieri Type-212A**

Timeline

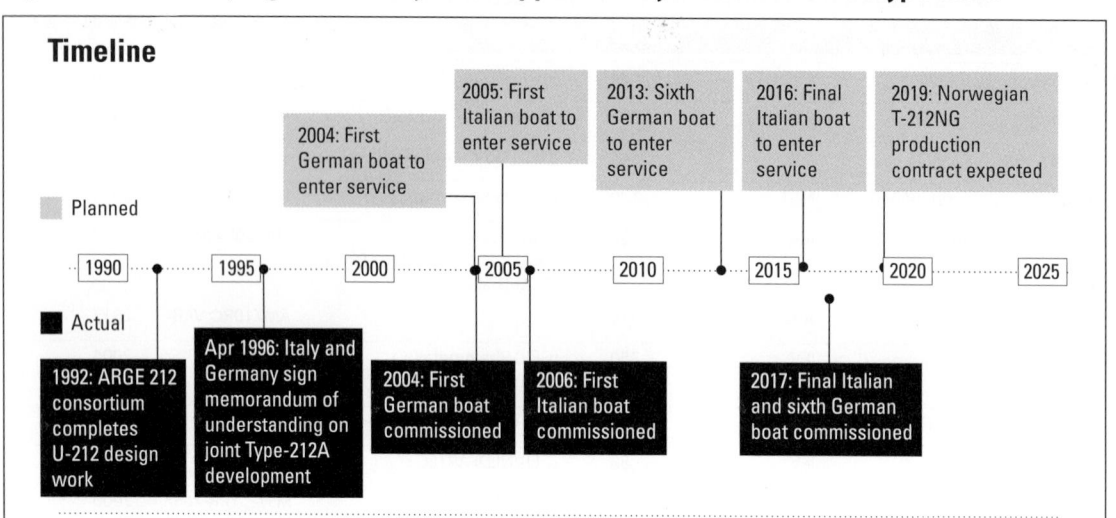

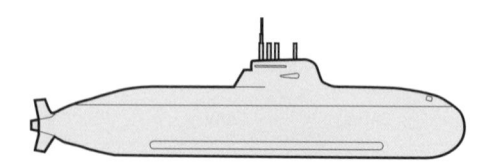

Planned
- 2004: First German boat to enter service
- 2005: First Italian boat to enter service
- 2013: Sixth German boat to enter service
- 2016: Final Italian boat to enter service
- 2019: Norwegian T-212NG production contract expected

Actual
- 1992: ARGE 212 consortium completes U-212 design work
- Apr 1996: Italy and Germany sign memorandum of understanding on joint Type-212A development
- 2004: First German boat commissioned
- 2006: First Italian boat commissioned
- 2017: Final Italian and sixth German boat commissioned

Following tests in the late 1980s on a Type-205 boat fitted with air-independent propulsion, Germany decided to order the U-212 design in 1994. An agreement in 1996 established the Type-212A joint programme that would see Germany and Italy acquire six and four boats respectively. Like other conventionally powered attack submarines, these boats are fitted with a diesel engine and batteries for propulsion. However, these are the only class of submarine in service to use a hydrogen fuel-cell system. Whilst more expensive and difficult to refuel than the commonly used Stirling engine system, it generates greater power and has far fewer moving parts, meaning greater speed and a reduced acoustic signature. Complex new technology, modifications to subsequent batches and budget cuts meant that the average production time was greater than for other SSKs. Norway's selection of the Type-212A in 2017 for its future-submarine requirement means that production of the type will almost certainly resume in the 2020s.

Type-212A production rates

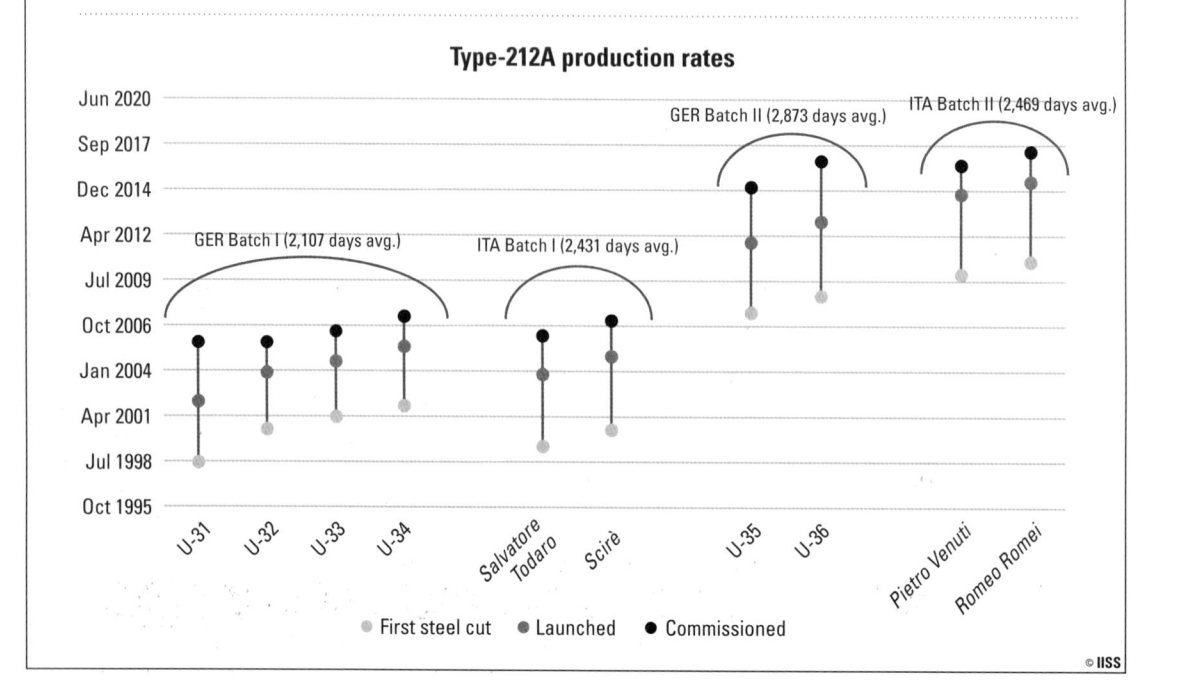

- GER Batch I (2,107 days avg.): U-31, U-32, U-33, U-34
- ITA Batch I (2,431 days avg.): Salvatore Todaro, Scirè
- GER Batch II (2,873 days avg.): U-35, U-36
- ITA Batch II (2,469 days avg.): Pietro Venuti, Romeo Romei

● First steel cut ● Launched ● Commissioned

© IISS

Chapter Five
Russia and Eurasia

In 2017 Russia continued to pursue its aspiration to field a more modern suite of military capabilities and more professional armed forces held at a higher state of readiness. Elements of these forces continue to maintain and sustain the deployment to Syria, where Russian combat forces remain engaged across land, sea and air, and have proven instrumental to the Assad regime's survival in the six-year-long civil war.

Meanwhile, there are further indications that Russia has moved away from important elements of the 'New Look' reforms, which began in late 2008. In March 2017 a presidential decree raised the upper limit on the total number of military personnel from one million to 1,013,628. This constituted the first notional increase in the size of the armed forces for some years. Limiting the maximum numerical strength of the Russian armed forces to one million had been one of the key principles of 'New Look', which continued a trend since the end of the Cold War of reducing personnel numbers. Indeed, in recent years the Russian armed forces have numbered under one million. The new requirement to increase personnel numbers is dictated by the accelerating shift from the land forces' 'New Look' brigade structure towards divisions and armies. In 2016 alone, one combined-arms army, four motor-rifle divisions and one tank division were reestablished. These new divisions draw on existing brigades and equipment-storage bases and, as such, this transformation process requires substantial additional personnel strength.

At the same time, a new naval doctrine was approved in July 2017 for the period up to 2030. It identified among the main dangers facing Russia 'the aspiration of a number of countries, primarily the United States and its allies, to dominate the world's oceans'. Its ambition included developing capabilities to act as a strategic conventional deterrent, including hypersonic missiles and autonomous systems, from 2025, and preserving Russia's position as the second global naval power. With the possible exception of its sub-surface capabilities, however, it would appear difficult for the Russian Navy fully to achieve these ambitions. Although Russia has stated its intention to continue its submarine-construction programme, and to develop the navy's capability to attack land targets with precision-guided, non-nuclear and nuclear weapons, funding for the navy will almost certainly be reduced in the new State Armament Programme (GPV) 2018–27. This makes no provision to build large surface combatants, such as a new aircraft carrier, cruisers and destroyers, before 2025. Despite this, the navy should still achieve some significant, if more limited, ability to pose major challenges to potential adversaries, at least close to home waters.

Overall, total spending under the period of the GPV 2018–27 is planned fall from 20 to 17 trillion roubles (US$318 billion to US$270bn) (see pp. 177–8). During this time, the aerospace forces and land forces will be prioritised. The need to upgrade equipment has led to a significant rise in costs for the land forces and the airborne troops (VDV), but it is expected that the pace of rearmament will slow and there will be greater focus on modernisation at the expense of new weapons purchases.

The merger of the Interior Troops and various law-enforcement agencies into the National Guard (Rosgvardiya) was completed in 2017, bringing the organisation's overall personnel strength to around 340,000. The new National Guard structure is intended to tackle internal threats, but has not received any additional heavy weapons except what had been issued to the Interior Troops (although this in itself is significant in terms of capability).

Under existing legislation, the National Guard can be used abroad for peacekeeping operations and to train foreign law-enforcement agencies. In Syria, however, Russia has instead used the military police for work with the civilian population. New legislation, which gave the military police additional functions, was adopted in 2015 with this purpose in mind.

The civilian Federal Agency for Special Construction (Spetsstroy) was disbanded by September 2017. Spetsstroy was responsible for the construction of military infrastructure; however, this function and some of the agency's personnel have now been transferred to the defence ministry.

Syria

Russia's military intervention in Syria continued into 2017, and there was little sign that it was causing overstretch. The operation has not led to large-scale strategic change in the Russian armed forces and, for the most part, remains a distant conflict involving limited numbers of forces and only moderate losses, even if some of these have been high-ranking officers. That said, the mission remains an important proving ground for new and existing weapons, forces and tactics.

Russian troops have trialled over 160 models of new and modernised weapons in Syria, including experimental systems and prototypes that had not yet completed their normal test-cycles. The defence minister said that at least ten weapons systems had been rejected and, though he did not elaborate on this point, it was reported separately that there had been problems with defensive systems deployed against man-portable air-defence systems and new radio-electronic equipment on Su-34 and Su-35 aircraft. In addition, some types of precision-guided munitions may have failed to demonstrate their effectiveness under operational conditions.

Nonetheless, there has been progress in the ministry's ability to operationally coordinate the armed services. For example, military operations in Syria have been coordinated by the National Defence Control Centre in Moscow – the first operational use of this organisation. This experience has also led to improvements in automated command-and-control systems at tactical and divisional levels; this should in turn improve efficiency in transmitting information and orders.

The further development of reconnaissance and strike systems, improved communications and inter-service cooperation have been prioritised by the armed forces as a result of its Syrian experience. Intensive work has gone into reducing the time from the detection of a target by reconnaissance systems, including unmanned aerial vehicles (UAVs) and satellites, to engagement

Russia's military exercises

The Russian armed forces have undertaken thousands of exercises during the last decade. These have grown considerably in both size and sophistication since 2010, and taken a variety of forms, from the annual strategic exercises that rotate quadrennially – *Kavkaz* ('Caucasus'), *Tsentr* ('Centre'), *Vostok* ('East') and *Zapad* ('West') – and all the preparatory exercises that accompany them, to surprise combat-readiness inspections, or 'snap exercises', which were reintroduced in 2013.

A lack of transparency, combined with some definitional variation, has meant that the precise number of the exercises is uncertain, and their exact size is prone to both exaggeration and understatement. But, along with other international deployments such as the resumption of strategic-aviation flights and the expeditionary campaign in Syria, they have given the Russian authorities a great deal of contemporary experience of operating in a wide range of conditions. They both illuminate Moscow's concerns about Russian security – particularly about countering regime change or 'colour revolution'-type operations and anti-terrorism preparations – and have helped to shape a military tool that facilitates the leadership's more assertive stance on the international stage.

The exercises serve a number of specific tasks. Perhaps that which is most often highlighted by officials and observers in the Euro-Atlantic community is their use as a coercive tool. They are interpreted as Moscow's use of military muscle to intimidate neighbours, including NATO allies in the Baltic region. Moscow has used exercises to concentrate force and apply pressure to neighbours, for instance, prior to the Russo-Georgian war in 2008 and again during the escalating crisis in Ukraine in early 2014. Weeks of exercises were conducted in Russia's Western Military District, neighbouring Ukraine, in early 2014, for instance, allowing Russia to mass forces on the border.

This served to increase uncertainty and conceal intentions, showing Moscow's own political resolve to discourage other actors from intervening in Ukraine, while obliging Ukraine to defend itself on multiple fronts, as well as distracting attention from the developments then under way in Crimea. Ukrainian officials, including President Petro Poroshenko, suggested that Russia sought to use *Zapad 2017* to similar effect, as cover for mobilisation for an invasion of Ukraine, and others suggested Moscow's intention was either to remain in Belarus or threaten the Baltic states.

At the same time, the exercises send a range of other signals. Russian officials emphasise that the exercises are defensive in nature – *Kavkaz 2016* was primarily about territorial defence, for instance, and *Zapad 2017* about defending against a 'colour revolution'- type emergency. Such exercises are also intended, therefore, to send deterrent signals to the Euro-Atlantic community by demonstrating that any intervention against Russian interests would bear heavy costs. Moscow has also conducted exercises with partners, such as Tajikistan in 2016 and 2017,

by an offensive system, a process that involves the extensive use of each service's automated systems.

Indeed, during the deployment of the *Admiral Kuznetsov* carrier group to the eastern Mediterranean, the aircraft carrier's command centre controlled not only its own air component, but also air-force Su-24 combat aircraft based at Khmeimim air base in Syria. The headquarters of the Russian forces in Syria could, in turn, control carrier-borne aircraft. However, Russia's use of naval aviation during the operation was not considered successful. Two combat aircraft from the carrier's air component, including one of the newest MiG-29KRs, were lost during recovery to the carrier. This led to the redeployment of the air group from the *Kuznetsov* to land. Of over 360 combat sorties flown by naval Su-33s during the deployment, just over 30 were made from the carrier.

The carrier group's deployment finished ahead of schedule, and, on return, the *Admiral Kuznetsov* was due to enter Zvezdochka Shipyard in Severodvinsk for a scheduled long-term refit. This is expected to take at least three years to complete, although at the time of writing the vessel had yet to enter the dock. However, the comparatively low effectiveness of the Russian carrier group during the Syria operation has jeopardised plans to develop new aircraft carriers and, more generally, larger blue-water naval vessels. This compounds the existing challenges in developing blue-water capability stemming from still-sclerotic surface-ship construction rates.

Nevertheless, Russia's use of long-range, conventionally armed cruise missiles has continued to prove effective. These have been launched by submarines and surface ships as well as Russia's strategic aviation fleet. This success appears to have been a significant factor in the decision to resume production of the Tu-160 *Blackjack* strategic bomber.

in order to practise combined operations but also to signal reassurance and long-term commitment to them, and illustrate that Russia should be their partner of choice in a crisis.

The exercises are also intended to deliver direct operational benefits for the armed forces themselves. Indeed, their primary purpose is internal, and they are an essential feature of the ongoing force modernisation and development that has followed many years of underinvestment and decline. They are being used both to reveal and address problems and shortfalls, as well as to integrate lessons learnt from the exercises themselves (and from experience in Ukraine and Syria) with new theories about contemporary and future warfare.

In the wake of Russia's post-2008 military-modernisation process, the exercises are also designed to improve essential training, and are a feature of how the leadership has sought to integrate these reforms and new structures, and to ensure that the Russian armed forces develop appropriately.

Three particular features stand out. Firstly, the exercises have been about training and testing both all-arms and joint operations, deploying increasingly substantial forces over long distances and commanding a mix of different types of forces in different theatres. *Vostok 2014* featured long-distance marches with heavy weapons and subsequent regrouping, for instance, and *Kavkaz 2016* deployed at-distance divisions from four armies, coordinating them with command units in a new operational theatre.

Secondly, the exercises are often coordinated with, or integrated into, other elements of Russia's security apparatus, including interior forces, such as the newly established National Guard, police and other paramilitary forces, and civil-defence capabilities. Although exercises usually begin in one military district, they often spread to or include other districts: in March 2015, the armed forces conducted a major snap exercise of the northern fleet and its reinforcement with elements from the Central, Southern, Western and Eastern military districts. This was followed by a major policing exercise, *Zaslon 2015*. All of Russia's armed forces, including the nuclear triad, have taken part in exercises.

Finally, the exercises are about testing command, control and coordination across regions and authorities. Defence Minister Sergei Shoigu has stated that the exercises are about checking mobilisation systems across Russia, including coordination between civilian and military agencies at federal, regional and local levels. Exercises have involved coordination not just with reserves, but with the ministries of health, communications and transport, for instance, as well as the Central Bank. *Kavkaz 2016* also involved the first real-time test of the Russian defence ministry taking direct command of regional and local authorities.

Weaving these threads together indicates that Russia is preparing and testing its entire state system to cope with a major emergency, including transitioning from peace and deterrence, through high-intensity conventional fighting and even escalating to nuclear deployment.

Russia's military leadership has also spoken of the need to increase the role of UAVs, robotic systems and precision weapons in the wake of operational lessons from Syria; these will be prioritised in the new GPV.

Contract service

A significant development in personnel management occurred with the long-heralded transition to a fully contract-manned, non-commissioned officer (NCO) corps, which was finally completed in 2017.

The continued growth in the number of contract-service personnel has led to a reduction in the size of planned conscription drafts. Whereas in each spring draft in 2014–16, 150,000 to 155,000 soldiers were called up, in the spring of 2017 just 142,000 were liable to be conscripted. The total for both drafts in 2016 was 275,000. At the same time, the number of contract-service personnel continues to grow and was just short of the target (stated in 2016) of 384,000 soldiers and NCOs by mid-2017; the target for the end of 2017 was 405,000 (which was revised down from 420,000 due to budget considerations). The overall personnel strength in the armed forces, comprising conscript and contract personnel, was stated as being at 93%.

Two new initiatives relating to terms of service are intended to further boost contract-personnel numbers. The first is the June 2017 presidential decree that allows conscripts to immediately sign up for at least two years of contract service, instead of being required to have served for at least six months after conscription. Other new legislation allows for short-term contracts, of under one year in duration, for reservists and conscripts in their final month of service, in an effort to increase the flexibility and efficiency of the manning system. Soldiers serving under these short-term contracts can be involved in operations abroad, including on special operations.

Ukraine

Russia's military presence along the border with Ukraine continues to be reinforced with both troops and infrastructure, while the motor-rifle brigades redeployed there from deep inside Russia were reorganised into divisions in 2016. The Western Military District's 20th Combined-Arms Army, based near the border with Ukraine, has also acquired two new motor-rifle divisions (the 3rd and 144th), a tank brigade in the process of formation, and support units.

Meanwhile, the Southern Military District's new 8th Combined-Arms Army, established near the southeastern borders of Ukraine, is still in the process of formation. It includes one motor-rifle division (150th) and a motor-rifle brigade (20th), which might also be converted into a division in the future. The formation of these new divisions and armies has required an unprecedented level of infrastructure development, in an area where previously almost no troops were based. As of late 2017, however, only priority work to build housing and barracks had been completed; the remaining infrastructure projects will require several more years to complete.

At the end of 2016, all ground troops stationed in Crimea were consolidated into the 22nd Army Corps, subordinated to the Black Sea Fleet. There have been no further increases in the numerical strength of the Russian group of forces in Crimea, but the rearmament of naval and air-force aviation – as well as the air defences deployed there – is now a priority.

New equipment

Land forces

Serial purchase of the land forces' new generation of armoured vehicles, which were first displayed at the Victory Day parade on 9 May 2015, has been delayed

Map 3 **Russia: army units near Ukraine's border**

by several years for financial and developmental reasons.

According to Deputy Defence Minister Yury Borisov, the plan is to procure just 100 T-14 *Armata* main battle tanks (MBTs) by 2020 for trials. Until 2022, the main effort will be directed to acquiring modernised versions of tanks already in service. In 2017, units began to take delivery of the first updated T-72B3 tanks with improved active-protection and fire-control systems. The T-72B3 will remain the most widely purchased MBT over the next few years, although after a pause of several years the defence ministry signed a contract to buy more T-90 MBTs in August 2017. This will amount to one battalion of the new T-90M version, which has been developed based on combat experience in Syria.

Similar decisions have been taken with Russia's light armour. A variant of the BMP-2 infantry fighting vehicle (IFV) with the *Berezhok* weapons system (a new turret with anti-armour missiles) was procured, whilst the *Kurganets* IFV is still in the development stage. Similarly, acquisition of the BTR-82A/AM IFV continues, in lieu of the new *Bumerang* armoured personnel carrier. Meanwhile, deliveries of the *Koalitsiya*-SV self-propelled gun are not scheduled to start before 2020.

In 2016, two VDV airborne-assault divisions and four separate airborne-assault brigades each acquired a T-72B3 tank company. It is planned that three of these companies will reorganise into tank battalions in 2018; it is possible that the other three tank companies could also increase in size. This move underscores the current trend towards making Russia's airborne troops 'heavier' and transforming them into mobile and expeditionary infantry.

Air force
Equipment for the Aerospace Forces (VKS) remains a priority for both the current and new GPVs, although while the VKS increasingly fields upgraded models of fourth-generation combat aircraft, the transition to fifth-generation designs remains elusive.

The air force has continued to benefit from the re-equipment programme laid down in the 2010–20 GPV. The delivery of new-build Su-35S and Su-30SM multi-role combat aircraft and the Su-34 tactical bomber was maintained during 2017. Additional upgraded MiG-31 *Foxhound* interceptors (MiG-31BM) also entered the inventory, as did a handful of modestly upgraded Tu-160 *Blackjack*, Tu-95 *Bear* and Tu-22M *Backfire* bombers.

However, the initial aspiration of the 2010–20 GPV to meet the air force's PAK-FA fifth-generation-fighter requirement by funding, as a first batch, the acquisition of 60 multi-role aircraft in 2015–20 has not been met. In 2016–17, three more PAK-FA T-50 fifth-generation fighter prototypes were built, bringing the number of airworthy prototypes to nine; the aircraft was officially designated as the Su-57 in 2017. In November 2016, ground tests began on the first example of Izdeliye (Article)-117: an improved, more powerful engine designed for the Su-57. Flight tests for the engine are supposed to take place by the end of 2017, and by 2019 the first serial-production Su-57 is supposed to be fitted with the Izdeliye-30 follow-on engine. The 2018–27 GPV, which was due to be released in the fourth quarter of 2017, should give a clearer indication of the pace and scale envisaged for the Su-57's introduction into service.

It may also provide greater clarity on the level of support to be provided in the near to medium term to meet the PAK-DA requirement for a new long-range bomber. The defence ministry has approved the draft design of the PAK-DA as a subsonic, low-observable aircraft. Although this allows development work to begin, PAK-DA is not expected to fly before 2025, with service entry not before the end of the 2020s at the earliest. In the meantime, the plan is to maintain the combat capability of the Tu-95MS *Bear* bomber and restart production of the Tu-160 bomber (as the upgraded Tu-160M2), together with renewed production of Tu-160 engines. The first 'transitional' prototype, using parts from an unfinished Soviet-era Tu-160 fuselage, is expected to fly in 2018, with a new-build airframe due to fly in 2021. Around 50 Tu-160M2s might be purchased.

The air force is also continuing to digest lessons from its ongoing operation in Syria. However, Russia has continued to rely, to a far greater extent than Western air powers, on unguided air-dropped munitions. The air force and Russian defence industry are keen to introduce into service a range of tactical air-launched guided weapons to replace ageing designs presently in the inventory. Development of the second variant of the Kh-38 family of medium-range air-to-surface missiles was due to be complete in 2017. The Kh-38ML semi-active laser version has already completed testing and is likely in production, while the Kh-38MT, fitted with an electro-optical seeker, was due to complete tests in 2017. Similarly, work on the KAB-250LG laser-guided bomb was also due to finish in the same time frame. This will be the smallest bomb in the KAB family when it is introduced into the air-force inventory. Additionally, a long-range dual-capable cruise missile, Kh-BD, is being developed for Russia's strategic bombers.

But while its combat-aircraft inventory is in the near term in comparatively good shape, the air force's tactical and heavy airlift fleets are increasingly old. Upgrade and successor projects are only slowly progressing.

Meanwhile, significant progress has been made in modernising Russia's air-defence systems. More S-400 systems are being produced each year, along with *Pantsir*-S units to protect them. Ten S-400 battalion sets were produced in 2016 and the same number was scheduled for 2017. However, entry into service of the system has been slower. As of October 2017, only three additional regiments were confirmed to have received regimental sets produced in 2016 (the 18th, 584th and 1528th air-defence regiments). Deliveries of S-400 sets produced in 2017 only began in the autumn; the first regiment (511th) was expected to take delivery in November. Meanwhile, testing has begun on the *Pantsir*-SM, which has been developed based on Russia's experiences in Syria. The system has a greater detection range and the ability to engage high-speed ballistic targets, including multiple-rocket-launcher munitions. A small, lightweight missile is being developed to specifically engage this type of target, as well as high-precision weapons and UAVs. This will increase the number of missiles in a single *Pantsir* loadout by up to a factor of four.

Navy

The elderly aircraft carrier *Admiral Kuznetsov* made its operational debut, launching missions against targets in Syria in the latter part of 2016. However, the high-profile deployment to the eastern Mediterranean ended in January 2017, having had only limited operational effect. A lack of trained pilots contributed to the fact that the carrier deployed with only about a dozen fixed-wing aircraft – made up of Su-33s and, for the first time, newer MiG-29KRs.

Of greater note, in terms of the navy's overall capability, were further sporadic strikes against targets in Syria with 3M14 *Kalibr* (SS-N-30) cruise missiles fired from surface ships and a Project 636.3 improved *Varshavyanka* (*Kilo*)-class submarine from the eastern Mediterranean. Russia's strategy to distribute *Kalibr* cruise missiles across the fleet, including to submarines and a variety of surface combatants, has given the Russian Navy (and air force) the capability to strike land targets located at a distance of up to 2,000 kilometres from the coast. This greatly enhances the navy's capability not just to project offensive power but also to support land operations. Indeed, the continuing proliferation of offensive missile capacity among large, medium and small surface combatants and submarines in the Russian inventory remains perhaps the most significant development in Russian naval capability, contributing to Russia's anti-access/area-denial potential and a defence-in-depth strategy.

Russia's shipbuilding industry continues to experience problems concerning the construction and testing of major naval combatants, while issues with the *Poliment-Redut* surface-to-air-missile system are causing delays. The first and name ship of the Project 22350 *Admiral Gorshkov* class of frigates was finally due to commission by the end of the year – 11 years after it was laid down. However, the construction of smaller ships with a displacement of up to 1,000 tonnes and armed with long-range cruise and anti-ship missiles has accelerated significantly. In addition, several older vessels (frigates and a cruiser) are being upgraded before being equipped with modern cruise-missile launchers.

Submarine construction is still a priority, although the production of diesel-electric boats is proceeding more smoothly than that of nuclear submarines. Upgrade work for the fleet of diesel-electric submarines is under way. In 2017, the Black Sea Fleet took delivery of the last three of six new Project 636.3 improved *Varshavyanka* (*Kilo*)-class submarines armed with *Kalibr* cruise missiles, in addition to torpedoes. Construction of the next batch of six *Kilos* has begun, with these planned to join the Pacific Fleet in 2019–21. Meanwhile, work has resumed on two Project 677 *Lada*-class torpedo- and missile-equipped submarines. The first Project 08851 improved *Yasen*-M-class nuclear-power guided-missile attack submarine was floated out in March 2017. But, again, progress on new hulls remains slow, and much effort continues to be devoted to modernising the combat capabilities of existing hulls.

The deployment of large surface warships or groups centred on, or consisting of, large legacy platforms like the *Kuznetsov* continues to allow Moscow to demonstrate force and to project status – and these platforms often pack a significant punch. Another such naval demonstration came in July, with the high-profile deployments of the *Kirov*-class cruiser *Pyotr Veliky* and *Typhoon*-class submarine *Dmitry Donskoi* (the world's largest submarine, but recently a missile-trials vessel), to the Baltic Sea for Navy Day celebrations in St Petersburg. However, this use of such vessels will become increasingly difficult as the prospects of sustaining, let alone replacing, these platforms in a timely fashion seem to be reducing – in large part due to renewed budgetary constraints.

Strategic forces
The Strategic Rocket Force (RVSN) continues to progressively rearm, with a number of regiments continuing to receive new *Yars* missiles and launchers in 2016. Meanwhile, tests of the heavy *Sarmat* liquid-fuel intercontinental ballistic missile (ICBM) have been postponed several times due to technical difficulties, and these are now expected to resume towards the end of 2017. Ejection tests of the rail-mobile *Barguzin* ICBM were first carried out in November 2016, but the future of the system has yet to be decided. It is not clear whether purchases of *Barguzin* will be included in the GPV 2018–27.

Although the first deliveries of the S-500 air- and missile-defence system are due to begin in 2020, so far only individual components have been tested. The system's official specifications and external appearance have not emerged in the public domain, which could indicate that it is not yet ready. However, it has been reported that the system's interceptor missile has been successfully tested. It is intended that this will have the capability to engage ballistic targets in the upper atmosphere. The S-500 is planned to be an air-portable system that can also provide theatre missile defence.

Work is also continuing on modernising the strategic-missile-defence shield around Moscow. Tests of interceptor missiles for the new A-235 system began in 2014. Meanwhile, one or two test launches of the A-135 system currently deployed in the Moscow region, and one A-235 test launch, are performed each year at a test site in Kazakhstan. The defence ministry has said that the tests will last for at least two to three years, although this timescale is considered to be optimistic. Related to this, construction work is also continuing on Russia's network of *Voronezh* radar stations. These are intended to form a key component of a missile-attack warning system, with detection ranges of up to 6,000km. It was reported in 2016 that all of Russia's borders were covered by the system. These radar stations will be used for both the strategic-level A-235 and the theatre-level S-500 missile-defence systems. In addition to seven radar sites already operational, three more are under construction and expected to be in service in 2019. A radar station for Crimea has also been announced, and this is intended to be operational in 2020–21. These additional radars, together with the *Voronezh* system's space-based sensors, should enable the detection of ICBMs at greater range and the possibility of over-the-horizon detection for medium-range and short-range ballistic-missile, and even cruise-missile, launches.

DEFENCE ECONOMICS

Defence spending
Although Russian defence spending appeared to increase sharply in 2016, this stemmed from a one-off settlement of debts that had been accumulated by defence industry under the government's scheme of state-guaranteed credits. If this exceptional payment of over 790 billion roubles (US$11.8bn) is excluded, military expenditure fell slightly in nominal terms.

Spending under the 'national defence' budget chapter in the 2016 budget, comprised mainly of funding for defence-ministry forces, amounted to over 2.980 trillion roubles (US$44.4bn), compared to 3.181trn roubles (US$52.2bn) in 2015. In real terms, using the annual GDP deflator, this represented a fall of almost 10%. In the 2017 budget, spending on 'national defence' was reduced further in nominal terms, to 2.835trn roubles (US$45.02bn), although this was increased to 2.872trn roubles (US$45.6bn) when the budget was amended in July. Meanwhile, defence spending relating to other budget chapters, and according to the standard NATO definition, meant that total military expenditure in 2016

Table 8 **Russian defence expenditure** as % of GDP

Year	'National defence'		Total military expenditure[1]	
	Trillion roubles	As % GDP	Trillion roubles	As % GDP
2018[2]	2.772	2.83	3.816	3.90
2017[3]	2.872	3.10	3.855	4.17
2016	2.982	3.47	3.835	4.46[4]
2015	3.181	3.82	4.026	4.84
2014	2.479	3.13	3.222	4.07
2013	2.106	2.88	2.783	3.81
2012	1.812	2.66	2.482	3.64
2011	1.516	2.51	2.028	3.36

1. According to NATO definition.
2. According to the draft budget.
3. Amended budget; other years actual spending.
4. Excluding a one-off payment to reduce accumulated debts of defence-industry enterprises under the scheme of state-guaranteed credits. If this debt payment is included in GDP, share rises to 5.4%.
2010–16: actual spending; 2017: amended federal budget for 2017.

176 THE MILITARY BALANCE 2018

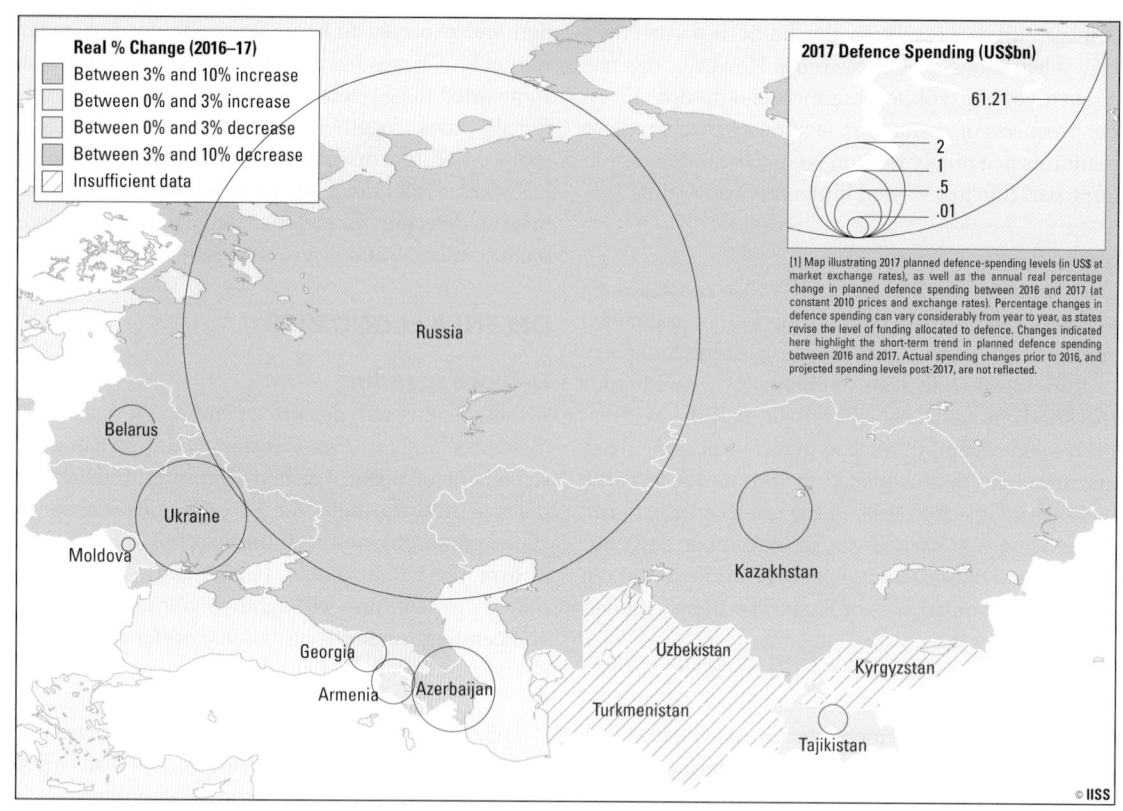

Map 4 **Russia and Eurasia regional defence spending**[1]

amounted to some 3.835trn roubles (US$57.2bn), with a modest increase to 3.855trn roubles (US$61.2bn) in the amended 2017 budget. In sum, Russia's defence spending has stabilised after a few years of rapid growth and, in real terms, is now falling.

Analysis of the scale of Russian military spending has been complicated for some time by the fact that the Federal Service for State Statistics (Rosstat) has been transitioning from a System of National Accounts (SNA) which adheres to the international standard of 1993, to SNA-2008. This has meant that published GDP data has been frequently amended. The new methodology also captures some economic activities previously excluded from the records, which has resulted in a decline in the share of GDP allocated to defence, as shown in Table 8. According to previously published data, Russian military expenditure peaked in 2015 at the high level of 5.5% of GDP. But, according to the new data, the share was actually closer to 4.84% of GDP, falling to 4.46% in 2016 (excluding debt repayment) and 4.17% in 2017. This is still a relatively high level by international standards (for example, the United States spent 3.1% of GDP in 2017) but not as exceptional as it earlier appeared.

This slower rate of military-spending growth should be viewed against the background of a faltering Russian economy, which in 2017 began to show some signs of recovery with an expected GDP growth rate of 1.8%. However, the principal factor underpinning this moderated growth is that levels of spending under the annual state defence order are

Figure 10 **Russia: estimated total military expenditure** as % of GDP

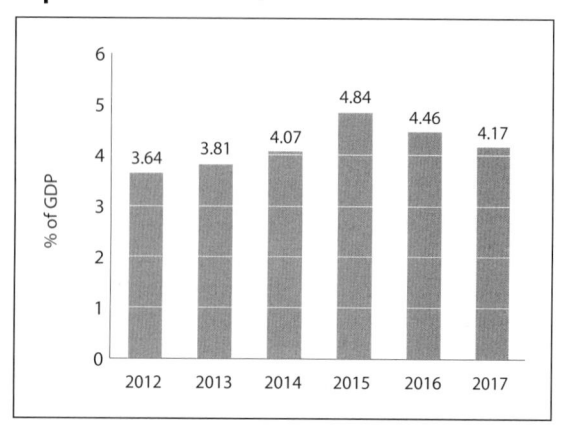

Year	% of GDP
2012	3.64
2013	3.81
2014	4.07
2015	4.84
2016	4.46
2017	4.17

no longer increasing, a trend that is likely to continue into the future. In August 2017, President Vladimir Putin stated firmly that military spending would fall in 2018, and a month later the ministry of finance's draft federal budget for 2018–20 gave 2018 spending on 'national defence' as 2.772trn roubles (US$43.1bn), 100bn roubles (US$1.6bn) less than expected spending in 2017 and only 2.83% of GDP. According to the draft budget, 'national defence' spending will thereafter be held at a fairly constant rate and by 2020 will be only 2.6% of GDP. This would bring the total share of military spending to approximately 3.5% of GDP, bringing Russia more in line with the US.

Since 2015, the defence ministry has been striving to optimise its spending under a programme known as 'Effective Army'. This covers many areas, including the better use of information technology, a reorganisation of logistics and reform of infrastructure construction. Substantial savings have been claimed, amounting to almost 37bn roubles (US$600m) in 2016. According to Tatyana Shevtsova, deputy defence minister for economic matters, when fully implemented the programme should provide annual savings of up to 47bn roubles (US$700m). If so, this will, to some degree, offset the more straitened defence-budget funding that is likely during the next few years. At the same time, a rigorous inter-agency system has been introduced to monitor all procurement spending under the state defence order. This permits the defence ministry to intervene directly if there is any evidence that funds are being diverted to other uses. Furthermore, it is claimed that corruption in defence procurement, formerly a serious problem, has been greatly reduced. There is little doubt that cost efficiency has improved in recent years, allowing the better use of budget funding. It is likely that the Syria campaign has been partly funded from such savings, as well as, it has been claimed by defence-ministry representatives, by the diversion of some funding from military exercises and investment.

State Armament Programme

As noted in *The Military Balance 2017* (p. 193), in early 2015 it became clear that the follow-on State Armament Programme (GPV) up to 2025 would be delayed. It was due to have started in 2016 but will now cover the years 2018–27. It was expected that the new GPV would be signed off by the president by the end of 2017 so that it could become operational from the beginning of 2018. While total funding under the new programme has not been confirmed officially, analysts claim that it will be 17trn roubles (US$270bn); this is less than the GPV 2011–20 allocation of 20trn roubles (US$318bn), but is for eight years instead of the previous programme's ten years. If confirmed, this will be a compromise that lands between the 12trn roubles (US$191bn) considered affordable by the finance ministry and the 24trn roubles (US$381bn) requested by the defence ministry.

Nonetheless, some features of the programme are already clear. There is likely to be more emphasis on research and development; the defence ministry is now taking seriously the need to strengthen its own research capability as the old Soviet-era stock of knowledge is exhausted. In addition, some new military technologies will be prioritised, in particular robotics and unmanned vehicles, including those for use underwater. The ministry's Main Research and Testing Centre for Robot Technology, established following a November 2012 decision, is now seen as a versatile unit that is undertaking a wide range of applied research on military robotics within the framework of the 'Robotizatsiya-2025' programme. Considerable progress is being made on the development of unmanned aerial vehicles (UAVs) intended for the reconnaissance role, with much practical experience gained from the intensive application of such systems under combat conditions in Syria. The defence ministry claims to now have at least 2,000 UAVs in its inventory. However, Russia still possesses no armed UAVs, although development work on medium and heavy systems has been under way for some time, with new propulsion units also under development. This is likely to be a priority feature of GPV 2018–27.

The funding of GPV 2011–20 initially prioritised the navy but was amended over the course of its implementation. The new programme will place a higher priority on equipping the ground forces, which have been comparatively starved of new equipment in recent years, partly because of delays and the high costs associated with the development of the new *Armata*, *Kurganets* and *Bumerang* armoured platforms. The army is now scheduled to receive a total of 100 T-14 *Armata* main battle tanks in the years 2019 and 2020 and then an as-yet-unknown quantity of these tanks by 2025. The rate of renewal of the Aerospace Forces' equipment looks set to slow, although the fifth-generation Su-57 combat aircraft should enter 'service' in small numbers from 2019 until its new upgraded engine is finally available. Russia's strategic nuclear forces will continue to be a high

Table 9 **Russian procurement of new weapons 2011–16 and goals of the State Armament Programme 2011–20 (approximate)**

	Total 2011–16	Total to 2020
Intercontinental ballistic missiles	91	400+
Submarine-launched ballistic missiles	c.113	100+
Military satellites	c.60	c.850
Fixed-wing aircraft	415	1,150
Helicopters	c.700	c.330
Including combat	c.170	4,000+
Unmanned aerial vehicles	c.860	56
S-400 air-defence systems (divisions)	21	8
Strategic nuclear submarines	4	7
Multi-role nuclear submarines	1	6–10
Diesel-electric submarines	5	50
Large surface-combat ships[a]	18	2,300+
Main battle tanks (new)	0[b]	10
Iskander missile systems[c]	8	

a. Mainly corvettes, frigates and small artillery ships.
b. Excluding a batch of T-14 *Armata* main battle tanks in trial use. Note that the army has received many modernised T-72B3 tanks.
c. Brigades.

priority, with the acquisition of new *Sarmat* heavy multi-warhead intercontinental ballistic missiles now scheduled from 2019 and possibly also the *Barguzin* rail-mounted-missile system.

Meanwhile, GPV 2011–20 remains in force and the armed forces continue to receive significant quantities of new weapons, although progress has been uneven when comparing the introduction of different equipment types (see Table 9). However, the programme's main success indicator – the share of modern weapons in the inventories of combat-ready equipment which is in active use – is being met ahead of schedule. The original equipment-modernisation goal was to have a proportion of 30% modern equipment in the inventory by the end of 2015; instead, a level of 47% has been claimed by officials. The target for the end of 2017 was 62%, while it appeared that the original goal to have a 70% proportion of modern equipment by 2020 could even be achieved by the end of 2018.

Defence industry

In 2016, defence-industrial output grew more moderately, at a level of 10.7%, compared to 13% growth in 2015 and 15.5% in 2014. This reflected a slower rate of growth in the annual state defence order. As a result, the defence industry's equipment output only increased by 9.5% in 2016, compared to approximately 20% in the two preceding years. This trend looked set to continue in 2017 and beyond.

As President Putin has been warning, defence-industrial firms will have to begin diversifying in order to maintain their levels of output and employment rates. For many, this has echoes of the 'conversion' policy pursued by Moscow with limited success in the late 1980s and early 1990s. But this time it is being underlined from the outset that defence companies are expected to manufacture high-technology civil and dual-use goods for domestic and export markets, not simply consumer items and other less demanding items. Targets have been issued for an increased share of civil-goods output. Indeed, following on from a 16.8% share of total output accounted for by civil goods in 2016, this is forecast to increase to 18.2% by 2020, and then rise to 30% by 2025 and 50% by 2030. Equipment for the energy sector, machine tools and other advanced production technology, medical equipment and civil electronic goods will be prioritised. Meanwhile, funding at low rates of interest will be made available through the Fund for Industrial Development, which launched the 'Konversiya' programme in June 2017.

Structural changes continue in the defence industry. The Rostec corporation, headed by Sergei Chemezov, which includes 700 enterprises grouped into 15 holding companies employing more than 450,000 people, has begun to implement a policy of partly privatising its assets. A pioneer in this move is Concern Kalashnikov, which is based in the Izhevsk machine-building works and is the country's largest producer of small arms. This firm is now diversifying into other fields, including shipbuilding and the development and manufacture of UAVs (under the Zala brand). Kalashnikov is now 49% privately owned and is undergoing rapid growth with a widening range of civil as well as military business activities.

Arms exports

Two of the most important recent Russian arms deals are now being realised: the delivery to China of 24 Su-35 combat aircraft, the first four of which were transferred in December 2016, and four divisions of S-400 air-defence systems. The S-400 will also be purchased by India, while Turkey and Russia reached agreement on a sale in November 2017. In late 2017, Indonesia and Russia were concluding the acquisition of 11 Su-35s.

According to the Federal Service for Military-Technical Cooperation, the total volume of armaments and military-services exports in 2016 was more than 914trn roubles (US$15bn) (compared with 884trn roubles (US$14.5bn) in 2015); the total was expected to be the same in 2017. Fixed-wing aircraft and helicopters accounted for half of total Russian exports, whilst ground-forces equipment accounted for 30%. It is now expected that air-defence systems (with a current share of 20%) will account for an increasing percentage of all exports, helped by the fact that the producer, Almaz-Antey, has introduced new production capacities. The use of Russian weaponry in Syria has also undoubtedly boosted international interest in Russian equipment, and this is beginning to influence the scale and pattern of new arms orders. According to Deputy Defence Minister Borisov, more than 600 different models of military hardware have been tested in Syria under combat conditions.

UKRAINE: MILITARY REFORM

Military reform continues in Ukraine, amid ongoing fighting in the east of the country and deployments by Russian forces close to the Russian–Ukrainian border. The security challenge from Russia has, in large measure, dictated the course of these reforms. They have led to the establishment of new military units, improved combat capabilities for existing units and development of the reserve system.

At the same time, Ukraine is aiming to make its armed forces interoperable with those of NATO member states, as outlined in its 2015 military doctrine (see *The Military Balance 2017*, p. 196) and develop them to Western standards. This goal has guided a key element of Ukraine's military reform: the implementation of processes aimed at standardising with NATO structures, from the command-and-control system and civilian control of the armed forces, to military medicine and tactical protocols. Those units that have been trained with the help of Western instructors, or are intended to participate in international peacekeeping missions, have been most affected by these processes. Overall, the principal priorities of Ukraine's defence planning are to:

1. Establish a joint command level, in accordance with NATO standards.
2. Establish a system for planning and resource management, again in accordance with NATO standards.
3. Construct a national military organisation capable of providing guaranteed defence against aggression and defence of the nation, and maintaining peace and international security.
4. Establish a unified logistics- and medical-support structure that is capable of providing support to all components of the nation's military organisation.
5. Establish professional armed forces with contract-service personnel, and to create a reserve system.

These are each overseen by specific subcommittees set up under the defence ministry's Reform Committee. Civilian activists and non-governmental advisory and expert groups are heavily involved in the committee, and this is seen as one of the ways in which Ukraine puts into practice the concept of civilian control of the armed forces. Within the ministry, the main thrust of reform has been to reduce the size of the administrative apparatus, reduce the number of departments (through a process of consolidation), improve the delegation of authority from the minister to deputies and department heads, and increase procurement transparency through the ProZorro system.

Armed-forces reform

Reform of the armed forces has centred on improving command and control, and reorganising and standardising unit establishments. A priority in developing command and control has been to restructure the Joint Operational Headquarters as an agency for inter-service and interdepartmental coordination during joint operations. At the same time, the general staff has also been restructured in accordance with NATO standards, with departments established and reorganised into a Western-style J-structure (where J-1 is the personnel function, J-2 is intelligence, J-5 is policy and plans, etc.).

With regard to the armed forces' organisational structure, reform efforts have been driven by the requirement to increase the proportion of combat personnel within overall establishment strength; reinforce reconnaissance capabilities and firepower, in the form of artillery (primarily anti-tank); and increase the autonomy of land-forces brigades.

The newly established Special Operations Forces have been further developed within the framework of these reforms, with the 3rd and 8th Special Purpose Regiments and special-operations centres at their core. More broadly, the influence of NATO and its member states on the reform process is illustrated by Ukraine's special-operations forces, particularly the number of psychological- and information-operations centres that have been established within them.

Meanwhile, Ukraine's Airborne Forces (VDV) have been moved from the land forces and are now a separate service arm in the military's strategic reserve. This stemmed from two factors: the relative weakness of Ukraine's airlift capability, and the nature of military operations in the Donbas region. In operational terms, the VDV serves as a rapid-reaction unit designed to contain crises on the front line. It consists of mobile land-force brigades, including tank units, and in function these are closer to US *Stryker* brigades than they are to Russian VDV airborne formations. In addition to the four pre-war brigades, three more VDV brigades are being formed. Overall, the large number of VDV units reflects the role assigned to them by the Ukrainian military leadership in its operational and strategic planning.

Personnel reform

Despite the establishment of new units, the total strength of the armed forces has remained relatively constant at around 204,000 military personnel and 46,000 civilians, which has led to shortages in some units. The problem of undermanning has been made worse by the decision not to proceed with the seventh wave of partial mobilisation as demobilisation from the previous six waves was completed, combined with the rather modest pace at which the army is being staffed with contract-service personnel. Because of the shortage of junior officers (at platoon-commander and company-commander level), officer reservists – graduates of military-training schemes in civilian higher-education establishments (akin to Western Officer Training Corps) – were called up for 18-month terms.

This model of personnel development was chosen in the expectation that units would be brought up to establishment strength with reservists. For instance, it is envisaged that the 4th Reserve Corps – with cadre brigades – would be brought up to establishment strength with the announcement of mobilisation. However, for this system to work effectively, a pool of trained reservists and a rapid mobilisation system are required.

The operational reserve (OR) is the most combat-capable component of the reserve system in Ukraine. It is subdivided into Stage One (OR-1) and Stage Two (OR-2). OR-1 includes former service personnel who were mainly mobilised during the six waves of partial mobilisation and discharged after one year of service. Many of these reservists have combat experience through their involvement in operations in the Donbas region. OR-1 reservists are assigned to specific military units (mostly those in which they previously served) and on mobilisation they are used to bring sub-units up to wartime strength, as attrition replacements or to create new sub-units. There are more than 100,000 OR-1 reservists in total, with this number seen as sufficient to bring the armed forces up to wartime strength. To maintain their professional skills, Ukraine's general staff and its subordinate structures periodically call up the OR-1 category of reservists for exercises at brigade bases and training centres.

OR-2 mainly consists of those liable for military service who are physically fit but have not yet served. This category of reservists can be used both to establish new units in the regular army, primarily the brigades of the 4th Reserve Corps, and to form Territorial Defence units, including rifle battalions, Territorial Defence detachments and conscription-centre guard companies. The Territorial Defence units comprise more than 400,000 personnel. However, because OR-2 reservists are liable only for partial mobilisation, and since conscription centres have found it difficult to find the required numbers liable for service, the general staff's targets for mobilised personnel have been consistently missed. As a result, many notional OR-2 reservists may not be available or even exist. A new electronic register of those liable for military service, set up in 2017, is expected to alleviate this situation, while cross-referencing with other government databases should improve the effectiveness of measures designed to tackle the evasion of military service.

Armenia ARM

Armenian Dram d		2016	2017	2018
GDP	d	5.08tr	5.39tr	
	US$	10.6bn	11.0bn	
per capita	US$	3,533	3,690	
Growth	%	0.2	3.5	
Inflation	%	-1.4	1.9	
Def bdgt [a]	d	207bn	210bn	
	US$	431m	429m	
FMA (US)	US$	1.4m	1m	0m
US$1=d		480.49	488.80	

[a] Includes imported military equipment, excludes military pensions

Population 3,045,191

Age	0–14	15–19	20–24	25–29	30–64	65 plus
Male	10.0%	3.1%	3.5%	4.4%	22.7%	4.5%
Female	8.8%	2.7%	3.4%	4.5%	25.0%	6.8%

Capabilities

The armed forces' main focus is territorial defence, given continuing tensions with neighbouring Azerbaijan over Nagorno-Karabakh. Overall military doctrine remains influenced strongly by Russian thinking, but overseas deployments, including to Afghanistan, Kosovo and Lebanon, have enabled personnel to learn from international counterparts. The country aims to develop its peacekeeping contingent into one brigade operating to NATO standards. Armenia is engaged in a NATO Individual Partnership Action Plan. Armenia is also a CSTO member and defence ties with Russia continue on a broad range of issues. In July 2017, Moscow ratified the concept for a Joint Group of Forces with Armenia, signed in December 2016. This grouping is intended to maintain security in the Caucasus. Conscription continues, but there is also a growing cohort of professional officers. Equipment is mainly of Russian origin, and agreements were reached in recent years to purchase modern Russian systems. Serviceability and maintenance of mainly ageing aircraft have been a problem for the air force. In June 2016, Armenia ratified a joint air-defence system with Russia.

ACTIVE 44,800 (Army 41,850 Air/AD Aviation Forces (Joint) 1,100 other Air Defence Forces 1,850)
Paramilitary 4,300
Conscript liability 24 months

RESERVE
Some mobilisation reported, possibly 210,000 with military service within 15 years

ORGANISATIONS BY SERVICE

Army 22,900; 18,950 conscripts (total 41,850)
FORCES BY ROLE
SPECIAL FORCES
　1 SF bde
MANOEUVRE
　Mechanised
　1 (1st) corps (1 recce bn, 1 tk bn, 2 MR regt, 1 maint bn)
　1 (2nd) corps (1 recce bn, 1 tk bn, 2 MR regt, 1 lt inf regt, 1 arty bn)
　1 (3rd) corps (1 recce bn, 1 tk bn, 4 MR regt, 1 lt inf regt, 1 arty bn, 1 MRL bn, 1 sigs bn, 1 maint bn)
　1 (4th) corps (4 MR regt; 1 SP arty bn; 1 sigs bn)
　1 (5th) corps (with 2 fortified areas) (1 MR regt)
　Other
　1 indep MR trg bde
COMBAT SUPPORT
　1 arty bde
　1 MRL bde
　1 AT regt
　1 AD bde
　2 AD regt
　2 (radiotech) AD regt
　1 engr regt
EQUIPMENT BY TYPE
ARMOURED FIGHTING VEHICLES
　MBT 109: 3 T-54; 5 T-55; 101 T-72
　RECCE 12 BRM-1K (CP)
　IFV 86: 75 BMP-1; 6 BMP-1K (CP); 5 BMP-2
　APC • APC (W) 130: 8 BTR-60; 100 BTR-60 look-a-like; 18 BTR-70; 4 BTR-80
ENGINEERING & MAINTENANCE VEHICLES
　AEV MT-LB
　ARV BREhM-D; BREM-1
ANTI-TANK/ANTI-INFRASTRUCTURE
　MSL • SP 22: 9 9P148 Konkurs (AT-5 Spandrel); 13 9P149 Shturm (AT-6 Spiral)
ARTILLERY 232
　SP 38: 122mm 10 2S1 Gvozdika; 152mm 28 2S3 Akatsiya
　TOWED 131: 122mm 69 D-30; 152mm 62: 26 2A36 Giatsint-B; 2 D-1; 34 D-20
　MRL 51: 122mm 47 BM-21 Grad; 273mm 4 WM-80
　MOR 120mm 12 M120
SURFACE-TO-SURFACE MISSILE LAUNCHERS
　SRBM • Conventional 16: 8 9K72 Elbrus (SS-1C Scud B); 4 9K79 Tochka (SS-21 Scarab); 4 9K720 Iskander-E
RADAR • LAND 6 SNAR-10
UNMANNED AERIAL VEHICLES
　ISR • Light 15 Krunk
AIR DEFENCE
　SAM
　　Medium-range 2K11 Krug (SA-4 Ganef); S-75 Dvina (SA-2 Guideline)
　　Short-range 2K12 Kub (SA-6 Gainful); S-125 Pechora (SA-3 Goa)
　　Point-defence 9K33 Osa (SA-8 Gecko); 9K310 Igla-1 (SA-16 Gimlet); 9K38 Igla (SA-18 Grouse); 9K333 Verba; 9K338 Igla-S (SA-24 Grinch)
　GUNS
　　SP 23mm ZSU-23-4
　　TOWED 23mm ZU-23-2

Air and Air Defence Aviation Forces 1,100
1 Air & AD Joint Command

FORCES BY ROLE
GROUND ATTACK
1 sqn with Su-25/Su-25UBK *Frogfoot*
EQUIPMENT BY TYPE
AIRCRAFT 15 combat capable
  ATK 15: 13 Su-25 *Frogfoot*; 2 Su-25UBK *Frogfoot*
  TPT 4: **Heavy** 3 Il-76 *Candid*; **PAX** 1 A319CJ
  TRG 14: 4 L-39 *Albatros*; 10 Yak-52
HELICOPTERS
  ATK 7 Mi-24P *Hind*
  ISR 4: 2 Mi-24K *Hind*; 2 Mi-24R *Hind* (cbt spt)
  MRH 10 Mi-8MT (cbt spt)
  C2 2 Mi-9 *Hip G* (cbt spt)
  TPT • **Light** 7 PZL Mi-2 *Hoplite*
AIR DEFENCE • SAM • Long-range S-300 (SA-10 *Grumble*); S-300PM (SA-20 *Gargoyle*)

Paramilitary 4,300

Police
FORCES BY ROLE
MANOEUVRE
  Other
  4 paramilitary bn
EQUIPMENT BY TYPE
ARMOURED FIGHTING VEHICLES
  RECCE 5 BRM-1K (CP)
  IFV 45: 44 BMP-1; 1 BMP-1K (CP)
  APC • **APC (W)** 24 BTR-60/BTR-70/BTR-152
  ABCV 5 BMD-1

Border Troops
Ministry of National Security
EQUIPMENT BY TYPE
ARMOURED FIGHTING VEHICLES
  RECCE 3 BRM-1K (CP)
  IFV 35 BMP-1
  APC • **APC (W)** 23: 5 BTR-60; 18 BTR-70
  ABCV 5 BMD-1

DEPLOYMENT

AFGHANISTAN
NATO • *Operation Resolute Support* 121
ALBANIA
OSCE • Albania 1
LEBANON
UN • UNIFIL 33
MALI
UN • MINUSMA 1
SERBIA
NATO • KFOR 35
UKRAINE
OSCE • Ukraine 2

FOREIGN FORCES
OSCE figures represent total Minsk Conference mission personnel in both Armenia and Azerbaijan

Bosnia-Herzegovina OSCE 1
Germany OSCE 1
Moldova OSCE 2
Poland OSCE 1
Russia 3,300: 1 mil base with (1 MR bde; 74 T-72; 80 BMP-1; 80 BMP-2; 12 2S1; 12 BM-21); 1 ftr sqn with 18 MiG-29 *Fulcrum*; 1 hel sqn with 8 Mi-24P *Hind*; 4 Mi-8MT *Hip*; 2 SAM bty with S-300V (SA-12 *Gladiator/Giant*); 1 SAM bty with 2K12 *Kub* (SA-6 *Gainful*)
United Kingdom OSCE 1

Azerbaijan AZE

Azerbaijani New Manat m		2016	2017	2018
GDP	m	60.0bn	66.7bn	
	US$	37.6bn	39.2bn	
per capita	US$	3,956.00	4,098	
Growth	%	-3.1	-1.04	
Inflation	%	12.4	12	
Def bdgt [a]	m	2.23bn	2.64bn	
	US$	1.40bn	1.55bn	
FMA (US)	US$	1.4m	1m	0m
US$1=m		1.60	1.70	

[a] Official defence budget. Excludes a significant proportion of procurement outlays

Population   9,961,396

Age	0–14	15–19	20–24	25–29	30–64	65 plus
Male	12.2%	3.5%	4.3%	4.9%	21.9%	2.5%
Female	10.7%	3.1%	3.9%	4.7%	23.8%	4.1%

Capabilities

The principal focus for Azerbaijan's armed forces is territorial defence, in light of continuing tensions with neighbouring Armenia over Nagorno-Karabakh. The armed forces rely on conscription, and readiness within the services varies between units. The air force also suffers from training and maintenance problems, and the armed forces cannot organically support external deployments. While forces have yet to fully transition from a Soviet-era model, oil revenues have in the recent past allowed an increase in defence expenditure. A number of combat-readiness exercises were held in 2017. Azerbaijan maintains a defence relationship with NATO and in 2016 the country was in the fourth cycle of its NATO Individual Partnership Action Plan. Azerbaijan is looking to deepen ties with Belarus, Serbia, the UK and the US through military-cooperation agreements. Peacekeeping deployments have included a small number of personnel in Afghanistan, as part of the NATO-led *Resolute Support* mission.

ACTIVE 66,950 (Army 56,850 Navy 2,200 Air 7,900)
Paramilitary 15,000
Conscript liability 18 months (12 for graduates)

RESERVE 300,000
Some mobilisation reported; 300,000 with military service within 15 years

ORGANISATIONS BY SERVICE

Army 56,850
FORCES BY ROLE
COMMAND
  5 corps HQ
MANOEUVRE
  Mechanised
  4 MR bde
  Light
  19 MR bde
  Other
  1 sy bde
COMBAT SUPPORT
  1 arty bde
  1 arty trg bde
  1 MRL bde
  1 AT bde
  1 engr bde
  1 sigs bde
COMBAT SERVICE SUPPORT
  1 log bde
EQUIPMENT BY TYPE
ARMOURED FIGHTING VEHICLES
  MBT 439: 95 T-55; 244 T-72; 100 T-90S
  RECCE 15 BRM-1
  IFV 181: 43 BMP-1; 33 BMP-2; 88 BMP-3; 7 BTR-80A; 10+ BTR-82A
  APC 568
    APC (T) 336 MT-LB
    APC (W) 142: 10 BTR-60; 132 BTR-70
    PPV 90: 45 *Marauder*; 45 *Matador*
  ABCV 20 BMD-1
ENGINEERING & MAINTENANCE VEHICLES
  AEV MT-LB
  MW *Bozena*
ANTI-TANK/ANTI-INFRASTRUCTURE
  SP 10 9P157-2 *Khrizantema-S* (AT-15 *Springer*)
  MSL • MANPATS 9K11 *Malyutka* (AT-3 *Sagger*); 9K111 *Fagot* (AT-4 *Spigot*); 9K111-1 *Konkurs* (AT-5 *Spandrel*); 9K115 *Metis* (AT-7 *Saxhorn*); *Spike*-LR
ARTILLERY 575
  SP 87: **122mm** 46 2S1 *Gvozdika*; **152mm** 24: 6 2S3 *Akatsiya*; 18 2S19 *Msta-S*; **155mm** 5 ATMOS 2000; **203mm** 12 2S7 *Pion*
  TOWED 207: **122mm** 129 D-30; **130mm** 36 M-46; **152mm** 42: 18 2A36 *Giatsint-B*; 24 D-20
  GUN/MOR 120mm 36: 18 2S9 NONA-S; 18 2S31 *Vena*
  MRL 133+: **122mm** 52+: 43 BM-21 Grad; 9+ IMI *Lynx*; **128mm** 12 RAK-12; **220mm** 18 TOS-1A; **300mm** 30 9A52 *Smerch*; **302mm** 21 T-300 *Kasirga*
  MOR 120mm 112: 5 *Cardom*; 107 M-1938 (PM-38)
SURFACE-TO-SURFACE MISSILE LAUNCHERS
  SRBM • Conventional ε4 9M79 *Tochka* (SS-21 *Scarab*)
RADAR • LAND SNAR-1 *Long Trough*/SNAR-2/-6 *Pork Trough* (arty); *Small Fred*/*Small Yawn*/SNAR-10 *Big Fred* (veh, arty); GS-13 *Long Eye* (veh)
UNMANNED AERIAL VEHICLES
  ISR • Medium 3 *Aerostar*

AIR DEFENCE • SAM
  Medium-range 2K11 *Krug* (SA-4 *Ganef*)
  Point-defence 9K33 *Osa* (SA-8 *Gecko*); 9K35 *Strela*-10 (SA-13 *Gopher*); 9K32 *Strela* (SA-7 *Grail*)‡; 9K34 *Strela-3* (SA-14 *Gremlin*); 9K310 *Igla*-1 (SA-16 *Gimlet*); 9K338 *Igla*-S (SA-24 *Grinch*)

Navy 2,200
EQUIPMENT BY TYPE
PATROL AND COASTAL COMBATANTS 11
  CORVETTES • FS 1 *Kusar* (ex-FSU *Petya II*) with 2 RBU 6000 *Smerch* 2 A/S mor, 2 twin 76mm gun
  PSO 1 *Luga* (*Wodnik* 2) (FSU Project 888; additional trg role)
  PCC 3: 2 *Petrushka* (FSU UK-3; additional trg role); 1 *Shelon* (ex-FSU Project 1388M)
  PB 3: 1 *Araz* (ex-TUR AB 25); 1 *Bryza* (ex-FSU Project 722); 1 *Poluchat* (ex-FSU Project 368)
  PBF 3 *Stenka*
MINE WARFARE • MINE COUNTERMEASURES 4
  MHC 4: 2 *Korund* (*Yevgenya*) (Project 1258); 2 *Yakhont* (FSU *Sonya*)
AMPHIBIOUS 6
  LSM 3: 1 *Polnochny A* (FSU Project 770) (capacity 6 MBT; 180 troops); 2 *Polnochny B* (FSU Project 771) (capacity 6 MBT; 180 troops)
  LCU 1 *Vydra*† (FSU) (capacity either 3 AMX-30 MBT or 200 troops)
  LCM 2 T-4 (FSU)
LOGISTICS AND SUPPORT • AGS 1 (FSU Project 10470)

Air Force and Air Defence 7,900
FORCES BY ROLE
FIGHTER
  1 sqn with MiG-29 *Fulcrum*; MiG-29UB *Fulcrum*
FIGHTER/GROUND ATTACK
  1 regt with Su-24 *Fencer*; Su-25 *Frogfoot*; Su-25UB *Frogfoot* B
TRANSPORT
  1 sqn with An-12 *Cub*; Yak-40 *Codling*
TRAINING
  1 sqn with L-39 *Albatros*
ATTACK/TRANSPORT HELICOPTER
  1 regt with Ka-32 *Helix* C; Mi-8 *Hip*; Mi-24 *Hind*; PZL Mi-2 *Hoplite*
EQUIPMENT BY TYPE
AIRCRAFT 37 combat capable
  FTR 16 MiG-29 *Fulcrum*; 2 MiG-29UB *Fulcrum*
  ATK 21: 2 Su-24 *Fencer*†; 16 Su-25 *Frogfoot*; 3 Su-25UB *Frogfoot* B
  TPT 4: **Medium** 1 An-12 *Cub*; **Light** 3 Yak-40 *Codling*
  TRG 12 L-39 *Albatros*
HELICOPTERS
  ATK 26 Mi-24 *Hind*
  MRH: 20+ Mi-17-IV *Hip*
  TPT 23: **Medium** 16: 3 Ka-32 *Helix* C; 13 Mi-8 *Hip* **Light** 7 PZL Mi-2 *Hoplite*
UAV • ISR 5: **Heavy** 1 *Heron*; **Medium** 4 *Aerostar*
AIR DEFENCE • SAM
  Long-range S-200 *Vega* (SA-5 *Gammon*); S-300PM/PMU2

Medium-range S-75 *Dvina* (SA-2 *Guideline*); 9K37M *Buk*-M1 (SA-11 *Gadfly*); *Buk*-MB; S-125-2TM *Pechora*-2TM (SA-26)

Short-range *Abisr*

AIR-LAUNCHED MISSILES • AAM • IR R-60 (AA-8 *Aphid*); R-73 (AA-11 *Archer*) IR/SARH R-27 (AA-10 *Alamo*)

Paramilitary ε15,000

State Border Service ε5,000

Ministry of Internal Affairs

EQUIPMENT BY TYPE
ARMOURED FIGHTING VEHICLES
  IFV 168 BMP-1/BMP-2
  APC • APC (W) 19 BTR-60/70/80
ARTILLERY • MRL 122mm 3 T-122
HELICOPTERS • ATK 24 Mi-35M *Hind*
UNMANNED AERIAL VEHICLES
  ISR • Medium *Hermes* 900

Coast Guard

The Coast Guard was established in 2005 as part of the State Border Service

EQUIPMENT BY TYPE
PATROL AND COASTAL COMBATANTS 16
  PCG 3 *Sa'ar* 62 with 1 8-cell lnchr with *Spike* NLOS SSM, 1 hel landing platform
  PBF 9: 1 *Osa* II (FSU Project 205); 6 *Shaldag* V; 2 Silver Ships 48ft
  PB 4: 2 Baltic 150; 1 *Point* (US); 1 *Grif* (FSU *Zhuk*)
LOGISTICS AND SUPPORT • ARS 1 *Iva* (FSU *Vikhr*)

Internal Troops 10,000+

Ministry of Internal Affairs

EQUIPMENT BY TYPE
ARMOURED FIGHTING VEHICLES
  APC • APC (W) 7 BTR-60/BTR-70/BTR-80

DEPLOYMENT

AFGHANISTAN
NATO • Operation Resolute Support 94

BOSNIA-HERZEGOVINA
OSCE • Bosnia and Herzegovina 1

UKRAINE
OSCE • Ukraine 1

FOREIGN FORCES

OSCE figures represent total Minsk Conference mission personnel in both Armenia and Azerbaijan

Bosnia-Herzegovina OSCE 1
Germany OSCE 1
Moldova OSCE 2
Poland OSCE 1
United Kingdom OSCE 1

TERRITORY WHERE THE GOVERNMENT DOES NOT EXERCISE EFFECTIVE CONTROL

Data presented here represents an assessment of the de facto situation. Nagorno-Karabakh was part of Azerbaijan, but mostly populated by ethnic Armenians. In 1988, when inter-ethnic clashes between Armenians and Azeris erupted in Azerbaijan, the local authorities declared their intention to secede and join Armenia. Baku rejected this and armed conflict erupted. A ceasefire was brokered in 1994; since then, Armenia has controlled most of Nagorno-Karabakh. While Armenia provides political, economic and military support to Nagorno-Karabakh, the region has declared itself independent – although this has not been recognised by any other state, including Armenia. Azerbaijan claims, and the rest of the international community generally regards, Nagorno-Karabakh and the occupied territories as part of Azerbaijan.

Nagorno-Karabakh

Available estimates vary with reference to military holdings in Nagorno-Karabakh. Main battle tanks are usually placed at around 200–300 in number, with similar numbers for other armoured combat vehicles and artillery pieces, and small numbers of helicopters. Overall personnel-strength estimates are between 18,000 and 20,000. Some of the equipment listed may belong to Armenian forces.

EQUIPMENT BY TYPE
ARMOURED FIGHTING VEHICLES
  MBT T-72
  RECCE BRDM-2
  IFV BMP-1; BMP-2
ANTI-TANK/ANTI-INFRASTRUCTURE
  MSL
    SP 9P148 *Konkurs* (AT-5 *Spandrel*); 9P149 *Shturm* (AT-6 *Spiral*)
    MANPATS 9K111-1 *Konkurs* (AT-5 *Spandrel*)
  RCL 73mm SPG-9
ARTILLERY 232
  SP 122mm 2S1 *Gvozdika*; 152mm 2S3 *Akatsiya*
  TOWED 122mm D-30; 152mm 2A36 *Giatsint*-B; D-20
  MRL 122mm BM-21 *Grad*; 273mm WM-80
  MOR 120mm M-74/M-75
SURFACE-TO-SURFACE MISSILE LAUNCHERS
  SRBM • Conventional 9K72 *Elbrus* (SS-1C *Scud* B)
HELICOPTERS
  ATK 5 Mi-24 *Hind*
  MRH 5 Mi-8MT *Hip*
AIR DEFENCE
  SAM
    Medium-range 2K11 *Krug* (SA-4 *Ganef*); S-75 *Dvina* (SA-2 *Guideline*)
    Short-range 2K12 *Kub* (SA-6 *Gainful*); S-125 *Pechora* (SA-3 *Goa*)
    Point-defence 9K33 *Osa* (SA-8 *Gecko*); 9K310 *Igla*-1 (SA-16 *Gimlet*); 9K38 *Igla* (SA-18 *Grouse*)
  GUNS
    SP 23mm ZSU-23-4
    TOWED 23mm ZU-23-2

Belarus BLR

Belarusian Ruble r		2016	2017	2018
GDP	r	94.3bn	103bn	
	US$	47.4bn	52.8bn	
per capita	US$	4,989	5,585	
Growth	%	-2.6	0.7	
Inflation	%	11.8	8.0	
Def bdgt	r	1.01bn	1.03bn	
	US$	506m	528m	
US$1=r		1.99	1.94	

Population 9,549,747

Age	0–14	15–19	20–24	25–29	30–64	65 plus
Male	8.1%	2.4%	2.8%	3.8%	24.4%	4.8%
Female	7.6%	2.3%	2.7%	3.7%	26.9%	10.2%

Capabilities

Maintaining territorial integrity is the fundamental task of the Belarusian armed forces. A new military doctrine was approved in July 2016; this identified security challenges including from 'hybrid methods' as well as 'colour revolutions'. The defence authorities aim to have smaller, more mobile forces with improved counter-terrorism capabilities, driven by a need for increased territorial-defence capability. Personnel reductions are being implemented as part of the country's revised defence policy. Russia is the country's principal defence partner, though Minsk has also looked to improve defence cooperation with China and Turkey. While Moscow would like to establish an air base in Belarus, there has been little real progress in this area. Russia does, however, deploy combat airpower to Baranovichi air base. Most multinational training is carried out within the context of the CSTO. The scenario for the September 2017 *Zapad* exercise was of a Russian intervention to support Belarusian action against external state-sponsored militants. The training and equipment of the territorial-defence troops have improved, with the aim of operating in cooperation with regular forces. Minsk received the final of four second-hand S-300PS SAM systems from Russia in mid-2016, and ordered a fifth battery of the 9K332 *Tor*-M2E SAM system. Belarus plans to replace its Soviet-era MiG-29 *Fulcrum* combat aircraft; a contract for Russian Su-30SMs was signed in June 2017. Military pay remains low. Belarus has an indigenous defence industry, manufacturing, among others, vehicles, guided weapons and electronic-warfare systems, while the sector also undertakes upgrades for foreign customers. Minsk aims to increase combat readiness, including through so-called readiness 'control checks'.

ACTIVE 45,350 (Army 10,700 Air 11,750 Special Operations Forces 5,900 Joint 17,000) **Paramilitary 110,000**

Conscript liability 18 months (alternative service option)

RESERVE 289,500 (Joint 289,500 with mil service within last 5 years)

ORGANISATIONS BY SERVICE

Army 16,500
FORCES BY ROLE
COMMAND
  2 comd HQ (West & North West)
MANOEUVRE
  Mechanised
  2 mech bde
  2 mech bde(-)
COMBAT SUPPORT
  4 arty bde
  3 engr bde
  1 engr regt
EQUIPMENT BY TYPE
ARMOURED FIGHTING VEHICLES
  MBT 532: 527 T-72; 5 T-72B3
  RECCE 132 BRM-1
  IFV 932 BMP-2
  APC • APC (T) 58 MT-LB
  AUV 5 CS/VN3B mod
ENGINEERING & MAINTENANCE VEHICLES
  AEV MT-LB
  VLB 24: 20 MTU-20; 4 MT-55A
ANTI-TANK/ANTI-INFRASTRUCTURE • MSL
  SP 160: 75 9P148 *Konkurs*; 85 9P149 *Shturm*
  MANPATS 9K111 *Fagot* (AT-4 *Spigot*); 9K111-1 *Konkurs* (AT-5 *Spandrel*); 9K115 *Metis* (AT-7 *Saxhorn*)
ARTILLERY 583
  SP 333: **122mm** 125 2S1 *Gvozdika*; **152mm** 208: 125 2S3 *Akatsiya*; 71 2S5; 12 2S19 *Msta-S*
  TOWED **152mm** 72 2A65 *Msta-B*
  MRL 164: **122mm** 128 BM-21 *Grad*; **220mm** 36 9P140 *Uragan*
  MOR **120mm** 14 2S12
RADAR • LAND GS-13 *Long Eye*/SNAR-1 *Long Trough*/SNAR-2/-6 *Pork Trough* (arty); some *Small Fred*/*Small Yawn*/SNAR-10 *Big Fred* (veh, arty)
AIR DEFENCE
  SAM Point-defence 2K22 *Tunguska* (SA-19 *Grison*)
  GUNS • SP **23mm** ZU-23-2 (tch)

Air Force and Air Defence Forces 15,000
Flying hours 15 hrs/yr
FORCES BY ROLE
FIGHTER
  2 sqn with MiG-29/S/UB *Fulcrum*
GROUND ATTACK
  2 sqn with Su-25K/UBK *Frogfoot* A/B
TRANSPORT
  1 base with An-12 *Cub*; An-24 *Coke*; An-26 *Curl*; Il-76 *Candid*; Tu-134 *Crusty*
TRAINING
  Some sqn with L-39 *Albatros*
ATTACK HELICOPTER
  Some sqn with Mi-24 *Hind*
TRANSPORT HELICOPTER
  Some (cbt spt) sqn with Mi-8 *Hip*; Mi-8MTV-5 *Hip*; Mi-26 *Halo*

EQUIPMENT BY TYPE
AIRCRAFT 64 combat capable
  FTR 34: 28 MiG-29 *Fulcrum*/MiG-29S *Fulcrum* C; 6 MiG-29UB *Fulcrum* B
  FGA (21 Su-27/UB *Flanker* B/C non-operational/stored)
  ATK 22 Su-25K/UBK *Frogfoot* A/B
  TPT 8: **Heavy** 2 Il-76 *Candid* (+9 civ Il-76 available for mil use); **Light** 6: 1 An-24 *Coke*; 4 An-26 *Curl*; 1 Tu-134 *Crusty*
  TRG 8+: Some L-39 *Albatros*; 8 Yak-130 *Mitten**
HELICOPTERS
  ATK 12 Mi-24 *Hind*
  TPT 26: **Heavy** 6 Mi-26 *Halo*; **Medium** 20: 8 Mi-8 *Hip*; 12 Mi-8MTV-5 *Hip*
AIR-LAUNCHED MISSILES
  AAM • IR R-60 (AA-8 *Aphid*); R-73 (AA-11 *Archer*)
  SARH R-27R (AA-10 *Alamo* A)
  ASM Kh-25 (AS-10 *Karen*); Kh-29 (AS-14 *Kedge*)
  ARM Kh-58 (AS-11 *Kilter*) (likely WFU)

Air Defence
AD data from Uzal Baranovichi EW radar
FORCES BY ROLE
AIR DEFENCE
  1 bde S-300PS (SA-10B *Grumble*)
  1 bde with S-300V(SA-12A *Gladiator*/SA-12B *Giant*)
  1 bde with 9K37 *Buk* (SA-11 *Gadfly*)
  1 bde with 9K37 *Buk* (SA-11 *Gadfly*); 9K332 *Tor*-M2E (SA-15 *Gauntlet*)
  1 bde with 9K33 *Osa* (SA-8 *Gecko*)
  1 bde with 9K33 *Osa* (SA-8 *Gecko*); 9K332 *Tor*-M2E (SA-15 *Gauntlet*)
  3 regt with S-300PS (SA-10B *Grumble*)
EQUIPMENT BY TYPE
AIR DEFENCE • SAM
  Long-range S-300PS (SA-10B *Grumble*); S-300V (SA-12A *Gladiator*/SA-12B *Giant*)
  Medium-range 9K37 *Buk* (SA-11 *Gadfly*)
  Short-range 17 9K332 *Tor*-M2E (SA-15 *Gauntlet*)
  Point-defence 9K33 *Osa* (SA-8 *Gecko*); 9K35 *Strela*-10 (SA-13 *Gopher*)

Special Operations Command 6,000
FORCES BY ROLE
SPECIAL FORCES
  1 SF bde
MANOEUVRE
  Mechanised
  2 (mobile) mech bde
EQUIPMENT BY TYPE
ARMOURED FIGHTING VEHICLES
  APC • APC (W) 192: 39 BTR-70; 153 BTR-80
ARTILLERY • TOWED 122mm 24 D-30
ANTI-TANK/ANTI-INFRASTRUCTURE • MSL
  MANPATS 9K111 *Fagot* (AT-4 *Spigot*); 9K111-1 *Konkurs* (AT-5 *Spandrel*); 9K115 *Metis* (AT-7 *Saxhorn*)

Joint 10,500 (Centrally controlled units and MoD staff)
FORCES BY ROLE
SURFACE-TO-SURFACE MISSILE
  2 SRBM bde
COMBAT SUPPORT
  1 arty gp
  1 MRL bde
  2 engr bde
  1 EW unit
  1 NBC regt
  1 ptn bridging regt
  2 sigs bde
EQUIPMENT BY TYPE
ARMOURED FIGHTING VEHICLES
  APC • APC (T) 20 MT-LB
ARTILLERY 196
  SP 152mm 70 2S5 *Giatsint*-S
  TOWED 152mm 90 2A65 *Msta*-B
  MRL 300mm 40: 36 9A52 *Smerch*; 4 *Polonez*
SURFACE-TO-SURFACE MISSILE LAUNCHERS
  SRBM • Conventional 96: 36 9M79 *Tochka* (SS-21 *Scarab*); 60 *Elbrus* (SS-1C *Scud* B)

Paramilitary 110,000

State Border Troops 12,000
Ministry of Interior

Militia 87,000
Ministry of Interior

Internal Troops 11,000

DEPLOYMENT
LEBANON
UN • UNIFIL 5

UKRAINE
OSCE • Ukraine 1

Georgia GEO

Georgian Lari		2016	2017	2018
GDP	lari	33.9bn	37.4bn	
	US$	14.3bn	15.2bn	
per capita	US$	3,872	4,123	
Growth	%	2.7	4.0	
Inflation	%	2.1	6.0	
Def bdgt	lari	670m	743m	
	US$	283m	303m	
FMA (US)	US$	30m	20m	0m
US$1=lari		2.37	2.45	

Population 4,926,330

Age	0–14	15–19	20–24	25–29	30–64	65 plus
Male	9.5%	2.9%	3.4%	4.1%	21.6%	6.3%
Female	8.6%	2.5%	3.2%	4.0%	24.2%	9.7%

Capabilities

Georgia's main security preoccupations concern Russian military deployments and the breakaway regions of Abkhazia and South Ossetia. The armed forces continue to make efforts to address lessons from the war with Russia in 2008, which revealed shortcomings, including in air defence. A Strategic Defence Review 2017–20 was published in April 2017. This said that 'Georgia must now be prepared for responding to the full spectrum of threats, including hybrid conflict scenarios'. The focus was on improving personnel structures, training facilities and equipment. A new white paper was also published in 2017. At the NATO Wales Summit in 2014, a 'Substantial NATO–Georgia Package' was approved to strengthen Georgian military capability. As part of this, a NATO Joint Training and Evaluation Centre was inaugurated near Tbilisi in mid-2015. Although Georgia abolished conscription in mid-2016, this was reinstated by a new defence minister in early 2017. Long-standing security cooperation with the US includes the Georgia Defence Readiness Program, designed to boost military capabilties. Georgia maintains its deployment to NATO's *Resolute Support* mission in Afghanistan and hosted the *Noble Partner 2017* multinational exercise.

ACTIVE 20,650 (Army 19,050 National Guard 1,600)
Paramilitary 5,400
Conscript liability 12 months

ORGANISATIONS BY SERVICE

Army 15,000; 4,050 conscript (total 19,050)
FORCES BY ROLE
SPECIAL FORCES
  1 SF bde
MANOEUVRE
  Light
  5 inf bde
  Amphibious
  2 mne bn (1 cadre)
COMBAT SUPPORT
  2 arty bde
  1 engr bde
  1 sigs bn
  1 SIGINT bn
  1 MP bn
COMBAT SERVICE SUPPORT
  1 med bn
EQUIPMENT BY TYPE
ARMOURED FIGHTING VEHICLES
  MBT 123: 23 T-55; 100 T-72
  RECCE 5: 1 BRM-1K; 4+ *Didgori*-2
  IFV 71: 25 BMP-1; 46 BMP-2
  APC 189+
    APC (T) 69+: 3+ *Lazika*; 66 MT-LB
    APC (W) 120+: 25 BTR-70; 19 BTR-80; 8+ *Didgori*-1; 3+ *Didgori*-3; 65 *Ejder*
  AUV 10 *Cougar*
ANTI-TANK/ANTI-INFRASTRUCTURE
  MSL • MANPATS 9K111 *Fagot* (AT-4 *Spigot*); 9K113 *Konkurs* (AT-5 *Spandrel*)
GUNS • TOWED ε40: **85mm** D-44; **100mm** T-12
ARTILLERY 240
  SP 67: **122mm** 20 2S1 *Gvozdika*; **152mm** 46: 32 M-77 *Dana*; 13 2S3 *Akatsiya*; 1 2S19 *Msta-S*; **203mm** 1 2S7 *Pion*
  TOWED 71: **122mm** 58 D-30; **152mm** 13: 3 2A36 *Giatsint*-B; 10 2A65 *Msta*-B
  MRL 122mm 37: 13 BM-21 *Grad*; 6 GradLAR; 18 RM-70
  MOR 120mm 65: 14 2S12 *Sani*; 33 M-75; 18 M120
AIR DEFENCE • SAM
  Short-range *Spyder*-SR
  Point-defence *Grom*; 9K32 *Strela*-2 (SA-7 *Grail*)‡; 9K35 *Strela*-10 (SA-13 *Gopher*); 9K36 *Strela*-3 (SA-14 *Gremlin*); 9K310 *Igla*-1 (SA-16 *Gimlet*)

Aviation and Air Defence Command 1,300 (incl 300 conscript)
1 avn base, 1 hel air base
EQUIPMENT BY TYPE
AIRCRAFT 3 combat capable
  ATK 3 Su-25KM *Frogfoot* (6 Su-25 *Frogfoot* in store)
  TPT • Light 9: 6 An-2 *Colt*; 1 Tu-134A *Crusty* (VIP); 2 Yak-40 *Codling*
  TRG 9 L-29 *Delfin*
HELICOPTERS
  ATK 6 Mi-24 *Hind*
  TPT 29: **Medium** 17 Mi-8T *Hip*; **Light** 12 Bell 205 (UH-1H *Iroquois*)
UNMANNED AERIAL VEHICLES
  ISR • Medium 1+ *Hermes* 450
AIR DEFENCE • SAM
  Medium 9K37 *Buk-M1* (SA-11 *Gadfly*) (1-2 bn)
  Point 8 9K33 *Osa* AK (SA-8B *Gecko*) (two bty); 9K33 *Osa* AKM (6-10 updated SAM systems)

National Guard 1,600 active reservists opcon Army
FORCES BY ROLE
MANOEUVRE
  Light
  1 inf bde

Paramilitary 5,400

Border Police 5,400

Coast Guard
HQ at Poti. The Navy was merged with the Coast Guard in 2009 under the auspices of the Georgian Border Police, within the Ministry of the Interior
EQUIPMENT BY TYPE
PATROL AND COASTAL COMBATANTS 21
  PBF 6: 4 *Ares 43m*; 1 *Kaan 33*; 1 *Kaan 20*
  PB 15: 1 *Akhmeta*; 2 *Dauntless*; 2 *Dilos* (ex-GRC); 1 *Kutaisi* (ex-TUR AB 25); 2 *Point*; 7 *Zhuk* (3 ex-UKR) (up to 20 patrol launches also in service)
AMPHIBIOUS • LANDING CRAFT • LCU 1 *Vydra* (ex-BLG)

DEPLOYMENT

AFGHANISTAN
NATO • *Operation Resolute Support* 870; 1 lt inf bn
UN • UNAMA 2 obs

CENTRAL AFRICAN REPUBLIC
EU • EUTM RCA 35

MALI
EU • EUTM Mali 1

SERBIA
OSCE • Kosovo 1

UKRAINE
OSCE • Ukraine 12

TERRITORY WHERE THE GOVERNMENT DOES NOT EXERCISE EFFECTIVE CONTROL

Following the August 2008 war between Russia and Georgia, the areas of Abkhazia and South Ossetia declared themselves independent. Data presented here represents the de facto situation and does not imply international recognition as sovereign states.

FOREIGN FORCES

Russia 7,000; 1 mil base at Gudauta (Abkhazia) with (1 MR bde; 40 T-90A; 120 BTR-82A; 18 2S3; 12 2S12; 18 BM-21; some S-300 SAM; some atk hel); 1 mil base at Djava/Tskhinvali (S. Ossetia) with (1 MR bde; 40 T-72; 120 BMP-2; 36 2S3; 12 2S12)

Kazakhstan KAZ

Kazakhstani Tenge t		2016	2017	2018
GDP	t	45.7tr	51.7tr	
	US$	134bn	156bn	
per capita	US$	7,456	8,585	
Growth	%	1.1	3.3	
Inflation	%	14.6	7.3	
Def bdgt	t	388bn	412bn	
	US$	1.13bn	1.25bn	
US$1=t		342.13	331.00	

Population 18,556,698

Ethnic groups: Kazakk 63.3%; Russian 23.7%; Uzbek 2.8%; Ukraninan 2.1%; Tatars 1.3%; German 1.1%; other or non-specified 5.7%

Age	0–14	15–19	20–24	25–29	30–64	65 plus
Male	12.8%	3.2%	3.9%	4.5%	20.5%	2.6%
Female	13.1%	3.1%	3.7%	4.4%	22.8%	4.9%

Capabilities

In October 2017, Kazakhstan adopted a new military doctrine, indicating a change in focus from countering violent extremism towards a wider concern for border security and hybrid threats to national security. In September, Kazakhstan entered a bilateral military agreement with Uzbekistan to cooperate on training and education, countering violent extremism and reducing militant flows. By regional standards, Kazakhstan's armed forces are both relatively sizeable and well equipped, following the acquisition of significant amounts of new and upgraded materiel in recent years. Kazakhstan's close defence relationship with Russia, reinforced by CSTO and SCO membership, has been a key part of this recapitalisation process. Moscow operates a radar station at Balkash. It has supplied Kazakhstan with five S-300PS self-propelled surface-to-air-missile systems as part of a Joint Air-Defence Agreement, boosting long-range air-defence capability. In the army, air-mobile units are held at the highest level of readiness. Deployment is concentrated in the country's eastern regions, with almost all combat formations based in either Almaty or East Kazakhstan. Airlift is being improved, with joint ventures and production envisaged with European companies for rotary-wing and medium-lift fixed-wing aircraft. However, airworthiness remains problematic. In 2016, in an effort to improve training, Kazakhstan broadened the curriculum taught in military academies. Kazakhstan took part in the multinational *Dushanbe Anti-Terror* exercise in May 2017 and the CSTO KSOR counter-terror exercise in November.

ACTIVE 39,000 (Army 20,000 Navy 3,000 Air 12,000 MoD 4,000) **Paramilitary 31,500**

Conscript liability 12 months (due to be abolished)

ORGANISATIONS BY SERVICE

Army 20,000
4 regional comd: Astana, East, West and Southern

FORCES BY ROLE
MANOEUVRE
  Armoured
    1 tk bde
  Mechanised
    3 mech bde
  Air Manoeuvre
    4 air aslt bde
COMBAT SUPPORT
  3 arty bde
  1 SSM unit
  3 cbt engr bde

EQUIPMENT BY TYPE
ARMOURED FIGHTING VEHICLES
  MBT 300 T-72BA
  RECCE 100: 40 BRDM-2; 60 BRM-1
  IFV 607: 500 BMP-2; 107 BTR-80A
  APC 369+
    APC (T) 150 MT-LB
    APC (W) 209: 2 BTR-3E; 190 BTR-80; 17 *Cobra*
    PPV 10+ *Arlan*
ENGINEERING & MAINTENANCE VEHICLES
  AEV MT-LB
ANTI-TANK/ANTI-INFRASTRUCTURE
  MSL
    SP 3+: 3 BMP-T; HMMWV with 9K111-1 *Konkurs* (AT-5 *Spandrel*); 9P149 *Shturm* (MT-LB with AT-6 *Spiral*)
    MANPATS 9K111 *Fagot* (AT-4 *Spigot*); 9K111-1 *Konkurs* (AT-5 *Spandrel*); 9K115 *Metis* (AT-7 *Saxhorn*)
  GUNS 100mm 68 MT-12/T-12
ARTILLERY 611
  SP 246: **122mm** 126: 120 2S1 *Gvozdika*; 6 *Semser*; **152mm** 120 2S3 *Akatsiya*

TOWED 150: **122mm** 100 D-30; **152mm** 50 2A65 *Msta*-B (**122mm** up to 300 D-30 in store)
GUN/MOR **120mm** 25 2S9 NONA-S
MRL 127: **122mm** 100 BM-21 *Grad*; **220mm** 3 TOS-1A; **300mm** 24: 6 BM-30 *Smerch*; 18 IMI *Lynx* (with 50 msl) (**122mm** 100 BM-21 *Grad*; **220mm** 180 9P140 *Uragan* all in store)
MOR 63 **SP 120mm** 18 *Cardom*; **120mm** 45 2B11 *Sani*/M120
SURFACE-TO-SURFACE MISSILE LAUNCHERS
SRBM • **Conventional** 12 9K79 *Tochka* (SS-21 *Scarab*)

Navy 3,000

EQUIPMENT BY TYPE
PATROL AND COASTAL COMBATANTS 24
PCGM 2 *Kazakhstan* with 1 *Barrier*-BK lnchr with 4 RK-2B SSM, 1 *Arbalet*-K lnchr with 4 9K38 *Igla* (SA-18 *Grouse*), 1 AK306 CIWS
PCC 1 *Kazakhstan* with 1 122mm MRL
PBF 5: 2 *Saygak*; 3 *Sea Dolphin*
PB 16: 4 *Almaty*; 3 *Archangel*; 1 *Dauntless*; 4 *Sardar*; 1 *Turk* (AB 25); 2 *Zhuk* (of which 1 may be operational); 1 Other
MINE WARFARE • MINE COUNTERMEASURES 1
MCC 1 *Alatau* (Project 10750E) with 1 AK306 CIWS
LOGISTICS AND SUPPORT • AGS 1 *Zhaik*

Coastal Defence

FORCES BY ROLE
MANOEUVRE
  Mechanised
  1 naval inf bde
EQUIPMENT BY TYPE
ARMOURED FIGHTING VEHICLES
  IFV 70 BTR-82A

Air Force 12,000 (incl Air Defence)

Flying hours   100 hrs/yr

FORCES BY ROLE
FIGHTER
  1 sqn with MiG-29/MiG-29UB *Fulcrum*
  2 sqn with MiG-31B/MiG-31BM *Foxhound*
FIGHTER/GROUND ATTACK
  1 sqn with MiG-27 *Flogger* D; MiG-23UB *Flogger* C
  1 sqn with Su-27/Su-27UB *Flanker*
  1 sqn with Su-27/Su-30SM *Flanker*
GROUND ATTACK
  1 sqn with Su-25 *Frogfoot*
TRANSPORT
  1 unit with Tu-134 *Crusty*; Tu-154 *Careless*
  1 sqn with An-12 *Cub*, An-26 *Curl*, An-30 *Clank*, An-72 *Coaler*, C295M
TRAINING
  1 sqn with L-39 *Albatros*
ATTACK HELICOPTER
  5 sqn with Mi-24V *Hind*
TRANSPORT HELICOPTER
  Some sqn with Bell 205 (UH-1H *Iroquois*); H145; Mi-8 *Hip*; Mi-17V-5 *Hip*; Mi-171Sh *Hip*; Mi-26 *Halo*
AIR DEFENCE
  Some regt with S-75M *Volkhov* (SA-2 *Guideline*); S-125 *Neva* (SA-3 *Goa*); S-300/S-300PS (SA-10/10B *Grumble*); 2K11 *Krug* (SA-4 *Ganef*); S-200 *Angara* (SA-5 *Gammon*); 2K12 *Kub* (SA-6 *Gainful*)

EQUIPMENT BY TYPE
AIRCRAFT 104 combat capable
  FTR 46: 12 MiG-29 *Fulcrum*; 2 MiG-29UB *Fulcrum*; 32 MiG-31/MiG-31BM *Foxhound*
  FGA 44: 12 MiG-27 *Flogger* D; 2 MiG-23UB *Flogger* C; 20 Su-27 *Flanker*; 4 Su-27UB *Flanker*; 6 Su-30SM
  ATK 14: 12 Su-25 *Frogfoot*; 2 Su-25UB *Frogfoot*
  ISR 1 An-30 *Clank*
  TPT 19: **Medium** 2 An-12 *Cub*; **Light** 16: 6 An-26 *Curl*, 2 An-72 *Coaler*; 6 C295; 2 Tu-134 *Crusty*; **PAX** 1 Tu-154 *Careless*
  TRG 18: 17 L-39 *Albatros*; 1 Z-242L
HELICOPTERS
  ATK 24: 20 Mi-24V *Hind* (some upgraded); 4 Mi-35M *Hind*
  MRH 26: 20 Mi-17V-5 *Hip*; 6 Mi-171Sh *Hip*
  TPT 14: **Heavy** 4 Mi-26 *Halo*; **Light** 10: 4 Bell 205 (UH-1H *Iroquois*); 6 H145
UNMANNED AERIAL VEHICLES
  CISR • **Heavy** 2 *Wing Loong* (GJ-1)
AIR DEFENCE • SAM
  Long-range S-200 *Angara* (SA-5 *Gammon*); S-300 (SA-10 *Grumble*); 40+ S-300PS (SA-10B *Grumble*)
  Medium-range 2K11 *Krug* (SA-4 *Ganef*); S-75M *Volkhov* (SA-2 *Guideline*)
  Short-range 2K12 *Kub* (SA-6 *Gainful*); S-125 *Neva* (SA-3 *Goa*)
  Point-defence 9K35 *Strela*-10 (SA-13 *Gopher*)
AIR-LAUNCHED MISSILES
  AAM • **IR** R-60 (AA-8 *Aphid*); R-73 (AA-11 *Archer*); **IR/SARH** R-27 (AA-10 *Alamo*); **SARH** R-33 (AA-9 *Amos*); **ARH** R-77 (AA-12A *Adder* – on MiG-31BM)
  ASM Kh-23 (AS-7 *Kerry*)‡; Kh-25 (AS-10 *Karen*); Kh-29 (AS-14 *Kedge*)
  ARM Kh-27 (AS-12 *Kegler*); Kh-58 (AS-11 *Kilter*)

Paramilitary 31,500

National Guard ε20,000
Ministry of Interior

State Security Service 2,500

Border Service ε9,000
Ministry of Interior
EQUIPMENT BY TYPE
AIRCRAFT 7: **Light** 6: 4 An-26 *Curl*; 1 An-74T; 1 An-74TK **PAX** 1 SSJ-100
HELICOPTERS • TPT • **Medium** 15: 1 Mi-171; 14 Mi-171Sh

DEPLOYMENT

WESTERN SAHARA
UN • MINURSO 4 obs

UKRAINE
OSCE • Ukraine 4

Kyrgyzstan KGZ

Kyrgyzstani Som s		2016	2017	2018
GDP	s	458bn	491bn	
	US$	6.55bn	7.06bn	
per capita	US$	1,073	1,140	
Growth	%	3.8	3.5	
Inflation	%	0.4	3.8	
Def bdgt	s	n.k.	n.k.	
	US$	n.k.	n.k.	
US$1=s		69.92	69.56	

Population 5,789,122

Ethnic groups: Kyrgyz 71.7%; Uzbek 14.3%; Russian 7.2%; Dungan 1.1%; Uygur 0.9%; other or unspecified 4.8%

Age	0–14	15–19	20–24	25–29	30–64	65 plus
Male	15.5%	4.0%	4.5%	4.7%	18.1%	2.0%
Female	14.7%	3.9%	4.3%	4.7%	20.0%	3.2%

Capabilities

Kyrgyzstan's armed forces generally possess ageing land equipment and limited air capabilities. A July 2013 military doctrine detailed plans to reform the armed forces, with enhanced command and control, effective military logistics and a modern air-defence system. To date, there appears to have been little progress, and combat readiness remains low with large numbers of conscripts. Kyrgyzstan maintains a close strategic relationship with Russia and is a member of both the CSTO and the SCO. Moscow also maintains a number of military bases in the country, including a squadron of Su-25SM ground-attack aircraft at Kant air base, which it has leased since 2003. As part of Kyrgyzstan's effort to counter terrorism, the government has ordered the creation of an inter-agency working group to devise an anti-extremism and anti-terrorism programme. Kyrgyzstan held a joint anti-terror exercise, *Khanjar*-IV, with India and participated in *Dushanbe Anti-Terror 2017* exercise and the CSTO KSOR counter-terror exercise in November.

ACTIVE 10,900 (Army 8,500 Air 2,400) **Paramilitary 9,500**

Conscript liability 18 months

ORGANISATIONS BY SERVICE

Army 8,500
FORCES BY ROLE
SPECIAL FORCES
 1 SF bde
MANOEUVRE
 Mechanised
 2 MR bde
 1 (mtn) MR bde
COMBAT SUPPORT
 1 arty bde
 1 AD bde

EQUIPMENT BY TYPE
ARMOURED FIGHTING VEHICLES
 MBT 150 T-72
 RECCE 30 BRDM-2
 IFV 320: 230 BMP-1; 90 BMP-2
 APC • APC (W) 55: 25 BTR-70; 20 BTR-70M; 10 BTR-80
ANTI-TANK/ANTI-INFRASTRUCTURE
 MSL • MANPATS 9K11 *Malyutka* (AT-3 *Sagger*); 9K111 *Fagot* (AT-4 *Spigot*); 9K111-1 *Konkurs* (AT-5 *Spandrel*)
 RCL 73mm SPG-9
 GUNS 100mm 36: 18 MT-12/T-12; 18 M-1944
ARTILLERY 228
 SP 122mm 18 2S1 *Gvozdika*
 TOWED 123: **122mm** 107: 72 D-30; 35 M-30 (M-1938); **152mm** 16 D-1
 GUN/MOR 120mm 12 2S9 NONA-S
 MRL 21: **122mm** 15 BM-21; **220mm** 6 9P140 *Uragan*
 MOR 120mm 54: 6 2S12; 48 M-120
AIR DEFENCE
 SAM • Point-defence 9K32 *Strela*-2 (SA-7 *Grail*)‡
 GUNS 48
  SP 23mm 24 ZSU-23-4
  TOWED 57mm 24 S-60

Air Force 2,400
FORCES BY ROLE
FIGHTER
 1 regt with L-39 *Albatros**
TRANSPORT
 1 regt with An-2 *Colt*; An-26 *Curl*
ATTACK/TRANSPORT HELICOPTER
 1 regt with Mi-24 *Hind*; Mi-8 *Hip*
AIR DEFENCE
 Some regt with S-125 *Pechora* (SA-3 *Goa*); S-75 *Dvina* (SA-2 *Guideline*); 2K11 *Krug* (SA-4 *Ganef*)
EQUIPMENT BY TYPE
AIRCRAFT 4 combat capable
 TPT • Light 6: 4 An-2 *Colt*; 2 An-26 *Curl*
 TRG 4 L-39 *Albatros**
HELICOPTERS
 ATK 2 Mi-24 *Hind*
 TPT • Medium 8 Mi-8 *Hip*
AIR DEFENCE • SAM
 Medium-range 2K11 *Krug* (SA-4 *Ganef*); S-75 *Dvina* (SA-2 *Guideline*)
 Short-range S-125 *Pechora* (SA-3 *Goa*)

Paramilitary 9,500

Border Guards 5,000 (KGZ conscript, RUS officers)

Internal Troops 3,500

National Guard 1,000

DEPLOYMENT

SERBIA
OSCE • Kosovo 2

SOUTH SUDAN
UN • UNMISS 2; 1 obs

SUDAN
UN • UNAMID 1 obs
UN • UNISFA 1 obs

UKRAINE
OSCE • Ukraine 17

FOREIGN FORCES

Russia ε500 Military Air Forces: 13 Su-25SM *Frogfoot*; 2 Mi-8 *Hip*

Moldova MDA

Moldovan Leu L		2016	2017	2018
GDP	L	135bn	150bn	
	US$	6.77bn	7.95bn	
per capita	US$	1,907	2,240	
Growth	%	4.3	4.0	
Inflation	%	6.4	6.5	
Def bdgt	L	538m	554m	609m
	US$	27m	29m	
FMA (US)	US$	12.75m	12.75m	0m
US$1=L		19.92	18.90	

Population   3,474,121

Age	0–14	15–19	20–24	25–29	30–64	65 plus
Male	9.4%	2.9%	3.5%	4.2%	23.8%	4.9%
Female	8.8%	2.7%	3.3%	3.9%	24.8%	7.7%

Capabilities

The primary role of Moldova's armed forces is to maintain territorial integrity. The forces are constitutionally neutral. In early 2017, a National Defence Strategy for 2017–21 was approved, covering border defence, airspace control and protection, and improvements to the military-training system and the national emergency-management system, as well as modernising military equipment. The MoD was also working on a military strategy. Chisinau has looked to continue to build relations with both European states and NATO, and signed up to the NATO Defence Capacity Building Initiative in September 2014. The dispute over the separatist region of Transdniestr continues, with Russian forces still present there. There is concern over a 'hybrid' threat from Moscow. The services exercise with NATO states and have deployed service members to KFOR.

ACTIVE 5,150 (Army 3,250 Air 600 Logistic Support 1,300) **Paramilitary 2,400**
Conscript liability 12 months (3 months for university graduates)

RESERVE 58,000 (Joint 58,000)

ORGANISATIONS BY SERVICE

Army 1,300; 1,950 conscript (total 3,250)
FORCES BY ROLE
SPECIAL FORCES
  1 SF bn
MANOEUVRE
  Light
  3 mot inf bde
  1 lt inf bn
  Other
  1 gd bn
COMBAT SUPPORT
  1 arty bn
  1 engr bn
  1 NBC coy
  1 sigs bn
EQUIPMENT BY TYPE
ARMOURED FIGHTING VEHICLES
  APC 163
    APC (T) 69: 9 BTR-D; 60 MT-LB (variants)
    APC (W) 94: 13 BTR-80; 81 TAB-71
  ABCV 44 BMD-1
ANTI-TANK/ANTI-INFRASTRUCTURE
  MSL • MANPATS 9K111 *Fagot* (AT-4 *Spigot*); 9K111-1 *Konkurs* (AT-5 *Spandrel*)
  RCL 73mm SPG-9
  GUNS 100mm 37 MT-12
ARTILLERY 221
  TOWED 69: **122mm** 17 (M-30) M-1938; **152mm** 52: 21 2A36 *Giatsint*-B; 31 D-20
  GUN/MOR • SP **120mm** 9 2S9 NONA-S
  MRL **220mm** 11 9P140 *Uragan*
  MOR 132: **82mm** 75 BM-37; **120mm** 57: 50 M-1989; 7 PM-38
RADAR • LAND 5: 2 ARK-1; 3 SNAR-10
AIR DEFENCE • GUNS • TOWED 39: **23mm** 28 ZU-23; **57mm** 11 S-60

Air Force 600 (incl 250 conscripts)
FORCES BY ROLE
TRANSPORT
  1 sqn with An-2 *Colt*; Mi-8MTV-1/PS *Hip*; Yak-18
AIR DEFENCE
  1 regt with S-125 *Neva* (SA-3 *Goa*)
EQUIPMENT BY TYPE
AIRCRAFT
  TPT • **Light** 3: 2 An-2 *Colt*; 1 Yak-18
HELICOPTERS
  TPT • **Medium** 6: 2 Mi-8PS *Hip*; 4 Mi-8MTV-1 *Hip*
AIR DEFENCE • SAM • Short-range 3 S-125 *Neva* (SA-3 *Goa*)

Paramilitary 2,400
Ministry of Interior

OPON 900 (riot police)
Ministry of Interior

DEPLOYMENT

ALBANIA
OSCE • Albania 1

ARMENIA/AZERBAIJAN
OSCE • Minsk Conference 2

BOSNIA-HERZEGOVINA
OSCE • Bosnia and Herzegovina 1

CENTRAL AFRICAN REPUBLIC
UN • MINUSCA 1; 2 obs

LIBERIA
UN • UNMIL 1 obs

SERBIA
NATO • KFOR 41
OSCE • Kosovo 1
UN • UNMIK 1 obs

SOUTH SUDAN
UN • UNMISS 1; 3 obs

UKRAINE
OSCE • Ukraine 33

FOREIGN FORCES

Estonia OSCE 1
Hungary OSCE 1
Russia ε1,500 (including 400 peacekeepers) 7 Mi-24 *Hind*/ Mi-8 *Hip*
Sweden OSCE 1
Ukraine 10 mil obs (Joint Peacekeeping Force)
United Kingdom OSCE 1
United States OSCE 3

Russia RUS

Russian Rouble r		2016	2017	2018
GDP	r	86.0tr	92.5tr	
	US$	1.28tr	1.47tr	
per capita	US$	8,946	10,248	
Growth	%	-0.2	1.8	
Inflation	%	7.0	4.2	
Def exp [a]	r	3.84tr	3.86tr	3.82tr
	US$	57.2bn	61.7bn	
Def bdgt	r	2.98tr	2.87tr	2.77tr
	US$	44.5bn	45.6bn	
US$1=r		67.06	62.98	

[a] Calculated to be comparable with the NATO definition of defence expenditure

Population 142,257,519

Ethnic groups: Tatar 3.71%; Armenian 0.8%; Bashkir 1.1%; Chechen 1%; Chuvash 1%

Age	0–14	15–19	20–24	25–29	30–64	65 plus
Male	8.8%	2.3%	2.5%	3.8%	24.3%	4.5%
Female	8.3%	2.2%	2.4%	3.7%	27.2%	9.8%

Capabilities

Russia continues to recapitalise both its nuclear and conventional forces, though economic difficulties are affecting spending plans. The overall aspiration of Russia's military modernisation is to field a more modern suite of military capabilities and more professional armed forces held at high readiness. The latest State Armament Plan (2018–27) was expected to be made public at the end of 2017 at the earliest. It was, however, widely trailed in the Russian press from mid-year. A number of high-profile projects for the navy and aerospace forces have reportedly been delayed or deferred, including the new aircraft carrier and the Project 23560 *Lider* destroyer for the navy, while there is a reduced emphasis on the air force's PAK-DA low-observable bomber project, and a mooted successor to the MiG-31 *Foxhound* appears to have been shelved. A new naval doctrine was approved but, with the possible exception of sub-surface capabilities, it would appear difficult for the navy fully to achieve the ambitions contained in the document. Russian forces remain on operational deployment in Syria in support of the Assad regime, with the conflict providing a testing ground for a variety of new or upgraded systems. However, the navy's decision to send its only aircraft carrier, *Admiral Kuznetsov*, to take part in the Syrian campaign during the fourth quarter of 2016 seems to have not been sufficient to secure enough support for significant investment in a future aircraft-carrier programme in the GPV 2018–27. While some of Russia's more ambitious projects have likely been reined in, core equipment-acquisition programmes are still supported, including the army's T-14 *Armata* main battle tank and the air force's PAK-FA requirement for a next-generation combat aircraft. Delivery rates and in-service dates could, however, be affected further. Improving readiness also remains a priority, with 'no-notice' exercises used to examine this. A major event in the exercise calendar was *Zapad 2017*, which took place in Belarus and the Western Military District in September. (See pp. 169–79.)

ACTIVE 900,000 (Army 280,000 Navy 150,000 Air 165,000 Strategic Rocket Force 50,000 Airborne 45,000 Special Operations Forces 1,000 Railway Troops 29,000 Command and Support 180,000) **Paramilitary 554,000**

Conscript liability 12 months (conscripts now can opt for contract service immediately, which entails a 24-month contract)

RESERVE 2,000,000 (all arms)

Some 2,000,000 with service within last 5 years; reserve obligation to age 50

ORGANISATIONS BY SERVICE

Strategic Deterrent Forces ε80,000 (incl personnel assigned from the Navy and Aerospace Forces)

Navy
EQUIPMENT BY TYPE
SUBMARINES • STRATEGIC • SSBN 13:
  3 *Kalmar* (*Delta* III) with 16 R-29RKU-02 *Statsiya*-02 (SS-N-18 *Stingray*) nuclear SLBM, 2 single 400mm TT with SET-72 LWT, 4 single 533mm TT with 53-65K HWT/SET-65K HWT/USET-80K *Keramika* HWT

6 *Delfin* (*Delta* IV) with 16 R-29RMU2 *Sineva*/R-29RMU2.1 *Layner* (SS-N-23 *Skiff*) nuclear SLBM, 4 single 533mm TT with 53-65K HWT/SET-65K HWT/USET-80K *Keramika* HWT (of which 1 in refit)

1 *Akula* (*Typhoon*)† in reserve for training with capacity for 20 *Bulava* (SS-N-32) nuclear SLBM, 6 single 533mm TT with 53-65K HWT/SET-65K HWT/USET-80K *Keramika* HWT

3 *Borey* (*Dolgorukiy*) with 16 *Bulava* (SS-N-32) nuclear SLBM, 6 single 533mm TT with USET-80K *Keramika* HWT/UGST *Fizikov* HWT

Strategic Rocket Force Troops 50,000

3 Rocket Armies operating silo and mobile launchers organised in 12 divs. Regt normally with 10 silos (6 for RS-20/SS-18), or 9 mobile lnchr, and one control centre

FORCES BY ROLE
SURFACE-TO-SURFACE MISSILE
  9 ICBM regt with RS-12M *Topol* (SS-25 *Sickle*)
  8 ICBM regt with RS-12M2 *Topol*-M (SS-27 mod 1)
  3 ICBM regt with RS-18 (SS-19 *Stiletto*)
  9 ICBM regt with RS-20 (SS-18 *Satan*)
  10 ICBM regt with RS-24 *Yars* (SS-27 mod 2)
  4 ICBM regt (forming) with RS-24 *Yars* (SS-27 mod 2)

EQUIPMENT BY TYPE
SURFACE-TO-SURFACE MISSILE LAUNCHERS
  ICBM • Nuclear 313: ε63 RS-12M *Topol* (SS-25 *Sickle*) (mobile single warhead); 60 RS-12M2 *Topol*-M (SS-27 mod 1) silo-based (single warhead); 18 RS-12M2 *Topol*-M (SS-27 mod 1) road mobile (single warhead); 30 RS-18 (SS-19 *Stiletto*) (mostly mod 3, 6 MIRV per msl) (being withdrawn); 46 RS-20 (SS-18 *Satan*) (mostly mod 5, 10 MIRV per msl); 84 RS-24 *Yars* (SS-27 mod 2; ε3 MIRV per msl) road mobile; 12 RS-24 *Yars* (SS-27 mod 2; ε3 MIRV per msl) silo-based

Long-Range Aviation Command

FORCES BY ROLE
BOMBER
  1 sqn with Tu-160/Tu-160M1 *Blackjack*
  3 sqn with Tu-95MS/MS mod/MSM *Bear*

EQUIPMENT BY TYPE
AIRCRAFT
  BBR 76: 10 Tu-160 *Blackjack* with Kh-55/Kh-55SM (AS-15A/B *Kent*); 6 Tu-160M1 *Blackjack* with Kh-55/Kh-55SM (AS-15A/B *Kent*)/Kh-102 nuclear LACM; 46 Tu-95MS/MS mod *Bear* H with Kh-55/Kh-55SM (AS-15A/B *Kent*)/Kh-102 nuclear ALCM; 14 Tu-95MSM *Bear* H with Kh-55/Kh-55SM (AS-15A/B *Kent*)/Kh-102 nuclear LACM

Space Command

EQUIPMENT BY TYPE
SATELLITES 99
  COMMUNICATIONS 58: 1 *Blagovest*; 2 *Garpun*; 13 *Gonets*-D/M (dual-use); 3 Mod *Globus* (*Raduga*-1M); 4 *Meridian*; 3 *Parus*; 3 *Raduga*; 21 *Rodnik* (*Strela*-3M); 8 *Strela*-3

EARLY WARNING 2 *Tundra*
NAVIGATION/POSITIONING/TIMING 25 GLONASS
ISR 10: 2 *Bars*-M; 1 GEO-IK 2; 1 *Kondor*; 1 *Kosmos*-2519; 2 *Persona*; 3 *Resurs*-P
ELINT/SIGINT 4: 3 *Liana* (*Lotos*-S); 1 *Tselina*-2
RADAR 12; Russia leases ground-based radar stations in Baranovichi (Belarus) and Balkhash (Kazakhstan). It also has radars on its own territory at Lekhtusi (St Petersburg); Armavir (Krasnodar); Olenegorsk (Murmansk); Mishelevka (Irkuts); Kaliningrad; Pechora (Komi); Yeniseysk (Krasnoyarsk); Baranul (Altayskiy); Orsk (Orenburg) and Gorodets/Kovylkino (OTH)

Aerospace Defence Command

FORCES BY ROLE
AIR DEFENCE
  2 AD div HQ
  4 SAM regt with S-300PM1/PM2 (SA-20 *Gargoyle*)
  5 SAM regt with S-400 (SA-21 *Growler*); 96K6 *Pantsir*-S1 (SA-22 *Greyhound*)

EQUIPMENT BY TYPE
AIR DEFENCE • SAM 222
  Long-range 186: 90 S-300PM1/PM2 (SA-20 *Gargoyle*); 96 S-400 (SA-21 *Growler*)
  Short-range 36 96K6 *Pantsir*-S1 (SA-22 *Greyhound*)
MISSILE DEFENCE 68 53T6 (ABM-3 *Gazelle*)
RADAR 1 ABM engagement system located at Sofrino (Moscow)

Army ε280,000 (incl conscripts)

4 military districts (West (HQ St Petersburg), Centre (HQ Yekaterinburg), South (HQ Rostov-on-Don) & East (HQ Khabarovsk), each with a unified Joint Strategic Command

FORCES BY ROLE
COMMAND
  12 army HQ
  1 corps HQ
SPECIAL FORCES
  8 (Spetsnaz) SF bde
  1 (Spetsnaz) SF regt
MANOEUVRE
  Reconnaissance
  2 recce bde
  Armoured
  1 (4th) tk div (1 armd recce bn, 2 tk regt, 1 MR regt, 1 arty regt, 1 AD regt)
  1 (90th) tk div (1 armd recce bn, 2 tk regt, 1 MR regt)
  2 tk bde (1 armd recce bn, 3 tk bn, 1 MR bn, 1 arty bn, 1 MRL bn, 2 AD bn, 1 engr bn, 1 EW coy, 1 NBC coy)
  1 (3rd) MR div (1 armd recce bn, 1 tk regt, 2 MR regt, 1 arty regt)
  1 (144th) MR div (1 armd recce bn, 1 MR regt, 1 arty regt)
  1 (150th) MR div (1 tk regt, 1 MR regt)
  14 (BMP) MR bde (1 armd recce bn, 1 tk bn, 3 armd inf bn, 2 arty bn, 1 MRL bn, 1 AT bn, 2 AD bn, 1 engr bn, 1 EW coy, 1 NBC coy)
  Mechanised
  1 (2nd) MR div (1 armd recce bn, 1 tk regt, 2 MR regt, 1 arty regt, 1 AD regt)

1 (42nd) MR div (1 armd recce bn, 3 MR regt, 1 arty regt)
9 (BTR/MT-LB) MR bde (1 recce bn; 1 tk bn; 3 mech inf bn; 2 arty bn; 1 MRL bn; 1 AT bn; 2 AD bn; 1 engr bn; 1 EW coy; 1 NBC coy)
2 MR bde (4–5 mech inf bn; 1 arty bn; 1 AD bn; 1 engr bn)
3 (lt/mtn) MR bde (1 recce bn; 2 mech inf bn; 1 arty bn)
1 (18th) MGA div (2 MGA regt; 1 arty regt; 1 tk bn; 2 AD bn)

SURFACE-TO-SURFACE MISSILE
10 SRBM/GLCM bde with 9K720 *Iskander*-M (SS-26 *Stone*/SSC-7)
1 SRBM bde with 9K79-1 *Tochka*-U (SS-21B *Scarab*)

COMBAT SUPPORT
9 arty bde
1 hy arty bde
4 MRL bde
4 engr bde
1 MP bde
5 NBC bde
10 NBC regt

COMBAT SERVICE SUPPORT
10 log bde

AIR DEFENCE
14 AD bde

EQUIPMENT BY TYPE
ARMOURED FIGHTING VEHICLES
  MBT 2,780: 1,100 T-72B/BA; 800 T-72B3; 80 T-73B3 mod; 450 T-80BV/U; 350 T-90/T-90A (10,200 in store: 7,000 T-72/T-72A/B; 3,000 T-80B/BV/U; 200 T-90)
  RECCE 1,700: 1,000 BRDM-2/2A (1,000+ BRDM-2 in store); 700 BRM-1K (CP)
  IFV 5,140: 500 BMP-1; 3,000 BMP-2; 540 BMP-3; 100 BTR-80A; 1,000 BTR-82A/AM (8,500 in store: 7,000 BMP-1; 1,500 BMP-2)
  APC 6,100+
    APC (T) 3,500+: some BMO-T; 3,500 MT-LB (2,000 MT-LB in store)
    APC (W) 2,600: 800 BTR-60 (all variants); 200 BTR-70 (all variants); 1,500 BTR-80; 100+ BPM-97 *Dozor* (4,000 BTR-60/70 in store)
    PPV *Typhoon*-K
  AUV 100+: 100+ GAZ *Tigr*; some IVECO LMV
ENGINEERING & MAINTENANCE VEHICLES
  AEV BAT-2; IMR; IMR-2; IMR-3; IRM; MT-LB
  ARV BMP-1; BREM-1/64/K/L; BTR-50PK(B); M1977; MTP-LB; RM-G; T-54/55; VT-72A
  VLB KMM; MT-55A; MTU; MTU-20; MTU-72; PMM-2
  MW BMR-3M; GMX-3; MCV-2 (reported); MTK; MTK-2
ANTI-TANK/ANTI-INFRASTRUCTURE
  MSL
    SP BMP-T with 9K120 *Ataka* (AT-9 *Spiral* 2); 9P149 with 9K114 *Shturm* (AT-6 *Spiral*); 9P149M with 9K132 *Shturm*-SM (AT-9 *Spiral*-2); 9P157-2 with 9K123 *Khrizantema* (AT-15 *Springer*); 9K128-1 *Kornet*-T
    MANPATS 9K111M *Fagot* (AT-4 *Spigot*); 9K111-1 *Konkurs* (AT-5 *Spandrel*); 9K115 *Metis* (AT-7 *Saxhorn*); 9K115-1 *Metis*-M (AT-13 *Saxhorn* 2); 9K115-2 *Metis*-M1 (AT-13 *Saxhorn* 2); 9K135 *Kornet* (AT-14 *Spriggan*)
  RCL 73mm SPG-9

GUNS • TOWED 100mm 526 MT-12 (**100mm** 2,000 T-12/MT-12 in store)
ARTILLERY 4,328+
  SP 1,596: **122mm** 150 2S1 *Gvozdika*; **152mm** 1,386: 800 2S3 *Akatsiya*; 100 2S5 *Giatsint*-S; 450 2S19 *Msta*-S; 36 2S33 *Msta*-SM; **203mm** 60 2S7M *Malka* (4,260 in store: **122mm** 2,000 2S1 *Gvozdika*; **152mm** 2,000: 1,000 2S3 *Akatsiya*; 850 2S5 *Giatsint*-S; 150 2S19 *Msta*-S; **203mm** 260 2S7 *Pion*)
  TOWED 150: **152mm** 150 2A65 *Msta*-B (12,415 in store: **122mm** 8,150: 4,400 D-30; 3,750 M-30 (M-1938); **130mm** 650 M-46; **152mm** 3,575: 1,100 2A36 *Giatsint*-B; 600 2A65 *Msta*-B; 1,075 D-20; 700 D-1 (M-1943); 100 M-1937 (ML-20); **203mm** 40 B-4M)
  GUN/MOR 180+
    SP 120mm 80+: 30 2S23 NONA-SVK; 50+ 2S34
    TOWED 120mm 100 2B16 NONA-K
  MRL 862+ **122mm** 550 BM-21 *Grad*/*Tornado*-G; **220mm** 200 9P140 *Uragan*; some TOS-1A; **300mm** 112: 100 9A52 *Smerch*; 12 9A54 *Tornado*-S (3,220 in store: **122mm** 2,420: 2,000 BM-21 *Grad*; 420 9P138; **132mm** 100 BM-13; **220mm** 700 9P140 *Uragan*)
  MOR 1,540+: **82mm** 800+ 2B14; **120mm** 700 2S12 *Sani*; **240mm** 40 2S4 *Tulpan* (2,590 in store: **120mm** 1,900: 1,000 2S12 *Sani*; 900 M-1938 (PM-38); **160mm** 300 M-160; **SP 240mm** 390 2S4 *Tulpan*)
SURFACE-TO-SURFACE MISSILE LAUNCHERS
  SRBM 144:
    Dual-capable 120 9K720 *Iskander*-M (SS-26 *Stone*)
    Conventional 24 9K79-1 *Tochka*-U (SS-21B *Scarab*) (some *Scud* in store)
  GLCM • Dual-capable Some 9M728 *Iskander*-K (SSC-7); some 9M729 (SSC-8) (reported)
UNMANNED AERIAL VEHICLES
  ISR • Heavy Tu-143 *Reys*; Tu-243 *Reys*/Tu-243 *Reys* D; **Light** BLA-07; *Pchela*-1; *Pchela*-2
AIR DEFENCE
  SAM 1,520+
    Long-range S-300V (SA-12 *Gladiator/Giant*); S-300V4 (SA-23)
    Medium-range 360: ε200 9K37M *Buk*-M1-2 (SA-11 *Gadfly*); ε90 9K317 *Buk*-M2 (SA-17 *Grizzly*); ε60 *Buk*-M3 (SA-17 *Grizzly*)
    Short-range 120+ 9K331/9K332 *Tor*-M/M1/M2/M2U (SA-15 *Gauntlet*) (9M338 msl entering service)
    Point-defence 1,050+: 250+ 2K22M *Tunguska* (SA-19 *Grison*); 400 9K33M3 *Osa*-AKM (SA-8B *Gecko*); 400 9K35M3 *Strela*-10 (SA-13 *Gopher*); 9K310 *Igla*-1 (SA-16 *Gimlet*); 9K34 *Strela*-3 (SA-14 *Gremlin*); 9K38 *Igla* (SA-18 *Grouse*); 9K333 *Verba*; 9K338 *Igla*-S (SA-24 *Grinch*)
  GUNS
    SP 23mm ZSU-23-4
    TOWED 23mm ZU-23-2; **57mm** S-60

Reserves
Cadre formations
FORCES BY ROLE
MANOEUVRE
  Mechanised
    13 MR bde

Navy ε150,000 (incl conscripts)

4 major fleet organisations (Northern Fleet, Pacific Fleet, Baltic Fleet, Black Sea Fleet) and Caspian Sea Flotilla

EQUIPMENT BY TYPE
SUBMARINES 62
STRATEGIC • SSBN 13:

3 *Kalmar* (*Delta* III) with 16 R-29RKU-02 *Statsiya*-02 (SS-N-18 *Stingray*) nuclear SLBM, 2 single 400mm TT with SET-72 LWT, 4 single 533mm TT with 53-65K HWT/SET-65K HWT/USET-80K *Keramika* HWT

6 *Delfin* (*Delta* IV) with 16 R-29RMU2 *Sineva*/R-29RMU2.1 *Layner* (SS-N-23 *Skiff*) nuclear SLBM, 4 single 533mm TT with 53-65K HWT/SET-65K HWT/USET-80K *Keramika* HWT (of which 1 in refit)

1 *Akula* (*Typhoon*)† in reserve for training with capacity for 20 *Bulava* (SS-N-32) nuclear SLBM, 6 single 533mm TT with 53-65K HWT/SET-65K HWT/USET-80K *Keramika* HWT

3 *Borey* (*Dolgorukiy*) with 16 *Bulava* (SS-N-32) nuclear SLBM, 6 single 533mm TT with USET-80K *Keramika* HWT/UGST *Fizikov* HWT

TACTICAL 49
SSGN 9:

8 *Antyey* (*Oscar* II) with 2 12-cell lnchr with 3M45 *Granit* (SS-N-19 *Shipwreck*) AShM, 2 single 650mm TT each with T-65 HWT/RPK-7 (SS-N-16 *Stallion*) ASW msl, 4 single 553mm TT with 53-65K HWT/SET-65K HWT/USET-80K *Keramika* HWT (of which 2 in refit)

1 *Yasen* (*Severodvinsk*) with 1 octuple VLS with 3M54 (SS-N-27 *Sizzler*) AShM/3M55 *Onyx* (SS-N-26 *Strobile*) AShM/3M14 *Kalibr* (SS-N-30) dual-capable LACM; 10 single 533mm TT with USET-80K *Keramika* HWT/UGST *Fizikov* HWT

SSN 17:

9 *Schuka*-B (*Akula* I) with 4 single 533mm TT with 53-65K HWT/TEST-71M HWT/USET-80K *Keramika* HWT/3M10 *Granat* (SS-N-21 *Sampson*) LACM (weapons in store), 4 single 650mm TT with T-65 HWT/RPK-7 (SS-N-16 *Stallion*) ASW msl (of which 6 in refit)

2 *Schuka*-B (*Akula* II) with 4 single 533mm TT with 53-65K HWT/TEST-71M HWT/USET-80K *Keramika* HWT/3M10 *Granat* (SS-N-21 *Sampson*) LACM (weapons in store), 4 single 650mm TT with T-65 HWT/RPK-7 (SS-N-16 *Stallion*) ASW msl (of which 1 in refit)

2 *Kondor* (*Sierra* II) with 4 single 533mm TT with TEST-71M HWT/USET-80K *Keramika* HWT/3M10 *Granat* (SS-N-21 *Sampson*) LACM (weapons in store), 4 single 650mm TT with T-65 HWT

1 *Barracuda* (*Sierra* I) (in reserve) with 6 single 533mm TT with TEST-71M HWT/USET-80K *Keramika* HWT/3M10 *Granat* (SS-N-21 *Sampson*) LACM (weapons in store)

3 *Schuka* (*Victor* III) with 4 single 533mm TT with 53-65K HWT/SET-65K HWT/USET-80K *Keramika* HWT/3M10 *Granat* (SS-N-21 *Sampson*) LACM (weapons in store), 2 single 650mm TT with T-65 HWT

SSK 23:

16 *Paltus* (*Kilo*) with 6 single 533mm TT with 53-65K HWT/TEST-71M HWT/USET-80K *Keramika* HWT

6 *Varshavyanka* (*Kilo*) with 6 single 533mm TT with 53-65K HWT/TEST-71M HWT/USET-80K *Keramika* HWT/3M54 (SS-N-27 *Sizzler*) AShM/3M14 *Kalibr* (SS-N-30) dual-capable LACM

1 *Lada* (*Petersburg*) (AIP fitted) with 6 single 533mm TT with USET-80K *Keramika* HWT

PRINCIPAL SURFACE COMBATANTS 34
AIRCRAFT CARRIERS • CV 1

Admiral Kuznetsov with 1 12-cell VLS with 3M45 *Granit* (SS-N-19 *Shipwreck*) AShM, 4 sextuple VLS with 3K95 *Kindzhal* (SA-N-9 *Gauntlet*) SAM, 2 RBU-12000 *Udav* 1 A/S mor, 8 *Kortik* (CADS-N-1) CIWS with 3M311 (SA-N-11 *Grison*) SAM, 6 AK630 CIWS (capacity 18–24 Su-33 *Flanker* D Ftr ac; MiG-29KR FGA ac; 15 Ka-27 *Helix* ASW hel, 2 Ka-31R *Helix* AEW hel)

CRUISERS 5
CGHMN 2:

2 *Orlan* (*Kirov*) with 2 10-cell VLS with 3M45 *Granit* (SS-N-19 *Shipwreck*) AShM, 2 octuple VLS with S-300F *Fort* (SA-N-6 *Grumble*) SAM/S-300FM *Fort* M (SA-N-20 *Gargoyle*) SAM, 2 8-cell VLS with 128 3S95 *Kindzhal* (SA-N-9 *Gauntlet*) SAM, 2 twin lnchr with *Osa*-M (SA-N-4 *Gecko*) SAM, 2 quintuple 533mm ASTT with SET-65K HWT, 1 RBU 6000 *Smerch* 2 A/S mor, 2 RBU 1000 *Smerch* 3 A/S mor, 6 *Kortik* (CADS-N-1) CIWS with 3M311 (SA-N-11 *Grison*) SAM, 1 twin 130mm gun (capacity 3 Ka-27 *Helix* ASW hel) (of which 1 non-operational; undergoing extensive refit and expected to return to service in 2018)

CGHM 3:

3 *Atlant* (*Slava*) with 8 twin lnchr with 3M70 *Vulkan* (SS-N-12 mod 2 *Sandbox*) AShM, 8 octuple VLS with S-300F *Fort* (SA-N-6 *Grumble*) SAM/S-300FM *Fort* M (SA-N-20 *Gargoyle*) SAM, 2 twin lnchr with *Osa*-M (SA-N-4 *Gecko*) SAM, 2 quintuple 533mm ASTT with SET-65K HWT, 2 RBU 6000 *Smerch* 2 A/S mor, 6 AK630 CIWS, 1 twin 130mm gun (capacity 1 Ka-27 *Helix* ASW hel)

DESTROYERS 15
DDGHM 14:

5 *Sarych* (*Sovremenny*) with 2 quad lnchr with 3M80 *Moskit* (SS-N-22 *Sunburn*) AShM, 2 twin lnchr with 3K90 *Uragan* (SA-N-7 *Gadfly*) SAM, 2 twin 533mm TT with 53-65K HWT/SET-65K HWT, 2 RBU 1000 *Smerch* 3 A/S mor, 4 AK630M CIWS, 2 twin 130mm guns (capacity 1 Ka-27 *Helix* ASW hel) (of which 2 in refit)

8 *Fregat* (*Udaloy* I) with 2 quad lnchr with *Rastrub* (SS-N-14 *Silex*) AShM/ASW, 8 octuple VLS with 3K95 *Kindzhal* (SA-N-9 *Gauntlet*) SAM, 2 quad 533mm ASTT with 53-65K HWT/SET-65K HWT, 2 RBU 6000 *Smerch* 2 A/S mor, 4 AK630 CIWS, 2 100mm guns (capacity 2 Ka-27 *Helix* ASW hel)

1 *Fregat* (*Udaloy* II) with 2 quad lnchr with 3M80 *Moskit* (SS-N-22 *Sunburn*) AShM, 8 octuple VLS with 3K95 *Kindzhal* (SA-N-9 *Gauntlet*) SAM, 2 *Kortik* (CADS-N-1) CIWS with 3M311 (SA-N-11

Grison) SAM, 2 quintuple 533mm ASTT with 53-65K HWT/SET-65K HWT, 2 RBU 6000 *Smerch* 2 A/S mor, 1 twin 130mm gun (capacity 2 Ka-27 *Helix* ASW hel)

DDGM 1:
1 *Komsomolets Ukrainy* (*Kashin* mod) with 2 quad lnchr with 3M24 *Uran* (SS-N-25 *Switchblade*) AShM, 2 twin lnchr with *Volnya* (SA-N-1 *Goa*) SAM, 5 single 533mm ASTT with 53-65K HWT/SET-65K HWT, 2 RBU 6000 *Smerch* 2 A/S mor, 1 twin 76mm gun

FRIGATES 13
FFGHM 9:
2 *Admiral Grigorovich* (*Krivak* V) with 1 8-cell VLS with 3M54 (SS-N-27 *Sizzler*) AShM/3M55 *Oniks* (SS-N-26 *Strobile*) AShM/3M14 *Kalibr* (SS-N-30) dual-capable LACM, 2 12-cell VLS with 9M317E *Shtil*-1 SAM, 2 twin 533mm TT with 53-65K HWT/SET-65K HWT, 1 RBU 6000 A/S mor, 2 AK630 CIWS, 1 100mm gun (capacity 1 Ka-27 *Helix* ASW hel)

2 *Jastreb* (*Neustrashimy*) with 2 quad lnchr with 3M24 *Uran* (SS-N-25 *Switchblade*) AShM, 4 octuple VLS with 3K95 *Kindzhal* (SA-N-9 *Gauntlet*) SAM, 6 single 533mm ASTT, 1 RBU 6000 *Smerch* 2 A/S mor, 2 *Kortik* (CADS-N-1) CIWS with 3M311 (SA-N-11 *Grison*) SAM, 1 100mm gun (capacity 1 Ka-27 *Helix* ASW hel) (of which 1 in refit)

1 *Steregushchiy* (Project 20380) with 2 quad lnchr with 3M24 *Uran* (SS-N-25 *Switchblade*) AShM, 2 quad 324mm ASTT with *Paket*-NK LWT, 1 *Kortik* (CADS-N-1) CIWS with 3M311 (SA-N-11 *Grison*) SAM, 2 AK630 CIWS, 1 100mm gun (capacity 1 Ka-27 *Helix* ASW hel)

4 *Steregushchiy* (Project 20380) with 2 quad lnchr with 3M24 *Uran* (SS-N-25 *Switchblade*) AShM, 1 12-cell VLS with 3K96 *Redut* (SA-NX-28) SAM (in test), 2 quad 324mm ASTT with *Paket*-NK LWT, 2 AK630 CIWS, 1 100mm gun (capacity 1 Ka-27 *Helix* ASW hel)

FFGM 4:
1 *Gepard* with 2 quad lnchr with 3M24 *Uran* (SS-N-25 *Switchblade*) AShM, 1 twin lnchr with *Osa*-M (SA-N-4 *Gecko*) SAM, 2 AK630 CIWS, 1 76mm gun

1 *Gepard* with 1 8-cell VLS with 3M14 *Kalibr* (SS-N-30) dual capable LACM, 2 quad lnchr with 3M24 *Uran* (SS-N-25 *Switchblade*) AShM, 1 twin lnchr with *Osa*-M (SA-N-4 *Gecko*) SAM, 1 AK630 CIWS, 1 76mm gun

1 *Burevestnik* (*Krivak* I mod)† with 1 quad lnchr with *Rastrub* (SS-N-14 *Silex*) AShM/ASW, 1 twin lnchr with *Osa*-M (SA-N-4 *Gecko*) SAM, 2 quad 533mm ASTT with 53-65K HWT/SET-65K HWT, 2 RBU 6000 *Smerch* 2 A/S mor, 2 twin 76mm guns

1 *Burevestnik* M (*Krivak* II) with 1 quad lnchr with RPK-3 *Rastrub* (SS-N-14 *Silex*) AShM/ASW, 2 twin lnchr with 10 *Osa*-M (SA-N-4 *Gecko* SAM), 2 quad 533mm ASTT with 53-65K HWT/SET-65K HWT, 2 RBU 6000 *Smerch* 2 A/S mor, 2 100mm guns

PATROL AND COASTAL COMBATANTS 100
CORVETTES 48
FSGM 19
5 *Buyan*-M (*Sviyazhsk*) with 1 octuple VLS with 3M54 (SS-N-27 *Sizzler*) AShM/3M14 *Kalibr* (SS-N-30) dual-capable LACM, 2 sextuple lnchr with 3M47 *Gibka* (SA-N-10 *Grouse*) SAM, 1 AK630-M2 CIWS, 1 100mm gun

2 *Sivuch* (*Dergach*) with 2 quad lnchr with 3M80 *Moskit* (SS-N-22 *Sunburn*) AShM, 1 twin lnchr with *Osa*-M (SA-N-4 *Gecko*) SAM, 2 AK630 CIWS, 1 76mm gun

12 *Ovod* (*Nanuchka* III) with 2 triple lnchr with P-120 *Malakhit* (SS-N-9 *Siren*) AShM, 1 twin lnchr with *Osa*-M (SA-N-4 *Gecko*) SAM, 1 AK630 CIWS, 1 76mm gun

FSM 29:
2 *Albatros* (*Grisha* III) with 1 twin lnchr with *Osa*-M (SA-N-4 *Gecko*) SAM, 2 twin 533mm ASTT, 2 RBU 6000 *Smerch* 2 A/S mor, 1 twin 57mm gun

18 *Albatros* (*Grisha* V) with 1 twin lnchr with *Osa*-M (SA-N-4 *Gecko*) SAM, 2 twin 533mm ASTT, 1 RBU 6000 *Smerch* 2 A/S mor, 1 76mm gun

3 *Buyan* (*Astrakhan*) with 1 sextuple lnchr with 3M47 *Gibka* (SA-N-10 *Grouse*) SAM, 1 A-215 *Grad*-M 122mm MRL, 2 AK306 CIWS, 1 100mm gun

6 *Parchim* II with 2 quad lnchr with *Strela*-2 (SA-N-5 *Grail*) SAM, 2 twin 533mm ASTT, 2 RBU 6000 *Smerch* 2 A/S mor, 1 AK630 CIWS, 1 76mm gun

PCFG 21:
3 *Molnya* (*Tarantul* II) with 2 twin lnchr with P-15M *Termit* (SS-N-2C/D *Styx*) AShM, 1 quad lnchr (manual aiming) with *Strela*-2 (SA-N-5 *Grail*) SAM, 2 AK630 CIWS, 1 76mm gun

18 *Molnya* (*Tarantul* III) with 2 twin lnchr with 3M80 *Moskit* (SS-N-22 *Sunburn*) AShM, 1 quad lnchr (manual aiming) with *Strela*-2 (SA-N-5 *Grail*) SAM, 2 AK630 CIWS, 1 76mm gun

PBM 14 *Grachonok* with 1 quad lnchr with 3M47 *Gibka* (SA-N-10 *Grouse*) (original design was as diving tender)
PBF 13: 11 *Raptor* (capacity 20 troops); 2 *Mangust*
PBR 4 *Shmel* with 1 76mm gun

MINE WARFARE • MINE COUNTERMEASURES 43
MCC 1 *Alexandrit* (Project 12700) with 1 AK306 CIWS
MHI 8: 7 *Sapfir* (*Lida*) with 1 AK306 CIWS; 1 *Malakhit* (*Olya*)
MHO 2 *Rubin* (*Gorya*) with 2 quad lnchr with *Strela*-2 (SA-N-5 *Grail*) SAM, 1 AK630 CIWS, 1 76mm gun
MSC 22: 20 *Yakhont* (*Sonya*) with 4 AK630 CIWS (some with 2 quad lnchr with *Strela*-2 (SA-N-5 *Grail*) SAM); 2 *Korund*-E (*Yevgenya*) (Project 1258E)
MSO 10: 9 *Akvamaren* (*Natya*); 1 *Agat* (*Natya* II) (all with 2 quad lnchr (manual aiming) with *Strela*-2 (SA-N-5 *Grail*) SAM, 2 RBU 1200 *Uragan* A/S mor, 2 twin AK230 CIWS

AMPHIBIOUS
LANDING SHIPS • LST 19:
12 Project 775 (*Ropucha* I/II) with 2 twin 57mm guns (capacity either 10 MBT and 190 troops or 24 APC (T) and 170 troops)

3 Project 775M (*Ropucha* III) with 2 AK630 CIWS, 1 76mm gun (capacity either 10 MBT and 190 troops or 24 APC (T) and 170 troops)

4 *Tapir* (*Alligator*) with 2-3 twin lnchr with *Strela-2* (SA-N-5 *Grail*) SAM, 2 twin 57mm guns (capacity 20 tanks; 300 troops)

LANDING CRAFT 28
  LCU 17:
    5 *Dyugon*
    12 Project 11770 (*Serna*) (capacity 100 troops)
  LCM 9 *Akula* (*Ondatra*) (capacity 1 MBT)
  LCAC 2 *Pomornik* (*Zubr*) with 2 AK630 CIWS (capacity 230 troops; either 3 MBT or 10 APC (T))

LOGISTICS AND SUPPORT 265
  SSAN 9: 1 *Orenburg* (*Delta* III Stretch); 1 *Losharik*; 1 *Nelma* (X-Ray) (Project 1851); 2 *Halibut* (*Paltus*) (Project 18511); 3 *Kashalot* (*Uniform*); 1 *Podmoskovye* (Project 09787)
  SSA 1 *Sarov* (Project 20120)
  ABU 12: 8 *Kashtan*; 4 Project 419 (*Sura*)
  AE 9: 7 *Muna*; 1 *Dubnyak*; *Akademik Kovalev* (Project 20181) with 1 hel landing platform
  AEM 2: 1 *Kalma-3* (Project 1791R); 1 *Lama*
  AG 1 *Potok*
  AGB 5: 1 *Dobrynya Mikitich*; 1 *Ilya Muromets*; 2 *Ivan Susanin*; 1 *Vladimir Kavraisky*
  AGE 1 *Tchusovoy*
  AGI 13: 2 *Alpinist*; 2 *Dubridium* (Project 1826); 1 *Moma*; 7 *Vishnya*; 1 *Yuri Ivanov*
  AGM 1 *Marshal Nedelin*
  AGOR 8: 1 *Akademik Krylov*; 1 *Igor Belousov*; 1 *Seliger*; 2 *Sibiriyakov*; 2 *Vinograd*; 1 *Yantar*
  AGS 69: 8 *Biya*; 19 *Finik*; 7 *Kamenka*; 5 *Moma*; 9 *Onega*; 5 *Baklan* (Project 19920); 4 *Baklan* (Project 19920B); 2 *Vaygach*; 10 *Yug*
  AGSH 1 *Samara*
  AH 3 *Ob*†
  AK 3: 2 *Irgiz*; 1 *Pevek* with 1 AK306 CIWS
  AOL 9: 2 *Dubna*; 3 *Uda*; 4 *Altay* (mod)
  AOR 3 *Boris Chilikin*
  AORL 2: 1 *Kaliningradneft*; 1 *Olekma*
  AOS 2 *Luza*
  AR ε7 *Amur*
  ARC 4: 3 *Emba*; 1 Improved *Klasma*
  ARS 30: 1 *Kommuna*; 6 *Goryn*; 4 *Mikhail Rudnitsky*; 18 Project 23040; 1 *Zvezdochka* (Project 20180)
  AS 3 Project 2020 (*Malina*)
  ASR 1 *Elbrus*
  ATF 55: 1 *Okhotsk*; 1 *Baklan*; ε3 *Katun*; 4 *Ingul*; 2 *Neftegaz*; 12 *Okhtensky*; 13 *Prometey*; 1 *Prut*; 4 *Sliva*; 14 *Sorum*
  AWT 1 *Manych*
  AXL 10: 8 *Petrushka*; 2 *Smolny* with 2 RBU 2500 A/S mor, 2 twin 76mm guns

Naval Aviation ε31,000
Flying hours 80+ hrs/yr
FORCES BY ROLE
FIGHTER
  1 sqn with MiG-31B/BS *Foxhound*
  1 sqn with Su-27/Su-27UB *Flanker*
  1 regt with Su-33 *Flanker* D; Su-25UTG *Frogfoot*

FIGHTER/GROUND ATTACK
  1 regt with MiG-29KR/KUBR *Fulcrum*
  1 regt with MiG-31BM *Foxhound*; Su-24M/M2/MR *Fencer*
ANTI-SURFACE WARFARE/ISR
  1 regt with Su-24M/MR *Fencer*; Su-30SM
  1 sqn with Su-24M/MR *Fencer*
ANTI-SUBMARINE WARFARE
  3 sqn with Il-38/Il-38N *May**; Il-18D; Il-20RT *Coot* A; Il-22 *Coot* B
  8 sqn with Ka-27/Ka-29 *Helix*
  1 sqn with Mi-14 *Haze* A
  2 sqn with Tu-142MK/MZ/MR *Bear* F/J*
  1 unit with Ka-31R *Helix*
MARITIME PATROL/TRANSPORT
  1 sqn with An-26 *Curl*; Be-12 *Mail**; Mi-8 *Hip*
SEARCH & RESCUE/TRANSPORT
  1 sqn with An-12PS *Cub*; An-26 *Curl*; Tu-134
TRANSPORT
  1 sqn with An-12BK *Cub*; An-24RV *Coke*; An-26 *Curl*; An-72 *Coaler*; An-140
  2 sqn with An-26 *Curl*; Tu-134
TRAINING
  1 sqn with L-39 *Albatros*; Su-25UTG *Frogfoot*
  1 sqn with An-140; Tu-134; Tu-154, Il-38 *May*
ATTACK/TRANSPORT HELICOPTER
  1 sqn with Mi-24P *Hind*; Mi-8 *Hip*
TRANSPORT HELICOPTER
  1 sqn with Mi-8 *Hip*
AIR DEFENCE
  1 SAM regt with S-300PM1 (SA-20 *Gargoyle*)
  1 SAM regt with S-300PM1 (SA-20 *Gargoyle*); S-300PS (SA-10B *Grumble*)
  1 SAM regt with S-300PM1 (SA-20 *Gargoyle*); S-400 (SA-21 *Growler*); 96K6 *Pantsir-S1* (SA-22 *Greyhound*)
  1 SAM regt with S-300PS (SA-10B *Grumble*); S-400 (SA-21 *Growler*); 96K6 *Pantsir-S1* (SA-22 *Greyhound*)

EQUIPMENT BY TYPE
AIRCRAFT 216 combat capable
  FTR 67: 12 MiG-31B/BS *Foxhound*; 20 MiG-31BM *Foxhound*; 17 Su-33 *Flanker* D; 18 Su-27/Su-27UB *Flanker*
  FGA 43: 19 MiG-29KR *Fulcrum*; 3 MiG-29KUBR *Fulcrum*; 21 Su-30SM
  ATK 46: 41 Su-24M *Fencer*; 5 Su-25UTG *Frogfoot* (trg role)
  ASW 44: 12 Tu-142MK/MZ *Bear* F; 10 Tu-142MR *Bear* J (comms); 15 Il-38 *May*; 7 Il-38N *May*
  MP 5: 4 Be-12PS *Mail**; 1 Il-18D
  ISR 12 Su-24MR *Fencer* E*
  SAR 3 An-12PS *Cub*
  ELINT 4: 2 Il-20RT *Coot* A; 2 Il-22 *Coot* B
  TPT 49: **Medium** 2 An-12BK *Cub*; **Light** 45: 1 An-24RV *Coke*; 24 An-26 *Curl*; 6 An-72 *Coaler*; 4 An-140; 9 Tu-134; 1 Tu-134UBL; **PAX** 2 Tu-154M *Careless*
  TRG 4 L-39 *Albatros*
HELICOPTERS
  ATK 8 Mi-24P *Hind*
  ASW 83: 63 Ka-27 *Helix*; 20 Mi-14 *Haze* A
  EW 8 Mi-8 *Hip* J
  AEW 2 Ka-31R *Helix*
  SAR 56: 16 Ka-27PS *Helix* D; 40 Mi-14PS *Haze* C

TPT • **Medium** 36: 28 Ka-29 *Helix*; 4 Mi-8T *Hip*; 4 Mi-8MT *Hip*
AIR DEFENCE • SAM
Long-range 120: 56 S-300PM1 (SA-20 *Gargoyle*); 40 S-300PS (SA-10B *Grumble*); 24 S-400 (SA-21 *Growler*)
Short-range 12 96K6 *Pantsir*-S1 (SA-22 *Greyhound*)
AIR-LAUNCHED MISSILES
AAM • IR R-27T/ET (AA-10B/D *Alamo*); R-60 (AA-8 *Aphid*); R-73 (AA-11 *Archer*); **SARH** R-27R/ER (AA-10A/C *Alamo*); R-33 (AA-9A *Amos*)
ASM Kh-25 (AS-10 *Karen*); Kh-59 (AS-13 *Kingbolt*); Kh-29T
ARM Kh-25MP (AS-12 *Kegler*); Kh-58 (AS-11 *Kilter*)

Naval Infantry (Marines) ε35,000

FORCES BY ROLE
COMMAND
3 corps HQ
SPECIAL FORCES
1 (fleet) SF bde (1 para bn, 2–3 underwater bn, 1 spt unit)
2 (fleet) SF bde (cadre) (1 para bn, 2–3 underwater bn, 1 spt unit)
MANOEUVRE
Reconnaissance
1 recce bde
Mechanised
3 MR bde
1 MR regt
6 indep naval inf bde
SURFACE-TO-SURFACE MISSILE
1 SRBM bde with 9K720 *Iskander*-M (SS-26 *Stone*)
COMBAT SUPPORT
2 arty bde
AIR DEFENCE
2 SAM regt with 9K33 *Osa* (SA-8 *Gecko*); *Strela*-1/*Strela*-10 (SA-9 *Gaskin*/SA-13 *Gopher*)
2 SAM regt with S-400 (SA-21 *Growler*); 96K6 *Pantsir*-S1 (SA-22 *Greyhound*)
1 SAM regt with S-300V4 (SA-23)
EQUIPMENT BY TYPE
ARMOURED FIGHTING VEHICLES
MBT 250: 50 T-72B; 200 T-72B3
IFV 1,000: 400 BMP-2; 600 BTR-82A
APC 400
  APC (T) 300 MT-LB
  APC (W) 100 BTR-80
ANTI-TANK/ANTI-INFRASTRUCTURE
MSL
  SP 60 9P148 with 9K111-1 *Konkurs* (AT-5 *Spandrel*); 9P149 with 9K114 *Shturm* (AT-6 *Spiral*); 9P157-2 with 9K123 *Khrisantema* (AT-15 *Springer*)
  MANPATS 9K111-1 *Konkurs* (AT-5 *Spandrel*); 9K135 *Kornet* (AT-14 *Spriggan*)
GUNS 100mm T-12
ARTILLERY 365
SP 163: **122mm** 95 2S1 *Gvozdika*; **152mm** 68: 50 2S3 *Akatsiya*; 18 2S19 *Msta*-S
TOWED 152mm 100: 50 2A36 *Giatsint*-B; 50 2A65 *Msta*-B
GUN/MOR 66

SP 120mm 42: 12 2S23 NONA-SVK; 30 2S9 NONA-S
TOWED 120mm 24 2B16 NONA-K
MRL 122mm 36 BM-21 *Grad*
SURFACE-TO-SURFACE MISSILE LAUNCHERS
SRBM • Conventional 12 9K720 *Iskander*-M (SS-26 *Stone*)
AIR DEFENCE
SAM
  Long-range 48+: 48 S-400 (SA-21 *Growler*); S-300V4 (SA-23)
  Short-range 12 96K6 *Pantsir*-S1 (SA-22 *Greyhound*)
  Point-defence 70+: 20 9K33 *Osa* (SA-8 *Gecko*); 50 9K31 *Strela*-1/9K35 *Strela*-10 (SA-9 *Gaskin*/SA-13 *Gopher*); 9K338 *Igla*-S (SA-24 *Grinch*)
GUNS 23mm 60 ZSU-23-4

Coastal Missile and Artillery Troops 2,000

FORCES BY ROLE
COASTAL DEFENCE
5 AShM bde
1 AShM regt
EQUIPMENT BY TYPE
COASTAL DEFENCE
ARTY • SP 130mm ε36 A-222 *Bereg*
AShM 76+: 36 3K60 *Bal* (SSC-6 *Sennight*); 40 3K55 *Bastion* (SSC-5 *Stooge*); some 4K44 *Redut* (SSC-1 *Sepal*); some 4K51 *Rubezh* (SSC-3 *Styx*)

Aerospace Forces ε165,000 (incl conscripts)

Flying hours 60–100 hrs/yr (combat aircraft) 120+ (transport aircraft)

A joint CIS Unified Air Defence System covers RUS, ARM, BLR, KAZ, KGZ, TJK, TKM and UZB

FORCES BY ROLE
BOMBER
3 regt with Tu-22M3 *Backfire* C
3 sqn with Tu-95MS/MS mod/MSM *Bear*
1 sqn with Tu-160/Tu-160M1 *Blackjack*
FIGHTER
1 sqn with MiG-29/MiG-29UB *Fulcrum* (Armenia)
1 regt with MiG-29SMT/UBT *Fulcrum*; Su-30SM
1 regt with MiG-31BM *Foxhound*
1 regt with MiG-31B/BS/BM *Foxhound*
1 regt with MiG-31B/BS/BM *Foxhound*; Su-27/Su-27UB *Flanker*
1 regt with Su-27/Su-27UB *Flanker*; Su-27SM *Flanker*; Su-35S *Flanker*
1 regt with Su-27/Su-27UB *Flanker*
1 regt with Su-30SM
FIGHTER/GROUND ATTACK
1 regt with MiG-31BM *Foxhound*; Su-27SM *Flanker*; Su-30M2; Su-30SM; Su-35S *Flanker*
1 regt with Su-35S *Flanker*; Su-30SM
1 regt with Su-27SM *Flanker*; Su-27SM3 *Flanker*; Su-30M2
1 regt with Su-25 *Frogfoot*; Su-30SM
GROUND ATTACK
1 regt with Su-24M/M2 *Fencer*; Su-34 *Fullback*
1 regt with Su-24M *Fencer*; Su-25SM *Frogfoot*
2 sqn with Su-24M/M2 *Fencer*
3 regt with Su-25SM/SM3 *Frogfoot*

1 sqn with Su-25SM *Frogfoot* (Kyrgyzstan)
2 regt with Su-34 *Fullback*
ELECTRONIC WARFARE
1 sqn with Mi-8PPA *Hip*
ISR
2 regt with Su-24MR *Fencer**
2 sqn with Su-24MR *Fencer**
1 flt with An-30 *Clank*
AIRBORNE EARLY WARNING & CONTROL
1 sqn with A-50/A-50U *Mainstay*
TANKER
1 sqn with Il-78/Il-78M *Midas*
TRANSPORT
6 regt/sqn with An-12BK *Cub*; An-26 *Curl*; Tu-134 *Crusty*; Tu-154 *Careless*; Mi-8 *Hip*
1 regt with An-124 *Condor*; Il-76MD *Candid*
1 regt with An-12BK *Cub*; Il-76MD *Candid*
1 sqn with An-22 *Cock*
3 regt with Il-76MD *Candid*
ATTACK/TRANSPORT HELICOPTER
1 bde with Ka-52A *Hokum* B; Mi-28N *Havoc* B; Mi-35 *Hind*; Mi-26 *Halo*; Mi-8MTV-5 *Hip*
1 bde with Ka-52A *Hokum* B; Mi-26 *Halo*; Mi-8 *Hip*
1 bde with Mi-28N *Havoc* B; Mi-35 *Hind*; Mi-26 *Halo*; Mi-8 *Hip*
1 bde with Mi-24P *Hind*; Mi-8 *Hip*
2 regt with Ka-52A *Hokum* B; Mi-28N *Havoc* B; Mi-35 *Hind*; Mi-8 *Hip*
1 regt with Ka-52A *Hokum* B; Mi-8 *Hip*
1 regt with Mi-28N *Havoc* B; Mi-35 *Hind*; Mi-8 *Hip*
1 regt with Mi-28N *Havoc* B; Mi-24P *Hind*; Mi-35 *Hind*; Mi-8 *Hip*
1 regt with Mi-24P *Hind*; Mi-8 *Hip*
2 sqn with Mi-24P *Hind*; Mi-8 *Hip*
ATTACK HELICOPTER
1 sqn with Ka-52A *Hokum* B
1 sqn with Mi-24P *Hind*
TRANSPORT HELICOPTER
1 sqn with Mi-8 *Hip*
AIR DEFENCE
9 AD div HQ
4 regt with 9K37M *Buk*-M1-2/9K317 *Buk*-M2 (SA-11 *Gadfly*/SA-17 *Grizzly*); S-300V (SA-12 *Gladiator/Giant*)
1 bde with S-300PS (SA-10B *Grumble*)
5 regt with S-300PS (SA-10 *Grumble*)
8 regt with S-300PM1/PM2 (SA-20 *Gargoyle*)
7 regt with S-400 (SA-21 *Growler*); 96K6 *Pantsir*-S1 (SA-22 *Greyhound*)
EQUIPMENT BY TYPE
AIRCRAFT 1,176 combat capable
BBR 139: 61 Tu-22M3 *Backfire* C; 1 Tu-22M3M *Backfire*; 1 Tu-22MR *Backfire* (1 in overhaul); 46 Tu-95MS/MS mod *Bear*; 14 Tu-95MSM *Bear*; 10 Tu-160 *Blackjack*; 6 Tu-160M1 *Blackjack*
FTR 222: 70 MiG-29/MiG-29UB *Fulcrum*; 12 MiG-31B/31BS *Foxhound*; 80 MiG-31BM *Foxhound*; 50 Su-27 *Flanker*; 10 Su-27UB *Flanker*
FGA 378: 44 MiG-29SMT *Fulcrum*; 6 MiG-29UBT *Fulcrum*; 47 Su-27SM *Flanker*; 14 Su-27SM3 *Flanker*; 20 Su-30M2; 79 Su-30SM; 98 Su-34 *Fullback*; 70 Su-35S *Flanker*

ATK 265: 70 Su-24M/M2 *Fencer*; 40 Su-25 *Frogfoot*; 140 Su-25SM/SM3 *Frogfoot*; 15 Su-25UB *Frogfoot*
ISR 87: 4 An-30 *Clank*; 79 Su-24MR *Fencer**; 2 Tu-214ON; 2 Tu-214R
EW 3 Il-22PP
ELINT 32: 15 Il-20M *Coot* A; 5 Il-22 *Coot* B; 12 Il-22M *Coot* B
AEW&C 18: 14 A-50 *Mainstay*; 4 A-50U *Mainstay*
C2 10: 4 Il-80 *Maxdome*; 2 Il-82; 4 Tu-214SR
TKR 15: 5 Il-78 *Midas*; 10 Il-78M *Midas*
TPT 428: **Heavy** 111: 9 An-124 *Condor*; 2 An-22 *Cock*; 100 Il-76MD *Candid*; **Medium** 65 An-12BK *Cub*; **Light** 235: 115 An-26 *Curl*; 25 An-72 *Coaler*; 5 An-140; 9 An-148-100E; 27 L-410; 54 Tu-134 *Crusty*; **PAX** 17 Tu-154 *Careless*
TRG 213: 120 L-39 *Albatros*; 93 Yak-130 *Mitten**
HELICOPTERS
ATK 376+: 118 Ka-52A *Hokum* B; 100 Mi-24D/V/P *Hind*; 90+ Mi-28N *Havoc* B; 8 Mi-28UB *Havoc*; 60+ Mi-35 *Hind*
EW 27: 20 Mi-8PPA *Hip*; 7 Mi-8MTRP-1 *Hip*
TPT 339: **Heavy** 33 Mi-26/Mi-26T *Halo*; **Medium** 306 Mi-8/Mi-8MT/Mi-8AMTSh/Mi-8AMTSh-VA/Mi-8MTV-5 *Hip*
TRG 64: 19 Ka-226; 45 *Ansat*-U
UNMANNED AERIAL VEHICLES
ISR • Medium *Forpost* (*Searcher* II)
AIR DEFENCE • SAM 612:
Long-range 490: 180 S-300PM1/PM2 (SA-20 *Gargoyle*); 170 S-300PS (SA-10B *Grumble*); 20 S-300V (SA-12 *Gladiator/Giant*); 120 S-400 (SA-21 *Growler*)
Medium-range 80 9K37M *Buk*-M1-2/9K317 *Buk*-M2 (SA-11 *Gadfly*/SA-17 *Grizzly*)
Short-range 42 96K6 *Pantsir*-S1/S2 (SA-22 *Greyhound*)
AIR-LAUNCHED MISSILES
AAM • IR R-27T/ET (AA-10B/D *Alamo*); R-73 (AA-11 *Archer*); R-60T (AA-8 *Aphid*); **SARH** R-27R/ER (AA-10A/C *Alamo*); R-33/33S (AA-9 *Amos* A/B); **ARH** R-77-1 (AA-12B *Adder*); R-37M (AA-13 *Axehead*); **PRH** R-27P/EP (AA-10E/F *Alamo*)
ARM Kh-25MP (AS-12 *Kegler*); Kh-31P/PM (AS-17A *Krypton*); Kh-58 (AS-11 *Kilter*)
ASM Kh-25 (AS-10 *Karen*); Kh-29 (AS-14 *Kedge*); Kh-31A/AM (AS-17B *Krypton*); Kh-38; Kh-59/Kh-59M (AS-13 *Kingbolt*/AS-18 *Kazoo*)
AShM Kh-22 (AS-4 *Kitchen*); Kh-32 (entering service); Kh-35U (AS-20 *Kayak*) (in test/entering service)
LACM
Nuclear Kh-55/Kh-55SM (AS-15A/B *Kent*); Kh-102
Conventional Kh-101; Kh-555
BOMBS
Laser-guided KAB-500; KAB-1500L
TV-guided KAB-500KR; KAB-1500KR; KAB-500OD; UPAB 1500
INS/GLONASS-guided KAB-500S

Airborne Troops ε45,000
FORCES BY ROLE
SPECIAL FORCES
1 (AB Recce) SF bde
MANOEUVRE
Air Manoeuvre
2 AB div (1 tk coy; 2 para/air aslt regt; 1 arty regt; 1 AD regt)

2 AB div (2 para/air aslt regt; 1 arty regt; 1 AD regt)
1 indep AB bde
3 air aslt bde

EQUIPMENT BY TYPE
ARMOURED FIGHTING VEHICLES
  MBT 60 T-72B3
  IFV 20 BTR-82AM
  APC • APC (T) 776: 700 BTR-D; 76 BTR-MDM
  AUV GAZ *Tigr*
  ABCV 1,291: 100 BMD-1; 1,000 BMD-2; 10 BMD-3; 30 BMD-4; 151 BMD-4M
ENGINEERING & MAINTENANCE VEHICLES
  ARV BREM-D; BREhM-D
ANTI-TANK/ANTI-INFRASTRUCTURE
  MSL
    SP 100 BTR-RD
    MANPATS 9K111 *Fagot* (AT-4 *Spigot*); 9K113 *Konkurs* (AT-5 *Spandrel*); 9K115 *Metis* (AT-7 *Saxhorn*); 9K115-1 *Metis*-M (AT-13 *Saxhorn 2*); 9K135 *Kornet* (AT-14 *Spriggan*)
  RCL 73mm SPG-9
  GUNS • SP 125mm 36+ 2S25 *Sprut*-SD
ARTILLERY 600+
  TOWED 122mm 150 D-30
  GUN/MOR • SP 120mm 250 2S9 NONA-S (500 in store: **120mm** 500 2S9 NONA-S)
  MOR • TOWED 200+ **82mm** 150 2B14; **120mm** 50+ 2B23 NONA-M1
AIR DEFENCE
  SAM • Point-defence 30+: 30 *Strela*-10MN; 9K310 *Igla*-1 (SA-16 *Gimlet*); 9K38 *Igla* (SA-18 *Grouse*); 9K333 *Verba*; 9K338 *Igla*-S (SA-24 *Grinch*); 9K34 *Strela*-3 (SA-14 *Gremlin*)
  GUNS • SP 23mm 150 BTR-ZD

Special Operations Forces ε1,000
FORCES BY ROLE
SPECIAL FORCES
  2 SF unit

Railway Troops ε29,000
4 regional commands
FORCES BY ROLE
COMBAT SERVICE SUPPORT
10 (railway) tpt bde

Russian Military Districts

Western Military District
HQ at St Petersburg

Army
FORCES BY ROLE
COMMAND
  3 army HQ
SPECIAL FORCES
  2 (Spetsnaz) SF bde
MANOEUVRE
  Reconnaissance
  1 recce bde
  Armoured
  1 tk div

1 tk bde
2 MR div
Mechanised
1 MR div
3 MR bde
SURFACE-TO-SURFACE MISSILE
2 SRBM/GLCM bde with *Iskander*-M/K
1 SRBM bde with *Tochka*-U
COMBAT SUPPORT
2 arty bde
1 (hy) arty bde
1 MRL bde
1 engr bde
1 MP bde
1 NBC bde
2 NBC regt
COMBAT SERVICE SUPPORT
2 log bde
AIR DEFENCE
3 AD bde

Reserves
FORCES BY ROLE
MANOEUVRE
  Mechanised
  2 MR bde

Northern Fleet
EQUIPMENT BY TYPE
SUBMARINES 30
  STRATEGIC 8 **SSBN** (of which 1 in refit and 1 in reserve)
  TACTICAL 22: 4 **SSGN**; 12 **SSN** (of which 4 in refit); 6 **SSK** (of which 1 in refit)
PRINCIPAL SURFACE COMBATANTS 10: 1 **CV** (in refit); 2 **CGHMN** (of which 1 in refit); 1 **CGHM**; 6 **DDGHM**
PATROL AND COASTAL COMBATANTS 10: 2 **FSGM**; 6 **FSM**; 2 **PBM**
MINE WARFARE • MINE COUNTERMEASURES 10: 1 **MHO**; 2 **MSO**; 7 **MSC**
AMPHIBIOUS 6: 4 **LST**; 2 **LCM**

Naval Aviation
FORCES BY ROLE
FIGHTER
  1 regt with Su-33 *Flanker* D; Su-25UTG *Frogfoot*
FIGHTER/GROUND ATTACK
  1 regt with MiG-29KR/KUBR *Fulcrum*
FIGHTER/GROUND ATTACK/ISR
  1 regt with MiG-31BM *Foxhound*; Su-24M/M2/MR *Fencer*
ANTI-SUBMARINE WARFARE
  1 sqn with Il-38 *May*; Il-20RT *Coot* A; Tu-134
  3 sqn with Ka-27/Ka-29 *Helix*
  1 sqn with Tu-142MK/MZ/MR *Bear* F/J
AIR DEFENCE
  3 SAM regt with S-300PS (SA-10B *Grumble*); S-300PM (SA-20 *Gargoyle*); S-400 (SA-21 *Growler*); 96K6 *Pantsir*-S1 (SA-22 *Greyhound*)

EQUIPMENT BY TYPE
AIRCRAFT
 FTR 38: 20 MiG-31BM *Foxhound*; 18 Su-33 *Flanker* D
 FGA 25: 19 MiG-29KR *Fulcrum*; 4 MiG-29KUBR *Fulcrum*; 2 Su-30SM
 ATK 18: 13 Su-24M *Fencer*; 5 Su-25UTG *Frogfoot* (trg role)
 ASW 21: 10 Il-38 *May*; 11 Tu-142MK/MZ/MR *Bear* F/J
 ISR 4 Su-24MR *Fencer**
 ELINT 3: 2 Il-20RT *Coot A*; 1 Il-22 *Coot B*
 TPT 9: 8 An-26 *Curl*; 1 Tu-134
HELICOPTERS
 ASW Ka-27 *Helix* A
 TPT • Medium Ka-29 *Helix* B; Mi-8 *Hip*
AIR DEFENCE • SAM
 Long-range S-300PS (SA-10B *Grumble*); S-300PM (SA-20 *Gargoyle*); S-400 (SA-21 *Growler*)
 Short-range 96K6 *Pantsir*-S1 (SA-22 *Greyhound*)

Naval Infantry
FORCES BY ROLE
COMMAND
 1 corps HQ
MANOEUVRE
 Mechanised
 2 MR bde
 1 naval inf bde

Coastal Artillery and Missile Troops
FORCES BY ROLE
COASTAL DEFENCE
 1 AShM bde

Baltic Fleet
EQUIPMENT BY TYPE
 SUBMARINES • TACTICAL • SSK 2
 PRINCIPAL SURFACE COMBATANTS 8: 2 DDGHM; 6 FFGHM
 PATROL AND COASTAL COMBATANTS 25: 6 FSGM; 6 FSM; 7 PCFG; 5 PBF; 1 PBM
 MINE WARFARE • MINE COUNTERMEASURES 12: 1 MCC; 5 MSC; 6 MHI
 AMPHIBIOUS 13: 4 LST; 6 LCU; 1 LCM; 2 LCAC

Naval Aviation
FORCES BY ROLE
FIGHTER
 1 sqn with Su-27 *Flanker*
ANTI-SURFACE WARFARE/ISR
 1 sqn with Su-24M/MR *Fencer*; Su-30SM
ANTI-SUBMARINE WARFARE
 1 sqn with Ka-27/Ka-29 *Helix*
TRANSPORT
 1 sqn with An-26 *Curl*; Tu-134 *Crusty*
ATTACK/TRANSPORT HELICOPTER
 1 sqn with Mi-24P *Hind*; Mi-8 *Hip*
TRANSPORT HELICOPTER
 1 sqn with Mi-8 *Hip*

EQUIPMENT BY TYPE
AIRCRAFT
 FTR 18 Su-27/Su-27UB *Flanker*
 FGA 7 Su-30SM
 ATK 10 Su-24M *Fencer*
 ISR 4 Su-24MR *Fencer**
 TPT 8: 6 An-26 *Curl*; 2 Tu-134 *Crusty*
HELICOPTERS
 ATK Mi-24P *Hind*
 ASW Ka-27 *Helix*
 TPT • Medium Ka-29 *Helix*; Mi-8 *Hip*

Naval Infantry
FORCES BY ROLE
COMMAND
 1 corps HQ
MANOEUVRE
 Mechanised
 1 MR bde
 1 MR regt
 1 naval inf bde
SURFACE-TO-SURFACE MISSILE
 1 SRBM bde with *Iskander*-M/K
COMBAT SUPPORT
 1 arty bde
AIR DEFENCE
 3 SAM regt

Coastal Artillery and Missile Troops
FORCES BY ROLE
COASTAL DEFENCE
 1 AShM regt

Military Air Force

6th Air Force & Air Defence Army
FORCES BY ROLE
FIGHTER
 1 regt with MiG-29SMT *Fulcrum*; Su-30SM
 1 regt with MiG-31B/BS/BM *Foxhound*; Su-27 *Flanker*
 1 regt with Su-27/Su-27SM *Flanker*; Su-35S *Flanker*
GROUND ATTACK
 1 regt with Su-34 *Fullback*
ISR
 1 sqn with Su-24MR *Fencer*
 1 flt with A-30 *Clank*
ELECTRONIC WARFARE
 1 sqn with Mi-8PPA *Hip*
TRANSPORT
 1 regt with An-12 *Cub*; An-26 *Curl*; Tu-134 *Crusty*
ATTACK HELICOPTER
 1 bde with Ka-52A *Hokum B*; Mi-28N *Havoc B*; Mi-35 *Hind*; Mi-26 *Halo*; Mi-8MTV-5 *Hip*
 1 regt with with Mi-24P/Mi-35 *Hind*; Mi-28N *Havoc B*; Mi-8 *Hip*
 1 sqn with Mi-24P *Hind*
TRANSPORT HELICOPTER
 1 sqn with Mi-8 *Hip*
AIR DEFENCE
 1 SAM regt with 9K37M *Buk*-M1-2 (SA-11 *Gadfly*); S-300V (SA-12 *Gladiator/Giant*)

5 SAM regt with S-300PM (SA-20 *Gargoyle*)
1 SAM regt with S-400 (SA-21 *Growler*); 96K6
Pantsir-S1 (SA-22 *Greyhound*)

EQUIPMENT BY TYPE
AIRCRAFT
FTR 61: 31 MiG-31B/BS/BM *Foxhound*; 30 Su-27/Su-27UB *Flanker*
FGA 96: 28 MiG-29SMT *Fulcrum*; 6 MiG-29UBT *Fulcrum*; 12 Su-27SM *Flanker*; 10 Su-30SM; 24 Su-34 *Fullback*; 16 Su-35S *Flanker*
ISR 19: 4 An-30 *Clank*; 15 Su-24MR *Fencer**
TPT 12 An-12/An-26/Tu-134
HELICOPTERS
ATK 64+: 12 Ka-52A *Hokum* B; 16 Mi-24P *Hind*; 24 Mi-28N *Havoc* B; 12+ Mi-35 *Hind*
EW 10 Mi-8PPA *Hip*
TPT • Medium 50 Mi-8 *Hip*
AIR DEFENCE • SAM
Long-range S-300PM (SA-20 *Gargoyle*); S-300V (SA-12 *Gladiator/Giant*); S-400 (SA-21 *Growler*)
Medium-range 9K37M *Buk*-M1-2 (SA-11 *Gadfly*)
Short-range 96K6 *Pantsir*-S1 (SA-22 *Greyhound*)

Airborne Troops
FORCES BY ROLE
SPECIAL FORCES
1 (AB Recce) SF bde
MANOEUVRE
Air Manoeuvre
3 AB div

Central Military District
HQ at Yekaterinburg

Army
FORCES BY ROLE
COMMAND
2 army HQ
SPECIAL FORCES
2 (Spetsnaz) SF bde
MANOEUVRE
Armoured
1 tk div
3 MR bde
Mechanised
2 MR bde
2 (lt/mtn) MR bde
SURFACE-TO-SURFACE MISSILE
2 SRBM/GLCM bde with *Iskander*-M/K
COMBAT SUPPORT
2 arty bde
1 MRL bde
1 engr bde
2 NBC bde
2 NBC regt
COMBAT SERVICE SUPPORT
2 log bde
AIR DEFENCE
3 AD bde

Reserves
FORCES BY ROLE
MANOEUVRE
Mechanised
3 MR bde

Military Air Force

14th Air Force & Air Defence Army
FORCES BY ROLE
FIGHTER
1 regt with MiG-31BM *Foxhound*
1 regt with MiG-31B/BS/BM *Foxhound*
GROUND ATTACK
2 sqn with Su-24M *Fencer*
1 sqn with Su-25SM *Frogfoot* (Kyrgyzstan)
ISR
1 sqn with Su-24MR *Fencer* E
TRANSPORT
1 regt with An-12 *Cub*; An-26 *Curl*; Tu-134 *Crusty*; Tu-154; Mi-8 *Hip*
ATTACK/TRANSPORT HELICOPTER
1 bde with Mi-24P *Hind*; Mi-8 *Hip*
1 sqn with Mi-24P *Hind*; Mi-8 *Hip* (Tajikistan)
AIR DEFENCE
3 regt with S-300PS (SA-10B *Grumble*)
1 bde with S-300PS (SA-10B *Grumble*)
1 regt with S-300PM (SA-20 *Gargoyle*)
2 regt with S-400 (SA-21 *Growler*); 96K6 Pantsir-S1 (SA-22 *Greyhound*)
EQUIPMENT BY TYPE
AIRCRAFT
FTR 40 MiG-31B/BS/BM *Foxhound*
ATK 39: 26 Su-24M *Fencer*; 13 Su-25SM *Frogfoot*
ISR 9 Su-24MR *Fencer* E
TPT 36 An-12 *Cub*/An-26 *Curl*/Tu-134 *Crusty*/Tu-154 *Careless*
HELICOPTERS
ATK 24 Mi-24 *Hind*
TPT 46: 6 Mi-26 *Halo*; 40 Mi-8 *Hip*
AIR DEFENCE • SAM
Long-range S-300PS (SA-10B *Grumble*); S-300PM (SA-20 *Gargoyle*); S-400 (SA-21 *Growler*)
Short-range 96K6 *Pantsir*-S1 (SA-22 *Greyhound*)

Airborne Troops
FORCES BY ROLE
MANOEUVRE
Air Manoeuvre
1 AB bde

Southern Military District
HQ located at Rostov-on-Don

Army
FORCES BY ROLE
COMMAND
3 army HQ
SPECIAL FORCES
3 (Spetsnaz) SF bde
1 (Spetsnaz) SF regt

MANOEUVRE
Reconnaissance
1 recce bde
Armoured
1 MR div
3 MR bde
1 MR bde (Armenia)
1 MR bde (South Ossetia)
Mechanised
1 MR div
1 MR bde
1 MR bde (Abkhazia)
1 (lt/mtn) MR bde
SURFACE-TO-SURFACE MISSILE
2 SRBM/GLCM bde with *Iskander*-M/K
COMBAT SUPPORT
2 arty bde
1 MRL bde
1 engr bde
1 NBC bde
2 NBC regt
COMBAT SERVICE SUPPORT
2 log bde
AIR DEFENCE
4 AD bde

Black Sea Fleet

The Black Sea Fleet is primarily based in Crimea, at Sevastopol, Karantinnaya Bay and Streletskaya Bay
EQUIPMENT BY TYPE
SUBMARINES • TACTICAL 7 SSK
PRINCIPAL SURFACE COMBATANTS 6: 1 CGHM; 1 DDGM; 2 FFGHM; 2 FFGM
PATROL AND COASTAL COMBATANTS 29: 4 FSGM; 6 FSM; 5 PCFG; 6 PBM; 8 PBF
MINE WARFARE • MINE COUNTERMEASURES 10: 1 MHO; 6 MSO; 2 MSC; 1 MHI
AMPHIBIOUS 10: 7 LST; 1 LCM; 2 LCU

Naval Aviation
FORCES BY ROLE
FIGHTER
ANTI-SURFACE WARFARE/ISR
1 regt with Su-24M/MR *Fencer*; Su-30SM
ANTI-SUBMARINE WARFARE
1 sqn with Ka-27 *Helix*
1 sqn with Mi-14 *Haze*
MARITIME PATROL/TRANSPORT
1 sqn with An-26 *Curl*; Be-12PS *Mail**; Mi-8
EQUIPMENT BY TYPE
AIRCRAFT
FGA 12 Su-30SM
ATK 13 Su-24M *Fencer*
ISR 4 Su-24MR *Fencer* E
MP 3 Be-12PS *Mail**
TPT 6 An-26
HELICOPTERS
ASW Ka-27 *Helix*
TPT • **Medium** Mi-8 *Hip* (MP/EW/Tpt)

Naval Infantry
FORCES BY ROLE
COMMAND
1 corps HQ
MANOEUVRE
Mechanised
2 naval inf bde
COMBAT SUPPORT
1 arty bde
AIR DEFENCE
1 SAM regt

Coastal Artillery and Missile Troops
FORCES BY ROLE
COASTAL DEFENCE
2 AShM bde

Caspian Sea Flotilla
EQUIPMENT BY TYPE
PRINCIPAL SURFACE COMBATANTS 2 FFGM
PATROL AND COASTAL COMBATANTS 12: 3 FSGM; 3 FSM; 1 PCFG; 1 PBM; 4 PBR
MINE WARFARE • MINE COUNTERMEASURES 3: 2 MSC; 1 MHI
AMPHIBIOUS 9: 2 LCM; 7 LCU

Military Air Force

4th Air Force & Air Defence Army
FORCES BY ROLE
FIGHTER
1 regt with Su-30SM
1 sqn with MiG-29 *Fulcrum* (Armenia)
FIGHTER/GROUND ATTACK
1 regt with Su-27 *Flanker*
1 regt with Su-27SM/SM3 *Flanker*; Su-30M2
GROUND ATTACK
1 regt with Su-24M *Fencer*; Su-25SM *Frogfoot*
2 regt with Su-25SM/SM3 *Frogfoot*
1 regt with Su-34 *Fullback*
ISR
1 regt with Su-24MR *Fencer* E
TRANSPORT
1 regt with An-12 *Cub*/Mi-8 *Hip*
ATTACK/TRANSPORT HELICOPTER
1 bde with Mi-28N *Havoc* B; Mi-35 *Hind*; Mi-8 *Hip*; Mi-26 *Halo*
1 regt with Mi-28N *Havoc* B; Mi-35 *Hind*; Mi-8 *Hip*
2 regt with Ka-52A *Hokum* B; Mi-28N *Havoc* B; Mi-35 *Hind*; Mi-8AMTSh *Hip*
1 sqn with Mi-24P *Hind*; Mi-8 *Hip* (Armenia)
AIR DEFENCE
1 regt with 9K317 *Buk*-M2 (SA-17 *Grizzly*)
2 regt with S-300PM (SA-20 *Gargoyle*)
2 regt with S-400 (SA-21 *Growler*); 96K6 *Pantsir*-S1 (SA-22 *Greyhound*)
EQUIPMENT BY TYPE
AIRCRAFT
FTR 46: 12 MiG-29 *Fulcrum*; 34 Su-27 *Flanker*
FGA 86: 12 Su-27SM *Flanker*; 12 Su-27SM3 *Flanker*; 4 Su-30M2; 22 Su-30SM; 36 Su-34 *Fullback*

ATK 97: 12 Su-24M *Fencer*; 85 Su-25SM/SM3 *Frogfoot*
ISR 24 Su-24MR *Fencer**
TPT 12 An-12 *Cub*
HELICOPTERS
ATK 117: 25 Ka-52A *Hokum* B; 44 Mi-28N *Havoc* B; 8 Mi-24P *Hind*; 40 Mi-35 *Hind*
TPT 72: **Heavy** 10 Mi-26 *Halo*; **Medium** 62 Mi-8 *Hip*
AIR DEFENCE • SAM
Long-range S-300PM (SA-20 *Gargoyle*); S-400 (SA-21 *Growler*)
Medium-range 9K317 *Buk*-M2 (SA-17 *Grizzly*)
Short-range 96K6 *Pantsir*-S1 (SA-22 *Greyhound*)

Airborne Troops
FORCES BY ROLE
MANOEUVRE
Air Manoeuvre
1 AB div
1 air aslt bde

Eastern Military District
HQ located at Khabarovsk

Army
FORCES BY ROLE
COMMAND
4 army HQ
SPECIAL FORCES
1 (Spetsnaz) SF bde
MANOEUVRE
Armoured
1 tk bde
6 MR bde
Mechanised
4 MR bde
1 MGA div
SURFACE-TO-SURFACE MISSILE
4 SRBM/GLCM bde with *Iskander*-M/K
COMBAT SUPPORT
3 arty bde
1 MRL bde
1 engr bde
1 NBC bde
4 NBC regt
COMBAT SERVICE SUPPORT
4 log bde
AIR DEFENCE
4 AD bde

Reserves
FORCES BY ROLE
MANOEUVRE
Mechanised
8 MR bde

Pacific Fleet
EQUIPMENT BY TYPE
SUBMARINES 23
STRATEGIC 5 SSBN
TACTICAL 18: 5 SSGN (of which 2 in refit); 5 SSN (of which 4 in refit); 8 SSK
PRINCIPAL SURFACE COMBATANTS 8: 1 CGHM; 6 DDGHM (of which 2 in refit); 1 FFGHM
PATROL AND COASTAL COMBATANTS 24: 4 FSGM; 8 FSM; 9 PCFG; 3 PBM
MINE WARFARE 8: 2 MSO; 6 MSC
AMPHIBIOUS 9: 4 LST; 3 LCM; 2 LCU

Naval Aviation
FORCES BY ROLE
FIGHTER
1 sqn with MiG-31B/BS *Foxhound*
ANTI-SUBMARINE WARFARE
3 sqn with Ka-27/Ka-29 *Helix*
2 sqn with Il-38 *May**; Il-18D; Il-22 *Coot* B
1 sqn with Tu-142MK/MZ/MR *Bear* F/J*
TRANSPORT
2 sqn with An-12BK *Cub*; An-26 *Curl*; Tu-134
EQUIPMENT BY TYPE
AIRCRAFT
FTR 12 MiG-31B/BS *Foxhound*
ASW 23: 11 Tu-142MK/MZ/MR *Bear* F/J; 12 Il-38 *May*
EW • ELINT 1 Il-22 *Coot* B
TPT 6: 2 An-12BK *Cub*; 3 An-26 *Curl*; 1 Tu-134
HELICOPTERS
ASW Ka-27 *Helix*
TPT • **Medium** Ka-29 *Helix*; Mi-8 *Hip*

Naval Infantry
FORCES BY ROLE
MANOEUVRE
Mechanised
2 naval inf bde
AIR DEFENCE
1 SAM regt

Coastal Artillery and Missile Troops
FORCES BY ROLE
COASTAL DEFENCE
2 AShM bde

Military Air Force

11th Air Force & Air Defence Army
FORCES BY ROLE
FIGHTER/GROUND ATTACK
1 regt with MiG-31BM *Foxhound*; Su-27SM *Flanker*; Su-30M2; Su-30SM; Su-35S *Flanker*
1 regt with Su-35S *Flanker*; Su-30SM
1 regt with Su-25 *Frogfoot*; Su-30SM
GROUND ATTACK
1 regt with Su-24M/M2 *Fencer*; Su-34 *Fullback*
1 regt with Su-25SM *Frogfoot*
ISR
1 regt with Su-24MR *Fencer* E
TRANSPORT
2 sqn with An-12 *Cub*/An-26 *Curl*/Tu-134 *Crusty*/Tu-154 *Careless*

ATTACK/TRANSPORT HELICOPTER
1 bde with Ka-52A *Hokum* B; Mi-8 *Hip*; Mi-26 *Halo*
1 regt with Ka-52A *Hokum* B; Mi-8 *Hip*; Mi-26 *Halo*
1 regt with Mi-24P *Hind*; Mi-8 *Hip*

AIR DEFENCE
2 regt with 9K37M *Buk*-M1-2 (SA-11 *Gadfly*); 9K317 Buk-M2 (SA-17 *Grizzly*); S-300V (SA-12 *Gladiator/Giant*)
2 regt with S-300PS (SA-10B *Grumble*)
2 regt with S-400 (SA-21 *Growler*); 96K6 *Pantsir*-S1 (SA-22 *Greyhound*)

EQUIPMENT BY TYPE
AIRCRAFT
FTR 20 MiG-31B/BS/BM *Foxhound*
FGA 112: 23 Su-27SM *Flanker*; 2 Su-30M2; 29 Su-30SM; 24 Su-34 *Fullback*; 34 Su-35S *Flanker*
ATK 102: 20 Su-24M *Fencer*; 10 Su-24M2 *Fencer*; 72 Su-25/Su-25SM *Frogfoot*
ISR 28 Su-24MR *Fencer* E
TPT 24: 22 An-12 *Cub*/An-26 *Curl*; 1 Tu-134 *Crusty*; 1 Tu-154 *Careless*

HELICOPTERS
ATK 36: 24 Ka-52A *Hokum* B; 12 Mi-24P *Hind*
TPT 60: **Heavy** 4 Mi-26 *Halo*; **Medium** 56 Mi-8 *Hip*

AIR DEFENCE • SAM
Long-range S-300PS (SA-10B *Grumble*); S-300V (SA-12 *Gladiator/Giant*); S-400 (SA-21 *Growler*)
Medium-range 9K317 *Buk*-M1-2 (SA-11 *Gadfly*); 9K317 *Buk*-M2 (SA-17 *Grizzly*)
Short-range 96K6 *Pantsir*-S1 (SA-22 *Greyhound*)

Airborne Troops
FORCES BY ROLE
MANOEUVRE
Air Manoeuvre
2 air aslt bde

Paramilitary 554,000

Border Guard Service ε160,000
Subordinate to Federal Security Service
FORCES BY ROLE
10 regional directorates
MANOEUVRE
Other
7 frontier gp

EQUIPMENT BY TYPE
ARMOURED FIGHTING VEHICLES
IFV/APC (W) 1,000 BMP/BTR
ARTILLERY 90:
SP 122mm 2S1 *Gvozdika*
GUN/MOR • SP 120mm 2S9 NONA-S
MOR 120mm 2S12 *Sani*

PRINCIPAL SURFACE COMBATANTS
FRIGATES • FFHM 3 *Nerey* (*Krivak* III) with 1 twin lnchr with *Osa*-M (SA-N-4 *Gecko*) SAM, 2 quad 533mm TT lnchr, 2 RBU 6000 *Smerch* 2 A/S mor, 1 100mm gun (capacity 1 Ka-27 *Helix* A ASW hel)

PATROL AND COASTAL COMBATANTS 187
PSO 5: 4 *Komandor*; 1 *Okean* (Project 22100) with 1 76mm gun, 1 hel landing platform
PCO 22: 8 *Alpinist* (Project 503); 1 *Sprut*; 11 *Okhotnik* (Project 22460) with 1 AK630 CIWS, 1 hel landing platform; 2 *Purga* with 1 hel landing platform
PCC 37: 5 *Molnya* II (*Pauk* II); 3 *Svetlyak* (Project 10410) with 2 AK306 CIWS; 20 *Svetlyak* (Project 10410) with 1 AK630M CIWS, 1 76mm gun; 8 *Svetlyak* (Project 10410) with 2 AK630M CIWS; 1 *Yakhont* with 2 AK306 CIWS
PCR 1 *Slepen* (*Yaz*) with 1 AK630 CIWS, 2 100mm guns
PBF 80: 50 *Mangust*; 3 *Mirazh* (Project 14310); 4 *Mustang*-2 (Project 18623); 21 *Sobol*; 2 *Sokzhoi* with 1 AK306 CIWS
PBR 30: 2 *Ogonek* with 1 AK306 CIWS; 2 *Ogonek* with 2 AK306 CIWS; 8 *Piyavka* with 1 AK630 CIWS; 18 *Moskit* (*Vosh*) with 1 AK630 CIWS, 1 100mm gun
PB 12: 2 *Morzh* (Project 1496M); 10 *Lamantin* (Project 1496M1)

LOGISTICS AND SUPPORT 37
AE 1 *Muna*
AGB 3 *Ivan Susanin* (primarily used as patrol ships) with 2AK630 CIWS, 1 76mm gun, 1 hel landing platform
AK 8 *Pevek* with 1 AK306 CIWS
AKSL 5 *Kanin*
AO 3: 1 *Ishim* (Project 15010); 2 *Envoron*
ATF 17: 16 *Sorum* (primarily used as patrol ships) with 2 AK230M CIWS; 1 *Sorum* (primarily used as patrol ship) with 2 AK306 CIWS

AIRCRAFT • TPT ε86: 70 An-24 *Coke*/An-26 *Curl*/An-72 *Coaler*/Il-76 *Candid*/Tu-134 *Crusty*/Yak-40 *Codling*; 16 SM-92

HELICOPTERS: ε200 Ka-28 (Ka-27) *Helix* ASW/Mi-24 *Hind* Atk/Mi-26 *Halo* Spt/Mi-8 *Hip* Spt

Federal Guard Service ε40,000–50,000
Org include elm of ground forces (mech inf bde and AB regt)
FORCES BY ROLE
MANOEUVRE
Mechanised
1 mech inf regt
Air Manoeuvre
1 AB regt
Other
1 (Presidential) gd regt

Federal Security Service Special Purpose Centre ε4,000
FORCES BY ROLE
SPECIAL FORCES
2 SF unit (Alfa and Vympel units)

National Guard ε340,000
FORCES BY ROLE
MANOEUVRE
Other
10 paramilitary div
(2–5 paramilitary regt)

17 paramilitary bde (3 mech bn, 1 mor bn)
36 indep paramilitary rgt
90 paramilitary bn (incl special motorised units)
Aviation
8 sqn
COMBAT SUPPORT
1 arty regt
EQUIPMENT BY TYPE
ARMOURED FIGHTING VEHICLES
RECCE some BRDM-2A
IFV/APC (W) 1,650 BMP-2/BTR-70M/BTR-80/BTR-82A/BTR-82AM
ARTILLERY 35
TOWED 122mm 20 D-30
MOR 120mm 15 M-1938 (PM-38)
AIRCRAFT • TPT 29: **Heavy** 9 Il-76 *Candid*; **Medium** 2 An-12 *Cub*; **Light** 12 An-26 *Curl*; 6 An-72 *Coaler*
HELICOPTERS • TPT 70: **Heavy** 10 Mi-26 *Halo*; **Medium** 60+: 60 Mi-8 *Hip*; some Mi-8AMTSh *Hip*

Cyber

The first official doctrinal statement on the role of the Russian military in cyberspace, the 'Conceptual Views on the Activity of the Russian Federation Armed Forces in Information Space', was released at the end of 2011, and described cyber-force tasks with little correlation to those of equivalent commands in the West. In particular, the document contains no mention of the possibility of offensive cyber activity. It is also entirely defensive in tone, and focuses on force protection and prevention of information war, including allowing for a military role in negotiating international treaties governing information security. In January 2012, then-CGS Makarov gave a different picture of the three main tasks for any new command: 'disrupting adversary information systems, including by introducing harmful software; defending our own communications and command systems'; and 'working on domestic and foreign public opinion using the media, Internet and more'. The third task is a reminder that, unlike some other nations with advanced cyber capabilities, Russia considers cyber warfare as an integral component of information warfare. Operations in Crimea from early 2014, in the wider information space concerning the conflict in Ukraine, and allegations of influence activity in Western countries' elections demonstrate that Russian thinking and capacity has matured in these areas. In February 2017, Defence Minister Shoigu provided the first official acknowledgement that Russia had formed a new information-warfare branch of the armed forces.

DEPLOYMENT

ARMENIA
3,300: 1 mil base with (1 MR bde; 74 T-72; 80 BMP-1; 80 BMP-2; 12 2S1; 12 BM-21); 1 sqn with 18 MiG-29 *Fulcrum*; 1 sqn with 8 Mi-24P *Hind*; 4 Mi-8MT *Hip*; 2 AD bty with S-300V (SA-12 *Gladiator/Giant*); 1 AD bty with 2K12 *Kub* (SA-6 *Gainful*)

BELARUS
1 radar station at Baranovichi (*Volga* system; leased); 1 naval comms site

BOSNIA-HERZEGOVINA
OSCE • Bosnia and Herzegovina 2

DEMOCRATIC REPUBLIC OF THE CONGO
UN • MONUSCO 1; 24 obs

GEORGIA
7,000; Abkhazia 1 mil base with (1 MR bde; 40 T-90A; 120 BTR-82A; 18 2S3; 12 2S12; 18 BM-21; some S-300 SAM; some atk hel); South Ossetia 1 mil base with (1 MR bde; 40 T-72; 120 BMP-2; 36 2S3; 12 2S12)

KAZAKHSTAN
1 radar station at Balkash (*Dnepr* system; leased)

KYRGYZSTAN
ε500; 13 Su-25SM *Frogfoot*; 2 Mi-8 *Hip* spt hel

LIBERIA
UN • UNMIL 1 obs

MEDITERRANEAN SEA
2 SSK; 1 FFGHM; 1 FFGM; 1 AGI

MIDDLE EAST
UN • UNTSO 3 obs

MOLDOVA/TRANSDNIESTR
ε1,500 (including 441 peacekeepers); 2 MR bn; 100 MBT/AIFV/APC; 7 Mi-24 *Hind*; some Mi-8 *Hip*

SERBIA
OSCE • Kosovo 1

SOUTH SUDAN
UN • UNMISS 4; 2 obs

SUDAN
UN • UNISFA 1 obs

SYRIA
6,000: 1 l inf BG; 4 MP bn; 1 engr unit; 7 T-90; ε20 BTR-82A; *Typhoon*-K; *Tigr*; 12 2A65; 4 9A52 *Smerch*; TOS-1A; 9K720 *Iskander*-M; 4 MiG-29SMT *Fulcrum*; 8 Su-24M *Fencer*; 6 Su-25SM; 4 Su-30SM; 10 Su-34; 5 Su-35S; 1 Il-20M; 4 Mi-28N *Havoc*; 4 Ka-52 *Hokum* B; 12 Mi-24P/Mi-35M *Hind*; 4 Mi-8AMTSh *Hip*; 3 *Pantsir*-S1/S2; 1 AShM bty with 3K55 *Bastion*; 1 SAM bty with S-400; 1 SAM bty with S-300V4; air base at Latakia; naval facility at Tartus

TAJIKISTAN
5,000; 1 (201st) mil base with (40 T-72B1; 60 BMP-2; 80 BTR-82A; 40 MT-LB; 18 2S1; 36 2S3; 6 2S12; 12 9P140 *Uragan*); 4 Mi-24P *Hind*; 4 Mi-8MTV *Hip*

UKRAINE
Crimea: 28,000; 1 recce bde, 2 naval inf bde; 1 arty bde; 1 NBC regt; 40 T-72B3 MBT; 80 BMP-2 AIFV; 200 BTR-82A; 20 BTR-80 APC: 150 MT-LB; 18 2S1 arty; 18 2S19 arty; 12 BM-21 MRL; 1 AShM bde with 3K60 *Bal*; 3K55 *Bastion*; 1 FGA regt with Su-24M/MR; Su-30SM; 1 FGA regt with Su-27SM/SM3; Su-30M2; 1 FGA regt with Su-24M/Su-25SM; 1 atk/tpt hel regt; 1 ASW hel regt; 1 AD regt with S-300PM;

1 AD regt with S-400; 1 Fleet HQ located at Sevastopol; 2 radar stations located at Sevastopol (*Dnepr* system) and Mukachevo (*Dnepr* system)
Donetsk/Luhansk: 3,000 (reported)
OSCE • Ukraine 36

WESTERN SAHARA
UN • MINURSO 15 obs

Tajikistan TJK

Tajikistani Somoni Tr		2016	2017	2018
GDP	Tr	54.5bn	62.6bn	
	US$	6.92bn	7.23bn	
per capita	US$	800	819	
Growth	%	6.9	4.5	
Inflation	%	5.9	8.9	
Def bdgt	Tr	1.52bn	1.66bn	
	US$	193m	192m	
US$1=Tr		7.87	8.66	

Population 8,468,555

Ethnic groups: Tajik 84.2%; Uzbek 12.2%; Kyrgyz 0.8%; Russian 0.5%; other or unspecified 2.3%

Age	0–14	15–19	20–24	25–29	30–64	65 plus
Male	16.4%	4.8%	4.6%	4.9%	17.5%	1.4%
Female	15.8%	4.7%	4.5%	4.8%	18.4%	1.9%

Capabilities

The Tajik armed forces have little capacity to deploy other than token forces and almost all equipment is of Soviet-era origin. Regional security and counter-terrorism is a concern, due to the possibility that violence could spill over from Afghanistan, especially with the recent expansion of ISIS there. Border deployments have been stepped up in response. Tajikistan is a member of the CSTO and a large Russian military presence remains at the 201st military base. A 2014 deal on military modernisation with Russia was followed in late 2016 by the signing of a 2017 Military Cooperation Plan. Russia is training Tajik military personnel, and Moscow indicated that Tajikistan was to receive military equipment, including aircraft. In May 2017, the US embassy in Tajikistan donated vehicles, radios and thermal cameras to the Tajik Border Guard. The same month, Tajikistan hosted the *Dushanbe Anti-Terror 2017* exercise, and in November the CSTO KSOR counter-terror exercise. Tajikistan has also been building counter-terrorism capability through US ties by hosting a counter-terrorism exercise supported by US CENTCOM.

ACTIVE 8,800 (Army 7,300 Air Force/Air Defence 1,500) **Paramilitary 7,500**
Conscript liability 24 months

ORGANISATIONS BY SERVICE

Army 7,300

FORCES BY ROLE
MANOEUVRE
  Mechanised
  3 MR bde
  Air Manoeuvre
  1 air aslt bde
COMBAT SUPPORT
  1 arty bde
AIR DEFENCE
  1 SAM regt
EQUIPMENT BY TYPE
ARMOURED FIGHTING VEHICLES
  MBT 37: 30 T-72; 7 T-62
  IFV 23: 8 BMP-1; 15 BMP-2
  APC • APC (W) 23 BTR-60/BTR-70/BTR-80
ARTILLERY 23
  TOWED 122mm 10 D-30
  MRL 122mm 3 BM-21 *Grad*
  MOR 120mm 10
AIR DEFENCE • SAM
  Medium-range S-75 *Dvina* (SA-2 *Guideline*); S-125 *Pechora*-2M (SA-26)
  Point-defence 9K32 *Strela*-2 (SA-7 *Grail*)‡

Air Force/Air Defence 1,500

FORCES BY ROLE
TRANSPORT
  1 sqn with Tu-134A *Crusty*
ATTACK/TRANSPORT HELICOPTER
  1 sqn with Mi-24 *Hind*; Mi-8 *Hip*; Mi-17TM *Hip* H
EQUIPMENT BY TYPE
AIRCRAFT
  TPT • Light 1 Tu-134A *Crusty*
  TRG 4+: 4 L-39 *Albatros*; some Yak-52
HELICOPTERS
  ATK 4 Mi-24 *Hind*
  TPT • Medium 11 Mi-8 *Hip*/Mi-17TM *Hip* H

Paramilitary 7,500

Internal Troops 3,800

National Guard 1,200

Emergencies Ministry 2,500

Border Guards

DEPLOYMENT

SERBIA
OSCE • Kosovo 1

UKRAINE
OSCE • Ukraine 14

FOREIGN FORCES

Russia 5,000; 1 (201st) mil base with (40 T-72B1; 60 BMP-2; 80 BTR-82A; 40 MT-LB; 18 2S1; 36 2S3; 6 2S12; 12 9P140 *Uragan*); 4 Mi-24P *Hind*; 4 Mi-8MTV *Hip*

Turkmenistan TKM

Turkmen New Manat TMM		2016	2017	2018
GDP	TMM	127bn	146bn	
	US$	36.2bn	41.7bn	
per capita	US$	6,622	7,522	
Growth	%	6.2	6.5	
Inflation	%	3.6	6.0	
Def exp	TMM	n.k.	n.k.	
	US$	n.k.	n.k.	
USD1=TMM		3.50	3.50	

Population   5,351,277

Ethnic groups: Turkmen 77%; Uzbek 9%; Russian 7%; Kazak 2%

Age	0–14	15–19	20–24	25–29	30–64	65 plus
Male	13.1%	4.3%	4.9%	4.9%	20.2%	2.0%
Female	12.7%	4.2%	4.9%	4.9%	20.9%	2.6%

Capabilities

Turkmenistan declared its neutrality in 1995 and confirmed this commitment in its 2016 military doctrine. This document aimed to increase defensive capability in order to safeguard national interests and territorial integrity. The security situation in Afghanistan, and any possibility that this might affect Turkmenistan, is of interest to the authorities. Turkmenistan is not a member of the CSTO. The largely conscript-based armed forces remain reliant on Soviet-era equipment and doctrine. While the ground forces are shifting from a Soviet-era divisional structure to a brigade system, progress is slow. The air force has a very modest capability; most of the aircraft are of Soviet-era origin, have been stored or scrapped, and no significant new procurement has occurred. The 2016 military doctrine was intended to partly redress these issues. The government has stated a requirement for equipment investment and improvements to conditions of service. The Border Guard service will be strengthened with new equipment and facilities. Plans to strengthen naval forces resulted in some procurements, leading to a moderate improvement in the naval presence in the Caspian Sea.

ACTIVE 36,500 (Army 33,000 Navy 500 Air 3,000)
Paramilitary 5,000
Conscript liability 24 months

ORGANISATIONS BY SERVICE

Army 33,000
5 Mil Districts
FORCES BY ROLE
SPECIAL FORCES
  1 spec ops regt
MANOEUVRE
  Armoured
  1 tk bde
  Mechanised
  1 (3rd) MR div (1 tk regt; 3 MR regt, 1 arty regt)
  1 (22nd) MR div (1 tk regt; 1 MR regt, 1 arty regt)
  4 MR bde
  1 naval inf bde
  Other
  1 MR trg div
SURFACE-TO-SURFACE MISSILE
  1 SRBM bde with SS-1 *Scud*
COMBAT SUPPORT
  1 arty bde
  1 (mixed) arty/AT regt
  1 MRL bde
  1 AT regt
  1 engr regt
AIR DEFENCE
  2 SAM bde

EQUIPMENT BY TYPE†
ARMOURED FIGHTING VEHICLES
  MBT 654: 4 T-90S; 650 T-72/T-72UMG
  RECCE 260+: 200 BRDM-2; 60 BRM-1; Nimr *Ajban*
  IFV 1,038: 600 BMP-1/BMP-1M; 430 BMP-2; 4 BMP-3; 4 BTR-80A
  APC 898+
    APC (W) 874+: 120 BTR-60 (all variants); 300 BTR-70; 450 BTR-80; 4+ *Cobra*
    PPV 28+ *Kirpi*
  AUV 8 Nimr *Ajban* 440A
  ABCV 8 BMD-1
ANTI-TANK/ANTI-INFRASTRUCTURE
  MSL
    SP 58+: 8 9P122 *Malyutka*-M (AT-3 *Sagger* on BRDM-2); 8 9P133 *Malyutka*-P (AT-3 *Sagger* on BRDM-2); 2 9P148 *Konkurs* (AT-5 *Spandrel* on BRDM-2); 36 9P149 *Shturm* (AT-6 *Spiral* on MT-LB); 4+ *Baryer* (on *Karakal*)
    MANPATS 9K11 *Malyutka* (AT-3 *Sagger*); 9K111 *Fagot* (AT-4 *Spigot*); 9K111-1 *Konkurs* (AT-5 *Spandrel*); 9K115 *Metis* (AT-7 *Saxhorn*)
  GUNS 100mm 60 MT-12/T-12
ARTILLERY 765
  SP 122mm 40 2S1
  TOWED 457: **122mm** 350 D-30; **130mm** 6 M-46; **152mm** 101: 17 D-1; 72 D-20; 6 2A36 *Giatsint*-B; 6 2A65 *Msta*-B
  GUN/MOR 120mm 17 2S9 NONA-S
  MRL 154+: **122mm** 88: 18 9P138; 70 BM-21 *Grad*; RM-70; **220mm** 60 9P140 *Uragan*; **300mm** 6 9A52 *Smerch*
  MOR 97: **82mm** 31; **120mm** 66 M-1938 (PM-38)
SURFACE-TO-SURFACE MISSILE LAUNCHERS
  SRBM • Conventional 16 SS-1 *Scud*
UNMANNED AERIAL VEHICLES
  CISR • Heavy CH-3A; WJ-600
  ISR • Medium *Falco*
AIR DEFENCE
  SAM
    Short-range: FM-90; 2K12 *Kub* (SA-6 *Gainful*)
    Point-defence 53+: 40 9K33 *Osa* (SA-8 *Gecko*); 13 9K35 *Strela*-10 mod (SA-13 *Gopher*); 9K38 *Igla* (SA-18 *Grouse*); 9K32 *Strela*-2 (SA-7 *Grail*)‡; 9K34 *Strela*-3 (SA-14 *Gremlin*); *Mistral* (reported)

GUNS 70
  SP 23mm 48 ZSU-23-4
  TOWED 22+: 23mm ZU-23-2; 57mm 22 S-60
AIR-LAUNCHED MISSILES
  ASM: CM-502KG

Navy 500
EQUIPMENT BY TYPE
PATROL AND COASTAL COMBATANTS 19
  PCFGM 2 *Edermen* (RUS *Molnya*) with 4 quad lnchr with 3M24E *Uran*-E (SS-N-25 *Switchblade*) AShM, 1 quad lnchr (manual aiming) with 9K32 *Strela*-2 (SA-N-5 *Grail*) SAM, 2 AK630 CIWS, 1 76mm gun
  PCC 4 *Arkadag*
  PBF 12: 5 *Grif*-T; 5 Dearsan 14: 2 *Sobol*
  PB 1 *Point*

Air Force 3,000
FORCES BY ROLE
FIGHTER
  2 sqn with MiG-29 *Fulcrum*; MiG-29UB *Fulcrum*;
GROUND ATTACK
  1 sqn with Su-25 *Frogfoot*
  1 sqn with Su-25MK *Frogfoot*
TRANSPORT
  1 sqn with An-26 *Curl*; Mi-8 *Hip*; Mi-24 *Hind*
TRAINING
  1 unit with L-39 *Albatros*
AIR DEFENCE
  Some sqn with S-75 *Dvina* (SA-2 *Guideline*); S-125 *Pechora* (SA-3 *Goa*); S-125 *Pechora*-2M (SA-26); S-200 *Angara* (SA-5 *Gammon*); FD-2000 (HQ-9); KS-1A (HQ-12)
EQUIPMENT BY TYPE
AIRCRAFT 55 combat capable
  FTR 24: 22 MiG-29A/S *Fulcrum*; 2 MiG-29UB *Fulcrum*
  ATK 31: 19 Su-25 *Frogfoot*; 12 Su-25MK *Frogfoot*
  TPT • Light 3: 1 An-26 *Curl*; 2 An-74TK *Coaler*
  TRG 2 L-39 *Albatros*
HELICOPTERS
  ATK 10 Mi-24P *Hind* F
  MRH 2+ AW139
  TPT 11: Medium 8: 6 Mi-8 *Hip*; 2 Mi-17V-V *Hip*; Light 3+ AW109
AIR-LAUNCHED MISSILES
  AAM • IR R-60 (AA-8 *Aphid*); R-73 (AA-11 *Archer*)
AIR DEFENCE • SAM
  Long-range S-200 *Angara* (SA-5 *Gammon*); FD-2000 (HQ-9)
  Medium-range S-75 *Dvina* (SA-2 *Guideline*); S-125 *Pechora*-2M (SA-26); KS-1A (HQ-12)
  Short-range S-125 *Pechora* (SA-3 *Goa*); S-125-2BM *Pechora*

Paramilitary 5,000

Federal Border Guard Service ε5,000
EQUIPMENT BY TYPE
HELICOPTERS
  MRH 2 AW139
  TPT 3+: Medium some Mi-8 *Hip*; Light 3 AW109

Ukraine UKR

Ukrainian Hryvnia h		2016	2017	2018
GDP	h	2.38tr	2.83tr	
	US$	93.3bn	104bn	
per capita	US$	2,199	2,459	
Growth	%	2.3	2.0	
Inflation	%	13.9	12.8	
Def bdgt [a]	h	65.3bn	74.4bn	
	US$	2.55bn	2.73bn	
FMA (US)	US$	85m	42m	0m
USD1=h		25.55	27.22	

[a] Includes military pensions

Population 44,033,874

Age	0–14	15–19	20–24	25–29	30–64	65 plus
Male	8.1%	2.2%	2.8%	3.7%	23.9%	5.5%
Female	7.6%	2.1%	2.7%	3.6%	26.8%	10.8%

Capabilities

Ukraine was not able to offer any resistance to Russia's seizure of Crimea in March 2014, and the country's armed forces have since been fighting Russian-supported separatist forces in the east, with continuing casualties. The security challenge from Russia has dictated the course of Ukraine's military-reform process. A key goal is to implement processes aimed at standardising with NATO structures. Indeed, NATO standards are being adopted and the general staff has also been restructured in accordance with NATO standards. The reform process has also centred on improving command and control, and reorganising and standardising unit establishments. New formations have been created, and volunteer units incorporated into the army and the national guard. Training has been increased, including developing a professional NCO education system. Organisational reforms are driven by the need to increase the proportion of combat personnel in the overall establishment strength. The influence of NATO and its member states on the reform process is illustrated by Ukraine's special-operations forces and the number of specialist supporting centres that have developed within them. Ukrainian defence industry was consolidated under the state-owned Ukroboronprom organisation in 2010. It is able to provide almost all of the armed forces' equipment, in particular armoured vehicles and fixed-wing transport aircraft, and has even resumed delivery of export orders. Much of the focus of the Ukrainian defence industry in the past couple of years has been on repairing and modernising equipment for use by the newly expanded armed forces. Ukraine receives training, advice and assistance from the US and other NATO countries. Ukraine has also increased participation in multinational exercises, and hosted the multinational *Rapid Trident 2017* exercise. Aircraft availability remains problematic; L-39 training aircraft have been attached to tactical-aviation brigades in order to increase flying hours for *Flanker* and *Fulcrum* pilots. The limited availability of fixed-wing transport aircraft and helicopters places restrictions on the rapid mobility of forces. (See pp. 179–80.)

ACTIVE 204,000 (Army 145,000 Navy 6,000 Air Force 45,000 Airborne 8,000 Special Operations Forces n.k.) Paramilitary 88,000

Conscript liability Army, Air Force 18 months, Navy 2 years. Minimum age for conscription raised from 18 to 20 in 2015

RESERVE 900,000 (Joint 900,000)
Military service within 5 years

ORGANISATIONS BY SERVICE

Army 145,000
4 regional HQ
FORCES BY ROLE
MANOEUVRE
  Reconnaissance
  5 recce bn
  Armoured
  2 tk bde
  Mechanised
  9 mech bde
  2 mtn bde
  Light
  4 mot inf bde
SURFACE-TO-SURFACE MISSILES
  1 SSM bde
COMBAT SUPPORT
  5 arty bde
  3 MRL regt
  1 engr regt
  1 EW regt
  1 EW bn
  2 EW coy
  1 CBRN regt
  4 sigs regt
COMBAT SERVICE SUPPORT
  3 maint regt
  1 maint coy
HELICOPTERS
  4 avn bde
  1 avn regt
AIR DEFENCE
  4 AD regt

Reserves
FORCES BY ROLE
MANOEUVRE
  Light
  25+ inf bn
EQUIPMENT BY TYPE
ARMOURED FIGHTING VEHICLES
  MBT 832: 710 T-64/T-64BV/BM; 100 T-72AV/B1; 22 T-80BV (10 T-84 *Oplot*; 100 T-80; 530 T-72; 588 T-64; 20 T-55 all in store)
  RECCE 548: 433 BRDM-2; 115 BRM-1K (CP)
  IFV 1,087: 193 BMP-1; 890 BMP-2; 4 BMP-3; some BTR-3DA; some BTR-3E1; some BTR-4E *Bucephalus*
  APC 338
    APC (T) 15+: 15 BTR-D; some MT-LB
    APC (W) 313: 5 BTR-60; 215 BTR-70; 93 BTR-80
    PPV 10 *Kozak*-2
  ABCV 30: 15 BMD-1, 15 BMD-2
ENGINEERING & MAINTENANCE VEHICLES
  AEV 53 BAT-2; MT-LB
  ARV BREM-1; BREM-2; BREM-64; T-54/T-55
  VLB MTU-20
ANTI-TANK/ANTI-INFRASTRUCTURE
  MSL • MANPATS 9K111 *Fagot* (AT-4 *Spigot*); 9K113 *Konkurs* (AT-5 *Spandrel*); 9K114 *Shturm* (AT-6 *Spiral*); *Stugna*-P
  GUNS 100mm ε500 MT-12/T-12
ARTILLERY 1,737
  SP 532+: **122mm** 238 2S1 *Gvozdika*; **152mm** 288: 235 2S3 *Akatsiya*; 18 2S5 *Giatsint*-S; 35 2S19 *Msta*-S; **203mm** 6+ 2S7 *Pion* (up to 90 2S7 *Pion* in store)
  TOWED 515+: **122mm** 75 D-30; **152mm** 440: 180 2A36 *Giatsint*-B; 130 2A65 *Msta*-B; 130+ D-20
  GUN/MOR • 120mm • TOWED 2 2B16 NONA-K
  MRL 348: **122mm** 203: 18 9P138; 185 BM-21 *Grad*; **220mm** 70 9P140 *Uragan*; **300mm** 75 9A52 *Smerch*
  MOR 120mm 340: 190 2S12 *Sani*; 30 M-1938 (PM-38); 120 M120-15
SURFACE-TO-SURFACE MISSILE LAUNCHERS
  SRBM • Conventional 90 9K79 *Tochka* (SS-21 *Scarab*)
RADAR • LAND AN/TPQ-36 *Firefinder* (arty); *Small Fred/Small Yawn*/SNAR-10 *Big Fred* (arty)
HELICOPTERS
  ATK ε35 Mi-24 *Hind*
  MRH 1 *Lev*-1
  TPT • Medium ε24 Mi-8 *Hip*
AIR DEFENCE
  SAM
    Long-range (Some S-300V (SA-12 *Gladiator*) in store)
    Point-defence 9K35 *Strela*-10 (SA-13 *Gopher*); 9K33 *Osa* (SA-8 *Gecko*)
  GUNS
    SP 30mm 70 2S6
    TOWED 23mm ZU-23-2; **57mm** S-60

Navy 6,000 (incl Naval Aviation and Naval Infantry)
After Russia's annexation of Crimea, HQ shifted to Odessa. Several additional vessels remain in Russian possession in Crimea

2 Regional HQ
EQUIPMENT BY TYPE
PRINCIPAL SURFACE COMBATANTS 1
  FRIGATES • FFHM 1 *Hetman Sagaidachny* (RUS *Krivak* III) with 1 twin lnchr with *Osa*-M (SA-N-4 *Gecko*) SAM, 2 quad 533mm ASTT with T-53 HWT, 1 100mm gun (capacity 1 Ka-27 *Helix* ASW hel)
PATROL AND COASTAL COMBATANTS 10
  CORVETTES • FSM 1 *Grisha* (II/V) with 1 twin lnchr with *Osa*-M (SA-N-4 *Gecko*) SAM, 2 twin 533mm ASTT with SAET-60 HWT, 2 RBU 6000 *Smerch* 2 A/S mor, 1 76mm gun

PCFGM 1 *Tarantul* II (FSU *Molnya*) with 2 twin lnchr with P-15 *Termit*-R (SS-N-2D *Styx*) AShM; 1 quad lnchr (manual aiming) with 9K32 *Strela*-2 (SA-N-5 *Grail*) SAM; 1 76mm gun
PHG 1 *Matka* (FSU *Vekhr*) with 2 single lnchr with P-15 *Termit*-M/R (SS-N-2C/D *Styx*) AShM, 1 76mm gun
PB 1 *Zhuk* (FSU *Grif*)
PBR 6 *Gyurza*-M (Project 51855) with 2 *Katran*-M IFV turret with 1 twin lnchr with *Baryer* ATGM
MINE WARFARE • MINE COUNTERMEASURES 1
MHI 1 *Korund* (*Yevgenya*) (Project 1258)
AMPHIBIOUS
LANDING SHIPS 2
LST 1 *Ropucha* I (Project 775)
LSM 1 *Polnochny* C (capacity 6 MBT; 180 troops)
LANDING CRAFT • LCU 3
LOGISTICS AND SUPPORT 11
ABU 1 Project 419 (*Sura*)
AG 1 *Bereza*
AGI 1 *Muna*
AGS 1 *Biya*
AKL 1
AO 2 *Toplivo*
AWT 1 *Sudak*
AXL 3 *Petrushka*

Naval Aviation ε1,000

EQUIPMENT BY TYPE
FIXED-WING AIRCRAFT
  ASW (2 Be-12 *Mail* non-operational)
  TPT • Light (2 An-26 *Curl* in store)
HELICOPTERS
  ASW 7+: 4+ Ka-27 *Helix* A; 3 Mi-14PS/PL *Haze* A/C
  TPT • Medium 1 Ka-29 *Helix*-B

Naval Infantry ε2,000

FORCES BY ROLE
MANOEUVRE
  Light
  1 nav inf bde
  1 nav inf bn
EQUIPMENT BY TYPE
ARMOURED FIGHTING VEHICLES
  MBT 31 T-80BV
  IFV some BMP-1
  APC • APC (W) some BTR-60; some BTR-80
ARTILLERY
  SP 122mm 2S1 *Gvozdika*
  TOWED 152mm some 2A36 *Giatsint*-B

Air Forces 45,000

Flying hours 40 hrs/yr

3 Regional HQ

FORCES BY ROLE
FIGHTER
  4 bde with MiG-29 *Fulcrum*; Su-27 *Flanker*; L-39 *Albatros*
FIGHTER/GROUND ATTACK
  2 bde with Su-24M *Fencer*; Su-25 *Frogfoot*
ISR
  2 sqn with Su-24MR *Fencer* E*

TRANSPORT
  3 bde with An-24; An-26; An-30; Il-76 *Candid*; Tu-134 *Crusty*
TRAINING
  Some sqn with L-39 *Albatros*
TRANSPORT HELICOPTER
  Some sqn with Mi-8; Mi-9; PZL Mi-2 *Hoplite*
AIR DEFENCE
  6 bde with 9K37M *Buk*-M1 (SA-11 *Gadfly*); S-300P/PS/PT (SA-10 *Grumble*)
  4 regt with 9K37M *Buk*-M1 (SA-11); S-300P/PS/PT (SA-10)

EQUIPMENT BY TYPE
AIRCRAFT ε125 combat capable
  FTR 71: ε37 MiG-29 *Fulcrum*; ε34 Su-27 *Flanker*
  FGA ε14 Su-24M *Fencer*
  ATK ε31 Su-25 *Frogfoot*
  ISR 12: 3 An-30 *Clank*; ε9 Su-24MR *Fencer* E*
  TPT 30: **Heavy** 5 Il-76 *Candid*; **Medium** 1 An-70; **Light** ε24: 3 An-24 *Coke*; ε20 An-26 *Curl*; 1 Tu-134 *Crusty*
  TRG ε32 L-39 *Albatros*
HELICOPTERS
  C2 ε14 Mi-9
  TPT 32: **Medium** ε30 Mi-8 *Hip*; **Light** 2 PZL Mi-2 *Hoplite*
AIR DEFENCE • SAM 322:
  Long-range 250 S-300P/PS/PT (SA-10 *Grumble*)
  Medium-range 72 9K37M *Buk*-M1 (SA-11 *Gadfly*)
AIR-LAUNCHED MISSILES
  AAM • IR R-60 (AA-8 *Aphid*); R-73 (AA-11 *Archer*)
  SARH R-27 (AA-10A *Alamo*)
  ASM Kh-25 (AS-10 *Karen*); Kh-29 (AS-14 *Kedge*)
  ARM Kh-25MP (AS-12 *Kegler*); Kh-58 (AS-11 *Kilter*); Kh-28 (AS-9 *Kyle*) (likely WFU)

High-Mobility Airborne Troops ε8,000

FORCES BY ROLE
MANOEUVRE
  Air Manoeuvre
  1 AB bde
  4 air mob bde
EQUIPMENT BY TYPE
ARMOURED FIGHTING VEHICLES
  IFV 75+: 30 BMD-1; 45 BMD-2; some BTR-3E1; some BTR-4 *Bucephalus*
  APC 160+
    APC (T) 25 BTR-D
    APC (W) 135+: 1 BTR-60; 2 BTR-70; 122 BTR-80; 10+ *Dozor*-B
ANTI-TANK/ANTI-INFRASTRUCTURE
  MSL • MANPATS 9K111 *Fagot* (AT-4 *Spigot*); 9K111-1 *Konkurs* (AT-5 *Spandrel*)
ARTILLERY 118
  TOWED • 122mm 54 D-30
  GUN/MOR • SP • 120mm 40 2S9 NONA-S
  MOR 120mm 24 2S12 *Sani*
AIR DEFENCE • GUNS • SP 23mm some ZU-23-2 (truck mounted)

Special Operations Forces n.k.

SPECIAL FORCES
  2 SF regt

Paramilitary 88,000

National Guard ε46,000
Ministry of Internal Affairs; 5 territorial comd
FORCES BY ROLE
MANOEUVRE
  Armoured
  Some tk bn
  Mechanised
  Some mech bn
  Light
  Some lt inf bn
EQUIPMENT BY TYPE
ARMOURED FIGHTING VEHICLES
  MBT T-64; T-64BV; T-64BM; T-72
  IFV 83: BTR-3; 32+ BTR-3E1; ε50 BTR-4 *Bucephalus*; 1 BMP-2
  APC 22+
    APC (W) BTR-70; BTR-80
    PPV 22+: Streit *Cougar*; Streit *Spartan*; 22 *Kozak-2*
ANTI-TANK/ANTI-INFRASTRUCTURE
  RCL 73mm some SPG-9
ARTILLERY
  TOWED 122mm some D-30
  MOR 120mm some
AIRCRAFT
  TPT • Light 24: 20 An-26 *Curl*; 2 An-72 *Coaler*; 2 Tu-134 *Crusty*
HELICOPTERS • TPT Medium 7 Mi-8 *Hip*
AIR DEFENCE
  SAM • Point-defence 9K38 *Igla* (SA-18 *Grouse*)
  GUNS • SP 23mm some ZU-23-2 (truck mounted)

Border Guard ε42,000
FORCES BY ROLE
MANOEUVRE
  Light
  some mot inf gp
EQUIPMENT BY TYPE
ARMOURED FIGHTING VEHICLES
  APC • PPV 17 *Kozak-2*

Maritime Border Guard
The Maritime Border Guard is an independent subdivision of the State Commission for Border Guards and is not part of the navy
FORCES BY ROLE
PATROL
  4 (cutter) bde
  2 rvn bde
MINE WARFARE
  1 MCM sqn
TRANSPORT
  3 sqn
TRANSPORT HELICOPTER
  1 sqn
COMBAT SERVICE SUPPORT
  1 trg div
  1 (aux ships) gp

EQUIPMENT BY TYPE
PATROL AND COASTAL COMBATANTS 26
  PCFT 6 *Stenka* with 4 single 406mm TT
  PCT 3 *Pauk* I with 4 single 406mm TT, 2 RBU-1200 A/S mor, 1 76mm gun
  PHT 1 *Muravey* with 2 single 406mm TT, 1 76mm gun
  PB 12: 11 *Zhuk*; 1 *Orlan*
  PBR 4 *Shmel*
LOGISTICS AND SUPPORT • AGF 1
AIRCRAFT • TPT Medium An-8 *Camp*; **Light** An-24 *Coke*; An-26 *Curl*; An-72 *Coaler*
HELICOPTERS • ASW: Ka-27 *Helix* A

Cyber
Ukraine remains the target of persistent and damaging cyber attacks, which have prompted greater state attention and international support. In June 2016, a National Cyber Security Coordination Centre was established, a year after the publication of the National Cyber Security Strategy. This centre is an agency of the National Security and Defence Council and will consist of representatives from MoD, armed forces and the SBU (security service), among others. Through a Cyber Defence Trust Fund, NATO states are extending help to Ukraine in developing its technical capability to counter cyber attack. According to NATO, this help will include establishing an Incident Management Centre. Ukraine has also received assistance from a number of member states in addressing cyber threats. In April 2017, Ukroboronprom announced plans to set up a cyber-security centre in cooperation with Turkish firm Havelsan.

DEPLOYMENT

AFGHANISTAN
NATO • *Operation Resolute Support* 10

CYPRUS
UN • UNFICYP 2

DEMOCRATIC REPUBLIC OF THE CONGO
UN • MONUSCO 255; 9 obs; 2 atk hel sqn; 1 hel sqn

LIBERIA
UN • UNMIL 107; 1 hel sqn

MOLDOVA
10 obs

SERBIA
NATO • KFOR 40
OSCE • Kosovo 1
UN • UNMIK 2 obs

SOUTH SUDAN
UN • UNMISS 1; 3 obs

SUDAN
UN • UNISFA 1; 3 obs

FOREIGN FORCES
Albania OSCE 3
Armenia OSCE 2

Austria OSCE 14
Azerbaijan OSCE 1
Belarus OSCE 1
Belgium OSCE 4
Bosnia-Herzegovina OSCE 37
Bulgaria OSCE 35
Canada OSCE 22 • *Operation Unifier* 200
Croatia OSCE 10
Czech Republic OSCE 15
Denmark OSCE 4
Estonia OSCE 5
Finland OSCE 17
France OSCE 14
Georgia OSCE 12
Germany OSCE 27
Greece OSCE 22
Hungary OSCE 30
Ireland OSCE 12
Italy OSCE 19
Kazakhstan OSCE 4
Kyrgyzstan OSCE 17
Latvia OSCE 4
Lithuania OSCE 3 • JMTG-U 16
Macedonia (FYROM) OSCE 24
Moldova OSCE 33
Montenegro OSCE 2
Netherlands OSCE 4
Norway OSCE 17
Poland OSCE 35
Portugal OSCE 4
Romania OSCE 32
Russia OSCE 36
Serbia OSCE 10
Slovakia OSCE 10
Slovenia OSCE 2
Spain OSCE 13
Sweden OSCE 10
Switzerland OSCE 11
Tajikistan OSCE 14
Turkey OSCE 11
United Kingdom OSCE 51 • *Operation Orbital* 100
United States OSCE 68 • JMTG-U 310

TERRITORY WHERE THE GOVERNMENT DOES NOT EXERCISE EFFECTIVE CONTROL

Following the overthrow of Ukraine's President Yanukovich in February 2014, the region of Crimea requested to join the Russian Federation after a referendum regarded as unconstitutional by the new Ukrainian government. Data presented here represents the de facto situation and does not imply international recognition.

EASTERN UKRAINE SEPARATIST FORCES

ORGANISATIONS BY SERVICE

Donetsk People's Republic ε20,000
FORCES BY ROLE
SPECIAL FORCES
  2 (Spetsnaz) SF bn
MANOEUVRE
  Reconnaissance
  1 recce bn
  Armoured
  1 tk bn
  Light
  6 mot inf bde
COMBAT SUPPORT
  1 arty bde
  1 engr coy
  1 EW coy
COMBAT SERVICE SUPPORT
  1 log bn
AIR DEFENCE
  1 AD bn

Luhansk People's Republic ε14,000
FORCES BY ROLE
MANOEUVRE
  Reconnaissance
  1 recce bn
  Armoured
  1 tk bn
  Light
  4 mot inf bde
COMBAT SUPPORT
  1 arty bde
  1 engr coy
  1 EW coy
COMBAT SERVICE SUPPORT
  1 log bn
AIR DEFENCE
  1 AD bn
EQUIPMENT BY TYPE
ARMOURED FIGHTING VEHICLES
  MBT T-64BV; T-64B; T-64BM†; T-72B1; T-72BA
  RECCE BDRM-2
  IFV BMP-1; BMP-2; BTR-4
  APC
    APC (T) BTR-D; MT-LB; GT-MU
    APC (W) BTR-60; BTR-70; BTR-80
  ABCV BMD-1, BMD-2
ANTI-TANK/ANTI-INFRASTRUCTURE
  MSL 9K115 *Metis* (AT-7 *Saxhorn*); 9K135 *Kornet* (AT-14 *Spriggan*)
  RCL 73mm SPG-9
  GUNS 100mm MT-12
ARTILLERY
  SP 122mm 2S1 *Gvozdika*; **152mm** 2S3 *Akatsiya*; 2S19 *Msta-S*†; **203mm** 2S7 *Pion*
  TOWED 122mm D-30; **152mm** 2A65 *Msta-B*

GUN/MOR
SP 120mm 2S9 NONA-S
TOWED 120mm 2B16 NONA-K
MRL 122mm BM-21 *Grad*
MOR 82mm 2B14; 120mm 2B11 *Sani*
AIR DEFENCE
SAM
Short-range 9K332 *Tor-M2* (SA-15 *Gauntlet*)
Point-defence 2K22 *Tunguska* (SA-19 *Grison*); 9K32M *Strela*-2M (SA-7B *Grail*); 9K33 *Osa* (SA-8 *Gecko*); 9K35 *Strela*-10 (SA-13 *Gopher*); 9K38 *Igla* (SA-18 *Grouse*); GROM
GUNS
SP 23mm ZU-23-2 (tch/on MT-LB)
TOWED 14.5mm ZPU-2; 57mm S-60

FOREIGN FORCES

Russia Crimea: 28,000; 1 recce bde, 2 naval inf bde; 1 arty bde; 1 NBC bde; 40 T-72B3 MBT; 80 BMP-2 AIFV; 200 BTR-82A; 20 BTR-80 APC: 150 MT-LB; 18 2S1 arty; 18 2S19 arty; 12 BM-21 MRL; 1 AShM bde with 3K60 Bal; 3K55 *Bastion*; 1 FGA regt with Su-24M/MR; Su-30SM; 1 FGA regt with Su-27SM/SM3; Su-30M2; 1 FGA regt with Su-24M/Su-25SM; 1 atk/tpt hel regt; 1 ASW hel regt; 1 AD regt with S-300PM; 1 AD regt with S-400; 1 Fleet HQ located at Sevastopol; 2 radar stations located at Sevastopol (*Dnepr* system) and Mukachevo (*Dnepr* system)
Donetsk/Luhansk: 3,000 (reported)

Uzbekistan UZB

Uzbekistani Som s		2016	2017	2018
GDP	s	199tr	245tr	
	US$	66.8bn	67.5bn	
per capita	US$	2,133	2,128	
Growth	%	7.8	6.0	
Inflation	%	8.0	13.0	
Def exp	s	n.k.	n.k.	
	US$	n.k.	n.k.	
FMA (US)	US$	0m	0m	
US$1=s		2,928.90	3,635.39	

Population 29,748,859

Ethnic groups: Uzbek 73%; Russian 6%; Tajik 5%; Kazakh 4%; Karakalpak 2%; Tatar 2%; Korean <1%; Ukrainian <1%

Age	0–14	15–19	20–24	25–29	30–64	65 plus
Male	12.2%	4.3%	5.1%	5.2%	20.6%	2.2%
Female	11.6%	4.1%	4.9%	5.2%	21.4%	3.0%

Capabilities

The security situation in neighbouring Afghanistan is a key concern, particularly the rise of ISIS there and the possibility of instability spilling over Uzbekistan's border. Although Uzbekistan is a member of the SCO, it suspended its membership of the CSTO in mid-2012. It maintains bilateral defence ties with Moscow and uses mainly Soviet-era equipment. A sizeable air capability was inherited from the Soviet Union, but minimal recapitalisation in the intervening period has substantially reduced the active inventory. However, in recent years there has been some procurement of rotary- and fixed-wing transport assets. Flying hours are reported to be low, with logistical and maintenance shortcomings affecting the availability of the remaining aircraft.

ACTIVE 48,000 (Army 24,500 Air 7,500 Joint 16,000)
Paramilitary 20,000
Conscript liability 12 months

ORGANISATIONS BY SERVICE

Army 24,500
4 Mil Districts; 2 op comd; 1 Tashkent Comd
FORCES BY ROLE
SPECIAL FORCES
  1 SF bde
MANOEUVRE
  Armoured
  1 tk bde
  Mechanised
  11 MR bde
  Air Manoeuvre
  1 air aslt bde
  1 AB bde
  Mountain
  1 lt mtn inf bde
COMBAT SUPPORT
  3 arty bde
  1 MRL bde
EQUIPMENT BY TYPE
ARMOURED FIGHTING VEHICLES
  MBT 340: 70 T-72; 100 T-64; 170 T-62
  RECCE 19: 13 BRDM-2; 6 BRM-1
  IFV 270 BMP-2
  APC 359
    APC (T) 50 BTR-D
    APC (W) 259: 24 BTR-60; 25 BTR-70; 210 BTR-80
    PPV 50 *Maxxpro*+
  ABCV 129: 120 BMD-1; 9 BMD-2
  AUV 7 *Cougar*
ENGINEERING & MAINTENANCE VEHICLES
  ARV 20 *Maxxpro* ARV
ANTI-TANK/ANTI-INFRASTRUCTURE
  MSL • MANPATS 9K11 *Malyutka* (AT-3 *Sagger*); 9K111 *Fagot* (AT-4 *Spigot*)
  GUNS 100mm 36 MT-12/T-12
ARTILLERY 487+
  SP 83+: 122mm 18 2S1 *Gvozdika*; 152mm 17+: 17 2S3 *Akatsiya*; 2S5 *Giatsint*-S (reported); 203mm 48 2S7 *Pion*
  TOWED 200: 122mm 60 D-30; 152mm 140 2A36 *Giatsint*-B
  GUN/MOR 120mm 54 2S9 NONA-S
  MRL 108: 122mm 60: 36 BM-21 *Grad*; 24 9P138; 220mm 48 9P140 *Uragan*
  MOR 120mm 42: 5 2B11 *Sani*; 19 2S12 *Sani*; 18 M-120

Air Force 7,500
FORCES BY ROLE
FIGHTER
 1 sqn with MiG-29/MiG-29UB *Fulcrum*;
 1 sqn with Su-27/Su-27UB *Flanker*
FIGHTER/GROUND ATTACK
 1 regt with Su-24 *Fencer*
GROUND ATTACK
 2 sqn with Su-25/Su-25BM *Frogfoot*
ELINT/TRANSPORT
 1 regt with An-12/An-12PP *Cub*; An-26/An-26RKR *Curl*
TRANSPORT
 Some sqn with An-24 *Coke*; C295W; Tu-134 *Crusty*
TRAINING
 1 sqn with L-39 *Albatros*
ATTACK/TRANSPORT HELICOPTER
 1 regt with Mi-24 *Hind*; Mi-26 *Halo*; Mi-8 *Hip*;
 1 regt with Mi-6 *Hook*; Mi-6AYa *Hook* C

EQUIPMENT BY TYPE
AIRCRAFT 45 combat capable
 FTR 12 MiG-29/MiG-29UB *Fulcrum* (18 more in store)
 FGA 13 Su-27/Su-27UB *Flanker* (11 more in store) (26 Su-17M (Su-17MZ)/Su-17UM-3 (Su-17UMZ) *Fitter* C/G non-operational)
 ATK 20 Su-25/Su-25BM *Frogfoot*
 EW/Tpt 26 An-12 *Cub* (med tpt)/An-12PP *Cub* (EW)
 ELINT/Tpt 13 An-26 *Curl* (lt tpt)/An-26RKR *Curl* (ELINT)
 TPT 7: **Heavy** 1 Il-76 *Candid*; **Light** 6: 1 An-24 *Coke*; 4 C295W; 1 Tu-134 *Crusty*
 TRG 14 L-39 *Albatros*
HELICOPTERS
 ATK 29 Mi-24 *Hind*
 TPT 69: **Heavy** 9: 8 H225M *Caracal*; 1 Mi-26 *Halo*; **Medium** 52 Mi-8 *Hip*; **Light** 8 AS350 *Ecureuil*
AIR DEFENCE • SAM 45
 Long-range S-200 *Angara* (SA-5 *Gammon*)
 Medium-range S-75 *Dvina* (SA-2 *Guideline*)
 Short-range S-125 *Pechora* (SA-3 *Goa*)
AIR-LAUNCHED MISSILES
 AAM • IR R-60 (AA-8 *Aphid*); R-73 (AA-11 *Archer*); **IR/SARH** R-27 (AA-10 *Alamo*)
 ASM Kh-23 (AS-7 *Kerry*); Kh-25 (AS-10 *Karen*)
 ARM Kh-25P (AS-12 *Kegler*); Kh-28 (AS-9 *Kyle*); Kh-58 (AS-11 *Kilter*)

Paramilitary up to 20,000

Internal Security Troops up to 19,000
Ministry of Interior

National Guard 1,000
Ministry of Defence

Arms procurements and deliveries – Russia and Eurasia

Significant events in 2017

- MiG unveiled its MiG-35 combat aircraft, which is a further upgrade of the MiG-29 *Fulcrum*. An initial batch of 24 aircraft is planned to be ordered in the next State Armament Programme for 2018–27.

- Missile manufacturer KTRV announced that it would complete development and testing of the infrared-guided Kh-38MT and *Grom*-1 air-to-surface missiles by the end of 2017.

- The Russian defence ministry ordered the first pair of production-standard Mi-38T transport helicopters for the Aerospace Forces.

- Russia's defence industry began to deliver MiG-29M2 fighter aircraft and Ka-52 attack helicopters to Egypt.

- Trials of the Yak-152 basic-training aircraft were due to be completed by the end of 2017.

- President Vladimir Putin signed a decree approving the transfer of defence company UralVagonZavod to Rostec in December 2016. The process was expected to be completed by the end of 2017 or early 2018.

- The head of Almaz-Antey was reportedly sacked after delays in the development of the *Poliment-Redut* and *Shtil* air-defence systems.

- Russia's deputy defence minister stated that a PAK-DA bomber prototype is now expected to undertake its maiden flight in 2025 or 2026, with series production beginning in 2028 or 2029.

- Russia's A-100 airborne early-warning-and-control aircraft prototype undertook its maiden flight in November 2017. The A-100 is based on the Il-76MD-90A airframe and is planned to replace Russia's A-50 and A-50U aircraft.

Table 10 **9K720 *Iskander*-M/-K (SS-26 *Stone*/SSC-7): brigade-set deliveries to Russia**

Contract	Date delivered	Unit	Location	Military District
2010	Mid-2011	26th Missile Brigade	Luga	Western
Aug 2011	Jul 2013	107th Missile Brigade	Birobidzhan	Eastern
Aug 2011	Nov 2013	1st Missile Brigade	Krasnodar	Southern
Aug 2011	Jul 2014	112th Missile Brigade	Shuya	Western
Aug 2011	Nov 2014	92nd Missile Brigade	Totskoye Vtorye	Central
Aug 2011	Jul 2015	103rd Missile Brigade	Ulan-Ude	Eastern
Aug 2011	Nov 2015	12th Missile Brigade	Mozdok	Southern
Aug 2011	Jun 2016	20th Missile Brigade	Ussuriysk	Eastern
Aug 2011	Nov 2016	119th Missile Brigade	Elanskiy	Central
Aug 2011	Jun 2017	3rd Missile Brigade (new formation; reported)	Gorny	Eastern
Aug 2011	Nov 2017	152nd Missile Brigade (Navy)	Kaliningrad	Western
Units yet to receive *Iskander*				
Aug 2017	2018*	448th Missile Brigade	Kursk	Western
Aug 2017	2018*	n.k. (new formation)	n.k.	n.k.

*Expected date of delivery

Table 11 **Russia: principal surface- and sub-surface-combatant commissioning, 2012–17**

With just over half of the principal surface-combatant fleet having entered service before 1991, the Russian Navy has a clear requirement for new aircraft carriers, cruisers, destroyers and frigates if it is to maintain its current size. As this table illustrates, the Russian shipbuilding industry has struggled to meet this need, with only six frigates entering service from 2012 to October 2017. Problems with the *Admiral Gorshkov* (Project 22350) destroyer's *Poliment-Redut* (SA-NX-28) air-defence system have prevented that class joining the fleet. It was originally planned to enter service in 2009. Other United Shipbuilding Corporation (USC) programmes that have struggled to enter service on time or are significantly delayed include the *Ivan Gren* (Project 11711) landing ships and the *Alexandrit*-class (Project 12700) mine-countermeasures vessels. Because of problems with USC, the Russian government has been increasingly turning to other shipyards, such as Pella, Vympel and Zelenodolsk, to provide smaller missile boats, often armed with the *Kalibr* land-attack cruise missile. One USC success story, however, has been Admiralty Shipyard's production of *Varshavyanka* (Project 636.3) conventionally powered submarines, variants of which are in service with Algeria, China and Vietnam.

Type	Class	Project No.	Shipyard	Vessel Name	ISD
FFGM	Gepard	11661K	Zelenodolsk Shipyard	Dagestan	28 Nov 2012
FSM	Buyan	21630	Almaz Shipbuilding Company	Makhachkala	04 Dec 2012
SSBN	Borey	955	Sevmash Shipyard	Yuri Dolgorukiy	29 Dec 2012
FFGHM	Steregushchiy	20380	Severnaya Verf	Boiky	16 May 2013
SSBN	Borey	955	Sevmash Shipyard	Alexander Nevsky	23 Dec 2013
SSGN	Yasen	885	Sevmash Shipyard	Severodvinsk	17 Jun 2014
FFGHM	Steregushchiy	20380	Severnaya Verf	Stoiky	18 Jul 2014
FSGM	Buyan-M	21631	Zelenodolsk Shipyard	Grad Sviyazhsk	27 Jul 2014
FSGM	Buyan-M	21631	Zelenodolsk Shipyard	Uglich	27 Jul 2014
SSK	Varshavyanka	636.3	Admiralty Shipyard	Novorossiysk	21 Aug 2014
SSBN	Borey	955	Sevmash Shipyard	Vladimir Monomakh	10 Dec 2014
FSGM	Buyan-M	21631	Zelenodolsk Shipyard	Velikiye Ustyug	19 Dec 2014
SSK	Varshavyanka	636.3	Admiralty Shipyard	Rostov on Don	26 Dec 2014
SSK	Varshavyanka	636.3	Admiralty Shipyard	Stary Oskol	25 Jun 2015
SSK	Varshavyanka	636.3	Admiralty Shipyard	Krasnodar	05 Nov 2015
FSGM	Buyan-M	21631	Zelenodolsk Shipyard	Zeleny Dol	12 Dec 2015
FSGM	Buyan-M	21631	Zelenodolsk Shipyard	Serpukhov	12 Dec 2015
FFGHM	Admiral Grigorovich	11356	Yantar Shipyard	Admiral Grigorovich	27 May 2016
FFGHM	Admiral Grigorovich	11356	Yantar Shipyard	Admiral Essen	07 Jun 2016
SSK	Varshavyanka	636.3	Admiralty Shipyard	Veliky Novgorod	26 Oct 2016
SSK	Varshavyanka	636.3	Admiralty Shipyard	Kolpino	24 Nov 2016
FFGHM	Steregushchiy	20380	Amur Shipbuilding Plant	Sovershenny	20 Jul 2017

Figure 11 **Russian Air Force: tactical-aircraft deliveries, 2010–16**

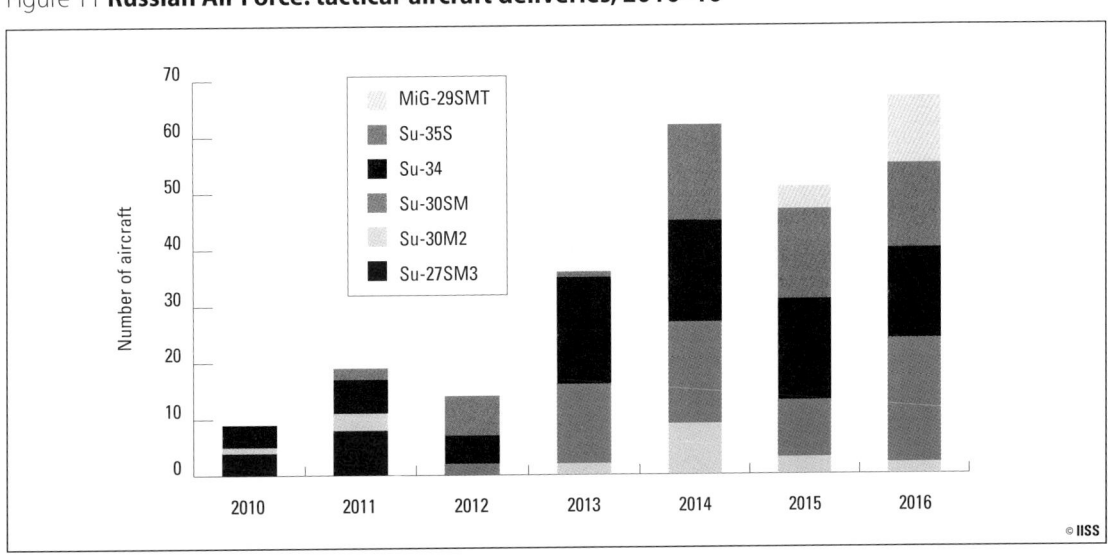

© IISS

Figure 12 **Russia: Sukhoi Su-57 (T-50)**

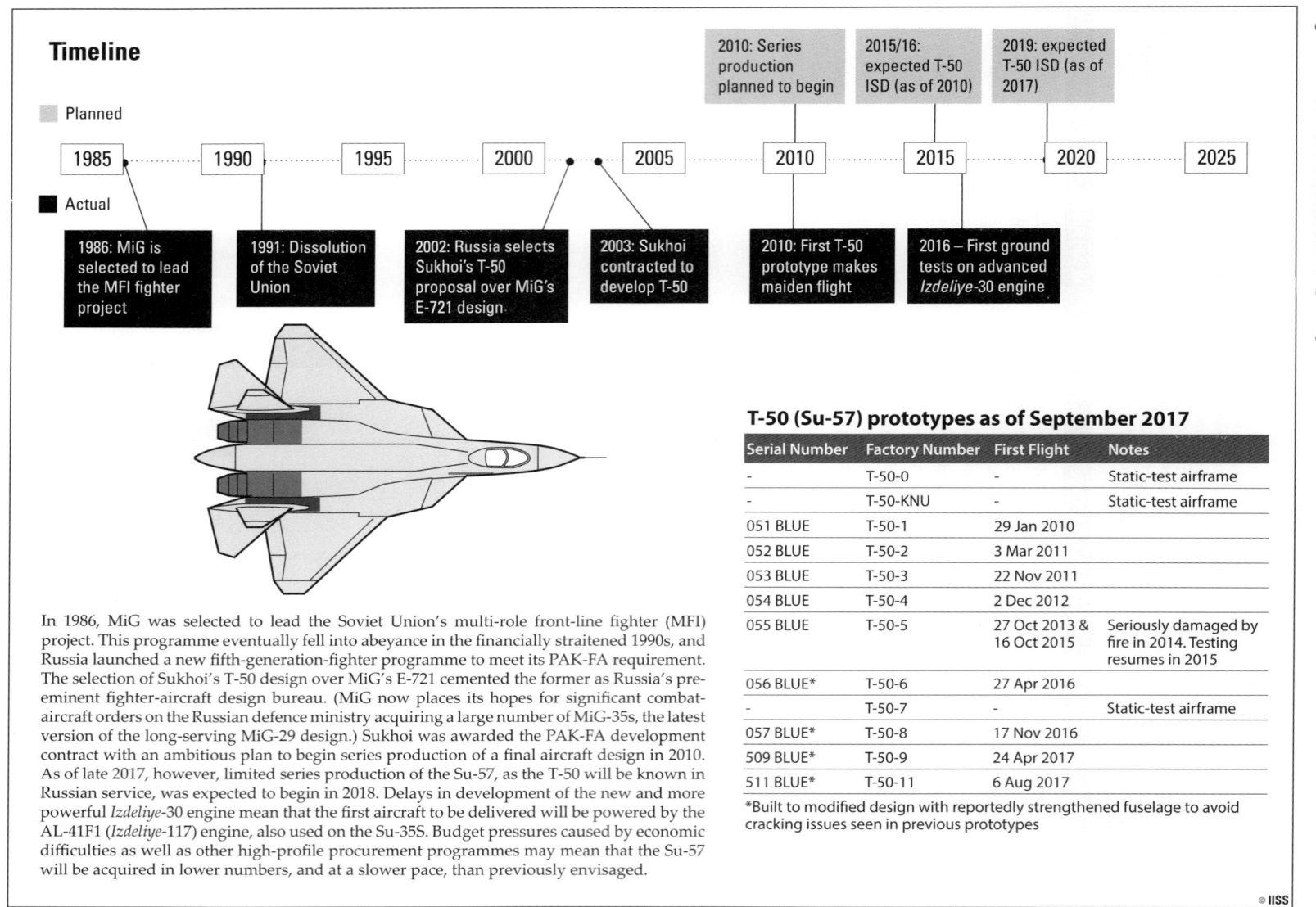

Timeline

- Planned
- Actual

1986: MiG is selected to lead the MFI fighter project

1991: Dissolution of the Soviet Union

2002: Russia selects Sukhoi's T-50 proposal over MiG's E-721 design

2003: Sukhoi contracted to develop T-50

2010: Series production planned to begin

2010: First T-50 prototype makes maiden flight

2015/16: expected T-50 ISD (as of 2010)

2016 – First ground tests on advanced *Izdeliye-30* engine

2019: expected T-50 ISD (as of 2017)

T-50 (Su-57) prototypes as of September 2017

Serial Number	Factory Number	First Flight	Notes
–	T-50-0	–	Static-test airframe
–	T-50-KNU	–	Static-test airframe
051 BLUE	T-50-1	29 Jan 2010	
052 BLUE	T-50-2	3 Mar 2011	
053 BLUE	T-50-3	22 Nov 2011	
054 BLUE	T-50-4	2 Dec 2012	
055 BLUE	T-50-5	27 Oct 2013 & 16 Oct 2015	Seriously damaged by fire in 2014. Testing resumes in 2015
056 BLUE*	T-50-6	27 Apr 2016	
–	T-50-7	–	Static-test airframe
057 BLUE*	T-50-8	17 Nov 2016	
509 BLUE*	T-50-9	24 Apr 2017	
511 BLUE*	T-50-11	6 Aug 2017	

*Built to modified design with reportedly strengthened fuselage to avoid cracking issues seen in previous prototypes

In 1986, MiG was selected to lead the Soviet Union's multi-role front-line fighter (MFI) project. This programme eventually fell into abeyance in the financially straitened 1990s, and Russia launched a new fifth-generation-fighter programme to meet its PAK-FA requirement. The selection of Sukhoi's T-50 design over MiG's E-721 cemented the former as Russia's pre-eminent fighter-aircraft design bureau. (MiG now places its hopes for significant combat-aircraft orders on the Russian defence ministry acquiring a large number of MiG-35s, the latest version of the long-serving MiG-29 design.) Sukhoi was awarded the PAK-FA development contract with an ambitious plan to begin series production of a final aircraft design in 2010. As of late 2017, however, limited series production of the Su-57, as the T-50 will be known in Russian service, was expected to begin in 2018. Delays in development of the new and more powerful *Izdeliye-30* engine mean that the first aircraft to be delivered will be powered by the AL-41F1 (*Izdeliye-117*) engine, also used on the Su-35S. Budget pressures caused by economic difficulties as well as other high-profile procurement programmes may mean that the Su-57 will be acquired in lower numbers, and at a slower pace, than previously envisaged.

Chapter Six
Asia

In the Asia-Pacific region, the influences on defence policy, military spending and equipment procurement, and on the development of armed forces' capabilities, were as wide-ranging as ever in 2017. However, the most important were pervasive and persistent insecurity; economic circumstances that allowed for a relatively high – and in some cases increasing – allocation of national resources to the armed forces; and domestic political circumstances, which often helped to support ambitious defence programmes.

The most important factors driving the region's sense of insecurity were evident at the 16th IISS Shangri-La Dialogue. In June 2017, this annual event again brought together in Singapore defence ministers and other senior representatives of Asia-Pacific defence establishments. Serious concern over the security ramifications of China's emergence as a major strategic actor in the Asia-Pacific and beyond was as apparent as it had been for the last half-decade – particularly in terms of its maritime assertiveness and the growing presence of the People's Liberation Army Navy (PLAN) in regional waters. Meanwhile, Australia, Japan, the Republic of Korea (ROK) and other regional states had good reason to view North Korea's accelerating development of nuclear weapons and long-range missiles as an acute threat. In addition, some Southeast Asian defence ministers and military chiefs viewed jihadi terrorism as an increasingly important challenge, particularly as the Islamic State, also known as ISIS or ISIL, lost territory in the Middle East and the risk increased that its fighters might disperse to Southeast Asia. A new concern for regional states was the uncertainty generated by the Trump administration, which had appeared to question the importance of the United States' alliances, and also seemed to have no clear strategy towards the region.

Concerns over China
Developments since the turn of 2017 only reinforced these concerns. Chinese government representatives claimed that the South China Sea was now 'quiet', particularly after senior officials from China and member states of the Association of Southeast Asian Nations agreed a framework for a code of conduct in the area, in May 2017. The reality, however, was that Beijing further strengthened its military bases in the South China Sea, on the features it had physically expanded after 2012. At the same time, it continued to engage in coercive behaviour there. For the Chinese Communist Party and the PLA, securing greater control of South China Sea features and surrounding waters was evidently a strategic priority, despite the unease that Beijing's actions were creating in Southeast Asia and beyond. In July, following Hanoi's refusal to yield to Chinese demands to halt drilling by a Spanish oil company on Vanguard Bank, an area that Vietnam claimed was within its exclusive economic zone, Beijing reportedly threatened to use force against a Vietnamese-occupied feature. In August, China deployed a flotilla of fishing vessels, accompanied by PLAN and coastguard ships, close to Pagasa, the largest feature occupied by the Philippines in the Spratly Islands.

While Southeast Asian governments emphasised the importance of diplomacy in managing regional maritime tensions, in these circumstances several states have continued their efforts to develop military capabilities that could help to deter potential future Chinese aggression. In February, Vietnam commissioned the last two of six Project 636.1 (improved *Kilo*-class) submarines supplied by Russia. At the commissioning ceremony, Prime Minister Nguyễn Xuân Phúc praised the Vietnamese Navy's willingness to defend 'every inch' of national territory including territorial waters. Later in the year, Vietnam received a third Russian *Gepard* 3.9-class frigate, with another due by year's end. Reflecting Hanoi's increasing sense of vulnerability to Chinese pressure, Minister of National Defence Ngo Xuan Lich visited Washington DC in August, where he met US Secretary of Defense James Mattis; the two sides reached an agreement on increased bilateral naval engagement and information-sharing, and more importantly that a US aircraft carrier would visit Vietnam during 2018, the first such visit since the Vietnamese communists' victory in 1975.

Five Power Defence Arrangements

The Five Power Defence Arrangements (FPDA) is a low-profile but important regional security institution established in 1971, based on a set of bilateral agreements between Australia, Malaysia, New Zealand, Singapore and the United Kingdom in the wake of the UK's withdrawal of most of its military forces from 'East of Suez'. While it does not involve formal alliance relations, its members are committed to consult in the event – or threat – of an attack on Malaysia or Singapore, with the aim of deciding how to respond. Originally intended to hedge against the resurgence of an unstable and threatening Indonesia, which had engaged in a politico-military campaign of *Konfrontasi* ('Confrontation') against Malaysia in 1963–66, the FPDA also provided channels of communication on defence matters between Malaysia and Singapore, as well as a degree of reassurance as communist victories in Indochina seemed ever more likely.

The subsequent transformation of Southeast Asia's strategic environment has rendered the original rationale for the FPDA much less compelling. However, Malaysia and Singapore have continued to face diverse security challenges and, over time, the FPDA's member governments have adapted the grouping in ways that transcend its origins. Organised from its small multinational permanent headquarters, HQ Integrated Area Defence System, at Butterworth air base in Malaysia, the FPDA's exercises – such as *Bersama Lima* in October 2016, which involved more than 3,000 personnel, 71 aircraft and 12 naval vessels – have evolved to reflect contemporary security concerns, including terrorism and humanitarian assistance and disaster relief.

At the FPDA's tenth defence ministers' meeting in Singapore on 2 June 2017, which was timed to coincide with the 16th IISS Shangri-La Dialogue, ministers agreed 'to continually enhance the operational value of the exercises including incorporating newer capabilities'. This apparently reflected a strong feeling on the part of members with more advanced capabilities, notably Australia and the UK, that 'high-end' exercises, which would provide opportunities to deploy their latest equipment, were vital if their armed forces were to continue deriving value from participation. UK officials, including Foreign Secretary Boris Johnson, have confirmed that the UK's new *Queen Elizabeth*-class aircraft carriers will be deployed to the Asia-Pacific region from the early 2020s; it is conceivable that such deployments could include participation in FPDA exercises.

The FPDA ministers also agreed in Singapore to enhance opportunities for non-member countries in the region to observe the grouping's exercises. Given its origins, the FPDA's members view the involvement of observers from the Indonesian armed forces as particularly important. Significantly, given the start of the urban uprising in Marawi in the southern Philippines a week earlier, the ministers additionally agreed to 'share intelligence to deal with terrorist threats against Malaysia and Singapore', as well as unspecified 'further measures to strengthen counter-terrorist activities'. All the indications are that the FPDA will maintain its usefulness as a security institution linking Australia, New Zealand and the UK to Southeast Asian security concerns.

Meanwhile, growing concern over the challenge posed by China's emergence as an assertive major power has continued to significantly influence Japan's defence policy and activity. While the Abe administration's August 2017 defence white paper was similar in content to the previous edition, it noted that the number of Japan Air Self-Defense Force interceptions of Chinese military aircraft close to national airspace reached a record level during the year preceding March 2017. Such Chinese missions – which Tokyo saw as 'provocative' – continued during 2017 and included a group of six H-6K bombers which, in late August, flew close to Japan's southern island of Okinawa.

One aspect of Japan's response was to strengthen defence and security relations with Southeast Asian partners. In November 2016, Japan's then-minister of defense, Tomomi Inada, highlighted Tokyo's commitment to regional defence cooperation when she launched the 'Vientiane Vision', intended to foster Southeast Asian defence establishments' understanding of international law, promote maritime security and build defence capacity. From May to August 2017, Tokyo underlined its commitment to protect its maritime interests, while reinforcing the maritime security of its key Southeast Asian partners, when it deployed the Japan Maritime Self-Defense Force's helicopter carrier *Izumo*, together with a destroyer, to the South China Sea and nearby waters. The ships made port calls in the Philippines, Singapore and Vietnam before participating in the *Malabar* exercise with the Indian and US navies.

Korean Peninsula

North Korea's nuclear and missile programmes have become more pressing concerns for the US and its Northeast Asian allies. In response to heightened anxiety caused by this threat, in March 2017 Itsunori Onodera (who became Japan's defence minister in August) and other Liberal Democratic Party (LDP) legislators urged Prime Minister Shinzo Abe to consider giving the Japan Self-Defense Force (JSDF) the capacity to attack enemy bases. Japan's defence white paper claimed that the North Korean threat had 'entered a new stage' following two nuclear tests and more than 20 ballistic-missile launches over the previous 12 months, and that North Korea might already have acquired nuclear warheads. In parliament, Onodera warned that Tokyo would be within its constitutional rights if it shot down North Korean missiles threatening its territory, and the defence ministry ordered the deployment of six *Patriot* PAC-3 surface-to-air missile batteries to southwestern Japan. Abe's conclusive victory in the October snap general election made it likely that the new government would seek to revise constitutional constraints that have limited the JSDF to defensive roles. Such a revision would allow the acquisition of the offensive capabilities favoured by Onodera.

Although South Korea's Moon administration evidently opposed the notion of preventive war against the North, fearing the calamitous impact of such a conflict on the South's population and economy, its deterrent strategy nevertheless required credible capabilities for preventive attacks in tandem with the US. Specifically, South Korea attempted to strengthen its deterrence of North Korea through its Korean Massive Punishment and Retaliation strategy, which emphasises precise long-range strikes into enemy territory. In July, following North Korea's second test of the *Hwasong*-14 intercontinental ballistic missile, US forces tested ATACMS (Army Tactical Missile System) missiles twice, and the ROK test-fired two *Hyonmu* II ballistic missiles. Following North Korea's nuclear test on 3 September, US President Donald Trump agreed during a telephone conversation with President Moon Jae-in on the removal of a bilaterally agreed restriction on the weight of the warheads on South Korea's ballistic missiles. This change would allow, for example, the new 800 kilometre-range version of South Korea's *Hyonmu* II missile to carry a payload weighing more than 500 kilograms. In late September, South Korea's air force tested, for the first time, a KEPD-350 *Taurus* air-launched cruise missile, further demonstrating precision-strike capability.

Regional insurgency and terrorism

While state-based challenges have become increasingly important over the last half-decade, non-state threats have also intensified. Insurgencies in Southeast Asia have continued to tax the armed forces of Myanmar, Thailand and – particularly – the Philippines. Although the southern Philippines has for around 45 years been the locus for armed struggles by a series of rebel groups drawing support from the Moro (Muslim) population of Basilan, Mindanao and Sulu, the eruption of a major urban conflict in the city of Marawi in late May 2017 represented a new challenge for security forces that had hitherto been focused on rural counter-insurgency. Even with substantial support from the US in the form of logistics, intelligence and special-forces advisers, it took the Philippine armed forces and police five months to win the battle, which resulted in the deaths of more than 900 insurgents. Those killed included members of the local Maute and Abu Sayyaf rebel groups, both of which had allied themselves with ISIS, and it was significant – and worrying for regional states' defence establishments – that the insurgents had been reinforced by foreign combatants from not only Indonesia and elsewhere in Southeast Asia, but also the Middle East. Other distinctive features of the Marawi battle included the militants' extensive use of powerful and effective weapons, particularly mortars and rocket-propelled grenades. They also employed snipers, improvised explosive devices and tunnel networks, suggesting the transfer of operational experience from ISIS operations in Iraq and Syria; there was also evidence of ISIS direction and funding.

As such, there was widespread concern among regional states over the potential for further outbreaks of jihadi rebellion supported by ISIS in Southeast Asia, and fuelled by Southeast Asian and other fighters with combat experience from the Middle East. This concern stimulated an intensification of counter-terrorism cooperation among some Southeast Asian states, and in June 2017 Indonesia, Malaysia and the Philippines – through their new Trilateral Cooperative Arrangement – began coordinated maritime patrols in the Sulu Sea. In October, they added Trilateral Air Patrols to the arrangement.

During 2017, US allies and security partners in the Asia-Pacific were concerned over the new US administration's apparent lack of a coherent strategy towards the region, and Trump's evident view of alliances and partnerships as essentially transactional. Early visits by the new administration's vice-president, secretary of state and secretary of defense, during which they reaffirmed Washington's commitment, did not entirely reassure sceptical and anxious regional policymakers. However, the substance of US security cooperation continued uninterrupted, in terms of exercises, such as *Cobra Gold*, held in Thailand from February to March; routine deployments of ships and aircraft; and the intensification of links with new security partners. In late October, the US Navy revealed that an exercise the following month would involve three of its carrier strike groups – the first exercise on such a scale since 2007 and a clear show of resolve in the face of the continuing crisis over North Korea.

It was unclear whether the Trump administration's muscular approach to North Korea reassured US allies and partners, though it was apparent that the change of administration in Washington had provided yet more reasons for them to take provision for their own national defence even more seriously.

DEFENCE ECONOMICS

Macroeconomics: the world's fastest-growing region

In 2017, Asia continued to be the fastest-growing region in the world in economic terms, with a rate of 5.6%. Some of the region's largest economies also achieved stronger than expected economic performances, with China realising 6.8% growth (0.2 percentage points higher than previously forecast) and Japan 1.5% (0.3 percentage points higher). However, growth in Australia and New Zealand, at 2.2% and 3.5% respectively, slowed in comparison to 2016 levels (2.5% and 3.6%).

Such regional growth was supported by strengthened global demand in 2017, while exports, including intra-Asian trade, were a key driver of growth. In particular, exports rebounded in the electronics sector, which favoured states such as Malaysia and Singapore. Furthermore, Asian currencies appreciated against the US dollar in 2017, with some exceptions (for example, the Philippines and Vietnam).

In addition to exports, Japan's improved growth was due to fiscal stimulus and private consumption. Indeed, as of the second quarter of 2017, Japan was experiencing a sixth consecutive quarter of growth. Growth over six consecutive quarters had not occurred since mid-2006. Besides the intensification of global trade, China's economy was driven by continuing high levels of public investment. Higher growth in China has also helped to improve other economies in the region. For instance, Indonesia's GDP rose from 5.0% in 2016 to 5.2% in 2017, Malaysia's from 4.2% to 5.4% and Thailand's from 3.2% to 3.7%. The Philippines' slowed from 6.9% to 6.6%, but remained one of the fastest-growing economies in Asia.

Among the economies slowing down this year was India's. In November 2016, the Modi government demonetised more than 86% of the Indian currency: from 8 November, all existing 500 and 1,000 rupee notes became invalid. The rationale was to limit shadow economic activities, but the move generated disruption, constraining small businesses and the availability of credit. Another Indian reform that temporarily affected growth was the new goods and services tax, introduced in mid-2017, which was designed to unify several taxes. Nevertheless, India's GDP grew by 6.7% in 2017, following a rate of 7.1% in 2016, and was forecast to rise to 7.4% in 2018.

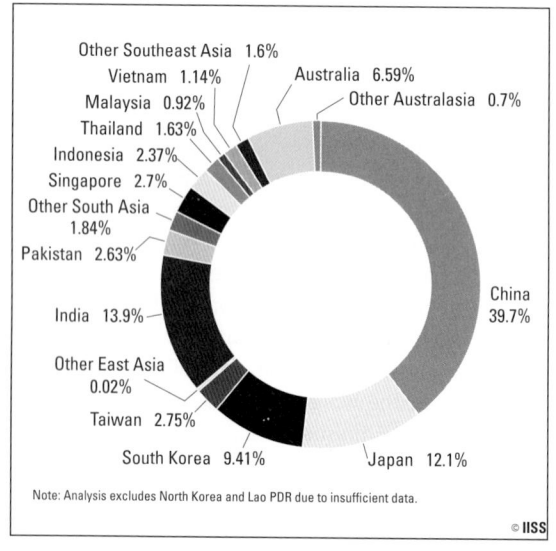

Figure 13 **Asia defence spending by country and sub-region, 2017**

- Other Southeast Asia 1.6%
- Vietnam 1.14%
- Malaysia 0.92%
- Thailand 1.63%
- Indonesia 2.37%
- Singapore 2.7%
- Other South Asia 1.84%
- Pakistan 2.63%
- India 13.9%
- Other East Asia 0.02%
- Taiwan 2.75%
- South Korea 9.41%
- Japan 12.1%
- China 39.7%
- Australia 6.59%
- Other Australasia 0.7%

Note: Analysis excludes North Korea and Lao PDR due to insufficient data.

© IISS

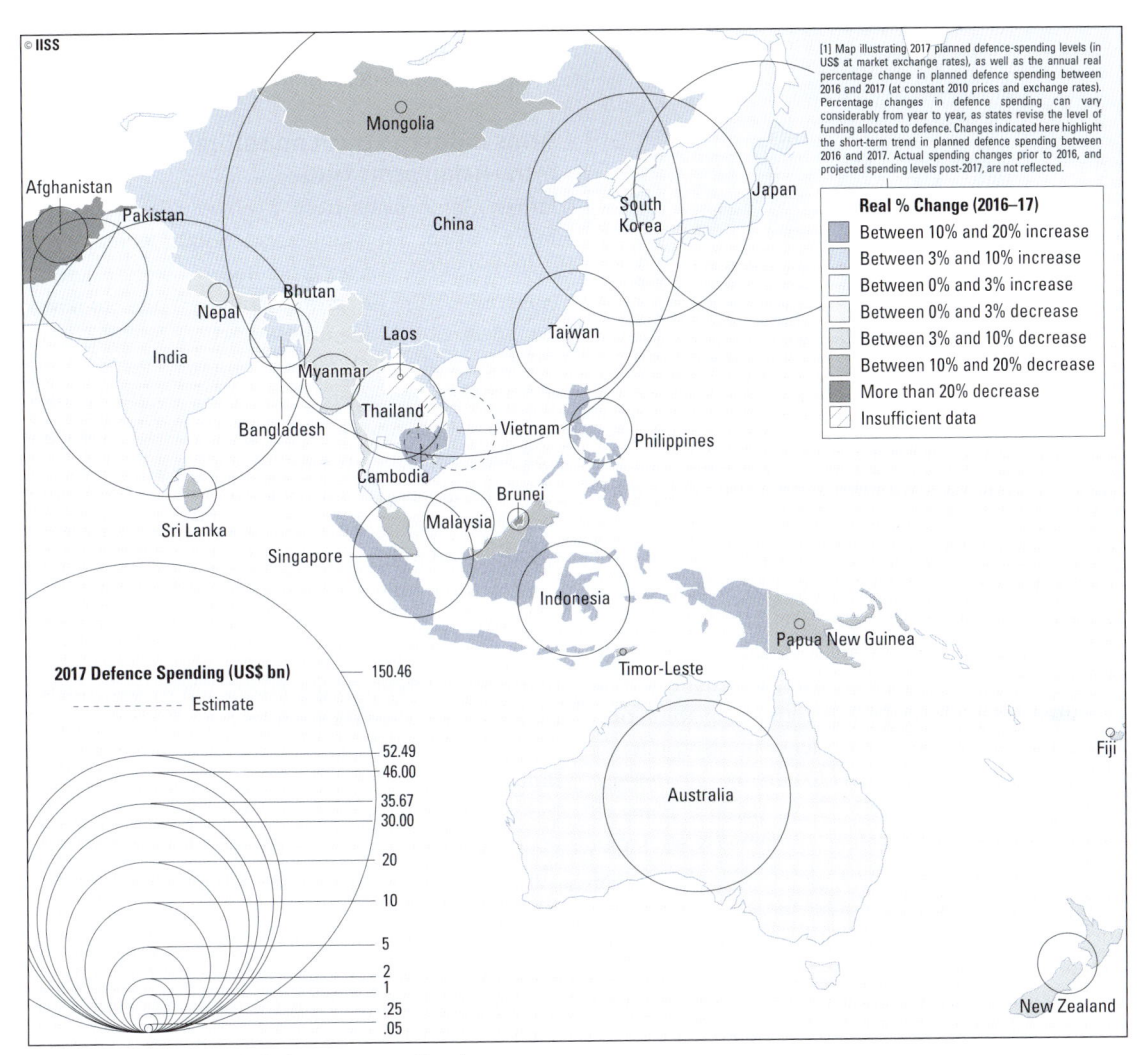

Map 5 **Asia regional defence spending**[1]

Defence budgets and procurement: responding to latent threats

This positive regional economic outlook did not automatically translate into similar rates of defence-spending growth. After several years of real-terms defence-spending growth above 5%, this slowed to 2.2% between 2016 and 2017. This did not necessarily reflect a shift of resources towards other outlays, as the share of GDP dedicated to defence within the total regional economy remained stable (1.46% in 2016 and 1.45% in 2017).

China officially earmarked RMB1.02 trillion (US$150 billion) in 2017 for defence, although this number is considered to exclude key expenses such as research and development (R&D) and arms imports. This represents a nominal increase of 7.1% compared to 2016, when China allocated RMB955bn (US$144bn) to defence. The next-largest defence spenders in Asia were India (R3.6trn, or US$52.5bn) and Japan (¥5.13trn, or US$46bn). While India's defence budget grew by 4.3% in nominal terms in 2017, this increase was mostly allocated to personnel expenses, notably pensions. Budgetary documents revealed that in 2016, as in previous years, the amount earmarked for procurement was underspent. This recurring problem hampers the Indian armed forces' modernisation goals. Furthermore, as India's personnel numbers are growing – unlike in China, where reforms are aimed at downsizing the armed forces – personnel costs are likely to continue to overtake efforts to better fund India's equipment upgrades.

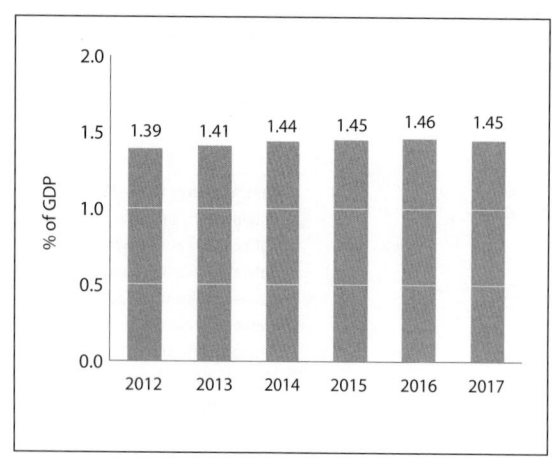

Figure 14 **Asia regional defence expenditure** as % of GDP

Year	% of GDP
2012	1.39
2013	1.41
2014	1.44
2015	1.45
2016	1.46
2017	1.45

Japan's defence budget also grew between 2016 and 2017, although only by 1.4%. The 2018 budget proposal plans a larger increase of 2.5%. This should allow the Japan Self-Defense Force to pursue several procurement plans geared at countering the North Korean threat. Notably, the defence ministry intends to acquire a land-based *Aegis* Ashore missile-defence system and advanced radar systems, and plans to upgrade its existing air-defence-radar network. Japan is also procuring three RQ-4 *Global Hawk* unmanned aerial vehicles. Facing a similar threat environment, South Korea is also bolstering its missile-defence capability. Although the US deployed its Terminal High-Altitude Area Defense missile system there in 2017, South Korea's Mid-Term Defense Program 2017–21 prioritises the Korea Air and Missile Defense programme, which will include PAC-2 and PAC-3 *Patriot* air-defence systems, L-SAM and M-SAM ground-to-air missiles and the 'Kill Chain' pre-emptive-strike system.

Another source of concern in the region, besides the North Korean threat, was China's maritime activities, which concerned nations such as Japan. Meanwhile, Indonesia attempted to improve its air and naval capabilities, despite budgeting difficulties (a decline of 11.8% between the proposed 2018 defence budget and the 2017 revised budget). Jakarta continued talks with Russia regarding the purchase of 11 Su-35 combat aircraft, and in August 2017 commissioned its first DSME-built Type-209/1400 submarine. At the same time, Malaysia's navy is pursuing its '15 to 5 Transformation Programme', under which French company Naval Group launched the country's first Gowind 2500 Littoral Combat Ship in August 2017, and an order was placed with China in April the same year for four Littoral Mission Ships.

Arms industry: push on self-reliance and intra-Asian arms trade

Fifteen Asian firms from five countries (Australia, India, Japan, Singapore and South Korea) were included in the *Defense News* 'top 100 largest defence companies' list in 2016. However, the rankings excluded China due to the lack of reliable data. China's NORINCO Group reported RMB403.8bn (US$60.8bn) in revenue in 2016, while Aviation Industry Corporation of China (AVIC) achieved RMB370.6bn (US$55.8bn) in sales the same year. These figures potentially place NORINCO and AVIC as the leading defence groups globally, ahead of Lockheed Martin and Boeing, although the proportion of their total revenue dedicated to defence is unknown.

Across the region, there were efforts to develop domestic defence-technology industrial bases (DTIBs). In third-tier defence-industrial states, reforms were focused on the institutional front. Building on existing legislation passed in 2012, Indonesia adopted new laws regarding offsets in order to increase technology transfer. The Philippines also looked to strengthen its offset mechanisms, with a new offset policy expected in 2018, while Manila also overhauled its procurement processes. Similarly, Thailand is looking to amend its procurement policy, including by revising partnership requirements with foreign firms. Bangkok published a 'Defence Industry Masterplan' intended to improve national defence-industry capabilities by 2020 and seeks to create a new agency dedicated to defence-industrial development. Southeast Asian states are also looking to foster cooperation in terms of armament procurement via the ASEAN Defence Industry Collaboration plan, but this is still at an early stage.

Meanwhile, states with more advanced DTIBs are also implementing reforms. Australia took steps to develop its domestic defence industry in 2017, notably in the shipbuilding sector, and the government launched defence R&D initiatives. The Centre for Defence Industry and Capability is overseeing two funding sources: the Next Generation Technologies Fund, which focuses on research, and the Defence Innovation Hub, which focuses on development. A$640 million (US$494m) will be allocated to the Defence Innovation Hub and A$730m

(US$564m) to the Next Generation Technologies Fund between 2017 and 2026.

Under President Tsai Ing-wen's push to develop the indigenous DTIB, Taiwan has also earmarked funding for defence innovation. In 2017, the government created a national investment company, with starting capital of NT$250m (US$8m) and a goal to raise NT$10bn (US$327m). Defence is one of the five focus sectors for this company. Furthermore, Taiwan is considering whether to set up a new department within its defence ministry modelled on the US Defense Advanced Research Projects Agency (DARPA). This comes after China announced in July 2017 the creation of a body also modelled on DARPA (see p. 233).

While many Southeast Asian countries are working to develop defence-industrial capabilities, for the time being they still rely on arms imports. In this context, China and Japan are competing to gain regional influence through arms transfers. This has accelerated since Japan relaxed its guidelines on arms exports in 2014.

For instance, Japan offered Malaysia some of its retired Lockheed Martin P-3 *Orion* anti-submarine-warfare aircraft, while China agreed to supply Littoral Mission Ships to be built in Malaysia. Meanwhile, Japan agreed to provide the Philippines with parts for its Bell UH-1 helicopters and had already supplied second-hand Beechcraft TC-90 *King Air* aircraft and vessels for the Philippines' coastguard. Tokyo provided Vietnam with six second-hand patrol vessels in 2014 and offered six more in early 2017. Japan has also pledged military aid worth US$500m in 2017–19 to Southeast Asian countries, including Vietnam and the Philippines. Further south, Japan is looking to strengthen ties with Indonesia and India, with the potential sale of – and defence-industrial cooperation regarding – US-2i amphibious search-and-rescue aircraft on the agenda.

CHINA

China's People's Liberation Army (PLA) continued to modernise its organisation, equipment and operational activities throughout 2017. Its broad-based approach has resulted in significant progress towards its goal to complete the first phase of modernisation, to blend mechanisation and informatisation, which was elaborated as one of three goals at the 19th Party Congress.

Policy developments

The range of activities observed in 2017 suggests that the PLA is on track to complete the first phase of its reform process by around 2020. As part of this, the theatre commands are being further reorganised, with new commanders already replacing those appointed in early 2016 when the theatre commands were activated. This has seen former North Sea Fleet commander Vice Admiral Yuan Yubai appointed to head the Southern Theatre Command, and Lieutenant General Li Qiaoming, formerly 41st Group Army commander, to head the Northern Theatre Command. President Xi Jinping had earlier approved multi-grade promotions, as in 2012 when General Fan Changlong rose from Jinan Military Region commander (Grade 3) to Vice Chairman of the Central Military Commission (Grade 1). This would seem to suggest that Xi is prepared to bypass established promotion processes, presumably in favour of talented and/or loyal officers.

Similar changes are already under way in terms of Central Military Commission (CMC) positions. The promotion of General Li Zuocheng to head the Joint Staff Department is notable, and not only because of the key role that the department is likely to play in the PLA. Li had previously been the inaugural head of the newly created PLA ground forces. His promotion, therefore, could be seen as underscoring the continued importance of the ground forces, despite the reorganisation's move towards joint operations and a greater emphasis on air and naval domains. However, as one of the few remaining PLA officers to have fought in the 1979 war with Vietnam, his promotion may also be intended to provide the Joint Staff Department with a leader who possesses combat experience.

Organisational reform

China's modernisation efforts in 2017 have resulted in organisational changes within the PLA, which supplement the sweeping changes announced at the end of 2015.

Complementing the PLA's new emphasis on joint operations has been the creation of a new Joint Logistics Support Force. This appears to be a series of joint facilities, established across China's new theatre commands. In September, President Xi presented flags to the commanders of the new joint logistics-support base in Wuhan, and new joint logistics-support centres in Guilin, Shenyang, Wuxi, Xining and Zhengzhou.

New CMC leadership changes

At the 19th Party Congress in Beijing in late October 2017, the Central Military Commission (CMC) was reduced from 11 to seven members, with President Xi Jinping as chairman, two vice-chairmen (seen as close allies of Xi) and four other members. Xi did not create more vice-chair positions, which would have reduced the total number of member positions. The four members of the CMC have strong ties to Xi, and are seen as rising stars with experience in military modernisation and reform. Xi will also have a stronger hand in disciplinary oversight through the appointment of Lieutenant-General Zhang Shengmin as secretary of the CMC Discipline Inspection Committee.

The first-ranked vice-chairman is General Xu Qiliang (aged 67). Xu worked with Xi in Fuzhou in the 1990s, after he became commander of the People's Liberation Army (PLA) Air Force's Eighth Army in 1989 and Xi became the city's party head in 1990. In his position as Fuzhou party head, Xi was also the Fuzhou military area's first party secretary, making Xu his direct subordinate. He is the first airforce general to be named vice-chairman, a post normally held by land-force officers – a reflection of the increasing emphasis on maritime and air capability within the PLA.

The second-ranked vice-chairman is General Zhang Youxia (also 67), who is one of the few senior military officers with combat experience. Zhang was previously the director of the CMC's Equipment Development Department and is considered by analysts to be one of Xi's most trusted allies.

The four members of the CMC are: Chief of the Joint Staff Department (appointed 2017) General Li Zuocheng (63), a combat veteran who is seen as a rising star after being named chief of the former Chengdu Military Region that borders India; Director of the Political Work Department (appointed 2017) Admiral Miao Hua, formerly political commissar of the PLA Navy; Commander of the PLA Rocket Force (appointed 2012) General Wei Fenghe (63); and Secretary of the CMC Discipline Inspection Committee Lieutenant-General Shengmin, who has a strong reformist track record, having served in several PLA departments that have seen significant reform since 2012.

One of the purposes of the new theatre commands, which replaced military regions in the PLA's 2015 reorganisation, is to effect further 'jointness' throughout the PLA. An example of this came in 2017, when control of the Southern Theatre Command passed to Vice Admiral Yubai; this was the first time that a non-ground-force commander had been appointed to lead this theatre command. Given that the Southern Theatre Command's area of responsibility includes the South China Sea, this is also the first time that a commander from outside the ground forces will oversee some of the most sensitive developments in China's security environment. This also perhaps reflects the greater importance of naval capabilities, and the maritime domain in general, in light of Beijing's Maritime Silk Road initiative, as well as the statement in the 2015 defence white paper that 'the traditional mentality that land outweighs sea must be abandoned'.

Meanwhile, the PLA's new Strategic Support Force has been steadily taking shape. Various Chinese media reports indicate that the force is integrating elements drawn from what had previously been the General Staff Department (GSD) intelligence and cyber-/network-warfare entities, including the GSD's 3rd Department (responsible for signals intelligence) and 4th Department (electronic warfare). It has also apparently absorbed many of the space capabilities that had previously resided with the General Armaments Department, and may have incorporated the political-warfare force of the previous General Political Department.

Space

The PLA Strategic Support Force (PLASSF) is responsible for Chinese military space activities, as well as electronic and network warfare. The PLASSF is arguably China's 'information warfare' force, responsible for attacking and defending not only cyber elements, but the key physical infrastructure associated with information, including space systems.

Specific Chinese military space programmes remain unclear, with the PLA providing little information about its ambitions or current satellite constellations. The 2016 Chinese space white paper, for instance, makes almost no mention of the PLA, and only obliquely references national security as a motivation for space activities. However, the white paper's discussion of major tasks over the next five years provides some possible indications of where the PLA is likely to develop greater capabilities. That said, China's nascent anti-satellite capability has been long-studied, as has Beijing's interest in directed-energy systems and micro-satellites.

The space white paper indicates that China will develop new medium-lift launch vehicles. These will probably supplement the new series of *Long March* rockets, which already include the *Long March*-5 (heavy), *Long March*-6 (light) and *Long March*-7 (medium). This recent series of rockets uses non-toxic kerosene and liquid oxygen, unlike the earlier generation, which rely on UDMH (often referred to as 'hydrazine'). Solid-fuel rockets mentioned in the text, such as the *Kuaizhou* and *Long March*-11, are associated with launches of small satellites and the rapid replenishment of various constellations.

Improving satellite networks
The space white paper also indicates that China wants to improve its space-based remote-sensing system; satellite communications; and its position, navigation and timing (PNT) satellites. Improvements to these would have military implications.

Most PLA military operations in the next decade will likely still occur near China's shores. As such, the majority of China's intelligence, surveillance and reconnaissance (ISR) requirements can be met by terrestrially based systems, including manned and unmanned aircraft and naval platforms, various types of signals intelligence, and human intelligence. However, as China seeks to operate farther afield, and the navy plans to meet potential adversary naval forces farther from its shores, it will increasingly have to call upon space-based remote-sensing platforms to provide additional early-warning capability and more precise information about force locations. Meanwhile, the ability to gather signals intelligence and electronic intelligence will be enabled by more space-based sensors, which are capable of monitoring activity on a global scale.

As PLA naval and air forces expand their footprint, including operations from Djibouti, there will be more reliance on space-based communications. There has been a steady increase in Indian Ocean deployments, as well as the now-routine counter-piracy deployments in the Gulf of Aden. If China's forces are to regularly operate in the Mediterranean and Baltic seas, the demand for greater satellite-communications support will grow even faster. There will be a similar demand for improved Chinese PNT support; China's *Beidou* satellite network provides an additional communications channel, as it has the ability to provide positioning and timing information, in addition to relaying limited data and text.

Improving infrastructure and support
The space white paper also indicates that China is prepared to make substantial investments in space-launch and space situational-awareness capabilities. The former presumably is focused on improving the new space-launch facility on Hainan Island, but might also include additional launch sites, especially for mobile solid-fuel rockets. Improvements to space situational awareness include a second-generation relay satellite system, more accurate space tracking, the incorporation of space-based tracking systems and the expansion of ground-based capabilities.

Expanding international presence

Part of the demand for increased space support is generated by China's growing global presence. China's establishment of its first official overseas military base in Djibouti attracted significant attention, but the escalating tempo of Chinese military exercises is also likely to be a consideration, as are developments associated with the Maritime Silk Road project.

Chinese naval forces have begun regular transits of the Miyako Strait separating Okinawa and the lower Ryukyus from Taiwan, involving surface ships and, sometimes, naval-aviation assets. The aircraft carrier *Liaoning* took part in one of these transits, passing through the Miyako Strait and sailing east of Taiwan before heading into the South China Sea. China's naval forces are now operating more routinely at a distance from the mainland. Whereas in 2000 China's armed forces rarely operated away from its shores, as of mid-2017, it had sustained 25 rotations of PLA Navy (PLAN) vessels conducting anti-piracy patrols off Somalia. During transit to these six-month deployments, PLAN task forces typically pay calls to a number of Indian Ocean ports for 'presence' and liaison tasks, much like the US and other navies before them.

China's maritime emphasis is matched by an increased tempo in out-of-area operations in 2017. Perhaps the most important was the formal opening of the Djibouti base, the first explicitly military facility that Chinese forces have established abroad. (China did construct facilities in Namibia and the Pacific island of Kiribati in the early 2000s, but these were to support their manned space programme; it maintains similar facilities in Kenya and Pakistan.) The facility in Djibouti is expected to support Chinese anti-piracy operations in the Gulf of Aden, but will also provide a replenishment facility for ships (and possibly, if an airstrip is constructed, aircraft) bound for the Mediterranean Sea and European waters.

In 2017, Chinese naval forces conducted exercises for the first time in the Baltic Sea. Three PLAN warships, including its newest destroyer and frigate designs, joined ten Russian vessels in the exercise *Joint Sea 2017*, which was directed from a Russian facility in Kaliningrad. This was part of a trend of closer cooperation between Chinese and Russian naval forces, which have also conducted bilateral exercises in the Mediterranean and the Pacific Ocean.

In addition to these rotations, the Chinese navy has begun a steady deployment of submarines and submarine tenders to the Indian Ocean. Indian press reports mentioned over a dozen Chinese warships in the Indian Ocean at a time during July, when tensions rose between India and China over the Doklam Plateau border, although this probably includes the Gulf of Aden task force.

All of these operations reflect not only an expanding presence in 2017, but also an indication that global activity by Chinese naval forces could soon be commonplace.

Meanwhile, PLA ground forces engaged in joint exercises with their Shanghai Cooperation Organisation (SCO) partners. Infantry forces from a number of countries were involved, drilling at PLA training facilities. In addition, the PLA dispatched a

Map 6 **China: the People's Liberation Army reorganises**

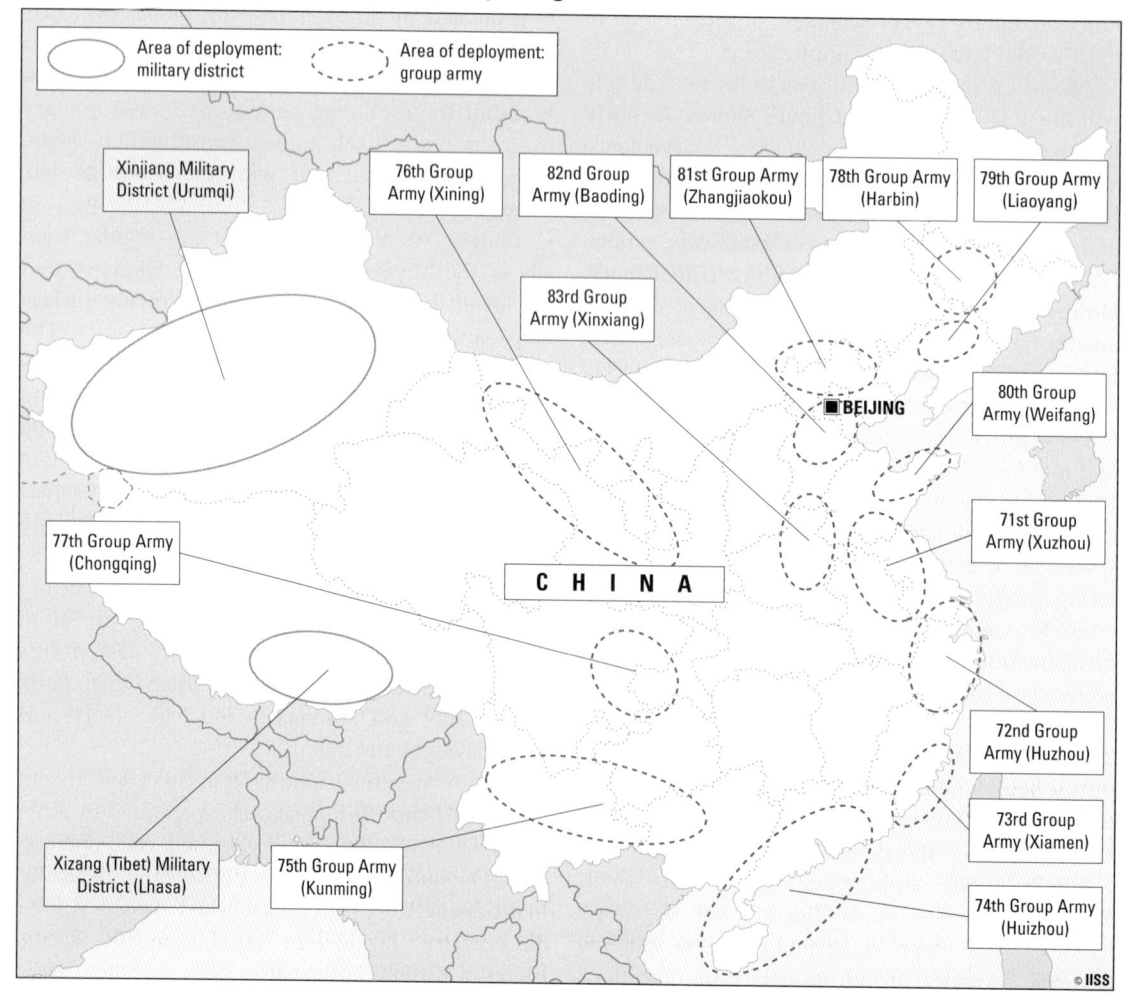

special-operations-force element to Nepal in April 2017, showing that Chinese interest in the subcontinent and Indian Ocean region is not only a maritime one.

This pattern of PLA engagements is consistent with broader Chinese interests. The PLA is used not only to indicate a military presence (and interest), but to reinforce certain messages. This includes China's efforts in countering terrorism (as reflected in Gulf of Aden anti-piracy operations), as well as humanitarian relief and international peacekeeping. At the same time, however, the PLA is gaining valuable experience in undertaking and supporting longer-range deployments and sustained operations.

People's Liberation Army

In 2017, there was a wholesale reorganisation of the PLA ground forces. Five of the existing 18 Group Armies were disbanded and the remaining 13 were renumbered. Meanwhile, significant numbers of the subordinate brigade- and divisional-level formations were reorganised, moved or disbanded in order to create a form of 'standard organisation' for the new armies.

Each group army is now assigned six 'combined arms' manoeuvre brigades: one artillery, one air-defence, one special-operations, one aviation (or, in the case of two of the Group Armies, air-assault), one engineer and chemical-defence (formed from pre-existing regiments), and one new service-support brigade. The PLA has been experimenting with combined-arms units at battalion level in exercises for years, but the establishment of them as the standard peacetime unit organisation across the board represents a radical departure from previous PLA battalion structures. The new combined brigades reportedly have two fewer manoeuvre battalions than their predecessors, but the surviving battalions appear to have doubled in effective size. In the heavy brigades at least, these combined-arms battalions appear to resemble a previous mechanised infantry battalion supplemented by tank companies and a 122mm artillery company.

Most of the divisions that had survived previous waves of 'brigadisation' have now been folded into new brigades – only the 112th Mechanised Division near Beijing remains, albeit with its subordinate battalions converted to combined-arms units. The status of the non-group army-assigned formations in Tibet and Xinjiang is currently unclear; it is probable that some of the divisions previously based in Xinjiang are also still extant.

Effectively, the manoeuvre forces of the PLA ground forces have changed from around 19 divisions and 76 brigades at the end of 2016 to around five divisions and 81 brigades at the end of 2017. Allowing for the organisational and battalion-size changes, this represents only about a 10% reduction in their overall force size. This reduction has, to some extent, been balanced by an increase in the number of special-operations and aviation/air-assault brigades, enabling each group army, as well as the forces in Tibet and Xinjiang, to have one brigade of each.

The final impact that these force-structure changes will have on the equipment holdings of the army remains to be seen. Some of the older tanks and artillery pieces may now be surplus to requirements and therefore will be transferred to reserve units, sold or scrapped. Otherwise, the PLA generally continues to take delivery of the range of armoured vehicles and artillery pieces that it has received for the past decade.

People's Liberation Army Rocket Force

Following its elevation to full service level, the People's Liberation Army Rocket Force (PLARF) has issued new military-unit cover designators (MUCDs) to all of its subordinate formations, indicating that it has also undergone some internal reorganisation and restructuring, The previous six missile bases (51 to 56) remain extant, but have been reprioritised and renumbered (now 61 to 66). Whilst most missile brigades remain subordinate to the same base as they were in 2016, several have been reassigned, and some may also have been rebased. The overall force size of the PLARF appears largely unchanged, for now, but at least four newly issued MUCDs in the same range as the existing missile brigades suggest that an expansion might be planned for the near future.

Any expansion plans might be linked to the status of a number of new ballistic-missile variants (and possibly one new type altogether) currently in test or being deployed with the PLARF. At least one, and possibly more, new versions of the DF-16 short- or medium-range ballistic missile are now in service with the existing DF-16-equipped brigades at Shaoguan, and possibly Shangrao. A newly modified version of the DF-31A intercontinental ballistic missile (ICBM) (CH-SS-10 mod 2), with the designation DF-31A(G), and a new transporter-erector-launcher were seen on exercise in 2017. This new missile is possibly the same weapon previously reported in the United States as DF-31B, and is believed to have entered service with one of the existing DF-31A brigades. The follow-on DF-41 (CH-SS-X-20) ICBM remains in test for now, although if the PLARF is indeed forming new missile brigades it is possible that one of them is intended to bring this new type into service.

People's Liberation Army Air Force: continuing reorganisation

In late November 2015, at the Work Conference on Reform of the CMC, changes were announced by President Xi, chairman of the CMC, to the organisational structure of the People's Liberation Army Air Force (PLAAF). These changes, formally implemented in January 2016, included reforms at PLAAF headquarters; the reduction from seven military regions (MRs) and military region air forces (MRAFs) to five theatre commands (TCs) and theatre command air forces (TCAFs); and changes at the unit (corps and below) level, with particular focus on new air brigades and the Airborne Corps. All of these moves are linked to the overall reduction by 300,000 personnel (half officers and half other ranks), across the whole of the PLA, that was planned to be completed by the end of 2017.

Overall, the PLAAF has reorganised and downsized the PLAAF headquarters and each TCAF headquarters. It has also upgraded several more air regiments and all of its airborne regiments to brigades and abolished several air-division headquarters and the airborne-division headquarters. It reportedly also renamed the 15th Airborne Corps simply as the PLA Airborne Corps, but it is still subordinate to the PLAAF. It has also created several bases from former command posts that are now responsible for all of the aviation, surface-to-air missile, anti-aircraft artillery and radar units in their area of responsibility (AOR).

PLAAF headquarters
The overall organisational structure of the PLAAF headquarters, whose grade was renamed from MR leader to TC leader, has essentially not changed. While several subordinate-organisation names and sizes have changed, their grades have remained the same. Specifically, the former Headquarters Department has become the 'Staff Department', and the Political Department has become the 'Political Work Department', both of which are TC deputy-leader-grade organisations. The Logistics Department and Equipment Department, each of which has a director and political commissar, have not changed their names and they remain corps leader-grade organisations.

As a general rule, with the exception of the General Office and the Military Theory Research Department, all previous second-level administrative and functional organisations (under the four first-level departments) are now bureaus and retain their division-leader grade, while all third-level bureaus have been renamed 'divisions', with the grade of regiment leader, or were merged or abolished. As a result, every first-, second- and third-level organisation has been reduced in size by up to a half.

The number of deputy commanders has been reduced from five, in 2013, to three, while the number of deputy political commissars has been reduced from three to one, with the addition of a Secretary of the Discipline Inspection Commission/Committee. In terms of responsibilities, the PLAAF headquarters is now solely responsible for 'pursuing the Air Force's construction', while command responsibilities have been shifted down to the five TCAFs. In addition, unlike his predecessors since 2004, the new commander of the PLAAF, Lieutenant General Ding Laihang, has not been added as a member of the Central Military Commission.

Theatre command headquarters
Under the reorganisation, unlike the previous MR headquarters, each TC headquarters has one PLAAF officer as a permanent deputy commander. The TCAF commanders, like their predecessors, serve concurrently as TC deputy commanders.

Theatre command air force headquarters
On 3 February 2016, the PLAAF held an official ceremony in Beijing, where then air-force commander Ma Xiaotian inaugurated all five TCAF headquarters, granting them the grade of TC deputy leader. (Ma was replaced as PLAAF commander by Lieutenant General Ding Laihang in August 2017, though Ma remained on the CMC until he retired in October.) The new headquarters replace five of the former MRAF headquarters: Eastern TCAF is in Nanjing (formerly Nanjing MRAF headquarters), Southern TCAF is in Guangzhou (formerly Guangzhou MRAF headquarters), Western TCAF

is in Chengdu (formerly Chengdu MRAF headquarters), Northern TCAF is in Shenyang (formerly Shenyang MRAF headquarters) and Central TCAF is in Beijing (formerly Beijing MRAF headquarters). The former Jinan and Lanzhou MRAF headquarters were downsized and became corps deputy-leader-grade bases in mid-2017. However, the two former commanders became permanent deputy commanders of the Central and Western TCs, respectively.

Since the new TCAF headquarters were formed, each now has a Staff Department (formerly Headquarters Department) and Political Work Department (formerly Political Department) with the grade of corps leader, a Logistics Department with a director and political commissar (no change) and an Equipment Department with a director and political commissar (no change) with the grade of corps deputy leader. All second-level organisations under the first-level departments are still divisions and have retained the same grade of division deputy leader, but they have been reduced in size. Some third-level branches may exist as battalion-leader-grade organisations, and have either been abolished or merged with other organisations. It is also possible that some third-level branches may exist.

In addition, each TCAF headquarters has only one or two deputy commanders and one or two deputy political commissars compared to the previous MRAFs, which had between two and five deputy commanders and two deputy political commissars. As in the Theatre Command headquarters, it is probable that one of the deputy commanders may also concurrently serve as the chief of staff (e.g. director of the Staff Department) and one deputy political commissar may concurrently serve as the director of the Political Work Department.

Air brigades
In late 2011 and 2012, the PLAAF merged its existing seven division-leader-grade flight colleges into three flight colleges, upgraded them to corps deputy-leader grade and created subordinate training brigades out of existing regiments. It also abolished at least four air-division headquarters, created four corps deputy-leader-grade bases (at Dalian, Nanning, Shanghai and Urumqi) from existing command posts, and upgraded about 15 regiments to brigades and subordinated them under the four bases.

This situation remained constant until late 2016 or early 2017, when the PLAAF created several more fighter and ground-attack brigades from existing regiments and created at least seven more corps deputy-leader-grade bases (Datong, Fuzhou, Jinan, Kunming, Lanzhou, Lhasa and Wuhan) from existing corps deputy-leader- and division-leader-grade command posts and two former MRAF HQs, each of which is most likely subordinate to its respective TC Air Force HQ. At the time of writing, the PLAAF had not abolished its bomber divisions or its three transport divisions or converted their subordinate regiments to brigades. It is not clear if this will happen in the future. The air force has also apparently created at least two unmanned-aerial-vehicle brigades, but it is not clear to whom they are subordinate. In addition, each TC Air Force now has one subordinate transport and search-and-rescue brigade to support disaster-relief efforts; these brigades are equipped with Z-8 and Mi-171 helicopters, and reportedly also Y-5 and Y-7 fixed-wing aircraft. (It is worth noting that when a regiment is upgraded to a brigade, every 'commanding officer' billet (i.e. all officers except staff officers) are also upgraded.)

Airborne Corps
In April 2017, the PLAAF reportedly held a ceremony to abolish the Airborne Corps' three existing airborne divisions (43rd, 44th and 45th) and to upgrade their six subordinate airborne regiments to brigades, and created a special-operations force brigade. In addition, the PLAAF upgraded the corps' existing transport regiment to a brigade. To date, it still has a single helicopter regiment; however, the regiment headquarters might be abolished and its battalion-leader-grade flight groups may be subordinated under the transport brigade.

Other issues
In 2016, the PLAAF and TCAF headquarters transitioned from a first-level Headquarters Department and Political Department to a Staff Department and Political Work Department, respectively. In 2017, each of the PLA's 84 main-body corps leader- and deputy-leader-grade organisations, including the PLAAF's Airborne Corps and bases noted above, also began to make the transition. As a result, the next likely step will be to see a transition at the division, brigade and regiment levels. When that takes place, the regiment level will have

a Political Work Division, not a Department, which will match the current Political Work Division at that level.

Hypersonic weapons and unmanned vehicles
The extent of Chinese research into hypersonic technologies has become increasingly clear. At the 21st AIAA International Space Planes and Hypersonics Technologies Conference, jointly sponsored by Chinese and US institutions, it was apparent that China had a wide range of engineering programmes examining hypersonic boost-glide vehicles and scramjet-engine technologies.

People's Liberation Army Navy

In late 2016 and early 2017, the aircraft carrier *Liaoning* carried out its most extensive deployment to date, including a first live-fire exercise in the Bohai Sea and its first flying operations in the South China Sea. In April, after a rapid construction period, China launched its first indigenously built carrier at Dalian shipyard. The new vessel is an evolutionary development of the *Liaoning*, which was itself purchased as an incomplete hull from Russia. The new vessel is believed to have larger hangar space, which might allow for a larger air wing, as well as more deck space and a modified island-superstructure design. A second ship should be available for service in about 2020.

The PLAN is moving from a situation in which its nascent carrier force has only a training and experimentation role, to one that yields a limited regional power-projection capability. This will also allow for an incremental increase in the navy's ability to operate independently at range in the next few years.

To reinforce these developments, China launched its first Type-055 cruiser-size surface combatant on 28 June, with at least three more under construction. These sophisticated vessels will further enhance the PLAN's potential in task-group and long-range independent operations. Likely displacing over 10,000 tonnes, they are the largest warships (bar aircraft and helicopter carriers and amphibious ships) launched from Asian shipyards since the Second World War. The commissioning of two Type-052D destroyers, two Type-054A frigates and seven Type-056A corvettes continued the consolidation and modernisation of the PLAN's surface forces. Meanwhile, in August, the first of the new Type-901 fast-replenishment ships, which at 40,000 tonnes is the largest yet for the PLAN, was commissioned. The month before, the second vessel of the class was launched.

The first of the new Type-093A *Shang* II-class nuclear-powered attack/guided-missile submarines began operating from Yalong Bay on Hainan Island by late 2017. However, the observed presence of all four Type-094 *Jin*-class nuclear-powered ballistic-missile submarines (SSBNs) in port at the same base earlier in the year suggests that the PLAN is not operating them on a continuous at-sea basis. It is not clear what production at Bohai shipyard has shifted to since the completion of the Type-093A batch. The US Department of Defense currently expects the next-generation SSBN (Type-096) to begin production in the early 2020s, a view supported by the missile-test Type-032 submarine undergoing modification work likely associated with a new submarine-launched ballistic-missile programme (believed to be JL-3) in early 2017. Production of the conventionally powered Type-039B *Yuan* II-class submarines has increased, but, for now, the priority appears to be modernisation rather than the expansion of the PLAN's submarine force.

As China continues to expand the capabilities of its coastguard with larger and more capable vessels, the second of its 10,000-tonne *Zhaotou*-class cutters undertook its first official patrol in the South China Sea in May (the first began deploying to the East China Sea in 2015).

August saw the formal opening of China's first overseas support base, at Djibouti, with plans for further development, including a new pier to accept vessels of up to 40,000 tonnes, also being unveiled. The PLAN also undertook its first joint exercise with Russia in the Baltic Sea (although this was not the PLAN's first deployment to the Baltic).

This ongoing effort to develop China's maritime capabilities, coupled with its expanding maritime operations in the Indian Ocean and elsewhere, indicates that Beijing is taking seriously the idea that its future security has a major maritime component. This is consistent with past directives from leaders such as Hu Jintao, more recently reinforced under Xi, which have made preserving China's maritime interests a 'new historic mission' for the PLA.

DEFENCE ECONOMICS

China's defence economy flourished in President Xi Jinping's first five-year term (2012 to 2017), and its prospects look similarly bright in his second term. The building of defence and civil–military science, technology and industrial capabilities intersect two of Xi's most prized policy priorities: strengthening China's defence capabilities and making innovation the primary locomotive of China's long-term development.

In October 2017, at the 19th Chinese Communist Party Congress, Xi spelled out his vision and time frame for turning China into a militarily powerful and technologically advanced country. China should, he said, reach the first tier of the world's most innovative countries by 2035 and, at the same time, the defence establishment would realise its objective of becoming a fully modernised, information-enabled force. By the middle of the century, China would challenge for global leadership, with its world-class armed forces a centrepiece of the country's national power.

Xi laid out some of the key steps required to achieve these ambitious goals: 'strengthen unified leadership, top-level design, reform, innovation, and the implementation of major projects; reform the defence science and technology industry; achieve greater civil–military integration; and build an integrated national strategic system and capabilities'. Xi's statement encapsulates many of the key initiatives that the defence authorities are implementing in their efforts to transition the Chinese defence economy from 'catching up' to innovating at the global frontier.

Reorganising the defence science and technology system

A far-reaching reorganisation of the top echelons of the Chinese defence science and technology system, especially the military component, has been under way since the beginning of 2016. The People's Liberation Army's (PLA's) armament system has been restructured into two distinct parts, in order to carry out Xi's dual requirement of accelerating the pace of development and the fielding of conventional armaments, while at the same time pursuing more advanced, higher-risk and longer-term research and development (R&D) in next-generation technologies.

Reform to the acquisition system for conventional weapons saw the PLA General Armament Department transformed into the Central Military Commission Equipment Development Department (CMC-EDD) in January 2016. The emphasis of the new body is on joint development programmes rather than the ground-forces focus of its predecessor.

A more significant overhaul has taken place in the management of the R&D of more strategic, cutting-edge or revolutionary capabilities with the establishment of the CMC Science and Technology Commission (CMC-STC), which was set up at the same time as the CMC-EDD. When the CMC-STC was unveiled, there was considerable speculation in Chinese and foreign media that it was modelled on the US Defense Advanced Research Projects Agency (DARPA). Indeed, there are similarities in the functions of the CMC-STC and DARPA, for instance they both actively engage with civilian universities to support basic research.

However, there are also important differences that suggest the Chinese approach in conducting disruptive innovation is distinctive from the US model. A key variance is that the CMC-STC is tightly integrated into the PLA hierarchy, with a two-star lieutenant-general in charge, whereas DARPA enjoys considerable autonomy by being outside of the uniformed chain of command. A CMC science-research steering committee has also been established to provide technical and strategic guidance to the CMC-STC.

These institutional developments demonstrate a clear commitment by the Chinese military authorities to engage seriously in higher-end, home-grown innovation, research and development.

Implementing major projects

The defence industry's relentless pace of output was maintained in 2017. Naval shipbuilders launched several high-profile projects including China's first indigenously built aircraft carrier in April 2017, and the first Type-055 cruiser-size surface combatant in June 2017. Both ships will likely take at least another two to three years to be fitted out before they are ready for operational service. Meanwhile, the aviation industry began low-rate production of the J-20 fighter aircraft.

The development pipeline for major weapons and dual-use projects appears to be full. This includes a larger and more advanced aircraft carrier, a new generation of nuclear submarines, ballistic-missile defence and satellite-navigation systems, next-generation exascale extremely high-performance computers and quantum-communications technology.

Defence-industry reform

The Chinese defence industry has posted robust annual growth in profits and revenues for the past 15 years. This continued into 2017, but the government is nonetheless seeking to implement major reforms to overcome deep-rooted structural bottlenecks caused by the industry's central-planning legacy.

One important reform initiative in 2017 was a pilot project to overhaul the ownership structure of wholly state-owned defence-research institutes and academies so they could list on the stock market. This would provide a lucrative source of capital since research institutes make up a significant proportion of defence corporations' fixed-asset stock. Defence companies have been engaged in this process, known as asset securitisation, since 2013 and have raised more than US$30 billion from initial public offerings and other financial vehicles, which has been reinvested into product development including weapons activities. Forty-one research institutes were part of the first batch to undergo ownership reform, a considerable number of which had come from the country's two principal space and missile corporations (China Aerospace Science and Technology Corp. and China Aerospace Science and Industry Corp.).

Another reform initiative, launched around the same time, was to establish a series of innovation centres located within the defence corporate-research system that would become critical centralised hubs to drive advanced original R&D in their industrial sectors. Ten of these system-design innovation centres have so far been established, the most prominent of which are in the missile, naval and aviation sectors.

Efforts also resumed in 2017 to consolidate the line-up of leading state-owned defence conglomerates with the merger of the two principal firms in the nuclear sector: China National Nuclear Corp. and China Nuclear Engineering and Construction Company. Each of the six sectors that make up the Chinese defence industry (aviation, aerospace and missiles, nuclear, shipbuilding, electronics and ordnance/land equipment) is controlled by one or two of the country's big ten state-owned defence conglomerates. Efforts to promote competition in the late 1990s by dividing these monopolistic giants into two competing entities failed badly because of poor institutional design.

Consequently, the Chinese authorities have been examining the possibility of once again merging these firms, especially so that they can compete with much larger foreign firms on the global arms and technology markets. The shipbuilding industry may be next in line for restructuring, as one of its two dominant conglomerates, China State Shipbuilding Corp., has been adversely affected by a sharp downturn in the global civilian-shipbuilding market. The company was the only one of the country's big ten defence corporations to post losses in the past couple of years.

Civil–military integration

Efforts to seriously push civil–military integration (CMI) began in 2015 when it was made a national priority. These efforts received further impetus in January 2017 with the formation of the Commission for Integrated Civilian–Military Development (CICMD). The importance of this organisation in leading CMI implementation was made clear with the appointment of President Xi as its chair and Premier Li Keqiang as a vice-chair. Xi presided over two CICMD meetings in June and September 2017 that laid out long-term strategic guidelines and development plans.

At the CICMD's June meeting, Xi said that there was a 'short period of strategic opportunity' to implement CMI, pointing out that the most fruitful areas included infrastructure, equipment procurement, training, military logistics and defence mobilisation. In its September meeting, the CICMD issued a series of plans and guidelines (tied to the 13th Five Year Plan) on CMI, defence-industrial development and military-logistics CMI.

In the creation of a working CMI system, the CMC-EDD is playing the lead role by setting up the critical mechanisms to allow for the two-way flow of goods, services and technologies between the civilian and defence sectors through market competition. It announced in February 2017 that it was in the process of setting up an acquisition system that would allow for the open sharing of procurement information, a robust market-pricing mechanism, an intellectual-property protection system, a contract-fulfilment supervision system, and a standards system for military and civilian products. If successful, this CMI acquisition system would represent a major improvement on the existing defence-acquisition system, which lacks fundamental capabilities such as pricing functions. The CMC-EDD said that it would solicit more than 800 research and technology development projects worth around RMB6bn (US$883 million) using this new CMI acquisition system.

Funding

In 2017, and for the second year in a row, the official Chinese defence budget received a single-digit increase of only 7.1%, which meant that total expenditures exceeded RMB1 trillion (US$147bn) for the first time to reach RMB1.02trn (US$150bn). This is equivalent to 1.26% of GDP, although many categories of defence spending are not included in the official Chinese defence budget, such as research and development and foreign-arms acquisitions. With the 2016 budget increasing by 7.6% over 2015, this suggests that the new normal rate of Chinese defence-budget growth is around 7% – a marked decline from the annual double-digit increases of the previous 25 years.

To fund the significant pick-up in the pace of China's defence-technological development and industrialisation, the authorities are looking to non-government sources, especially corporate and market inputs. Besides the asset-securitisation initiative, another new fundraising channel to emerge in the past few years has been investment funds established by a consortium of state and private companies. Over the past few years, more than 30 defence- and dual-use-related investment vehicles have been publicly established. They include the RMB150bn (US$22bn) China Innovation Fund and RMB30bn (US$4.4bn) Sino CMI Industry Development Fund, both led by China Aerospace Investment Holdings, one of China's big ten defence corporations.

TAIWAN

Cross-Strait relations entered a new period of uncertainty following the election of Tsai Ing-wen of the Democratic Progressive Party (DPP) in January 2016. Despite Tsai's commitment to maintaining the 'status quo' in the Taiwan Strait, Beijing has regarded her policies, particularly the refusal to acknowledge the so-called '1992 consensus', as evidence of a pro-independence agenda and therefore justification for increasing political and military pressure on the island nation. All-time-low support in Taiwan for unification with China, the failure of the 'one country, two systems' formula in Hong Kong and an intensifying crackdown on civil society in China have also contributed to tensions by increasing resistance to China within Taiwanese society. These tensions come as China, under President Xi Jinping, becomes more assertive and expansive in its territorial claims within the region, placing Taiwan amid a surge in People's Liberation Army (PLA) activity in the East and South China seas.

China, which claims sovereignty over Taiwan, is the island nation's sole credible external threat. In the past year, China's armed forces have greatly increased the frequency of their activity north and south of Taiwan, through the Miyako Strait and Bashi Channel respectively, to conduct exercises in the western Pacific. PLA aircraft, including H-6K bombers, have crossed into Taiwan's air-defence identification zone, forcing the scramble of interceptors. China's aircraft carrier, *Liaoning*, has also transited the Taiwan Strait and sailed by Taiwan's east coast. Besides exposing Taiwan to attacks on several fronts, and notwithstanding the fact that such transits are part of China's 'natural' push beyond the 'first island chain', this increased military activity has allowed the PLA to familiarise itself with the environment surrounding Taiwan, which will be crucial in any Taiwan Strait military contingency.

As Taiwan's Ministry of National Defense (MND) stated in its 2017 Quadrennial Defense Review (QDR), China's 'obvious improvement in military operational capabilities, by expediting military organisational reform and maintaining R&D [research and development] on advanced arms and their conversions, is the major factor that affects security in the Taiwan Strait'. Following a reorganisation, multi-year double-digit growth in defence spending and improved training, the PLA now possesses sufficient capabilities to impose a blockade on Taiwan and conduct multidimensional operations to seize its offshore islands (Kinmen, Matsu and Penghu). Improvements to the PLA Rocket Force in terms of manoeuvrability, accuracy and lethality now give China the ability to conduct precision strikes against political, military and economic high-value targets across Taiwan. Additionally, the PLA has deployed capabilities to achieve 'multi-layered firepower, joint air defence, anti-missile operations', and can now achieve 'air supremacy west of the first island chain', which greatly complicates Taiwan's security environment.

With some US analysts arguing that Taiwan would now need to hold on for as much as a month before the US armed forces could intervene during a military confrontation in the Taiwan Strait – up from what was previously a two-day wait – Taipei's security challenge has become all the more daunting. Besides making preparations for countering limited strikes, embargoes or an amphibious assault, Taiwan's armed forces also play a major role in humanitarian assistance and disaster relief in a region that is prone to typhoons and earthquakes.

Bolstering defence capability

Responding to the 'complex regional strategic environment and multiple security challenges', Taiwan's MND has adopted a strategy of 'resolute defence' and 'multi-domain deterrence' to create a military force 'capable of delivering deterrence and defence to keep the enemy at bay'. Overarching this is a strategy built on five pillars: 'Safeguard the Nation', 'Cultivate a Professional Military', 'Realise Defence Self-Reliance', 'Protect the People's Wellbeing' and 'Strengthen Regional Stability'.

As in the past, Taiwan continues to rely on the US security umbrella, particularly the provisions of the Taiwan Relations Act, which aims to ensure Taipei has the capabilities it needs to defend itself against external aggression through a foreign military sales (FMS) programme. The latest US arms package for Taiwan, announced in late June 2017 and which ended a period of 562 days since the last package, included the Standard Missile-2 (SM-2) Block IIIA, MK 54 Lightweight Torpedo conversion kits, the MK48 Mod 6 Advanced Technology Heavyweight Torpedo, the AGM-154C Joint Standoff Weapon air-to-ground missile and the AGM-88B High-Speed Anti-Radiation Missile.

Given uncertainties surrounding the future role of the US armed forces in the region, and added to the additional challenges posed by China's growing anti-access/area-denial capabilities, Taiwan has taken a more proactive approach in order to bolster its defence self-reliance by prioritising the indigenous development of various platforms. It is also increasingly relying on an asymmetrical 'counterforce' capability, as well as its own area-denial capabilities in the Taiwan Strait. Although economics are undoubtedly a factor in this decision, uncertainty over Washington's continued willingness to sell advanced weapons systems to Taiwan, and the refusal of other states to do so, has also been a rationale for this shift.

Taiwan has, therefore, embarked on a multi-year Indigenous Defense Submarine programme, in which a total of eight diesel-electric submarines are to be produced to supplement its two combat-ready *Hai Lung*-class submarines, a major endeavour that is likely to require assistance from other countries. It is also developing and producing a variety of fast-attack vessels, a new-generation frigate and high-speed minelayers, as well as automated coastal-defence systems (the 'Tan An' Coastal Defense Rocket System and the XTR-102 system, which employs two T-75 20mm automatic guns), which will likely be deployed on its outlying islands as well as on Taiping (Itu Aba) in the South China Sea. Taiwanese road-mobile anti-ship missiles (*Hsiung Feng* III) and land-attack cruise missiles (*Hsiung Feng* IIE), as well as various air-to-ground missiles procured from the US or produced domestically, constitute the main elements of Taiwan's counterforce capability. Greater emphasis is now also being placed on anti-radiation missiles and unmanned aerial vehicles (UAVs) – unveiled at the 2017 Taipei Aerospace & Defense Technology Exhibition and ostensibly based on Israel's IAI *Harop* – to target Chinese radar sites.

Meanwhile, Taiwan's first domestically produced satellite, *Formosat*-5, was successfully launched on 24 August 2017. Developed by a consortium led by the National Space Organisation, the satellite will provide two-metre panchromatic and four-metre multispectral resolution images, which, according to the government, will have a national-security application.

Bringing improvements to air defence and the survivability of fixed early-warning radar systems remains a priority for the Taiwanese armed forces, which currently rely on US-made *Patriot* PAC-2/-3 and domestically produced *Tien Kung* surface-to-air missile systems for the first line of defence against missile and air attack from China. Some US analysts have begun arguing in favour of Taiwan's procurement of the road-mobile Terminal High-Altitude Area Defense (THAAD) system deployed in South Korea. However, given China's reaction to the deployment of this in South Korea, its possible reaction to any Taiwanese purchase is likely to weigh heavily on any procurement decision.

In addition to ongoing upgrades to its fleet of 145 F-16A/B fighter aircraft and mid-life upgrades to the F-CK-1 *Ching Kuo* fighter/ground-attack aircraft, Taiwan has embarked on a programme to develop 66 new jet trainers to replace its legacy AT-3 trainer, produced by Aerospace Industrial Development Corp. In August 2017, Taiwan also announced it would submit a 'Letter of Request' to the US for the F-35 Joint Strike Fighter, though the likelihood that such a request will succeed remains slim, and Taiwan will probably have to consider developing its own four-and-a-half-/fifth-generation aircraft, admittedly with US assistance.

In light of the current geostrategic environment, Taipei has also redoubled efforts to form closer ties with Tokyo, which is also locked in a territorial dispute with Beijing in the East China Sea over the Senkaku/Diaoyu islands. The prospect of the PLA seizing control of Taiwan, and the consequences of such an outcome for Japan's security, have also contributed to greater willingness on the part of Shinzo Abe's government to explore opportunities for cooperation with Taiwan. However, contact has largely occurred behind the scenes and cooperation remains constrained by Japan's constitution, as well as its need to avoid further destabilising its relations with China.

Amid efforts to refine its force structure, Taiwan's defence ministry is now aiming for a military force characterised by 'organisational flexibility, flattened command and control [and] full jointness across services'. Among other things, this includes implementing a single chain of command for air defence and improvements in, and integration of, major command-and-control – as well as intelligence, surveillance and reconnaissance – centres. Throughout, emphasis has been placed on joint operational training, with increased responsibility for theatres of operations to ensure operational readiness.

Upon entering office, President Tsai made it clear that she intended to allocate a larger share of the defence budget to improve conditions, salaries and benefits for members of the armed forces. Furthermore, to improve military professionalism for the active forces, the MND has established a Graduate Institute of Chinese Military Affairs Studies and Leadership Excellence Course, and will eventually offer PhD courses on Strategic Security and Defence Management. The ministry is also seeking to improve interactions between members of the armed forces and civilians by recruiting 'specialists in defence affairs' from the civilian sector. At the same time, a campaign has been launched to improve the public image of the military – a long-standing handicap in Taiwan, in part due to its history of martial law – through stricter military discipline and more interactions with civilians. Such efforts are intended to improve morale, which suffered under the Ma Ying-jeou administration; and to bolster recruitment rates, a long-term challenge since an all-volunteer-force programme was launched in 2013. Minister of National Defense Feng Shih-kuan announced in December 2016 that compulsory military service could end in 2018, as planned, if the ministry succeeds in recruiting enough volunteer soldiers and officers, adding that recruitment had increased steadily.

However, Taiwan's reserve force remains under-trained, underprepared and underutilised, with serious doubt as to its ability to muster should it be called upon to defend the nation. Revisions to the reservist-mobilisation policy have been made to promote voluntary short-term active duty, with emphasis on reservists with 'high-demand military occupational specialties', and technical and combat skills. Reserve units of retired volunteer-service members will also now be combined with regular forces to enhance the skills base. More regular training is being considered, and a mobilisation-information system is planned to be set up to manage recall messages and quickly assemble Taiwan's reserve forces.

Taiwan faces a growing cyber threat from China and has for several years been a principal target of Chinese cyber attacks. To combat this, Taiwan's Executive Yuan upgraded its Office of Information and Communication Security on 1 August 2016 and created a Department of Cyber Security (DCS). Serving as a strategic centre for national information security, the DCS also manages cyber security throughout the government. The DCS will also look to increase cooperation with the private sector, among other initiatives. Additionally, on 29 June 2017 the MND launched its Information and Electronic Warfare Command, which will work in conjunction with the National Chung-Shan Institute of Science and Technology (NCSIST) to defend Taiwan's digital territory.

Defence economics

As stated in the MND's 2017 QDR, the armed forces will 'seek to obtain a reasonable and adequate defence budget appropriate to national budget allocations, and allocate and manage these resources appropriately'.

In August 2017, the Tsai administration announced it would seek NT$331.8 billion (US$10.8bn) for national defence for 2018, a 3.9% year-on-year increase on the 2017 budget and the largest share of the nation's total budget (16.71%) for any government agency. Of this amount, NT$151.8bn (US$4.9bn), or 46% of the total, will be allocated to personnel costs, an increase of 5% on the previous year. Although this means reductions in other areas – including NT$7.3bn (US$238m) less for equipment acquisition

– the reallocation is intended to help remedy long-standing issues relating to morale and preparedness, and to help boost recruitment rates. The 2018 budget will continue to fall short of 3% of GDP, which is regarded by Washington as the 'baseline' for Taiwan to demonstrate its commitment to national defence. The Tsai government has nevertheless indicated that it will seek a more substantial increase for the next year.

Although marginal compared with China's official defence budget, which at RNB1.022 trillion (US$150bn) in 2017 is in US dollars about 14 times that of Taiwan, the Tsai government's ability to reach the 3% benchmark would nevertheless be a small victory given the country's relatively sluggish economy (GDP growth for 2018 is expected to be 1.9%) and other major infrastructure and social-welfare projects that require substantial investment. That success, which Tsai's predecessor never achieved, is in part attributable to growing consciousness among the Taiwanese public of the challenge from China. This has become less abstract in recent years amid increased PLA activity in the region and growing pressure on Taiwan under President Xi.

While personnel costs account for 46% of the total open defence budget, military investments (including acquisitions) account for an estimated 30%, followed by more than 20% for operations and maintenance.

If reformers win the argument, Taiwan's long-standing FMS procurement process with the US could also undergo revisions, including the 'de-packaging' of arms sales to ensure a more streamlined acquisition mechanism and a more timely delivery of necessary defence articles.

Defence industry

Despite the slightly smaller share of the defence budget allocated to acquisitions, local companies are expected to benefit from the Tsai administration's greater focus on the indigenous development and production of defence articles for Taiwan. These include Aerospace Industrial Development Corp., which is developing the new jet trainer; CSBC Corp., which is responsible for the Indigenous Defence Submarine and a variety of surface combatants; the Ordnance Readiness Development Centre (ORDC), which produces various armoured vehicles; and the semi-private NCSIST, which produces missiles, UAVs and other platforms.

Taiwan has 'national champions' in the defence sector for the land, air and sea services. For the land sector, the ORDC and the Armaments Bureau under the MND are the key developers of land platforms and ammunition for the army. The ORDC is the manufacturer of the CM-32 *Yunpao* armoured vehicle, the CM-21 armoured infantry fighting vehicle (an indigenous design based on the US M113 armoured personnel carrier) and self-propelled howitzers. More recently, the ORDC has been developing the M1 *Cloud Leopard* II armoured fighting vehicle. Besides providing ammunition to the Taiwanese armed forces, the Armaments Bureau's 205th Factory is also a major producer of ammunition for the US armed forces. The ORDC and Armaments Bureau rely on a number of local contractors (Chung Hsin Electric and Machinery Manufacturing Corp., Yi Rong Technology Co., Wei Shuan Co. and Chi Fu Industry among them) for various parts.

Of all three, the land sector is the one that has the least international positioning and exposure in Taiwan's defence-manufacturing sector. However, as the Tsai government tries to revitalise Taiwan's defence industry, and the related private sector, some foreign defence manufacturers have been exploring the possibility of co-developing and -manufacturing various land platforms, including a new main battle tank, though there has been no progress so far.

For the naval sector, the national champion is CSBC Corporation. Headquartered in Kaohsiung, southern Taiwan, with shipyards in Kaohsiung and in Keelung in northern Taiwan, CSBC Corp. is a former state-owned enterprise that develops and manufactures various sea vessels for civilian and military use, including fast-attack boats, transport ships, support vessels, guided-missile frigates and coast-guard ships. CSBC has been awarded the contract to oversee, through its Submarine Development Center, the Taiwan Indigenous Defense Submarine programme, whose success will be contingent on collaboration with various foreign defence manufacturers. Other smaller players include Lung Teh Shipbuilding, manufacturer of the *Tuo Jiang*-class corvette, and Ching Fu Shipbuilding Co.

Taiwan's leading aircraft designer for the military and civilian sector is the Aerospace Industrial Development Corp. (AIDC). AIDC is the designer of the F-CK-1 *Ching Kuo* combat aircraft and, through a memorandum of understanding with Lockheed Martin, has been awarded the contract to complete upgrades on Taiwan's F-16A/Bs. It is also the developer of the soon-to-be-retired AT-3 trainer and has been awarded the contract to develop a second-generation trainer for the Taiwan Air Force.

However, Taiwan's real national defence-industry champion is the Taoyuan-based NCSIST, the state's main defence-research institute, with facilities at various locations in northern and southern parts of the country. Among other things, the NCSIST produces the *Tien Kung* (I, II and III) air-defence system, the *Tien Chien* (I, II) air-to-air missile, the *Antelope* air-defence system, *Hsiung Feng* (I, II and III) anti-ship cruise missiles, the *Hsiung Feng* IIE land-attack cruise missile, the *Wan Chien* stand-off air-to-ground cruise missile, the *Ray-Ting* 2000 artillery multiple-launch rocket system, UAVs and various automated coastal-defence systems.

Under its defence-industrial development strategy, Taiwan is focusing on the three key fields of aerospace, shipbuilding and information security. This will be accomplished by incorporating capacities in the private sector, supervised by a 'technology management mechanism' aimed at developing indigenous weapon systems and lifecycle support with 'critical and advanced technologies', and by leading the development of relevant industries, with the purpose of 'attaining mutual support between national defence and economic development'.

For the information-security sector, the government will push for R&D on new-generation technologies by forming a strategic alliance with industry, academia and the research sector, as well as establishing national information-security test and training facilities. The Taiwanese government has also said it will improve counter-espionage measures to ensure information integrity and prevent the proliferation of dual-use technologies from its programmes. These efforts will also be crucial in securing foreign participation in Taiwan's defence-related projects amid active attempts by China to compromise the island's defence architecture and likely also discredit it in the eyes of potential allies.

Afghanistan AFG

New Afghan Afghani Afs		2016	2017	2018
GDP	Afs	1.32tr	1.44tr	
	US$	19.5bn	21.1bn	
per capita	US$	582	572	
Growth	%	2.4	2.5	
Inflation	%	4.4	6.0	
Def bdgt [a]	Afs	176bn	148bn	
	US$	2.59bn	2.17bn	
US$1=Afs		67.86	68.19	

[a] Security expenditure. Includes expenditure on Ministry of Defence, Ministry of Interior, Ministry of Foreign Affairs, National Security Council and the General Directorate of National Security. Also includes donor funding

Population 34,124,811

Ethnic groups: Pashtun 38%; Tajik 25%; Hazara 19%; Uzbek 12%; Aimaq 4%; Baluchi 0.5%

Age	0–14	15–19	20–24	25–29	30–64	65 plus
Male	20.8%	6.0%	5.3%	4.2%	13.2%	1.2%
Female	20.1%	5.8%	5.1%	4.1%	12.8%	1.4%

Capabilities

The Afghan National Defence and Security Forces (ANDSF) are still building capability to counter ISIS, the Taliban and other insurgent and terrorist groups. The ANDSF largely succeeded in countering major insurgent attacks in 2017, but the government lost control of some rural territory and the force was tested by Taliban activity. The forces continue to suffer a high attrition rate due to casualties and desertions. Insurgent forces retain significant influence in rural areas, also demonstrating their ability to conduct spectacular attacks in population centres. Although at the tactical level the Taliban has often overmatched the army and police, they have eventually been able to organise tactical- and operational-level counter attacks. Army and police special forces are well regarded by NATO and bear the brunt of intelligence-led strike operations against insurgent networks. NATO advisers remain embedded in the defence and interior ministries, although the ANDSF are now responsible for the majority of training, albeit with NATO support. Indigenous logistic support is slowly improving but remains a source of weakness. Efforts are also under way to improve leadership, intelligence, logistics and coordination between different service arms. An 'ANDSF Road Map' contains ambitious plans to improve capability, but depends on continued international funding. In August 2017, a new US strategy for Afghanistan was announced, which would increase US troop levels and is expected to include additional tactical advisers and trainers and increase air and artillery strikes.

ACTIVE 174,300 (Army 167,000 Air Force 7,300)
Paramilitary 148,700

ORGANISATIONS BY SERVICE

Afghan National Army (ANA) 167,00
5 regional comd

FORCES BY ROLE
SPECIAL FORCES
1 spec ops div (1 (National Mission) SF bde (1 SF gp; 1 mech inf bn (2 mech inf coy)); 2 cdo bde (1 mech inf coy, 4 cdo bn); 1 (1st MSF) mech bde (2 mech inf bn); 1 (2nd MSF) mech bde (3 mech inf bn))

MANOEUVRE
Light
1 (201st) corps (3 inf bde (4 inf bn, 1 sy coy, 1 cbt spt bn, 1 CSS bn), 1 inf bde (3 inf bn, 1 sy coy, 1 cbt spt bn, 1 CSS bn), 1 engr bn, 1 int bn, 2 MP coy, 1 sigs bn)
1 (203rd) corps (2 inf bde (5 inf bn, 1 sy coy, 1 cbt spt bn, 1 CSS bn), 2 inf bde (4 inf bn, 1 sy coy, 1 cbt spt bn, 1 CSS bn), 1 engr bn, 1 int bn, 2 MP coy, 1 sigs bn)
1 (205th) corps (4 inf bde (4 inf bn, 1 sy coy, 1 cbt spt bn, 1 CSS bn), 1 engr bn, 1 int bn, 2 MP coy, 1 sigs bn)
2 (207th & 209th) corps (1 div HQ (209th only) 3 inf bde (4 inf bn, 1 sy coy, 1 cbt spt bn, 1 CSS bn), 1 engr bn, 1 int bn, 2 MP coy, 1 sigs bn)
1 (215th) corps (3 inf bde (4 inf bn, 1 sy coy, 1 cbt spt bn, 1 CSS bn), 1 inf bde (2 inf bn, 1 cbt spt bn, 1 CSS bn), 1 engr bn, 1 int bn, 2 MP coy, 1 sigs bn)
1 (111st Capital) div (1 inf bde (1 tk bn, 1 mech inf bn, 2 inf bn, 1 sy coy, 1 cbt spt bn, 1 CSS bn), 1 inf bde (4 inf bn, 1 sy coy, 1 cbt spt bn, 1 CSS bn), 1 int bn)

EQUIPMENT BY TYPE
ARMOURED FIGHTING VEHICLES
  MBT 20 T-55/T-62 (24 more in store†)
  APC 996
    APC (T) 173 M113A2†
    APC (W) 623 MSFV (inc variants)
    PPV 200 Maxxpro
ENGINEERING & MAINTENANCE VEHICLES
  ARV 20 Maxxpro ARV
  MW Bozena
ARTILLERY 775
  TOWED 109: **122mm** 85 D-30†; **155mm** 24 M114A1†
  MOR 82mm 666: 521 2B14†; 105 M-69†; 40 M252†

Afghan Air Force (AAF) 7,300
Including Special Mission Wing

EQUIPMENT BY TYPE
AIRCRAFT 19 combat capable
  TPT 47: **Medium** 4 C-130H Hercules; **Light** 42: 24 Cessna 208B; 18 PC-12 (Special Mission Wing); **PAX** 1 B-727 (2 more in store)
  TRG 19 EMB-314 Super Tucano* (of which 7 in the US for trg)
HELICOPTERS
  ATK 4 Mi-35 Hind
  MRH 102: 3 Cheetal; 25 MD-530F (11 armed); 74 Mi-17 Hip H (incl 28 Special Mission Wing hel)
  TPT • Medium 4 UH-60A+ Black Hawk

Paramilitary 148,700

Afghan National Police 148,700

Under control of Interior Ministry. Includes Afghan Uniformed Police (AUP), Afghan National Civil Order Police (ANCOP), Afghan Border Police (ABP), Police Special Forces (GDPSU) and Afghan Anti-Crime Police (AACP)

FOREIGN FORCES

All *Operation Resolute Support* unless otherwise specified
Albania 83
Armenia 121
Australia 270; 1 SF unit; 1 sy unit; 1 sigs unit
Austria 9
Azerbaijan 94
Belgium 60
Bosnia-Herzegovina 55
Bulgaria 160
Croatia 94
Czech Republic 267; 1 sy coy; 1 MP unit
Denmark 100
Estonia 6
Finland 37
Georgia 870; 1 lt inf bn • UNAMA 2 obs
Germany 980; 1 bde HQ; 1 recce bn; 1 hel ft with CH-53G *Stallion*; 1 ISR UAV flt with *Heron* UAV • UNAMA 1 obs
Greece 4
Hungary 110
India Indo-Tibetan Border Police 335 (facilities protection)
Italy 1,037; 1 mtn inf bde HQ; 1 mtn inf regt(-); 1 avn regt(-) with AW129 *Mangusta*; CH-47 *Chinook*; NH90
Latvia 22
Lithuania 29
Luxembourg 1
Mongolia 120 • UNAMA 1 obs
Montenegro 18
Netherlands 100
New Zealand 10
Norway 50
Poland 220 • UNAMA 1 obs
Portugal 10 • UNAMA 2 obs
Romania 683 • UNAMA 4 obs
Slovakia 40
Slovenia 7
Spain 16
Sweden 25
Turkey 659; 1 mot inf bn(-)
Ukraine 10
United Kingdom 500; 1 inf bn(-)
United States 7,000; 1 div HQ; 1 div HQ (fwd); 1 spec ops bn; 2 AB bde; 1 EOD bn; 1 cbt avn bde; F-16C *Fighting Falcon*; MC-12W *Liberty*; RC-12X *Guardrail*; EC-130H *Compass Call*, C-130 *Hercules*, AH-64 *Apache*; CH-47 *Chinook*; UH-60 *Black Hawk*; HH-60 *Pave Hawk*; RQ-7B *Shadow*; MQ-1 *Predator*; MQ-9 *Reaper* • *Operation Freedom's Sentinel* 8,000

Australia AUS

Australian Dollar A$		2016	2017	2018
GDP	A$	1.70tr	1.80tr	
	US$	1.26tr	1.39tr	
per capita	US$	51,737	56,135	
Growth	%	2.5	2.2	
Inflation	%	1.3	2.0	
Def bdgt	A$	31.7bn	32.3bn	34.6bn
	US$	23.6bn	25.0bn	
US$1=A$		1.34	1.30	

Population 23,232,413

Age	0–14	15–19	20–24	25–29	30–64	65 plus
Male	9.1%	3.1%	3.5%	3.6%	23.3%	7.5%
Female	8.6%	3.0%	3.3%	3.5%	22.7%	8.6%

Capabilities

Australia possesses capable, well-trained and -equipped armed forces, with strong doctrine, logistic support, C4ISR and the capacity for deployment over long distances. They also have considerable recent operational experience. Canberra's primary ally remains the United States, but it is also forging closer defence ties with India, Japan and South Korea, while remaining committed to the Five Power Defence Arrangements in Southeast Asia and close defence relations with New Zealand. In March 2016, the government published Australia's third defence white paper in seven years. This identified China's growing regional role, regional military modernisation and inter-state rivalry, the threat of terrorism from the Middle East and cyber attacks as important influences shaping Australia's defence policy. The defence of Australia, securing maritime Southeast Asia and the Pacific, and contributing to stability and the 'rules-based order' across the wider Indo-Pacific region are the country's three main 'defence objectives'. The Australian Defence Force (ADF) continued to be involved in the Middle East training Iraq's security forces and in the counter-ISIS coalition. The government has promised to increase the defence budget to 2% of projected GDP by 2020–21, enabling the procurement of high-end equipment. The white paper confirmed that Australia is still committed to buying 72 F-35A Joint Strike Fighters, and that from the early 2020s the air force will also acquire MQ-4C *Triton* unmanned aerial vehicles for maritime reconnaissance. In the meantime, deliveries of P-8A maritime-patrol aircraft began in late 2016.

ACTIVE 57,800 (Army 29,000 Navy 14,400 Air 14,400)

RESERVE 21,100 (Army 13,200 Navy 3,150 Air 4,750)

Integrated units are formed from a mix of reserve and regular personnel. All ADF operations are now controlled by Headquarters Joint Operations Command (HQJOC)

ORGANISATIONS BY SERVICE

Space
EQUIPMENT BY TYPE
SATELLITES • COMMUNICATIONS 1 *Optus* C1 (dual use for civil/mil comms)

Army 29,000

Forces Command
FORCES BY ROLE
COMMAND
  1 (1st) div HQ (1 sigs regt)
MANOEUVRE
  Mechanised
  1 (1st) mech inf bde (1 armd cav regt, 1 mech inf bn, 1 lt mech inf bn, 1 arty regt, 1 cbt engr regt, 1 sigs regt, 1 CSS bn)
  2 (3rd & 7th) mech inf bde (1 armd cav regt, 2 mech inf bn, 1 arty regt, 1 cbt engr regt, 1 sigs regt, 1 CSS bn)
  Amphibious
  1 (2nd RAR) amph bn
  Aviation
  1 (16th) avn bde (1 regt (2 ISR hel sqn), 1 regt (3 tpt hel sqn), 1 regt (2 spec ops hel sqn, 1 avn sqn))
COMBAT SUPPORT
  1 (6th) cbt spt bde (1 STA regt (1 STA bty, 1 UAV bty, 1 CSS bty), 1 AD/FAC regt (integrated), 1 engr regt (2 construction sqn, 1 EOD sqn), 1 EW regt, 1 int bn)
COMBAT SERVICE SUPPORT
  1 (17th) CSS bde (3 log bn, 3 med bn, 1 MP bn)

Special Operations Command
FORCES BY ROLE
SPECIAL FORCES
  1 (SAS) SF regt
  1 (SF Engr) SF regt
  2 cdo regt
COMBAT SUPPORT
  3 sigs sqn (incl 1 reserve sqn)
COMBAT SERVICE SUPPORT
  1 CSS sqn

Reserve Organisations 13,200 reservists

Force Command
FORCES BY ROLE
COMMAND
  1 (2nd) div HQ
MANOEUVRE
  Reconnaissance
  3 (regional force) surv unit (integrated)
  Light
  6 inf bde (total: 3 recce regt, 3 recce sqn, 12 inf bn, 6 arty bty)
COMBAT SUPPORT
  3 cbt engr regt
  1 sigs regt

COMBAT SERVICE SUPPORT
  6 CSS bn

Special Operations Command
FORCES BY ROLE
SPECIAL FORCES
  1 cdo regt
EQUIPMENT BY TYPE
ARMOURED FIGHTING VEHICLES
  MBT 59 M1A1 *Abrams*
  IFV 253 ASLAV-25 (all variants)
  APC • APC (T) 431 M113AS4
  AUV 1,030: 1,020 *Bushmaster* IMV; 10 *Hawkei*
ENGINEERING & MAINTENANCE VEHICLES
  ARV 45: 15 ASLAV-F; 17 ASLAV-R; 13 M88A2
  VLB 5 *Biber*
  MW 20: 12 *Husky*; 8 MV-10
ANTI-TANK/ANTI-INFRASTRUCTURE
  MSL • MANPATS FGM-148 *Javelin*
  RCL • 84mm *Carl Gustav*
ARTILLERY 239
  TOWED 155mm 54 M777A2
  MOR 81mm 185
RADAR • LAND 33: 3 *Giraffe*; 30 LCMR
AMPHIBIOUS 15 LCM-8 (capacity either 1 MBT or 200 troops)
HELICOPTERS
  ATK 22 *Tiger*
  TPT 105: **Heavy** 10 CH-47F *Chinook*; **Medium** 72: 38 NH90 TTH (MRH90 TTH); 34 S-70A *Black Hawk*; **Light** 23 Bell 206B1 *Kiowa*
UNMANNED AERIAL VEHICLES
  ISR • Medium 15 RQ-7B *Shadow* 200
AIR DEFENCE • SAM • Point-defence RBS-70

Navy 14,400
Fleet Comd HQ located at Sydney. Naval Strategic Comd HQ located at Canberra
EQUIPMENT BY TYPE
SUBMARINES • TACTICAL • SSK 6 *Collins* with 6 single 533mm TT with Mk48 *Sea Arrow* ADCAP HWT/UGM-84C *Harpoon* AShM
PRINCIPAL SURFACE COMBATANTS 12
DESTROYERS • DDGHM 1 *Hobart* with *Aegis* Baseline 7.1 C2, 2 quad lnchr with RGM-84D *Harpoon* AShM, 6 8-cell Mk41 VLS with SM-2 Block IIIB SAM/RIM-162 ESSM SAM, 2 twin 324mm ASTT with MU90 LWT, 1 *Phalanx* CIWS, 1 127mm gun (capacity 1 MH-60R *Seahawk*)
FRIGATES • FFGHM 11
  3 *Adelaide* (Mod) with 1 Mk13 GMLS with RGM-84C *Harpoon* AShM/SM-2 MR SAM, 1 8 cell Mk41 VLS with RIM-162 ESSM SAM, 2 triple Mk32 324mm ASTT with MU90 LWT, 1 *Phalanx* Block 1B CIWS, 1 76mm gun (capacity 2 S-70B *Seahawk* ASW hel/MH-60R *Seahawk* ASW hel))
  8 *Anzac* (GER MEKO 200) with 2 quad Mk141 lnchr with RGM-84C *Harpoon* Block 2 AShM, 1 8 cell Mk41 VLS with RIM-162 ESSM SAM, 2 triple 324mm ASTT with MU90 LWT, 1 127mm gun (capacity 1 S-70B *Seahawk* ASW hel) (capability upgrades in progress)

PATROL AND COASTAL COMBATANTS 14
    PCO 14: 13 *Armidale* (*Bay* mod); 1 *Cape* (leased)
MINE WARFARE • MINE COUNTERMEASURES •
MHO 6 *Huon* (of which 2 in reserve)
AMPHIBIOUS
    PRINCIPAL AMPHIBIOUS SHIPS 3
        LHD 2 *Canberra* (capacity 8 hel; 4 LCM; 100 veh; 1,000 troops)
        LSD 1 *Choules* (UK *Bay*) (capacity 1 med hel; 2 LCVP; 24 MBT; 350 troops)
    LANDING CRAFT 17
        LCM 12 LCM-1E
        LCVP 5
LOGISTICS AND SUPPORT 14
    AGHS 2 *Leeuwin* with 1 hel landing platform
    AGS 4 *Paluma*
    AORH 1 *Success*
    AOR 1 *Sirius*
The following vessels are operated by a private company, DMS Maritime:
    ASR 2: 1 *Besant*; 1 *Stoker*
    AX 2: 1 *Seahorse Horizon*; 1 *Seahorse Standard*
    AXL 1 *Seahorse Mercator*
    AXS 1 *Young Endeavour*

Naval Aviation 1,350

FORCES BY ROLE
ANTI SUBMARINE WARFARE
    1 sqn with NH90 (MRH90)
    1 sqn with MH-60R *Seahawk*
TRAINING
    1 OCU sqn with MH-60R *Seahawk*
    1 sqn with AS350BA *Ecureuil*; Bell 429; H135
EQUIPMENT BY TYPE
HELICOPTERS
    ASW 24 MH-60R *Seahawk*
    TPT 25: **Medium** 6 NH90 (MRH90); **Light** 19: 4 Bell 429; 15 H135

Clearance Diving Branch

FORCES BY ROLE
SPECIAL FORCES
    2 diving unit

Air Force 14,400

Flying hours   175 hrs/yr on F/A-18 *Hornet*

FORCES BY ROLE
FIGHTER/GROUND ATTACK
    3 sqn with F/A-18A/B *Hornet*
    1 sqn with F/A-18F *Super Hornet*
    1 sqn (forming) with F-35A *Lightning* II
ANTI SUBMARINE WARFARE
    1 sqn with AP-3C *Orion*
    1 sqn (forming) with P-8A *Poseidon*
ELECTRONIC WARFARE
    1 sqn with EA-18G *Growler*
ISR
    1 (FAC) sqn with PC-9/A(F)
AIRBORNE EARLY WARNING & CONTROL
    1 sqn with B-737-700 *Wedgetail* (E-7A)
TANKER/TRANSPORT
    1 sqn with A330 MRTT (KC-30A)
TRANSPORT
    1 VIP sqn with B-737BBJ; CL-604 *Challenger*
    1 sqn with Beech 350 *King Air*
    1 sqn with C-17A *Globemaster* III
    1 sqn with C-27J *Spartan*
    1 sqn with C-130J-30 *Hercules*
TRAINING
    1 OCU with F/A-18A/B *Hornet*
    1 sqn with Beech 350 *King Air*
    2 (LIFT) sqn with *Hawk* MK127*
EQUIPMENT BY TYPE
AIRCRAFT 163 combat capable
    FGA 98: 55 F/A-18A *Hornet*; 16 F/A-18B *Hornet*; 24 F/A-18F *Super Hornet*; 3 F-35A *Lightning* II (in test)
    ASW 20: 15 AP-3C *Orion*; 5 P-8A *Poseidon*
    EW 12 EA-18G *Growler**
    AEW&C 6 B-737-700 *Wedgetail* (E-7A)
    TKR/TPT 5 A330 MRTT (KC-30A)
    TPT 49: **Heavy** 8 C-17A *Globemaster* III; **Medium** 20: 8 C-27J *Spartan*; 12 C-130J-30 *Hercules*; **Light** 16 Beech 300 *King Air*;
    PAX 5: 2 B-737BBJ (VIP); 3 CL-604 *Challenger* (VIP)
    TRG 105: 33 *Hawk* Mk127*; 62 PC-9/A (incl 4 PC-9/A(F) for tgt marking); 10 PC-21
RADAR • AD RADAR 7
    OTH-B 3 *Jindalee*
    Tactical 4 AN/TPS-77
AIR-LAUNCHED MISSILES
    AAM • IIR AIM-9X *Sidewinder* II; ASRAAM; **ARH** AIM-120B/C-5/C-7 AMRAAM
    AShM AGM-84A *Harpoon*
    LACM Conventional AGM-158 JASSM
BOMBS
    Laser-guided *Paveway* II/IV; Laser JDAM
    INS/GPS-guided AGM-154C JSOW; JDAM; JDAM-ER

Paramilitary

Maritime Border Command

Has responsibility for operational coordination and control of both civil and military maritime-enforcement activities within Australia's EEZ. At any one time, between 5 and 7 *Armidale*-class patrol boats and 2 AP-3C *Orion* aircraft are also assigned

EQUIPMENT BY TYPE
PATROL AND COASTAL COMBATANTS 14
    PSO 2: 1 *Ocean Protector* with 1 hel landing platform; 1 *Ocean Shield* with 1 hel landing platform
    PCO 10: 1 *Thaiyuk*; 1 *Triton* (leased) with 1 hel landing platform; 8 *Cape*
    PCC 2 *Bay*
AIRCRAFT • TPT • Light 10 DHC-8
HELICOPTERS • TPT 2: **Medium** 1 Bell 214; **Light** 1 AS350 *Ecureuil*

Cyber

The Australian Cyber Security Centre was officially opened on 27 November 2014 and brings cyber-security capabilities from across the Australian government into a single location. On 21 April 2016, the Australian Government Cyber Security Strategy was launched. During the launch, the government publicly announced Australia's offensive cyber capabilities to respond to cyber intrusions against Australian networks. This capability is housed in the Australian Signals Directorate (ASD) and this public recognition brings Australia in line with international partners who have already announced their capability. The 2016 Defence White Paper acknowledged the importance of cyber security to the future of Australia's security environment and announced growth for the ASD's cyber capabilities. An Information Warfare Division was formed in July 2017, and comes under the Joint Capabilities Group of the Australian Defence Force Headquarters. The division consists of four separate branches: Information Warfare Capability, C4 and Battle Management Capability, Capability Support Directorate and the Joint Cyber Unit and will be responsible for offensive and defensive cyber operations. The Armed Forces are also recruiting skilled reservists to boost ADF cyber capability.

DEPLOYMENT

AFGHANISTAN
NATO • ISAF *Operation Resolute Support (Highroad)* 270; 1 SF unit; 1 sy unit; 1 sigs unit

ARABIAN SEA
Combined Maritime Forces • CTF-150 1 FFGHM

EGYPT
MFO (*Operation Mazurka*) 25

IRAQ
Operation Inherent Resolve (Okra) 380; 1 SF gp; 1 trg unit

MALAYSIA
120; 1 inf coy (on 3-month rotational tours); 2 AP-3C *Orion* (on rotation)

MIDDLE EAST
UN • UNTSO 11 obs

SOUTH SUDAN
UN • UNMISS 23; 1 obs

UNITED ARAB EMIRATES
Operation Accordion 400: 1 tpt det with 2 C-130J-30 *Hercules*
Operation Inherent Resolve (Okra) 300; 1 FGA det with 6 F/A-18A *Hornet*; 1 B-737-700 *Wedgetail* (E-7A); 1 A330 MRTT (KC-30A)

FOREIGN FORCES
New Zealand 9 (air navigation trg)
Singapore 230: 1 trg sqn at Pearce with PC-21 trg ac; 1 trg sqn at Oakey with 12 AS332 *Super Puma*; AS532 *Cougar*
United States US Pacific Command: 1,250; 1 SEWS at Pine Gap; 1 comms facility at NW Cape; 1 SIGINT stn at Pine Gap • US Strategic Command: 1 detection and tracking radar at Naval Communication Station Harold E. Holt

Bangladesh BGD

Bangladeshi Taka Tk		2016	2017	2018
GDP	Tk	18.4tr	20.9tr	
	US$	228bn	250bn	
per capita	US$	1,414	1,532	
Growth	%	7.2	7.1	
Inflation	%	5.7	5.7	
Def bdgt	Tk	207bn	232bn	258bn
	US$	2.56bn	2.78bn	
FMA (US)	US$	2m	2m	0m
US$1=Tk		80.76	83.54	

Population 157,826,578

Religious groups: Muslim 90%; Hindu 9%; Buddhist 1%

Age	0–14	15–19	20–24	25–29	30–64	65 plus
Male	14.1%	5.0%	4.6%	4.1%	18.4%	2.9%
Female	13.6%	4.9%	4.7%	4.4%	19.8%	3.3%

Capabilities

Bangladesh has a limited military capability optimised for border and domestic security, and its forces have shown themselves capable of mobilising and deploying quickly to tackle internal-security tasks. Autumn 2017 saw the army deployed to the country's eastern border to provide humanitarian assistance to Rohingya refugees fleeing Myanmar. The armed forces reportedly retain extensive business interests, in real estate, banks and other businesses. Counter-terrorism operations increased following a July 2016 attack. A major naval-recapitalisation and expansion programme is under way, in order to protect the country's large EEZ. In the recent past, Bangladesh has relied on Chinese and Russian aid and credit to overcome its limited procurement funding. It has increased defence collaboration with India. A requirement for modern howitzers has been announced. Substantial efforts have been made to strengthen a nascent shipbuilding industry, and work has begun on a new submarine-support facility. The country has a long record of UN peacekeeping deployments, with UN payments reportedly providing an important income source.

ACTIVE 157,050 (Army 126,150 Navy 16,900 Air 14,000) **Paramilitary 63,900**

ORGANISATIONS BY SERVICE

Army 126,150
FORCES BY ROLE
COMMAND
 9 inf div HQ
SPECIAL FORCES
 1 cdo bn
MANOEUVRE
 Armoured
 1 armd bde
 3 indep armd regt

Light
23 inf bde
1 (composite) bde
COMBAT SUPPORT
9 arty bde
1 engr bde
1 sigs bde
AVIATION
1 avn regt (1 avn sqn; 1 hel sqn)
AIR DEFENCE
1 AD bde
EQUIPMENT BY TYPE
ARMOURED FIGHTING VEHICLES
MBT 276: 174 Type-59; 58 Type-69/Type-69G; 44 Type-90-II (MBT-2000)
LT TK 8 Type-62
RECCE 8+ BOV M11
APC 476
  APC (T) 134 MT-LB
  APC (W) 342: 325 BTR-80; 17 Cobra
ENGINEERING & MAINTENANCE VEHICLES
AEV MT-LB
ARV 3+: T-54/T-55; Type-84; 3 Type-654
VLB MTU
ANTI-TANK/ANTI-INFRASTRUCTURE
MSL • MANPATS 9K115-2 Metis M1 (AT-13 Saxhorn-2)
RCL 106mm 238 M40A1
ARTILLERY 853+
SP 155mm 12 NORA B-52
TOWED 363+: 105mm 170 Model 56 pack howitzer; 122mm 131: 57 Type-54/54-1 (M-30); 20 Type-83; 54 Type-96 (D-30), 130mm 62 Type-59-1 (M-46)
MRL 122mm 6 (PRC)
MOR 472: 81mm 11 M29A1; 82mm 366 Type-53/type-87/M-31 (M-1937); 120mm 95 AM-50/UBM 52
RADAR • LAND 2 SLC-2 (arty)
AMPHIBIOUS • LANDING CRAFT 3: 1 LCT; 2 LCVP
AIRCRAFT • TPT • Light 7: 1 C295; 5 Cessna 152; 1 PA-31T Cheyenne
HELICOPTERS
MRH 2 AS365N3 Dauphin
TPT 6: **Medium** 3 Mi-171Sh **Light** 3 Bell 206L-4 Long Ranger
AIR DEFENCE
SAM
  Short-range FM-90
  Point-defence QW-2; HN-5A (being replaced by QW-2)
GUNS • TOWED 166: 37mm 132 Type-65/74; 57mm 34 Type-59 (S-60)

Navy 16,900
EQUIPMENT BY TYPE
SUBMARINES • TACTICAL • SSK 2 Nabajatra (ex-PRC Ming Type-035G) with 8 single 533mm TT
PRINCIPAL SURFACE COMBATANTS • FRIGATES 5
  FFGHM 1 Bangabandhu (ROK modified Ulsan) with 2 twin lnchr with Otomat Mk2 AShM, 1 octuple HQ-7 SAM, 2 triple 324mm TT with A244 LWT, 1 76mm gun (capacity: 1 AW109E hel)
  FFG 3:
    2 Abu Bakr (ex-PRC Jianghu III) with 2 twin lnchr with C-802A AShM, 2 RBU 1200 A/S mor, 2 twin 100mm gun
    1 Osman (ex-PRC Jianghu I) with 2 quad lnchr with C-802 (CH-SS-N-8 Saccade) AShM, 2 RBU 1200 A/S mor, 2 twin 100mm gun
  FF 1 Umar Farooq† (UK Salisbury – trg role) with 3 Squid A/S Mor, 1 twin 115mm gun
PATROL AND COASTAL COMBATANTS 50
  CORVETTES 6
  FSGM 2 Shadhinota (PRC C13B) with 2 twin lnchr with C-802 AShM, 1 octuple FL-3000N lnchr with HHQ-10 SAM, 1 76mm gun, 1 hel landing platform
  FSG 4:
    2 Durjoy with 2 twin lnchr with C-704 AShM, 1 76mm gun
    2 Bijoy (ex-UK Castle) with 2 twin lnchr with C-704 AShM, 1 76mm gun, 1 hel landing platform
  PSOH 2 Somudra Joy (ex-USCG Hero) with 1 76mm gun, hel landing platform
  PCFG 4 Durdarsha (ex-PRC Huangfeng) with 4 single lnchr with HY-2 (CH-SS-N-2 Safflower) AShM
  PCO 6: 1 Madhumati (Sea Dragon) with 1 57mm gun; 5 Kapatakhaya (ex-UK Island)
  PCC 8:
    2 Meghna with 1 57mm gun (fishery protection)
    1 Nirbhoy (ex-PRC Hainan) with 4 RBU 1200 A/S mor; 2 twin 57mm gun
    5 Padma
  PBFG 5 Durbar (PRC Hegu) with 2 single lnchr with SY-1 AShM
  PBFT 4 Huchuan (PRC) with 2 single 533mm TT each with YU-1 Type-53 HWT
  PBF 4 Titas (ROK Sea Dolphin)
  PB 11: 1 Barkat (ex-PRC Shanghai III); 2 Karnaphuli; 1 Salam (ex-PRC Huangfen); 7 Shaheed Daulat (PRC Shanghai II)
MINE WARFARE • MINE COUNTERMEASURES 5
  MSO 5: 1 Sagar; 4 Shapla (ex-UK River)
AMPHIBIOUS
  LANDING SHIPS • LSL 1
  LANDING CRAFT 14
    LCT 2
    LCU 4 (of which 2†)
    LCVP 3†
    LCM 5 Darshak (Yuchin)
LOGISTICS AND SUPPORT 9
  AG 1
  AGHS 2: 1 Agradoot; 1 Anushandhan
  AOR 2 (coastal)
  AOT 1 Khan Jahangir Ali
  AR 1†
  ATF 1†
  AX 1 Shaheed Ruhul Amin

Naval Aviation
EQUIPMENT BY TYPE
AIRCRAFT • TPT • Light 2 Do-228NG (MP)
HELICOPTERS • TPT • Light 2 AW109E *Power*

Special Warfare and Diving Command 300

Air Force 14,000
FORCES BY ROLE
FIGHTER
1 sqn with MiG-29B/UB *Fulcrum*
FIGHTER/GROUND ATTACK
1 sqn with F-7MB/FT-7B *Airguard*
1 sqn with F-7BG/FT-7BG *Airguard*
1 sqn with F-7BGI/FT-7BGI *Airguard*
GROUND ATTACK
1 sqn with Yak-130 *Mitten**
TRANSPORT
1 sqn with An-32 *Cline*
1 sqn with C-130B *Hercules*
1 sqn with L-410UVP
TRAINING
1 sqn with K-8W *Karakorum**; L-39ZA *Albatros**
1 sqn with PT-6
TRANSPORT HELICOPTER
1 sqn with AW139; Mi-17 *Hip* H; Mi-17-1V *Hip* H; Mi-171Sh
1 sqn with Mi-17 *Hip* H; Mi-17-1V *Hip* H; Mi-171Sh
1 sqn with Bell 212
1 trg sqn with Bell 206L *Long Ranger*; AW119 *Koala*
EQUIPMENT BY TYPE
AIRCRAFT 84 combat capable
  FTR 53: 9 F-7MB *Airguard*; 11 F-7BG *Airguard*; 12 F-7BGI *Airguard*; 5 FT-7B *Airguard*; 4 FT-7BG *Airguard*; 4 FT-7BGI *Airguard*; 6 MiG-29 *Fulcrum*; 2 MiG-29UB *Fulcrum*
  TPT 10: **Medium** 4 C-130B *Hercules*; **Light** 6: 3 An-32 *Cline*†; 3 L-410UVP
  TRG 41: 9 K-8W *Karakorum**; 7 L-39ZA *Albatros**; 10 PT-6; 15 Yak-130 *Mitten**
HELICOPTERS
  MRH 16: 2 AW139 (SAR); 12 Mi-17 *Hip* H; 2 Mi-17-1V *Hip* H (VIP)
  TPT 15: **Medium** 7 Mi-171Sh; **Light** 8: 2 Bell 206L *Long Ranger*; 4 Bell 212; 2 AW119 *Koala*
AIR-LAUNCHED MISSILES
  AAM • IR R-3 (AA-2 *Atoll*)‡; R-73 (AA-11 *Archer*); PL-5; PL-7; **SARH** R-27R (AA-10A *Alamo*)

Paramilitary 63,900

Ansars 20,000+
Security Guards

Rapid Action Battalions 5,000
Ministry of Home Affairs
FORCES BY ROLE
MANOEUVRE
  Other
  14 paramilitary bn

Border Guard Bangladesh 38,000
FORCES BY ROLE
MANOEUVRE
  Amphibious
  1 rvn coy
  Other
  54 paramilitary bn

Coast Guard 900
EQUIPMENT BY TYPE
PATROL AND COASTAL COMBATANTS 13
  PSO 4 *Syed Nazrul* (ex-ITA *Minerva*) with 1 hel landing platform
  PB 4: 1 *Ruposhi Bangla*; 1 *Shaheed Daulat*; 2 *Shetgang*
  PBR 5 *Pabna*

DEPLOYMENT

CENTRAL AFRICAN REPUBLIC
UN • MINUSCA 1,008; 10 obs; 1 cdo coy; 1 inf bn; 1 med coy

CYPRUS
UN • UNFICYP 3

DEMOCRATIC REPUBLIC OF THE CONGO
UN • MONUSCO 1,710; 13 obs; 1 inf bn; 1 engr coy; 1 avn coy; 2 hel coy

LEBANON
UN • UNIFIL 275; 1 FFG; 1 FSG

MALI
UN • MINUSMA 1,531; 2 obs; 1 inf bn; 1 engr coy; 1 sigs coy; 1 tpt coy; 1 hel sqn

SOMALIA
UN • UNSOM 1 obs

SOUTH SUDAN
UN • UNMISS 1,604; 20 obs; 1 inf bn; 1 rvn coy; 2 engr coy

SUDAN
UN • UNAMID 371; 8 obs; 2 inf coy

WESTERN SAHARA
UN • MINURSO 20; 8 obs; 1 fd hospital

Brunei BRN

Brunei Dollar B$		2016	2017	2018
GDP	B$	15.7bn	16.7bn	
	US$	11.4bn	12.0bn	
per capita	US$	26,935	27,893	
Growth	%	-2.5	-1.3	
Inflation	%	-0.7	-0.2	
Def bdgt	B$	565m	452m	
	US$	409m	324m	
US$1=B$		1.38	1.39	

Population 443,593

Ethnic groups: Malay 65.7%; Chinese 10.3%; Indigenous 3.4%; other or unspecified 23.6%

Age	0–14	15–19	20–24	25–29	30–64	65 plus
Male	11.9%	4.1%	4.4%	4.5%	22.0%	2.3%
Female	11.2%	4.0%	4.6%	4.9%	23.6%	2.5%

Capabilities

While professional and well trained, the limited size of the Royal Brunei Armed Forces (RBAF) means they could offer little resistance to a determined aggressor. Since 2015/16 (when defence spending was significantly reduced) funding shortfalls resulting primarily from the impact of declining energy prices on the national budget have challenged the RBAF's efforts to implement its Defence Capability Enhancement Project. The defence ministry announced a preliminary study on the development of a defence-support industry, as part of the June 2016 Defence Science and Technology Policy Framework that is designed to improve performance in defence science and technology. However, Brunei has always depended on external support for its defence. The sultanate has long-established and close defence relations with the UK, and in February 2015 the long-standing agreement under which the sultanate hosts a British Army garrison, including a Gurkha battalion and a jungle-warfare school, was renewed for a further five years. There is also a long-term Singapore Armed Forces presence. Brunei continues to deploy small peacekeeping contingents, under Malaysian command, in Lebanon (UNIFIL) and the southern Philippines (IMT).

ACTIVE 7,200 (Army 4,900 Navy 1,200 Air 1,100)
Paramilitary 4,900

RESERVE 700 (Army 700)

ORGANISATIONS BY SERVICE

Army 4,900
FORCES BY ROLE
MANOEUVRE
  Light
  3 inf bn
COMBAT SUPPORT
  1 cbt spt bn (1 armd recce sqn, 1 engr sqn)

Reserves 700
FORCES BY ROLE
MANOEUVRE
  Light
  1 inf bn
EQUIPMENT BY TYPE
ARMOURED FIGHTING VEHICLES
  LT TK 20 *Scorpion* (16 to be upgraded)
  APC • APC (W) 45 VAB
ENGINEERING & MAINTENANCE VEHICLES
  ARV 2 *Samson*
ARTILLERY • MOR 81mm 24

Navy 1,200
FORCES BY ROLE
SPECIAL FORCES
  1 SF sqn
EQUIPMENT BY TYPE
PATROL AND COASTAL COMBATANTS 10
  CORVETTES • FSG 4 *Darussalam* with 2 twin lnchr with MM40 *Exocet* Block 2 AShM, 1 57mm gun, 1 hel landing platform
  PCC 4 *Ijtihad*
  PBF 1 *Mustaed*
  PB 1 *Perwira*
AMPHIBIOUS • LANDING CRAFT • LCU 4: 2 *Teraban*; 2 *Cheverton Loadmaster*

Air Force 1,100
FORCES BY ROLE
MARITIME PATROL
  1 sqn with CN235M
TRAINING
  1 sqn with PC-7; Bell 206B *Jet Ranger* II
TRANSPORT HELICOPTER
  1 sqn with Bell 214 (SAR)
  1 sqn with Bo-105
  1 sqn with S-70i *Black Hawk*
AIR DEFENCE
  1 sqn with *Rapier*
  1 sqn with *Mistral*
EQUIPMENT BY TYPE
AIRCRAFT
  MP 1 CN235M
  TRG 4 PC-7
HELICOPTERS
  TPT 21: **Medium** 13: 1 Bell 214 (SAR); 12 S-70i *Black Hawk*; **Light** 8: 2 Bell 206B *Jet Ranger* II; 6 Bo-105 (armed, 81mm rockets)
AIR DEFENCE • SAM • Point-defence *Rapier*; *Mistral*

Paramilitary ε4,900

Gurkha Reserve Unit 400–500
FORCES BY ROLE
MANOEUVRE
  Light
  2 inf bn(-)

Royal Brunei Police 4,400

EQUIPMENT BY TYPE
PATROL AND COASTAL COMBATANTS • PB 10: 3 *Bendaharu*; 7 PDB-type

DEPLOYMENT

LEBANON
UN • UNIFIL 30

PHILIPPINES
IMT 9

FOREIGN FORCES

Singapore 1 trg camp with infantry units on rotation; 1 trg school; 1 hel det with AS332 *Super Puma*

United Kingdom 1,000; 1 Gurkha bn; 1 jungle trg centre; 1 hel flt with 3 Bell 212

Cambodia CAM

Cambodian Riel r		2016	2017	2018
GDP	r	81.7tr	90.3tr	
	US$	20.2bn	22.3bn	
per capita	US$	1,278	1,390	
Growth	%	7.0	6.9	
Inflation	%	3.0	3.7	
Def bdgt [a]	r	ε2.66tr	ε3.20tr	
	US$	ε656m	ε788m	
US$1=r		4,053.33	4,059.17	

[a] Defence and security budget

Population 16,204,486

Ethnic groups: Khmer 90%; Vietnamese 5%; Chinese 1%

Age	0–14	15–19	20–24	25–29	30–64	65 plus
Male	15.6%	4.4%	4.7%	5.1%	17.1%	1.6%
Female	15.3%	4.5%	4.8%	5.2%	18.8%	2.6%

Capabilities

Despite their name, which reflects Cambodia's formal status as a constitutional monarchy – and the integration in the early 1990s of two non-communist resistance armies – the Royal Cambodian Armed Forces (RCAF) are essentially the modern manifestation of the armed forces of the former People's Republic of Kampuchea, established in 1979 following Vietnam's invasion. In terms of organisation, the RCAF has an excessive number of senior officers, while many formations and units appear to be of only nominal status. Skirmishes on the border with Thailand since 2008 provide little indication of capacity for high-intensity combat. Cambodia's most important international links are with the Chinese and Vietnamese armed forces. It was reported that an agreement was reached in late 2016 to increase Chinese military assistance to Cambodia. A training relationship with the US was suspended in 2017, also ending the deployment of US Naval Construction Force. In 2017, Cambodia participated in the *Shanti Prayas-III* peacekeeping-training exercise. Cambodia contributes personnel to UN peacekeeping missions.

ACTIVE 124,300 (Army 75,000 Navy 2,800 Air 1,500 Provincial Forces 45,000) **Paramilitary 67,000**

Conscript liability 18 months service authorised but not implemented since 1993

ORGANISATIONS BY SERVICE

Army ε75,000

6 Military Regions (incl 1 special zone for capital)
FORCES BY ROLE
SPECIAL FORCES
  1 (911th) AB/SF Bde
MANOEUVRE
  Light
  2 (2nd & 3rd Intervention) inf div (3 inf bde)
  5 (Intervention) indep inf bde
  8 indep inf bde
  Other
  1 (70th) sy bde (4 sy bn)
  17 (border) sy bn
COMBAT SUPPORT
  2 arty bn
  4 fd engr regt
COMBAT SERVICE SUPPORT
  1 (construction) engr regt
  2 tpt bde
AIR DEFENCE
  1 AD bn
EQUIPMENT BY TYPE
ARMOURED FIGHTING VEHICLES
  MBT 200+: 50 Type-59; 150+ T-54/T-55
  LT TK 20+: Type-62; 20 Type-63
  RECCE 4+ BRDM-2
  IFV 70 BMP-1
  APC 230+
    APC (T) M113
    APC (W) 230: 200 BTR-60/BTR-152; 30 OT-64
ENGINEERING & MAINTENANCE VEHICLES
  ARV T-54/T-55
  MW *Bozena*; RA-140 DS
ANTI-TANK/ANTI-INFRASTRUCTURE
  RCL 82mm B-10; **107mm** B-11
ARTILLERY 433+
  TOWED 400+ **76mm** ZIS-3 (M-1942)/**122mm** D-30/**122mm** M-30 (M-1938)/**130mm** Type-59-I
  MRL 33+: **107mm** Type-63; **122mm** 13: 8 BM-21; 5 RM-70; **132mm** BM-13-16 (BM-13); **140mm** 20 BM-14-16 (BM-14)
  MOR 82mm M-37; **120mm** M-43; **160mm** M-160
AIR DEFENCE
  SAM • Point-defence FN-6; FN-16 (reported)
  GUNS • TOWED 14.5mm ZPU-1/ZPU-2/ZPU-4; **37mm** M-1939; **57mm** S-60

Navy ε2,800 (incl 1,500 Naval Infantry)
EQUIPMENT BY TYPE
PATROL AND COASTAL COMBATANTS 14
  PBF 3 *Stenka*

PB 9: 4 (PRC 46m); 3 (PRC 20m); 2 *Shershen*
PBR 2 *Kaoh Chhlam*
AMPHIBIOUS • LANDING CRAFT
  LCU 1
LOGISTICS AND SUPPORT • AFDL 1

Naval Infantry 1,500
FORCES BY ROLE
MANOEUVRE
  Light
    1 (31st) nav inf bde
  COMBAT SUPPORT
    1 arty bn

Air Force 1,500
FORCES BY ROLE
ISR/TRAINING
  1 sqn with P-92 *Echo* (L-39 *Albatros** in store)
TRANSPORT
  1 VIP sqn (reporting to Council of Ministers) with An-24RV *Coke*; AS350 *Ecureuil*; AS355F2 *Ecureuil* II
  1 sqn with BN-2 *Islander*; Y-12 (II)
TRANSPORT HELICOPTER
  1 sqn with Mi-17 *Hip* H; Mi-8 *Hip*; Z-9; (Mi-26 *Halo* in store)
EQUIPMENT BY TYPE
AIRCRAFT
  TPT • **Light** 12: 2 An-24RV *Coke*; 1 BN-2 *Islander*; 2 MA60; 5 P-92 *Echo* (pilot trg/recce); 2 Y-12 (II)
  TRG (5 L-39 *Albatros** in store)
HELICOPTERS
  MRH 14: 3 Mi-17 *Hip* H; 11 Z-9
  TPT 8: **Heavy** (2 Mi-26 *Halo* in store); **Medium** 4 Mi-8 *Hip*; **Light** 4: 2 AS350 *Ecureuil*; 2 AS355F2 *Ecureuil* II

Provincial Forces 45,000+
Reports of at least 1 inf regt per province, with varying numbers of inf bn (with lt wpn)

Paramilitary
  Police 67,000 (including gendarmerie)

DEPLOYMENT
CENTRAL AFRICAN REPUBLIC
UN • MINUSCA 216; 6 obs; 1 engr coy

LEBANON
UN • UNIFIL 185; 1 engr coy

MALI
UN • MINUSMA 304; 1 EOD coy

SOUTH SUDAN
UN • UNMISS 77; 6 obs; 1 MP unit

SUDAN
UN • UNAMID 2 obs
UN • UNISFA 1; 2 obs

China, People's Republic of PRC

Chinese Yuan Renminbi Y		2016	2017	2018
GDP	Y	74.6tr	81.1tr	
	US$	11.2tr	11.9tr	
per capita	US$	8,123	8,583	
Growth	%	6.7	6.8	
Inflation	%	2.0	1.8	
Def exp	Y	1.31tr	n.k.	
	US$	197bn	n.k.	
Def bdgt [a]	Y	955bn	1.02tr	
	US$	144bn	150bn	
US$1=Y		6.64	6.80	

[a] Central Expenditure budget

Population   1,387,096,243

Ethnic groups: Han 91.5%; Zhuang 1.3%; Hui 0.8%; Manchu 0.8%; Uygur 0.7%; Tibetan 0.5%; other or unspecified 4.4%

Age	0–14	15–19	20–24	25–29	30–64	65 plus
Male	9.2%	3.1%	3.7%	4.5%	25.7%	5.2%
Female	7.9%	2.7%	3.3%	4.3%	24.8%	5.7%

Capabilities

China's most recent defence white paper, published in English in 2015, outlined the importance of power-projection capabilities, emphasising the requirements for offensive and defensive air operations, and 'open seas protection'. At the 19th Chinese Communist Party National Congress, President Xi outlined a development path for the People's Liberation Army (PLA) to become a global 'top tier' military by 2050. To this end, the major restructuring of the PLA begun in late 2015 is now mostly in effect, and will probably be complete by 2020. Whilst a key objective of this reform is improving the PLA's readiness for combat operations, it remains unclear how effective the newly established structures will be at generating and controlling high-intensity combined-arms capabilities, as efforts to improve operational effectiveness will remain tempered by the political requirement to maintain control. The establishment of the Strategic Support Force underscores the importance placed upon the further development of China's already advanced cyber, space and information-dominance capabilities, a key objective set by Xi for 2020. Recent deals for Su-35 combat aircraft and S-400 air-defence systems demonstrate the willingness to buy limited amounts of foreign equipment to help develop the domestic defence industry. China is capable of indigenously producing advanced equipment across all domains, although questions persist over quality. While a significant amount of old PLA equipment remains in service, the reduction in overall force size as part of the restructuring process may see outdated designs finally withdrawn over the next few years. The armed forces have some experience in extended out-of-area maritime deployments, and China is constructing facilities in Djibouti to support such missions. There is less experience of this in the other services; however, incremental growth in limited deployments to UN peacekeeping missions indicates developing intent in this area. (See pp. 225–35.)

ACTIVE 2,035,000 (Ground Forces 975,000 Navy 240,000 Air Force 395,000 Strategic Missile Forces 100,000 Strategic Support Force 175,000 Other 150,000) **Paramilitary 660,000**
Conscript liability Selective conscription; all services 2 years

RESERVE ε510,000

ORGANISATIONS BY SERVICE

Strategic Missile Forces 100,000+

People's Liberation Army Rocket Force

The People's Liberation Army Rocket Force (formerly the Second Artillery Force) organises and commands its own troops to launch nuclear counter-attacks with strategic missiles and to conduct operations with conventional missiles. Organised as launch bdes subordinate to 6 army-level msl bases. Org varies by msl type

FORCES BY ROLE
SURFACE-TO-SURFACE MISSILE
  1 ICBM bde with DF-4
  2 ICBM bde with DF-5A
  1 ICBM bde with DF-5B
  1 ICBM bde with DF-31
  2 ICBM bde with DF-31A/A(G)
  1 IRBM bde with DF-26
  2 MRBM bde with DF-16
  1 MRBM bde with DF-21
  5 MRBM bde with DF-21A
  2 MRBM bde with DF-21C
  2 MRBM bde with DF-21D
  4 SRBM bde with DF-11A
  2 SRBM bde with DF-15B
  2 GLCM bde with CJ-10
  2 SSM trg bde
  4+ SSM bde (forming)

EQUIPMENT BY TYPE
SURFACE-TO-SURFACE MISSILE LAUNCHERS
  ICBM • Nuclear 70: ε10 DF-4 (CH-SS-3); ε20 DF-5A/B (CH-SS-4 Mod 2/3); ε8 DF-31 (CH-SS-10 Mod 1); ε24 DF-31A (CH-SS-10 Mod 2); ε8 DF-31A(G) (CH-SS-10 Mod 3)
  IRBM • Dual-capable ε16 DF-26
  MRBM 146: **Nuclear** ε80 DF-21/DF-21A/DF-21E (CH-SS-5 Mod 1/2/6); **Conventional** 66: ε24 DF-16 (CH-SS-11 Mod 1/2); ε24 DF-21C (CH-SS-5 Mod 4); ε18 DF-21D (CH-SS-5 Mod 5 – ASBM)
  SRBM • Conventional 189: ε108 DF-11A (CH-SS-7 Mod 2); ε81 DF-15B (CH-SS-6 Mod 3)
  GLCM • Dual-capable ε54 CJ-10

Navy

EQUIPMENT BY TYPE
SUBMARINES • STRATEGIC • SSBN 4:
  4 *Jin* (Type-094) with up to 12 JL-2 (CH-SS-N-14) strategic SLBM, 6 single 533mm TT with Yu-6 HWT

Defensive

EQUIPMENT BY TYPE
RADAR • STRATEGIC: 4+ large phased array radars; some detection and tracking radars

Space

EQUIPMENT BY TYPE
SATELLITES 77
  COMMUNICATIONS 6 *Zhongxing* (dual-use telecom satellites for civ/mil comms)
  NAVIGATION/POSITIONING/TIMING 23: 7 *Beidou-2*(M); 5 *Beidou-2*(G); 9 *Beidou-2*(IGSO); 2 *Beidou-3*(M)
  ISR 33: 32 *Yaogan Weixing* (remote sensing); 1 *Ziyuan* (ZY-2 – remote sensing)
  ELINT/SIGINT 15: 8 *Shijian* 6 (4 pairs – reported ELINT/SIGINT role); 7 *Shijian* 11 (reported ELINT/SIGINT role)

Ground Forces ε975,000

In late 2015, a single, separate headquarters was established for the People's Liberation Army (PLA) ground forces, in place of the four general departments

FORCES BY ROLE
COMMAND
  13 (Group) army HQ
SPECIAL FORCES
  15 spec ops bde
MANOEUVRE
  Armoured
  23 (cbd arms) armd bde
  1 hy mech inf div (1 armd regt, 2 mech inf regt, 1 arty regt, 1 AD regt)
  Mechanised
  1 (high alt) mech inf div (1 armd regt, 2 mech inf regt, 1 arty regt, 1 AD regt)
  23 (cbd arms) mech inf bde
  Light
  3 (high alt) mot inf div (1 armd regt, 2 mot inf regt, 1 arty regt, 1 AD regt)
  27 (cbd arms) inf bde
  Air Manoeuvre
  2 air aslt bde
  Amphibious
  6 amph aslt bde
  Other
  1 (OPFOR) mech inf bde
  1 mech gd div (1 armd regt, 2 mech inf regt, 1 arty regt, 1 AD regt)
  1 sy gd div (4 sy regt)
  16 (border) sy bde
  15 (border) sy regt
  1 (border) sy gp
COMBAT SUPPORT
  14 arty bde
  13 engr/NBC bde
  2 engr regt
  10 EW regt
  50 sigs regt
COMBAT SERVICE SUPPORT
  13 spt bde

COASTAL DEFENCE
19 coastal arty/AShM bde
AVIATION
1 mixed avn bde
HELICOPTER
12 hel bde
TRAINING
4 hel trg regt
AIR DEFENCE
15 AD bde

Reserves
FORCES BY ROLE
MANOEUVRE
  Armoured
  2 armd regt
  Light
  18 inf div
  4 inf bde
  3 indep inf regt
COMBAT SUPPORT
  3 arty div
  7 arty bde
  15 engr regt
  1 ptn br bde
  3 ptn br regt
  10 chem regt
  10 sigs regt
COMBAT SERVICE SUPPORT
  9 log bde
  1 log regt
AIR DEFENCE
  17 AD div
  8 AD bde
  8 AD regt
EQUIPMENT BY TYPE
ARMOURED FIGHTING VEHICLES
  MBT 6,740+: 1,600 ZTZ-59; 650 ZTZ-59-II; 600 ZTZ-59D; 200 ZTZ-79; 300 ZTZ-88A/B; 1,000 ZTZ-96; 1,500 ZTZ-96A; 40 ZTZ-98A; 600 ZTZ-99; 250 ZTZ-99A; some ZTQ-15
  LT TK 650: 250 ZTD-05; 250 ZTQ-62; 150 ZTS-63A
  ASLT 400 ZTL-11
  IFV 3,800: 400 ZBD-04; 500 ZBD-04A; 500 ZBL-08; 600 ZBD-86; 650 ZBD-86A; 550 ZSL-92; 600 ZSL-92B
  APC 5,020+
    APC (T) 4,150: 2,400 ZSD-63/ZSD-63C; 1,750 ZSD-89
    APC (W) 870+: 700 ZSL-92A; 120 ZBL-11; 50 ZSL-93; some EQ2050F
  AAV 300 ZBD-05
  AUV *Tiger* 4×4
ENGINEERING & MAINTENANCE VEHICLES
  ARV Type-73; Type-84; Type-85; Type-97; Type-654
  VLB KMM; MTU; TMM; Type-84A
  MW Type-74; Type-79; Type-81-II; Type-84
ANTI-TANK/ANTI-INFRASTRUCTURE
  MSL
    SP 924: 450 HJ-8 (veh mounted); 24 HJ-10; 450 ZSL-02B
    MANPATS HJ-73A/B/C; HJ-8A/C/E
  RCL 3,966: **75mm** PF-56; **82mm** PF-65 (B-10); PF-78; **105mm** PF-75; **120mm** PF-98

GUNS 1,788
  SP 480: **100mm** 250 PTL-02; **120mm** 230 PTZ-89
  TOWED • **100mm** 1,308 PT-73 (T-12)/PT-86
ARTILLERY 13,218+
  SP 2,320: **122mm** 1,650: 700 PLZ-89; 300 PLZ-07; 150 PLZ-07B; 300 PLC-09; 200 PLL-09; **152mm** 350 PLZ-83A/B; **155mm** 320 PLZ-05
  TOWED 6,140: **122mm** 3,800 PL-54-1 (M-1938)/PL-83/PL-60 (D-74)/PL-96 (D-30); **130mm** 234 PL-59 (M-46)/PL-59-I; **152mm** 2,106 PL-54 (D-1)/PL-66 (D-20)
  GUN/MOR 120mm 300: 200 PLL-05; 100 PLZ-05A
  MRL 1,872+ **107mm** 54+ PH-63; **122mm** 1,643: 1,250 PHL-81/PHL-90/SR4; 375 PHZ-89; 18 PHZ-10; **300mm** 175 PHL-03
  MOR 2,586: **82mm** PP-53 (M-37)/PP-67/PP-82/PP-87; **100mm** PP-89
RADAR • LAND *Cheetah*; RASIT; Type-378
COASTAL DEFENCE
  AShM HY-1 (CH-SSC-2 *Silkworm*); HY-2 (CH-SSC-3 *Seersucker*); HY-4 (CH-SSC-7 *Sadsack*); YJ-62
PATROL AND COASTAL COMBATANTS 25
  PB 25: 9 *Huzong*; 16 *Shenyang*
AMPHIBIOUS 148+
  LCM 117+: 1+ *Yunnan*; 100+ *Yunnan* II; 16+ *Yupen*
  LCU 31+: 30 *Yuwei*; 1 other
LOGISTICS AND SUPPORT 18
  AK 5 *Leizhuang*
  AKR 1 PLA Logistics Support Vessel (capacity 1 MBT; 1 med hel)
  ARC 1
  AOT 8: 1 *Fuzhong*; 7 *Fubing*
  ATF 2 *Huntao*
  AX 1 *Haixun* III
AIRCRAFT • TPT 9: **Medium** 5: 4 Y-8; 1 Y-9; **Light** 4 Y-7
HELICOPTERS
  ATK 240: 120 WZ-10; 120 WZ-19
  MRH 351: 22 Mi-17 *Hip* H; 3 Mi-17-1V *Hip* H; 38 Mi-17V-5 *Hip* H; 25 Mi-17V-7 *Hip* H; 8 SA342L *Gazelle*; 21 Z-9A; 31 Z-9W; 10 Z-9WA; 193 Z-9WZ
  TPT 382: **Heavy** 105: 9 Z-8A; 96 Z-8B; **Medium** 209: 50 Mi-8T *Hip*; 140 Mi-171; 19 S-70C2 (S-70C) *Black Hawk*; **Light** 68: 53 AS350 *Ecureuil*; 15 H120 *Colibri*
UNMANNED AERIAL VEHICLES
  ISR • Heavy BZK-005; BZK-009 (reported); **Medium** BZK-006; BZK-007; BZK-008; **Light** *Harpy* (anti-radiation)
AIR DEFENCE
  SAM
    Medium-range 90: 72 HQ-16A; 18 HQ-17
    Short-range 254: 24 9K331 *Tor*-M1 (SA-15 *Gauntlet*); 30 HQ-6D; 200 HQ-7A/B
    Point-defence HN-5A/HN-5B; FN-6/QW-1/QW-2
  GUNS 7,376+
    SP 376: **25mm** 270 PGZ-04A; **35mm** 100 PGZ-07; **37mm** 6 PGZ-88
    TOWED 7,000+: **25mm** PG-87; **35mm** PG-99 (GDF-002); **37mm** PG-55 (M-1939)/PG-65/PG-74; **57mm** PG-59 (S-60); **100mm** PG-59 (KS-19)
AIR-LAUNCHED MISSILES
  ASM AKD-8; AKD-9; AKD-10

Navy ε240,000

The PLA Navy is organised into five service arms: submarine, surface, naval aviation, coastal defence and marine corps, as well as other specialised units. There are three fleets: the Beihai Fleet (North Sea), Donghai Fleet (East Sea) and Nanhai Fleet (South Sea)

EQUIPMENT BY TYPE
SUBMARINES 62
  STRATEGIC • SSBN 4:
    4 *Jin* (Type-094) with up to 12 JL-2 (CH-SS-N-14) strategic SLBM, 6 single 533mm TT with Yu-6 HWT
  TACTICAL 58
  SSN 9:
    3 *Han* (Type-091) with 6 single 533mm TT with Yu-3 HWT/YJ-82 (CH-SS-N-7) AShM (operational status unclear)
    2 *Shang* I (Type-093) with 6 single 533mm TT with Yu-3 HWT/Yu-6 HWT/YJ-82 (CH-SS-N-7) AShM or YJ-18 (CH-SS-N-13) AShM
    4 *Shang* II (Type-093A) with 6 single 533mm TT with Yu-3 HWT/Yu-6 HWT/YJ-82 (CH-SS-N-7) AShM or YJ-18 (CH-SS-N-13) AShM (operational status unclear)
  SSK 48:
    4 *Kilo* (2 Project 877 & 2 Project 636) with 6 single 533mm TT with TEST-71ME HWT/53-65KE HWT
    8 *Kilo* (Project 636M) with 6 single 533mm TT with TEST-71ME HWT/53-65KE HWT/3M54E *Klub* (SS-N-27B *Sizzler*) AShM
    11 *Ming* (7 Type-035(G), 4 Type-035B) with 8 single 533mm TT with Yu-3 HWT/Yu-4 HWT
    12 *Song* (Type-039(G)) with 6 single 533mm TT with Yu-3 HWT/Yu-6 HWT/YJ-82 (CH-SS-N-7) AShM or YJ-18 (CH-SS-N-13) AShM
    4 *Yuan* (Type-039A) with 6 533mm TT with Yu-3 HWT/Yu-6 HWT/YJ-82 (CH-SS-N-7) AShM or YJ-18 (CH-SS-N-13) AShM
    9 *Yuan* II (Type-039B) with 6 533mm TT with Yu-3 HWT/Yu-6 HWT/YJ-82 (CH-SS-N-7) AShM or YJ-18 (CH-SS-N-13) AShM
  SSB 1 *Qing* (Type-032) (SLBM trials)
PRINCIPAL SURFACE COMBATANTS 83
  AIRCRAFT CARRIERS • CV 1
    1 *Liaoning* (RUS *Kuznetsov*) with 4 18-cell GMLS with HHQ-10 SAM, 2 RBU 6000 *Smerch* 2 A/S mor, 3 H/PJ-11 CIWS (capacity 18–24 J-15 ac; 17 Ka-28/Ka-31/Z-8S/Z-8JH/Z-8AEW hel)
DESTROYERS 23
  DDGHM 21:
    2 *Hangzhou* (RUS *Sovremenny*) with 2 quad lnchr with 3M80/3M82 *Moskit* (SS-N-22A/B *Sunburn*) AShM, 2 3K90 *Uragan* (SA-N-7 *Gadfly*) SAM, 2 twin 533mm ASTT, 2 RBU 1000 *Smerch* 3 A/S mor, 2 CADS-N-1 *Kashtan* CIWS, 2 twin 130mm gun (capacity 1 Z-9C/Ka-28 *Helix* A hel)
    2 *Hangzhou* (RUS *Sovremenny*) with 2 quad lnchr with 3M80/3M82 *Moskit* (SS-N-22A/B *Sunburn*) AShM, 2 *Yezh* (SA-N-12 *Grizzly*) SAM, 2 twin 533mm ASTT, 2 RBU 1000 *Smerch* 3 A/S mor, 4 AK630 CIWS, 1 twin 130mm gun (capacity 1 Z-9C/Ka-28 *Helix* A hel) (of which 1 in refit)
    1 *Luhai* (Type-051B) with 4 quad lnchr with YJ-83 AShM, 1 octuple lnchr with HHQ-7 SAM, 2 triple 324mm ASTT with Yu-7 LWT, 1 twin 100mm gun (capacity 2 Z-9C/Ka-28 *Helix* A hel) (in refit)
    2 *Luhu* (Type-052) with 4 quad lnchr with YJ-83 AShM, 1 octuple lnchr with HHQ-7 SAM, 2 triple 324mm ASTT with Yu-7 LWT, 2 FQF 2500 A/S mor, 2 H/PJ-12 CIWS, 1 twin 100mm gun (capacity 2 Z-9C hel)
    2 *Luyang* (Type-052B) with 4 quad lnchr with YJ-83 AShM, 2 single lnchr with *Yezh* (SA-N-12 *Grizzly*) SAM, 2 triple 324mm TT with Yu-7 LWT, 2 H/PJ-12 CIWS, 1 100mm gun (capacity 1 Ka-28 *Helix* A hel)
    6 *Luyang* II (Type-052C) with 2 quad lnchr with YJ-62 AShM, 8 sextuple VLS with HHQ-9 SAM, 2 triple 324mm TT with Yu-7 LWT, 2 H/PJ-12 CIWS, 1 100mm gun (capacity 2 Ka-28 *Helix* A hel)
    6 *Luyang* III (Type-052D) with 8 octuple VLS with YJ-18A (CH-SS-N-13) AShM/HHQ-9ER SAM/Yu-8 A/S msl, 1 24-cell GMLS with HHQ-10 SAM, 2 triple 324mm TT with Yu-7 LWT, 1 H/PJ-12 CIWS, 1 130mm gun (capacity 2 Ka-28 *Helix* A hel)
  DDGM 2:
    2 *Luzhou* (Type-051C) with 2 quad lnchr with YJ-83 AShM; 6 sextuple VLS with S-300FM (SA-N-20 *Grumble*) SAM, 2 H/PJ-12 CIWS, 1 100mm gun, 1 hel landing platform
FRIGATES 59
  FFGHM 37:
    2 *Jiangkai* (Type-054) with 2 quad lnchr with YJ-83 AShM, 1 octuple lnchr with HHQ-7 SAM, 2 triple 324mm TT with Yu-7 LWT, 2 RBU 1200 A/S mor, 4 AK630 CIWS, 1 100mm gun (capacity 1 Ka-28 *Helix* A/Z-9C hel)
    16 *Jiangkai* II (Type-054A) with 2 quad lnchr with YJ-83 AShM, 1 32-cell VLS with Yu-8 A/S msl/HHQ-16 SAM, 2 triple 324mm TT with Yu-7 LWT, 2 FQF 2300 A/S mor, 2 H/PJ-12 CIWS, 1 76mm gun (capacity 1 Ka-28 *Helix* A/Z-9C hel)
    9 *Jiangkai* II (Type-054A) with 2 quad lnchr with YJ-83 AShM, 1 32-cell VLS with Yu-8 A/S msl/HHQ-16 SAM, 2 triple 324mm TT with Yu-7 LWT, 2 FQF 2300 A/S mor, 2 H/PJ-11 CIWS, 1 76mm gun (capacity 1 Ka-28 *Helix* A/Z-9C hel)
    7 *Jiangwei* II (Type-053H3) with 2 quad lnchr with YJ-83 AShM, 1 octuple lnchr with HHQ-7 SAM, 2 RBU 1200 A/S mor, 1 twin 100mm gun (capacity 2 Z-9C hel)
    3 *Jiangwei* II (Type-053H3) with 2 quad lnchr with YJ-83 AShM, 1 8-cell GMLS with HHQ-10 SAM, 2 RBU 1200 A/S mor, 1 twin 100mm gun (capacity 2 Z-9C hel)
  FFGH 1:
    1 *Jianghu* IV (Type-053H1Q – trg role) with 1 triple lnchr with HY-2 (CH-SS-N-2) AShM, 4 RBU 1200 A/S mor, 1 100mm gun (capacity 1 Z-9C hel)
  FFGM 4:
    2 *Luda* IV (Type-051DT) with 4 quad lnchr with YJ-83 AShM, 1 octuple lnchr with HHQ-7 SAM, 2 FQF 2500 A/S mor, 2 130mm gun, 3 twin 57mm gun

2 *Luda* III (Type-051G) with 4 quad lnchr with YJ-83 AShM, 1 octuple lnchr with HHQ-7 SAM, 2 FQF 2500 A/S mor, 2 triple 324mm ASTT, 2 twin 100mm gun

FFG 17:

2 *Jianghu* I (Type-053H) with 2 twin lnchr with SY-1 (CH-SS-N-1) AShM, 4 RBU 1200 A/S mor, 2 100mm gun

6 *Jianghu* II (Type-053H1) with 2 twin lnchr with HY-2 (CH-SS-N-2) AShM, 2 RBU 1200 A/S mor, 1 twin 100mm gun (capacity 1 Z-9C hel)

1 *Jianghu* III (Type-053H2) with 2 quad lnchr with YJ-83 AShM, 2 RBU 1200, 2 twin 100mm gun

6 *Jianghu* V (Type-053H1G) with 2 quad lnchr with YJ-83 AShM, 2 RBU 1200, 2 twin 100mm gun

2 *Luda* II (Type-051) with 2 triple lnchr with HY-2 (CH-SS-N-2) AShM, 2 triple 324mm ASTT, 2 FQF 2500 A/S mor, 2 twin 130mm gun (minelaying capability)

PATROL AND COASTAL COMBATANTS ε206

CORVETTES • FSGM 37:

21 *Jiangdao* I (Type-056) with 2 twin lnchr with YJ-83 AShM, 1 8-cell GMLS with HHQ-10 SAM, 2 triple 324mm ASTT with Yu-7 LWT, 1 76mm gun, 1 hel landing platform

16 *Jiangdao* II (Type-056A) with 2 twin lnchr with YJ-83 AShM, 1 8-cell GMLS with HHQ-10 SAM, 2 triple 324mm ASTT with Yu-7 LWT, 1 76mm gun, 1 hel landing platform

PCFG ε65 *Houbei* (Type-022) with 2 quad lnchr with YJ-83 AShM, 1 H/PJ-13 CIWS

PCG 26

6 *Houjian* (Type-037-II) with 2 triple lnchr with YJ-8 (CH-SS-N-4) AShM, 1 76mm gun

20 *Houxin* (Type-037-IG) with 2 twin lnchr with YJ-8 (CH-SS-N-4) AShM

PCC 48

2 *Haijiu* (Type-037-I) with 4 RBU 1200 A/S mor, 1 twin 57mm gun

30 *Hainan* (Type-037) with ε4 RBU 1200 A/S mor, 2 twin 57mm gun

16 *Haiqing* (Type-037-IS) with 2 FQF-3200 A/S mor

PB ε30 *Shanghai* III (Type-062-1)

MINE WARFARE 42

MINE COUNTERMEASURES 42

MCO 15: 4 *Wochi* (Type-081); 6 *Wochi* mod (Type-081A); 5 *Wozang*

MSO ε5 T-43 (Type-010/6610)

MSC 16: 4 *Wosao* I (Type-082); 12 *Wosao* II (Type-082-II)

MSD 6 *Wonang* (Type-529)

AMPHIBIOUS

PRINCIPAL AMPHIBIOUS SHIPS • LPD 4 *Yuzhao* (Type-071) with 4 AK630 CIWS, 1 76mm gun (capacity 4 *Yuyi* LCAC plus supporting vehicles; 800 troops; 60 armoured vehs; 4 hel)

LANDING SHIPS 53

LSM 23:

1 *Yudeng* (Type-073-II) (capacity 5 tk or 500 troops)

12 *Yuhai* (Type-074) (capacity 2 tk; 250 troops)

10 *Yunshu* (Type-073A) (capacity 6 tk)

LST 30:

4 *Yukan* (Type-072-IIG) (capacity 2 LCVP; 10 tk; 200 troops)

11 *Yuting* I (Type-072-II/III) (capacity 10 tk; 250 troops; 2 hel)

9 *Yuting* II (Type-072A) (capacity 4 LCVP; 10 tk; 250 troops)

6 *Yuting* III (Type-072B) (capacity 4 LCVP; 10 tk; 250 troops)

LANDING CRAFT 87

LCU 67: 11 *Yubei* (Type-074A) (capacity 10 tanks or 150 troops); 56 *Yunnan*

LCAC 8: 6 *Yuyi*; 2 *Zubr*

UCAC 12 *Payi* (Type-724)

LOGISTICS AND SUPPORT 186

ABU 5: 4 *Yannan* (Type-744); 1 Type-744A

AFS 3: 2 *Dayun* (Type-904); 1 *Danyao* (Type-904A)

AFSH 2 *Junshanhu* (Type-904B)

AG 5: 1 *Darong*; 3 *Kanhai*; 1 *Kanwu*

AGB 3: 2 *Haibing* (Type-272) with 1 hel landing platform; 1 *Yanha*

AGE 7: 2 *Dahua* (Type-909) with 1 hel landing platform (weapons test platform); 1 *Kantan*; 2 *Shupang* (Type-636); 1 *Yanqian* (Type-904I); 1 *Yanqian* (Type-904II)

AGI 8: 1 *Dadie*; 1 *Dongdiao* (Type-815) with 1 hel landing platform; 5 *Dongdiao* (Type-815A) with 1 hel landing platform; 1 *Hai Yang* (Type-625C)

AGM 4 *Yuan Wang* (Type-718) (space and missile tracking)

AGOR 2 *Dahua*

AGS 13: 1 *Kandao*; 2 *Kanyang*; 4 *Shupang* (Type-636A) with 1 hel landing platform; 2 *Yanjiu*; 4 *Yanlai* (Type-635A/B/C)

AH 8: 5 *Ankang*; 1 *Anwei* (Type-920); 2 *Qiongsha* (hospital conversion)

AK 5: 4 *Hongqi*; 1 *Yudao*

AOEH 1 Type-901 with 2 H/PJ-13 CIWS

AORH 11: 2 *Fuchi* (Type-903); 6 *Fuchi* mod (Type-903A); 2 *Fuqing* (Type-905); 1 *Fusu*

AOT 32: 4 *Fubai*; 6 *Fuchang*; 13 *Fujian* (Type-632); 8 *Fulin*; 1 *Shengli*

AP 1 *Daguan*

ARC 6 *Youdian* (Type-991)

ARS 11: 1 *Dadao*; 1 *Dadong*; 1 *Dalang* II (Type-922III); 3 *Dalang* III (Type-922IIIA); 3 *Dasan*; 2 *Dazhou*

ASR 6: 3 *Dalao* (Type-926); 3 *Dajiang* (Type-925) (capacity 2 Z-8)

ATF 33: ε17 *Hujiu*; ε13 *Roslavl*; 3 *Tuqiang*

AWT 14: 3 *Fujian*; 4 *Fulin*; 3 *Fushi*; 3 *Guangzhou*; 1 *Jinyou*

AX 4:

1 *Dashi* (Type-0891A) with 2 hel landing platforms

1 *Daxin* with 2 FQF 1200 A/S mor, 2 Type-69 CIWS, 1 57mm gun, 1 hel landing platform

1 *Qi Ji Guang* (Type-927) with 1 76mm gun, 1 hel landing platform

1 *Yudao*

ESD 1 *Donghaidao*

COASTAL DEFENCE • AShM 72 YJ-62 (3 regt)

Naval Aviation 26,000
FORCES BY ROLE
Naval aviation may be shifting from a division/regimental structure to a brigade-based structure
BOMBER
  2 regt with H-6DU/G
FIGHTER
  1 regt with J-8F *Finback*
FIGHTER/GROUND ATTACK
  1 regt with J-10A/S *Firebird*
  3 regt with J-11B/BS *Flanker* L
  1 regt with J-15 *Flanker*
  1 regt with Su-30MK2 *Flanker* G
ATTACK
  2 regt with JH-7 *Flounder*
  3 regt with JH-7A *Flounder*
ASW/AEW
  1 regt (forming) with Y-8Q; KJ-500
ELINT/ISR/AEW
  1 regt with Y-8J/JB/W/X; Y-9JB
TRANSPORT
  1 regt with Y-7H; Y-8C; CRJ-200/700
TRAINING
  1 regt with CJ-6A
  1 regt with HY-7
  1 regt with JL-8
  1 regt with JL-8/JL-9G
  1 regt with JL-9
  1 regt with Y-5
HELICOPTER
  1 regt with Ka-27PS; Ka-28; Ka-31
  1 regt with SH-5; A3565N; Z-9C/D; Z-8J/JH
  1 regt with Y-7G; Z-8; Z-8J; Z-8S; Z-9C/D
AIR DEFENCE
  1 SAM bde with HQ-9
EQUIPMENT BY TYPE
AIRCRAFT 374 combat capable
  BBR 27 H-6G
  FTR 24 J-8F *Finback*
  FGA 139: 16 J-10A *Firebird*; 7 J-10S *Firebird*; 72 J-11B/BS *Flanker* L; 20 J-15 *Flanker*; 24 Su-30MK2 *Flanker* G
  ATK 120: 48 JH-7; 72 JH-7A *Flounder*
  ASW 7+: 3 SH-5; 4+ Y-8Q
  ELINT 7: 4 Y-8JB *High New* 2; 3 Y-8X
  AEW&C 17: 4 Y-8J *Mask*; 6 Y-8W *High New* 5; 4 Y-9JB; 3+ KJ-500
  TKR 5 H-6DU
  TPT 36: **Medium** 6 Y-8C; **Light** 28: 20 Y-5; 2 Y-7G; 6 Y-7H; **PAX** 4: 2 CRJ-200; 2 CRJ-700
  TRG 107: 38 CJ-6; 12 HY-7; 16 JL-8*; 28 JL-9*; 12 JL-9GJ*; 1+ JL-10*
HELICOPTERS
  ASW 28: 14 Ka-28 *Helix* A; 14 Z-9C
  AEW 10+: 9 Ka-31; 1+ Z-18 AEW
  MRH 18: 7 AS365N; 11 Z-9D
  SAR 11: 3 Ka-27PS; 4 Z-8JH; 2 Z-8S; 2 Z-9S
  TPT 38: **Heavy** 30: 8 SA321 *Super Frelon*; 9 Z-8; 13 Z-8J; **Medium** 8 Mi-8 *Hip*
UNMANNED AERIAL VEHICLES
  ISR Heavy BZK-005; **Medium** BZK-007

AIR DEFENCE
  SAM • **Long-range** HQ-9
AIR-LAUNCHED MISSILES
  AAM • **IR** PL-5; PL-8; PL-9; R-73 (AA-11 *Archer*); **IR/SARH** R-27 (AA-10 *Alamo*); **SARH** PL-11; **ARH** R-77 (AA-12A *Adder*); PL-12
  ASM Kh-31A (AS-17B *Krypton*); KD-88
  AShM YJ-12; YJ-61; YJ-8K; YJ-83K; YJ-9
  ARM YJ-91
BOMBS
  Laser-guided: LS-500J
  TV-guided: KAB-500KR; KAB-1500KR

Marines ε15,000
FORCES BY ROLE
MANOEUVRE
  Amphibious
  3 mne bde (1 spec ops bn, 1 SF amph recce bn, 1 recce bn, 1 tk bn, 2 mech inf bn, 1 arty bn, 1 AT/AD bn, 1 engr bn, 1 sigs bn)
EQUIPMENT BY TYPE
ARMOURED FIGHTING VEHICLES
  LT TK 73 ZTD-05
  ASLT 30 ZTL-11
  IFV 60 ZBL-08
  AAV 152 ZBD-05
ANTI-TANK/ANTI-INFRASTRUCTURE
  MSL • **MANPATS** HJ-73; HJ-8
  RCL 120mm Type-98
ARTILLERY 40+
  SP 122mm 40+: 20+ PLZ-07; 20+ PLZ-89
  MRL 107mm PH-63
  MOR 82mm
AIR DEFENCE • **SAM** • **Point-defence** HN-5

Air Force 395,000

Flying hours Ftr, ground attack and bbr pilots average 100–150 hrs/yr. Tpt pilots average 200+ per year. Each regt has two quotas to meet during the year – a total number of hours, and the percentage of flight time dedicated to tactics trg

FORCES BY ROLE
Air Force fighter/ground-attack units shifting to brigade structure from 2017. Remaining J-7 and Q-5 regiments may be disbanded/being disbanded.
BOMBER
  1 regt with H-6M
  2 regt with H-6H
  5 regt with H-6K
FIGHTER
  6 regt with J-7 *Fishbed*
  2 regt with J-7E *Fishbed*
  2 bde with J-7E *Fishbed*
  3 regt with J-7G *Fishbed*
  1 regt with J-8B *Finback*
  1 bde with J-8F *Finback*
  2 regt with J-8H *Finback*
  2 bde with J-8H *Finback*
  7 bde with J-11/Su-27SK/Su-27UBK *Flanker*

FIGHTER/GROUND ATTACK
  2 regt with J-10/J-10A/J-10S *Firebird*
  6 bde with J-10/J-10A/J-10S *Firebird*
  3 bde with J-10B/S *Firebird*
  1 bde with J-10C/S *Firebird*
  3 bde with J-11B/BS *Flanker* L
  1 bde with J-11/Su-35 *Flanker*
  1 bde with J-16 *Flanker*
  3 bde with Su-30MKK *Flanker*
GROUND ATTACK
  1 regt with JH-7A *Flounder*
  5 bde with JH-7A *Flounder*
  3 regt with Q-5D/E *Fantan*
  1 bde with Q-5D/E *Fantan*
ELECTRONIC WARFARE
  2 regt with Y-8CB/G/XZ
ISR
  1 regt with JZ-8F *Finback*
  1 bde with JZ-8F *Finback*
  1 regt with Y-8H1
AIRBORNE EARLY WARNING & CONTROL
  1 regt with KJ-200 *Moth*; KJ-500; KJ-2000; Y-8T
COMBAT SEARCH & RESCUE
  5 bde with Mi-171E; Z-8
TANKER
  1 regt with H-6U
TRANSPORT
  1 (VIP) regt with B-737; CRJ-200/700
  1 (VIP) regt with B-737; Tu-154M; Tu-154M/D
  1 regt with Il-76MD/TD *Candid*
  1 regt with Il-76MD *Candid*; Il-78 *Midas*
  1 regt with Mi-17V-5; Y-7
  1 regt with Y-5/Y-7/Z-9
  1 regt with Y-5/Y-7
  3 regt with Y-7
  1 regt with Y-8
  1 regt with Y-8; Y-9
TRAINING
  2 regt with J-7; JJ-7
  13 bde with CJ-6/6A/6B; H-6; HY-7; JL-8*; Y-5; Y-7; Z-9
TRANSPORT HELICOPTER
  1 regt with AS332 *Super Puma*; H225 (VIP)
ISR UAV
  2 bde with GJ-1
AIR DEFENCE
  3 SAM div
  2 mixed SAM/ADA div
  9 SAM bde
  2 mixed SAM/ADA bde
  2 ADA bde
  9 indep SAM regt
  1 indep ADA regt
  4 indep SAM bn
EQUIPMENT BY TYPE
  AIRCRAFT 2,397 combat capable
    BBR 162: ε12 H-6 (trg role); ε60 H-6H/M; ε90 H-6K
    FTR 819: 216 J-7 *Fishbed*; 192 J-7E *Fishbed*; 120 J-7G *Fishbed*; 24 J-8B *Finback*; 24 J-8F *Finback*; 96 J-8H *Finback*; 95 J-11; 20 Su-27SK *Flanker*; 32 Su-27UBK *Flanker*
    FGA 566: 78 J-10 *Firebird*; 142 J-10A *Firebird*; 55+ J-10B *Firebird*; 24 J-10C *Firebird*; 48 J-10S *Firebird*; 110 J-11B/BS *Flanker* L; 16 J-16 *Flanker*; 6 J-20A (in test); 73 Su-30MKK *Flanker*; 14 Su-35 *Flanker*
    ATK 240: 140 JH-7A; 100 Q-5D/E *Fantan*
    EW 13: 4 Y-8CB *High New* 1; 7 Y-8G *High New* 3; 2 Y-8XZ *High New* 7
    ELINT 4 Tu-154M/D *Careless*
    ISR 51: 24 JZ-8 *Finback**; 24 JZ-8F *Finback**; 3 Y-8H1
    AEW&C 10: 4 KJ-200 *Moth*; 2 KJ-500; 4 KJ-2000
    C2 5: 2 B-737; 3 Y-8T *High New* 4
    TKR 13: 10 H-6U; 3 Il-78 *Midas*
    TPT 333+ **Heavy** 25: 20 Il-76MD/TD *Candid*; 5 Y-20; **Medium** 42+: 30 Y-8; 12+ Y-9; **Light** 239: 170 Y-5; 41 Y-7/Y-7H; 20 Y-11; 8 Y-12; **PAX** 27: 9 B-737 (VIP); 5 CRJ-200; 5 CRJ-700; 8 Tu-154M *Careless*
    TRG 974+: 400 CJ-6/6A/6B; 12+ H-Y7; 200 JJ-7*; 350 JL-8*; some JL-9*; 12+ JL-10*
  HELICOPTERS
    MRH 22: 20 Z-9; 2 Mi-17V-5 *Hip* H
    TPT 31+: **Heavy** 18+ Z-8; **Medium** 13+: 6+ AS332 *Super Puma* (VIP); 3 H225 (VIP); 4+ Mi-171
  UNMANNED AERIAL VEHICLES
    CISR • Heavy 12+ GJ-1
    ISR • Heavy 3+ EA-03
  AIR DEFENCE
    SAM 600+
      Long-range 192+: 32+ HQ-9/HQ-9B; 32 S-300PMU (SA-10 *Grumble*); 64 S-300PMU1 (SA-20 *Gargoyle*); 64 S-300PMU2 (SA-20 *Gargoyle*)
      Medium-range 324: 300+ HQ-2/HQ-2A/HQ-2B(A); 24 HQ-12 (KS-1A); HQ-22
      Short-range 84+: 24 HQ-6D; 60+ HQ-7
    GUNS 16,000 **100mm/85mm**
  AIR-LAUNCHED MISSILES
    AAM • IR PL-5B/C; PL-8; R-73 (AA-11 *Archer*); **IIR** PL-10; **IR/SARH** R-27 (AA-10 *Alamo*); **SARH** PL-11; **ARH** PL-12; R-77 (AA-12A *Adder*)
    ASM AKD-9; AKD-10; KD-88; Kh-29 (AS-14 *Kedge*); Kh-31A/P (AS-17B/A *Krypton*); Kh-59M (AS-18 *Kazoo*); AKD-9; AKD-10
    ARM YJ-91 (Domestically produced Kh-31P variant)
    ALCM • Conventional CJ-20; YJ(KD)-63
  BOMBS
    Laser-guided: LS-500J; LT-2
    TV-guided: KAB-500KR; KAB-1500KR

Airborne Corps
FORCES BY ROLE
SPECIAL FORCES
  1 spec ops bde
MANOEUVRE
  Air Manoeuvre
    6 AB bde
  Aviation
    1 hel regt
COMBAT SERVICE SUPPORT
  1 spt bde
TRANSPORT
  1 bde with Y-7; Y-8
EQUIPMENT BY TYPE
ARMOURED FIGHTING VEHICLES
  ABCV 180 ZBD-03
  APC • APC (T) 4 ZZZ-03 (CP)

ANTI-TANK/ANTI-INFRASTRUCTURE
SP some HJ-9
ARTILLERY 162+
TOWED 122mm ε54 PL-96 (D-30)
MRL 107mm ε54 PH-63
MOR 54+: 82mm some; 100mm 54
AIRCRAFT • TPT 20: Medium 6 Y-8; Light 14: 2 Y-7; 12 Y-12D
HELICOPTERS
ATK 6 WZ-10
CSAR 8 Z-8KA
MRH 12 Z-9WZ
AIR DEFENCE
SAM • Point-defence QW-1
GUNS • TOWED 25mm 54 PG-87

Strategic Support Force ε175,000

At the end of 2015, a new Strategic Support Force was established by drawing upon capabilities previously exercised by the PLA's 3rd and 4th departments and other central functions. It reports to the Central Military Commission and is believed to be responsible for the PLA's space and cyber capabilities

Theatre Commands

In early 2016, the previous seven military regions were consolidated into five new theatre commands

Northern Theatre Command

(Former Shenyang and parts of Beijing & Jinan MRs)

Northern Theatre Ground Forces
78th Group Army
(1 spec ops bde, 2 armd bde, 3 mech inf bde, 1 inf bde, 1 arty bde, 1 engr/NBC bde, 1 spt bde, 1 hel bde, 1 AD bde)
79th Group Army
(1 spec ops bde, 1 armd bde, 3 mech inf bde, 2 inf bde, 1 arty bde, 1 engr/NBC bde, 1 spt bde, 1 hel bde, 1 AD bde)
80th Group Army
(1 spec ops bde, 1 mech inf bde, 5 inf bde, 1 arty bde, 1 engr/NBC bde, 1 spt bde, 1 hel bde, 1 AD bde)

North Sea Fleet
Coastal defence from the DPRK border (Yalu River) to south of Lianyungang (approx 35°10′N), and to seaward; HQ at Qingdao; support bases at Lushun, Qingdao. 9 coastal-defence districts
5 SSN; 15 SSK; 1 CV; 3 DDGHM; 2 DDGM; 9 FFGHM; 2 FFGM; 1 FFGH; 4 FFG; 7 FSGM; ε18 PCFG/PCG; ε7 LS; ε6 MCMV

North Sea Fleet Naval Aviation
2nd Naval Air Division
(2 EW/ISR/AEW regt with Y-8J/JB/W/X; Y-9JB; 1 MP/hel regt with SH-5; AS365N; Ka-28; SA321; Z-8J/JH; Z-9C/D)
5th Naval Air Division
(2 FGA regt with JH-7A; 1 ftr regt with J-8F)

Other Forces
(1 ftr regt with J-15; 1 tpt regt with Y-7H/Y-8C/CRJ-200/CRJ-700; 1 trg regt with CJ-6A; 1 trg regt with HY-7; 1 trg regt with JL-8; 1 trg regt with JL-8/JL-9G; 1 trg regt with JL-9; 1 trg regt with Y-5)

Nothern Theatre Air Force
5th & 11th Attack Divisions
(2 atk regt with Q-5)
12th & 21st Fighter Divisions
(1 ftr regt with J-7G; 1 ftr regt with J-7H; 1 ftr regt with J-8B; 1 ftr regt with J-8H)
16th Special Mission Division
(1 EW regt with Y-8/Y-8CB/Y-8G; 1 ISR regt with JZ-8F; 1 tpt regt with Y-5/Y-7)
Dalian Base
(1 FGA bde with J-10/J-10A; 1 ftr bde with J-8F; 1 atk bde with JH-7A; 1 FGA bde with J-10B; 1 FGA bde with J-7E; 2 FGA bde with J-11B; 1 atk bde with Q-5; 1 ftr bde with J-7H)
Jinan Base
(1 FGA bde with J-10/J-10A; 1 atk bde with JH-7A)
Harbin Flying Academy
(5 trg bde with CJ-6; H-6; H-7; JL-8; Y-5)
Other Forces
(1 (mixed) SAM/ADA bde; 1 SAM bde; 4 SAM bn)

Other Forces
Marines
(1 mne bde)

Central Theatre Command
(Former Beijing & part Jinan MRs)

Central Theatre Ground Forces
81st Group Army
(1 spec ops bde, 2 armd bde, 2 mech inf bde, 1 (OPFOR) mech inf bde, 1 inf bde, 1 arty bde, 1 engr/NBC bde, 1 spt bde, 1 avn bde, 1 AD bde)
82nd Group Army
(1 spec ops bde, 1 armd bde, 3 mech bde, 1 inf bde, 1 arty bde, 1 engr/NBC bde, 1 spt bde, 1 hel bde, 1 AD bde)
83rd Group Army
(1 spec ops bde, 1 armd bde, 5 mech inf bde, 1 air aslt bde, 1 arty bde, 1 engr/NBC bde, 1 spt bde, 1 AD bde)
Other Forces
(1 hy mech inf div, 2 (Beijing) gd div)

Central Theatre Air Force
7th & 19th Fighter Divisions
(2 ftr regt with J-7; 1 trg regt with J-7/JJ-7)
15th Fighter/Attack Division
(1 FGA regt with J-10A; 1 ftr regt with J-7G)
24th Fighter Division
(1 ftr regt with J-7G; 1 FGA regt with J-10/J-10A)
Datong Base
(1 ftr bde with J-11)
Wuhan Base
(1 ftr bde with Su-27SK; 1 FGA bde with J-10B)
Shijiazhuang Flying Academy
(3 trg bde with JL-8)

Other Forces
(1 Flight Test Centre; 3 SAM div; 1 (mixed) SAM/ADA div)

Other Forces
34th VIP Transport Division
(1 tpt regt with B-737; CRJ200/700; 1 tpt regt with B-737; Tu-154M; Tu-154M/D; 1 tpt regt with Y-7; 1 hel regt with AS332; H225)

Western Theatre Command
(Former Lanzhou & part Chengdu MRs)

Western Theatre Ground Forces
(Command relationship between Western Theatre Command and Xinjiang/Xizang Military District forces unclear)
76th Group Army
(1 spec ops bde, 4 armd bde, 2 inf bde, 1 arty bde, 1 engr/NBC bde, 1 spt bde, 1 hel bde, 1 AD bde)
77th Group Army
(1 spec ops bde, 2 armd bde, 4 inf bde, 1 arty bde, 1 engr/NBC bde, 1 spt bde, 1 hel bde, 1 AD bde)
Xinjiang Military District
(1 spec ops bde, 1 (high alt) mech div, 3 (high alt) mot div, 1 arty bde, 1 AD bde, 1 engr regt, 1 EW regt, 1 hel bde)
Xizang Military District
(1 spec ops bde; 1 (high alt) mech inf bde; 2 mtn inf bde; 1 arty regt, 1 AD bde, 1 engr bde, 1 EW regt)

Western Theatre Air Force
4th Transport Division
(1 tpt regt with Y-8/Y-9; 1 tpt regt with Y-7; 1 tpt regt with Mi-17V-5/Y-7/Y-20)
6th & 33rd Fighter Divisions
(2 ftr regt with J-7E; 1 ftr regt with J-7)
36th Bomber Division
(2 bbr regt with H-6K; 1 bbr regt with H-6H)
Lanzhou Base
(2 ftr bde with J-11)
Urumqi Base
(1 ftr bde with J-8H; 1 ftr bde with J-11B; 1 atk bde with JH-7A)
Xi'an Flying Academy
(5 trg bde with JL-8; Y-7; Z-9)
Other Forces
(1 surv regt with Y-8H1; 1 (mixed) SAM/ADA div; 1 (mixed) SAM/ADA bde; 1 SAM bde; 4 indep SAM regt)

Eastern Theatre Command
(Former Nanjing MR)

Eastern Theatre Ground Forces
71st Group Army
(1 spec ops bde, 4 armd bde, 1 mech inf bde, 1 inf bde, 1 arty bde, 1 engr/NBC bde regt, 1 spt bde, 1 hel bde, 1 AD bde)
72nd Group Army
(1 spec ops bde, 1 armd bde, 1 mech inf bde, 2 inf bde, 2 amph bde, 1 arty bde, 1 engr/NBC bde, 1 spt bde, 1 hel bde, 1 AD bde)

73rd Group Army
(1 spec ops bde, 1 armd bde, 3 inf bde, 2 amph bde, 1 arty bde, 1 engr/NBC bde, 1 spt bde, 1 hel bde, 1 AD bde)

East Sea Fleet
Coastal defence from south of Lianyungang to Dongshan (approx. 35°10′N to 23°30′N), and to seaward; HQ at Ningbo; support bases at Fujian, Zhoushan, Ningbo. 7 coastal-defence districts
16 **SSK**; 9 **DDGHM**; 17 **FFGHM**; 2 **FFG**; 17 **FSGM**; ε30 **PCFG/PCG**; 1 **LPD**; ε22 **LS**; ε18 **MCMV**

East Sea Fleet Naval Aviation
4th Naval Aviation Division
(1 FGA regt with Su-30MK2; 1 hel regt with Ka-27PS; Ka-28; Ka-31; 1 FGA regt with J-10A)
6th Naval Aviation Division
(2 FGA regt with JH-7; 1 bbr regt with H-6DU/G)

Eastern Theatre Air Force
10th Bomber Division
(1 bbr regt with H-6H; 1 bbr regt with H-6K; 1 bbr regt with H-6M)
14th & 32nd Fighter Divisions
(1 ftr regt with J-7E; 1 tpt regt with Y-5/Y-7/Z-9; 1 trg regt with J-7/JJ-7)
26th Special Mission Division
(1 AEW&C regt with KJ-200/KJ-500/Y-8T; 1 AEW&C regt with KJ-2000/Y-8T)
28th Attack Division
(1 atk regt with JH-7A; 1 atk regt with Q-5D/E)
Fuzhou Base
(2 ftr bde with J-11; 1 FGA bde with Su-30MKK)
Shanghai Base
(1 FGA bde with J-16; 1 FGA bde with J-10/J-10A; 1 FGA bde with J-11B; 1 FGA bde with Su-30MKK; 1 atk bde with JH-7A; 1 ftr bde with J-8H; 1 FGA bde with J-7E)
Other Forces
(1 ISR bde with JZ-8F; 1 CSAR bde with M-171; Z-8; 3 SAM bde; 1 ADA bde; 2 indep SAM regt; 1 Flight Instructor Training Base with CJ-6; JL-8)

Southern Theatre Command
(Former Guangzhou and part Chengdu MRs)

Southern Theatre Ground Forces
74th Group Army
(1 spec ops bde, 1 armd bde, 1 mech inf bde, 2 inf bde, 2 amph bde, 1 arty bde, 1 engr/NBC bde, 1 spt bde, 1 hel bde, 1 AD bde)
75th Group Army
(1 spec ops bde, 3 armd bde, 2 mech inf bde, 1 inf bde, 1 air aslt bde, 1 arty bde, 1 engr/NBC bde, 1 spt bde, 1 AD bde)
Other Forces
(1 (composite) inf bde (Hong Kong); 1 hel sqn (Hong Kong), 1 AD bn (Hong Kong))

South Sea Fleet
Coastal defence from Dongshan (approx. 23°30´N) to VNM border, and to seaward (including Paracel and Spratly islands); HQ at Zhanjiang; support bases at Yulin, Guangzhou
4 **SSBN**; 4 **SSN**; 16 **SSK**; 9 **DDGHM**; 11 **FFGHM**; 2 **FFGM**; 10 **FFG**; 13 **FSGM**; ε38 **PCFG/PCG**; 3 **LPD**; ε22 **LS**; ε18 **MCMV**

South Sea Fleet Naval Aviation
8th Naval Aviation Division
(2 FGA regt with J-11B; 1 bbr regt with H-6DU/G)
9th Naval Aviation Division
(1 FGA regt with J-11B, 1 FGA regt with JH-7A; 1 tpt/hel regt with Y-7G; Z-8; Z-8J; Z-8S; Z-9C/D; 1 ASW/AEW&C regt with KJ-500; Y-8Q)
Other Forces
1 SAM bde

Southern Theatre Air Force
2nd, 9th & 18th Fighter Divisions
(2 ftr regt with J-7; 1 ftr regt with J-8H)
8th Bomber Division
(1 tkr regt with H-6U; 2 bbr regt with H-6K)
13th Transport Division
(1 tpt regt with Y-8C; 1 tpt regt with Il-76MD/TD; 1 tpt regt with Il-76MD; Il-78)
20th Special Mission Division
(1 tpt regt with Y-7; 1 EW regt with Y-8CB/G/XZ)
Kunming Base
(1 FGA bde with J-10/J-10A; 1 FGA bde with J-10B)
Nanning Base
(2 FGA bde with J-10A; 1 FGA bde with J-10B; 1 FGA bde with J-11/Su-35; 1 FGA bde with J-7; 1 FGA bde with Su-30MKK; 1 atk bde with JH-7A)
Other Forces
(4 SAM Bde; 3 indep SAM regt; 1 ADA bde; 1 indep ADA regt)

Other Forces
Marines
(2 mne bde)
Airborne Corps
(6 AB bde)

Paramilitary 660,000+ active

People's Armed Police ε660,000

Internal Security Forces ε400,000
FORCES BY ROLE
MANOEUVRE
  Other
  14 (mobile) paramilitary div
  22 (mobile) indep paramilitary regt
  Some (firefighting/garrison) unit

Border Defence Force ε260,000
FORCES BY ROLE
COMMAND
  30 div HQ
MANOEUVRE
  Other
  110 (border) paramilitary regt
  20 (marine) paramilitary regt

China Coast Guard (CCG)
In March 2013, four of China's maritime law-enforcement agencies were unified under the State Oceanic Administration and renamed the China Coast Guard
EQUIPMENT BY TYPE
PATROL AND COASTAL COMBATANTS 448
  PSOH 38:
    2 *Zhaotou* with 1 76mm gun (capacity 2 med hel)
    3 Type-818 (Type-054 mod) with 1 76mm gun (capacity 1 med hel)
    3 *Jiangwei* I (Type-053H2G) (capacity 1 med hel) (ex-PLAN)
    4 *Shuoshi* II (capacity 1 med hel)
    2 *Shucha* I (capacity 1 med hel)
    10 *Shucha* II (capacity 1 med hel)
    12 *Zhaoyu* (capacity 1 med hel)
    1 *Zhoachang* (capacity 1 med hel)
    1 *Zhongyang* (capacity 1 med hel)
  PSO 47:
    8 Type-718B with 1 76mm gun, 1 hel landing platform
    1 *Dalang* I (Type-922) (ex-PLAN)
    1 *Haixun* II with 1 hel landing platform
    1 *Hai Jian* 73
    1 *Hai Yang* (Type-625C) (ex-PLAN)
    1 *Jianghu* I (Type-053H) (ex-PLAN)
    1 *Kanjie* (Type-636A) with 1 hel landing platform (ex-PLAN)
    6 *Shusheng* with 1 hel landing platform
    3 *Shuwu*
    1 *Shuyang*
    3 *Tuzhong* (ex-PLAN)
    1 *Wolei* (Type-918) (ex-PLAN)
    1 *Xiang Yang Hong* 9 (ex-PLAN)
    4 *Zhaolai* with 1 hel landing platform
    14 *Zhaotim*
  PCO 33: 4 *Jiangdao* (Type-056 mod) with 1 hel landing platform; 1 *Shuke* I; 4 *Shuke* II; 13 *Shuke* III; 3 *Shuyou*; 1 *Youdian* (Type-991-II) (ex-PLAN); 4 *Zhaodai*; 3 *Zhaoming*
  PCC 130: 24 Type-618B-II; 77 *Hailin* I/II; 1 *Shuzao* II; 14 *Shuzao* III; 9 *Zhongeng*; 2 *Zhongmei*; 3 *Zhongsui*
  PB/PBF ε200
AMPHIBIOUS • **LST** 2 *Yuting* I (Type-072-II) (Ex-PLAN; used as hospital vessels and island supply)
LOGISTICS AND SUPPORT 21
  AGB 1 *Yanbing* (Type-071) (ex-PLAN)
  AGOR 9: 4 *Haijian*; 3 *Shuguang* 04 (ex-PLAN); 2 *Xiang Yang Hong* 9
  ATF 11
AIRCRAFT
  MP 1+ MA60H
  TPT • **Light** Y-12 (MP role)
HELICOPTERS
  TPT • **Light** Z-9

Maritime Militia

Made up of full- and part-time personnel. Reports to PLA command and trains to assist PLAN and CCG in a variety of military roles. These include ISR, maritime law enforcement, island supply, troop transport and supporting sovereignty claims. The Maritime Militia operates a variety of civilian vessels including fishing boats and oil tankers.

Cyber

The PLA has devoted much attention to information warfare over the past decade, in terms of both battlefield electronic warfare (EW) and wider cyber-warfare capabilities. The main doctrine is the 'Integrated Network Electronic Warfare' (INEW) document, which guides PLA computer-network operations. PLA thinking appears to have moved beyond INEW, towards a new concept of 'information confrontation' (*xinxi duikang*), which aims to integrate both electronic and non-electronic aspects of information warfare within a single command authority. PLA thinking sees warfare under informationised conditions as characterised by opposing sides using complete systems of ground, naval, air, space and electromagnetic forces. Since 2008, major PLA military exercises have had cyber and information-operations components that have been both offensive and defensive in nature. The PLA reorganised in 2015, and established three new support branches including the Strategic Support Force (SSF). Although precise responsibilities remain unclear, the SSF reportedly has three sections: the first dealing with intelligence and military operations in cyberspace (defensive and offensive); the second responsible for military space operations (surveillance and satellite); and the third in charge of defensive and offensive EW and electronic intelligence. In March 2017, China released an International Strategy for Cooperation in Cyberspace, which stated that the PLA will play an 'important role' in cyberspace. The strategy also stated that the country would 'expedite the development of a cyber force and enhance capabilities in terms of situational awareness, cyber defense, supporting state activities and participating in international cooperation, to prevent major cyber crisis, safeguard cyber security and maintain national security and social stability'. China is investing in quantum technology, and announced in September 2017 that it would build the largest quantum-research facility in the world to support technology developments that can be used by the armed forces, including code-breaking capabilities and covert navigational capacities for submarines.

DEPLOYMENT

DEMOCRATIC REPUBLIC OF THE CONGO
UN • MONUSCO 220; 12 obs; 1 engr coy; 1 fd hospital

DJIBOUTI
240; 1 mne coy(-); 1 med unit; 2 ZTL-11; 8 ZBL-08; 1 LPD; 1 ESD

GULF OF ADEN
1 DDGHM; 1 FFGHM; 1 AORH

LEBANON
UN • UNIFIL 413; 2 engr coy; 1 med coy

LIBERIA
UN • UNMIL 1

MALI
UN • MINUSMA 403; 1 sy coy; 1 engr coy; 1 fd hospital

MIDDLE EAST
UN • UNTSO 4 obs

SOUTH SUDAN
UN • UNMISS 1,047; 4 obs; 1 inf bn; 1 engr coy; 1 fd hospital

SUDAN
UN • UNAMID 370; 1 engr coy

WESTERN SAHARA
UN • MINURSO 12 obs

Fiji FJI

Fijian Dollar F$		2016	2017	2018
GDP	F$	9.79bn	10.5bn	
	US$	4.68bn	5.05bn	
per capita	US$	5,357	5,761	
Growth	%	0.4	3.8	
Inflation	%	3.9	3.8	
Def bdgt	F$	108m	105m	
	US$	52m	51m	
US$1=F$		2.09	2.07	

Population 920,938

Ethnic groups: Fijian 51%; Indian 44%; European/others 5%

Age	0–14	15–19	20–24	25–29	30–64	65 plus
Male	14.2%	4.0%	4.2%	4.0%	21.3%	3.0%
Female	13.5%	3.9%	4.0%	3.9%	20.4%	3.5%

Capabilities

The Republic of Fiji Military Forces (RFMF) are an infantry-dominated defence force with a small naval element. Work began on a National Security Strategy in February 2017, but a planned white paper had yet to be published by November 2017. The main roles of the infantry regiment are international peacekeeping (an important revenue source) and home defence. Peacekeeping training has modernised with support from New Zealand. Such international deployments have provided the RFMF with considerable operational experience; its professionalism is widely recognised. However, the RFMF has intervened heavily in domestic politics and between a third coup in 2006 and 2014 democracy was effectively suspended, leading to a rift in relations with Australia and other Western states. This opened the way for China (which signed a bilateral memorandum of understanding on defence cooperation in 2014) and Russia (which donated equipment in January 2016) to develop closer military relations with Fiji. Nevertheless, Fiji conducts joint maritime-surveillance patrols with the New Zealand Navy to monitor its EEZ.

ACTIVE 3,500 (Army 3,200 Navy 300)

RESERVE ε6,000
(to age 45)

ORGANISATIONS BY SERVICE

Army 3,200 (incl 300 recalled reserves)
FORCES BY ROLE
SPECIAL FORCES
  1 spec ops coy
MANOEUVRE
  Light
  3 inf bn
COMBAT SUPPORT
  1 arty bty
  1 engr bn
COMBAT SUPPORT
  1 log bn

Reserves 6,000
FORCES BY ROLE
MANOEUVRE
  Light
  3 inf bn
EQUIPMENT BY TYPE
ARMOURED FIGHTING VEHICLES
  AUV 10 *Bushmaster* IMV
ARTILLERY 16
  TOWED 85mm 4 25-pdr (ceremonial)
  MOR 81mm 12

Navy 300
EQUIPMENT BY TYPE
PATROL AND COASTAL COMBATANTS • PB 5: 3 *Kula* (AUS *Pacific*); 2 *Levuka*

DEPLOYMENT

EGYPT
MFO 203; elm 1 inf bn

IRAQ
UN • UNAMI 168; 2 sy unit

LEBANON
UN • UNIFIL 145; 1 inf coy

MIDDLE EAST
UN • UNTSO 2 obs

SOUTH SUDAN
UN • UNMISS 4: 2 obs

SYRIA/ISRAEL
UN • UNDOF 302; 1 inf bn(-)

India IND

Indian Rupee Rs		2016	2017	2018
GDP	Rs	152tr	167tr	
	US$	2.26tr	2.44tr	
per capita	US$	1,742	1,852	
Growth	%	7.1	6.7	
Inflation	%	4.5	3.8	
Def bdgt [a]	Rs	3.45tr	3.60tr	
	US$	51.5bn	52.5bn	
US$1=Rs		67.07	68.55	

[a] Includes defence civil estimates, which include military pensions

Population   1,281,935,911

Religious groups: Hindu 80%; Muslim 14%; Christian 2%; Sikh 2%

Age	0–14	15–19	20–24	25–29	30–64	65 plus
Male	14.5%	4.8%	4.7%	4.3%	20.6%	3.0%
Female	12.8%	4.3%	4.1%	3.9%	19.7%	3.3%

Capabilities

India continues to modernise its military capabilities. The armed forces are subordinated to the civilian political leadership and orientated against both China and Pakistan. Though internal security is the responsibility of civilian police at state level, large numbers of paramilitary forces are employed in this role. India does not have a chief of defence staff or a system of joint operational-level theatre command and control (C2). A new Indian Joint Armed Forces Doctrine was issued in 2017. Much is consistent with similar US and NATO doctrines. It sets out joint doctrine for Indian nuclear C2, and sees an 'emerging triad' of space, cyber and special-operations capabilities complementing conventional land, sea and air capabilities. A defence space agency, defence cyber agency and special-operations division are to be formed. India continues to modernise its strategic forces, particularly its delivery systems. The overall capability of the army is limited by inadequate logistics, and shortages of ammunition and spare parts. Defence cooperation with the US continues to grow, with an increasing level of exercising and sales of US equipment. Development and procurement programmes across the services are aimed at replacing ageing equipment, but many projects have experienced significant delays and cost overruns, particularly indigenous systems. The government's 'Make in India' policy aims to strengthen the defence-industrial base through measures including reforming the cap on foreign direct investment. Indian personnel participate in numerous bilateral and multilateral exercises, and the country is one of the top troop contributors to UN peacekeeping operations.

ACTIVE 1,395,100 (Army 1,200,000 Navy 58,350 Air 127,200 Coast Guard 9,550) Paramilitary 1,585,950

RESERVE 1,155,000 (Army 960,000 Navy 55,000 Air 140,000) Paramilitary 941,000

Army first-line reserves (300,000) within 5 years of full-time service, further 500,000 have commitment to age 50

ORGANISATIONS BY SERVICE

Strategic Forces Command

Strategic Forces Command (SFC) is a tri-service command established in 2003. The commander-in-chief of SFC, a senior three-star military officer, manages and administers all strategic forces through separate army and air-force chains of command

FORCES BY ROLE
SURFACE-TO-SURFACE MISSILE
  1 SRBM gp with *Agni* I
  1 MRBM gp with *Agni* II
  1 IRBM gp (reported forming) with *Agni* III
  2 SRBM gp with SS-250 *Prithvi* II
EQUIPMENT BY TYPE
SURFACE-TO-SURFACE MISSILE LAUNCHERS 54
  ICBM • **Nuclear** *Agni* V (in test)
  IRBM • **Nuclear** *Agni* III (entering service); *Agni* IV (in test)
  MRBM • **Nuclear** ε12 *Agni* II
  SRBM • **Nuclear** 42: ε12 *Agni* I; ε30 SS-250 *Prithvi* II; some SS-350 *Dhanush* (naval testbed)
AIR-LAUNCHED MISSILES
  ALCM • **Nuclear** *Nirbhay* (likely nuclear capable; in development)
Some Indian Air Force assets (such as *Mirage* 2000H or Su-30MKI) may be tasked with a strategic role

Space

EQUIPMENT BY TYPE
SATELLITES 12
  NAVIGATION, POSITONING, TIMING: 7 IRNSS
  COMMUNICATIONS: 2 GSAT
  ISR 3: 1 *Cartosat* 2C; 2 RISAT

Army 1,200,000

6 Regional Comd HQ (Northern, Western, Central, Southern, Eastern, Southwestern), 1 Training Comd (ARTRAC)

FORCES BY ROLE
COMMAND
  4 (strike) corps HQ
  10 (holding) corps HQ
SPECIAL FORCES
  8 SF bn
MANOEUVRE
  Armoured
  3 armd div (2–3 armd bde, 1 arty bde (2 arty regt))
  8 indep armd bde
  Mechanised
  6 (RAPID) mech inf div (1 armd bde, 2 mech inf bde, 1 arty bde)
  2 indep mech bde
  Light
  15 inf div (2–5 inf bde, 1 arty bde)
  1 inf div (forming)
  7 indep inf bde
  12 mtn div (3-4 mtn inf bde, 3–4 arty regt)
  2 indep mtn bde
  Air Manoeuvre
  1 para bde
SURFACE-TO-SURFACE MISSILE
  1 SRBM gp with *Agni* I
  1 MRBM gp with *Agni* II
  1 IRBM gp (reported forming) with *Agni* III
  2 SRBM gp with SS-250 *Prithvi* II
  3 GLCM regt with PJ-10 *Brahmos*
COMBAT SUPPORT
  3 arty div (2 arty bde, 1 MRL bde)
  2 indep arty bde
  4 engr bde
HELICOPTER
  14 hel sqn
AIR DEFENCE
  8 AD bde

Reserve Organisations

Reserves 300,000 reservists (first-line reserve within 5 years full-time service); 500,000 reservists (commitment until age 50) (total 800,000)

Territorial Army 160,000 reservists (only 40,000 regular establishment)

FORCES BY ROLE
MANOEUVRE
  Light
  42 inf bn
COMBAT SUPPORT
  6 (Railway) engr regt
  2 engr regt
  1 sigs regt
COMBAT SERVICE SUPPORT
  6 ecological bn
EQUIPMENT BY TYPE
ARMOURED FIGHTING VEHICLES
  MBT 3,097+: 122 *Arjun*; 1,950 T-72M1; 1,025+ T-90S (ε1,100 various models in store)
  RECCE *Ferret* (used for internal-security duties along with some indigenously built armd cars)
  IFV 2,500: 700 BMP-1; 1,800 BMP-2 *Sarath* (incl some BMP-2K CP)
  APC 336+
    APC (W) 157+ OT-64
    PPV 179: 165 *Casspir*; 14+ *Yukthirath* MPV
ENGINEERING & MAINTENANCE VEHICLES
  AEV BMP-2; FV180
  ARV T-54/T-55; VT-72B; WZT-2; WZT-3
  VLB AM-50; BLG-60; BLG T-72; *Kartik*; MTU-20; MT-55; *Sarvatra*
  MW 24 910 MCV-2
ANTI-TANK/ANTI-INFRASTRUCTURE
  MSL
    SP 110 9P148 *Konkurs* (AT-5 *Spandrel*)
    MANPATS 9K11 *Malyutka* (AT-3 *Sagger*) (being phased out); 9K111 *Fagot* (AT-4 *Spigot*); 9K113 *Konkurs* (AT-5 *Spandrel*); *Milan* 2
  RCL 3,000+: **84mm** *Carl Gustav*; **106mm** 3,000+ M40A1 (10 per inf bn)

ARTILLERY 9,684+
  TOWED 2,972+: **105mm** 1,350+: 600+ IFG Mk1/Mk2/Mk3 (being replaced); up to 700 LFG; 50 M-56; **122mm** 520 D-30; **130mm** ε600 M-46 (500 in store) **155mm** 502: ε300 FH-77B; ε200 M-46 (mod); 2 M777
  MRL 192: **122mm** ε150 BM-21/LRAR **214mm** 14 *Pinaka* (non-operational) **300mm** 28 9A52 *Smerch*
  MOR 6,520+: **81mm** 5,000+ E1; **120mm** ε1,500 AM-50/E1; **SP 120mm** E1; **160mm** 20 M-58 Tampella
SURFACE-TO-SURFACE MISSILE LAUNCHERS
  IRBM • **Nuclear** some *Agni-III* (entering service)
  MRBM • **Nuclear** ε12 *Agni-II*
  SRBM • **Nuclear** 42: ε12 *Agni-I*; ε30 250 *Prithvi* II
  GLCM • **Conventional** 15 PJ-10 *Brahmos*
RADAR • **LAND** 38+: 14 AN/TPQ-37 *Firefinder*; BSR Mk.2; 24 *Cymbeline*; EL/M-2140; M113 A1GE *Green Archer* (mor); MUFAR; *Stentor*
AMPHIBIOUS 2 LCVP
HELICOPTERS
  MRH 275+: 80 *Dhruv*; 12 *Lancer*; 3+ *Rudra*; 120 SA315B *Lama* (*Cheetah*); 60 SA316B *Alouette* III (*Chetak*)
UNMANNED AERIAL VEHICLES
  ISR • **Medium** 25: 13 *Nishant*; 12 *Searcher* Mk I/II
AIR DEFENCE
  SAM
    Medium-range *Akash*
    Short-range 180 2K12 *Kub* (SA-6 *Gainful*)
    Point-defence 500+: 50+ 9K33 *Osa* (SA-8B *Gecko*); 200 9K31 *Strela-1* (SA-9 *Gaskin*); 250 9K35 *Strela-10* (SA-13 *Gopher*); 9K32 *Strela-2* (SA-7 *Grail* – being phased out)‡; 9K310 *Igla-1* (SA-16 *Gimlet*); 9K38 *Igla* (SA-18 *Grouse*)
  GUNS 2,395+
    SP 155+: 23mm 75 ZSU-23-4; ZU-23-2 (truck-mounted); **30mm** 20-80 2S6 *Tunguska*
    TOWED 2,240+: **20mm** Oerlikon (reported); **23mm** 320 ZU-23-2; **40mm** 1,920 L40/70

Navy 58,350 (incl 7,000 Naval Avn and 1,200 Marines)

Fleet HQ New Delhi. Commands located at Mumbai, Vishakhapatnam, Kochi & Port Blair
EQUIPMENT BY TYPE
SUBMARINES • TACTICAL 14
  SSN 1 *Chakra* (ex-RUS *Akula* II) with 4 single 533mm TT with 3M54E *Klub* (SS-N-27B *Sizzler*) AShM, 4 single 650mm TT with T-65 HWT (RUS lease agreement)
  SSK 13:
    4 *Shishumar* (GER T-209/1500) with 8 single 533mm TT with AEG SUT mod 1 HWT
    2 *Sindhughosh* (FSU *Kilo*) with 6 single 533mm TT with 53-65KE HWT/TEST-71ME HWT/SET-65E HWT
    7 *Sindhughosh* (FSU *Kilo*) with 6 single 533mm TT with 53-65KE HWT/TEST-71ME HWT/SET-65E HWT/3M54E *Klub* (SS-N-27B *Sizzler*) AShM
PRINCIPAL SURFACE COMBATANTS 28
  AIRCRAFT CARRIERS 1
    CV 1 *Vikramaditya* (ex-FSU *Kiev* mod) with 3 octuple VLS with *Barak-1* SAM, 4 AK630 CIWS (capacity: 12 MiG-29K/KUB *Fulcrum* FGA ac; 6 Ka-28 *Helix* A ASW hel/Ka-31 *Helix* B AEW hel)
  DESTROYERS 14
    DDGHM 9:
      3 *Delhi* with 4 quad lnchr with 3M24E *Uran-E* (SS-N-25 *Switchblade*) AShM, 2 single lnchr with 3K90 *Uragan* (SA-N-7 *Gadfly*) SAM, 4 octuple VLS with *Barak-1* SAM, 5 single 533mm ASTT, 2 RBU 6000 A/S mor; 2 AK630 CIWS, 1 100mm gun (capacity either 2 *Dhruv* hel/*Sea King* Mk42A ASW hel)
      3 *Kolkata* with 2 octuple VLS with *Brahmos* AShM; 4 octuple VLS fitted for *Barak-8* SAM; 2 twin 533mm TT with SET-65E HWT, 2 RBU 6000 *Smerch* 2 A/S mor, 4 AK630 CIWS, 1 76mm gun (capacity 2 *Dhruv*/*Sea King* Mk42B hel)
      3 *Shivalik* with 1 octuple VLS with 3M54E *Klub* (SS-N-27B *Sizzler*) AShM; *Brahmos* AShM, 4 octuple VLS with *Barak-1* SAM, 1 single lnchr with 3K90 *Uragan* (SA-N-7 *Gadfly*) SAM, 2 triple 324mm ASTT, 2 RBU 6000 *Smerch* 2 A/S mor, 2 AK630 CIWS, 1 76mm gun (capacity 1 *Sea King* Mk42B ASW hel)
    DDGM 5:
      2 *Rajput* (FSU *Kashin*) with 2 twin lnchr with P-15M *Termit* (SS-N-2C *Styx*) AShM, 2 twin lnchr with M-1 *Volna* (SA-N-1 *Goa*) SAM, 5 single 533mm ASTT, 2 RBU 6000 *Smerch* 2 A/S mor, 2 AK630 CIWS, 1 76mm gun (capacity Ka-28 *Helix* A hel)
      1 *Rajput* (FSU *Kashin*) with 2 twin lnchr with *Brahmos* AShM, 2 single lnchr with P-15M *Termit* (SS-N-2C *Styx*) AShM, 2 twin lnchr with M-1 *Volna* (SA-N-1 *Goa*) SAM, 5 single 533mm ASTT with SET-65E HWT, 2 RBU 6000 *Smerch* 2 A/S mor, 4 AK630 CIWS, 1 76mm gun (capacity 1 Ka-28 *Helix* A hel)
      2 *Rajput* (FSU *Kashin*) with 1 octuple VLS with *Brahmos* AShM, 2 twin lnchr with P-15M *Termit* (SS-N-2C *Styx*) AShM, 2 octuple VLS with *Barak* SAM. 1 twin lnchr with M-1 *Volna* (SA-N-1 *Goa*) SAM, 5 single 533mm ASTT with SET-65E HWT, 2 RBU 6000 *Smerch* 2 A/S mor, 4 AK630 CIWS, 1 76mm gun (capacity 1 Ka-28 *Helix* A hel)
  FRIGATES 13
    FFGHM 10:
      3 *Brahmaputra* with 4 quad lnchr with 3M24E *Uran-E* (SS-N-25 *Switchblade*) AShM, 3 octuple VLS with *Barak-1* SAM, 2 triple 324mm ASTT with A244 LWT, 4 AK630 CIWS, 1 76mm gun (capacity 2 SA316B *Alouette* III (*Chetak*)/*Sea King* Mk42 ASW hel) (of which 1 non-operational)
      1 *Godavari* with 4 single lnchr with P-15M *Termit* (SS-N-2D *Styx*) AShM, 1 octuple VLS with *Barak-1* SAM, 2 triple 324mm ASTT with A244 LWT, 4 AK630 CIWS, 1 76mm gun (capacity 2 SA316B *Alouette* III (*Chetak*)/*Sea King* Mk42 ASW hel)
      3 *Talwar* I with 1 octuple VLS with 3M54E *Klub* (SS-N-27B *Sizzler*) AShM, 1 single lnchr with 3K90 *Uragan* (SA-N-7 *Gadfly*) SAM, 2 twin 533mm ASTT with SET-65E HWT, 2 RBU 6000 *Smerch* 2 A/S mor, 2 *Kashtan* (CADS-N-1) CIWS, 1 100mm gun (capacity 1 *Dhruv*/Ka-28 *Helix* A ASW hel)
      3 *Talwar* II with 1 octuple VLS with *Brahmos* AShM, 1 single lnchr with 3K90 *Uragan* (SA-N-7 *Gadfly*)

SAM, 2 twin 533mm ASTT with SET-65E HWT, 2 RBU 6000 *Smerch* 2 A/S mor, 2 AK630 CIWS, 1 100mm gun (capacity 1 *Dhruv*/Ka-28 *Helix* A ASW hel)

FFH 3:

3 *Kamorta* with 2 twin 533mm TT, 2 RBU 6000 *Smerch* 2 A/S mor, 2 AK630 CIWS, 1 76mm gun (capacity 1 *Dhruv*/Ka-28 *Helix* A ASW hel)

PATROL AND COASTAL COMBATANTS 108

CORVETTES • FSGM 8:

4 *Khukri* with 2 twin lnchr with P-15M *Termit* (SS-N-2C *Styx*) AShM, 2 twin lnchr (manual aiming) with 9K32M *Strela*-2M (SA-N-5 *Grail*) SAM, 2 AK630 CIWS, 1 76mm gun, 1 hel landing platform (for *Dhruv*/SA316 *Alouette* III (*Chetak*))

4 *Kora* with 4 quad lnchr with 3M24E *Uran*-E (SS-N-25 *Switchblade*) AShM, 1 quad lnchr (manual aiming) with 9K32M *Strela*-2M (SA-N-5 *Grail*) SAM, 2 AK630 CIWS, 1 76mm gun, 1 hel landing platform (for *Dhruv*/SA316 *Alouette* III (*Chetak*))

PSOH 10: 4 *Saryu* with 2 AK630 CIWS, 1 76mm gun (capacity 1 *Dhruv*); 6 *Sukanya* with 4 RBU 2500 A/S mor (capacity 1 SA316 *Alouette* III (*Chetak*))

PCFGM 10

8 *Veer* (FSU *Tarantul*) with 4 single lnchr with P-15M *Termit* (SS-N-2D *Styx*) AShM, 2 quad lnchr (manual aiming) with 9K32M *Strela*-2M (SA-N-5 *Grail*), 2 AK630 CIWS, 1 76mm gun

2 *Prabal* (mod *Veer*) each with 4 quad lnchr with 3M24E *Uran*-E (SS-N-25 *Switchblade*) AShM, 1 quad lnchr (manual aiming) with 9K32M *Strela*-2M (SA-N-5 *Grail*) SAM, 2 AK630 CIWS, 1 76mm gun

PCMT 3 *Abhay* (FSU *Pauk* II) with 1 quad lnchr (manual aiming) with 9K32M *Strela*-2M (SA-N-5 *Grail*) SAM, 2 twin 533mm ASTT, 2 RBU 1200 A/S mor, 1 76mm gun

PCC 15: 4 *Bangaram*; 10 *Car Nicobar*; 1 *Trinkat* (SDB Mk5)

PCF 4 *Tarmugli* (*Car Nicobar* mod)

PBF 58: 9 Immediate Support Vessel (Rodman 78); 13 Immediate Support Vessel (Craftway); 15 Plascoa 1300 (SPB); 5 *Super Dvora*; 16 Solas Marine Interceptor (additional vessels in build)

MINE WARFARE • MINE COUNTERMEASURES 4

MSO 4 *Pondicherry* (FSU *Natya*) with 2 RBU 1200 A/S mor

AMPHIBIOUS

PRINCIPAL AMPHIBIOUS VESSELS 1

LPD 1 *Jalashwa* (ex-US *Austin*) with 1 *Phalanx* CIWS (capacity up to 6 med spt hel; either 9 LCM or 4 LCM and 2 LCAC; 4 LCVP; 930 troops)

LANDING SHIPS 8

LSM 3 *Kumbhir* (FSU *Polnocny* C) (capacity 5 MBT or 5 APC; 160 troops)

LST 5:

2 *Magar* (capacity 15 MBT or 8 APC or 10 trucks; 500 troops)

3 *Magar* mod (capacity 11 MBT or 8 APC or 10 trucks; 500 troops)

LANDING CRAFT 10

LCM 4 LCM 8 (for use in *Jalashwa*)

LCT 6: 2 LCU Mk-IV; 4 LCU Mk-3 (capacity 2 APC; 120 troops)

LOGISTICS AND SUPPORT 31

AGOR 1 *Sagardhwani* with 1 hel landing platform

AGHS 7 *Sandhayak*

AGS 1 *Makar*

AOL 7: 6 *Poshak*; 1 *Ambika*

AOR 1 *Jyoti* with 1 hel landing platform

AORH 3: 1 *Aditya* (based on *Deepak* (1967) Bremer Vulkan design); 2 *Deepak* with 4 AK630 CIWS

AP 3 *Nicobar* with 1 hel landing platform

ASR 1

ATF 1

AWT 2

AX 1 *Tir*

AXS 3

Naval Aviation 7,000

FORCES BY ROLE

FIGHTER/GROUND ATTACK

2 sqn with MiG-29K/KUB *Fulcrum*

ANTI-SUBMARINE WARFARE

4 sqn with Ka-28 *Helix* A; SA316B *Alouette* III (*Chetak*); *Sea King* Mk42A/B

MARITIME PATROL

2 sqn with BN-2 *Islander*; Do-228-101; Il-38SD *May*

1 sqn with P-8I *Neptune*

AIRBORNE EARLY WARNING & CONTROL

1 sqn with Ka-31 *Helix* B

SEARCH & RESCUE

1 sqn with SA316B *Alouette* III (*Chetak*); *Sea King* Mk42C

1 sqn with *Dhruv*

TRANSPORT

1 sqn with HS-748M (HAL-748M)

TRAINING

1 sqn with Do-228

1 sqn with HJT-16 *Kiran* MkI/II, *Hawk* Mk132

TRANSPORT HELICOPTER

1 sqn with UH-3H *Sea King*

ISR UAV

1 sqn with *Heron*; *Searcher* MkII

EQUIPMENT BY TYPE

AIRCRAFT 69 combat capable

FTR 45 MiG-29K/KUB *Fulcrum*

ASW 13: 5 Il-38SD *May*; 8 P-8I *Neptune*

MP 13 Do-228-101

TPT 37:

Light 27: 17 BN-2 *Islander*; 10 Do-228

PAX 10 HS-748M (HAL-748M)

TRG 23: 6 HJT-16 *Kiran* MkI; 6 HJT-16 *Kiran* MkII; 11 *Hawk* Mk132*

HELICOPTERS

ASW 47: 12 Ka-28 *Helix* A; 21 *Sea King* Mk42A; 14 *Sea King* Mk42B

MRH 58: 10 *Dhruv*; 25 SA316B *Alouette* III (*Chetak*); 23 SA319 *Alouette* III

AEW 9 Ka-31 *Helix* B

TPT

Medium 11: 5 *Sea King* Mk42C; up to 6 UH-3H *Sea King*

UNMANNED AERIAL VEHICLES
ISR 10: **Heavy** 4 *Heron*; **Medium** 6 *Searcher* Mk II
AIR-LAUNCHED MISSILES
AAM • **IR** R-550 *Magic/Magic* 2; R-73 (AA-11 *Archer*) **IR/SARH** R-27 (AA-10 *Alamo*); **ARH** R-77 (AA-12A *Adder*)
AShM AGM-84 *Harpoon* (on P-8I ac); Kh-35 (AS-20 *Kayak*; on *Bear* and *May* ac); *Sea Eagle* (service status unclear)

Marines ε1,200 (Additional 1,000 for SPB duties)

After the Mumbai attacks, the Sagar Prahari Bal (SPB), with 80 PBF, was established to protect critical maritime infrastructure

FORCES BY ROLE
SPECIAL FORCES
1 (marine) cdo force
MANOEUVRE
Amphibious
1 amph bde

Air Force 127,200

5 regional air comds: Western (New Delhi), Southwestern (Gandhinagar), Eastern (Shillong), Central (Allahabad), Southern (Trivandrum). 2 support comds: Maintenance (Nagpur) and Training (Bangalore)

Flying hours   180 hrs/yr

FORCES BY ROLE
FIGHTER
3 sqn with MiG-29 *Fulcrum*; MiG-29UB *Fulcrum*
FIGHTER/GROUND ATTACK
4 sqn with *Jaguar* IB/IS
6 sqn with MiG-21 *Bison*
1 sqn with MiG-21M/MF *Fishbed*
4 sqn with MiG-27ML/MiG-23UB *Flogger*
3 sqn with *Mirage* 2000E/ED/I/IT (2000H/TH – secondary ECM role)
11 sqn with Su-30MKI *Flanker*
ANTI SURFACE WARFARE
1 sqn with *Jaguar* IM
ISR
1 unit with Gulfstream IV SRA-4
AIRBORNE EARLY WARNING & CONTROL
1 sqn with Il-76TD *Phalcon*
TANKER
1 sqn with Il-78 *Midas*
TRANSPORT
1 sqn with C-130J-30 *Hercules*
1 sqn with C-17A *Globemaster* III
5 sqn with An-32/An-32RE *Cline*
1 (comms) sqn with B-737; B-737BBJ; EMB-135BJ
4 sqn with Do-228; HS-748
1 sqn with Il-76MD *Candid*
1 flt with HS-748
TRAINING
1 OCU sqn with Su-30MKI *Flanker*
1 sqn (forming) with *Tejas*
Some units with An-32; Do-228; *Hawk* Mk 132*; HJT-16 *Kiran* MkI/II; *Jaguar* IS/IM; MiG-21bis; MiG-21FL; MiG-21M/MF; MiG-27ML; PC-7 *Turbo Trainer* MkII; SA316B *Alouette* III (*Chetak*)
ATTACK HELICOPTER
2 sqn with Mi-25 *Hind*; Mi-35 *Hind*
TRANSPORT HELICOPTER
5 sqn with *Dhruv*
1 sqn with Mi-8 *Hip*
7 sqn with Mi-17/Mi-17-1V *Hip* H
12 sqn with Mi-17V-5 *Hip* H
2 sqn with SA316B *Alouette* III (*Chetak*)
1 flt with Mi-8 *Hip*
1 flt with Mi-26 *Halo*
2 flt with SA315B *Lama* (*Cheetah*)
2 flt with SA316B *Alouette* III (*Chetak*)
ISR UAV
5 sqn with *Heron*; *Searcher* MkII
AIR DEFENCE
25 sqn with S-125 *Pechora* (SA-3B *Goa*)
6 sqn with 9K33 Osa-AK (SA-8B *Gecko*)
2 sqn with *Akash*
10 flt with 9K38 Igla-1 (SA-18 *Grouse*)

EQUIPMENT BY TYPE
AIRCRAFT 849 combat capable
FTR 62: 55 MiG-29 *Fulcrum* (incl 12+ MiG-29UPG); 7 MiG-29UB *Fulcrum*
FGA 561: 115 MiG-21 *Bison*; 20 MiG-21M/MF *Fishbed*; 39 MiG-21U/UM *Mongol*; 65 MiG-27ML *Flogger*; 20 MiG-23UB *Flogger*; 40 *Mirage* 2000E/I (2000H); 10 *Mirage* 2000ED/IT (2000TH); ε250 Su-30MKI *Flanker*; 2 *Tejas*
ATK 117: 28 *Jaguar* IB; 79 *Jaguar* IS; 10 *Jaguar* IM
ISR 3 Gulfstream IV SRA-4
AEW&C 4: 1 EMB-145AEW *Netra* (2 more in test); 3 Il-76TD *Phalcon*
TKR 6 Il-78 *Midas*
TPT 241: **Heavy** 27: 10 C-17A *Globemaster* III; 17 Il-76MD *Candid*; **Medium** 9 C-130J-30 *Hercules*; **Light** 141: 57 An-32; 45 An-32RE *Cline*; 35 Do-228; 4 EMB-135BJ; **PAX** 64: 1 B-707; 4 B-737; 3 B-737BBJ; 56 HS-748
TRG 339: 89 *Hawk* Mk132*; 120 HJT-16 *Kiran* MkI/IA; 55 HJT-16 *Kiran* MkII; 20 MiG-23UB*; 75 PC-7 *Turbo Trainer* MkII
HELICOPTERS
ATK 19 Mi-25/Mi-35 *Hind*
MRH 387: 60 *Dhruv*; 35 Mi-17 *Hip* H; 45 Mi-17-1V *Hip* H; 149 Mi-17V-5 *Hip* H; 59 SA315B *Lama* (*Cheetah*); 39 SA316B *Alouette* III (*Chetak*)
TPT 56+: **Heavy** 1+ Mi-26 *Halo*; **Medium** 55+ Mi-8 *Hip*
UNMANNED AERIAL VEHICLES
ISR • **Heavy** 9 *Heron*; **Medium** some *Searcher* MkII
AIR DEFENCE • SAM
Medium-range *Akash*
Short-range S-125 *Pechora* (SA-3B *Goa*)
Point-defence 9K33 Osa-AK (SA-8B *Gecko*); 9K38 Igla (SA-18 *Grouse*)
AIR-LAUNCHED MISSILES
AAM • **IR** R-60 (AA-8 *Aphid*); R-73 (AA-11 *Archer*) R-550 *Magic*; **IIR** *Mica* IR; **IR/SARH** R-27 (AA-10 *Alamo*); **SARH** Super 530D **ARH** R-77 (AA-12A *Adder*); *Mica* RF
AShM AGM-84 *Harpoon*; AM39 *Exocet*; *Sea Eagle*†

ASM Kh-29 (AS-14 *Kedge*); Kh-59 (AS-13 *Kingbolt*); Kh-59M (AS-18 *Kazoo*); Kh-31A (AS-17B *Krypton*); AS-30; Kh-23 (AS-7 *Kerry*)‡; *Popeye* II (*Crystal Maze*)
ARM Kh-25MP (AS-12 *Kegler*); Kh-31P (AS-17A *Krypton*)
ALCM • **Nuclear** *Nirbhay* (likely nuclear capable; in development)
BOMBS • **Laser-guided** *Paveway* II

Coast Guard 9,550

EQUIPMENT BY TYPE
PATROL AND COASTAL COMBATANTS 110
PSOH 14: 2 *Sankalp* (capacity 1 *Chetak/Dhruv* hel); 4 *Samar* with 1 76mm gun (capacity 1 *Chetak/Dhruv* hel); 5 *Samarth*; 3 *Vishwast* (capacity 1 *Dhruv* hel)
PSO 3 *Samudra Prahari* with 1 hel landing platform
PCO 2 *Vikram* with 1 hel landing platform
PCC 39: 20 *Aadesh*; 8 *Rajshree*; 4 *Rani Abbakka*; 7 *Sarojini Naidu*
PBF 48: 4 C-154; 2 C-141; 11 C-143; 31 C-401
PB 4 *Priyadarshini*
AMPHIBIOUS
UCAC 18: 6 H-181 (*Griffon* 8000TD); 12 H-187 (*Griffon* 8000TD)
AIRCRAFT • **TPT** • **Light** 23 Do-228
HELICOPTERS • **MRH** 21: 4 *Dhruv*; 17 SA316B *Alouette* III (*Chetak*)

Paramilitary 1,585,950

Rashtriya Rifles 65,000
Ministry of Defence. 15 sector HQ
FORCES BY ROLE
MANOEUVRE
  Other
  65 paramilitary bn

Assam Rifles 63,750
Ministry of Home Affairs. Security within northeastern states, mainly army-officered; better trained than BSF
FORCES BY ROLE
Equipped to roughly same standard as an army inf bn
COMMAND
  7 HQ
MANOEUVRE
  Other
  46 paramilitary bn
EQUIPMENT BY TYPE
ARTILLERY • **MOR 81mm** 252

Border Security Force 257,350
Ministry of Home Affairs
FORCES BY ROLE
MANOEUVRE
  Other
  186 paramilitary bn
EQUIPMENT BY TYPE
Small arms, lt arty, some anti-tank weapons
ARTILLERY • **MOR 81mm** 942+
AIRCRAFT • **TPT** some (air spt)
HELICOPTERS • **MRH** 2 Mi-17V-5 *Hip*

Central Industrial Security Force 144,400 (lightly armed security guards)
Ministry of Home Affairs. Guards public-sector locations

Central Reserve Police Force 313,650
Ministry of Home Affairs. Internal-security duties, only lightly armed, deployable throughout the country
FORCES BY ROLE
MANOEUVRE
  Other
  236 paramilitary bn
  10 (rapid action force) paramilitary bn
  10 (CoBRA) paramilitary bn
  6 (Mahila) paramilitary bn (female)
  2 sy gp
COMBAT SUPPORT
  5 sigs bn

Defence Security Corps 31,000
Provides security at Defence Ministry sites

Indo-Tibetan Border Police 89,450
Ministry of Home Affairs. Tibetan border security SF/guerrilla-warfare and high-altitude-warfare specialists
FORCES BY ROLE
MANOEUVRE
  Other
  56 paramilitary bn

National Security Guards 12,000
Anti-terrorism contingency deployment force, comprising elements of the armed forces, CRPF and Border Security Force

Railway Protection Forces 70,000

Sashastra Seema Bal 76,350
Guards the borders with Nepal and Bhutan

Special Frontier Force 10,000
Mainly ethnic Tibetans

Special Protection Group 3,000
Protection of ministers and senior officials

State Armed Police 450,000
For duty primarily in home state only, but can be moved to other states. Some bn with GPMG and army-standard infantry weapons and equipment
FORCES BY ROLE
MANOEUVRE
  Other
  144 (India Reserve Police) paramilitary bn

Reserve Organisations

Civil Defence 500,000 reservists
Operate in 225 categorised towns in 32 states. Some units for NBC defence

Home Guard 441,000 reservists (547,000 authorised str)

In all states except Arunachal Pradesh and Kerala; men on reserve lists, no trg. Not armed in peacetime. Used for civil defence, rescue and firefighting provision in wartime; 6 bn (created to protect tea plantations in Assam)

Cyber

National agencies include the Computer Emergency Response Team (CERT-In), which has authorised designated individuals to carry out penetration tests against infrastructure. The Defence Information Assurance and Research Agency (DIARA) is mandated to deal with cyber-security-related issues for the armed services. All services have their own cyber-security policies and CERT teams, and headquarters maintain information-security policies. The Indian Army raised the Army Cyber Security Establishment in 2005 and set up the Cyber Security Laboratory at the Military College of Telecommunication Engineering (under the Corps of Signals) in April 2010. The services have their own cyber groups, and the defence minister announced in July 2017 that a long-awaited proposal to establish a tri-service command for cyberspace had been approved.

DEPLOYMENT

AFGHANISTAN
335 (Indo-Tibetan Border Police paramilitary: facilities protection)

DEMOCRATIC REPUBLIC OF THE CONGO
UN • MONUSCO 2,640; 39 obs; 4 inf bn; 1 fd hospital

LEBANON
UN • UNIFIL 902; 1 inf bn; 1 med coy

MIDDLE EAST
UN • UNTSO 1 obs

SOUTH SUDAN
UN • UNMISS 2,373; 11 obs; 2 inf bn; 1 engr coy; 1 fd hospital

SUDAN
UN • UNISFA 3; 2 obs

SYRIA/ISRAEL
UN • UNDOF 204; 1 log bn

WESTERN SAHARA
UN • MINURSO 3 obs

FOREIGN FORCES

Total numbers for UNMOGIP mission in India and Pakistan
Chile 2 obs
Croatia 9 obs
Italy 2 obs
Korea, Republic of 7 obs
Philippines 7 obs
Romania 2 obs
Sweden 6 obs
Switzerland 3 obs
Thailand 4 obs
Uruguay 2 obs

Indonesia IDN

Indonesian Rupiah Rp		2016	2017	2018
GDP	Rp	12,407tr	13,505tr	
	US$	932bn	1.01tr	
per capita	US$	3,604	3,859	
Growth	%	5.0	5.2	
Inflation	%	3.5	4.0	
Def bdgt	Rp	98.2tr	120tr	106tr
	US$	7.38bn	8.98bn	
FMA (US)	US$	14m	10m	0m
US$1=Rp		13,305.63	13,358.77	

Population 260,580,739

Ethnic groups: Jawa 40.2%; Sunda, Priangan 15.5%; Banjar, Melayu Banjar 4%; other or unspecified 40.5%

Age	0–14	15–19	20–24	25–29	30–64	65 plus
Male	12.7%	4.4%	4.2%	3,9%	21.6%	3.0%
Female	12.3%	4.3%	4.1%	3.7%	21.6%	3.9%

Capabilities

The Indonesian National Defence Force (TNI) has traditionally been concerned primarily with internal security and counter-insurgency. The army remains the dominant service and is deployed operationally in West Papua and on counter-terrorist operations in central Sulawesi and elsewhere. However, the emergence of clearer threats to Jakarta's extensive maritime interests have contributed to a drive to restructure and modernise the TNI. The current modernisation plan calls for the establishment by 2024 of a 'Minimum Essential Force', including strengthened air, naval and maritime-paramilitary capabilities. Increased defence spending has enabled military modernisation and restructuring, and has allowed for significant equipment acquisitions, including the first new *Nagapasa*-class attack submarine, and the construction of new infrastructure. However, continuing budget pressures are likely to slow efforts to strengthen capabilities. Indonesia has bought military equipment from diverse sources, while using technology-transfer agreements with foreign suppliers to develop its own defence industry. The TNI has contributed to international peacekeeping operations, and exercises with the Australian and US armed forces and those of several other Southeast Asian states. In 2017, Indonesia began trilateral joint maritime patrols and joint Sulu Sea air patrols with the Philippines and Malaysia to counter movement and attacks by ISIS-linked militants in regional waterways.

ACTIVE 395,500 (Army 300,400 Navy 65,000 Air 30,100) **Paramilitary 280,000**

Conscription liability 2 years selective conscription authorised (not required by law)

RESERVE 400,000

Army cadre units; numerical str n.k., obligation to age 45 for officers

ORGANISATIONS BY SERVICE

Army ε300,400

Mil Area Commands (KODAM)
13 comd (I, II, III, IV, V, VI, VII, IX, XII, XVI, XVII, Jaya & Iskandar Muda)

FORCES BY ROLE
MANOEUVRE
  Mechanised
    3 armd cav bn
    5 cav bn
  Light
    1 inf bde (1 cav bn, 3 inf bn)
    4 inf bde (1 cdo bn, 2 inf bn)
    3 inf bde (3 inf bn)
    36 indep inf bn
    15 cdo bn
COMBAT SUPPORT
  12 fd arty bn
  7 cbt engr bn
COMBAT SERVICE SUPPORT
  4 construction bn
AVIATION
  1 composite avn sqn
HELICOPTER
  1 hel sqn
AIR DEFENCE
  1 AD regt (2 ADA bn, 1 SAM unit)
  6 ADA bn
  3 SAM unit

Special Forces Command (KOPASSUS)
FORCES BY ROLE
SPECIAL FORCES
  3 SF gp (total: 2 cdo/para unit, 1 CT unit, 1 int unit)

Strategic Reserve Command (KOSTRAD)
FORCES BY ROLE
COMMAND
  2 div HQ
MANOEUVRE
  Armoured
    2 armd bn
  Light
    3 inf bde (total: 1 mech inf bn; 7 cdo bn)
  Air Manoeuvre
    3 AB bde (3 AB bn)
COMBAT SUPPORT
  2 fd arty regt (1 SP arty bn; 2 arty bn)
  1 arty bn
  2 cbt engr bn

AIR DEFENCE
  2 AD bn

EQUIPMENT BY TYPE
ARMOURED FIGHTING VEHICLES
  MBT 79: 42 *Leopard* 2A4; 37 *Leopard* 2RI
  LT TK 350: 275 AMX-13 (partially upgraded); 15 PT-76; 60 *Scorpion* 90
  RECCE 142: 55 *Ferret* (13 upgraded); 69 *Saladin* (16 upgraded); 18 VBL
  IFV 64: 22 *Black Fox*; 42 *Marder* 1A3
  APC 584+
    APC (T) 217: 75 AMX-VCI; 34 BTR-50PK; 15 FV4333 *Stormer*; 93 M113A1-B
    APC (W) 367+: ε150 *Anoa*; some *Barracuda*; 40 BTR-40; 45 FV603 *Saracen* (14 upgraded); 100 LAV-150 *Commando*; 32 VAB-VTT
    PPV some *Casspir*
  AUV 39: 14 APR-1; 3 *Bushmaster*; 22 *Commando Ranger*;
ENGINEERING & MAINTENANCE VEHICLES
  AEV 4: 3 *Leopard* 2; 1 M113A1-B-GN
  ARV 15+: 2 AMX-13; 6 AMX-VCI; 3 BREM-2; 4 *Leopard* 2; *Stormer*; T-54/T-55
  VLB 16+: 10 AMX-13; *Leguan*; 4 *Leopard* 2; 2 *Stormer*
ANTI-TANK/ANTI-INFRASTRUCTURE
  MSL • **MANPATS** SS.11; *Milan*; 9K11 *Malyutka* (AT-3 *Sagger*)
  RCL 90mm M67; **106mm** M40A1
  RL 89mm LRAC
ARTILLERY 1,160+
  SP 155mm 36 CAESAR
  TOWED 133+: **105mm** 110+: some KH-178; 60 M101; 50 M-56; **155mm** 23: 5 FH-88; 18 KH-179
  MRL 127mm 36 ASTROS II Mk6
  MOR 955: **81mm** 800; **120mm** 155: 75 Brandt; 80 UBM 52
AMPHIBIOUS • **LCU** 17
  1 ADRI XXXII
  4 ADRI XXXIII
  1 ADRI XXXIX
  1 ADRI XL
  3 ADRI XLI
  2 ADRI XLIV
  2 ADRI XLVI
  2 ADRI XLVIII
  1 ADRI L
AIRCRAFT • **TPT** • **Light** 9: 1 BN-2A *Islander*; 6 C-212 *Aviocar* (NC-212); 2 *Turbo Commander* 680
HELICOPTERS
  ATK 6 Mi-35P *Hind*
  MRH 37: 3 H125M *Fennec*; 17 Bell 412 *Twin Huey* (NB-412); 17 Mi-17V-5 *Hip* H
  TPT • **Light** 29: 7 Bell 205A; 20 Bo-105 (NBo-105); 2 H120 *Colibri*
  TRG 12 Hughes 300C
AIR DEFENCE
  SAM • **Point-defence** 95+: 2 *Kobra* (with 125 GROM-2 msl); TD-2000B (*Giant Bow* II); 51 *Rapier*; 42 RBS-70; QW-3
  GUNS • **TOWED** 411: **20mm** 121 Rh 202; **23mm** *Giant Bow*; **40mm** 90 L/70; **57mm** 200 S-60

Navy ε65,000 (including Marines and Aviation)

Two fleets: East (Surabaya), West (Jakarta). It is currently planned to change to three commands: Riau (West); Papua (East); Makassar (Central). Two Forward Operating Bases at Kupang (West Timor) and Tahuna (North Sulawesi)

EQUIPMENT BY TYPE
SUBMARINES • TACTICAL • SSK 3:
  2 *Cakra†* (Type-209/1300) with 8 single 533mm TT with SUT HWT
  1 *Nagapasa* (Type-209/1400) with 8 single 533mm TT with *Black Shark* HWT

PRINCIPAL SURFACE COMBATANTS 13
  FRIGATES 13
    FFGHM 8:
      3 *Ahmad Yani* (ex-NLD *Van Speijk*) fitted for 2 quad Mk 141 lnchr with RGM-84A *Harpoon* AShM, 2 SIMBAD twin lnchr (manual) with *Mistral* SAM, 2 triple 324mm ASTT with Mk46 LWT, 1 76mm gun (capacity 1 Bo-105 (NBo-105) hel)
      1 *Ahmad Yani* (ex-NLD *Van Speijk*) with 2 twin-cell VLS with 3M55E *Yakhont* (SS-N-26 *Strobile*) AShM, 2 SIMBAD twin lnchr (manual) with *Mistral* SAM, 2 triple 324mm ASTT with Mk46 LWT, 1 76mm gun (capacity 1 Bo-105 (NBo-105) hel)
      2 *Ahmad Yani* (ex-NLD *Van Speijk*) with 2 twin lnchr with C-802 (CH-SS-N-8 *Saccade*) AShM, 2 SIMBAD twin lnchr (manual) with *Mistral* SAM, 2 triple 324mm ASTT with Mk46 LWT, 1 76mm gun (capacity 1 Bo-105 (NBo-105) hel)
      2 *R.E. Martadinata* (SIGMA 10514) with 2 quad lnchr with MM40 *Exocet* Block 3 AShM, 2 6-cell VLS with VL-*MICA* SAM, 2 triple 324mm ASTT with A244/S LWT, 1 *Millennium* CIWS, 1 76mm gun (1 med hel)
    FFGM
      4 *Diponegoro* (SIGMA 9113) with 2 twin lnchr with MM40 *Exocet* Block 2 AShM, 2 quad *Tetral* lnchr with *Mistral* SAM, 2 triple 324mm ASTT with MU90 LWT, 1 76mm gun, 1 hel landing platform
    FFG
      1 *Hajar Dewantara* (trg role) with 2 twin lnchr with MM38 *Exocet* AShM, 2 single 533mm ASTT with SUT HWT, 1 57mm gun (capacity 1 Bo-105 (NBo-105) hel)

PATROL AND COASTAL COMBATANTS 108
  CORVETTES 20
    FSGM 3 *Bung Tomo* with 2 quad lnchr with MM40 *Exocet* Block 2 AShM, 1 18-cell VLS with *Sea Wolf* SAM, 2 triple 324mm ASTT, 1 76mm gun (capacity: 1 Bo-105 hel)
    FSGH 1 *Nala* with 2 twin lnchr with MM38 *Exocet* AShM, 1 twin 375mm A/S mor, 1 120mm gun (capacity 1 lt hel)
    FSG 2 *Fatahillah* with 2 twin lnchr with MM38 *Exocet* AShM, 2 triple B515 *ILAS*-3/Mk32 324mm ASTT with A244/Mk46 LWT, 1 twin 375mm A/S mor, 1 120mm gun

    FS 14 *Kapitan Pattimura* (GDR *Parchim* I) with 4 single 400mm ASTT, 2 RBU 6000 *Smerch* 2 A/S mor, 1 twin 57mm gun
  PCFG 4 *Mandau* with 4 single lnchr with MM38 *Exocet* AShM, 1 57mm gun
  PCG 5:
    3 *Sampari* (KCR-60M) with 2 twin lnchr for C-705 AShM
    2 *Todak* with 2 single lnchr with C-802 (CH-SS-N-8 *Saccade*), 1 57mm gun
  PCT 2 *Singa* with 2 single 533mm TT, 1 57mm gun
  PCC 11: 4 *Kakap*; 2 *Pandrong*; 3 *Pari* with 1 57mm gun; 2 *Todak* with 1 57mm gun
  PBG 10:
    2 *Clurit* with 2 single lnchr with C-705 AShM, 1 AK630 CIWS
    6 *Clurit* with 2 single lnchr with C-705 AShM
    2 *Badau* (ex-BRN *Waspada*) with 2 twin lnchr for MM38 *Exocet* AShM
  PB 56: 9 *Boa*; 1 *Cucut* (ex-*SGP Jupiter*); 4 *Kobra*; 1 *Krait*; 8 *Sibarau*; 18 *Sinabang* (KAL 28); 4 *Tarihu*; 6 *Tatihu* (PC-40); 5 *Viper*

MINE WARFARE • MINE COUNTERMEASURES 8
  MCO 2 *Pulau Rengat*
  MSC 6 *Pulau Rote* (ex-GDR *Wolgast*)

AMPHIBIOUS
  PRINCIPAL AMPHIBIOUS VESSELS • LPD 5:
    1 *Dr Soeharso* (ex-*Tanjung Dalpele*; capacity 2 LCU/LCVP; 13 tanks; 500 troops; 2 AS332L *Super Puma*) (used in AH role)
    4 *Makassar* (capacity 2 LCU or 4 LCVP; 13 tanks; 500 troops; 2 AS332L *Super Puma*)
  LANDING SHIPS • LST 19
    1 *Teluk Amboina* (capacity 16 tanks; 800 troops)
    1 *Teluk Bintuni* (capacity 10 MBT)
    10 *Teluk Gilimanuk* (ex-GDR *Frosch*)
    2 *Teluk Langsa* (capacity 16 tanks; 200 troops)
    5 *Teluk Semangka* (capacity 17 tanks; 200 troops)
  LANDING CRAFT 55
    LCM 20
    LCU 5
    LCVP 30

LOGISTICS AND SUPPORT 24
  AGF 1 *Multatuli* with 1 hel landing platform
  AGOR 2 *Rigel*
  AGOS 1 *Leuser*
  AGHS 1
  AGS 3 *Pulau Rote* (ex-GDR *Wolgast*)
  AKSL 4
  AORLH 1 *Arun* (ex-UK *Rover*)
  AOT 3: 2 *Khobi*; 1 *Sorong*
  AP 4: 1 *Tanjung Kambani* (troop transport) with 1 hel landing platform; 1 *Tanjung Nusanive* (troop transport); 2 *Karang Pilang* (troop transport)
  ATF 1
  AXS 3

Naval Aviation ε1,000

EQUIPMENT BY TYPE
AIRCRAFT
  MP 26: 3 C212-200; 3 CN235 MPA; 14 N-22B *Searchmaster* B; 6 N-22SL *Searchmaster* L

TPT • Light 32: 8 Beech G36 *Bonanza*; 2 Beech G38 *Baron*; 17 C-212-200 *Aviocar*; 3 TB-9 *Tampico*; 2 TB-10
HELICOPTERS
  MRH 4 Bell 412 (NB-412) *Twin Huey*
  CSAR 4 H225M *Caracal*
  TPT 15: **Medium** 3 AS332L *Super Puma* (NAS322L); **Light** 12: 3 H120 *Colibri*; 9 Bo-105 (NBo-105)

Marines ε20,000
FORCES BY ROLE
SPECIAL FORCES
  1 SF bn
MANOEUVRE
  Amphibious
  2 mne gp (1 cav regt, 3 mne bn, 1 arty regt, 1 cbt spt regt, 1 CSS regt)
  1 mne bde (3 mne bn)
EQUIPMENT BY TYPE
ARMOURED FIGHTING VEHICLES
  LT TK 65: 10 AMX-10 PAC 90; 55 PT-76†
  RECCE 21 BRDM-2
  IFV 114: 24 AMX-10P; 22 BMP-2; 54 BMP-3F; 2 BTR-4; 12 BTR-80A
  APC 103: • **APC (T)** 100 BTR-50P; **APC (W)** 3 BTR-4M
  AAV 10 LVTP-7A1
  ARTILLERY 71+
  TOWED 50: **105mm** 22 LG1 MK II; **122mm** 28 M-38
  MRL 122mm 21: 4 PHL-90B; 9 RM-70; 8 RM-70 *Vampir*
  MOR 81mm
  AIR DEFENCE • GUNS • 40mm 5 L/60/L/70; **57mm** S-60

Air Force 30,100
2 operational comd (East and West) plus trg comd
FORCES BY ROLE
FIGHTER
  1 sqn with F-5E/F *Tiger* II
  1 sqn with F-16A/B/C/D *Fighting Falcon*
FIGHTER/GROUND ATTACK
  1 sqn with F-16C/D *Fighting Falcon*
  1 sqn with Su-27SK/SKM *Flanker*; Su-30MK/MK2 *Flanker*
  2 sqn with *Hawk* Mk109*/Mk209*
  1 sqn with T-50i *Golden Eagle**
GROUND ATTACK
  1 sqn with EMB-314 (A-29) *Super Tucano**
MARITIME PATROL
  1 sqn with B-737-200; CN235M-220 MPA
TANKER/TRANSPORT
  1 sqn with C-130B/KC-130B *Hercules*
TRANSPORT
  1 VIP sqn with B-737-200; C-130H/H-30 *Hercules*; L-100-30; F-27-400M *Troopship*; F-28-1000/3000; AS332L *Super Puma* (NAS332L); SA330SM *Puma* (NAS300SM)
  1 sqn with C-130H/H-30 *Hercules*; L-100-30
  1 sqn with C-212 *Aviocar* (NC-212)
  1 sqn with CN235M-110; C295M
TRAINING
  1 sqn with Grob 120TP
  1 sqn with KT-1B
  1 sqn with SF-260M; SF-260W *Warrior*

TRANSPORT HELICOPTER
  2 sqn with H225M; AS332L *Super Puma* (NAS332L); SA330J/L *Puma* (NAS330J/L); H120 *Colibri*
EQUIPMENT BY TYPE
Only 45% of ac op
AIRCRAFT 102 combat capable
  FTR 9: 7 F-16A *Fighting Falcon*; 2 F-16B *Fighting Falcon* (8 F-5E *Tiger* II; 4 F-5F *Tiger* II non-operational)
  FGA 33: 12 F-16C *Fighting Falcon*; 5 F-16D *Fighting Falcon*; 2 Su-27SK; 3 Su-27SKM; 2 Su-30MK; 9 Su-30MK2
  MP 6: 3 B-737-200; 3 CN235M-220 MPA
  TKR 1 KC-130B *Hercules*
  TPT 49: **Medium** 16: 4 C-130B *Hercules*; 4 C-130H *Hercules*; 6 C-130H-30 *Hercules*; 2 L-100-30; **Light** 24: 9 C295; 9 C-212 *Aviocar* (NC-212); 5 CN235-110; 1 F-27-400M *Troopship*; **PAX** 9: 1 B-737-200; 3 B-737-400; 1 B-737-500; 1 B-737-800BBJ; 1 F-28-1000; 2 F-28-3000
  TRG 109: 15 EMB-314 (A-29) *Super Tucano**; 18 Grob 120TP; 7 *Hawk* Mk109*; 23 *Hawk* Mk209*; 14 KT-1B; 10 SF-260M; 7 SF-260W *Warrior*; 15 T-50i *Golden Eagle**
HELICOPTERS
  TPT 36: **Heavy** 6 H225M (CSAR); **Medium** 18: 9 AS332 *Super Puma* (NAS332L) (VIP/CSAR); 1 SA330SM *Puma* (NAS330SM) (VIP); 4 SA330J *Puma* (NAS330J); 4 SA330L *Puma* (NAS330L); **Light** 12 H120 *Colibri*
AIR-LAUNCHED MISSILES
  AAM • **IR** AIM-9P *Sidewinder*; R-73 (AA-11 *Archer*); **IR/SARH** R-27 (AA-10 *Alamo*)
  ARH R-77 (AA-12A *Adder*)
  ASM AGM-65G *Maverick*
  ARM Kh-31P (AS-17A *Krypton*)

Special Forces (Paskhasau)
FORCES BY ROLE
SPECIAL FORCES
  3 (PASKHASAU) SF wg (total: 6 spec ops sqn)
  4 indep SF coy
EQUIPMENT BY TYPE
AIR DEFENCE
  SAM • Point QW-3
  GUNS • TOWED 35mm 6 Oerlikon *Skyshield*

Paramilitary 280,000+

Customs
EQUIPMENT BY TYPE
PATROL AND COASTAL COMBATANTS 59
  PCO 2 PT Dumas 60m
  PCF 9 BC Speed Craft
  PBF 14
  PB 34

Marine Police
EQUIPMENT BY TYPE
PATROL AND COASTAL COMBATANTS 37
  PSO 2 *Bisma*
  PCC 5
  PBF 3 *Gagak*
  PB 27: 14 *Bango*; 13 (various)
LOGISTICS AND SUPPORT • AP 1

Police ε280,000 (including 14,000 police 'mobile bde' (BRIMOB) org in 56 coy, incl CT unit (Gegana))

EQUIPMENT BY TYPE
ARMOURED FIGHTING VEHICLES
  APC (W) 34 *Tactica*
AIRCRAFT • TPT • Light 5: 2 Beech 18; 2 C-212 *Aviocar* (NC-212); 1 *Turbo Commander* 680
HELICOPTERS • TPT • Light 22: 3 Bell 206 *Jet Ranger*; 19 Bo-105 (NBo-105)

KPLP (Coast and Seaward Defence Command)

Responsible to Military Sea Communications Agency

EQUIPMENT BY TYPE
PATROL AND COASTAL COMBATANTS 31
  PCO 4: 2 *Arda Dedali*; 2 *Trisula*
  PB 27: 4 *Golok* (SAR); 5 *Kujang*; 3 *Rantos*; 15 (various)
LOGISTICS AND SUPPORT • ABU 1 *Jadayat*

Bakamla (Maritime Security Agency)

EQUIPMENT BY TYPE
PATROL AND COASTAL COMBATANTS 6
  PB 6 *Bintang Laut* (KCR-40 mod)

Reserve Organisations

Kamra People's Security ε40,000 (report for 3 weeks' basic training each year; part-time police auxiliary)

DEPLOYMENT

CENTRAL AFRICAN REPUBLIC
UN • MINUSCA 207; 6 obs; 1 engr coy

DEMOCRATIC REPUBLIC OF THE CONGO
UN • MONUSCO 175; 4 obs; 1 engr coy

LEBANON
UN • UNIFIL 1,288; 1 mech inf bn; 1 FSGHM

MALI
UN • MINUSMA 8

PHILIPPINES
IMT 9

SOUTH SUDAN
UN • UNMISS 1; 2 obs

SUDAN
UN • UNAMID 810; 7 obs; 1 inf bn
UN • UNISFA 2; 1 obs

WESTERN SAHARA
UN • MINURSO 5 obs

Japan JPN

Japanese Yen ¥		2016	2017	2018
GDP	¥	537tr	544tr	
	US$	4.94tr	4.88tr	
per capita	US$	38,883	38,550	
Growth	%	1.0	1.5	
Inflation	%	-0.1	0.4	
Def bdgt	¥	5.05tr	5.13tr	5.26tr
	US$	46.5bn	46.0bn	
US$1=¥		108.79	111.41	

Population 126,451,398
Ethnic groups: Korean <1%

Age	0–14	15–19	20–24	25–29	30–64	65 plus
Male	6.6%	2.5%	2.6%	2.5%	22.1%	12.2%
Female	6.2%	2.3%	2.3%	2.5%	22.6%	15.7%

Capabilities

Japan's alliance with the United States remains the cornerstone of its defence policy, reflected by continued US basing on Honshu, Kyushu and Okinawa; the widespread use of US equipment across all three services; and regular training with US forces. While the Self-Defense Forces' offensive capacity remains weak, the navy has strengths in anti-submarine warfare and air defence. As evidenced in its 2017 defence white paper, Tokyo's concerns over its deteriorating regional security environment have escalated, principally relating to an emerging threat from China and an established concern over North Korea. This has stimulated budget increases and defence-policy and legislative reforms to enable it to play a more active international security role, as well as to strengthen the US–Japan alliance. The country's ongoing military-procurement drive has for the first time focused on power projection, mobility and ISR, with the first domestically produced F-35 combat aircraft rolled out in mid-2017. Japan has expressed a desire to boost its ballistic-missile-defence capability, with reported interest in the *Aegis* Ashore system. Japan continues plans to develop an amphibious force. The defence minister noted in November 2017 that the SDF was researching technologies relating to extending the range of anti-ship missile capability 'intended for the defense of remote islands', with this included in the FY2018 budget request. Japan also continues its efforts to develop a more internationally focused defence industry to promote its products in the region.

ACTIVE 247,150 (Ground Self-Defense Force 150,850 Maritime Self-Defense Force 45,350 Air Self-Defense Force 46,950 Central Staff 4,000) **Paramilitary 13,740**

RESERVE 56,000 (General Reserve Army (GSDF) 46,000 Ready Reserve Army (GSDF) 8,100 Navy 1,100 Air 800)

ORGANISATIONS BY SERVICE

Space
EQUIPMENT BY TYPE
SATELLITES 8
  COMMUNICATIONS 1 *Kirameki-2*
  ISR 7 IGS

Ground Self-Defense Force 150,850
FORCES BY ROLE
COMMAND
  5 army HQ (regional comd)
SPECIAL FORCES
  1 spec ops unit (bn)
MANOEUVRE
  Armoured
    1 (7th) armd div (1 armd recce sqn, 3 tk regt, 1 armd inf regt, 1 avn sqn, 1 SP arty regt, 1 AD regt, 1 cbt engr bn, 1 sigs bn, 1 NBC bn, 1 log regt)
  Mechanised
    1 (2nd) inf div (1 armd recce sqn, 1 tk regt, 1 mech inf regt, 2 inf regt, 1 avn sqn, 1 SP arty regt, 1 AT coy, 1 AD bn, 1 cbt engr bn, 1 sigs bn, 1 NBC bn, 1 log regt)
    1 (4th) inf div (1 armd recce sqn, 1 tk bn, 1 mech inf regt, 2 inf regt, 1 inf coy, 1 avn sqn, 1 arty regt, 1 AT coy, 1 AD bn, 1 cbt engr bn, 1 sigs bn, 1 NBC bn, 1 log regt)
    1 (9th) inf div (1 armd recce sqn, 1 tk bn, 3 mech inf regt, 1 avn sqn, 1 arty regt, 1 AD bn, 1 cbt engr bn, 1 sigs bn, 1 NBC bn, 1 log regt) 2 (5th & 11th) inf bde (1 armd recce sqn, 1 tk bn, 3 mech inf regt, 1 avn sqn, 1 SP arty bn, 1 AD coy, 1 cbt engr coy, 1 sigs coy, 1 NBC coy, 1 log bn)
  Light
    1 (8th) inf div (1 recce sqn, 1 tk bn, 4 inf regt, 1 avn sqn, 1 arty regt, 1 AD bn, 1 cbt engr bn, 1 sigs bn, 1 NBC bn, 1 log regt)
    4 (1st, 3rd, 6th & 10th) inf div (1 recce sqn, 1 tk bn, 3 inf regt, 1 avn sqn, 1 arty regt, 1 AD bn, 1 cbt engr bn, 1 sigs bn, 1 NBC bn, 1 log regt)
    1 (13th) inf bde (1 recce sqn, 1 tk coy, 3 inf regt, 1 avn sqn, 1 arty bn, 1 AD coy, 1 cbt engr coy, 1 NBC coy, 1 sigs coy, 1 log bn)
    1 (14th) inf bde (1 recce sqn, 1 tk coy, 2 inf regt, 1 avn sqn, 1 arty bn, 1 AD coy, 1 cbt engr coy, 1 NBC coy, 1 sigs coy, 1 log bn)
    1 (15th) inf bde (1 recce sqn, 1 inf regt, 1 avn sqn, 1 AD regt, 1 cbt engr coy, 1 NBC coy, 1 sigs coy, 1 log bn)
  Air Manoeuvre
    1 (1st) AB bde (3 AB bn, 1 arty bn, 1 cbt engr coy, 1 sigs coy, 1 log bn)
    1 (12th) air mob inf bde (1 recce sqn, 3 inf regt, 1 avn sqn, 1 SP arty bn, 1 AD coy, 1 cbt engr coy, 1 NBC coy, 1 sigs coy, 1 log bn)
COMBAT SUPPORT
  1 arty bde
  2 arty unit (bde)
  4 engr bde
  1 engr unit
  1 EW bn
  5 int bn
  1 MP bde
  1 sigs bde
COMBAT SERVICE SUPPORT
  5 log unit (bde)
  5 trg bde
HELICOPTER
  1 hel bde
  5 hel gp (1 atk hel bn, 1 hel bn)
AIR DEFENCE
  2 AD bde
  4 AD gp
EQUIPMENT BY TYPE
ARMOURED FIGHTING VEHICLES
  MBT 690: 66 Type-10; 283 Type-74; 341 Type-90
  RECCE 111 Type-87
  IFV 68 Type-89
  APC 795
    APC (T) 226 Type-73
    APC (W) 569: 204 Type-82; 365 Type-96
  AAV 4 AAV-7
  AUV 4 *Bushmaster*
ENGINEERING & MAINTENANCE VEHICLES
  ARV 70: 4 Type-11; 36 Type-78; 30 Type-90
  VLB 22 Type-91
NBC VEHICLES 57: 41 Chemical Reconnaissance Vehicle; 16 NBC Reconnaissance Vehicle
ANTI-TANK/ANTI-INFRASTRUCTURE
  MSL
    SP 37 Type-96 MPMS
    MANPATS Type-79 *Jyu*-MAT; Type-87 *Chu*-MAT; Type-01 LMAT
  RCL • 84mm *Carl Gustav*
ARTILLERY 1,774
  SP 172: 155mm 105 Type-99; 203mm 67 M110A2
  TOWED 155mm 398 FH-70
  MRL 227mm 99 M270 MLRS
  MOR 1,105: 81mm 652 L16 120mm 429; SP 120mm 24 Type-96
COASTAL DEFENCE • AShM 88: 6 Type-12; 82 Type-88
AIRCRAFT
  TPT • Light 7 Beech 350 *King Air* (LR-2)
HELICOPTERS
  ATK 104: 59 AH-1S *Cobra*; 12 AH-64D *Apache*; 33 OH-1
  ISR 44 OH-6D
  TPT 272: Heavy 69: 24 CH-47D *Chinook* (CH-47J); 45 CH-47JA *Chinook*; Medium 42: 3 H225 *Super Puma* MkII+ (VIP); 39 UH-60L *Black Hawk* (UH-60JA); Light 161: 131 Bell 205 (UH-1J); 30 Enstrom 480B (TH-480B)
AIR DEFENCE
  SAM
    Medium-range 163: 43 Type-03 *Chu*-SAM; 120 MIM-23B I-*Hawk*
    Short-range 5 Type-11 *Tan*-SAM
    Point-defence 159+: 46 Type-81 *Tan*-SAM; 113 Type-93 *Kin*-SAM; Type-91 *Kei*-SAM
  GUNS • SP 35mm 52 Type-87

Maritime Self-Defense Force 45,350

Surface units organised into 4 Escort Flotillas with a mix of 8 warships each. Bases at Yokosuka, Kure, Sasebo, Maizuru, Ominato. SSK organised into two flotillas with bases at Kure and Yokosuka

EQUIPMENT BY TYPE
SUBMARINES • TACTICAL • SSK 19:
  2 *Oyashio* (trg role) with 6 single 533mm TT with T-89 HWT/UGM-84C *Harpoon* AShM
  9 *Oyashio* with 6 single 533mm TT with T-89 HWT/UGM-84C *Harpoon* AShM
  8 *Soryu* (AIP fitted) with 6 single 533mm TT with T-89 HWT/UGM-84C *Harpoon* AShM

PRINCIPAL SURFACE COMBATANTS 47
  AIRCRAFT CARRIERS • CVH 4:
    2 *Hyuga* with 1 16-cell Mk41 VLS with ASROC/RIM-162 ESSM SAM, 2 triple 324mm ASTT with Mk46/Type-97 LWT, 2 *Phalanx* Block 1B CIWS (normal ac capacity 3 SH-60 *Seahawk* ASW hel; plus additional ac embarkation up to 7 SH-60 *Seahawk* or 7 MCH-101)
    2 *Izumo* with 2 11-cell SeaRAM lnchr with RIM-116 SAM, 2 *Phalanx* Block 1B CIWS (normal ac capacity 7 SH-60 *Seahawk* ASW hel; plus additional ac embarkation up to 5 SH-60 *Seahawk*/MCH-101 hel)
  CRUISERS • CGHM 2 *Atago* with *Aegis* Baseline 7 C2, 2 quad lnchr with SSM-1B AShM, 1 64-cell Mk41 VLS with SM-2 MR SAM/ASROC, 1 32-cell Mk41 VLS with SM-2 MR SAM, 2 triple 324mm ASTT with Mk46 LWT, 2 *Phalanx* Block 1B CIWS, 1 127mm gun (capacity 1 SH-60 *Seahawk* ASW hel)
  DESTROYERS 32
    DDGHM 26:
      8 *Asagiri* with 2 quad Mk141 lnchr with RGM-84C *Harpoon* AShM, 1 octuple Mk29 lnchr with *Sea Sparrow* SAM, 2 triple 324mm ASTT with Mk46 LWT, 1 octuple Mk112 lnchr with ASROC, 2 *Phalanx* CIWS, 1 76mm gun (capacity 1 SH-60 *Seahawk* ASW hel)
      4 *Akizuki* with 2 quad lnchr with SSM-1B AShM, 1 32-cell Mk41 VLS with ASROC/ESSM SAM, 2 triple 324mm ASTT with Type-97 LWT, 2 *Phalanx* CIWS, 1 127mm gun (capacity 1 SH-60 *Seahawk* ASW hel)
      9 *Murasame* with 2 quad lnchr with SSM-1B AShM, 1 16-cell Mk48 VLS with ESSM SAM, 2 triple 324mm TT with Mk46 LWT, 1 16-cell Mk41 VLS with ASROC, 2 *Phalanx* CIWS, 2 76mm gun (capacity 1 SH-60 *Seahawk* ASW hel)
      5 *Takanami* (improved *Murasame*) with 2 quad lnchr with SSM-1B AShM, 1 32-cell Mk41 VLS with ASROC/RIM-7M/ESSM SAM, 2 triple 324mm TT with Mk46 LWT, 2 *Phalanx* CIWS, 1 127mm gun (capacity 1 SH-60 *Seahawk* ASW hel)
    DDGM 6:
      2 *Hatakaze* with 2 quad Mk141 lnchr with RGM-84C *Harpoon* AShM, 1 Mk13 GMLS with SM-1 MR SAM, 2 triple 324mm ASTT with Mk46 LWT, 1 octuple Mk112 lnchr with ASROC, 2 *Phalanx* CIWS, 2 127mm gun, 1 hel landing platform
      4 *Kongou* with *Aegis* Baseline 4/5 C2, 2 quad Mk141 lnchr with RGM-84C *Harpoon* AShM, 1 29-cell Mk41 VLS with SM-2/3 SAM/ASROC, 1 61-cell Mk41 VLS with SM-2/3 SAM/ASROC, 2 triple 324mm ASTT, 2 *Phalanx* Block 1B CIWS, 1 127mm gun
  FRIGATES 9
    FFGHM 3 *Hatsuyuki* with 2 quad Mk141 lnchr with RGM-84C *Harpoon* AShM, 1 octuple Mk29 lnchr with RIM-7F/M *Sea Sparrow* SAM, 2 triple ASTT with Mk46 LWT, 1 octuple Mk112 lnchr with ASROC, 2 *Phalanx* CIWS, 1 76mm gun (capacity 1 SH-60 *Seahawk* ASW hel)
    FFG 6 *Abukuma* with 2 quad Mk141 lnchr with RGM-84C *Harpoon* AShM, 2 triple ASTT with Mk 46 LWT, 1 octuple Mk112 lnchr with ASROC, 1 *Phalanx* CIWS, 1 76mm gun

PATROL AND COASTAL COMBATANTS 6
  PBFG 6 *Hayabusa* with 4 SSM-1B AShM, 1 76mm gun

MINE WARFARE • MINE COUNTERMEASURES 26
  MCCS 5:
    1 *Ieshima*
    1 *Uraga* with 1 76mm gun, 1 hel landing platform (for MCH-101 hel)
    1 *Uraga* with 1 hel landing platform (for MCH-101)
    2 *Uwajima*
  MSC 19: 3 *Hirashima*; 12 *Sugashima*; 1 *Uwajima*; 3 *Enoshima*
  MSO 2: 1 *Awaji*; 1 *Yaeyama*

AMPHIBIOUS
  PRINCIPAL AMPHIBIOUS SHIPS • LHD 3 *Osumi* with 2 *Phalanx* CIWS (capacity for 2 CH-47 hel) (capacity 10 Type-90 MBT; 2 LCAC(L) ACV; 330 troops)
  LANDING CRAFT 8
    LCU 2 *Yusotei*
    LCAC 6 LCAC(L) (capacity either 1 MBT or 60 troops)

LOGISTICS AND SUPPORT 21
  AGBH 1 *Shirase* (capacity 2 AW101 *Merlin* hel)
  AGEH 1 *Asuka* with 1 8-cell VLS (wpn trials) (capacity 1 SH-60 *Seahawk* hel)
  AGOS 2 *Hibiki* with 1 hel landing platform
  AGS 3: 1 *Futami*; 1 *Nichinan*; 1 *Shonan*
  AOE 5: 2 *Mashu* (capacity 1 med hel); 3 *Towada* with 1 hel landing platform
  ARC 1 *Muroto*
  ASR 2: 1 *Chihaya* with 1 hel landing platform; 1 *Chiyoda* with 1 hel landing platform
  AX 6:
    1 *Kashima* with 2 triple 324mm ASTT, 1 76mm gun, 1 hel landing platform
    1 *Kurobe* with 1 76mm gun (trg spt ship)
    3 *Shimayuki* with 2 quad lnchr with RGM-84 *Harpoon* AShM, 1 octuple Mk29 lnchr with RIM-7M *Sea Sparrow* SAM, 1 octuple Mk112 lnchr with ASROC, 2 triple 324mm ASTT with Mk46 LWT, 2 *Phalanx* CIWS, 1 76mm gun
    1 *Tenryu* (trg spt ship); with 1 76mm gun (capacity: 1 med hel)

Naval Aviation ε9,800

7 Air Groups

FORCES BY ROLE
ANTI SUBMARINE/SURFACE WARFARE
  5 sqn with SH-60B (SH-60J)/SH-60K *Seahawk*
MARITIME PATROL
  1 sqn with P-1; P-3C *Orion*
  3 sqn with P-3C *Orion*
ELECTRONIC WARFARE
  1 sqn with EP-3 *Orion*
MINE COUNTERMEASURES
  1 sqn with MCH-101
SEARCH & RESCUE
  1 sqn with *Shin Meiwa* US-1A/US-2
  2 sqn with UH-60J *Black Hawk*
TRANSPORT
  1 sqn with AW101 *Merlin* (CH-101); Beech 90 *King Air* (LC-90); KC-130R *Hercules*
TRAINING
  1 sqn with Beech 90 *King Air* (TC-90)
  1 sqn with P-3C *Orion*
  1 sqn with T-5J
  1 hel sqn with H135 (TH-135); OH-6DA; SH-60B (SH-60J) *Seahawk*

EQUIPMENT BY TYPE
AIRCRAFT 74 combat capable
  ASW 74: 12 P-1; 62 P-3C *Orion*
  ELINT 5 EP-3C *Orion*
  SAR 5: 1 *Shin Meiwa* US-1A; 4 *Shin Meiwa* US-2
  TPT 27: **Medium** 6 C-130R *Hercules*; **Light** 21: 5 Beech 90 *King Air* (LC-90); 16 Beech 90 *King Air* (TC-90)
  TRG 30 T-5J
HELICOPTERS
  ASW 87: 35 SH-60B *Seahawk* (SH-60J); 52 SH-60K *Seahawk*
  MCM 10 MCH-101
  SAR 15 UH-60J *Black Hawk*
  TPT 18: **Medium** 3 AW101 *Merlin* (CH-101); **Light** 15 H135 (TH-135)

Air Self-Defense Force 46,950

Flying hours 150 hrs/yr

7 cbt wg

FORCES BY ROLE
FIGHTER
  7 sqn with F-15J *Eagle*
  2 sqn with F-4EJ (F-4E) *Phantom* II
  3 sqn with Mitsubishi F-2
ELECTRONIC WARFARE
  2 sqn with Kawasaki EC-1; YS-11E
ISR
  1 sqn with RF-4EJ (RF-4E) *Phantom* II*
AIRBORNE EARLY WARNING & CONTROL
  2 sqn with E-2C *Hawkeye*
  1 sqn with E-767
SEARCH & RESCUE
  1 wg with U-125A *Peace Krypton*; UH-60J *Black Hawk*
TANKER
  1 sqn with KC-767J
TRANSPORT
  1 (VIP) sqn with B-747-400
  2 sqn with C-1; C-2
  1 sqn with C-130H *Hercules*
  Some (liaison) sqn with Gulfstream IV (U-4); T-4*
TRAINING
  1 (aggressor) sqn with F-15J *Eagle*
TEST
  1 wg with F-15J *Eagle*; T-4*
TRANSPORT HELICOPTER
  4 flt with CH-47JA *Chinook*

EQUIPMENT BY TYPE
AIRCRAFT 542 combat capable
  FTR 189: 147 F-15J *Eagle*; 42 F-15DJ *Eagle*
  FGA 143: 58 F-2A; 30 F-2B; 51 F-4E *Phantom* II (F-4EJ); 4 F-35A *Lightning* II (in test)
  EW 3: 1 Kawasaki EC-1; 2 YS-11EA
  ISR 17: 13 RF-4E *Phantom* II* (RF-4J); 4 YS-11EB
  AEW&C 17: 13 E-2C *Hawkeye*; 4 E-767
  SAR 26 U-125A *Peace Krypton*
  TKR 6: 2 KC-130H *Hercules*; 4 KC-767J
  TPT 57: **Medium** 16: 13 C-130H *Hercules*; 3 C-2; **PAX** 39: 2 B-747-400; 13 Beech T-400; 19 C-1; 5 Gulfstream IV (U-4)
  TRG 246: 197 T-4*; 49 T-7
HELICOPTERS
  SAR 36 UH-60J *Black Hawk*
  TPT • **Heavy** 15 CH-47JA *Chinook*
AIR-LAUNCHED MISSILES
  AAM • **IR** AAM-3 (Type-90); AIM-9 *Sidewinder*; **IIR** AAM-5 (Type-04); **SARH** AIM-7 *Sparrow*; **ARH** AAM-4 (Type-99); AIM-120C5/C7 AMRAAM (limited numbers)
  ASM ASM-1 (Type-80); ASM-2 (Type-93)

Air Defence

Ac control and warning. 4 wg; 28 radar sites

FORCES BY ROLE
AIR DEFENCE
  6 SAM gp (total: 24 SAM bty with MIM-104D/F *Patriot* PAC-2/3)
  1 AD gp with Type-81 *Tan*-SAM; M167 *Vulcan*

EQUIPMENT BY TYPE
AIR DEFENCE
  SAM
    Long-range 120 MIM-104D/F *Patriot* PAC-2 GEM/PAC-3
    Point-defence Type-81 *Tan*-SAM
  GUNS • **TOWED 20mm** M167 *Vulcan*

Paramilitary 13,740

Coast Guard 13,740

Ministry of Land, Transport, Infrastructure and Tourism (no cbt role)

EQUIPMENT BY TYPE
PATROL AND COASTAL COMBATANTS 367
  PSOH 14: 2 *Mizuho* (capacity 2 hels); 2 *Shikishima* (capacity 2 hels); 10 *Soya* (capacity 1 hel)
  PSO 43:
    3 *Hida* with 1 hel landing platform
    1 *Izu* with 1 hel landing platform
    9 *Hateruma* with 1 hel landing platform

6 *Iwami*
1 *Kojima* (trg) with 1 hel landing platform
2 *Kunigami* with 1 hel landing platform
1 *Miura* with 1 hel landing platform
6 *Ojika* with 1 hel landing platform
14 *Taketomi* with 1 hel landing platform
PCO 17: 3 *Aso*; 2 *Katori*; 2 *Takatori*; 10 *Teshio*
PCC 26: 4 *Amami*; 22 *Tokara*
PBF 47: 20 *Hayagumo*; 5 *Mihashi*; 14 *Raizan*; 2 *Takatsuki*; 6 *Tsuruugi*
PB 52: 2 *Akizuki*; 4 *Asogiri*; 4 *Hamagumo*; 11 *Hayanami*; 8 *Katonami*; 1 *Matsunami*; 4 *Murakumo*; 2 *Natsugiri*; 3 *Shimagiri*; 3 *Shimoji*; 10 *Yodo*
PBI 168: 2 *Hakubai*; 1 *Hayagiku*; 163 *Himegiku*; 2 *Nadaka*
LOGISTICS AND SUPPORT 17
ABU 1 *Teshio*
AGS 13: 7 *Hamashio*; 1 *Jinbei*; 2 *Meiyo*; 1 *Shoyo*; 1 *Takuyo*; 1 *Tenyo*
AX 3
AIRCRAFT
MP 2 *Falcon* 900 MPAT
TPT 27: **Light** 18: 9 Beech 350 *King Air* (LR-2); 9 DHC *Dash-7* (Bombardier 300) (MP); **PAX** 9: 3 CL-300; 2 Gulfstream V (MP); 4 Saab 340B
HELICOPTERS
MRH 5 Bell 412 *Twin Huey*
SAR 11 S-76D
TPT 38: **Medium** 8: 3 AS332 *Super Puma*; 5 H225 *Super Puma*; **Light** 30: 18 AW139; 3 Bell 206B *Jet Ranger* II; 6 Bell 212; 3 S-76C

Cyber

In 2012 a 'Cyber Planning Office' was established in the C4 Systems Planning Division, Joint Staff Office (JSO) of the Ministry of Defense to consolidate the cyber-planning functions of the JSO and to create a more systematic structure for responding to cyber attacks. The National Defense Program Guidelines for FY2014 and beyond stated that 'Japan will build up persistent ISR [intelligence, surveillance and reconnaissance] capabilities to prevent any acts that could impede efficient action by the SDF'. The 2014 Mid-Term Defense Program (FY2014–18) said that the Self-Defense Forces would develop specialist training for cyber personnel. The document also said that 'through its efforts to secure response capabilities in cyberspace where attackers have an overwhelming advantage, the SDF may consider the acquisition of capabilities to prevent them from using cyberspace'. A Cyber Defense Group, which integrates the cyber-warfare functions of the three armed services, was launched in March 2014 to respond to cyber threats. The group monitors defence-ministry and SDF networks, and provides responses to cyber attacks. A revised Cybersecurity Strategy was developed in mid-2015.

DEPLOYMENT

DJIBOUTI
170; 2 P-3C *Orion*

GULF OF ADEN & INDIAN OCEAN
2 DDGHM

SOUTH SUDAN
UN • UNMISS 4

FOREIGN FORCES

United States
US Pacific Command: 39,950
Army 2,750; 1 corps HQ (fwd); 1 SF gp; 1 avn bn; 1 SAM bn
Navy 11,700; 1 CVN; 3 CGHM; 2 DDGHM; 7 DDGM (2 non-op); 1 LCC; 4 MCO; 1 LHD; 1 LPD; 2 LSD; 3 FGA sqn with 10 F/A-18E *Super Hornet*; 1 FGA sqn with 10 F/A-18F *Super Hornet*; 1 EW sqn with 5 EA-18G *Growler*; 1 AEW&C sqn with 5 E-2D *Hawkeye*; 2 ASW hel sqn with 12 MH-60R *Seahawk*; 1 tpt hel sqn with MH-60S *Knight Hawk*; 1 base at Sasebo; 1 base at Yokosuka
USAF: 11,900; 1 HQ (5th Air Force) at Okinawa–Kadena AB; 1 ftr wg at Misawa AB (2 ftr sqn with 22 F-16C/D *Fighting Falcon*); 1 ftr wg at Okinawa–Kadena AB (2 ftr sqn with total of 54 F-15C/D *Eagle*; 1 FGA sqn with 12 F-35A *Lightning* II; 1 tkr sqn with 15 KC-135R *Stratotanker*; 1 AEW sqn with 2 E-3B *Sentry*; 1 CSAR sqn with 10 HH-60G *Pave Hawk*); 1 tpt wg at Yokota AB with 5 C-130J-30 *Hercules*; 2 Beech 1900C (C-12J); 1 spec ops gp at Okinawa–Kadena AB with (1 sqn with 5 MC-130H *Combat Talon*; 1 sqn with 5 MC-130J *Commando* II); 1 ISR sqn with RC-135 *Rivet Joint*; 1 ISR UAV flt with 5 RQ-4A *Global Hawk*
USMC 20,700; 1 mne div; 1 mne regt HQ; 1 arty regt HQ; 1 recce bn; 1 mne bn; 1 amph aslt bn; 1 arty bn; 1 FGA sqn at Iwakuni with 12 F/A-18D *Hornet*; 1 FGA sqn at Iwakuni with 12 F/A-18C *Hornet*; 1 FGA sqn at Iwakuni with 12 F-35B *Lightning* II; 1 tkr sqn at Iwakuni with 15 KC-130J *Hercules*; 2 tpt sqn at Futenma with 12 MV-22B *Osprey*
US Strategic Command: 1 AN/TPY-2 X-band radar at Shariki; 1 AN/TPY-2 X-band radar at Kyogamisaki

Korea, Democratic People's Republic of DPRK

North Korean Won		2016	2017	2018
GDP	US$			
per capita	US$			
Def exp	won			
	US$			

US$1=won
*definitive economic data not available

Population   25,248,140

Age	0–14	15–19	20–24	25–29	30–64	65 plus
Male	10.6%	3.8%	4.0%	4.0%	22.8%	3.3%
Female	10.2%	3.7%	3.9%	3.8%	23.3%	6.3%

Capabilities

Despite international sanctions, North Korea continues to define the development of nuclear weapons and ballistic missiles as central to its military power and survival. While questions remain over the extent of progress in the miniaturisation and integration of warheads, North Korea's missile programme continues apace, and the country continues its ambition of fielding a credible operational capability in the future. The higher frequency of ballistic-missile and associated ground-system tests conducted in 2016 continued into 2017, revealing four new successfully tested road-mobile systems. This includes the first testing of ICBM-categorised systems, the *Hwasong*-14 and *Hwasong*-15. However, other North Korean ICBM designs previously observed remain untested. Development of at-sea systems also reportedly continues, with successors to the *Gorae*-class trial submarine and the initial *Bukkeukseong*-1 SLBM believed to be in development. A shore-based mobile version, the *Bukkeukseong*-2 MRBM, was also tested for the first time in 2017. Whilst North Korea has shown clear progress in developing more capable and credible delivery systems, a number of technical hurdles may still exist before these systems – particularly those with a longer range – are operationally fielded. In contrast, the country's conventional forces remain reliant on increasingly obsolete equipment, with limited evidence of modernisation across the armed services. Capability is arguably more reliant on personnel strength and asymmetric warfare. Exercises are conducted regularly, but often appear staged and are not necessarily representative of wider operational capability.

ACTIVE 1,280,000 (Army 1,100,000 Navy 60,000 Air 110,000 Strategic Forces 10,000) **Paramilitary 189,000**

Conscript liability Army 5–12 years, Navy 5–10 years, Air Force 3–4 years, followed by compulsory part-time service to age 40. Thereafter service in the Worker/Peasant Red Guard to age 60

RESERVE ε600,000 (Armed Forces ε600,000), **Paramilitary 5,700,000**

Reservists are assigned to units (see also Paramilitary)

ORGANISATIONS BY SERVICE

Strategic Forces ε10,000

North Korea's ballistic missiles and obsolete H-5 (Il-28) bombers could be used to deliver nuclear warheads or bombs. At present, however, there is no conclusive evidence to verify that North Korea has successfully produced a warhead or bomb capable of being delivered by these systems

EQUIPMENT BY TYPE (ε)
SURFACE-TO-SURFACE MISSILE LAUNCHERS
  ICBM 6+: *Hwasong*-13/*Hwasong*-13 mod/*Hwasong*-14 (in test); *Hwasong*-15 (in test)
  IRBM *Hwasong*-12 (in test)
  MRBM ε10 *Nodong* mod 1/mod 2 (ε90+ msl); some *Scud-ER*; *Bukkeukseong*-2 (in test); *Hwasong*-10 (*Musudan*) (in test)
  SRBM 30+ *Hwasong*-5 (SS-1C *Scud*-B)/*Hwasong*-6 (SS-1D *Scud*-C) (ε200+ msl); some *Scud* (mod) (in test)

Army ε1,100,000
FORCES BY ROLE
COMMAND
  2 mech corps HQ
  10 inf corps HQ
  1 (Capital Defence) corps HQ
MANOEUVRE
  Armoured
  1 armd div
  15 armd bde
  Mechanised
  4 mech div
  Light
  27 inf div
  14 inf bde
COMBAT SUPPORT
  1 arty div
  21 arty bde
  9 MRL bde
  5–8 engr river crossing/amphibious regt
  1 engr river crossing bde

Special Purpose Forces Command 88,000
FORCES BY ROLE
SPECIAL FORCES
  8 (Reconnaissance General Bureau) SF bn
MANOEUVRE
  Reconnaissance
  17 recce bn
  Light
  9 lt inf bde
  6 sniper bde
  Air Manoeuvre
  3 AB bde
  1 AB bn
  2 sniper bde
  Amphibious
  2 sniper bde

Reserves 600,000
FORCES BY ROLE
MANOEUVRE
  Light
  40 inf div
  18 inf bde
EQUIPMENT BY TYPE (ε)
ARMOURED FIGHTING VEHICLES
  MBT 3,500+ T-34/T-54/T-55/T-62/Type-59/*Chonma*/*Pokpoong*
  LT TK 560+: 560 PT-76; M-1985
  IFV 32 BTR-80A
  APC 2,500+
    APC (T) BTR-50; Type-531 (Type-63); VTT-323
    APC (W) 2,500 BTR-40/BTR-60/M-1992/1/BTR-152/M-2010 (6×6)/M-2010 (8×8)
ANTI-TANK/ANTI-INFRASTRUCTURE
  MSL
    SP 9K11 *Malyutka* (AT-3 *Sagger*)
    MANPATS 2K15 *Shmel* (AT-1 *Snapper*); 9K111 *Fagot* (AT-4 *Spigot*); 9K113 *Konkurs* (AT-5 *Spandrel*)
  RCL 82mm 1,700 B-10

ARTILLERY 21,100+
SP/TOWED 8,500: SP 122mm M-1977/M-1981/M-1985/M-1991; 130mm M-1975/M-1981/M-1991; 152mm M-1974/M-1977; 170mm M-1978/M-1989
TOWED 122mm D-30/D-74/M-1931/37; 130mm M-46; 152mm M-1937/M-1938/M-1943
GUN/MOR 120mm (reported)
MRL 5,100: 107mm Type-63; 122mm BM-11/M-1977 (BM-21)/M-1985/M-1992/M-1993; 200mm BMD-20; 240mm BM-24/M-1985/M-1989/M-1991; 300mm some
MOR 7,500: 82mm M-37; 120mm M-43; 160mm M-43
SURFACE-TO-SURFACE MISSILE LAUNCHERS
SRBM 24 FROG-3/5/7; some Toksa (SS-21B Scarab mod)
AIR DEFENCE
SAM • Point-defence 9K35 Strela-10 (SA-13 Gopher); 9K310 Igla-1 (SA-16 Gimlet); 9K32 Strela-2 (SA-7 Grail)‡
GUNS 11,000
SP 14.5mm M-1984; 23mm M-1992; 37mm M-1992; 57mm M-1985
TOWED 11,000: 14.5mm ZPU-1/ZPU-2/ZPU-4; 23mm ZU-23; 37mm M-1939; 57mm S-60; 85mm M-1939 KS-12; 100mm KS-19

Navy ε60,000
EQUIPMENT BY TYPE
SUBMARINES • TACTICAL 73
SSB 1 *Gorae* with 1 *Bukkeukseong*-1 SLBM (SLBM trials)
SSK 20 PRC Type-033/FSU *Romeo*† with 8 single 533mm TT with 14 SAET-60 HWT
SSC 32+:
ε30 *Sang-O* some with 2 single 533mm TT with 53–65 HWT
2+ *Sang-O* II with 4 single 533mm TT with 53–65 HWT
SSW ε20† (some *Yugo* some with 2 single 406mm TT; some *Yeono* some with 2 single 533mm TT)
PRINCIPAL SURFACE COMBATANTS 2
FRIGATES • FFG 2:
1 *Najin* with 2 single lnchr with P-15 *Termit* (SS-N-2) AShM, 2 RBU 1200 A/S mor, 2 100mm gun, 2 twin 57mm gun
1 *Najin* with 2 twin lnchr with *Kumsong*-3 mod (KN-SS-N-2 *Stormpetrel*) AShM, 2 RBU 1200 A/S mor, 2 100mm gun, 2 twin 57mm gun (operational status unclear)
PATROL AND COASTAL COMBATANTS 383+
PCG 18:
8 *Osa* I with 4 single lnchr with P-15 *Termit* (SS-N-2) AShM, 2 twin AK230 CIWS
10 *Soju* with 4 single lnchr with P-15 *Termit* (SS-N-2) AShM
PCO 5:
4 *Sariwon* with 2 twin 57mm gun
1 *Tral* with 1 85mm gun
PCC 18:
6 *Hainan* with 4 RBU 1200 A/S mor, 2 twin 57mm gun
7 *Taechong* I with 2 RBU 1200 A/S mor, 1 85mm gun, 1 twin 57mm gun
5 *Taechong* II with 2 RBU 1200 A/S mor, 1 100mm gun, 1 twin 57mm gun

PBFG 17+:
4 *Huangfen* with 4 single lnchr with P-15 *Termit* (SS-N-2) AShM, 2 twin AK230 CIWS
6 *Komar* with 2 single lnchr with P-15 *Termit* (SS-N-2) AShM
6 *Sohung* with 2 single lnchr with P-15 *Termit* (SS-N-2) AShM
1+ *Nongo* with 2 twin lnchr with *Kumsong*-3 mod (KN-SS-N-2 *Stormpetrel*) AShM, 2 30mm CIWS (operational status unknown)
PBF 229:
54 *Chong-Jin* with 1 85mm gun
142 *Ku Song/Sin Hung/Sin Hung* (mod)
33 *Sinpo*
PB 96:
59 *Chaho*
6 *Chong-Ju* with 2 RBU 1200 A/S mor, 1 85mm gun
13 *Shanghai* II
18 SO-1 with 4 RBU 1200 A/S mor, 2 twin 57mm gun
MINE WARFARE • MINE COUNTERMEASURES 24
MSC 24: 19 *Yukto* I; 5 *Yukto* II
AMPHIBIOUS
LANDING SHIPS • LSM 10 *Hantae* (capacity 3 tanks; 350 troops)
LANDING CRAFT 257
LCPL 96 *Nampo* (capacity 35 troops)
LCM 25
UCAC 136 *Kongbang* (capacity 50 troops)
LOGISTICS AND SUPPORT 23:
AGI 14 (converted fishing vessels)
AS 8 (converted cargo ships)
ASR 1 *Kowan*

Coastal Defence
FORCES BY ROLE
COASTAL DEFENCE
2 AShM regt with HY-1/*Kumsong*-3 (6 sites, some mobile launchers)
EQUIPMENT BY TYPE
COASTAL DEFENCE
ARTY 130mm M-1992; SM-4-1
AShM HY-1; *Kumsong*-3
ARTILLERY • TOWED 122mm M-1931/37; 152mm M-1937

Air Force 110,000
4 air divs. 1st, 2nd and 3rd Air Divs (cbt) responsible for N, E and S air-defence sectors respectively; 8th Air Div (trg) responsible for NE sector. The AF controls the national airline

Flying hours 20 hrs/yr on ac

FORCES BY ROLE
BOMBER
3 lt regt with H-5; Il-28 *Beagle*
FIGHTER
1 regt with MiG-15 *Fagot*
6 regt with J-5; MiG-17 *Fresco*
4 regt with J-6; MiG-19 *Farmer*
5 regt with J-7; MiG-21F-13/PFM *Fishbed*
1 regt with MiG-21bis *Fishbed*

1 regt with MiG-23ML/P *Flogger*
1 regt with MiG-29A/S/UB *Fulcrum*
GROUND ATTACK
1 regt with Su-25/Su-25UBK *Frogfoot*
TRANSPORT
Some regt with An-2 *Colt*/Y-5 (to infiltrate 2 air-force sniper brigades deep into ROK rear areas); An-24 *Coke*; Il-18 *Coot*; Il-62M *Classic*; Tu-134 *Crusty*; Tu-154 *Careless*
TRAINING
Some regt with CJ-6; FT-2; MiG-21U/UM
TRANSPORT HELICOPTER
Some regt with Hughes 500D/E; Mi-8 *Hip*; Mi-17 *Hip* H; Mil-26 *Halo*; PZL Mi-2 *Hoplite*; Z-5
AIR DEFENCE
19 bde with S-125 *Pechora* (SA-3 *Goa*); S-75 *Dvina* (SA-2 *Guideline*); S-200 *Angara* (SA-5 *Gammon*); 9K36 *Strela*-3 (SA-14 *Gremlin*); 9K310 *Igla*-1 (SA-16 *Gimlet*); 9K32 *Strela*-2 (SA-7 *Grail*)‡; *Pongae*-5

EQUIPMENT BY TYPE
AIRCRAFT 545 combat capable
BBR 80 Il-28 *Beagle*/H-5†
FTR 401+: MiG-15 *Fagot*; 107 MiG-17 *Fresco*/J-5; 100 MiG-19 *Farmer*/J-6; 120 MiG-21F-13 *Fishbed*/J-7; MiG-21PFM *Fishbed*; 46 MiG-23ML *Flogger*; 10 MiG-23P *Flogger*; 18+ MiG-29A/S/UB *Fulcrum*
FGA 30 MiG-21bis *Fishbed* (18 Su-7 *Fitter* in store)
ATK 34 Su-25/Su-25UBK *Frogfoot*
TPT 217+: **Heavy** some Il-76 (operated by state airline); **Light** 208: 6 An-24 *Coke*; 2 Tu-134 *Crusty*; ε200 An-2 *Colt*/Y-5; **PAX** 9: 2 Il-18 *Coot*; 2 Il-62M *Classic*; 4 Tu-154 *Careless*; 1 Tu-204-300
TRG 215+: 180 CJ-6; 35 FT-2; some MiG-21U/UM
HELICOPTERS
MRH 80 Hughes 500D/E†
TPT 206: **Heavy** 4 Mi-26 *Halo*; **Medium** 63: 15 Mi-8 *Hip*/Mi-17 *Hip* H; 48 Mi-4 *Hound*/Z-5; **Light** 139 PZL Mi-2 *Hoplite*
UNMANNED AERIAL VEHICLES
ISR • Medium some (unidentified indigenous type); **Light** *Pchela*-1 (*Shmel*) (reported)
AIR DEFENCE • SAM
Long-range 38 S-200 *Angara* (SA-5 *Gammon*)
Medium-range 179+: some *Pongae*-5 (status unknown); 179+ S-75 *Dvina* (SA-2 *Guideline*)
Short-range 133 S-125 *Pechora* (SA-3 *Goa*)
Point-defence 9K32 *Strela*-2 (SA-7 *Grail*)‡; 9K36 *Strela*-3 (SA-14 *Gremlin*); 9K310 *Igla*-1 (SA-16 *Gimlet*)
AIR-LAUNCHED MISSILES
AAM • IR R-3 (AA-2 *Atoll*)‡; R-60 (AA-8 *Aphid*); R-73 (AA-11 *Archer*); PL-5; PL-7; **SARH** R-23/24 (AA-7 *Apex*); R-27R/ER (AA-10 A/C *Alamo*)
ASM Kh-23 (AS-7 *Kerry*)‡; Kh-25 (AS-10 *Karen*)

Paramilitary 189,000 active

Security Troops 189,000 (incl border guards, public-safety personnel)
Ministry of Public Security

Worker/Peasant Red Guard ε5,700,000 reservists
Org on a province/town/village basis; comd structure is bde–bn–coy–pl; small arms with some mor and AD guns (but many units unarmed)

Cyber

Since the 1970s, the North Korean military (the Korean People's Army or KPA) has maintained a modest electronic-warfare (EW) capability. As a result of strategic reviews following *Operation Desert Storm*, the KPA established an information-warfare (IW) capability under the concept of 'electronic intelligence warfare' (EIW). The two key organisations are the Reconnaissance General Bureau (RGB), which conducts covert operations in peacetime, and the General Staff Department (GSD), which is responsible for cyber operations in support of conventional military efforts. The General Staff Department is responsible for operational command and oversees cyber, EW and psychological operations. This includes the Electronic Warfare Bureau, which was reportedly established in the mid-1980s. Experts assess North Korea as conceiving of cyber capabilities as useful tools for 'coercive diplomacy' and 'disruptive actions' in the South in the case of war. North Korea has launched distributed-denial-of-service attacks on South Korean institutions and pursues cyber infiltration against military and other government agencies. The attack on Sony Pictures in 2014 was attributed to North Korea. The incident illustrated that while attribution of North Korean activity may have been possible in this case, the country has also invested significant capacity in cyber operations. South Korea estimates that North Korea has a near 7,000-strong unit of cyber-warfare specialists.

Korea, Republic of ROK

South Korean Won		2016	2017	2018
GDP	won	1,637tr	1,739tr	
	US$	1.41tr	1.53tr	
per capita	US$	27,535	29,730	
Growth	%	2.8	3.0	
Inflation	%	1.0	1.9	
Def bdgt	won	39.0tr	40.6tr	43.7tr
	US$	33.6bn	35.7bn	
US$1=won		1,160.43	1,136.82	
Population	51,181,299			

Age	0–14	15–19	20–24	25–29	30–64	65 plus
Male	6.8%	3.0%	3.7%	3.5%	27.1%	6.0%
Female	6.4%	2.8%	3.2%	3.1%	26.4%	8.1%

Capabilities

South Korea's primary military concern remains its troubled relationship with North Korea. This has led to a defence policy aimed at recapitalising conventional military capabilities in order to maintain Seoul's qualitative edge, while simultaneously pursuing the niche capabilities required to deter North Korea's artillery, ballistic-missile and littoral-submarine threats. Military procurement includes new armoured vehicles and artillery, tactical and tanker aircraft, UAVs, precision munitions, ballistic and cruise missiles, satellites, and cyber- and missile-defence equipment. While most acquisitions are from local defence industry, the lengthy timelines of key programmes such as Korean Air and Missile Defence and 'Kill Chain' have led to the import of key items. Another strategy, 'Korea Massive Punishment and Retaliation', was outlined in late 2016 after the North's fifth nuclear test. Ongoing nuclear and missile testing by the North led to the US deployment in 2017 of the THAAD missile-defence system. Also in 2017, the US and South Korea agreed in principle to remove current warhead limitations on the South's ballistic missiles. Japan, South Korea and the US conducted missile-defence drills in 2017. In late 2016, Tokyo and Seoul agreed to share intelligence on North Korea. The US alliance remains a major element of South Korea's defence strategy, and the transfer of wartime operational control of forces to Seoul, planned for the end of 2015, is now 'conditions based', with no firm date set.

ACTIVE 625,000 (Army 490,000 Navy 70,000 Air 65,000) Paramilitary 9,000
Conscript liability 20–24 months depending on branch

RESERVE 3,100,000
Reserve obligation of three days per year. First Combat Forces (Mobilisation Reserve Forces) or Regional Combat Forces (Homeland Defence Forces) to age 33

Reserve Paramilitary 3,000,000
Being reorganised

ORGANISATIONS BY SERVICE

Army 490,000
FORCES BY ROLE
COMMAND
  2 army HQ
  8 corps HQ
  1 (Capital Defence) comd HQ
SPECIAL FORCES
  1 (Special Warfare) SF comd
  6 SF bde
  1 indep SF bn
  2 cdo bde
  6 cdo regt
  2 indep cdo bn
MANOEUVRE
  Armoured
  5 armd bde
  3 mech inf div (1 recce bn, 1 armd bde, 2 armd inf bde, 1 fd arty bde, 1 engr bn)
  Mechanised
  3 mech inf div (1 recce bn, 1 armd bde, 2 mech inf bde, 1 fd arty bde, 1 engr bn)
  Light
  16 inf div (1 recce bn, 1 tk bn, 3 inf regt, 1 arty regt (4 arty bn), 1 engr bn)
  2 indep inf bde

Air Manoeuvre
1 air aslt bde
Other
5 sy regt
SURFACE-TO-SURFACE MISSILE
3 SSM bn
COMBAT SUPPORT
6 engr bde
5 engr gp
1 CBRN defence bde
8 sigs bde
COMBAT SERVICE SUPPORT
4 log spt comd
HELICOPTER
1 (army avn) comd
AIR DEFENCE
1 ADA bde
5 ADA bn

Reserves
FORCES BY ROLE
COMMAND
  1 army HQ
MANOEUVRE
  Light
  24 inf div
EQUIPMENT BY TYPE
ARMOURED FIGHTING VEHICLES
  MBT 2,514: 1,000 K1; 484 K1A1; 100 K2; 253 M48; 597 M48A5; 80 T-80U (400 M47 in store)
  IFV 540: ε500 K21; 40 BMP-3
  APC 2,790
    APC (T) 2,560: 300 Bv 206; 1,700 KIFV; 420 M113; 140 M577 (CP)
    APC (W) 220; 20 BTR-80; 200 KM-900/-901 (Fiat 6614)
  PPV 10 *MaxxPro*
ENGINEERING & MAINTENANCE VEHICLES
  AEV 207 M9
  ARV 238+: 200 K1; K21 ARV; K288A1; M47; 38 M88A1
  VLB 56 K1
ANTI-TANK/ANTI-INFRASTRUCTURE
  MSL • MANPATS 9K115 *Metis* (AT-7 *Saxhorn*); TOW-2A
  RCL 57mm; 75mm; 90mm M67; 106mm M40A2
  GUNS 58
    SP 90mm 50 M36
    TOWED 76mm 8 M18 *Hellcat* (AT gun)
ARTILLERY 11,067+
  SP 1,353+: 155mm 1,340: ε300 K9 *Thunder*; 1,040 M109A2 (K55/K55A1); 175mm some M107; 203mm 13 M110
  TOWED 3,500+: 105mm 1,700 M101/KH-178; 155mm/203mm 1,800+ KH-179/M114/M115
  MRL 214+: 130mm 156 K136 *Kooryong*; 227mm 58: 48 M270 MLRS; 10 M270A1 MLRS; 239mm some *Chunmoo*
  MOR 6,000: 81mm KM29 (M29); 107mm M30
SURFACE-TO-SURFACE MISSILE LAUNCHERS
  SRBM • Conventional 30 *Hyonmu* I/IIA/IIB; MGM-140A/B ATACMS (launched from M270/M270A1 MLRS)
  GLCM • Conventional *Hyonmu* III
RADAR • LAND AN/TPQ-36 *Firefinder* (arty, mor); AN/TPQ-37 *Firefinder* (arty); RASIT (veh, arty)

HELICOPTERS
ATK 96: 60 AH-1F/J *Cobra*; 36 AH-64E *Apache*
MRH 175: 130 Hughes 500D; 45 MD-500
TPT 301: **Heavy** 37: 31 CH-47D *Chinook*; 6 MH-47E *Chinook*; **Medium** 152: 65 KUH-1 *Surion*; 87 UH-60P *Black Hawk*; **Light** 112: ε100 Bell 205 (UH-1H *Iroquois*); 12 Bo-105

AIR DEFENCE
SAM • **Point-defence** *Chun Ma* (*Pegasus*); FIM-92 *Stinger*; *Javelin*; *Mistral*; 9K310 *Igla-1* (SA-16 *Gimlet*)
GUNS 330+
SP 170: **20mm** ε150 KIFV *Vulcan* SPAAG; **30mm** 20 BIHO *Flying Tiger*
TOWED 160: **20mm** 60 M167 *Vulcan*; **35mm** 20 GDF-003; **40mm** 80 L/60/L/70; M1

AIR-LAUNCHED MISSILES
ASM AGM-114R1 *Hellfire*

Navy 70,000 (incl marines)

Three separate fleet elements: 1st Fleet Donghae (East Sea/Sea of Japan); 2nd Fleet Pyeongtaek (West Sea/Yellow Sea); 3rd Fleet Busan (South Sea/Korea Strait); independent submarine command; three additional flotillas (incl SF, mine warfare, amphibious and spt elements) and 1 Naval Air Wing (3 gp plus spt gp)

EQUIPMENT BY TYPE
SUBMARINES • TACTICAL 24
  SSK 15:
    6 *Chang Bogo* (GER Type-209/1200; KSS-1) with 8 single 533mm TT with SUT HWT/*White Shark* HWT
    3 *Chang Bogo* (GER Type-209/1200; KSS-1) with 8 single 533mm TT with SUT HWT/*White Shark* HWT/UGM-84B *Harpoon* AShM
    6 *Son Won-il* (GER Type-214; KSS-2; AIP fitted) with 8 single 533mm TT with SUT HWT/*White Shark* HWT/*Hae Sung* I AShM/*Hae Sung* III LACM
  SSC 9 *Cosmos*
PRINCIPAL SURFACE COMBATANTS 25
  CRUISERS • CGHM 3:
    3 *Sejong* (KDD-III) with *Aegis* Baseline 7 C2, 2 quad Mk141 lnchr with RGM-84 *Harpoon* AShM, 1 48-cell Mk41 VLS with SM-2MR SAM, 1 32-cell Mk41 VLS with SM-2MR SAM, 1 Mk49 GMLS with RIM-116 SAM, 2 triple Mk32 324mm ASTT with K745 LWT, 1 32-cell VLS with ASROC, 1 *Goalkeeper* CIWS, 1 127mm gun (capacity 2 *Lynx* Mk99 hel)
  DESTROYERS • DDGHM 6:
    6 *Chungmugong Yi Sun-Sin* (KDD-II) with 2 quad Mk141 lnchr with RGM-84C *Harpoon* AShM/*Hae Sung* I AShM, 1 32-cell Mk41 VLS with SM-2MR SAM/ASROC/*Hae Sung* II LACM, 1 Mk49 GMLS with RIM-116 SAM, 2 triple Mk32 324mm ASTT with Mk46 LWT, 1 *Goalkeeper* CIWS, 1 127mm gun (capacity 1 *Lynx* Mk99 hel)
  FRIGATES 16
    FFGHM 9:
      3 *Gwanggaeto Daewang* (KDD-I) with 2 quad Mk141 lnchr with RGM-84 *Harpoon* AShM, 1 16 cell Mk48 VLS with *Sea Sparrow* SAM, 2 triple Mk32 324mm ASTT with Mk46 LWT, 1 *Goalkeeper* CIWS, 1 127mm gun (capacity 1 *Lynx* Mk99 hel)
      6 *Incheon* with 2 quad lnchr with *Hae Sung* I AShM/TSLM LACM, 1 21-cell Mk49 lnchr with RIM-116 SAM, 2 triple 324mm ASTT with K745 *Blue Shark* LWT, 1 MK15 1B *Phalanx* CIWS, 1 127 mm gun
    FFGM 7 *Ulsan* with 2 quad Mk141 lnchr with RGM-84C *Harpoon* AShM, 2 triple Mk32 324mm ASTT with Mk46 LWT, 2 76mm gun
PATROL AND COASTAL COMBATANTS ε104
  CORVETTES • FSG 33:
    17 *Gumdoksuri* with 2 twin lnchr with *Hae Sung* I AShM, 1 76mm gun
    16 *Po Hang* with 2 twin lnchr with RGM-84 *Harpoon* AShM, 2 triple 324mm ASTT with Mk46 LWT, 2 76mm gun
  PBF ε71 *Sea Dolphin*
MINE WARFARE 10
  MINE COUNTERMEASURES 9
    MHO 6 *Kan Kyeong*
    MSO 3 *Yang Yang*
  MINELAYERS • ML 1 *Won San* with 2 triple Mk32 324mm ASTT, 1 76mm gun, 1 hel landing platform
AMPHIBIOUS
  PRINCIPAL AMPHIBIOUS SHIPS 3
    LHD
      1 *Dokdo* with 1 Mk49 GMLS with RIM-116 SAM, 2 *Goalkeeper* CIWS (capacity 2 LCAC; 10 tanks; 700 troops; 10 UH-60 hel)
    LPD 2:
      2 *Cheonwangbong* (LST-II) (capacity 2 LCM; 300 troops; 2 UH-60 hel)
  LANDING SHIPS • LST 4 *Go Jun Bong* with 1 hel landing platform (capacity 20 tanks; 300 troops)
  LANDING CRAFT 22
    LCAC 5: 3 *Tsaplya* (capacity 1 MBT; 130 troops); 2 LSF-II (capacity 150 troops or 1 MBT & 24 troops)
    LCM 10 LCM-8
    LCT 3 *Mulgae* II
    LCU 4 *Mulgae* I
LOGISTICS AND SUPPORT 7
  AG 1 *Sunjin* (trials spt)
  AORH 3 *Chun Jee*
  ARS 2: 1 *Cheong Hae Jin*; 1 *Pyong Taek* (ex-US *Edenton*)
  ASR 1 *Tongyeong*

Naval Aviation

EQUIPMENT BY TYPE
AIRCRAFT 16 combat capable
  ASW 16: 8 P-3C *Orion*; 8 P-3CK *Orion*
  TPT • Light 5 Cessna F406 *Caravan* II
HELICOPTERS
  ASW 31: 11 *Lynx* Mk99; 12 *Lynx* Mk99A; 8 AW159 *Wildcat*
  MRH 3 SA319B *Alouette* III
  TPT 15: **Medium** 8 UH-60P *Black Hawk* **Light** 7 Bell 205 (UH-1H *Iroquois*)

Marines 29,000

FORCES BY ROLE
SPECIAL FORCES
  1 SF regt

MANOEUVRE
  Amphibious
    2 mne div (1 recce bn, 1 tk bn, 3 mne regt, 1 amph bn, 1 arty regt, 1 engr bn)
    1 mne bde
COMBAT SUPPORT
  Some cbt spt unit
EQUIPMENT BY TYPE
ARMOURED FIGHTING VEHICLES
  MBT 100: 50 K1A1; 50 M48
  AAV 166 AAV-7A1
ANTI-TANK/ANTI-INFRASTUCTURE
  MSL • SP Spike NLOS
ARTILLERY • TOWED 105mm; 155mm
COASTAL DEFENCE • AShM RGM-84A Harpoon (truck mounted)

Naval Special Warfare Flotilla

Air Force 65,000

4 Comd (Ops, Southern Combat, Logs, Trg)
FORCES BY ROLE
FIGHTER/GROUND ATTACK
  2 sqn with F-4E Phantom II
  6 sqn with F-5E/F Tiger II
  3 sqn with F-15K Eagle
  10 sqn with F-16C/D Fighting Falcon (KF-16C/D)
  2 sqn with FA-50 Fighting Eagle
ISR
  1 wg with KO-1
SIGINT
  1 sqn with Hawker 800RA/XP
SEARCH & RESCUE
  2 sqn with AS332L Super Puma; Bell 412EP; HH-47D Chinook; HH-60P Black Hawk; Ka-32 Helix C
TRANSPORT
  1 VIP sqn with B-737-300; B-747; CN235-220; S-92A Superhawk; VH-60P Black Hawk (VIP)
  3 sqn (incl 1 Spec Ops) with C-130H/H-30/J-30 Hercules
  2 sqn with CN235M-100/220
TRAINING
  2 sqn with F-5E/F Tiger II
  1 sqn with F-16C/D Fighting Falcon
  4 sqn with KT-1
  1 sqn with Il-103
  3 sqn with T-50/TA-50 Golden Eagle*
TRANSPORT HELICOPTER
  1 sqn with UH-60P Black Hawk (Spec Ops)
AIR DEFENCE
  3 AD bde (total: 3 SAM bn with MIM-23B I-HAWK; 2 SAM bn with MIM-104E Patriot PAC-2 GEM-T)
EQUIPMENT BY TYPE
AIRCRAFT 587 combat capable
  FTR 174: 142 F-5E Tiger II; 32 F-5F Tiger II
  FGA 333: 60 F-4E Phantom II; 60 F-15K Eagle; 118 F-16C Fighting Falcon (KF-16C); 45 F-16D Fighting Falcon (KF-16D); 50 FA-50 Fighting Eagle
  AEW&C 4 B-737 AEW
  ISR 24: 4 Hawker 800RA; 20 KO-1
  SIGINT 6: 4 Hawker 800SIG; 2 Falcon 2000 (COMINT/SIGINT)
  TPT 38: **Medium** 16: 8 C-130H Hercules; 4 C-130H-30 Hercules; 4 C-130J-30 Hercules; **Light** 20: 12 CN235M-100; 8 CN235M-220 (incl 2 VIP); **PAX** 2: 1 B-737-300; 1 B-747
  TRG 186: 23 Il-103; 83 KT-1; 49 T-50 Golden Eagle*; 9 T-50B Black Eagle* (aerobatics); 22 TA-50 Golden Eagle*
HELICOPTERS
  SAR 16: 5 HH-47D Chinook; 11 HH-60P Black Hawk
  MRH 3 Bell 412EP
  TPT • **Medium** 30: 2 AS332L Super Puma; 8 Ka-32 Helix C; 3 S-92A Super Hawk; 7 UH-60P Black Hawk; 10 VH-60P Black Hawk (VIP)
UNMANNED AERIAL VEHICLES • ISR 103+: **Medium** 3+: some Night Intruder; 3 Searcher **Light** 100 Harpy (anti-radiation)
AIR DEFENCE • SAM 206
  Long-range 48 MIM-104E Patriot PAC-2 GEM-T
  Medium-range 158 MIM-23B I-HAWK
AIR-LAUNCHED MISSILES
  AAM • **IR** AIM-9 Sidewinder; **IIR** AIM-9X Sidewinder II; **SARH** AIM-7 Sparrow; **ARH** AIM-120B/C-5/7 AMRAAM
  ASM AGM-65A Maverick; AGM-130
  AShM AGM-84 Harpoon; AGM-142 Popeye
  ARM AGM-88 HARM
  ALCM AGM-84H SLAM-ER; KEPD-350 Taurus
BOMBS • Laser-guided Paveway II

Paramilitary 9,000 active

Civilian Defence Corps 3,000,000 reservists (to age 50)

Coast Guard 9,000

Part of the Ministry of Public Safety and Secuity. Five regional headquarters and 17 coastguard stations
EQUIPMENT BY TYPE
PATROL AND COASTAL COMBATANTS 79
  PSOH 15: 1 Lee Cheong-ho with 1 76mm gun; 1 Sambongho; 13 Tae Pung Yang with 1 med hel
  PSO 21: 3 Han Kang with 1 76mm gun, 1 hel landing platform; 5 Han Kang II with 1 76mm gun, 1 hel landing pllatform; 12 Jaemin with 1 hel landing platform; 1 Sumjinkang
  PCO 15 Tae Geuk
  PCC 10: 4 Bukhansan; 6 (430 tonne)
  PB 18: 14 Hae Uri; ε4 (various)
AMPHIBIOUS
  LANDING CRAFT • UCAC 8: 1 BHT-150; 4 Griffon 470TD; 3 Griffon 8000TD
AIRCRAFT
  MP 5: 1 C-212-400 MP; 4 CN235-110 MPA
  TPT • **PAX** 1 CL-604
HELICOPTERS
  MRH 7: 5 AS565MB Panther; 1 AW139; 1 Bell 412SP
  SAR 1 S-92
  TPT • **Medium** 8 Ka-32 Helix C

Cyber

The MND commands Defense Cyber Command, which was established in February 2015. (South Korea had earlier, in 2010, established a Cyber Warfare Command Centre.) A Korea–US National Cyber Defense Cooperation Working Group shares information and enhances cooperation including over policy, strategy, doctrine and training. In 2015 a unit responsible for overseeing cyber operations was established within the Joint Chiefs of Staff (JCS), and the Chairman of the JCS was also given command and control authority for cyber operations. The Joint Cyber Operations Manual describes the cyber-operations structure within the JCS. The defence ministry is preparing a National Defence Cybersecurity Strategy, and announced in April 2017 that it would allocate US$218 million for spending on cyber capabilities from 2018–22.

DEPLOYMENT

AFGHANISTAN
NATO • *Operation Resolute Support* 50

ARABIAN SEA
Combined Maritime Forces • CTF-151: 1 DDGHM

INDIA/PAKISTAN
UN • UNMOGIP 7 obs

LEBANON
UN • UNIFIL 332; 1 mech inf coy; 1 engr coy; 1 sigs coy; 1 maint coy

SOUTH SUDAN
UN • UNMISS 299; 2 obs; 1 engr coy

SUDAN
UN • UNAMID 2

UNITED ARAB EMIRATES
139 (trg activities at UAE Spec Ops School)

WESTERN SAHARA
UN • MINURSO 4 obs

FOREIGN FORCES

Sweden NNSC: 5 obs
Switzerland NNSC: 5 obs
United States US Pacific Command: 28,500
  Army 19,200; 1 HQ (8th Army) at Seoul; 1 div HQ at Tongduchon; 1 armd bde with M1 *Abrams*; M2/M3 *Bradley*; M109; 1 (cbt avn) hel bde with AH-64 *Apache*; CH-47 *Chinook*; UH-60 *Black Hawk*; 1 MRL bde with M270A1 MLRS; 1 AD bde with MIM 104 *Patriot*/FIM-92A *Avenger*; 1 SAM bty with THAAD; 1 (APS) armd bde eqpt set
  Navy 250
  USAF 8,800; 1 HQ (7th Air Force) at Osan AB; 1 ftr wg at Kunsan AB (2 ftr sqn with 20 F-16C/D *Fighting Falcon*); 1 ftr wg at Osan AB (1 ftr sqn with 20 F-16C/D *Fighting Falcon*, 1 atk sqn with 24 A-10C *Thunderbolt* II); 1 ISR sqn at Osan AB with U-2S
  USMC 250

Laos LAO

New Lao Kip		2016	2017	2018
GDP	kip	129tr	142tr	
	US$	15.8bn	17.2bn	
per capita	US$	2,394	2,568	
Growth	%	7.0	6.9	
Inflation	%	2.0	2.3	
Def exp	kip	n.k.	n.k.	
	US$	n.k.	n.k.	
FMA	US$	0.2m	0m	0m
US$1=kip		8,175.13	8,254.97	

Population 7,126,706
Ethnic groups: Lao 55%; Khmou 11%; Hmong 8%

Age	0–14	15–19	20–24	25–29	30–64	65 plus
Male	16.6%	5.6%	4.9%	4.5%	16.3%	1.8%
Female	16.2%	5.6%	5.1%	4.6%	16.8%	2.1%

Capabilities

The Lao People's Armed Forces (LPAF) have considerable military experience from the Second Indo-China War and the 1988 border war with Thailand. However, defence spending and military procurement have been limited for more than 20 years. The armed forces remain closely linked to the ruling Communist Party, and their primary role is internal security. Maintenance capacity is limited, reflected in a support contract for a Russian firm to maintain the air force's Mi-17 helicopters. Contacts with the Chinese and Vietnamese armed forces continue. Laos participates in ADMM–Plus military exercises, and in 2014–15 was co-chair with Japan of the ADMM–Plus expert working group on HADR. However, the LPAF have made no international deployments and have little capacity for sustained high-intensity operations.

ACTIVE 29,100 (Army 25,600 Air 3,500) **Paramilitary 100,000**

Conscript liability 18 months minimum

ORGANISATIONS BY SERVICE

Space
EQUIPMENT BY TYPE
SATELLITES • ISR 1 LaoSat-1

Army 25,600
FORCES BY ROLE
4 mil regions
MANOEUVRE
  Armoured
  1 armd bn
  Light
  5 inf div
  7 indep inf regt
  65 indep inf coy

COMBAT SUPPORT
5 arty bn
1 engr regt
2 (construction) engr regt
AIR DEFENCE
9 ADA bn
EQUIPMENT BY TYPE
ARMOURED FIGHTING VEHICLES
  MBT 25: 15 T-54/T-55; 10 T-34/85
  LT TK 10 PT-76
  APC • APC (W) 50: 30 BTR-40/BTR-60; 20 BTR-152
  AUV ZYZ-8002 (VN3)
ENGINEERING & MAINTENANCE VEHICLES
  ARV T-54/T-55
  VLB MTU
ANTI-TANK/ANTI-INFRASTRUCTURE • RCL 57mm M18/A1; **75mm** M20; **106mm** M40; **107mm** B-11
ARTILLERY 62+
  TOWED 62: **105mm** 20 M101; **122mm** 20 D-30/M-30 M-1938; **130mm** 10 M-46; **155mm** 12 M114
  MOR **81mm**; **82mm**; **107mm** M-1938/M2A1; **120mm** M-43
AIR DEFENCE
  SAM • Point-defence 9K32 *Strela*-2 (SA-7 *Grail*)‡; 25 9K310 *Igla*-1 (SA-16 *Gimlet*)
  GUNS
    SP **23mm** ZSU-23-4
    TOWED **14.5mm** ZPU-1/ZPU-4; **23mm** ZU-23; **37mm** M-1939; **57mm** S-60

Army Marine Section ε600
EQUIPMENT BY TYPE
PATROL AND COASTAL COMBATANTS • PBR some
AMPHIBIOUS LCM some

Air Force 3,500
FORCES BY ROLE
TRANSPORT
1 regt with MA60; MA600; Mi-17 *Hip* H
EQUIPMENT BY TYPE
AIRCRAFT
  TPT • **Light** 5: 1 An-74TK *Coaler*; 2 MA60; 2 MA600
HELICOPTERS
  MRH 15: 6 Mi-17 *Hip* H; 5 Mi-17V-5 *Hip*; 4 Z-9A
  TPT 4: **Medium** 1 Ka-32T *Helix* C; **Light** 3 SA360 *Dauphin*

Paramilitary

Militia Self-Defence Forces 100,000+
Village 'home guard' or local defence

Malaysia MYS

Malaysian Ringgit RM		2016	2017	2018
GDP	RM	1.23tr	1.34tr	
	US$	297bn	310bn	
per capita	US$	9,374	9,660	
Growth	%	4.2	5.4	
Inflation	%	2.1	3.8	
Def bdgt	RM	17.3bn	15.1bn	15.9bn
	US$	4.17bn	3.48bn	
US$1=RM		4.15	4.33	

Population 31,381,992

Ethnic groups: Malay 50.1%; Chinese 22.5%; Indian 6.5%; other or unspecified 20.9%

Age	0–14	15–19	20–24	25–29	30–64	65 plus
Male	14.3%	4.4%	4.1%	3.9%	21.0%	2.9%
Female	13.5%	4.2%	4.0%	3.8%	20.5%	3.2%

Capabilities

Modernisation programmes in recent decades have developed the armed forces' capacity for external defence, notably by strengthening air and naval capabilities and moving the army's operational focus away from counter-insurgency and towards conventional warfare. The 2013 armed intrusion at Lahad Datu, the aftermath of the March 2014 disappearance of MH370 and Chinese naval intrusions into Malaysia's EEZ in 2015–16 all revealed serious capability shortcomings, particularly in air and maritime surveillance. Addressing these is a high priority, but budgetary constraints have slowed equipment procurement and infrastructural improvements. In 2017, the navy announced an ambitious modernisation plan to reduce the number of vessel classes from 15 to five and boost local shipbuilding. As part of this, Malaysia awarded China a contract for four littoral-mission ships, two of which are to be built in-country, despite reported misgivings by some officers. In 2017, Malaysia began trilateral joint maritime patrols and joint Sulu Sea air patrols with Indonesia and the Philippines to counter movements and attacks by ISIS-linked militants in regional waterways. Army units have deployed on UN peacekeeping operations and the navy has achieved successes with its anti-piracy patrols in the Gulf of Aden. Malaysian forces regularly participate in the Five Power Defence Arrangements, ADMM–Plus and other exercises with regional and international partners, including the US.

ACTIVE 109,000 (Army 80,000 Navy 14,000 Air 15,000) Paramilitary 24,600

RESERVE 51,600 (Army 50,000, Navy 1,000 Air Force 600) Paramilitary 244,700

ORGANISATIONS BY SERVICE

Army 80,000 (to be 60–70,000)
2 mil region, 4 area comd (div)

FORCES BY ROLE
SPECIAL FORCES
 1 SF bde (3 SF bn)
MANOEUVRE
 Armoured
  1 tk regt (5 armd bn)
 Mechanised
  5 armd regt
  1 mech inf bde (3 mech bn, 1 cbt engr sqn)
 Light
  1 inf bde (4 inf bn, 1 arty regt)
  5 inf bde (3 inf bn, 1 arty regt)
  2 inf bde (2 inf bn)
  1 inf bde (2 inf bn)
 Air Manoeuvre
  1 (Rapid Deployment Force) AB bde (1 lt tk sqn, 3 AB bn, 1 lt arty regt, 1 engr sqn)
 Other
  1 (border) sy bde (5 bn)
  1 (border) sy bde (forming)
COMBAT SUPPORT
 9 arty regt
 1 STA regt
 1 MRL regt
 1 cbt engr sqn
 3 fd engr regt (total: 7 cbt engr sqn, 3 engr spt sqn)
 1 construction regt
 1 int unit
 4 MP regt
 1 sigs regt
HELICOPTER
 1 hel sqn
 1 tpt sqn with S-61A-4 *Nuri* (forming)
AIR DEFENCE
 3 ADA regt
EQUIPMENT BY TYPE
ARMOURED FIGHTING VEHICLES
 MBT 48 PT-91M *Twardy*
 LT TK 21 *Scorpion*-90
 RECCE 214: 130 AML-60/90; 74 SIBMAS (some†); 10 VBL
 IFV 71+: 31 ACV300 *Adnan* (25mm *Bushmaster*); 13 ACV300 *Adnan* AGL; 27+ AV8 *Gempita* IFV25/IFV30
 APC 777
  APC (T) 265: 149 ACV300 *Adnan* (incl 69 variants); 13 FV4333 *Stormer* (upgraded); 63 K200A; 40 K200A1
  APC (W) 512: 32 *Anoa*; 300 *Condor* (incl variants); 150 LAV-150 *Commando*; 30 M3 Panhard
ENGINEERING & MAINTENANCE VEHICLES
 AEV 3 MID-M
 ARV 47+: *Condor*; 15 ACV300; 4 K288A1; 22 SIBMAS; 6 WZT-4
 VLB 5+: *Leguan*; 5 PMCz-90
NBC VEHICLES K216A1
ANTI-TANK/ANTI-INFRASTRUCTURE • MSL
 SP 8 ACV300 *Baktar Shikan*
 MANPATS 9K115 *Metis* (AT-7 *Saxhorn*); 9K115-2 *Metis-M* (AT-13 *Saxhorn 2*); *Eryx*; *Baktar Shihan* (HJ-8); SS.11
 RCL 260: **84mm** 236 *Carl Gustav*; **106mm** 24 M40

ARTILLERY 424
 TOWED 134: **105mm** 100 Model 56 pack howitzer; **155mm** 34: 12 FH-70; 22 G-5
 MRL 36 ASTROS II (equipped with 127mm SS-30)
 MOR 254: **81mm** 232; **SP 81mm** 14: 4 K281A1; 10 ACV300-S; **SP 120mm** 8 ACV-S
AMPHIBIOUS • LANDING CRAFT
 LCA 165 Damen Assault Craft 540 (capacity 10 troops)
HELICOPTERS • TPT 12: **Medium** 2 S-61A-4 *Nuri*; **Light** 10 AW109
AIR DEFENCE
 SAM • **Point-defence** 15+: 15 *Jernas* (*Rapier* 2000); *Anza*; HY-6 (FN-6); 9K38 *Igla* (SA-18 *Grouse*); QW-1 *Vanguard*;
 GUNS 52+
  SP 20mm K263
  TOWED 52: **35mm** 16 GDF-005; **40mm** 36 L40/70

Reserves

Territorial Army
Some paramilitary forces to be incorporated into a re-organised territorial organisation
FORCES BY ROLE
MANOEUVRE
 Mechanised
  4 armd sqn
 Light
  16 inf regt (3 inf bn)
 Other
  5 (highway) sy bn
COMBAT SUPPORT
 5 arty bty
 2 fd engr regt
 1 int unit
 3 sigs sqn
COMBAT SUPPORT
 4 med coy
 5 tpt coy

Navy 14,000

3 Regional Commands: Kuantan (East Coast), Kinabalu (Borneo) and Langkawi (West Coast)
EQUIPMENT BY TYPE
SUBMARINES • TACTICAL • SSK 2 *Tunku Abdul Rahman* (FRA *Scorpene*) with 6 single 533mm TT with WASS *Black Shark* HWT/SM39 *Exocet* AShM
PRINCIPAL SURFACE COMBATANTS 10
 FRIGATES 10
  FFGHM 2:
   2 *Lekiu* with 2 quad lnchr with MM40 *Exocet* Block 2 AShM, 1 16-cell VLS with *Sea Wolf* SAM, 2 B515 ILAS-3 triple 324mm ASTT with *Sting Ray* LWT, 1 57mm gun (capacity 1 *Super Lynx* hel)
  FFG 2:
   2 *Kasturi* with 2 quad lnchr with MM40 *Exocet* Block 2 AShM, 1 twin 375mm A/S mor, 1 100mm gun, 1 57mm gun, 1 hel landing platform
  FF 6:
   6 *Kedah* (GER MEKO) with 1 76mm gun, 1 hel landing platform (fitted for MM40 *Exocet* AShM & RAM CIWS)

PATROL AND COASTAL COMBATANTS 37
    CORVETTES • FSGM 4 *Laksamana* with 3 twin lnchr with Mk 2 *Otomat* AShM, 1 *Albatros* quad lnchr with *Aspide* SAM, 1 76mm gun
    PCFG 4 *Perdana* (FRA *Combattante* II) with 2 single lnchr with MM38 *Exocet* AShM, 1 57mm gun
    PBG 4 *Handalan* (SWE *Spica*-M) with 2 twin lnchr with MM38 *Exocet* AShM , 1 57mm gun
    PBF 17 *Tempur* (SWE CB90)
    PB 8: 6 *Jerong* (Lurssen 45) with 1 57mm gun; 2 *Sri Perlis*
MINE WARFARE • MINE COUNTERMEASURES 4
    MCO 4 *Mahamiru* (ITA *Lerici*)
LOGISTICS AND SUPPORT 13
    AFS 2: 1 *Mahawangsa* with 2 57mm guns, 1 hel landing platform; 1 *Sri Indera Sakti* with 1 57mm gun, 1 hel landing platform
    AG 2 *Bunga Mas Lima* with 1 hel landing platform
    AGS 2: 1 *Mutiara* with 1 hel landing platform; 1 *Perantau*
    AP 2 *Sri Gaya*
    ASR 1 *Mega Bakti*
    ATF 1
    AX 2: 1 *Hang Tuah* with 1 57mm gun, 1 hel landing platform; 1 *Gagah Samudera* with 1 hel landing platform
    AXS 1

Naval Aviation 160

EQUIPMENT BY TYPE
HELICOPTERS
    ASW 6 *Super Lynx* 300
    MRH 6 AS555 *Fennec*
    AIR-LAUNCHED MISSILES • AShM *Sea Skua*

Special Forces

FORCES BY ROLE
SPECIAL FORCES
    1 (mne cdo) SF unit

Air Force 15,000

1 air op HQ, 2 air div, 1 trg and log comd, 1 Intergrated Area Def Systems HQ

Flying hours 60 hrs/yr

FORCES BY ROLE
FIGHTER
    2 sqn with MiG-29/MiG-29UB *Fulcrum*
FIGHTER/GROUND ATTACK
    1 sqn with F/A-18D *Hornet*
    1 sqn with Su-30MKM *Flanker*
    2 sqn with *Hawk* Mk108*/Mk208*
FIGHTER/GROUND ATTACK/ISR
    1 sqn with F-5E/F *Tiger* II; RF-5E *Tigereye**
MARITIME PATROL
    1 sqn with Beech 200T
TANKER/TRANSPORT
    2 sqn with KC-130H *Hercules*; C-130H *Hercules*; C-130H-30 *Hercules*; Cessna 402B
TRANSPORT
    1 (VIP) sqn with A319CT; AW109; B-737-700 BBJ; BD700 *Global Express*; F-28 *Fellowship*; *Falcon* 900
    1 sqn with CN235

TRAINING
    1 unit with PC-7; SA316 *Alouette* III
TRANSPORT HELICOPTER
    4 (tpt/SAR) sqn with H225M *Super Cougar*; S-61A-4 *Nuri*; S-61N; S-70A *Black Hawk*
AIR DEFENCE
    1 sqn with *Starburst*
SPECIAL FORCES
    1 (Air Force Commando) unit (airfield defence/SAR)
EQUIPMENT BY TYPE
AIRCRAFT 66 combat capable
    FTR 21: 8 F-5E *Tiger* II; 3 F-5F *Tiger* II; 8 MiG-29 *Fulcrum* (MiG-29N); 2 MiG-29UB *Fulcrum* (MIG-29NUB)
    FGA 26: 8 F/A-18D *Hornet*; 18 Su-30MKM
    ISR 5: 3 Beech 200T; 2 RF-5E *Tigereye**
    TKR 4 KC-130H *Hercules*
    TPT 37: **Heavy** 4 A400M *Atlas*; **Medium** 10: 2 C-130H *Hercules*; 8 C-130H-30 *Hercules*; **Light** 18: 9 CN235M-220 (incl 1 VIP); 9 Cessna 402B (2 modified for aerial survey); **PAX** 5: 1 A319CT; 1 B-737-700 BBJ; 1 BD700 *Global Express*; 1 F-28 *Fellowship*; 1 *Falcon* 900
    TRG 78: 5 *Hawk* Mk108*; 12 *Hawk* Mk208*; 7 MB-339C; 7 MD3-160 *Aero Tiga*; 30 PC-7; 17 PC-7 Mk II *Turbo Trainer*
HELICOPTERS
    MRH 17 SA316 *Alouette* III
    TPT 42: **Heavy** 12 H225M *Super Cougar*; **Medium** 29: 25 S-61A-4 *Nuri*; 2 S-61N; 2 S-70A *Black Hawk*; **Light** 1 AW109
UNMANNED AERIAL VEHICLES
    ISR • Medium *Aludra*
AIR DEFENCE • SAM • Point-defence *Starburst*
AIR-LAUNCHED MISSILES
    AAM • IR AIM-9 *Sidewinder*; R-73 (AA-11 *Archer*); **IIR** AIM-9X *Sidewinder* II; **IR/SARH** R-27 (AA-10 *Alamo*); **SARH** AIM-7 *Sparrow*; **ARH** AIM-120C AMRAAM; R-77 (AA-12A *Adder*)
    ASM AGM-65 *Maverick*
    AShM AGM-84D *Harpoon*
BOMBS • Laser-guided *Paveway* II

Paramilitary ε24,600

Police–General Ops Force 18,000

FORCES BY ROLE
COMMAND
    5 bde HQ
SPECIAL FORCES
    1 spec ops bn
MANOEUVRE
    Other
    19 paramilitary bn
    2 (Aboriginal) paramilitary bn
    4 indep paramilitary coy
EQUIPMENT BY TYPE
ARMOURED FIGHTING VEHICLES
    RECCE 192: ε100 S52 *Shorland*; 92 FV701 *Ferret* (60 mod)
    APC • APC (W) 140 AT105 *Saxon*
    AUV ε30 SB-301

Malaysian Maritime Enforcement Agency (MMEA) ε4,500

Controls 5 Maritime Regions (Northern Peninsula; Southern Peninsula; Eastern Peninsula; Sarawak; Sabah), subdivided into a further 18 Maritime Districts. Supported by one provisional MMEA Air Unit

EQUIPMENT BY TYPE
PATROL AND COASTAL COMBATANTS 129
  PSO 4: 1 *Arau* (ex-JPN *Nojima*) with 1 hel landing platform; 2 *Langkawi* with 1 57mm gun, 1 hel landing platform; 1 *Pekan* (ex-JPN *Ojika*) with 1 hel landing platform
  PCC 1 *Bagan Datuk*
  PBF 57: 18 *Penggalang 17* (TUR MRTP 16); 2 *Penggalang 18*; 6 *Penyelamat 20*; 16 *Penggalang 16*; 15 *Tugau*
  PB 67: 15 *Gagah*; 4 *Malawali*; 2 *Nusa*; 3 *Nusa 28*; 1 *Peninjau*; 7 *Ramunia*; 2 *Rhu*; 4 *Semilang*; 8 *Sipadan* (ex-*Kris/Sabah*); 8 *Icarus 1650*; 10 *Pengawal*; 4 *Penyelamat*; 2 *Perwira*
LOGISTICS AND SUPPORT • **AX** 1 *Marlin*
AIRCRAFT • **MP** 2 Bombardier 415MP
HELICOPTERS • **MRH** 3 AS365 *Dauphin*

Marine Police 2,100

EQUIPMENT BY TYPE
PATROL AND COASTAL COMBATANTS 132
  PBF 12: 6 *Sangitan*; 6 Stan Patrol 1500
  PB/PBR 120

Police Air Unit

EQUIPMENT BY TYPE
AIRCRAFT
  TPT • **Light** 17: 4 Cessna 206 *Stationair*; 6 Cessna 208 *Caravan*; 7 PC-6 *Turbo-Porter*
HELICOPTERS
  TPT • **Light** 2: 1 Bell 206L *Long Ranger*; 1 AS355F *Ecureuil* II

Area Security Units 3,500 reservists

(Auxiliary General Ops Force)
FORCES BY ROLE
MANOEUVRE
  Other
    89 paramilitary unit

Border Scouts 1,200 reservists

in Sabah, Sarawak

People's Volunteer Corps 240,000 reservists (some 17,500 armed)

RELA

Customs Service

EQUIPMENT BY TYPE
PATROL AND COASTAL COMBATANTS 23
  PBF 10
  PB 13

DEPLOYMENT

DEMOCRATIC REPUBLIC OF THE CONGO
UN • MONUSCO 3; 10 obs

LEBANON
UN • UNIFIL 828; 1 mech inf bn

PHILIPPINES
IMT 16

SUDAN
UN • UNAMID 11
UN • UNISFA 1 obs

WESTERN SAHARA
UN • MINURSO 10 obs

FOREIGN FORCES

Australia 130; 1 inf coy (on 3-month rotational tours); 1 AP-3C *Orion* on occasion

Mongolia MNG

Mongolian Tugrik t		2016	2017	2018
GDP	t	23.9tr	26.8tr	
	US$	11.0bn	10.9bn	
per capita	US$	3,660	3,553	
Growth	%	1.0	2.0	
Inflation	%	0.6	4.4	
Def bdgt	t	216bn	207bn	257bn
	US$	100m	84m	
FMA (US)	US$	1.6m	1.6m	0m
US$1=t		2,165.39	2,469.92	

Population 3,068,243

Ethnic groups: Khalkh 81.9%; Kazak 3.8%; Dorvod 2.7%; other or unspecified 11.6%

Age	0–14	15–19	20–24	25–29	30–64	65 plus
Male	13.7%	3.9%	4.2%	5.1%	20.2%	1.7%
Female	13.2%	3.8%	4.1%	5.2%	22.1%	2.5%

Capabilities

Mongolia pursues defence ties and bilateral training with multiple regional powers, as well as the US. The country has been discussing the adoption of permanent neutrality since 2015. The armed forces focus on peacekeeping missions and remain reliant on Soviet-era equipment, although this has been supplemented by deliveries of second-hand Russian weapons, including T-72 MBTs and BTR-70 APCs. Mongolia hosts the annual *Khaan Quest* multinational exercise, but its main exercise partners are India and Russia, with each country running regular bilateral exercises (*Nomadic Elephant* and *Selenga* respectively).

ACTIVE 9,700 (Army 8,900 Air 800) **Paramilitary 7,500**

Conscript liability One year for males aged 18–25

RESERVE 137,000 (Army 137,000)

ORGANISATIONS BY SERVICE

Army 5,600; 3,300 conscript (total 8,900)

FORCES BY ROLE
MANOEUVRE
Mechanised
1 MR bde
Light
1 (rapid deployment) lt inf bn (2nd bn to form)
Air Manoeuvre
1 AB bn
COMBAT SUPPORT
1 arty regt
EQUIPMENT BY TYPE
ARMOURED FIGHTING VEHICLES
MBT 420: 370 T-54/T-55; 50 T-72A
RECCE 120 BRDM-2
IFV 310 BMP-1
APC • APC (W) 210: 150 BTR-60; 40 BTR-70M; 20 BTR-80
ENGINEERING & MAINTENANCE VEHICLES
ARV T-54/T-55
ANTI-TANK/ANTI-INFRASTRUCTURE
GUNS • TOWED 200: **85mm** D-44/D-48; **100mm** M-1944/MT-12
ARTILLERY 570
TOWED ε300: **122mm** D-30/M-30 (M-1938); **130mm** M-46; **152mm** ML-20 (M-1937)
MRL **122mm** 130 BM-21
MOR 140: **120mm**; **160mm**; **82mm**
AIR DEFENCE
SAM Medium-range 2+ S-125 *Pechora*-2M (SA-26)
GUNS • TOWED 23mm ZU-23-2

Air Force 800

FORCES BY ROLE
TRANSPORT
1 sqn with An-24 *Coke*; An-26 *Curl*
ATTACK/TRANSPORT HELICOPTER
1 sqn with Mi-8 *Hip*; Mi-171
AIR DEFENCE
2 regt with S-60/ZPU-4/ZU-23
EQUIPMENT BY TYPE
AIRCRAFT • TPT • Light 3: 2 An-24 *Coke*; 1 An-26 *Curl*
HELICOPTERS
TPT • Medium 12: 10 Mi-8 *Hip*; 2 Mi-171
AIR DEFENCE • GUNS • TOWED 150: **14.5mm** ZPU-4; **23mm** ZU-23; **57mm** S-60

Paramilitary 7,500 active

Border Guard 1,300; 4,700 conscript (total 6,000)

Internal Security Troops 400; 800 conscript (total 1,200)
FORCES BY ROLE
MANOEUVRE
Other
4 gd unit

Construction Troops 300

DEPLOYMENT

AFGHANISTAN
NATO • *Operation Resolute Support* 120
UN • UNAMA 1 obs

DEMOCRATIC REPUBLIC OF THE CONGO
UN • MONUSCO 1 obs

SOUTH SUDAN
UN • UNMISS 866; 6 obs; 1 inf bn

SUDAN
UN • UNAMID 70; 1 fd hospital
UN • UNISFA 1; 2 obs

WESTERN SAHARA
UN • MINURSO 4 obs

Myanmar MMR

Myanmar Kyat K		2016	2017	2018
GDP	K	81.1tr	93.2tr	
	US$	64.4bn	67.0bn	
per capita	US$	1,232	1,272	
Growth	%	6.1	7.2	
Inflation	%	6.8	6.5	
Def bdgt	K	2.88tr	2.92tr	
	US$	2.28bn	2.10bn	
US$1=K		1,260.42	1,391.35	

Population 55,123,814

Ethnic groups: Burman 68%; Shan 9%; Karen 7%; Rakhine 4%; Chinese 3+%; other Chin, Kachin, Kayan, Lahu, Mon, Palaung, Pao, Wa 9%

Age	0–14	15–19	20–24	25–29	30–64	65 plus
Male	13.7%	4.5%	4.4%	4.0%	20.2%	2.4%
Female	13.1%	4.4%	4.4%	4.2%	21.5%	3.1%

Capabilities

Since the country's independence struggle in the 1940s, Myanmar's large, army-dominated Tatmadaw (armed forces) has been intimately involved in domestic politics. Even though the National League for Democracy (NLD) won the November 2015 election, the armed forces remain politically important, with control of key ministries (including defence) and the automatic right to 25% of parliamentary seats. The primary focus of the Tatmadaw has always been maintaining internal security, particularly in the face of one of the world's longest-running insurgencies. In late 2016, fighting continued with several 'non-ceasefire groups', and the armed forces were heavily criticised internationally in 2017 for their military actions against the Rohingya minority. While the army grew substantially after the military seized power in 1988, its counter-insurgency focus means it remains essentially a light-infantry force. Nevertheless, since the

1990s, the armed forces have attempted to develop limited conventional-warfare capabilities and have brought into service new armoured vehicles, air-defence weapons, artillery, combat aircraft and ships procured from China, Russia and other diverse sources. The NLD government's dependence on military goodwill implies that defence spending is likely to continue increasing. However, in light of the absence of a comprehensive peace settlement with ethnic-minority armed groups, Western arms embargoes were not planned to be lifted until 2018.

ACTIVE 406,000 (Army 375,000 Navy 16,000 Air 15,000) **Paramilitary 107,250**

Conscript liability 24–36 months

ORGANISATIONS BY SERVICE

Army ε375,000
14 military regions, 7 regional op comd
FORCES BY ROLE
COMMAND
  20 div HQ (military op comd)
  10 inf div HQ
  34+ bde HQ (tactical op comd)
MANOEUVRE
  Armoured
    10 armd bn
  Light
    100 inf bn (coy)
    337 inf bn (coy) (regional comd)
COMBAT SUPPORT
  7 arty bn
  37 indep arty coy
  6 cbt engr bn
  54 fd engr bn
  40 int coy
  45 sigs bn
AIR DEFENCE
  7 AD bn
EQUIPMENT BY TYPE
ARMOURED FIGHTING VEHICLES
  MBT 185+: 10 T-55; 50 T-72S; 25+ Type-59D; 100 Type-69-II
  LT TK 105 Type-63 (ε60 serviceable)
  ASLT 24 PTL-02 mod
  RECCE 87+: 12+ EE-9 *Cascavel*; 45 *Ferret*; 30 Mazda; MAV-1
  IFV 10+ BTR-3U
  APC 431+
    APC (T) 331: 26 MT-LB; 250 Type-85; 55 Type-90
    APC (W) 90+: 20 Hino; 40 Humber *Pig*; 30+ Type-92
    PPV 10 MPV
ENGINEERING & MAINTENANCE VEHICLES
  ARV Type-72
  VLB MT-55A
ANTI-TANK/ANTI-INFRASTRUCTURE
  RCL 1,000+: **84mm** ε1,000 *Carl Gustav*; **106mm** M40A1
  GUNS • TOWED 60: **57mm** 6-pdr; **76mm** 17-pdr
ARTILLERY 422+
  SP 155mm 42: 30 NORA B-52; 12 SH-1
  TOWED 264+: **105mm** 132: 36 M-56; 96 M101; **122mm** 100 D-30; **130mm** 16 M-46; **140mm**; **155mm** 16 Soltam M-845P
  MRL 36+: **107mm** 30 Type-63; **122mm** BM-21 *Grad* (reported); Type-81; **240mm** 6+ M-1985 mod
  MOR 80+: **82mm** Type-53 (M-37); **120mm** 80+: 80 Soltam; Type-53 (M-1943)
SURFACE-TO-SURFACE MISSILE LAUNCHERS
  SRBM • Conventional some *Hwasong*-6 (reported)
AIR DEFENCE
  SAM
    Medium-range 4+: 4 KS-1A (HQ-12); S-125 *Pechora*-2M (SA-26); 2K12 *Kvadrat*-M (SA-6 *Gainful*)
    Point-defence Some 2K22 *Tunguska* (SA-19 *Grison*); HN-5 *Hong Nu/Red Cherry* (reported); 9K310 *Igla*-1 (SA-16 *Gimlet*)
  GUNS 46 **SP 57mm** 12 Type-80
  TOWED 34: **37mm** 24 Type-74; **40mm** 10 M1

Navy ε16,000
EQUIPMENT BY TYPE
PRINCIPAL SURFACE COMBATANTS • FRIGATES 5
  FFGH 2 *Kyansitthar* with 2 twin lnchr with DPRK AShM (possibly KN-SS-N-02 *Storm Petrel*), 4 AK630 CIWS, 1 76mm gun (capacity 1 med hel)
  FFG 3:
    1 *Aung Zeya* with 2 twin lnchr with DPRK AShM (possibly KN-SS-N-01), 4 AK630 CIWS, 1 76mm gun, 1 hel landing platform
    2 *Mahar Bandoola* (PRC Type-053H1) with 2 quad lnchr with C-802 (CH-SS-N-8 *Saccade*) AShM, 2 RBU 1200 A/S mor, 2 twin 100mm gun
PATROL AND COASTAL COMBATANTS 115
  CORVETTES 3
    FSGHM 1 *Tabinshwethi* (*Anawrahta* mod) with 2 twin lnchr with C-802 (CH-SS-N-8 *Saccade*), 1 sectuple lnchr with unknown MANPADs, 2 RBU 1200 A/S mor, 2 AK630 CIWS, 1 76mm gun (capacity 1 med hel)
    FSG 2 *Anawrahta* with 2 twin lnchr with C-802 (CH-SS-N-8 *Saccade*) AShM; 1 76mm gun, 1 hel landing platform
  PCG 7: 6 *Houxin* with 2 twin lnchr with C-801 (CH-SS-N-4 *Sardine*) AShM; 1 FAC(M) mod with 2 twin lnchr with C-802 (CH-SS-N-8 *Saccade*) AShM, 1 AK630 CIWS
  PCO 2 *Indaw*
  PCC 11: 2 *Admirable* (ex-US); 9 *Hainan* with 4 RBU 1200 A/S mor, 2 twin 57mm gun
  PBG 4 *Myanmar* with 2 twin lnchr with C-801 (CH-SS-N-4 *Sardine*) AShM
  PBF 1 Type-201
  PB 31: 3 PB-90; 6 PGM 401; 6 PGM 412; 13 *Myanmar*; 3 *Swift*
  PBR 57: 4 *Sagu*; 9 Y-301†; 1 Y-301 (Imp); 43 (various)
AMPHIBIOUS • CRAFT 9: 3 **LCU** 6 **LCM**
LOGISTICS AND SUPPORT 20
  ABU 1; **AGS** 1; **AH** 2; **AK** 1; **AKSL** 5; **AP** 10

Naval Infantry 800
FORCES BY ROLE
MANOEUVRE
  Light
    1 inf bn

Air Force ε15,000

FORCES BY ROLE
FIGHTER
  4 sqn with F-7 *Airguard*; FT-7; MiG-29B *Fulcrum*; MiG-29SM *Fulcrum*; MiG-29UB *Fulcrum*
GROUND ATTACK
  2 sqn with A-5M *Fantan*
TRANSPORT
  1 sqn with An-12 *Cub*; F-27 *Friendship*; FH-227; PC-6A/B *Turbo Porter*
TRAINING
  2 sqn with G-4 *Super Galeb**; PC-7 *Turbo Trainer**; PC-9*
  1 (trg/liaison) sqn with Cessna 550 *Citation* II; Cessna 180 *Skywagon*; K-8 *Karakorum**
TRANSPORT HELICOPTER
  4 sqn with Bell 205; Bell 206 *Jet Ranger*; Mi-17 *Hip* H; Mi-35P *Hind*; PZL Mi-2 *Hoplite*; PZL W-3 *Sokol*; SA316 *Alouette* III

EQUIPMENT BY TYPE
AIRCRAFT 150 combat capable
  FTR 66: 24 F-7 *Airguard*; 10 FT-7; 11 MiG-29 *Fulcrum*; 6 MiG-29SE *Fulcrum*; 10 MiG-29SM *Fulcrum*; 5 MiG-29UB *Fulcrum*
  ATK 22 A-5M *Fantan*
  TPT 20: **Medium** 5: 4 Y-8D; 1 Y-8F-200W **Light** 16: 3 Beech 1900D; 4 Cessna 180 *Skywagon*; 1 Cessna 550 *Citation* II; 3 F-27 *Friendship*; 5 PC-6A/B *Turbo Porter*; **PAX** 1+ FH-227
  TRG 82: 11 G-4 *Super Galeb**; 20 Grob G120; 24+ K-8 *Karakorum**; 12 PC-7 *Turbo Trainer**; 9 PC-9*; 6 Yak-130 *Mitten**
HELICOPTERS
  ATK 10 Mi-35P *Hind*
  MRH 23: 3 AS365; 11 Mi-17 *Hip* H; 9 SA316 *Alouette* III
  TPT 45: **Medium** 10 PZL W-3 *Sokol*; **Light** 35: 12 Bell 205; 6 Bell 206 *Jet Ranger*; 17 PZL Mi-2 *Hoplite*
UNMANNED AERIAL VEHICLES
  CISR • Heavy 4 CH-3
AIR-LAUNCHED MISSILES • AAM • IR PL-5; R-73 (AA-11 *Archer*); **IR/SARH** R-27 (AA-10 *Alamo*)

Paramilitary 107,250

People's Police Force 72,000

People's Militia 35,000

People's Pearl and Fishery Ministry ε250
EQUIPMENT BY TYPE
PATROL AND COASTAL COMBATANTS • PBR 6 *Carpentaria*

DEPLOYMENT
SOUTH SUDAN
UN • UNMISS 2

Nepal NPL

Nepalese Rupee NR		2016	2017	2018
GDP	NR	2.25tr	2.60tr	
	US$	21.1bn	24.1bn	
per capita	US$	733	824	
Growth	%	0.4	7.5	
Inflation	%	9.9	4.5	
Def bdgt	NR	33.3bn	35.7bn	45.0bn
	US$	314m	330m	
FMA (US)	US$	18m	1.7m	0m
US$1=NR		106.30	108.01	

Population 29,384,297

Religious groups: Hindu 90%; Buddhist 5%; Muslim 3%

Age	0–14	15–19	20–24	25–29	30–64	65 plus
Male	15.7%	5.6%	5.4%	3.9%	15.5%	2.5%
Female	14.5%	5.4%	5.4%	4.7%	18.6%	2.6%

Capabilities

The principal role of Nepal's armed forces is maintaining territorial integrity, but they have also traditionally focused on internal security and humanitarian relief. Following a 2006 peace accord with the Maoist People's Liberation Army, Maoist personnel underwent a process of demobilisation or integration into the armed forces. Nepal's logistic capability appears to be sufficient for internal-security operations, including countering IEDs, however its contingents on UN peacekeeping operations appear to largely depend on contracted logistic support. Gurkhas continue to be recruited by the British and Indian armed forces and the Singaporean police. In 2016, India increased the size of its Gurkha Rifles unit, comprising Gurkhas resident in India. The small air wing provides a limited transport and support capacity but mobility remains a challenge, in part because of the country's topography. This deficit was highlighted by Nepal's considerable dependence on foreign military assistance following the earthquake in April 2015. Training support is provided by several countries, including China, India and the US.

ACTIVE 96,600 (Army 96,600) **Paramilitary 62,000**

ORGANISATIONS BY SERVICE

Army 96,600
FORCES BY ROLE
COMMAND
  6 inf div HQ
  1 (valley) comd
SPECIAL FORCES
  1 bde (1 SF bn, 1 AB bn, 1 cdo bn, 1 ranger bn, 1 mech inf bn)

MANOEUVRE

Light
16 inf bde (total: 62 inf bn; 32 indep inf coy)

COMBAT SUPPORT
4 arty regt
5 engr bn

AIR DEFENCE
2 AD regt
4 indep AD coy

EQUIPMENT BY TYPE
ARMOURED FIGHTING VEHICLES
RECCE 40 *Ferret*
APC 253
    APC (W) 13: 8 OT-64C; 5 WZ-551
    PPV 240: 90 *Casspir*; 150 MPV
ARTILLERY 92+
    TOWED 105mm 22: 8 L118 Light Gun; 14 pack howitzer (6 non-operational)
    MOR 70+: 81mm; 120mm 70 M-43 (est 12 op)
AIR DEFENCE • GUNS • TOWED 32+: 14.5mm 30 Type-56 (ZPU-4); 37mm (PRC); 40mm 2 L/60

Air Wing 320

EQUIPMENT BY TYPE†
AIRCRAFT • TPT 2: **Light** 2: 1 BN-2T *Islander*; 1 M-28 *Skytruck*
HELICOPTERS
    MRH 12: 2 *Dhruv*; 2 *Lancer*; 3 Mi-17-1V *Hip* H; 2 Mi-17V-5 *Hip*; 1 SA315B *Lama (Cheetah)*; 2 SA316B *Alouette* III
    TPT 3: **Medium** 1 SA330J *Puma*; **Light** 2 AS350B2 *Ecureuil*

Paramilitary 62,000

Armed Police Force 15,000
Ministry of Home Affairs

Police Force 47,000

DEPLOYMENT

CENTRAL AFRICAN REPUBLIC
UN • MINUSCA 128; 3 obs; 1 MP pl

DEMOCRATIC REPUBLIC OF THE CONGO
UN • MONUSCO 1,029; 17 obs; 1 inf bn; 1 engr coy

IRAQ
UN • UNAMI 76; 1 sy unit

LEBANON
UN • UNIFIL 869; 1 mech inf bn

LIBERIA
UN • UNMIL 1 obs

MALI
UN • MINUSMA 153; 2 obs; 1 EOD coy

MIDDLE EAST
UN • UNTSO 3 obs

SOUTH SUDAN
UN • UNMISS 1,710; 11 obs; 2 inf bn

SUDAN
UN • UNAMID 366; 10 obs; 2 inf coy
UN • UNISFA 4; 2 obs

SYRIA/ISRAEL
UN • UNDOF 344; 1 mech inf coy; 1 inf coy

WESTERN SAHARA
UN • MINURSO 4 obs

FOREIGN FORCES
United Kingdom 60 (Gurkha trg org)

New Zealand NZL

New Zealand Dollar NZ$		2016	2017	2018
GDP	NZ$	261bn	278bn	
	US$	182bn	201bn	
per capita	US$	38,278	41,629	
Growth	%	3.6	3.5	
Inflation	%	0.6	2.2	
Def bdgt	NZ$	3.70bn	3.49bn	3.67bn
	US$	2.58bn	2.52bn	
US$1=NZ$		1.43	1.38	

Population 4,510,327

Age	0–14	15–19	20–24	25–29	30–64	65 plus
Male	10.1%	3.4%	3.5%	3.4%	22.3%	7.0%
Female	9.6%	3.2%	3.3%	3.4%	22.6%	8.2%

Capabilities

Reflecting its geographical isolation and the absence of immediate threats, limited defence spending has restricted the size of the New Zealand Defence Force (NZDF). Nevertheless, New Zealand has a strong military tradition. The NZDF is well trained and has operational experience, taking part, for example, in coalition operations in Afghanistan and Iraq. Australia is New Zealand's closest defence partner but defence relations with the United States have revived since 2010. New Zealand also maintains ties with other regional partners such as Singapore, with which it conducts regular military training. The June 2016 defence white paper – the first since 2010 – foresaw a range of challenges likely to affect New Zealand's security in the period to 2040. In response, the country's updated defence policy places greater emphasis on maritime-domain awareness and response; New Zealand's interests in Antarctica and the Southern Ocean; and the need to maintain the international 'rules-based order'. The white paper indicated there would be future investment in improved maritime air-surveillance capability; new cyber-support capability for deployed operations; and additional intelligence personnel, among others. The effect on defence policy of the 2017 change in government has yet to be ascertained. New Zealand has a relatively small defence industry, preferring to buy 'off-the-shelf' from international defence companies, including a fleet-replenishment oiler from Hyundai Heavy Industries. New Zealand operates a small number of life-extended C-130H medium transport aircraft, giving it some capability to deploy abroad. Since 2010, New Zealand has joined other Five Eyes nations on annual cyber exercises in the US.

ACTIVE 9,000 (Army 4,500 Navy 2,050 Air 2,450)
RESERVE 2,300 (Army 1,650 Navy 450 Air Force 200)

ORGANISATIONS BY SERVICE

Army 4,500
FORCES BY ROLE
SPECIAL FORCES
  1 SF gp
MANOEUVRE
  Light
  1 inf bde (1 armd recce regt, 2 lt inf bn, 1 arty regt (2 arty bty, 1 AD tp), 1 engr regt(-), 1 MI coy, 1 MP coy, 1 sigs regt, 2 log bn, 1 med bn)
COMBAT SUPPORT
  1 EOD sqn
EQUIPMENT BY TYPE
ARMOURED FIGHTING VEHICLES
  IFV 93 NZLAV-25
ENGINEERING & MAINTENANCE VEHICLES
  AEV 7 NZLAV
  ARV 3 LAV-R
ANTI-TANK/ANTI-INFRASTRUCTURE
  MSL • MANPATS FGM-148 *Javelin*
  RCL 84mm 40 *Carl Gustav*
ARTILLERY 60
  TOWED 105mm 24 L118 *Light Gun*
  MOR 81mm 36

Reserves

Territorial Force 1,650 reservists
Responsible for providing trained individuals for augmenting deployed forces
FORCES BY ROLE
COMBAT SERVICE SUPPORT
  3 (Territorial Force Regional) trg regt

Navy 2,050
Fleet HQ at Auckland
EQUIPMENT BY TYPE
PRINCIPAL SURFACE COMBATANTS • FRIGATES • FFHM 2:
  2 *Anzac* (GER MEKO 200) with 1 octuple Mk41 VLS with RIM-7M *Sea Sparrow* SAM, 2 triple Mk32 324mm TT with Mk46 mod 5 LWT, 1 Mk15 *Phalanx* Block 1B CIWS, 1 127mm gun (capacity 1 SH-2G(I) *Super Seasprite* ASW hel)
PATROL AND COASTAL COMBATANTS 6
  PSOH 2 *Otago* (capacity 1 SH-2G(I) *Super Seasprite* ASW hel)
  PCC 4 *Lake*

AMPHIBIOUS • LANDING CRAFT • LCM 2
LOGISTICS AND SUPPORT 2
  AKRH 1 *Canterbury* (capacity 4 NH90 tpt hel; 1 SH-2G(I) *Super Seasprite* ASW hel; 2 LCM; 16 NZLAV; 14 NZLAV; 20 trucks; 250 troops)
  AOR 1 *Endeavour* with 1 hel landing platform

Air Force 2,450
Flying hours 190 hrs/yr
FORCES BY ROLE
MARITIME PATROL
  1 sqn with P-3K2 *Orion*
TRANSPORT
  1 sqn with B-757-200 (upgraded); C-130H *Hercules* (upgraded)
ANTI-SUBMARINE/SURFACE WARFARE
  1 (RNZAF/RNZN) sqn with SH-2G(I) *Super Seasprite*
TRAINING
  1 sqn with T-6C *Texan* II
  1 sqn with Beech 200 *King Air* (leased)
TRANSPORT HELICOPTER
  1 sqn with AW109; NH90
EQUIPMENT BY TYPE
AIRCRAFT 6 combat capable
  ASW 6 P-3K2 *Orion*
  TPT 11: **Medium** 5 C-130H *Hercules* (upgraded); **Light** 4 Beech 200 *King Air* (leased); **PAX** 2 B-757-200 (upgraded)
  TRG 11 T-6C *Texan* II
HELICOPTERS
  ASW 8 SH-2G(I) *Super Seasprite*
  TPT 13: **Medium** 8 NH90; **Light** 5 AW109
AIR-LAUNCHED MISSILES • AShM AGM-119 *Penguin* Mk2 mod7

DEPLOYMENT

AFGHANISTAN
NATO • *Operation Resolute Support* 10

EGYPT
MFO 26; 1 trg unit; 1 tpt unit

IRAQ
Operation Inherent Resolve 154; 1 trg unit

MIDDLE EAST
UN • UNTSO 6 obs

SOUTH SUDAN
UN • UNMISS 1; 3 obs

Pakistan PAK

Pakistani Rupee Rs		2016	2017	2018
GDP	Rs	29.1tr	31.9tr	
	US$	279bn	n.k.	
per capita	US$	1,441	n.k.	
Growth	%	4.5	5.3	
Inflation	%	2.9	4.1	
Def bdgt [a]	Rs	959bn	1.02tr	1.11tr
	US$	9.19bn	9.72bn	
FMA (US)	US$	255m	265m	100m
US$1=Rs		104.34	105.10	

[a] Includes defence allocations to the Public Sector Development Programme (PSDP), including funding to the Defence Division and the Defence Production Division

Population 204,924,861

Religious groups: Hindu less than 3%

Age	0–14	15–19	20–24	25–29	30–64	65 plus
Male	16.1%	5.6%	5.3%	4.8%	17.4%	2.1%
Female	15.2%	5.2%	5.0%	4.5%	16.2%	2.4%

Capabilities

Pakistan's nuclear and conventional forces have traditionally been oriented and structured against a prospective threat from India. Since 2008, however, counter-insurgency and counter-terrorism have been of increasing importance and are now the forces' main effort. While an army-led counter-terrorism operation has improved domestic security, terrorist attacks continue. As part of the China–Pakistan Economic Corridor initiative, the army is raising a two-division dedicated security force to protect the project and the navy has formed Task Force-88 to protect Gwadar Port and its sea lines of communication. China is Pakistan's main defence partner, with all three services employing a large amount of Chinese equipment. Major investment in military nuclear programmes continue, including the commissioning of a VLF submarine-communications facility and the testing in 2017 of a submarine-launched cruise missile. The air force is modernising its inventory while improving its precision-strike and ISR capabilities. Recent and likely future naval investment in Chinese-supplied frigates, missile craft and submarines could improve sea-denial capabilities. According to the minister for defence production, Pakistan has significantly reduced its reliance on external defence suppliers; the indigenous defence industry exports defence materiel. The army continues to contribute to UN peacekeeping operations. The army and air force have considerable operational experience from a decade of counter-insurgency operations in Pakistan's tribal areas and the navy has consistently supported US-led maritime counter-terrorism missions.

ACTIVE 653,800 (Army 560,000 Navy 23,800 Air 70,000) **Paramilitary 282,000**

ORGANISATIONS BY SERVICE

Strategic Forces

Operational control rests with the National Command Authority. The Strategic Plans Directorate (SPD) manages and commands all of Pakistan's military nuclear capability. The SPD also commands a reportedly 25,000-strong military security force responsible for guarding military nuclear infrastructure

Army Strategic Forces Command 12,000–15,000

Commands all land-based strategic nuclear forces

EQUIPMENT BY TYPE
SURFACE-TO-SURFACE MISSILE LAUNCHERS 60+
  MRBM • **Nuclear** ε30 *Ghauri/Ghauri* II (*Hatf*-5)/ *Shaheen*-2 (*Hatf*-6 – in test); *Shaheen*-3 (in test)
  SRBM • **Nuclear** 30+: ε30 *Ghaznavi* (*Hatf*-3 – PRC M-11)/*Shaheen*-1 (*Hatf*-4); some *Abdali* (*Hatf*-2); some *Nasr* (*Hatf*-9)
  GLCM • **Nuclear** *Babur* (*Hatf*-7); *Ra'ad* (*Hatf*-8 – in test)

Air Force

1–2 sqn of F-16A/B or *Mirage* 5 may be assigned a nuclear-strike role

Army 560,000

FORCES BY ROLE
COMMAND
  9 corps HQ
  1 (area) comd
SPECIAL FORCES
  2 SF gp (total: 4 SF bn)
MANOEUVRE
  Armoured
  2 armd div
  7 indep armd bde
  Mechanised
  2 mech inf div
  1 indep mech bde
  Light
  18 inf div
  5 indep inf bde
  Other
  1 sy div (1 more div forming)
COMBAT SUPPORT
  1 arty div
  14 arty bde
  7 engr bde
AVIATION
  1 VIP avn sqn
  4 avn sqn
HELICOPTER
  3 atk hel sqn
  2 ISR hel sqn
  2 SAR hel sqn
  2 tpt hel sqn
  1 spec ops hel sqn
AIR DEFENCE
  1 AD comd (3 AD gp (total: 8 AD bn))

EQUIPMENT BY TYPE
ARMOURED FIGHTING VEHICLES
MBT 2,467+: 300 *Al-Khalid* (MBT 2000); 21 *Al-Khalid* I; 320 T-80UD; 51 T-54/T-55; 1,100 Type-59/*Al-Zarrar*; 400 Type-69; 275+ Type-85 (270 M48A5 in store)
APC 1,605
    APC (T) 1,260: 1,160 M113/*Talha*; ε100 Type-63
    APC (W) 120 BTR-70/BTR-80
    PPV 225 *Maxxpro*
    AUV 10 *Dingo* 2
ENGINEERING & MAINTENANCE VEHICLES
ARV 117+: 65 Type-653; *Al-Hadeed*; 52 M88A1; T-54/T-55
VLB M47M; M48/60
MW *Aardvark* Mk II
ANTI-TANK/ANTI-INFRASTRUCTURE
MSL
    SP M901 TOW
    MANPATS HJ-8; TOW
RCL 75mm Type-52; **106mm** M40A1 **RL 89mm** M20
GUNS 85mm 200 Type-56 (D-44)
ARTILLERY 4,472+
SP 375: **155mm** 315: 200 M109A2; ε115 M109A5 **203mm** 60 M110/M110A2
TOWED 1,659: **105mm** 329: 216 M101; 113 M-56; **122mm** 570: 80 D-30 (PRC); 490 Type-54 (M-1938); **130mm** 410 Type-59-I; **155mm** 322: 144 M114; 148 M198; ε30 *Panter*; **203mm** 28 M115
MRL 88+: **107mm** Type-81; **122mm** 52+: 52 *Azar* (Type-83); some KRL-122; **300mm** 36 A100
MOR 2,350+: **81mm**; **120mm** AM-50
SURFACE-TO-SURFACE MISSILE LAUNCHERS
    MRBM • Nuclear ε30 *Ghauri/Ghauri* II (*Hatf-5*); some *Shaheen-2* (*Hatf-6* – in test); *Shaheen-3* (in test)
    SRBM 135+: **Nuclear** 30+: ε30 *Ghaznavi* (*Hatf-3* – PRC M-11)/*Shaheen-1* (*Hatf-4*); some *Abdali* (*Hatf-2*); some *Nasr* (*Hatf-9*); **Conventional** 105 *Hatf-1*
    GLCM • Nuclear some *Babur* (*Hatf-7*)
RADAR • LAND AN/TPQ-36 *Firefinder* (arty, mor); RASIT (veh, arty); SLC-2
AIRCRAFT
TPT • Light 14: 1 Beech 200 *King Air*; 1 Beech 350 *King Air*; 3 Cessna 208B; 1 Cessna 421; 1 Cessna 550 *Citation*; 1 Cessna 560 *Citation*; 2 Turbo Commander 690; 4 Y-12(II)
TRG 87 MFI-17B *Mushshak*
HELICOPTERS
ATK 42: 38 AH-1F/S *Cobra* with TOW; 4 Mi-35M *Hind* (1 Mi-24 *Hind* in store)
MRH 115+: 10 H125M *Fennec*; 7 AW139; 26 Bell 412EP *Twin Huey*; 38+ Mi-17 *Hip* H; 2 Mi-171E *Hip*; 12 SA315B *Lama*; 20 SA319 *Alouette* III
TPT 76: **Medium** 36: 31 SA330 *Puma*; 4 Mi-171; 1 Mi-172; **Light** 40: 17 H125 *Ecureuil* (SAR); 5 Bell 205 (UH-1H *Iroquois*); 5 Bell 205A-1 (AB-205A-1); 13 Bell 206B *Jet Ranger* II
TRG 10 Hughes 300C
UNMANNED AERIAL VEHICLES
ISR • Light *Bravo*; *Jasoos*; *Vector*
AIR DEFENCE
SAM
    Medium-range LY-80
    Short-range FM-90
    Point-defence M113 with RBS-70; *Anza* Mk1/Mk2; FIM-92 *Stinger*; HN-5A; *Mistral*; RBS-70
GUNS • TOWED 1,933: **14.5mm** 981; **35mm** 248 GDF-002/GDF-005 (with 134 *Skyguard* radar units); **37mm** 310 Type-55 (M-1939)/Type-65; **40mm** 50 L/60; **57mm** 144 Type-59 (S-60); **85mm** 200 Type-72 (M-1939) KS-12

Navy 23,800 (incl ε3,200 Marines and ε2,000 Maritime Security Agency (see Paramilitary))
EQUIPMENT BY TYPE
SUBMARINES • TACTICAL 8
SSK 5:
    2 *Hashmat* (FRA *Agosta* 70) with 4 single 533mm ASTT with F17P HWT/UGM-84 *Harpoon* AShM
    3 *Khalid* (FRA *Agosta* 90B – 1 with AIP) with 4 single 533mm ASTT with F17 Mod 2 HWT/SM39 *Exocet* AShM
SSI 3 MG110 (SF delivery) each with 2 single 533mm TT
PRINCIPAL SURFACE COMBATANTS • FRIGATES 10
FFGHM 4 *Sword* (F-22P) with 2 quad lnchr with C-802A AShM, 1 octuple lnchr with HHQ-7 SAM, 2 triple 324mm ASTT with Mk 46 LWT, 2 sextuple Type 87 A/S mor, 1 Type 730B CIWS, 1 76mm gun (capacity 1 Z-9C *Haitun* hel)
FFGH 3:
    1 *Alamgir* (US *Oliver Hazard Perry*) with 2 quad lnchr with RGM-84D *Harpoon* AShM, 2 triple 324mm ASTT with Mk46 LWT, 1 *Phalanx* CIWS, 1 76mm gun
    1 *Tariq* (UK *Amazon*) with 2 twin Mk141 lnchr with RGM-84D *Harpoon* AShM, 2 triple 324mm ASTT with Mk 46 LWT, 1 *Phalanx* Block 1B CIWS, 1 114mm gun (capacity 1 hel)
    1 *Tariq* (UK *Amazon*) with 2 quad Mk141 lnchr with RGM-84D *Harpoon* AShM, 2 single 400mm TT with TP 45 LWT, 1 *Phalanx* Block 1B CIWS, 1 114mm gun (capacity 1 hel)
FFHM 3 *Tariq* (UK *Amazon*) with 1 sextuple lnchr with LY-60 (*Aspide*) SAM, 2 single 400mm TT with TP 45 LWT, 1 *Phalanx* Block 1B CIWS, 1 114mm gun (capacity 1 hel)
PATROL AND COASTAL COMBATANTS 17
PCG 3:
    2 *Azmat* (FAC(M)) with 2 quad lnchr with C-802A AShM, 1 AK630 CIWS
    1 *Azmat* (FAC(M)) with 2 triple lnchr with C-602 AShM, 1 AK630 CIWS
PBFG 2 *Zarrar* (33) with 4 single lnchr each with RGM-84 *Harpoon* AShM
PBG 4:
    2 *Jalalat* with 2 twin lnchr with C-802 (CH-SS-N-8 *Saccade*) AShM
    2 *Jurrat* with 2 twin lnchr with C-802 (CH-SS-N-8 *Saccade*) AShM
PBF 2 *Kaan* 15
PB 6: 1 *Larkana*; 1 *Rajshahi*; 4 M16 *Fast Assault Boat*
MINE WARFARE • MINE COUNTERMEASURES
MCC 3 *Munsif* (FRA *Eridan*)
AMPHIBIOUS • LANDING CRAFT 8
LCM 2
LCAC 2 *Griffon* 8100TD
UCAC 4 *Griffon* 2000

LOGISTICS AND SUPPORT 9
  AGS 1 *Behr Paima*
  AOL 2 *Madagar*
  AORH 2:
    1 *Fuqing* with 1 *Phalanx* CIWS (capacity 1 SA319 *Alouette* III hel)
    1 *Moawin* with 1 *Phalanx* CIWS (capacity 1 *Sea King* Mk45 ASW hel)
  AOT 3: 1 *Attock*; 2 *Gwadar*
  AXS 1

Marines ε3,200
FORCES BY ROLE
SPECIAL FORCES
  1 cdo gp
MANOEUVRE
  Amphibious
    3 mne bn
  AIR DEFENCE
    1 AD bn

Naval Aviation
EQUIPMENT BY TYPE
AIRCRAFT 7 combat capable
  ASW 7 P-3B/C *Orion*
  MP 6 F-27-200 MPA
  TPT 4: **Light** 3 ATR-72-500 (MP); **PAX** 1 Hawker 850XP
HELICOPTERS
  ASW 12: 5 *Sea King* Mk45; 7 Z-9C *Haitun*
  MRH 6 SA319B *Alouette* III
AIR-LAUNCHED MISSILES • AShM AM39 *Exocet*

Air Force 70,000

3 regional comds: Northern (Peshawar), Central (Sargodha), Southern (Masroor). The Composite Air Tpt Wg, Combat Cadres School and PAF Academy are Direct Reporting Units

FORCES BY ROLE
FIGHTER
  3 sqn with F-7PG/FT-7PG *Airguard*
  1 sqn with F-16A/B MLU *Fighting Falcon*
  1 sqn with F-16A/B ADF *Fighting Falcon*
  1 sqn with *Mirage* IIID/E (IIIOD/EP)
FIGHTER/GROUND ATTACK
  2 sqn with JF-17 *Thunder*
  2 sqn with JF-17 *Thunder* Block II
  1 sqn with F-16C/D Block 52 *Fighting Falcon*
  3 sqn with *Mirage* 5 (5PA)
ANTI-SURFACE WARFARE
  1 sqn with *Mirage* 5PA2/5PA3 with AM-39 *Exocet* AShM
ELECTRONIC WARFARE/ELINT
  1 sqn with *Falcon* 20F
AIRBORNE EARLY WARNING & CONTROL
  1 sqn with Saab 2000; Saab 2000 *Erieye*
  1 sqn with ZDK-03
SEARCH & RESCUE
  1 sqn with Mi-171Sh (SAR/liaison)
  6 sqn with SA316 *Alouette* III
TANKER
  1 sqn with Il-78 *Midas*
TRANSPORT
  1 sqn with C-130B/E *Hercules*; CN235M-220; L-100-20
  1 VIP sqn with B-707; Cessna 560XL *Citation Excel*; CN235M-220; F-27-200 *Friendship*; *Falcon* 20E; Gulfstream IVSP
  1 (comms) sqn with EMB-500 *Phenom* 100; Y-12 (II)
TRAINING
  1 OCU sqn with F-7P/FT-7P *Skybolt*
  1 OCU sqn with *Mirage* III/*Mirage* 5
  1 OCU sqn with F-16A/B MLU *Fighting Falcon*
  2 sqn with K-8 *Karakorum**
  2 sqn with MFI-17
  2 sqn with T-37C *Tweet*
AIR DEFENCE
  1 bty with HQ-2 (SA-2 *Guideline*); 9K310 *Igla*-1 (SA-16 *Gimlet*)
  6 bty with *Crotale*
  10 bty with SPADA 2000

EQUIPMENT BY TYPE
AIRCRAFT 425 combat capable
  FTR 153: 46 F-7PG *Airguard*; 20 F-7P *Skybolt*; 24 F-16A MLU *Fighting Falcon*; 21 F-16B MLU *Fighting Falcon*; 9 F-16A ADF *Fighting Falcon*; 4 F-16B ADF *Fighting Falcon*; 21 FT-7; 6 FT-7PG; 2 *Mirage* IIIB
  FGA 224: 12 F-16C Block 52 *Fighting Falcon*; 6 F-16D Block 52 *Fighting Falcon*; 49 JF-17 *Thunder* (FC-1 Block 1); 36 JF-17 *Thunder* (FC-1 Block 2); 7 *Mirage* IIID (*Mirage* IIIOD); 63 *Mirage* IIIE (IIIEP); 39 *Mirage* 5 (5PA)/5PA2; 2 *Mirage* 5D (5DPA)/5DPA2; 10 *Mirage* 5PA3 (ASuW)
  ISR 10 *Mirage* IIIR* (*Mirage* IIIRP)
  ELINT 2 *Falcon* 20F
  AEW&C 7: 3 Saab 2000 *Erieye*; 4 ZDK-03
  TKR 4 Il-78 *Midas*
  TPT 35: **Medium** 16: 5 C-130B *Hercules*; 10 C-130E *Hercules*; 1 L-100-20; **Light** 14: 2 Cessna 208B; 1 Cessna 560XL *Citation Excel*; 4 CN235M-220; 4 EMB-500 *Phenom* 100; 1 F-27-200 *Friendship*; 2 Y-12 (II); **PAX** 5: 1 B-707; 1 *Falcon* 20E; 2 Gulfstream IVSP; 1 Saab 2000
  TRG 142: 38 K-8 *Karakorum**; 80 MFI-17B *Mushshak*; 24 T-37C *Tweet*
HELICOPTERS
  MRH 15 SA316 *Alouette* III
  TPT • Medium 4 Mi-171Sh
UNMANNED AERIAL VEHICLES
  CISR • Heavy CH-3 (*Burraq*)
  ISR • Medium *Falco*
AIR DEFENCE • SAM 190+
  Medium-range 6 HQ-2 (SA-2 *Guideline*)
  Short-range 184: 144 *Crotale*; ε40 SPADA 2000
  Point-defence 9K310 *Igla*-1 (SA-16 *Gimlet*)
RADAR • AD 6+: 6 AR-1 (AD radar low level); some *Condor* (AD radar high level); some FPS-89/100 (AD radar high level); MPDR 45/MPDR 60/MPDR 90 (AD radar low level); Type-514 (AD radar high level)
AIR-LAUNCHED MISSILES
  AAM • IR AIM-9L/P *Sidewinder*; *U-Darter*; PL-5; **SARH** Super 530; **ARH** PL-12; AIM-120C AMRAAM
  ASM AGM-65 *Maverick*; *Raptor* II
  AShM AM39 *Exocet*

ARM MAR-1
ALCM • **Nuclear** *Ra'ad* (in test)
BOMBS
INS/SAT-guided FT-6 (REK)
Laser-guided *Paveway* II

Paramilitary 282,000 active

Coast Guard
EQUIPMENT BY TYPE
PATROL AND COASTAL COMBATANTS 5
  PBF 4
  PB 1

Frontier Corps 70,000
Ministry of Interior
FORCES BY ROLE
MANOEUVRE
  Reconnaissance
    1 armd recce sqn
  Other
    11 paramilitary regt (total: 40 paramilitary bn)
EQUIPMENT BY TYPE
ARMOURED FIGHTING VEHICLES
  APC (W) 45 UR-416

Maritime Security Agency ε2,000
EQUIPMENT BY TYPE
PATROL AND COASTAL COMBATANTS 14
  PCC 6: 4 *Barkat*; 2 *Hingol*
  PBF 5
  PB 3 *Guns*

National Guard 185,000
Incl Janbaz Force; Mujahid Force; National Cadet Corps; Women Guards

Pakistan Rangers 25,000
Ministry of Interior

DEPLOYMENT

ARABIAN SEA
Combined Maritime Forces • 1 FFGH

CENTRAL AFRICAN REPUBLIC
UN • MINUSCA 1,126; 10 obs; 1 inf bn; 1 engr coy; 1 hel sqn

DEMOCRATIC REPUBLIC OF THE CONGO
UN • MONUSCO 3,447; 35 obs; 4 inf bn; 1 hel sqn

LIBERIA
UN • UNMIL 71; 1 obs; 1 fd hospital

SOMALIA
UN • UNSOM 1 obs
UN • UNSOS 1 obs

SOUTH SUDAN
UN • UNMISS 1; 1 obs

SUDAN
UN • UNAMID 1,412; 8 obs; 1 inf bn, 1 engr coy

WESTERN SAHARA
UN • MINURSO 14 obs

FOREIGN FORCES
Figures represent total numbers for UNMOGIP mission in India and Pakistan
Chile 2 obs
Croatia 9 obs
Italy 2 obs
Korea, Republic of 7 obs
Philippines 7 obs
Romania 2 obs
Sweden 6 obs
Switzerland 3 obs
Thailand 4 obs
Uruguay 2 obs

Papua New Guinea PNG

Papua New Guinea Kina K		2016	2017	2018
GDP	K	63.3bn	70.6bn	
	US$	20.5bn	21.8bn	
per capita	US$	2,589	2,690	
Growth	%	2.4	3.1	
Inflation	%	6.7	5.8	
Def bdgt	K	256m	229m	
	US$	83m	71m	
US$1=K		3.09	3.23	

Population 6,909,701

Age	0–14	15–19	20–24	25–29	30–64	65 plus
Male	17.0%	5.3%	4.7%	4.1%	17.6%	2.1%
Female	16.4%	5.2%	4.6%	4.0%	16.6%	2.1%

Capabilities

Since independence in 1975, the Papua New Guinea Defence Force (PNGDF) has suffered from chronic underfunding and lack of capacity to perform its core roles. Mainly for budgetary reasons, a PNGDF Reform Program reduced personnel strength to 2,100 between 2002 and 2007. However, during the current decade, the government has made efforts to revive PNGDF capability, increasing defence spending from 2010. The 2013 defence white paper identified core PNGDF roles, including defending the state and civil-emergency assistance. It called for the strengthening of defence capability on an ambitious scale, with personnel increases projected by 2017, though the authorities reportedly acknowledged in late 2017 that personnel growth remained slightly short of the planned number. In the meantime, the PNGDF continues to receive substantial external military assistance, not only from Australia but also from China, which donated some transport vehicles in 2015.

ACTIVE 3,600 (Army 3,300 Maritime Element 200 Air 100)

ORGANISATIONS BY SERVICE

Army ε3,300
FORCES BY ROLE
SPECIAL FORCES
 1 spec ops unit
MANOEUVRE
 Light
  2 inf bn
COMBAT SUPPORT
 1 engr bn
 1 EOD unit
 1 sigs sqn
EQUIPMENT BY TYPE
ARTILLERY • MOR 3+: **81mm** Some; **120mm** 3

Maritime Element ε200
1 HQ located at Port Moresby
EQUIPMENT BY TYPE
PATROL AND COASTAL COMBATANTS • PB 4 *Rabaul* (*Pacific*)
AMPHIBIOUS • LANDING SHIPS • LCT 3 *Salamaua* (ex-AUS *Balikpapan*) (of which 1 in trg role)

Air Force ε100
FORCES BY ROLE
TRANSPORT
 1 sqn with CN235M-100; IAI-201 *Arava*
TRANSPORT HELICOPTER
 1 sqn with Bell 205 (UH-1H *Iroquois*)†
EQUIPMENT BY TYPE
AIRCRAFT • TPT • **Light** 3: 1 CN235M-100 (1 more in store); 2 IAI-201 *Arava*
HELICOPTERS • TPT • **Light** 3: 2 Bell 412 (leased); 1 Bell 212 (leased) (2 Bell 205 (UH-1H *Iroquois*) non-operational)

DEPLOYMENT

SUDAN
UN • UNAMID 1; 1 obs

Philippines PHL

Philippine Peso P		2016	2017	2018
GDP	P	14.5tr	15.9tr	
	US$	305bn	321bn	
per capita	US$	2,927	3,022	
Growth	%	6.9	6.6	
Inflation	%	1.8	3.1	
Def bdgt [a]	P	118bn	137bn	145bn
	US$	2.47bn	2.78bn	
FMA (US)	US$	40m	40m	0m
US$1=P		47.49	49.41	

[a] Excludes military pensions

Population 104,256,076

Age	0–14	15–19	20–24	25–29	30–64	65 plus
Male	17.0%	5.1%	4.7%	4.2%	17.3%	1.8%
Female	16.3%	4.9%	4.4%	4.0%	17.4%	2.6%

Capabilities

Despite modest increases in defence funding, mainly in response to rising tensions in the South China Sea, the capabilities and procurement plans of the Armed Forces of the Philippines (AFP) remain limited. The AFP has benefited from some new equipment, including delivery in 2017 of its first FA-50PH fighter/ground-attack aircraft and two additional landing platform docks, but the Philippines would still struggle to be able to provide more than a token national capability to defend its maritime claims. For this reason, under the Aquino administration the country relied heavily on revived alliance relations with the US for its external defence. In October 2016, President Duterte announced a 'separation' from the US and the pursuit of closer relations with China but in September 2017 he described the US as an important security ally, especially in support to counter-terrorism. The 2014 US–Philippines Enhanced Defence Cooperation Agreement continues, as does military training. The army and marines continue to deploy extensively, with air-force support, on internal-security duties in the south, where Manila faces continuing challenges from insurgent groups. In 2017, the Philippines began trilateral joint maritime patrols and joint Sulu Sea air patrols with Indonesia and Malaysia to counter movement and attacks by ISIS-linked militants in regional waterways.

ACTIVE 125,000 (Army 86,000 Navy 24,000 Air 15,000) Paramilitary 40,500

RESERVE 131,000 (Army 100,000 Navy 15,000 Air 16,000) Paramilitary 50,000 (to age 49)

ORGANISATIONS BY SERVICE

Army 86,000
5 Area Unified Comd (joint service), 1 National Capital Region Comd

FORCES BY ROLE
SPECIAL FORCES
  1 spec ops comd (1 ranger regt, 1 SF regt, 1 CT regt)
MANOEUVRE
  Mechanised
  1 mech inf div (2 mech bde (total: 3 lt armd sqn; 7 armd cav tp; 4 mech inf bn; 1 cbt engr coy; 1 avn bn; 1 cbt engr coy, 1 sigs coy))
  Light
  1 div (4 inf bde; 1 arty bn, 1 int bn, 1 sigs bn)
  9 div (3 inf bde; 1 arty bn, 1 int bn, 1 sigs bn)
  Other
  1 (Presidential) gd gp
COMBAT SUPPORT
  1 arty regt HQ
  5 engr bde
EQUIPMENT BY TYPE
ARMOURED FIGHTING VEHICLES
  LT TK 7 FV101 *Scorpion*
  IFV 54: 2 YPR-765; 34 M113A1 FSV; 18 M113A2 FSV
  APC 387
    APC (T) 168: 6 ACV300; 42 M113A1; 120 M113A2
    APC (W) 219: 73 LAV-150 *Commando*; 146 *Simba*
ENGINEERING & MAINTENANCE VEHICLES
  ARV ACV-300; *Samson*; M578; 4 M113 ARV
ANTI-TANK-ANTI-INFRASTRUCTURE • RCL 75mm M20; **90mm** M67; **106mm** M40A1
ARTILLERY 260+
  TOWED 220: **105mm** 204 M101/M102/Model 56 pack howitzer; **155mm** 16: 10 M114/M-68; 6 Soltam M-71
  MOR 40+: **81mm** M29; **107mm** 40 M30
AIRCRAFT
  TPT • Light 4: 1 Beech 80 *Queen Air*; 1 Cessna 170; 1 Cessna 172; 1 Cessna P206A
UNMANNED AERIAL VEHICLES • ISR • Medium *Blue Horizon*

Navy 24,000

EQUIPMENT BY TYPE
PRINCIPAL SURFACE COMBATANTS • FRIGATES
  FF 1 *Rajah Humabon* (ex-US *Cannon*) with 3 76mm gun
PATROL AND COASTAL COMBATANTS 68
  PSOH 3 *Gregorio del Pilar* (ex-US *Hamilton*) with 1 76mm gun (capacity 1 Bo 105)
  PCF 1 *General Mariano Alvares* (ex-US *Cyclone*)
  PCO 11:
    3 *Emilio Jacinto* (ex-UK *Peacock*) with 1 76mm gun
    6 *Miguel Malvar* (ex-US) with 1 76mm gun
    2 *Rizal* (ex-US *Auk*) with 2 76mm gun
  PBF 17: 2 *Conrado Yap* (ex-ROK *Sea Hawk*); 6 *Tomas Batilo* (ex-ROK *Chamsuri*); 6 MPAC Mk1/2; 3 MPAC Mk3 (to be fitted with *Spike*-ER SSM)
  PB 31: 1 *Aguinaldo*; 22 *Jose Andrada*; 2 *Kagitingan*; 2 *Point* (ex-US); 4 *Swift* Mk3 (ex-US)
  PBR 6 Silver Ships
AMPHIBIOUS
  PRINCIPAL AMPHIBIOUS SHIPS 2
    LPD 2 *Tarlac* (IDN *Makassar*) (capacity 2 LCU; 2 hels; 13 tanks; 500 troops)

LANDING SHIPS • LST 4:
    2 *Bacolod City* (US *Besson*) with 1 hel landing platform (capacity 32 tanks; 150 troops)
    2 LST-1/542 (ex-US) (capacity 16 tanks; 200 troops)
LANDING CRAFT 11
  LCM 2: 1 *Manobo*; 1 *Tagbanua* (capacity 100 tons; 200 troops)
  LCT 5 *Ivatan* (ex-AUS *Balikpapan*)
  LCU 4: 3 LCU Mk 6 (ex-US); 1 *Mulgae* I (ex-RoK)
LOGISTICS AND SUPPORT 6
  AGOR 1 *Gregorio Velasquez* (ex-US *Melville*)
  AOL 1
  AO 1 *Lake Caliraya*
  AP 1
  AWT 2

Naval Aviation
EQUIPMENT BY TYPE
  AIRCRAFT • TPT • Light 8: 4 BN-2A *Defender*; 2 Cessna 177 *Cardinal*; 2 Beech 90 *King Air* (TC-90) (leased)
  HELICOPTERS • TPT 13: **Medium** 4 Mi-171Sh; **Light** 9: 3 AW109; 2 AW109E; 4 Bo-105

Marines 8,300
FORCES BY ROLE
SPECIAL FORCES
  1 (force recon) spec ops bn
MANOEUVRE
  Amphibious
  4 mne bde (total: 12 mne bn)
COMBAT SUPPORT
  1 CSS bde (6 CSS bn)
EQUIPMENT BY TYPE
ARMOURED FIGHTING VEHICLES
  APC • APC (W) 42: 19 LAV-150 *Commando*; 23 LAV-300
  AAV 59: 4 LVTH-6†; 55 LVTP-7
ARTILLERY 37+
  TOWED 37: **105mm** 31: 23 M101; 8 M-26; **155mm** 6 Soltam M-71
  MOR 107mm M30

Naval Special Operations Group
FORCES BY ROLE
SPECIAL FORCES
  1 SEAL unit
  1 diving unit
  10 naval spec ops unit
  1 special boat unit
COMBAT SUPPORT
  1 EOD unit

Air Force 15,000
FORCES BY ROLE
FIGHTER
  1 sqn with FA-50PH *Fighting Eagle**
GROUND ATTACK
  1 sqn with OV-10A/C *Bronco**
ISR
  1 sqn with *Turbo Commander* 690A

SEARCH & RESCUE
4 (SAR/Comms) sqn with Bell 205 (UH-1M *Iroquois*); AUH-76
TRANSPORT
1 sqn with C-130B/H/T *Hercules*; L-100-20
1 sqn with N-22B *Nomad*; N-22SL *Searchmaster*
1 sqn with F-27-200 MPA; F-27-500 *Friendship*
1 VIP sqn with F-28 *Fellowship*
TRAINING
1 sqn with SF-260F/TP
1 sqn with T-41B/D/K *Mescalero*
ATTACK HELICOPTER
1 sqn with MD-520MG
TRANSPORT HELICOPTER
1 sqn with AUH-76
1 sqn with W-3 *Sokol*
4 sqn with Bell 205 (UH-1H *Iroquois*)
1 (VIP) sqn with Bell 412EP *Twin Huey*; S-70A *Black Hawk* (S-70A-5)

EQUIPMENT BY TYPE
AIRCRAFT 34 combat capable
FGA 12 FA-50PH *Fighting Eagle*
MP 2: 1 F-27-200 MPA; 1 N-22SL *Searchmaster*
ISR 12: 2 Cessna 208B *Grand Caravan*; 10 OV-10A/C *Bronco*
TPT 15: **Medium** 6: 1 C-130B *Hercules*; 3 C-130H *Hercules*; 2 C-130T *Hercules* **Light** 6: 3 C295; 1 F-27-500 *Friendship*; 1 N-22B *Nomad*; 1 Turbo Commander 690A; **PAX** 1 F-28 *Fellowship* (VIP)
TRG 39: 12 S-211*; 7 SF-260F; 10 SF-260TP; 10 T-41B/D/K *Mescalero*
HELICOPTERS
MRH 32: 8 W-3 *Sokol*; 3 AUH-76; 8 Bell 412EP *Twin Huey*; 2 Bell 412HP *Twin Huey*; 11 MD-520MG
TPT 34: **Medium** 1 S-70A *Black Hawk* (S-70A-5); **Light** 33: 2 AW109E; 11 Bell 205 (UH-1D); 20 Bell 205 (UH-1H *Iroquois*) (25 more non-operational)
UNMANNED AERIAL VEHICLES
ISR • **Medium** 2 *Blue Horizon* II
AIR-LAUNCHED MISSILES
AAM • IR AIM-9 *Sidewinder*
ASM AGM-65D *Maverick*

Paramilitary

Philippine National Police 40,500
Department of Interior and Local Government. 15 regional & 73 provincial comd. 62,000 auxiliaries
EQUIPMENT BY TYPE
AIRCRAFT
TPT • **Light** 5: 2 BN-2; 3 Lancair 320

Coast Guard
EQUIPMENT BY TYPE
Rodman 38 and Rodman 101 owned by Bureau of Fisheries and Aquatic Resources
PATROL AND COASTAL COMBATANTS 78
PCO 5: 4 *San Juan* with 1 hel landing platform; 1 *Balsam*
PCC 2 *Tirad*
PB 60: 3 *De Haviland*; 4 *Ilocos Norte*; 1 *Palawan*; 12 PCF 50 (US *Swift* Mk1/2); 10 PCF 46; 10 PCF 65 (US *Swift* Mk3); 4 Rodman 38; 10 Rodman 101; 6 *Tubbatah*
PBR 11
LOGISTICS AND SUPPORT • ABU 1 *Corregidor*
AIRCRAFT • TPT • **Light** 2 BN-2 *Islander*
HELICOPTERS • TPT • **Light** 2 Bo-105

Citizen Armed Force Geographical Units
50,000 reservists
MANOEUVRE
Other 56 militia bn (part-time units which can be called up for extended periods)

DEPLOYMENT

INDIA/PAKISTAN
UN • UNMOGIP 7 obs

FOREIGN FORCES
Brunei IMT 9
Indonesia IMT 9
Malaysia IMT 16
United States US Pacific Command 100

Singapore SGP

Singapore Dollar S$		2016	2017	2018
GDP	S$	410bn	425bn	
	US$	297bn	306bn	
per capita	US$	52,961	53,880	
Growth	%	2.0	2.5	
Inflation	%	-0.5	0.9	
Def bdgt	S$	13.8bn	14.2bn	
	US$	10.0bn	10.2bn	
US$1=S$		1.38	1.390	

Population 5,888,926

Ethnic groups: Chinese 74.1%; Malay 13.4%; Indian 9.2%; other or unspecified 3.3%

Age	0–14	15–19	20–24	25–29	30–64	65 plus
Male	6.6%	3.5%	4.8%	5.3%	24.5%	4.4%
Female	6.3%	3.3%	5.2%	5.7%	25.4%	5.2%

Capabilities

The Singapore Armed Forces (SAF) are the best equipped in Southeast Asia. The air force and navy are staffed mainly by professionals while the much larger army, apart from a small regular core, is based on conscripts and reservists. It is presumed that the SAF's primary role is to deter attacks on the city-state or interference with its vital interests – particularly its sea lines of communication – by potential regional adversaries. There is an additional focus on counter-terrorist operations. There is a looming personnel challenge, with an ageing population and declining conscript cohort; and in response the SAF plans to utilise lean personnel levels and more technology. Tracking its economic growth,

Singapore's defence budget has increased to the extent that the city-state spends more than any of its Southeast Asian counterparts. Equipment modernisation continues, with the first of eight littoral mission vessels commissioned and new protected patrol vehicles brought into service, as well as progress on the procurement of armoured vehicles and surface-to-air missiles. In March 2017, the defence minister announced funding for two new laboratories to promote technological innovation: a robotics lab under the Defence Science Organisation and an analytics and artificial-intelligence laboratory set up by the Defence Science and Technology Agency. Training is routinely carried out overseas, notably in Australia, Brunei, Germany, Taiwan, Thailand and the United States, as well as through the Five Power Defence Arrangements and the ADMM–Plus. Singaporean forces have gradually become more involved in multinational operations. These deployments have provided some operational experience. Training standards and operational readiness are high, but the reliance on conscripts and reservists limits the army's capacity for sustained operations away from Singapore.

ACTIVE 72,500 (Army 50,000 Navy 9,000 Air 13,500)
Paramilitary 19,900
Conscription liability 22–24 months

RESERVE 312,500 (Army 300,000 Navy 5,000 Air 7,500)
Annual trg to age 40 for army other ranks, 50 for officers

ORGANISATIONS BY SERVICE

Army 15,000; 35,000 conscript (total 50,000)
FORCES BY ROLE
COMMAND
  3 (combined arms) div HQ
  1 (rapid reaction) div HQ
  3 armd bde HQ
  9 inf bde HQ
  1 air mob bde HQ
  1 amph bde HQ
SPECIAL FORCES
  1 cdo bn
MANOEUVRE
  Reconnaissance
  3 lt armd/recce bn
  Armoured
  1 armd bn
  Mechanised
  6 mech inf bn
  Light
  2 (gds) inf bn
  Other
  2 sy bn
COMBAT SUPPORT
  2 arty bn
  1 STA bn
  2 engr bn
  1 EOD bn
  1 ptn br bn

  1 int bn
  2 ISR bn
  1 CBRN bn
  3 sigs bn
COMBAT SERVICE SUPPORT
  3 med bn
  2 tpt bn
  3 spt bn

Reserves
Activated units form part of divisions and brigades listed above; 1 op reserve div with additional inf bde; People's Defence Force Comd (homeland defence) with 12 inf bn
FORCES BY ROLE
SPECIAL FORCES
  1 cdo bn
MANOEUVRE
  Reconnaissance
  6 lt armd/recce bn
  Mechanised
  6 mech inf bn
  Light
  ε56 inf bn
COMBAT SUPPORT
  ε12 arty bn
  ε8 engr bn

EQUIPMENT BY TYPE
ARMOURED FIGHTING VEHICLES
  MBT 96 *Leopard* 2SG (80–100 *Tempest* (upgraded *Centurion*) reported in store)
  LT TK 372: 22 AMX-10 PAC 90; ε350 AMX-13 SM1
  IFV 572+: 22 AMX-10P; 250 *Bionix* IFV-25; 250 *Bionix* IFV-40/50; 50+ M113A1/A2 (some with 40mm AGL, some with 25mm gun)
  APC 1,576+
    APC (T) 1,100+: 700+ M113A1/A2; 400+ ATTC *Bronco*
    APC (W) 415: 250 LAV-150 *Commando*/V-200 *Commando*; 135 *Terrex* ICV; 30 V-100 *Commando*
    PPV 61+: 6+ *Belrex*; 15 *MaxxPro Dash*; 40 *Peacekeeper*
ENGINEERING & MAINTENANCE VEHICLES
  AEV 94: 18 CET; 54 FV180; 14 *Kodiak*; 8 M728
  ARV *Bionix*; *Büffel*; LAV-150; LAV-300
  VLB 72+: *Bionix*; LAB 30; *Leguan*; M2; 60 M3; 12 M60
  MW 910-MCV-2; *Trailblazer*
ANTI-TANK/ANTI-INFRASTRUCTURE
  MSL • MANPATS *Milan*; *Spike*-SR; *Spike*-MR
  RCL 290: **84mm** ε200 *Carl Gustav*; **106mm** 90 M40A1
ARTILLERY 798+
  SP 155mm 54 SSPH-1 *Primus*
  TOWED 88: **105mm** (37 LG1 in store); **155mm** 88: 18 FH-2000; ε18 *Pegasus*; 52 FH-88
  MRL 227mm 18 M142 HIMARS
  MOR 638+
    SP 90+: **81mm**; **120mm** 90: 40 on *Bronco*; 50 on M113
    TOWED 548: **81mm** 500 **120mm** 36 M-65; **160mm** 12 M-58 Tampella
RADAR • LAND AN/TPQ-36 *Firefinder*; AN/TPQ-37 *Firefinder* (arty, mor); 3 ARTHUR (arty)
UNMANNED AERIAL VEHICLES • ISR • Light *Skylark*

Navy 3,000; 1,000 conscript; ε5,000 active reservists (total 9,000)

EQUIPMENT BY TYPE
SUBMARINES • TACTICAL • SSK 4:
  2 *Challenger* (ex-SWE *Sjoormen*) with 2 single 400mm TT, 4 single 533mm TT
  2 *Archer* (ex-SWE *Västergötland*) (AIP fitted) with 3 single 400mm TT, 6 single 533mm TT for WASS *Black Shark* HWT
PRINCIPAL SURFACE COMBATANTS 6:
  FRIGATES • FFGHM 6 *Formidable* with 2 quad lnchr with RGM-84 *Harpoon* AShM, 4 octuple VLS with *Aster* 15 SAM, 2 triple B515 324mm ASTT with A244 LWT, 1 76mm gun (capacity 1 S-70B *Sea Hawk* hel)
PATROL AND COASTAL COMBATANTS 22
  CORVETTES 9
  FSGM 6 *Victory* with 2 quad Mk140 lnchr with RGM-84C *Harpoon* AShM, 2 octuple lnchr with *Barak* SAM, 2 triple B515 324mm ASTT with A244S LWT, 1 76mm gun
  FSM 3 *Independence* (Littoral Mission Vessel) with 1 12-cell CLA VLS with VL-*MICA*, 1 76mm gun, 1 hel landing platform
  PCO 7 *Fearless* with 1 76mm gun (can be fitted with 2 sextuple *Sadral* lnchr with *Mistral* SAM)
  PBF 6
MINE WARFARE • MINE COUNTERMEASURES
  MCC 4 *Bedok*
AMPHIBIOUS
  PRINCIPAL AMPHIBIOUS SHIPS • LPD 4 *Endurance* with 2 twin lnchr with *Mistral* SAM, 1 76mm gun (capacity 2 hel; 4 LCVP; 18 MBT; 350 troops)
  LANDING CRAFT 23
    LCVP 23: ε17 FCEP; 6 FCU
LOGISTICS AND SUPPORT 2
  ASR 1 *Swift Rescue*
  AX 1

Naval Diving Unit
FORCES BY ROLE
SPECIAL FORCES
  1 SF gp
  1 (diving) SF gp
COMBAT SUPPORT
  1 EOD gp

Air Force 13,500 (incl 3,000 conscript)
5 comds
FORCES BY ROLE
FIGHTER/GROUND ATTACK
  1 sqn with F-5S/T *Tiger* II
  2 sqn with F-15SG *Eagle*
  3 sqn with F-16C/D *Fighting Falcon* (some used for ISR with pods)
ANTI-SUBMARINE WARFARE
  1 sqn with S-70B *Seahawk*
MARITIME PATROL/TRANSPORT
  1 sqn with F-50
AIRBORNE EARLY WARNING & CONTROL
  1 sqn with G550-AEW
TANKER 1 sqn with KC-135R *Stratotanker*
TANKER/TRANSPORT
  1 sqn with KC-130B/H *Hercules*; C-130H *Hercules*
TRAINING
  1 (FRA-based) sqn with M-346 *Master*
  4 (US-based) units with AH-64D *Apache*; CH-47D *Chinook*; F-15SG: F-16C/D
  1 (AUS-based) sqn with PC-21
  1 hel sqn with H120 *Colibri*
ATTACK HELICOPTER
  1 sqn with AH-64D *Apache*
TRANSPORT HELICOPTER
  1 sqn with CH-47SD *Super D Chinook*
  2 sqn with AS332M *Super Puma*; AS532UL *Cougar*
ISR UAV
  1 sqn with *Hermes* 450
  1 sqn with *Heron* 1
  1 sqn with *Searcher* MkII
AIR DEFENCE
  1 AD bn with *Mistral* opcon Army
  3 AD bn with RBS-70; 9K38 *Igla* (SA-18 *Grouse*) opcon Army
  1 ADA sqn with Oerlikon
  1 AD sqn with MIM-23 HAWK
  1 AD sqn with *Spyder*
  1 radar sqn with radar (mobile)
  1 radar sqn with LORADS
MANOEUVRE
  Other
  4 (field def) sy sqn

EQUIPMENT BY TYPE
AIRCRAFT 134 combat capable
  FTR 29: 20 F-5S *Tiger* II; 9 F-5T *Tiger* II
  FGA 100: 40 F-15SG *Eagle*; 20 F-16C *Fighting Falcon*; 40 F-16D *Fighting Falcon* (incl reserves)
  ATK (4 A-4SU *Super Skyhawk*; 10 TA-4SU *Super Skyhawk* in store)
  MP 5 F-50 *Maritime Enforcer**
  AEW&C 4 G550-AEW
  TKR 5: 1 KC-130H *Hercules*; 4 KC-135R *Stratotanker*
  TKR/TPT 4 KC-130B *Hercules*
  TPT 9: **Medium** 5 C-130H *Hercules* (2 ELINT); **PAX** 4 F-50
  TRG 31: 12 M-346 *Master*; 19 PC-21
HELICOPTERS
  ATK 19 AH-64D *Apache*
  ASW 10 S-70B *Seahawk*
  TPT 51: **Heavy** 16: 6 CH-47 *Chinook*; 10 CH-47SD *Super D Chinook*; **Medium** 30: 18 AS332M *Super Puma* (incl 5 SAR); 12 AS532UL *Cougar*; **Light** 5 H120 *Colibri* (leased)
UNMANNED AERIAL VEHICLES
  ISR 37+: **Heavy** 8+ *Heron* 1; **Medium** 29: 9+ *Hermes* 450; 20 *Searcher* MkII
AIR DEFENCE
  SAM
    Medium-range MIM-23 *Hawk*
    Short-range *Spyder*-SR
    Point-defence 9K38 *Igla* (SA-18 *Grouse*) (some on V-200/M113); *Mistral*; RBS-70
  GUNS 34
    SP 20mm GAI-C01
    TOWED 34 **20mm** GAI-C01; **35mm** 34 GDF (with 25 *Super-Fledermaus* fire control radar)

AIR-LAUNCHED MISSILES
AAM • **IR** AIM-9N/P *Sidewinder*; *Python* 4 (reported);
IIR AIM-9X *Sidewinder* II; **SARH** AIM-7P *Sparrow*; **ARH**
(AIM-120C5/7 AMRAAM in store in US)
ASM: AGM-65B/G *Maverick*; AGM-114 *Hellfire*; AGM-154A/C JSOW
AShM AGM-84 *Harpoon*; AM39 *Exocet*
ARM AGM-45 *Shrike*
BOMBS
INS/GPS guided GBU-31 JDAM
Laser-guided *Paveway* II

Paramilitary 19,900 active

Civil Defence Force 5,600 (incl conscripts); 500 auxiliaries (total 6,100)

Singapore Police Force (including Coast Guard) 8,500; 3,500 conscript (total 12,000)
EQUIPMENT BY TYPE
PATROL AND COASTAL COMBATANTS 102
  PBF 81: 25 *Angler Ray*; 2 *Atlantic Ray*; 1 *Marlin*; 11 *Sailfish*; 10 *Shark*; 32 other
  PB 21: 19 *Amberjack*; 2 *Manta Ray*

Singapore Gurkha Contingent (under police) 1,800
FORCES BY ROLE
MANOEUVRE
  Other
    6 paramilitary coy

Cyber
The Singapore Ministry of Defence has long identified the potential damage that could be caused by cyber attacks, with this concern perhaps more acute following its adoption of the Integrated Knowledge-based Command-and-Control (IKC2) doctrine, designed to aid the transition of Singapore's armed forces to a 'third-generation' force. In March 2017, Singapore's defence minister announced the country would establish a new cyber command, the Defence Cyber Organisation, consisting of four formations and responsible for overseeing cyber policy, training and defending military networks. When fully staffed DCO will have 2,600 soldiers. The armed forces announced in mid-2017 that a C4 Command would be stood up in November 2017. C4 Command comprises a Cyber Defence Group and a C4 Operations Group.

DEPLOYMENT

AUSTRALIA
2 trg schools – 1 with 12 AS332 *Super Puma*/AS532 *Cougar* (flying trg) located at Oakey; 1 with PC-21 (flying trg) located at Pearce. Army: prepositioned AFVs and heavy equipment at Shoalwater Bay training area

BRUNEI
1 trg camp with inf units on rotation; 1 hel det with AS332 *Super Puma*

FRANCE
200: 1 trg sqn with 12 M-346 *Master*

KUWAIT
Operation Inherent Resolve 11

TAIWAN
3 trg camp (incl inf and arty)

THAILAND
1 trg camp (arty, cbt engr)

UNITED STATES
Trg units with F-16C/D; 12 F-15SG; AH-64D *Apache*; 6+ CH-47D *Chinook*

FOREIGN FORCES
United States US Pacific Command: 220; 1 naval spt facility at Changi naval base; 1 USAF log spt sqn at Paya Lebar air base

Sri Lanka LKA

Sri Lankan Rupee Rs		2016	2017	2018
GDP	Rs	11.8tr	13.1tr	
	US$	80.5bn	83.6bn	
per capita	US$	3,789	3,906	
Growth	%	4.4	4.7	
Inflation	%	4.0	6.0	
Def bdgt	Rs	293bn	267bn	
	US$	1.99bn	1.70bn	
FMA (US)	US$	0m	0.4m	0m
US$1=Rs		147.04	156.73	

Population 22,409,381

Age	0–14	15–19	20–24	25–29	30–64	65 plus
Male	12.3%	3.7%	3.7%	3.6%	21.4%	4.1%
Female	11.8%	3.6%	3.6%	3.6%	23.0%	5.6%

Capabilities
Since the defeat of the Tamil Tigers, the armed forces have reoriented to a peacetime internal-security role. The army is reducing in size and there appears to have been little spending on new equipment since the end of the civil war, although Sri Lanka is looking to begin a series of procurements to fill key capability gaps. The navy's littoral capability, based on fast-attack and patrol boats, is being strengthened with the acquisition of offshore-patrol vessels. Its first *Vikram*-class OPV entered service in October 2017. Military support has been provided by China, in an indication of a growing military-to-military relationship. The US has eased its long-standing military-trade restrictions on Sri Lanka, and US foreign-military financing is expected to rise over the coming years. Colombo is developing a national cyber-security centre. Sri Lanka has little capacity for force projection beyond its national territory, but has sent small numbers of troops on UN missions. Sri Lanka hosted a multinational maritime-security exercise in 2017.

ACTIVE 243,000 (Army 200,000 Navy 15,000 Air 28,000) Paramilitary 62,200

RESERVE 5,500 (Army 1,100 Navy 2,400 Air Force 2,000) Paramilitary 30,400

ORGANISATIONS BY SERVICE

Army 140,000; 60,00 active reservists (recalled) (total 200,000)

Regt are bn sized

FORCES BY ROLE
COMMAND
 7 region HQ
 21 div HQ
SPECIAL FORCES
 1 indep SF bde
MANOEUVRE
 Reconnaissance
 3 armd recce regt
 Armoured
 1 armd bde(-)
 Mechanised
 1 mech inf bde
 Light
 55 inf bde
 1 cdo bde
 Air Manoeuvre
 1 air mob bde
COMBAT SUPPORT
 7 arty regt
 1 MRL regt
 8 engr regt
 6 sigs regt
EQUIPMENT BY TYPE
ARMOURED FIGHTING VEHICLES
 MBT 62 T-55A/T-55AM2
 RECCE 15 *Saladin*
 IFV 62: 13 BMP-1; 49 BMP-2
 APC 211+
 APC (T) 30+: some Type-63; 30 Type-85; some Type-89
 APC (W) 181: 25 BTR-80/BTR-80A; 31 *Buffel*; 20 Type-92; 105 *Unicorn*
ENGINEERING & MAINTENANCE VEHICLES
 ARV 16 VT-55
 VLB 2 MT-55
ANTI-TANK/ANTI-INFRASTRUCTURE
 RCL 40: **105mm** ε10 M-65; **106mm** ε30 M40
 GUNS **85mm** 8 Type-56 (D-44)
ARTILLERY 908
 TOWED 96: **122mm** 20; **130mm** 30 Type-59-I; **152mm** 46 Type-66 (D-20)
 MRL **122mm** 28: 6 KRL-122; 22 RM-70
 MOR 784: **81mm** 520; **82mm** 209; **120mm** 55 M-43
 RADAR • LAND 4 AN/TPQ-36 *Firefinder* (arty)
UNMANNED AERIAL VEHICLES
 ISR • Medium 1 *Seeker*

Navy 15,000 (incl 2,400 recalled reservists)
EQUIPMENT BY TYPE
PATROL AND COASTAL COMBATANTS 132
 PSOH 2: 1 *Sayura* (IND *Vigraha*); 1 *Sayurala* (IND *Samarth*)
 PCG 2 *Nandimithra* (ISR *Sa'ar* 4) with 3 single lnchr with *Gabriel* II AShM, 1 76mm gun
 PCO 2: 1 *Samadura* (ex-US *Reliance*); 1 *Sagara* (IND *Vikram*) with 1 hel landing platform
 PCC 1 *Jayesagara*
 PBF 79: 26 *Colombo*; 2 *Dvora*; 3 *Killer* (ROK); 6 *Shaldag*; 10 *Super Dvora* MkII/III; 5 *Trinity Marine*; 27 *Wave Rider*
 PB 20: 4 *Cheverton*; 2 *Oshadi* (ex-AUS *Bay*); 2 *Prathapa* (PRC mod *Haizhui*); 3 *Ranajaya* (PRC *Haizhui*); 1 *Ranarisi* (PRC mod *Shanghai* II); 5 *Weeraya* (PRC *Shanghai* II); 3 (various)
 PBR 26
AMPHIBIOUS
 LANDING SHIPS • LSM 1 *Shakthi* (PRC *Yuhai*) (capacity 2 tanks; 250 troops)
 LANDING CRAFT 8
  LCM 2
  LCP 3 *Hansaya*
  LCU 2 *Yunnan*
  UCAC 1 M 10 (capacity 56 troops)
LOGISTICS AND SUPPORT 2: 1 AP; 1 AX

Air Force 28,000 (incl SLAF Regt)
FORCES BY ROLE
FIGHTER
 1 sqn with F-7BS/G; FT-7
FIGHTER/GROUND ATTACK
 1 sqn with MiG-23UB *Flogger* C; MiG-27M *Flogger* J2
 1 sqn with *Kfir* C-2/C-7/TC-2
 1 sqn with K-8 *Karakorum**
TRANSPORT
 1 sqn with An-32B *Cline*; C-130K *Hercules*; Cessna 421C *Golden Eagle*
 1 sqn with Beech B200 *King Air*; Y-12 (II)
TRAINING
 1 wg with PT-6, Cessna 150L
ATTACK HELICOPTER
 1 sqn with Mi-24V *Hind* E; Mi-35P *Hind*
TRANSPORT HELICOPTER
 1 sqn with Mi-17 *Hip* H; Mi-171Sh
 1 sqn with Bell 206A/B (incl basic trg), Bell 212
 1 (VIP) sqn with Bell 212; Bell 412 *Twin Huey*
ISR UAV
 1 sqn with *Blue Horizon* II
 1 sqn with *Searcher* MkII
MANOEUVRE
 Other
 1 (SLAF) sy regt
EQUIPMENT BY TYPE
AIRCRAFT 30 combat capable
 FTR 8: 3 F-7BS; 4 F-7GS; 1 FT-7
 FGA 15: 4 *Kfir* C-2; 2 *Kfir* C-7; 2 *Kfir* TC-2; 6 MiG-27M *Flogger* J2; 1 MiG-23UB *Flogger* C (conversion trg)
 TPT 21: **Medium** 2 C-130K *Hercules*; **Light** 19: 3 An-32B *Cline*; 6 Cessna 150L; 1 Cessna 421C *Golden Eagle*; 7 Y-12 (II); 2 Y-12 (IV)

TRG 14: 7 K-8 *Karakoram**; 7 PT-6
HELICOPTERS
  ATK 11: 6 Mi-24P *Hind*; 3 Mi-24V *Hind* E; 2 Mi-35V *Hind*
  MRH 18: 6 Bell 412 *Twin Huey* (VIP); 2 Bell 412EP (VIP); 10 Mi-17 *Hip* H
  TPT 16: **Medium** 4 Mi-171Sh; **Light** 12: 2 Bell 206A *Jet Ranger*; 2 Bell 206B *Jet Ranger*; 8 Bell 212
UNMANNED AERIAL VEHICLES
  ISR • Medium 2+: some *Blue Horizon* II; 2 *Searcher* MkII
AIR DEFENCE • GUNS • TOWED 27: 40mm 24 L/40; 94mm 3 (3.7in)
AIR-LAUNCHED MISSILES
  AAM • IR PL-5E

Paramilitary ε62,200

Home Guard 13,000

National Guard ε15,000

Police Force 30,200; 1,000 (women) (total 31,200) 30,400 reservists

Ministry of Defence Special Task Force 3,000
Anti-guerrilla unit

Coast Guard n/k
EQUIPMENT BY TYPE
PATROL AND COASTAL COMBATANTS 12
  PCO 1 *Suraksha* (ex-IND *Vikram*) with 1 hel landing platform
  PBF 8: 1 *Dvora*; 4 *Super Dvora* MkI; 3 *Killer* (ROK)
  PB 2 Simonneau Type-508
  PBR 1

DEPLOYMENT

CENTRAL AFRICAN REPUBLIC
UN • MINUSCA 116; 5 obs; 1 avn unit

DEMOCRATIC REPUBLIC OF THE CONGO
UN • MONUSCO 4 obs

LEBANON
UN • UNIFIL 151; 1 inf coy

MALI
UN • MINUSMA 7

SOUTH SUDAN
UN • UNMISS 178; 4 obs; 1 fd hospital; 1 hel sqn

SUDAN
UN • UNISFA 2; 5 obs

WESTERN SAHARA
UN • MINURSO 4 obs

Taiwan (Republic of China) ROC

New Taiwan Dollar NT$		2016	2017	2018
GDP	NT$	17.1tr	17.5tr	
	US$	530	571	
per capita	US$	22,497	24,227	
Growth	%	1.5	2.0	
Inflation	%	1.4	1.0	
Def bdgt	NT$	320bn	319bn	332bn
	US$	9.90bn	10.4bn	
US$1=NT$		32.33	30.61	

Population 23,508,428

Ethnic groups: Taiwanese 84%; mainland Chinese 14%

Age	0–14	15–19	20–24	25–29	30–64	65 plus
Male	6.6%	3.1%	3.5%	3.5%	26.6%	6.3%
Female	6.2%	2.9%	3.4%	3.4%	27.1%	7.4%

Capabilities

Taiwan's relationship with China and its attempts to sustain a credible military capability dominate its security policy. Taiwan published a Quadrennial Defense Review in March 2017, which highlighted the challenge from Beijing and saw the defence guidelines shift from 'solid defence and effective deterrence' to 'solid defence and multi-layered deterrence'. The armed forces remain well trained and exercise regularly, but China's ongoing military recapitalisation continues to undermine Taiwan's historic qualitative military advantage over the PLA. As a result, procurement efforts have been directed towards asymmetric and defensive items, such as development programmes for indigenous anti-ship missiles and land-attack cruise missiles. Despite persistent US refusal to sanction the transfer of new combat aircraft, Taiwan has still obtained US assistance to modernise its current fleet of F-16s to F-16V standard. Nevertheless, in 2017 Taipei announced an interest in the F-35. Due to the lack of potential foreign equipment suppliers, Taiwan has focused on modernising its existing holdings, and refocused on developing its domestic defence-industry capabilities. The indigenous-submarine programme was officially launched in 2017, with the aim to locally build eight submarines. Demographic pressure has influenced plans for force reductions and a shift towards an all-volunteer force. The current government has announced plans to terminate conscription in 2018. (See pp. 235–39.)

ACTIVE 215,000 (Army 130,000 Navy 40,000 Air 45,000) **Paramilitary 11,450**

Conscript liability (19–40 years) 12 months for those born before 1993; four months for those born after 1994 (alternative service available)

RESERVE 1,657,000 (Army 1,500,000 Navy 67,000 Air Force 90,000)

Some obligation to age 30

ORGANISATIONS BY SERVICE

Army ε130,000 (incl ε10,000 MP)
FORCES BY ROLE
COMMAND
 3 corps HQ
 5 defence comd HQ
SPECIAL FORCES/HELICOPTER
 1 SF/hel comd (2 spec ops gp, 2 hel bde)
MANOEUVRE
 Armoured
  4 armd bde
 Mechanised
  3 mech inf bde
 Light
  6 inf bde
COMBAT SUPPORT
 3 arty gp
 3 engr gp
 3 CBRN gp
 3 sigs gp
COASTAL DEFENCE
 1 AShM bn

Reserves
FORCES BY ROLE
MANOEUVRE
 Light
  21 inf bde
EQUIPMENT BY TYPE
ARMOURED FIGHTING VEHICLES
 MBT 565: 200 M60A3; 100 M48A5; 265 M48H *Brave Tiger*
 LT TK 625 M41/Type-64 (230 M24 *Chaffee* (90mm gun) in store)
 IFV 225 CM-25 (M113 with 20–30mm cannon)
 APC 1,220
  APC (T) 650 M113
  APC (W) 570: ε270 CM-32 *Yunpao*; 300 LAV-150 *Commando*
ENGINEERING & MAINTENANCE VEHICLES
 AEV 18 M9
 ARV CM-27/A1; 37 M88A1
 VLB 22 M3; M48A5
NBC VEHICLES 48+: BIDS; 48 K216A1; KM453
ANTI-TANK/ANTI-INFRASTRUCTURE
 MSL
  SP TOW
  MANPATS FGM-148 *Javelin*; TOW
 RCL 500+: **90mm** M67; **106mm** 500+: 500 M40A1; Type-51
 ARTILLERY 2,200
  SP 488: **105mm** 100 M108; **155mm** 318: 225 M109A2/A5; 48 M44T; 45 T-69; **203mm** 70 M110
  TOWED 1,060+: **105mm** 650 T-64 (M101); **155mm** 340+: 90 M59; 250 T-65 (M114); M44; XT-69; **203mm** 70 M115
  MRL 330: **117mm** 120 *Kung Feng* VI; **126mm** 210: 60 *Kung Feng* III/*Kung Feng* IV; 150 RT 2000 *Thunder* (KF towed and SP)
  MOR 322+
   SP 162+: **81mm** 72+: M29; 72 M125; **107mm** 90 M106A2
   TOWED **81mm** 160 M29; T-75; **107mm** M30; **120mm** K5; XT-86

RADAR 1 AN/TPQ-37 *Firefinder*
COASTAL DEFENCE
 ARTY 54: **127mm** ε50 US Mk32 (reported); **240mm** 4 M1
 AShM *Ching Feng*
HELICOPTERS
 ATK 96: 67 AH-1W *Cobra*; 29 AH-64E *Apache*
 MRH 38 OH-58D *Kiowa Warrior*
 TPT 96: **Heavy** 8 CH-47SD *Super D Chinook*; **Medium** 12 UH-60M *Black Hawk*; **Light** 76 Bell 205 (UH-1H *Iroquois*)
 TRG 29 TH-67 *Creek*
UNMANNED AERIAL VEHICLES
 ISR • Light *Mastiff* III
AIR DEFENCE
 SAM • **Point-defence** 76: 74 M1097 *Avenger*; 2 M48 *Chaparral*; FIM-92 *Stinger*
 GUNS 400
  SP **40mm** M42
  TOWED 20: **35mm** 20 GDF-001 (30 systems with 20 guns) **40mm** L/70

Navy 40,000
3 district; 1 (ASW) HQ located at Hualien; 1 Fleet HQ located at Tsoying; 1 New East Coast Fleet
EQUIPMENT BY TYPE
SUBMARINES • TACTICAL • SSK 4:
 2 *Hai Lung* with 6 single 533mm TT with SUT HWT/UGM-84L *Harpoon* AShM
 2 *Hai Shih*† (ex-US *Guppy* II – trg role) with 10 single 533mm TT (6 fwd, 4 aft) with SUT HWT
PRINCIPAL SURFACE COMBATANTS 24
 CRUISERS • CGHM 4 *Keelung* (ex-US *Kidd*) with 1 quad lnchr with RGM-84L *Harpoon* AShM, 2 twin Mk26 lnchr with SM-2MR SAM, 2 triple Mk32 324mm ASTT with Mk46 LWT, 2 *Phalanx* Block 1B CIWS, 2 127mm gun (capacity 1 S-70 ASW hel)
 FRIGATES 20
 FFGHM 19:
  8 *Cheng Kung* with 2 quad lnchr with *Hsiung Feng* II/III AShM, 1 Mk13 GMLS with SM-1MR SAM, 2 triple 324mm ASTT with Mk 46 LWT, 1 *Phalanx* Block 1B CIWS, 1 76mm gun (capacity 2 S-70C ASW hel)
  5 *Chin Yang* (ex-US *Knox*) with 1 octuple Mk16 lnchr with ASROC/RGM-84C *Harpoon* AShM, 2 triple lnchr with SM-1MR SAM, 2 twin lnchr with SM-1MR SAM, 2 twin 324mm ASTT with Mk 46 LWT, 1 *Phalanx* Block 1B CIWS, 1 127mm gun (capacity 1 MD-500 hel)
  6 *Kang Ding* with 2 quad lnchr with *Hsiung Feng* II AShM, 1 quad lnchr with *Sea Chaparral* SAM, 2 Mk32 triple 324mm ASTT with Mk 46 LWT, 1 *Phalanx* Block 1B CIWS, 1 76mm gun (capacity 1 S-70C ASW hel)
 FFGH • 1 *Chin Yang* (ex-US *Knox*) with 1 octuple Mk112 lnchr with ASROC/RGM-84C *Harpoon* AShM, 2 twin 324mm ASTT with Mk 46 LWT, 1 *Phalanx* Block 1B CIWS, 1 127mm gun (capacity 1 MD-500 hel)

PATROL AND COASTAL COMBATANTS 43
  CORVETTES • FSG 1 *Tuo Jiang (Hsun Hai)* with 4 twin lnchr with *Hsiung Feng* II AShM, 4 twin lnchr with *Hisung Feng* III AShM, 1 *Phalanx* Block 1B CIWS; 1 76mm gun
  PCG 11:
    1 *Jin Chiang* with 1 quad lnchr with *Hsiung Feng* II AShM
    4 *Jin Chiang* with 2 twin lnchr with *Hsiung Feng* II AShM, 1 76mm gun
    6 *Jin Chiang* with 1 quad lnchr with *Hsiung Feng* III AShM, 1 76mm gun
  PCC 1 *Jin Chiang* (test platform)
  PBG 31 *Kwang Hua* with 2 twin lnchr with *Hsiung Feng* II AShM
MINE WARFARE • MINE COUNTERMEASURES 10
  MHC 6: 4 *Yung Feng*; 2 *Yung Jin* (ex-US *Osprey*)
  MSO 4 *Yung Yang* (ex-US *Aggressive*)
COMMAND SHIPS • LCC 1 *Kao Hsiung*
AMPHIBIOUS
  PRINCIPAL AMPHIBIOUS SHIPS • LSD 1 *Shiu Hai* (ex-US *Anchorage*) with 2 *Phalanx* CIWS, 1 hel landing platform (capacity either 2 LCU or 18 LCM; 360 troops)
  LANDING SHIPS
    LST 8:
      6 *Chung Hai* (capacity 16 tanks; 200 troops)
      2 *Chung Ho* (ex-US *Newport*) with 1 *Phalanx* CIWS , 1 hel landing platform (capacity 3 LCVP, 400 troops)
  LANDING CRAFT • LCU 12 LCU 1610 (capacity 2 M60A3 or 400 troops) (minelaying capability)
LOGISTICS AND SUPPORT 10
  AGOR 1 *Ta Kuan*
  AK 1 *Wu Kang* with 1 hel landing platform (capacity 1,400 troops)
  AOEH 1 *Panshih* with 1 quad lnchr with *Sea Chaparral* SAM, 2 *Phalanx* CIWS (capacity 3 med hel)
  AOE 1 *Wu Yi* with 1 quad lnchr with *Sea Chaparral* SAM, 1 hel landing platform
  ARS 6

Marines 10,000
FORCES BY ROLE
MANOEUVRE
  Amphibious
  3 mne bde
COMBAT SUPPORT
  Some cbt spt unit
EQUIPMENT BY TYPE
ARMOURED FIGHITNG VEHICLES
  AAV 202: 52 AAV-7A1; 150 LVTP-5A1
ENGINEERING & MAINTENANCE VEHICLES
  ARV 2 AAVR-7
ANIT-TANK/ANTI-INFRASTRUCTURE
  RCL 106mm
ARTILLERY • TOWED 105mm; 155mm

Naval Aviation
FORCES BY ROLE
ANTI SUBMARINE WARFARE
  2 sqn with S-70C *Seahawk* (S-70C *Defender*)
  1 sqn with MD-500 *Defender*

EQUIPMENT BY TYPE
HELICOPTERS
  ASW 20 S-70C *Seahawk* (S-70C *Defender*)
  MRH 10 MD-500 *Defender*

Air Force 45,000
Flying hours   180 hrs/yr

FORCES BY ROLE
FIGHTER
  3 sqn with *Mirage* 2000-5E/D (2000-5EI/DI)
FIGHTER/GROUND ATTACK
  3 sqn with F-5E/F *Tiger* II
  6 sqn with F-16A/B *Fighting Falcon*
  5 sqn with F-CK-1A/B/C/D *Ching Kuo*
ANTI-SUBMARINE WARFARE
  1 sqn with P-3C *Orion*
ELECTRONIC WARFARE
  1 sqn with C-130HE *Tien Gian*
ISR
  1 sqn with RF-5E *Tigereye*
AIRBORNE EARLY WARNING & CONTROL
  1 sqn with E-2T *Hawkeye*
SEARCH & RESCUE
  1 sqn with H225; S-70C *Black Hawk*
TRANSPORT
  2 sqn with C-130H *Hercules*
  1 (VIP) sqn with B-727-100; B-737-800; Beech 1900; F-50; S-70C *Black Hawk*
TRAINING
  1 sqn with AT-3A/B *Tzu-Chung**
  1 sqn with Beech 1900
  1 (basic) sqn with T-34C *Turbo Mentor*
EQUIPMENT BY TYPE
AIRCRAFT 481 combat capable
  FTR 286: 87 F-5E/F *Tiger* II (some in store); 144 F-16A/B *Fighting Falcon*; 9 *Mirage* 2000-5D (2000-5DI); 46 *Mirage* 2000-5E (2000-5EI)
  FGA 128: 57 F-CK-1A/B *Ching Kuo*; 71 F-CK-1C/D *Ching Kuo*
  ASW 12 P-3C *Orion*
  EW 1 C-130HE *Tien Gian*
  ISR 7 RF-5E *Tigereye*
  AEW&C 6 E-2T *Hawkeye*
  TPT 33: **Medium** 19 C-130H *Hercules*; **Light** 10 Beech 1900; **PAX** 4: 1 B-737-800; 3 F-50
  TRG 97: 55 AT-3A/B *Tzu-Chung**; 42 T-34C *Turbo Mentor*
HELICOPTERS
  TPT • Medium 19: 3 H225; 16 S-70C *Black Hawk*
AIR DEFENCE
  SAM • Point-defence *Antelope*
AIR-LAUNCHED MISSILES
  AAM • IR AIM-9J/P *Sidewinder*; R-550 *Magic* 2; *Shafrir*; *Sky Sword* I; **IR/ARH** *Mica*; **ARH** AIM-120C AMRAAM; *Sky Sword* II
  ASM AGM-65A *Maverick*
  AShM AGM-84 *Harpoon*
  ARM *Sky Sword* IIA
  LACM Conventional *Wan Chien*
BOMBS • Laser-guided *Paveway* II

Air Defence and Missile Command
FORCES BY ROLE
SURFACE-TO-SURFACE MISSILE
  3 SSM bty with *Hsiung Feng* IIE
AIR DEFENCE
  2 AD/SAM gp (total: 13 bty with MIM-23 HAWK; 4 bty with MIM-104F *Patriot* PAC-3; 6 bty with *Tien Kung* I *Sky Bow/Tien Kung* II *Sky Bow*)
EQUIPMENT BY TYPE
SURFACE-TO-SURFACE MISSILE LAUNCHERS
  GLCM • **Conventional** ε12 *Hsiung Feng* IIE
AIR DEFENCE • SAM • Medium-range 600+: 100 MIM-23 HAWK; ε500 *Tien Kung* I *Sky Bow/Tien Kung* II *Sky Bow*
MISSILE DEFENCE • Medium-range 24+ MIM-104F *Patriot* PAC-3

Paramilitary 11,450

Coast Guard 11,450
EQUIPMENT BY TYPE
PATROL AND COASTAL COMBATANTS 161
  PSOH 4: 2 *Tainan*; 2 *Yilan*
  PSO 6: 4 *Miaoli* with 1 hel landing platform; 2 *Ho Hsing*
  PCO 13: 2 *Kinmen*; 2 *Mou Hsing*; 3 *Shun Hu 7*; 4 *Taichung*; 2 *Taipei*
  PBF ε56 (various)
  PB 82: 1 *Shun Hu 6*; ε81 (various)

Directorate General (Customs)
EQUIPMENT BY TYPE
PATROL AND COASTAL COMBATANTS 9
  PCO 1 *Yun Hsing*
  PB 8: 4 *Hai Cheng*; 4 *Hai Ying*

Cyber
Although Taiwan has a highly developed civilian IT sector, the Taiwanese government has been relatively slow to exploit this advantage for national-defence purposes. But for the past decade, Taipei has worked on its Po Sheng – Broad Victory – C4ISR programme, an all-hazards-defence system with a significant defence component. The main focus of the military component of this programme is countering PLA IW and EW attacks. The authorities responsible for cyber activity include the National Security Bureau (NSB), the defence ministry, and the Research, Development and Evaluation Commission (RDEC). In 2015 a Defence Policy Paper recommended that an independent fourth service branch combining cyber and electronic-warfare capabilities should be established. The Information and Electronic Warfare Command was established in mid-2017 and is responsible for coordinating cyber defence and directing R&D efforts in cyber and EW.

FOREIGN FORCES
Singapore 3 trg camp (incl inf and arty)

Thailand THA

Thai Baht b		2016	2017	2018
GDP	b	14.4tr	15.2tr	
	US$	407bn	438bn	
per capita	US$	5,902	6,336	
Growth	%	3.2	3.7	
Inflation	%	0.2	0.6	
Def bdgt	b	205bn	214bn	222bn
	US$	5.82bn	6.16bn	
US$1=b		35.29	34.65	

Population 68,414,135

Ethnic and religious groups: Thai 75%; Chinese 14%; Muslim 4%

Age	0–14	15–19	20–24	25–29	30–64	65 plus
Male	8.7%	3.4%	3.8%	3.7%	24.8%	4.7%
Female	8.3%	3.2%	3.7%	3.6%	26.2%	5.9%

Capabilities
Thailand has large, well-funded armed forces. In particular, its air force is one of the best equipped and trained in Southeast Asia: the introduction into service of *Gripen* combat aircraft and Saab 340 airborne early-warning platforms has boosted the effectiveness of Thailand's airpower. However, despite the fact that they have benefited from substantially increased budgets during the present decade and from engagement in bilateral and multinational exercises with regional partners and the US, the armed forces remain army-dominated. In early 2017, the armed forces approved a ten-year modernisation programme called 'Vision 2026', which is understood to include plans for restructuring and increased defence spending. The armed forces' involvement in domestic politics has often overshadowed efforts to sustain and modernise operational capability. The May 2014 coup again brought the armed forces into a central political role, undermining Thailand's defence relations with the US, which reduced its participation in the annual exercise *Cobra Gold* in 2015 and 2016. However, defence relations with Beijing have warmed and, in 2017, Thailand signed a contract for the acquisition of a first Chinese S26T submarine.

ACTIVE 360,850 (Army 245,000 Navy 69,850 Air 46,000) **Paramilitary 93,700**
Conscription liability 2 years

RESERVE 200,000 Paramilitary 45,000

ORGANISATIONS BY SERVICE

Army 130,000; ε115,000 conscript (total 245,000)
FORCES BY ROLE
COMMAND
  4 (regional) army HQ
  3 corps HQ
SPECIAL FORCES
  1 SF div
  1 SF regt

MANOEUVRE
    Armoured
    3 cav div (1 recce bn; 3 tk regt (3 tk bn); 1 indep tk bn; 1 sigs bn; 1 maint bn; 1 hel sqn)
    Mechanised
    1 mech inf div (1 recce coy; 1 recce sqn; 1 tk bn; 1 inf regt (4 inf bn); 3 inf regt; 1 engr bn; 1 sigs bn)
    Light
    8 inf div (1 recce sqn; 3 inf regt (3 inf bn); 1 engr bn; 1 sigs bn)
COMBAT SUPPORT
    1 arty div
    1 engr div
COMBAT SERVICE SUPPORT
    4 economic development div
HELICOPTER
    Some hel flt
AIR DEFENCE
    1 ADA div (6 bn)
EQUIPMENT BY TYPE
ARMOURED FIGHTING VEHICLE
    MBT 318: 53 M60A1; 125 M60A3; (50 Type-69 in store); 105 M48A5; 25 T-84 *Oplot*; 10 VT-4
    LT TK 194: 24 M41; 104 *Scorpion* (50 in store); 66 *Stingray*
    RECCE 32 S52 *Shorland*
    IFV 168 BTR-3E1
    APC 1,140
        APC (T) 880: *Bronco*; 430 M113A1/A3; 450 Type-85
        APC (W) 160: 9 BTR-3K (CP); 6 BTR-3C (amb); 18 *Condor*; 142 LAV-150 *Commando*
        PPV 100 REVA
ENGINEERING & MAINTENANCE VEHICLES
    ARV 56: 13 BTR-3BR; 22 M88A1; 6 M88A2; 10 M113; 5 Type-653; WZT-4
    VLB Type-84
    MW *Bozena*; *Giant Viper*
ANTI-TANK/ANTI-INFRASTRUCTURE
    MSL
        SP 30+: 18+ M901A5 (TOW); 12 BTR-3RK
        MANPATS M47 *Dragon*
    RCL 180: 75mm 30 M20; 106mm 150 M40
ARTILLERY 2,643
    SP 155mm 32: 6 ATMOS-2000; 6 CAESAR; 20 M109A5
    TOWED 617: 105mm 340: 24 LG1 MkII; 12 M-56; 200 M101/M425; 12 M102; 32 M618A2; 60 L119 Light Gun; 155mm 277: 90 GHN-45 A1; 48 M114; 118 M198; 21 M-71
    MRL 68: 122mm 4 SR-4; 130mm 60 PHZ-85; 302mm 4: 1 DTI-1 (WS-1B); 3 DTI-1G (WS-32)
    MOR 1,926+: SP 81mm 39: 18 BTR-3M1; 21 M125A3; SP 107mm M106A3; SP 120mm 20: 8 BTR-3M2; 12 M1064A3; 1,867 81mm/107mm/120mm
RADAR • LAND AN/TPQ-36 *Firefinder* (arty, mor); RASIT (veh, arty)
AIRCRAFT
    TPT • Light 20: 2 Beech 200 *King Air*; 2 Beech 1900C; 1 C-212 *Aviocar*; 1 C295W; 10 Cessna A185E (U-17B); 2 ERJ-135LR; 2 *Jetstream* 41
    TRG 33: 11 MX-7-235 *Star Rocket*; 22 T-41B *Mescalero*
HELICOPTERS
    ATK 7 AH-1F *Cobra*
    MRH 15: 8 AS550 *Fennec*; 2 AW139; 5 Mi-17V-5 *Hip H*
    TPT 210: Heavy 5 CH-47D *Chinook*; Medium 12: 9 UH-60L *Black Hawk*; 3 UH-60M *Black Hawk*; Light 193: 93 Bell 205 (UH-1H *Iroquois*); 27 Bell 206 *Jet Ranger*; 52 Bell 212 (AB-212); 16 Enstrom 480B; 5 UH-72A *Lakota*
    TRG 53 Hughes 300C
UNMANNED AERIAL VEHICLES
    ISR • Medium *Searcher*; *Searcher* II
AIR DEFENCE
    SAM
        Short-range *Aspide*
        Point-defence 8+: 8 *Starstreak*; 9K338 *Igla*-S (SA-24 *Grinch*)
    GUNS 184
        SP 54: 20mm 24 M163 *Vulcan*; 40mm 30 M1/M42 SP
        TOWED 130: 20mm 24 M167 *Vulcan*; 37mm 52 Type-74; 40mm 48 L/70; 57mm ε6 Type-59 (S-60) (18+ more non-operational)

Reserves

FORCES BY ROLE
COMMAND
    1 inf div HQ

Navy 44,000 (incl Naval Aviation, Marines, Coastal Defence); 25,850 conscript (total 69,850)

EQUIPMENT BY TYPE
PRINCIPAL SURFACE COMBATANTS 9
    AIRCRAFT CARRIERS • CVH 1:
        1 *Chakri Naruebet* with 2 sextuple *Sadral* lnchr with *Mistral* SAM (capacity 6 S-70B *Seahawk* ASW hel)
    FRIGATES 8
    FFGHM 2:
        2 *Naresuan* with 2 quad Mk141 lnchr with RGM-84A *Harpoon* AShM, 1 8 cell Mk41 VLS with RIM-7M *Sea Sparrow* SAM, 2 triple Mk32 324mm TT, 1 127mm gun (capacity 1 *Super Lynx* 300 hel)
    FFGM 4:
        2 *Chao Phraya* (trg role) with 4 twin lnchr with C-802A AShM, 2 twin lnchr with HHQ-61 (CH-SA-N-2) SAM (non-operational), 2 RBU 1200 A/S mor, 2 twin 100mm gun
        2 *Kraburi* with 4 twin lnchr with C-802A AShM, 2 twin lnchr with HHQ-61 (CH-SA-N-2) SAM, 2 RBU 1200 A/S mor, 1 twin 100mm gun, 1 hel landing platform
    FF 2:
        1 *Makut Rajakumarn* with 2 triple 324mm ASTT, 2 114mm gun
        1 *Pin Klao* (ex-US *Cannon*) (trg role) with 6 single 324mm ASTT, 3 76mm gun
PATROL AND COASTAL COMBATANTS 95
    CORVETTES 7
        FSGM 2 *Rattanakosin* with 2 twin Mk140 lnchr with RGM-84A *Harpoon* AShM, 1 octuple *Albatros* lnchr with *Aspide* SAM, 2 triple Mk32 324mm ASTT with *Stingray* LWT, 1 76mm gun
        FS 5:
            3 *Khamronsin* with 2 triple 324mm ASTT with *Stingray* LWT, 1 76mm gun

2 *Tapi* with 2 triple 324mm ASTT with Mk46 LWT, 1 76mm gun
PSO 1 *Krabi* (UK *River* mod) with 1 76mm gun
PCFG 6:
  3 *Prabparapak* with 2 single lnchr with *Gabriel* I AShM, 1 triple lnchr with *Gabriel* I AShM, 1 57mm gun
  3 *Ratcharit* with 2 twin lnchr with MM38 *Exocet* AShM, 1 76mm gun
PCOH 2 *Pattani* (1 in trg role) with 1 76mm gun
PCO 4: 3 *Hua Hin* with 1 76mm gun; 1 M58 Patrol Gun Boat with 1 76mm gun
PCC 9: 3 *Chon Buri* with 2 76mm gun; 6 *Sattahip* with 1 76mm gun
PBF 4 M18 Fast Assault Craft (capacity 18 troops)
PB 62: 7 T-11; 4 *Swift*; 3 T-81; 9 T-91; 3 M36 Patrol Boat; 3 T-210; 13 T-213; 1 T-227; 13 M21 Patrol Boat; 3 T-991; 3 T-994
MINE WARFARE • MINE COUNTERMEASURES 17
  MCCS 1 *Thalang*
  MCO 2 *Lat Ya*
  MCC 2 *Bang Rachan*
  MSR 12: 7 T1; 5 T6
AMPHIBIOUS
  PRINCIPAL AMPHIBIOUS SHIPS 1
    LPD 1 *Anthong* (SGP *Endurance*) with 1 76mm gun (capacity 2 hel; 19 MBT; 500 troops)
  LANDING SHIPS 2
    LST 2 *Sichang* with 2 hel landing platform (capacity 14 MBT; 300 troops)
  LANDING CRAFT 14
    LCU 9: 3 *Man Nok*; 2 *Mataphun* (capacity either 3–4 MBT or 250 troops); 4 *Thong Kaeo*
    LCM 2
    UCAC 3 *Griffon* 1000TD
  LOGISTICS AND SUPPORT 13
    ABU 1 *Suriya*
    AGOR 1 *Sok*
    AGS 2
    AOL 6: 1 *Matra* with 1 hel landing platform; 3 *Proet*; 1 *Prong*; 1 *Samui*
    AOR 1 *Chula*
    AORH 1 *Similan* (capacity 1 hel)
    AWT 1

Naval Aviation 1,200
EQUIPMENT BY TYPE
AIRCRAFT 3 combat capable
  ASW 2 P-3A *Orion* (P-3T)
  ISR 9 *Sentry* O-2-337
  MP 1 F-27-200 MPA*
  TPT • Light 15: 7 Do-228-212; 2 ERJ-135LR; 2 F-27-400M *Troopship*; 3 N-24A *Searchmaster*; 1 UP-3A *Orion* (UP-3T)
HELICOPTERS
  ASW 8: 6 S-70B *Seahawk*; 2 *Super Lynx* 300
  MRH 2 MH-60S *Knight Hawk*
  TPT 15: **Medium** 2 Bell 214ST (AB-214ST); **Light** 13: 6 Bell 212 (AB-212); 2 H145M; 5 S-76B
AIR-LAUNCHED MISSILES • AShM AGM-84 *Harpoon*

Marines 23,000
FORCES BY ROLE
COMMAND
  1 mne div HQ
MANOEUVRE
  Reconnaissance
  1 recce bn
  Light
  2 inf regt (total: 6 bn)
  Amphibious
  1 amph aslt bn
COMBAT SUPPORT
  1 arty regt (3 fd arty bn, 1 ADA bn)
EQUIPMENT BY TYPE
ARMOURED FIGHTING VEHICLES
  IFV 14 BTR-3E1
  APC (W) 24 LAV-150 *Commando*
  AAV 33 LVTP-7
ENGINEERING & MAINTENANCE VEHICLES
  ARV 1 AAVR-7
ANTI-TANK/ANTI-INFRASTRUCTURE • MSL
  SP 10 M1045A2 HMMWV with TOW
  MANPATS M47 *Dragon*; TOW
ARTILLERY • TOWED 48: **105mm** 36 (reported); **155mm** 12 GC-45
AIR DEFENCE • GUNS 12.7mm 14

Naval Special Warfare Command

Air Force ε46,000
4 air divs, one flying trg school
Flying hours   100 hrs/yr
FORCES BY ROLE
FIGHTER
  2 sqn with F-5E/5F *Tiger* II
  3 sqn with F-16A/B *Fighting Falcon*
FIGHTER/GROUND ATTACK
  1 sqn with *Gripen* C/D
GROUND ATTACK
  1 sqn with *Alpha Jet**
  1 sqn with AU-23A *Peacemaker*
  1 sqn with L-39ZA *Albatros**
ELINT/ISR
  1 sqn with DA42 MPP *Guardian*
AIRBORNE EARLY WARNING & CONTROL
  1 sqn with Saab 340B; Saab 340 *Erieye*
TRANSPORT
  1 (Royal Flight) sqn with A319CJ; A340-500; B-737-800
  1 sqn with ATR-72; BAe-748
  1 sqn with BT-67
  1 sqn with C-130H/H-30 *Hercules*
TRAINING
  1 sqn with L-39ZA *Albatros**
  1 sqn with CT-4A/B *Airtrainer*; T-41D *Mescalero*
  1 sqn with CT-4E *Airtrainer*
  1 sqn with PC-9
TRANSPORT HELICOPTER
  1 sqn with Bell 205 (UH-1H *Iroquois*)
  1 sqn with Bell 412 *Twin Huey*; S-92A

EQUIPMENT BY TYPE
AIRCRAFT 149 combat capable
  FTR 78: 1 F-5B *Freedom Fighter*; 21 F-5E *Tiger* II; 3 F-5F *Tiger* II (F-5E/F being upgraded); 38 F-16A *Fighting Falcon*; 15 F-16B *Fighting Falcon*
  FGA 11: 7 *Gripen* C; 4 *Gripen* D
  ATK 17 AU-23A *Peacemaker*
  ISR 5 DA42 MPP *Guardian*
  AEW&C 2 Saab 340 *Erieye*
  ELINT 2 Saab 340 *Erieye* (COMINT/ELINT)
  TPT 43: **Medium** 14: 6 C-130H *Hercules*; 6 C-130H-30 *Hercules*; 2 Saab 340B; **Light** 21: 3 ATR-72; 3 Beech 200 *King Air*; 8 BT-67; 1 *Commander* 690; 6 DA42M; **PAX** 8: 1 A319CJ; 1 A320CJ; 1 A340-500; 1 B-737-800; 2 SSJ-100-95LR (1 A310-324 in store)
  TRG 110: 16 *Alpha Jet**; 13 CT-4A *Airtrainer*; 6 CT-4B *Airtrainer*; 20 CT-4E *Airtrainer*; 27 L-39ZA *Albatros**; 21 PC-9; 7 T-41D *Mescalero*
HELICOPTERS
  MRH 11: 2 Bell 412 *Twin Huey*; 2 Bell 412SP *Twin Huey*; 1 Bell 412HP *Twin Huey*; 6 Bell 412EP *Twin Huey*
  CSAR 4 H225M *Super Cougar*
  TPT 20: **Medium** 3 S-92A *Super Hawk*; **Light** 17 Bell 205 (UH-1H *Iroquois*)
AIR-LAUNCHED MISSILES
  AAM • IR AIM-9P/S *Sidewinder*; *Python* 3; ARH AIM-120 AMRAAM
  ASM AGM-65 *Maverick*
BOMBS • Laser-guided *Paveway* II

Paramilitary ε93,700

Border Patrol Police 20,000

Marine Police 2,200
EQUIPMENT BY TYPE
PATROL AND COASTAL COMBATANTS 93
  PCO 1 *Srinakrin*
  PCC 2 *Hameln*
  PB 44: 2 *Chasanyabadee*; 3 *Cutlass*; 2 *Ratayapibanbancha* (*Reef Ranger*); 1 *Sriyanont*; 36 (various)
  PBR 46

National Security Volunteer Corps 45,000 – Reserves

Police Aviation 500
EQUIPMENT BY TYPE
AIRCRAFT 6 combat capable
  ATK 6 AU-23A *Peacemaker*
  TPT 16: **Light** 15: 2 CN235; 8 PC-6 *Turbo-Porter*; 3 SC-7 3M *Skyvan*; 2 Short 330UTT; **PAX** 1 F-50
HELICOPTERS
  MRH 12: 6 Bell 412 *Twin Huey*; 6 Bell 429
  TPT • **Light** 61: 27 Bell 205A; 14 Bell 206 *Jet Ranger*; 20 Bell 212 (AB-212)

Provincial Police 50,000 (incl ε500 Special Action Force)

Thahan Phran (Hunter Soldiers) 21,000
Volunteer irregular force
FORCES BY ROLE
MANOEUVRE
  Other
    22 paramilitary regt (total: 275 paramilitary coy)

DEPLOYMENT

INDIA/PAKISTAN
UN • UNMOGIP 4 obs

SUDAN
UN • UNAMID 10; 4 obs

FOREIGN FORCES
United States US Pacific Command: 300

Timor-Leste TLS

US$		2016	2017	2018
GDP	US$	2.70bn	2.72bn	
per capita	US$	2,230	2,190	
Growth	%	5.0	4.0	
Inflation	%	-1.3	1.0	
Def bdgt	US$	26m	25m	

Population 1,291,358

Age	0–14	15–19	20–24	25–29	30–64	65 plus
Male	21.0%	5.8%	4.5%	3.7%	13.2%	1.8%
Female	19.8%	5.5%	4.5%	3.9%	14.1%	2.0%

Capabilities

The Timor-Leste Defence Force (F-FDTL) has been affected by funding, personnel and morale challenges since it was established in 2001. It is responsible for external defence, but the parallel internal-security role has sometimes brought it into conflict with the national police force. The F-FDTL has been reconstituted with outside help, mainly from Australia and Portugal, but is still a long way from meeting the force-structure goals set out in the Force 2020 plan published in 2007. The origins of the F-FDTL in the Falintil national resistance force and continued training and doctrinal emphasis on low-intensity infantry tactics mean that the force provides a deterrent to invasion. In 2014 and 2016, Australia offered to boost the F-FDTL naval component's capability by providing 'a complete patrol boat capability', though this offer was not taken up. Australian forces still support F-FDTL force development, including by support to exercises.

ACTIVE 1,330 (Army 1,250 Naval Element 80)

ORGANISATIONS BY SERVICE

Army 1,250
Training began in January 2001 with the aim of deploying 1,500 full-time personnel and 1,500 reservists. Authorities

are engaged in developing security structures with international assistance

FORCES BY ROLE
MANOEUVRE
  Light
    2 inf bn
COMBAT SUPPORT
  1 MP pl
COMBAT SERVICE SUPPORT
  1 log spt coy

Naval Element 80
EQUIPMENT BY TYPE
PATROL AND COASTAL COMBATANTS 7
  PB 7: 2 *Albatros*; 2 *Dili* (ex-ROK); 2 *Shanghai* II; 1 *Kamenassa* (ex-ROK *Chamsuri*)

Vietnam VNM

Vietnamese Dong d		2016	2017	2018
GDP	d	4,503tr	4,965tr	
	US$	201bn	216bn	
per capita	US$	2,172	2,306	
Growth	%	6.2	6.3	
Inflation	%	2.7	4.4	
Def bdgt	d	ε91.1tr	ε99.3tr	
	US$	ε4.07bn	ε4.32bn	
FMA (US)	US$	12m	10m	0m
US$1=d		22,367.27	22,991.82	

Population 96,160,163

Ethnic groups: Kinh 85.7%; Tay 1.9%; Thai 1.8%; Khome 1.4%; Hmong 1.3%; other or unspecified 7.1%

Age	0–14	15–19	20–24	25–29	30–64	65 plus
Male	12.4%	4.0%	4.4%	4.8%	21.1%	2.4%
Female	11.2%	3.7%	4.1%	4.5%	22.6%	3.7%

Capabilities

Vietnam has a stronger military tradition and its armed forces have more operational experience than any of its Southeast Asian neighbours. Its defence efforts and conscript-based armed forces also benefit from broad popular support, particularly in the context of current tensions with China over conflicting claims in the South China Sea. With rapid economic growth over the last decade, defence spending has increased and particular efforts have been made to re-equip the navy and air force, mainly with a view to deterring Chinese military pressure in the disputed Spratly Islands. While Hanoi cannot hope to balance China's power on its own, the recent development of a submarine capability, based on six improved *Kilo*-class boats, and the procurement of additional Su-30MK2 combat aircraft and new air-defence capabilities would complicate Beijing's military options. Improved relations with India, Japan and Russia are a stated priority for Vietnam, which has signed a series of cooperation agreements with these countries. However, residual sensitivities and restrictions on both sides have meant that US–Vietnam defence relations have been slow to develop, although the 'joint vision statement' of June 2015 declared the intent to expand defence trade and to strengthen maritime-security collaboration.

ACTIVE 482,000 (Army 412,000 Navy 40,000 Air 30,000) **Paramilitary 40,000**

Conscript liability 2 years army and air defence, 3 years air force and navy, specialists 3 years, some ethnic minorities 2 years

RESERVES Paramilitary 5,000,000

ORGANISATIONS BY SERVICE

Space
EQUIPMENT BY TYPE
SATELLITES • ISR 1 VNREDSat

Army ε412,000
8 Mil Regions (incl capital)
FORCES BY ROLE
COMMAND
  4 corps HQ
SPECIAL FORCES
  1 SF bde (1 AB bde, 1 demolition engr regt)
MANOEUVRE
  Armoured
    6 armd bde
    3 armd regt
  Mechanised
    2 mech inf div
  Light
    23 inf div
SURFACE-TO-SURFACE MISSILE
  1 SRBM bde
COMBAT SUPPORT
  13 arty bde
  1 arty regt
  10 engr bde
  1 engr regt
  1 EW unit
  3 sigs bde
  2 sigs regt
COMBAT SERVICE SUPPORT
  9 economic construction div
  1 log regt
  1 med unit
  1 trg regt
AIR DEFENCE
  11 AD bde

Reserve
MANOEUVRE
  Light
    9 inf div
EQUIPMENT BY TYPE
ARMOURED FIGHTING VEHICLES
  MBT 1,270: 70 T-62; 350 Type-59; 850 T-54/T-55 (45 T-34† in store)

LT TK 620: 300 PT-76; 320 Type-62/Type-63
RECCE 100 BRDM-1/BRDM-2
IFV 300 BMP-1/BMP-2
APC 1,380+
  APC (T) 280+: Some BTR-50; 200 M113 (to be upgraded); 80 Type-63
  APC (W) 1,100 BTR-40/BTR-60/BTR-152
ANTI-TANK/ANTI-INFRASTRUCTURE
  MSL • MANPATS 9K11 *Malyutka* (AT-3 *Sagger*)
  RCL 75mm Type-56; **82mm** Type-65 (B-10); **87mm** Type-51
  GUNS
    SP 100mm SU-100; **122mm** SU-122
    TOWED 100mm T-12 (arty); M-1944
ARTILLERY 3,040+
  SP 30+: **122mm** 2S1 *Gvozdika*; **152mm** 30 2S3 *Akatsiya*; **175mm** M107
  TOWED 2,300: **105mm** M101/M102; **122mm** D-30/Type-54 (M-1938)/Type-60 (D-74); **130mm** M-46; **152mm** D-20; **155mm** M114
  MRL 710+: **107mm** 360 Type-63; **122mm** 350 BM-21 *Grad*; **140mm** BM-14
  MOR 82mm; **120mm** M-1943; **160mm** M-1943
SURFACE-TO-SURFACE MISSILE LAUNCHERS
  SRBM • Coventional *Scud*-B/C
AIR DEFENCE
  SAM • Point-defence 9K32 *Strela*-2 (SA-7 *Grail*)‡; 9K310 *Igla*-1 (SA-16 *Gimlet*); 9K38 *Igla* (SA-18 *Grouse*)
  GUNS 12,000
    SP 23mm ZSU-23-4
    TOWED 14.5mm/30mm/37mm/57mm/85mm/100mm

Navy ε40,000 (incl ε27,000 Naval Infantry)

EQUIPMENT BY TYPE
SUBMARINES • TACTICAL 8
  SSK 6 *Hanoi* (RUS *Varshavyanka*) with 6 533mm TT with 53-65KE HWT/TEST-71ME HWT/3M54E *Klub* (SS-N-27B *Sizzler*) AShM
  SSI 2 *Yugo* (DPRK)
PRINCIPAL SURFACE COMBATANTS 2
  FRIGATES • FFGM 2
    2 *Dinh Tien Hoang* (RUS *Gepard* 3.9) with 2 quad lnchr with 3M24E *Uran*-E (SS-N-25 *Switchblade*) AShM, 1 *Palma* lnchr with *Sosna*-R SAM, 1 RBU 6000 *Smerch* 2 A/S mor, 2 AK630 CIWS, 1 76mm gun, 1 hel landing platform
PATROL AND COASTAL COMBATANTS 68
  CORVETTES 6:
    FSGM 1 BPS-500 with 2 quad lnchr with 3M24E *Uran*-E (SS-N-25 *Switchblade*) AShM, 9K32 *Strela*-2M (SA-N-5 *Grail*) SAM (manually operated), 2 twin 533mm TT, 1 RBU-1600 A/S mor, 1 AK630 CIWS, 1 76mm gun
    FS 5:
      3 *Petya* II (FSU) with 1 quintuple 406mm ASTT, 4 RBU 6000 *Smerch* 2 A/S mor, 2 twin 76mm gun
      2 *Petya* III (FSU) with 1 triple 533mm ASTT with SET-53ME HWT, 4 RBU 2500 *Smerch* 1 A/S mor, 2 twin 76mm gun

  PCFGM 12:
    4 *Tarantul* (FSU) with 2 twin lnchr with P-15 *Termit* (SS-N-2D *Styx*) AShM, 1 quad lnchr with 9K32 *Strela*-2M (SA-N-5 *Grail*) SAM (manually operated), 2 AK630 CIWS, 1 76mm gun
    8 *Tarantul* V with 4 quad lnchr with 3M24E *Uran*-E (SS-N-25 *Switchblade*) AShM; 1 quad lnchr with 9K32 *Strela*-2M (SA-N-5 *Grail*) SAM (manually operated), 2 AK630 CIWS, 1 76mm gun
  PCO 5: 1 Project FC264; 4 TT-400TP with 2 AK630 CIWS, 1 76mm gun
  PCC 6 *Svetlyak* with 1 AK630 CIWS, 1 76mm gun
  PBFG 8 *Osa* II with 4 single lnchr with P-15 *Termit* AShM
  PBFT 2 *Shershen*† (FSU) with 4 single 533mm TT
  PH 2 *Turya*† with 1 twin 57mm gun
  PHT 3 *Turya*† with 4 single 533mm TT, 1 twin 57mm gun
  PB 20: 14 *Zhuk*†; 4 *Zhuk* (mod); 2 TP-01
  PBR 4 *Stolkraft*
MINE WARFARE • MINE COUNTERMEASURES 13
  MSO 2 *Yurka*
  MSC 4 *Sonya*
  MHI 2 *Korund* (*Yevgenya*) (Project 1258)
  MSR 5 K-8
AMPHIBIOUS
  LANDING SHIPS 7
    LSM 5:
      1 *Polnochny* A (capacity 6 Lt Tk/APC; 200 troops)
      2 *Polnochny* B (capacity 6 Lt Tk/APC; 200 troops)
      2 *Nau Dinh*
    LST 2 *Tran Khanh Du* (ex-US LST 542) with 1 hel landing platform (capacity 16 Lt Tk/APC; 140 troops)
  LANDING CRAFT • LCM 12
    8 LCM 6 (capacity 1 Lt Tk or 80 troops)
    4 LCM 8 (capacity 1 MBT or 200 troops)
LOGISTICS AND SUPPORT 27
  AFD 2
  AGS 1 *Tran Dai Nia* (Damen Research Vessel 6613)
  AGSH 1
  AKSL 18
  AP 1 *Truong Sa*
  AT 2
  AWT 1
  AXS 1 *Le Quy Don*
COASTAL DEFENCE • AShM 4K44 *Redut* (SSC-1B *Sepal*); 4K51 *Rubezh* (SS-C-3 *Styx*); K-300P *Bastion*-P (SSC-5 *Stooge*)

Naval Infantry ε27,000

EQUIPMENT BY TYPE
ARMOURED FIGHTING VEHICLES
  LT TK PT-76; Type-63
  APC • APC (W) BTR-60
ARTILLERY • MRL 306mm EXTRA

Navy Air Wing

FORCES BY ROLE
ASW/SAR
1 regt with H225; Ka-28 (Ka-27PL) *Helix* A; Ka-32 *Helix* C

EQUIPMENT BY TYPE
AIRCRAFT • TPT • Light 6 DHC-6-400 *Twin Otter*
HELICOPTERS

ASW 10 Ka-28 *Helix* A
TPT • **Medium** 4: 2 H225; 2 Ka-32 *Helix* C

Air Force 30,000

3 air div, 1 tpt bde
FORCES BY ROLE
FIGHTER/GROUND ATTACK
 1 regt with Su-22M3/M4/UM *Fitter* (some ISR)
 1 regt with Su-27SK/Su-27UBK *Flanker*
 1 regt with Su-27SK/Su-27UBK *Flanker*; Su-30MK2
 1 regt with Su-30MK2
TRANSPORT
 2 regt with An-2 *Colt*; An-26 *Curl*; Bell 205 (UH-1H *Iroquois*); Mi-8 *Hip*; Mi-17 *Hip* H; M-28 *Bryza*
TRAINING
 1 regt with L-39 *Albatros*
 1 regt with Yak-52
ATTACK/TRANSPORT HELICOPTER
 2 regt with Mi-8 *Hip*; Mi-17 *Hip* H; Mi-171; Mi-24 *Hind*
AIR DEFENCE
 4 ADA bde
 Some (People's Regional) force (total: ε1,000 AD unit, 6 radar bde with 100 radar stn)
EQUIPMENT BY TYPE
AIRCRAFT 74 combat capable
 FGA 74: 28 Su-22M3/M4/UM *Fitter* (some ISR); 6 Su-27SK *Flanker*; 5 Su-27UBK *Flanker*; 35 Su-30MK2 *Flanker*
 TPT • **Light** 23: 6 An-2 *Colt*; 12 An-26 *Curl*; 3 C-295M; 1 M-28 *Bryza*
 TRG 47: 17 L-39 *Albatros*; 30 Yak-52
HELICOPTERS
 ATK 26 Mi-24 *Hind*
 MRH 6 Mi-17 *Hip* H
 TPT 28: **Medium** 17: 14 Mi-8 *Hip*; 3 Mi-171; **Light** 11 Bell 205 (UH-1H *Iroquois*)
AIR DEFENCE
 SAM 12+:
  Long-range 12 S-300PMU1 (SA-20 *Gargoyle*)
  Medium-range S-75 *Dvina* (SA-2 *Guideline*); S-125-2TM *Pechora* (SA-26), *Spyder*-MR
  Short-range 2K12 *Kub* (SA-6 *Gainful*);
  Point-defence 9K32 *Strela*-2 (SA-7 *Grail*)‡; 9K310 *Igla*-1 (SA-16 *Gimlet*)
 GUNS 37mm; 57mm; 85mm; 100mm; 130mm

AIR-LAUNCHED MISSILES
 AAM • **IR** R-3 (AA-2 *Atoll*)‡; R-60 (AA-8 *Aphid*); R-73 (AA-11 *Archer*); **IR/SARH** R-27 (AA-10 *Alamo*); **ARH** R-77 (AA-12 *Adder*)
 ASM Kh-29L/T (AS-14 *Kedge*); Kh-31A (AS-17B *Krypton*); Kh-59M (AS-18 *Kazoo*)
 ARM Kh-28 (AS-9 *Kyle*); Kh-31P (AS-17A *Krypton*)

Paramilitary 40,000+ active

Border Defence Corps ε40,000

Coast Guard
EQUIPMENT BY TYPE
PATROL AND COASTAL COMBATANTS 69+
 PSO 4 DN2000 (Damen 9014)
 PCO 13+: 1 *Mazinger* (ex-ROK); 9 TT-400; 3+ other
 PBF 24: 22 MS-50S; 2 *Shershen*
 PB 28: 2 *Hae Uri* (ex-ROK); 1 MS-50; 12 TT-200; 13 TT-120
LOGISTICS AND SUPPORT 5
 AFS 1
 ATF 4 Damen Salvage Tug
 AIRCRAFT • **MP** 3 C-212-400 MPA

Fisheries Surveillance Force
EQUIPMENT BY TYPE
PATROL AND COASTAL COMBATANTS 32
 PSO 3 DN2000 (Damen 9014)
 PCO 2: 1 *Hayato* (ex-JPN); 1 *Yuhzan Maru* (ex-JPN)
 PB ε27

Local Forces ε5,000,000 reservists

Incl People's Self-Defence Force (urban units) and People's Militia (rural units); comprises static and mobile cbt units, log spt and village protection pl; some arty, mor and AD guns; acts as reserve

DEPLOYMENT

CENTRAL AFRICAN REPUBLIC
UN • MINUSCA 4; 1 obs

SOUTH SUDAN
UN • UNMISS 2 obs

Arms procurements and deliveries – Asia

Selected events in 2017

- Australia issued a tender to three shortlisted shipyards to provide final designs for its Future Frigate programme. The three yards and designs were:
    - (ESP) Navantia – F100 mod
    - (ITA) Fincantieri – FREMM
    - (UK) BAE Systems – Type-26

- China launched the first Type-055 cruiser. A total of four are currently under construction at two shipyards. China also launched its first indigenously built aircraft carrier.

- China announced that the J-20 twin-engined fighter has entered service with the People's Liberation Army Air Force. Chinese company Chengdu Aerospace Corporation had been working on designs for an aircraft of this type since the 1990s.

- South Korea fast-tracked a number of naval-vessel orders to assist its shipbuilding industry. The sector has suffered a downturn in recent years.

- Taiwan launched its Indigenous Defense Submarine programme. Taiwan plans to design and build eight boats with the first entering service in 2027.

- Malaysian company Boustead and Germany's Rheinmetall formed a joint venture called BHIC Defence Technologies. The company will offer project management and other services to the Malaysian defence industry. This is Rheinmetall's second joint venture with Boustead.

- India reportedly issued a request for information (RFI) for six locally built conventionally powered submarines for its Project 75(I) programme. An RFI was first issued for this programme in 2010. However, at that time, it was envisaged that two of the boats would be built abroad.

- Malaysia's Multi-Role Combat Aircraft programme to acquire a new fighter aircraft has reportedly been suspended as the country looks to prioritise the acquisition of airborne intelligence, surveillance and reconnaissance capabilities instead.

Figure 15 **Asia: selected ongoing or completed procurement priorities in 2017**

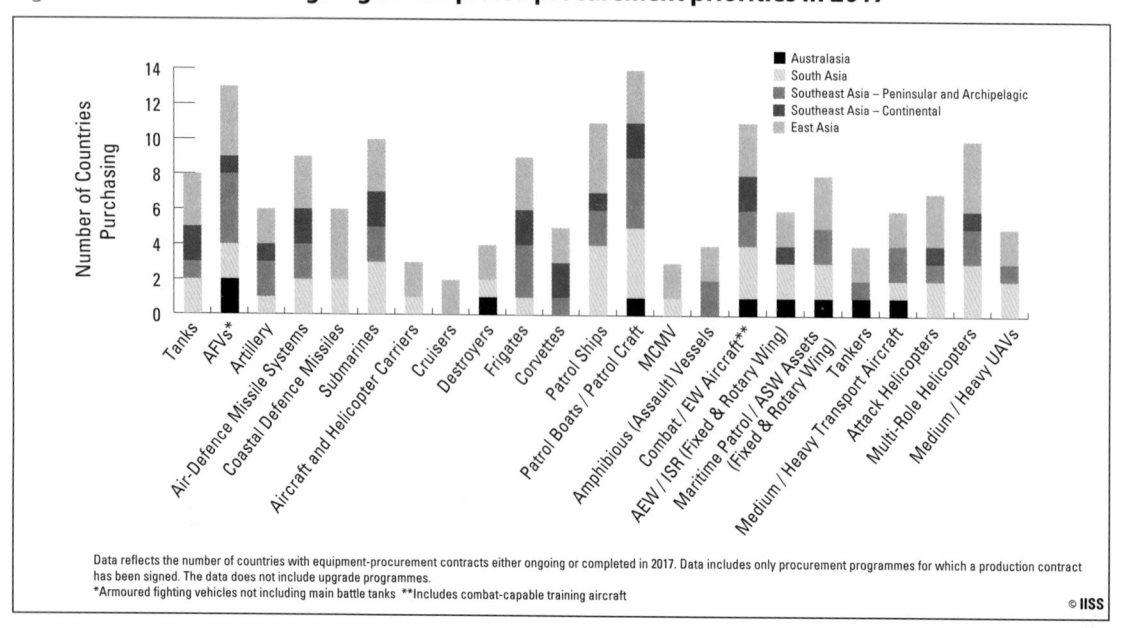

Data reflects the number of countries with equipment-procurement contracts either ongoing or completed in 2017. Data includes only procurement programmes for which a production contract has been signed. The data does not include upgrade programmes.
*Armoured fighting vehicles not including main battle tanks **Includes combat-capable training aircraft

© IISS

Table 12 **Asia: ongoing submarine procurements**

Country	Class	Type	Quantity	Value	Shipyard(s)	First order date	First of class entered/ planned to enter service	Notes
Australia	*Shortfin Barracuda*	SSK	12	εUS$37.4bn (total lifetime costs)	(FRA) Naval Group (formerly DCNS) (AUS) ASC	2016	Early 2030s	Design contract
China	*Shang* II (Type-093A)	SSN	4	n.k.	(PRC) BSHIC	n.k.	n.k.	Four boats built. Operational status unclear
	Yuan I/II (Type-039A/B)	SSK	ε16	n.k.	(PRC) WSIC (PRC) Jiangnan Shipyard	n.k.	2006	
India	*Arihant*	SSBN	ε3	εUS$4.96bn	(IND) DRDO (IND) Visakhapatnam Dockyard	n.k.	n.k.	First of class in trials. Status unclear
	Kalvari (*Scorpene*)	SSK	6	US$2.94bn	(FRA) Naval Group (IND) Mazagon Dock Limited	2005	2017/18	
Indonesia	*Nagapasa* (Type-209/1400)	SSK	3	US$1.1bn	(ROK) DSME (IDN) PT PAL	2012	2017	Third boat to be built in Indonesia
Japan	*Soryu*	SSK	13	US$7.37bn	(JPN) MHI (JPN) KHI	2004	2009	
Korea, Republic of	KSS-III	SSG	3	US$2.06bn	(ROK) DSME (ROK) HHI	2012	2020	
	Son Won-il (Type-214)	SSK	9	εUS$4.5bn	(ROK) DSME (ROK) HHI	2000	2007	
Pakistan	S20 (Type-039 mod)	SSK	8	n.k.	(PRC) CSIC (PAK) KSEW	2015	2022	Four to be built in Pakistan
Singapore	Type-218SG	SSK	4	n.k.	(GER) TKMS	2013	2020	Two more ordered in 2017
Taiwan	Indigenous Defense Submarine	SSK	t.b.d.	n.k.	(ROC) CSBC	2017	2027	Development contract
Thailand	S26T (Type-039 mod)	SSK	1	US$386.27m	(PRC) CSIC	2017	2023	

Table 13 **Japan FY2018 defence-budget request: top ten equipment-procurement programmes by value**

Equipment	Type	Quantity	Value (JPY)	Value (US$)	Prime Contractor(s)
3,900t Escort Vessel with MCM capability	FFGHM	2	96.4bn	865.31m	(JPN) MHI & MES
F-35A *Lightning* II	FGA ac	6	88.1bn	790.81m	(USA) Lockheed Martin (JPN) MHI
X-Band Comms Satellite	Comms Satellite	1	73bn	655.27m	(JPN) DSN Corporation
Soryu class	SSK	1	71.5bn	589.74m	(JPN) KHI & MHI
SM-3 Block IIA & SM-3 Block IB	Ship-launched SAM	n.k.	65.7bn	589.74m	(USA) Raytheon
E-2D *Hawkeye*	AEW&C ac	2	49.1bn	440.73m	(USA) Northrop Grumman
V-22 *Osprey*	Tilt-rotor ac	4	45.7bn	410.21m	(USA) Bell Helicopter (USA) Boeing
C-2	Hy Tpt ac	2	45bn	403.93m	(JPN) KHI
KC-46A *Pegasus*	Tkr ac	1	27.7bn	248.64m	(USA) Boeing
Patriot PAC-3MSE	Long-range SAM	n.k.	20.5bn	184.01m	(USA) Lockheed Martin

Figure 16 Australia: AWD Alliance *Hobart*-class Air Warfare Destroyer

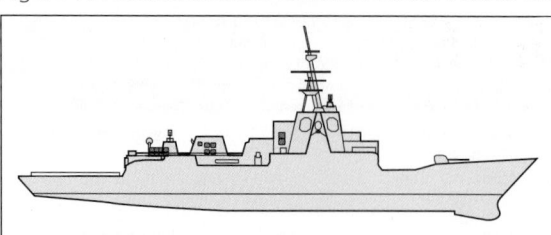

The Air Warfare Destroyer (AWD) project is the second-largest procurement programme the Australian defence department has ever conducted and also one of the most complex. It has involved the modification of an acquired design with construction distributed among several companies. A 2014 national audit report on the programme stated that risks in design and construction were underestimated. For example, the report said the designer, Spanish company Navantia, had never sold a surface-naval-vessel design to a foreign shipyard before and the buyer, ASC, had never built a complex warship before. The design was still being modified by ASC and Navantia after the first of class had been laid down. Australian shipbuilding productivity has been lower than anticipated and errors in the construction of vessel blocks have resulted in higher costs. However, some risk was avoided by acquiring the long-serving and proven US *Aegis* combat system. Development and upgrades of this system will be largely paid for by the United States itself which Australia can then buy into. With other very large naval shipbuilding programmes about to begin, recommendations have been made in government audit reports, such as involving industry more in the design stage to mitigate risks. Despite the delays, the *Hobart* class is likely to be one of the most capable naval vessels in the region into the near future.

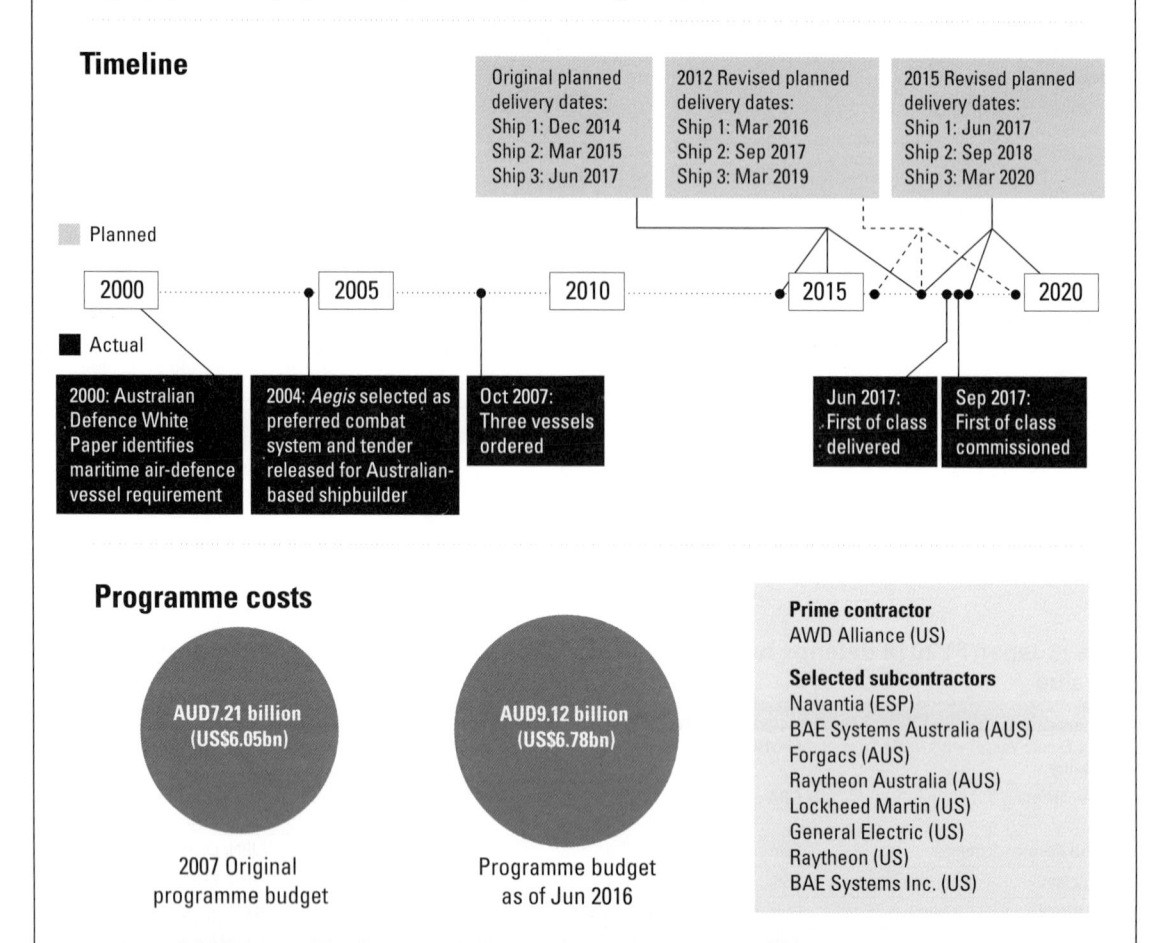

Timeline

Original planned delivery dates:
Ship 1: Dec 2014
Ship 2: Mar 2015
Ship 3: Jun 2017

2012 Revised planned delivery dates:
Ship 1: Mar 2016
Ship 2: Sep 2017
Ship 3: Mar 2019

2015 Revised planned delivery dates:
Ship 1: Jun 2017
Ship 2: Sep 2018
Ship 3: Mar 2020

- 2000: Australian Defence White Paper identifies maritime air-defence vessel requirement
- 2004: *Aegis* selected as preferred combat system and tender released for Australian-based shipbuilder
- Oct 2007: Three vessels ordered
- Jun 2017: First of class delivered
- Sep 2017: First of class commissioned

Programme costs

- AUD7.21 billion (US$6.05bn) — 2007 Original programme budget
- AUD9.12 billion (US$6.78bn) — Programme budget as of Jun 2016

Prime contractor
AWD Alliance (US)

Selected subcontractors
Navantia (ESP)
BAE Systems Australia (AUS)
Forgacs (AUS)
Raytheon Australia (AUS)
Lockheed Martin (US)
General Electric (US)
Raytheon (US)
BAE Systems Inc. (US)

Vessel name	Pennant number	Laid down	Launched	Original planned delivery	Delivered	Commissioned
Hobart	39	06 Sep 2012	23 May 2015	Dec 2014	16 Jun 2017	23 Sep 2017
Brisbane	41	02 Mar 2014	15 Dec 2016	Mar 2015		
Sydney	42	19 Nov 2015		Jun 2017		

© IISS

Chapter Seven
Middle East and North Africa

The region remains dominated by the ongoing conflicts in Iraq, Syria and Yemen, while regional governments also have to address threats from transnational terror groups. At the same time, states in the Gulf are increasingly concerned by Iran, particularly its support for Houthi forces in Yemen, and also its destabilising activities in the region more broadly, to say nothing of its continuing effort to develop its ballistic-missile capability. The fight against the Islamic State, also known as ISIS or ISIL, accelerated considerably during 2017, as various forces concentrated their assault on the jihadi organisation in both Iraq and Syria. These efforts, supported by coalition airpower, special-forces activity and other military support, resulted in the territorial contraction and military attrition of the caliphate.

Countering ISIS
Principal local actors in the fight against ISIS in Syria have included Assad-regime forces (with deployed Russian forces playing a significant role) in addition to some Syrian opposition groups. In Iraq, the armed forces, particularly Iraq's Counter-Terrorism Service (also known as the Golden Division, which has suffered heavy casualties in the campaign), have engaged ISIS.

In both countries, Kurdish groups have been heavily involved in combat, fighting ISIS in the north of both Iraq and Syria from 2014. After Iraq's armed forces collapsed in the north, Kurdish fighters were for a time the main bulwark against further ISIS expansion. For the United States, the major dilemma in Syria was whether to rely increasingly on forces operating under the umbrella of the Kurdistan Workers' Party (PKK)-linked People's Protection Units (YPG), which could jeopardise the relationship with Turkey, a NATO ally. After internal deliberation, the Trump administration chose to continue the Obama administration's military strategy, which relied on the YPG-dominated Syrian Democratic Forces (SDF) and US airpower to liberate the city of Raqqa and defeat ISIS along the Euphrates river valley, although the rules of engagement were relaxed and the tempo of operations increased. The US provided light vehicles, weapons and other equipment to the SDF and deployed ground-targeting units, as well as special-operations forces. The SDF, meanwhile, sought to enrol more local people to provide security as a core of Kurdish and Arab fighters. As US-backed forces advanced, the US built forward-operating bases and airstrips, providing better support to ground-combat operations and also decreasing reliance on its base at Incirlik in Turkey.

Consequently, ISIS has suffered significantly in the ongoing military campaign to oust it from territory in Iraq and Syria. The near-consecutive US-backed campaigns in the cities of Mosul (which took nine months) and Raqqa (which lasted less than five months) overwhelmed the group. While eastern Mosul was liberated relatively quickly, the more densely populated western part of the city witnessed intense, devastating combat. Iraq's Counter-Terrorism Service spearheaded the ground-combat operation. It fielded battle-hardened, well-equipped troops and deployed light and heavy armour to enter the city's narrow streets (also deploying armoured construction vehicles in order to build fortifications against car bombs as its troops moved forward) but suffered high casualties. Western special forces played a discreet yet active role, while US targeting was essential in both the Mosul and Raqqa battles.

ISIS fiercely defended these cities, aided by the length of time the group had had to construct fortifications and work on defensive plans during its occupation. It was no longer able to field large units or conduct stealthy operations to outflank enemy forces, instead resorting to snipers, improvised explosive devices (IEDs), vehicle-borne IEDs, unmanned aerial vehicles and other asymmetric tactics. In Mosul and Raqqa, ISIS also deployed civilians as human shields, contributing to the considerable death toll among the civilian population. This slowed the coalition's advances and increased its reliance on airpower.

Meanwhile, the end of major combat operations against rebel factions allowed the Syrian regime and its Iranian and Russian supporters to redirect their firepower against ISIS. Together, they retook significant ISIS-controlled areas and cities, including Deir ez-Zor, Mayadin and other towns on the border with Iraq. Foreign Shia militiamen and Russian fighters, both military and contractors, played a pivotal combat role, which served to expose the Assad regime's enduring personnel shortfall.

It became clear that the fight against ISIS was at the same time a race to secure influence over former ISIS-held territory by various local and regional forces in the theatre. As ISIS-controlled territory shrank and combatant forces operated closer to each other, their plans and strategies were tested. This led to small-scale skirmishes and subsequent attempts to control escalation. For example, in June, US aircraft shot down a Syrian combat aircraft after it targeted US-backed personnel in northern Syria. Deconfliction mechanisms to secure zones of control were also tested. Over the summer and autumn, as regime and Russian forces moved to seize Deir ez-Zor, the US expected them to stay east of the Euphrates River. However, they subsequently crossed the river and sought to secure oilfields and territory there.

By October 2017, ISIS-held territory had shrunk considerably; the group had no territorial control over any major city or town, except for Abu Kamal in Syria. But the group, and its ideology, had not been totally eradicated. The expectation was that ISIS would transform into a lethal rural insurgency in its former heartland, while ISIS 'provinces' in Afghanistan, Libya, the Philippines and elsewhere would attempt to expand.

The war in Syria

The capture of eastern Aleppo by the Assad regime, backed by Iran and Russia, was the culmination of a year of setbacks for the rebel forces. It heralded a new phase of the Syrian conflict, characterised by the US focus on fighting ISIS, Russian management of the Syrian battlefield, regime advances and rebel disarray.

The loss of Aleppo debilitated the mainstream rebellion, which effectively transformed into a rebel insurgency. It also led the rebels' patrons to reconsider their objectives, commitment and the resources dedicated to the conflict. As a consequence, financial and material support for the rebellion has decreased, as evidenced by the reduced availability of quality munitions, such as TOW anti-armour weapons, and the overall weakening of the rebellion. In summer 2017, meanwhile, the US announced that it would discontinue its training and support for mainstream rebels, except those fighting ISIS.

Regime forces have recaptured significant territory, using sieges and offers of local ceasefires to break pockets of resistance. In support of this strategy, Russia has continued to deploy combat airpower, despite announcements of de-escalation zones. The Assad regime has tried to use this position of relative dominance to rebuild some of its military institutions. For instance, it has attempted to impose government authority on the various pro-regime militias that emerged after 2012. Many National Defence Forces, which served as auxiliary forces, have progressively been brought under military command. At the same time, Russia has attempted to form a new Syrian Army corps, as part of a strategy of reforming and building up the country's conventional forces. A continuing challenge for Assad-regime forces is not just organisation (and equipment) deficiencies after years of war, but rebuilding personnel strength. Indeed, personnel has remained a major concern, as demonstrated by mandatory conscription and the forced recruitment of former rebels into military ranks.

Although the war between the regime and the mainstream rebellion has largely subsided, other fronts remain active. Israel conducted several strikes against Hizbullah targets and weapons shipments from Iran throughout 2017, destroying a suspected rocket factory in northern Syria in September. There was no Syrian or Iranian retaliation, perhaps in part for fear of further escalation, but also because both remained focused on rebel and ISIS threats. US military forces conducted precision strikes on Shayrat air base using cruise missiles in April 2017, in response to an airborne chemical attack (using sarin) by the regime against the town of Khan Sheikhoun. The strikes destroyed some targets but in effect constituted a punitive operation that was not a prelude to any US escalation in Syria; as such it did not affect the overall trajectory of the conflict.

As ground combat against ISIS entered its final phase in the region, attention shifted to the al-Qaeda affiliate Jabhat al-Nusra, which rebranded itself as Hayat Tahrir al-Sham (HTS) in early 2017. HTS's defeat of rebel rivals owed much to the committed and organised fighters in its ranks. The group was effectively in control of much of Idlib province, where more than two million residents and internally displaced people lived. The presence of this jihadi statelet close to Europe posed a dilemma for all actors. Idlib borders Turkey, which was concerned that a combined Russia–Assad-regime push to reconquer the province, or any US move to destroy the group, would result in large numbers of refugees and increase the terrorist threat. By the end of the

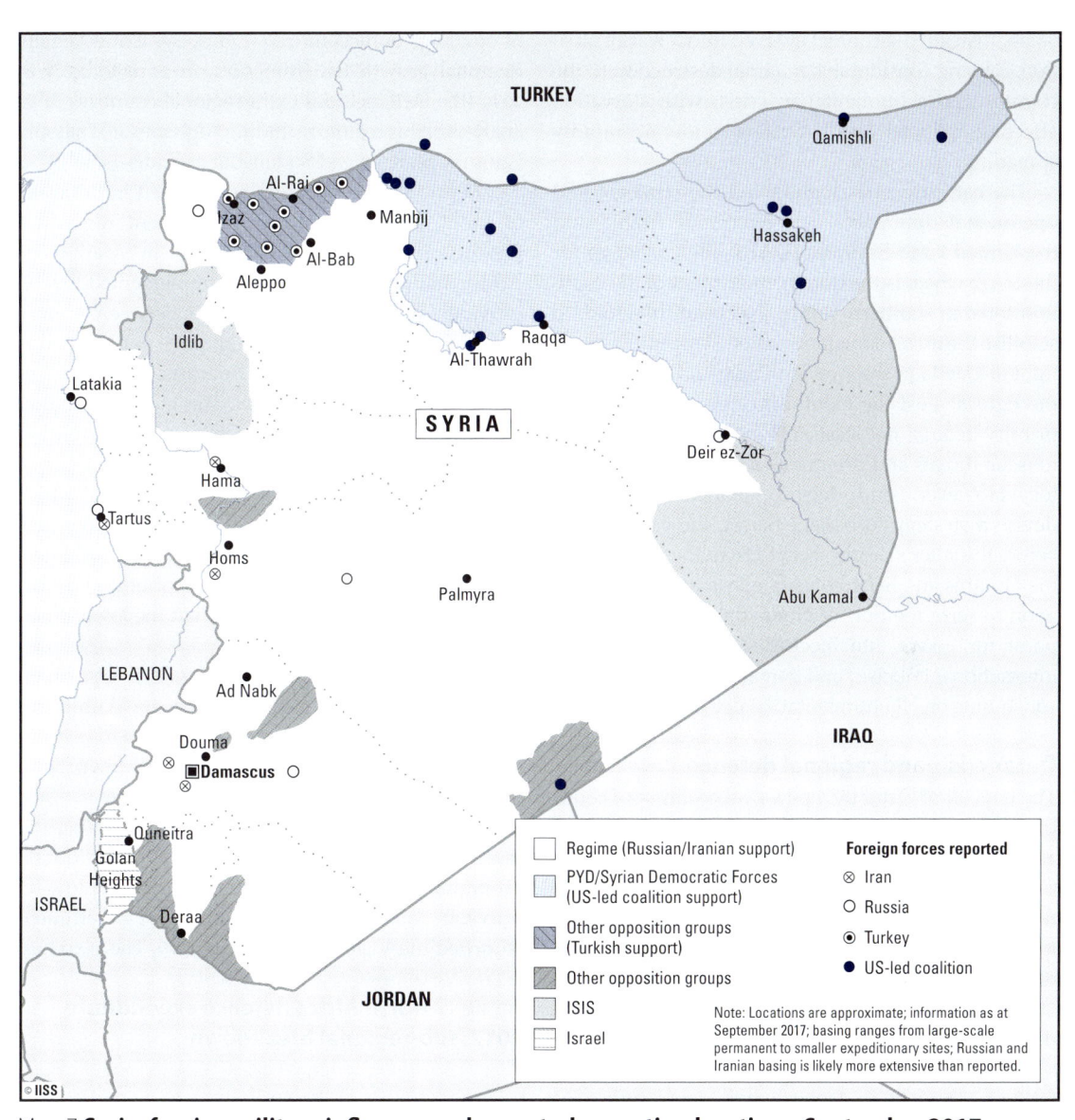

Map 7 **Syria: foreign military influence and reported operating locations, September 2017**

year, Idlib was effectively besieged, starving HTS of resources.

Meanwhile, Iran and Russia have either established or extended their military facilities in Syria. These facilities, combined with land lines of supply from Iran to Lebanon, and transnational Shia militias operating under Iranian command, have changed the military and strategic landscape in the northern Middle East. At the same time, Moscow continues to deploy advanced military systems to Syria, testing and showcasing these on the battlefield. In northern Syria, Turkey sought to contain Kurdish ambitions and minimise its losses there. To enable this, it built a military presence alongside allied rebel groups in a small pocket north of Aleppo, where it sponsored and trained local forces, and assisted Russia in establishing ceasefire zones in Syria.

Yemen

Three years after the fighting began in Yemen, the war remains in a stalemate. The Saudi-led coalition, comprising forces from the internationally recognised but beleaguered government of President Abd Rabbo Mansour Hadi, failed to significantly advance the front lines or deliver fatal blows to Houthi rebel forces that had allied with former president Ali Abdullah

Saleh. Instead, the conflict evolved into a war of attrition, causing considerable material destruction to the country and a humanitarian crisis, with starvation affecting millions and a cholera epidemic rapidly spreading.

The campaign has highlighted the strategic and operational differences between Saudi Arabia and the United Arab Emirates (UAE). The challenge for the UAE, which is the dominant element of the coalition force in southern Yemen, has been threefold: to stabilise the area, manage secessionist aspirations and fight al-Qaeda in the Arabian Peninsula. For Riyadh, the fight against the Houthi insurgency remained a priority in 2017, not least as Houthi forces continued to issue threats and fire missiles towards Saudi territory. However, Saudi defence planners struggled to devise a strategy to besiege Sanaa, the capital, or – before the latter's death – benefit from the rift between the Houthis and Saleh. Meanwhile, a proposed operation to seize the port of Hudaydah (the main entry point for goods into blockaded Yemen) met with international criticism and demands that Riyadh lifts constraints on UN humanitarian deliveries.

Qatar crisis and regional defence

The boycott of Qatar by a powerful coalition of countries led by Saudi Arabia and the UAE threatened to end the already dim prospect of Gulf Cooperation Council (GCC) military cooperation and integration. The boycott ended all political, diplomatic and military relations with Qatar and weakened the role of the GCC. At the same time, the crisis complicated US-led military efforts in the region in terms of maritime security, missile defence and joint exercises.

Qatar used defence diplomacy to ward off any military intervention. It conducted high-profile joint exercises with US and United Kingdom forces, and announced its intention to purchase 24 *Typhoon* combat aircraft from the UK and F-15QA combat aircraft from the US, naval vessels from Italy and other US weaponry. Qatar also sought and obtained an increase in the number of Turkish troops at a base in the country, although Saudi Arabia and the UAE in turn demanded the dismantling of this facility and the departure of Turkish forces.

DEFENCE ECONOMICS

Economic outlook: uncertain times

The economic outlook for the region remained unsettled in 2017, caused by lower oil prices and the impact of ongoing conflicts in Iraq, Libya, Syria and Yemen. Regional growth fell from 5.0% in 2016 to 2.6% in 2017 (the IMF includes extra-regional countries in its analysis of this region, including Afghanistan, Djibouti, Pakistan, Somalia and Sudan, but excludes Israel).

Oil prices have not risen as expected in the wake of OPEC's November 2016 agreement to reduce production, which was extended in May 2017. Additionally, production cuts implemented by oil providers weighed on their growth. Between January and August 2017, the average oil price per barrel was US$49.4. For 2018, the IMF forecasts that oil prices will average US$50.17 a barrel. This is slightly higher than the average 2016 price (US$43.3 per barrel) but still significantly below Gulf Cooperation Council (GCC) states' average fiscal break-even point, which is estimated at US$70–80 per barrel. Stronger US shale production, and stronger recovery in Libya and Nigeria (these countries were not bound by the OPEC agreement), helped to explain the lower-than-expected price.

Oil exporters experienced low GDP growth in 2017, at 1.7%, down from 5.6% in 2016. Within this group, Saudi Arabia slowed from 1.7% in 2016 to 0.1% in 2017. Iran also drove the slowdown, with growth declining from 12.5% in 2016 to 3.5% in 2017. As a consequence, most oil-exporting states in the region continued to pursue fiscal-consolidation programmes to adjust to the environment of low oil prices. In Saudi Arabia, for instance, the government launched the Vision 2030 plan in 2016. The plan has,

Figure 17 **North Africa defence expenditure 2017: sub-regional breakdown**

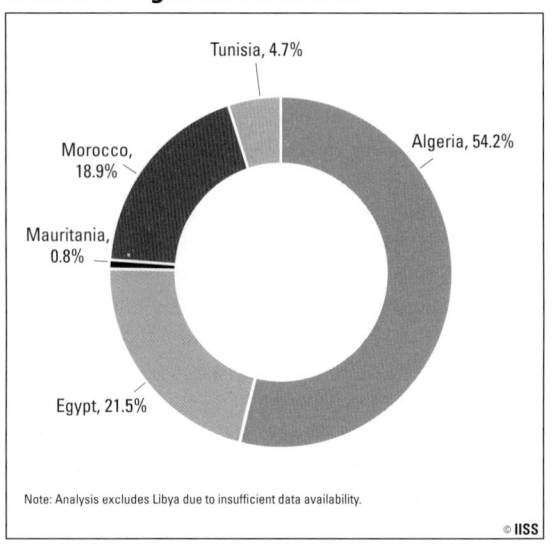

- Algeria, 54.2%
- Egypt, 21.5%
- Morocco, 18.9%
- Tunisia, 4.7%
- Mauritania, 0.8%

Note: Analysis excludes Libya due to insufficient data availability.

© IISS

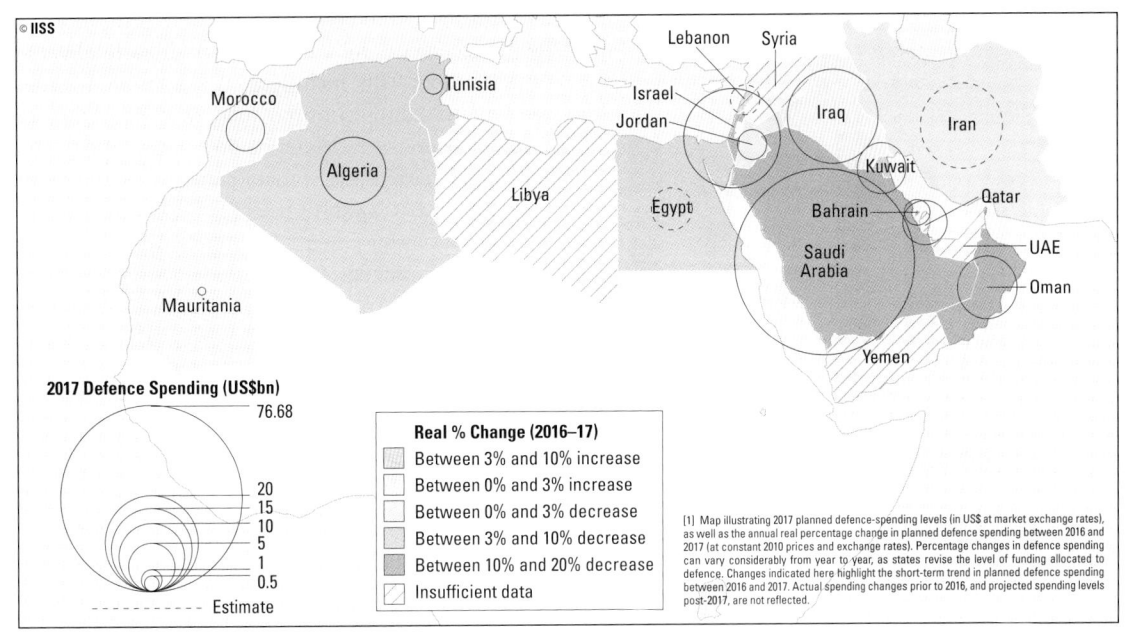

Map 8 **Middle East and North Africa regional defence spending**[1]

[1] Map illustrating 2017 planned defence-spending levels (in US$ at market exchange rates), as well as the annual real percentage change in planned defence spending between 2016 and 2017 (at constant 2010 prices and exchange rates). Percentage changes in defence spending can vary considerably from year to year, as states revise the level of funding allocated to defence. Changes indicated here highlight the short-term trend in planned defence spending between 2016 and 2017. Actual spending changes prior to 2016, and projected spending levels post-2017, are not reflected.

however, already hit some roadblocks: the administration reinstated benefits to civil servants and military personnel that were cut the previous year as part of an austerity agenda.

Conversely, the GDP of regional oil importers grew from 3.6% in 2016 to 4.3% in 2017. In line with this trend, Egypt's growth was strong in 2017 at 4.1%, but the country's underlying economic structures remained fragile. In November 2016, in exchange for an IMF loan, the government applied tough reforms: the currency was devalued, subsidies were cut and new taxes implemented. While these measures began to reassure international investors and to increase exports, they also pushed up inflation (23.5% in 2017). Among oil importers, Morocco in particular rebounded, from 1.2% GDP growth in 2016 to 4.8% in 2017, after a year of drought. However, challenges for countries within this group are tied to concerns over ongoing conflict-related instability, with a consequent decline in tourism and disruption to trade routes.

Defence spending: opacity prevails

Problems in obtaining accurate defence-spending data mean it is not possible to provide a figure for total regional defence spending. Nonetheless, key states provide clues about defence-spending trends, particularly Saudi Arabia, which has the largest defence budget in the region. Financial documents published in 2016 announced cuts of 30.5% to the Kingdom's defence budget between 2015 and 2016. However, 2016 defence spending was revised upwards in subsequent official data releases. While there was a fall in defence spending, this was at an incremental pace: R307 billion (US$81.9bn) in 2015, R305.7bn (US$81.5bn) in 2016 and R287.5bn (US$76.7bn) in 2017.

Given the arms procurements announced by Qatar and the United Arab Emirates (UAE), these countries are very likely the region's other top spenders, besides Israel. However, the lack of reliable information makes this conclusion difficult to validate. Meanwhile, smaller countries in the Gulf signal a downward trend. In Oman, defence and security expenditures declined from R3.5bn (US$9.1bn) in 2016 to R3.34bn (US$8.69bn) in 2017. However, this does not include procurement spending. Bahrain's defence budget was also set to decline from D573 million (US$1.53bn) in 2016 to D557m (US$1.49bn) in 2017, and should remain stable in 2018 also at D557m (estimated at US$1.48bn), but, like for Oman, this figure is likely to include current expenditures only.

On the other side of the Gulf, Iran's nominal defence spending rose from an estimated r499 trillion (US$15.9bn) in 2016 to r544trn (US$16bn) in 2017, although this still meant a slight decline of 1.2% in real terms. However, total military-related expenditure is unknown. For instance, the parliament in 2017 reportedly approved additional funding of

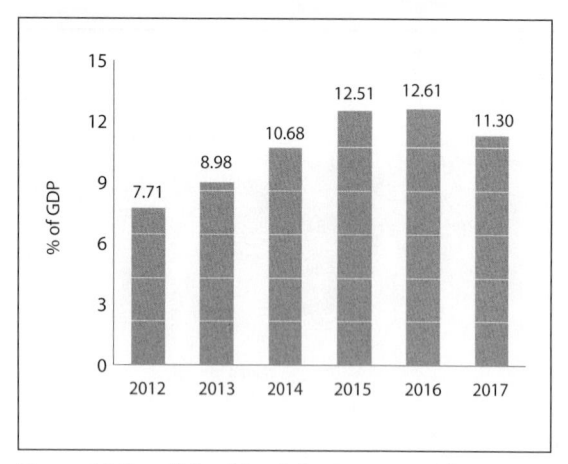

Figure 18 **Saudi Arabia defence expenditure** as % of GDP

Year	% of GDP
2012	7.71
2013	8.98
2014	10.68
2015	12.51
2016	12.61
2017	11.30

US$609m, in part to boost the country's ballistic-missile programme.

Egypt's budget increased slightly between 2016 and 2017, from E£43.2bn (US$5.3bn) to E£47.1bn (US$2.7bn), excluding US Foreign Military Assistance. However, given currency devaluation, this meant a significant drop in US dollar terms (-50%). It is difficult to assess whether this actually was detrimental to the Egyptian armed forces: since President Abdel Fattah Al-Sisi seized power, the role of the military in Egypt's economy has strengthened. It is deeply involved in key sectors such as food, energy and construction, and may derive additional funding from such activities.

Defence procurement and industry

There are modernisation and recapitalisation needs throughout the region, as Gulf states aim to boost their military capability and enhance their strategic autonomy. Areas of focus include improved intelligence, surveillance and reconnaissance (ISR) and command-and-control resources, and precision-guided munitions. The desire to reduce reliance on external support can also be seen in regional powers' diversification strategy regarding their arms imports. Even those who traditionally looked to Western suppliers are now also looking to suppliers such as China and Russia.

Saudi Arabia exemplified this diversification strategy in 2017, using military procurement both as political leverage and as a way to further its own defence-industry ambitions. Ties with the United States were reaffirmed after Donald Trump's inauguration as president. His visit to Riyadh in May 2017 resulted in the proclamation of a 'historic' arms deal; agreements were announced with a total value of US$110bn. This included sales approved under the Obama administration, such as US$11.25bn for multi-mission surface combatant ships; US$1.15bn for more M1A2S *Abrams* main battle tanks and other vehicles; and US$3.5bn for CH-47F *Chinook* helicopters. Intentions for potential contracts were expressed for (among others): US$15bn for seven Terminal High-Altitude Area Defense (THAAD) batteries; US$4.46bn for 104,000 air-to-ground munitions; US$6.65bn for enhancements to the *Patriot* air-defence system; and US$6bn for four frigates. However, at the time of writing, these remain letters of intent only, as the State Department and Congress first need to authorise those purchases. At the same time, Saudi Arabia began to turn to Russia. In October 2017, the Kingdom was talking to Moscow about the possible procurement of S-400 air-defence systems. Should the deal come through, this would be a breakthrough for Russia, which has never exported major conventional weapons systems to Riyadh. The next day, the US State Department's Defense Security Cooperation Agency cleared the sale of seven THAAD batteries – although this still needs to be approved by Congress.

Qatar also looked to diversify its suppliers in 2017. Since the GCC crisis broke out in June 2017, Qatar has signed defence contracts with Italy's Fincantieri and Leonardo for four corvettes, two offshore-patrol vessels and one landing platform dock, estimated at US$5.91bn (including the weapons package). It has also signed a letter of intent to procure 24 *Typhoon* combat aircraft from BAE Systems, after moving to purchase 72 F-15QA fighter aircraft from Boeing for US$21.1bn in late 2016. A deal to buy 24 *Rafale* fighter aircraft from Dassault Aviation for US$7.48bn was signed in 2015. These various procurements reflect Qatar's traditional strategy of gaining security guarantees through arms deals with Western powers. However, Qatar, like Saudi Arabia, signed a memorandum of understanding with Russia for 'air defence and military supplies' in October 2017.

Beyond the Gulf, 2017 was a crucial year for Egypt, which has received significant equipment deliveries, in particular for the navy. In April, the first German Type-209/1400 submarine, out of an order of four, was commissioned by the Egyptian Navy. The previous year, two French *Mistral*-class amphibious-assault ships had been commissioned. In mid-2017, Egypt received the first delivery of Russian Ka-52A attack helicopters. Another order is expected for the Ka-52K naval version, to be deployed on the *Mistral*-class vessels. These deliveries highlight the government's plan to reinforce its strength in the Red Sea, in order to protect the Suez Canal. Meanwhile, the air force accepted a first batch of MiG-29M/M2 fighter aircraft in 2016 and continued to receive deliveries of *Rafale* combat aircraft. As of October 2017, the Egyptian Air Force had received 11 out of 24 *Rafale*s.

While Egypt and most regional states depend on external suppliers, efforts to develop local defence firms have increased due to the fall in oil prices and requirements to diversify the economy. In 2017, Saudi Arabia met important milestones towards its goal to develop a domestic defence-industrial base, in relation to the Vision 2030 plan. In May, the Kingdom established a national company for defence-equipment development and manufacturing, the Saudi Arabian Military Industries (SAMI), to be led by a former Airbus and Rheinmetall executive. SAMI is tied to the Public Investment Fund, the state's sovereign fund, chaired by Crown Prince Mohammed bin Salman. In the medium term, the new entity will likely oversee or regroup existing Saudi Arabian defence groups such as Taqnia and the Military Industries Corporation. In August, the government announced the creation of a new procurement body, the General Authority of Military Industries. It will be in charge of defence procurement, research and development, the expansion of the local defence-technology industrial base (DTIB) and, relatedly, offsets. This organisation will also be headed by the Crown Prince.

Saudi Arabia's new defence-industrial strategy has interested defence manufacturers around the world. Key emerging partners, besides the Kingdom's traditional Western partners, include Ukraine and South Africa. A number of partnerships were signed with Asian countries, including Indonesia, India and Pakistan, in 2017, while South Korean companies are looking to open local joint ventures. Cooperation has also advanced with China. Not only has Saudi Arabia procured Chinese-built CH-4 and *Wing-Loong* 1 unmanned aerial vehicles (UAVs), but it has also signed partnerships with China Aerospace Science and Technology Corporation to develop the local manufacture of armed UAVs.

To develop its own DTIB, Saudi Arabia is following the path of the UAE, which is at a more advanced stage in this process. Not only is the UAE producing weapons for its own armed forces, but it is starting to export as well. For instance, Abu Dhabi Ship Building Company is providing landing craft to Oman and Kuwait. NIMR, a vehicle manufacturer, signed an agreement with a Czech firm in 2017 for the sale of its products to Central and Eastern Europe. The UAE has also begun to offer licenced-production agreements to its customers, as evidenced by the NIMR production line that was set up in Algeria. Furthermore, like traditional Western arms suppliers, the UAE is also using the arms trade in support of its political goals: Abu Dhabi reportedly donated M1248 *Caiman* vehicles to the Libyan National Army and other military vehicles to Iraqi Kurds.

QATAR

Qatar gained independence from the United Kingdom in 1971, the same year as Bahrain and the United Arab Emirates (UAE). Geopolitically, like Oman, Qatar is removed from the Gulf Cooperation Council (GCC) mainstream. In 2014, Bahrain, Saudi Arabia and the UAE withdrew their ambassadors from Doha in protest at alleged Qatari 'meddling in their internal affairs', its alleged support to certain Islamist groups and its 'allowing' the Qatar-based Al-Jazeera media network to be used as a mouthpiece for these groups. Kuwait and, eventually, King Salman of Saudi Arabia later brokered a deal that outwardly demonstrated unity.

In early June 2017, Bahrain, Egypt, Saudi Arabia and the UAE imposed a 'blockade' on Qatar, with extensive bans on a broad range of vital services, including air movement, and the closure of the land border with Saudi Arabia. At the time of writing, the blockade had no military element; however, it comes at a time when the Qatari armed forces (QAF) are still in 'catch-up' mode in comparison with their neighbours – especially Saudi Arabia and the UAE – in terms of military capability. There is an extensive procurement drive in place across all the military domains and a commensurate increase in cooperation with Turkey.

Since its independence Qatar, like other Gulf states, has also participated to some degree in regional military activities, for example, coalition operations in Kuwait during the First Gulf War (1991) and the conflict in Yemen (2016), as well as, more controversially, deploying air elements to Libya and training Libyan personnel. With the possible exception of the Kuwait campaign, where a Qatari AMX-30 tank battalion was primarily manned by Pakistani personnel, the Qatari military commitment to each of these endeavours has been modest, reflecting the size, experience and capability of the QAF and its ability to operate outside its own territorial boundaries. In addition to operational deployments, the Qatar Emiri Navy (QEN) has also made small periodic contributions to the US-led Combined Maritime Forces.

Defence policy

Qatar has not published any defence-policy goals, although the following are understood to feature in its thinking: firstly, to protect Qatari territorial integrity, including its exclusive economic zone and oil and gas infrastructure, from internal and external threats; secondly, to participate in the defence of GCC member states, as necessary; thirdly, to contribute to coalition operations to maintain peace and security in accordance with the provisions of international law; and fourthly, to provide international humanitarian aid in times of disaster.

In common with its GCC neighbours, Qatar also has no published defence budget. The UK Defence and Security Organisation assesses that Qatar was the world's third-largest importer of defence items between 2007 and 2016, behind India and Saudi Arabia – a position that predates a recent Eurofighter *Typhoon* combat-aircraft letter of intent. Some estimates state that Qatar spent US$4.4 billion on defence materiel in 2016, and was expected to spend US$7bn by 2020, although these forecasts may now be affected by the present regional crisis. That said, the figures are less important than the significant challenges that the country will face in generating capability from its impressive future equipment inventory.

Until May 2017, Qatar participated in collective-defence discussions and initiatives with, and made a small contribution to, the GCC military secretariat in Riyadh. It has also taken part in the periodic GCC set-piece collective-defence exercises, although the QAF was absent from the large exercise *Saif Abdullah* in 2014. In common with all other Gulf states, except Saudi Arabia, Qatar is also home to substantial external armed forces – in this case, the US CENTCOM forward HQ, its Air Operations Center and a major US air base at Al Udeid, as well as a significant US Army base at Al Sayliyah. Since 2016, Qatar has also hosted an increasing number of Turkish forces, primarily land and naval, which is an element in the dispute with Qatar's neighbours. Qatar has also taken a more open approach to dealing with Iran, and has reinstated full diplomatic relations at a time when Saudi Arabia, in particular, is minimising Saudi–Iranian ties.

Internally, considerable overlaps remain between the perceived roles and responsibilities of the defence and interior ministries. In common with other GCC countries, Qatar also possesses a 'third force': the Emiri Guard.

Armed forces

Qatar has one of the smallest armed forces by overall size in the Gulf region, although GCC countries rarely publish official personnel figures. The armed forces include a sizeable Emiri Guard force and there is also an Internal Security Force of some 5,000 paramilitary personnel separate from the armed forces. It is estimated that less than 30% of QAF personnel are native Qataris, mainly officers. Among this officer corps, there are thought to be in excess of 350 brigadiers/officers of one-star rank (considerably more than the United States and UK armed forces). This has resulted in outsourcing some elements of the defence ministry.

Structurally, Qatar has a conventional defence-ministry headquarters, with three individual domain headquarters and associated forces: the Qatar Emiri Land Forces (QELF), the Qatar Emiri Air Forces (QEAF) and the QEN, with a special-forces group and a border guard/frontier force. A chief of staff looks after the defence-ministry staff, advises the defence minister, and is responsible for the preparation and readiness of units, but the individual services report directly to the minister. A joint headquarters coordinates defence-ministry capabilities and also has liaison cells with the interior ministry, the Emiri Guard and major gas companies.

Air forces
The QEAF is estimated to comprise some 2,000 personnel at two main bases, Doha Airport and Al Udeid, with the present capability built around an ageing squadron of 12 French *Mirage* 2000 combat aircraft. In 2015 an order was placed with Dassault for 24 *Rafale*s (18 single and six twin seaters) that are reportedly due to enter service from 2018. The US Congress cleared the sale of up to 72 F-15 *Eagle* aircraft in 2016, and in September 2017 a letter of intent was signed with BAE Systems for the potential purchase of 24 Eurofighter *Typhoon*s. This future air-force inventory presents significant challenges for Qatar, especially given its personnel shortages.

Early indications from the *Rafale* purchase, the most advanced of these procurements, is that training will be a major challenge, with early batches of potential pilots below the required standard. The QEAF has not invested in training with other air forces to the same extent as the Saudi and Emirati air arms; it lacks not only pilots, but also other essential supporting capabilities that make modern air platforms effective. The experience required to deliver such vital supporting capabilities cannot be created quickly; it usually takes years to develop.

The QEAF also operates the armed forces' rotary-wing capability, which is undergoing a significant upgrade programme. AH-64E *Apache* attack helicopters are joining a number of AW139 utility and medevac helicopters, and an ageing fleet of *Gazelle*s and *Sea King*s. Meanwhile, a letter of intent has been issued for NH90 transport helicopters. The combat air and aviation fleet is supported by C-17A *Globemaster* III heavy transport aircraft, while a contract has been signed for three US airborne early-warning aircraft (based on the Boeing 737 airframe). In 2014, Airbus announced that Qatar had selected its A330 Multi Role Tanker Transport.

Underpinning these acquisitions are discussions about the construction of a new military air base at Dhukan on the western coast. At a conservative estimate of 1.5 pilots trained per aircraft, this will mean that, in due course, the QEAF will need a minimum steady state of over 300 trained pilots, plus the requisite engineers, weapons experts and other personnel, which will likely prove a significant challenge.

At the same time, Qatar's air-defence capability sits within the QEAF and comprises US *Patriot* and French *Roland* systems. The US approved the Terminal High-Altitude Area Defense system for sale to Qatar in 2012, but the deal has yet to be finalised. Given the country's limited size, any response to a direct threat will probably rely heavily on the US systems that protect Al Udeid air base, where a substantial number of aircraft are based.

Navy
The QEN is estimated to possesses some 2,500 personnel, including coastguard personnel. It too is entering a period of change, updating its ageing fleet of fast-attack craft and patrol boats with a recent agreement to buy a landing platform dock, four corvettes and two offshore-patrol vessels from Italian company Fincantieri. This programme will give the navy the platforms necessary to operate a full littoral navy. However, in common with the challenges facing the air force, bringing these vessels into service and crewing them effectively will be difficult.

Qatar lacks its own naval academy, and even if it had one, officers would be hard pressed to assimilate the specialist training and experience that will be required to operate the navy's new ships to their full capability. As such, the QEN will likely need to approach other nations for training support and personnel. A new base is due to be built for the QEN as part of the port development project to the south of Doha.

Land forces
The QLF is the largest service component, and is undertaking a major equipment-modernisation programme, primarily through the purchase of *Leopard* 2A7 main battle tanks and PzH 2000 self-propelled artillery pieces from Germany. *Leopard* deliveries are under way, and are due to be complete in 2018. This is being used to equip the tank battalion in the Jassim Bin Mohammed Brigade and the independent artillery battalion.

Qatar's combat inventory (which includes a modest special-forces group) also requires a wide range of supporting capabilities that will be essential for it to be militarily effective, not least a fully integrated command-and-control system, and training, maintenance and logistics requirements.

Defence and security cooperation

Qatar has not made the same investment in coalition training as its neighbours, notably the UAE but also increasingly Saudi Arabia, despite a substantial US presence in-country. This is most notable in the air domain, where Saudi Arabia and the UAE regularly exercise with the UK, the US and sometimes NATO. The QAF has participated in GCC exercises, but these tend to be time-limited showpiece events, with little real substance or military value. The QEN has made occasional contributions to the Combined Maritime Forces, but these too have been small and time-limited. There is little real internal cooperation between the services, not least because this would highlight the considerable duplication of roles and capabilities between elements of the defence and interior ministries and the Emiri Guard.

In contrast to Oman, Saudi Arabia and the UAE, where extensive relationships with foreign armed forces, and military and ex-military advisers, are employed, as well as links with international training academies, Qatar has employed modest numbers of individual contract officers, including from France, the UK and the US, and operated a short-lived commercially run staff-college programme with UK defence-ministry support.

Operational experience

Qatar has contributed military forces to a small number of operations in the region, notably with other Gulf allies at Khafji in 1991, where an AMX-30 tank battalion participated, and in the Yemen campaign; Qatar is presently 'suspended' although its contribution was very small. Qatar was involved in the conflict in Libya in 2011, where it contributed six *Mirage* fighters and two C-17A transport aircraft to coalition no-fly-zone enforcement efforts. At later stages in the operation, Qatari special forces assisted in the training of the Tripoli Brigade and rebel forces in Benghazi and the Nafusa mountains. In addition, it also brought small groups of Libyans to Qatar for small-unit leadership training in preparation for the rebel advance on Tripoli in August 2011. Unseen funding and influence activities may also have had more effect than the overt military contributions.

Personnel and training

Personnel costs constitute a significant part of Qatar's commitment to military spending. Overall, the priority will be to man and sustain the new equipment that is being delivered, taking it from initial operating capability to full operating capability, and maintaining it through-life, which will be upwards of 20 years in many cases. However, scant attention appears to have been paid to looking at all of the defence lines of development. This UK term describes a way of coordinating the elements needed to generate military capability (training, equipment, personnel, information, concepts and doctrine, organisation, infrastructure and logistics) for individual platforms or collective activity.

However, retrospective measures are being taken, such as the introduction of a national military-service programme (including three to four months of training) and employing small numbers of military contract officers. A remaining challenge is to convey a sense that the armed forces can constitute a profession for Qatari citizens. Indeed, the expectation that others will provide security is no longer sustainable, and much needs to be done to professionalise the services. Given the country's national personnel limitations, a review of duplicated capabilities, including transferring personnel back into front-line posts, may be necessary.

There have also been small positive steps in terms of force development, but these have not been sustained. For instance, the standing up in 2013 of a joint staff college course by a private UK company, backed by the UK Ministry of Defence, only lasted three years before the QAF took it back in house. Qatar's in-house replacement is, according to experts, suffering from a lack of experienced staff.

Nevertheless, training will be at the heart of assimilating and integrating Qatar's new capabilities over the coming years. The present regional dispute could work in favour of the armed forces, if sufficient pride in military service can be generated in order to drive a process of improvement. However, Qatar's small population will likely result in more foreign nationals (such as Pakistanis, Palestinians and Syrians) bolstering the QAF ranks.

Defence economics and industry

Qatar's defence procurement in the past five years has been considerable, and while not all of the agreements and negotiations have yet to translate into contracts, it indicates that the government has allocated significant sums for defence. However, as in some other regional states, obtaining accurate figures on defence disbursements is extremely difficult. Some measure can be obtained by looking at signed contracts, though a contract value is not given in all cases. At the same time, some of the significant costs will fall outside these parameters, namely personnel costs and necessary sums for training and maintenance contracts.

Qatar has no indigenous defence industry, nor are there any indications that the government intends to develop one. As such, it is reliant on original equipment manufacturers and other contractors for defence-equipment support; there is not the same pressure to industrialise as in Qatar's neighbours, or to employ Qatari nationals in manufacturing jobs. Indeed, the size of the population – and even the most optimistic of growth forecasts – mean that there is little prospect of Qatar ever needing to develop an indigenous defence-industrial capability to meet any need for job creation; national-security or security-of-supply requirements would be the likely prompts for any moves in this direction.

Taken together, the individual challenges of lower gas prices, the regional dispute with its neighbours, a changing defence posture and lessons from Yemen will impose huge demands on a relatively inexperienced defence ministry. These factors highlight the need for significant defence reform, including outside help to resolve major equipment-integration challenges. Harnessing coherent and considered external assistance is likely to be the best way to address this challenge.

Algeria ALG

Algerian Dinar D		2016	2017	2018
GDP	D		17.4tr	19.6tr
	US$		159bn	175bn
per capita	US$		3,902	4,225
Growth	%		3.3	1.5
Inflation	%		6.4	5.5
Def bdgt	D		1.12tr	1.12tr
	US$		10.2bn	10.0bn
US$1=D			109.45	111.63

Population 40,969,443

Age	0–14	15–19	20–24	25–29	30–64	65 plus
Male	15.0%	3.6%	4.2%	4.5%	20.7%	2.6%
Female	14.3%	3.4%	4.0%	4.3%	20.3%	3.0%

Capabilities

Territorial integrity, internal security and regional stability are the primary roles of the Algerian armed forces. Islamist extremism continues to be an internal and a regional security issue. The armed forces train regularly, including on combined-operations exercises, have substantial counter-insurgency experience and in 2013 took on the task of counter narcotics trafficking. Algeria is part of the African Union's North African Regional Capability Standby Force, hosting the force's logistics base in Algiers. Its forces are the best equipped in northern Africa, following a period of recapitalisation, with much equipment sourced from Russia. Recent deliveries include the *Iskander*-E short-range ballistic-missile system, which will improve the army's deep-strike capacity. The *Buk*-M2E medium-range surface-to-air-missile system was also introduced into the inventory. China has also been a source of some equipment, including self-propelled artillery. The security of its border with Libya remained a concern throughout 2017, with a large number of army and gendarmerie personnel deployed in this area.

ACTIVE 130,000 (Army 110,000 Navy 6,000 Air 14,000) **Paramilitary 187,200**
Conscript liability 18 months, only in the army (6 months basic, 12 months with regular army often involving civil projects)

RESERVE 150,000 (Army 150,000) to age 50

ORGANISATIONS BY SERVICE

Army 35,000; 75,000 conscript (total 110,000)
FORCES BY ROLE
6 Mil Regions
MANOEUVRE
  Armoured
  2 (1st & 8th) armd div (3 tk regt; 1 mech regt, 1 arty gp)
  1 indep armd bde
  Mechanised
  2 (12th & 40th) mech div (1 tk regt; 3 mech regt, 1 arty gp)
  3 indep mech bde
  Light
  2 indep mot bde
  Air Manoeuvre
  1 AB div (4 para regt; 1 SF regt)
COMBAT SUPPORT
2 arty bn
4 engr bn
AIR DEFENCE
7 AD bn
EQUIPMENT BY TYPE
ARMOURED FIGHTING VEHICLES
  MBT 1,295: 400 T-90SA; 325 T-72; 300 T-62; 270 T-54/T-55
  RECCE 134: 44 AML-60; 26 BRDM-2; 64 BRDM-2M with 9M133 *Kornet* (AT-14 *Spriggan*)
  IFV 1,089: 685 BMP-1; 304 BMP-2M with 9M133 *Kornet* (AT-14 *Spriggan*); 100 BMP-3
  APC 883+
    APC (W) 881+: 250 BTR-60; 150 BTR-80; 150 OT-64; 55 M3 Panhard; 176+ *Fuchs* 2; 100 *Fahd*
  PPV 2 *Marauder*
ANTI-TANK/ANTI-INFRASTRUCTURE
  MSL • MANPATS 9K11 *Malyutka* (AT-3 *Sagger*); 9K111 *Fagot* (AT-4 *Spigot*); 9K111-1 *Konkurs* (AT-5 *Spandrel*); 9K115-2 *Metis*-M1 (AT-13 *Saxhorn*-2); 9K135 *Kornet*-E (AT-14 *Spriggan*); *Milan*
  RCL 180: **82mm** 120 B-10; **107mm** 60 B-11
  GUNS 250: **57mm** 160 ZIS-2 (M-1943); **85mm** 80 D-44; **100mm** 10 T-12
ARTILLERY 1,091
  SP 224: **122mm** 140 2S1 *Gvozdika*; **152mm** 30 2S3 *Akatsiya*; **155mm** ε54 PLZ-45
  TOWED 393: **122mm** 345: 160 D-30; 25 D-74; 100 M-1931/37; 60 M-30; **130mm** 10 M-46; **152mm** 20 M-1937 (ML-20); **155mm** 18 Type-88 (PLL-01)
  MRL 144: **122mm** 48 BM-21 *Grad*; **140mm** 48 BM-14; **240mm** 30 BM-24; **300mm** 18 9A52 *Smerch*
  MOR 330: **82mm** 150 M-37; **120mm** 120 M-1943; **160mm** 60 M-1943
SURFACE-TO-SURFACE MISSILE LAUNCHERS
  SRBM 4 *Iskander*-E
AIR DEFENCE
  SAM 106+
    Short-range 38 96K6 *Pantsir*-S1 (SA-22 *Greyhound*)
    Point-defence 68+: ε48 9K33M *Osa* (SA-8B *Gecko*); ε20 9K31 *Strela*-1 (SA-9 *Gaskin*); 9K32 *Strela*-2 (SA-7A/B *Grail*)‡
  GUNS ε830
    SP 23mm ε225 ZSU-23-4
    TOWED ε605: **14.5mm** 100: 60 ZPU-2; 40 ZPU-4; **23mm** 100 ZU-23; **37mm** ε150 M-1939; **57mm** 75 S-60; **85mm** 20 M-1939 (KS-12); **100mm** 150 KS-19; **130mm** 10 KS-30

Navy ε6,000
EQUIPMENT BY TYPE
SUBMARINES • TACTICAL • SSK 4:
  2 *Kilo* (FSU *Paltus*) with 6 single 533mm TT with Test-71ME HWT/3M54E *Klub*-S (SS-N-27B *Sizzler*) AShM
  2 Improved *Kilo* (RUS *Varshavyanka*) with 6 single 533mm TT with Test-71ME HWT/3M54E *Klub*-S (SS-N-27B) AShM

PRINCIPAL SURFACE COMBATANTS • FRIGATES 8
FFGHM 5:
  3 *Adhafer* (C28A) with 2 quad lnchr with C-802A AShM, 1 FM-90 lnchr with HHQ-7 SAM, 2 triple 324mm ASTT, 2 Type-730B CIWS, 1 76mm gun (capacity 1 hel)
  2 *Erradii* (MEKO 200AN) with 2 octuple lnchrs with RBS-15 Mk3 AShM, 4 8-cell VLS with *Umkhonto*-IR SAM, 2 twin 324mm TT with MU90 LWT, 1 127mm gun (capacity 1 *Super Lynx* 300)
FF 3 *Mourad Rais* (FSU *Koni*) with 2 twin 533mm TT, 2 RBU 6000 *Smerch* 2 A/S mor, 2 twin 76mm gun
PATROL AND COASTAL COMBATANTS 25
  CORVETTES 7
    FSGM 3 *Rais Hamidou* (FSU *Nanuchka* II) with up to 4 twin lnchr with 3M24E *Uran*-E (SS-N-25 *Switchblade*) AShM, 1 twin lnchr with 9M33 *Osa*-M (SA-N-4 *Gecko*) SAM, 1 AK630 CIWS, 1 twin 57mm gun
    FSG 4:
      3 *Djebel Chenoua* with 2 twin lnchr with C-802 (CH-SS-N-8 *Saccade*) AShM, 1 AK630 CIWS, 1 76mm gun
      1 *Rais Hassen Barbiar* (*Djebel Chenoua* mod) with 2 twin lnchr with C-802 (CH-SS-N-8 *Saccade*) AShM, 1 Type-730 CIWS, 1 76mm gun
  PBFG 9 *Osa* II (3†) with 4 single lnchr with P-15 *Termit* (SS-N-2B *Styx*) AShM
  PB 9 *Kebir* with 1 76mm gun
MINE WARFARE • MINE COUNTERMEASURES 1
  MCC 1 *El-Kasseh* (ITA *Gaeta* mod)
AMPHIBIOUS 7
  PRINCIPAL AMPHIBIOUS SHIPS • LHD 1 *Kalaat Beni Abbes* with 1 8-cell A50 VLS with *Aster*-15 SAM, 1 76mm gun (capacity 5 med hel; 3 LCVP; 15 MBT; 350 troops)
  LANDING SHIPS 3:
    LSM 1 *Polnochny* B with 1 twin AK230 CIWS (capacity 6 MBT; 180 troops)
    LST 2 *Kalaat beni Hammad* (capacity 7 MBT; 240 troops) with 1 med hel landing platform
  LANDING CRAFT • LCVP 3
LOGISTICS AND SUPPORT 3
  AGS 1 *El Idrissi*
  AX 1 *Daxin* with 2 twin AK230 CIWS, 1 76mm gun, 1 hel landing platform
  AXS 1 *El Mellah*

Naval Infantry
FORCES BY ROLE
MANOEUVRE
  Amphibious
    1 naval inf bn

Naval Aviation
EQUIPMENT BY TYPE
HELICOPTERS
  MRH 9: 3 AW139 (SAR); 6 *Super Lynx* 300
  SAR 9: 5 AW101 SAR; 4 *Super Lynx* Mk130

Coastal Defence
EQUIPMENT BY TYPE
COASTAL DEFENCE
  AShM 4K51 *Rubezh* (SSC-3 *Styx*)

Coast Guard ε500
EQUIPMENT BY TYPE
PATROL AND COASTAL COMBATANTS 55
  PBF 6 *Baglietto* 20
  PB 49: 6 *Baglietto Mangusta*; 12 *Jebel Antar*; 21 *Deneb*; 4 *El Mounkid*; 6 *Kebir* with 1 76mm gun
LOGISTICS AND SUPPORT 9
  AR 1 *El Mourafek*
  ARS 3 *El Moundjid*
  AXL 5 *El Mouderrib* (PRC *Chui*-E) (2 more in reserve†)

Air Force 14,000
Flying hours 150 hrs/yr
FORCES BY ROLE
FIGHTER
  1 sqn with MiG-25PDS/RU *Foxbat*
  4 sqn with MiG-29C/UB *Fulcrum*
FIGHTER/GROUND ATTACK
  3 sqn with Su-30MKA *Flanker*
GROUND ATTACK
  2 sqn with Su-24M/MK *Fencer* D
ELINT
  1 sqn with Beech 1900D
MARITIME PATROL
  2 sqn with Beech 200T/300 *King Air*
ISR
  1 sqn with Su-24MR *Fencer* E*; MiG-25RBSh *Foxbat* D*
TANKER
  1 sqn with Il-78 *Midas*
TRANSPORT
  1 sqn with C-130H/H-30 *Hercules*; L-100-30
  1 sqn with C-295M
  1 sqn with Gulfstream IV-SP; Gulfstream V
  1 sqn with Il-76MD/TD *Candid*
TRAINING
  2 sqn with Z-142
  1 sqn with Yak-130 *Mitten**
  2 sqn with L-39C/ZA *Albatros*
  1 hel sqn with PZL Mi-2 *Hoplite*
ATTACK HELICOPTER
  3 sqn with Mi-24 *Hind* (one re-equipping with Mi-28NE *Havoc*)
TRANSPORT HELICOPTER
  1 sqn with AS355 *Ecureuil*
  5 sqn with Mi-8 *Hip*; Mi-17 *Hip* H
  1 sqn with Ka-27PS *Helix* D; Ka-32T *Helix*
ISR UAV
  1 sqn with *Seeker* II
AIR DEFENCE
  3 ADA bde
  3 SAM regt with S-125 *Neva* (SA-3 *Goa*); 2K12 *Kub* (SA-6 *Gainful*); S-300PMU2 (SA-20 *Gargoyle*)
EQUIPMENT BY TYPE
AIRCRAFT 135 combat capable
  FTR 34: 11 MiG-25PDS/RU *Foxbat*; 23 MiG-29C/UB *Fulcrum*
  FGA 44 Su-30MKA
  ATK 33 Su-24M/MK *Fencer* D
  ISR 8: 4 MiG-25RBSh *Foxbat* D*; 4 Su-24MR *Fencer* E*

TKR 6 Il-78 *Midas*
TPT 67: **Heavy** 12: 3 Il-76MD *Candid* B; 9 Il-76TD *Candid*;
Medium 17: 9 C-130H *Hercules*; 6 C-130H-30 *Hercules*; 2 L-100-30; **Light** 32: 3 Beech C90B *King Air*; 5 Beech 200T *King Air*; 6 Beech 300 *King Air*; 12 Beech 1900D (electronic surv); 5 C-295M; 1 F-27 *Friendship*; **PAX** 6: 1 A340; 4 Gulfstream IV-SP; 1 Gulfstream V
TRG 99: 36 L-39ZA *Albatros*; 7 L-39C *Albatros*; 16 Yak-130 *Mitten**; 40 Z-142
HELICOPTERS
  ATK 37: 31 Mi-24 *Hind*; 6 Mi-28NE *Havoc*
  SAR 3 Ka-27PS *Helix* D
  MRH 11: 8 AW139 (SAR); 3 Bell 412EP
  MRH/TPT 74 Mi-8 *Hip* (med tpt)/Mi-17 *Hip* H
  TPT 48: **Heavy** 8 Mi-26T2 *Halo*; **Medium** 4 Ka-32T *Helix*; **Light** 36: 8 AW119KE *Koala*; 8 AS355 *Ecureuil*; 28 PZL Mi-2 *Hoplite*
UNMANNED AERIAL VEHICLES
  ISR • Medium *Seeker* II
AIR DEFENCE
  Long-range S-300PMU2 (SA-20 *Gargoyle*)
  Medium-range 9K317 *Buk*-M2E (SA-17 *Grizzly*); S-125 *Pechora*-M (SA-3 *Goa*)
  Short-range 2K12 *Kvadrat* (SA-6 *Gainful*)
  GUNS 725 **100mm/130mm/85mm**
AIR-LAUNCHED MISSILES
  AAM • IR R-60 (AA-8 *Aphid*); R-73 (A-11 *Archer*); **IR/SARH** R-40/46 (AA-6 *Acrid*); R-23/24 (AA-7 *Apex*); R-27 (AA-10 *Alamo*); **ARH** R-77 (AA-12A *Adder*);
  ASM Kh-25 (AS-10 *Karen*); Kh-29 (AS-14 *Kedge*); Kh-31P/A (AS-17A/B *Krypton*); Kh-59ME (AS-18 *Kazoo*); ZT-35 *Ingwe*
  ARM Kh-25MP (AS-12 *Kegler*)

Paramilitary ε187,200

Gendarmerie 20,000
Ministry of Defence control; 6 regions
EQUIPMENT BY TYPE
ARMOURED FIGHTING VEHICLES
  RECCE AML-60
  APC • APC (W) 210: 100 TH-390 *Fahd*; 110 Panhard M3
HELICOPTERS • TPT • Light 12+: 12 AW109; Some PZL Mi-2 *Hoplite*

National Security Forces 16,000
Directorate of National Security. Small arms

Republican Guard 1,200
EQUIPMENT BY TYPE
ARMOURED FIGHTING VEHICLES
  RECCE AML-60
  APC • APC (T) M3 half-track

Legitimate Defence Groups ε150,000
Self-defence militia, communal guards (60,000)

DEPLOYMENT

DEMOCRATIC REPUBLIC OF THE CONGO
UN • MONUSCO 5 obs

Bahrain BHR

Bahraini Dinar D		2016	2017	2018
GDP	D	12.0bn	12.7bn	
	US$	31.9bn	33.9bn	
per capita	US$	24,146	25,170	
Growth	%	3.0	2.5	
Inflation	%	2.8	0.9	
Def bdgt [a]	D	573m	557m	557m
	US$	1.52bn	1.48bn	
FMA (US)	US$	7.5m	5m	0m
US$1=D		0.38	0.38	

[a] Excludes funds allocated to the Ministry of the Interior

Population 1,410,942

Ethnic groups: Nationals 46%; Asian 45.5%; African 1.5%; other or unspecified 7%

Age	0–14	15–19	20–24	25–29	30–64	65 plus
Male	9.7%	3.8%	5.1%	6.2%	34.3%	1.4%
Female	9.4%	3.2%	3.6%	3.8%	17.8%	1.5%

Capabilities

Bahrain has small but comparatively well-equipped and -trained armed forces. The core role of the military is to protect territorial integrity, although this is fundamentally underpinned by the presence of the US 5th Fleet and Bahrain's membership of the Gulf Cooperation Council (GCC). It has contributed both ground and air units to the Saudi-led coalition of GCC states that intervened in Yemen in 2015 to counter the Houthi-led insurgency – notably units from the Royal Guard. Bahraini forces have suffered combat losses during the operation. The navy has in the past also assisted in the naval blockade. The Royal Bahrain Air Force has also supported the air campaign against ISIS in Syria. As part of a major air-force modernisation, Bahrain announced in late 2017 an intention to buy 16 F-16V fighters and to upgrade its existing F-16C/Ds to that configuration. Upgrade work approved by the US DoD includes the sale of active electronically scanned array radars and SNIPER targeting pods, which should enhance its tactical-combat capabilities. In a major enhancement to Bahrain's air mobility, it has bought two ex-UK C-130J transport aircraft. In late 2017, Bahrain assumed command of CTF-151, marking, according to Combined Maritime Forces command, the first time that a GCC nation has assumed command of a CTF outside the Arabian Gulf.

ACTIVE 8,200 (Army 6,000 Navy 700 Air 1,500)
Paramilitary 11,260

ORGANISATIONS BY SERVICE

Army 6,000
FORCES BY ROLE
SPECIAL FORCES
  1 SF bn

MANOEUVRE
Armoured
1 armd bde(-) (1 recce bn, 2 armd bn)
Mechanised
1 inf bde (2 mech bn, 1 mot bn)
Light
1 (Amiri) gd bn
COMBAT SUPPORT
1 arty bde (1 hvy arty bty, 2 med arty bty, 1 lt arty bty, 1 MRL bty)
1 engr coy
COMBAT SERVICE SUPPORT
1 log coy
1 tpt coy
1 med coy
AIR DEFENCE
1 AD bn (1 ADA bty, 2 SAM bty)
EQUIPMENT BY TYPE
ARMOURED FIGHTING VEHICLES
MBT 180 M60A3
RECCE 22 AML-90
IFV 67: 25 YPR-765 PRI; 42 AIFV-B-C25
APC 203+
  APC (T) 203: 200 M113A2; 3 AIFV-B
  APC (W) *Arma* 6×6
ENGINEERING & MAINTENANCE VEHICLES
ARV 53 *Fahd* 240
ANTI-TANK/ANTI-INFRASTRUCTURE
MSL
  SP 5 AIFV-B-*Milan*; HMMWV with BGM-71A TOW
  MANPATS BGM-71A TOW
RCL 31: **106mm** 25 M40A1; **120mm** 6 MOBAT
ARTILLERY 161
SP 82: **155mm** 20 M109A5; **203mm** 62 M110A2
TOWED 36: **105mm** 8 L118 Light Gun; **155mm** 28 M198
MRL 13: **122mm** 4 SR5; **227mm** 9 M270 MLRS
MOR 30: **81mm** 18: 12 L16; 6 EIMOS; **SP 120mm** 12 M113A2
SURFACE-TO-SURFACE MISSILE LAUNCHERS
SRBM • Conventional MGM-140A ATACMS (launched from M270 MLRS)
AIR DEFENCE
SAM
  Medium-range 6 MIM-23B I-*Hawk*
  Short-range 7 *Crotale*
  Point-defence FIM-92 *Stinger*; RBS-70
GUNS 24: **35mm** 12 Oerlikon; **40mm** 12 L/70

Navy 700

EQUIPMENT BY TYPE
PRINCIPAL SURFACE COMBATANTS 1
  FRIGATES • FFGHM 1 *Sabha* (ex-US *Oliver Hazard Perry*) with 1 Mk13 GMLS with SM-1MR SAM/RGM-84C *Harpoon* AShM, 2 triple 324mm Mk32 ASTT with Mk46 LWT, 1 *Phalanx* Block 1B CIWS, 1 76mm gun (capacity 1 Bo-105 hel)
PATROL AND COASTAL COMBATANTS 12
  CORVETTES • FSG 2 *Al Manama* (GER Lurssen 62m) with 2 twin lnchr with MM40 *Exocet* AShM, 2 76mm guns, 1 hel landing platform
  PCFG 4 *Ahmed el Fateh* (GER Lurssen 45m) with 2 twin lnchr with MM40 *Exocet* AShM, 1 76mm gun
  PB 4: 2 *Al Jarim* (US *Swift* FPB-20); 2 *Al Riffa* (GER Lurssen 38m)
  PBF 2 Mk V SOC
AMPHIBIOUS • LANDING CRAFT 9
  LCU 7: 1 *Loadmaster*; 4 *Mashtan*; 2 *Dinar* (ADSB 42m)
  LCVP 2 *Sea Keeper*

Naval Aviation

EQUIPMENT BY TYPE
HELICOPTERS • TPT • Light 2 Bo-105

Air Force 1,500

FORCES BY ROLE
FIGHTER
2 sqn with F-16C/D *Fighting Falcon*
FIGHTER/GROUND ATTACK
1 sqn with F-5E/F *Tiger* II
TRANSPORT
1 (Royal) flt with B-727; B-747; BAe-146; Gulfstream II; Gulfstream IV; Gulfstream 450; Gulfstream 550; S-92A
TRAINING
1 sqn with *Hawk* Mk129*
1 sqn with T-67M *Firefly*
ATTACK HELICOPTER
2 sqn with AH-1E/F *Cobra*; TAH-1P *Cobra*
TRANSPORT HELICOPTER
1 sqn with Bell 212 (AB-212)
1 sqn with UH-60M *Black Hawk*
1 (VIP) sqn with Bo-105; S-70A *Black Hawk*; UH-60L *Black Hawk*
EQUIPMENT BY TYPE
AIRCRAFT 38 combat capable
  FTR 12: 8 F-5E *Tiger* II; 4 F-5F *Tiger* II
  FGA 20: 16 F-16C Block 40 *Fighting Falcon*; 4 F-16D Block 40 *Fighting Falcon*
  TPT • PAX 10: 1 B-727; 2 B-747; 1 Gulfstream II; 1 Gulfstream IV; 1 Gulfstream 450; 1 Gulfstream 550; 3 BAe-146
  TRG 9: 6 *Hawk* Mk129*; 3 T-67M *Firefly*
HELICOPTERS
  ATK 28: 16 AH-1E *Cobra*; 12 AH-1F *Cobra*
  TPT 27: **Medium** 13: 3 S-70A *Black Hawk*; 1 S-92A (VIP); 1 UH-60L *Black Hawk*; 8 UH-60M *Black Hawk*; **Light** 14: 11 Bell 212 (AB-212); 3 Bo-105
  TRG 6 TAH-1P *Cobra*
AIR-LAUNCHED MISSILES
  AAM • IR AIM-9P *Sidewinder*; SARH AIM-7 *Sparrow*; ARH AIM-120B/C AMRAAM
  ASM AGM-65D/G *Maverick*; some TOW
BOMBS
  Laser-guided GBU-10/12 *Paveway* II

Paramilitary ε11,260

Police 9,000
Ministry of Interior

EQUIPMENT BY TYPE
ARMOURED FIGHTING VEHICLES
  RECCE 8 S52 *Shorland*
  APC • APC (W) Otokar ISV; *Cobra*
HELICOPTERS
  MRH 2 Bell 412 *Twin Huey*
  ISR 2 Hughes 500
  TPT • Light 1 Bo-105

National Guard ε2,000
FORCES BY ROLE
MANOEUVRE
  Other
  3 paramilitary bn
EQUIPMENT BY TYPE
ARMOURED FIGHTING VEHICLES
  APC • APC (W) *Arma* 6×6; *Cobra*

Coast Guard ε260
Ministry of Interior
PATROL AND COASTAL COMBATANTS 52
  PBF 23: 2 *Ares* 18; 4 *Jaris*; 6 *Saham*; 6 *Fajr*; 5 *Jarada*
  PB 29: 6 *Haris*; 1 *Al Muharraq*; 10 *Deraa* (of which 4 *Halmatic* 20, 2 *Souter* 20, 4 *Rodman* 20); 10 *Saif* (of which 4 *Fairey Sword*, 6 *Halmatic* 160); 2 *Hawar*
AMPHIBIOUS • LANDING CRAFT • LCU 1 *Loadmaster* II

DEPLOYMENT

PERSIAN GULF
Combined Maritime Forces • CTF-152: 1 PCFG

SAUDI ARABIA
Operation Restoring Hope 250; 1 SF gp; 6 F-16C *Fighting Falcon*

FOREIGN FORCES

Saudi Arabia GCC (SANG): Peninsula Shield ε1,500
United Kingdom Air Force 80: 1 naval base
United States US Central Command 5,000; 1 HQ (5th Fleet); 2 AD bty with MIM-104E/F *Patriot* PAC-2/3

Egypt EGY

Egyptian Pound E£		2016	2017	2018
GDP	E£	2.71tr	3.47tr	
	US$	332bn	n.k.	
per capita	US$	3,685	n.k.	
Growth	%	4.3	4.1	
Inflation	%	10.2	23.5	
Def bdgt	E£	43.2bn	47.1bn	51.9bn
	US$	5.30bn	2.67bn	
FMA (US)	US$	1.3bn	1.3bn	1.3bn
US$1=E£		8.15	17.65	

Population 97,041,072

Age	0–14	15–19	20–24	25–29	30–64	65 plus
Male	17.2%	4.8%	4.8%	4.8%	17.2%	2.0%
Female	16.0%	4.5%	4.6%	4.6%	16.8%	2.1%

Capabilities

Territorial integrity and internal security are the two principal tasks for the Egyptian armed forces, although emphasis has recently been on the latter: the armed forces have been fighting ISIS-affiliated groups in the northern Sinai for several years. Notwithstanding this, the military is also undertaking an equipment-recapitalisation programme, significant elements of which have been sourced from Russia. Deliveries of the MiG-29M/M2 multi-role fighter aircraft, the Ka-52 attack helicopter and the S-300V4 SAM system began in 2017. Deliveries of the *Rafale* to the air force continued, while Egypt and France appeared close to concluding a deal for a further 12 aircraft in late 2017. Egypt also hosted its first joint exercise with Russia in 2016, followed by a comparatively large-scale joint airborne exercise in 2017. The re-equipment programme has reportedly been characterised by President Al-Sisi as allowing the country to be able to address regional security issues. Egypt regularly exercises its two new *Mistral*-class amphibious-assault vessels. These have the potential to support future regional deployments, though as yet neither vessel has integrated defences or a dedicated air wing. The delivery of the first two of four Type-209/1400 submarines from Germany serves to further highlight the range of Egypt's ongoing naval recapitalisation.

ACTIVE 438,500 (Army 310,000 Navy 18,500 Air 30,000 Air Defence Command 80,000) **Paramilitary 397,000**

Conscription liability 12 months–3 years (followed by refresher training over a period of up to 9 years)

RESERVE 479,000 (Army 375,000 Navy 14,000 Air 20,000 Air Defence 70,000)

ORGANISATIONS BY SERVICE

Army 90,000–120,000; 190,000–220,000 conscript (total 310,000)

FORCES BY ROLE
SPECIAL FORCES
5 cdo gp
1 counter-terrorist unit
MANOEUVRE
Armoured
4 armd div (2 armd bde, 1 mech bde, 1 arty bde)
4 indep armd bde
1 Republican Guard bde
Mechanised
8 mech div (1 armd bde, 2 mech bde, 1 arty bde)
4 indep mech bde
Light
1 inf div
2 indep inf bde
Air Manoeuvre
2 air mob bde
1 para bde
SURFACE-TO-SURFACE MISSILE
1 SRBM bde with FROG-7
1 SRBM bde with *Scud*-B
COMBAT SUPPORT
15 arty bde
6 engr bde (3 engr bn)
2 spec ops engr bn
6 salvage engr bn
24 MP bn
18 sigs bn
COMBAT SERVICE SUPPORT
36 log bn
27 med bn

EQUIPMENT BY TYPE
ARMOURED FIGHTING VEHICLES
MBT 2,460: 1,110 M1A1 *Abrams*; 300 M60A1; 850 M60A3; 200 T-62 (260 *Ramses* II (mod T-54/55); 840 T-54/T-55; 300 T-62 all in store)
RECCE 412: 300 BRDM-2; 112 *Commando Scout*
IFV 405+: 390 YPR-765 25mm; 15+ BMP-1 (205 BMP-1 in store)
APC 4,701+
  APC (T) 2,700: 2,000 M113A2/YPR-765 (incl variants); 500 BTR-50; 200 OT-62
  APC (W) 1,560: 250 BMR-600P; 250 BTR-60; 410 *Fahd*-30/TH 390 *Fahd*; 650 *Walid*
  PPV 441+: 92 *Caiman*; some REVA III; some REVA V LWB; 349 RG-33L (incl 89 amb)
  AUV *Panthera* T6; *Sherpa Light Scout*
ENGINEERING & MAINTENANCE VEHICLES
ARV 607+: *Fahd* 240; BMR 3560.55; 12 *Maxxpro* ARV; 220 M88A1; 90 M88A2; M113 ARV; 45 M578; T-54/55 ARV
VLB KMM; MTU; MTU-20
MW *Aardvark* JFSU Mk4
ANTI-TANK/ANTI-INFRASTRUCTURE • MSL
SP 352+: 52 M901, 300 YPR-765 PRAT; HMMWV with TOW-2
MANPATS 9K11 *Malyutka* (AT-3 *Sagger*) (incl BRDM-2); HJ-73; *Milan*; TOW-2
ARTILLERY 4,468
SP 492+: **122mm** 124+: 124 SP 122; D-30 mod; **130mm** M-46 mod; **155mm** 368: 164 M109A2; 204 M109A5
TOWED 962: **122mm** 526: 190 D-30M; 36 M-1931/37; 300 M-30; **130mm** 420 M-46; **155mm** 16 GH-52
MRL 450: **122mm** 356: 96 BM-11; 60 BM-21; 50 Sakr-10; 50 Sakr-18; 100 Sakr-36; **130mm** 36 K136 *Kooryong*; **140mm** 32 BM-14; **227mm** 26 M270 MLRS; **240mm** (48 BM-24 in store)
MOR 2,564: **81mm** 50 M125A2; **82mm** 500; **SP 107mm** 100: 65 M106A1; 35 M106A2; **120mm** 1,848: 1,800 M-1943; 48 Brandt; **SP 120mm** 36 M1064A3; **160mm** 30 M-160
SURFACE-TO-SURFACE MISSILE LAUNCHERS
SRBM • Conventional 42+: 9 FROG-7; 24 *Sakr*-80; 9 *Scud*-B
RADAR • LAND AN/TPQ-36 *Firefinder*; AN/TPQ-37 *Firefinder* (arty/mor)
UNMANNED AERIAL VEHICLES
ISR • Medium R4E-50 *Skyeye*; ASN-209
AIR DEFENCE
SAM
  Point-defence 96+: 50 M1097 *Avenger*; 26 M48 *Chaparral*; 20 9K31 *Strela*-1 (SA-9 *Gaskin*); *Ayn al-Saqr*; 9K32 *Strela*-2 (SA-7 *Grail*)‡; FIM-92 *Stinger*; 9K38 *Igla* (SA-18 *Grouse*)
GUNS
  SP 205: **23mm** 165: 45 *Sinai*-23; 120 ZSU-23-4; **57mm** 40 ZSU-57-2
  TOWED 700: **14.5mm** 300 ZPU-4; **23mm** 200 ZU-23-2; **57mm** 200 S-60

Navy ε8,500 (incl 2,000 Coast Guard); 10,000 conscript (total 18,500)

EQUIPMENT BY TYPE
SUBMARINES • TACTICAL • SSK 6
4 *Romeo*† (PRC Type-033) with 8 single 533mm TT with UGM-84C *Harpoon* AShM/Mk37 HWT (being replaced by Type-209/1400)
2 Type-209/1400 with 8 single 533mm TT with DM2A4/*SeaHake* Mod 4 HWT
PRINCIPAL SURFACE COMBATANTS 9
DESTROYERS • DDGHM 1 *Tahya Misr* (FRA *Aquitaine*) with 2 quad lnchr with MM40 *Exocet* Block 3 AShM, 2 octuple A43 VLS with *Aster* 15 SAM, 2 twin B515 324mm ASTT with MU90 LWT, 1 76mm gun (capacity 1 med hel)
FRIGATES 9
  FFGHM 5:
    4 *Alexandria* (ex-US *Oliver Hazard Perry*) with 1 Mk13 GMLS with RGM-84C *Harpoon* AShM/SM-1MP SAM, 2 triple 324mm ASTT with Mk 46 LWT, 1 *Phalanx* CIWS, 1 76mm gun (capacity 2 SH-2G *Super Seasprite* ASW hel)
    1 *El Fateh* (*Gowind* 2500) with 2 quad lnchrs with MM40 *Exocet* Blk 3 AShM, 1 16-cell VLS with VL-MICA SAM, 2 triple 324mm ASTT with MU90 LWT, 1 76mm gun (capacity 1 med hel)
  FFGH 2 *Damyat* (ex-US *Knox*) with 1 octuple Mk16 GMLS with RGM-84C *Harpoon* AShM/ASROC, 2 twin 324mm Mk 32 TT with Mk 46 LWT, 1 *Phalanx* CIWS, 1 127mm gun (capacity 1 SH-2G *Super Seasprite* ASW hel)

FFG 2 *Najim Al Zaffer* (PRC *Jianghu* I) with 2 twin lnchr with HY-2 (CH-SS-N-2 *Safflower*) AShM, 4 RBU 1200 A/S mor, 2 twin 57mm guns

PATROL AND COASTAL COMBATANTS 61
  CORVETTES 3
    FSGM 2 *Abu Qir* (ESP *Descubierta* – 1†) with 2 quad Mk141 lnchr with RGM-84C *Harpoon* AShM, 1 octuple *Albatros* lnchr with *Aspide* SAM, 2 triple Mk32 324mm ASTT with *Sting Ray* LWT, 1 twin 375mm A/S mor, 1 76mm gun
    FS 1 *Shabab Misr* (ex-RoK *Po Hang*) with 2 76mm guns
  PCFGM 4:
    4 *Ezzat* (US *Ambassador* IV) with 2 quad lnchr with RGM-84L *Harpoon* Block II AShM, 1 21-cell Mk49 lnchr with RAM Block 1A SAM, 1 Mk15 Mod 21 Block 1B *Phalanx* CIWS 1 76mm gun
  PCFG 12:
    1 *Molnya* (RUS *Tarantul* IV) with 2 twin lnchr with 3M80E *Moskit* (SS-N-22 *Sunburn*), 2 AK630 CIWS, 1 76mm gun
    6 *Ramadan* with 4 single lnchr with *Otomat* MkII AShM, 1 76mm gun
    5 *Tiger* with 2 twin lnchr with MM38 *Exocet* AShM, 1 76mm gun
  PCC 5:
    5 *Al-Nour* (ex-PRC *Hainan* – 3 more in reserve†) with 2 triple 324mm TT, 4 RBU 1200 A/S mor, 2 twin 57mm guns
  PBFG 17:
    4 *Hegu* (PRC – *Komar* type) with 2 single lnchr with SY-1 AShM (2 additional vessels in reserve)
    5 *October* (FSU *Komar* – 1†) with 2 single lnchr with *Otomat* MkII AShM (1 additional vessel in reserve)
    8 *Osa* I (ex-YUG – 3†) with 1 9K32 *Strela*-2 (SA-N-5 *Grail*) SAM (manual aiming), 4 single lnchr with P-15 *Termit* (SS-N-2A *Styx*) AShM
  PBFM 4:
    4 *Shershen* (FSU) with 1 9K32 *Strela*-2 (SA-N-5 *Grail*) SAM (manual aiming), 1 12-tube BM-24 MRL
  PBF 10:
    6 *Kaan* 20 (TUR MRTP 20)
    4 *Osa* II (ex-FIN)
  PB 6:
    4 *Shanghai* II (PRC)
    2 *Shershen* (FSU – 1†) with 4 single 533mm TT, 1 8-tube BM-21 MRL

MINE WARFARE • MINE COUNTERMEASURES 14
  MHC 5: 2 *Al Siddiq* (ex-US *Osprey*); 3 *Dat Assawari* (US Swiftships)
  MSI 2 *Safaga* (US Swiftships)
  MSO 7: 3 *Assiout* (FSU T-43 class); 4 *Aswan* (FSU *Yurka*)

AMPHIBIOUS 20
  PRINCIPAL AMPHIBIOUS SHIPS • LHD 2 *Gamal Abdel Nasser* (FRA *Mistral*) (capacity 16 med hel; 2 LCT or 4 LCM; 13 MBTs; 50 AFVs; 450 troops)
  LANDING SHIPS • LSM 3 *Polnochny* A (FSU) (capacity 6 MBT; 180 troops)
  LANDING CRAFT 15:
    LCM 4 CTM NG
    LCT 2 EDA-R
    LCU 9 *Vydra* (FSU) (capacity either 3 AMX-30 MBT or 100 troops)

LOGISTICS AND SUPPORT 24
  AOT 7 *Ayeda* (FSU *Toplivo* – 1 additional in reserve)
  AE 1 *Halaib* (ex-GER *Westerwald*-class)
  AKR 3 *Al Hurreya*
  AR 1 *Shaledin* (ex-GER *Luneberg*-class)
  ARS 2 *Al Areesh*
  ATF 5 *Al Maks*† (FSU *Okhtensky*)
  AX 5: 1 *El Fateh*† (ex-UK 'Z' class); 1 *El Horriya* (also used as the presidential yacht); 1 *Al Kousser*; 1 *Intishat*; 1 other

Coastal Defence

Army tps, Navy control
EQUIPMENT BY TYPE
COASTAL DEFENCE
  ARTY 100mm; **130mm** SM-4-1; **152mm**
  AShM 4K87 (SS-C-2B *Samlet*); *Otomat* MkII

Naval Aviation

All aircraft operated by Air Force
AIRCRAFT • TPT • Light 4 Beech 1900C (maritime surveillance)
HELICOPTERS
  ASW 10 SH-2G *Super Seasprite* with Mk 46 LWT
  MRH 5 SA342L *Gazelle*
UNMANNED AERIAL VEHICLES
  ISR • Light 2 *Camcopter* 5.1

Coast Guard 2,000

EQUIPMENT BY TYPE
PATROL AND COASTAL COMBATANTS 79
  PBF 14: 6 *Crestitalia*; 5 *Swift Protector*; 3 *Peterson*
  PB 65: 5 *Nisr*; 12 *Sea Spectre* MkIII; 15 *Swiftships*; 21 *Timsah*; 3 Type-83; 9 *Peterson*

Air Force 30,000 (incl 10,000 conscript)

FORCES BY ROLE
FIGHTER
  1 sqn with F-16A/B *Fighting Falcon*
  8 sqn with F-16C/D *Fighting Falcon*
  1 sqn with J-7
  3 sqn with MiG-21 *Fishbed*/MiG-21U *Mongol* A
  2 sqn with *Mirage* 5D/E
  1 sqn with *Mirage* 2000B/C
FIGHTER/GROUND ATTACK
  1 sqn with *Mirage* 5E2
  1 sqn (forming) with *Rafale* DM
  1 sqn (forming) with MiG-29M/M2 *Fulcrum*
ANTI-SUBMARINE WARFARE
  1 sqn with SH-2G *Super Seasprite*
MARITIME PATROL
  1 sqn with Beech 1900C
ELECTRONIC WARFARE
  1 sqn with Beech 1900 (ELINT); *Commando* Mk2E (ECM)
ELECTRONIC WARFARE/TRANSPORT
  1 sqn with C-130H/VC-130H *Hercules*
AIRBORNE EARLY WARNING
  1 sqn with E-2C *Hawkeye*

SEARCH & RESCUE
  1 unit with AW139
TRANSPORT
  1 sqn with An-74TK-200A
  1 sqn with C-130H/C-130H-30 *Hercules*
  1 sqn with C295M
  1 sqn with DHC-5D *Buffalo*
  1 sqn with B-707-366C; B-737-100; Beech 200 *Super King Air*; *Falcon* 20; Gulfstream III; Gulfstream IV; Gulfstream IV-SP
TRAINING
  1 sqn with *Alpha Jet**
  1 sqn with DHC-5 *Buffalo*
  3 sqn with EMB-312 *Tucano*
  1 sqn with Grob 115EG
  ε6 sqn with K-8 *Karakorum**
  1 sqn with L-39 *Albatros*; L-59E *Albatros**
ATTACK HELICOPTER
  2 sqn with AH-64D *Apache*
  2 sqn with SA-342K *Gazelle* (with HOT)
  1 sqn with SA-342L *Gazelle*
TRANSPORT HELICOPTER
  1 sqn with CH-47C/D *Chinook*
  1 sqn with Mi-8
  1 sqn with Mi-8/Mi-17-V1 *Hip*
  1 sqn with S-70 *Black Hawk*; UH-60A/L *Black Hawk*
UAV
  Some sqn with R4E-50 *Skyeye*; Teledyne-Ryan 324 *Scarab*; *Wing Loong* (GJ-1)*

EQUIPMENT BY TYPE
AIRCRAFT 557 combat capable
  FTR 62: 26 F-16A *Fighting Falcon*; 6 F-16B *Fighting Falcon*; ε30 J-7
  FGA 298+: 139 F-16C *Fighting Falcon*; 37 F-16D *Fighting Falcon*; 3 *Mirage* 2000B; 15 *Mirage* 2000C; 36 *Mirage* 5D/E; 12 *Mirage* 5E2; ε40 MiG-21 *Fishbed*/MiG-21U *Mongol* A; 4+ MiG-29M/M2 *Fulcrum*; 6 *Rafale* DM, 5 *Rafale* EM
  ELINT 2 VC-130H *Hercules*
  ISR 6 *Mirage* 5R (5SDR)*
  AEW&C 7 E-2C *Hawkeye*
  TPT 77: Medium 24: 21 C-130H *Hercules*; 3 C-130H-30 *Hercules*; Light 42: 3 An-74TK-200A; 1 Beech 200 *King Air*; 4 Beech 1900 (ELINT); 4 Beech 1900C; 21 C295M; 9 DHC-5D *Buffalo* (being withdrawn) PAX 11: 1 B-707-366C; 3 *Falcon* 20; 2 Gulfstream III; 1 Gulfstream IV; 4 Gulfstream IV-SP
  TRG 329: 36 *Alpha Jet**; 54 EMB-312 *Tucano*; 74 Grob 115EG; 120 K-8 *Karakorum**; 10 L-39 *Albatros*; 35 L-59E*
HELICOPTERS
  ATK 48: 45 AH-64D *Apache*; 3 Ka-52A *Hokum* B
  ASW 10 SH-2G *Super Seasprite* (opcon Navy)
  ELINT 4 *Commando* Mk2E (ECM)
  MRH 72: 2 AW139 (SAR); 65 SA342K *Gazelle* (some with HOT); 5 SA342L *Gazelle* (opcon Navy)
  TPT 96: Heavy 19: 3 CH-47C *Chinook*; 16 CH-47D *Chinook*; Medium 77: 2 AS-61; 24 *Commando* (of which 3 VIP); 40 Mi-8T *Hip*; 3 Mi-17-1V *Hip*; 4 S-70 *Black Hawk* (VIP); 4 UH-60L *Black Hawk* (VIP)
  TRG 17 UH-12E
UNMANNED AERIAL VEHICLES
  CISR • Heavy 4+ *Wing Loong* (GJ-1)

ISR • Medium R4E-50 *Skyeye*
AIR LAUNCHED MISSILES
  AAM • IR R-3 (AA-2 *Atoll*)‡; AIM-9M/P *Sidewinder*; R-550 *Magic*; IIR *Mica* IR; ARH *Mica* RF; SARH AIM-7E/F/M *Sparrow*; R-530
  ASM AGM-65A/D/F/G *Maverick*; AGM-114F/K *Hellfire*; AS-30L; HOT
  AShM AGM-84 *Harpoon*; AM39 *Exocet*;
  ARM *Armat*; Kh-25MP (AS-12 *Kegler*)
BOMBS
  Laser-guided GBU-10/12 *Paveway* II

Air Defence Command 80,000 conscript; 70,000 reservists (total 150,000)

FORCES BY ROLE
AIR DEFENCE
  5 AD div (geographically based) (total: 12 SAM bty with M48 *Chaparral*, 12 radar bn, 12 ADA bde (total: 100 ADA bn), 12 SAM bty with MIM-23B I-*Hawk*, 14 SAM bty with *Crotale*, 18 AD bn with RIM-7M *Sea Sparrow* with *Skyguard*/GDF-003 with *Skyguard*, 110 SAM bn with S-125 *Pechora-M* (SA-3A *Goa*); 2K12 *Kub* (SA-6 *Gainful*); S-75M *Volkhov* (SA-2 *Guideline*))

EQUIPMENT BY TYPE
AIR DEFENCE
  SAM 812+
    Long-range S-300V4 (SA-23)
    Medium-range 612+: 40+ *Buk*-M1-2/M2E (SA-11/SA-17); 78+ MIM-23B I-*Hawk*; 282 S-75M *Volkhov* (SA-2 *Guideline*); 212+ S-125 *Pechora-M* (SA-3A *Goa*)
    Short-range 150+: 56+ 2K12 *Kub* (SA-6 *Gainful*); 10 9K331M *Tor*-M1 (SA-15 *Gauntlet*); 24+ *Crotale*; 80 RIM-7M *Sea Sparrow* with *Skyguard*
    Point-defence 50+ M48 *Chaparral*
  GUNS 1,646+
    SP • 23mm 266+: 36+ *Sinai*-23 with *Ayn al-Saqr* MANPAD; 230 ZSU-23-4
    TOWED 1,380: 35mm 80 GDF-003 with *Skyguard*; 57mm 600 S-60; 85mm 400 M-1939 (KS-12); 100mm 300 KS-19

Paramilitary ε397,000 active

Central Security Forces ε325,000
Ministry of Interior; includes conscripts
ARMOURED FIGHTING VEHICLES
  APC • APC (W) *Walid*

National Guard ε60,000
Lt wpns only
FORCES BY ROLE
MANOEUVRE
  Other
    8 paramilitary bde (cadre) (3 paramilitary bn)
EQUIPMENT BY TYPE
  ARMOURED FIGHTING VEHICLES APC • APC (W) 250 *Walid*

Border Guard Forces ε12,000
Ministry of Interior; lt wpns only

FORCES BY ROLE
MANOEUVRE
Other
18 Border Guard regt

DEPLOYMENT

CENTRAL AFRICAN REPUBLIC
UN • MINUSCA 1,014; 5 obs; 1 inf bn; 1 tpt coy

DEMOCRATIC REPUBLIC OF THE CONGO
UN • MONUSCO 154; 19 obs; 1 SF coy

LIBERIA
UN • UNMIL 2 obs

MALI
UN • MINUSMA 74; 3 obs; 1 MP coy

SOUTH SUDAN
UN • UNMISS 1; 3 obs

SUDAN
UN • UNAMID 847; 18 obs; 1 inf bn

UNITED ARAB EMIRATES
Operation Restoring Hope 6 F-16C *Fighting Falcon*

WESTERN SAHARA
UN • MINURSO 23 obs

FOREIGN FORCES

Australia MFO (*Operation Mazurka*) 25
Canada MFO 70
Colombia MFO 354; 1 inf bn
Czech Republic MFO 18; 1 C295M
Fiji MFO 203; elm 1 inf bn
France MFO 1
Italy MFO 75; 3 PB
New Zealand MFO 26; 1 trg unit; 1 tpt unit
Norway MFO 3
United Kingdom MFO 2
United States MFO 410; elm 1 ARNG inf bn; 1 ARNG spt bn (1 EOD coy, 1 medical coy, 1 hel coy)
Uruguay MFO 58 1 engr/tpt unit

Iran IRN

Iranian Rial r		2016	2017	2018
GDP	r	12,723tr	14,522tr	
	US$	404bn	428bn	
per capita	US$	5,027	5,252	
Growth	%	12.5	3.5	
Inflation	%	9.0	10.5	
Def bdgt	r	ε499tr	ε544tr	
	US$	ε15.9bn	ε16.0	
US$1=r		31,457.39	33,955.668	

Population 82,021,564

Ethnic groups: Persian 51%; Azeri 24%; Gilaki/Mazandarani 8%; Kurdish 7%; Arab 3%; Lur 2%; Baloch 2%; Turkmen 2%

Age	0–14	15–19	20–24	25–29	30–64	65 plus
Male	12.4%	3.5%	4.0%	5.4%	22.9%	2.5%
Female	11.8%	3.3%	4.8%	5.1%	22.4%	2.8%

Capabilities

Iran continues to rely on a mix of ageing combat equipment, reasonably well-trained regular and Islamic Revolutionary Guard Corps (IRGC) forces, and its ballistic-missile inventory to underpin the security of the regime. The IRGC, including senior military leaders, has been increasingly involved in the civil war in Syria, supporting President Assad's regular and irregular forces. It was first deployed to Syria in an 'advisory' role in 2012; deployments of the army began in 2016. Iran's role in Syria escalated with ballistic-missile strikes in June, in response to attacks on sites in Tehran claimed by ISIS. Further development activity in this area was highlighted by tests of a missile and launch vehicle, as well as the parading in September of the new 2,000km-range *Khorramshahr* missile. The IRGC's Quds Force is a principal element of Iran's military power abroad, while elements of the Basij militia also play a foreign role (as well as operating domestically) – as do Iranian-supported contingents of other nationalities. The armed forces continue to struggle with an ageing inventory of primary combat equipment that ingenuity and asymmetric-warfare techniques can only partially offset. In regional terms, Iran has a well-developed defence-industrial base, which has displayed the capacity to support and sustain equipment when access to the original manufacturer is blocked. Key sectors continue to develop, including missiles and guided weapons, but Iran's defence industry is still incapable of meeting the armed forces' need for modern weapons systems. Iran will increasingly seek these through imports; co-development and technology transfer will likely also feature in major deals. Although the Trump administration decertified Iranian compliance with the 2015 nuclear agreement with the P5+1 and the European Union, for now the agreement still opens the way for Iran to revamp its equipment inventory. China and Russia are potentially major suppliers, although sales of conventional systems remain embargoed for a five-year period after the agreement's 'adoption day'. Following the nuclear agreement, Tehran and Moscow re-engaged on the sale of a version of the S-300 long-range surface-to-air missile system; what is believed to be the S-300PMU2 (SA-20 *Gargoyle*) variant has now been introduced into service.

ACTIVE 523,000 (Army 350,000 Islamic Revolutionary Guard Corps 125,000 Navy 18,000 Air 30,000) Paramilitary 40,000

Armed Forces General Staff coordinates two parallel organisations: the regular armed forces and the Islamic Revolutionary Guard Corps

Conscript liability 21 months (reported, with variations depending on location in which service is performed)

RESERVE 350,000 (Army 350,000, ex-service volunteers)

ORGANISATIONS BY SERVICE

Army 130,000; 220,000 conscript (total 350,000)
FORCES BY ROLE
5 corps-level regional HQ
COMMAND
  1 cdo div HQ
  4 armd div HQ
  2 mech div HQ
  4 inf div HQ
SPECIAL FORCES
  1 cdo div (3 cdo bde)
  6 cdo bde
  1 SF bde
MANOEUVRE
  Armoured
    8 armd bde
  Mechanised
    14 mech bde
  Light
    12 inf bde
  Air Manoeuvre
    1 AB bde
  Aviation
    Some avn gp
COMBAT SUPPORT
  5 arty gp
EQUIPMENT BY TYPE
Totals incl those held by IRGC Ground Forces. Some equipment serviceability in doubt
ARMOURED FIGHTING VEHICLES
  MBT 1,513+: 480 T-72S; 150 M60A1; 75+ T-62; 100 Chieftain Mk3/Mk5; 540 T-54/T-55/Type-59/*Safir*-74; 168 M47/M48; *Zulfiqar*
  LT TK 80+: 80 *Scorpion*; *Towsan*
  RECCE 35 EE-9 *Cascavel*
  IFV 610+: 210 BMP-1; 400 BMP-2 with 9K111 *Fagot* (AT-4 *Spigot*); BMT-2 *Cobra*
  APC 640+
    APC (T) 340: 140 *Boragh* with 9K111 *Fagot* (AT-4 *Spigot*); 200 M113
    APC (W) 300+: 300 BTR-50/BTR-60; *Rakhsh*

ENGINEERING & MAINTENANCE VEHICLES
  ARV 20+: BREM-1 reported; 20 *Chieftain* ARV; M578; T-54/55 ARV reported
  VLB 15: 15 *Chieftain* AVLB **MW** *Taftan* 1
ANTI-TANK/ANTI-INFRASTRUCTURE
  MSL • **MANPATS** 9K11 *Malyutka* (AT-3 *Sagger*/I-*Raad*); 9K111 *Fagot* (AT-4 *Spigot*); 9K111-1 *Konkurs* (AT-5 *Spandrel*/*Towsan*-1); *Saeqhe* 1; *Saeqhe* 2; *Toophan*; *Toophan* 2
  RCL 200+: **75mm** M20; **82mm** B-10; **106mm** ε200 M40; **107mm** B-11
ARTILLERY 6,798+
  SP 292+: **122mm** 60+: 60 2S1 *Gvozdika*; *Raad*-1 (*Thunder* 1); **155mm** 150+: 150 M109; *Raad*-2 (*Thunder* 2); **170mm** 30 M-1978; **175mm** 22 M107; **203mm** 30 M110
  TOWED 2,030+; **105mm** 150: 130 M101A1; 20 M-56; **122mm** 640: 540 D-30, 100 Type-54 (M-30); **130mm** 985 M-46; **152mm** 30 D-20; **155mm** 205: 120 GHN-45; 70 M114; 15 Type-88 WAC-21; **203mm** 20 M115
  MRL 1,476+: **107mm** 1,300: 700 Type-63; 600 HASEB *Fadjr* 1; **122mm** 157: 7 BM-11; 100 BM-21 *Grad*; 50 *Arash*/*Hadid*/*Noor*; **240mm** 19+: ε10 *Fadjr* 3; 9 M-1985; **330mm** *Fadjr* 5
  MOR 3,000: **81mm**; **82mm**; **107mm** M30; **120mm** M-65
SURFACE-TO-SURFACE MISSILE LAUNCHERS
  SRBM • **Conventional** ε30 CH-SS-8 (175 msl); *Shahin*-1/*Shahin*-2; *Nazeat*; *Oghab*
AIRCRAFT • **TPT** 17 **Light** 16: 10 Cessna 185; 2 F-27 *Friendship*; 4 *Turbo Commander* 690; **PAX** 1 *Falcon* 20
HELICOPTERS
  ATK 50 AH-1J *Cobra*
  TPT 167: **Heavy** 20 CH-47C *Chinook*; **Medium** 69: 49 Bell 214; 20 Mi-171; **Light** 78: 68 Bell 205A (AB-205A); 10 Bell 206 *Jet Ranger* (AB-206)
UNMANNED AERIAL VEHICLES
  CISR • **Medium** *Shahed* 129
  ISR • **Medium** *Mohajer* 3/4; **Light** *Mohajer* 2; *Ababil*
AIR DEFENCE
  SAM
    Short-range FM-80
    Point-defence 9K36 *Strela*-3 (SA-14 *Gremlin*); 9K32 *Strela*-2 (SA-7 *Grail*)‡; *Misaq* 1 (QW-1 *Vanguard*); *Misaq* 2 (QW-18); 9K338 *Igla*-S (SA-24 *Grinch*) (reported); HN-5A
  GUNS 1,122
    SP 180: **23mm** 100 ZSU-23-4; **57mm** 80 ZSU-57-2
    TOWED 942+: **14.5mm** ZPU-2; ZPU-4; **23mm** 300 ZU-23-2; **35mm** 92 *Skyguard*; **37mm** M-1939; **40mm** 50 L/70; **57mm** 200 S-60; **85mm** 300 M-1939

Islamic Revolutionary Guard Corps 125,000+

Islamic Revolutionary Guard Corps Ground Forces 100,000+

Controls Basij paramilitary forces. Lightly manned in peacetime. Primary role: internal security; secondary role: external defence, in conjunction with regular armed forces

FORCES BY ROLE
COMMAND
  31 provincial corps HQ (2 in Tehran)

SPECIAL FORCES
  3 spec ops div
MANOEUVRE
  Armoured
    2 armd div
    3 armd bde
  Light
    8+ inf div
    5+ inf bde
  Air Manoeuvre
    1 AB bde

Islamic Revolutionary Guard Corps Naval Forces 20,000+ (incl 5,000 Marines)

FORCES BY ROLE
COMBAT SUPPORT
  Some arty bty
  Some AShM bty with HY-2 (CH-SSC-3 *Seersucker*) AShM

EQUIPMENT BY TYPE
In addition to the vessels listed, the IRGC operates a substantial number of patrol boats with a full-load displacement below 10 tonnes, including ε40 *Boghammar*-class vessels and small *Bavar*-class wing-in-ground effect air vehicles
PATROL AND COASTAL COMBATANTS 126
  PBFG 56:
    5 C14 with 2 twin lnchr with C-701 (*Kosar*)/C-704 (*Nasr*) AShM
    10 Mk13 with 2 single lnchr with C-704 (*Nasr*) AShM, 2 single 324mm TT
    10 *Thondor* (PRC *Houdong*) with 2 twin lnchr with C-802A (*Ghader*) AShM, 2 twin AK230 CIWS
    25 *Peykaap* II (IPS-16 mod) with 2 single lnchr with C-701 (*Kosar*) AShM/C-704 (*Nasr*), 2 single 324mm TT
    6 *Zolfaghar* (*Peykaap* III/IPS-16 mod) with 2 single lnchr with C-701 (*Kosar*)/C-704 (*Nasr*) AShM
  PBFT 15 *Peykaap* I (IPS -16) with 2 single 324mm TT
  PBF 35: 15 *Kashdom* II; 10 *Tir* (IPS-18); ε10 *Pashe* (MIG-G-1900)
  PB ε20 *Ghaem*
AMPHIBIOUS
  LANDING SHIPS • LST 3 *Hormuz* 24 (*Hejaz* design for commercial use)
  LANDING CRAFT • LCT 2 *Hormuz* 21 (minelaying capacity)
  LOGISTICS AND SUPPORT • AP 3 *Naser*
  COASTAL DEFENCE • AShM C-701 (*Kosar*); C-704 (*Nasr*); C-802; HY-2 (CH-SSC-3 *Seersucker*)
HELICOPTERS
  TPT 5+: **Medium** 5 Mi-171 *Hip*; **Light** some Bell 206 (AB-206) *Jet Ranger*

Islamic Revolutionary Guard Corps Marines 5,000+

FORCES BY ROLE
MANOEUVRE
  Amphibious
    1 marine bde

Islamic Revolutionary Guard Corps Air Force
Controls Iran's strategic-missile force
FORCES BY ROLE
MISSILE
  ε1 bde with *Shahab*-1/2
  ε1 bn with *Shahab*-3; *Ghadr*-1; *Sajjil*-2 (in devt)
EQUIPMENT BY TYPE
SURFACE-TO-SURFACE MISSILE LAUNCHERS
  MRBM • **Conventional** 22+: 12+ *Shahab*-3/*Ghadr*-1 (mobile); 10 *Shahab*-3/*Ghadr*-1 (silo); some *Sajjil*-2 (in devt)
  SRBM • **Conventional** 18+: some *Fateh* 110; 12–18 *Shahab*-1/2 (ε200–300 msl); some *Zelzal*
UNMANNED AERIAL VEHICLES
  CISR • **Medium** *Shahed* 129

Navy 18,000
HQ at Bandar Abbas
EQUIPMENT BY TYPE
In addition to the vessels listed, the Iranian Navy operates a substantial number of patrol boats with a full-load displacement below 10 tonnes
SUBMARINES 21
  TACTICAL 21
    SSK 3 *Taregh* (RUS *Paltus* Project-877EKM) with 6 single 533mm TT
    SSC 1 *Fateh* (in trials)
    SSW 17: 16 *Qadir* with 2 single 533mm TT with *Valfajar* HWT (additional vessels in build); 1 *Nahang*
PATROL AND COASTAL COMBATANTS 67 (+ε50 small craft under 10 tonnes)
  CORVETTES 7
    FSGM 2 *Jamaran* (UK Vosper Mk 5 derivative – 1 more undergoing sea trials) with 2 twin lnchr with C-802 (*Noor*) (CH-SS-N-8 *Saccade*) AShM, 2 single lnchr with SM-1 SAM, 2 triple 324mm Mk32 ASTT, 1 76mm gun, 1 hel landing platform
    FSG 5:
      3 *Alvand* (UK Vosper Mk 5) with 2 twin lnchr with C-802 (CH-SS-N-8 *Saccade*) AShM, 2 triple Mk32 324mm ASTT, 1 114mm gun
      2 *Bayandor* (US PF-103) with 2 twin lnchr with C-802 (CH-SS-N-8 *Saccade*) AShM, 2 triple 324mm Mk32 ASTT, 1 76mm gun
  PCFG 13 *Kaman* (FRA *Combattante* II) with 1–2 twin lnchr with C-802 (*Noor*) (CH-SS-N-8 *Saccade*) AShM, 1 76mm gun
  PBG 9:
    3 *Hendijan* with 2 twin lnchr with C-802 (*Noor*) (CH-SS-N-8 *Saccade*) AShM
    3 *Kayvan* with 2 single lnchr with C-704 (*Nasr*) AShM
    3 *Parvin* with 2 single lnchr with C-704 (*Nasr*) AShM
  PBFT 3 *Kajami* (semi-submersible) with 2 324mm TT
  PBF 1 MIL55
  PB 34: 9 C14; 9 *Hendijan*; 6 MkII; 10 MkIII
AMPHIBIOUS
  LANDING SHIPS 12
    LSM 3 *Farsi* (ROK) (capacity 9 tanks; 140 troops)

LST 3 *Hengam* with 1 hel landing platform (capacity 9 tanks; 225 troops)
LSL 6 *Fouque*
LANDING CRAFT 11
  LCT 2
  LCU 1 *Liyan 110*
  UCAC 8: 2 *Wellington* Mk 4; 4 *Wellington* Mk 5; 2 *Tondar* (UK *Winchester*)
LOGISTICS AND SUPPORT 18
  AE 2 *Delvar*
  AFD 2 *Dolphin*
  AG 1 *Hamzah* with 2 single lnchr with C-802 (*Noor*) (CH-55-N-8 *Saccade*) AShM
  AK 3 *Delvar*
  AORH 3: 2 *Bandar Abbas*; 1 *Kharg* with 1 76mm gun
  AWT 5: 4 *Kangan*; 1 *Delvar*
  AX 2 *Kialas*
COASTAL DEFENCE • AShM C-701 (*Kosar*); C-704 (*Nasr*); C-802 (*Noor*); C-802A (*Ghader*); *Ra'ad* (reported)

Marines 2,600
FORCES BY ROLE
MANOEUVRE
  Amphibious
    2 marine bde

Naval Aviation 2,600
EQUIPMENT BY TYPE
AIRCRAFT 3 combat capable
  ASW 3 P-3F *Orion*
  TPT 16: **Light** 13: 5 Do-228; 4 F-27 *Friendship*; 4 Turbo Commander 680; **PAX** 3 Falcon 20 (ELINT)
HELICOPTERS
  ASW ε10 SH-3D *Sea King*
  MCM 3 RH-53D *Sea Stallion*
  TPT • Light 17: 5 Bell 205A (AB-205A); 2 Bell 206 *Jet Ranger* (AB-206); 10 Bell 212 (AB-212)

Air Force 30,000 (incl 12,000 Air Defence)
FORCES BY ROLE
Serviceability probably about 60% for US ac types and about 80% for PRC/Russian ac. Includes IRGC AF equipment
FIGHTER
  1 sqn with F-7M *Airguard*; JJ-7*
  2 sqn with F-14 *Tomcat*
  2 sqn with MiG-29A/UB *Fulcrum*
FIGHTER/GROUND ATTACK
  1 sqn with Mirage F-1E; F-5E/F *Tiger* II
  5 sqn with F-4D/E *Phantom* II
  3 sqn with F-5E/F *Tiger* II
  1 sqn (forming) with Su-22M4 *Fitter K*; Su-22UM-3K *Fitter G*
GROUND ATTACK
  1 sqn with Su-24MK *Fencer D*
MARITIME PATROL
  1 sqn with P-3MP *Orion**
ISR
  1 (det) sqn with RF-4E *Phantom* II*
SEARCH & RESCUE
  Some flt with Bell 214C (AB-214C)

TANKER/TRANSPORT
  1 sqn with B-707; B-747; B-747F
TRANSPORT
  1 sqn with B-707; Falcon 50; L-1329 *Jetstar*; Bell 412
  2 sqn with C-130E/H *Hercules*
  1 sqn with F-27 *Friendship*; Falcon 20
  1 sqn with Il-76 *Candid*; An-140 (Iran-140 *Faraz*)
TRAINING
  1 sqn with Beech F33A/C *Bonanza*
  1 sqn with F-5B *Freedom Fighter*
  1 sqn with PC-6
  1 sqn with PC-7 *Turbo Trainer*
  Some units with EMB-312 *Tucano*; MFI-17 *Mushshak*; TB-21 *Trinidad*; TB-200 *Tobago*
TRANSPORT HELICOPTER
  1 sqn with CH-47 *Chinook*
  Some units with Bell 206A *Jet Ranger* (AB-206A); *Shabaviz* 2-75; *Shabaviz* 2061
AIR DEFENCE
  16 bn with MIM-23B I-*Hawk/Shahin*
  4 bn with S-300PMU2 (SA-20 *Gargoyle*)
  5 sqn with FM-80 (*Crotale*); *Rapier*; *Tigercat*; S-75M *Volkhov* (SA-2 *Guideline*); S-200 *Angara* (SA-5 *Gammon*); FIM-92A *Stinger*; 9K32 *Strela-2* (SA-7 *Grail*)‡; 9K331 *Tor-M1* (SA-15 *Gauntlet*) (reported)

EQUIPMENT BY TYPE
AIRCRAFT 334 combat capable
  FTR 184+: 20 F-5B *Freedom Fighter*; 55+ F-5E/F *Tiger* II 24 F-7M *Airguard*; 43 F-14 *Tomcat*; 36 MiG-29A/U/UB *Fulcrum*; up to 6 *Azarakhsh* (reported)
  FGA 85: 64 F-4D/E *Phantom* II; 10 Mirage F-1E; up to 6 *Saegheh* (reported); 3 Su-22M4 *Fitter K*; 2 Su-22UM-3K *Fitter G*
  ATK 39: 29 Su-24MK *Fencer D*; 7 Su-25K *Frogfoot* (status unknown); 3 Su-25UBK *Frogfoot* (status unknown)
  ASW 5 P-3MP *Orion*
  ISR: 6+ RF-4E *Phantom* II*
  TKR/TPT 3: ε1 B-707; ε2 B-747
  TPT 117: **Heavy** 12 Il-76 *Candid*; **Medium** ε19 C-130E/H *Hercules*; **Light** 75: 11 An-74TK-200; 5 An-140 (Iran-140 *Faraz*) (45 projected); 10 F-27 *Friendship*; 1 L-1329 *Jetstar*; 10 PC-6B *Turbo Porter*; 8 TB-21 *Trinidad*; 4 TB-200 *Tobago*; 3 Turbo Commander 680; 14 Y-7; 9 Y-12; **PAX** 11: 2 B-707; 1 B-747; 4 B-747F; 1 Falcon 20; 3 Falcon 50
  TRG 151: 25 Beech F33A/C *Bonanza*; 15 EMB-312 *Tucano*; 15 JJ-7*; 25 MFI-17 *Mushshak*; 12 *Parastu*; 15 PC-6; 35 PC-7 *Turbo Trainer*; 9 T-33
HELICOPTERS
  MRH 2 Bell 412
  TPT 34+: **Heavy** 2+ CH-47 *Chinook*; **Medium** 30 Bell 214C (AB-214C); **Light** 2+: 2 Bell 206A *Jet Ranger* (AB-206A); some *Shabaviz* 2-75 (indigenous versions in production); some *Shabaviz* 2061
AIR DEFENCE •
  SAM 514+:
    Long-range 10 S-200 *Angara* (SA-5 *Gammon*); 32 S-300PMU2 (SA-20 *Gargoyle*)
    Medium-range 195+: 150+ MIM-23B I-*Hawk/Shahin*; 45 S-75 *Dvina* (SA-2 *Guideline*);
    Short-range 279: 250 FM-80 (*Crotale*); 29 9K331 *Tor-M1* (SA-15 *Gauntlet*) (reported)

Point-defence 30+: 30 *Rapier*; FIM-92 *Stinger*; 9K32 *Strela*-2 (SA-7 *Grail*)‡
GUNS • TOWED 23mm ZU-23-2; **35mm** Oerlikon
AIR-LAUNCHED MISSILES
AAM • IR PL-2A‡; PL-7; R-60 (AA-8 *Aphid*); R-73 (AA-11 *Archer*); AIM-9 *Sidewinder*; **IR/SARH** R-27 (AA-10 *Alamo*); **SARH** AIM-7 *Sparrow*; **ARH** AIM-54 *Phoenix*†
ASM AGM-65A *Maverick*; Kh-25 (AS-10 *Karen*); Kh-29 (AS-14 *Kedge*)
AShM C-801K
ARM Kh-58 (AS-11 *Kilter*)

Air Defence Command
Established to coordinate army, air-force and IRGC air-defence assets. Precise composition unclear

Paramilitary 40,000–60,000

Law-Enforcement Forces 40,000–60,000 (border and security troops); 450,000 on mobilisation (incl conscripts)
Part of armed forces in wartime
EQUIPMENT BY TYPE
PATROL AND COASTAL COMBATANTS • PB ε90
AIRCRAFT • TPT • Light 2+: 2 An-140; some Cessna 185/Cessna 310
HELICOPTERS • TPT • Light ε24 AB-205 (Bell 205)/AB-206 (Bell 206) *Jet Ranger*

Basij Resistance Force up to ε1,000,000 on mobilisation
Paramilitary militia with claimed membership of 12.6 million; perhaps 1 million combat capable; in the process of closer integration with IRGC Ground Forces
FORCES BY ROLE
MANOEUVRE
Other
2,500 militia bn(-) (claimed, limited permanent membership)

Cyber
Iran has a well-developed capacity for cyber operations. It has a well-educated and computer-literate young population. In September 2015, Ayatollah Ali Khamenei appointed members to a Supreme Council for Cyberspace, reportedly a policymaking and supervisory body. The Stuxnet incident in 2010 is reported to have been a turning point in Iran's approach to cyber capabilities. In 2011–12, Tehran established a Joint Chiefs of Staff Cyber Command with emphasis on thwarting attacks against Iranian nuclear facilities and coordinating national cyber warfare and information security. The IRGC has its own Cyber Defence Command; IRGC civilian business interests will aid its activities in this area. The precise relationship of groups such as the 'Iranian Cyber Army' to regime and military organisations is unclear, but the former has launched hacking attacks against a number of foreign organisations. There are continued reports of increasing investment in cyber capabilities, used not only for propaganda and intelligence exploitation but also as a means for Iran to attempt to offset its conventional military weakness vis-à-vis its neighbours and the US. Reports in 2017 alleged that a series of targeted cyber attacks, including against the UK Parliament and companies in Saudi Arabia and the US, originated in Iran. But Iran also remains aware of its own potential vulnerabilities, not least in terms of infrastructure protection: it was reported in May that a senior official was advising that Iran should identify 'vital points' in infrastructure so as to boost passive defences, while another reportedly said in February that Iran should 'adopt a pre-emptive approach towards future cyber risks'.

DEPLOYMENT

GULF OF ADEN AND SOMALI BASIN
Navy: 1 FSG; 1 AORH

SUDAN
UN • UNAMID 1 obs

SYRIA
5,000 (incl up to 2,000 IRGC)

Iraq IRQ

Iraqi Dinar D		2016	2017	2018
GDP	D	20.0tr	22.8tr	
	US$	172bn	193bn	
per capita	US$	4,533	4,958	
Growth	%	11.0	-0.4	
Inflation	%	0.4	2.0	
Def bdgt [a]	D	20.0tr	22.8tr	
	US$	17.0bn	19.3bn	
FMA (US$)	US$	250m	150m	0m
US$1=D		1,180.17	1,182.00	

[a] Defence and security budget

Population 39,192,111

Ethnic and religious groups: Arab 75–80% (of which Shia Muslim 55%, Sunni Muslim 45%); Kurdish 20–25%

Age	0–14	15–19	20–24	25–29	30–64	65 plus
Male	20.1%	5.3%	4.4%	3.8%	15.1%	1.5%
Female	19.3%	5.1%	4.3%	3.7%	15.0%	1.9%

Capabilities

Army capabilities and morale have improved since the collapse of several divisions in the face of the ISIS advance in the north in 2014. The recapture of Mosul in October 2017 demonstrated the incremental growth in capability, in terms of both combat power and tactics, as the force adapted to fight ISIS's asymmetric tactics in urban areas. However, the level of attrition among Iraqi forces caused concern, particularly that of the Counter Terrorist Service, which was often used as a spearhead force. There was also improved inter-service coordination. After defeating ISIS in Mosul, and amid a broader rollback of ISIS forces, questions arose as to the place of Kurdish forces within the Iraqi state, and their relationship with Iraq's military, as reports of friction persisted. The Iraqi Army continues to benefit from training and equipment support from Western supporters, as does the air force, which is being rebuilt, primarily for the counter-insurgency role. F-16 deliveries continued during 2017, marking a notable capability improvement for the air force. The campaign to retake Mosul and other northern areas benefited from US air and intelligence support, suggesting continuing capability limitations within the Iraqi armed forces in these areas.

ACTIVE 64,000 (Army 54,000 Navy 3,000 Air 4,000 Air Defence 3,000) Paramilitary 145,000

ORGANISATIONS BY SERVICE

Army 54,000

Due to ongoing conflict with ISIS insurgents, there have been significant personnel and equipment losses in the Iraqi Army. Many formations are now under-strength. Military capability has been bolstered by the activity of Shia militias and Kurdish Peshmerga forces

FORCES BY ROLE
SPECIAL FORCES
  2 SF bde
MANOEUVRE
  Armoured
  1 armd div (2 armd bde, 2 mech bde, 1 engr bn, 1 sigs regt, 1 log bde)
  Mechanised
  2 mech div (4 mech inf bde, 1 engr bn, 1 sigs regt, 1 log bde)
  1 mech div (3 mech inf bde, 1 engr bn, 1 sigs regt, 1 log bde)
  1 mech div (2 mech inf bde, 1 inf bde, 1 engr bn, 1 sigs regt, 1 log bde)
  Light
  1 mot div (1 mech bde, 3 mot inf bde, 2 inf bde, 1 engr bn, 1 sigs regt, 1 log bde)
  1 mot div (2 mot inf bde, 3 inf bde, 1 engr bn, 1 sigs regt, 1 log bde)
  1 inf div (4 lt inf bde, 1 engr bn, 1 sigs regt, 1 log bde)
  1 inf div (3 inf bde)
  1 inf div (2 inf bde)
  1 inf div (1 inf bde)
  1 cdo div (5 lt inf bde, 1 engr bn, 1 sigs regt, 1 log bde)
  1 inf bde
  Aviation
  1 atk hel sqn with Mi-28NE *Havoc*
  1 atk hel sqn with Mi-35M *Hind*
  1 sqn with Bell 205 (UH-1H *Huey* II)
  3 atk hel sqn with Bell T407; H135M
  3 sqn with Mi-17 *Hip* H; Mi-171Sh
  1 ISR sqn with SA342M *Gazelle*
  2 trg sqn with Bell 206; OH-58C *Kiowa*
  1 trg sqn with Bell 205 (UH-1H *Huey* II)
  1 trg sqn with Mi-17 *Hip*
EQUIPMENT BY TYPE
ARMOURED FIGHTING VEHICLES
  MBT 318+: ε100 M1A1 *Abrams*; 168+ T-72; ε50 T-55;
  RECCE 435: ε400 *Akrep*; 18 BRDM 2; 35 EE-9 *Cascavel*;

IFV 240: ε80 BMP-1; ε60 BTR-4 (inc variants); 100 BTR-80A
APC 2,102+
  APC (T) 900: ε500 M113A2/*Talha*; ε400 MT-LB
  APC (W) 10 *Cobra*
  PPV 1,192+: 12 *Barracuda*; 250 *Caiman*; ε500 *Dzik-3*; ε400 ILAV *Badger*; *Mamba*; 30 *Maxxpro*
  AUV M-ATV
ENGINEERING & MAINTENANCE VEHICLES
  ARV 215+: 180 BREM; 35+ M88A1/2; T-54/55 ARV; Type-653; VT-55A
NBC VEHICLES 20 *Fuchs* NBC
ANTI-TANK/ANTI-INFRASTRUCTURE
  MSL • MANPATS 9K135 *Kornet* (AT-14 *Spriggan*) (reported)
ARTILLERY 1,085+
  SP 72+: **152mm** 18+ Type-83; **155mm** 30: 6 M109A1; 24 M109A5
  TOWED 60+: **130mm** M-46/Type-59; **152mm** D-20; Type-83; **155mm** ε60 M198
  MRL 3+: **122mm** some BM-21 *Grad*; **220mm** 3+ TOS-1A
  MOR 950+: **81mm** ε500 M252; **120mm** ε450 M120; **240mm** M-240
HELICOPTERS
  ATK 28: 11 Mi-28NE *Havoc*; 4 Mi-28UB *Havoc*; 13 Mi-35M *Hind*
  MRH 51+: 4+ SA342 *Gazelle*; 24 Bell IA407; 23 H135M
  MRH/TPT ε19 Mi-17 *Hip* H/Mi-171Sh
  ISR 10 OH-58C *Kiowa*
  TPT • Light 44: 16 Bell 205 (UH-1H *Huey* II); 10 Bell 206B3 *Jet Ranger*; ε18 Bell T407
UNMANNED AERIAL VEHICLES • CISR Heavy CH-4
AIR-LAUNCHED MISSILES • ASM 9K114 *Shturm* (AT-6 *Spiral*); AR-1; *Ingwe*

Navy 3,000

EQUIPMENT BY TYPE
PATROL AND COASTAL COMBATANTS 32+
  PCO 2 *Al Basra* (US River Hawk)
  PCC 4 *Fateh* (ITA Diciotti)
  PB 20: 12 Swiftships 35; 5 *Predator* (PRC 27m); 3 *Al Faw*
  PBR 6: 2 Type-200; 4 Type-2010

Marines 1,000

FORCES BY ROLE
MANOEUVRE
  Amphibious
  2 mne bn

Air Force ε4,000

FORCES BY ROLE
FIGHTER/GROUND ATTACK
  1 sqn with F-16C/D *Fighting Falcon*
GROUND ATTACK
  1 sqn with Su-25/Su-25K/Su-25UBK *Frogfoot*
  1 sqn with L-159
ISR
  1 sqn with CH-2000 *Sama*; SB7L-360 *Seeker*
  1 sqn with Cessna 208B *Grand Caravan*; Cessna AC-208B *Combat Caravan**
  1 sqn with Beech 350 *King Air*

TRANSPORT
1 sqn with An-32B *Cline*
1 sqn with C-130E/J-30 *Hercules*
TRAINING
1 sqn with Cessna 172, Cessna 208B
1 sqn with *Lasta*-95
1 sqn with T-6A
EQUIPMENT BY TYPE
AIRCRAFT 60 combat capable
FGA 27: 18 F-16C *Fighting Falcon*; 3 F-16D *Fighting Falcon*; 6 T-50IQ
ATK 29: 10 L-159; ε19 Su-25/Su-25K/Su-25UBK *Frogfoot*
ISR 10: 2 Cessna AC-208B *Combat Caravan**; 2 SB7L-360 *Seeker*; 6 Beech 350ER *King Air*
TPT 29: **Medium** 15: 3 C-130E *Hercules*; 6 C-130J-30 *Hercules*; 6 An-32B *Cline* (of which 2 combat capable); **Light** 17: 1 Beech 350 *King Air*; 5 Cessna 208B *Grand Caravan*; 8 Cessna 172
TRG 33+: 8 CH-2000 *Sama*; 10+ *Lasta*-95; 15 T-6A
AIR-LAUNCHED MISSILES
AAM • IR AIM-9L *Sidewinder*; AIM-9M *Sidewinder*
ASM AGM-114 *Hellfire*
BOMBS • **Laser-Guided** GBU-12 *Paveway* II

Air Defence Command ε3,000

FORCES BY ROLE
AIR DEFENCE
1 bn with 96K6 *Pantsir*-S1 (SA-22 *Greyhound*)
1 bn with M1097 *Avenger*
1 bn with 9K338 *Igla*-S (SA-24 *Grinch*)
1 bn with ZU-23-2; S-60
EQUIPMENT BY TYPE
AIR DEFENCE
SAM
  Short-range 24 96K6 *Pantsir*-S1 (SA-22 *Greyhound*)
  Point-defence M1097 *Avenger*; 9K338 *Igla*-S (SA-24 *Grinch*)
GUNS • **TOWED** **23mm** ZU-23-2; **57mm** S-60

Paramilitary ε145,000

Iraqi Federal Police ε36,000

Border Enforcement ε9,000

Militias ε100,000
Popular Mobilisation Forces include: Kata'ib Sayyid al-Shuhada Brigade; Kata'ib Hizbullah; Badr Brigades; Peace Brigades and Imam Ali Battalions

FOREIGN FORCES
Australia *Operation Inherent Resolve (Okra)* 380
Belgium *Operation Inherent Resolve (Valiant Phoenix)* 30
Canada *Operation Inherent Resolve (Impact)* 280; 1 SF gp; 1 med unit; 1 hel flt with 4 Bell 412 (CH-146 *Griffon*)
Czech Republic *Operation Inherent Resolve* 30
Denmark *Operation Inherent Resolve* 190; 1 SF gp; 1 trg team
Estonia *Operation Inherent Resolve* 7
Fiji UNAMI 168; 2 sy unit
Finland *Operation Inherent Resolve* 100; 1 trg unit
France *Operation Inherent Resolve (Chammal)* 500; 1 SF gp; 1 trg unit; 1 SP arty bty with 4 CAESAR
Germany *Operation Inherent Resolve* 145; some trg unit
Hungary *Operation Inherent Resolve* 140
Italy *Operation Inherent Resolve (Prima Parthica)* 1,220; 1 inf regt; 1 trg unit; 1 hel sqn with 4 AW129 *Mangusta*; 4 NH90
Latvia *Operation Inherent Resolve* 6
Nepal UNAMI 76; 1 sy unit
Netherlands *Operation Inherent Resolve* 150; 3 trg units
New Zealand *Operation Inherent Resolve* 154; 1 trg unit
Norway *Operation Inherent Resolve* 60; 1 trg unit
Poland *Operation Inherent Resolve* 60
Portugal *Operation Inherent Resolve* 31
Romania *Operation Inherent Resolve* 50
Slovenia *Operation Inherent Resolve* 6
Spain *Operation Inherent Resolve* 400; 2 trg units
Sweden *Operation Inherent Resolve* 70
Turkey Army 2,000; 1 armd BG
United Kingdom *Operation Inherent Resolve (Shader)* 600; 2 inf bn(-); 1 engr sqn(-)
United States *Operation Inherent Resolve* 9,000; 1 armd div HQ; 2 inf coy; 1 mne coy; 1 EOD pl; 1 SP arty bty with 4 M109A6; 1 fd arty bty with 4 M777A2; 1 MRL bty with 4 M142 HIMARS; 1 atk hel sqn with AH-64D *Apache*

Israel ISR

New Israeli Shekel NS		2016	2017	2018
GDP	NS	1.2tr	1.26tr	
	US$	318bn	348bn	
per capita	US$	37,192	39,974	
Growth	%	4.0	3.1	
Inflation	%	-0.5	0.2	
Def bdgt	NS	76.3bn	67.3bn	
	US$	19.9bn	18.5bn	
FMA (US)	US$	3.1bn	3.1bn	3.1bn
US$1=NS		3.84	3.63	

Population 8,299,706

Age	0–14	15–19	20–24	25–29	30–64	65 plus
Male	14.0%	4.1%	3.8%	3.6%	19.5%	5.0%
Female	13.4%	3.9%	3.6%	3.4%	19.0%	6.2%

Capabilities

The Israel Defense Forces (IDF) remain the most capable military forces in the region, with the motivation, equipment and training to considerably overmatch the conventional capability of other regional armed forces. Israel's defence policy prioritises homeland defence but with the ability to intervene in Lebanon and Syria. The requirement for power projection further afield appears limited to ISR, precision strikes and special-forces operations as far away as Iran. Training and readiness are priority areas. Currently preoccupied by threats posed by Hamas,

Hizbullah and Iran's proxies in Syria, the IDF retains the capability to launch strikes in Syria. Israel must also be assumed to have the military capability for a unilateral attack on Iran. There is an emphasis on maintaining Israel's regional technological superiority, especially in missile-defence, intelligence-gathering, precision-weapons and cyber capabilities. Israel continues to improve its air-defence network, with the *David's Sling* medium-range SAM system declared operational in 2017. In 2016, the IDF started to implement its five-year 'Gideon' modernisation plan to improve combat capability and administrative efficiency, while reducing costs and overheads. To date, this has included removing two army divisions, and the retirement of F-16A/B combat aircraft as more F-35s are delivered. The plan also calls for career-soldier numbers to reduce to 40,000; in 2015, the length of compulsory service for men was reduced from 36 to 32 months. A new artillery doctrine focused on swift precision strikes was introduced in 2016 and a new artillery brigade has been formed, as well as an improved network for the coordination of air, land and sea attack. Logistics capability appears adequate to support military operations and plans. Israel has a capable defence industry, with aerospace, ISR, missile and armoured-vehicle sectors particular strengths, as are counter-rocket systems and active-protection systems for armoured vehicles. A major exercise in late 2017 focused on defeating an attack by Hizbullah, and service- and reserve-force integration.

ACTIVE 176,500 (Army 133,000 Navy 9,500 Air 34,000) **Paramilitary 8,000**

Conscript liability Officers 48 months, other ranks 32 months, women 24 months (Jews and Druze only; Christians, Circassians and Muslims may volunteer)

RESERVE 465,000 (Army 400,000 Navy 10,000 Air 55,000)

Annual trg as cbt reservists to age 40 (some specialists to age 54) for male other ranks, 38 (or marriage/pregnancy) for women

ORGANISATIONS BY SERVICE

Strategic Forces

Israel is widely believed to have a nuclear capability – delivery means include F-15I and F-16I ac, *Jericho* 2 IRBM and, reportedly, *Dolphin/Tanin*-class SSKs with LACM

FORCES BY ROLE
SURFACE-TO-SURFACE MISSILE
  3 IRBM sqn with *Jericho* 2

EQUIPMENT BY TYPE
SURFACE-TO-SURFACE MISSILE LAUNCHERS
  IRBM • Nuclear: ε24 *Jericho* 2

Strategic Defences

FORCES BY ROLE
AIR DEFENCE
  3 bty with *Arrow* 2 ATBM with *Green Pine/Super Green Pine* radar and *Citrus Tree* command post
  10 bty with *Iron Dome* (incl reserve bty)
  17 bty with MIM-23B I-*Hawk*
  6 bty with MIM-104C *Patriot* PAC-2

Space

EQUIPMENT BY TYPE
SATELLITES 9
  COMMUNICATIONS 3 *Amos*
  ISR 6: 1 EROS; 4 *Ofeq* (7, 9, 10 & 11); 1 TecSAR-1 (*Polaris*)

Army 26,000; 107,000 conscript (total 133,000)

Organisation and structure of formations may vary according to op situations. Equipment includes that required for reserve forces on mobilisation

FORCES BY ROLE
COMMAND
  3 (regional comd) corps HQ
  2 armd div HQ
  5 (territorial) inf div HQ
  1 (home defence) comd HQ
SPECIAL FORCES
  3 SF bn
  1 spec ops bde (4 spec ops unit)
MANOEUVRE
  Reconnaissance
  1 indep recce bn
  Armoured
  3 armd bde (1 armd recce coy, 3 armd bn, 1 AT coy, 1 cbt engr bn)
  Mechanised
  3 mech inf bde (3 mech inf bn, 1 cbt spt bn, 1 sigs coy)
  1 mech inf bde (5 mech inf bn)
  1 indep mech inf bn
  Light
  2 indep inf bn
  Air Manoeuvre
  1 para bde (3 para bn, 1 cbt spt bn, 1 sigs coy)
  Other
  1 armd trg bde (3 armd bn)
COMBAT SUPPORT
  3 arty bde
  3 engr bn
  1 EOD coy
  1 CBRN bn
  1 int bde (3 int bn)
  1 SIGINT unit
  2 MP bn

Reserves 400,000+ on mobilisation

FORCES BY ROLE
COMMAND
  3 armd div HQ
  1 AB div HQ
MANOEUVRE
  Armoured
  9 armd bde
  Mechanised
  8 mech inf bde
  Light
  16 (territorial/regional) inf bde
  Air Manoeuvre
  4 para bde

Mountain
  1 mtn inf bn
COMBAT SUPPORT
  5 arty bde
COMBAT SERVICE SUPPORT
  6 log unit
EQUIPMENT BY TYPE
ARMOURED FIGHTING VEHICLES
  MBT 460: ε160 *Merkava* MkIII; ε300 *Merkava* MkIV (ε370 *Merkava* MkII; ε570 *Merkava* MkIII; ε180 *Merkava* MkIV all in store)
  RECCE ε300 RBY-1 RAMTA
  APC • APC (T) 1,200: ε100 *Namer*; ε200 *Achzarit* (modified T-55 chassis); 500 M113A2; ε400 *Nagmachon* (*Centurion* chassis); *Nakpadon* (5,000 M113A1/A2 in store)
  AUV 100 *Ze'ev*
ENGINEERING & MAINTENANCE VEHICLES
  AEV D9R; *Puma*
  ARV *Centurion* Mk2; *Eyal*; *Merkava*; M88A1; M113 ARV
  VLB *Alligator* MAB; M48/60; MTU
NBC VEHICLES ε8 TPz-1 *Fuchs* NBC
ANTI-TANK/ANTI-INFRASTRUCTURE • MSL
  SP M113 with *Spike*; *Tamuz* (*Spike* NLOS); *Magach* mod with *Spike*
  MANPATS IMI MAPATS; *Spike* MR/LR/ER
ARTILLERY 530
  SP 250: **155mm** 250 M109A5 (**155mm** 148 Soltam L-33; 30 M109A1; 50 M-50; **175mm** 36 M107; **203mm** 36 M110 all in store)
  TOWED (**122mm** 5 D-30; **130mm** 100 M-46; **155mm** 171: 40 M-46 mod; 50 M-68/M-71; 81 M-839P/M-845P all in store)
  MRL 30: **227mm** 30 M270 MLRS (**122mm** 58 BM-21 *Grad*; **160mm** 50 LAR-160; **227mm** 18 M270 MLRS; **240mm** 36 BM-24; **290mm** 20 LAR-290 all in store)
  MOR 250: **81mm** 250 (**81mm** 1,100; **120mm** 650; **160mm** 18 Soltam M-66 all in store)
SURFACE-TO-SURFACE MISSILE LAUNCHERS
  IRBM • Nuclear ε24 *Jericho* 2
  SRBM • Dual-capable (7 *Lance* in store)
  RADAR • LAND AN/PPS-15 (arty); AN/TPQ-37 *Firefinder* (arty); EL/M-2140 (veh)
  AIR DEFENCE • SAM • Point-defence 20 *Machbet*; FIM-92 *Stinger*

Navy 7,000; 2,500 conscript (total 9,500)

EQUIPMENT BY TYPE
SUBMARINES • TACTICAL
  SSK 5:
    3 *Dolphin* (GER HDW design) with 6 single 533mm TT with DM2A3/4 HWT/UGM-84C *Harpoon* AShM, 4 single 650mm TT
    2 *Tanin* (GER HDW design with AIP) with 6 single 533mm TT with DM2A3/4 HWT/UGM-84C *Harpoon* AShM, 4 single 650mm TT
PATROL AND COASTAL COMBATANTS 45
  CORVETTES • FSGHM 3:
    2 *Eilat* (*Sa'ar* 5) with 2 quad Mk140 lnchr with RGM-84C *Harpoon* AShM, 2 32-cell VLS with *Barak*-1 SAM (being upgraded to *Barak*-8), 2 triple 324mm TT with Mk 46 LWT, 1 *Sea Vulcan* CIWS, 1 76mm gun (capacity 1 AS565SA *Panther* ASW hel)
    1 *Eilat* (*Sa'ar* 5) with 2 quad Mk140 lnchr with RGM-84C *Harpoon* AShM, 2 32-cell VLS with *Barak*-8 SAM, 2 triple 324mm TT with Mk 46 LWT, 1 *Sea Vulcan* CIWS, 1 76mm gun (capacity 1 AS565SA *Panther* ASW hel)
  PCGM 8 *Hetz* (*Sa'ar* 4.5) with 6 single lnchr with *Gabriel* II AShM, 2 twin Mk140 lnchr with RGM-84C *Harpoon* AShM, 2 8-cell Mk56 VLS with *Barak*-1 SAM, 1 *Vulcan* CIWS, 1 *Typhoon* CIWS, 1 76mm gun
  PBF 34: 5 *Shaldag* with 1 *Typhoon* CIWS; 3 *Stingray*; 9 *Super Dvora* Mk I (SSM & TT may be fitted); 4 *Super Dvora* Mk II (SSM & TT may be fitted); 6 *Super Dvora* Mk II-I (SSM & TT may be fitted); 4 *Super Dvora* Mk III (SSM & TT may be fitted); 3 *Super Dvora* Mk III with 1 *Typhoon* CIWS (SSM may be fitted)
AMPHIBIOUS • LANDING CRAFT • LCVP 2 *Manta*
LOGISTICS AND SUPPORT 3
  AG 2 *Bat Yam* (ex-GER Type-745)
  AX 1 *Queshet*

Naval Commandos ε300
FORCES BY ROLE
SPECIAL FORCES
  1 cdo unit

Air Force 34,000

Responsible for Air and Space Coordination
FORCES BY ROLE
FIGHTER & FIGHTER/GROUND ATTACK
  1 sqn with F-15A/B/D *Eagle*
  1 sqn with F-15B/C/D *Eagle*
  1 sqn with F-15I *Ra'am*
  6 sqn with F-16C/D *Fighting Falcon*
  4 sqn with F-16I *Sufa*
  1 sqn (forming) with F-35I *Adir*
ANTI-SUBMARINE WARFARE
  1 sqn with AS565SA *Panther* (missions flown by IAF but with non-rated aircrew)
ELECTRONIC WARFARE
  2 sqn with RC-12D *Guardrail*; Beech A36 *Bonanza* (*Hofit*); Beech 200 *King Air*; Beech 200T *King Air*; Beech 200CT *King Air*
AIRBORNE EARLY WARNING & CONTROL
  1 sqn with Gulfstream G550 *Eitam*; Gulfstream G550 *Shavit*
TANKER/TRANSPORT
  1 sqn with C-130E/H *Hercules*; KC-130H *Hercules*
  1 sqn with C-130J-30 *Hercules*
  1 sqn with KC-707
TRAINING
  1 OPFOR sqn with F-16C/D *Fighting Falcon*
  1 sqn with M-346 *Master* (*Lavi*)
ATTACK HELICOPTER
  1 sqn with AH-64A *Apache*
  1 sqn with AH-64D *Apache*
TRANSPORT HELICOPTER
  2 sqn with CH-53D *Sea Stallion*
  2 sqn with S-70A *Black Hawk*; UH-60A *Black Hawk*
  1 medevac unit with CH-53D *Sea Stallion*

UAV
  1 ISR sqn with *Hermes* 450
  1 ISR sqn with *Heron* (*Shoval*); *Heron* TP (*Eitan*)
  1 ISR sqn with *Heron* (*Shoval*) (MP role)
AIR DEFENCE
  3 bty with *Arrow* 2
  10 bty with *Iron Dome*
  15 bty with MIM-23 I-*Hawk*
  6 bty with MIM-104C *Patriot* PAC-2
  2 bty with *David's Sling*
SPECIAL FORCES
  1 SF unit
  1 spec ops unit
EQUIPMENT BY TYPE
AIRCRAFT 347 combat capable
  FTR 58: 16 F-15A *Eagle*; 6 F-15B *Eagle*; 17 F-15C *Eagle*; 19 F-15D *Eagle*
  FGA 259: 25 F-15I *Ra'am*; 78 F-16C *Fighting Falcon*; 49 F-16D *Fighting Falcon*; 98 F-16I *Sufa*; 9 F-35I *Adir*
  ISR 6 RC-12D *Guardrail*
  ELINT 4: 1 EC-707; 3 Gulfstream G550 *Shavit*
  AEW 4: 2 B-707 *Phalcon*; 2 Gulfstream G550 *Eitam* (1 more on order)
  TKR/TPT 11: 4 KC-130H *Hercules*; 7 KC-707
  TPT 62: **Medium** 15: 5 C-130E *Hercules*; 6 C-130H *Hercules*; 4 C-130J-30 *Hercules*; **Light** 47: 3 AT-802 *Air Tractor*; 9 Beech 200 *King Air*; 8 Beech 200T *King Air*; 5 Beech 200CT *King Air*; 22 Beech A36 *Bonanza* (*Hofit*)
  TRG 67: 17 Grob G-120; 30 M-346 *Master* (*Lavi*)*; 20 T-6A
HELICOPTERS
  ATK 43: 26 AH-64A *Apache*; 17 AH-64D *Apache* (*Sarat*)
  ASW 7 AS565SA *Panther* (missions flown by IAF but with non-rated aircrew)
  ISR 12 OH-58B *Kiowa*
  TPT 81: **Heavy** 26 CH-53D *Sea Stallion*; **Medium** 49: 39 S-70A *Black Hawk*; 10 UH-60A *Black Hawk*; **Light** 6 Bell 206 *Jet Ranger*
UNMANNED AERIAL VEHICLES
  ISR 3+: **Heavy** 3+: *Heron* (*Shoval*); 3 *Heron* TP (*Eitan*); RQ-5A *Hunter*; **Medium** *Hermes* 450; *Hermes* 900 (22+ *Searcher* MkII in store); **Light** *Harpy* (anti-radiation UAV)
AIR DEFENCE
  SAM 54+:
    Long-range MIM-104C *Patriot* PAC-2; **Medium-range** 24 *Arrow* 2; some MIM-23B I-*Hawk*; some *David's Sling*; **Short-range** ε30 *Iron Dome*
  GUNS 920
    SP 165: **20mm** 105 M163 *Machbet Vulcan*; **23mm** 60 ZSU-23-4
    TOWED 755: **23mm** 150 ZU-23-2; **20mm/37mm** 455 M167 *Vulcan* towed 20mm/M-1939 towed 37mm/TCM-20 towed 20mm; **40mm** 150 L/70
AIR-LAUNCHED MISSILES
  AAM • IR AIM-9 *Sidewinder*; *Python* 4; **IIR** *Python* 5; **ARH** AIM-120C AMRAAM
  ASM AGM-114 *Hellfire*; AGM-62B *Walleye*; AGM-65 *Maverick*; *Delilah* AL; *Popeye* I/*Popeye* II; *Spike* NLOS
BOMBS
  IIR guided *Opher*
  Laser-guided *Griffin*; *Lizard*; *Paveway* II
  INS/GPS guided GBU-31 JDAM; GBU-39 Small Diameter Bomb (*Barad Had*); *Spice*

Airfield Defence 3,000 active (15,000 reservists)

Paramilitary ε8,000

Border Police ε8,000

Cyber

Israel has a substantial capacity for cyber operations. In early 2012, the National Cyber Bureau (NCB) was created in the prime minister's office to develop technology, human resources and international collaboration. It is reported that the IDF's 'Unit 8200' is responsible for ELINT and some cyber operations. In 2012, according to the IDF, the C4I Directorate and Unit 8200 were combined into a new task force 'tasked with developing offensive capabilities and operations'. Specialist training courses exist, including the four-month 'Cyber Shield' activity. In April 2016, the National Cyber Defense Authority was created, consolidating cyber defences into one body. Although the IDF's Gideon plan called for a Joint Cyber Command, in January 2017 the IDF announced it would not take this step. The cyber-defence unit of the C4I Directorate will reportedly be turned into an operational command in late 2017, and Unit 8200 will retain its remit.

FOREIGN FORCES

UNTSO unless specified. UNTSO figures represent total numbers for mission.
Argentina 3 obs
Australia 11 obs
Austria 4 obs
Belgium 2 obs
Bhutan 2 obs • UNDOF 3
Canada 4 obs
Chile 3 obs
China 4 obs
Czech Republic UNDOF 2
Denmark 12 obs
Estonia 3 obs
Fiji 2 obs • UNDOF 302; 1 inf bn(-)
Finland 19 obs • UNDOF 2
India 1 obs • UNDOF 204; 1 log bn
Ireland 12 obs • UNDOF 136; 1 inf coy
Nepal 3 obs • UNDOF 344; 1 mech inf coy; 1 inf coy
Netherlands 13 obs • UNDOF 2
New Zealand 6 obs
Norway 13 obs
Russia 3 obs
Serbia 1 obs
Slovakia 2 obs
Slovenia 3 obs
Sweden 7 obs
Switzerland 12 obs
United States 2 obs • US Strategic Command; 1 AN/TPY-2 X-band radar at Mount Keren

Jordan JOR

Jordanian Dinar D		2016	2017	2018
GDP	D	27.4bn	28.7bn	
	US$	38.7bn	40.5bn	
per capita	US$	5,549	5,678	
Growth	%	2.0	2.3	
Inflation	%	-0.8	3.3	
Def bdgt [a]	D	1.04bn	1.16bn	
	US$	1.47bn	1.63bn	
FMA (US)	US$	450m	350m	350m
US$1=D		0.71	0.71	

[a] Excludes expenditure on public order and safety

Population 10,248,069

Ethnic groups: Palestinian ε50–60%

Age	0–14	15–19	20–24	25–29	30–64	65 plus
Male	17.8%	5.5%	5.5%	4.7%	17.8%	1.7%
Female	16.8%	4.8%	4.4%	3.9%	15.3%	1.7%

Capabilities

Jordan's armed forces benefit from a fairly high level of defence spending relative to GDP, and strong defence relationships with the UK and the US that have boosted training. The main roles of the fully professional armed forces are border and internal security. The services are combat capable and have contributed to international expeditionary operations. Security preoccupations include the threat from ISIS, conflict in Syria and Iraq, and resulting refugee flows. In 2016 a new Quick Reaction Force was formed to support activity by Jordanian special forces. Most military equipment is externally supplied, and a batch of *Marder* IFVs was received from Germany in late 2016. However, state-owned KADDB produces some light armoured vehicles and reportedly tested a new 8x8 wheeled AFV in 2017. Personnel are well trained, particularly aircrew and special forces, who are highly regarded and have served alongside ISAF in Afghanistan and participated in UN missions. The country has developed a bespoke special-forces training centre, which regularly plays host to various special-forces contingents and continues to host annual exercise *Eager Lion*. UK and US forces also regularly exercise in the country, and Syrian opposition groups have been trained in-country. Jordan has significantly stepped up border security in light of ISIS activity on its periphery, including a complex border-security project funded by the US, which includes a communications, command and control package, sensors, watchtowers and a command centre.

ACTIVE 100,500 (Army 74,000 Navy 500 Air 12,000 Special Operations 14,000) Paramilitary 15,000

RESERVE 65,000 (Army 60,000 Joint 5,000) Paramilitary 35,000

ORGANISATIONS BY SERVICE

Army 74,000
FORCES BY ROLE
MANOEUVRE
  Armoured
  1 (strategic reserve) armd div (3 armd bde, 1 arty bde, 1 AD bde)
  1 armd bde
  Mechanised
  5 mech bde
  Light
  3 lt inf bde
COMBAT SUPPORT
  3 arty bde
  3 AD bde
  1 MRL bn
EQUIPMENT BY TYPE
ARMOURED FIGHTING VEHICLES
  MBT 572: 390 FV4034 *Challenger* 1 (*Al Hussein*); 182 M60 *Phoenix* (274 FV4030/2 *Khalid* in store)
  LT TK (19 FV101 *Scorpion* in store)
  ASLT 141 B1 *Centauro*
  RECCE 153: 103 FV107 *Scimitar*; 50 FV701 *Ferret*
  IFV 717: 13 AIFV-B-C25; 31 BMP-2; 16 *Marder* 1A3; 321 *Ratel*-20; 336 YPR-765 PRI
  APC 879+
    APC (T) 729+: 370 M113A1/A2 Mk1J; 269 M577A2 (CP); some *Temsah*; 87 YPR-765 PRCO (CP); 3 AIFV-B
    PPV 150: 25 *Marauder*; 25 *Matador*; 100 *MaxxPro*
  AUV 35 *Cougar*
ENGINEERING & MAINTENANCE VEHICLES
  ARV 155+: *Al Monjed*; 55 *Chieftain* ARV; *Centurion* Mk2; 20 M47; 32 M88A1; 30 M578; 18 YPR-806
  MW 12 *Aardvark* Mk2
ANTI-TANK/ANTI-INFRASTRUCTURE • MSL
  SP 115: 70 M901; 45 AIFV-B-*Milan*
  MANPATS FGM-148 *Javelin*; TOW/TOW-2A; 9K135 *Kornet* (AT-14 *Spriggan*)
ARTILLERY 1,429+
  SP 574: **105mm** 48: 30 M52; 18 MOBAT; **155mm** 78: 358 M109A1/A2; 20 M44; **203mm** 148 M110A2
  TOWED 82: **105mm** 54 M102; **155mm** 28: 10 M1/M59; 18 M114; **203mm** (4 M115 in store)
  MRL 14+: **227mm** 12 M142 HIMARS; **273mm** 2+ WM-80
  MOR 759: **81mm** 359; **SP 81mm** 50; **107mm** 50 M30; **120mm** 300 Brandt
RADAR • LAND 7 AN/TPQ-36 *Firefinder*/AN/TPQ-37 *Firefinder* (arty, mor)
AIR DEFENCE
  SAM • Point-defence 140+: 92 9K35 *Strela*-10 (SA-13 *Gopher*); 48 9K33 *Osa*-M (SA-8 *Gecko*); 9K32M *Strela*-2M (SA-7B *Grail*)‡; 9K36 *Strela*-3 (SA-14 *Gremlin*); 9K310 *Igla*-1 (SA-16 *Gimlet*); 9K38 *Igla* (SA-18 *Grouse*)
  GUNS • SP 416: **20mm** 100 M163 *Vulcan*; **23mm** 40 ZSU-23-4; **35mm** 60 *Cheetah* (*Gepard*); **40mm** 216 M42 (not all op)

Navy ε500
EQUIPMENT BY TYPE
PATROL AND COASTAL COMBATANTS 7
  PB 7: 3 *Al Hussein* (UK Vosper 30m); 4 *Abdullah* (US *Dauntless*)

Air Force 12,000
Flying hours 180 hrs/yr

FORCES BY ROLE
FIGHTER/GROUND ATTACK
  2 sqn with F-16AM/BM *Fighting Falcon*
GROUND ATTACK
  1 sqn with AC-235
ISR
  1 sqn with AT-802U *Air Tractor*; Cessna 208B
TRANSPORT
  1 sqn with C-130E/H *Hercules*
  1 unit with Il-76MF *Candid*
TRAINING
  1 OCU with F-16AM/BM *Fighting Falcon*
  1 OCU with *Hawk* Mk63
  1 sqn with C-101 *Aviojet*
  1 sqn with T-67M *Firefly*
  1 hel sqn with AS350B3; Hughes 500
ATTACK HELICOPTER
  2 sqn with AH-1F *Cobra* (with TOW)
TRANSPORT HELICOPTER
  1 sqn with AS332M *Super Puma*
  1 sqn with Bell 205 (UH-1H *Iroquois*); UH-60A *Black Hawk*
  1 sqn with H135M (Tpt/SAR)
  1 (Royal) flt with S-70A *Black Hawk*; UH-60L/M *Black Hawk*; AW139
AIR DEFENCE
  2 bde with MIM-104C *Patriot* PAC-2; MIM-23B Phase III *I-Hawk*

EQUIPMENT BY TYPE
AIRCRAFT 67 combat capable
  FGA 47: 33 F-16AM *Fighting Falcon*; 14 F-16BM *Fighting Falcon*
  ATK 2 AC235
  ISR 6 AT-802U *Air Tractor**
  TPT 21: **Heavy** 2 Il-76MF *Candid*; **Medium** 7: 3 C-130E *Hercules*; 4 C-130H *Hercules*; **Light** 6: 5 Cessna 208B; 1 M-28 *Skytruck* (2 C295M in store being converted into gunships)
  TRG 40+: 12 *Hawk* Mk63*; 14 T-67M *Firefly*; 10 C-101 *Aviojet*; 4+ PC-21
HELICOPTERS
  ATK 24+ AH-1F *Cobra*
  MRH 14: 3 AW139; 11 H135M (Tpt/SAR)
  TPT 45: **Medium** 35: 10 AS332M *Super Puma*; 25 S-70A/UH-60A/UH-60L/VH-60M *Black Hawk*; **Light** 10: 4+ Bell 205 (UH-1H *Iroquois*); 6 AS350B3; 8 R-44 *Raven* II
UNMANNED AERIAL VEHICLES
  ISR • Light some *Falco*; S-100 *Camcopter*
AIR DEFENCE • SAM 64:
  Long-range 40 MIM-104C *Patriot* PAC-2
  Medium-range 24 MIM-23B Phase III *I-Hawk*

AIR-LAUNCHED MISSILES
  AAM • IR AIM-9J/N/P *Sidewinder*; **SARH** AIM-7 *Sparrow*; **ARH** AIM-120C AMRAAM
  ASM AGM-65D/G *Maverick*; BGM-71 TOW
BOMBS
  Laser-guided GBU-10/12 *Paveway* II

Joint Special Operations Command 14,000
FORCES BY ROLE
SPECIAL FORCES
  1 (Royal Guard) SF bde (1 SF regt, 2 SF bn, 1 CT bn)
  1 ranger bde (1 SF bn, 3 ranger bn)
MANOEUVRE
  Air Manoeuvre
  1 AB bde (2 SF bn, 2 AB bn, 1 AB arty bn, 1 psyops unit)
ISR
  1 sqn with AT-802U *Air Tractor*
TRANSPORT
  1 sqn with An-32B
TRANSPORT HELICOPTER
  1 sqn with MD-530F
  1 sqn with UH-60L *Black Hawk*

EQUIPMENT BY TYPE
AIRCRAFT
  ISR 10 AT-802U *Air Tractor*
  TPT Light 3 An-32B *Cline*
HELICOPTERS
  MRH 6 MD-530F
  TPT • Medium 8 UH-60L *Black Hawk*

Paramilitary ε15,000 active

Gendarmerie ε15,000 active
3 regional comd
FORCES BY ROLE
SPECIAL FORCES
  2 SF unit
MANOEUVRE
  Other
  10 sy bn
EQUIPMENT BY TYPE
ARMOURED FIGHTING VEHICLES
  APC • APC (W) 25+: AT105 *Saxon* (reported); 25+ EE-11 *Urutu*
  AUV AB2 *Al-Jawad*

Reserve Organisations ε35,000 reservists

Civil Militia 'People's Army' ε35,000 reservists
Men 16–65, women 16–45

DEPLOYMENT

CENTRAL AFRICAN REPUBLIC
UN • MINUSCA 7; 3 obs

DEMOCRATIC REPUBLIC OF THE CONGO
UN • MONUSCO 9; 13 obs

MALI
UN • MINUSMA 4; 1 obs

SOUTH SUDAN
UN • UNMISS 2

SUDAN
UN • UNAMID 17; 7 obs

UNITED ARAB EMIRATES
Operation Restoring Hope 6 F-16C *Fighting Falcon*

FOREIGN FORCES

Belgium Operation Inherent Resovle (*Desert Falcon*) 110: 4 F-16AM *Fighting Falcon*
France Operation Inherent Resolve (*Chammal*) 8 *Rafale* F3; 1 *Atlantique* 2
Germany Operation Inherent Resolve 284; 4 *Tornado* ECR; 1 A310 MRTT
Netherlands Operation Inherent Resolve 35
Norway Operation Inherent Resolve 60
United States Central Command: *Operation Inherent Resolve* 2,000; 1 FGA sqn with 12 F-15E *Strike Eagle*; 1 AD bty with MIM-104E/F *Patriot* PAC-2/3; MQ-9A; MQ-1B

Kuwait KWT

Kuwaiti Dinar D		2016	2017	2018
GDP	D	33.5bn	36.2bn	
	US$	111bn	118bn	
per capita	US$	26,245	27,237	
Growth	%	2.5	-2.1	
Inflation	%	3.5	2.5	
Def bdgt	D	1.74bn	1.75bn	
	US$	5.74bn	5.71bn	
US$1=D		0.30	0.31	

Population 2,875,422

Ethnic groups: Nationals 35.5%; other non-Arab Asian countries 37.7%; other Arab countries 17.5%; other or unspecified 9.3%

Age	0–14	15–19	20–24	25–29	30–64	65 plus
Male	13.0%	3.2%	5.1%	7.2%	28.6%	1.2%
Female	12.0%	2.9%	3.8%	4.3%	17.1%	1.4%

Capabilities

The armed forces' primary role is ensuring the territorial integrity of the state, although in practice the limited size of the country, and of the armed forces, would make this task a challenge in the face of a larger committed aggressor. With this in mind, Kuwait has sought security through a close relationship with the US and its membership of the Gulf Cooperation Council. A range of US equipment is prepositioned in the country, including armoured vehicles. The second US–Kuwait Strategic Dialogue, in September 2017, included an agreement to modernise military facilities in Kuwait. The tenth UK–Kuwait Joint Steering Group, meeting in July, noted deepening defence cooperation, and reiterated a commitment to 'refresh the Defence Cooperation Accord' between the two states. Regular exercises continue, including with US forces. Decisions in 2016 regarding the recapitalisation of its combat aircraft saw the country select the F/A-18E/F *Super Hornet* and the *Typhoon*, while the focus in 2017 shifted toward land systems. The army intends to upgrade its M1A2 main battle tanks, while it was reported that discussions continued regarding the possible purchase of Russian T-90MS tanks.

ACTIVE 15,500 (Army 11,000 Navy 2,000 Air 2,500)
Paramilitary 7,100

RESERVE 23,700 (Joint 23,700)
Reserve obligation to age 40; 1 month annual trg

ORGANISATIONS BY SERVICE

Army 11,000
FORCES BY ROLE
SPECIAL FORCES
  1 SF unit (forming)
MANOEUVRE
  Reconnaissance
  1 mech/recce bde
  Armoured
  3 armd bde
  Mechanised
  2 mech inf bde
  Light
  1 cdo bn
  Other
  1 (Amiri) gd bde
COMBAT SUPPORT
  1 arty bde
  1 engr bde
  1 MP bn
COMBAT SERVICE SUPPORT
  1 log gp
  1 fd hospital

Reserve
FORCES BY ROLE
MANOEUVRE
  Mechanised
  1 bde
EQUIPMENT BY TYPE
ARMOURED FIGHTING VEHICLES
  MBT 293: 218 M1A2 *Abrams*; 75 M-84 (75 more in store)
  IFV 465: 76 BMP-2; 153 BMP-3; 236 *Desert Warrior*† (incl variants)
  APC 260
    APC (T) 260: 230 M113A2; 30 M577 (CP)
    APC (W) (40 TH 390 *Fahd* in store)
ENGINEERING & MAINTENANCE VEHICLES
  ARV 24+: 24 M88A1/2; Type-653A; *Warrior*
  MW *Aardvark* Mk2
NBC VEHICLES 11 TPz-1 *Fuchs* NBC
ARTY 211
  SP 155mm 106: 37 M109A3; 18 Mk F3; 51 PLZ-45 (18 AU-F-1 in store)
  MRL 300mm 27 9A52 *Smerch*

MOR 78: **81mm** 60; **107mm** 6 M30; **120mm** ε12 RT-F1
ANTI-TANK/ANTI-INFRASTRUCTURE
  MSL
    SP 74: 66 HMMWV TOW; 8 M901
    MANPATS TOW-2; M47 *Dragon*
  RCL 84mm ε200 *Carl Gustav*
AIR DEFENCE
  SAM
    Short-range 12 *Aspide*
    Point-defence *Starburst*; FIM-92 *Stinger*
  GUNS • TOWED 35mm 12+ Oerlikon

Navy ε2,000 (incl 500 Coast Guard)

EQUIPMENT BY TYPE
PATROL AND COASTAL COMBATANTS 20
  PCFG 2:
    1 *Al Sanbouk* (GER Lurssen TNC-45) with 2 twin lnchr with MM40 *Exocet* AShM, 1 76mm gun
    1 *Istiqlal* (GER Lurssen FPB-57) with 2 twin lnchr with MM40 *Exocet* AShM, 1 76mm gun
  PBF 10 *Al Nokatha* (US Mk V *Pegasus*)
  PBG 8 *Um Almaradim* (FRA P-37 BRL) with 2 twin lnchr with *Sea Skua* AShM
LOGISTICS AND SUPPORT • AG 1 *Sawahil* with 1 hel landing platform

Air Force 2,500

Flying hours 210 hrs/yr

FORCES BY ROLE
FIGHTER/GROUND ATTACK
  2 sqn with F/A-18C/D *Hornet*
TRANSPORT
  1 sqn with C-17A *Globemaster* III; KC-130J *Hercules*; L-100-30
TRAINING
  1 unit with EMB-312 *Tucano**; *Hawk* Mk64*
ATTACK HELICOPTER
  1 sqn with AH-64D *Apache*
  1 atk/trg sqn with SA342 *Gazelle* with HOT
TRANSPORT HELICOPTER
  1 sqn with AS532 *Cougar*; SA330 *Puma*; S-92
EQUIPMENT BY TYPE
AIRCRAFT 66 combat capable
  FGA 39: 31 F/A-18C *Hornet*; 8 F/A-18D *Hornet*
  TKR 3 KC-130J *Hercules*
  TPT 5: **Heavy** 2 C-17A *Globemaster* III; **Medium** 3 L-100-30
  TRG 27: 11 *Hawk* Mk64*; 16 EMB-312 *Tucano**
HELICOPTERS
  ATK 16 AH-64D *Apache*
  MRH 13 SA342 *Gazelle* with HOT
  TPT • Medium 13: 3 AS532 *Cougar*; 7 SA330 *Puma*; 3 S-92
AIR-LAUNCHED MISSILES
  AAM • IR AIM-9L *Sidewinder*; R-550 *Magic*; **SARH** AIM-7F *Sparrow*; **ARH** AIM-120C7 AMRAAM
  ASM AGM-65G *Maverick*; AGM-114K *Hellfire*
  AShM AGM-84A *Harpoon*

Air Defence Command

FORCES BY ROLE
AIR DEFENCE
  1 SAM bde (7 SAM bty with MIM-104D *Patriot* PAC-2 GEM)
  1 SAM bde (6 SAM bty with *Skyguard/Aspide*)
EQUIPMENT BY TYPE
AIR DEFENCE • SAM 52:
  Long-range 40 MIM-104D *Patriot* PAC-2 GEM
  Short-range 12 *Skyguard/Aspide*

Paramilitary ε7,100 active

National Guard ε6,600 active
FORCES BY ROLE
SPECIAL FORCES
  1 SF bn
MANOEUVRE
  Reconnaissance
  1 armd car bn
  Other
  3 security bn
COMBAT SUPPORT
  1 MP bn
EQUIPMENT BY TYPE
ARMOURED FIGHTING VEHICLES
  RECCE 20 VBL
  APC • APC (W) 97+: 5+ *Desert Chameleon*; 70 *Pandur*; 22 S600 (incl variants)
ENGINEERING & MAINTENANCE VEHICLES
  ARV *Pandur*

Coast Guard 500
EQUIPMENT BY TYPE
PATROL AND COASTAL COMBATANTS 32
  PBF 12 *Manta*
  PB 20: 3 *Al Shaheed*; 4 *Inttisar* (Austal 31.5m); 3 *Kassir* (Austal 22m); 10 *Subahi*
AMPHIBIOUS • LANDING CRAFT • LCU 4: 2 *Al Tahaddy*; 1 *Saffar*; 1 other
LOGISTICS AND SUPPORT • AG 1 *Sawahil*

DEPLOYMENT

SAUDI ARABIA
Operation Restoring Hope 4 F/A-18A *Hornet*

FOREIGN FORCES

Canada *Operation Inherent Resolve (Impact)* 1 P-3 *Orion* (CP-140); 1 A310 MRTT (C-150T); 1 C-130J-30 *Hercules* (CC-130J)
Denmark *Operation Inherent Resolve* 20
Italy *Operation Inherent Resolve (Prima Parthica)* 280; 4 AMX; 2 MQ-9A *Reaper*; 1 KC-767A
Poland *Operation Inherent Resolve* 4 F-16C *Fighting Falcon*
Singapore *Operation Inherent Resolve* 11
United Kingdom 30 (trg team) • *Operation Inherent Resolve (Shader)* MQ-9A *Reaper*

United States Central Command: 14,300; 1 armd bde; 1 ARNG cbt avn bde; 1 spt bde; 4 AD bty with MIM-104E/F *Patriot* PAC-2/3; 1 CISR UAV sqn with MQ-9A *Reaper*; 1 (APS) armd bde eqpt set; 1 (APS) inf bde eqpt set

Lebanon LBN

Lebanese Pound LP		2016	2017	2018
GDP	LP	76.1tr	79.4tr	
	US$	50.5bn	52.7bn	
per capita	US$	11,295	11,684	
Growth	%	1.0	1.5	
Inflation	%	-0.8	3.1	
Def bdgt	LP	2.62tr	ε2.81tr	
	US$	1.74bn	ε1.87bn	
FMA (US)	US$	86m	105m	0m
US$1=LP		1,507.49	1,507.50	

Population 6,229,794

Ethnic and religious groups: Christian 30%; Druze 6%; Armenian 4%, excl ε300,000 Syrians and ε350,000 Palestinian refugees

Age	0–14	15–19	20–24	25–29	30–64	65 plus
Male	12.3%	4.2%	4.2%	4.4%	21.9%	2.8%
Female	11.7%	3.9%	4.0%	4.2%	22.0%	3.8%

Capabilities

The destabilising effects of the complex war in Syria have seen the Lebanese Armed Forces (LAF) increasingly tested in their principal roles of internal and border security. Hizbullah plays a key role in Lebanese politics and operates throughout southern and eastern Lebanon; the group has also been involved in pro-regime military operations in Syria since 2013. In 2016 and 2017, ISIS and other jihadi groups mounted attacks along the eastern border. In summer 2017, the LAF conducted large-scale operations there to expel ISIS. Due to Western and Arab concerns about Hizbullah, these were conducted separately from (but deconflicted with) Hizbullah operations against ISIS and other militant groups in the border area. Despite the sensitivities arising from Hizbullah's role in complimentary operations, LAF operations against ISIS have demonstrated improved capability. This included the ability to conduct complex combined-arms operations led by relatively well-equipped special-operations forces, benefiting from the training and support of Western partners. The Lebanese Army has traditionally been stretched by internal-security operations and has had to rely on outdated equipment. Modernisation efforts are under way but funding is a challenge. Though Saudi Arabia cancelled a military-aid package in 2016, some deliveries of French equipment had already taken place and, in 2017, France donated 15 VAB armoured vehicles with HOT anti-tank guided missiles. Separately, in 2017 the US delivered the first eight of 32 M2A2 *Bradley* APCs, on top of earlier deliveries including artillery and C-208B aircraft. The UK has pledged assistance for training, communications equipment, light vehicles and body armour, and in January 2017 updated and developed agreements to support border security and train Land Border regiments. These deliveries are aimed at boosting firepower and counter-insurgency capabilities in order to better tackle militants and improve border security.

ACTIVE 60,000 (Army 56,600 Navy 1,800 Air 1,600)
Paramilitary 20,000

ORGANISATIONS BY SERVICE

Army 56,600
FORCES BY ROLE
5 regional comd (Beirut, Bekaa Valley, Mount Lebanon, North, South)
SPECIAL FORCES
  1 cdo regt
MANOEUVRE
  Armoured
  1 armd regt
  Mechanised
  11 mech inf bde
  Air Manoeuvre
  1 AB regt
  Amphibious
  1 mne cdo regt
  Other
  1 Presidential Guard bde
  6 intervention regt
  4 border sy regt
COMBAT SUPPORT
  2 arty regt
  1 cbt spt bde (1 engr regt, 1 AT regt, 1 sigs regt; 1 log bn)
  1 MP gp
COMBAT SERVICE SUPPORT
  1 log bde
  1 med gp
  1 construction regt
EQUIPMENT BY TYPE
MBT 324: 92 M48A1/A5; 185 T-54; 47 T-55
RECCE 55 AML
IFV 24: 16 AIFV-B-C25; 8 M2A2 *Bradley*
APC 1,370
  APC (T) 1,274 M113A1/A2 (incl variants)
  APC (W) 96: 86 VAB VCT; 10 VBPT-MR *Guarani*
ENGINEERING & MAINTENANCE VEHICLES
  ARV M113 ARV; T-54/55 ARV reported
  VLB MTU-72 reported
  MW *Bozena*
ARTILLERY 571
  SP 155mm 12 M109
  TOWED 313: **105mm** 13 M101A1; **122mm** 35: 9 D-30; 26 M-30; **130mm** 15 M-46; **155mm** 250: 18 M114A1; 218 M198; 14 Model-50
  MRL 122mm 11 BM-21
  MOR 275: **81mm** 134; **82mm** 112; **120mm** 29 Brandt
ANTI-TANK/ANTI-INFRASTRUCTURE
  MSL
    SP 15 VAB with HOT
    MANPATS *Milan*; TOW
  RCL 106mm 113 M40A1

UNMANNED AERIAL VEHICLES
ISR • **Medium** 8 *Mohajer* 4
AIR DEFENCE
SAM • **Point-defence** 9K32 *Strela*-2/2M (SA-7A *Grail*/SA-7B *Grail*)‡
GUNS • **TOWED** 77: **20mm** 20; **23mm** 57 ZU-23-2

Navy 1,800
EQUIPMENT BY TYPE
PATROL AND COASTAL COMBATANTS 13
 PCC 1 *Trablous*
 PB 11: 1 *Aamchit* (ex-GER *Bremen*); 1 *Al Kalamoun* (ex-FRA *Avel Gwarlarn*); 7 *Tripoli* (ex-UK *Attacker/Tracker* Mk 2); 1 *Naquora* (ex-GER *Bremen*); 1 *Tabarja* (ex-GER *Bergen*)
 PBF 1
AMPHIBIOUS • **LANDING CRAFT** • **LCT** 2 *Sour* (ex-FRA EDIC – capacity 8 APC; 96 troops)

Air Force 1,600
4 air bases
FORCES BY ROLE
FIGHTER/GROUND ATTACK
 1 sqn with Cessna AC-208 *Combat Caravan**
ATTACK HELICOPTER
 1 sqn with SA342L *Gazelle*
TRANSPORT HELICOPTER
 4 sqn with Bell 205 (UH-1H)
 1 sqn with SA330/IAR330SM *Puma*
 1 trg sqn with R-44 *Raven* II
EQUIPMENT BY TYPE
AIRCRAFT 5 combat capable
 ISR 3 Cessna AC-208 *Combat Caravan**
 TRG 5: 3 *Bulldog*; 2 A-29 *Super Tucano**
HELICOPTERS
 MRH 9: 1 AW139; 8 SA342L *Gazelle* (5 SA342L *Gazelle*; 5 SA316 *Alouette* III; 1 SA318 *Alouette* II all non-operational)
 TPT 38: **Medium** 13: 3 S-61N (fire fighting); 10 SA330/IAR330 *Puma*; **Light** 25: 18 Bell 205 (UH-1H *Huey*); 3 Bell 205 (UH-1H *Huey* II); 4 R-44 *Raven* II (basic trg) (11 Bell 205; 7 Bell 212 all non-operational)

Paramilitary ε20,000 active
Internal Security Force ε20,000
Ministry of Interior
FORCES BY ROLE
Other Combat Forces
 1 (police) judicial unit
 1 regional sy coy
 1 (Beirut Gendarmerie) sy coy
EQUIPMENT BY TYPE
ARMOURED FIGHTING VEHICLES
 APC • **APC (W)** 60 V-200 *Chaimite*

Customs
EQUIPMENT BY TYPE
PATROL AND COASTAL COMBATANTS 7
 PB 7: 5 *Aztec*; 2 *Tracker*

FOREIGN FORCES
Unless specified, figures refer to UNTSO and represent total numbers for the mission
Argentina 3 obs
Armenia UNIFIL 33
Australia 11 obs
Austria 4 obs • UNIFIL 183: 1 log coy
Bangladesh UNIFIL 275: 1 FFG; 1 FSG
Belarus UNIFIL 5
Belgium 2 obs • UNIFIL 1
Bhutan 2 obs
Brazil UNIFIL 207: 1 FFGH
Brunei UNIFIL 30
Cambodia UNIFIL 185: 1 engr coy
Canada 4 obs (*Operation Jade*)
Chile 3 obs
China, People's Republic of 4 obs • UNIFIL 413: 1 engr coy
Colombia UNIFIL 1
Croatia UNIFIL 1
Cyprus UNIFIL 2
Denmark 12 obs
El Salvador UNIFIL 52: 1 inf pl
Estonia 3 obs • UNIFIL 38
Fiji 2 obs • UNIFIL 145; 1 inf coy
Finland 19 obs • UNIFIL 301; elm 1 inf bn
France UNIFIL 661: 1 mech inf bn(-); VBL; VBCI; VAB; *Mistral*
Germany UNIFIL 122: 1 FFGM
Ghana UNIFIL 870: 1 mech inf bn
Greece UNIFIL 49: 1 PCFG
Guatemala UNIFIL 2
Hungary UNIFIL 4
India 1 obs • UNIFIL 902: 1 inf bn; 1 med coy
Indonesia UNIFIL 1,288: 1 mech inf bn; 1 FSGHM
Ireland 12 obs • UNIFIL 374: elm 1 inf bn
Italy UNIFIL 1,077: 1 AB bde HQ; 1 mech inf bn; 1 engr coy; 1 sigs coy; 1 hel bn
Kenya UNIFIL 1
Korea, Republic of UNIFIL 332: 1 mech inf coy; 1 engr coy; 1 sigs coy; 1 maint coy
Malaysia UNIFIL 828: 1 mech inf bn
Nepal 3 obs • UNIFIL 869: 1 mech inf bn
Netherlands 13 obs • UNIFIL 1
New Zealand 6 obs
Norway 13 obs
Qatar UNIFIL 2
Russia 3 obs
Serbia 1 obs • UNIFIL 174; 1 mech inf coy
Sierra Leone UNIFIL 3
Slovakia 2 obs

Slovenia 3 obs • UNIFIL 15
Spain UNIFIL 628: 1 lt inf bde HQ; 1 mech inf bn(-); 1 engr coy; 1 sigs coy
Sri Lanka UNIFIL 151: 1 inf coy
Sweden 7 obs
Switzerland 12 obs
Tanzania UNIFIL 157: 2 MP coy
Turkey UNIFIL 49: 1 PCFG
United States 2 obs

Libya LBY

Libyan Dinar D		2016	2017	2018
GDP	D	28.4bn	46.2bn	
	US$	20.5bn	33.3bn	
per capita	US$	3,205	5,166	
Growth	%	-3.0	55.1	
Inflation	%	27.1	32.8	
Def exp	D	n.k.	n.k.	
	US$	n.k.	n.k.	
US$1=D		1.39	1.39	

Population   6,653,210

Age	0–14	15–19	20–24	25–29	30–64	65 plus
Male	13.2%	4.4%	4.4%	4.7%	22.8%	2.1%
Female	12.6%	4.2%	4.1%	4.3%	20.8%	2.2%

Capabilities

Two rival administrations and their respective military forces continued to struggle for supremacy in Libya. The internationally recognised Tripoli-based Government of National Accord and the Tobruk-headquartered House of Representatives agreed to a conditional ceasefire in July 2017, in part to allow them to focus on fighting ISIS and other Islamist extremist groups. However, the ceasefire has been breached repeatedly. The forces of the rival governments have limited capabilities. While each faction's military arm has a small number of combat aircraft, availability is an issue, as is attrition, with pilot readiness a concern. Although reportedly in receipt of foreign assistance, the forces remain dependent on the arms stockpiles of the former Gadhafi regime. The EUNAVFOR naval mission has provided training for the Libyan coastguard and the navy in an effort to stem the flow of refugees from the Libyan coast.

Forces loyal to the Government of National Accord (Tripoli-based)

ACTIVE n.k.

ORGANISATIONS BY SERVICE

Ground Forces n.k.
EQUIPMENT BY TYPE
ARMOURED FIGHTING VEHICLES
  MBT T-55; T-72
  IFV BMP-2
  APC • APC (T) 4K-7FA *Steyr*
  AUV Nimr *Ajban*
ENGINEERING & MAINTENANCE VEHICLES
  ARV *Centurion* 105 AVRE
ANTI-TANK/ANTI-INFRASTRUCTURE
  MSL • SP 9P157-2 *Khrizantema*-S (AT-15 *Springer*)
ARTILLERY
  SP 155mm *Palmaria*
  TOWED 122mm D-30

Navy n.k.
A number of intact naval vessels remain in Tripoli, although serviceability is questionable
EQUIPMENT BY TYPE
PRINCIPAL SURFACE COMBATANTS 1
  FRIGATES • FFGM 1 *Al Hani* (FSU *Koni*) (in Italy for refit since 2013) with 2 twin lnchr with P-15 *Termit*-M (SS-N-2C *Styx*) AShM, 1 twin lnchr with 9K33 *Osa*-M (SA-N-4 *Gecko*) SAM, 2 twin 406mm ASTT with USET-95 Type-40 LWT, 1 RBU 6000 *Smerch* 2 A/S mor, 2 twin 76mm gun†
PATROL AND COASTAL COMBATANTS 3+
  PBFG 1 *Sharaba* (FRA *Combattante* II) with 4 single lnchr with *Otomat* Mk2 AShM, 1 76mm gun†
  PB 2+ PV30
AMPHIBIOUS
  LANDING SHIPS • LST 1 *Ibn Harissa* with 3 twin 40mm DARDO CIWS† (capacity 1 hel; 11 MBT; 240 troops)
LOGISTICS AND SUPPORT 2
  AFD 1
  ARS 1 *Al Munjed* (YUG *Spasilac*)†

Air Force n.k.
EQUIPMENT BY TYPE
AIRCRAFT 14+ combat capable
  FGA 2 MiG-23BN
  ATK 1 J-21 *Jastreb*†
  TRG 11+: 3 G-2 *Galeb**; up to 8 L-39ZO*; some SF-260
HELICOPTERS
  ATK Mi-24 *Hind*
  TPT • Medium Mi-17 *Hip*
AIR-LAUNCHED MISSILES • AAM • IR R-3 (AA-2 *Atoll*)‡; R-60 (AA-8 *Aphid*); R-24 (AA-7 *Apex*)

Paramilitary n.k.

Coast Guard n.k.
EQUIPMENT BY TYPE
PATROL AND COASTAL COMBATANTS 7+
  PCC Damen Stan 2909 (YTB armed with with 14.5mm ZSU-2 AD GUNS and 122mm MRL)
  PBF 4 *Bigliani*
  PB 3: 1 *Burdi* (Damen Stan 1605); 1 *Hamelin*; 1 *Ikrimah* (FRA RPB 20)

TERRITORY WHERE THE RECOGNISED AUTHORITY DOES NOT EXERCISE EFFECTIVE CONTROL

Data here represents the de facto situation. This does not imply international recognition

ACTIVE n.k.

ORGANISATIONS BY SERVICE

Libya National Army n.k.
EQUIPMENT BY TYPE
ARMOURED FIGHTING VEHICLES
  MBT T-55; T-72
  RECCE BRDM-2; EE-9 *Cascavel*
  IFV BMP-1; *Ratel*-20
  APC
    APC (T) M113
    APC (W) BTR-60PB; *Puma*
    PPV *Caiman*; Streit *Typhoon*
    AUV *Panthera* T6
ANTI-TANK/ANTI-INFRASTRUCTURE
  MSL
    SP 10 9P157-2 *Khryzantema*-S (status unknown)
    MANPATS 9K11 *Malyutka* (AT-3 *Sagger*); 9K111 *Fagot* (AT-4 *Spigot*); 9K111-1 *Konkurs* (AT-5 *Spandrel*); *Milan*
  RCL some: **106mm** M40A1; **84mm** *Carl Gustav*
ARTILLERY
  TOWED 122mm D-30
  MRL 107mm Type-63; **122mm** BM-21 *Grad*
  MOR M106
AIR DEFENCE
  SAM • Point-defence 9K338 *Igla*-S (SA-24 *Grinch*)
  GUNS • SP 14.5mm ZPU-2 (on tch); **23mm** ZSU-23-4 *Shilka*; ZU-23-2 (on tch)

Navy n.k.
EQUIPMENT BY TYPE
PATROL AND COASTAL COMBATANTS 7+
  PB: 7+: 1 *Burdi* (Damen Stan 1605) with 1 23mm gun; 1 *Burdi* (Damen Stan 1605) with 1 76mm gun; 1 *Burdi* (Damen Stan 1605); 2 *Ikrimah* (FRA RPB20); 1 *Hamelin*; 1+ PV30
LOGISTICS AND SUPPORT 1
  AFD 1

Air Force n.k.
EQUIPMENT BY TYPE
AIRCRAFT 5+ combat capable
  FTR MiG-23 *Flogger*
  FGA 5+: 3+ MiG-21bis/MF *Fishbed*; 1 *Mirage* F-1ED; 1 Su-22UM-3K *Fitter*
  TRG 1+ MiG-21UM *Mongol* B
HELICOPTERS
  ATK Mi-24/35 *Hind*
  TPT Medium Mi-8/Mi-17 *Hip*
AIR-LAUNCHED MISSILES • AAM • IR R-3 (AA-2 *Atoll*)‡; R-60 (AA-8 *Aphid*)

FOREIGN FORCES

Italy Operation *Ippocrate* 300; 1 inf coy; 1 log unit; 1 fd hospital • UNSMIL 2 obs
United Arab Emirates 6 AT-802; 2 UH-60M; 2 *Wing Loong* I (GJ-1) UAV
United Kingdom UNSMIL 1 obs
United States UNSMIL 1 obs

Mauritania MRT

Mauritanian Ouguiya OM		2016	2017	2018
GDP	OM	1.66tr	1.81tr	
	US$	4.73bn	4.99bn	
per capita	US$	1,247	1,284	
Growth	%	1.7	3.8	
Inflation	%	1.5	2.1	
Def bdgt	OM	48.4bn	51.6bn	
	US$	138m	142m	
US$1=OM		351.53	362.51	

Population 3,758,571

Age	0–14	15–19	20–24	25–29	30–64	65 plus
Male	19.4%	5.2%	4.5%	3.9%	13.6%	1.6%
Female	19.2%	5.3%	4.8%	4.3%	16.1%	2.2%

Capabilities

The country's small and modestly equipped military is tasked with territorial integrity and internal security. Its ability to execute these tasks is challenged by a limited and ageing equipment inventory and a lack of adequate training. Due to Mauritania's position in the fight against ISIS and other Islamist extremists in the region, the training requirement has been recognised by the US, NATO and, most recently, Morocco. In early 2017, Mauritania again took part in the US-led special-operations *Flintlock* training exercise, while in September Morocco offered training support to all of the G5 Sahel states. The G5 Sahel agreed in 2017 to form a regional force to operate with French troops in countering Islamist terrorists in the region, which could provide the Mauritanian military with further valuable experience of operating alongside capable and operationally experienced armed forces. In July 2017, Mauritania declared the country's northeastern border region with Algeria a 'no-go' zone for civilians as it attempted to tackle terrorism and drug smuggling there.

ACTIVE 15,850 (Army 15,000 Navy 600 Air 250)
Paramilitary 5,000
Conscript liability 24 months authorised

ORGANISATIONS BY SERVICE

Army 15,000
FORCES BY ROLE
6 mil regions

MANOEUVRE
Reconnaissance
1 armd recce sqn
Armoured
1 armd bn
Light
7 mot inf bn
8 (garrison) inf bn
Air Manoeuvre
1 cdo/para bn
Other
2 (camel corps) bn
1 gd bn
COMBAT SUPPORT
3 arty bn
4 ADA bty
1 engr coy
EQUIPMENT BY TYPE
ARMOURED FIGHTING VEHICLES
MBT 35 T-54/T-55
RECCE 70: 20 AML-60; 40 AML-90; 10 *Saladin*
APC • APC (W) 37: 12 *Cobra*; 5 FV603 *Saracen*; ε20 Panhard M3
ENGINEERING & MAINTENANCE VEHICLES
ARV T-54/55 ARV reported
ANTI-TANK/ANTI-INFRASTRUCTURE
MSL • MANPATS *Milan*
RCL 114: **75mm** ε24 M20; **106mm** ε90 M40A1
ARTILLERY 180
TOWED 80: **105mm** 36 HM-2/M101A1; **122mm** 44: 20 D-30; 24 D-74
MRL 10: **107mm** 4 Type-63; **122mm** 6 Type-81
MOR 90: **81mm** 60; **120mm** 30 Brandt
AIR DEFENCE
SAM • Point-defence ε4 SA-9 *Gaskin* (reported); 9K32 *Strela-2 (SA-7 Grail)*‡
GUNS • TOWED 82: **14.5mm** 28: 16 ZPU-2; 12 ZPU-4; **23mm** 20 ZU-23-2; **37mm** 10 M-1939; **57mm** 12 S-60; **100mm** 12 KS-19

Navy ε600
EQUIPMENT BY TYPE
PATROL AND COASTAL COMBATANTS 17
PCO 1 *Voum-Legleita*
PCC 7: 1 *Aboubekr Ben Amer* (FRA OPV 54); 1 *Arguin*; 2 *Conejera*; 1 *Limam El Hidrami* (PRC); 2 *Timbédra* (PRC *Huangpu* Mod)
PB 9: 1 *El Nasr*† (FRA *Patra*); 4 *Mandovi*; 2 *Saeta-12*; 2 *Megsem Bakkar* (FRA RPB20 – for SAR duties)

Air Force 250
EQUIPMENT BY TYPE
AIRCRAFT 4 combat capable
ISR 2 Cessna 208B *Grand Caravan*
TPT 8: **Light** 7: 2 BN-2 *Defender*; 1 C-212; 2 PA-31T *Cheyenne* II; 2 Y-12(II); **PAX** 1 BT-67 (with sensor turret)
TRG 11: 3 EMB-312 *Tucano*; 4 EMB-314 *Super Tucano**; 4 SF-260E
HELICOPTERS • MRH 3: 1 SA313B *Alouette* II; 2 Z-9

Paramilitary ε5,000 active
Gendarmerie ε3,000
Ministry of Interior
FORCES BY ROLE
MANOEUVRE
Other
6 regional sy coy
EQUIPMENT BY TYPE
ARMOURED FIGHTING VEHICLES
APC • APC (W) 12 *Cobra*
PATROL AND COASTAL COMBATANTS • 2 Rodman 55M

National Guard 2,000
Ministry of Interior

Customs
EQUIPMENT BY TYPE
PATROL AND COASTAL COMBATANTS • **PB** 2: 1 *Dah Ould Bah* (FRA *Amgram* 14); 1 *Yaboub Ould Rajel* (FRA RPB18)

DEPLOYMENT
CENTRAL AFRICAN REPUBLIC
UN • MINUSCA 754; 9 obs; 1 inf bn

MALI
UN • MINUSMA 5

MAURITANIA
UN • UNSOS 1 obs

Morocco MOR

Moroccan Dirham D		2016	2017	2018
GDP	D	1.02tr	1.07tr	
	US$	104bn	111bn	
per capita	US$	3,004	3,177	
Growth	%	1.2	4.8	
Inflation	%	1.6	0.9	
Def bdgt	D	32.6bn	33.8bn	
	US$	3.33bn	3.49bn	
FMA (US)	US$	10m	5m	0m
US$1=D		9.81	9.70	

Population 33,986,655

Age	0–14	15–19	20–24	25–29	30–64	65 plus
Male	13.1%	4.3%	4.2%	4.1%	20.4%	3.0%
Female	12.7%	4.3%	4.3%	4.3%	21.7%	3.7%

Capabilities

Regional security challenges will rank highly for Morocco's armed forces, though they have also been deployed on missions abroad. The armed forces have gained extensive experience in operations in Western Sahara, and have deployed overseas in peacekeeping roles. In 2015, Morocco deployed forces overseas in a combat role, with the dispatch of F-16s to operate as part of the Saudi-led coalition during the conflict in Yemen. The defence budget continues to rise in order to modernise and re-equip the services, partly in response to regional security contingencies; orders for US Army surplus M1A1 *Abrams* MBTs, refurbished to SA standard, were placed in 2015 and deliveries continue. Airforce equipment is ageing overall, bar the delivery of F-16s in 2012. Significant investment in the navy is now taking place. Moroccan troops took part in the US-led *Flintlock 2017* special-forces exercise, training alongside over 20 African and European states. In December 2015, it was reported that Saudi Arabia had pledged US$22bn of financing over 2015–19 to develop Morocco's defence industry, as well as to provide training and exercises. Western defence companies such as Airbus and Thales have a presence in the country. In early 2016, the Moroccan armed forces were incorporated into NATO's Interoperability Platform, in order to strengthen Morocco's defence and security sectors and to bring its forces up to NATO standard. November 2017 saw Arianespace launch the *Mohammed* VI Earth-observation satellite for Morocco.

ACTIVE 195,800 (Army 175,000 Navy 7,800 Air 13,000) Paramilitary 50,000

Conscript liability 18 months authorised; most enlisted personnel are volunteers

RESERVE 150,000 (Army 150,000)
Reserve obligation to age 50

ORGANISATIONS BY SERVICE

Army ε75,000; 100,000 conscript (total 175,000)

FORCES BY ROLE
2 comd (Northern Zone, Southern Zone)
MANOEUVRE
  Armoured
    1 armd bde
    11 armd bn
  Mechanised
    3 mech inf bde
  Mechanised/Light
    8 mech/mot inf regt (2–3 bn)
  Light
    1 lt sy bde
    3 (camel corps) mot inf bn
    35 lt inf bn
    4 cdo unit
  Air Manoeuvre
    2 para bde
    2 AB bn
  Mountain
    1 mtn inf bn
COMBAT SUPPORT
  11 arty bn
  7 engr bn
AIR DEFENCE
  1 AD bn

Royal Guard 1,500

FORCES BY ROLE
MANOEUVRE
  Other
    1 gd bn
    2 cav sqn
EQUIPMENT BY TYPE
ARMOURED FIGHTING VEHICLES
  MBT 407: 27+ M1A1SA *Abrams*; 220 M60A1 *Patton*; 120 M60A3 *Patton*; 40 T-72 (ε200 M48A5 *Patton* in store)
  LT TK 116: 5 AMX-13; 111 SK-105 *Kuerassier*
  ASLT 80 AMX-10RC
  RECCE 284: 38 AML-60-7; 190 AML-90; 40 EBR-75; 16 *Eland*
  IFV 135: 10 AMX-10P; 30 *Ratel* Mk3-20; 30 *Ratel* Mk3-90; 45 VAB VCI
  APC 808
    APC (T) 488: 400 M113A1/A2; 2+ M113A3; 86 M577A2 (CP)
    APC (W) 320 VAB VTT
ENGINEERING & MAINTENANCE VEHICLES
  ARV 48+: 10 *Greif*; 18 M88A1; M578; 20 VAB-ECH
ANTI-TANK/ANTI-INFRASTRUCTURE
  MSL
    SP 80 M901
    MANPATS 9K11 *Malyutka* (AT-3 *Sagger*); M47 *Dragon*; *Milan*; TOW
  RCL 106mm 350 M40A1
  RL 89mm 200 M20
  GUNS • SP 36: **90mm** 28 M56; **100mm** 8 SU-100
ARTILLERY 2,306
  SP 357: **105mm** 5 AMX Mk 61; **155mm** 292: 84 M109A1/A1B; 43 M109A2; 4 M109A3; 1 M109A4; 70 M109A5; 90 Mk F3; **203mm** 60 M110
  TOWED 118: **105mm** 50: 30 L118 Light Gun; 20 M101; **130mm** 18 M-46; **155mm** 50: 30 FH-70; 20 M114
  MRL 122mm 35 BM-21 *Grad*
  MOR 1,796: **81mm** 1,100 Expal model LN; **SP 107mm** 36 M106A2; **120mm** 550 Brandt; **SP 120mm** 110: 20 (VAB APC); 90 M1064A3
RADAR • LAND RASIT (veh, arty)
UNMANNED AERIAL VEHICLES
  ISR • Medium R4E-50 *Skyeye*
AIR DEFENCE
  SAM
    Point-defence 49+: 12 2K22M *Tunguska*-M (SA-19 *Grison*); 37 M48 *Chaparral*; 9K32 *Strela*-2 (SA-7 *Grail*)‡
  GUNS 407
    SP 20mm 60 M163 *Vulcan*
    TOWED 347: **14.5mm** 200: 150–180 ZPU-2; 20 ZPU-4; **20mm** 40 M167 *Vulcan*; **23mm** 75–90 ZU-23-2; **100mm** 17 KS-19

Navy 7,800 (incl 1,500 Marines)

EQUIPMENT BY TYPE
PRINCIPAL SURFACE COMBATANTS 6
  DESTROYERS 1
    DDGHM 1 *Mohammed* VI-class (FRA FREMM) with 2 quad lnchr with MM40 *Exocet* Block 3 AShM, 2 octuple A43 VLS with *Aster* 15 SAM, 2 triple

B515 324mm ASTT with MU90 LWT, 1 76mm gun (capacity 1 AS565SA *Panther*)
FRIGATES 5
  FFGHM 3 *Tarik ben Ziyad* (NLD SIGMA 9813/10513) with 4 single lnchr with MM40 *Exocet* Block 2/3 AShM, 2 6-cell VLS with VL-MICA SAM, 2 triple 324mm ASTT with MU90 LWT, 1 76mm gun (capacity 1 AS565SA *Panther*)
  FFGH 2 *Mohammed V* (FRA *Floreal*) with 2 single lnchr with MM38 *Exocet* AShM, 1 76mm gun (can be fitted with *Simbad* SAM) (capacity 1 AS565SA *Panther*)
PATROL AND COASTAL COMBATANTS 50
  CORVETTES • FSGM 1
    1 *Lt Col Errhamani* (ESP *Descubierto*) with 2 twin lnchr with MM38 *Exocet* AShM, 1 octuple *Albatros* lnchr with *Aspide* SAM, 2 triple 324mm ASTT with Mk46 LWT, 1 76mm gun
  PSO 1 *Bin an Zaran* (OPV 70) with 1 76mm gun
  PCG 4 *Cdt El Khattabi* (ESP *Lazaga* 58m) with 4 single lnchr with MM38 *Exocet* AShM, 1 76mm gun
  PCO 5 *Rais Bargach* (under control of fisheries dept)
  PCC 12:
    4 *El Hahiq* (DNK *Osprey* 55, incl 2 with customs)
    6 *LV Rabhi* (ESP 58m B-200D)
    2 *Okba* (FRA PR-72) each with 1 76mm gun
  PB 27: 6 *El Wacil* (FRA P-32); 10 VCSM (RPB 20); 10 Rodman 101; 1 other (UK *Bird*)
AMPHIBIOUS 5
  LANDING SHIPS 4:
    LSM 3 *Ben Aicha* (FRA *Champlain* BATRAL) (capacity 7 tanks; 140 troops)
    LST 1 *Sidi Mohammed Ben Abdallah* (US *Newport*) (capacity 3 LCVP; 400 troops)
  LANDING CRAFT 2:
    LCM 1 CTM (FRA CTM-5)
    LCT 1 *Sidi Ifni*
LOGISTICS AND SUPPORT 8
  AG 1 Damen 3011
  AGOR 1 *Abou Barakat Albarbari†* (ex-US *Robert D. Conrad*)
  AGS 1 Stan 1504
  AK 2
  AX 1 *Essaouira*
  AXS 2

Marines 1,500

FORCES BY ROLE
MANOEUVRE
  Amphibious
  2 naval inf bn

Naval Aviation

EQUIPMENT BY TYPE
HELICOPTERS • ASW/ASUW 3 AS565SA *Panther*

Air Force 13,000

Flying hours 100 hrs/yr on *Mirage* F-1/F-5E/F *Tiger* II/F-16C/D *Fighting Falcon*

FORCES BY ROLE
FIGHTER/GROUND ATTACK
  2 sqn with F-5E/F-5F *Tiger* II
  3 sqn with F-16C/D *Fighting Falcon*
  1 sqn with *Mirage* F-1C (F-1CH)
  1 sqn with *Mirage* F-1E (F-1EH)
ELECTRONIC WARFARE
  1 sqn with EC-130H *Hercules*; *Falcon* 20 (ELINT)
MARITIME PATROL
  1 flt with Do-28
TANKER/TRANSPORT
  1 sqn with C-130/KC-130H *Hercules*
TRANSPORT
  1 sqn with CN235
  1 VIP sqn with B-737BBJ; Beech 200/300 *King Air*; *Falcon* 50; Gulfstream II/III/V-SP/G550
TRAINING
  1 sqn with *Alpha Jet**
  1 sqn T-6C
ATTACK HELICOPTER
  1 sqn with SA342L *Gazelle* (some with HOT)
TRANSPORT HELICOPTER
  1 sqn with Bell 205A (AB-205A); Bell 206 *Jet Ranger* (AB-206); Bell 212 (AB-212)
  1 sqn with CH-47D *Chinook*
  1 sqn with SA330 *Puma*

EQUIPMENT BY TYPE
AIRCRAFT 90 combat capable
  FTR 22: 19 F-5E *Tiger* II; 3 F-5F *Tiger* II
  FGA 49: 15 F-16C *Fighting Falcon*; 8 F-16D *Fighting Falcon*; 15 *Mirage* F-1C (F-1CH); 11 *Mirage* F-1E (F-1EH)
  ELINT 1 EC-130H *Hercules*
  TKR/TPT 2 KC-130H *Hercules*
  TPT 47: **Medium** 17: 4 C-27J *Spartan*; 13 C-130H *Hercules*; **Light** 19: 4 Beech 100 *King Air*; 2 Beech 200 *King Air*; 1 Beech 200C *King Air*; 2 Beech 300 *King Air*; 3 Beech 350 *King Air*; 5 CN235; 2 Do-28; **PAX** 11: 1 B-737BBJ; 2 *Falcon* 20; 2 *Falcon* 20 (ELINT); 1 *Falcon* 50 (VIP); 1 Gulfstream II (VIP); 1 Gulfstream III; 1 Gulfstream V-SP; 2 Gulfstream G550
  TRG 80: 12 AS-202 *Bravo*; 19 *Alpha Jet**; 2 CAP-10; 24 T-6C *Texan*; 9 T-34C *Turbo Mentor*; 14 T-37B *Tweet*
  FF 4 CL-415
HELICOPTERS
  MRH 19 SA342L *Gazelle* (7 with HOT, 12 with cannon)
  TPT 77: **Heavy** 10 CH-47D *Chinook*; **Medium** 24 SA330 *Puma*; **Light** 43: 25 Bell 205A (AB-205A); 11 Bell 206 *Jet Ranger* (AB-206); 3 Bell 212 (AB-212); 4 Bell 429
AIR-LAUNCHED MISSILES
  AAM • IR AIM-9J *Sidewinder*; R-550 *Magic*; **IIR** AIM-9X *Sidewinder* II; **SARH** R-530; **ARH** AIM-120C7 AMRAAM
  ASM AASM; AGM-65 *Maverick*; HOT
  ARM AGM-88B HARM
BOMBS • Laser-guided *Paveway* II

Paramilitary 50,000 active

Gendarmerie Royale 20,000

FORCES BY ROLE
MANOEUVRE
  Air Manoeuvre
  1 para sqn

Other
  1 paramilitary bde
  4 (mobile) paramilitary gp
  1 coast guard unit
TRANSPORT HELICOPTER
  1 sqn
EQUIPMENT BY TYPE
PATROL AND COASTAL COMBATANTS • PB 15
Arcor 53
AIRCRAFT • TRG 2 R-235 *Guerrier*
HELICOPTERS
  MRH 14: 3 SA315B *Lama*; 2 SA316 *Alouette* III; 3 SA318 *Alouette* II; 6 SA342K *Gazelle*
  TPT 8: **Medium** 6 SA330 *Puma*; **Light** 2 SA360 *Dauphin*

Force Auxiliaire 30,000 (incl 5,000 Mobile Intervention Corps)

Customs/Coast Guard

EQUIPMENT BY TYPE
PATROL AND COASTAL COMBATANTS • PB 36: 4 *Erraid*; 18 *Arcor* 46; 14 (other SAR craft)

DEPLOYMENT

CENTRAL AFRICAN REPUBLIC
UN • MINUSCA 765; 2 obs; 1 inf bn
DEMOCRATIC REPUBLIC OF THE CONGO
UN • MONUSCO 836; 3 obs; 1 inf bn; 1 fd hospital
UNITED ARAB EMIRATES
Operation Restoring Hope 6 F-16C *Fighting Falcon*

Oman OMN

Omani Rial R		2016	2017	2018
GDP	R	25.5bn	27.7bn	
	US$	66.3bn	71.9bn	
per capita	US$	16,535	17,406	
Growth	%	3.0	0.0	
Inflation	%	1.1	3.2	
Def bdgt	R	3.50bn	3.34bn	
	US$	9.10bn	8.69bn	
FMA (US)	US$	2m	0m	0m
US$1=R		0.38	0.38	

Population 3,424,386
Expatriates: 27%

Age	0–14	15–19	20–24	25–29	30–64	65 plus
Male	15.4%	4.5%	5.2%	5.9%	21.4%	1.7%
Female	14.6%	4.3%	4.6%	4.6%	15.7%	1.7%

Capabilities

Oman supports small but well-trained and -equipped armed forces whose principal task is ensuring territorial integrity. Membership of the Gulf Cooperation Council (GCC) and ties with the UK and the US are also intended to act as security guarantors. The forces are in the process of recapitalising core inventory elements with air- and naval-systems purchases. The air force has taken delivery of the last of a batch of F-16 Block 40s that have replaced the *Jaguar*, and received the first of eight *Hawk* and 12 *Typhoon* aircraft. Naval recapitalisation is also under way, with the delivery in 2016 of patrol and high-speed support vessels. Oman is making a significant investment in infrastructure, such as at the port of Duqm. In August 2017, the UK and Oman signed a memorandum of understanding over use of the port, and its strategic importance will deepen the interest of other navies. The US Navy has already carried out extensive examination of the facilities. Although a GCC member, Oman has not contributed any forces to the Saudi-led military intervention in Yemen.

ACTIVE 42,600 (Army 25,000 Navy 4,200 Air 5,000 Foreign Forces 2,000 Royal Household 6,400) **Paramilitary 4,400**

ORGANISATIONS BY SERVICE

Army 25,000

FORCES BY ROLE
(Regt are bn size)
MANOEUVRE
  Armoured
  1 armd bde (2 armd regt, 1 recce regt)
  Light
  1 inf bde (5 inf regt, 1 arty regt, 1 fd engr regt, 1 engr regt, 1 sigs regt)
  1 inf bde (3 inf regt, 2 arty regt)
  1 indep inf coy (Musandam Security Force)
  Air Manoeuvre
  1 AB regt
COMBAT SERVICE SUPPORT
  1 tpt regt
AIR DEFENCE
  1 ADA regt (2 ADA bty)
EQUIPMENT BY TYPE
ARMOURED FIGHTING VEHICLES
  MBT 117: 38 *Challenger* 2; 6 M60A1 *Patton*; 73 M60A3 *Patton*
  LT TK 37 FV101 *Scorpion*
  RECCE 137: 13 FV105 *Sultan* (CP); 124 VBL
  IFV some *Pars* III 8×8 (reported)
  APC 200
    APC (T) 10 FV4333 *Stormer*
    APC (W) 190: 175 *Piranha* (incl variants); 15 AT-105 *Saxon*
  AUV 6 FV103 *Spartan*
ENGINEERING & MAINTENANCE VEHICLES
  ARV 11: 4 *Challenger*; 2 M88A1; 2 *Piranha*; 3 *Samson*
ARTILLERY 233
  SP 155mm 24 G-6
  TOWED 108: **105mm** 42 L118 Light Gun; **122mm** 30 D-30; **130mm** 24: 12 M-46; 12 Type-59-I; **155mm** 12 FH-70

MOR 101: **81mm** 69; **107mm** 20 M30; **120mm** 12 Brandt
ANTI-TANK/ANTI-INFRASTRUCTURE • MSL
SP 8 VBL with TOW
MANPATS FGM-148 *Javelin*; *Milan*; TOW/TOW-2A
AIR DEFENCE
SAM • Point-defence 8 *Mistral 2*; FGM-148 *Javelin*; 9K32 *Strela-2* (SA-7 *Grail*)‡
GUNS 26: **23mm** 4 ZU-23-2; **35mm** 10 GDF-005 (with *Skyguard*); **40mm** 12 L/60 (Towed)

Navy 4,200
EQUIPMENT BY TYPE
PRIMARY SURFACE COMBATANTS 3
FFGHM 3 *Al-Shamikh* with 2 twin lnchr with MM40 *Exocet* Block 3 AShM, 2 6-cell VLS with VL-*MICA* SAM, 1 76mm gun
PATROL AND COASTAL COMBATANTS 12
CORVETTES • FSGM 2:
2 *Qahir Al Amwaj* with 2 quad lnchr with MM40 *Exocet* AShM, 1 octuple lnchr with *Crotale* SAM, 1 76mm gun, 1 hel landing platform
PCFG 3 *Dhofar* with 2 quad lnchr with MM40 *Exocet* AShM, 1 76mm gun
PCO 4 *Al Ofouq* with 1 76mm gun, 1 hel landing platform
PCC 3 *Al Bushra* (FRA P-400) with 1 76mm gun
AMPHIBIOUS 6
LANDING SHIPS • LST 1 *Nasr el Bahr* with 1 hel landing platform (capacity 7 tanks; 240 troops)
LANDING CRAFT 5: 1 LCU; 3 LCM; 1 LCT
LOGISTICS AND SUPPORT 8
AGS 1 *Al Makhirah*
AK 1 *Al Sultana*
AP 2 *Shinas* (commercial tpt – auxiliary military role only) (capacity 56 veh; 200 tps)
AXS 1 *Shabab Oman* II
EPF 2 *Al Mubshir* (High Speed Support Vessel 72) with 1 hel landing platform (capacity 260 troops)

Air Force 5,000
FORCES BY ROLE
FIGHTER/GROUND ATTACK
2 sqn with F-16C/D Block 50 *Fighting Falcon*
1 sqn with *Hawk* Mk103; *Hawk* Mk203
1 sqn (forming) with *Typhoon*
MARITIME PATROL
1 sqn with C295MPA; SC.7 3M *Skyvan*
TRANSPORT
1 sqn with C-130H/J/J-30 *Hercules*
1 sqn with C295M
TRAINING
1 sqn with MFI-17B *Mushshak*; PC-9*; Bell 206 (AB-206) *Jet Ranger*
TRANSPORT HELICOPTER
4 (med) sqn; Bell 212 (AB-212); NH-90; *Super Lynx* Mk300 (maritime/SAR)
AIR DEFENCE
2 sqn with *Rapier*; *Blindfire*; S713 *Martello*
EQUIPMENT BY TYPE
AIRCRAFT 58 combat capable

FGA 30: 18 F-16C Block 50 *Fighting Falcon*; 6 F-16D Block 50 *Fighting Falcon*; 6 *Typhoon*
MP 4 C295MPA
TPT 20: **Medium** 6: 3 C-130H *Hercules*; 2 C-130J *Hercules*; 1 C-130J-30 *Hercules* (VIP); **Light** 12: 5 C295M; 7 SC.7 3M *Skyvan* (radar-equipped, for MP); **PAX** 2 A320-300
TRG 40: 4 *Hawk* Mk103*; 4 *Hawk* Mk166; 12 *Hawk* Mk203*; 8 MFI-17B *Mushshak*; 12 PC-9*
HELICOPTERS
MRH 15 *Super Lynx* Mk300 (maritime/SAR)
TPT 36+: **Medium** 20 NH90 TTH; **Light** 6: 3 Bell 206 (AB-206) *Jet Ranger*; 3 Bell 212 (AB-212)
AIR DEFENCE • SAM • Point-defence 40 *Rapier*
RADAR • AIR DEFENCE 6+: 6 *Blindfire*; S713 *Martello*
MSL
AAM • IR AIM-9/M/P *Sidewinder*; IIR AIM-9X *Sidewinder* II; ARH AIM-120C7 AMRAAM
ASM AGM-65D/G *Maverick*
AShM AGM-84D *Harpoon*
BOMBS
Laser-guided EGBU-10 *Paveway* II; EGBU-12 *Paveway* II
INS/GPS guided GBU-31 JDAM

Royal Household 6,400
(incl HQ staff)
FORCES BY ROLE
SPECIAL FORCES
2 SF regt

Royal Guard Brigade 5,000
FORCES BY ROLE
MANOEUVRE
Other
1 gd bde (1 armd sqn, 2 gd regt, 1 cbt spt bn)
EQUIPMENT BY TYPE
ARMOURED FIGHTING VEHICLES
ASLT 9 *Centauro* MGS (9 VBC-90 in store)
IFV 14 VAB VCI
APC • APC (W) ε50 Type-92
ANTI-TANK/ANTI-INFRASTRUCTURE
MSL • MANPATS *Milan*
ARTILLERY • MRL **122mm** 6 Type-90A
AIR DEFENCE
SAM • Point-defence 14 *Javelin*
GUNS • SP 9: **20mm** 9 VAB VDAA

Royal Yacht Squadron 150
EQUIPMENT BY TYPE
LOGISTICS AND SUPPORT 3
AP 1 *Fulk Al Salamah* (also veh tpt) with up to 2 AS332 *Super Puma* hel

Royal Flight 250
EQUIPMENT BY TYPE
AIRCRAFT • TPT • PAX 5: 2 B-747SP; 1 DC-8-73CF; 2 Gulfstream IV
HELICOPTERS • TPT • Medium 6: 3 SA330 (AS330) *Puma*; 2 AS332F *Super Puma*; 1 AS332L *Super Puma*

Paramilitary 4,400 active

Tribal Home Guard 4,000
org in teams of ε100

Police Coast Guard 400
EQUIPMENT BY TYPE
PATROL AND COASTAL COMBATANTS 33
  PCO 2 *Haras*
  PBF 3 *Haras* (US Mk V *Pegasus*)
  PB 27: 3 Rodman 101; 1 *Haras* (SWE CG27); 3 *Haras* (SWE CG29); 14 Rodman 58; 1 D59116; 5 *Zahra*

Police Air Wing
EQUIPMENT BY TYPE
AIRCRAFT • TPT • Light 4: 1 BN-2T *Turbine Islander*; 2 CN235M; 1 Do-228
HELICOPTERS • TPT • Light 5: 2 Bell 205A; 3 Bell 214ST (AB-214ST)

FOREIGN FORCES
United Kingdom 90; 1 hel flt with AW101 ASW *Merlin* HM2; AW159 *Wildcat* HMA2

Palestinian Territories PT

New Israeli Shekel NS		2016	2017	2018
GDP	US$			
per capita	US$			
Growth	%			
Inflation	%			

US$1=NS
*definitive economic data unavailable

Population 4,543,126

Age	0–14	15–19	20–24	25–29	30–64	65 plus
Male	20.4%	5.7%	5.1%	4.3%	13.7%	1.4%
Female	19.3%	5.5%	4.9%	4.2%	13.5%	1.6%

Capabilities

The Palestinian Authority's National Security Force (NSF) is a paramilitary organisation designed to provide internal-security support within Gaza and the West Bank. The NSF only has real authority within the West Bank, where it has generally proved capable of maintaining internal security. In October 2017, Hamas and Fatah reached agreement to hand administrative control of Gaza to a Fatah-backed unity government; since 2007, Hamas had controlled Gaza. The agreement did not address the fate of Hamas's military wing, which has a strong, well-developed rocket-artillery capability. Hamas brigades also engage in innovative asymmetric attacks. Israel's military actions in recent years have periodically degraded the command and control of, as well as the physical infrastructure used by, Hamas forces, but have seemingly had little effect on the long-term ability of the brigades to produce, import, store and launch rockets. In late 2016, the then-Hamas-led administration in Gaza announced a new maritime-police force, separate from other security forces in Gaza, to enhance coastal security. Full security coordination between Israel and the Palestinian Authority resumed in late 2017. International partners remain engaged in support and development of the security sector; the EU, for instance, has maintained a police-support mission headquartered in Ramallah since 2006.

ACTIVE 0 Paramilitary n.k.
Precise personnel-strength figures for the various Palestinian groups are not known

ORGANISATIONS BY SERVICE

There is little available data on the status of the organisations mentioned below. Following internal fighting in June 2007, Gaza has been under the de facto control of Hamas, while the West Bank is controlled by the Palestinian Authority. In October 2017, both sides agreed a preliminary reconciliation deal on control of Gaza.

Paramilitary

Palestinian Authority n.k.

Presidential Security ε3,000

Special Forces ε1,200

Police ε9,000

National Security Force ε10,000
FORCES BY ROLE
MANOEUVRE
  Other
  9 paramilitary bn

Preventative Security ε4,000

Civil Defence ε1,000

The al-Aqsa Brigades n.k.
Profess loyalty to the Fatah group that dominates the Palestinian Authority

Hamas n.k.

Izz al-Din al-Qassam Brigades ε15,000–20,000
FORCES BY ROLE
COMMAND
  6 bde HQ (regional)
MANOEUVRE
  Other
  1 cdo unit (Nukhba)
  27 paramilitary bn
  100 paramilitary coy
COMBAT SUPPORT
  Some engr units
COMBAT SERVICE SUPPORT
  Some log units
EQUIPMENT BY TYPE
ANTI-TANK/ANTI-INFRASTRUCTURE • MSL •
MANPATS 9K11 *Malyutka* (AT-3 *Sagger*) (reported)

ARTILLERY
MRL • *Qassam* rockets (multiple calibres); **122mm** *Grad*
MOR some (multiple calibres)

Martime Police ε600

Qatar QTR

Qatari Riyal R		2016	2017	2018
GDP	R	567bn	606bn	
	US$	156bn	166bn	
per capita	US$	59,514	60,812	
Growth	%	2.2	2.5	
Inflation	%	2.7	0.9	
Def exp	R	n.k.	n.k.	
	US$	n.k.	n.k.	
US$1=R		3.64	3.64	

Population 2,314,307

Ethnic groups: Nationals 25%; expatriates 75% of which Indian 18%; Iranian 10%; Pakistani 18%

Age	0–14	15–19	20–24	25–29	30–64	65 plus
Male	6.4%	2.4%	6.5%	11.3%	50.0%	0.6%
Female	6.2%	1.5%	1.9%	2.8%	9.8%	0.3%

Capabilities

The diplomatic crisis between Qatar and several of its neighbours raises questions about the emirate's future cooperation and integration with the rest of the Gulf Cooperation Council (GCC). But it seems to have brought Qatar and Turkey closer together in their limited but significant defence cooperation, which includes a small Turkish military presence in-country. Neither the crisis, nor Washington's response to it, appear to have affected the significant Qatar–US military relationship, including the presence of forces from the US and other Western states at Al-Udeid air base. Qatar continues its ambitious re-equipment and expansion programme and has procured, or plans to procure, platforms with potentially significant power-projection capability. With the delivery of C-17A *Globemaster*s complete, only the UAE has a larger strategic-transport fleet in the GCC. Following approval for the sale of F-15QA aircraft in late 2016, Qatar signed an agreement with the US in June 2017 towards the purchase of a batch of 36, while a letter of intent for *Typhoon* aircraft was signed with the UK in September. Both of these agreements follow the signing of a contract in 2015 for *Rafale* aircraft from France. These procurements would, when combined, dramatically increase the size of the air force; this raises questions about Qatar's ability to procure the necessary infrastructure, maintenance and personnel. Contracts are also proceeding for naval expansion, after four corvettes, two offshore-patrol vessels and an amphibious platform were ordered from Italy in June 2016. *Marte* ER and *Exocet* MM40 Block 3 missiles are being acquired for coastal defence, which will provide a layered engagement field out to 200km. In March, Raytheon was awarded a US$1.07bn contract to install an AN/FPS-132 early-warning radar. (See pp. 321–24.)

ACTIVE 11,800 (Army 8,500 Navy 1,800 Air 1,500)
Paramilitary up to 5,000

Conscript liability 4 months national service for those aged 18–35; reduced to 3 months for graduates. Reserve commitment for 10 years or to age 40

ORGANISATIONS BY SERVICE

Army 12,000 (including Emiri Guard)
FORCES BY ROLE
SPECIAL FORCES
1 SF coy
MANOEUVRE
Armoured
1 armd bde (1 tk bn, 1 mech inf bn, 1 mor sqn, 1 AT bn)
Mechanised
3 mech inf bn
Light
1 (Emiri Guard) bde (3 inf regt)
COMBAT SUPPORT
1 fd arty bn
EQUIPMENT BY TYPE
ARMOURED FIGHTING VEHICLES
MBT 73: 30 AMX-30; 43 *Leopard* 2A7
ASLT 48: 12 AMX-10RC; 36 *Piranha* II 90mm
RECCE 44: 20 EE-9 *Cascavel*; 8 V-150 *Chaimite*; 16 VBL
IFV 40 AMX-10P
APC 190
APC (T) 30 AMX-VCI
APC (W) 160 VAB
ENGINEERING & MAINTENANCE VEHICLES
ARV 3: 1 AMX-30D; 2 *Piranha*
ANTI-TANK/ANTI-INFRASTRUCTURE
MSL
SP 24 VAB VCAC HOT
MANPATS *Milan*
RCL **84mm** ε40 *Carl Gustav*
ARTILLERY 115+
SP **155mm** 52: 28 Mk F3; 24 PzH 2000
TOWED **155mm** 12 G-5
MRL 6+: **122mm** 2+ (30-tube); **127mm** 4 ASTROS II Mk3
MOR 45: **81mm** 26 L16; SP **81mm** 4 VAB VPM 81; **120mm** 15 Brandt

Navy 2,500 (incl Coast Guard)
EQUIPMENT BY TYPE
PATROL AND COASTAL COMBATANTS 11
PCFGM 4 *Barzan* (UK *Vita*) with 2 quad lnchr with MM40 *Exocet* Block 3 AShM, 1 sextuple lnchr with *Mistral* SAM, 1 *Goalkeeper* CIWS, 1 76mm gun
PCFG 3 *Damsah* (FRA *Combattante* III) with 2 quad lnchr with MM40 *Exocet* AShM, 1 76mm gun
PBF 3 MRTP 16
PB 1 MRTP 34
AMPHIBIOUS • LANDING CRAFT • LCT 1 *Rabha* (capacity 3 MBT; 110 troops)

Coast Guard

EQUIPMENT BY TYPE
PATROL AND COASTAL COMBATANTS 12
  PBF 4 DV 15
  PB 8: 4 *Crestitalia* MV-45; 3 *Halmatic* M160; 1 other

Coastal Defence

FORCES BY ROLE
COASTAL DEFENCE
  1 bty with 3 quad lnchr with MM40 *Exocet* AShM
EQUIPMENT BY TYPE
COASTAL DEFENCE • AShM 12 MM40 *Exocet* AShM

Air Force 2,000

FORCES BY ROLE
FIGHTER/GROUND ATTACK
  1 sqn with *Alpha Jet**
  1 sqn with *Mirage* 2000ED; *Mirage* 2000D
TRANSPORT
  1 sqn with C-17A *Globemaster* III; C-130J-30 *Hercules*
  1 sqn with A340; B-707; B-727; *Falcon* 900
ATTACK HELICOPTER
  1 ASuW sqn with *Commando* Mk3 with *Exocet*
  1 sqn with SA341 *Gazelle*; SA342L *Gazelle* with HOT
TRANSPORT HELICOPTER
  1 sqn with *Commando* Mk2A; *Commando* Mk2C
  1 sqn with AW139
EQUIPMENT BY TYPE
AIRCRAFT 18 combat capable
  FGA 12: 9 *Mirage* 2000ED; 3 *Mirage* 2000D
  TPT 18: **Heavy** 8 C-17A *Globemaster* III; **Medium** 4 C-130J-30 *Hercules*; **PAX** 6: 1 A340; 2 B-707; 1 B-727; 2 *Falcon* 900
  TRG 27: 6 *Alpha Jet**; 21 PC-21
HELICOPTERS
  ASuW 8 *Commando* Mk3
  MRH 34: 21 AW139 (incl 3 for medevac); 2 SA341 *Gazelle*; 11 SA342L *Gazelle*
  TPT • Medium 4: 3 *Commando* Mk2A; 1 *Commando* Mk2C
AIR DEFENCE • SAM
  Long-Range MIM-104E *Patriot* PAC-2 GEM-T
  Short-Range 9 *Roland* II
  Point-defence *Mistral*; *Blowpipe*; FIM-92 *Stinger*; 9K32 *Strela*-2 (SA-7 *Grail*)‡
AIR-LAUNCHED MISSILES
  AAM • IR R-550 *Magic* 2; **ARH** *Mica* RF
  ASM *Apache*; HOT
  AShM AM39 *Exocet*

Paramilitary up to 5,000 active

Internal Security Force up to 5,000

DEPLOYMENT

LEBANON
UN • UNIFIL 2

FOREIGN FORCES

Turkey 150 (trg team)
United States US Central Command: 8,000; USAF CAOC; 1 bbr sqn with 6 B-52H *Stratofortress*; 1 ISR sqn with 4 RC-135 *Rivet Joint*; 1 ISR sqn with 4 E-8C JSTARS; 1 tkr sqn with 24 KC-135R/T *Straotanker*; 1 tpt sqn with 4 C-17A *Globemaster*; 4 C-130H/J-30 *Hercules*; 2 AD bty with MIM-104E/F *Patriot* PAC-2/3 • US Strategic Command: 1 AN/TPY-2 X-band radar

Saudi Arabia SAU

Saudi Riyal R		2016	2017	2018
GDP	R	2.42tr	2.54tr	
	US$	646bn	679bn	
per capita	US$	20,365	20,957	
Growth	%	1.7	0.1	
Inflation	%	3.5	-0.2	
Def exp	R	306bn	288bn	
	US$	81.5bn	76.7bn	
US$1=R		3.75	3.75	

Population 28,571,770

Ethnic groups: Nationals 73%, of which Bedouin up to 10%, Shia 6%; expatriates 27% of which Asian 20%, Arab 6%, African 1%, European <1%

Age	0–14	15–19	20–24	25–29	30–64	65 plus
Male	13.4%	4.5%	5.4%	5.9%	23.2%	1.7%
Female	12.7%	4.2%	4.4%	4.6%	18.1%	1.7%

Capabilities

Saudi Arabia retains the region's best-equipped military forces, with the exception of Israel. Principal roles are securing territorial integrity, internal security and regional stability. Its armed forces are continuing to gain combat experience in its war with the Houthi and allied Saleh-loyalist opposition in Yemen, although the operation, begun in 2015, has also exposed areas of comparative weakness and capability gaps. The fourth quarter of 2017 saw a series of leadership changes initiated by King Salman and Crown Prince Mohammed bin Salman, the defence minister, which included the replacement of National Guard (SANG) commander Prince Miteb with Prince Khaled bin Ayyaf, who has long experience with the SANG. The fighting in Yemen continued to see Houthi forces fire *Scud*-based ballistic missiles at Saudi Arabia, with the Kingdom's *Patriot* PAC-2/PAC-3 batteries being used to intercept them. A diplomatic row involving Saudi Arabia and Qatar has stymied, for the moment at least, aspirations for closer defence ties among GCC states, particularly in the area of missile defence. The UK and the US remain the country's two main sources of advanced military equipment and will be a focus of defence-industrial support as Riyadh attempts to implement elements of the Vision 2030 programme, which aims to diversify the Saudi economy and reduce the country's reliance on hydrocarbons. The UK and Saudi Arabia signed a new Military and Security Cooperation

Agreement in September 2017. During President Trump's visit to Riyadh in May, the two countries agreed to establish a Strategic Joint Consultative Group, and furthered existing defence and security cooperation.

ACTIVE 227,000 (Army 75,000 Navy 13,500 Air 20,000 Air Defence 16,000 Strategic Missile Forces 2,500 National Guard 100,000) Paramilitary 24,500

ORGANISATIONS BY SERVICE

Army 75,000
FORCES BY ROLE
MANOEUVRE
  Armoured
    4 armd bde (1 recce coy, 3 tk bn, 1 mech bn, 1 fd arty bn, 1 AD bn, 1 AT bn, 1 engr coy, 1 log bn, 1 maint coy, 1 med coy)
  Mechanised
    5 mech bde (1 recce coy, 1 tk bn, 3 mech bn, 1 fd arty bn, 1 AD bn, 1 AT bn, 1 engr coy, 1 log bn, 1 maint coy, 1 med coy)
  Light
    2 lt inf bde
    1 (Royal Guard) regt (3 lt inf bn)
  Air Manoeuvre
    1 AB bde (2 AB bn, 3 SF coy)
  Aviation
    1 comd (3 hel gp)
COMBAT SUPPORT
  3 arty bde
EQUIPMENT BY TYPE
  MBT 900: 140 AMX-30; 370 M1A2/A2S *Abrams*; 390 M60A3 *Patton*
  RECCE 300 AML-60/AML-90
  IFV 765: 380 AMX-10P; 385 M2A2 *Bradley*
  APC 1,573
    APC (T) 1,190 M113A1/A2/A3 (incl variants)
    APC (W) 150 Panhard M3 (ε40 AF-40-8-1 *Al-Fahd* in store)
  AUV 233: 73 *Aravis*; 160 M-ATV
  ENGINEERING & MAINTENANCE VEHICLES
    AEV 15 M728
    ARV 278+: 8 ACV ARV; AMX-10EHC; 55 AMX-30D; *Leclerc* ARV; 125 M88A1; 90 M578
    VLB 10 AMX-30
    MW *Aardvark* Mk2
  NBC VEHICLES 10 TPz-1 *Fuchs* NBC
  ANTI-TANK/ANTI-INFRASTRUCTURE
    MSL
      SP 290+: 90+ AMX-10P (HOT); 200 VCC-1 ITOW
      MANPATS M47 *Dragon*; TOW-2A
    RCL 84mm *Carl Gustav*; **90mm** M67; **106mm** M40A1
  ARTILLERY 761
    SP 155mm 224: 60 AU-F-1; 110 M109A1B/A2; 54 PLZ-45
    TOWED 110: **105mm** (100 M101/M102 in store); **155mm** 110: 50 M114; 60 M198; **203mm** (8 M115 in store)
    MRL 127mm 60 ASTROS II Mk3
    MOR 367: **SP 81mm** 70; **SP 107mm** 150 M30; **120mm** 147: 110 Brandt; 37 M12-1535

RADAR • LAND AN/TPQ-36 *Firefinder*/AN/TPQ-37 *Firefinder* (arty, mor)
HELICOPTERS
  ATK 35: 11 AH-64D *Apache*; 24 AH-64E *Apache*
  MRH 21: 6 AS365N *Dauphin* 2 (medevac); 15 Bell 406CS *Combat Scout*
  TPT • Medium 58: 12 S-70A1 *Desert Hawk*; 22 UH-60A *Black Hawk* (4 medevac); 24 UH-60L *Black Hawk*
AIR DEFENCE • SAM
  Short-range *Crotale*
  Point-defence FIM-92 *Stinger*

Navy 13,500
Navy HQ at Riyadh; Eastern Fleet HQ at Jubail; Western Fleet HQ at Jeddah
EQUIPMENT BY TYPE
PRINCIPAL SURFACE COMBATANTS 7
  DESTROYERS • DDGHM 3 *Al Riyadh* (FRA *La Fayette* mod) with 2 quad lnchr with MM40 *Exocet* Block 2 AShM, 2 8-cell A43 VLS with *Aster* 15 SAM, 4 single 533mm TT with F17P HWT, 1 76mm gun (capacity 1 AS365N *Dauphin* 2 hel)
  FRIGATES • FFGHM 4 *Madina* (FRA F-2000) with 2 quad lnchr with *Otomat* Mk2 AShM, 1 octuple lnchr with *Crotale* SAM, 4 single 533mm TT with F17P HWT, 1 100mm gun (capacity 1 AS365N *Dauphin* 2 hel)
PATROL AND COASTAL COMBATANTS 30
  CORVETTES • FSG 4 *Badr* (US *Tacoma*) with 2 quad Mk140 lnchr with RGM-84C *Harpoon* AShM, 2 triple 324mm ASTT with Mk 46 LWT, 1 *Phalanx* CIWS, 1 76mm gun
  PCFG 9 *Al Siddiq* (US 58m) with 2 twin Mk140 lnchr with RGM-84C *Harpoon* AShM, 1 *Phalanx* CIWS, 1 76mm gun
  PB 17 (US *Halter Marine*)
MINE WARFARE • MINE COUNTERMEASURES 3
  MHC 3 *Al Jawf* (UK *Sandown*)
AMPHIBIOUS • LANDING CRAFT 5
  LCM 3 LCM 6 (capacity 80 troops)
  LCU ε2 *Al Qiaq* (US LCU 1610) (capacity 120 troops)
LOGISTICS AND SUPPORT 2
  AORH 2 *Boraida* (mod FRA *Durance*) (capacity either 2 AS365F *Dauphin* 2 hel or 1 AS332C *Super Puma*)

Naval Aviation
EQUIPMENT BY TYPE
HELICOPTERS
  MRH 34: 6 AS365N *Dauphin* 2; 15 AS565; 13 Bell 406CS *Combat Scout*
  TPT • Medium 12 AS332B/F *Super Puma*
AIR-LAUNCHED MISSILES
  AShM AM39 *Exocet*; AS-15TT

Marines 3,000
FORCES BY ROLE
SPECIAL FORCES
  1 spec ops regt with (2 spec ops bn)
EQUIPMENT BY TYPE
ARMOURED FIGHTING VEHICLES
  RECCE *Bastion Patsas*
  APC • APC (W) 140 BMR-600P

Air Force 20,000
FORCES BY ROLE
FIGHTER
4 sqn with F-15C/D *Eagle*
FIGHTER/GROUND ATTACK
2 sqn with F-15S *Eagle*
3 sqn with *Typhoon*
GROUND ATTACK
3 sqn with *Tornado* IDS; *Tornado* GR1A
AIRBORNE EARLY WARNING & CONTROL
1 sqn with E-3A *Sentry*
1 sqn with Saab 2000 *Erieye*
ELINT
1 sqn with RE-3A/B; Beech 350ER *King Air*
TANKER
1 sqn with KE-3A
TANKER/TRANSPORT
1 sqn with KC-130H/J *Hercules*
1 sqn with A330 MRTT
TRANSPORT
3 sqn with C-130H *Hercules*; C-130H-30 *Hercules*; CN-235; L-100-30HS (hospital ac)
2 sqn with Beech 350 *King Air* (forming)
TRAINING
1 OCU sqn with F-15SA *Eagle*
3 sqn with *Hawk* Mk65*; *Hawk* Mk65A*; *Hawk* Mk165*
1 sqn with *Jetstream* Mk31
1 sqn with MFI-17 *Mushshak*; SR22T
2 sqn with PC-9; PC-21
TRANSPORT HELICOPTER
4 sqn with AS532 *Cougar* (CSAR); Bell 212 (AB-212); Bell 412 (AB-412) *Twin Huey* (SAR)
EQUIPMENT BY TYPE
AIRCRAFT 365 combat capable
  FTR 81: 56 F-15C *Eagle*; 25 F-15D *Eagle*
  FGA 161: 67 F-15S *Eagle*; 23 F-15SA *Eagle*; 71 *Typhoon*
  ATK 69 *Tornado* IDS
  ISR 14+: 12 *Tornado* GR1A*; 2+ Beech 350ER *King Air*
  AEW&C 7: 5 E-3A *Sentry*; 2 Saab 2000 *Erieye*
  ELINT 2: 1 RE-3A; 1 RE-3B
  TKR/TPT 15: 6 A330 MRTT; 7 KC-130H *Hercules*; 2 KC-130J *Hercules*
  TKR 7 KE-3A
  TPT 51+: **Medium** 36: 30 C-130H *Hercules*; 3 C-130H-30 *Hercules*; 3 L-100-30; **Light** 15+: 10+ Beech 350 *King Air*; 1 *Jetstream* Mk31
  TRG 161: 24 *Hawk* Mk65* (incl aerobatic team); 16 *Hawk* Mk65A*; 2 *Hawk* Mk165*; 20 MFI-17 *Mushshak*; 20 PC-9; 55 PC-21; 24 SR22T
HELICOPTERS
  MRH 15 Bell 412 (AB-412) *Twin Huey* (SAR)
  TPT 30: **Medium** 10 AS532 *Cougar* (CSAR); **Light** 20 Bell 212 (AB-212)
UNMANNED AERIAL VEHICLES
  CISR • Heavy some *Wing Loong* 1 (GJ-1) (reported); some CH-4
AIR-LAUNCHED MISSILES
  AAM • IR AIM-9P/L *Sidewinder*; **IIR** AIM-9X *Sidewinder* II; IRIS-T; **SARH** AIM-7 *Sparrow*; AIM-7M *Sparrow*; **ARH** AIM-120C AMRAAM
  ASM AGM-65 *Maverick*; AR-1
  AShM *Sea Eagle*
  ARM ALARM
  ALCM *Storm Shadow*
BOMBS
  Laser-guided GBU-10/12 *Paveway* II; *Paveway* IV
  INS/GPS-guided GBU-31 JDAM; FT-9

Royal Flt
EQUIPMENT BY TYPE
AIRCRAFT • TPT 24: **Medium** 8: 5 C-130H *Hercules*; 3 L-100-30; **Light** 3: 1 Cessna 310; 2 Learjet 35; **PAX** 13: 1 A340; 1 B-737-200; 2 B-737BBJ; 2 B-747SP; 4 BAe-125-800; 2 Gulfstream III; 1 Gulfstream IV
HELICOPTERS • TPT 3+: **Medium** 3: 2 AS-61; 1 S-70 *Black Hawk*; **Light** some Bell 212 (AB-212)

Air Defence Forces 16,000
FORCES BY ROLE
AIR DEFENCE
6 bn with MIM-104D/F *Patriot* PAC-2 GEM/PAC-3
17 bty with *Shahine*/AMX-30SA
16 bty with MIM-23B I-*Hawk*
73 units (static defence) with *Crotale*/*Shahine*
EQUIPMENT BY TYPE
AIR DEFENCE
  SAM
    Long-range 108 MIM-104D/F *Patriot* PAC-2 GEM/PAC-3
    Medium-range 128 MIM-23B I-*Hawk*
    Short-range 181: 40 *Crotale*; 73 *Shahine*; 68 *Crotale*/*Shahine*
    Point-defence 400+: 400 M1097 *Avenger*; *Mistral*
  GUNS 1,070
    SP 942: **20mm** 92 M163 *Vulcan*; **30mm** 850 AMX-30SA
    TOWED 128: **35mm** 128 GDF Oerlikon; **40mm** (150 L/70 in store)
RADARS • AIR DEFENCE 80: 17 AN/FPS-117; 28 AN/TPS-43; AN/TPS-59; 35 AN/TPS-63; AN/TPS-70

Strategic Missile Forces 2,500
EQUIPMENT BY TYPE
MSL • TACTICAL
  IRBM 10+ DF-3 (CH-SS-2) (service status unclear)
  MRBM Some DF-21 (CH-SS-5 – variant unclear) (reported)

National Guard 73,000 active; 27,000 (tribal levies) (total 100,000)
FORCES BY ROLE
MANOEUVRE
  Mechanised
  5 mech bde (1 recce coy, 3 mech inf bn, 1 SP arty bn, 1 cbt engr coy, 1 sigs coy, 1 log bn)
  Light
  5 inf bde (3 combined arms bn, 1 arty bn, 1 log bn)
  3 indep lt inf bn
  Other
  1 (Special Security) sy bde (3 sy bn)
  1 (ceremonial) cav sqn

COMBAT SUPPORT
1 MP bn

EQUIPMENT BY TYPE
ARMOURED FIGHTING VEHICLES
ASLT 214 LAV-AG (90mm)
IFV 647 LAV-25
APC • APC (W) 808: 119 LAV-A; 30 LAV-AC; 296 LAV-CC; 73 LAV-PC; 290 V-150 *Commando* (810 in store)
ENGINEERING & MAINTENANCE VEHICLES
AEV 58 LAV-E
ARV 111 LAV-R; V-150 ARV
ANTI-TANK/ANTI-INFRASTRUCTURE
 MSL
  SP 183 LAV-AT
  MANPATS TOW-2A; M47 *Dragon*
 RCL • 106mm M40A1
ARTILLERY 359+
 SP 155mm 132 CAESAR
 TOWED 108: 105mm 50 M102; 155mm 58 M198
 MOR 119+: 81mm some; 120mm 119 LAV-M
HELICOPTERS
 ATK 12 AH-64E *Apache*
 MRH 6 AH-6i *Little Bird*
 TPT • Medium 23 UH-60M *Black Hawk*
 TRG 12 MD530F
AIR DEFENCE
 GUNS • TOWED 160: 20mm 30 M167 *Vulcan*; 90mm 130 M2
AIR-LAUNCHED MISSILES
 ASM AGM-114R *Hellfire* II

Paramilitary 24,500+ active

Border Guard 10,500

FORCES BY ROLE
Subordinate to Ministry of Interior. HQ in Riyadh. 9 subordinate regional commands
MANOEUVRE
 Other
  Some mobile def (long-range patrol/spt) units
  2 border def (patrol) units
  12 infrastructure def units
  18 harbour def units
  Some coastal def units
COMBAT SUPPORT
 Some MP units
EQUIPMENT BY TYPE
ARMOURED FIGHTING VEHICLES
 APC • PPV *Caprivi* Mk3

Coast Guard 4,500

EQUIPMENT BY TYPE
PATROL AND COASTAL COMBATANTS 17+
 PCC 3 CSB 40
 PBF 6+: 4 *Al Jouf*; 2 *Sea Guard*; some *Plascoa* FIC 1650
 PB 8: 6 Damen Stan Patrol 2606; 2 *Al Jubatel*
AMPHIBIOUS • LANDING CRAFT 8: 5 UCAC *Griffon* 8000; 3 other
LOGISTICS AND SUPPORT 4: 1 AXL; 3 AO

Facilities Security Force 9,000+
Subordinate to Ministry of Interior

General Civil Defence Administration Units
EQUIPMENT BY TYPE
HELICOPTERS • TPT • Medium 10 Boeing *Vertol* 107

Special Security Force 500
EQUIPMENT BY TYPE
ARMOURED FIGHTING VEHICLES
 APC • APC (W) UR-416
 AUV *Gurkha* LAPV

DEPLOYMENT

BAHRAIN
GCC • *Peninsula Shield* ε1,500 (National Guard)

TURKEY
Operation Inherent Resolve 6 F-15S *Eagle*

YEMEN
Operation Restoring Hope 750; M-ATV; 2+ MIM-104D/F *Patriot* PAC-2/3

FOREIGN FORCES

Bahrain *Operation Restoring Hope* 250; 1 SF gp; 6 F-16C *Fighting Falcon*
Kuwait *Operation Restoring Hope* 4 F/A-18A *Hornet*
Sudan *Operation Restoring Hope* 3 Su-24 *Fencer*
United Arab Emirates *Operation Restoring Hope* 12 F-16E *Fighting Falcon*
United States US Central Command: 500

Syria SYR

Syrian Pound S£		2016	2017	2018
GDP	S£			
	US$			
per capita	US$			
Growth	%			
Inflation	%			
Def exp	S£			
	US$			

US$1=S£

*definitive economic data unavailable

Population   18,028,549

Age	0–14	15–19	20–24	25–29	30–64	65 plus
Male	16.2%	4.7%	4.7%	4.5%	17.7%	1.9%
Female	15.4%	5.0%	4.6%	4.5%	17.8%	2.3%

Capabilities

After over six years of war, government forces have suffered considerable attrition. The army is short of personnel, resulting in increased efforts to conscript young men, many of whom try to avoid service. In many areas, conventional forces have been supplanted by or work alongside militias over which the government often has varying levels of control. In 2017, the regime had some success in increasing its control of militias and building up its own forces, including through the formation, in late 2016, of the 'Fifth Assault Corps', a volunteer organisation that recruits new members as well as integrating existing fighters into the army command structure. The corps has been involved in operations in Palmyra and west Hama. During 2017, de-escalation zones were set up between regime and opposition forces across Syria after Russian-backed talks in Astana. Freezing the fighting has allowed regime forces, with support from Lebanese Hizbullah, Iran and Russia, to make significant gains in the east, especially in Raqqa and Deir ez-Zor governorates. Iran and Russia have provided financial as well as materiel support, whilst Hizbullah and Iran have helped field militia forces. Russian airstrikes have been decisive in reversing rebel momentum and ending their threat to the regime. Both Iran and Russia have assisted with fixed- and rotary-wing airlift. Most army formations are believed to be under-strength. Their ability to coordinate operations has been greatly improved by Russian advisers. (See pp. 316–17.)

ACTIVE 142,500 (Army 105,000 Navy 2,500 Air 15,000 Air Defence 20,000) **Paramilitary 150,000**
Conscript liability 30 months (there is widespread avoidance of military service)

ORGANISATIONS BY SERVICE

Army ε105,000
FORCES BY ROLE
The Syrian Arab Army is a heterogeneous force, combining conventional formations, special forces and auxiliary militias. The main fighting units are the 4th Armoured Division, the Republican Guard, the paratroopers and the Special Forces (including Tiger Forces); they receive the most attention and training. Much of the remainder performs static functions across regime-held areas. Many formations are under-strength, at an estimated 500–1,000 personnel in brigades and regiments.
COMMAND
 4 corps HQ
 1 (5th Assault) corps HQ
SPECIAL FORCES
 2 SF div (total: 11 SF regt; 1 tk regt)
MANOEUVRE
 Armoured
 1 (4th) armd div (1 SF regt, 2 armd bde, 2 mech bde, 1 arty regt, 1 SSM bde (3 SSM bn with *Scud*-B/C))
 5 armd div(-)
 Mechanised
 1 (Republican Guard) mech div (3 mech bde, 2 sy regt, 1 arty regt)
 3 mech div(-)
 2 indep inf bde(-)
 Amphibious
 1 mne unit

COMBAT SUPPORT
 2 arty bde
 2 AT bde
 1 SSM bde (3 SSM bn with FROG-7)
 1 SSM bde (3 SSM bn with SS-21)
EQUIPMENT BY TYPE
Attrition during the civil war has severely reduced equipment numbers for almost all types. It is unclear how much remains available for operations
ARMOURED FIGHTING VEHICLES
 MBT T-55A; T-55AM; T-55AMV; T-62; T-62M; T-72; T-72AV; T-72B; T-72M1; T-90
 RECCE BRDM-2
 IFV BMP-1; BMP-2; BTR-82A
 APC
  APC (T) BTR-50
  APC (W) BTR-152; BTR-60; BTR-70; BTR-80
 APC IVECO LMV
ENGINEERING & MAINTENANCE VEHICLES
 ARV BREM-1 reported; T-54/55
 VLB MTU; MTU-20
 MW UR-77
ANTI-TANK/ANTI-INFRASTRUCTURE • MSL
 SP 9P133 *Malyutka*-P (BRDM-2 with AT-3C *Sagger*); 9P148 *Konkurs* (BRDM-2 with AT-5 *Spandrel*)
 MANPATS 9K111 *Fagot* (AT-4 *Spigot*); 9K111-1 *Konkurs* (AT-5 *Spandrel*); 9K115 *Metis* (AT-7 *Saxhorn*); 9K115-2 *Metis*-M (AT-13 *Saxhorn* 2); 9K116-1 *Bastion* (AT-10 *Stabber*); 9K135 *Kornet* (AT-14 *Spriggan*); Milan
ARTILLERY
 SP 122mm 2S1 *Gvozdika*; D-30 (mounted on T34/85 chassis); **130mm** M-46 (truck–mounted); **152mm** 2S3 *Akatsiya*
 TOWED 122mm D-30; M-30 (M1938); **130mm** M-46; **152mm** D-20; ML-20 (M-1937); **180mm** S-23
 GUN/MOR 120mm 2S9 NONA-S
 MRL 107mm Type-63; **122mm** BM-21 *Grad*; **140mm** BM-14; **220mm** 9P140 *Uragan*; **300mm** 9A52 *Smerch*; **330mm** some (also improvised systems of various calibres)
 MOR 82mm some; **120mm** M-1943; **160mm** M-160; **240mm** M-240
SURFACE-TO-SURFACE MISSILE LAUNCHERS
 SRBM • Conventional *Scud*-B/C/D; *Scud* look-a-like; 9K79 *Tochka* (SS-21 *Scarab*); *Fateh*-110/M-600
UNMANNED AERIAL VEHICLES
 ISR • Medium *Mohajer* 3/4; **Light** *Ababil*
AIR DEFENCE
 SAM
  Medium-range 9K37 *Buk* (SA-11 *Gadfly*); 9K317 *Buk*-M2 (SA-17 *Grizzly*)
  Short-range 96K6 *Pantsir*-S1 (SA-22 *Greyhound*)
  Point-defence 9K31 *Strela*-1 (SA-9 *Gaskin*); 9K33 *Osa* (SA-8 *Gecko*); 9K35 *Strela*-10 (SA-13 *Gopher*); 9K32 *Strela*-2 (SA-7 *Grail*)‡; 9K38 *Igla* (SA-18 *Grouse*); 9K36 *Strela*-3 (SA-14 *Gremlin*); 9K338 *Igla*-S (SA-24 *Grinch*)
 GUNS
  SP 23mm ZSU-23-4; **57mm** ZSU-57-2; S-60 (on 2K12 chassis)
  TOWED 23mm ZU-23-2; **37mm** M-1939; **57mm** S-60; **100mm** KS-19

Navy ε4,000

Some personnel are likely to have been drafted into other services

EQUIPMENT BY TYPE
PATROL AND COASTAL COMBATANTS 32†:
  CORVETTES • FS 2 *Petya* III (1†) with 1 triple 533mm ASTT with SAET-60 HWT, 4 RBU 2500 *Smerch* 1† A/S mor, 2 twin 76mm gun
  PBFG 22:
    16 *Osa* I/II with 4 single lnchr with P-15M *Termit*-M (SS-N-2C *Styx*) AShM
    6 *Tir* with 2 single lnchr with C-802 (CH-SS-N-8 *Saccade*) AShM
  PB 8 *Zhuk*†
MINE WARFARE • MINE COUNTERMEASURES 7
  MHC 1 *Sonya* with 2 quad lnchr with 9K32 *Strela*-2 (SA-N-5 *Grail*)‡ SAM, 2 AK630 CIWS
  MSO 1 *Natya* with 2 quad lnchr with 9K32 *Strela*-2 (SA-N-5 *Grail*)‡ SAM
  MSI 5 *Korund* (*Yevgenya*) (Project 1258)
AMPHIBIOUS • LANDING SHIPS • LSM 3 *Polnochny* B (capacity 6 MBT; 180 troops)
LOGISTICS AND SUPPORT • AX 1 *Al Assad*

Coastal Defence

FORCES BY ROLE
COASTAL DEFENCE
  1 AShM bde with P-35 (SSC-1B *Sepal*); P-15M *Termit*-R (SSC-3 *Styx*); C-802; K-300P *Bastion* (SSC-5 *Stooge*)

EQUIPMENT BY TYPE
COASTAL DEFENCE • AShM P-35 (SSC-1B *Sepal*); P-15M *Termit*-R (SSC-3 *Styx*); C-802; K-300P *Bastion* (SSC-5 *Stooge*)

Naval Aviation

All possibly non-operational after vacating base for Russian deployment

EQUIPMENT BY TYPE
HELICOPTERS • ASW 10: 4 Ka-28 *Helix* A; 6 Mi-14 *Haze*

Air Force ε15,000(-)

FORCES BY ROLE
FIGHTER
  2 sqn with MiG-23 MF/ML/UM *Flogger*
  2 sqn with MiG-29A/U *Fulcrum*
FIGHTER/GROUND ATTACK
  4 sqn with MiG-21MF/bis *Fishbed*; MiG-21U *Mongol* A
  2 sqn with MiG-23BN/UB *Flogger*
GROUND ATTACK
  4 sqn with Su-22 *Fitter* D
  1 sqn with Su-24 *Fencer*
  1 sqn with L-39 *Albatros**
TRANSPORT
  1 sqn with An-24 *Coke*; An-26 *Curl*; Il-76 *Candid*
  1 sqn with *Falcon* 20; *Falcon* 900
  1 sqn with Tu-134B-3
  1 sqn with Yak-40 *Codling*

ATTACK HELICOPTER
  3 sqn with Mi-25 *Hind* D
  2 sqn with SA342L *Gazelle*
TRANSPORT HELICOPTER
  6 sqn with Mi-8 *Hip*/Mi-17 *Hip* H

EQUIPMENT BY TYPE
Heavy use of both fixed- and rotary-wing assets has likely reduced readiness and availability to very low levels. It is estimated that no more than 30–40% of the inventory is operational
AIRCRAFT
  FTR 70: 34 MiG-23MF/ML/UM *Flogger*; 30 MiG-29A/SM/UB *Fulcrum*
  FGA 128: 68 MiG-21MF/bis *Fishbed*; 9 MiG-21U *Mongol* A; 41 MiG-23BN/UB *Flogger*;
  ATK 39: 28 Su-22 *Fitter* D; 11 Su-24 *Fencer*
  TPT 23: **Heavy** 3 Il-76 *Candid*; **Light** 13: 1 An-24 *Coke*; 6 An-26 *Curl*; 2 PA-31 *Navajo*; 4 Yak-40 *Codling*; **PAX** 7: 2 *Falcon* 20; 1 *Falcon* 900; 4 Tu-134B-3
  TRG 15 L-39 *Albatros**
HELICOPTERS
  ATK 24 Mi-25 *Hind* D
  MRH 54: 26 Mi-17 *Hip* H; 28 SA342L *Gazelle*
  TPT • Medium 27 Mi-8 *Hip*
AIR-LAUNCHED MISSILES
  AAM • IR R-3 (AA-2 *Atoll*)‡; R-60 (AA-8 *Aphid*); R-73 (AA-11 *Archer*); **IR/SARH** R-23/24 (AA-7 *Apex*); R-27 (AA-10 *Alamo*); **ARH** R-77 (AA-12A *Adder*) reported
  ASM Kh-25 (AS-10 *Karen*); Kh-29T/L (AS-14 *Kedge*) HOT
  ARM Kh-31P (AS-17A *Krypton*)

Air Defence Command ε20,000 (-)

FORCES BY ROLE
AIR DEFENCE
  4 AD div with S-125 *Pechora* (SA-3 *Goa*); 2K12 *Kub* (SA-6 *Gainful*); S-75 *Dvina* (SA-2 *Guideline*)
  3 AD regt with S-200 *Angara* (SA-5 *Gammon*)
EQUIPMENT BY TYPE
AIR DEFENCE • SAM
  Long-range S-200 *Angara* (SA-5 *Gammon*)
  Medium-range S-75 *Dvina* (SA-2 *Guideline*)
  Short-range 2K12 *Kub* (SA-6 *Gainful*); S-125 *Pechora* (SA-3 *Goa*)
  Point-defence 9K32 *Strela*-2/2M (SA-7A/B *Grail*)‡

Paramilitary ε150,000

National Defence Force ε100,000

An umbrella of disparate regime militias performing a variety of roles, including territorial control

Other Militias ε50,000

Numerous military groups fighting for the Assad regime, including Afghan, Iraqi, Pakistani and sectarian organisations. Some receive significant Iranian support

Coast Guard

EQUIPMENT BY TYPE
PATROL AND COASTAL COMBATANTS 6
  PBF 2 *Mawani*
  PB 4

TERRITORY WHERE THE GOVERNMENT DOES NOT EXERCISE EFFECTIVE CONTROL

Data here represents the de facto situation for selected armed opposition groups and their observed equipment

Free Syrian Army (Coalition) ε35,000

The Free Syrian Army (FSA) is a coalition that includes all FSA affiliates not associated with the FSA Southern Front. The FSA is a broad anti-regime grouping comprising local defence forces, anti-regime militias, moderate and hardline Islamists, secularists and others.

EQUIPMENT BY TYPE
ARMOURED FIGHTING VEHICLES
  MBT T-55; T-62; T-72AV
  IFV BMP-1
ANTI-TANK/ANTI-INFRASTRUCTURE
  MSL • MANPATS 9K11 *Malyutka* (AT-3 *Sagger*); 9K111 *Fagot* (AT-4 *Spigot*); 9K113 *Konkurs* (AT-5 *Spandrel*); 9K115-2 *Metis*-M (AT-13 *Saxhorn* 2); 9K135 *Kornet* (AT-14 *Spriggan*); BGM-71 TOW; *Milan*
ARTILLERY
  TOWED 122mm D-30
  MRL 107mm Type-63; **122mm** BM-21 *Grad*; *Grad* (6-tube tech)
  MOR 82mm some
AIR DEFENCE
  SAM
    Point-defence MANPADS some
  GUNS
    SP 14.5mm ZPU-1; ZPU-2 **23mm** ZU-23-2; ZSU-23-4 *Shilka*

Free Syrian Army – Southern Front (Coalition) 25,000+

The FSA Southern Front is a capable coalition almost entirely concentrated in the provinces of Daraa and Quneitra, south of Damascus. The coalition includes mainstream Islamist factions as well as tribal forces. It was reported in July 2017 that the US-funded provision of weapons and training to moderate rebel groups had stopped; this will affect FSA capabilities.

EQUIPMENT BY TYPE
ARMOURED FIGHTING VEHICLES
  MBT T-55; T-54B/M; T-54-3; T-72AV
  IFV BMP-1
  APC • APC(W) OT-64
ANTI-TANK/ANTI-INFRASTRUCTURE
  MSL • MANPATS 9K11 *Malyutka* (AT-3 *Sagger*); 9K111 *Fagot* (AT-4 *Spigot*); 9K115-2 *Metis*-M (AT-13 *Saxhorn* 2); BGM-71 TOW
  RCL 106mm M40
ARTILLERY
  SP 122mm 2S1 *Gvozdika*
  TOWED 122mm D-30
  MOR 120mm some; others of varying calibre

AIR DEFENCE
  SAM
    Point-defence 9K32 *Strela*-2 (SA-7 *Grail*)‡
  GUNS
    SP 14.5mm ZPU-2 (tch); **23mm** ZU-23-2 (tch); ZSU-23-4

Syrian Democratic Forces (Coalition) ε50,000

The Syrian Democratic Forces (SDF) benefit from considerable US and coalition air support as well as weaponry. Embedded US special-operations forces train, assist and even fight alongside the SDF. Kurdish forces from the YPG/J (People's Protection Units/Women's Protection Units) provide military leadership and main combat power. Arab forces complement these units, often at the insistence of the US to promote a cross-ethnic image. In 2017, the SDF made gains against ISIS in Raqqa and Deir ez-Zor provinces, coming into close rivalry with regime forces in the area of Deir ez-Zor City.

EQUIPMENT BY TYPE
ARMOURED FIGHTING VEHICLES
  MBT T-55; T-72 (reported)
  IFV BMP-1
  APC • PPV *Guardian*
  AUV M-ATV
ANTI-TANK/ANTI-INFRASTRUCTURE
  MSL • MANPATS 9K111-1 *Konkurs*
  RCL 73mm SPG-9; **90mm** M-79 *Osa*
ARTILLERY
  MRL 122mm BM-21 *Grad*; 9K132 *Grad*-P
  MOR 82mm 82-BM-37; M-1938; **120mm** M-1943; improvised mortars of varying calibre
AIR DEFENCE • GUNS
  SP 14.5mm ZPU-4 (tch); ZPU-2 (tch); ZPU-1 (tch); 1 ZPU-2 (tch/on T-55); **23mm** ZSU-23-4 *Shilka*; ZU-23-2 (tch); **57mm** AZP S-60
  TOWED 14.5mm ZPU-2; ZPU-1; **23mm** ZU-23-2

Euphrates Shield Forces ε10,000

These rebel factions (including the Syrian Turkmen Brigades) operate under Turkish command in the northwestern area that Turkey has controlled since 2016.

EQUIPMENT BY TYPE
ARMOURED FIGHTING VEHICLES
  MBT T-54; T-55; T-62
  IFV BMP-1
ANTI-TANK/ANTI-INFRASTRUCTURE
  MSL • MANPATS BGM-71 TOW; 9K115 *Metis* (AT-7 *Saxhorn*)
  RCL 73mm SPG-9; **82mm** B-10
ARTILLERY
  MRL 107mm Type-63; **122mm** 9K132 *Grad*-P
  MOR 82mm 2B9 *Vasilek*; improvised mortars of varying calibre
AIR DEFENCE • GUNS
  SP 14.5mm ZPU-4 (tch); ZPU-2 (tch); ZPU-1 (tch); **23mm** ZU-23-2 (tch); **57mm** AZP S-60
  TOWED 14.5mm ZPU-1; ZPU-2; ZPU-4; **23mm** ZU-23-2

Hayat Tahrir al-Sham (HTS) ε20,000

HTS was formed by Jabhat Fateh al-Sham (formerly known as Jabhat al-Nusra) in January 2017 by absorbing other hardline groups. HTS has been one of the most effective and capable rebel groups; it is designated a terrorist organisation by the US for its links to al-Qaeda. It is active throughout Syria, particularly in the north. It made significant gains against rival group Ahrar al-Sham in Idlib province. HTS remains opposed to all de-escalation efforts, thereby appealing to rebel fighters seeking to continue the fight against the regime.

EQUIPMENT BY TYPE
ARMOURED FIGHTING VEHICLES
  MBT T-55; T-62; T-72; T-72AV
  IFV BMP-1
ANTI-TANK/ANTI-INFRASTRUCTURE
  MSL • MANPATS 9K11 *Malyutka* (AT-3 *Sagger*); 9K113 *Konkurs* (AT-5 *Spandrel*); 9K115-2 *Metis*-M (AT-13 *Saxhorn 2*); 9K135 *Kornet* (AT-14 *Spriggan*)
  RCL 73mm SPG-9; 106mm M-40
ARTILLERY
  SP 122mm 2S1 *Gvozdika*
  TOWED 122mm D-30; 130mm M-46
  MRL 107mm Type-63
  MOR 120mm some; improvised mortars of varying calibres
AIR DEFENCE
  SAM
    Point-defence 9K37 *Strela*-2 (SA-7 *Grail*)‡
  GUNS
    SP 14.5mm ZPU-1; ZPU-2; 23mm ZU-23-2; 57mm AZP S-60

Jaysh al-Islam ε10,000

Jaysh al-Islam is one of the few remaining significant independent Islamist groups. The bulk of its forces are thought to be based in the East Ghouta suburbs of Damascus. Recently its Northern Sector transferred allegiance to Ahrar al-Sham.

EQUIPMENT BY TYPE
ARMOURED FIGHTING VEHICLES
  MBT T-72; T-55
  IFV BMP-1
ANTI-TANK/ANTI-INFRASTRUCTURE
  MSL • MANPATS 9K113 *Konkurs* (AT-5 *Spandrel*)
  RCL 106mm M-40
ARTILLERY
  SP 122mm 2S1 *Gvozdika*
  MRL 107mm Type-63; 122mm BM-21 *Grad*
SURFACE-TO-SURFACE MISSILE LAUNCHERS
  SRBM *Zelzal*-2
AIR DEFENCE • SAM
  Point-defence 9K33 *Osa* (SA-8 *Gecko*)

Ahrar al-Sham ε15,000

Ahrar al-Sham was once considered one of the strongest Salafist organisations in Syria, but it has been in increasing rivalry with Hayat Tahrir al-Sham. Ahrar sought to build a rival front, appealing to other Islamist factions. Following conflict with HTS over the summer, Ahrar al-Sham withdrew from strategic locations in Idlib near the Turkish border.

EQUIPMENT BY TYPE
ARMOURED FIGHTING VEHICLES
  MBT T-55
  IFV BMP-1
ANTI-TANK/ANTI-INFRASTRUCTURE
  MSL • MANPATS 9K113 *Konkurs* (AT-5 *Spandrel*); 9K115-2 *Metis*-M (AT-13 *Saxhorn 2*); 9K135 *Kornet* (AT-14 *Spriggan*)
  RCL 106mm M40
ARTILLERY
  SP 122mm 2S1 *Gvozdika*
  TOWED 130mm some M-46
  MRL 107mm 5+ Type-63
  MOR improvised mortars of varying calibre

FOREIGN FORCES

France *Operation Inherent Resolve* (*Chammal*) 1 SF unit

Hizbullah 7,000–8,000

Iran 5,000 (incl 2,000 IRGC)

Russia 6,000: 1 inf BG; 4 MP bn; 1 engr unit; 7 T-90; ε20 BTR-82A; 12 2A65; 4 9A52 *Smerch*; TOS-1A; 9K720 *Iskander*-M; 4 MiG-29SMT *Fulcrum*; 8 Su-24M *Fencer*; 6 Su-25SM; 4 Su-30SM; 10 Su-34; 4 Su-35S; 1 Il-20M; 4 Mi-28N *Havoc*; 4 Ka-52 *Hokum* B; 12 Mi-24P/Mi-35M *Hind*; 4 Mi-8AMTSh *Hip*; 3 *Pantsir*-S1/S2; 1 AShM bty with 3K55 *Bastion* (SSC-5 *Stooge*); 1 SAM bty with S-400 (SA-21 *Growler*); 1 SAM bty with S-300V4 (SA-23); air base at Latakia; naval facility at Tartus

Turkey 500+; 1 SF coy; 1 armd coy(+); 1 arty unit

United States *Operation Inherent Resolve* 1,700+; 1 ranger unit; 1 arty bty with M777A2; 1 MRL bty with M142 HIMARS

Tunisia TUN

Tunisian Dinar D		2016	2017	2018
GDP	D	90.4bn	97.4bn	
	US$	42.1bn	39.9bn	
per capita	US$	3,749	3,518	
Growth	%	1.0	2.3	
Inflation	%	3.7	4.5	
Def bgt	D	2.09bn	2.02bn	2.33bn
	US$	975m	826m	
FMA (US)	US$	65m	45m	0m
US$1=D		2.15	2.44	

Population 11,403,800

Age	0–14	15–19	20–24	25–29	30–64	65 plus
Male	12.9%	3.4%	3.7%	4.0%	21.9%	3.7%
Female	12.1%	3.2%	3.7%	4.2%	22.8%	4.2%

Capabilities

Territorial sovereignty and internal security are the main tasks of the Tunisian armed forces. During 2017, the government and armed forces worked on a revised defence and security policy for a yet to be published 'white book'. The civil war in neighbouring Libya and Islamist terrorist groups operating from this territory continue to loom large as a security concern. Tunisian forces have been working with and have benefited from training from Algeria as part of their counter-terrorism efforts. The country's overall military capability is limited by its comparatively aged inventory of equipment, although it has been the recipient of surplus US systems, including the OH-58D *Kiowa Warrior* armed utility helicopter, delivery of which began in early 2017. This acquisition reflects wider and closer military relations between Tunisia and the US. In May 2017, the government deployed the armed forces to protect oil-, gas- and phosphate-production sites in the face of industrial unrest.

ACTIVE 35,800 (Army 27,000 Navy 4,800 Air 4,000)
Paramilitary 12,000
Conscript liability 12 months selective

ORGANISATIONS BY SERVICE

Army 5,000; 22,000 conscript (total 27,000)
FORCES BY ROLE
SPECIAL FORCES
  1 SF bde
  1 (Sahara) SF bde
MANOEUVRE
  Reconnaissance
  1 recce regt
  Mechanised
  3 mech bde (1 armd regt, 2 mech inf regt, 1 arty regt, 1 AD regt, 1 engr regt, 1 sigs regt, 1 log gp)
COMBAT SUPPORT
  1 engr regt
EQUIPMENT BY TYPE
ARMOURED FIGHTING VEHICLES
  MBT 84: 30 M60A1; 54 M60A3
  LT TK 48 SK-105 *Kuerassier*
  RECCE 60: 40 AML-90; 20 FV601 *Saladin*
  APC 350
    APC (T) 140 M113A1/A2
    APC (W) 110 Fiat 6614
    PPV 100+: *Ejder Yalcin*; 100+ *Kirpi*
ENGINEERING & MAINTENANCE VEHICLES
  AEV 2 *Greif*
  ARV 3 *Greif*; 6 M88A1
ANTI-TANK/ANTI-INFRASTRUCTURE • MSL
  SP 35 M901 ITV TOW
  MANPATS *Milan*; TOW
ARTILLERY 276
  TOWED 115: **105mm** 48 M101A1/A2; **155mm** 67: 12 M114A1; 55 M198
  MOR 161: **81mm** 95; **SP 107mm** 48 M106; **120mm** 18 Brandt
RADAR • LAND RASIT (veh, arty)
AIR DEFENCE
  SAM • Point-defence 26 M48 *Chaparral*; RBS-70

GUNS 127
  SP 40mm 12 M42
  TOWED 115: **20mm** 100 M-55; **37mm** 15 Type-55 (M-1939)/Type-65

Navy ε4,800
EQUIPMENT BY TYPE
PATROL AND COASTAL COMBATANTS 29
  PCFG 3 *La Galite* (FRA *Combattante* III) with 2 quad Mk140 lnchr with MM40 *Exocet* AShM, 1 76mm gun
  PCG 3 *Bizerte* (FRA P-48) with 8 SS 12M AShM
  PCF 6 *Albatros* (GER Type-143B) with 2 single 533mm TT, 2 76mm guns
  PBF 2 20m Fast Patrol Boat
  PB 15: 1 *Istiklal*; 3 *Utique* (mod PRC *Haizhui* II); 5 *Joumhouria*; 6 V Series
LOGISTICS AND SUPPORT 7:
  ABU 3: 2 *Tabarka* (ex-US *White Sumac*); 1 *Sisi Bou Said*
  AGE 1 *Hannibal*
  AGS 1 *Khaireddine* (ex-US *Wilkes*)
  AWT 1 *Ain Zaghouan* (ex-ITA *Simeto*)
  AX 1 *Salambo* (ex-US *Conrad*, survey)

Air Force 4,000
FORCES BY ROLE
FIGHTER/GROUND ATTACK
  1 sqn with F-5E/F-5F *Tiger* II
TRANSPORT
  1 sqn with C-130B/H/J-30 *Hercules*; G.222; L-410 *Turbolet*
  1 liaison unit with S-208A
TRAINING
  2 sqn with L-59 *Albatros**; MB-326B; SF-260
  1 sqn with MB-326K; MB-326L
TRANSPORT HELICOPTER
  2 sqn with AS350B *Ecureuil*; AS365 *Dauphin* 2; AB-205 (Bell 205); SA313; SA316 *Alouette* III; UH-1H *Iroquois*; UH-1N *Iroquois*
  1 sqn with HH-3E
EQUIPMENT BY TYPE
AIRCRAFT 24 combat capable
  FTR 12: 10 F-5E *Tiger* II; 2 F-5F *Tiger* II
  ATK 3 MB-326K
  ISR 12 Maule MX-7-180B
  TPT 18: **Medium** 13: 5 C-130B *Hercules*; 1 C-130H *Hercules*; 2 C-130J-30 *Hercules*; 5 G.222; **Light** 5: 3 L-410 *Turbolet*; 2 S-208A
  TRG 30: 9 L-59 *Albatros**; 4 MB-326B; 3 MB-326L; 14 SF-260
HELICOPTERS
  MRH 16: 1 AS365 *Dauphin* 2; 6 SA313; 3 SA316 *Alouette* III; 6 OH-58D *Kiowa Warrior*
  SAR 11 HH-3E
  TPT • Light 31: 6 AS350B *Ecureuil*; 15 Bell 205 (AB-205); 8 Bell 205 (UH-1H *Iroquois*); 2 Bell 212 (UH-1N *Iroquois*)
AIR-LAUNCHED MISSILES
  AAM • IR AIM-9P *Sidewinder*
  ASM AGM-114R *Hellfire*

Paramilitary 12,000

National Guard 12,000
Ministry of Interior
EQUIPMENT BY TYPE
ARMOURED FIGHTING VEHICLES
  ASLT 2 EE-11 *Urutu* FSV
  APC • APC (W) 16 EE-11 *Urutu* (anti-riot); VAB Mk3
PATROL AND COASTAL COMBATANTS 24
  PCC 6 *Rais el Blais* (ex-GDR *Kondor* I)
  PBF 7: 4 *Gabes*; 3 *Patrouiller*
  PB 11: 5 *Breitla* (ex-GDR *Bremse*); 4 Rodman 38; 2 *Socomena*
HELICOPTERS
  MRH 8 SA318 *Alouette* II/SA319 *Alouette* III

DEPLOYMENT

DEMOCRATIC REPUBLIC OF THE CONGO
UN • MONUSCO 32 obs

United Arab Emirates UAE

Emirati Dirham D		2016	2017	2018
GDP	D	1.28tr	1.39tr	
	US$	349bn	379bn	
per capita	US$	35,384	37,346	
Growth	%	3.0	1.3	
Inflation	%	1.8	2.1	
Def exp	D	n.k.	n.k.	
	US$	n.k.	n.k.	
US$1=D		3.67	3.67	

Population 6,072,475

Ethnic groups: Nationals 24%; expatriates 76% of which Indian 30%, Pakistani 20%; other Arab 12%; other Asian 10%; UK 2%; other European 1%

Age	0–14	15–19	20–24	25–29	30–64	65 plus
Male	10.7%	2.8%	5.2%	10.5%	38.5%	0.6%
Female	10.2%	2.3%	3.1%	3.9%	11.4%	0.4%

Capabilities

The UAE's armed forces are arguably the best trained and most capable among the GCC states. In recent years, the UAE has shown a growing willingness to take part in operations, including sending an F-16 detachment to Afghanistan, and participating in the air campaign in Libya, the counter-ISIS air campaign and the Saudi-led effort to defeat Houthi rebels in Yemen. In the case of Yemen, the UAE has committed air and ground forces, particularly but not exclusively the presidential guard, and has incurred significant casualties. In part as a reflection of these activities, the US and the UAE signed a new defence agreement in May designed to deepen military-to-military cooperation. The UAE's involvement in the Yemen campaign is also offering combat lessons, not least of all in littoral operations and the threat from coastal-defence missiles, after an Emirati vessel was hit by an anti-ship missile in late 2016. A request in May for additional *Patriot* air-defence missiles is an indicator of a high use rate. The UAE is reportedly developing a number of regional staging posts in Eritrea, Somaliland and in the Bab al-Mandab to support the Yemen operation. This also demonstrated the country's developing approach to the use of force and there are signs of an acceptance of military risk. The UAE has deployed armour during the campaign and demonstrated the use of a range of air munitions, including precision-guidance kits. Efforts to purchase a successor to the *Mirage* 2000 aircraft have slowed, although the French *Rafale* is the preferred option. In 2016, the UAE began to receive US-manufactured THAAD ballistic-missile-defence batteries. The UAE continues to develop its defence-industrial base to maintain and support military equipment; parent company EDIC oversees a variety of subsidiaries, including in the UAV, support, munitions, guided-weapons and defence-electronic sectors. The UAE remains reliant, however, on external providers for major weapons systems.

ACTIVE 63,000 (Army 44,000 Navy 2,500 Air 4,500 Presidential Guard 12,000)

Conscript liability 2 years National Service for men aged 18–30; reduced to 9 months for those completing secondary school. Voluntary 9 months service for women

ORGANISATIONS BY SERVICE

Space
EQUIPMENT BY TYPE
SATELLITES • COMMUNICATIONS 2 *Yahsat*

Army 44,000
FORCES BY ROLE
MANOEUVRE
  Armoured
    2 armd bde
  Mechanised
    2 mech bde
  Light
    1 inf bde
COMBAT SUPPORT
  1 arty bde (3 SP arty regt)
  1 engr gp
EQUIPMENT BY TYPE
ARMOURED FIGHTING VEHICLES
  MBT 421: 45 AMX-30; 340 *Leclerc*; 36 OF-40 Mk2 (*Lion*)
  LT TK 76 FV101 *Scorpion*
  RECCE 73: 49 AML-90; 24 VBL (20 FV701 *Ferret* in store; 20 FV601 *Saladin* in store)
  IFV 405: 15 AMX-10P; 390 BMP-3
  APC 1,245+
    APC (T) 136 AAPC (incl 53 engr plus other variants)
    APC (W) 630: 40 AMV 8×8; 120 EE-11 *Urutu*; 370 Panhard M3; 80 VCR (incl variants); 20 VAB
    PPV 479+: 450+ *Caiman*; 29 *Maxxpro* LWB
  AUV 750 M-ATV; Nimr

ENGINEERING & MAINTENANCE VEHICLES
  AEV 53 ACV-AESV
  ARV 143: 8 ACV-AESV Recovery; 4 AMX-30D; 85 BREM-L; 46 *Leclerc* ARV
NBC VEHICLES 32 TPz-1 *Fuchs* NBC
ANTI-TANK/ANTI-INFRASTRUCTURE
  MSL
    SP 20 HOT
    MANPATS FGM-148 *Javelin*; *Milan*; TOW; (*Vigilant* in store)
  RCL 262: **84mm** 250 *Carl Gustav*; **106mm** 12 M40
ARTILLERY 600+
  SP 155mm 181: 78 G-6; 85 M109A3; 18 Mk F3
  TOWED 93: **105mm** 73 L118 Light Gun; **130mm** 20 Type-59-I
  MRL 75+: **122mm** 48+: 48 Firos-25 (est 24 op); Type-90 (reported); **227mm** 21+ M142 HIMARS; **300mm** 6 9A52 *Smerch*
  MOR 251: **81mm** 134: 20 Brandt; 114 L16; **120mm** 21 Brandt; **SP 120mm** 96 RG-31 MMP *Agrab* Mk2
SURFACE-TO-SURFACE MISSILE LAUNCHERS
  SRBM • **Conventional** 6 *Scud*-B (up to 20 msl); MGM-140A/B ATACMS (launched from M142 HIMARS)
UNMANNED AERIAL VEHICLES
  ISR • **Medium** *Seeker* II
AIR DEFENCE
  SAM • **Point-defence** *Blowpipe*; *Mistral*
  GUNS 62
    SP 20mm 42 M3 VDAA
    TOWED 30mm 20 GCF-BM2

Navy 2,500
EQUIPMENT BY TYPE
PRINCIPAL SURFACE COMBATANTS 1
  FRIGATES • **FFGH** 1
    1 *Abu Dhabi* with 2 twin lnchr with MM40 *Exocet* Block 3 AShM, 1 76mm gun
PATROL AND COASTAL COMBATANTS 42
  CORVETTES 10
    FSGHM 6:
      6 *Baynunah* with 2 quad lnchr with MM40 *Exocet* Block 3 AShM, 1 8-cell Mk56 VLS with RIM-162 ESSM SAM, 1 21-cell Mk49 GMLS with RIM-116B SAM, 1 76mm gun
    FSGM 4:
      2 *Muray Jib* (GER Lurssen 62m) with 2 quad lnchr with MM40 *Exocet* Block 2 AShM, 1 octuple lnchr with *Crotale* SAM, 1 *Goalkeeper* CIWS, 1 76mm gun, 1 hel landing platform
      2 *Ganthoot* with 2 twin lnchr with MM40 *Exocet* Block 3 AShM, 2 3-cell VLS with VL-*MICA* SAM, 1 76mm gun, 1 hel landing platform
  PCFGM 2 *Mubarraz* (GER Lurssen 45m) with 2 twin lnchr with MM40 *Exocet* AShM, 1 sextuple lnchr with *Mistral* SAM, 1 76mm gun
  PCFG 6 *Ban Yas* (GER Lurssen TNC-45) with 2 twin lnchr with MM40 *Exocet* Block 3 AShM, 1 76mm gun
  PBFG 12 *Butinah* (*Ghannatha* mod) with 4 single lnchr with *Marte* Mk2/N AShM
  PBF 12: 6 *Ghannatha* with 120mm mor (capacity 42 troops); 6 *Ghannatha* (capacity 42 troops)

MINE WARFARE • **MINE COUNTERMEASURES** 2
  MHO 2 *Al Murjan* (ex-GER *Frankenthal*-class Type-332)
AMPHIBIOUS 29
  LANDING SHIPS • **LST** 2 *Alquwaisat* with 1 hel landing platform
  LANDING CRAFT 16
    LCP 4 Fast Supply Vessel (multipurpose)
    LCU 5: 3 *Al Feyi* (capacity 56 troops); 2 (capacity 40 troops and additional vehicles)
    LCT 7
LOGISTICS AND SUPPORT 2:
  AFS 2 *Rmah* with 4 single 533mm TT

Air Force 4,500
Flying hours 110 hrs/yr
FORCES BY ROLE
FIGHTER/GROUND ATTACK
  3 sqn with F-16E/F Block 60 *Fighting Falcon*
  3 sqn with *Mirage* 2000-9DAD/EAD/RAD
AIRBORNE EARLY WARNING AND CONTROL
  1 flt with Saab 340 *Erieye*
SEARCH & RESCUE
  2 flt with AW109K2; AW139
TANKER
  1 flt with A330 MRTT
TRANSPORT
  1 sqn with C-17A *Globemaster*
  1 sqn with C-130H/H-30 *Hercules*; L-100-30
  1 sqn with CN235M-100
TRAINING
  1 sqn with Grob 115TA
  1 sqn with *Hawk* Mk102*
  1 sqn with PC-7 *Turbo Trainer*
  1 sqn with PC-21
TRANSPORT HELICOPTER
  1 sqn with Bell 412 *Twin Huey*
EQUIPMENT BY TYPE
AIRCRAFT 156 combat capable
  FGA 137: 54 F-16E Block 60 *Fighting Falcon* (*Desert Eagle*); 24 F-16F Block 60 *Fighting Falcon* (13 to remain in US for trg); 15 *Mirage* 2000-9DAD; 44 *Mirage* 2000-9EAD
  ISR 7 *Mirage* 2000 RAD*
  AEW&C 2 Saab 340 *Erieye*
  TPT/TKR 3 A330 MRTT
  TPT 23: **Heavy** 7 C-17 *Globemaster* III; **Medium** 6: 3 C-130H *Hercules*; 1 C-130H-30 *Hercules*; 2 L-100-30; **Light** 10: 6 CN235; 4 DHC-8 *Dash* 8 (MP)
  TRG 79: 12 Grob 115TA; 12 *Hawk* Mk102*; 30 PC-7 *Turbo Trainer*; 25 PC-21
HELICOPTERS
  MRH 21: 12 AW139; 9 Bell 412 *Twin Huey*
  TPT • **Light** 4: 3 AW109K2; 1 Bell 407
UNMANNED AERIAL VEHICLES
  CISR • **Heavy** *Wing Loong* 1 (GJ-1)
AIR-LAUNCHED MISSILES
  AAM • **IR** AIM-9L *Sidewinder*; R-550 *Magic*; **IIR** AIM-9X *Sidewinder* II; **IIR/ARH** *Mica*; **ARH** AIM-120B/C AMRAAM
  ASM AGM-65G *Maverick*; *Hakeem* 1/2/3 (A/B)
  ARM AGM-88C HARM
  ALCM *Black Shaheen* (*Storm Shadow*/SCALP EG variant)

BOMBS
   INS/SAT guided *Al Tariq*
   Laser-guided GBU-12/58 *Paveway* II

Air Defence
FORCES BY ROLE
AIR DEFENCE
   2 AD bde (3 bn with MIM-23B *I-Hawk*; MIM-104F *Patriot* PAC-3)
   3 (short range) AD bn with *Crotale*; *Mistral*; *Rapier*; RB-70; *Javelin*; 9K38 *Igla* (SA-18 *Grouse*); 96K6 *Pantsir*-S1
   1 SAM bty with THAAD
EQUIPMENT BY TYPE
AIR DEFENCE • SAM
   Medium-range MIM-23B *I-Hawk*; MIM-104F *Patriot* PAC-3
   Short-range *Crotale*; 50 96K6 *Pantsir*-S1
   Point-defence RBS-70; *Rapier*; *Javelin*; 9K38 *Igla* (SA-18 *Grouse*); *Mistral*
   MISSILE DEFENCE 6+ THAAD

Presidential Guard Command 12,000
FORCES BY ROLE
MANOEUVRE
   Reconaissance
   1 recce sqn
   Mechanised
   1 mech bde (1 tk bn, 4 mech inf bn, 1 AT coy, 1 cbt engr coy, 1 CSS bn)
   Amphibious
   1 mne bn
EQUIPMENT BY TYPE
ARMOURED FIGHTING VEHICLES
   MBT 50 *Leclerc*
   IFV 290: 200 BMP-3; 90 BTR-3U *Guardian*
ANTI-TANK/ANTI-INFRASTRUCTURE
   MSL • SP HMMWV with 9M133 *Kornet*

Joint Aviation Command
FORCES BY ROLE
GROUND ATTACK
   1 sqn with *Archangel*; AT802 *Air Tractor*
ANTI-SURFACE/ANTI-SUBMARINE WARFARE
   1 sqn with AS332F *Super Puma*; AS565 *Panther*
TRANSPORT
   1 (Spec Ops) gp with AS365F *Dauphin* 2; H125M *Fennec*; AW139; Bell 407MRH; Cessna 208B *Grand Caravan*; CH-47C/F *Chinook*; DHC-6-300/400 *Twin Otter*; UH-60L/M *Black Hawk*
ATTACK HELICOPTER
   1 gp with AH-64D *Apache*
EQUIPMENT BY TYPE
AIRCRAFT 39 combat capable
   ATK 23 *Archangel*
   ISR 8 AT802 *Air Tractor**
   TPT • **Light** 15: 2 Beech 350 *King Air*; 8 Cessna 208B *Grand Caravan**; 1 DHC-6-300 *Twin Otter*; 4 DHC-6-400 *Twin Otter*
HELICOPTERS
   ATK 28 AH-64D *Apache*
   ASW 7 AS332F *Super Puma* (5 in ASuW role)
   MRH 55: 4 AS365F *Dauphin* 2 (VIP); 18 H125M *Fennec*; 7 AS565 *Panther*; 3 AW139 (VIP); 20 Bell 407MRH; 4 SA316 *Alouette* III
   TPT 63+: **Heavy** 22 CH-47F *Chinook*; **Medium** 41+: 11 UH-60L *Black Hawk*; 29+ UH-60M *Black Hawk*
AIR-LAUNCHED MISSILES
   ASM AGM-114 *Hellfire*; *Cirit* (reported); *Hydra*-70; HOT
   AShM AS-15TT; AM39 *Exocet*

Paramilitary
Coast Guard
Ministry of Interior
EQUIPMENT BY TYPE
PATROL AND COASTAL COMBATANTS 112
   PSO 1 *Al Watid*
   PBF 58: 6 *Baglietto* GC23; 3 *Baglietto* 59; 15 DV-15; 34 MRTP 16
   PB 53: 2 *Protector*; 16 (US Camcraft 65); 5 (US Camcraft 77); 6 Watercraft 45; 12 *Halmatic Work*; 12 *Al Saber*

DEPLOYMENT
ERITREA
Operation Restoring Hope 1,000; 1 armd BG; *Leclerc*; BMP-3; G-6; *Agrab* Mk2; 2 *Archangel*; 3 AH-64D *Apache*; 2 CH-47F *Chinook*; 4 UH-60M *Black Hawk*; *Wing Loong* 1 (GJ-1) UAV; 4 MIM-104F *Patriot* PAC-3

LIBYA
6 AT-802; 2 UH-60M; 2 *Wing Loong* 1 (GJ-1) UAV

SAUDI ARABIA
Operation Restoring Hope 12 F-16E *Fighting Falcon*

YEMEN
Operation Restoring Hope 3,000 1 bde HQ; 2 armd BG; *Leclerc*; BMP-3; M-ATV; G-6; M109A3; *Agrab* Mk2; 4 AH-64D *Apache*; 2 CH-47F *Chinook*; 4 UH-60M *Black Hawk*; 96K6 *Pantsir*-S1; 4 MIM-104F *Patriot* PAC-3

FOREIGN FORCES
Australia 700; 1 FGA det with 6 F/A-18A *Hornet*; 1 B-737-700 *Wedgetail* (E-7A); 1 A330 MRTT (KC-30A); 1 tpt det with 2 C-130J-30 *Hercules*
Denmark Operation Inherent Resolve 20
Egypt Operation Restoring Hope 6 F-16C *Fighting Falcon*
France 650: 1 armd BG (1 tk sqn, 1 aty bty); *Leclerc*; VBCI; CASEAR; 6 *Rafale*, 1 C-135FR
Italy 120; 1 tpt flt with 2 C-130J *Hercules*
Jordan Operation Restoring Hope 6 F-16C *Fighting Falcon*
Korea, Republic of: 139 (trg activities at UAE Spec Ops School)
Morocco Operation Restoring Hope 6 F-16C *Fighting Falcon*
United Kingdom 1 tkr/tpt flt with C-17A *Globemaster*; C-130J *Hercules*; A330 MRTT *Voyager*
United States: 5,000; 1 ftr sqn with 6 F-22A *Raptor*; 1 ISR

sqn with 4 U-2; 1 AEW&C sqn with 4 E-3 *Sentry*; 1 tkr sqn with 12 KC-10A; 1 ISR UAV sqn with RQ-4 *Global Hawk*; 2 AD bty with MIM-104E/F *Patriot* PAC-2/3

Yemen, Republic of YEM

Yemeni Rial R		2016	2017	2018
GDP	R	7.65tr	8.99tr	
	US$	27.3bn	25.7bn	
per capita	US$	938	856	
Growth	%	-9.8	-2.0	
Inflation	%	5.0	20.0	
Def bdgt	R	n.k.	n.k.	
	US$	n.k.	n.k.	
US$1=R		280.00	349.99	

Population 28,036,829

Ethnic groups: Majority Arab, some African and South Asian

Age	0–14	15–19	20–24	25–29	30–64	65 plus
Male	20.3%	5.7%	5.0%	4.4%	13.9%	1.2%
Female	19.6%	5.6%	4.8%	4.3%	13.6%	1.5%

Capabilities

The civil war in Yemen continued unabated with Houthi rebels and Saleh-loyalist troops continuing to fight the armed forces of President Hadi's government, allied militias and the Saudi-led coalition supporting his regime. Cholera outbreaks have exacerbated a humanitarian situation where, according to the UN, '17 million Yemenis are hungry, nearly seven million facing famine, and about 16 million lack access to water or sanitation'. Opposition forces remained strongest in the northwest of the country, while the government controlled the central and eastern areas of Yemen. Al-Qaeda affiliates were active in the central and southern regions. Insurgent activities include the use of targeted IED attacks. The Saudi-led coalition continued to provide ground and air support for the Hadi government. Greater use is reportedly being made of strategies designed to secure the allegiance of local militias and tribal groupings, which reportedly helped the ejection of al-Qaeda-affiliated groups from the eastern port town of Mukalla in 2016. Government troops and local affiliated forces, reportedly backed by the UAE and US, continued to target al-Qaeda in Shabwa governorate in late 2017. Civilian casualties resulting from coalition air and artillery strikes remain an area subject to international attention and concern. The insurgents appear to retain the majority of the more capable heavy armour and armoured fighting vehicles, although the effect of the apparent Houthi split with Saleh-loyalist forces, and his death in late 2017, remained uncertain. Insurgent forces have maintained their ability to launch surface-to-air missiles at Saudi Arabia. With regard to this capability, and other insurgent military capabilities, international and regional states continue to allege direct involvement by Iran in supplying weaponry to the rebels. Yemeni special forces have been deployed in the current campaign, operating closely with coalition forces. The air force has effectively ceased to function, except for a small number of aircraft apparently stored at Al-Anad Air Base and AT-802 aircraft provided by the UAE.

ACTIVE 10,000–20,000 (Army 10,000–20,000 Navy n.k. Air Force n.k., Air Defence n.k.) Paramilitary n.k.

ORGANISATIONS BY SERVICE

Army 10,000–20,000 (incl militia)
FORCES BY ROLE
MANOEUVRE
  Mechanised
    up to 10 bde(-)
EQUIPMENT BY TYPE
ARMOURED FIGHTING VEHICLES
  MBT Some M60A1; T-34†; T-54/55; T-62; T-72
  RECCE some BRDM-2
  APC • APC (W) BTR-60
ANTI-TANK/ANTI-INFRASTRUCTURE
  MSL • MANPATS 9K11 *Malyutka* (AT-3 *Sagger*); M47 *Dragon*; TOW
  GUNS • SP 100mm SU-100†
ARTILLERY • SP 122mm 2S1 *Gvozdika*
AIR DEFENCE • SAM systems heavily degraded during coalition air attacks

Navy n.k.
Yemen's naval forces have no operational capability

Air Force n.k.
The air force has no operational capability, and most of its aircraft appear to have been destroyed. Coalition forces have provided the AT-802s and training for Yemeni pilots
EQUIPMENT BY TYPE 14 combat capable
AIRCRAFT
  FTR/FGA 8: 6 MiG-21 *Fishbed*; 2 Su-22 *Fitter*
  ISR 6 AT-802 *Air Tractor**
  TRG 3 L-39C *Albatros*

TERRITORY WHERE THE GOVERNMENT DOES NOT EXERCISE EFFECTIVE CONTROL

Insurgent forces 20,000 (incl Republican Guard, Houthi and tribes)
FORCES BY ROLE
MANOEUVRE
  Mechanised
    up to 20 bde(-)
EQUIPMENT BY TYPE
ARMOURED FIGHTING VEHICLES
  MBT Some T-72; T-55; T-80
  IFV BTR-80A; *Ratel*
  APC • APC (W) Some BTR-40; BTR-60
ANTI-TANK/ANTI-INFRASTRUCTURE
  MSL • MANPATS M47 *Dragon*; 9K111-1 *Konkurs* (AT-5B *Spandrel/Towsan*-1); 9K115 *Metis* (AT-7 *Saxhorn*)

SURFACE-TO-SURFACE MISSILE LAUNCHERS
SRBM • Conventional (most fired or destroyed) 9K79 *Tochka* (SS-21 *Scarab*); *Scud*-B/*Hwasong*-5; *Borkan*-1 (possible extended-range *Scud* derivative); *Qaher*-1 (possible *Tondar*-69 derivative)
COASTAL DEFENCE • AShM some C-801/C-802 (reported)

DEPLOYMENT

CENTRAL AFRICAN REPUBLIC
UN • MINUSCA 5 obs

MALI
UN • MINUSMA 4

SOUTH SUDAN
UN • UNMISS 3; 2 obs

SUDAN
UN • UNAMID 3; 3 obs

WESTERN SAHARA
UN • MINURSO 6 obs

FOREIGN FORCES

All *Operation Restoring Hope* unless stated

Saudi Arabia 750; M-ATV; AH-64 *Apache*; 2+ MIM-104D/F *Patriot* PAC-2/3

Sudan 950; 1 mech BG; T-72AV; BTR-70M *Kobra* 2

United Arab Emirates 3,000 1 bde HQ; 2 armd BG; *Leclerc*; BMP-3; M-ATV; G-6; M109A3; *Agrab* Mk2; 4 AH-64D *Apache*; 2 CH-47F *Chinook*; 4 UH-60M *Black Hawk*; 96K6 *Pantsir*-S1; 4 MIM-104F *Patriot* PAC-3

Arms procurements and deliveries – Middle East and North Africa

Significant events in 2017

- Israel began tests of an upgraded infantry fighting vehicle variant of its *Namer* armoured vehicle. The prototype has an unmanned turret with a 30mm gun. The vehicle will also be fitted with the *Trophy* active protection system.

- Germany approved the sale of three more submarines to Israel. The deal had been delayed by a corruption investigation in Germany. These will replace the *Dolphin*-class boats delivered to Israel in 1999 and 2000.

- Deliveries of *Typhoon* fighter aircraft from the United Kingdom to Saudi Arabia, under the 2005 *Project Salam* deal, were completed.

- Saudi Arabia formed the General Authority of Military Industries (GAMI) to oversee areas such as defence procurement, research and development, and the local defence industry. GAMI is headed by Crown Prince Mohammed bin Salman al Saud.

- Israel signed an agreement with Indian companies Dynamatic Technologies and Elcom Systems concerning the transfer of unmanned-aerial-vehicle technology to India.

- Saudi Arabia's KACST signed an agreement with China's China Aerospace Science and Technology Corporation to build a 'CH' UAV series-production line in the country.

Figure 19 **Middle East and North Africa: selected ongoing or completed procurement priorities in 2017**

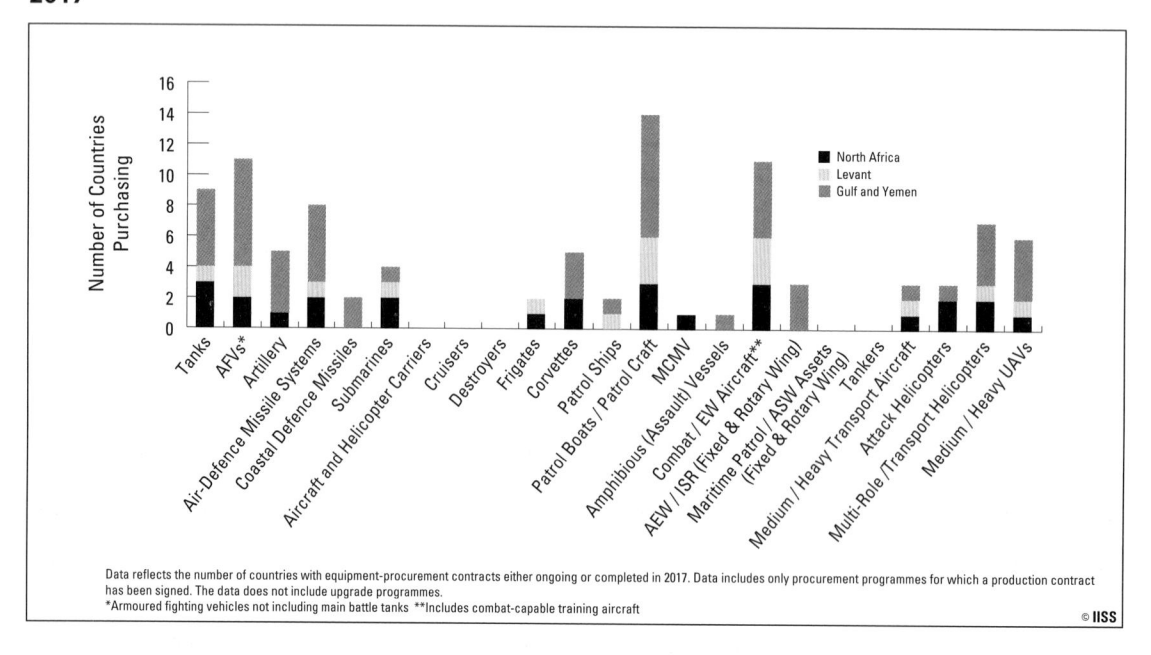

Data reflects the number of countries with equipment-procurement contracts either ongoing or completed in 2017. Data includes only procurement programmes for which a production contract has been signed. The data does not include upgrade programmes.
*Armoured fighting vehicles not including main battle tanks **Includes combat-capable training aircraft

© IISS

Over the past five years, Qatar has signed contracts with Western defence companies for new equipment worth over US$20 billion and has signed initial agreements, the majority with the United States, on well over US$30bn of other equipment. Noteworthy quantities of high-quality equipment are being acquired at significant cost. For example, the order of 62 *Leopard* 2A7 main battle tanks (MBTs) is double that of Qatar's current AMX-30 MBT inventory. As intriguing are the agreements made concerning fighter aircraft. Qatar currently operates a squadron of 12 *Mirage* 2000 fighter aircraft and signed a deal with Dassault for 24 *Rafale*s in 2015 that would double its fleet size. If more contracts are signed, either for 24 *Typhoon*s or a large number of F-15QA fighter aircraft, it is unclear from where the Qataris would secure and train the personnel to operate and maintain them, only having a population of 2.2 million and an air force of around 2,000 personnel. The tensions in Qatar–Gulf Cooperation Council relations may well drive Qatar to finalise more of the pending deals listed below as it seeks to broaden its defence ties with nations outside the region.

Table 14 Qatar: selected ongoing defence contracts

Order Date	Equipment	Type	Quantity	Value	Contractor(s)	Notes
Apr 2013	*Leopard* 2A7 PzH 2000	MBT 155mm SP Arty	62 24	US$2.21bn	(GER) KMW	
Mar 2014	B-737 AEW	AEW&C ac	3	n.k.	(US) Boeing	
Dec 2014	MIM-104F *Patriot* PAC-3	Long-range SAM	10 Fire Units	US$2.4bn	(US) Raytheon	
May 2015	*Rafale*	FGA ac	24	US$7.48bn	(FRA) Dassault Aviation	
Jun 2016	AH-64E *Apache Guardian*	ATK hel	24	US$667.52m	(US) Boeing	
Jun 2016	*Exocet* MM40 Block 3 *Aster* Block 1 VL MICA	AShM SAM SAM	n.k.	US$1.12bn	(Int'l) MBDA	For navy corvettes
Sep 2016	*Marte*-ER *Exocet* MM40 Block 3	Ground-launched AShM	n.k.	εUS$714.54m	(Int'l) MBDA	
Feb 2017	AN/FPS-132 Upgraded Early Warning Radar	Ballistic Missile Early Warning Radar	1	US$1.07bn	(US) Raytheon	
Aug 2017	Corvette OPV LPD	FSGHM PSO LPD	4 2 1	US$4.47bn	(ITA) Fincantieri (ITA) Leonardo	Agreed Jun 2016; finalised in 2017
		Total		εUS$20.13bn+		

Table 15 Qatar: selected defence-equipment procurements pending contract signature

Date	Equipment	Type	Quantity	Est. value	Contractor(s)	Notes
Sep 2011	MH-60R *Seahawk*	ASW hel	6	US$750m	(US) Sikorsky	Approved by US State Dept
Jun 2012	UH-60M *Black Hawk*	Med Tpt hel	12	US$1.11bn	(US) Sikorsky	Approved by US State Dept
Nov 2012	THAAD	SAM	2 fire units	US$6.5bn	(US) Lockheed Martin	Approved by US State Dept
Mar 2013	*Javelin*	MANPATS	50 lnchrs & 500 msls	US$122m	(US) Lockheed Martin (US) Raytheon	Approved by US State Dept; LoA signed Jul 2014
Mar 2014	A330 MRTT	Tkr/Tpt ac	2	n.k.	(Int'l) Airbus Defence and Space	Selected in 2014
Mar 2014	NH90 TTH NH90 NFH	Med Tpt hel ASW hel	12 10	US$2.8bn	(Int'l) NH Industries	LoI signed in 2014
May 2016	*Javelin*	MANPATS	10 lnchrs & 50 msls	US$20m	(US) Lockheed Martin (US) Raytheon	Approved by US State Dept
Nov 2016	F-15QA	FGA ac	72	US$21.1bn	(US) Boeing	Approved by US State Dept; LoA signed Jun 2017
Sep 2017	*Typhoon*	FGA ac	24	n.k.	(Int'l) Eurofighter	LoI signed with UK
		Total		US$32.4bn+		

Over the past decade, several North African nations have established substantial surface and sub-surface fleets, largely sourced from European shipyards. Morocco began by acquiring several SIGMA frigates from the Netherlands before becoming the first export customer of the Franco-Italian FREMM. Prior to this acquisition, the Moroccan Navy had operated a small number of light frigates and a corvette. Egypt also bought a FREMM destroyer from France, as well as four *Gowind* 2500 frigates. Three are to be built in Egypt, giving the country a new industrial capability. Algeria has acquired two classes of frigates from China and Germany, with different anti-ship missiles, surface-to-air missiles and naval guns. Furthermore, Algeria's corvettes operate Russian systems. It is not yet clear how the Algerian Navy will handle the logistics and maintenance for these different types of systems. Both Algeria and Egypt have each bought a large amphibious-assault vessel, suggesting that these countries may want to project power further from their coastlines in the future. Meanwhile, a first pair of *Varshavyanka*-class submarines from Russia arrived in Algeria in 2009. They will be followed by a second batch to replace the two *Kilo*s acquired in the 1980s. The two batches will lead to an Algerian submarine fleet twice the size of ten years ago. Egypt is replacing its Chinese-origin *Romeo*s with German Type-209/1400 submarines.

Table 16 **North Africa: selected naval deliveries since 2011**

Country	Class	Type	Shipyard	Vessel name	Pennant number	ISD
Algeria	El-Kasseh 1 (ITA *Gaeta* mod)	MCC	(ITA) Intermarine	El-Kasseh 1	501	Sep 2017
	Rais Hassen Barbiar (*Djebel Chenoua* mod)	FSG	(ALG) ECRN	Rais Hassen Barbiar	807	Aug 2017
	Erraddii (MEKO 200AN)	FFGHM	(GER) TKMS	El Moudamir	911	May 2017
	Adhafer (C28A)	FFGHM	(PRC) Hudong-Zhonghua Shipbuilding	Ezzadjer	922	Aug 2016
	Erraddii (MEKO 200AN)	FFGHM	(GER) TKMS	Erraddii	910	Apr 2016
	Adhafer (C28A)	FFGHM	(PRC) Hudong-Zhonghua Shipbuilding	El Fateh	921	Mar 2016
	Adhafer (C28A)	FFGHM	(PRC) Hudong-Zhonghua Shipbuilding	Adhafer	920	Nov 2015
	Kalaat Beni Abbes	LHD	(ITA) Fincantieri	Kalaat Beni Abbes	474	Mar 2015
Egypt	El Fateh (*Gowind* 2500)	FFGHM	(FRA) Naval Group (Formerly DCNS)	El Fateh	971	Oct 2017
	Type-209/1400	SSK	(GER) TKMS	S42	862	Oct 2017
	Type-209/1400	SSK	(GER) TKMS	S41	861	Apr 2017
	Gamal Abdel Nasser (FRA *Mistral*)	LHD	(FRA) DCNS	Anwar Sadat	1020	Sep 2016
	Gamal Abdel Nasser (FRA *Mistral*)	LHD	(FRA) DCNS	Gamal Abdel Nasser	1010	Jun 2016
	Tahya Misr (FREMM)	DDGHM	(FRA) DCNS	Tahya Misr	1001	Jun 2015
Morocco	Mohammed VI (FREMM)	DDGHM	(FRA) DCNS	Mohammed VI	701	Jan 2014
	Tarik Ben Ziyad (SIGMA 9813)	FFGHM	(NLD) Damen Schelde	Allal Ben Abdellah	615	Sep 2012
	Tarik Ben Ziyad (SIGMA 9813)	FFGHM	(NLD) Damen Schelde	Sultan Moulay Ismail	614	Mar 2012
	Tarik Ben Ziyad (SIGMA 10513)	FFGHM	(NLD) Damen Schelde	Tarik Ben Ziyad	613	Sep 2011

Table 17 **North Africa: selected future naval deliveries**

Country	Class	Type	Shipyard	Vessel name	Pennant number	Likely ISD
Algeria	Kilo (Pr. 636.1)	SSK	(RUS) Admiralty Shipyards	n.k.	n.k.	2018
	Kilo (Pr. 636.1)	SSK	(RUS) Admiralty Shipyards	n.k.	n.k.	2018
Egypt	Type-209/1400	SSK	(GER) TKMS	S43	863	2019
	Type-209/1400	SSK	(GER) TKMS	S44	864	2020
	El Fateh (*Gowind* 2500)	FFGHM	(EGY) Alexandria Shipyard	n.k.	972	n.k.
	El Fateh (*Gowind* 2500)	FFGHM	(EGY) Alexandria Shipyard	n.k.	973	n.k.
	El Fateh (*Gowind* 2500)	FFGHM	(EGY) Alexandria Shipyard	n.k.	974	n.k.

Chapter Eight
Latin America and the Caribbean

The increasingly unstable political, economic and social situation in Venezuela has highlighted not just the domestic actions of the government's security and armed forces, and militias, but also tensions with neighbouring countries, such as Colombia and Guyana. For some states, worries about the situation in Venezuela were prompted not just by the domestic problems there, and the outflow into neighbouring states of some Venezuelan citizens fleeing the country, but also the activities of the Venezuelan armed forces and militias, which included military deployments to the country's border areas. These issues added to the enduring security challenges facing regional governments, such as the threat from narco-trafficking and organised crime, and the requirement for humanitarian assistance and disaster-relief tasks; across the region, armed forces remain centrally involved in such missions.

In May 2017, Venezuela announced that it would deploy 2,000 members of the Venezuelan National Guard (National Bolivarian Guard, GNB) and 600 regular troops to the border with Colombia, and a month later it announced the delivery of NORINCO *Lynx* 8x8 all-terrain vehicles to equip its marine-infantry forces deployed along the border with Brazil. Venezuela criticised the presence of Colombian armoured units close to its border and, while Colombia acknowledged that such units were deployed to its La Guajira region, it said that these were deployed there in 2015 and that the units were located 11 kilometres from the border.

Meanwhile, Colombia's government has raised concerns over the militarisation of Venezuelan society, including President Nicolás Maduro's call to boost the GNB militia by an additional 500,000 armed personnel. On 9 August, Venezuelan Defence Minister Vladimir Padrino Lopez participated in a ceremony to commemorate the 30th anniversary of the 1987 'Corvette Crisis', when a Colombian corvette crossed into maritime territory disputed with Venezuela, and announced that the armed forces were ready to respond if Colombian forces ventured into Venezuelan territory. While tensions may have increased, however, the Colombian government distanced itself – as did a number of other regional governments – from US President Donald Trump's comments that he would not rule out military action against Venezuela.

Central America and the role of the armed forces

Central American armed forces remain, for the most part, significantly involved in operations to counter organised crime and narco-trafficking.

In 2017, **Honduras** stood up an additional two 500-strong Military Police battalions. These units are specifically tasked with supporting law-enforcement operations. The government has also announced an objective to establish a 10,000-strong military-police corps that is specifically designated to internal-security tasks. At the same time, Honduras is also expanding its marine-infantry force, with a second 250-strong unit stood up during 2017 and a third planned for 2018. Meanwhile, the air force is looking to overhaul and repair its fleet of F-5 *Tiger* II and A-37B *Dragonfly* fighter/ground-attack aircraft and EMB-312 *Tucano* armed trainers, and it was announced that a US$200 million contract was being negotiated with Israel to this end. Maintaining cooperation with its southern neighbour Nicaragua, Honduran and Nicaraguan armed forces continued joint border-security patrols under *Operation Morazan-Sandino*. This cooperation has been pursued intermittently for three years. Additionally, Honduras expects to procure between two and six unmanned aerial vehicles for border surveillance and internal-security operations.

Costa Rica has focused on continued expansion of its National Coast Guard (SNG) and plans to increase personnel by up to 25% during 2018. The US announced in 2016 that two former US Coast Guard cutters would be transferred to the SNG, and it is anticipated that these will be delivered in 2018. Meanwhile, US SOUTHCOM has approved a US$30m budget to continue supporting the SNG. **El Salvador** announced that in 2017 it had allocated 13,000 troops to support the National Police in operations against organised crime. This is an increase from the previous reported figure of 10,400, and confirms the upwards trend in the armed forces' contribution to internal security. The Salvadorean Air Force also expects to take delivery of four UH-1H helicopters donated by Taiwan and plans to convert up to ten of its existing fleet of UH-1Hs to the *Huey*-II standard. Taiwan has also provided financing for an additional Damen Interceptor 1102 for **Panama**'s aeronaval service; this would bring the number of boats in service to eight, three of which have been financed by Taiwan. **Guatemala**'s armed forces are changing roles and missions, focusing on border surveillance and a new role supporting national development projects, including the repair and reconstruction of public infrastructure. This shift seeks to refocus the armed forces, ahead of a potential move by the government to withdraw them from internal-security roles in 2018.

Post-FARC Colombia

Colombia's armed forces have begun a significant transformation process to a post-conflict military force. The objective is to move from a counter-insurgency focus towards a multi-mission force; this transition will include changes to organisation and equipment. As part of this long-term transformation process, Colombia concluded an individual partnership agreement with NATO in May 2017. Negotiations on the agreement began in 2013. It is meant to foster Colombia's participation in a broad range of defence and security matters with the Alliance. The Colombian Army has established the Comando de Transformación Ejército del Futuro (COTEF), or Future Army Transformation Command, to guide its transformation, laying out three distinct phases towards 2030. Phase 1, from 2014 to 2018, has been focused on supporting the peace process and envisages the army providing stabilisation operations. Operational capabilities will be strengthened under Phase 2, from 2018 to 2022, while in Phase 3 – planned to begin in 2023 – the army will consolidate its skills in order to become a multi-mission force capable of deploying both inside Colombia and externally.

Meanwhile, the navy is pressing ahead with plans to procure four new-generation frigates under the Strategic Surface Platform programme; these are due to join the fleet in the early 2020s. The programme has attracted significant attention, with multiple international firms offering production licences and technology transfer. The ships will be built locally by COTECMAR. The company launched the third licence-built OPV-80-class ocean-patrol vessel (OPV) in 2017, which entered service in July, and announced plans to switch construction to the OPV-93C, a vessel designed in Colombia. COTECMAR is emerging as a regional supplier, having closed contracts with Honduras and Panama to build logistics vessels. The Colombian Air Force (FAC) announced in 2017 the procurement of two *Kfir* TC12 two-seater combat-capable trainers as attrition replacements; this was an interim measure pending the selection of a new-generation fighter, which is currently scheduled to take place in 2019. The FAC took delivery in 2017 of the first TADER tactical air-defence radar indigenously developed by the defence-ministry-run CODALTEC.

Military developments in Mexico

It is likely that Mexico's armed forces will, for the foreseeable future, continue to deploy in the internal-security role.

The army has begun to expand its Military Police Corps, with a 4th brigade formed in 2016 and a new brigade forming in Guanajuato from 2017. The plan is to reach a strength of 12 brigades, one for each military region, composed of three infantry and one special-forces battalion. These units are being equipped with *SandCat* light combat vehicles, as well as the locally manufactured DN-XI protected patrol vehicle.

Regular army (and marine) units continue to receive HMMWV light vehicles, part of an order for over 3,300, and the army has launched a programme to procure new armoured vehicles and light artillery. The Mexican Air Force placed orders for 12 Beechcraft T-6C+ turboprop armed trainers, raising total T-6C+ procurement to 60, plus a single *King Air* 350i and three S-45 *Baalam* tactical unmanned aerial vehicles during 2017. It also launched a programme to procure a new early-warning-radar system for the northwest of the country. Notwithstanding political rhetoric, tension and threats from Trump to end the North American Free Trade Agreement, the military-to-military relationship has grown closer, with more joint exercises.

The Mexican Navy decommissioned one of its four *Allende*-class frigates (formerly US *Knox* class) and both former Israeli *Sa'ar*-class missile boats, and as part of the country's decades-old ongoing naval-shipbuilding project announced a programme to begin the replacement of its surface-warfare fleet. The navy has selected the Damen 10514 light frigate; the keel was laid on the first vessel in June 2017 in the Netherlands, and the vessel will be completed in Mexico. It expects to launch the first of eight frigates from its shipyards in Salina Cruz in December

2018. Naval construction continues at a steady pace, including the launch of the tenth Damen Stan Patrol 4207-class coastal-patrol craft and the seventh *Oaxaca*-class OPV. The navy also boosted its aviation capacity in 2017, with the delivery of five AS565MBe *Panther* helicopters, more UH-60M *Black Hawk*s, a single maritime-surveillance-configured *King Air* 350 and seven T-6C+ aircraft configured for close-air support, after which it was able to retire the last of its L-90TP *Redigo* armed trainers.

Other developments

There are few large defence-procurement programmes under way in the region, principally as a result of economic challenges. For example, Brazil has been hit by a deteriorating financial situation, which led Michel Temer's administration to apply various measures including cutting military-procurement spending by about 30%. This resulted in the cancellation or delay of multiple programmes. Nonetheless, initial deliveries of the *Gripen*-E/-F fighter and KC-390 cargo/tanker aircraft are expected in 2019. The navy has postponed its new surface-ship programme PROSUPER, which originally called for five 6,000-tonne frigates, five 1,800-tonne OPVs and a single replenishment ship, and is currently reassessing its requirements. Its short-term focus has shifted to procuring four *Tamandaré*-class corvettes. The army, meanwhile, has turned to second-hand opportunity buys, including M113 armoured personnel carriers, M109A5 self-propelled guns and C-23B *Sherpa* short-take-off-and-landing transports from US Army stocks.

Argentina selected the T-6C+ *Texan* and placed an initial order for four of the 12 aircraft making up the requirement. Deliveries began in 2017, but the fact that the air force has not yet been able to secure funding for a next-generation fighter to replace either its now-retired *Mirage*-III fleet or its A-4AR *Fighting Hawk*s represents a broader challenge. Recent administrations have reportedly explored a number of possible replacements since 2013. Reconstituting Argentina's fast-jet air-combat capabilities will rely as much on retaining and growing its cadre of fast-jet pilots as it will on procuring new equipment. Meanwhile, roll-out of the upgraded IA-63 *Pampa* III advanced jet trainer took place in 2017, with three expected to join the air force. The navy has now prioritised the long-awaited procurement of four or five OPVs; funding for this was approved in 2017. The navy came under renewed scrutiny in late year with the loss of the submarine ARA *San Juan* while on exercise.

In early 2017, Chile selected Lockheed Martin Canada to modernise its three former UK Type-23 frigates and will in August 2018 begin to take delivery of six S-70i *Black Hawk*s procured from Sikorsky's PZL Mielec production line in Poland. However, the defence ministry is yet to make a decision on several pending requirements. The Chilean Navy has announced that it will transfer three Cessna O-2A *Skymaster* search-and-rescue and maritime-patrol aircraft to Uruguay as part of a government-to-government project that will support Uruguay's naval-surveillance requirements. Uruguay's air force retired its last IA-58 *Pucara* attack aircraft in early 2017, with the outcome that its air-combat capability now lies in a small number of A-37B *Dragonfly*s.

DEFENCE ECONOMICS

Macroeconomics: a modest recovery

After a year of contraction, the region returned to growth in 2017. This modest recovery – the growth rate was 1.1% – was particularly welcome in South America, where there had been two years of negative growth (-1.2% in 2015 and -2.6% in 2016). Conversely, Central American and Caribbean states fared better in recent years. The highest growth rates in 2017 were in Central America, with Panama reaching 5.3%, the Dominican Republic 4.8% and Nicaragua 4.5%. The success story in South America was Bolivia, where the economy grew by 4.2%.

The region benefited from the upturn in global trade in 2017, which bolstered Latin American

Figure 20 **Latin America and the Caribbean defence spending by country and sub-region**

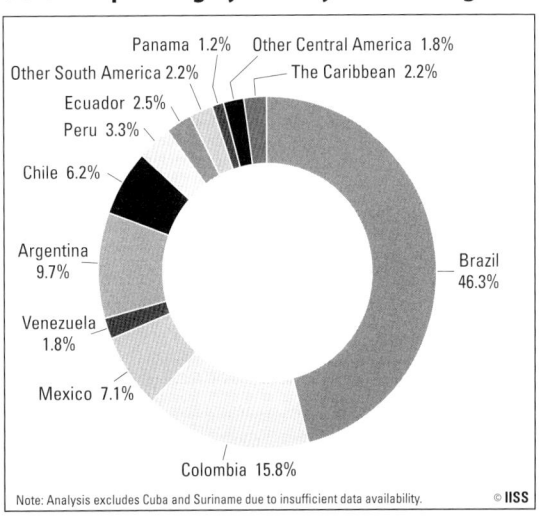

- Panama 1.2%
- Other Central America 1.8%
- Other South America 2.2%
- The Caribbean 2.2%
- Ecuador 2.5%
- Peru 3.3%
- Chile 6.2%
- Argentina 9.7%
- Venezuela 1.8%
- Mexico 7.1%
- Colombia 15.8%
- Brazil 46.3%

Note: Analysis excludes Cuba and Suriname due to insufficient data availability. © IISS

and Caribbean exports. Additionally, the increase in raw-materials prices during the year benefited commodity exporters in the region; that said, commodity prices remain low compared to previous years. Inflation rates have also eased in many countries, except for Venezuela, where it is above 650%. In the Caribbean, tourism continued to support growth, including in Belize and Jamaica, although the costs of recovery after Hurricane Irma in September will have hit sub-regional finances and projected tourism revenues.

Despite this improved outlook, there are still important negative trends and risks concerning regional economic performance. Political uncertainties remain, mainly because of pending decisions from the Trump administration about the possible renegotiation of trade agreements, including the North American Free Trade Agreement. This uncertainty has weighed heavily on the Mexican economy in particular. For instance, after Trump's election, Mexico's exchange rate depreciated significantly. Other uncertainties involve upcoming elections, in Argentina and Chile in late 2017 and in Brazil, Colombia and Venezuela in 2018. These could alter current economic trajectories.

Commodity exporters, despite the modest recovery, still need to respond to the consequences of

Map 9 **Latin America and the Caribbean regional defence spending**[1]

[1] Map illustrating 2017 planned defence-spending levels (in US$ at market exchange rates), as well as the annual real percentage change in planned defence spending between 2016 and 2017 (at constant 2010 prices and exchange rates). Percentage changes in defence spending can vary considerably from year to year, as states revise the level of funding allocated to defence. Changes indicated here highlight the short-term trend in planned defence spending between 2016 and 2017. Actual spending changes prior to 2016, and projected spending levels post-2017, are not reflected.

the drop in commodity prices. In Ecuador, fiscal space remains limited and in Venezuela in particular the fall in oil prices has contributed to an economic and political crisis. Venezuela's GDP is expected to contract by 12% in 2017, after falling by 16% in 2016. According to a survey conducted by a Venezuelan foundation (Fundación Bengoa para la Alimentación y Nutrición), poverty has increased significantly in recent years. In 2014, 48% of Venezuelan households lived in poverty, but this number had risen to 81.8% in 2016.

Defence spending and procurement: budget constraints limit modernisation

After contracting in real terms by 4.7% in 2015 and 5.1% in 2016, the trend in Latin American defence spending reversed, increasing by 3.2% in 2017 (in real terms, in constant 2010 US$). Although still a reduction compared to 2015, this figure seems to reflect the region's slow macroeconomic improvement. The lack of significant external threats also contributes to lower defence spending than in other regions. However, the overall regional total is still an estimate, as some major countries purchase equipment using off-budget funding mechanisms. This is the case in Chile, Ecuador, Peru and Venezuela. In 2017, in current dollar terms, the region's top defence spenders were Brazil (US$29.4 billion), Colombia (US$10bn) and Argentina (US$6.1bn). Two regional states spent more than 2% of GDP on defence in 2017: Colombia (3.26%) and Trinidad and Tobago (2.93%).

Defence investments (including procurement and maintenance) were estimated to comprise only 9% of regional defence budgets in 2016. This figure is low in light of the modernisation requirements of Latin American armed forces. As there are no major external threats to the region, and no major inter-state conflicts, domestic challenges are driving military procurement needs. Principally these relate to threats from organised crime, narco-trafficking, and potential insurgent or guerrilla groups, as well as tasks relating to humanitarian assistance and disaster relief or support to police forces.

Procurements in Argentina and Brazil illustrate how, despite small steps towards recovery, defence spending in these two countries will likely remain limited in coming years. In Argentina, despite a

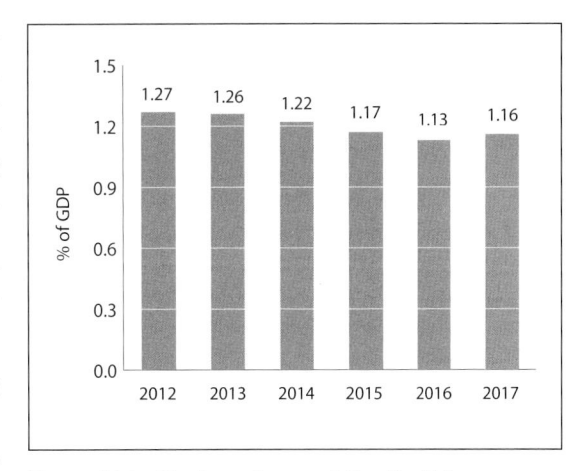

Figure 21 **Latin America and the Caribbean regional defence expenditure** as % of GDP

return to nominal defence-budget growth following the election of President Mauricio Macri in 2015 (US$5.2bn in 2016 and US$6.1bn (actual spending) in 2017), military budgets remain constrained. In 2018 the proposed budget will actually decline in US dollar terms to US$5.9bn, which will hinder any new procurement planning, such as a replacement for Argentina's fast-jet combat-aircraft fleet.

Similarly, in Brazil, even though the budget increased in 2017 (from US$23.6bn in 2016 to US$29.4bn in 2017), the armed forces will still feel the effects of previous years of restricted funding. For 2018, the budget proposal foresees a slight decline compared to 2017 (US$29bn). As a consequence, the defence budget in 2018 will still be lower than that in 2010, measured either in current or real terms (see Table 18).

Brazil's budget constraints have affected important programmes, such as PROSUB (the ongoing programme to build four conventional submarines and one nuclear-powered boat), which has suffered delays. Initially, the first of class was supposed to enter service in 2017. But by late 2016 the launch of this conventional boat had been pushed back to July 2018, the second to September 2020, the third to December 2021 and the fourth to December 2022. It has been reported that the nuclear-submarine programme may also be postponed. Meanwhile, the army cancelled negotiations for 12 *Pantsir* S-1 air-defence systems, while in late 2016 the air force

Table 18 **Brazil: defence spending, 2010–18 (US$bn)**

	2010	2011	2012	2013	2014	2015	2016	2017	2018
US$ billion current	33.9	36.0	33.2	31.4	31.0	23.7	23.6	29.4	29.0
US$ billion constant	33.9	31.6	31.5	30.7	30.6	30.6	29.4	32.0	30.3

suspended the procurement of two second-hand Boeing 767-300ER transport/tanker aircraft.

VENEZUELA

Venezuela's late president Hugo Chávez dreamed of transforming Venezuela into a major military power, but instead the Bolivarian National Armed Forces (FANB) face tough prospects in the near term due to two crucial factors: its increasing involvement in politics and an abrupt decline in its operational capabilities.

The country's political and economic crisis has prompted President Nicolás Maduro to expand the scope of the armed forces' influence in order to ensure continued control, leading to increased military involvement in the government. Venezuela has close to 200 generals, many of whom are managing public companies in strategic sectors. Meanwhile, 37.5% of the executive branch is under military control – 12 of 32 ministries – and a significant number of state governors are active or retired officers.

Although Maduro has tried to prevent direct military involvement in suppressing opposition protests, in order not to fuel discontent among the military, this could be unavoidable if the political and economic situation continues to deteriorate. Indeed, the armed forces have already taken part in some activities against opposition-inspired protests. Since July 2017, 600 special-operations troops have been deployed in the border state of Táchira to strengthen control over a region where anti-regime protests have been particularly violent.

Under these circumstances, there is an increasing risk of fragmentation within the armed forces. By July 2017, the security forces had detained more than 100 FANB personnel on charges of treason, rebellion, theft, desertion and insubordination. At the same time, there have been several cases of dissent within the armed forces. Significant examples include the attack on the Supreme Court of Justice and the Ministry of the Interior by an army officer using a Judicial Police helicopter in June 2017 and an assault on the base of the 41st Armoured Brigade, at Fuerte Paramacay, by a group of military rebels in August.

Meanwhile, the conventional capabilities of the FANB are rapidly deteriorating because of a combination of mismanagement, corruption and the parlous state of Venezuela's economy. Many of the sophisticated weapon systems acquired from China and Russia have low readiness due to a lack of spare parts and broader technical maintenance deficiencies within the FANB. In addition, there are only minimum levels of fuel stocks and other basic supplies needed to sustain military operations, perhaps reflective of the broader crisis affecting the country.

In this context, one of the main security risks is access to some of the key assets of the FANB equipment inventory, notably the almost 2,000 KBM 9K338 *Igla*-S man-portable air-defence systems acquired from Russia. Given the level of corruption alleged in the Venezuelan military system, there is fear over the possibility of an illegal transfer of these weapons to criminal groups. As such, after years of efforts to modernise the country's defence apparatus, the main threat posed by the Venezuelan armed forces might not be related to their strength but instead to their decline.

Command and control

Venezuela's defence system has a dual command structure. The defence ministry is the administrative body responsible for formulating policies and managing resources, while the Operational Strategic Command of the Bolivarian National Armed Forces (CEOFANB) is in charge of the operational direction and control of the armed forces through a chain of subordinate territorial commands. These include the Strategic Integral Defence Regions, the Integral Defence Operational Zones and the Integral Defence Areas. However, the defence minister sometimes makes operational decisions (theoretically an exclusive responsibility of the CEOFANB).

The Venezuelan defence ministry also has administrative control over the FANB and the Bolivarian Militia. The FANB comprises the three traditional armed services – army, navy and air force – as well as the National Guard, a paramilitary force responsible for internal security and border protection. The Bolivarian Militia has a large number of territorial units distributed throughout the country.

The security establishment also includes the corps of the Bolivarian National Police, which is commanded by the interior ministry, and state- and municipal-level police forces. Given that the armed forces, the National Guard, the Bolivarian Militia and police forces all have some responsibility for maintaining public order, the division of roles is unclear and there are problems of inter-service friction and rivalry.

The Bolivarian Militia was created in 2007, and after this Venezuela's security apparatus became one of the largest in the region. Although the FANB is around 123,000 strong, the total number of personnel

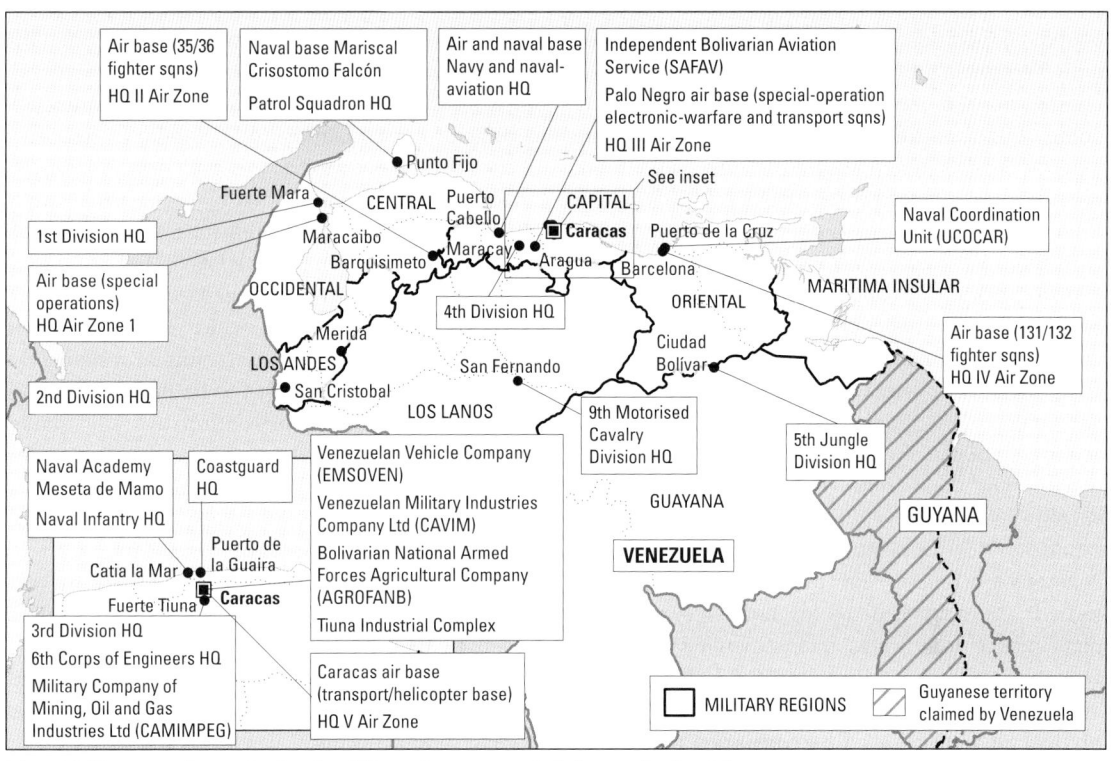

Map 10 **Venezuela: principal military bases and defence industries**

within the security forces has increased exponentially with the incorporation of more than 220,000 militia. Although this number is. far below the goal of 500,000 militia members that was established by the Bolivarian regime, it places the total size of Venezuela's military personnel close to 345,000. However, the operational relevance of the militia force is undermined by minimal investment in equipment and training, and questionable levels of morale.

Defence-doctrine changes

Under the Chavista regime, now headed by Maduro, the force structure of the FANB has remained fundamentally unchanged. However, Venezuela's security apparatus has been subject to radical changes in terms of doctrine and equipment.

In the 1970s, the focus of the Venezuelan armed forces shifted from counter-insurgency to deterrence (vis-à-vis Colombia), oil-infrastructure protection and power-projection in the Caribbean. However, when Hugo Chávez came to power in 1998 he began a process of military transformation. This included implementing the so-called 'Doctrine of Integral Defense', which defined the relationship between the FANB and Venezuelan society as the crucial factor guaranteeing national security and enabling the success of the Bolivarian revolution.

Under this new concept, the Chavista regime implemented three key changes. Firstly, the armed forces were strengthened by increasing their size and modernising their equipment. Secondly, in a move to extend the military's influence into the political sphere, high-ranking officers were appointed to key positions in the civilian public administration. Thirdly, popular participation in national defence was encouraged, based on the idea that it was the joint responsibility of civil society and the FANB.

The regime launched an effort to improve the conventional defence capabilities of the FANB. However, the policies and rhetoric of the administration increased tensions with Western governments, which progressively blocked access to their weapons manufacturers, forcing Caracas to find alternative sources. Consequently, Western manufacturers with a long tradition of cooperation with Venezuela, such as Israel and the United States, were replaced by suppliers in countries such as Belarus, China, Cuba, Iran and Russia.

At the same time, and as a part of its nationalistic ideology, the regime emphasised the need to build an independent defence posture. This stimulated cooperation with partners closely aligned with Venezuela's political position, and who were willing to take part in joint ventures and technology-transfer schemes. The result was a set of joint defence projects aimed at increasing the capabilities of the Venezuelan national defence industry. For example, memoranda of understanding were signed with Russia to build a factory for the production of AK-103 assault rifles and to establish a maintenance centre for Mi-17 helicopters. This policy also triggered the production of a coastal-patrol vessel by state-owned shipyard DIANCA as part of the 2005 agreement with Spanish shipbuilder Navantia to acquire eight patrol vessels.

However, this new twin-track procurement strategy has failed overall to deliver comprehensive capability development. The introduction of new Belarusian, Chinese and Russian equipment has caused serious difficulties, as both operators and maintenance technicians lack experience in these weapons systems. At the same time, the regime's attempts to increase indigenous capacity for weapons production were derailed by corruption (such as in the case of the Russian-made assault-rifle factory) or technical problems (as happened with the plan to build the Mi-17 helicopter-maintenance plant). These difficulties are among the key factors hampering Venezuelan military capabilities.

Meanwhile, in conjunction with the plans to modernise the FANB's conventional capabilities, the Venezuelan regime formed the Bolivarian Militia in order to try and politically mobilise the population, maintain internal security and sustain a guerrilla campaign in case of foreign invasion. Inspired by the model of the Cuban Territorial Militia Troops, it comprises armed civilians who receive periodic training in exchange for a small stipend. The regime planned to equip it with heavy weapons and transform it into a powerful armed force to balance the influence of the regular armed forces. However, mismanagement, a lack of resources and army misgivings have prevented this from happening.

Consequently, the Bolivarian Militia has become a collection of undisciplined and poorly trained units with very limited military value. However, it has played a critical role in repressing the political opposition. It has been used to organise and arm gangs of radical Chavista militants known as *colectivos*. These groups use violence to suppress anti-government marches and are accused of human-rights violations.

Economic crisis and defence acquisitions

Venezuela's economic crisis has seriously affected the government's ability to sustain its military expenditure. However, due to low levels of transparency, it is difficult to estimate the total amount of resources allocated to the armed forces and how it is spent. This problem is compounded by the fact that funds allocated to military procurement are not managed by the defence ministry or the FANB, but by a set of state-owned companies (such as Veximca) and financial funds such as FONDEN, which do not make their records public and lack clear accounting systems.

Nevertheless, even with the limited information available, it is possible to confirm two key trends. Firstly, there has been a sweeping reduction in the amount of money allocated for the acquisition of new weapons. According to the Venezuelan non-governmental organisation Control Ciudadano, Caracas reduced its arms and equipment purchases by 90% between 2013–14 and 2015–16. This has been caused largely by factors such as the fall in global oil prices, which affected Venezuela significantly. Meanwhile, the country is also experiencing broader financial instability. For instance, Venezuela has experienced high inflation rates (of over 250% in 2016 and 650% in 2017, according to the IMF) and currency depreciation (in 2013, one US dollar was exchanged for less than ten bolivars; in 2017, one US dollar was worth more than 900 bolivars).

Secondly, equipment procurement has shifted from conventional weapons to riot-control and internal-security equipment, given the increase in protests and riots driven by the dire economic situation and the regime's authoritarianism. Consequently, in recent years, the National Guard and the Bolivarian National Police have been the main beneficiaries of Caracas's military-procurement policy. Both organisations have received large numbers of crowd-control vehicles and significant amounts of personal equipment.

Outside such internal-security purchases, the air force has acquired nine Chinese Hongdu K-8W *Karakorum* light attack/training aircraft. At the same time, the Venezuelan Marines have incorporated a number of Chinese armoured vehicles into their inventory, including the NORINCO VN1, VN18 and VN16. However, the military acquisitions made by Maduro look modest in comparison to those of his predecessor. Under Chávez, Venezuela acquired Russian Su-30MKV *Flanker* fighter/ground-attack aircraft and T-72M main battle tanks, as well as a large number of air-defence systems.

Antigua and Barbuda ATG

East Caribbean Dollar EC$		2016	2017	2018
GDP	EC$	3.94bn	4.15bn	
	US$	1.46bn	1.54bn	
per capita	US$	16,176	16,826	
Growth	%	5.3	2.7	
Inflation	%	-0.5	2.4	
Def bdgt [a]	EC$	71m	73m	
	US$	26m	27m	
US$1=EC$		2.70	2.70	

[a] Budget for the Ministry of Legal Affairs, Public Safety, Immigration and Labour

Population 94,731

Age	0–14	15–19	20–24	25–29	30–64	65 plus
Male	11.7%	4.3%	4.1%	3.5%	20.2%	3.4%
Female	11.3%	4.3%	4.1%	3.8%	24.4%	4.6%

Capabilities

The damage caused by Hurricane Irma, particularly to Barbuda, has tested the small Antigua and Barbuda Defence Force's (ABDF's) disaster-response capacity, practised in the 2017 iteration of the annual *Tradewinds* exercise series. Personnel have also been deployed to nearby Dominica to assist other Caribbean states in relief efforts there after Hurricane Maria. The ABDF also provides internal-security support and takes part in regional cooperation efforts to counter the trade in illicit narcotics.

ACTIVE 180 (Army 130 Coast Guard 50)
(all services form combined Antigua and Barbuda Defence Force)

RESERVE 80 (Joint 80)

ORGANISATIONS BY SERVICE

Army 130
FORCES BY ROLE
MANOEUVRE
  Light
  1 inf bn HQ
  1 inf coy
COMBAT SERVICE SUPPORT
  1 spt gp (1 engr unit, 1 med unit)

Coast Guard 50
EQUIPMENT BY TYPE
PATROL AND COASTAL COMBATANTS • PB 2: 1 *Dauntless*; 1 *Swift*

Argentina ARG

Argentine Peso P		2016	2017	2018
GDP	P	8.05tr	10.3tr	
	US$	545bn	620bn	
per capita	US$	12,494	14,062	
Growth	%	-2.2	2.5	
Inflation	%	n.k.	26.9	
Def bdgt	P	76.9bn	102bn	116bn
	US$	5.20bn	6.13bn	
US$1=P		14.78	16.68	

Population 44,293,293

Age	0–14	15–19	20–24	25–29	30–64	65 plus
Male	12.6%	3.9%	3.8%	3.8%	20.2%	4.8%
Female	11.9%	3.8%	3.7%	3.7%	20.6%	6.7%

Capabilities

Argentina's armed forces principally focus on border security, surveillance and counter-narcotics operations, in part due to the increase in drug-trafficking activity in and around the country. Buenos Aires cooperates with Bolivia and Paraguay on border-security and counter-narcotics operations. Argentina's equipment inventory is increasingly obsolete, with modernisation hampered by limited funding. According to the 2016 defence-spending review and 2017 projections, most of the budget will be allocated to aircraft maintenance and modernisation and for the procurement of new types. Air-force capability has been in serious decline, with the entire A-4 *Skyhawk* fleet essentially non-operational, although the purchase of five ex-French Dassault *Super Etandard Modernisée* could allow the regeneration of Argentina's own *Super Etendard*s. The air force has begun receiving the first of a dozen Beechcraft *Texan* II trainers as another part of the effort to regain air capability. The naval fleet has also seen its capability decline in areas such as anti-submarine warfare, mine warfare and airborne early warning. The loss of the submarine ARA *San Juan* highlighted challenges for Argentina's naval operations. The return to sea of the icebreaker ARA *Almirante Irizar* after ten years of repairs should improve Argentina's ability to support operations in Antarctica. Argentina relies on foreign suppliers for most of its equipment. Aviation firm FAdeA conducts some aircraft maintenance, but faces restructuring as it has struggled to manufacture and win orders for aircraft beyond the domestic market, itself starved of resources. The armed forces train with Brazil and Chile and participate in UN peacekeeping missions. A 'state partnership' agreement was signed with the US Georgia National Guard in late 2016; this military-to-military relationship will include sharing expertise in enhancing readiness as well as in disaster-response, border-security and peacekeeping missions.

ACTIVE 74,200 (Army 42,800 Navy 18,500 Air 12,900) **Paramilitary 31,250**

ORGANISATIONS BY SERVICE

Army 42,800; 7,000 civilian
Regt and gp are usually bn-sized

FORCES BY ROLE
SPECIAL FORCES
  1 SF gp
MANOEUVRE
  Mechanised
  1 (1st) div (1 armd bde (4 tk regt, 1 mech inf regt, 1 SP arty gp, 1 cbt engr bn, 1 int coy, 1 sigs coy, 1 log coy), 1 (3rd) jungle bde (2 jungle inf regt, 1 arty gp, 1 engr bn, 1 int coy, 1 sigs coy, 1 log coy, 1 med coy); 1 (12th) jungle bde (3 jungle inf regt, 1 arty gp, 1 engr bn, 1 int coy, 1 sigs coy, 1 log coy, 1 med coy), 2 engr bn, 1 sigs bn, 1 log coy)
  1 (3rd) div (1 mech bde (1 armd recce regt, 1 tk regt, 2 mech inf regt, 1 SP arty gp, 1 cbt engr bn, 1 int coy, 1 sigs coy, 1 log coy), 1 mech bde (1 armd recce tp, 1 tk regt, 2 mech inf regt, 1 SP arty gp, 1 cbt engr bn, 1 int coy, 1 sigs coy, 1 log coy), 1 int bn, 1 sigs bn, 1 log coy))
  1 (Rapid Deployment) force (1 armd bde (1 recce sqn, 3 tk regt, 1 mech inf regt, 1 SP arty gp, 1 cbt engr coy, 1 int coy, 1 sigs coy, 1 log coy), 1 mech bde (1 armd recce regt, 3 mech inf regt, 1 arty gp, 1 cbt engr coy, 1 int coy, 1 sigs coy,1 log coy), 1 AB bde (1 recce tp, 2 para regt, 1 arty gp, 1 cbt engr coy, 1 sigs coy, 1 log coy), 1 AD gp (2 AD bn))
  Light
  1 (2nd) mtn inf div (2 mtn inf bde (1 armd recce regt, 3 mtn inf regt, 2 arty gp, 1 cbt engr bn, 1 sigs coy, 1 log coy), 1 mtn inf bde (1 armd recce bn, 2 mtn inf regt, 1 jungle inf regt, 2 arty gp, 1 cbt engr bn, 1 sigs coy, 1 construction coy, 1 log coy), 1 AD gp, 1 sigs bn)
  1 mot cav regt (presidential escort)
  Air Manoeuvre
  1 air aslt regt
COMBAT SUPPORT
  1 arty gp (bn)
  1 engr bn
  1 sigs gp (1 EW bn, 1 sigs bn, 1 maint bn)
  1 sigs bn
  1 sigs coy
COMBAT SERVICE SUPPORT
  5 maint bn
HELICOPTER
  1 avn gp (bde) (1 avn bn, 1 hel bn)
EQUIPMENT BY TYPE
ARMOURED FIGHTING VEHICLES
  MBT 231: 225 TAM, 6 TAM S21
  LT TK 117: 107 SK-105A1 *Kuerassier*; 6 SK-105A2 *Kuerassier*; 4 *Patagón*
  RECCE 47 AML-90
  IFV 232: 118 VCTP (incl variants); 114 M113A2 (20mm cannon)
  APC 278
    APC (T) 274: 70 M113A1-ACAV; 204 M113A2
    APC (W) 4 WZ-551B1

ENGINEERING & MAINTENANCE VEHICLES
  ARV *Greif*
ANTI-TANK/ANTI-INFRASTRUCTURE
  MSL • SP 3 M1025 HMMWV with TOW-2A
  RCL 105mm 150 M-1968
ARTILLERY 1,085
  SP 155mm 19 VCA 155 *Palmaria*
  TOWED 172: **105mm** 64 Model 56 pack howitzer; **155mm** 108: 28 CITEFA M-77/CITEFA M-81; 80 SOFMA L-33
  MRL 8: **105mm** 4 SLAM *Pampero*; **127mm** 4 CP-30
  MOR 886: **81mm** 492; **SP 107mm** 25 M106A2; **120mm** 330 Brandt; **SP 120mm** 39 TAM-VCTM
RADAR • LAND 18+: M113A1GE *Green Archer* (mor); 18 RATRAS (veh, arty)
AIRCRAFT
  TPT • Light 17: 1 Beech 80 *Queen Air*; 3 C-212-200 *Aviocar*; 3 Cessna 207 *Stationair*; 2 Cessna 208EX *Grand Caravan*; 1 Cessna 500 *Citation* (survey); 1 Cessna 550 *Citation Bravo*; 3 DA42 (to be converted to ISR role); 2 DHC-6 *Twin Otter*; 1 Sabreliner 75A (*Gaviao* 75A)
  TRG 5 T-41 *Mescalero*
HELICOPTERS
  MRH 5: 4 SA315B *Lama*; 1 Z-11
  TPT 67: **Medium** 3 AS332B *Super Puma*; **Light** 64: 1 Bell 212; 25 Bell 205 (UH-1H *Iroquois* – 6 armed); 5 Bell 206B3; 13 UH-1H-II *Huey* II; 20 AB206B1
AIR DEFENCE
  SAM • Point-defence RBS-70
  GUNS • TOWED 229: **20mm** 200 GAI-B01; **30mm** 21 HS L81; **35mm** 8 GDF Oerlikon (*Skyguard* fire control)
RADAR • AIR DEFENCE 11: 5 Cardion AN/TPS-44; 6 *Skyguard*

Navy 18,500; 7,200 civilian
Commands: Surface Fleet, Submarines, Naval Avn, Marines

FORCES BY ROLE
SPECIAL FORCES
  1 (diver) SF gp
EQUIPMENT BY TYPE
SUBMARINES • TACTICAL • SSK 2:
  1 *Salta* (GER T-209/1100) with 8 single 533mm TT with Mk 37/SST-4 HWT
  1 *Santa Cruz* (GER TR-1700) with 6 single 533mm TT with SST-4 HWT (undergoing MLU)
PRINCIPAL SURFACE COMBATANTS 11
  DESTROYERS • DDH 1 *Hercules* (UK Type-42 – utilised as a fast troop-transport ship), with 1 114mm gun (capacity 2 SH-3H *Sea King* hel)
  FRIGATES • FFGHM 10:
    4 *Almirante Brown* (GER MEKO 360) with 2 quad lnchr with MM40 *Exocet* AShM, 1 octuple *Albatros* lnchr with *Aspide* SAM, 2 triple B515 ILAS-3 324mm TT with A244 LWT, 1 127mm gun (capacity 1 AS555 *Fennec* hel)
    6 *Espora* (GER MEKO 140) with 2 twin lnchr with MM38 *Exocet* AShM, 2 triple B515 ILAS-3 324mm ASTT with A244 LWT, 1 76mm gun (capacity 1 AS555 *Fennec* hel) (1 vessel damaged in 2016, in repair)

PATROL AND COASTAL COMBATANTS 16
CORVETTES • FSG 3 *Drummond* (FRA A-69) with 2 twin lnchr with MM38 *Exocet* AShM, 2 triple Mk32 324mm ASTT with A244 LWT, 1 100mm gun
PSO 3:
2 *Irigoyen* (ex-US *Cherokee*)
1 *Teniente Olivieri* (ex-US oilfield tug)
PCO 2:
1 *Murature* (ex-US *King* – trg/river patrol role) with 3 105mm gun
1 *Sobral* (ex-US *Sotoyomo*)
PCGT 1 *Intrepida* (GER Lurssen 45m) with 2 single lnchr with MM38 *Exocet* AShM, 2 single 533mm TT with SST-4 HWT, 1 76mm gun
PCC 1 *Intrepida* (GER Lurssen 45m) with 1 76mm gun
PB 6: 4 *Baradero* (*Dabur*); 2 *Point*
AMPHIBIOUS 6 LCVP
LOGISTICS AND SUPPORT 18
ABU 3 *Red*
AFS 4 *Puerto Argentina* (ex-RUS *Neftegaz*)
AGB 1 *Almirante Irizar* (damaged by fire in 2007; returned to service in mid-2017)
AGHS 3: 1 *Austral*; 1 *Cormoran*; 1 *Puerto Deseado* (ice-breaking capability, used for polar research)
AGOR 1 *Commodoro Rivadavia*
AK 3 *Costa Sur* (capacity 4 LCVP)
AOR 1 *Patagonia* (FRA *Durance*) with 1 hel platform
AORL 1 *Ingeniero Julio Krause*
AXS 1 *Libertad*

Naval Aviation 2,000

EQUIPMENT BY TYPE
AIRCRAFT 20 combat capable
FGA 2 *Super Etendard* (9 more in store)
ATK 1 AU-23 *Turbo Porter*
ASW 7: 3 S-2T *Tracker†*; 4 P-3B *Orion*
TPT • Light 7 Beech 200F/M *King Air*
TRG 10 T-34C *Turbo Mentor**
HELICOPTERS
ASW 2 SH-3H (ASH-3H) *Sea King*
MRH 4 AS555 *Fennec*
TPT • Medium 4 UH-3H *Sea King*
AIR-LAUNCHED MISSILES
AAM • IR R-550 *Magic*
AShM AM39 *Exocet*

Marines 2,500

FORCES BY ROLE
MANOEUVRE
Amphibious
1 (fleet) force (1 cdo gp, 1 (AAV) amph bn, 1 mne bn, 1 arty bn, 1 ADA bn)
1 (fleet) force (2 mne bn, 2 navy det)
1 force (1 mne bn)
EQUIPMENT BY TYPE
ARMOURED FIGHTING VEHICLES
RECCE 12 ERC-90F *Sagaie*
APC • APC (W) 31 VCR
AAV 24: 13 LARC-5; 11 LVTP-7
ENGINEERING & MAINTENANCE VEHICLES
ARV AAVR 7

ANTI-TANK/ANTI-INFRASTRUCTURE
RCL 105mm 30 M-1974 FMK-1
ARTILLERY 89
TOWED 19: **105mm** 13 Model 56 pack howitzer; **155mm** 6 M114
MOR 70: **81mm** 58; **120mm** 12
AIR DEFENCE
SAM • Point-defence RBS-70
GUNS 40mm 4 Bofors 40L

Air Force 12,900; 6,900 civilian

4 Major Comds – Air Operations, Personnel, Air Regions, Logistics, 8 air bde

Air Operations Command
FORCES BY ROLE
GROUND ATTACK
2 sqn with A-4/OA-4 (A-4AR/OA-4AR) *Skyhawk*
2 (tac air) sqn with IA-58 *Pucara*; EMB-312 *Tucano* (on loan for border surv/interdiction)
ISR
1 sqn with Learjet 35A
SEARCH & RESCUE/TRANSPORT HELICOPTER
2 sqn with Bell 212; Bell 212 (UH-1N); Mi-171, SA-315B *Lama*
TANKER/TRANSPORT
1 sqn with C-130H *Hercules*; KC-130H *Hercules*; L-100-30
TRANSPORT
1 sqn with B-707
1 sqn with DHC-6 *Twin Otter*; Saab 340
1 sqn with F-27 *Friendship*
1 sqn with F-28 *Fellowship*; Learjet 60
1 (Pres) flt with B-757-23ER; S-70A *Black Hawk*, S-76B
TRAINING
1 sqn with AT-63 *Pampa*
1 sqn with EMB-312 *Tucano*
1 sqn with Grob 120TP
1 hel sqn with Hughes 369; SA-315B *Lama*
TRANSPORT HELICOPTER
1 sqn with Hughes 369; MD-500; MD500D
EQUIPMENT BY TYPE
AIRCRAFT 72 combat capable
ATK 52: 20 A-4 (A-4AR) *Skyhawk†*; 2 OA-4 (OA-4AR) *Skyhawk†*; 21 IA-58 *Pucara*; 9 IA-58M *Pucara*
ELINT 1 Cessna 210
TKR 2 KC-130H *Hercules*
TPT 27: **Medium** 4: 3 C-130H *Hercules*; 1 L-100-30; **Light** 16: 1 Cessna 310; 6 DHC-6 *Twin Otter*; 4 Learjet 35A (test and calibration); 1 Learjet 60 (VIP); 4 Saab 340; **PAX** 7: 1 B-737; 1 B-757-23ER; 5 F-28 *Fellowship*
TRG 57: 20 AT-63 *Pampa** (LIFT); 19 EMB-312 *Tucano*; 8 Grob 120TP; 6 P2002JF *Sierra*; 4 T-6C *Texan* II
HELICOPTERS
MRH 25: 2 Bell 412EP; 11 Hughes 369; 3 MD-500; 4 MD-500D; 5 SA315B *Lama*
TPT 12: **Medium** 3: 2 Mi-171E; 1 S-70A *Black Hawk*; **Light** 9: 7 Bell 212; 2 S-76B (VIP)
AIR DEFENCE
GUNS 88: **20mm**: 86 Oerlikon/Rh-202 with 9 Elta EL/M-2106 radar; **35mm**: 2 Oerlikon GDF-001 with *Skyguard* radar

RADAR • AIR DEFENCE 6: 5 AN/TPS-43; 1 BPS-1000
AIR-LAUNCHED MISSILES
AAM • IR AIM-9L *Sidewinder*; R-550 *Magic*; *Shafrir* 2‡

Paramilitary 31,250

Gendarmerie 18,000
Ministry of Security
FORCES BY ROLE
COMMAND
  7 regional comd
SPECIAL FORCES
  1 SF unit
MANOEUVRE
  Other
  17 paramilitary bn
  Aviation
  1 (mixed) avn bn
EQUIPMENT BY TYPE
ARMOURED FIGHTING VEHICLES
  RECCE S52 *Shorland*
  APC (W) 87: 47 *Grenadier*; 40 UR-416
ARTILLERY • MOR 81mm
AIRCRAFT
  TPT • Light 12: 3 Cessna 152; 3 Cessna 206; 1 Cessna 336; 1 PA-28 *Cherokee*; 2 PC-6B *Turbo Porter*; 2 PC-12
HELICOPTERS
  MRH 2 MD-500C
  TPT • Light 16: 5 Bell 205 (UH-1H *Iroquois*); 7 AS350 *Ecureuil*; 1 H135; 3 R-44 *Raven* II
  TRG 1 S-300C

Prefectura Naval (Coast Guard) 13,250
Ministry of Security
EQUIPMENT BY TYPE
PATROL AND COASTAL COMBATANTS 67
  PCO 7: 1 *Correa Falcon*; 1 *Delfin*; 5 *Mantilla* (F30 *Halcón* – undergoing modernisation)
  PCC 1 *Mariano Moreno*
  PB 58: 1 *Dorado*; 25 *Estrellemar*; 2 *Lynch* (US *Cape*); 18 *Mar del Plata* (Z-28); 1 *Surel*; 8 Damen Stan 2200; 3 Stan Tender 1750
  PBR 1 *Tonina*
LOGISTICS & SUPPORT 11
  AAR 1 *Tango*
  AFS 1 *Prefecto Garcia*
  AG 2
  ARS 1 *Prefecto Mansilla*
  AX 5: 1 *Mandubi*; 4 other
  AXS 1 *Dr Bernardo Houssay*
AIRCRAFT
  MP 1 Beech 350ER *King Air*
  TPT • Light 6: 5 C-212 *Aviocar*; 1 Beech 350ER *King Air*
  TRG 2 Piper PA-28 *Archer* III
HELICOPTERS
  SAR 3 AS565MA *Panther*
  MRH 1 AS365 *Dauphin* 2
  TPT 5: Medium 3: 1 H225 *Puma*; 2 SA330L (AS330L) *Puma*; Light 2 AS355 *Ecureuil* II
  TRG 4 S-300C

DEPLOYMENT

CYPRUS
UN • UNFICYP 277; 2 inf coy; 1 hel flt; 2 Bell 212

MIDDLE EAST
UN • UNTSO 3 obs

WESTERN SAHARA
UN • MINURSO 3 obs

Bahamas BHS

Bahamian Dollar B$		2016	2017	2018
GDP	B$	8.72bn	9.13bn	
	US$	8.72bn	9.13bn	
per capita	US$	23,671	24,516	
Growth	%	-0.3	1.8	
Inflation	%	0.8	2.4	
Def bdgt	B$	121m	99m	91m
	US$	121m	99m	
US$1=B$		1.00	1.00	

Population 329,988

Age	0–14	15–19	20–24	25–29	30–64	65 plus
Male	11.4%	4.0%	4.3%	4.1%	22.1%	2.9%
Female	11.1%	3.9%	4.2%	4.0%	23.0%	4.7%

Capabilities

In addition to the disaster-relief capacity demonstrated in the aftermath of Hurricane Irma, the Royal Bahamas Defence Force (RBDF) is primarily tasked with maritime security and countering narcotics trafficking. The second phase of the Sandy Bottom Project was completed in April 2017; the final phase of the project will now see further infrastructure improvements and an increase in RBDF personnel numbers. The final vessel acquired under the project, HMBS *Madeira*, is undergoing renovation work, after being rammed by a Dominican-flagged fishing vessel in 2016, whilst both *Bahamas*-class patrol vessels have now completed refits with the support of Damen Group, one in the Netherlands and the other locally. A new permanent naval base on Grand Bahama is also currently under discussion to bolster the RBDF's counter-narcotics work. The country is a regular participant in the *Tradewinds* exercise series and has a training relationship with the US armed forces.

ACTIVE 1,300

ORGANISATIONS BY SERVICE

Royal Bahamian Defence Force 1,300
FORCES BY ROLE
MANOEUVRE
  Amphibious
  1 mne coy (incl marines with internal- and base-security duties)

EQUIPMENT BY TYPE
PATROL AND COASTAL COMBATANTS 23
  PCC 2 *Bahamas*
  PBF 6 Nor-Tech
  PB 15: 4 *Arthur Dion Hanna*; 2 *Dauntless*; 1 *Eleuthera*; 3 *Lignum Vitae* (Damen 3007); 1 *Protector*; 2 Sea Ark 12m; 2 Sea Ark 15m
LOGISTICS & SUPPORT 1
  AKR 1 *Lawrence Major* (Damen 5612)
AIRCRAFT • TPT • **Light** 3: 1 Beech A350 *King Air*; 1 Cessna 208 *Caravan*; 1 P-68 *Observer*

FOREIGN FORCES

Guyana Navy: Base located at New Providence Island

Barbados BRB

Barbados Dollar B$		2016	2017	2018
GDP	B$	9.10bn	9.64bn	
	US$	4.55bn	4.82bn	
per capita	US$	16,237	17,159	
Growth	%	1.6	0.9	
Inflation	%	1.3	5.0	
Def bdgt [a]	B$	78m	76m	
	US$	39m	38m	
US$1=B$		2.00	2.00	

[a] Defence and security expenditure

Population 292,336

Age	0–14	15–19	20–24	25–29	30–64	65 plus
Male	8.9%	3.1%	3.2%	3.6%	24.7%	4.7%
Female	8.9%	3.1%	3.2%	3.5%	25.7%	7.0%

Capabilities

Maritime security and resource protection are the main tasks of the Barbados Defence Force (BDF), but it also has a secondary public-safety role in support of the Royal Barbados Police Force. Both the coastguard and the Barbados Regiment have been active in counter-narcotics work in recent years, and the latter may in future be tasked with law-enforcement patrols. In 2017, the BDF participated in regional disaster-relief efforts in the northern Caribbean in the wake of hurricanes Irma and Maria, and hosted the annual iteration of the *Tradewinds* exercise series. Barbados hosts the headquarters of the Regional Security System (RSS), a grouping of Caribbean nations' police and security forces – and military capabilities – that can be called on to address threats to regional security and to undertake counter-narcotics and disaster-relief tasks. The US, in collaboration with Canada, recently overhauled the RSS's two maritime-patrol aircraft.

ACTIVE 610 (Army 500 Coast Guard 110)
RESERVE 430 (Joint 430)

ORGANISATIONS BY SERVICE

Army 500
FORCES BY ROLE
MANOEUVRE
  Light
  1 inf bn (cadre)

Coast Guard 110
HQ located at HMBS Pelican, Spring Garden
EQUIPMENT BY TYPE
PATROL AND COASTAL COMBATANTS • PB 6: 1 *Dauntless*; 2 *Enterprise* (Damen Stan 1204); 3 *Trident* (Damen Stan Patrol 4207)
LOGISTICS & SUPPORT • AX 1

Belize BLZ

Belize Dollar BZ$		2016	2017	2018
GDP	BZ$	3.48bn	3.64bn	
	US$	1.74bn	1.82bn	
per capita	US$	4,630	4,699	
Growth	%	-0.8	2.5	
Inflation	%	0.6	1.8	
Def bdgt [a]	BZ$	42m	46m	
	US$	21m	23m	
FMA (US)	US$	1m	1m	0m
US$1=BZ$		2.00	2.00	

[a] Excludes funds allocated to Coast Guard and Police Service

Population 360,346

Age	0–14	15–19	20–24	25–29	30–64	65 plus
Male	17.3%	5.4%	5.1%	4.6%	16.4%	1.8%
Female	16.6%	5.2%	4.9%	4.4%	16.1%	2.0%

Capabilities

The principal task for Belize's small armed forces is territorial defence, particularly along the border with Guatemala, where security incidents continued in 2017. Recent activity has focused on countering narcotics smuggling, although this is hampered by insufficient maritime-patrol or aerial-surveillance and interdiction capacity. The first pilots for the air wing's newly acquired UH-1H helicopters completed conversion training in 2017; with these helicopters now in service, the defence force's ability to deploy and operate in the country's jungles has seen a significant boost. An update of the national defence and security strategy was planned for 2016, but it is not clear if this process has concluded. There are established training relationships with the UK, the US (including maintenance support) and regional states. There are plans to invite foreign states to carry out jungle training with the defence force.

ACTIVE 1,500 (Army 1,500) Paramilitary 150
RESERVE 700 (Joint 700)

ORGANISATIONS BY SERVICE

Army ε1,500
FORCES BY ROLE
MANOEUVRE
  Light
  2 inf bn (3 inf coy)
COMBAT SERVICE SUPPORT
  1 spt gp
EQUIPMENT BY TYPE
ANTI-TANK/ANTI-INFRASTRUCTURE • RCL 84mm
  8 *Carl Gustav*
ARTILLERY • MOR 81mm 6

Air Wing
EQUIPMENT BY TYPE
AIRCRAFT
  TPT • Light 3: 1 BN-2A *Defender*; 1 BN-2B *Defender*; 1 Cessna 182 *Skylane*
  TRG 1 T-67M-200 *Firefly*
HELICOPTERS
  TPT • Light 3: 2 Bell 205 (UH-1H *Iroquois*); 1 Bell 407

Reserve
FORCES BY ROLE
MANOEUVRE
  Light
  1 inf bn (3 inf coy)

Paramilitary 150

Coast Guard 150
EQUIPMENT BY TYPE
All operational patrol vessels under 10t FLD

FOREIGN FORCES
United Kingdom Army 20

Bolivia BOL

Bolivian Boliviano B		2016	2017	2018
GDP	B	234bn	259bn	
	US$	34.1bn	37.8bn	
per capita	US$	3,125	3,412	
Growth	%	4.3	4.2	
Inflation	%	3.6	3.2	
Def bdgt	B	3.04bn	3.73bn	
	US$	442m	543m	
US$1=B		6.86	6.86	
Population	11,138,234			

Age	0–14	15–19	20–24	25–29	30–64	65 plus
Male	16.2%	5.1%	4.7%	4.4%	16.6%	2.3%
Female	15.6%	4.9%	4.6%	4.4%	17.9%	2.9%

Capabilities

Counter-narcotics and internal and border security are the main tasks of the armed forces. Modest procurement programmes are intended to improve the services' ability to undertake these roles. In June 2017, Bolivia introduced a new military-volunteer initiative, aimed in part at improving the gender balance within the armed forces. In August 2017, Bolivia and Russia agreed to expand a 2016 agreement on defence-technology collaboration following a Bolivian defence-delegation visit to Moscow, but China remains a significant supplier of military materiel. Airspace control is an emerging strategic priority, and construction began in September 2017 on the first of 13 civilian and military radars that Bolivia is acquiring to help address this requirement. There is also increasing cooperation with Peru on border security and countering narcotics trafficking, while exercises in this area have taken place with Argentina's air force. There is some local maintenance capacity for the services, with refurbished aircraft delivered in late 2016. Bolivian personnel deploy on UN peacekeeping missions.

ACTIVE 34,100 (Army 22,800 Navy 4,800 Air 6,500)
Paramilitary 37,100
Conscript liability 12 months (18–22 years of age)

ORGANISATIONS BY SERVICE

Army 9,800; 13,000 conscript (total 22,800)
FORCES BY ROLE
COMMAND
  6 mil region HQ
  10 div HQ
SPECIAL FORCES
  3 SF regt
MANOEUVRE
  Reconnaissance
  1 mot cav gp
  Armoured
  1 armd bn
  Mechanised
  1 mech cav regt
  2 mech inf regt
  Light
  1 (aslt) cav gp
  5 (horsed) cav gp
  3 mot inf regt
  21 inf regt
  Air Manoeuvre
  2 AB regt (bn)
  Other
  1 (Presidential Guard) inf regt
COMBAT SUPPORT
  6 arty regt (bn)
  6 engr bn
  1 int coy
  1 MP bn
  1 sigs bn
COMBAT SERVICE SUPPORT
  2 log bn
AVIATION
  2 avn coy
AIR DEFENCE
  1 ADA regt

EQUIPMENT BY TYPE
ARMOURED FIGHTING VEHICLES
LT TK 54: 36 SK-105A1 *Kuerassier*; 18 SK-105A2 *Kuerassier*
RECCE 24 EE-9 *Cascavel*
APC 148+
  APC (T) 87+: 50+ M113, 37 M9 half-track
  APC (W) 61: 24 EE-11 *Urutu*; 22 MOWAG *Roland*; 15 V-100 *Commando*
  AUV 19 *Tiger* 4×4
ENGINEERING & MAINTENANCE VEHICLES
ARV 4 *Greif*; M578 LARV
ANTI-TANK/ANTI-INFRASTRUCTURE
MSL
  SP 2 *Koyak* with HJ-8
  MANPATS HJ-8
RCL 90mm M67; **106mm** M40A1
ARTILLERY 311+
  TOWED 61: **105mm** 25 M101A1; **122mm** 36 M-30 (M-1938)
  MOR 250+: **81mm** 250 M29; Type-W87; **107mm** M30; **120mm** M120
AIRCRAFT
  TPT • Light 4: 1 Fokker F-27-200; 1 Beech 90 *King Air*; 1 C-212 *Aviocar*; 1 Cessna 210 *Centurion*
HELICOPTERS
  MRH 6 H425
  TRG 1 Robinson R55
AIR DEFENCE • GUNS • TOWED **37mm** 18 Type-65

Navy 4,800
Organised into six naval districts with HQ located at Puerto Guayaramerín
EQUIPMENT BY TYPE
PATROL AND COASTAL COMBATANTS • PBR 3: 1 *Santa Cruz*; 2 others
LOGISTICS AND SUPPORT 3
  AG 1
  AH 2

Marines 1,700 (incl 1,000 Naval Military Police)
FORCES BY ROLE
MANOEUVRE
  Mechanised
    1 mech inf bn
  Amphibious
    6 mne bn (1 in each Naval District)
COMBAT SUPPORT
  4 (naval) MP bn

Air Force 6,500 (incl conscripts)
FORCES BY ROLE
GROUND ATTACK
  1 sqn with K-8WB *Karakorum*
ISR
  1 sqn with Cessna 206; Cessna 402; Learjet 25B/25D (secondary VIP role)
SEARCH & RESCUE
  1 sqn with AS332B *Super Puma*; H125 *Ecureuil*; H145

TRANSPORT
  1 sqn with BAe-146-100; CV-580; MA60
  1 (TAB) sqn with C-130A *Hercules*; MD-10-30F
  1 sqn with C-130B/H *Hercules*
  1 sqn with F-27-400M *Troopship*
  1 (VIP) sqn with Beech 90 *King Air*; Beech 200 *King Air* Beech 1900; *Falcon* 900EX; *Sabreliner* 60
  6 sqn with Cessna 152/206; IAI-201 *Arava*, PA-32 *Saratoga*; PA-34 *Seneca*
TRAINING
  1 sqn with DA40; T-25
  1 sqn with Cessna 152/172
  1 sqn with PC-7 *Turbo Trainer*
  1 hel sqn with R-44 *Raven* II
TRANSPORT HELICOPTER
  1 (anti-drug) sqn with Bell 205 (UH-1H *Iroquois*)
AIR DEFENCE
  1 regt with Oerlikon; Type-65
EQUIPMENT BY TYPE
AIRCRAFT 22 combat capable
  TPT 85: **Heavy** 1 MD-10-30F; **Medium** 4: 1 C-130A *Hercules*; 2 C-130B *Hercules*; 1 C-130H *Hercules*; **Light** 70: 1 Aero Commander 690; 3 Beech 90 *King Air*; 2 Beech 200 *King Air*; 1 Beech 1900; 5 C-212-100; 10 Cessna 152; 2 Cessna 172, 19 Cessna 206; 1 Cessna 402; 1 CV-580; 9 DA40; 3 F-27-400M *Troopship*; 4 IAI-201 *Arava*; 2 Learjet 25B/D; 2 MA60†; 1 PA-32 *Saratoga*; 3 PA-34 *Seneca*; 1 *Sabreliner* 60; **PAX** 10: 1 B-727; 3 B-737-200; 5 BAe-146-100; 1 *Falcon* 900EX (VIP)
  TRG 30: 6 K-8WB *Karakorum**; 6 T-25; 16 PC-7 *Turbo Trainer**; 2 Z-242L
HELICOPTERS
  MRH 1 SA316 *Alouette* III
  TPT 35: **Medium** 6 H215 *Super Puma*; **Light** 29: 2 H125 *Ecureuil*; 19 Bell 205 (UH-1H *Iroquois*); 2 H145; 6 R-44 *Raven* II
AIR DEFENCE • GUNS 18+: **20mm** Oerlikon; **37mm** 18 Type-65

Paramilitary 37,100+

National Police 31,100+
FORCES BY ROLE
MANOEUVRE
  Other
    27 frontier sy unit
    9 paramilitary bde
    2 (rapid action) paramilitary regt

Narcotics Police 6,000+
FOE (700) – Special Operations Forces

DEPLOYMENT

CENTRAL AFRICAN REPUBLIC
UN • MINUSCA 1; 3 obs

DEMOCRATIC REPUBLIC OF THE CONGO
UN • MONUSCO 7 obs

SOUTH SUDAN
UN • UNMISS 1; 3 obs

Brazil BRZ

Brazilian Real R		2016	2017	2018
GDP	R	6.27tr	6.60tr	
	US$	1.80tr	2.08tr	
per capita	US$	8,727	10,020	
Growth	%	-3.6	0.7	
Inflation	%	8.7	3.7	
Def bdgt [a]	R	82.1bn	93.3bn	92.6bn
	US$	23.6bn	29.4bn	
US$1=R		3.48	3.17	

[a] Includes military pensions

Population 207,353,391

Age	0–14	15–19	20–24	25–29	30–64	65 plus
Male	11.4%	4.2%	4.0%	4.0%	22.0%	3.5%
Female	10.9%	4.1%	3.9%	3.9%	22.9%	4.7%

Capabilities

Brazil still wishes to enhance power-projection capabilities, boost surveillance of the Amazon region and coastal waters, and further develop its defence industry. However, economic difficulties continue to affect its ability to develop these ambitions; procurements have decreased and modernisation plans have slowed. Funding and internal deployments associated with the major sporting events of recent years have also had a budgetary impact. Key programmes, including KC-390, FX-2, SISFRON and PROSUB, have all suffered funding challenges. Brazil has a well-developed defence-industrial base, across the land, sea and air domains. It is looking to further its capabilities in terms of aerospace manufacturing and shipbuilding through the *Gripen* combat-aircraft procurement and the PROSUB programme, which is intended to lead to the construction in Brazil of nuclear- and conventionally powered submarines. The air force saw organisational change in 2017, with new wings and squadrons created and two commands deactivated. The armed forces continue to work towards a national cyber-defence capability and regularly participate in domestic and international exercises; its deployment to Haiti concluded with the end of the UN MINUSTAH mission.

ACTIVE 334,500 (Army 198,000 Navy 69,000 Air 67,500) **Paramilitary 395,000**
Conscript liability 12 months (can go to 18; often waived)

RESERVE 1,340,000

ORGANISATIONS BY SERVICE

Army 128,000; 70,000 conscript (total 198,000)
FORCES BY ROLE
COMMAND
  8 mil comd HQ
  12 mil region HQ
  7 div HQ (2 with regional HQ)

SPECIAL FORCES
  1 SF bde (1 SF bn, 1 cdo bn)
  1 SF coy
MANOEUVRE
  Reconnaissance
  3 mech cav regt
  Armoured
  1 (5th) armd bde (1 mech cav sqn, 2 armd bn, 2 armd inf bn, 1 SP arty bn, 1 engr bn, 1 sigs coy, 1 log bn)
  1 (6th) armd bde (1 mech cav sqn, 2 armd bn, 2 armd inf bn, 1 SP arty bn, 1 AD bty, 1 engr bn, 1 sigs coy, 1 log bn)
  Mechanised
  3 (1st, 2nd & 4th) mech cav bde (1 armd cav bn, 3 mech cav bn, 1 arty bn, 1 engr coy, 1 sigs coy, 1 log bn)
  1 (3rd) mech cav bde (1 armd cav bn, 2 mech cav bn, 1 arty bn, 1 engr coy, 1 sigs coy, 1 log bn)
  1 (15th) mech inf bde (3 mech inf bn, 1 arty bn, 1 engr coy, 1 log bn)
  Light
  1 (3rd) mot inf bde (1 mech cav sqn, 2 mot inf bn, 1 inf bn, 1 arty bn, 1 engr coy, 1 sigs coy, 1 log bn)
  1 (4th) mot inf bde (1 mech cav sqn, 1 mot inf bn, 1 inf bn, 1 mtn inf bn, 1 arty bn, 1 sigs coy, 1 log bn)
  1 (7th) mot inf bde (3 mot inf bn, 1 arty bn)
  1 (8th) mot inf bde (1 mech cav sqn, 3 mot inf bn, 1 arty bn, 1 log bn)
  1 (10th) mot inf bde (1 mech cav sqn, 4 mot inf bn, 1 inf coy, 1 arty bn, 1 engr coy, 1 sigs coy)
  1 (13th) mot inf bde (1 mot inf bn, 2 inf bn, 1 inf coy, 1 arty bn)
  1 (14th) mot inf bde (1 mech cav sqn, 3 inf bn, 1 arty bn)
  1 (11th) lt inf bde (1 mech cav regt, 3 inf bn, 1 arty bn, 1 engr coy, 1 sigs coy, 1 MP coy, 1 log bn)
  11 inf bn
  1 (1st) jungle inf bde (1 mech cav sqn, 2 jungle inf bn, 1 arty bn)
  3 (2nd, 16th & 17th) jungle inf bde (3 jungle inf bn)
  1 (23rd) jungle inf bde (1 cav sqn, 4 jungle inf bn, 1 arty bn, 1 sigs coy, 1 log bn)
  2 jungle inf bn
  Air Manoeuvre
  1 AB bde (1 cav sqn, 3 AB bn, 1 arty bn, 1 engr coy, 1 sigs coy, 1 log bn)
  1 (12th) air mob bde (1 cav sqn, 3 air mob bn, 1 arty bn, 1 engr coy, 1 sigs coy, 1 log bn)
  Other
  1 (9th) mot trg bde (3 mot inf bn, 1 arty bn, 1 log bn)
  1 (18th) sy bde (2 sy bn, 2 sy coy)
  1 sy bn
  7 sy coy
  3 gd cav regt
  1 gd inf bn
COMBAT SUPPORT
  3 SP arty bn
  6 fd arty bn
  1 MRL bn
  1 STA bty
  6 engr bn
  1 engr gp (1 engr bn, 4 construction bn)
  1 engr gp (4 construction bn, 1 construction coy)

2 construction bn
1 EW coy
1 int coy
6 MP bn
3 MP coy
4 sigs bn
2 sigs coy
COMBAT SERVICE SUPPORT
  5 log bn
  1 tpt bn
  4 spt bn
HELICOPTER
  1 avn bde (3 hel bn, 1 maint bn)
  1 hel bn
AIR DEFENCE
  1 ADA bde (5 ADA bn)
EQUIPMENT BY TYPE
ARMOURED FIGHTING VEHICLES
  MBT 393: 128 *Leopard* 1A1BE; 220 *Leopard* 1A5BR; 45 M60A3/TTS
  LT TK 50 M41C
  RECCE 408 EE-9 *Cascavel*
  IFV 6 VBTP-MR *Guarani* 30mm
  APC 1,013
    APC (T) 630: 584 M113; 12 M113A2; 34 M577A2
    APC (W) 383: 223 EE-11 *Urutu*; 160 VBTP-MR *Guarani* 6×6
ENGINEERING & MAINTENANCE VEHICLES
  AEV 4+: *Greif*; HART; 4+ *Leopard* 1
  ARV 4+: *Leopard* 1; 4 M88A1; M578 LARV
  VLB 4+: XLP-10; 4 *Leopard* 1
ANTI-TANK/ANTI-INFRASTRUCTURE
  MSL • MANPATS *Eryx*; *Milan*; MSS-1.2 AC
  RCL 343: **84mm** 149 *Carl Gustav*; **106mm** 194 M40A1
ARTILLERY 1,855
  SP 149: **105mm** 72 M7/108; **155mm** 77: 37 M109A3; 40 M109A5/A5+
  TOWED 431
    105mm 336: 233 M101/M102; 40 L118 Light Gun; 63 Model 56 pack howitzer
    155mm 95 M114
  MRL 127mm 30: 18 ASTROS II Mk3M; 12 ASTROS II Mk6
  MOR 1,245: **81mm** 1,168: 453 L16, 715 M936 AGR; **120mm** 77 M2
HELICOPTERS
  MRH 51: 29 AS565 *Panther* (HM-1); 5 AS565 K2 *Panther* (HM-1); 17 AS550U2 *Fennec* (HA-1 – armed)
  TPT 36: **Heavy** 9 H225M *Caracal* (HM-4); **Medium** 12: 8 AS532 *Cougar* (HM-3); 4 S-70A-36 *Black Hawk* (HM-2); **Light** 15 AS350L1 *Ecureuil* (HA-1)
AIR DEFENCE
  SAM • Point-defence RBS-70; 9K38 *Igla* (SA-18 *Grouse*); 9K338 *Igla*-S (SA-24 *Grinch*)
  GUNS 100:
    SP 35mm 34 *Gepard* 1A2
    TOWED 66: **35mm** 39 GDF-001 towed (some with *Super Fledermaus* radar); **40mm** 27 L/70 (some with BOFI)
RADAR • AIR DEFENCE 5 SABER M60

Navy 69,000
Organised into 9 districts with HQ I Rio de Janeiro, HQ II Salvador, HQ III Natal, HQ IV Belém, HQ V Rio Grande, HQ VI Ladario, HQ VII Brasilia, HQ VIII Sao Paulo, HQ IX Manaus
FORCES BY ROLE
SPECIAL FORCES
  1 (diver) SF gp
EQUIPMENT BY TYPE
SUBMARINES • TACTICAL • SSK 5:
  4 *Tupi* (GER T-209/1400) with 8 single 533mm TT with Mk48 HWT
  1 *Tikuna* with 8 single 533mm TT with Mk48 HWT
PRINCIPAL SURFACE COMBATANTS 11
  DESTROYERS • DDGHM 2:
    1 *Greenhalgh* (ex-UK *Broadsword*) with 4 single lnchr with MM38 *Exocet* AShM, 2 sextuple lnchr with *Sea Wolf* SAM, 6 single STWS Mk2 324mm ASTT with Mk 46 LWT (capacity 2 *Super Lynx* Mk21A hel)
    1 *Greenhalgh* (ex-UK *Broadsword*) with 4 single lnchr with MM40 *Exocet* Block 2 AShM, 2 sextuple lnchr with *Sea Wolf* SAM, 6 single STWS Mk2 324mm ASTT with Mk 46 LWT (capacity 2 *Super Lynx* Mk21A hel)
  FRIGATES 9
    FFGHM 6 *Niterói* with 2 twin lnchr with MM40 *Exocet* Block 2 AShM, 1 octuple *Albatros* lnchr with *Aspide* SAM, 2 triple Mk32 324mm ASTT with Mk 46 LWT, 1 twin 375mm A/S mor, 2 *Sea Trinity* Mk3 CIWS, 1 115mm gun (capacity 1 *Super Lynx* Mk21A hel)
    FFGH 3:
      2 *Inhaúma* with 2 twin lnchr with MM40 *Exocet* Block 2 AShM, 2 triple Mk32 324mm ASTT with Mk 46 LWT, 1 115mm gun (1 *Super Lynx* Mk21A hel)
      1 *Barroso* with 2 twin lnchr with MM40 *Exocet* Block 2 AShM, 2 triple 324mm ASTT with Mk 46 LWT, 1 *Sea Trinity* CIWS, 1 115mm gun (capacity 1 *Super Lynx* Mk21A hel)
PATROL AND COASTAL COMBATANTS 44
  PSO 3 *Amazonas* with 1 hel landing platform
  PCO 6: 4 *Bracui* (ex-UK *River*); 1 *Imperial Marinheiro* with 1 76mm gun; 1 *Parnaiba* with 1 hel landing platform
  PCC 2 *Macaé*
  PCR 5: 2 *Pedro Teixeira* with 1 hel landing platform; 3 *Roraima*
  PB 24: 12 *Grajau*; 6 *Marlim*; 6 *Piratini* (US PGM)
  PBR 4 LPR-40
MINE WARFARE • MINE COUNTERMEASURES • MSC 4 *Aratu* (GER *Schutze*)
AMPHIBIOUS
  PRINCIPAL AMPHIBIOUS SHIPS • LPD 1 *Bahia* (ex-FRA *Foudre*) (capacity 4 hels; 8 LCM, 450 troops)
  LANDING SHIPS 3
    LST 1 *Mattoso Maia* (ex-US *Newport*) with 1 *Phalanx* CIWS (capacity 3 LCVP; 1 LCPL; 400 troops)
    LSLH 2: 1 *Garcia D'Avila* (ex-UK *Sir Galahad*) (capacity 1 hel; 16 MBT; 340 troops); 1 *Almirante Saboia* (ex-UK *Sir Bedivere*) (capacity 1 med hel; 18 MBT; 340 troops)
  LANDING CRAFT 16:
    LCM 12: 10 EDVM-25; 2 *Icarai* (ex-FRA CTM)
    LCT 1 *Marambaia* (ex-FRA CDIC)
    LCU 3 *Guarapari* (LCU 1610)

LOGISTICS AND SUPPORT 44
    ABU 5: 4 *Comandante Varella*; 1 *Faroleiro Mario Seixas*
    ABUH 1 *Almirante Graca Aranah* (lighthouse tender)
    AFS 1 *Potengi*
    AGHS 5: 1 *Caravelas* (riverine); 4 *Rio Tocantin*
    AGOS 2: 1 *Ary Rongel* with 1 hel landing platform; 1 *Almirante Maximiano* (capacity 2 AS350/AS355 *Ecureuil* hel)
    AGS 8: 1 *Aspirante Moura*; 1 *Cruzeiro do Sul*; 1 *Antares*; 3 *Amorim do Valle* (ex-UK *Rover*); 1 *Rio Branco*; 1 *Vital de Oliveira*
    AGSH 1 *Sirius*
    AH 5: 2 *Oswaldo Cruz* with 1 hel landing platform; 1 *Dr Montenegro*; 1 *Tenente Maximianol* with 1 hel landing platform; 1 *Soares de Meirelles*
    AOR 2: 1 *Almirante Gastão Motta*; 1 *Marajó*
    AP 3: 1 *Almirante Leverger*; 1 *Paraguassu*; 1 *Pará* (all river transports)
    ASR 1 *Felinto Perry* (NOR *Wildrake*) with 1 hel landing platform
    ATF 5: 3 *Triunfo*; 2 *Almirante Guihem*
    AX 1 *Brasil* (*Niterói* mod) with 1 hel landing platform
    AXL 3 *Nascimento*
    AXS 1 *Cisne Barco*

Naval Aviation 2,100
FORCES BY ROLE
GROUND ATTACK
    1 sqn with A-4/4M (AF-1) *Skyhawk*; TA-4/4M (AF-1A) *Skyhawk*
ANTI SURFACE WARFARE
    1 sqn with *Super Lynx* Mk21A
ANTI SUBMARINE WARFARE
    1 sqn with S-70B *Seahawk* (MH-16)
TRAINING
    1 sqn with Bell 206B3 *Jet Ranger* III
TRANSPORT HELICOPTER
    1 sqn with AS332 *Super Puma*; AS532 *Cougar*
    1 sqn with AS350 *Ecureuil* (armed); AS355 *Ecureuil* II (armed); H225M *Caracal* (UH-15A)
    3 sqn with AS350 *Ecureuil* (armed); AS355 *Ecureuil* II (armed)
EQUIPMENT BY TYPE
AIRCRAFT 11 combat capable
    ATK 11: 8 A-4/4M (AF-1/1B) *Skyhawk*; 3 TA-4/4M (AF-1A) *Skyhawk*
HELICOPTERS
    ASW 18: 11 *Super Lynx* Mk21A; 1 *Super Lynx* Mk21B; 6 S-70B *Seahawk* (MH-16)
    CSAR 2 H225M *Caracal* (UH-15A)
    TPT 52: **Heavy** 7 H225M *Caracal* (UH-15); **Medium** 7: 5 AS332 *Super Puma*; 2 AS532 *Cougar* (UH-14); **Light** 38: 15 AS350 *Ecureuil* (armed); 8 AS355 *Ecureuil* II (armed); 15 Bell 206B3 *Jet Ranger* III (IH-6B)
AIR-LAUNCHED MISSILES • AShM: AM39 *Exocet*; *Sea Skua*; AGM-119 *Penguin*

Marines 16,000
FORCES BY ROLE
SPECIAL FORCES
    1 SF bn
MANOEUVRE
  Amphibious
    1 amph div (1 lt armd bn, 3 mne bn, 1 arty bn)
    1 amph aslt bn
    7 (regional) mne gp
    1 rvn bn
COMBAT SUPPORT
    1 engr bn
COMBAT SERVICE SUPPORT
    1 log bn
EQUIPMENT BY TYPE
ARMOURED FIGHTING VEHICLES
    LT TK 18 SK-105 *Kuerassier*
    APC 60
        APC (T) 30 M113A1 (incl variants)
        APC (W) 30 *Piranha* IIIC
    AAV 27: 13 AAV-7A1; 1 AAV-7A1 RAM/RS; 1 AAV-7A1 RAM/RS; 12 LVTP-7
ENGINEERING VEHICLES • ARV 1 AAVR-7
ANTI-TANK/ANTI-INFRASTRUCTURE
    MSL• MANPATS RB-56 *Bill*; MSS-1.2 AC
ARTILLERY 65
    TOWED 41: **105mm** 33: 18 L118 Light Gun; 15 M101; **155mm** 8 M114
    MRL 127mm 6 ASTROS II Mk6
    MOR 81mm 18 M29
AIR DEFENCE • GUNS 40mm 6 L/70 (with BOFI)

Air Force 67,500
Brazilian airspace is divided into 7 air regions, each of which is responsible for its designated air bases. Air assets are divided among 4 designated air forces (I, II, III & V) for operations (IV Air Force temporarily deactivated)

FORCES BY ROLE
FIGHTER
    4 sqn with F-5EM/FM *Tiger* II
FIGHTER/GROUND ATTACK
    2 sqn with AMX (A-1A/B)
GROUND ATTACK/ISR
    4 sqn with EMB-314 *Super Tucano* (A-29A/B)*
MARITIME PATROL
    1 sqn with P-3AM *Orion*
    2 sqn with EMB-111 (P-95A/B/M)
ISR
    1 sqn with AMX-R (RA-1)*
    1 sqn with Learjet 35 (R-35A); EMB-110B (R-95)
AIRBORNE EARLY WARNING & CONTROL
    1 sqn with EMB-145RS (R-99); EMB-145SA (E-99)
TANKER/TRANSPORT
    1 sqn with C-130H/KC-130H *Hercules*
TRANSPORT
    1 VIP sqn with A319 (VC-1A); EMB-190 (VC-2); AS355 *Ecureuil* II (VH-55); H135M (VH-35); H225M *Caracal* (VH-36)
    1 VIP sqn with EMB-135BJ (VC-99B); ERJ-135LR (VC-99C); ERJ-145LR (VC-99A); Learjet 35A (VU-35); Learjet 55C (VU-55C)
    2 sqn with C-130E/H *Hercules*
    2 sqn with C295M (C-105A)

7 (regional) sqn with Cessna 208/208B (C-98); Cessna 208-G1000 (C-98A); EMB-110 (C-95); EMB-120 (C-97)
1 sqn with ERJ-145 (C-99A)
1 sqn with EMB-120RT (VC-97), EMB-121 (VU-9)

TRAINING
1 sqn with EMB-110 (C-95)
2 sqn with EMB-312 *Tucano* (T-27) (incl 1 air show sqn)
1 sqn with T-25A/C

ATTACK HELICOPTER
1 sqn with Mi-35M *Hind* (AH-2)

TRANSPORT HELICOPTER
1 sqn with H225M *Caracal* (H-36)
1 sqn with AS350B *Ecureuil* (H-50); AS355 *Ecureuil* II (H-55)
1 sqn with Bell 205 (H-1H); H225M *Caracal* (H-36)
2 sqn with UH-60L *Black Hawk* (H-60L)

ISR UAV
1 sqn with *Hermes* 450/900

EQUIPMENT BY TYPE
AIRCRAFT 202 combat capable
  FTR 47: 43 F-5EM *Tiger* II; 4 F-5FM *Tiger* II
  FGA 49: 38 AMX (A-1); 11 AMX-T (A-1B)
  ASW 9 P-3AM *Orion*
  MP 19: 10 EMB-111 (P-95A *Bandeirulha*)*; 9 EMB-111 (P-95BM *Bandeirulha*)*
  ISR: 8: 4 AMX-R (RA-1)*; 4 EMB-110B (R-95)
  ELINT 6: 3 EMB-145RS (R-99); 3 Learjet 35A (R-35A)
  AEW&C 5 EMB-145SA (E-99)
  SAR 7: 1 C295M *Amazonas* (SC-105); 4 EMB-110 (SC-95B), 1 SC-130E *Hercules*
  TKR/TPT 2 KC-130H
  TPT 198: **Medium** 20: 4 C-130E *Hercules*; 16 C-130H *Hercules*; **Light** 170: 11 C295M (C-105A); 7 Cessna 208 (C-98); 9 Cessna 208B (C-98); 13 Cessna 208-G1000 (C-98A); 52 EMB-110 (C-95A/B/C/M); 16 EMB-120 (C-97); 4 EMB-120RT (VC-97); 5 EMB-121 (VU-9); 7 EMB-135BJ (VC-99B); 3 EMB-201R *Ipanema* (G-19); 2 EMB-202A *Ipanema* (G-19A); 2 ERJ-135LR (VC-99C); 7 ERJ-145 (C-99A); 1 ERJ-145LR (VC-99A); 9 Learjet 35A (VU-35); 1 Learjet 55C (VU-55); 9 PA-34 *Seneca* (U-7); 12 U-42 *Regente*; **PAX** 8: 1 A319 (VC-1A); 3 EMB-190 (VC-2); 4 Hawker 800XP (EU-93A – calibration)
  TRG 264: 100 EMB-312 *Tucano* (T-27); 39 EMB-314 *Super Tucano* (A-29A)*; 44 EMB-314 *Super Tucano* (A-29B)*; 81 T-25A/C

HELICOPTERS
  ATK 12 Mi-35M *Hind* (AH-2)
  MRH 2 H135M (VH-35)
  TPT 81: **Heavy** 13 H225M *Caracal* (11 H-36 & 2 VH-36); **Medium** 16 UH-60L *Black Hawk* (H-60L); **Light** 52: 24 AS350B *Ecureuil* (H-50); 4 AS355 *Ecureuil* II (H-55/VH-55); 24 Bell 205 (H-1H)

UNMANNED AERIAL VEHICLES
  ISR • **Medium** 5: 4 *Hermes* 450; 1 *Hermes* 900

AIR-LAUNCHED MISSILES
  AAM • **IR** MAA-1 *Piranha*; R-550 *Magic* 2; *Python* 3; **IIR** *Python* 4; **SARH** Super 530F; **ARH** *Derby*
  AShM AM39 *Exocet*
  ARM MAR-1 (in development)

Paramilitary 395,000 opcon Army

Public Security Forces 395,000

State police organisation technically under army control. However, military control is reducing, with authority reverting to individual states

EQUIPMENT BY TYPE
UNMANNED AERIAL VEHICLES
  ISR • **Heavy** 3 *Heron* (deployed by Federal Police for Amazon and border patrols)

Cyber

Cyber was a key component of the 2008 National Defence Strategy and the July 2012 Defence White Paper. In 2011, the army inaugurated Brazil's cyber-defence centre (CDCiber) to coordinate existing army, navy and air-force activities. There is an active training programme, run by the Institute of Cyber Defence among others, and a Cyber Operations Simulator (SIMOC) was set up in 2013, within the Integrated Electronic Warfare Centre. In July 2015, the army acticivated two provisional cyber-defence units under CDCiber, a cyber-defence command and a national school of cyber defence. In December 2016, the army approved the establishment of a permanent cyber-defence command (ComDCiber), reporting to the Department of Science and Technology.

DEPLOYMENT

CENTRAL AFRICAN REPUBLIC
UN • MINUSCA 2; 4 obs

CYPRUS
UN • UNFICYP 2

LEBANON
UN • UNIFIL 207; 1 FFGH

LIBERIA
UN • UNMIL 1; 1 obs

SOUTH SUDAN
UN • UNMISS 6; 5 obs

SUDAN
UN • UNAMID 3 obs
UN • UNISFA 2 obs

WESTERN SAHARA
UN • MINURSO 10 obs

Chile CHL

Chilean Peso pCh		2016	2017	2018
GDP	pCh	167tr	174tr	
	US$	247bn	263bn	
per capita	US$	13,576	14,315	
Growth	%	1.6	1.4	
Inflation	%	3.8	2.3	
Def bdgt [a]	pCh	2.33tr	2.60tr	
	US$	3.44bn	3.93bn	
US$1=pCh		676.94	661.907	

[a] Includes military pensions

Population   17,789,267

Age	0–14	15–19	20–24	25–29	30–64	65 plus
Male	10.2%	3.6%	4.0%	4.2%	22.5%	4.5%
Female	9.8%	3.5%	3.8%	4.0%	23.3%	6.2%

Capabilities

Assuring sovereignty, territorial integrity and internal security remain core roles for the armed forces, which have spent the past decade recapitalising the inventories of all three services with second-hand US and European equipment. However, there is an increasing focus on non-traditional military roles, such as disaster relief, illustrated by deployments in response to flooding and an earthquake in 2015. A new defence white paper was scheduled for 2017 but it had not been released by November. Procurement priorities have changed to reflect the new focus on littoral and blue-water surveillance capabilities and helicopters, although slower economic growth may delay or reduce the scope of some of these plans. Chile has a developed defence-industrial base, with ENAER conducting aircraft maintenance. ASMAR and FAMAE are key industries in the maritime and land sectors respectively, with the former completing four OPVs for the navy, and set to begin full construction on a new icebreaker in 2018 that will enhance Chile's ability to support operations in Antarctica. Training takes place regularly on a national basis, and the armed forces routinely participate in exercises with international and regional partners. Santiago is looking to increase its contributions to international peace operations following the end of the UN MINUSTAH mission in Haiti.

ACTIVE 77,200 (Army 46,350 Navy 19,800 Air 11,050) **Paramilitary 44,700**

Conscript liability Army 1 year; Navy 18 months; Air Force 12 months. Legally, conscription can last for 2 years

RESERVE 40,000 (Army 40,000)

ORGANISATIONS BY SERVICE

Space
EQUIPMENT BY TYPE
SATELLITES
  ISR 1 SSOT (Sistema Satelital del la Observación de la Tierra)

Army 46,350
6 military administrative regions
FORCES BY ROLE
Currently being reorganised into 1 SF bde, 4 armd bde, 1 armd det, 3 mot bde, 2 mot det, 4 mtn det and 1 avn bde
COMMAND
  6 div HQ
SPECIAL FORCES
  1 SF bde (1 SF bn, 1 (mtn) SF gp, 1 para bn, 3 cdo coy, 1 log coy)
MANOEUVRE
  Reconnaissance
  4 cav sqn
  2 recce sqn
  2 recce pl
  Armoured
  3 (1st, 2nd & 3rd) armd bde (1 armd recce pl, 1 armd cav gp, 1 mech inf bn, 1 arty gp, 1 AT coy, 1 engr coy, 1 sigs coy)
  1 (4th) armd bde (1 armd recce pl, 1 armd cav gp, 1 mech inf bn, 1 arty gp, 1 engr coy)
  1 (5th) armd det (1 armd cav gp, 1 mech inf coy, 1 arty gp)
  Mechanised
  1 (1st) mech inf regt
  Light
  1 (1st) mot inf bde (1 recce coy, 1 mot inf bn, 1 arty gp, 3 AT coy, 1 engr bn)
  1 (4th) mot inf bde (1 mot inf bn, 1 MRL gp, 2 AT coy, 1 engr bn)
  1 (24th) mot inf bde (1 mot inf bn, 1 arty gp, 1 AT coy)
  1 (6th) reinforced regt (1 mot inf bn, 1 arty gp, 1 sigs coy)
  1 (10th) reinforced regt (1 mot inf bn, 2 AT coy, 1 engr bn)
  1 (11th) mot inf det (1 inf bn, 1 arty gp)
  1 (14th) mot inf det (1 mot inf bn, 1 arty gp, 1 sigs coy, 1 AT coy)
  7 mot inf regt
  1 (3rd) mtn det (1 mtn inf bn, 1 arty gp, 1 engr coy)
  1 (9th) mtn det (1 mtn inf bn, 1 engr coy, 1 construction bn)
  2 (8th & 17th) mtn det (1 mtn inf bn, 1 arty coy)
COMBAT SUPPORT
  1 arty regt
  1 engr regt
  4 sigs bn
  1 sigs coy
  2 int regt
  1 MP regt
COMBAT SERVICE SUPPORT
  1 log div (2 log regt)
  4 log regt
  6 log coy
  1 maint div (1 maint regt)
AVIATION
  1 avn bde (1 tpt avn bn, 1 hel bn, 1 spt bn)
EQUIPMENT BY TYPE
ARMOURED FIGHTING VEHICLES
  MBT 246: 115 *Leopard* 1; 131 *Leopard* 2A4
  IFV 191: 173 *Marder* 1A3; 18 YPR-765 PRI

APC 548
   APC (T) 369 M113A1/A2
   APC (W) 179 *Piranha*
ENGINEERING & MAINTENANCE VEHICLES
   AEV 9 *Leopard 1*
   ARV 35 *Leopard 1*
   VLB 16 *Leopard 1*
   MW 3 *Leopard 1*
ANTI-TANK/ANTI-INFRASTRUCTURE
   MSL • MANPATS *Spike*-LR; *Spike*-ER
   RCL **84mm** *Carl Gustav*; **106mm** 213 M40A1
ARTILLERY 1,407
   SP **155mm** 48: 24 M109A3; 24 M109A5+
   TOWED 240: **105mm** 192: 88 M101; 104 Model 56 pack howitzer; **155mm** 48 M-68
   MRL **160mm** 12 LAR-160
   MOR 1,107: **81mm** 743: 303 ECIA L65/81; 175 FAMAE; 265 Soltam; **120mm** 293: 173 ECIA L65/120; 17 FAMAE; 93 M-65; **SP 120mm** 71: 35 FAMAE (on *Piranha* 6x6); 36 Soltam (on M113A2)
AIRCRAFT
   TPT • **Light** 8: 2 C-212-300 *Aviocar*; 3 Cessna 208 *Caravan*; 3 CN235
HELICOPTERS
   ISR 9 MD-530F *Lifter* (armed)
   TPT 17: **Medium** 12: 8 AS532AL *Cougar*; 2 AS532ALe *Cougar*; 2 SA330 *Puma*; **Light** 5: 4 H125 *Ecureuil*; 1 AS355F *Ecureuil* II
AIR DEFENCE
   SAM • **Point-defence** *Mistral*
   GUNS 41:
     SP **20mm** 17 *Piranha*/TCM-20
     TOWED **20mm** 24 TCM-20

Navy 19,800

5 Naval Zones; 1st Naval Zone and main HQ at Valparaiso; 2nd Naval Zone at Talcahuano; 3rd Naval Zone at Punta Arenas; 4th Naval Zone at Iquique; 5th Naval Zone at Puerto Montt

FORCES BY ROLE
SPECIAL FORCES
   1 (diver) SF comd
EQUIPMENT BY TYPE
SUBMARINES • TACTICAL • SSK 4:
   2 *O'Higgins* (*Scorpene*) with 6 single 533mm TT with A-184 *Black Shark* HWT/SUT HWT/SM39 *Exocet* Block 2 AShM (1 currently in repair)
   2 *Thomson* (GER T-209/1400) with 8 single 533mm TT A-184 *Black Shark* HWT/SUT HWT/SM39 *Exocet* Block 2 AShM
PRINCIPAL SURFACE COMBATANTS 8
   DESTROYERS • DDGHM 1 *Almirante Williams* (ex-UK *Broadsword* Type-22) with 2 quad Mk141 lnchr with RGM-84 *Harpoon* AShM, 2 octuple VLS with *Barak* SAM; 2 triple 324mm ASTT with Mk46 LWT, 1 76mm gun (capacity 1 AS532SC *Cougar*)
   FRIGATES 7:
     FFGHM 5:
       3 *Almirante Cochrane* (ex-UK *Duke* Type-23) with 2 quad Mk141 lnchr with RGM-84C *Harpoon* AShM,
1 32-cell VLS with *Sea Wolf* SAM, 2 twin 324mm ASTT with Mk46 Mod 2 LWT, 1 114mm gun (capacity 1 AS-532SC *Cougar*)
       2 *Almirante Riveros* (NLD *Karel Doorman*-class) with 2 quad lnchr with MM40 *Exocet* Block 3 AShM, 1 octuple Mk48 lnchr with RIM-7P *Sea Sparrow* SAM, 4 single Mk32 Mod 9 324mm ASTT with Mk46 Mod 5 HWT, 1 76mm gun (capacity 1 AS532SC *Cougar*)
     FFGM 2:
       2 *Almirante Lattore* (NLD *Jacob Van Heemskerck*-class) with 2 twin Mk141 lnchr with RGM-84 *Harpoon* AShM, 1 Mk13 GMLS with SM-1MR SAM, 1 octuple Mk48 lnchr with RIM-7P *Sea Sparrow* SAM, 2 twin Mk32 324mm ASTT with Mk46 LWT, 1 *Goalkeeper* CIWS
PATROL AND COASTAL COMBATANTS 14
   PSOH 4: 2 *Piloto Pardo*; 2 *Piloto Pardo* with 1 76mm gun (ice-strengthened hull)
   PCG 5:
     3 *Casma* (ISR *Sa'ar* 4) with 4 GI *Gabriel* I AShM, 2 76mm guns
     2 *Tiger* (GER Type-148) with 4 single lnchr with MM38 *Exocet* AShM, 1 76mm gun
   PCO 5 *Micalvi*
AMPHIBIOUS
PRINCIPAL AMPHIBIOUS SHIPS
   LPD 1 *Sargento Aldea* (FRA *Foudre*) with 3 twin *Simbad* lnchr with *Mistral* SAM (capacity 4 med hel; 1 LCT; 2 LCM; 22 tanks; 470 troops)
LANDING SHIPS 3
   LSM 1 *Elicura*
   LST 2 *Maipo* (FRA *Batral*) with 1 hel landing platform (capacity 7 tanks; 140 troops)
LANDING CRAFT 3
   LCT 1 CDIC (for use in *Sargento Aldea*)
   LCM 2 (for use in *Sargento Aldea*)
LOGISTICS AND SUPPORT 14
   ABU 1 *George Slight Marshall* with 1 hel landing platform
   AFD 3
   AG 1 *Almirante Jose Toribio Merino Castro* (also used as general spt ship) with 1 hel landing platform
   AGOR 1 *Cabo de Hornos*
   AGHS 1 *Micalvi*
   AGS 1 Type-1200 (ice-strengthened hull, ex-CAN) with 1 hel landing platform
   AOR 2: 1 *Almirante Montt* with 1 hel landing platform; 1 *Araucano*
   AP 1 *Aguiles* (1 hel landing platform)
   ATF 2 *Veritas*
   AXS 1 *Esmeralda*

Naval Aviation 600

EQUIPMENT BY TYPE
AIRCRAFT 14 combat capable
   ASW 4: 2 C295ASW *Persuader*; 2 P-3ACH *Orion*
   MP 4: 1 C295MPA *Persuader*; 3 EMB-111 *Bandeirante**
   ISR 7 P-68
   TRG 7 PC-7 *Turbo Trainer**
HELICOPTERS
   ASW 5 AS532SC *Cougar*
   MRH 8 AS365 *Dauphin*

TPT • Light 7: 3 Bell 206 *Jet Ranger*; 4 Bo-105S
AIR-LAUNCHED MISSILES • AShM AM39 *Exocet*

Marines 3,600
FORCES BY ROLE
MANOEUVRE
Amphibious
1 amph bde (2 mne bn, 1 cbt spt bn, 1 log bn)
2 coastal def unit
EQUIPMENT BY TYPE
ARMOURED FIGHTING VEHICLES
LT TK 15 FV101 *Scorpion*
APC • APC (W) 25 MOWAG *Roland*
AAV 12 AAV-7
ARTILLERY 39
TOWED 23: **105mm** 7 KH-178; **155mm** 16 M-71
MOR **81mm** 16
COASTAL DEFENCE • AShM MM38 *Exocet*
AIR DEFENCE • SAM • Point-defence 14: 4 M998 *Avenger*; 10 M1097 *Avenger*

Coast Guard
Integral part of the Navy
EQUIPMENT BY TYPE
PATROL AND COASTAL COMBATANTS 55
PBF 26 *Archangel*
PB 29: 18 *Alacalufe* (*Protector*-class); 4 *Grumete Diaz* (*Dabor*-class); 6 *Pelluhue*; 1 *Ona*

Air Force 11,050
Flying hours 100 hrs/yr
FORCES BY ROLE
FIGHTER
1 sqn with F-5E/F *Tiger* III+
2 sqn with F-16AM/BM *Fighting Falcon*
FIGHTER/GROUND ATTACK
1 sqn with F-16C/D Block 50 *Fighting Falcon* (*Puma*)
ISR
1 (photo) flt with; DHC-6-300 *Twin Otter*; Learjet 35A
AIRBORNE EARLY WARNING
1 flt with B-707 *Phalcon*
TANKER/TRANSPORT
1 sqn with B-737-300; C-130B/H *Hercules*; KC-130R *Hercules*; KC-135 *Stratotanker*
TRANSPORT
3 sqn with Bell 205 (UH-1H *Iroquois*); C-212-200/300 *Aviocar*; Cessna O-2A; Cessna 525 *Citation* CJ1; DHC-6-100/300 *Twin Otter*; PA-28-236 *Dakota*; Bell 205 (UH-1H *Iroquois*)
1 VIP flt with B-737-500 (VIP); Gulfstream IV
TRAINING
1 sqn with EMB-314 *Super Tucano**
1 sqn with PA-28-236 *Dakota*; T-35A/B *Pillan*
TRANSPORT HELICOPTER
1 sqn with Bell 205 (UH-1H *Iroquois*); Bell 206B (trg); Bell 412 *Twin Huey*; Bo-105CBS-4; S-70A *Black Hawk*
AIR DEFENCE
1 AD regt (5 AD sqn) with *Crotale*; *Mistral*; M163/M167 *Vulcan*; Oerlikon GDF-005

EQUIPMENT BY TYPE
AIRCRAFT 79 combat capable
FTR 48: 10 F-5E *Tigre* III+; 2 F-5F *Tigre* III+; 29 F-16AM *Fighting Falcon*; 7 F-16BM *Fighting Falcon*
FGA 10: 6 F-16C Block 50 *Fighting Falcon*; 4 F-16D Block 50 *Fighting Falcon*
ATK 9 C-101CC *Aviojet* (A-36 *Halcón*)
ISR 3 Cessna O-2A
AEW&C 1 B-707 *Phalcon*
TKR 5: 2 KC-130R *Hercules*; 3 KC-135 *Stratotanker*
TPT 37: **Medium** 3: 1 C-130B *Hercules*; 2 C-130H *Hercules*; **Light** 29: 2 C-212-200 *Aviocar*; 1 C-212-300 *Aviocar*; 4 Cessna 525 *Citation* CJ1; 3 DHC-6-100 *Twin Otter*; 7 DHC-6-300 *Twin Otter*; 2 Learjet 35A; 10 PA-28-236 *Dakota*; **PAX** 5: 1 B-737-300; 1 B-737-500; 1 B-767-300ER; 2 Gulfstream IV
TRG 45: 4 Cirrus SR-22T; 12 EMB-314 *Super Tucano**; 29 T-35A/B *Pillan*
HELICOPTERS
MRH 12 Bell 412EP *Twin Huey*
TPT 22: **Medium** 1 S-70A *Black Hawk*; **Light** 21: 13 Bell 205 (UH-1H *Iroquois*); 5 Bell 206B (trg); 2 BK-117; 1 Bo-105CBS-4
UNMANNED AERIAL VEHICLES
ISR • Medium 3 *Hermes* 900
AIR DEFENCE
SAM
Short-range 5 *Crotale*
Point-defence *Mistral* (including some *Mygale*/*Aspic*)
GUNS • TOWED **20mm** M163/M167 *Vulcan*; **35mm** Oerlikon GDF-005
AIR-LAUNCHED MISSILES
AAM • IR AIM-9J/M *Sidewinder*; *Python* 3; *Shafrir*‡; IIR *Python* 4; ARH AIM-120C AMRAAM; *Derby*
ASM AGM-65G *Maverick*
BOMBS
Laser-guided *Paveway* II
INS/GPS guided JDAM

Paramilitary 44,700

Carabineros 44,700
Ministry of Interior; 15 zones, 36 districts, 179 *comisaria*
EQUIPMENT BY TYPE
ARMOURED FIGHTING VEHICLES
APC • APC (W) 20 MOWAG *Roland*
ARTILLERY • MOR **81mm**
AIRCRAFT
TPT • Light 4: 1 Beech 200 *King Air*; 1 Cessna 208; 1 Cessna 550 *Citation* V; 1 PA-31T *Cheyenne* II
HELICOPTERS • TPT • Light 15: 5 AW109E *Power*; 1 Bell 206 *Jet Ranger*; 2 BK-117; 5 Bo-105; 2 H135

Cyber
The Joint Staff coordinates cyber-security policies for the Ministry of National Defence and the armed forces. Each service has a cyber-security organisation. The Ministry of Interior and Public Security (Internal Affairs) released a National Cyber Security Strategy in 2017. This states that the Ministry of National Defence will be responsible

for developing cyber-security policy to protect military networks and information systems and will establish its own CSIRT.

DEPLOYMENT

Legal provisions for foreign deployment:
Constitution: Constitution (1980, since amended)
Decision on deployment of troops abroad: Article 63, number 13 of the constitution, concerning matters of law, states that the procedures for foreign deployment are a matter that must be established by law by congress. Law Number 19.067 regulates matters concerning the foreign deployment of Chilean troops and deployment of foreign troops in Chile. It states that the government needs to request congressional approval

BOSNIA-HERZEGOVINA
EU • EUFOR • *Operation Althea* 15

CENTRAL AFRICAN REPUBLIC
UN • MINUSCA 4

CYPRUS
UN • UNFICYP 14

INDIA/PAKISTAN
UN • UNMOGIP 2 obs

MIDDLE EAST
UN • UNTSO 3 obs

Colombia COL

Colombian Peso pC		2016	2017	2018
GDP	pC	863tr	921tr	
	US$	282bn	307bn	
per capita	US$	5,792	6,238	
Growth	%	2.0	1.7	
Inflation	%	7.5	4.3	
Def bdgt [a]	pC	28.1tr	30.0tr	32.4tr
	US$	9.20bn	10.0bn	
FMA (US)	US$	27m	38.5m	0m
US$1=pC		3,055.26	2,996.035	

[a] Includes defence and security

Population   47,698,524

Age	0–14	15–19	20–24	25–29	30–64	65 plus
Male	12.4%	4.3%	4.4%	4.3%	20.8%	3.1%
Female	11.8%	4.1%	4.3%	4.2%	21.7%	4.3%

Capabilities

Colombia's security and defence requirements continue to be dominated by counter-insurgency and counter-narcotics operations. Demobilising and reintegrating former FARC combatants remains a significant challenge. The government reached a ceasefire with ELN guerrillas in September 2017. This period of transformation will see a reduction in personnel and likely also see the police transferring from the defence ministry to the interior ministry. Colombia's armed forces have in recent years been planning for new security roles, and new organisational structures for the post-FARC era. The army's 'Damascus' doctrine emphasises roles such as disaster relief and assistance to rural communities, but a strong focus on combat capabilities remains. The navy has increased its international activities, but it will likely see its marine forces reduced as part of the transformation plans. The air force is due to undergo organisational change, and three new commands will likely be created. Colombia has a defence industry active across all domains, with COTECMAR building vessels including amphibious ships and patrol boats, CIAC active in the aerospace sector as a maintenance and manufacturing firm, and INDUMIL fabricating arms and ammunition. The strong relationship with the US continues and has been particularly valuable in terms of training and equipment support, although this has reduced in recent years due to the improved security situation.

ACTIVE 293,200 (Army 223,150, Navy 56,400 Air 13,650) **Paramilitary 187,900**

RESERVE 34,950 (Army 25,050 Navy 6,500 Air 3,400)

ORGANISATIONS BY SERVICE

Army 223,150

FORCES BY ROLE
SPECIAL FORCES
  1 SF div (3 SF regt)
  1 (anti-terrorist) SF bn
MANOEUVRE
  Mechanised
  1 (1st) div (1 (2nd) mech bde (2 mech inf bn, 1 mtn inf bn, 1 engr bn, 1 MP bn, 1 cbt spt bn, 1 log bn, 1 Gaula anti-kidnap gp); 1 (10th) mech bde (1 armd recce bn, 1 mech cav bn, 1 mech inf bn, 1 mtn inf bn, 2 sy bn, 2 arty bn, 1 engr bn, 1 cbt spt bn, 2 Gaula anti-kidnap gp); 2 sy bn; 1 log bn)
  Light
  1 (2nd) div (1 (5th) lt inf bde (2 lt inf bn, 1 jungle inf bn, 1 sy bn, 1 arty bn, 1 AD bn, 1 engr bn, 1 cbt spt bn, 1 Gaula anti-kidnap gp); 1 (30th) lt inf bde (1 cav recce bn, 2 lt inf bn, 1 sy bn, 1 arty bn, 1 engr bn, 1 cbt spt bn, 1 log bn); 1 rapid reaction force (3 mobile sy bde))
  1 (3rd) div (1 (3rd) lt inf bde (2 lt inf bn, 1 mtn inf bn, 1 COIN bn, 1 arty bn, 1 engr bn, 1 cbt spt bn, 1 MP bn, 1 log bn, 1 Gaula anti-kidnap gp); 1 (23rd) lt inf bde (1 cav gp, 1 lt inf bn, 1 jungle inf bn, 1 cbt spt bn, 1 log bn); 1 (29th) mtn bde (1 mtn inf bn, 1 lt inf bn, 2 COIN bn, 1 cbt spt bn, 1 log bn); 2 rapid reaction force (total: 7 mobile sy bde))
  1 (4th) div (1 (7th) air mob bde (2 air mob inf bn, 1 lt inf bn, 1 COIN bn, 1 engr bn, 1 cbt spt bn, 1 log bn, 1 Gaula anti-kidnap gp); 1 (22nd) jungle bde (1 air mob inf bn, 1 lt inf bn, 1 jungle inf bn, 1 COIN bn, 1 cbt spt bn, 1 log bn); 1 (31st) jungle bde (1 lt inf bn, 1 jungle inf bn))

1 (5th) div (1 (6th) lt inf bde (2 lt inf bn,1 mtn inf bn, 2 COIN bn, 1 cbt spt bn, 1 log bn, 1 Gaula anti-kidnap gp); 1 (8th) lt inf bde (1 lt inf bn, 1 mtn inf bn, 1 arty bn, 1 engr bn, 1 cbt spt bn, 1 Gaula anti-kidnap gp); 1 (9th) lt inf bde (1 SF bn, 2 lt inf bn, 1 arty bn, 1 COIN bn, 1 cbt spt bn, 1 sy bn, 1 log bn, 1 Gaula anti-kidnap gp); 1 (13th) lt inf bde (2 cav recce bn, 1 airmob inf bn, 3 lt inf bn, 1 COIN bn, 1 arty bn, 1 engr bn, 1 cbt spt bn, 2 MP bn, 1 log bn, 2 Gaula anti-kidnap gp); 1 rapid reaction force (3 mobile sy bde))

1 (6th) div (1 (12th) lt inf bde (2 lt inf bn, 2 jungle inf bn, 1 COIN bn, 1 engr bn, 1 cbt spt bn, 1 Gaula anti-kidnap gp); 1 (13th) mobile sy bde (4 COIN bn); 1 (26th) jungle bde (1 lt jungle inf bn, 1 COIN bn, 1 cbt spt bn); 1 (27th) lt inf bde (2 lt inf bn, 1 jungle inf bn, 1 arty bn, 1 cbt spt bn, 1 log bn))

1 (7th) div (1 (4th) lt inf bde (1 (urban) spec ops bn; 1 cav recce bn, 3 lt inf bn, 1 sy bn, 1 arty bn, 1 engr bn, 1 MP bn, 1 cbt spt bn, 1 log bn); 1 (11th) lt inf bde (2 lt inf bn, 1 sy bn, 1 engr bn, 1 cbt spt bn); 1 (14th) lt inf bde (3 lt inf bn, 1 sy bn, 1 engr bn, 1 cbt spt bn, 1 log bn); 1 (15th) jungle bde (1 lt inf bn, 1 COIN bn, 1 engr bn, 1 log bn); 1 (17th) lt inf bde (2 lt inf bn, 1 COIN bn, 1 engr bn, 1 cbt spt bn, 1 log bn); 1 rapid reaction force (1 (11th) mobile sy bde (3 COIN bn)))

1 (8th) div (1 (16th) lt inf bde (1 mech cav recce bn, 1 lt inf bn, 1 log bn, 1 Gaula anti-kidnap gp); 1 (18th) lt inf bde (1 air mob gp, 1 sy bn, 1 arty bn, 1 engr bn, 1 cbt spt bn, 1 log bn); 1 (28th) jungle bde (2 inf, 2 COIN, 1 cbt spt bn); 1 rapid reaction force (1 (5th) mobile sy bde (3 COIN bn); 1 (31st) mobile sy bde (5 COIN bn)))

3 COIN mobile bde (each: 4 COIN bn, 1 cbt spt bn)

Other
1 indep rapid reaction force (1 SF bde, 3 mobile sy bde)

COMBAT SUPPORT
1 cbt engr bde (1 SF engr bn, 1 (emergency response) engr bn, 1 EOD bn, 1 construction bn, 1 demining bn, 1 maint bn)
1 int bde (2 SIGINT bn, 1 log bn, 1 maint bn)

COMBAT SERVICE SUPPORT
2 spt/log bde (each: 1 spt bn, 1 maint bn, 1 supply bn, 1 tpt bn, 1 medical bn, 1 log bn)

AVIATION
1 air aslt div (1 counter-narcotics bde (3 counter-narcotics bn, 1 spt bn); 1 (25th) avn bde (4 hel bn; 5 avn bn; 1 avn log bn); 1 (32nd) avn bde (1 avn bn, 2 maint bn, 1 trg bn, 1 spt bn); 1 SF avn bn)

EQUIPMENT BY TYPE
ARMOURED FIGHTING VEHICLES
RECCE 121 EE-9 *Cascavel*
IFV 60: 28 *Commando Advanced*; 32 LAV III
APC 114
    APC (T) 54: 28 M113A1 (TPM-113A1); 26 M113A2 (TPM-113A2)
    APC (W) 56 EE-11 *Urutu*
PPV 4 RG-31 *Nyala*
AUV 38 M1117 *Guardian*
ANTI-TANK/ANTI-INFRASTRUCTURE
MSL
    SP 77 *Nimrod*
    MANPATS TOW; *Spike*-ER
RCL 106mm 73 M40A1
ARTILLERY 1,796
    TOWED 120: **105mm** 107: 22 LG1 MkIII; 85 M101; **155mm** 13 155/52 APU SBT-1
    MOR 1,676: **81mm** 1,507; **120mm** 169
AIRCRAFT
    ELINT 3: 2 Beech B200 *King Air*; 1 Beech 350 *King Air*
    TPT • **Light** 22: 2 An-32B; 2 Beech B200 *King Air*; 3 Beech 350 *King Air*; 1 Beech C90 *King Air*; 2 C-212 *Aviocar* (Medevac); 7 Cessna 208B *Grand Caravan*; 1 Cessna 208B-EX *Grand Caravan*; 4 Turbo Commander 695A
HELICOPTERS
    MRH 18: 7 Mi-17-1V *Hip*; 6 Mi-17MD; 5 Mi-17V-5 *Hip*
    TPT 93: **Medium** 54: 47 UH-60L *Black Hawk*; 7 S-70i *Black Hawk*; **Light** 39: 24 Bell 205 (UH-1H *Iroquois*); 15 Bell 212 (UH-1N *Twin Huey*)
AIR DEFENCE • GUNS • TOWED 40mm 4 M1A1

Navy 56,400 (incl 12,100 conscript)

HQ located at Puerto Carreño
EQUIPMENT BY TYPE
SUBMARINES • TACTICAL • SSK 4:
    2 *Pijao* (GER T-209/1200) each with 8 single 533mm TT each with HWT
    2 *Intrepido* (GER T-206A) each with 8 single 533mm TT each with HWT
PRINCIPAL SURFACE COMBATANTS 4
    FRIGATES • FFGHM 4 *Almirante Padilla* with 2 twin lnchr with MM40 *Exocet* AShM, 2 twin *Simbad* lnchr with *Mistral* SAM, 2 triple B515 ILAS-3 324mm ASTT each with A244 LWT, 1 76mm gun (capacity 1 Bo-105/AS555SN *Fennec* hel)
PATROL AND COASTAL COMBATANTS 59
    CORVETTES • FS 1 *Narino* (ex-ROK *Dong Hae*) with 2 triple 324mm ASTT with Mk46 LWT, 1 76mm gun
    PSOH 3 *20 de Julio*
    PCO 2: 1 *Valle del Cauca Durable* (ex-US *Reliance*) with 1 hel landing platform; 1 *San Andres* (ex-US *Balsam*)
    PCC 3 *Punta Espada* (CPV-46)
    PCR 10: 2 *Arauca* with 2 76mm guns; 8 *Nodriza* (PAF-II) with hel landing platform
    PB 12: 1 *11 de Noviembre* (CPV-40) with 1 *Typhoon* CIWS; 2 *Castillo y Rada* (Swiftships 105); 2 *Jaime Gomez*; 1 *José Maria Palas* (Swiftships 110); 4 *Point*; 2 *Toledo*
    PBR 31: 6 *Diligente*; 7 LPR-40; 3 Swiftships; 9 *Tenerife*; 2 PAF-L; 4 others
AMPHIBIOUS 22
    LCM 3 LCM-8
    LCU 11: 4 *Golfo de Tribuga*; 7 *Morrosquillo* (LCU 1466)
    UCAC 8 *Griffon* 2000TD
LOGISTICS AND SUPPORT 8
    ABU 1 *Quindio*
    AG 3: 1 *Inirida*; 2 *Luneburg* (ex-GER, depot ship for patrol vessels)
    AGOR 2 *Providencia*
    AGS 1 *Gorgona*
    AXS 1 *Gloria*

Naval Aviation 150
EQUIPMENT BY TYPE
AIRCRAFT
MP 3 CN235 MPA *Persuader*
ISR 1 PA-31 *Navajo* (upgraded for ISR)
TPT • **Light** 11: 1 C-212 (Medevac); 4 Cessna 206; 3 Cessna 208 *Caravan*; 1 PA-31 *Navajo*; 1 PA-34 *Seneca*; 1 Beech 350 *King Air*
HELICOPTERS
MRH 8: 1 AS555SN *Fennec*; 3 Bell 412 *Twin Huey*; 4 Bell 412EP *Twin Huey*
TPT • **Light** 9: 1 Bell 212; 5 Bell 212 (UH-1N); 1 BK-117; 2 Bo-105

Marines 22,250
FORCES BY ROLE
SPECIAL FORCES
1 SF bde (4 SF bn)
MANOEUVRE
Amphibious
1 mne bde (1 SF (Gaula) bn, 5 mne bn, 2 rvn bn, 1 spt bn)
1 mne bde (1 SF bn, 2 mne bn, 2 rvn bn, 1 spt bn)
1 rvn bde (1 SF bn, 1 mne bn, 2 rvn bn, 1 spt bn)
1 rvn bde (4 rvn bn)
1 rvn bde (3 rvn bn)
COMBAT SERVICE SUPPORT
1 log bde (6 spt bn)
1 trg bde (7 trg bn, 1 spt bn)
EQUIPMENT BY TYPE
ARTILLERY • MOR 82: **81mm** 74; **120mm** 8
AIR DEFENCE • SAM **Point-defence** *Mistral*

Air Force 13,650
FORCES BY ROLE
FIGHTER/GROUND ATTACK
2 sqn with *Kfir* C-10/C-12/TC-12
GROUND ATTACK/ISR
1 sqn with A-37B/OA-37B *Dragonfly*
1 sqn with AC-47T
1 sqn with EMB-312 *Tucano**
2 sqn with EMB-314 *Super Tucano** (A-29)
EW/ELINT
2 sqn with Beech 350 *King Air*; Cessna 208; Cessna 560; C-26B *Metroliner*; SA 2-37; 1 *Turbo Commander* 695
TRANSPORT
1 (Presidential) sqn with B-737BBJ; EMB-600 *Legacy*; Bell 412EP; F-28 *Fellowship*; UH-60L *Black Hawk*
1 sqn with B-727; B-737-400; C-130B/H *Hercules*; C-212; C295M; CN235M; ; IAI *Arava*; KC-767
1 sqn with Beech C90 *King Air*; Beech 350C *King Air*; Cessna 208B; Cessna 550; EMB-110P1 (C-95)
TRAINING
1 sqn with Lancair *Synergy* (T-90 *Calima*)
1 sqn with T-37B
1 hel sqn with Bell 206B3
1 hel sqn with TH-67
HELICOPTER
1 sqn with AH-60L *Arpia* III
1 sqn with UH-60L *Black Hawk* (CSAR)

1 sqn with Hughes 500M
1 sqn with Bell 205 (UH-1H)
1 sqn with Bell 212
EQUIPMENT BY TYPE
AIRCRAFT 72 combat capable
FGA 22: 10 *Kfir* C-10; 9 *Kfir* C-12; 3 *Kfir* TC-12
ATK 12: 6 A-37B/OA-37B *Dragonfly*; 6 AC-47T *Spooky* (*Fantasma*)
ISR 13: 1 Beech C90 *King Air*; 1 C-26B *Metroliner*; 5 Cessna 560 *Citation* II; 6 SA 2-37
ELINT 13: 4 Beech 350 *King Air*; 6 Cessna 208 *Grand Caravan*; 2 Cessna 337G; 1 *Turbo Commander* 695
TKR/TPT 1 KC-767
TPT 64: **Medium** 7: 3 C-130B *Hercules* (3 more in store); 3 C-130H *Hercules*; 1 B-737F; **Light** 49: 10 ATR-42; 2 Beech 300 *King Air*; 2 Beech 350C *King Air*; 1 Beech 350i *King Air* (VIP); 4 Beech C90 *King Air*; 4 C-212; 6 C295M; 1 Cessna 182R; 12 Cessna 208B (medevac); 1 Cessna 550; 2 CN235M; 2 EMB-110P1 (C-95); 1 EMB-170-100LR; 1 IAI-201 *Arava*; **PAX** 8: 2 B-727; 1 B-737-400; 1 B-737BBJ; 1 EMB-600 *Legacy*; 1 F-28-1000 *Fellowship*; 1 F-28-3000 *Fellowship*; 1 Learjet 60
TRG 78: 14 EMB-312 *Tucano**; 24 EMB-314 *Super Tucano* (A-29)*; 23 Lancair *Synergy* (T-90 *Calima*); 17 T-37B
HELICOPTERS
MRH 18: 6 AH-60L *Arpia* III; 8 AH-60L *Arpia* IV; 2 Bell 412EP *Twin Huey* (VIP); 2 Hughes 500M
TPT 48: **Medium** 13 UH-60L *Black Hawk* (incl 1 VIP hel); **Light** 35: 12 Bell 205 (UH-1H *Iroquois*); 12 Bell 206B3 *Jet Ranger* III; 11 Bell 212
TRG 30 TH-67
UNAMMED AERIAL VEHICLES • ISR • **Medium** 8: 6 *Hermes* 450; 2 *Hermes* 900
AIR-LAUNCHED MISSILES
AAM • **IR** *Python* 3; **IIR** *Python* 4; *Python* 5; **ARH** *Derby*; I-*Derby* ER (reported)
ASM *Spike*-ER; *Spike*-NLOS
BOMBS
Laser-guided *Paveway* II
INS/GPS guided *Spice*

Paramilitary 187,900

National Police Force 187,900
EQUIPMENT BY TYPE
AIRCRAFT
ELINT 5 C-26B *Metroliner*
TPT • **Light** 40: 3 ATR-42; 3 Beech 200 *King Air*; 2 Beech 300 *King Air*; 2 Beech 1900; 1 Beech C99; 4 BT-67; 2 C-26 *Metroliner*; 3 Cessna 152; 3 Cessna 172; 9 Cessna 206; 2 Cessna 208 *Caravan*; 2 DHC-6 *Twin Otter*; 1 DHC-8; 3 PA-31 *Navajo*
HELICOPTERS
MRH 3: 1 Bell 412EP; 2 MD-500D
TPT 72: **Medium** 14: 5 UH-60A *Black Hawk*; 9 UH-60L *Black Hawk*; **Light** 58: 34 Bell 205 (UH-1H-II *Huey* II); 6 Bell 206B; 5 Bell 206L/L3/L4 *Long Ranger*; 8 Bell 212; 5 Bell 407

Cyber

Colombia publicised policy guidelines for cyber security and cyber defence in 2011. There are three main organisations: the CERT team (colCERT); the Police Cyber Centre; and the armed forces' Joint Cyber Command. The defence ministry is the coordinating body for cyber defence, and Colombia has an active training and simulation programme in cyber defence, with the Higher War College also organising courses in cyber warfare for military (a staff course) and civil personnel. The armed forces are reported to be in the process of devolving cyber capability to the tactical level. An initial cyber cell was formed by linking the Joint Cyber Command, the National Police Cyber Center and the MoD's CERT team.

DEPLOYMENT

CENTRAL AFRICAN REPUBLIC
UN • MINUSCA 2 obs

EGYPT
MFO 354; 1 inf bn

LEBANON
UN • UNIFIL 1

FOREIGN FORCES

United States US Southern Command: 50

Costa Rica CRI

Costa Rican Colon C		2016	2017	2018
GDP	C	31.3tr	33.3tr	
	US$	58.1bn	58.9bn	
per capita	US$	11,836	11,857	
Growth	%	4.3	3.8	
Inflation	%	0	1.7	
Sy bdgt [a]	C	220bn	220bn	259bn
	US$	409m	389m	
FMA (US)	US$	1.4m	1.4m	0m
US$1=C		538.43	564.62	

[a] Paramilitary budget

Population 4,930,258

Age	0–14	15–19	20–24	25–29	30–64	65 plus
Male	11.5%	4.0%	4.3%	4.4%	22.2%	3.6%
Female	11.0%	3.8%	4.1%	4.3%	22.3%	4.2%

Capabilities

Costa Rica's armed forces were constitutionally abolished in 1949, and the country relies on paramilitary-type police organisations for internal-security, counter-narcotics and counter-criminal tasks, as well as participation in regional peacekeeping operations. More recently, Costa Rica has utilised these organisations to counter illegal immigration on its southern border with Panama. In May 2014 the country launched a joint-services initiative (known as OPMAT) to improve cooperation between the Public Force, Coast Guard and Air Surveillance Unit. Some elements, such as the Special Intervention Unit (UEI), have received training from non-regional states, including the US. The UEI has also conducted small-scale training with regional allies. The air wing is relatively well equipped with light aircraft. Coast Guard vessels have a relatively limited range, impeding operations at reach. Both the Public Force and the Coast Guard have plans to expand personnel numbers in the near future and the delivery of two ex-US Coast Guard patrol boats, expected in 2018, will significantly increase the Coast Guard's operational capability.

PARAMILITARY 9,800

ORGANISATIONS BY SERVICE

Paramilitary 9,800

Special Intervention Unit
FORCES BY ROLE
SPECIAL FORCES
1 spec ops unit

Public Force 9,000
11 regional directorates

Coast Guard Unit 400
EQUIPMENT BY TYPE
PATROL AND COASTAL COMBATANTS 8:
PB 8: 2 *Cabo Blanco* (US *Swift* 65); 1 *Isla del Coco* (US *Swift* 105); 3 *Point*; 1 *Primera Dama* (US *Swift* 42); 1 *Puerto Quebos* (US *Swift* 36)

Air Surveillance Unit 400
EQUIPMENT BY TYPE
AIRCRAFT • TPT • **Light** 17: 4 Cessna T210 *Centurion*; 4 Cessna U206G *Stationair*; 1 DHC-7 *Caribou*; 2 PA-31 *Navajo*; 2 PA-34 *Seneca*; 1 Piper PA-23 *Aztec*; 1 Cessna 182RG; 2 Y-12E
HELICOPTERS • **MRH** 3: 2 MD-500E; 1 MD-600N

Cuba CUB

Cuban Peso P		2016	2017	2018
GDP	P			
per capita	US$			
Def bdgt	P			
	US$			

US$1=P

*definitive economic data unavailable

Population 11,147,407

Age	0–14	15–19	20–24	25–29	30–64	65 plus
Male	8.5%	3.2%	3.1%	3.7%	24.4%	6.8%
Female	8.0%	2.9%	2.9%	3.4%	24.7%	8.1%

Capabilities

Cuba's defence forces are principally focused on protecting territorial integrity, with a strategy of mass mobilisation. They are hampered by an ageing and predominantly Soviet-era equipment inventory and by a reliance on continual maintenance instead of modernisation. The US has imposed new restrictions on trade and travel, particularly directed at the armed forces' business interests, which include ports, hotels and restaurants. Cuba maintains military ties with China and Russia, and the latter has stepped in to supply oil and diesel fuel to Cuba following the economic collapse in Venezuela. It is unlikely that Havana will be in a position to finance significant equipment recapitalisation in the near term. In tough economic conditions, desertion reportedly remains a problem for the largely conscript-based forces.

ACTIVE 49,000 (Army 38,000 Navy 3,000 Air 8,000) **Paramilitary 26,500**
Conscript liability 3 years (or 2 if studying for a profession)

RESERVE 39,000 (Army 39,000) **Paramilitary 1,120,000**
Ready Reserves (serve 45 days per year) to fill out Active and Reserve units; see also Paramilitary

ORGANISATIONS BY SERVICE

Army ε38,000
FORCES BY ROLE
COMMAND
 3 regional comd HQ
 3 army comd HQ
COMMAND
 3 SF regt
MANOEUVRE
 Armoured
 1 tk div (3 tk bde)
 Mechanised
 2 (mixed) mech bde
 Light
 2 (frontier) bde
 Air Manoeuvre
 1 AB bde
AIR DEFENCE
 1 ADA regt
 1 SAM bde

Reserves 39,000
FORCES BY ROLE
MANOEUVRE
 Light
 14 inf bde
EQUIPMENT BY TYPE†
ARMOURED FIGHTING VEHICLES
 MBT ε900 T-34/T-54/T-55/T-62
 LT TK PT-76
 ASLT BTR-60 100mm
 RECCE BRDM-2;
 AIFV ε50 BMP-1/1P
 APC ε500 BTR-152/BTR-50/BTR-60
ANTI-TANK/ANTI-INFRASTRUCTURE
 MSL
  SP 2K16 *Shmel* (AT-1 *Snapper*)
  MANPATS 9K11 *Malyutka* (AT-3 *Sagger*)
 GUNS 600+: **57mm** 600 ZIS-2 (M-1943); **85mm** D-44
ARTILLERY 1,715+
 SP 40+: **100mm** AAPMP-100; CATAP-100; **122mm** 2S1 *Gvozdika*; AAP-T-122; AAP-BMP-122; *Jupiter* III; *Jupiter* IV; **130mm** AAP-T-130; *Jupiter* V; **152mm** 2S3 *Akatsiya*
 TOWED 500: **122mm** D-30; M-30 (M-1938); **130mm** M-46; **152mm** D-1; M-1937 (ML-20)
 MRL • SP 175: **122mm** BM-21 *Grad*; **140mm** BM-14
 MOR 1,000: **82mm** M-41; **82mm** M-43; **120mm** M-43; M-38
AIR DEFENCE
 SAM
  Short-range 2K12 *Kub* (SA-6 *Gainful*)
  Pont-defence 200+: 200 9K35 *Strela*-10 (SA-13 *Gopher*); 9K33 *Osa* (SA-8 *Gecko*); 9K31 *Strela*-1 (SA-9 *Gaskin*); 9K36 *Strela*-3 (SA-14 *Gremlin*); 9K310 *Igla*-1 (SA-16 *Gimlet*); 9K32 *Strela*-2 (SA-7 *Grail*)‡
 GUNS 400
  SP **23mm** ZSU-23-4; **30mm** BTR-60P SP; **57mm** ZSU-57-2
  TOWED **100mm** KS-19/M-1939/**85mm** KS-12/**57mm** S-60/**37mm** M-1939/**30mm** M-53/**23mm** ZU-23

Navy ε3,000
Western Comd HQ at Cabanas; Eastern Comd HQ at Holquin
EQUIPMENT BY TYPE
PATROL AND COASTAL COMBATANTS 8
 PSO 1 *Rio Damuji* with two single P-15M *Termit* (SS-N-2C *Styx*) AShM, 2 57mm guns, 1 hel landing platform
 PCM 1 *Pauk* II† (FSU) with 1 quad lnchr (manual aiming) with 9K32 *Strela*-2 (SA-N-5 *Grail*) SAM, 4 single ASTT, 2 RBU 1200 A/S mor, 1 76mm gun
 PBF 6 *Osa* II† (FSU) each with 4 single lnchr (for P-15 *Termit* (SS-N-2B *Styx*) AShM – missiles removed to coastal-defence units)
MINE WARFARE AND MINE COUNTERMEASURES 5
 MHI 3 *Korund* (*Yevgenya*) (Project 1258)†
 MSC 2 *Sonya*† (FSU)
LOGISTICS AND SUPPORT 2
 ABU 1
 AX 1

Coastal Defence
ARTILLERY • TOWED **122mm** M-1931/37; **130mm** M-46; **152mm** M-1937
COASTAL DEFENCE • AShM 4+: *Bandera* IV (reported); 4 4K51 *Rubezh* (SSC-3 *Styx*)

Naval Infantry 550+
FORCES BY ROLE
MANOEUVRE
 Amphibious
 2 amph aslt bn

Anti-aircraft Defence and Revolutionary Air Force ε8,000 (incl conscripts)

Air assets divided between Western Air Zone and Eastern Air Zone

Flying hours 50 hrs/yr

FORCES BY ROLE
FIGHTER/GROUND ATTACK
  3 sqn with MiG-21ML *Fishbed*; MiG-23ML/MF/UM *Flogger*; MiG-29A/UB *Fulcrum*
TRANSPORT
  1 (VIP) tpt sqn with An-24 *Coke*; Mi-8P *Hip*; Yak-40
ATTACK HELICOPTER
  2 sqn with Mi-17 *Hip H*; Mi-35 *Hind*
TRAINING
  2 (tac trg) sqn with L-39C *Albatros* (basic); Z-142 (primary)

EQUIPMENT BY TYPE
AIRCRAFT 45 combat capable
  FTR 33: 16 MiG-23ML *Flogger*; 4 MiG-23MF *Flogger*; 4 MiG-23U *Flogger*; 4 MiG-23UM *Flogger*; 2 MiG-29A *Fulcrum*; 3 MiG-29UB *Fulcrum* (6 MiG-15UTI *Midget*; 4+ MiG-17 *Fresco*; 4 MiG-23MF *Flogger*; 6 MiG-23ML *Flogger*; 2 MiG-23UM *Flogger*; 2 MiG-29 *Fulcrum* in store)
  FGA 12: 4 MiG-21ML *Fishbed*; 8 MiG-21U *Mongol* A (up to 70 MiG-21bis *Fishbed*; 30 MiG-21F *Fishbed*; 28 MiG-21PFM *Fishbed*; 7 MiG-21UM *Fishbed*; 20 MiG-23BN *Flogger* in store)
  ISR 1 An-30 *Clank*
  TPT 11: **Heavy** 2 Il-76 *Candid*; **Light** 9: 1 An-2 *Colt*; 3 An-24 *Coke*; 2 An-32 *Cline*; 3 Yak-40 (8 An-2 *Colt*; 17 An-26 *Curl* in store)
  TRG 45: 25 L-39 *Albatros*; 20 Z-326 *Trener Master*
HELICOPTERS
  ATK 4 Mi-35 *Hind* (8 more in store)
  ASW (5 Mi-14 in store)
  MRH 8 Mi-17 *Hip H* (12 more in store)
  TPT • Medium 2 Mi-8P *Hip*
AIR DEFENCE • SAM
  Medium-range S-75 *Dvina* (SA-2 *Guideline*); S-75 *Dvina* mod (SA-2 *Guideline* – on T-55 chassis)
  Short-range S-125 *Pechora* (SA-3 *Goa*); S-125 *Pechora* mod (SA-3 *Goa* – on T-55 chassis)
AIR-LAUNCHED MISSILES
  AAM • IR R-3‡ (AA-2 *Atoll*); R-60 (AA-8 *Aphid*); R-73 (AA-11 *Archer*); **IR/SARH** R-23/24‡ (AA-7 *Apex*); R-27 (AA-10 *Alamo*)
  ASM Kh-23‡ (AS-7 *Kerry*)

Paramilitary 26,500 active

State Security 20,000
Ministry of Interior

Border Guards 6,500
Ministry of Interior
PATROL AND COASTAL COMBATANTS 20
  PCC 2 *Stenka*
  PB 18 *Zhuk*

Youth Labour Army 70,000 reservists

Civil Defence Force 50,000 reservists

Territorial Militia ε1,000,000 reservists

FOREIGN FORCES

United States US Southern Command: 950 (JTF-GTMO) at Guantanamo Bay

Dominican Republic DOM

Dominican Peso pRD		2016	2017	2018
GDP	pRD	3.30tr	356tr	
	US$	71.7bn	74.9bn	
per capita	US$	7,114	7,361	
Growth	%	6.6	4.8	
Inflation	%	1.6	3.0	
Def bdgt	pRD	21.1bn	23.5bn	
	US$	458m	496m	
US$1=pRD		46.02	47.52	

Population 10,734,247

Age	0–14	15–19	20–24	25–29	30–64	65 plus
Male	13.5%	4.7%	4.5%	4.2%	20.0%	3.5%
Female	13.1%	4.5%	4.3%	4.0%	19.2%	4.1%

Capabilities

The principal tasks for the Dominican armed forces include internal- and border-security missions, as well as disaster relief. Training and operations increasingly focus on counter-narcotics, and include collaboration with the police in an inter-agency task force. The army has strengthened its presence along the border with Haiti, establishing new surveillance posts and increasing its monitoring activities. The US continues to send training teams to the country under the terms of the 2015 military-partnership agreement. The armed forces continue regional military and security cooperation, including with Colombia in the *Caribe* VI air-force exercise. Personnel challenges continue, however, with reports of around 1,000 troops deserting in 2015 and 2016, including several officers.

ACTIVE 56,050 (Army 28,750 Navy 11,200 Air 16,100) **Paramilitary 15,000**

ORGANISATIONS BY SERVICE

Army 28,750
5 Defence Zones
FORCES BY ROLE
SPECIAL FORCES
  3 SF bn
MANOEUVRE
  Light
  4 (1st, 2nd, 3rd & 4th) inf bde (3 inf bn)
  2 (5th & 6th) inf bde (2 inf bn)

Air Manoeuvre
1 air cav bde (1 cdo bn, 1 (6th) mtn bn, 1 hel sqn with Bell 205 (op by Air Force); OH-58 *Kiowa*; R-22; R-44 *Raven* II)
Other
1 (Presidential Guard) gd regt
1 (MoD) sy bn
COMBAT SUPPORT
1 cbt spt bde (1 lt armd bn; 1 arty bn; 1 engr bn; 1 sigs bn)
EQUIPMENT BY TYPE
ARMOURED FIGHTING VEHICLES
LT TK 12 M41B (76mm)
APC • APC (W) 8 LAV-150 *Commando*
ANTI-TANK/ANTI-INFRASTRUCTURE
RCL 106mm 20 M40A1
GUNS 37mm 20 M3
ARTILLERY 104
TOWED 105mm 16: 4 M101; 12 *Reinosa* 105/26
MOR 88: **81mm** 60 M1; **107mm** 4 M30; **120mm** 24 Expal Model L
HELICOPTERS
ISR 8: 4 OH-58A *Kiowa*; 4 OH-58C *Kiowa*
TPT • Light 6: 4 R-22; 2 R-44 *Raven* II

Navy 11,200
HQ located at Santo Domingo
FORCES BY ROLE
SPECIAL FORCES
1 (SEAL) SF unit
MANOEUVRE
Amphibious
1 mne sy unit
EQUIPMENT BY TYPE
PATROL AND COASTAL COMBATANTS 17
PCO 1 *Almirante Didiez Burgos* (ex-US *Balsam*)
PCC 2 *Tortuguero* (ex-US *White Sumac*)
PB 14: 2 *Altair* (Swiftships 35m); 4 *Bellatrix* (US Sewart Seacraft); 2 *Canopus* (Swiftships 101); 3 *Hamal* (Damen Stan 1505); 3 *Point*
AMPHIBIOUS • LCU 1 *Neyba* (ex-US LCU 1675)
LOGISTICS AND SUPPORT 8
AG 8

Air Force 16,100
Flying hours 60 hrs/yr
FORCES BY ROLE
GROUND ATTACK
1 sqn with EMB-314 *Super Tucano**
SEARCH & RESCUE
1 sqn with Bell 205 (UH-1H *Huey II*); Bell 205 (UH-1H *Iroquois*); Bell 430 (VIP); OH-58 *Kiowa* (CH-136); S-333
TRANSPORT
1 sqn with C-212-400 *Aviocar*; PA-31 *Navajo*
TRAINING
1 sqn with T-35B *Pillan*
AIR DEFENCE
1 ADA bn with 20mm guns
EQUIPMENT BY TYPE
AIRCRAFT 8 combat capable

ISR 1 AMT-200 *Super Ximango*
TPT • Light 13: 3 C-212-400 *Aviocar*; 1 Cessna 172; 1 Cessna 182; 1 Cessna 206; 1 Cessna 207; 1 *Commander* 690; 3 EA-100; 1 PA-31 *Navajo*; 1 P2006T
TRG 13: 8 EMB-314 *Super Tucano**; 5 T-35B *Pillan*
HELICOPTERS
ISR 9 OH-58 *Kiowa* (CH-136)
TPT • Light 16: 8 Bell 205 (UH-1H *Huey* II); 5 Bell 205 (UH-1H *Iroquois*); 1 H155 (VIP); 2 S-333
AIR DEFENCE • GUNS 20mm 4

Paramilitary 15,000

National Police 15,000

Ecuador ECU

United States Dollar $		2016	2017	2018
GDP	US$	97.8bn	98.6bn	
per capita	US$	5,917	5,876	
Growth	%	-1.5	0.2	
Inflation	%	1.7	0.7	
Def bdgt	US$	1.57bn	1.57bn	

Population   16,290,913

Age	0–14	15–19	20–24	25–29	30–64	65 plus
Male	13.8%	4.7%	4.6%	4.2%	18.8%	3.5%
Female	13.3%	4.5%	4.4%	4.2%	19.9%	3.9%

Capabilities

Defence policy is aimed at guaranteeing sovereignty and territorial integrity, and allows the armed forces to participate in international peacekeeping operations. In 2015, the armed forces' role was expanded to include law-enforcement support. Border security has long been a priority but there has been a growing emphasis on maritime security in recent years, although there remains little capacity for sustained power projection beyond national borders. An earthquake in April 2016 devastated areas on Ecuador's Pacific coast, and prompted a large-scale HADR response from Ecuador and regional states. Extra-regional states including China also provided assistance. China and Ecuador signed a defence-cooperation agreement in November 2016. Major equipment maintenance is outsourced, but some low-level upgrades can be conducted in-country. The defence ministry announced that an integrated radar system was due to go into service in 2016, and that Ecuador was making progress in the field of cyber defence. The services take part in regular exercises, both domestically and with international partners.

ACTIVE 40,250 (Army 24,750 Navy 9,100 Air 6,400)
Paramilitary 500
Conscript liability Voluntary conscription

RESERVE 118,000 (Joint 118,000)
Ages 18–55

ORGANISATIONS BY SERVICE

Army 24,750
FORCES BY ROLE
gp are bn sized
COMMAND
  4 div HQ
SPECIAL FORCES
  1 (9th) SF bde (3 SF gp, 1 SF sqn, 1 para bn, 1 sigs sqn, 1 log comd)
MANOEUVRE
  Mechanised
  1 (11th) armd cav bde (3 armd cav gp, 1 mech inf bn, 1 SP arty gp, 1 engr gp)
  1 (5th) inf bde (1 SF sqn, 2 mech cav gp, 2 inf bn, 1 cbt engr coy, 1 sigs coy, 1 log coy)
  Light
  1 (1st) inf bde (1 SF sqn, 1 armd cav gp, 1 armd recce sqn, 3 inf bn, 1 med coy)
  1 (3rd) inf bde (1 SF gp, 1 mech cav gp, 1 inf bn, 1 arty gp, 1 hvy mor coy, 1 cbt engr coy, 1 sigs coy, 1 log coy)
  1 (7th) inf bde (1 SF sqn, 1 armd recce sqn, 1 mech cav gp, 3 inf bn, 1 jungle bn, 1 arty gp, 1 cbt engr coy, 1 sigs coy, 1 log coy, 1 med coy)
  1 (13th) inf bde (1 SF sqn, 1 armd recce sqn, 1 mot cav gp, 3 inf bn, 1 arty gp, 1 hvy mor coy, 1 cbt engr coy, 1sigs coy, 1 log coy)
  2 (17th & 21st) jungle bde (3 jungle bn, 1 cbt engr coy, 1 sigs coy, 1 log coy)
  1 (19th) jungle bde (3 jungle bn, 1 jungle trg bn, 1 cbt engr coy, 1 sigs coy, 1 log coy)
COMBAT SUPPORT
  1 (27th) arty bde (1 SP arty gp, 1 MRL gp, 1 ADA gp, 1 cbt engr coy, 1 sigs coy, 1 log coy)
  1 (23rd) engr bde (3 engr bn)
  2 indep MP coy
  1 indep sigs coy
COMBAT SERVICE SUPPORT
  1 (25th) log bde
  2 log bn
  2 indep med coy
AVIATION
  1 (15th) avn bde (2 tpt avn gp, 2 hel gp, 1 mixed avn gp)
AIR DEFENCE
  1 ADA gp
EQUIPMENT BY TYPE
ARMOURED FIGHTING VEHICLES
  LT TK 24 AMX-13
  RECCE 67: 25 AML-90; 10 EE-3 *Jararaca*; 32 EE-9 *Cascavel*
  APC 123
    APC (T) 95: 80 AMX-VCI; 15 M113
    APC (W) 28: 18 EE-11 *Urutu*; 10 UR-416
ANTI-TANK/ANTI-INFRASTRUCTURE
  RCL 404: **90mm** 380 M67; **106mm** 24 M40A1
ARTILLERY 541+
  SP 155mm 5 Mk F3
  TOWED 100: **105mm** 78: 30 M101; 24 M2A2; 24 Model 56 pack howitzer; **155mm** 22: 12 M114; 10 M198
  MRL 122mm 24: 18 BM-21 *Grad*; 6 RM-70
  MOR 412+: **81mm** 400 M29; **107mm** M30; **160mm** 12 M-66
AIRCRAFT
  TPT • Light 14: 1 Beech 200 *King Air*; 2 C-212; 1 CN235; 4 Cessna 172; 2 Cessna 206; 1 Cessna 500 *Citation* I; 3 IAI-201 *Arava*
  TRG 6: 2 MX-7-235 *Star Rocket*; 2 T-41D *Mescalero*; 2 CJ-6A
HELICOPTERS
  MRH 33: 7 H125M *Fennec*; 6 Mi-17-1V *Hip*; 2 SA315B *Lama*; 18 SA342L *Gazelle* (13 with HOT for anti-armour role)
  TPT 13: **Medium** 7: 5 AS332B *Super Puma*; 2 Mi-171E; (3 SA330 *Puma* in store); **Light** 6: 2 AS350B *Ecureuil*; 4 AS350B2 *Ecureuil*
AIR DEFENCE
  SAM • Point-defence *Blowpipe*; 9K32 *Strela*-2 (SA-7 *Grail*)‡; 9K38 *Igla* (SA-18 *Grouse*)
  GUNS 240
    SP 20mm 44 M163 *Vulcan*
    TOWED 196: **14.5mm** 128 ZPU-1/-2; **20mm** 38: 28 M-1935, 10 M167 *Vulcan*; **40mm** 30 L/70/M1A1

Navy 9,100 (incl Naval Aviation, Marines and Coast Guard)
EQUIPMENT BY TYPE
SUBMARINES • TACTICAL • SSK 2:
  2 *Shyri* (GER T-209/1300) with 8 single 533mm TT each with SUT HWT (1 undergoing refit in Chile)
PRINCIPAL SURFACE COMBATANTS • FRIGATES 1
  FFGHM 1 *Moran Valverde*† (ex-UK *Leander* batch II) with 4 single lnchr with MM40 *Exocet* AShM, 3 twin lnchr with *Mistral* SAM, 1 *Phalanx* CIWS, 1 twin 114mm gun (capacity 1 Bell 206B *Jet Ranger* II hel)
PATROL AND COASTAL COMBATANTS 9
  CORVETTES • FSGM 6 *Esmeraldas* (3†) with 2 triple lnchr with MM40 *Exocet* AShM, 1 quad *Albatros* lnchr with *Aspide* SAM, 2 triple B515 ILAS-3 324mm ASTT with A244 LWT (removed from two vessels), 1 76mm gun, 1 hel landing platform (upgrade programme ongoing)
  PCFG 3 *Quito* (GER Lurssen TNC-45 45m) with 4 single lnchr with MM38 *Exocet* AShM, 1 76mm gun (upgrade programme ongoing)
LOGISTICS AND SUPPORT 8
  AE 1 *Calicuchima*
  AGOS 1 *Orion* with 1 hel landing platform
  AGS 1 *Sirius*
  AK 1 *Galapagos*
  ATF 1
  AWT 2: 1 *Quisquis*; 1 *Atahualpa*
  AXS 1 *Guayas*

Naval Aviation 380
EQUIPMENT BY TYPE
AIRCRAFT
  MP 1 CN235-300M
  ISR 3: 2 Beech 200T *King Air*; 1 Beech 300 *Catpass King Air*

TPT • **Light** 3: 1 Beech 200 *King Air*; 1 Beech 300 *King Air*; 1 CN235-100
TRG 6: 2 T-34C *Turbo Mentor*; 4 T-35B *Pillan*
HELICOPTERS
TPT • **Light** 9: 3 Bell 206A; 3 Bell 206B; 1 Bell 230; 2 Bell 430
UNMANNED AERIAL VEHICLES
ISR 5: **Heavy** 2 *Heron*; **Medium** 3 *Searcher* Mk.II

Marines 2,150

FORCES BY ROLE
SPECIAL FORCES
  1 cdo unit
MANOEUVRE
  Amphibious
  5 mne bn (on garrison duties)
EQUIPMENT BY TYPE
ARTILLERY • MOR 32+ 60mm/81mm/120mm
AIR DEFENCE • SAM • **Point-defence** *Mistral*; 9K38 *Igla* (SA-18 *Grouse*)

Air Force 6,400

Operational Command
FORCES BY ROLE
FIGHTER
  1 sqn with *Cheetah* C/D
FIGHTER/GROUND ATTACK
  2 sqn with EMB-314 *Super Tucano**
  1 sqn with *Kfir* C-10 (CE); *Kfir* C-2; *Kfir* TC-2

Military Air Transport Group
FORCES BY ROLE
SEARCH & RESCUE/TRANSPORT HELICOPTER
  1 sqn with Bell 206B *Jet Ranger* II
  1 sqn with PA-34 *Seneca*
TRANSPORT
  1 sqn with C-130/H *Hercules*; L-100-30
  1 sqn with HS-748
  1 sqn with DHC-6-300 *Twin Otter*
  1 sqn with B-727; EMB-135BJ *Legacy* 600; *Sabreliner* 40
TRAINING
  1 sqn with Cessna 206; DA20-C1; MXP-650; T-34C *Turbo Mentor*
EQUIPMENT BY TYPE
AIRCRAFT 42 combat capable
  FGA 25: 10 *Cheetah* C; 2 *Cheetah* D; 4 *Kfir* C-2; 7 *Kfir* C-10 (CE); 2 *Kfir* TC-2
  TPT 29: **Medium** 4: 2 C-130B *Hercules*; 1 C-130H *Hercules*; 1 L-100-30; **Light** 15: 1 Beech E90 *King Air*; 3 C295M; 1 Cessna 206; 3 DHC-6 *Twin Otter*; 1 EMB-135BJ *Legacy* 600; 2 EMB-170; 2 EMB-190; 1 MXP-650; 1 PA-34 *Seneca*; **PAX** 10: 2 A320; 2 B-727; 1 Gulfstream G-1159; 5 HS-748
  TRG 39: 11 DA20-C1; 17 EMB-314 *Super Tucano**; 11 T-34C *Turbo Mentor*
HELICOPTERS • TPT • **Light** 7 Bell 206B *Jet Ranger* II
AIR-LAUNCHED MISSILES • AAM • **IR** *Python* 3; R-550 *Magic*; *Shafrir*‡; **IIR** *Python* 4; **SARH** *Super* 530

AIR DEFENCE
SAM • **Point-defence** 13+: 6 9K33 *Osa* (SA-8 *Gecko*); 7 M48 *Chaparral*; *Blowpipe*; 9K32 *Strela*-2 (SA-7 *Grail*)‡; 9K310 *Igla*-1 (SA-16 *Gimlet*); 9K38 *Igla* (SA-18 *Grouse*)
GUNS
  SP 20mm 28 M35
  TOWED 64: **23mm** 34 ZU-23; **35mm** 30 GDF-002 (twin)
RADAR • AIR DEFENCE 2 CFTC gap fillers; 2 CETC 2D

Paramilitary 500

All police forces; 39,500

Police Air Service
EQUIPMENT BY TYPE
HELICOPTERS
  ISR 3 MD-530F *Lifter*
  TPT • **Light** 6: 2 AS350B *Ecureuil*; 1 Bell 206B *Jet Ranger*; 3 R-44

Coast Guard 500
EQUIPMENT BY TYPE
PATROL AND COASTAL COMBATANTS 21
  PCC 4: 3 *Isla Fernandina* (*Vigilante*); 1 *Isla San Cristóbal* (Damen Stan Patrol 5009)
  PB 14: 1 *10 de Agosto*; 2 *Espada*; 2 *Manta* (GER Lurssen 36m); 1 *Point*; 4 *Rio Coca*; 4 *Isla Santa Cruz* (Damen Stan 2606)
  PBR 3: 2 *Río Esmeraldas*; 1 *Rio Puyango*

DEPLOYMENT

SUDAN
UN • UNAMID 1; 3 obs
UN • UNISFA 1; 1 obs

WESTERN SAHARA
UN • MIUNRSO 4 obs

El Salvador SLV

United States Dollar $		2016	2017	2018
GDP	US$	26.8bn	27.4bn	
per capita	US$	4,227	4,303	
Growth	%	2.4	2.3	
Inflation	%	0.6	0.8	
Def bdgt	US$	146m	146m	
FMA (US)	US$	2m	2m	0m
Population	6,172,011			

Age	0–14	15–19	20–24	25–29	30–64	65 plus
Male	13.3%	5.2%	5.0%	4.3%	17.0%	3.3%
Female	12.6%	5.0%	5.0%	4.5%	20.6%	4.2%

Capabilities

Principal roles for El Salvador's armed forces include territorial defence, support to civilian authorities, disaster relief and combating non-traditional threats.

Current challenges include boosting professionalisation – conscription accounts for a little under half of all recruits – and tackling organised crime and narcotics trafficking. The army deploys in support of National Civil Police security operations, particularly in San Salvador. In 2016, El Salvador, Guatemala and Honduras signed a memorandum of understanding to increase cooperation in counter-gang operations, and the three countries participate in a tri-national border task force. The armed forces have long-standing training programmes, including with regional states and with the US. While the Salvadorean forces are reasonably well equipped, there is a desire to upgrade equipment, including that held by the small (self-sustaining) contingent to the UN's MINUSMA mission in Mali.

ACTIVE 24,500 (Army 20,500 Navy 2,000 Air 2,000)
Paramilitary 17,000
Conscript liability 12 months (selective); 11 months for officers and NCOs

RESERVE 9,900 (Joint 9,900)

ORGANISATIONS BY SERVICE

Army 20,500
FORCES BY ROLE
SPECIAL FORCES
  1 spec ops gp (1 SF coy, 1 para bn, 1 (naval inf) coy)
MANOEUVRE
  Reconnaissance
  1 armd cav regt (2 armd cav bn)
  Light
  6 inf bde (3 inf bn)
  Other
  1 (special) sy bde (2 border gd bn, 2 MP bn)
COMBAT SUPPORT
  1 arty bde (2 fd arty bn, 1 AD bn)
  1 engr comd (2 engr bn)
EQUIPMENT BY TYPE
ARMOURED FIGHTING VEHICLES
  RECCE 5 AML-90 (4 more in store)
  APC • APC (W) 38: 30 VAL *Cashuat* (mod); 8 UR-416
ANTI-TANK/ANTI-INFRASTRUCTURE
  RCL 399: **106mm** 20 M40A1 (incl 16 SP); **90mm** 379 M67
ARTILLERY 217+
  TOWED **105mm** 54: 36 M102; 18 M-56 (FRY)
  MOR 163+: **81mm** 151 M29; **120mm** 12+: 12 UBM 52; (some M-74 in store)
  AIR DEFENCE • GUNS 35: **20mm** 31 M-55; 4 TCM-20

Navy 2,000
EQUIPMENT BY TYPE
PATROL AND COASTAL COMBATANTS 10
  PB 10: 3 Camcraft (30m); 1 *Point*; 1 Swiftships 77; 1 Swiftships 65; 4 Type-44 (ex-USCG)
AMPHIBIOUS • LANDING CRAFT • LCM 4

Naval Inf (SF Commandos) 90
FORCES BY ROLE
SPECIAL FORCES
  1 SF coy

Air Force 2,000
Flying hours 90 hrs/yr on A-37 *Dragonfly*
FORCES BY ROLE
FIGHTER/GROUND ATTACK/ISR
  1 sqn with A-37B/OA-37B *Dragonfly*; O-2A/B *Skymaster*
TRANSPORT
  1 sqn with BT-67; Cessna 210 *Centurion*; Cessna 337G; Commander 114; IAI-202 *Arava*; SA-226T *Merlin* IIIB
TRAINING
  1 sqn with R-235GT *Guerrier*; T-35 *Pillan*; T-41D *Mescalero*; TH-300
TRANSPORT HELICOPTER
  1 sqn with Bell 205 (UH-1H *Iroquois*); Bell 407; Bell 412EP *Twin Huey*; MD-500E; UH-1M *Iroquois*
EQUIPMENT BY TYPE
AIRCRAFT 25 combat capable
  ATK 14 A-37B *Dragonfly*
  ISR 11: 6 O-2A/B *Skymaster*; 5 OA-37B *Dragonfly*
  TPT • Light 10: 2 BT-67; 2 Cessna 210 *Centurion*; 1 Cessna 337G *Skymaster*; 1 Commander 114; 3 IAI-201 *Arava*; 1 SA-226T *Merlin* IIIB
  TRG 11: 5 R-235GT *Guerrier*; 5 T-35 *Pillan*; 1 T-41D *Mescalero*
HELICOPTERS
  MRH 14: 4 Bell 412EP *Twin Huey*; 8 MD-500E; 2 UH-1M *Iroquois*
  TPT• Light 9: 8 Bell 205 (UH-1H *Iroquois*); 1 Bell 407 (VIP tpt, govt owned)
  TRG 5 TH-300
AIR-LAUNCHED MISSILES • AAM • IR *Shafrir*‡

Paramilitary 17,000

National Civilian Police 17,000
Ministry of Public Security
AIRCRAFT
  ISR 1 O-2A *Skymaster*
  TPT • Light 1 Cessna 310
HELICOPTERS
  MRH 2 MD-520N
  TPT • Light 3: 1 Bell 205 (UH-1H *Iroquois*); 2 R-44 *Raven* II

DEPLOYMENT

LEBANON
UN • UNIFIL 52; 1 inf pl

MALI
UN • MINUSMA 104; 1 hel sqn

SOUTH SUDAN
UN • UNMISS 1; 2 obs

WESTERN SAHARA
UN • MINURSO 3 obs

FOREIGN FORCES

United States US Southern Command: 1 Forward Operating Location (Military, DEA, USCG and Customs personnel)

Guatemala GUA

Guatemalan Quetzal q		2016	2017	2018
GDP	q	523bn	559bn	
	US$	67.5bn	70.8bn	
per capita	US$	4,070	4,185	
Growth	%	3.1	3.2	
Inflation	%	4.4	4.4	
Def bdgt	q	2.19bn	1.91bn	2.25bn
	US$	283m	242m	
FMA (US)	US$	2m	2m	0m
US$1=q		7.74	7.89	

Population 15,460,732

Age	0–14	15–19	20–24	25–29	30–64	65 plus
Male	17.6%	5.5%	5.3%	4.5%	14.2%	2.1%
Female	16.9%	5.4%	5.3%	4.6%	15.9%	2.4%

Capabilities

The primary task of Guatemala's armed forces is territorial defence, though they retain limited capability to participate in international operations and disaster-relief tasks. By the beginning of 2018 the army plans to draw back from internal-security tasks, handing responsibility for operations against organised crime back to the National Civil Police. This move is intended to allow the armed forces to devote more resources to border security, as part of a wider interagency effort called Plan Fortaleza. As part of this endeavour, Guatemala already maintains a tri-national border task force with neighbouring El Salvador and Honduras. The army has recently trained with US SOUTHCOM and regional partners, including Brazil, Colombia and the Dominican Republic. Equipment recapitalisation is expected to be a focus of the 2018 budget, after a long hiatus, and requirements include aerial-surveillance radars and coastal-patrol craft to monitor littoral waters, light armoured vehicles and light attack/training aircraft.

ACTIVE 18,050 (Army 15,550 Navy 1,500 Air 1,000) Paramilitary 25,000

RESERVE 63,850 (Navy 650 Air 900 Armed Forces 62,300)

(National Armed Forces are combined; the army provides log spt for navy and air force)

ORGANISATIONS BY SERVICE

Army 15,550
15 Military Zones
FORCES BY ROLE
SPECIAL FORCES
  1 SF bde (1 SF bn, 1 trg bn)
  1 SF bde (1 SF coy, 1 ranger bn)
  1 SF mtn bde
MANOEUVRE
  Light
  1 (strategic reserve) mech bde (1 inf bn, 1 cav regt, 1 log coy)
  6 inf bde (1 inf bn)
  Air Manoeuvre
  1 AB bde with (2 AB bn)
  Amphibious
  1 mne bde
  Other
  1 (Presidential) gd bde (1 gd bn, 1 MP bn, 1 CSS coy)
COMBAT SUPPORT
  1 engr comd (1 engr bn, 1 construction bn)
  2 MP bde with (1 MP bn)

Reserves
FORCES BY ROLE
MANOEUVRE
  Light
  ε19 inf bn
EQUIPMENT BY TYPE
ARMOURED FIGHTING VEHICLES
  RECCE (7 M8 in store)
  APC 47
    APC (T) 10 M113 (5 more in store)
    APC (W) 37: 30 *Armadillo*; 7 V-100 *Commando*
ANTI-TANK/ANTI-INFRASTRUCTURE
  RCL 120+: **75mm** M20; **105mm** 64 M-1974 FMK-1 (ARG); **106mm** 56 M40A1
ARTILLERY 149
  TOWED **105mm** 76: 12 M101; 8 M102; 56 M-56
  MOR 73: **81mm** 55 M1; **107mm** (12 M30 in store); **120mm** 18 ECIA
AIR DEFENCE • **GUNS** • **TOWED** 32: **20mm** 16 GAI-D01; 16 M-55

Navy 1,500
EQUIPMENT BY TYPE
PATROL AND COASTAL COMBATANTS 10
  PB 10: 6 *Cutlass*; 1 *Dauntless*; 1 *Kukulkan* (US *Broadsword* 32m); 2 *Utatlan* (US *Sewart*)
AMPHIBIOUS • **LANDING CRAFT** • **LCP** 2 *Machete*
LOGISTICS AND SUPPORT • **AXS** 3

Marines 650 reservists
FORCES BY ROLE
MANOEUVRE
  Amphibious
  2 mne bn(-)

Air Force 1,000

2 air comd

FORCES BY ROLE
FIGHTER/GROUND ATTACK/ISR
  1 sqn with A-37B *Dragonfly*
  1 sqn with PC-7 *Turbo Trainer**
TRANSPORT
  1 sqn with BT-67; Beech 90/100/200/300 *King Air*; IAI-201 *Arava*
  1 (tactical support) sqn with Cessna 206; PA-31 *Navajo*
TRAINING
  1 sqn with Cessna R172K *Hawk XP*; T-35B *Pillan*
TRANSPORT HELICOPTER
  1 sqn with Bell 206 *Jet Ranger*; Bell 212 (armed); Bell 412 *Twin Huey* (armed); UH-1H *Iroquois*

EQUIPMENT BY TYPE
Serviceability of ac is less than 50%
AIRCRAFT 9 combat capable
  ATK 2 A-37B *Dragonfly*
  TPT • Light 27: 5 Beech 90 *King Air*; 1 Beech 100 *King Air*; 2 Beech 200 *King Air*; 2 Beech 300 *King Air*; 4 BT-67; 2 Cessna 206; 1 Cessna 208B; 5 Cessna R172K *Hawk XP*; 4 IAI-201 *Arava*; 1 PA-31 *Navajo*
  TRG 11: 7 PC-7 *Turbo Trainer**; 4 T-35B *Pillan*
HELICOPTERS
  MRH 2 Bell 412 *Twin Huey* (armed)
  TPT • Light 17: 2 Bell 205 (UH-1H *Iroquois*); 8 Bell 206 *Jet Ranger*; 7 Bell 212 (armed)

Tactical Security Group
Air Military Police

Paramilitary 25,000

National Civil Police 25,000
FORCES BY ROLE
SPECIAL FORCES
  1 SF bn
MANOEUVRE
  Other
    1 (integrated task force) paramilitary unit (incl mil and treasury police)

DEPLOYMENT

CENTRAL AFRICAN REPUBLIC
UN • MINUSCA 2; 2 obs

DEMOCRATIC REPUBLIC OF THE CONGO
UN • MONUSCO 152; 1 obs; 1 SF coy

LEBANON
UN • UNIFIL 2

SOUTH SUDAN
UN • UNMISS 4; 3 obs

SUDAN
UN • UNISFA 1; 2 obs

Guyana GUY

Guyanese Dollar G$		2016	2017	2018
GDP	G$	710bn	755bn	
	US$	3.44bn	3.59bn	
per capita	US$	4,475	4,662	
Growth	%	3.3	3.5	
Inflation	%	0.8	2.3	
Def bdgt	G$	10.6bn	11.8bn	
	US$	51m	56m	
US$1=G$		206.48	210.27	

Population 737,718

Age	0–14	15–19	20–24	25–29	30–64	65 plus
Male	13.3%	5.7%	5.3%	4.2%	19.3%	2.5%
Female	12.8%	5.5%	4.9%	3.8%	18.7%	3.6%

Capabilities

The Guyana Defence Force (GDF) has minimal military capability and its activities are limited to border control and support for law-enforcement operations. It also assists the civilian authorities and contributes to economic development. Guyana has close ties with Brazil, with whom it cooperates on safeguarding the security of the shared border via the annual military regional exchange meeting. The country also has bilateral agreements with France and China, who provide military training and equipment. Guyana is also part of the Caribbean Basin Security Initiative. The defence ministry plans to make increasing use of reservists in order to bolster the GDF and increase its ability to patrol Guyana's territory. The GDF took part in the US-led *Tradewinds* exercise in 2017 and *Integración 2017* in Chile, which drew together a number of regional armed forces in a HADR exercise scenario.

ACTIVE 3,400 (Army 3,000 Navy 200 Air 200)
Active numbers combined Guyana Defence Force

RESERVE 670 (Army 500 Navy 170)

ORGANISATIONS BY SERVICE

Army 3,000
FORCES BY ROLE
SPECIAL FORCES
  1 SF coy
MANOEUVRE
  Light
    1 inf bn
  Other
    1 (Presidential) gd bn
COMBAT SUPPORT
  1 arty coy
  1 (spt wpn) cbt spt coy
  1 engr coy

EQUIPMENT BY TYPE
ARMOURED FIGHTING VEHICLES
  RECCE 9: 6 EE-9 *Cascavel* (reported); 3 S52 *Shorland*
ARTILLERY 54
  TOWED 130mm 6 M-46†
  MOR 48: **81mm** 12 L16A1; **82mm** 18 M-43; **120mm** 18 M-43

Navy 200
EQUIPMENT BY TYPE
PATROL AND COASTAL COMBATANTS 5
  PCO 1 *Essequibo* (ex-UK *River*)
  PB 4 *Barracuda* (ex-US Type-44)

Air Force 200
FORCES BY ROLE
TRANSPORT
  1 unit with Bell 206; Cessna 206; Y-12 (II)
EQUIPMENT BY TYPE
AIRCRAFT • **TPT** • **Light** 2: 1 Cessna 206; 1 Y-12 (II)
HELICOPTERS
  MRH 1 Bell 412 *Twin Huey*†
  TPT • **Light** 2 Bell 206

Haiti HTI

Haitian Gourde G		2016	2017	2018
GDP	G	484bn	548bn	
	US$	8.23bn	8.36bn	
per capita	US$	759	761	
Growth	%	1.4	1.0	
Inflation	%	13.4	14.7	
Def bdgt	G	420m	435m	
	US$	7m	7m	
FMA (US)	US$	1.2m	1.2m	0m
US$1=G		58.84	65.54	

Population 10,646,714

Age	0–14	15–19	20–24	25–29	30–64	65 plus
Male	16.3%	5.4%	5.2%	4.5%	16.1%	1.8%
Female	16.4%	5.4%	5.2%	4.5%	16.6%	2.3%

Capabilities

The embryonic army is focused on providing an engineering capability for disaster-relief tasks. Plans for military expansion were outlined in the 2015 White Paper on Security and Defence. A road map for the re-establishment of the Haitian armed forces was distributed to ministers in early 2017. It is not clear, however, whether the current modest budgetary provision for the new armed forces will be sufficient to fund the level of capability required. The military component of the UN MINUSTAH mission completed its departure in October 2017. Although a new UN police mission (MINUJUSTH) remains, the MINUSTAH withdrawal, combined with the nascent nature of the Haitian armed forces, has raised concerns of a security vacuum within the country.

ACTIVE 150 (Army 150) **Paramilitary 50**

ORGANISATIONS BY SERVICE

Army 150

Paramilitary 50

  Coast Guard ε50
  EQUIPMENT BY TYPE
  PATROL AND COASTAL COMBATANTS • **PB** 8: 5 *Dauntless*; 3 3812-VCF

Honduras HND

Honduran Lempira L		2016	2017	2018
GDP	L	491bn	541bn	
	US$	21.4bn	22.7bn	
per capita	US$	2,609	2,730	
Growth	%	3.6	4.0	
Inflation	%	2.7	4.0	
Def bdgt [a]	L	6.78bn	6.28bn	
	US$	295m	263m	
FMA (US)	US$	4.5m	4.5m	0m
US$1=L		23.00	23.86	

[a] Defence and national-security budget

Population 9,038,741

Age	0–14	15–19	20–24	25–29	30–64	65 plus
Male	16.8%	5.5%	5.1%	4.6%	16.3%	1.8%
Female	16.1%	5.3%	4.9%	4.4%	16.3%	2.4%

Capabilities

Honduras retains a broad range of capabilities, but in many cases equipment is old, with serviceability in doubt. An agreement signed with Israel in late 2016 is expected to modernise the ageing air-force inventory, and supply new equipment for the Public Order Military Police (PMOP) and a new offshore patrol vessel for the navy. In 2011, the armed forces began to deploy in a paramilitary role, in conjunction with the police, to combat organised crime and narcotics trafficking. The PMOP, the primary force involved in this role, completed the raising of two additional battalions in 2017. The Honduran Navy is also active in counter-narcotics activities and operates in coordination with Colombia on *Operation Swordfish*, among other multilateral security initiatives. The navy's small marine contingent added a second battalion in 2017, and has plans for a third. In 2016, El Salvador, Guatemala and Honduras signed a memorandum of understanding to increase cooperation in counter-gang operations, and the three countries participate in a tri-national border task force. Honduras has also now established a similar task force with its southern neighbour, Nicaragua.

ACTIVE 14,950 (Army 7,300 Navy 1,350 Air 2,300 Military Police 4,000) **Paramilitary 8,000**

RESERVE 60,000 (Joint 60,000; Ex-servicemen registered)

ORGANISATIONS BY SERVICE

Army 7,300
FORCES BY ROLE
SPECIAL FORCES
  1 (special tac) spec ops gp (2 spec ops bn, 1 inf bn; 1 AB bn; 1 arty bn)
MANOEUVRE
  Mechanised
  1 inf bde (1 mech cav regt, 1 inf bn, 1 arty bn)
  Light
  1 inf bde (3 inf bn, 1 arty bn)
  3 inf bde (2 inf bn)
  1 indep inf bn
  Other
  1 (Presidential) gd coy
COMBAT SUPPORT
  1 engr bn
  1 sigs bn
AIR DEFENCE
  1 ADA bn
EQUIPMENT BY TYPE
ARMOURED FIGHTING VEHICLES
  LT TK 12 FV101 *Scorpion*
  RECCE 57: 1 FV105 *Sultan* (CP); 3 FV107 *Scimitar*; 40 FV601 *Saladin*; 13 RBY-1
ANTI-TANK/ANTI-INFRASTRUCTURE
  RCL 170: **84mm** 120 *Carl Gustav*; **106mm** 50 M40A1
ARTILLERY 118+
  TOWED 28: **105mm**: 24 M102; **155mm**: 4 M198
  MOR 90+: **81mm**; **120mm** 60 FMK-2; **160mm** 30 M-66
AIR DEFENCE • GUNS 20mm 48: 24 M-55A2; 24 TCM-20

Navy 1,350
EQUIPMENT BY TYPE
PATROL AND COASTAL COMBATANTS 17
  PB 17: 2 *Lempira* (Damen Stan Patrol 4207 – leased); 1 *Chamelecon* (Swiftships 85); 1 *Tegucilgalpa* (US *Guardian* 32m); 4 *Guanaja* (ex-US Type-44); 3 *Guaymuras* (Swiftships 105); 5 *Nacaome* (Swiftships 65); 1 *Rio Coco* (US PB Mk III)
AMPHIBIOUS • LANDING CRAFT 4
  LCU 2: 1 *Gracias a Dios* (COL *Golfo de Tribuga*); 1 *Punta Caxinas*
  LCM 2 LCM 8

Marines 1,000
FORCES BY ROLE
MANOEUVRE
  Amphibious
  2 mne bn

Air Force 2,300
FORCES BY ROLE
FIGHTER/GROUND ATTACK
  1 sqn with A-37B *Dragonfly*
  1 sqn with F-5E/F *Tiger* II
GROUND ATTACK/ISR/TRAINING
  1 unit with Cessna 182 *Skylane*; EMB-312 *Tucano*; MXT-7-180 *Star Rocket*
TRANSPORT
  1 sqn with Beech 200 *King Air*; C-130A *Hercules*; Cessna 185/210; IAI-201 *Arava*; PA-42 *Cheyenne*; Turbo Commander 690
  1 VIP flt with PA-31 *Navajo*; Bell 412EP/SP *Twin Huey*
TRANSPORT HELICOPTER
  1 sqn with Bell 205 (UH-1H *Iroquois*); Bell 412SP *Twin Huey*
EQUIPMENT BY TYPE
AIRCRAFT 17 combat capable
  FTR 11: 9 F-5E *Tiger* II†; 2 F-5F *Tiger* II†
  ATK 6 A-37B *Dragonfly*
  TPT 17: **Medium** 1 C-130A *Hercules*; **Light** 16: 1 Beech 200 *King Air*; 2 Cessna 172 *Skyhawk*; 2 Cessna 182 *Skylane*; 1 Cessna 185; 2 Cessna 208B *Grand Caravan*; 2 Cessna 210; 1 EMB-135 *Legacy* 600; 1 IAI-201 *Arava*; 1 L-410 (leased); 1 PA-31 *Navajo*; 1 PA-42 *Cheyenne*; 1 Turbo Commander 690
  TRG 16: 9 EMB-312 *Tucano*; 7 MXT-7-180 *Star Rocket*
HELICOPTERS
  MRH 8: 1 Bell 412EP *Twin Huey* (VIP); 5 Bell 412SP *Twin Huey*; 2 Hughes 500
  TPT • Light 7: 6 Bell 205 (UH-1H *Iroquois*); 1 H125 *Ecureuil*
AIR-LAUNCHED MISSILES • AAM • IR *Shafrir*‡

Military Police 4,000
FORCES BY ROLE
MANOEUVRE
  Other
  8 sy bn

Paramilitary 8,000

Public Security Forces 8,000
Ministry of Public Security and Defence; 11 regional comd

DEPLOYMENT

WESTERN SAHARA
UN • MINURSO 12 obs

FOREIGN FORCES

United States US Southern Command: 380; 1 avn bn with CH-47F *Chinook*; UH-60 *Black Hawk*

Jamaica JAM

Jamaican Dollar J$		2016	2017	2018
GDP	J$	1.75tr	1.86tr	
	US$	14.0bn	14.3bn	
per capita	US$	4,934	5,024	
Growth	%	1.3	1.7	
Inflation	%	2.3	3.4	
Def bdgt	J$	17.5bn	15.6bn	
	US$	139m	120m	
US$1=J$		125.58	130.247	

Population   2,990,561

Age	0–14	15–19	20–24	25–29	30–64	65 plus
Male	13.8%	5.1%	5.3%	4.8%	16.8%	3.6%
Female	13.3%	5.0%	5.3%	4.9%	17.4%	4.4%

Capabilities

The Jamaican Defence Force is focused principally on its maritime-security and internal-security capability, including support to police operations. Although Jamaica maintains relatively small military forces, these benefit from training with larger armed services, including those of Canada, the UK and the US. The Coast Guard and Air Wing have received additional funding in the 2017 budget to improve airborne-surveillance and coastal-patrol capabilities. As part of a fleet-modernisation programme, two new Damen 4207 patrol vessels were acquired in early 2017 to replace the three older 4207 boats in service. Increased funding will also allow for the procurement of a maritime-patrol aircraft. The armed forces plan to recruit 250 personnel per year in 2017 and 2018 in order to support a planned new battalion-sized deployment in western Jamaica.

ACTIVE 3,950 (Army 3,400 Coast Guard 300 Air 250)
(combined Jamaican Defence Force)

RESERVE 980 (Army 900 Coast Guard 60 Air 20)

ORGANISATIONS BY SERVICE

Army 3,400
FORCES BY ROLE
MANOEUVRE
  Mechanised
    1 (PMV) lt mech inf coy
  Light
    2 inf bn
COMBAT SUPPORT
  1 engr regt (4 engr sqn)
COMBAT SERVICE SUPPORT
  1 spt bn (1 MP coy, 1 med coy, 1 log coy, 1 tpt coy)
EQUIPMENT BY TYPE
ARMOURED FIGHTING VEHICLES
  AUV 12 *Bushmaster*
ARTILLERY • MOR 81mm 12 L16A1

Reserves
FORCES BY ROLE
MANOEUVRE
  Light
    1 inf bn

Coast Guard 300
EQUIPMENT BY TYPE
PATROL AND COASTAL COMBATANTS 10
  PBF 3
  PB 7: 2 *County* (Damen Stan Patrol 4207); 4 *Dauntless*; 1 *Paul Bogle* (US 31m)

Air Wing 250
Plus National Reserve
FORCES BY ROLE
MARITIME PATROL/TRANSPORT
  1 flt with BN-2A *Defender*; Cessna 210M *Centurion*
SEARCH & RESCUE/TRANSPORT HELICOPTER
  1 flt with Bell 407
  1 flt with Bell 412EP
TRAINING
  1 unit with Bell 206B3; DA40-180FP *Diamond Star*
EQUIPMENT BY TYPE
AIRCRAFT
  TPT • Light 4: 1 BN-2A *Defender*; 1 Cessna 210M *Centurion*; 2 DA40-180FP *Diamond Star*
HELICOPTERS
  MRH 2 Bell 412EP
  TPT • Light 5: 2 Bell 206B3 *Jet Ranger*; 3 Bell 407

Mexico MEX

Mexican Peso NP		2016	2017	2018
GDP	NP	19.5tr	21.8tr	
	US$	1.05tr	1.14tr	
per capita	US$	8,562	9,249	
Growth	%	2.3	2.1	
Inflation	%	2.8	5.9	
Def bdgt [a]	NP	91.8bn	86.4bn	102bn
	US$	4.92bn	4.53bn	
FMA (US)	US$	7m	3m	0m
US$1=NP		18.66	19.08	

[a] National-security expenditure

Population   124,574,795

Age	0–14	15–19	20–24	25–29	30–64	65 plus
Male	13.7%	4.5%	4.4%	4.2%	19.0%	3.2%
Female	13.1%	4.3%	4.3%	4.2%	21.0%	3.9%

Capabilities

Mexico has the most capable armed forces in Central America. They are tasked with defending state sovereignty and territorial integrity, internal security and extending aid to civilian authorities. Operations against drug cartels and other organised crime remain the army's primary activity, and the Military Police Corps has been significantly expanded in recent years to allow it to take on a wider role as part of this tasking. The navy retains well-equipped frigates, but the majority of its forces are dedicated to maritime security, though there are plans to reorganise the navy into coastal and blue-water forces. Both the air force and naval aviation have devoted substantial resources to the recapitalisation of their light attack-, surveillance- and training-aircraft fleets, and their transport helicopters, principally sourced from the US. The retirement of the air force's remaining F-5 fighter aircraft in late 2016 has, however, left the country without any airborne air-defence capability.

ACTIVE 277,150 (Army 208,350 Navy 60,300 Air 8,500) Paramilitary 58,900

RESERVE 81,500 (National Military Service)

ORGANISATIONS BY SERVICE

Space
EQUIPMENT BY TYPE
SATELLITES • COMMUNICATIONS 2 *Mexsat*

Army 208,350
12 regions (total: 46 army zones)
FORCES BY ROLE
SPECIAL FORCES
  1 (1st) SF bde (5 SF bn)
  1 (2nd) SF bde (7 SF bn)
  1 (3rd) SF bde (4 SF bn)
MANOEUVRE
  Reconnaissance
  3 (2nd, 3rd & 4th Armd) mech bde (2 armd recce bn, 2 lt mech bn, 1 arty bn, 1 (Canon) AT gp)
  25 mot recce regt
  Light
  1 (1st) inf corps (1 (1st Armd) mech bde (2 armd recce bn, 2 lt mech bn, 1 arty bn, 1 (Canon) AT gp), 3 (2nd, 3rd & 6th) inf bde (each: 3 inf bn, 1 arty regt, 1 (Canon) AT gp), 1 cbt engr bde (3 engr bn))
  3 (1st, 4th & 5th) indep lt inf bde (2 lt inf bn, 1 (Canon) AT gp)
  92 indep inf bn
  25 indep inf coy
  Air Manoeuvre
  1 para bde with (1 (GAFE) SF gp, 3 bn, 1 (Canon) AT gp)
  Other
  1 (Presidential) gd corps (1 SF gp, 1 mech inf bde (2 inf bn, 1 aslt bn), 1 mne bn (Navy), 1 cbt engr bn, 1 MP bde (3 bn, 1 special ops anti-riot coy))
COMBAT SUPPORT
  1 indep arty regt
  7 MP bde (3 MP bn)
  2 MP bde (forming)
EQUIPMENT BY TYPE
ARMOURED FIGHTING VEHICLES
  RECCE 255: 19 DN-5 *Toro*; 127 ERC-90F1 *Lynx* (7 trg); 40 M8; 37 MAC-1; 32 VBL

  IFV 390 DNC-1 (mod AMX-VCI)
  APC 309
    APC (T) 73: 40 HWK-11; 33 M5A1 half-track
    APC (W) 236: 95 BDX; 16 DN-4; 2 DN-6; 28 LAV-100 (*Pantera*); 26 LAV-150 ST; 25 MOWAG *Roland*; 44 VCR (3 amb; 5 cmd post)
ENGINEERING & MAINTENANCE VEHICLES
  ARV 7: 3 M32 *Recovery Sherman*; 4 VCR ARV
ANTI-TANK/ANTI-INFRASTRUCTURE
  MSL • SP 8 VBL with *Milan*
  RCL • 106mm 1,187+ M40A1 (incl some SP)
  GUNS 37mm 30 M3
ARTILLERY 1,390
  TOWED 123: **105mm** 123: 40 M101; 40 M-56; 16 M2A1; 14 M3; 13 NORINCO M90
  MOR 1,267: **81mm** 1,100: 400 M1; 400 Brandt; 300 SB **120mm** 167: 75 Brandt; 60 M-65; 32 RT-61
AIR DEFENCE • GUNS • TOWED 80: **12.7mm** 40 M55; **20mm** 40 GAI-B01

Navy 60,300
Two Fleet Commands: Gulf (6 zones), Pacific (11 zones)
EQUIPMENT BY TYPE
PRINCIPAL SURFACE COMBATANTS 5
  FRIGATES 5
    FFGHM 3 *Allende* (ex-US *Knox*) with 1 octuple Mk16 lnchr with ASROC/RGM-84C *Harpoon* AShM, 1 Mk25 GMLS with RIM-7 *Sea Sparrow* SAM, 2 twin Mk32 324mm ASTT with Mk46 LWT, 1 127mm gun (capacity 1 MD-902 hel)
    FF 2 *Bravo* (ex-US *Bronstein*) with 1 octuple Mk112 lnchr with ASROC†, 2 triple Mk32 324mm ASTT with Mk46 LWT, 1 twin 76mm gun, 1 hel landing platform
PATROL AND COASTAL COMBATANTS 125
  PSOH 5:
    4 *Oaxaca* with 1 76mm gun (capacity 1 AS565MB *Panther* hel)
    1 *Oaxaca* (mod) with 1 57mm gun (capacity 1 AS565MB *Panther* hel)
  PCOH 16:
    4 *Durango* with 1 57mm gun (capacity 1 Bo-105 hel)
    4 *Holzinger* (capacity 1 MD-902 *Explorer*)
    3 *Sierra* with 1 57mm gun (capacity 1 MD-902 *Explorer*)
    5 *Uribe* (ESP *Halcon*) (capacity 1 Bo-105 hel)
  PCO 10 *Leandro Valle* (US *Auk* MSF) with 1 76mm gun
  PCG 2 *Huracan* (ISR *Aliya*) with 4 single lnchr with *Gabriel* II AShM, 1 Phalanx CIWS
  PCC 2 *Democrata*
  PBF 73: 6 *Acuario*; 2 *Acuario* B; 48 *Polaris* (SWE CB90); 17 *Polaris* II (SWE IC 16M)
  PB 17: 3 *Azteca*; 3 *Cabo* (US *Cape Higgon*); 2 *Punta* (US *Point*); 9 *Tenochtitlan* (Damen Stan Patrol 4207)
AMPHIBIOUS • LS • LST 4: 2 *Monte Azule*s with 1 hel landing platform; 2 *Papaloapan* (US *Newport*) with 4 76mm guns, 1 hel landing platform
LOGISTICS AND SUPPORT 23
  AG 2
  AGOR 3: 2 *Altair* (ex-US *Robert D. Conrad*); 1 *Humboldt*
  AGS 8: 4 *Arrecife*; 1 *Onjuku*; 1 *Rio Hondo*; 1 *Rio Tuxpan*; 1 *Moctezuma* II (also used as AXS)

AK 2: 1 *Tarasco*; 1 *Rio Suchiate*
AP 1 *Isla Maria Madre* (Damen Fast Crew Supplier 5009)
ATF 4 *Otomi* with 1 76mm gun
AX 2 *Huasteco* (also serve as troop transport, supply and hospital ships)
AXS 1 *Cuauhtemoc* with 2 65mm saluting guns

Naval Aviation 1,250
FORCES BY ROLE
MARITIME PATROL
 5 sqn with Cessna 404 *Titan*; MX-7 *Star Rocket*; Lancair IV-P; T-6C+ *Texan* II
 1 sqn with Beech 350ER *King Air*; C-212PM *Aviocar*; CN235-300 MPA *Persuader*
 1 sqn with L-90 *Redigo*
TRANSPORT
 1 sqn with An-32B *Cline*
 1 (VIP) sqn with DHC-8 *Dash 8*; Learjet 24; *Turbo Commander* 1000
TRANSPORT HELICOPTER
 2 sqn with AS555 *Fennec*; AS565MB/AS565MBe *Panther*; MD-902
 2 sqn with Bo-105 CBS-5
 5 sqn with Mi-17-1V/V-5 *Hip*
TRAINING
 1 sqn with Z-242L
EQUIPMENT BY TYPE
AIRCRAFT 3 combat capable
 MP 6 CN235-300 MPA *Persuader*
 ISR 2 C-212PM *Aviocar*
 TPT 29: **Light** 27: 5 Beech 350ER *King Air* (4 used for ISR); 4 C295M; 2 C295W; 1 Cessna 404 *Titan*; 1 DHC-8 *Dash 8*; 6 Lancair IV-P; 3 Learjet 24; 5 *Turbo Commander* 1000; **PAX** 2: 1 CL-605 *Challenger*; 1 Gulfstream 550
 TRG 47: 3 L-90TP *Redigo**; 4 MX-7 *Star Rocket*; 13 T-6C+ *Texan* II; 27 Z-242L
HELICOPTERS
 MRH 29: 2 AS555 *Fennec*; 4 MD-500E; 19 Mi-17-1V *Hip*; 4 Mi-17V-5 *Hip*
 SAR 10: 4 AS565MB *Panther*; 6 AS565MBe *Panther*
 TPT 39: **Heavy** 3 H225M *Caracal*; **Medium** 9 UH-60M *Black Hawk*; **Light** 27: 1 AW109SP; 11 Bo-105 CBS-5; 5 MD-902 (SAR role); 10 S-333
 TRG 4 Schweizer 300C

Marines 21,500 (Expanding to 26,560)
FORCES BY ROLE
SPECIAL FORCES
 3 SF unit
MANOEUVRE
 Light
  32 inf bn(-)
 Air Manoeuvre
  1 AB bn
 Amphibious
  2 amph bde (4 inf bn, 1 amph bn, 1 arty gp)
 Other
  1 (Presidential) gd bn (included in army above)
COMBAT SERVICE SUPPORT
 2 spt bn

EQUIPMENT BY TYPE
ARMOURED FIGHTING VEHICLES
 APC • APC (W) 29: 3 BTR-60 (APC-60); 26 BTR-70 (APC-70)
ANTI-TANK/ANTI-INFRASTRUCTURE
 RCL 106mm M40A1
ARTILLERY 22+
 TOWED 105mm 16 M-56
 MRL 122mm 6 Firos-25
 MOR 81mm some
AIR DEFENCE • SAM • Point-defence 9K38 *Igla* (SA-18 *Grouse*)

Air Force 8,500
FORCES BY ROLE
GROUND ATTACK/ISR
 4 sqn with T-6C+ *Texan* II
 1 sqn with PC-7/PC-9M
ISR/AEW
 1 sqn with Beech 350ER *King Air*; EMB-145AEW *Erieye*; EMB-145RS; SA-2-37B; SA-227-BC *Metro* III (C-26B)
TRANSPORT
 1 sqn with C295M; PC-6B
 1 sqn with B-737; Beech 90
 1 sqn with C-27J *Spartan*; C-130E/K-30 *Hercules*; L-100-30
 5 (liaison) sqn with Cessna 182/206
 1 (anti-narcotic spraying) sqn with Bell 206; Cessna T206H;
 1 (Presidential) gp with AS332L *Super Puma*; AW109SP; B-737; B-757; B-787; Gulfstream 150/450/550; H225; Learjet 35A; Learjet 36; *Turbo Commander* 680
 1 (VIP) gp with B-737; Beech 200 *King Air*; Beech 350i *King Air*; Cessna 501/680 *Citation*; CL-605 *Challenger*; Gulfstream 550; Learjet 35A; Learjet 45; S-70A-24
TRAINING
 1 sqn with Cessna 182
 1 sqn with PC-7; T-6C+ *Texan* II
 1 sqn with Beech F33C *Bonanza*; Grob G120TP; SF-260EU
TRANSPORT HELICOPTER
 4 sqn with Bell 206B; Bell 212; Bell 407GX
 1 sqn with MD-530MF/MG
 1 sqn with Mi-17 *Hip*
 1 sqn with H225M *Caracal*; Bell 412EP *Twin Huey*; S-70A-24 *Black Hawk*
 1 sqn with UH-60M *Black Hawk*
ISR UAV
 1 unit with *Hermes* 450; S4 *Ehécatl*
EQUIPMENT BY TYPE
AIRCRAFT 57 combat capable
 ISR 8: 2 Cessna 501 *Citation*; 2 SA-2-37A; 4 SA-227-BC *Metro* III (C-26B)
 ELINT 8: 6 Beech 350ER *King Air*; 2 EMB-145RS
 AEW&C 1 EMB-145AEW *Erieye*
 TPT 112: **Medium** 9: 4 C-27J *Spartan*; 2 C-130E *Hercules*; 2 C-130K-30 *Hercules*; 1 L-100-30; **Light** 90: 2 Beech 90 *King Air*; 1 Beech 200 *King Air*; 1 Beech 350i *King Air*; 6 C295M; 59 Cessna 182; 3 Cessna 206; 8 Cessna T206H; 1 Cessna 501 *Citation*; 1 Cessna 680 *Citation*; 2 Learjet 35A; 1 Learjet 36; 1 Learjet 45XP; 3 PC-6B; 1 *Turbo*

Commander 680; **PAX** 13: 6 B-737; 1 B-757; 1 B-787; 1 CL-605 *Challenger*; 2 Gulfstream 150; 1 Gulfstream 450; 1 Gulfstream 550
TRG 145: 4 Beech F33C *Bonanza*; 25 Grob G120TP; 20 PC-7* (30 more possibly in store); 1 PC-9M*; 4 PT-17; 25 SF-260EU; 36 T-6C+ *Texan* II*
HELICOPTERS
MRH 44: 15 Bell 407GXP; 11 Bell 412EP *Twin Huey*; 18 Mi-17 *Hip* H
ISR 13: 4 MD-530MF; 9 MD-530MG
TPT 125: **Heavy** 11 H225M *Caracal*; **Medium** 31: 3 AS332L *Super Puma* (VIP); 2 H225 (VIP); 2 Mi-8T *Hip*; 6 S-70A-24 *Black Hawk*; 18 UH-60M *Black Hawk* **Light** 83: 5 AW109SP; 45 Bell 206; 13 Bell 206B *Jet Ranger* II; 7 Bell 206L; 13 Bell 212
UNMANNED AERIAL VEHICLES • ISR 8: **Medium** 3 *Hermes* 450; **Light** 5 S4 *Ehécatl*
AIR-LAUNCHED MISSILES • AAM • IR AIM-9J *Sidewinder*

Paramilitary 62,900

Federal Police 41,000 (Incl 5,000 Gendarmerie)
Public Security Secretariat
EQUIPMENT BY TYPE
AIRCRAFT
TPT 13: **Light** 7: 2 CN235M; 2 Cessna 182 *Skylane*; 1 Cessna 500 *Citation*; 2 Turbo Commander 695; **PAX** 6: 4 B-727; 1 *Falcon* 20; 1 Gulfstream II
HELICOPTERS
MRH 3 Mi-17 *Hip* H
TPT 27: **Medium** 13: 1 SA330J *Puma*; 6 UH-60L *Black Hawk*; 6 UH-60M *Black Hawk*; **Light** 14: 2 AS350B *Ecureuil*; 1 AS355 *Ecureuil* II; 6 Bell 206B; 5 H120 *Colibri*
UNMANNED AERIAL VEHICLES
ISR 12: **Medium** 2 *Hermes* 900; **Light** 10 S4 *Ehécatl*

Federal Ministerial Police 4,500
EQUIPMENT BY TYPE
HELICOPTERS
TPT • Light 25: 18 Bell 205 (UH-1H); 7 Bell 212
UNMANNED AERIAL VEHICLES
ISR • Heavy 2 *Dominator* XP

Rural Defense Militia 17,400
FORCES BY ROLE
MANOEUVRE
Light
  13 inf unit
  13 (horsed) cav unit

Cyber

It was announced that two Cyberspace Operations centres would be created by 2018, one for the army and one for the navy, to address and better coordinate defence work on cyber security and in cyberspace. Key documentation includes the 2013–18 National Defence Sector Programme, the 2013–18 National Development Programme and the 2014–18 National Security Programme. In 2013 it was reported that a Center for Cyber Security and Cyber Defense Control would be created within naval intelligence.

DEPLOYMENT

CENTRAL AFRICAN REPUBLIC
UN • MINUSCA 1

WESTERN SAHARA
UN • MINURSO 4 obs

Nicaragua NIC

Nicaraguan Gold Cordoba Co		2016	2017	2018
GDP	Co	379bn	411bn	
	US$	13.2bn	13.7bn	
per capita	US$	2,151	2,201	
Growth	%	4.7	4.5	
Inflation	%	3.5	4.0	
Def bdgt	Co	2.08bn	2.51bn	2.58bn
	US$	73m	84m	
US$1=Co		28.62	30.05	

Population 6,025,951

Age	0–14	15–19	20–24	25–29	30–64	65 plus
Male	13.9%	5.2%	5.5%	4.7%	17.1%	2.3%
Female	13.7%	5.1%	5.5%	4.9%	19.4%	2.9%

Capabilities

Nicaragua's armed forces provide assistance to border- and internal-security operations, with a central reserve based around a single mechanised brigade, although there is increasing focus on disaster-relief, coastal-security and counter-narcotics activities. Most equipment is of Cold War-era vintage and the government has approached Russia for equipment support and recapitalisation, which has led to the supply of refurbished main battle tanks and armoured personnel carriers. Despite speculation, however, there do not currently appear to be any definite procurement plans for broader assets such as fixed- and rotary-wing aircraft and coastal-patrol vessels suitable for the border- and maritime-security roles. Nicaragua has training relationships with both Russia and the US, as well as with neighbouring and regional states, including Cuba and Venezuela.

ACTIVE 12,000 (Army 10,000 Navy 800 Air 1,200)

ORGANISATIONS BY SERVICE

Army ε10,000
FORCES BY ROLE
SPECIAL FORCES
  1 SF bde (2 SF bn)
MANOEUVRE
Mechanised
  1 mech inf bde (1 armd recce bn, 1 tk bn, 1 mech inf bn, 1 arty bn, 1 MRL bn, 1 AT coy)

Light
1 regional comd (3 lt inf bn)
1 regional comd (2 lt inf bn; 1 arty bn)
3 regional comd (2 lt inf bn)
2 indep lt inf bn
Other
1 comd regt (1 inf bn, 1 sy bn, 1 int unit, 1 sigs bn)
1 (ecological) sy bn
COMBAT SUPPORT
1 engr bn
COMBAT SERVICE SUPPORT
1 med bn
1 tpt regt
EQUIPMENT BY TYPE
ARMOURED FIGHTING VEHICLES
MBT 82: 62 T-55 (65 more in store); 20 T-72B1
LT TK (10 PT-76 in store)
RECCE 20 BRDM-2
IFV 17+ BMP-1
APC • APC (W) 90+: 41 BTR-152 (61 more in store); 45 BTR-60 (15 more in store); 4+ BTR-70M
ENGINEERING & MAINTENANCE VEHICLES
AEV T-54/T-55
VLB TMM-3
ANTI-TANK/ANTI-INFRASTRUCTURE
MSL
  SP 12 9P133 *Malyutka* (AT-3 *Sagger*)
  MANPATS 9K11 *Malyutka* (AT-3 *Sagger*)
RCL 82mm B-10
GUNS 281: **57mm** 174 ZIS-2; (90 more in store); **76mm** 83 ZIS-3; **100mm** 24 M-1944
ARTILLERY 766
  TOWED 12: **122mm** 12 D-30; (**152mm** 30 D-20 in store)
  MRL 151: **107mm** 33 Type-63: **122mm** 118: 18 BM-21 *Grad*; 100 *Grad* 1P (BM-21P) (single-tube rocket launcher, man portable)
  MOR 603: **82mm** 579; **120mm** 24 M-43; (**160mm** 4 M-160 in store)
AIR DEFENCE • SAM • Point-defence 9K36 *Strela*-3 (SA-14 *Gremlin*); 9K310 *Igla*-1 (SA-16 *Gimlet*); 9K32 *Strela*-2 (SA-7 *Grail*)‡

Navy ε800
EQUIPMENT BY TYPE
PATROL AND COASTAL COMBATANTS • PB 8: 3 *Dabur*; 4 Rodman 101, 1 *Zhuk*

Marines
FORCES BY ROLE
MANOEUVRE
  Amphibious
  1 mne bn

Air Force 1,200
FORCES BY ROLE
TRANSPORT
  1 sqn with An-26 *Curl*; Beech 90 *King Air*; Cessna U206; Cessna 404 *Titan* (VIP)
TRAINING
  1 unit with Cessna 172; PA-18 *Super Cub*; PA-28 *Cherokee*

TRANSPORT HELICOPTER
  1 sqn with Mi-17 *Hip* H (armed)
AIR DEFENCE
  1 gp with ZU-23
EQUIPMENT BY TYPE
AIRCRAFT
  TPT • Light 9: 3 An-26 *Curl*; 1 Beech 90 *King Air*; 1 Cessna 172; 1 Cessna U206; 1 Cessna 404 *Titan* (VIP); 2 PA-28 *Cherokee*
  TRG 2 PA-18 *Super Cub*
HELICOPTERS
  MRH 7 Mi-17 *Hip* H (armed)†
  TPT • Medium 2 Mi-171E
AIR DEFENCE • GUNS 23mm 18 ZU-23
AIR-LAUNCHED MISSILES • ASM 9M17 *Skorpion* (AT-2 *Swatter*)

Panama PAN

Panamanian Balboa B		2016	2017	2018
GDP	B	55.2bn	59.1bn	
	US$	55.2bn	59.1bn	
per capita	US$	13,670	14,409	
Growth	%	4.9	5.3	
Inflation	%	0.7	1.6	
Def bdgt [a]	B	751m	746m	
	US$	751m	746m	
FMA (US)	US$	2m	2m	0m
US$1=B		1.00	1.00	

[a] Public-security expenditure

Population   3,753,142

Age	0–14	15–19	20–24	25–29	30–64	65 plus
Male	13.5%	4.4%	4.2%	4.0%	20.3%	3.8%
Female	12.9%	4.2%	4.1%	3.8%	20.0%	4.5%

Capabilities

Panama's armed forces were abolished in 1990; however, a border service, police force and an air/maritime organisation were retained for low-level security activities. Disaster relief, internal security and combating narcotics trafficking and other transnational organised crime are key priorities. The border service is principally deployed along the country's southern border, and has trained with both Colombian and US personnel. Colombia and Panama reached an agreement to activate a number of new border posts in early 2018 to strengthen mutual control of crossing points. After a clash between the border service and Costa Rican police, Panama has also resumed mutual training and security operations with its northern neighbour. In 2017, the National Aeronaval Service received equipment donations from the US to bolster its maritime-surveillance capabilities, including two small interceptor boats.

Paramilitary 22,050

ORGANISATIONS BY SERVICE

Paramilitary 22,050

National Border Service 3,600
FORCES BY ROLE
SPECIAL FORCES
  1 SF gp
MANOEUVRE
  Other
  1 sy bde (5 sy bn(-))
  1 indep sy bn

National Police Force 16,150
No hvy mil eqpt, small arms only
FORCES BY ROLE
SPECIAL FORCES
  1 SF unit
MANOEUVRE
  Other
  1 (presidential) gd bn(-)

National Aeronaval Service ε2,300
FORCES BY ROLE
TRANSPORT
  1 sqn with C-212M *Aviocar*; Cessna 210; PA-31 *Navajo*; PA-34 *Seneca*
  1 (Presidential) flt with ERJ-135BJ; S-76C
TRAINING
  1 unit with Cessna 152; Cessna 172; T-35D *Pillan*
TRANSPORT HELICOPTER
  1 sqn with AW139; Bell 205; Bell 205 (UH-1H *Iroquois*); Bell 212; Bell 407; Bell 412EP; H145; MD-500E
EQUIPMENT BY TYPE
PATROL AND COASTAL COMBATANTS 17
  PCO 1 *Independencia* (ex-US *Balsam*)
  PCC 2 *Saettia*
  PB 14: 1 *Cocle*; 1 *Chiriqui* (ex-US PB MkIV); 2 *Panquiaco* (UK Vosper 31.5m); 5 *3 De Noviembre* (ex-US *Point*), 1 *Taboga*; 4 Type-200
AMPHIBIOUS • LANDING CRAFT • LCU 1 *General Estaban Huertas*
LOGISTICS AND SUPPORT • AG 2
AIRCRAFT
  TPT • Light 10: 3 C-212M *Aviocar*; 1 Cessna 152, 1 Cessna 172; 1 Cessna 210; 1 ERJ-135BJ; 1 PA-31 *Navajo*; 2 PA-34 *Seneca*
  TRG 6 T-35D *Pillan*
HELICOPTERS
  MRH 8: 6 AW139; 1 Bell 412EP; 1 MD-500E
  TPT • Light 21: 2 Bell 205; 13 Bell 205 (UH-1H *Iroquois*); 2 Bell 212; 2 Bell 407; 1 H145; 1 S-76C

Paraguay PRY

Paraguayan Guarani Pg		2016	2017	2018
GDP	Pg	156tr	167tr	
	US$	27.4bn	28.8bn	
per capita	US$	4,003	4,139	
Growth	%	4.1	3.9	
Inflation	%	4.1	3.5	
Def bdgt	Pg	1.52tr	1.53tr	1.78tr
	US$	268m	264m	
US$1=Pg		5,670.44	5,797.70	

Population 6,943,739

Age	0–14	15–19	20–24	25–29	30–64	65 plus
Male	12.5%	4.6%	5.1%	4.6%	19.9%	3.3%
Female	12.1%	4.5%	5.0%	4.6%	19.7%	3.7%

Capabilities

The armed forces are small by regional standards and the equipment inventory for all services is ageing and largely obsolete. They have been mainly involved in internal-security operations and humanitarian peacekeeping missions. The country faces growing internal challenges from insurgency and transnational organised crime, chiefly drug trafficking. Although landlocked, Paraguay supports a small force of river-patrol craft, reflecting the importance of its riverine systems, and the navy has also contributed a small force – alongside army personnel and troops from the air force's airborne formation – to the National Anti-Drug Secretariat's Joint Special Forces Battalion, a unit organised for counter-narcotics missions. The US has trained Paraguayan troops since 2001 as part of the State Partnership Program, and continued to send instructors in 2017, but Paraguayan hopes for greater cooperation with the US remained unfulfilled. Paraguay has had a consistent if limited tradition of contributing to UN peacekeeping operations since 2001.

ACTIVE 10,650 (Army 7,600 Navy 1,950 Air 1,100)
Paramilitary 14,800
Conscript liability 12 months

RESERVE 164,500 (Joint 164,500)

ORGANISATIONS BY SERVICE

Army 6,100; 1,500 conscript (total 7,600)

Much of the Paraguayan army is maintained in a cadre state during peacetime; the nominal inf and cav divs are effectively only at coy strength. Active gp/regt are usually coy sized

FORCES BY ROLE
MANOEUVRE
  Light
  3 inf corps (total: 6 inf div(-), 3 cav div(-), 6 arty bty)
  Other
  1 (Presidential) gd regt (1 SF bn, 1 inf bn, 1 sy bn, 1 log gp)

COMBAT SUPPORT
1 arty bde with (2 arty gp, 1 ADA gp)
1 engr bde with (1 engr regt, 3 construction regt)
1 sigs bn

Reserves
FORCES BY ROLE
MANOEUVRE
  Light
  14 inf regt (cadre)
  4 cav regt (cadre)
EQUIPMENT BY TYPE
ARMOURED FIGHTING VEHICLES
  MBT 3 M4A3 *Sherman*
  RECCE 28 EE-9 *Cascavel*
  APC • APC (W) 12 EE-11 *Urutu*
ARTILLERY 99
  TOWED 105mm 19 M101
  MOR 81mm 80
AIR DEFENCE • GUNS 22:
  SP 20mm 3 M9 half track
  TOWED 19: 40mm 13 M1A1, 6 L/60

Navy 1,100; 850 conscript (total 1,950)
EQUIPMENT BY TYPE
PATROL AND COASTAL COMBATANTS 22
  PCR 3: 1 *Itaipú*; 1 *Nanawa*†; 1 *Paraguay*† with 2 twin 120mm gun, 3 76mm gun
  PBR 19: 1 *Capitan Cabral*; 2 *Capitan Ortiz* (ROC *Hai Ou*); 2 *Novatec*; 6 Type-701; 3 Croq 15; 5 others
AMPHIBIOUS • LANDING CRAFT • LCVP 3

Naval Aviation 100
FORCES BY ROLE
TRANSPORT
  1 (liaison) sqn with Cessna 150; Cessna 210 *Centurion*; Cessna 310; Cessna 401
TRANSPORT HELICOPTER
  1 sqn with AS350 *Ecureuil* (HB350 *Esquilo*)
EQUIPMENT BY TYPE
  AIRCRAFT • TPT • Light 6: 2 Cessna 150; 1 Cessna 210 *Centurion*; 2 Cessna 310; 1 Cessna 401
  HELICOPTERS • TPT • Light 2 AS350 *Ecureuil* (HB350 *Esquilo*)

Marines 700; 200 conscript (total 900)
FORCES BY ROLE
MANOEUVRE
  Amphibious
  3 mne bn(-)
ARTILLERY • TOWED 105mm 2 M101

Air Force 900; 200 conscript (total 1,100)
FORCES BY ROLE
GROUND ATTACK/ISR
  1 sqn with EMB-312 *Tucano**
TRANSPORT
  1 gp with C-212-200/400 *Aviocar*; DHC-6 *Twin Otter*
  1 VIP gp with Beech 58 *Baron*; Bell 427; Cessna U206 *Stationair*; Cessna 208B *Grand Caravan*; Cessna 210 *Centurion*; Cessna 402B; PA-32R *Saratoga* (EMB-721C *Sertanejo*); PZL-104 *Wilga* 80
TRAINING
  1 sqn with T-25 *Universal*; T-35A/B *Pillan*
TRANSPORT HELICOPTER
  1 gp with AS350 *Ecureuil* (HB350 *Esquilo*); Bell 205 (UH-1H *Iroquois*)
MANOEUVRE
  Air Manoeuvre
  1 AB bde
EQUIPMENT BY TYPE
  AIRCRAFT 6 combat capable
  TPT • Light 18: 1 Beech 58 *Baron*; 4 C-212-200 *Aviocar*; 1 C-212-400 *Aviocar*; 2 Cessna 208B *Grand Caravan*; 1 Cessna 210 *Centurion*; 1 Cessna 310; 2 Cessna 402B; 2 Cessna U206 *Stationair*; 1 DHC-6 *Twin Otter*; 1 PA-32R *Saratoga* (EMB-721C *Sertanejo*); 2 PZL-104 *Wilga* 80
  TRG 21: 6 EMB-312 *Tucano**; 6 T-25 *Universal*; 6 T-35A *Pillan*; 3 T-35B *Pillan*
  HELICOPTERS • TPT • Light 9: 3 AS350 *Ecureuil* (HB350 *Esquilo*); 5 Bell 205 (UH-1H *Iroquois*); 1 Bell 427 (VIP)

Paramilitary 14,800

Special Police Service 10,800; 4,000 conscript (total 14,800)

DEPLOYMENT

CENTRAL AFRICAN REPUBLIC
UN • MINUSCA 2; 1 obs

CYPRUS
UN • UNFICYP 14

DEMOCRATIC REPUBLIC OF THE CONGO
UN • MONUSCO 14 obs

SOUTH SUDAN
UN • UNMISS 2 obs

Peru PER

Peruvian Nuevo Sol NS		2016	2017	2018
GDP	NS	659bn	708bn	
	US$	195bn	210bn	
per capita	US$	6,204	6,598	
Growth	%	4.0	2.7	
Inflation	%	3.6	3.2	
Def bdgt	NS	7.51bn	7.06bn	7.51bn
	US$	2.22bn	2.10bn	
FMA (US)	US$	1m	1m	0m
US$1=NS		3.38	3.37	

Population 31,036,656

Age	0–14	15–19	20–24	25–29	30–64	65 plus
Male	13.4%	4.5%	4.7%	4.3%	18.8%	3.5%
Female	12.9%	4.4%	4.7%	4.1%	20.5%	3.9%

Capabilities

The armed forces remain primarily orientated towards internal-security tasks, undertaking operations against guerrillas and narcotics traffickers, as well as tackling other challenges, such as illegal mining. As part of the fight against drug trafficking, the defence ministry is planning to improve military bases in the VRAEM region, which encompasses the Apurimac, Ene and Mantaro rivers and is associated with coca production. The SIVAN monitoring-and-surveillance system, intended to cover Peru's Amazon border regions, received government approval in late 2014; Peru's Earth-observation satellite (PERÚSAT-1) successfully launched in September 2016. Some modernisation of conventional equipment has been possible in recent years, but a substantial proportion of the inventories of all three services remain unmodernised. No replacement has been selected so far for the army's ageing T-55 main battle tanks and armoured fighting vehicles, although a number of platforms were being assessed in late 2016. A naval-modernisation programme is under way, including the construction of landing-platform-dock vessels. Peru is looking to improve its maintenance capabilities. A new army-aviation maintenance facility is scheduled to be fully operational by March 2018; a helicopter-maintenance centre was due to be operational from October 2017. In cooperation with Korean Aerospace Industries, Peru manufactures the KT-1 turboprop aircraft at its Las Palmas facility; South Korea is also interested in marketing its FA-50 combat aircraft to Peru. The armed forces continue to train regularly, and participate in multinational exercises and UN deployments.

ACTIVE 81,000 (Army 47,500 Navy 24,000 Air 9,500)
Paramilitary 77,000

RESERVE 188,000 (Army 188,000)

ORGANISATIONS BY SERVICE

Space
EQUIPMENT BY TYPE
SATELLITES • ISR PERÚSAT-1

Army 47,500
4 mil region
FORCES BY ROLE
SPECIAL FORCES
  1 (1st) SF bde (4 cdo bn, 1 airmob arty gp, 1 MP Coy, 1 cbt spt bn)
  1 (3rd) SF bde (3 cdo bn, 1 airmob arty gp, 1 MP coy)
  1 SF gp (regional troops)
MANOEUVRE
  Armoured
  1 (3rd) armd bde (2 tk bn, 1 armd inf bn, 1 arty gp, 1 AT coy, 1 AD gp, 1 engr bn, 1 cbt spt bn)
  1 (9th) armd bde (2 tk bn, 1 armd inf bn, 1 SP arty gp, 1 ADA gp)
  Mechanised
  1 (3rd) armd cav bde (3 mech cav bn, 1 mot inf bn, 1 arty gp, 1 AD gp, 1 engr bn, 1 cbt spt bn)
  1 (1st) cav bde (4 mech cav bn, 1 MP coy, 1 cbt spt bn)
  Light
  2 (2nd & 31st) mot inf bde (3 mot inf bn, 1 arty gp, 1 MP coy, 1 log bn)
  3 (1st, 7th & 32nd) inf bde (3 inf bn, 1 MP coy, 1 cbt spt bn)
  1 (4th) mtn bde (1 armd regt, 3 mot inf bn, 1 arty gp, 1 MP coy, 1 cbt spt bn)
  1 (5th) mtn bde (1 armd regt, 2 mot inf bn, 3 jungle coy, 1 arty gp, 1 MP coy, 1 cbt spt bn)
  1 (5th) jungle inf bde (1 SF gp, 3 jungle bn, 3 jungle coy, 1 jungle arty gp, 1 AT coy, 1 AD gp, 1 jungle engr bn)
  1 (6th) jungle inf bde (4 jungle bn, 1 engr bn, 1 MP coy, 1 cbt spt bn)
  Other
  1 (18th) armd trg bde (1 mech cav regt, 1 armd regt, 2 tk bn, 1 armd inf bn, 1 engr bn, 1 MP coy, 1 cbt spt bn)
COMBAT SUPPORT
  1 (1st) arty bde (4 arty gp, 2 AD gp, 1 sigs gp)
  1 (3rd) arty bde (4 arty gp, 1 AD gp, 1 sigs gp)
  1 (22nd) engr bde (3 engr bn, 1 demining coy)
AVIATION
  1 (1st) avn bde (1 atk hel/recce hel bn, 1 avn bn, 2 aslt hel/tpt hel bn)
AIR DEFENCE
  1 AD gp (regional troops)
EQUIPMENT BY TYPE
ARMOURED FIGHTING VEHICLES
  MBT 165 T-55; (75† in store)
  LT TK 96 AMX-13
  RECCE 95: 30 BRDM-2; 15 Fiat 6616; 50 M9A1
  APC 295
    APC (T) 120 M113A1
    APC (W) 175: 150 UR-416; 25 Fiat 6614
ENGINEERING & MAINTENANCE VEHICLES
  ARV M578
ANTI-TANK-ANTI-INFRASTRUCTURE
  MSL
    SP 22 M1165A2 HMMWV with 9K135 *Kornet* E (AT-14 *Spriggan*)
    MANPATS 9K11 *Malyutka* (AT-3 *Sagger*); HJ-73C; 9K135 *Kornet* E (AT-14 *Spriggan*); Spike-ER
  RCL 106mm M40A1
ARTILLERY 1,011
  SP 155mm 12 M109A2
  TOWED 290: 105mm 152: 44 M101; 24 M2A1; 60 M-56; 24 Model 56 pack howitzer; 122mm; 36 D-30; 130mm 36 M-46; 155mm 66: 36 M114, 30 Model 50
  MRL 122mm 35: 22 BM-21 *Grad*; 13 Type-90B
  MOR 674+: 81mm/107mm 350; SP 107mm 24 M106A1; 120mm 300+ Brandt/Expal Model L
AIRCRAFT
  TPT • Light 16: 2 An-28 *Cash*; 3 An-32B *Cline*; 1 Beech 350 *King Air*; 1 Beech 1900D; 4 Cessna 152; 1 Cessna 208 *Caravan* I; 2 Cessna U206 *Stationair*; 1 PA-31T *Cheyenne* II; 1 PA-34 *Seneca*
  TRG 4 IL-103
HELICOPTERS
  MRH 7 Mi-17 *Hip* H
  TPT 36: Heavy (3 Mi-26T *Halo* in store); Medium 23 Mi-171Sh; Light 13: 2 AW109K2; 9 PZL Mi-2 *Hoplite*; 2 R-44
  TRG 5 F-28F

AIR DEFENCE
SAM • Point-defence 9K36 *Strela*-3 (SA-14 *Gremlin*); 9K310 *Igla*-1 (SA-16 *Gimlet*); 9K32 *Strela*-2 (SA-7 *Grail*)‡
GUNS 165
SP 23mm 35 ZSU-23-4
TOWED 23mm 130: 80 ZU-23-2; 50 ZU-23

Navy 24,000 (incl 1,000 Coast Guard)

Commands: Pacific, Lake Titicaca, Amazon River
EQUIPMENT BY TYPE
SUBMARINES • TACTICAL • SSK 6:
4 *Angamos* (GER T-209/1200) with 8 single 533mm TT with AEG SST-4 HWT
2 *Islay* (GER T-209/1100) with 8 single 533mm TT with AEG SUT-264 HWT
PRINCIPAL SURFACE COMBATANTS 7
FRIGATES 7
FFGHM 6:
3 *Aguirre* (ex-ITA *Lupo*) with 8 single lnchr with *Otomat* Mk2 AShM, 1 octuple Mk29 lnchr with RIM-7P *Sea Sparrow* SAM, 2 triple 324mm ASTT with A244 LWT, 1 127mm gun (capacity 1 Bell 212 (AB-212)/SH-3D *Sea King*)
3 *Carvajal* (mod ITA *Lupo*) with 8 single lnchr with *Otomat* Mk2 AShM, 1 octuple *Albatros* lnchr with *Aspide* SAM, 2 triple 324mm ASTT with A244 LWT, 1 127mm gun (capacity 1 Bell 212 (AB-212)/SH-3D *Sea King*)
FFHM 1:
1 *Aguirre* (ex-ITA *Lupo*) with 1 octuple Mk29 lnchr with RIM-7P *Sea Sparrow* SAM, 2 triple 324mm ASTT with A244 LWT, 1 127mm gun (capacity 1 Bell 212 (AB-212)/SH-3D *Sea King*) (is being fit with MM40 *Exocet* Block 3)
PATROL AND COASTAL COMBATANTS 12
CORVETTES • FSG 6 *Velarde* (FRA PR-72 64m) with 4 single lnchr with MM38 *Exocet* AShM, 1 76mm gun
PCR 6:
2 *Amazonas* with 1 76mm gun
2 *Manuel Clavero*
2 *Marañon* with 2 76mm guns
AMPHIBIOUS
LANDING SHIPS • LST 2 *Paita* (capacity 395 troops) (US *Terrebonne Parish*)
LANDING CRAFT • UCAC 7 *Griffon* 2000TD (capacity 22 troops)
LOGISTICS AND SUPPORT 25
AG 4 *Rio Napo*
AGOR 1 *Humboldt*
AGORH 1 *Carrasco*
AGS 5: 1 *Carrasco* (ex-NLD *Dokkum*); 2 *Van Straelen*; 1 *La Macha*, 1 *Stiglich* (river survey vessel for the upper Amazon)
AH 4 (river hospital craft)
AO 2 *Noguera*
AOR 1 *Mollendo*
AORH 1 *Tacna* (ex-NLD *Amsterdam*)
AOT 2 *Bayovar*
ATF 1
AWT 1 *Caloyeras*
AXS 2: 1 *Marte*; 1 *Union*

Naval Aviation ε800

FORCES BY ROLE
MARITIME PATROL
1 sqn with Beech 200T; Bell 212 ASW (AB-212 ASW); F-27 *Friendship*; Fokker 60; SH-3D *Sea King*
TRANSPORT
1 flt with An-32B *Cline*; Cessna 206; Fokker 50
TRAINING
1 sqn with F-28F; T-34C *Turbo Mentor*
TRANSPORT HELICOPTER
1 (liaison) sqn with Bell 206B *Jet Ranger II*; Mi-8 *Hip*
EQUIPMENT BY TYPE
AIRCRAFT
MP 8: 4 Beech 200T; 4 Fokker 60
ELINT 1 F-27 *Friendship*
TPT • Light 6: 3 An-32B *Cline*; 1 Cessna 206; 2 Fokker 50
TRG 5 T-34C *Turbo Mentor*
HELICOPTERS
ASW 5: 2 Bell 212 ASW (AB-212 ASW); 3 SH-3D *Sea King*
MRH 3 Bell 412SP
TPT 11: **Medium** 8: 2 Mi-8 *Hip*; 6 UH-3H *Sea King*; **Light** 3 Bell 206B *Jet Ranger* II
TRG 5 F-28F
MSL • AShM AM39 *Exocet*

Marines 4,000

FORCES BY ROLE
SPECIAL FORCES
3 cdo gp
MANOEUVRE
Light
2 inf bn
1 inf gp
Amphibious
1 mne bde (1 SF gp, 1 recce bn, 2 inf bn, 1 amph bn, 1 arty gp)
Jungle
1 jungle inf bn
EQUIPMENT BY TYPE
ARMOURED FIGHTING VEHICLES
APC • APC (W) 47+: 32 LAV II; V-100 *Commando*; 15 V-200 *Chaimite*
ANTI-TANK/ANTI-INFRASTRUCTURE
RCL 84mm *Carl Gustav*; **106mm** M40A1
ARTILLERY 18+
TOWED 122mm D-30
MOR 18+: **81mm** some; **120mm** ε18
AIR DEFENCE • GUNS 20mm SP (twin)

Air Force 9,500

Divided into five regions – North, Lima, South, Central and Amazon
FORCES BY ROLE
FIGHTER
1 sqn with MiG-29S/SE *Fulcrum* C; MiG-29UB *Fulcrum* B
FIGHTER/GROUND ATTACK
1 sqn with *Mirage* 2000E/ED (2000P/DP)
2 sqn with A-37B *Dragonfly*
1 sqn with Su-25A *Frogfoot* A†; Su-25UB *Frogfoot* B†

ISR
1 (photo-survey) sqn with Learjet 36A; SA-227-BC *Metro III* (C-26B)
TRANSPORT
1 sqn with B-737; An-32 *Cline*
1 sqn with DHC-6 *Twin Otter*; DHC-6-400 *Twin Otter*; PC-6 *Turbo Porter*
1 sqn with L-100-20
TRAINING
2 (drug interdiction) sqn with EMB-312 *Tucano*
1 sqn with MB-339A*
1 sqn with Z-242
1 hel sqn with Schweizer 300C
ATTACK HELICOPTER
1 sqn with Mi-25/Mi-35P *Hind*
TRANSPORT HELICOPTER
1 sqn with Mi-17 *Hip* H
1 sqn with Bell 206 *Jet Ranger*; Bell 212 (AB-212); Bell 412 *Twin Huey*
1 sqn with Bo-105C/LS
AIR DEFENCE
6 bn with S-125 *Pechora* (SA-3 *Goa*)
EQUIPMENT BY TYPE
AIRCRAFT 78 combat capable
  FTR 20: 9 MiG-29S *Fulcrum* C; 3 MiG-29SE *Fulcrum* C; 6 MiG-29SMP *Fulcrum*; 2 MiG-29UBM *Fulcrum* B
  FGA 12: 2 *Mirage* 2000ED (2000DP); 10 *Mirage* 2000E (2000P) (some†)
  ATK 36: 18 A-37B *Dragonfly*; 10 Su-25A *Frogfoot* A†; 8 Su-25UB *Frogfoot* B†
  ISR 6: 2 Learjet 36A; 4 SA-227-BC *Metro* III (C-26B)
  TPT 36: **Medium** 5: 3 C-27J *Spartan*; 2 L-100-20; **Light** 27: 4 An-32 *Cline*; 7 Cessna 172 *Skyhawk*; 3 DHC-6 *Twin Otter*; 12 DHC-6-400 *Twin Otter*; 1 PC-6 *Turbo-Porter*; **PAX** 4 B-737
  TRG 68: 19 EMB-312 *Tucano*; 20 KT-1P; 10 MB-339A*; 6 T-41A/D *Mescalero*; 13 Z-242
HELICOPTERS
  ATK 18: 16 Mi-25 *Hind* D; 2 Mi-35P *Hind* E
  MRH 20: 2 Bell 412 *Twin Huey*; 18 Mi-17 *Hip* H
  TPT 28: **Medium** 7 Mi-171Sh; **Light** 21: 8 Bell 206 *Jet Ranger*; 6 Bell 212 (AB-212); 1 Bo-105C; 6 Bo-105LS
  TRG 4 Schweizer 300C
AIR DEFENCE • SAM
  Short-range S-125 *Pechora* (SA-3 *Goa*)
  Point-defence *Javelin*
AIR-LAUNCHED MISSILES
  AAM • IR R-3 (AA-2 *Atoll*)‡; R-60 (AA-8 *Aphid*)‡; R-73 (AA-11 *Archer*); R-550 *Magic*; **IR/SARH** R-27 (AA-10 *Alamo*); **ARH** R-77 (AA-12 *Adder*)
  ASM AS-30; Kh-29L (AS-14A *Kedge*)
  ARM Kh-58 (AS-11 *Kilter*)

Paramilitary 77,000

National Police 77,000 (100,000 reported)
EQUIPMENT BY TYPE
ARMOURED FIGHTING VEHICLES
  APC (W) 120: 20 BMR-600; 100 MOWAG *Roland*
HELICOPTERS
  MRH 1 Mi-17 *Hip* H

General Police 43,000

Security Police 21,000

Technical Police 13,000

Coast Guard 1,000
Personnel included as part of Navy
EQUIPMENT BY TYPE
PATROL AND COASTAL COMBATANTS 38
  PSOH 1 *Carvajal* (mod ITA *Lupo*) with 1 127mm gun (capacity 1 Bell 212 (AB-212)/SH-3D *Sea King*)
  PCC 8: 1 *Ferré* (ex-ROK *Po Hang*) with 1 76mm gun; 2 *Río Cañete* (ROK *Tae Geuk*); 5 *Río Nepena*
  PB 10: 6 *Chicama* (US *Dauntless*); 1 *Río Chira*; 3 *Río Santa*
  PBR 19: 1 *Río Viru*; 8 *Parachique*; 10 *Zorritos*
LOGISTICS AND SUPPORT • AH 1 *Puno*
AIRCRAFT
  TPT • Light 3: 1 DHC-6 *Twin Otter*; 2 F-27 *Friendship*

Rondas Campesinas
Peasant self-defence force. Perhaps 7,000 rondas 'gp', up to pl strength, some with small arms. Deployed mainly in emergency zone

DEPLOYMENT

CENTRAL AFRICAN REPUBLIC
UN • MINUSCA 209; 5 obs; 1 engr coy

DEMOCRATIC REPUBLIC OF THE CONGO
UN • MONUSCO 1; 11 obs

SOUTH SUDAN
UN • UNMISS 1; 2 obs

SUDAN
UN • UNAMID 1; 1 obs
UN • UNISFA 2 obs

Suriname SUR

Suriname Dollar srd		2016	2017	2018
GDP	srd	22.6bn	27.5bn	
	US$	3.63bn	3.67bn	
per capita	US$	6,430	6,416	
Growth	%	-10.5	-1.2	
Inflation	%	55.5	22.3	
Def exp	srd	n.k.	n.k.	
	US$	n.k.	n.k.	
US$1=srd		6.23	7.51	
Population	591,919			

Age	0–14	15–19	20–24	25–29	30–64	65 plus
Male	12.9%	4.7%	4.2%	4.2%	22.1%	2.6%
Female	12.1%	4.5%	4.0%	4.0%	21.6%	3.4%

Capabilities

The armed forces are principally intended to assure sovereignty and territorial integrity, but in practice their main activities are related to border security and tackling transnational criminal and terrorist activity. They have no ability to project power beyond the country's borders. Suriname has bilateral agreements with the US and other regional and extra-regional states regarding maritime counter-narcotics activities. Ties with larger countries, particularly Brazil, China and India, have been crucial to the supply of more costly equipment, including a limited number of armoured vehicles and helicopters, as well as training activity. Training is also delivered through participation in multinational exercises such as the *Tradewinds* series, in which Suriname participated in 2017. Suriname is also part of the US-led Caribbean Basin Security Initiative.

ACTIVE 1,840 (Army 1,400 Navy 240 Air 200)
Paramilitary 100
(All services form part of the army)

ORGANISATIONS BY SERVICE

Army 1,400
FORCES BY ROLE
MANOEUVRE
 Mechanised
  1 mech cav sqn
 Light
  1 inf bn (4 coy)
COMBAT SUPPORT
 1 MP bn (coy)
EQUIPMENT BY TYPE
ARMOURED FIGHTING VEHICLES
 RECCE 6 EE-9 *Cascavel*
 APC • **APC (W)** 15 EE-11 *Urutu*
ANTI-TANK/ANTI-INFRASTRUCTURE
 RCL 106mm M40A1
ARTILLERY • MOR 81mm 6

Navy ε240
EQUIPMENT BY TYPE
 PATROL AND COASTAL COMBATANTS 10 **PB** 5: 3 Rodman 101†; 2 others
 PBR 5 Rodman 55

Air Force ε200
EQUIPMENT BY TYPE
 AIRCRAFT 2 combat capable
  TPT • **Light** 2: 1 BN-2 *Defender**; 1 Cessna 182
  TRG 1 PC-7 *Turbo Trainer**
 HELICOPTERS • **MRH** 3 SA316B *Alouette* III (*Chetak*)

Paramilitary ε100

Coast Guard ε100
Formed in November 2013; 3 Coast Guard stations to be formed; HQ at Paramaribo

EQUIPMENT BY TYPE
PATROL AND COASTAL COMBATANTS • **PB** 3: 1 OCEA FPB 98; 2 OCEA FPB 72 MkII

Trinidad and Tobago TTO

Trinidad and Tobago Dollar TT$		2016	2017	2018
GDP	TT$	141bn	139bn	
	US$	21.1bn	20.3bn	
per capita	US$	15,459	14,784	
Growth	%	-5.4	-3.2	
Inflation	%	3.1	3.2	
Def bdgt	TT$	4.04bn	4.09bn	6.24bn
	US$	605m	596m	
US$1=TT$		6.67	6.87	

Population 1,218,208

Age	0–14	15–19	20–24	25–29	30–64	65 plus
Male	9.8%	3.1%	3.1%	3.8%	26.2%	4.6%
Female	9.5%	2.8%	2.8%	3.5%	24.6%	6.0%

Capabilities

The Trinidad and Tobago Defence Force (TTDF) focuses on border protection and maritime security, as well as counter-narcotics tasks. A larger role in law-enforcement support is planned for the army. A new national-security policy for 2018–23 has been prepared for submission to the National Security Council. TTDF personnel and vessels were deployed to Dominica in late 2017 to assist in disaster-relief efforts in the aftermath of Hurricane Maria, including two coastguard vessels ordered from Damen in 2015. The majority of these have now been delivered, bolstering maritime-security capacity. Trinidad and Tobago was one of the first Caribbean states to publish a cyber strategy, in 2012, which noted potential defence vulnerabilities arising from compromised critical national infrastructure.

ACTIVE 4,050 (Army 3,000 Coast Guard 1,050)
(All services form the Trinidad and Tobago Defence Force)

ORGANISATIONS BY SERVICE

Army ε3,000
FORCES BY ROLE
SPECIAL FORCES
 1 SF unit
MANOEUVRE
 Light
 2 inf bn
COMBAT SUPPORT
 1 engr bn
COMBAT SERVICE SUPPORT
 1 log bn
EQUIPMENT BY TYPE
ANTI-TANK/ANTI-INFRASTRUCTURE
 RCL 84mm ε24 *Carl Gustav*
ARTILLERY • MOR 81mm 6 L16A1

Coast Guard 1,050
FORCES BY ROLE
COMMAND
1 mne HQ
EQUIPMENT BY TYPE
PATROL AND COASTAL COMBATANTS 26
  PCO 1 *Nelson II* (ex-PRC)
  PCC 6: 2 *Point Lisas* (Damen Fast Crew Supplier 5009); 4 *Speyside* (Damen Stan Patrol 5009)
  PB 19: 2 *Gasper Grande*; 1 *Matelot*; 4 *Plymouth*; 4 *Point*; 6 *Scarlet Ibis* (Austal 30m); 2 *Wasp*; (1 *Cascadura* (SWE *Karlskrona* 40m) non-operational)

Air Wing 50
EQUIPMENT BY TYPE
AIRCRAFT
  TPT • Light 2 SA-227 *Metro* III (C-26)
HELICOPTERS
  MRH 2 AW139
  TPT • Light 1 S-76

Uruguay URY

Uruguayan Peso pU		2016	2017	2018
GDP	pU	1.58tr	1.73tr	
	US$	52.4bn	60.3bn	
per capita	US$	15,062	17,252	
Growth	%	1.5	3.5	
Inflation	%	9.6	6.1	
Def bdgt	pU	14.8bn	14.8bn	14.8bn
	US$	489m	513m	
US$1=pU		30.16	28.78	

Population 3,360,148

Age	0–14	15–19	20–24	25–29	30–64	65 plus
Male	10.3%	3.9%	4.0%	3.8%	20.6%	5.7%
Female	9.9%	3.8%	3.9%	3.7%	21.7%	8.5%

Capabilities

While the principal tasks for the armed forces are assuring sovereignty and territorial integrity, troops have in recent years deployed on peacekeeping missions, most notably in Haiti, as well as on domestic disaster-relief missions. Much of the equipment inventory is second-hand, which increases the maintenance burden, and there is little capacity for independent power projection. Much maintenance work is outsourced to foreign companies, such as Chile's ENAER. The air force is focused on the counter-insurgency role, but ambitions to purchase a light fighter aircraft remain hampered by funding problems. In March 2017, Uruguay retired all its ageing *Pucara* attack aircraft, resulting in even more limited combat power. While the acquisition of air-defence radars may have improved the military's ability to monitor domestic airspace, the lack of interdiction capability will continue to limit the capacity to respond to contingencies. The armed forces train regularly and participate in multinational exercises and deployments, notably on UN missions.

ACTIVE 24,650 (Army 16,250 Navy 5,400 Air 3,000)
Paramilitary 800

ORGANISATIONS BY SERVICE

Army 16,250
Uruguayan units are substandard size, mostly around 30%. Div are at most bde size, while bn are of reinforced coy strength. Regts are also coy size, some bn size, with the largest formation being the 2nd armd cav regt
FORCES BY ROLE
COMMAND
  4 mil region/div HQ
MANOEUVRE
  Mechanised
  2 armd regt
  1 armd cav regt
  5 mech cav regt
  8 mech inf regt
  Light
  1 mot inf bn
  5 inf bn
  Air Manoeuvre
  1 para bn
COMBAT SUPPORT
  1 (strategic reserve) arty regt
  5 fd arty gp
  1 (1st) engr bde (2 engr bn)
  4 cbt engr bn
AIR DEFENCE
  1 AD gp
EQUIPMENT BY TYPE
ARMOURED FIGHTING VEHICLES
  MBT 15 *Tiran-5*
  LT TK 38: 16 M24 *Chaffee*; 22 M41A1UR
  RECCE 15 EE-9 *Cascavel*
  IFV 18 BMP-1
  APC 376
    APC (T) 27: 24 M113A1UR; 3 MT-LB
    APC (W) 349: 54 *Condor*; 48 GAZ-39371 *Vodnik*; 53 OT-64; 47 OT-93; 147 *Piranha*
ENGINEERING & MAINTENANCE VEHICLES
  AEV MT-LB
ANTI-TANK/ANTI-INFRASTRUCTURE
  MSL • MANPATS *Milan*
  RCL 69: **106mm** 69 M40A1
ARTILLERY 185
  SP 122mm 6 2S1 *Gvozdika*
  TOWED 44: **105mm** 36: 28 M101A1; 8 M102; **155mm** 8 M114A1
  MOR 135: **81mm** 91: 35 M1, 56 Expal Model LN; **120mm** 44 Model SL
UNMANNED AERIAL VEHICLES • ISR • Light 1 *Charrua*
AIR DEFENCE • GUNS • TOWED 14: **20mm** 14: 6 M167 *Vulcan*; 8 TCM-20 (w/Elta M-2106 radar)

Navy 5,400 (incl 1,800 Prefectura Naval Coast Guard)

HQ at Montevideo

EQUIPMENT BY TYPE
PRINCIPAL SURFACE COMBATANTS • FRIGATES 2
  FF 2 *Uruguay* (PRT *Joao Belo*) with 2 triple Mk32 324mm ASTT with Mk46 LWT, 2 100mm gun
PATROL AND COASTAL COMBATANTS 15
  PB 15: 2 *Colonia* (US *Cape*); 1 *Paysandu*; 9 Type-44 (coast guard); 3 PS (coast guard)
MINE WARFARE • MINE COUNTERMEASURES 3
  MSO 3 *Temerario* (*Kondor* II)
AMPHIBIOUS 3: 2 **LCVP**; 1 **LCM**
LOGISTICS AND SUPPORT 9
  ABU 2
  AG 2: 1 *Artigas* (GER *Freiburg*, general spt ship with replenishment capabilities); 1 *Maldonado* (also used as patrol craft)
  AGS 2: 1 *Helgoland*; 1 *Trieste*
  ARS 1 *Vanguardia*
  AXS 2: 1 *Capitan Miranda*; 1 *Bonanza*

Naval Aviation 210

FORCES BY ROLE
ANTI-SUBMARINE WARFARE
  1 flt with Beech 200T*; *Jetstream* Mk2
SEARCH & RESCUE/TRANSPORT HELICOPTER
  1 sqn with AS350B2 *Ecureuil* (*Esquilo*); Bo-105M
TRANSPORT/TRAINING
  1 flt with T-34C *Turbo Mentor*

EQUIPMENT BY TYPE
AIRCRAFT 2 combat capable
  MP 2 *Jetstream* Mk2
  ISR 2 Beech 200T*
  TRG 2 T-34C *Turbo Mentor*
HELICOPTERS
  MRH 6 Bo-105M
  TPT • **Light** 1 AS350B2 *Ecureuil* (*Esquilo*)

Naval Infantry 450
FORCES BY ROLE
MANOEUVRE
  Amphibious
    1 mne bn(-)

Air Force 3,000

Flying hours   120 hrs/yr

FORCES BY ROLE
FIGHTER/GROUND ATTACK
  1 sqn with A-37B *Dragonfly*
ISR
  1 flt with EMB-110 *Bandeirante*
TRANSPORT
  1 sqn with C-130B *Hercules*; C-212 *Aviocar*; EMB–110C *Bandeirante*; EMB-120 *Brasilia*
  1 (liaison) sqn with Cessna 206H; T-41D
  1 (liaison) flt with Cessna 206H
TRAINING
  1 sqn with PC-7U *Turbo Trainer*
  1 sqn with Beech 58 *Baron* (UB-58); SF-260EU

TRANSPORT HELICOPTER
  1 sqn with AS365 *Dauphin*; Bell 205 (UH–1H *Iroquois*); Bell 212

EQUIPMENT BY TYPE
AIRCRAFT 13 combat capable
  ATK 12 A-37B *Dragonfly*
  ISR 1 EMB-110 *Bandeirante**
  TPT 23: **Medium** 2 C-130B *Hercules*; **Light** 21: 2 Beech 58 *Baron* (UB-58); 6 C-212 *Aviocar*; 9 Cessna 206H; 1 Cessna 210; 2 EMB-110C *Bandeirante*; 1 EMB-120 *Brasilia*
  TRG 21: 5 PC-7U *Turbo Trainer*; 12 SF-260EU; 4 T-41D *Mescalero*
HELICOPTERS
  MRH 2 AS365N2 *Dauphin* II
  TPT • **Light** 9: 5 Bell 205 (UH–1H *Iroquois*); 4 Bell 212

Paramilitary 800

Guardia de Coraceros 350 (under Interior Ministry)

Guardia de Granaderos 450

DEPLOYMENT

CENTRAL AFRICAN REPUBLIC
UN • MINUSCA 1

DEMOCRATIC REPUBLIC OF THE CONGO
UN • MONUSCO 1,165; 12 obs; 1 inf bn; 1 mne coy(-); 1 engr coy; 1 hel flt

EGYPT
MFO 58; 1 engr/tpt unit

INDIA/PAKISTAN
UN • UNMOGIP 2 obs

Venezuela VEN

Venezuelan Bolivar Fuerte Bs		2016	2017	2018
GDP	Bs	23.8tr	199tr	
	US$	236bn	215bn	
per capita	US$	7,620	6,850	
Growth	%	-16.5	-12.0	
Inflation	%	254	653	
Def bdgt	Bs	128bn	1.03tr	
	US$ [a]	1.28bn	1.12bn	
US$1=Bs		100.45	923.36	

[a] US dollar figures should be treated with caution due to high levels of currency volatility as well as wide differentials between official and parallel exchange rates

Population   31,304,016

Age	0–14	15–19	20–24	25–29	30–64	65 plus
Male	14.0%	4.3%	4.3%	4.2%	19.7%	3.2%
Female	13.3%	4.2%	4.3%	4.2%	20.4%	3.8%

Capabilities

The armed forces, including the National Guard, are tasked with protecting the sovereignty of the state, assuring territorial integrity and assisting with internal-security and counter-narcotics operations. The National Guard has seen its resources grow as it has become more involved in internal-security and counter-narcotics operations. In 2016, by presidential decree, the government initiated a process of formally giving public-order roles to paramilitary groups. In April 2017, after having declared a state of emergency, the government implemented Plan Zamora, which led to an increased military presence across the country, and has afforded the armed forces direct control over the distribution of some essential goods. Increased funds have in recent years been allocated to strengthen the National Guard and military capabilities amid broader economic difficulties that have seen inflation rise significantly. Despite these serious economic problems, the armed and security forces continue to receive significant funding, due to their role in regime protection and in helping suppress anti-government protests. A series of contracts with China and Russia have overhauled ageing army, marine and air-force inventories and are crucial for training as well as procurement; Venezuela possesses one of the region's most capable air and air-defence structures. (See pp. 380–82.)

ACTIVE 123,000 (Army 63,000 Navy 25,500 Air 11,500 National Guard 23,000) **Paramilitary 220,000**
Conscript liability 30 months selective, varies by region for all services

RESERVE 8,000 (Army 8,000)

ORGANISATIONS BY SERVICE

Space
EQUIPMENT BY TYPE
SATELLITES • COMMUNICATIONS 1 *Venesat*-1

Army ε63,000
FORCES BY ROLE
MANOEUVRE
　Armoured
　1 (4th) armd div (1 armd bde, 1 lt armd bde, 1 AB bde, 1 arty bde)
　Mechanised
　1 (9th) mot cav div (1 mot cav bde, 1 ranger bde, 1 sy bde)
　Light
　1 (1st) inf div (1 SF bn, 1 armd bde, 1 mech inf bde, 1 ranger bde, 1 inf bde, 1 arty unit, 1 spt unit)
　1 (2nd) inf div (1 mech inf bde, 1 inf bde, 1 mtn inf bde)
　1 (3rd) inf div (1 inf bde, 1 ranger bde, 1 sigs bde, 1 MP bde)
　1 (5th) inf div (1 SF bn, 1 cav sqn, 2 jungle inf bde, 1 engr bn)
COMBAT SUPPORT
　1 cbt engr corps (3 engr regt)
COMBAT SERVICE SUPPORT
　1 log comd (2 log regt)
AVIATION
　1 avn comd (1 tpt avn bn, 1 atk hel bn, 1 ISR avn bn)

Reserve Organisations 8,000
FORCES BY ROLE
MANOEUVRE
　Armoured
　1 armd bn
　Light
　4 inf bn
　1 ranger bn
COMBAT SUPPORT
　1 arty bn
　2 engr regt
EQUIPMENT BY TYPE
ARMOURED FIGHTING VEHICLES
　MBT 173: 81 AMX-30V; 92 T-72B1
　LT TK 109: 31 AMX-13; 78 *Scorpion*-90
　RECCE 121: 42 *Dragoon* 300 LFV2; 79 V-100/V-150
　IFV 237: 123 BMP-3 (incl variants); 114 BTR-80A (incl variants)
　APC 81
　　APC (T) 45: 25 AMX-VCI; 12 AMX-PC (CP); 8 AMX-VCTB (Amb)
　　APC (W) 36 *Dragoon* 300
ENGINEERING & MAINTENANCE VEHICLES
　ARV 5: 3 AMX-30D; BREM-1; 2 *Dragoon* 300RV; *Samson*
　VLB *Leguan*
NBC VEHICLES 10 TPz-1 *Fuchs* NBC
ANTI-TANK/ANTI-INFRASTRUCTURE
　MSL • MANPATS IMI MAPATS
　RCL 106mm 175 M40A1
　GUNS • SP 76mm 75 M18 *Hellcat*
ARTILLERY 515+
　SP 60: **152mm** 48 2S19 *Msta-S* (replacing Mk F3s); **155mm** 12 Mk F3
　TOWED 92: **105mm** 80: 40 M101A1; 40 Model 56 pack howitzer; **155mm** 12 M114A1
　MRL 56: **122mm** 24 BM-21 *Grad*; **160mm** 20 LAR SP (LAR-160); **300mm** 12 9A52 *Smerch*
　GUN/MOR 120mm 13 2S23 NONA-SVK
　MOR 294+: **81mm** 165; **SP 81mm** 21 *Dragoon* 300PM; AMX-VTT; **120mm** 108: 60 Brandt; 48 2S12
RADAR • LAND RASIT (veh, arty)
AIRCRAFT
　TPT • Light 28: 1 Beech 90 *King Air*; 1 Beech 200 *King Air*; 1 Beech 300 *King Air*; 1 Cessna 172; 6 Cessna 182 *Skylane*; 2 Cessna 206; 2 Cessna 207 *Stationair*; 1 IAI-201 *Arava*; 2 IAI-202 *Arava*; 11 M-28 *Skytruck*
HELICOPTERS
　ATK 10 Mi-35M2 *Hind*
　MRH 32: 10 Bell 412EP; 2 Bell 412SP; 20 Mi-17V-5 *Hip* H
　TPT 9: **Heavy** 3 Mi-26T2 *Halo*; **Medium** 2 AS-61D; **Light** 4: 3 Bell 206B *Jet Ranger*, 1 Bell 206L3 *Long Ranger* II

Navy ε22,300; ε3,200 conscript (total ε25,500)
EQUIPMENT BY TYPE
SUBMARINES • TACTICAL • SSK 2:
　2 *Sabalo* (GER T-209/1300) with 8 single 533mm TT with SST-4 HWT

Latin America and the Caribbean

PRINCIPAL SURFACE COMBATANTS • FRIGATES 6
  FFGHM 6 *Mariscal Sucre* (ITA mod *Lupo*) with 8 single lnchr with *Otomat* Mk2 AShM, 1 octuple *Albatros* lnchr with *Aspide* SAM, 2 triple 324mm ASTT with A244 LWT, 1 127mm gun (capacity 1 Bell 212 (AB-212) hel)
PATROL AND COASTAL COMBATANTS 10
  PSOH 3 *Guaiqueri* with 1 *Millennium* CIWS, 1 76mm gun (1 damaged in explosion in 2016)
  PBG 3 *Federación* (UK Vosper 37m) with 2 single lnchr with *Otomat* Mk2 AShM
  PB 3 *Constitucion* (UK Vosper 37m) with 1 76mm gun; 1 *Fernando Gomez de Saa* (Damen 4207)
AMPHIBIOUS
  LANDING SHIPS • LST 4 *Capana* (capacity 12 tanks; 200 troops) (FSU *Alligator*)
  LANDING CRAFT 3:
    LCU 2 *Margarita* (river comd)
    UCAC 1 *Griffon* 2000TD
LOGISTICS AND SUPPORT 10
  AGOR 1 *Punta Brava*
  AGS 2
  AKL 4 *Los Frailes*
  AORH 1 *Ciudad Bolivar*
  ATF 1
  AXS 1 *Simon Bolivar*

Naval Aviation 500
FORCES BY ROLE
ANTI-SUBMARINE WARFARE
  1 sqn with Bell 212 (AB-212)
MARITIME PATROL
  1 flt with C-212-200 MPA
TRANSPORT
  1 sqn with Beech 200 *King Air*; C-212 *Aviocar*; Turbo Commander 980C
TRAINING
  1 hel sqn with Bell 206B *Jet Ranger* II; TH-57A *Sea Ranger*
TRANSPORT HELICOPTER
  1 sqn with Bell 412EP *Twin Huey*; Mi-17V-5 *Hip H*
EQUIPMENT BY TYPE
AIRCRAFT 2 combat capable
  MP 2 C-212-200 MPA*
  TPT • Light 7: 1 Beech C90 *King Air*; 1 Beech 200 *King Air*; 4 C-212 *Aviocar*; 1 Turbo Commander 980C
HELICOPTERS
  ASW 5 Bell 212 ASW (AB-212 ASW)
  MRH 12: 6 Bell 412EP *Twin Huey*; 6 Mi-17V-5 *Hip*
  TPT • Light 1 Bell 206B *Jet Ranger* II (trg)
  TRG 1 TH-57A *Sea Ranger*

Marines ε15,000
FORCES BY ROLE
COMMAND
  1 div HQ
SPECIAL FORCES
  1 spec ops bde
MANOEUVRE
  Amphibious
    1 amph aslt bde
    3 mne bde
    3 (rvn) mne bde

COMBAT SUPPORT
  1 cbt engr bn
  1 MP bde
  1 sigs bn
COMBAT SERVICE SUPPORT
  1 log bn
EQUIPMENT BY TYPE
ARMOURED FIGHTING VEHICLES
  LT TK 10 VN-16
  IFV 21: 11 VN-1; 10 VN-18
  APC • APC (W) 37 EE-11 *Urutu*
  AAV 11 LVTP-7
ENGINEERING & MAINTENANCE VEHICLES
  ARV 1 VN-16 ARV
  AEV 1 AAVR7
ANTI-TANK/ANTI-INFRASTRUCTURE
  RCL 84mm *Carl Gustav*; **106mm** M40A1
ARTILLERY 30
  TOWED 105mm 18 M-56
  MOR 120mm 12 Brandt
PATROL AND COASTAL COMBATANTS • PBR 23: 18 *Constancia*; 2 *Manaure*; 3 *Terepaima* (*Cougar*)
AMPHIBIOUS • LANDING CRAFT • 1 LCM; 1 LCU; 12 LCVP

Coast Guard 1,000
EQUIPMENT BY TYPE
PATROL AND COASTAL COMBATANTS 22
  PSO 3 *Guaicamacuto* with 1 *Millennium* CIWS, 1 76 mm gun (capacity 1 Bell 212 (AB-212) hel) (1 additional vessel in build)
  PB 19: 12 *Gavion*; 1 *Pagalo* (Damen Stan 2606); 4 *Petrel* (US *Point*); 2 *Protector*
LOGISTICS AND SUPPORT 5
  AG 2 *Los Tanques* (salvage ship)
  AKSL 1
  AP 2

Air Force 11,500
Flying hours 155 hrs/yr
FORCES BY ROLE
FIGHTER/GROUND ATTACK
  1 sqn with F-5 *Freedom Fighter* (VF-5)
  2 sqn with F-16A/B *Fighting Falcon*
  4 sqn with Su-30MKV
  2 sqn with K-8W *Karakorum**
GROUND ATTACK/ISR
  1 sqn with EMB-312 *Tucano**; OV-10A *Bronco*
ELECTRONIC WARFARE
  1 sqn with *Falcon* 20DC; SA-227 *Metro* III (C-26B)
TRANSPORT
  1 sqn with Y-8; C-130H *Hercules*; KC-137
  1 sqn with A319CJ; B-737
  4 sqn with Cessna T206H; Cessna 750
  1 sqn with Cessna 500/550/551; *Falcon* 20F; *Falcon* 900
  1 sqn with G-222; Short 360 *Sherpa*
TRAINING
  1 sqn with Cessna 182N; SF-260E
  2 sqn with DA40NG; DA42VI
  1 sqn with EMB-312 *Tucano**

TRANSPORT HELICOPTER
1 VIP sqn with AS532UL *Cougar*; Mi-172
3 sqn with AS332B *Super Puma*; AS532 *Cougar*
2 sqn with Mi-17 *Hip* H

EQUIPMENT BY TYPE
AIRCRAFT 93 combat capable
  FTR 21: 17 F-16A *Fighting Falcon*; 4 F-16B *Fighting Falcon*
  FGA 23 Su-30MKV
  ATK 7 OV-10A *Bronco*
  EW 4: 2 *Falcon* 20DC; 2 SA-227 *Metro* III (C-26B)
  TKR 1 KC-137
  TPT 75: **Medium** 14: 5 C-130H *Hercules* (some in store); 1 G-222; 8 Y-8; **Light** 56: 6 Beech 200 *King Air*; 2 Beech 350 *King Air*; 10 Cessna 182N *Skylane*; 12 Cessna 206 *Stationair*; 4 Cessna 208B *Caravan*; 1 Cessna 500 *Citation* I; 3 Cessna 550 *Citation* II; 1 Cessna 551; 1 Cessna 750 *Citation* X; 2 Do-228-212; 1 Do-228-212NG; 11 Quad City *Challenger* II; 2 Short 360 *Sherpa*; **PAX** 5: 1 A319CJ; 1 B-737; 1 *Falcon* 20F; 2 *Falcon* 900
  TRG 84: 24 DA40NG; 6 DA42VI; 18 EMB-312 *Tucano**; 24 K-8W *Karakorum**; 12 SF-260E
HELICOPTERS
  MRH 8 Mi-17 (Mi-17VS) *Hip* H
  TPT • **Medium** 15: 3 AS332B *Super Puma*; 8 AS532 *Cougar*; 2 AS532UL *Cougar*; 2 Mi-172 (VIP)
AIR-LAUNCHED MISSILES
  AAM • **IR** AIM-9L/P *Sidewinder*; R-73 (AA-11 *Archer*); PL-5E; R-27T/ET (AA-10B/D *Alamo*); **IIR** *Python* 4; **SARH** R-27R/ER (AA-10A/C *Alamo*); **ARH** R-77 (AA-12 *Adder*)
  ASM Kh-29L/T (AS-14A/B *Kedge*); Kh-31A (AS-17B *Krypton*); Kh-59M (AS-18 *Kazoo*)
  AShM AM39 *Exocet*
  ARM Kh-31P (AS-17A *Krypton*)

Air Defence Command (CODAI)
Joint service command with personnel drawn from other services

FORCES BY ROLE
AIR DEFENCE
  5 AD bde

COMBAT SERVICE SUPPORT
  1 log bde (5 log gp)

EQUIPMENT BY TYPE
AIR DEFENCE
  SAM
    Long-range S-300VM
    Medium-range 9K317M2 *Buk*-M2E (SA-17 *Grizzly*); S-125 *Pechora*-2M (SA-26)
    Point-defence 9K338 *Igla*-S (SA-24 *Grinch*); ADAMS; *Mistral*; RBS-70
  GUNS 440+
    SP 40mm 12+: 6+ AMX-13 *Rafaga*; 6 M42
    TOWED 428+: **20mm**: 114 TCM-20; **23mm** ε200 ZU-23-2; **35mm**; **40mm** 114+: 114+ L/70; Some M1
RADARS • **AIR DEFENCE** *Flycatcher*

National Guard (Fuerzas Armadas de Cooperacion) 23,000
(Internal sy, customs) 9 regional comd

EQUIPMENT BY TYPE
ARMOURED FIGHTING VEHICLES
  APC • **APC (W)** 44: 24 Fiat 6614; 20 UR-416
ARTILLERY • **MOR** 50 81mm
PATROL AND COASTAL COMBATANTS • **PB** 34: 12 *Protector*; 12 *Punta*; 10 *Rio Orinoco* II
AIRCRAFT
  TPT • **Light** 34: 1 Beech 55 *Baron*; 1 Beech 80 *Queen Air*; 1 Beech 90 *King Air*; 1 Beech 200C *King Air*; 3 Cessna 152 *Aerobat*; 2 Cessna 172; 2 Cessna 402C; 4 Cessna U206 *Stationair*; 6 DA42 MPP; 1 IAI-201 *Arava*; 12 M-28 *Skytruck*
  TRG 3: 1 PZL 106 *Kruk*; 2 PLZ M2-6 *Isquierka*
HELICOPTERS
  MRH 13: 8 Bell 412EP; 5 Mi-17V-5 *Hip* H
  TPT • **Light** 19: 9 AS355F *Ecureuil* II; 4 AW109; 5 Bell 206B/L *Jet Ranger/Long Ranger*; 1 Bell 212 (AB 212);
  TRG 5 F-280C

Paramilitary ε220,000

Bolivarian National Militia ε220,000

Arms procurements and deliveries – Latin America and the Caribbean

Significant events in 2017

- Fábrica Argentina de Aviones (FAdeA) rolled out the first series production IA-63 *Pampa* III light attack aircraft destined for the Argentine Air Force.

- Argentina signed for and took delivery of four T-6C+ *Texan* II training aircraft from US company Beechcraft. The US approved the sale of 24 aircraft for US$300 million in 2016, but Argentina now plans to only purchase a total of 12.

- Argentina and France agreed the sale of five *Super Etendard Modernisé* fighter/ground-attack aircraft. Argentina will use some of these to repair and return to service some of its inactive *Super Etendard* aircraft.

- Brazil and Indonesia signed an agreement to enhance defence-industry support for Indonesian-operated military equipment supplied by Brazil.

- Brazil's KC-390 programme gained its first international customer after the Portuguese government authorised the purchase of at least five of the aircraft to replace the C-130H *Hercules*.

- Brazilian Army Aviation announced plans for the future procurement of light transport aircraft, utility helicopters and attack helicopters. The Brazilian Army has not had fixed-wing transport capability in over 70 years.

- Mexico purchased a new SIGMA 10514 frigate for ocean surveillance. The final stage of construction, before launch, is planned to be carried out at a yet-to-be-chosen Mexican shipyard.

- Venezuela signed a deal with China to arm its two operational *Guaiqueri*-class OPVs with C-802A (CH-SS-N-8 *Saccade*) anti-ship missiles. The vessels were originally to be armed as corvettes but the ships were delivered unarmed.

Figure 22 **Latin America and the Caribbean: selected ongoing or completed procurement priorities in 2017**

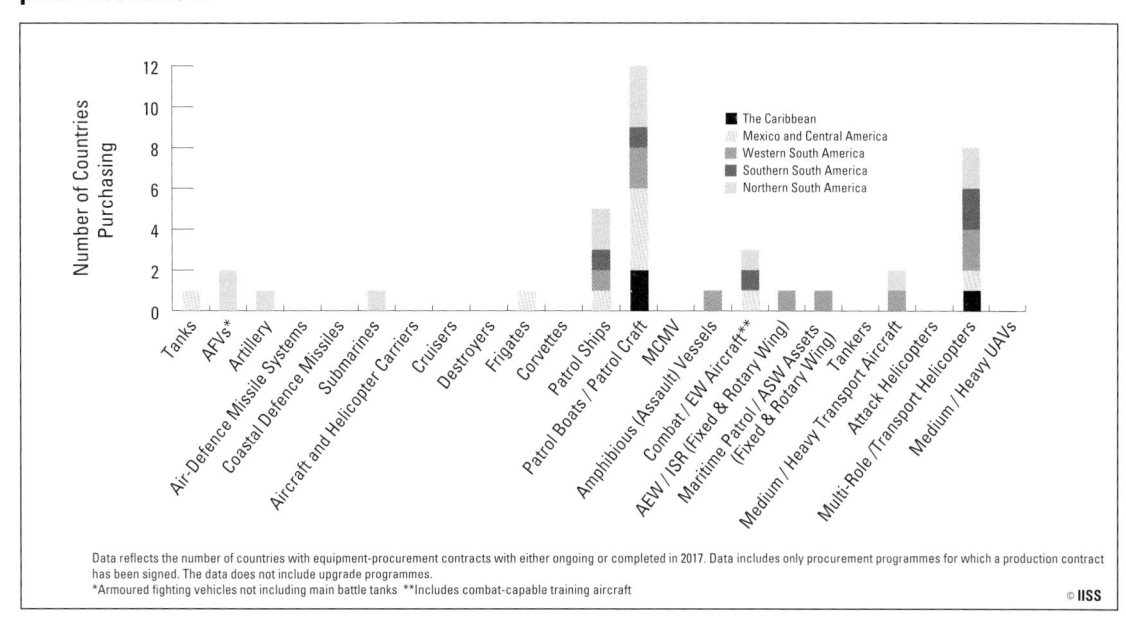

Data reflects the number of countries with equipment-procurement contracts with either ongoing or completed in 2017. Data includes only procurement programmes for which a production contract has been signed. The data does not include upgrade programmes.
*Armoured fighting vehicles not including main battle tanks **Includes combat-capable training aircraft

© IISS

Table 19 **Patrol vessels in Latin America: selected completed and ongoing contracts**

Country	Class	Type	Quantity	Contract value	Shipyard(s)	Order date
		Recently completed				
Chile	Piloto Pardo (OPV-80)	PSOH	4	n.k.	(CHL) ASMAR	2005
Colombia	20 de Julio (OPV-80)	PSOH	3	n.k.	(COL) COTECMAR	2008
Peru	Río Cañete	PCO	5	US$50m	(ROK) STX Offshore & Shipbuilding (PER) SIMA	2013
		Ongoing				
Argentina	Shaldag	PB	4	US$49m	(ISR) Israel Shipyards	Dec 2016
Chile	n.k.	AGB	1	US$217m	(CHL) ASMAR	2016
Costa Rica	n.k. (ex-US Island)	PB	2	Donation	(US) Govt surplus	2016
Ecuador	Damen Stan Patrol 5009	PCC	2	n.k.	(ECU) ASTINAVE	Aug 2014
Mexico	SIGMA 10514	FFHM	1	n.k.	(NLD) Damen Schelde (MEX) t.b.d.	2017
	Oaxaca	PSOH	4	n.k.	(MEX) ASTIMAR	2014
	Tenochtitlan (Damen Stan Patrol 4207)	PB	10	n.k.	(MEX) ASTIMAR	n.k.
Venezuela	Guaicamacuto	PSO	4	n.k.	(NLD) Damen Schelde (VEN) DIANCA	Nov 2005
	TN Fernando Gómez de Saa (Damen Stan Patrol 4207)	PB	8	n.k.	(NLD) Damen Schelde (CUB) DAMEX (VNM) Song Thu Shipyard (VEN) UCOCAR	Mar 2014

Table 20 **Transport helicopters in Latin America: selected completed and ongoing contracts**

Country	Equipment	Type	Quantity	Contract value	Contractor(s)	Order date	Service
		Recently completed					
Bolivia	H425	MRH	6	n.k.	(PRC) HAIG	2011	Army
	H215	Med Tpt hel	6	n.k.	(Int'l) Airbus Helicopters	2014	Air force
Chile	H215M	Med Tpt hel	10	n.k.	(Int'l) Airbus Helicopters	2008	Army
Colombia	Bell 412EP Twin Huey	MRH	4	US$120m	(US) Bell Helicopter	2013	Navy
Mexico	UH-60M Black Hawk	Med Tpt hel	3	US$83.9m	(US) Sikorsky	2010	Navy
Peru	Mi-171Sh Terminator	MRH	24	US$528m	(RUS) Ulan-Ude Aviation Plant	2011	Army, air force
		Ongoing					
Argentina	H225	Hvy Tpt hel	2	n.k.	(Int'l) Airbus Helicopters	2013	Coastguard
	AB-206B1	Lt Tpt hel	20	US$2.9m	(ITA) Govt surplus	2016	Army
Bolivia	MD-530F	MRH	2	n.k.	(US) MD Helicopters	2014	Police
Brazil	H225M	Hvy Tpt hel	50	US$2.72bn	(Int'l) Airbus Helicopters (BRZ) Helibras	Dec 2008	Army, navy and air force
Chile	S-70i Black Hawk	Med Tpt hel	6	US$180m	(US) Sikorsky (POL) PZL Mielec	Dec 2016	Air force
Colombia	UH-60A Black Hawk	Med Tpt hel	10	Donation	(US) Govt surplus	Apr 2017	Police
Mexico	UH-60M Black Hawk	Med Tpt hel	18	US$462.2m	(US) Sikorsky	Jul 2014	Air force
	UH-60M Black Hawk	Med Tpt hel	7	US$163.6m	(US) Sikorsky	Aug 2014	Navy
	AS565MBe Panther	SAR hel	10	US$433m	(Int'l) Airbus Helicopters	Jun 2014	Navy

Chapter Nine
Sub-Saharan Africa

Conflict and instability across parts of sub-Saharan Africa still constitute significant challenges to regional governments. A problem for regional states is that the requirement to deal with current threats risks absorbing the attention of defence establishments, possibly forestalling the defence-reform processes that might make responses to continental security threats more efficient. International involvement in these reform processes is important in terms of funding and organisational support.

Meanwhile, the fact that some of the continent's security challenges are transnational in cause and effect means that international attention remains focused on the continent. This focus is not just in terms of generating diplomatic support and helping to enable conflict and dispute resolution; it involves continuing material assistance to African nations and regional multilateral institutions, as they look to develop domestic capacity to tackle these crises. The move to develop such local capacity has been under way for some time, driven in large part by regional states and organisations such as the African Union (AU). However, defence spending across the region declined in real terms between 2016 and 2017. The risk is that this downward trend could affect more than just the money available for reforms and modernisation plans. Given the draws on government finances required by other sectors, and in light of the greater activism that some states have demonstrated in recent years, it could also affect their broader will and capacity to act.

Regional approaches

These financial challenges emphasise the potential benefits of more closely integrating responses to the continent's security challenges. Improving African states' ability to respond rapidly to crises is central to the African Standby Force (ASF) and African Capacity for Immediate Response to Crises initiatives. However, ad hoc responses have overall proven more practical, and perhaps more successful.

Tackling the Lord's Resistance Army
One example is the initiative to tackle the Lord's Resistance Army (LRA). The AU-authorised Regional Cooperation Initiative for the Elimination of the Lord's Resistance Army saw its mandate renewed until 22 May 2018. However, the deployment has changed: Uganda withdrew its troops in mid-2017 and the US drew down its special-forces contribution, saying that the LRA had been 'dramatically weakened in numbers and overall effectiveness'. Nonetheless, the US has said that it will still support regional forces tackling the LRA with intelligence and training. LRA leader Joseph Kony, however, has yet to be apprehended and some analysts fear that his reduced band of followers could cause further trouble across Central Africa should they regroup sufficiently. Meanwhile, the Central African Republic (CAR) – one of the countries where the LRA is still active – continues to be wracked by violence, and the government remains weakened.

A key driver for the continuing conflict in the CAR is the general lack of progress in the disarmament, demobilisation and reintegration (DDR) of the non-state groups that proliferate there. While the anti-LRA initiative did succeed in tamping down the activity of that group regionally and in the CAR, broader challenges there to the state and continuing capacity deficits risked undermining progress. It was feared that the withdrawal of the Ugandan and US contingents would leave a security vacuum ripe for exploitation by non-state actors.

Somalia
Another example of the ad hoc nature of integrated responses to continental security challenges is the AU Mission in Somalia (AMISOM). Although militant attacks continue, aimed at destabilising the Somali government and targeting the security forces, AMISOM and the Somali National Army made progress in the south against al-Shabaab.

Forces deployed to AMISOM have been learning under fire for many years. The troops have developed their ability to live in the field, as well as their soldiering skills such as patrolling and explosive-ordnance disposal. A number of nations, both local and international, have conducted AMISOM pre-deployment training and delivered broader assistance, such as in mobility support. This training and cumulative operational experience has led to capability benefits for the deployed forces, despite that fact that the mission has borne significant casualties. In time, this should make local forces more capable of addressing wider national and regional security challenges, should states wish to do so and if necessary. The main training effort, focused on the Somali forces, remains well supported internationally by the European Union and, most recently, Turkey.

Meanwhile, the international military support effort to tackle al-Shabaab has seen more US involvement. One characteristic of this has been support to AMISOM and troop-contributing countries. In early 2017, it was announced that US President Donald Trump had 'approved a Department of Defense proposal to provide additional precision fires in support of [AMISOM] and Somali security forces operations to defeat al-Shabaab in Somalia'. Secretary of Defense James Mattis said in May 2017 that US assistance to AMISOM had now been 'joined by training for select Somali soldiers, the provision of basic equipment to the Somalia National Army, and capacity-building so that [the] army can better sustain its forces in the field'.

Tackling Boko Haram
US assistance has continued to boost the capability of local forces to tackle the Boko Haram terror group; in August 2017 the US announced the possible sale of 12 *Super Tucano* aircraft to Nigeria (yet to be approved by Congress). Boko Haram continues to not only mount attacks inside Nigeria, but also absorb the security attention of neighbouring states. In early 2015 this led the AU to mandate the Lake Chad Basin Commission (which comprises regional states) plan to reinvigorate the Multinational Joint Task Force (MNJTF) concept. International assistance has included some funding. While the MNJTF has had an effect on degrading Boko Haram's operations, the group remains highly dangerous. Nonetheless, regional forces are working together to tackle a common adversary, which means that this may in effect constitute a confidence- and security-building mechanism, augmenting the improvements that the mission brings to national-defence capabilities and bilateral military-to-military ties.

Gambia
In Gambia, the December 2016 presidential election led to a stalemate. Following expressions of 'deep concern' by international organisations, particularly the Economic Community of West African States (ECOWAS), and the incumbent president's refusal to stand down, military forces from ECOWAS states intervened on 19 January. Constituting the ECOWAS Mission in Gambia (ECOMIG), troops from Ghana, Nigeria and Senegal secured key infrastructure in Gambia, and the former president soon left. Although the force wound down in early 2017, its mandate was extended until mid-2018.

The Sahel
Facing continued insurgent activity, states of the G5 Sahel grouping (Burkina Faso, Chad, Mali, Mauritania and Niger) decided in mid-2017 to deploy a force to tackle mainly Islamist insurgent groups. The operation had been authorised by these regional states two years previously and is due to grow to around 5,000 military and police personnel. With an operational headquarters in Mali, the force reportedly began operations in late October 2017.

The force will coordinate with the UN Mission in Mali (MINUSMA), and with French forces engaged in *Operation Barkhane*. These are deployed at a range of bases across the Sahel in order to tackle insurgent and terrorist activity there, while also training partner forces, such as those from the G5 Sahel. The US supports the G5 Sahel initiative, and the security capacities of each state, through funding assistance, training, equipment and intelligence support.

Some sub-Saharan African states are demonstrating greater activism in tackling these security challenges. While local forces are improving their capabilities to undertake these missions, international support remains vital. Most procurement needs derive more from the everyday challenges of insurgency, terrorism and criminality than the potential demands of inter-state warfare (see pp. 432–34). At the same time, measures to improve local military institutions and personnel quality remain important, as does security-sector reform and post-conflict-related DDR. Over time, progress in these areas may increase the chance of developing accountable and resilient armed and security forces to match the development in military will now exhibited by some states. Such forces may be able to exert greater control over ungoverned spaces or, at a minimum, extend governance to reassure and support vulnerable populations. Achieving these outcomes will, for the foreseeable future, require long-term international engagement and support.

DEFENCE ECONOMICS

Macroeconomic trends

Sub-Saharan African economic growth accelerated in 2017 to reach 2.6%, up from 1.4% in 2016. However, this regional figure masked significant disparities between slower-growing economies in larger states, and more dynamic growth observed in smaller nations.

Indeed, growth in the three largest economies was slower than in the region as a whole: Nigeria emerged from recession to reach 0.8% GDP growth in 2017 (up from -1.6%), while South Africa's GDP grew by 0.7% (up from 0.3%) and Angola's by 1.5% (up from -0.7%). The positive outcome was that Angola and Nigeria, the region's two principal oil exporters, continued their climb out of the economic difficulties that had been compounded by the fall in global oil prices. However, these two states apart, other regional oil exporters found themselves in a difficult position. For instance, after a severe recession in 2016 (when the country's GDP declined by 6.4%), Chad posted a figure of 0.6% in 2017. For the Republic of Congo, 2017 (with a figure of -3.6%) was even worse than 2016 (-2.8%).

Still-low oil prices meant that fiscal balances continued to worsen in oil-exporting countries in 2017, while fiscal deficits in oil-importing states remained broadly stable. Oil prices have slightly rebounded since OPEC's November 2016 agreement to cut production rates, but not by as much as expected. The IMF forecasted an average of US$50.17 per barrel for oil prices for 2018. Besides oil, other key commodity prices for sub-Saharan African economies experienced differing trends in 2017. Metal prices surged during the year: in the third quarter, zinc and nickel rose by 14%, iron ore by 13% and copper by 12%. Zimbabwe and South Africa are among the world's top exporters of nickel ore, while South Africa is the third-biggest exporter of iron ore. However, agricultural prices declined, due to improved food production in 2017. For example, cocoa prices were expected to decline by 30% by the end of 2017.

Smaller, non-oil-dependent economies experienced dynamic growth in 2017. Lower cocoa prices had a limited effect on Côte d'Ivoire, whose growth dipped only slightly, from 7.7% in 2016 to 7.6% in 2017. In Senegal, growth reached 6.8%, in part due to the implementation of the 20-year 'Plan Sénégal Emergent', an economic-modernisation plan that is being enacted in five-year increments.

Meanwhile, Mali's economy grew by 5.3% and Niger's by 4.2%, supported by strong public investment and agricultural output. Ethiopia, however, experienced the region's strongest growth in 2017. At 8.5%, this was a further increase on the 8.0% achieved in 2016. While Kenya decelerated from 5.8% in 2016 to 5.0% in 2017, it remained one of sub-Saharan Africa's fastest-growing economies. The same was true for Tanzania, which saw 6.5% GDP growth in 2017. But conflict, insecurity and development challenges continue to act as a brake on economic development in many areas. Indeed, famine was declared in South Sudan, and could reach northeastern parts of Nigeria.

South Africa's still-limited growth was caused mainly by internal political factors, with high levels of uncertainty undermining overall confidence in the economy. In April, President Jacob Zuma sacked finance minister Pravin Gordhan, in a dispute over the management of public spending. The value of the Rand fell shortly thereafter, and South Africa's credit rating was reduced by credit-rating agencies, further eroding confidence in the country's economy.

Nevertheless, although growth was slow in South Africa, the country still has firm underlying economic foundations. In contrast, Zimbabwe – which, at 2.8% in 2017, posted a higher growth rate than Nigeria and South Africa – has continued to de-industrialise. The economy is more reliant on commodity production and exports and has become dominated by the informal sector. Indeed, informal employment is believed to have grown by 30% between 2011 and 2014, constituting up to 94.5% of total employment. A shortage of hard currency also hit the country in late 2017. Meanwhile, Chad, where the government

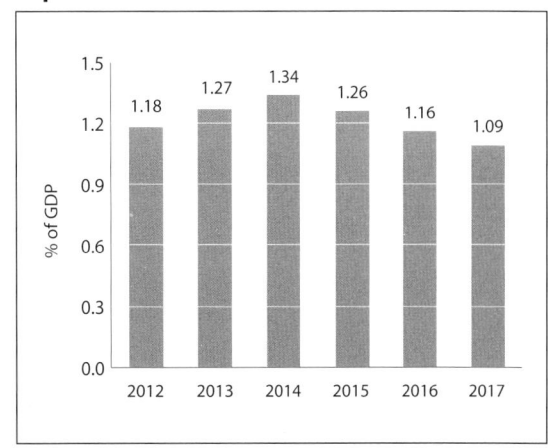

Figure 23 **Sub-Saharan Africa regional defence expenditure** as % of GDP

Year	% of GDP
2012	1.18
2013	1.27
2014	1.34
2015	1.26
2016	1.16
2017	1.09

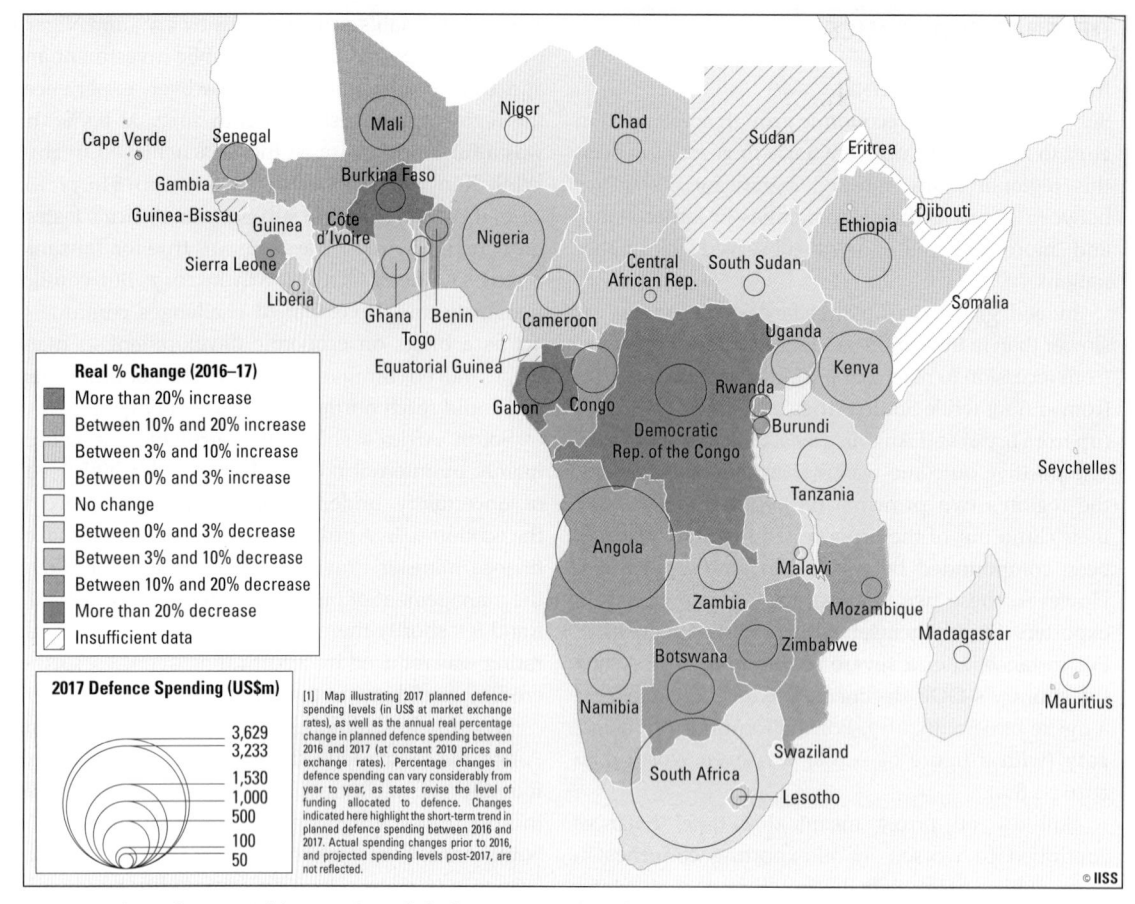

Map 11 Sub-Saharan Africa regional defence spending[1]

Real % Change (2016–17)
- More than 20% increase
- Between 10% and 20% increase
- Between 3% and 10% increase
- Between 0% and 3% increase
- No change
- Between 0% and 3% decrease
- Between 3% and 10% decrease
- Between 10% and 20% decrease
- More than 20% decrease
- Insufficient data

2017 Defence Spending (US$m)
3,629
3,233
1,530
1,000
500
100
50

[1] Map illustrating 2017 planned defence-spending levels (in US$ at market exchange rates), as well as the annual real percentage change in planned defence spending between 2016 and 2017 (at constant 2010 prices and exchange rates). Percentage changes in defence spending can vary considerably from year to year, as states revise the level of funding allocated to defence. Changes indicated here highlight the short-term trend in planned defence spending between 2016 and 2017. Actual spending changes prior to 2016, and projected spending levels post-2017, are not reflected.

derives most of its revenue from oil, also found itself in a difficult situation due to still-low oil prices. Austerity measures have been implemented, such as reductions to civil-service pay. This has led to greater reliance on international assistance in order to fulfil budgetary priorities. Defence spending, however, has been ring-fenced, given Chad's defence priorities and commitments, which include regional deployments. Indeed, in current terms, its defence spending increased by 3.6% between 2016 (US$160 million) and 2017 (US$165m).

Defence budgets and procurement: air-force recapitalisation

Total defence spending across sub-Saharan Africa declined by 5.2%, in real terms, between 2016 and 2017. This was driven by strong reductions in Angola (-15.1%), where inflation reached more than 30% in 2017; Kenya, where spending fell by 7.7% and inflation reached 8.0%; and the Democratic Republic of the Congo, where defence spending fell by 23.2% in real terms and inflation reached 41.7%. Overall, defence spending across the region mirrored broader economic conditions, with larger countries experiencing budget problems and delays to defence programmes, notwithstanding their allocation of increased nominal funds to defence, while smaller countries progressed with modernisation plans. Significantly, regional modernisation efforts focused on air-force recapitalisation.

Botswana, with defence spending of US$492m in 2017, placing it tenth in sub-Saharan Africa's defence-budget league table, made progress with its requirement to replace ageing F-5 fighter aircraft, with the Saab *Gripen* being a likely candidate. The evolution of Botswana's defence-budget breakdown shows an increasing share dedicated to 'development', overtaking 'recurrent' expenses (such as salaries) in 2016 (see Figure 24). Botswana has also procured VL-MICA surface-to-air missile systems and missiles for *Mistral* MANPADs from MBDA for €304.2m (US$343.1m).

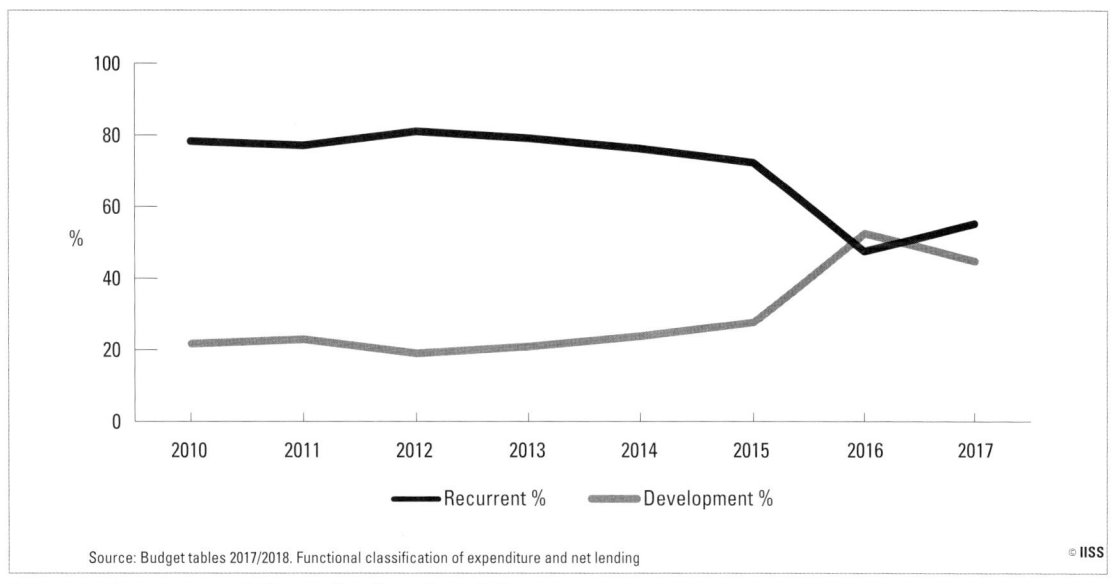

Figure 24 **Botswana: defence-budget breakdown, 2010–17**

Burkina Faso, which has a more modest budget (US$189m in 2017), expanded its rotary-wing fleet in 2017, thanks to Taiwan's donation of two second-hand UH-1H helicopters, worth an estimated US$8m. In addition, Burkina Faso signed agreements in 2017 with Russia for two Mi-171Sh transport helicopters, to be delivered in 2018. When these four aircraft enter service, they will increase Burkina Faso's air-force holdings by over 15% (from 24 fixed- and rotary-wing platforms to 28). Côte d'Ivoire also acquired two Mi-24s from Russia in 2017. French forces destroyed most air-force equipment during the civil war in 2004, and since then the country had been subject to an arms embargo. Prior to these new arrivals, the air force had operated only one Boeing-727 transport aircraft, and three SA330L *Puma* transport helicopters.

The Nigerian Air Force (NAF) saw new equipment delivered in 2017, particularly relating to training capability. The purchase of ten *Super Mushshak* trainers was earmarked in the 2016 budget, and receipt of the first five will reportedly allow NAF cadets to graduate in flight training from the Kaduna Defence Academy for the first time in 30 years, before commissioning as officers. NAF strength was modestly bolstered in 2017 by the receipt of two new Mi-35M attack helicopters and the refurbishment of two transport aircraft. In addition, the United States' Defense Security Cooperation Agency approved the sale to Nigeria of 12 A-29/EMB-314 *Super Tucano* light attack aircraft in a US$593m package including training, munitions and related support. However, this deal remains subject to US congressional authorisation.

Nevertheless, the modernisation of Nigeria's armed forces has been hindered by institutional failings. For instance, there remain allegations of corruption. Transparency International reported in 2017 that former military leaders are suspected of stealing up to US$15 billion from military-procurement programmes between 2007 and 2015. An ongoing investigation, opened in 2015 and led by the country's Economic and Financial Crimes Commission, has charged more than 300 individuals and companies with corruption. They are suspected of funnelling substantial funds from fake procurement orders to the then-ruling People's Democratic Party.

In South Africa, the armed forces have been battling real-term defence-spending declines for years, although the budget may have nominally increased. South African defence spending decreased by 2.5% between 2016 and 2017, and is expected to decline by another 1.3% between 2017 and 2018. Accordingly, the share of defence spending as a percentage of South Africa's GDP is on a downward trajectory, from 1.13% in 2014 to 1.05% in 2017; the figure is projected to fall to 1.03% in 2018 (see Figure 25).

In 2017, personnel costs constituted 80% of total South African defence spending. As the defence ministry seeks to reduce expenses related to the 'compensation of employees', it foresees a reduction in military personnel to 66,016 by 2019. Some

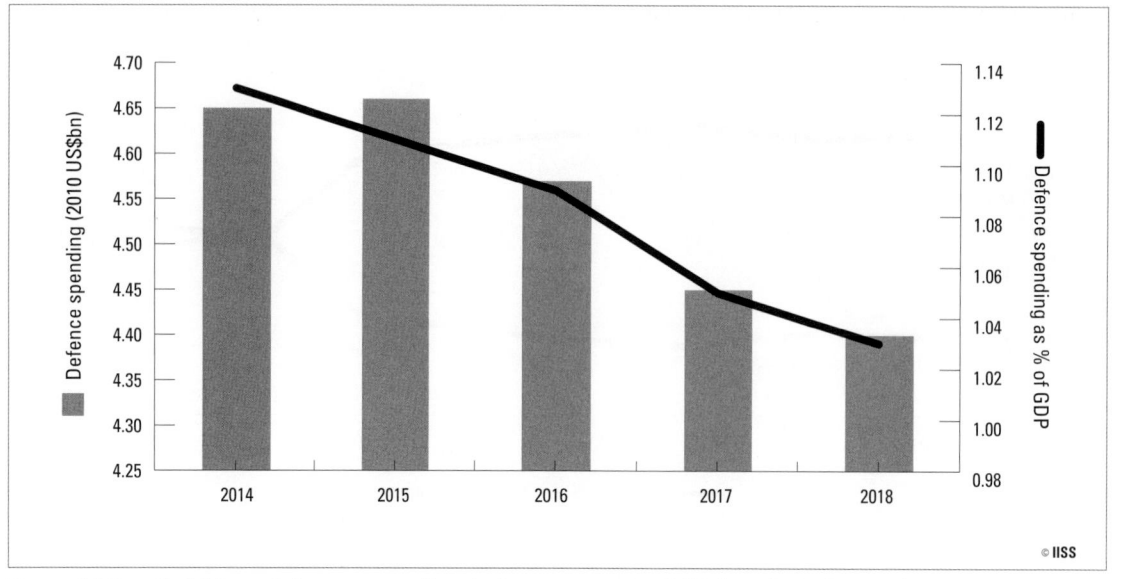

Figure 25 **South Africa: defence spending in (constant 2010) US$ and as share of GDP**

procurement programmes have also been delayed; for example, the acquisition of precision-guided air munitions has been postponed from 2018 to 2019. However, the procurement for the navy of a hydrographic vessel and patrol vessels was brought forward to 2017 and 2018 respectively, reflecting the increased prioritisation of maritime assets in defence planning.

DJIBOUTI

In 1977, France deployed an unprecedented air–sea task force off the coast of Djibouti to ensure the territorial integrity of this newly independent state. Previously, it had been a French Overseas Territory. The fear of invasion by Ethiopia or Somalia, which both had expansionist designs on the nascent country, became a determinant of Djibouti's defence policy, and 40 years later, Djibouti remains under the French defence umbrella. Yet over the past 15 years, Djibouti has begun to redefine its foreign-policy outlook by diversifying its security partners.

Foreign basing

Djibouti generates significant income from several foreign military bases in its territory. These have increased in number since 2001. Indeed, the global 'war on terror' and the fight against maritime piracy in and around the Gulf of Aden have raised demand for access to facilities in Djibouti and, for the government, provided opportunities for new funding.

For the United States, Djibouti is a crucial ally in the Horn of Africa. In 2002, the US established the Combined Joint Task Force–Horn of Africa (CJTF–HOA) at Camp Lemonnier (formerly a French facility), for which it signed a new 20-year lease in 2014. Lemonnier houses around 5,000 personnel, from CJTF–HOA and other units. The annual rent for this facility could be as high as US$63 million, according to experts. France retains facilities in Djibouti and uses the country as a power-projection base for its military activities in East Africa and further afield (such as Mali), as well as a training ground for desert combat. France is estimated to pay in the region of US$40m per year.

The EU has a small presence in the country under the framework of the European Union military counter-piracy operation *Atalanta* and civil training operation EUCAP *Nestor*, using Djibouti to support its operations. Germany and Spain, meanwhile, are among the countries that station maritime-patrol aircraft (MPA) there. (NATO did have a presence, although its *Ocean Shield* counter-piracy mission was wound up in December 2016.) Japan also maintains an MPA contingent in the country, and is understood to pay significant sums to use Djibouti's military facilities. Meanwhile, Djibouti and China signed a 'security and defence strategic partnership' agreement in 2014, which led to the establishment in 2017 of China's first overseas support base, near the new Doraleh Multi-Purpose Port. It has also been reported that Saudi Arabia might establish a facility in the country, in the wake of Djibouti's commitment to the Islamic Military Alliance to Fight Terrorism.

Commenting on this trend of foreign basing, Djibouti's President Ismail Omar Guelleh recently claimed that: 'The principle of military base concessions to foreign powers [should be seen] not as the chosen process to earn foreign currencies, but rather as a way to render the country more visible at the international level.'

Military capability

The main responsibilities of Djibouti's armed forces, gendarmerie and republican guard are to defend against external aggression and illicit trafficking; to ensure civilian security in non-military crisis situations (for example, humanitarian disasters); and to participate in peace operations, including those in Somalia.

In order to achieve these objectives, the president, who is also commander-in-chief of the armed forces, has initiated a major modernisation process. A White Paper on Defence and National Security was published in June 2017 to coincide with the 40th anniversary of the establishment of the armed forces. This document sets operational and financial objectives for the next three years (2017–20), including the modernisation of intelligence, command, air, maritime and land capabilities.

Two battalions are deployed to the African Union Mission in Somalia (AMISOM), an operation that is being led by Lieutenant-General Osman Nour Soubagleh of Djibouti from 2016–18. Two thousand personnel from Djibouti's armed forces are engaged in the operation, with another 1,000 held in reserve; this equates to approximately 33–34% of army strength. In recognition of the strain that this deployment could cause in the long run, the effort is backed by a recruitment policy that seeks to increase personnel numbers from 8,000 to 15,000.

Investments are needed in equipment, operational readiness and infrastructure. The armed forces operate mostly with equipment donated by foreign states. As such, the wide variety of equipment in the inventory presents challenges in terms of maintenance and interoperability. In addition, more than one-third of Djibouti's equipment has been deployed in Somalia since December 2011, which will again lead to a heavy maintenance requirement. Meanwhile, an overarching concept for military operations is lacking, which impedes operational readiness.

The success of the modernisation plan will depend on how Djibouti manages its external-debt levels; these reached an all-time high of 87% of GDP in 2017 (increasing from 85% of GDP in 2016 and 70% in 2015). Djibouti may be forced to confront the challenges of debt sustainability in the short term, which may come at the expense of longer-term investment in the armed forces, let alone broader areas of government spending.

SUDAN

Sudan's national-security policy is driven by one overriding objective: to maintain the rule of the Islamist/National Congress Party (NCP) regime. The NCP has existed in various guises since 1989. Linked to this is the determination of President Omar al-Bashir to avoid trial for his two war-crimes indictments by the International Criminal Court. He was first indicted in Darfur in 2009, and then for genocide in 2010.

The regime faces internal security threats from ongoing insurgencies at the country's periphery, in Darfur, and in Southern Kordofan and Blue Nile. These are linked to external security challenges on Sudan's borders with Chad, Libya and South Sudan. There are also periodic disagreements over the border with Egypt. Migrants from other parts of Africa seeking to reach Libya and the Mediterranean route to Europe present another range of challenges, particularly on the borders with Eritrea and Libya. However, Sudan's policy on all these issues is driven by how Khartoum perceives that they will affect the regime's chances of survival.

Regime survival

The roots of the NCP regime lie in the military coup of 1989. This was instigated by an alliance of Islamist-oriented army officers, led by current President Bashir and current first Vice-President and Prime Minister Bakri Hassan Saleh, and the Sudanese Muslim Brotherhood/National Islamic Front, whose chief ideologue was Hassan Turabi. In the 1990s, the regime's foreign and security policies reflected Turabi's inclinations: a close relationship with Iran; a bloody and ultimately unsuccessful 'jihad' against Sudan People's Liberation Army (SPLA) rebels in the south; hostility towards the secular regime in Egypt, leading to the involvement of Sudanese intelligence officers in an attempt to assassinate President Hosni Mubarak in 1995; and hosting international terrorists, including Osama bin Laden. As a result of these issues,

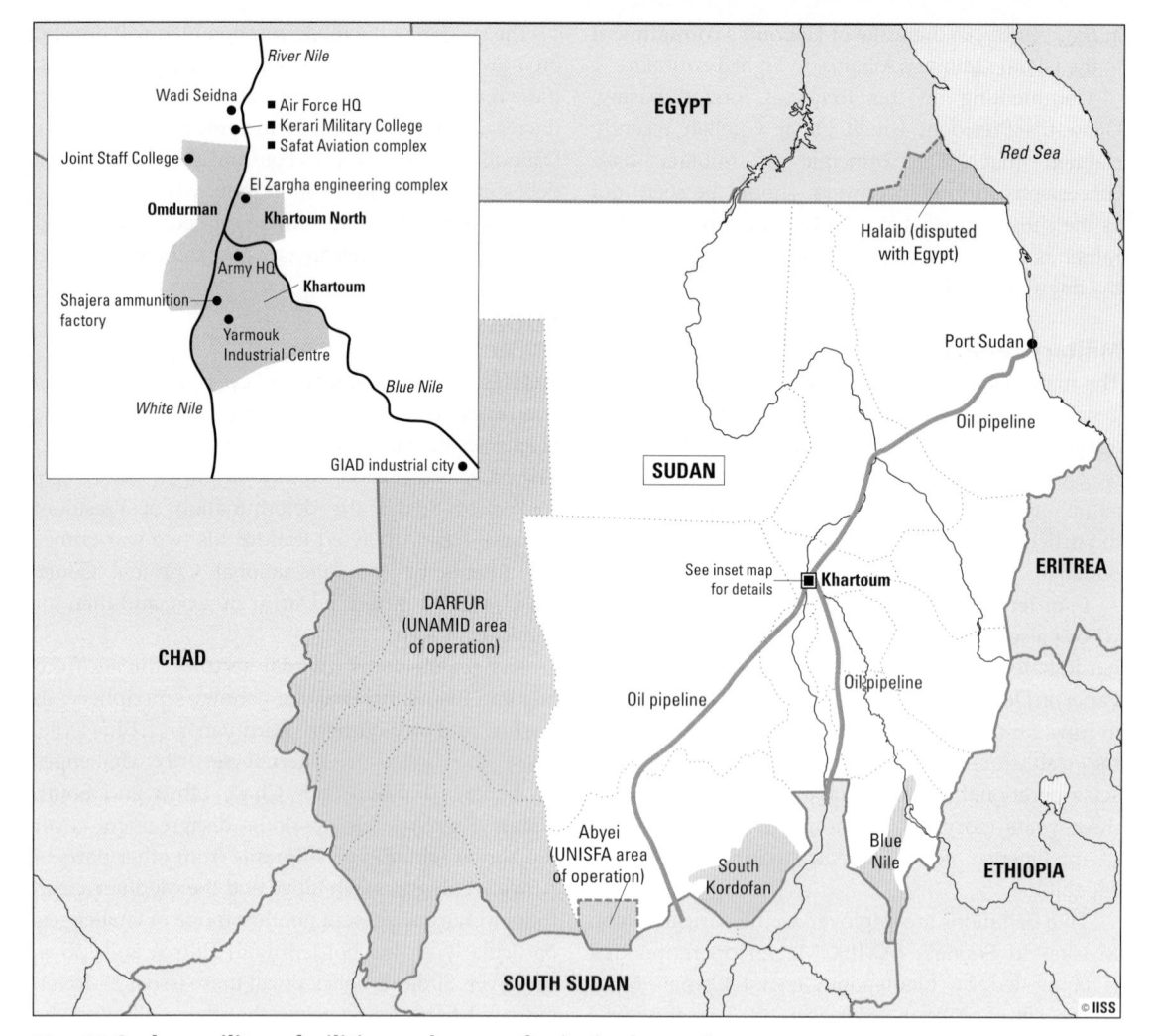

Map 12 **Sudan: military facilities and areas of principal security concern**

and human-rights concerns, in 1997 Washington imposed comprehensive economic sanctions on Khartoum. Following the terrorist attacks on the United States' embassies in Kenya and Tanzania in 1998, the US responded by launching cruise-missile strikes on a pharmaceutical factory in Khartoum North, alleged by US intelligence at the time to have been linked to bin Laden and to the processing of VX nerve agent. These developments led Bashir and a group of pragmatists to conclude that Turabi's policies were threatening the regime's existence; Turabi was ejected from all his official positions in 1999. The NCP began a policy of ending the war in the south and seeking engagement with the West.

This more collaborative approach led to the Comprehensive Peace Agreement (CPA) of 2005, which ended the war in the south by providing for an independence referendum and for the democratisation of the whole of Sudan. Although the Sudan National Intelligence and Security Service (NISS) began providing counter-terrorism information to Western intelligence agencies, the prospects for a fuller accommodation with the US and European Union were undermined by the regime's brutal handling of the Darfur uprising, which started in 2003. This produced an international outcry and led to the indictment of Bashir and senior figures in the regime and its associated militias. Even though the south was able to vote for and gain independence in 2011, US sanctions remained in place and were in effect extended, which made it impossible for European banks and companies with interests in the US to do business with Sudan.

The regime relied mainly on Chinese petrochemical companies for the exploitation of Sudan's oil reserves, which came on stream in 1999. Meanwhile, Sudan became increasingly dependent on China, and to a lesser extent Iran, for weapons, trade and infrastructure investment, and the development of the country's nascent arms industry. Sudan's continuing links with Iran and, in particular, its supply of weapons to Hamas led to a presumed Israeli airstrike on the Yarmouk arms factory near Khartoum in 2012.

However, there has been a significant shift in Sudan's alliance relationships since 2014. As the loss of oil revenues from South Sudan began to bite, and with poor economic conditions sparking serious riots in Khartoum and other cities in 2013, the regime began to pivot towards Saudi Arabia and the United Arab Emirates (UAE) for financial support to ensure its survival. This meant breaking with Tehran. Iranian cultural centres in Sudan were closed in 2014, and in September 2015 Sudan committed forces to the Saudi-led *Operation Decisive Storm* against the Iranian-backed Houthi rebels in Yemen. In early 2016, Sudan broke off diplomatic relations with Iran, following the ransacking of the Saudi embassy in Tehran.

This shift enabled the regime to renew its efforts to reach an accommodation with the EU and the US. The NISS intensified its cooperation with Western intelligence agencies, reportedly providing useful information on groups linked to the Islamic State, also known as ISIS or ISIL, and al-Qaeda in the Islamic Maghreb. As the rebellions in Darfur and in Southern Kordofan and Blue Nile began to falter, the regime signed an African Union (AU)-sponsored road-map agreement in 2016, leading to a ceasefire in these conflicts (not always honoured in full). The US began to loosen its sanctions in 2016, leading to their suspension in January 2017 and lifting in October 2017. The US asserted that the regime was broadly adhering to its main conditions, including working towards a permanent ceasefire in Darfur and in Southern Kordofan and Blue Nile; maintaining improved humanitarian access to the conflict zones; cooperating to find a solution to the internal conflict in South Sudan and other regional conflicts; cooperating on counter-terrorism; respecting freedom of religion; and ending links with North Korea. The United Kingdom started 'phased engagement' talks with the regime in March 2016.

Meanwhile, as migration became an increasingly crucial issue for the EU, Sudan undertook to provide intelligence on people-smuggling gangs and to stem the flow of migrants from Eritrea and other countries in the Horn of Africa towards Libya and the Mediterranean. The EU pledged a US$100 million aid package to help reduce the refugee flow as part of the EU–Horn of Africa Migration Route Initiative, which became known as the 'Khartoum Process'.

At the same time, Sudan has managed to stay neutral in the dispute between Saudi Arabia, the UAE and other Gulf states, and Qatar. It has no interest in upsetting its new allies, but also wants to maintain good relations with Qatar, which played an important role in trying to end the Darfur conflict and has long provided substantial development aid and investment.

Regional relations

Relations with South Sudan have been tense since the latter's independence in 2011. This is partly because of the unresolved border issue of Abyei, an area close to important oil fields and a flashpoint between northern Misseriya nomads and southern Ngok Dinka. Abyei essentially remains a frozen conflict, with the area under de facto control of the government in Khartoum, and a United Nations force (UNISFA) providing security. It is also partly a result of disputes over revenues from South Sudan's oil, which has to be pumped up the 1,400-kilometre pipeline to Port Sudan in the north for export. Sudan has also accused South Sudan of supporting their former comrades-in-arms of the Sudan People's Liberation Movement–North (SPLM–N) in the ongoing conflict in Southern Kordofan and Blue Nile, while South Sudan has accused the north of supporting the rebel Lord's Resistance Army (LRA), which has a long history of committing atrocities in the south. When South Sudan descended into full-scale civil war in 2013, the NISS began supplying weapons to the SPLM–Internal Opposition (SPLM–IO). However, the US made it clear that cooperation on finding a solution in South Sudan was crucial for lifting sanctions, and Sudan appears to have cut off the supply of arms to the SPLM–IO.

Historically, Sudan's strategic importance has stemmed from its control of the Nile waters flowing into Egypt. Egypt's regional significance has meant that most governments in Khartoum have regarded it as essential to maintain good bilateral relations. However, the NCP's sympathy for the

Egyptian Muslim Brotherhood has created a difficult relationship with Cairo, except for the brief period of the Morsi government in 2012–13. The present government accuses Sudan of harbouring Egyptian Muslim Brotherhood extremists. In addition, there are disputes over the construction of dams on the Nile; Sudan intermittently raises the question of the Halaib Triangle, a disputed border area under de facto Egyptian control; and Khartoum has accused Egypt of arming Darfur rebels that conducted an incursion from Libya in May 2017.

The Sudanese regime also periodically sees Eritrea as a threat. At various points in the past, Eritrea has supported the SPLA, and the Darfur and Eastern Front rebels. However, since 2012 the relationship has been more amicable. The main issue on the border is now people smuggling – principally of Eritreans heading across Sudan to Libya and Europe. This is largely controlled by the well-armed Rashaida tribe, who formed part of the Eastern Front rebellion until 2006 and are seen as a potential threat by the NCP regime. Reports that the Sudan government might use its Rapid Support Forces, made up of Darfur tribesmen, to interdict irregular migration across the frontier from Eritrea have not so far materialised.

The porous border between Chad and Sudan has also been a major source of instability. Relations were tense between 2006 and 2009, when Chad supported the Darfur rebels and Sudan backed insurgents fighting against the regime of President Idriss Déby. Following mediation by the UAE, Sudan and Chad reconciled and established joint border patrols, which now appear to be effective in controlling this remote frontier where there is potential for militant Islamist infiltration from West Africa.

Armed forces

The Sudan Armed Forces (SAF) comprise an army, navy and air force. Personnel numbers are not published, but it is estimated that the regular army has in excess of 100,000 soldiers, the navy about 1,300 sailors and the air force some 3,000 personnel. The army contains at least 20 divisions: 15 infantry plus armoured, mechanised, artillery, engineering and marine units. There are also presidential guard, special-forces, air-assault and counter-terrorism formations.

In theory, men and women aged between 18 and 33 are conscripted for one to two years, but implementation of this is haphazard. There is a core of volunteer soldiers, traditionally from the economically deprived areas of the south and Darfur. Officers have tended to come from the riverain tribes north of Khartoum, who have generally dominated Sudanese political life, while a number also come from Kordofan in the west. However, reports suggest that the ethnic balance in the SAF is changing, especially with the secession of the south reducing the number of southern troops.

Before 1989, the SAF was generally regarded as a professional force in which promotion was on merit and tribal influences minimised. It was proud of the role it had played in siding with the people in the uprisings that overthrew the Abboud and Nimeiri regimes in 1964 and 1985 respectively. Under the NCP regime, though, officers who do not pay lip service to its Islamist agenda have been removed. There are reports of Islamist 'Saihun' officers, who were prominent in the 1990s 'jihad' in the south, receiving preferment in recent years. Senior officers have benefited from regime privileges to the extent that many observers question whether the SAF would side with the people if popular uprisings like those in 1964 and 1985 were to occur. Nevertheless, the SAF generally remained uninvolved during the violent suppression of protests in 2013. The current chief of staff, General Imad Adawi, is regarded by some analysts as an outward-looking professional officer. He has publicly criticised the effects of tribalism on the army's coherence.

Basic military training takes place at the Kerari Military College at Wadi Seidna, north of Khartoum. There is a Joint Staff College and Higher Academy in Omdurman. Recently, considerable resources have been devoted to an English-language training programme delivered through the British Council. At the strategic level there is a defence college containing a war college and a research-studies centre.

Accurate information on SAF platforms and equipment is scarce. The Sudanese Military Industrial Corporation (MIC) claims to locally produce ZTZ-85-II (*Al-Bashir*), T-54/T-55 (*Digna*), T-72AV (*Al-Zubair* 1) and ZTZ-59D (*Al-Zubair* 2) main battle tanks. The MIC catalogue also advertises locally produced BTR-80A (*Shareef* 1), WZ-523 (*Shareef* 2) and BMP-2 (*Khatim* 2) armoured vehicles, amongst others, plus ZFB-05 (*Amir* 1) and BRDM-2 (*Amir* 2) reconnaissance vehicles. Whilst Sudan has imported varying quantities of all of these vehicles at some point in its history, it is unclear if the MIC has ever produced any of these designs, or how many remain operational with the SAF.

The Sudanese Navy is mainly focused on interdicting smuggling on the Red Sea coast and is equipped with around 11 patrol boats. The air force has Russian Su-24 and Su-25 attack aircraft (three Su-24s are deployed in Yemen) obtained from Belarus. It also has a number of MiG-29SE fighters, but many of these appear to be grounded for lack of spare parts. It is equipped with Antonov transport aircraft, which were reportedly improvised to conduct bombing missions during the Darfur conflict. The air force is reported to possess more than 50 Russian attack and 30 transport helicopters.

The NCP regime relies for its security on a range of forces in addition to the SAF. These include the NISS and various local and tribal militias. The use of tribal militias by the government in the conflicts in southern and western Sudan stretches back to the democratic government of Sadiq al-Mahdi in 1986–89. In part, it stems from fears in Khartoum that the large number of ordinary SAF soldiers from Darfur and the south might not be prepared to fire on their own people. After 1989, the Islamist/military regime established the Popular Defence Forces (PDF). These were militias of Muslim Brotherhood-oriented civilians, given military training to protect the regime against uprisings. PDF units served alongside the SAF in the south in the 1990s and in Darfur after 2003. In theory, the PDF still exist in most towns and villages as a vanguard to protect the regime. Their numbers are estimated at 20,000–40,000, but, in practice, they have been eclipsed by other irregular forces.

During the war in the south in the 1990s, the Sudanese regime backed breakaway groups from the SPLA, which were brought together under the umbrella of the Southern Sudan Defence Force. The regime also supported the LRA, who attacked the south from bases in the Democratic Republic of the Congo and Uganda. Even recently, the South Sudanese government has accused Sudan of supporting the LRA. When war broke out in Darfur in 2003, Khartoum supported 'Janjaweed' militias from the nomadic pastoralist Arab tribes, who were encouraged to seize land from the Fur and other settled non-Arab tribes regarded as sympathetic to the rebels of the Sudan Liberation Movement and the Justice and Equality Movement. From about 2006, some of the Janjaweed were moved by SAF military intelligence into the more formal structure of the border guard. Other Janjaweed were recruited by the NISS into the Central Reserve Police, known in Darfur as 'police soldiers'. When the removal of fuel subsidies led to protests in Khartoum and other cities in 2013, police soldiers directed by the NISS were accused of killing 200 demonstrators.

Shortly afterwards, elements of the border guard and the Central Reserve Police appear to have been amalgamated by the NISS into the Rapid Support Forces (RSF), which operated against the Darfur rebel movements and the SPLM–N in Southern Kordofan and Blue Nile. The RSF seem to have made a major contribution alongside the SAF to the significant degrading of the rebel effort since 2014. The RSF, believed to number more than 10,000, are also used to patrol the border with Libya, in order to reduce the flow of migrants under the Khartoum Process. There are reports, denied by the Sudan government, that the RSF are deployed as part of Sudan's contribution to the Saudi-led coalition in Yemen. There have been numerous reports of RSF brutality and indiscipline, including clashes with the SAF. In January 2017, the Sudanese parliament passed legislation removing the RSF from NISS control and integrating them into the SAF, but as a semi-autonomous force under a commander appointed by the president. There is now an official budget line for the RSF. Recently the government has embarked on a weapons-collection operation, ostensibly to reduce insecurity in Darfur. In reality, this appears to be designed to reduce the number of weapons in the hands of the remaining border guards and tribal militias, thereby further strengthening the hand of the RSF. The weapons-collection programme is opposed by those former Janjaweed commanders who did not join the RSF.

The regime's overall strategy in Darfur, Southern Kordofan and Blue Nile appears to be to express support for the AU road-map agreement while blaming divisions among the rebels for its non-implementation; to maintain the temporary ceasefire while using force to deny the armed movements control of any more territory; and, where possible, to win over rebel soldiers with offers of salaries and food, with the ultimate objective of integrating them into the SAF.

Very little detail is known about Sudan's contribution to the Saudi-led coalition in Yemen beyond the provision of several hundred ground troops and three Su-24 aircraft. Some analysts believe that Sudan's involvement is greater than generally acknowledged, in part because Sudanese troops have more combat experience than those from other countries in the coalition.

Defence economics and industry

Funding for Sudan's extensive defence and security structures is set against a complex and uncertain economic background. Traditionally, Sudan's economy was based on agriculture, livestock and related agribusiness, such as sugar production. But it has an enormous external-debt overhang from over-ambitious projects in the 1970s, totalling up to US$50 billion, equivalent to 61% of GDP (and 84% of it is in arrears). Furthermore, Sudan was subject to US sanctions from 1997 to 2017. Separate US and EU embargoes on arms sales to Sudan have been in force since 1993–94.

Sudanese oil production commenced in 1999, prompting a mini-boom in Khartoum. Oil revenues averaged nearly US$5bn a year between 2004 and 2008. However, with the independence of South Sudan in 2011, Sudan lost 75% of its oil reserves and 50% of its oil revenues. Under the CPA, South Sudan is supposed to pay Sudan transit fees for use of the pipeline to Port Sudan, plus transitional payments linked to its loss of oil wells. But, initially, South Sudan made no payments, leading to a damaging closure of the pipeline. Although production resumed in 2013, the drop in global oil prices and the civil war in South Sudan have kept revenues for Sudan low (under US$400m in 2017). Khartoum failed to use oil revenues to invest in agriculture, instead selling off tracts of land to Gulf investors who then employed small numbers of Sudanese workers. It hopes to replace some of the oil revenues it used to receive with earnings from gold production, which has increased significantly in recent years. However, this sector is not well regulated and the revenues are considerably less than those from oil in the boom years (under US$1.5bn in 2016).

In 2016, Sudan's balance-of-payments deficit amounted to US$5.1bn. Some of this has been made up by undisclosed bailouts from Saudi Arabia and the UAE, a reward for the regime's break with Iran and participation in the war in Yemen. However, Sudan cannot rely on Gulf handouts indefinitely. Inflation was 30.5% in 2016 and 21% in 2017, and the value of the Sudanese pound has dropped significantly over time (from 2.67 Sudanese pounds to one US dollar in 2011, to 6.48 in 2017). The situation is complicated by the existence of official, parallel and black-market exchange rates, with members of the defence and security establishment apparently benefiting from trading between the different rates. Information on Sudan's defence and security budgeting is difficult to obtain, although some analysts believe that as well as specific government disbursements, the defence and security establishment likely receives funding from off-budget sources.

Since 1989, with Chinese, Iranian and, initially, Bulgarian help, Sudan has developed the third-largest defence industry in Africa (after Egypt and South Africa). Its impressive and relatively low-cost items were on display at IDEX in Abu Dhabi in February 2017. The industry is coordinated by the MIC, but some plants are 'privately' owned (possibly by the NISS). The Yarmouk Industrial Centre produces rockets, heavy artillery, machine guns and light weapons. It was rebuilt with Iranian assistance after being bombed by Israel in 2012. The Safat Aviation Complex maintains aircraft and helicopters, while the Al Zarqa Engineering Complex produces communications equipment. The large GIAD plant, located 50km south of Khartoum, produces tanks, armoured personnel carriers and self-propelled guns, as well as assembling civilian vehicles.

A number of civilian companies are believed to be strongly linked to the armed forces, notably Danfodio (construction, furniture), Al Hiloul al Mutakamila (restaurants, media) and Alaia Pharmacology (medicines). The regime ensures the continuing loyalty of former SAF and NISS officers by awarding them lucrative positions in the MIC and its associated companies.

UGANDA

Uganda's national-security policy is determined by broader regional security dynamics. Its geographical position in a continually fragile setting means that Uganda needs to be able to respond to border threats and internal issues caused by regional instability. Furthermore, as a small, landlocked country, it risks pressures from its larger regional neighbours, including the Democratic Republic of the Congo (DRC), Ethiopia, Kenya, Sudan and Tanzania. In addition, Uganda contains multiple ethnic groups, which straddle its borders with fragile neighbours, and the country now hosts Africa's largest refugee population at over 1.2 million people, including 950,000 from South Sudan, 227,000 from the DRC and 45,000 from Burundi.

The last decade has seen a proliferation of defence agreements between Uganda and its neighbours and more distant allies. These include Rwanda in 2012 and 2014, Kenya in 2014, South Sudan in 2014,

Ethiopia in 2015, Qatar in 2017 and a still-to-be-signed agreement with Tanzania in 2017. In addition, Uganda has a well-developed security relationship with Djibouti and Somalia, through their engagement in the African Union Mission in Somalia (AMISOM). Uganda's leading role in AMISOM means that the country has received extensive external assistance, notably from the United States through the Africa Contingency Operations Training and Assistance (ACOTA) programme, from the United Kingdom through the Africa Conflict Prevention Pool (now renamed the Conflict, Stability and Security Fund (CSSF)) and from the European Union through the EU Training Mission (EUTM) for Somalia, which was based at Bihanga Camp in Uganda before it moved to the Somali capital, Mogadishu. In addition, like many of its neighbours, Uganda has become a major customer for Chinese defence sales.

Regional deployments

The ongoing civil war in South Sudan prompted an early response from Uganda, with the deployment of troops to Bor in 2013–14 in order to prevent the collapse of the ruling Sudan People's Liberation Movement (SPLM). Whether this was done to protect Ugandan nationals in South Sudan, or to preserve political and personal relationships between the two regimes and leaders, it had the effect of keeping the SPLM in power in South Sudan.

However, steadily increasing foreign and regional security engagement through the United Nations Mission in South Sudan (UNMISS) and, from summer 2017, the first deployment of the long-awaited Intergovernmental Authority on Development (IGAD) Regional Protection Force (comprising Ethiopia, Kenya and Rwanda) has limited Uganda's military freedom of action in South Sudan.

Up to 2,000 Uganda People's Defence Force (UPDF) troops from the African Union Regional Cooperation Initiative against the Lord's Resistance Army (RCI–LRA) have been withdrawn. The move was carried out in concert with the withdrawal of US special forces that had been deployed under *Operation Observant Compass*, established by the Obama administration in 2013. This withdrawal followed the decision by South Sudan to stop hosting the headquarters of the RCI. The move again limited the UPDF's external operations, leaving the focus of these on the UPDF's AMISOM contributions.

The UPDF has withdrawn almost all its troops from UN operations, except missions related to Somalia. It maintains a 530-strong UN guard unit in Somalia, essentially based at Mogadishu airport and mandated to protect UN personnel and installations. The other UPDF UN peacekeeping contingent is in UNMISS, again highlighting the now local focus of UPDF operations.

Internal threats

Amongst Uganda's internal security threats, the rebel Allied Democratic Forces (ADF) rank highest. This group was formerly based in western Uganda, and is now largely in the eastern DRC, particularly North Kivu. It was reported in April 2013 that the ADF had started a recruitment campaign in Kampala and other parts of the country. The DRC government, citing civil-society groups in North Kivu, has claimed that al-Shabaab fighters from Somalia are collaborating with the ADF. Given the Islamist nature of the ADF and al-Shabaab's focus on Uganda, as a result of UPDF operations in Somalia, this is a plausible link. Similar claims of al-Shabaab links with Boko Haram have been made and substantiated in the past.

In August 2016, Ugandan President Yoweri Museveni and DRC President Joseph Kabila announced a coordinated military strategy against the ADF. The UPDF continues to closely coordinate with the DRC armed forces on their side of the border, but, as of summer 2017, UPDF operations appeared to be limited to liaison and security duties in the border areas. Should the ADF present a significant threat or target in the future, relations between the DRC and Uganda are such that some form of coordinated response is possible, but a major cross-border operation between the two seems unlikely.

Operational capability

Uganda's purchase of six Su-30 *Flanker* fighter aircraft from Russia in 2011–12, at a cost of US$740m, reflects Uganda's need to be able to influence the security situation around its new oil-exploration and -exploitation activities in the Lake Albert region. The purchase is said by Uganda to be a purely defensive acquisition, but its newly enhanced ability to project power on and across its eastern border with the DRC may have been a factor in Kinshasa's recent acquisition of 25 modernised T-64BV-1 main battle tanks from Ukraine. It is unclear where else the DRC would need to deploy such assets.

The political and defence commitment to engaging in Somalia has also brought a number of significant

442 THE MILITARY BALANCE 2018

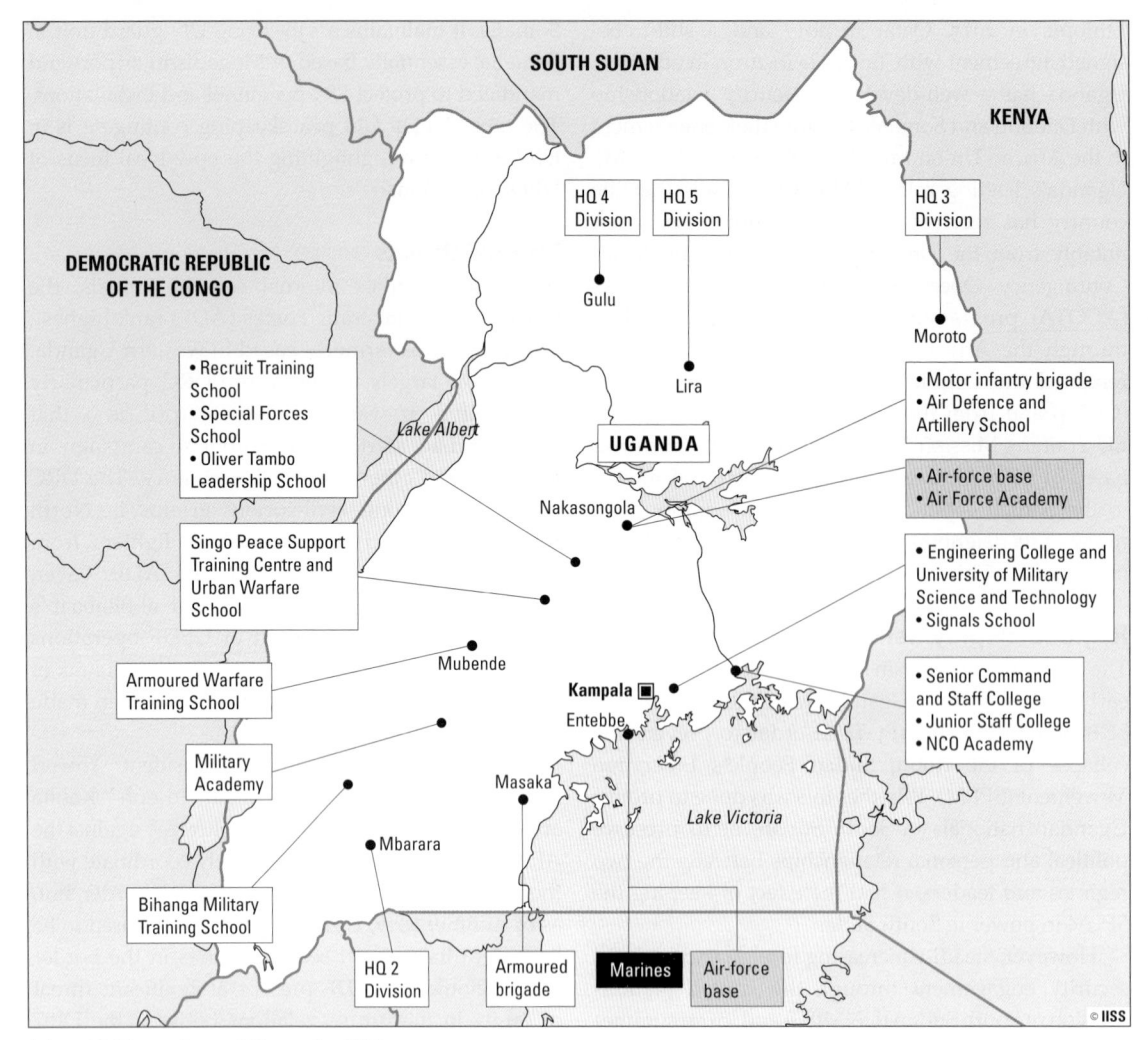

Map 13 **Uganda: military facilities**

improvements in UPDF equipment and capabilities from international partners, in particular in areas that have relevance to the UPDF's internal-security and border-protection roles. A case in point is the US Army's provision of five Bell *Huey* II helicopters, in a programme valued at US$35m. (These aircraft were due to be delivered by the end of 2017.) The UPDF currently has only limited helicopter assets for a country in which military deployment by road can be slow and dangerous. Although these helicopters are intended to improve the delivery of supplies and personnel to Uganda's operations in Somalia, their presence will have a knock-on effect throughout the UPDF system, maturing and enhancing capabilities such as air-force maintenance and servicing. The air force's small size and the central location of its main base at Nakasongola, north of Kampala, mean that improvements could in time have an effect throughout the force.

For the Ugandan Army and the Marines – the latter a small, 400-strong capability based on Lake Victoria but deployed in Somalia since 2008 – training such as that provided by the US ACOTA programme, the US AFRICOM *Cutlass Express* and *Flintlock* exercises, the UK CSSF and the EUTM assistance to Uganda in training the Somali National Army has changed the nature of service in the UPDF. Every UPDF soldier is familiar with engaging and training with international partners and allies in the fight against extremism. Although focused on Somalia, this professionalisation of training has become the norm within the Ugandan system. A very comprehensive series of military schools, largely based on the UK model, has been established and is functioning well.

The leaderships of the principal schools, for example the Senior and Junior Staff Colleges and the Military Academy, have been selected for their extensive command and staff experience in AMISOM and with the UN. This has resulted in a well-developed system of training and education, which has itself had an effect upon recruitment and retention and on the standing of the UPDF as a national institution.

The past ten years of operations in Somalia have brought a maturity and a level of international experience to the UPDF that is unusual in an African setting for such a small army (only 45,000 strong). Continuous international support to the UPDF, support that is improving in quantity and quality, has seen the UPDF develop into one of Africa's most capable forces, particularly on land. Operations in Somalia have taught the UPDF the value of night-vision aids, body armour, mine-protected vehicles, counter-improvised-explosive-device systems and unmanned aerial vehicles (UAVs). The provision of these items has come in tandem with training in their use, both in terms of doctrine, tactics, techniques and procedures, and in planning and conducting effective, intelligence-led counter-insurgency operations. The UPDF is now the key driver of the AU's AMISOM lessons-identified/-learned process. Given the international reliance on Uganda as the backbone of AMISOM, the UPDF and its international partners probably assimilate and act on the lessons from Somalia better than any other AMISOM contributor.

This ten-year period of development and maturation has put Uganda in an advantageous position for future engagement in international missions, when the UPDF's commitment to Somalia is reduced. These operations may come under the auspices of the African Union under its African Standby Force structure, such as the Rapid Deployment Capability in the regional Eastern African Standby Force, or the stopgap African Capacity for Immediate Response to Crises initiated in 2013, of which Uganda was a founding member. Or they may come under the UN or in coalitions of the willing, perhaps even outside Africa. It remains to be seen how the AU, EU and UN intend to draw down the AMISOM/Somalia operations, but one of their legacies will be to leave a deployable and effective regional capability in the form of the UPDF.

Defence economics

According to the IMF, Uganda's economy grew at a rate of 2.3% in 2016. However, since then the country has experienced a drought, leading to lower agricultural output. In response, the IMF revised its 2017 growth estimate downwards, from 5.0% to 4.4%.

In the next ten years, oil revenues and taxes are expected to become a larger source of government funding. However, lower oil prices, combined with protracted negotiations and legal disputes between the Ugandan government and oil companies, may prove a stumbling block to further exploration and development. In addition, instability in South Sudan has led to a sharp increase in Sudanese refugees and has disrupted Uganda's main export market.

Uganda's budget is dominated by energy- and road-infrastructure spending, while relying on donor support for long-term drivers of growth, including agriculture, health and education. The largest infrastructure projects are externally financed through low-interest concessional loans; debt servicing for these loans is expected to increase and to absorb an increasing proportion of available foreign exchange in the coming five years.

In this increasingly unfavourable economic outlook, defence expenditure declined from Ush1.64 trillion (US$478m) in 2016 to Ush1.58trn (US$436m) in 2017. The government planned a further decline in 2018 to Ush1.12trn (estimated at US$299m). The defence budget is expected to rise again only in 2019, to Ush1.29trn (estimated at US$336m).

While the bulk of the UPDF is relatively cheap to accommodate, pay, train and equip, the increasing appetite and need for sophisticated capabilities, highlighted by the lessons learned from AMISOM, and developments and acquisitions by regional competitors such as the DRC, Ethiopia and Kenya, will continue. Some of this will be met by donors and allies in the context of AMISOM/Somalia, as shown by the US provision of armoured personnel carriers, helicopters and UAVs, while others, such as new aircraft not committed to operations in Somalia, will have to be funded from the domestic defence budget.

Engagement in UN peacekeeping operations normally brings considerable revenues directly into the national defence budget. However, relatively few Ugandan troops are paid via this income stream. Meanwhile, 80% of the EU's reimbursement for AMISOM operations, through the EU's Africa Peace Facility, goes directly to the troops, without passing through the national defence budget. This may be good for recruitment and retention, but allows little flexibility for the UPDF.

Defence industry

Uganda's defence industry, in the form of the National Enterprise Corporation (NEC), was established in 1989 to serve as the industrial and commercial arm of the defence ministry and the UPDF, and to produce goods and services beneficial to the defence forces and the general public. In this regard, it was similar to the Ethiopian Defence Industry Sector established in the same period, and has to an extent developed in the same way as a national industry serving not only defence but also a wider civil requirement. In the Ugandan case in particular, this framework was intended to directly support the UPDF with a view to redeploying and providing employment to soldiers who were involved in the 1978–79 liberation war, and to produce goods and services for the army, with profits being used to improve the welfare of soldiers. In 1995, the Ugandan parliament mandated the NEC to produce goods and services for the UPDF's consumption.

The corporation now consists of five subsidiaries: NEC Construction Works and Engineering, Luwero Industries, NEC Tractor Hire Scheme and NEC Farm Katonga, plus a new subsidiary, NEC Uzima Ltd, involved in the production of mineral water in a factory located in Kakiri barracks, Wakiso district. In addition, the NEC has developed two joint ventures with foreign companies, including UgIran Company Limited, which was founded in 2008 in Kampala (and is 60% Iranian- and 40% Ugandan-owned) to manufacture and assemble tractors using licensed design kits delivered from the Iran Tractor Manufacturing Company's Iranian factories.

Of the NEC's subsidiaries, Luwero Industries, established in 1992, is the most important provider of domestic defence production and repair. The factory at Nakasongola produces ammunition and low-velocity armour-piercing and anti-personnel grenades, and reportedly has the capacity to rebuild 60 varying types of infantry fighting vehicles, 200 soft-skin vehicles, 20,000 small-calibre rifles and 300 large-calibre weapons per year. Luwero Industries is the main manufacturer of spare parts for UPDF equipment.

Given that the local defence sector lacks technologically advanced capabilities, Ugandan defence exports will remain negligible, and virtually all new Ugandan defence procurements will continue to be sourced from abroad. However, Uganda sees Luwero Industries as a centre of excellence in the East African Community, and it has established regional partnerships with defence industries in other IGAD member states. Ethiopia, Kenya and Sudan, when political conditions permit, offer opportunities for regional defence-industry cooperation. For example, Ethiopia has undertaken servicing work on Ugandan aircraft and refurbished Ugandan large-calibre ammunition in the past.

Given the economic constraints outlined above, Uganda's defence industry is likely to grow only slowly in the coming five years. However, regional defence industries, when taken as a whole, are beginning to amount to a considerable and comprehensive, if not yet technologically leading-edge, capability. IGAD nations should be expected to continue to build on the synergy offered by this cluster, and to fulfil each other's niche requirements when possible.

Angola ANG

New Angolan Kwanza AOA		2016	2017	2018
GDP	AOA	15.6tr	20.6tr	
	US$	95.3bn	124bn	
per capita	US$	3,485	4,401	
Growth	%	-0.7	1.5	
Inflation	%	32.4	30.9	
Def bdgt	AOA	486bn	536bn	
	US$	2.97bn	3.23bn	
USD1=AOA		163.59	165.89	

Population 29,310,273

Ethnic groups: Ovimbundu 37%; Kimbundu 25%; Bakongo 13%

Age	0–14	15–19	20–24	25–29	30–64	65 plus
Male	23.0%	4.9%	4.0%	3.3%	11.5%	1.0%
Female	24.2%	5.1%	4.3%	3.7%	12.7%	1.4%

Capabilities

The armed forces' role is to ensure sovereignty and territorial integrity, while maritime security and the protection of offshore resources is an increasing focus. Angola held defence discussions with South Korea in late 2016, with the focus on the potential for naval cooperation. A main security concern comes from secessionists in the Cabinda enclave. Force health and education have been investment priorities. Improving the military-logistics system has also been identified as a key requirement; however, it is not clear that significant improvements have been made. The armed forces train regularly and in the past year have participated in multinational exercises with the US and others, including *Obangame Express 2017*. Angola also participated in the *Utulivu Africa* III with the ACIRC. On paper, the army and air force constitute a significant force, but equipment availability and serviceability remain questionable; nonetheless, Angola is the only state in the region with strategic-airlift capacity in the form of Il-76s. In September 2017 it began to take delivery of the first of 12 second-hand Su-30K *Flanker* fighter aircraft, which will improve its multi-role air capability. There are plans to modernise equipment, particularly that associated with the maritime-security capability, in light of security concerns in the Gulf of Guinea, but these ambitions have been hit by the fall in oil prices.

ACTIVE 107,000 (Army 100,000 Navy 1,000 Air 6,000) Paramilitary 10,000

ORGANISATIONS BY SERVICE

Army 100,000

FORCES BY ROLE
MANOEUVRE
  Armoured
  1 tk bde
  Light
  1 SF bde
  1 (1st) div (1 mot inf bde, 2 inf bde)
  1 (2nd) div (3 mot inf bde, 3 inf bde, 1 arty regt)
  1 (3rd) div (2 mot inf bde, 3 inf bde)
  1 (4th) div (1 tk regt, 5 mot inf bde, 2 inf bde, 1 engr bde)
  1 (5th) div (2 inf bde)
  1 (6th) div (1 mot inf bde, 2 inf bde, 1 engr bde)
COMBAT SUPPORT
  Some engr units
COMBAT SERVICE SUPPORT
  Some log units
EQUIPMENT BY TYPE†
ARMOURED FIGHTING VEHICLES
  MBT 300: ε200 T-54/T-55; 50 T-62; 50 T-72
  LT TK 10 PT-76
  ASLT 3+ PTL-02 *Assaulter*
  RECCE 600 BRDM-2
  IFV 250 BMP-1/BMP-2
  APC 246
    APC (T) 31 MT-LB
    APC (W) 170+: ε170 BTR-152/BTR-60/BTR-80; WZ-551 (CP)
  PPV 45 *Casspir* NG2000
  ABCV BMD-3
ENGINEERING & MAINTENANCE VEHICLES
  ARV T-54/T-55
  MW *Bozena*
ARTILLERY 1,408+
  SP 16+: **122mm** 2S1 *Gvozdika*; **152mm** 4 2S3 *Akatsiya*; **203mm** 12 2S7 *Pion*
  TOWED 552: **122mm** 500 D-30; **130mm** 48 M-46; **152mm** 4 D-20
  MRL 90+: **122mm** 90: 50 BM-21 *Grad*; 40 RM-70; **240mm** BM-24
  MOR 750: **82mm** 250; **120mm** 500
ANTI-TANK/ANTI-INFRASTRUCTURE
  MSL • MANPATS 9K11 (AT-3 *Sagger*)
  RCL 500: 400 **82mm** B-10/**107mm** B-11†; **106mm** 100†
  GUNS • SP 100mm SU-100†
AIR DEFENCE
  SAM • Point-defence 9K32 *Strela*-2 (SA-7 *Grail*)‡; 9K36 *Strela*-3 (SA-14 *Gremlin*); 9K310 *Igla*-1 (SA-16 *Gimlet*)
  GUNS
    SP 23mm ZSU-23-4
    TOWED 450+: **14.5mm** ZPU-4; **23mm** ZU-23-2; **37mm** M-1939; **57mm** S-60

Navy ε1,000

EQUIPMENT BY TYPE
PATROL AND COASTAL COMBATANTS 21
  PCO 2 *Ngola Kiluange* with 1 hel landing platform (Ministry of Fisheries)
  PCC 5 *Rei Bula Matadi* (Ministry of Fisheries)
  PBF 5 PVC-170
  PB 9: 4 *Mandume*; 5 *Comandante Imperial Santana* (Ministry of Fisheries)

Coastal Defence

EQUIPMENT BY TYPE
COASTAL DEFENCE • AShM 4K44 *Utyos* (SS-C-1B *Sepal* – at Luanda)

Air Force/Air Defence 6,000

FORCES BY ROLE
FIGHTER
  1 sqn with MiG-21bis/MF *Fishbed*
  1 sqn with Su-27/Su-27UB/Su-30K *Flanker*
FIGHTER/GROUND ATTACK
  1 sqn with MiG-23BN/ML/UB *Flogger*
  1 sqn with Su-22 *Fitter* D
  1 sqn with Su-25 *Frogfoot*
MARITIME PATROL
  1 sqn with F-27-200 MPA; C-212 *Aviocar*
TRANSPORT
  3 sqn with An-12 *Cub*; An-26 *Curl*; An-32 *Cline*; An-72 *Coaler*; BN-2A *Islander*; C-212 *Aviocar*; Do-28D *Skyservant*; EMB-135BJ *Legacy* 600 (VIP); Il-76TD *Candid*
TRAINING
  1 sqn with Cessna 172K/R
  1 sqn with EMB-312 *Tucano*
  1 sqn with L-29 *Delfin*; L-39 *Albatros*
  1 sqn with PC-7 *Turbo Trainer*; PC-9*
  1 sqn with Z-142
ATTACK HELICOPTER
  2 sqn with Mi-24/Mi-35 *Hind*; SA342M *Gazelle* (with HOT)
TRANSPORT HELICOPTER
  2 sqn with AS565; SA316 *Alouette* III (IAR-316) (trg)
  1 sqn with Bell 212
  1 sqn with Mi-8 *Hip*; Mi-17 *Hip* H
  1 sqn with Mi-171Sh
AIR DEFENCE
  5 bn/10 bty with S-125 *Pechora* (SA-3 *Goa*); 9K35 *Strela*-10 (SA-13 *Gopher*)†; 2K12 *Kub* (SA-6 *Gainful*); 9K33 *Osa* (SA-8 *Gecko*); 9K31 *Strela*-1 (SA-9 *Gaskin*); S-75M *Volkhov* (SA-2 *Guideline*)

EQUIPMENT BY TYPE†
AIRCRAFT 88 combat capable
  FTR 26: 6 Su-27/Su-27UB *Flanker*; 2 Su-30K *Flanker*; 18 MiG-23ML *Flogger*
  FGA 42+: 20 MiG-21bis/MF *Fishbed*; 8 MiG-23BN/UB *Flogger*; 13 Su-22 *Fitter* D; 1+ Su-24 *Fencer*
  ATK 10: 8 Su-25 *Frogfoot*; 2 Su-25UB *Frogfoot*
  ELINT 1 B-707
  TPT 56: **Heavy** 4 Il-76TD *Candid*; **Medium** 6 An-12 *Cub*; **Light** 46: 12 An-26 *Curl*; 2 An-32 *Cline*; 8 An-72 *Coaler*; 8 BN-2A *Islander*; 2 C-212; 5 Cessna 172K; 6 Cessna 172R; 1 Do-28D *Skyservant*; 1 EMB-135BJ *Legacy* 600 (VIP); 1 Yak-40
  TRG 42: 13 EMB-312 *Tucano*; 6 EMB-314 *Super Tucano**; 6 L-29 *Delfin*; 2 L-39C *Albatros*; 5 PC-7 *Turbo Trainer*; 4 PC-9*; 6 Z-142
HELICOPTERS
  ATK 56: 34 Mi-24 *Hind*; 22 Mi-35 *Hind*
  MRH 25: 8 AS565 *Panther*; 9 SA316 *Alouette* III (IAR-316) (incl trg); 8 SA342M *Gazelle*
  MRH/TPT 35: 27 Mi-8 *Hip*/Mi-17 *Hip* H; 8 Mi-171Sh *Terminator*
  TPT • Light 8 Bell 212
AIR DEFENCE • SAM 122
  Medium-range 40 S-75M *Volkhov* (SA-2 *Guideline*)‡

Short-range 37: 25 2K12 *Kub* (SA-6 *Gainful*); 12 S-125 *Pechora* (SA-3 *Goa*)
Point-defence 45: 10 9K35 *Strela*-10 (SA-13 *Gopher*)†; 15 9K33 *Osa* (SA-8 *Gecko*); 20 9K31 *Strela*-1 (SA-9 *Gaskin*)
AIR-LAUNCHED MISSILES
  AAM • IR R-3 (AA-2 *Atoll*)‡; R-60 (AA-8 *Aphid*); R-73 (AA-11 *Archer*); **IR/SARH** R-23/24 (AA-7 *Apex*)‡; R-27 (AA-10 *Alamo*)
  ASM AT-2 *Swatter*; HOT
  ARM Kh-28 (AS-9 *Kyle*)

Paramilitary 10,000

Rapid-Reaction Police 10,000

Benin BEN

CFA Franc BCEAO fr		2016	2017	2018
GDP	fr	5.08tr	5.47tr	
	US$	8.58bn	9.41bn	
per capita	US$	771	826	
Growth	%	4.0	5.4	
Inflation	%	-0.8	2.0	
Def bdgt	fr	58.2bn	67.9bn	
	US$	98m	117m	
US$1=fr		592.73	581.55	

Population 11,038,805

Age	0–14	15–19	20–24	25–29	30–64	65 plus
Male	21.8%	5.6%	4.7%	3.8%	13.0%	1.1%
Female	20.8%	5.4%	4.6%	3.8%	13.3%	1.7%

Capabilities

The country's small armed forces mainly focus on border and internal security, as well as combating illicit trafficking. Benin took steps to increase border patrols and security, following increased concern over the threat from Boko Haram and al-Qaeda in the Islamic Maghreb. Maritime security is a priority in light of continuing piracy in the Gulf of Guinea. Benin's small navy has been trying to bolster its anti-piracy capability by acquiring high-speed craft. The air force is developing a surveillance role. The army and national police have received training from the US to boost border-surveillance capacity, while French forces based in Senegal are also heavily involved in similar assistance. As part of the France–Benin military-cooperation agreement, France trained personnel from the Military Engineering corps in 2017. Benin contributes 750 troops to the Multi-National Joint Task Force fighting Boko Haram. In April 2017, Benin joined the counter-Boko Haram *Unified Focus* tabletop exercise. The government is looking to merge the police and gendarmerie in 2018.

ACTIVE 7,250 (Army 6,500 Navy 500 Air 250)
Paramilitary 2,500
Conscript liability 18 months (selective)

ORGANISATIONS BY SERVICE

Army 6,500
FORCES BY ROLE
MANOEUVRE
  Armoured
   2 armd sqn
  Light
   1 (rapid reaction) mot inf bn
   8 inf bn
  Air Manoeuvre
   1 AB bn
COMBAT SUPPORT
  2 arty bn
  1 engr bn
  1 sigs bn
COMBAT SERVICE SUPPORT
  1 log bn
  1 spt bn
EQUIPMENT BY TYPE
ARMOURED FIGHTING VEHICLES
  LT TK 18 PT-76†
  RECCE 34: 3 AML-90; 14 BRDM-2; 7 M8; 10 VBL
  APC 34
     APC (T) 22 M113
     PPV 12: 2 *Bastion* APC; 10 *Casspir* NG
ARTILLERY 16+
  TOWED 105mm 16: 12 L118 Light Gun; 4 M101
  MOR 81mm some; **120mm** some

Navy ε500
EQUIPMENT BY TYPE
PATROL AND COASTAL COMBATANTS
  PB 6: 2 *Matelot Brice Kpomasse* (ex-PRC); 3 FPB 98; 1 27m (PRC)

Air Force 250
EQUIPMENT BY TYPE
AIRCRAFT
  TPT 3: **Light** 1 DHC-6 *Twin Otter*†; **PAX** 2: 1 B-727; 1 HS-748†
  TRG 2 LH-10 *Ellipse*
HELICOPTERS
  TPT • **Light** 5: 4 AW109BA; 1 AS350B *Ecureuil*†

Paramilitary 2,500

Gendarmerie 2,500
FORCES BY ROLE
MANOEUVRE
  Other
   4 (mobile) paramilitary coy

DEPLOYMENT

CENTRAL AFRICAN REPUBLIC
UN • MINUSCA 5; 3 obs

CHAD
Lake Chad Basin Commission • MNJTF 150

DEMOCRATIC REPUBLIC OF THE CONGO
UN • MONUSCO 453; 5 obs; 1 inf bn(-)

LIBERIA
UN • UNMIL 1 obs

MALI
UN • MINUSMA 260; 2 obs; 1 mech inf coy(+)

SOUTH SUDAN
UN • UNMISS 2; 1 obs

SUDAN
UN • UNISFA 2 obs

Botswana BWA

Botswana Pula P		2016	2017	2018
GDP	P	170bn	180bn	
	US$	15.6bn	16.7bn	
per capita	US$	7,227	7,674	
Growth	%	4.3	4.5	
Inflation	%	2.8	3.7	
Def bdgt [a]	P	6.11bn	5.30bn	
	US$	561m	492m	
US$1=P		10.90	10.78	

[a] Defence, justice and security budget

Population   2,214,858

Age	0–14	15–19	20–24	25–29	30–64	65 plus
Male	16.1%	4.7%	4.6%	4.1%	16.3%	2.3%
Female	15.8%	4.8%	4.7%	4.5%	18.9%	3.0%

Capabilities

Key tasks for the Botswana Defence Force (BDF) include ensuring territorial integrity, coupled with domestic tasks such as anti-poaching, and there is a history of involvement in peacekeeping operations. Botswana has a good relationship with the US and regularly sends its officers to train there. Military forces also train with other African nations, including taking part in the *Blue Kunene 2017* humanitarian-aid and disaster-relief exercise. The air force is looking to replace its ageing F-5 fighter aircraft, with the Swedish *Gripen* and South Korean FA-50 reportedly being considered. In January 2017, Botswana and South Korea signed a military-cooperation umbrella agreement. Delivery of short-range ground-based air-defence systems from MBDA may also have begun during 2017. The replacement of the F-5, when combined with improved ground-based air defences, would enhance Botswana's ability to defend its own air space. The latest BDF commander, when appointed in September 2016, identified priorities including improving conditions of service, a focus on overhauling retirement ages and boosting capability. The BDF has also been working on a doctrine that is believed to be heavily influenced by US concepts and practice. Local reports suggest a limited capacity in armoured-vehicle maintenance. Growing relations with Beijing have seen some military personnel travel to China for training. The operations centre for the SADC Standby Force is located in Gaborone. Botswana holds biannual exercises with Namibia; the most recent was in August 2016 and practised joint peacekeeping missions and other support operations for the SADC.

ACTIVE 9,000 (Army 8,500 Air 500)

ORGANISATIONS BY SERVICE

Army 8,500
FORCES BY ROLE
MANOEUVRE
  Armoured
  1 armd bde(-)
  Light
  2 inf bde (1 armd recce regt, 4 inf bn, 1 cdo unit, 1 engr regt, 1 log bn, 2 ADA regt)
COMBAT SUPPORT
  1 arty bde
  1 engr coy
  1 sigs coy
COMBAT SERVICE SUPPORT
  1 log gp
AIR DEFENCE
  1 AD bde(-)
EQUIPMENT BY TYPE
ARMOURED FIGHTING VEHICLES
  LT TK 45: ε20 SK-105 *Kuerassier*; 25 FV101 *Scorpion*
  RECCE 72+: RAM-V-1; ε8 RAM-V-2; 64 VBL
  APC • APC (W) 145: 50 BTR-60; 50 LAV-150 *Commando* (some with 90mm gun); 45 MOWAG *Piranha* III
  AUV 6 FV103 *Spartan*
ENGINEERING & MAINTENANCE VEHICLES
  ARV 2 *Greif*; M578
  MW *Aardvark* Mk2
ANTI-TANK/ANTI-INFRASTRUCTURE
  MSL
    SP V-150 TOW
    MANPATS TOW
  RCL 84mm *Carl Gustav*
ARTILLERY 78
  TOWED 30: **105mm** 18: 12 L118 Light Gun; 6 Model 56 pack howitzer; **155mm** 12 Soltam
  MRL 122mm 20 APRA-40
  MOR 28: **81mm** 22; **120mm** 6 M-43
AIR DEFENCE
  SAM • Point-defence *Javelin*; 9K310 *Igla*-1 (SA-16 *Gimlet*); 9K32 *Strela*-2 (SA-7 *Grail*)‡
  GUNS • TOWED 20mm 7 M167 *Vulcan*

Air Wing 500
FORCES BY ROLE
FIGHTER/GROUND ATTACK
  1 sqn with F-5A *Freedom Fighter*; F-5D *Tiger* II
ISR
  1 sqn with O-2 *Skymaster*

TRANSPORT
  2 sqn with BD-700 *Global Express*; BN-2A/B *Defender**; Beech 200 *Super King Air* (VIP); C-130B *Hercules*; C-212-300 *Aviocar*; CN-235M-100; Do-328-110 (VIP)
TRAINING
  1 sqn with PC-7 MkII *Turbo Trainer**
TRANSPORT HELICOPTER
  1 sqn with AS350B *Ecureuil*; Bell 412EP/SP *Twin Huey*; EC225LP *Super Puma*
EQUIPMENT BY TYPE
AIRCRAFT 29 combat capable
  FTR 14: 9 F-5A *Freedom Fighter*; 5 F-5D *Tiger* II
  ISR 5 O-2 *Skymaster*
  TPT 19: **Medium** 3 C-130B *Hercules*; **Light** 15: 4 BN-2 *Defender**; 6 BN-2B *Defender**; 1 Beech 200 *King Air* (VIP); 1 C-212-300 *Aviocar*; 2 CN-235M-100; 1 Do-328-110 (VIP); **PAX** 1 BD700 *Global Express*
  TRG 5 PC-7 MkII *Turbo Trainer**
HELICOPTERS
  MRH 7: 2 Bell 412EP *Twin Huey*; 5 Bell 412SP *Twin Huey*
  TPT 9: **Medium** 1 EC225LP *Super Puma*; **Light** 8 AS350B *Ecureuil*

Burkina Faso BFA

CFA Franc BCEAO fr		2016	2017	2018
GDP	fr	7.19tr	7.80tr	
	US$	12.1bn	13.2bn	
per capita	US$	658	696	
Growth	%	5.9	6.4	
Inflation	%	-0.2	1.5	
Def bdgt	fr	88.6bn	112bn	
	US$	150m	189m	
US$1=fr		592.73	591.28	

Population 20,107,509

Age	0–14	15–19	20–24	25–29	30–64	65 plus
Male	22.5%	5.4%	4.6%	3.8%	12.5%	0.9%
Female	22.4%	5.4%	4.6%	3.8%	12.5%	1.5%

Capabilities

In August 2017, a terrorist attack in Ouagadougou underscored the country's continuing security challenges, with the conflict in Mali spilling out into Burkina Faso. The country is participating in the G-5 Sahel initiative supported by European countries, notably France and Germany. As part of this, France has supplied armed pick-up trucks. The al-Qaeda in the Islamic Maghreb threat has led Ouagadougou to refocus its military efforts to the north. There is cooperation with France and Mali aimed at tackling the Islamist threat, as seen in *Operation Panga* in April 2017, in the area straddling the border shared by Burkina Faso and Mali. President Kaboré has stated that overhauling the army is a priority, in order to ensure that it is independent, apolitical and more effective, particularly in the counter-terrorism role. However, the armed forces have struggled with funding issues, which is reflected in the equipment inventory. Air-force rotary-wing capacity is developing, with the arrival of ex-Taiwanese UH-1 helicopters, for which the US is providing training, and an order for Mi-171Sh helicopters from Russia. The army has deployed personnel on a range of UN peacekeeping operations, including in Mali. But in order to help deal with domestic-security challenges, in 2017 Burkina Faso began to withdraw its forces deployed to the UN mission in Darfur.

ACTIVE 11,200 (Army 6,400 Air 600 Gendarmerie 4,200) Paramilitary 250

ORGANISATIONS BY SERVICE

Army 6,400

Three military regions. In 2011, several regiments were disbanded and merged into other formations, including the new 24th and 34th *régiments interarmes*

FORCES BY ROLE
MANOEUVRE
  Mechanised
    1 cbd arms regt
  Light
    1 cbd arms regt
    6 inf regt
  Air Manoeuvre
    1 AB regt (1 CT coy)
COMBAT SUPPORT
  1 arty bn (2 arty tp)
  1 engr bn

EQUIPMENT BY TYPE
ARMOURED FIGHTING VEHICLES
  RECCE 91+: 19 AML-60/AML-90; 8+ *Bastion Patsas*; 24 EE-9 *Cascavel*; 30 *Ferret*; 2 M20; 8 M8
  APC 44+
    APC (W) 13+: 13 Panhard M3; Some *Bastion* APC
    PPV 31 *Puma* M26-15
ANTI-TANK/ANTI-INFRASTRUCTURE
  RCL 75mm Type-52 (M20); **84mm** *Carl Gustav*
ARTILLERY 50+
  TOWED 14: **105mm** 8 M101; **122mm** 6
  MRL 9: **107mm** ɛ4 Type-63; **122mm** 5 APR-40
  MOR 27+: **81mm** Brandt; **82mm** 15; **120mm** 12
AIR DEFENCE
  SAM • Point-defence 9K32 *Strela*-2 (SA-7 *Grail*)‡
  GUNS • TOWED 42: **14.5mm** 30 ZPU; **20mm** 12 TCM-20

Air Force 600

FORCES BY ROLE
GROUND ATTACK/TRAINING
  1 sqn with SF-260WL *Warrior**; Embraer EMB-314 *Super Tucano**
TRANSPORT
  1 sqn with AT-802 *Air Tractor*; B-727 (VIP); Beech 200 *King Air*; CN235-220; PA-34 *Seneca*
ATTACK/TRANSPORT HELICOPTER
  1 sqn with AS350 *Ecureuil*; Mi-8 *Hip*; Mi-17 *Hip* H; Mi-35 *Hind*

EQUIPMENT BY TYPE
AIRCRAFT 5 combat capable
  ISR 1 DA42M (reported)
  TPT 9: **Light** 8: 1 AT-802 *Air Tractor*; 2 Beech 200 *King Air*; 1 CN235-220; 1 PA-34 *Seneca*; 3 *Tetras*; **PAX** 1 B-727 (VIP)
  TRG 5: 3 EMB-314 *Super Tucano**; 2 SF-260WL *Warrior**
HELICOPTERS
  ATK 2 Mi-35 *Hind*
  MRH 3: 2 Mi-17 *Hip* H; 1 AW139
  TPT 4: **Medium** 1 Mi-8 *Hip*; **Light** 3: 1 AS350 *Ecureuil*; 2 UH-1H *Huey*

Gendarmerie 4,200

Paramilitary 250

  People's Militia (R) 45,000 reservists (trained)

  Security Company 250

DEPLOYMENT

CENTRAL AFRICAN REPUBLIC
UN • MINUSCA 7; 1 obs

DEMOCRATIC REPUBLIC OF THE CONGO
UN • MONUSCO 7 obs

MALI
UN • MINUSMA 1,716; 2 inf bn

SUDAN
UN • UNAMID 73; 4 obs
UN • UNISFA 1 obs

FOREIGN FORCES
France *Operation Barkhane* 250; 1 SF gp

Burundi BDI

Burundi Franc fr		2016	2017	2018
GDP	fr	5.19tr	5.87tr	
	US$	3.14bn	3.39bn	
per capita	US$	325	343	
Growth	%	-1.04	0.0	
Inflation	%	5.5	18.0	
Def bdgt	fr	110bn	110bn	
	US$	66m	63m	
US$1=fr		1,654.66	1,730.71	

Population 11,466,756

Ethnic groups: Hutu 85%; Tutsi 14%

Age	0–14	15–19	20–24	25–29	30–64	65 plus
Male	22.9%	5.2%	4.3%	3.7%	12.4%	1.1%
Female	22.6%	5.2%	4.4%	3.7%	12.7%	1.5%

Capabilities

Burundi's armed forces retain a limited capability to deploy externally, and maintain a deployment to the AMISOM mission in Somalia. In 2015, the cohesiveness of the armed forces and the wider security and intelligence machinery was tested by the attempted coup against incumbent President Nkurunziza. Previous military training activity with international partners largely stalled in 2015 as a result of this situation. Intermittent violence, and targeted attacks, continue in the country, particularly in urban areas, and refugee flows continue to neighbouring countries. Notwithstanding the effect on the armed forces of the coup attempt and its aftermath, they have benefited from this training support as well as from their recent deployments, including to the UN mission in the CAR and to AMISOM, where they have gained valuable combat experience and specialist military skills. Burundi suffered combat losses in Somalia in 2017, and rotated a new battalion into the AMISOM deployment in August. A dispute over funding for Burundi's AMISOM mission (where EU concern over human-rights issues meant that Brussels reportedly routed these payments through the AU) was seemingly resolved in early 2017, with the EU now disbursing funds to a private bank in Burundi. Other foreign donors have curtailed or cut aid following the 2015 election result.

ACTIVE 30,050 (Army 30,000 Navy 50) **Paramilitary 21,000**

DDR efforts continue, while activities directed at professionalising the security forces have taken place, some sponsored by BNUB, the UN mission

ORGANISATIONS BY SERVICE

Army 30,000
FORCES BY ROLE
MANOEUVRE
  Mechanised
  2 lt armd bn (sqn)
  Light
  7 inf bn
  Some indep inf coy
COMBAT SUPPORT
  1 arty bn
  1 engr bn
AIR DEFENCE
  1 AD bn

Reserves
FORCES BY ROLE
MANOEUVRE
  Light
  10 inf bn (reported)

EQUIPMENT BY TYPE
ARMOURED FIGHTING VEHICLES
  RECCE 55: 6 AML-60; 12 AML-90; 30 BRDM-2; 7 S52 *Shorland*
  APC 82
    APC (W) 60: 20 BTR-40; 10 BTR-80; 9 Panhard M3; 15 Type-92; 6 *Walid*
    PPV 34: 12 *Casspir*; 12 RG-31 *Nyala*; 10 RG-33L
  AUV 15 *Cougar* 4×4
ARTILLERY 120
  TOWED 122mm 18 D-30
  MRL 122mm 12 BM-21 *Grad*
  MOR 90: 82mm 15 M-43; 120mm ε75
ANTI-TANK/ANTI-INFRASTRUCTURE
  MSL • MANPATS *Milan* (reported)
  RCL 75mm Type-52 (M20)
AIR DEFENCE
  SAM • Point-defence 9K32 *Strela*-2 (SA-7 *Grail*)‡
  GUNS • TOWED 150+: **14.5mm** 15 ZPU-4; 135+ **23mm** ZU-23/**37mm** Type-55 (M-1939)

Navy 50
EQUIPMENT BY TYPE
PATROL AND COASTAL COMBATANTS • PB 4
AMPHIBIOUS • LCT 2

Air Wing 200
EQUIPMENT BY TYPE
AIRCRAFT 1 combat capable
  TPT 2: **Light** 2 Cessna 150L†
  TRG 1 SF-260W *Warrior**
HELICOPTERS
  ATK 2 Mi-24 *Hind*
  MRH 2 SA342L *Gazelle*
  TPT • **Medium** (2 Mi-8 *Hip* non-op)

Paramilitary ε21,000

General Administration of State Security ε1,000

Imbonerakure ε20,000

DEPLOYMENT

CENTRAL AFRICAN REPUBLIC
UN • MINUSCA 761; 8 obs; 1 inf bn

SOMALIA
AU • AMISOM 5,432; 6 inf bn
UN • UNSOM 1 obs

SUDAN
UN • UNAMID 4; 4 obs
UN • UNISFA 2 obs

Cameroon CMR

CFA Franc BEAC fr		2016	2017	2018
GDP	fr	17.4tr	18.1tr	
	US$	29.3bn	30.7bn	
per capita	US$	1,238	1,263	
Growth	%	4.7	4.0	
Inflation	%	0.9	0.7	
Def bdgt	fr	230bn	239bn	
	US$	388m	404m	
US$1=fr		592.71	591.27	

Population 24,994,885

Age	0–14	15–19	20–24	25–29	30–64	65 plus
Male	21.3%	5.3%	4.5%	4.0%	13.4%	1.5%
Female	21.0%	5.2%	4.5%	3.9%	13.4%	1.7%

Capabilities

Although internal stability has long been a focus for Cameroon's armed forces, the threat from Boko Haram has generated a significant response, particularly in the northern area of the country bordering Nigeria. Many elements of Cameroon's equipment inventory are ageing, but infantry fighting vehicles and other armour were in recent years acquired from China and South Africa. Improving ISR capability is a priority that the government is hoping to address by buying aircraft and UAVs. The government is looking to increase the size of its armed forces by over 1,000 personnel in order to intensify the fight against Boko Haram. France, the US and others continue to provide support and training for the armed forces and gendarmerie. The US has also trained naval personnel as part of the Africa Maritime Law Enforcement Partnership. In 2017, three coastal-surveillance centres supported by US AFRICOM were opened, which will contribute to Cameroon's efforts to secure its maritime environment. In 2017, Cameroon hosted the *Unified Focus* Multi-National Joint Task Force table-top exercise. The army has contributed personnel to UN peacekeeping operations and in 2017 strengthened its participation to deployments in the CAR.

ACTIVE 14,400 (Army 12,500 Navy 1,500 Air 400)
Paramilitary 9,000

ORGANISATIONS BY SERVICE

Army 12,500
3 Mil Regions
FORCES BY ROLE
MANOEUVRE
  Light
  1 rapid reaction bde (1 armd recce bn, 1 AB bn, 1 amph bn)
  3 mot inf bde (3 mot inf bn, 1 spt bn)
  1 mot inf bde (2 mot inf bn, 1 spt bn)
  3 (rapid reaction) inf bn
  Air Manoeuvre
  1 cdo/AB bn
  Other
  1 (Presidential Guard) gd bn
COMBAT SUPPORT
  1 arty regt (5 arty bty)
  3 engr regt
AIR DEFENCE
  1 AD regt (6 AD bty)
EQUIPMENT BY TYPE
ARMOURED FIGHTING VEHICLES
  ASLT 18: 6 AMX-10RC; ε12 PTL-02 mod (*Cara* 105)
  RECCE 64: 31 AML-90; 15 *Ferret*; 8 M8; 5 RAM Mk3; 5 VBL
  IFV 42: 8 LAV-150 *Commando* with 20mm gun; 14 LAV-150 *Commando* with 90mm gun; 12 *Ratel*-20 (Engr); ε8 Type-07P
  APC 49
    APC (T) 12 M3 half-track
    APC (W) 21 LAV-150 *Commando*
    PPV 16 Gaia *Thunder*
    AUV 6 *Cougar* 4×4
ENGINEERING & MAINTENANCE VEHICLES
  ARV WZ-551 ARV
ANTI-TANK/ANTI-INFRASTRUCTURE
  MSL
    SP 24 TOW (on Jeeps)
    MANPATS *Milan*
  RCL 53: **75mm** 13 Type-52 (M20); **106mm** 40 M40A2
ARTILLERY 106+
  SP 155mm 18 ATMOS 2000
  TOWED 52: **105mm** 20 M101; **130mm** 24: 12 M-1982 (reported); 12 Type-59 (M-46); **155mm** 8 M-71
  MRL 122mm 20 BM-21 *Grad*
  MOR 16+: **81mm** (some SP); **120mm** 16 Brandt
AIR DEFENCE • GUNS
  SP 20mm RBY-1 with TCM-20
  TOWED 54: **14.5mm** 18 Type-58 (ZPU-2); **35mm** 18 GDF-002; **37mm** 18 Type-63

Navy ε1,500
HQ located at Douala
EQUIPMENT BY TYPE
PATROL AND COASTAL COMBATANTS 17
  PCC 4: 1 *Bakassi* (FRA P-48); 1 *Dipikar* (ex-FRA *Flamant*); 2 *Le Ntem* (PRC *Limam El Hidrami*) with 1 76mm gun
  PB 11: 2 Aresa 2400; 2 Aresa 3200; 2 Rodman 101; 4 Rodman 46; 1 *Quartier Maître Alfred Motto*
  PBR 2 *Swift*-38
AMPHIBIOUS • LANDING CRAFT 4
  LCM 2: 1 Aresa 2300; 1 *Le Moungo*
  LCU 2 *Yunnan*

Fusiliers Marin
FORCES BY ROLE
MANOEUVRE
  Amphibious
  3 mne bn

Air Force 300–400
FORCES BY ROLE
FIGHTER/GROUND ATTACK
  1 sqn with MB-326K; *Alpha Jet**†
TRANSPORT
  1 sqn with C-130H/H-30 *Hercules*; DHC-4 *Caribou*; DHC-5D *Buffalo*; IAI-201 *Arava*; PA-23 *Aztec*
  1 VIP unit with AS332 *Super Puma*; AS365 *Dauphin 2*; Bell 206B *Jet Ranger*; Gulfstream III
TRAINING
  1 unit with *Tetras*
ATTACK HELICOPTER
  1 sqn with SA342 *Gazelle* (with HOT); Mi-24 *Hind*
TRANSPORT HELICOPTER
  1 sqn with Bell 206L-3; Bell 412; SA319 *Alouette* III
EQUIPMENT BY TYPE
AIRCRAFT 9 combat capable
  ATK 5: 1 MB-326K *Impala* I; 4 MB-326K *Impala* II
  TPT 18: **Medium** 3: 2 C-130H *Hercules*; 1 C-130H-30 *Hercules*; **Light** 14: 1 CN235; 1 IAI-201 *Arava* (in store); 2 J.300 *Joker*; 1 MA60; 2 PA-23 *Aztec*; 7 *Tetras*; **PAX** 1 Gulfstream III
  TRG 4 *Alpha Jet**†
HELICOPTERS
  ATK 2 Mi-24 *Hind*
  MRH 13: 1 AS365 *Dauphin 2*; 1 Bell 412 *Twin Huey*; 2 Mi-17 *Hip* H; 2 SA319 *Alouette* III; 4 SA342 *Gazelle* (with HOT); 3 Z-9
  TPT 7: **Medium** 4: 2 AS332 *Super Puma*; 2 SA330J *Puma*; **Light** 3: 2 Bell 206B *Jet Ranger*; 1 Bell 206L3 *Long Ranger*

Fusiliers de l'Air
FORCES BY ROLE
MANOEUVRE
  Other
    1 sy bn

Paramilitary 9,000

Gendarmerie 9,000
FORCES BY ROLE
MANOEUVRE
  Reconnaissance
    3 (regional spt) paramilitary gp

DEPLOYMENT

CENTRAL AFRICAN REPUBLIC
UN • MINUSCA 777; 1 obs; 1 inf bn
MALI
UN • MINUSMA 2; 1 obs
DEMOCRATIC REPUBLIC OF THE CONGO
UN • MONUSCO 1; 4 obs

FOREIGN FORCES
United States 300; MQ-1C *Gray Eagle*

Cape Verde CPV

Cape Verde Escudo E		2016	2017	2018
GDP	E	163bn	172bn	
	US$	1.64bn	1.73bn	
per capita	US$	3,086	3,213	
Growth	%	3.8	4.0	
Inflation	%	-1.4	1.0	
Def bdgt	E	1.05bn	954m	
	US$	11m	10m	
US$1=E		99.62	99.40	

Population 560,899

Age	0–14	15–19	20–24	25–29	30–64	65 plus
Male	14.6%	5.0%	5.0%	4.7%	17.1%	1.9%
Female	14.5%	5.0%	5.0%	4.8%	18.8%	3.2%

Capabilities

In its Legislative Programme for 2016–21, the government outlined the priorities for Cape Verde's defence forces, including territorial defence and maritime security, EEZ and airspace protection. Although the armed forces are small and presently have limited capability, the government has suggested reorganising around marines and engineering and paramilitary national-guard units. The government is interested in greater regional and international defence engagement; some maritime-security training support is provided by international partners. The armed forces take part in multinational regional exercises, including in 2017 the US AFRICOM-led *Flintlock* and *Obangame Express*.

ACTIVE 1,200 (Army 1,000 Coast Guard 100 Air 100)
Conscript liability Selective conscription (14 months)

ORGANISATIONS BY SERVICE

Army 1,000
FORCES BY ROLE
MANOEUVRE
  Light
    2 inf bn (gp)
COMBAT SUPPORT
  1 engr bn
EQUIPMENT BY TYPE
ARMOURED FIGHTING VEHICLES
  RECCE 10 BRDM-2
ARTILLERY • **MOR** 18: **82mm** 12; **120mm** 6 M-1943
AIR DEFENCE
  SAM • **Point-defence** 9K32 *Strela* (SA-7 *Grail*)‡
  GUNS • **TOWED** 30: **14.5mm** 18 ZPU-1; **23mm** 12 ZU-23

Coast Guard ε100
EQUIPMENT BY TYPE
PATROL AND COASTAL COMBATANTS 5
  PCC 2: 1 *Guardião*; 1 *Kondor* I

PB 2: 1 *Espadarte*; 1 *Tainha* (PRC-27m)
PBF 1 *Archangel*
AIRCRAFT • TPT • Light 1 Do-228

Air Force up to 100
FORCES BY ROLE
MARITIME PATROL
  1 sqn with An-26 *Curl*
EQUIPMENT BY TYPE
AIRCRAFT • TPT • Light 3 An-26 *Curl*†

Central African Republic CAR

CFA Franc BEAC fr		2016	2017	2018
GDP	fr	1.04tr	1.15tr	
	US$	1.78bn	1.99bn	
per capita	US$	364	400	
Growth	%	4.5	4.7	
Inflation	%	4.6	3.8	
Def exp	fr	15.9bn	17.7bn	
	US$	27m	31m	
US$1=fr		585.05	578.12	

Population 5,625,118

Age	0–14	15–19	20–24	25–29	30–64	65 plus
Male	20.1%	5.3%	4.7%	4.2%	13.9%	1.3%
Female	19.9%	5.2%	4.6%	4.2%	14.2%	2.1%

Capabilities

Effective military and security organisations still remain largely absent in the wake of the violence in 2013. Instability continues to affect the country and – due to refugee flows – neighbouring states. Some military equipment remains held by government military forces, but inventory numbers are difficult to verify. The May 2015 Bangui Forum on National Reconciliation agreed principles governing DDR. Under the National Recovery and Peacebuilding Plan 2017–21, written by CAR officials with support from the EU, UN and World Bank, steps to improve security would focus on DDR, SSR, justice reforms, broader reconciliation and improving social cohesion. A National Superior Council on Security would be set up to oversee the overall reform process. The UN's MINUSCA mission remains the principal security provider in the country, and the UN secretary-general in 2017 asked for additional capacity. The EU released fresh development funding in late 2017, on top of international pledges made in December 2016 at the Brussels International Conference for the CAR.

ACTIVE 7,150 (Army 7,000 Air 150) **Paramilitary 1,000**

Conscript liability Selective conscription 2 years; reserve obligation thereafter, term n.k.

ORGANISATIONS BY SERVICE

Army ε7,000
FORCES BY ROLE
MANOEUVRE
  Light
    1 inf bn
EQUIPMENT BY TYPE
ARMOURED FIGHTING VEHICLES
  MBT 3 T-55†
  RECCE 9: 8 *Ferret*†; 1 BRDM-2
  IFV 18 *Ratel*
  APC • APC (W) 14+: 4 BTR-152†; 10+ VAB†
ARTILLERY • MOR 12+: **81mm**†; **120mm** 12 M-1943†
ANTI-TANK/ANTI-INFRASTRUCTURE
  RCL **106mm** 14 M40†
PATROL AND COASTAL COMBATANTS • PBR 9†

Air Force 150
EQUIPMENT BY TYPE
AIRCRAFT • TPT 7: **Medium** 1 C-130A *Hercules*; **Light** 6: 3 BN-2 *Islander*; 1 Cessna 172RJ *Skyhawk*; 2 J.300 *Joker*
HELICOPTERS • TPT • Light 1 AS350 *Ecureuil*

FOREIGN FORCES

MINUSCA unless stated
Austria EUTM RCA 3
Bangladesh 1,008; 10 obs; 1 cdo coy; 1 inf bn; 1 med coy
Belgium EUTM RCA 9
Benin 5; 3 obs
Bhutan 2; 1 obs
Bolivia 1; 3 obs
Bosnia-Herzegovina EUTM RCA 2
Brazil 2; 4 obs
Burkina Faso 7; 1 obs
Burundi 761; 8 obs; 1 inf bn
Cambodia 216; 6 obs; 1 engr coy
Cameroon 777; 1 obs; 1 inf bn
Chile 4
Colombia 2
Congo 19; 3 obs
Egypt 1,014; 5 obs; 1 inf bn; 1 tpt coy
France 91; 1 UAV unit • EUTM RCA 53
Gabon 445; 1 inf bn(-)
Gambia 2; 2 obs
Georgia EUTM RCA 35
Ghana 4; 3 obs
Guatemala 2; 2 obs
Hungary 2; 2 obs
Indonesia 207; 6 obs; 1 engr coy
Jordan 7; 3 obs
Kenya 8; 6 obs
Lithuania EUTM RCA 1
Mauritania 754; 9 obs; 1 inf bn
Mexico 1 obs
Moldova 1; 2 obs
Morocco 765; 2 obs; 1 inf bn
Nepal 128; 3 obs; 1 MP pl
Niger 130; 4 obs; 1 sigs coy

Nigeria 2
Pakistan 1,126; 10 obs; 1 inf bn; 1 engr coy; 1 hel sqn
Paraguay 2; 1 obs
Peru 209; 5 obs; 1 engr coy
Poland EUTM RCA 1
Portugal 150; 1 cdo coy • EUTM RCA 11
Romania EUTM RCA 9
Rwanda 977; 11 obs; 1 inf bn; 1 fd hospital
Senegal 114; 1 atk hel sqn
Serbia 69; 1 med coy • EUTM RCA 7
Spain EUTM RCA 30
Sri Lanka 116; 5 obs; 1 avn unit
Sweden EUTM RCA 9
Tanzania 201; 1 inf bn(-)
Togo 6; 4 obs
United States 8
Uruguay 1
Vietnam 4; 1 obs
Zambia 943; 7 obs; 1 inf bn

Chad CHA

CFA Franc BEAC fr		2016	2017	2018
GDP	fr	5.98tr	6.02tr	
	US$	10.1bn	9.74bn	
per capita	US$	852	799	
Growth	%	-6.4	0.6	
Inflation	%	-1.1	0.2	
Def bdgt	fr	94.6bn	102bn	
	US$	160m	165m	
US$1=fr		592.72	618.42	

Population 12,075,985

Age	0–14	15–19	20–24	25–29	30–64	65 plus
Male	21.8%	5.9%	4.6%	3.7%	11.1%	1.2%
Female	21.2%	5.9%	4.9%	4.1%	13.6%	1.7%

Capabilities

Chad's most pressing security concerns are instability in West Africa and the Sahel and the need to prosecute counter-insurgency operations against Boko Haram. Chad engaged in extensive joint operations with Niger and Nigeria against Boko Haram in 2016. The country is one of the G-5 Sahel nations, and has encouraged African armed forces to take greater ownership of regional security. The country's ISR capability should be improved by the receipt of aircraft from the US, coming after improvements in ground-attack and medium-airlift capability. However, in mid-2017, Chad's air force suffered from the effects of a storm, which damaged aircraft at N'Djamena air base. Chad's ground forces have recent combat experience in Mali in 2013, and as part of more recent operations against Boko Haram. France's *Operation Barkhane* is headquartered in N'Djamena. In October 2017, Chad reportedly redeployed troops previously in Niger to Chad's northern border area with Libya, which will affect the combat capability of forces ranged against insurgents in Niger.

ACTIVE 30,350 (Army 25,000 Air 350 Republican Guard 5,000) **Paramilitary 9,500**
Conscript liability Conscription authorised

ORGANISATIONS BY SERVICE

Army ε25,000
7 Mil Regions
FORCES BY ROLE
MANOEUVRE
 Armoured
  1 armd bn
 Light
  7 inf bn
COMBAT SUPPORT
 1 arty bn
 1 engr bn
 1 sigs bn
COMBAT SERVICE SUPPORT
 1 log gp
EQUIPMENT BY TYPE
ARMOURED FIGHTING VEHICLES
 MBT 60 T-55
 ASLT 30 PTL-02 *Assaulter*
 RECCE 309+: 132 AML-60/AML-90; 22 *Bastion Patsas*; ε100 BRDM-2; 20 EE-9 *Cascavel*; 4 ERC-90F *Sagaie*; 31+ RAM Mk3
 IFV 131: 80 BMP-1; 42 BMP-1U; 9 LAV-150 *Commando* with 90mm gun
 APC • APC (W) 99: 24 BTR-80; 12 BTR-3E; ε20 BTR-60; ε10 *Black Scorpion*; 25 VAB-VTT; 8 WZ-523
ARTILLERY 26+
 SP 122mm 10 2S1 *Gvozdika*
 TOWED 105mm 5 M2
 MRL 11+: **107mm** some Type-63; **122mm** 11: 6 BM-21 *Grad*; 5 Type-81
 MOR 81mm some; **120mm** AM-50
ANTI-TANK/ANTI-INFRASTRUCTURE
 MSL • MANPATS *Eryx*; *Milan*
 RCL 106mm M40A1
AIR DEFENCE
 SAM
  Short-range 2K12 *Kub* (SA-6 *Gainful*)
  Point-defence 9K310 *Igla*-1 (SA-16 *Gimlet*)
 GUNS • TOWED 14.5mm ZPU-1/ZPU-2/ZPU-4; **23mm** ZU-23

Air Force 350
FORCES BY ROLE
GROUND ATTACK
 1 unit with PC-7; PC-9*; SF-260WL *Warrior**; Su-25 *Frogfoot*
TRANSPORT
 1 sqn with An-26 *Curl*; C-130H-30 *Hercules*; Mi-17 *Hip H*; Mi-171
 1 (Presidential) Flt with B-737BBJ; Beech 1900; DC-9-87; Gulfstream II

ATTACK HELICOPTER
1 sqn with AS550C *Fennec*; Mi-24V *Hind*; SA316 *Alouette* III

EQUIPMENT BY TYPE
AIRCRAFT 14 combat capable
FTR 1 MiG-29 *Fulcrum*
ATK 10: 8 Su-25 *Frogfoot*; 2 Su-25UB *Frogfoot* B
TPT 10: **Medium** 3: 2 C-27J *Spartan*; 1 C-130H-30 *Hercules*; **Light** 4: 3 An-26 *Curl*; 1 Beech 1900; **PAX** 3: 1 B-737BBJ; 1 DC-9-87; 1 Gulfstream II
TRG 4: 2 PC-7 (only 1*); 1 PC-9 *Turbo Trainer**; 1 SF-260WL *Warrior**
HELICOPTERS
ATK 5 Mi-24V *Hind*
MRH 8: 3 AS550C *Fennec*; 3 Mi-17 *Hip* H; 2 SA316 *Alouette* III
TPT • **Medium** 2 Mi-171

Paramilitary 9,500 active

State Security Service General Direction (DGSSIE) 5,000

Gendarmerie 4,500

DEPLOYMENT

MALI
UN • MINUSMA 1,398; 2 obs; 1 SF coy; 2 inf bn

FOREIGN FORCES

Benin MNJTF 150
France Operation Barkhane 1,500; 1 mech inf BG; 1 FGA det with 2 *Mirage* 2000D; 2 *Mirage* 2000N; 1 tpt det with 1 C-130H; 2 CN-235M

Congo, Republic of COG

CFA Franc BEAC fr		2016	2017	2018
GDP	fr	4.66tr	4.61tr	
	US$	7.87bn	7.80bn	
per capita	US$	1,855	1,794	
Growth	%	-2.8	-3.6	
Inflation	%	3.6	-0.5	
Def bdgt	fr	333bn	284bn	
	US$	562m	481m	
US$1=fr		592.73	591.25	

Population 4,954,674

Age	0–14	15–19	20–24	25–29	30–64	65 plus
Male	21.0%	4.5%	4.1%	3.6%	15.6%	1.3%
Female	20.6%	4.4%	4.1%	3.8%	15.1%	1.7%

Capabilities

Congo's armed forces are small, utilise aged equipment, and have low levels of training and limited overall capability. They have struggled to recover from the brief but devastating civil war in the late 1990s. The troop contingent deployed to the CAR was withdrawn by the government in mid-2017, amid allegations of indiscipline levelled against the troops. Though the defence budget is not small in relation to those of its neighbours, the air force is effectively grounded for lack of spares and serviceable equipment. The navy is little more than a riverine force, despite the need for maritime security on the country's small coastline. France provides defence and security support in the form of advisory assistance and capacity building in areas including administration and accounting, as well as military and police capability. Reports in late 2017 also indicated Chinese security assistance in the form of communications equipment.

ACTIVE 10,000 (Army 8,000 Navy 800 Air 1,200)
Paramilitary 2,000

ORGANISATIONS BY SERVICE

Army 8,000
FORCES BY ROLE
MANOEUVRE
  Armoured
  2 armd bn
  Light
  2 inf bn (gp) each with (1 lt tk tp, 1 arty bty)
  1 inf bn
  Air Manoeuvre
  1 cdo/AB bn
COMBAT SUPPORT
  1 arty gp (with MRL)
  1 engr bn
EQUIPMENT BY TYPE†
ARMOURED FIGHTING VEHICLES
MBT 40: 25 T-54/T-55; 15 Type-59; (some T-34 in store)
LT TK 13: 3 PT-76; 10 Type-62
RECCE 25 BRDM-1/BRDM-2
APC 133+
  APC (W) 78+: 28 AT-105 *Saxon*; 20 BTR-152; 30 BTR-60; Panhard M3
  PPV 55: 18 *Mamba*; 37 *Marauder*
ARTILLERY 56+
  SP 122mm 3 2S1 *Gvozdika*
  TOWED 15+: 122mm 10 D-30; 130mm 5 M-46; 152mm D-20
  MRL 10+: 122mm 10 BM-21 *Grad*; 140mm BM-14; 140mm BM-16
  MOR 28+: 82mm; 120mm 28 M-43
ANTI-TANK/ANTI-INFRASTRUCTURE
  RCL 57mm M18
  GUNS 15: 57mm 5 ZIS-2 (M-1943); 100mm 10 M-1944
AIR DEFENCE • GUNS
    SP 23mm ZSU-23-4
    TOWED 14.5mm ZPU-2/ZPU-4; 37mm 28 M-1939; 57mm S-60; 100mm KS-19

Navy ε800
EQUIPMENT BY TYPE
PATROL AND COASTAL COMBATANTS 8
  PCC 4 *Février*
  PBR 4

Air Force 1,200
FORCES BY ROLE
FIGHTER/GROUND ATTACK
  1 sqn with *Mirage* F-1AZ
TRANSPORT
  1 sqn with An-24 *Coke*; An-32 *Cline*; CN235M-100
ATTACK/TRANSPORT HELICOPTER
  1 sqn with Mi-8 *Hip*; Mi-35P *Hind*
EQUIPMENT BY TYPE†
AIRCRAFT
  FGA 2 *Mirage* F-1AZ
  TPT • **Light** 4: 1 An-24 *Coke*; 2 An-32 *Cline*;
  1 CN235M-100
HELICOPTERS†
  ATK (2 Mi-35P *Hind* in store)
  TPT • **Medium** (3 Mi-8 *Hip* in store)
AIR-LAUNCHED MISSILES • AAM • IR R-3 (AA-2 *Atoll*)‡

Paramilitary 2,000 active

Gendarmerie 2,000
FORCES BY ROLE
MANOEUVRE
  Other
  20 paramilitary coy

Presidential Guard some
FORCES BY ROLE
MANOEUVRE
  Other
  1 paramilitary bn

DEPLOYMENT

CENTRAL AFRICAN REPUBLIC
UN • MINUSCA 19; 3 obs

Côte d'Ivoire CIV

CFA Franc BCEAO fr		2016	2017	2018
GDP	fr	21.1tr	23.2tr	
	US$	35.7bn	39.9bn	
per capita	US$	1,466	1,599	
Growth	%	7.7	7.6	
Inflation	%	0.7	1.0	
Def bdgt [a]	fr	448bn	482bn	
	US$	755m	829m	
US$1=fr		592.77	581.55	

[a] Defence, order and security expenses

Population 24,184,810

Age	0–14	15–19	20–24	25–29	30–64	65 plus
Male	18.6%	5.6%	4.9%	4.5%	15.2%	1.6%
Female	18.3%	5.5%	4.8%	4.4%	14.5%	1.8%

Capabilities

The armed forces are still undergoing reconstruction, and SSR initiatives remain in place. A law on the defence forces' organisation was enacted in 2015. This detailed defence zones and military regions, the creation of a general staff and general inspectorate for the armed forces, and stressed the armed forces' role in assisting Ivorian society. In 2016 a Military Programme Law for 2016–20 was adopted, planning for an incremental reduction in military strength up to 2020, to enable an increase in the gendarmerie. In April 2016, the United Nations lifted the arms embargo that had previously been imposed on the country. This allowed Côte d'Ivoire to start recapitalising its air force, notably with the delivery of Mi-24 helicopters from Russia. As part of the SSR process, an aviation academy was established in Abidjan, with limited rotary-wing pilot and maintenance training. The latter is also an issue for the small naval unit. The administration has moved to regulate promotion and salary structures to aid professionalisation, and also improve military infrastructure. France has a significant training mission in the country, and trained Ivorian naval personnel in October 2017. France increased its personnel presence in 2016. The UN peacekeeping mission, UNOCI, ended in June 2017.

ACTIVE 25,400 (Army 23,000 Navy 1,000 Air 1,400)
Paramilitary n.k.

Moves to restructure and reform the armed forces continue

ORGANISATIONS BY SERVICE

Army ε23,000
FORCES BY ROLE
MANOEUVRE
  Armoured
  1 armd bn
  Light
  4 inf bn
  Air Manoeuvre
  1 cdo/AB bn
COMBAT SUPPORT
  1 arty bn
  1 engr bn
COMBAT SERVICE SUPPORT
  1 log bn
AIR DEFENCE
  1 AD bn
EQUIPMENT BY TYPE
ARMOURED FIGHTING VEHICLES
  MBT 10 T-55†
  LT TK 5 AMX-13
  RECCE 34: 15 AML-60/AML-90; 13 BRDM-2; 6 ERC-90F4 *Sagaie*
  IFV 10 BMP-1/BMP-2†
  APC • APC (W) 31: 12 Panhard M3; 13 VAB; 6 BTR-80
ENGINEERING & MAINTENANCE VEHICLES
  VLB MTU

ANTI-TANK/ANTI-INFRASTRUCTURE
    MSL • MANPATS 9K111-1 *Konkurs* (AT-5 *Spandrel*)
    (reported); 9K135 *Kornet* (AT-14 *Spriggan*) (reported)
    RCL 106mm ε12 M40A1
ARTILLERY 36+
    TOWED 4+: **105mm** 4 M-1950; **122mm** (reported)
    MRL **122mm** 6 BM-21
    MOR 26+: **81mm**; **82mm** 10 M-37; **120mm** 16 AM-50
AIRCRAFT • TPT • Medium 1 An-12 *Cub*†
AIR DEFENCE
    SAM • Point-defence 9K32 *Strela*-2 (SA-7 *Grail*)‡
    (reported)
    GUNS 21+
        SP **20mm** 6 M3 VDAA
        TOWED 15+: **20mm** 10; **23mm** ZU-23-2; **40mm** 5 L/60

Navy ε1,000
EQUIPMENT BY TYPE
PATROL AND COASTAL COMBATANTS 7
    PB 5: 3 *L'Emergence*; 1 *Intrepide*† (FRA *Patra*); 1 27m
    (PRC)
    PBR 2 Rodman (fishery-protection duties)
AMPHIBIOUS • LANDING CRAFT • LCM 2 *Aby*†

Air Force ε1,400
EQUIPMENT BY TYPE†
AIRCRAFT
    TPT • PAX 1 B-727
HELICOPTERS
    ATK 1 Mi-24
    TPT • Medium 2 SA330L *Puma* (IAR-330L)

Paramilitary n.k.

Republican Guard n.k.
EQUIPMENT BY TYPE†
ARMOURED FIGHTING VEHICLES
    APC • APC (W) 4 *Mamba*

Gendarmerie n.k.
EQUIPMENT BY TYPE†
ARMOURED FIGHTING VEHICLES
    APC • APC (W) some VAB
PATROL AND COASTAL COMBATANTS • PB 1 *Bian*

DEPLOYMENT

MALI
UN • MINUSMA 150; 1 obs; 1 sy coy

FOREIGN FORCES

France 950; 1 (Marine) inf bn

Democratic Republic of the Congo DRC

Congolese Franc fr		2016	2017	2018
GDP	fr	42.2tr	61.4tr	
	US$	39.3bn	40.4bn	
per capita	US$	467	466	
Growth	%	2.4	2.8	
Inflation	%	18.2	41.7	
Def bdgt	fr	817bn	890bn	
	US$	762m	586m	
US$1=fr		1,072.14	1,518.95	

Population 83,301,151

Age	0–14	15–19	20–24	25–29	30–64	65 plus
Male	21.0%	5.7%	5.0%	4.1%	12.8%	1.1%
Female	20.7%	5.6%	5.0%	4.1%	13.1%	1.5%

Capabilities

On paper, the DRC has the largest armed forces in Central Africa. However, given the country's size and the poor levels of training, morale and equipment, the armed forces are unable to provide security throughout the country. The DRC has suffered the most protracted conflict since the end of the Cold War. Much military equipment is in poor repair and the armed forces, which have since incorporated a number of non-state armed groups, struggle with conflicting loyalties. The mandate of the UN mission was renewed in March for another 12 months. The UN's Force Intervention Brigade (FIB) remains active in the east of the country. Training will have improved for units operating with the FIB, while external-partner training and capacity-building assistance is also commonplace. However, the 13-year-long defence relationship with Belgium ended in July 2017, a period in which Belgian troops had trained three DRC rapid-intervention battalions, among other units. When conflict finally abates in the east, significant attention to wide-ranging DDR and SSR will be required, to continue the work intermittently undertaken over the past decade.

ACTIVE ε134,250 (Central Staffs ε14,000, Army 103,000 Republican Guard 8,000 Navy 6,700 Air 2,550)

ORGANISATIONS BY SERVICE

Army (Forces du Terre) ε103,000

The DRC has 11 Military Regions. In 2011, all brigades in North and South Kivu provinces were consolidated into 27 new regiments, the latest in a sequence of reorganisations designed to integrate non-state armed groups. The actual combat effectiveness of many formations is doubtful

FORCES BY ROLE
MANOEUVRE
    Light
    6 (integrated) inf bde
    ε3 inf bde (non-integrated)
    27+ inf regt

COMBAT SUPPORT
1 arty regt
1 MP bn

EQUIPMENT BY TYPE†
(includes Republican Guard eqpt)

ARMOURED FIGHTING VEHICLES
MBT 174: 12–17 Type-59†; 32 T-55; 25 T-64BV-1; 100 T-72AV
LT TK 40: 10 PT-76; 30 Type-62† (reportedly being refurbished)
RECCE up to 52: up to 17 AML-60; 14 AML-90; 19 EE-9 *Cascavel*; 2 RAM-V-2
IFV 20 BMP-1
APC 144:
  APC (T) 9: 3 BTR-50; 6 MT-LB
  APC (W) 135: 30-70 BTR-60PB; 58 Panhard M3†; 7 TH 390 *Fahd*

ANTI-TANK/ANTI-INFRASTRUCTURE
RCL 57mm M18; 73mm; 75mm M20; 106mm M40A1
GUNS 85mm 10 Type-56 (D-44)

ARTILLERY 726+
SP 16: 122mm 6 2S1 *Gvozdika*; 152mm 10 2S3 *Akatsiya*
TOWED 125: 122mm 77 M-30 (M-1938)/D-30/Type-60; 130mm 42 Type-59 (M-46)/Type-59-I; 152mm 6 D-20 (reported)
MRL 57+: 107mm 12 Type-63; 122mm 24+: 24 BM-21 *Grad*; some RM-70; 128mm 6 M-51; 130mm 3 Type-82; 132mm 12
MOR 528+: 81mm 100; 82mm 400; 107mm M30; 120mm 28: 10 Brandt; 18 other

AIR DEFENCE
SAM • Point-defence 9K32 *Strela*-2 (SA-7 *Grail*)‡
GUNS • TOWED 114: 14.5mm 12 ZPU-4; 37mm 52 M-1939

Republican Guard 8,000

FORCES BY ROLE
MANOEUVRE
  Armoured
    1 armd regt
  Light
    3 gd bde
COMBAT SUPPORT
  1 arty regt

Navy 6,700 (incl infantry and marines)

EQUIPMENT BY TYPE
PATROL AND COASTAL COMBATANTS 16
  PB 16: 1 *Shanghai* II; ε15 various (all under 15m)

Air Force 2,550

EQUIPMENT BY TYPE
AIRCRAFT 4 combat capable
  ATK 4 Su-25 *Frogfoot*
  TPT 5: Medium 1 C-130H *Hercules*; Light 2 An-26 *Curl*; PAX 2 B-727
HELICOPTERS
  ATK 7: 4 Mi-24 *Hind*; 3 Mi-24V *Hind*
  TPT • Medium 3: 1 AS332L *Super Puma*; 2 Mi-8 *Hip*

Paramilitary

National Police Force
Incl Rapid Intervention Police (National and Provincial forces)

People's Defence Force

FOREIGN FORCES
All part of MONUSCO unless otherwise specified
Algeria 5 obs
Bangladesh 1,710; 13 obs; 1 inf bn; 1 engr coy; 1 avn coy; 2 hel coy
Belgium 2
Benin 453; 5 obs; 1 inf bn(-)
Bhutan 1 obs
Bolivia 7 obs
Bosnia-Herzegovina 5 obs
Burkina Faso 7 obs
Cameroon 1; 4 obs
Canada (*Operation Crocodile*) 8
China, People's Republic of 220; 12 obs; 1 engr coy; 1 fd hospital
Czech Republic 3 obs
Egypt 154; 19 obs; 1 SF coy
France 2
Ghana 463; 21 obs; 1 mech inf bn(-)
Guatemala 152; 1 obs; 1 SF coy
India 2,640; 39 obs; 4 inf bn; 1 med coy
Indonesia 175; 4 obs; 1 engr coy
Ireland 4
Jordan 9; 13 obs
Kenya 13; 9 obs
Malawi 855; 2 obs; 1 inf bn
Malaysia 3; 10 obs
Mali 1 obs
Mongolia 1 obs
Morocco 836; 3 obs; 1 inf bn; 1 fd hospital
Nepal 1,029; 17 obs; 1 inf bn; 1 engr coy
Niger 4; 12 obs
Nigeria 1; 15 obs
Pakistan 3,447; 35 obs; 4 inf bn; 1 hel sqn
Paraguay 14 obs
Peru 1; 11 obs
Poland 2 obs
Romania 17 obs
Russia 1; 24 obs
Senegal 2; 2 obs
Serbia 8
South Africa (*Operation Mistral*) 1,358; 4 obs; 1 inf bn; 1 engr coy; 1 atk hel sqn; 1 hel sqn
Sri Lanka 4 obs
Sweden 2 obs
Switzerland 3
Tanzania 1,266; 1 SF coy; 1 inf bn
Tunisia 1; 31 obs

Ukraine 255: 9 obs; 2 atk hel sqn; 1 hel sqn
United Kingdom 6
United States 3
Uruguay 1,165; 12 obs; 1 inf bn; 1 mne coy(-); 1 engr coy; 1 hel sqn
Zambia 2; 17 obs

Djibouti DJB

Djiboutian Franc fr		2016	2017	2018
GDP	fr	336bn	370bn	
	US$	1.89bn	2.08bn	
per capita	US$	1,903	2,040	
Growth	%	6.5	7.0	
Inflation	%	2.7	3.0	
Def exp	fr	n.k	n.k	
	US$	n.k	n.k	
FMA (US)	US$	0.6m	0.5m	0m
US$1=fr		177.70	177.68	

Population 865,267
Ethnic groups: Somali 60%; Afar 35%

Age	0-14	15-19	20-24	25-29	30-64	65 plus
Male	15.6%	5.1%	4.8%	4.5%	13.8%	1.7%
Female	15.5%	5.4%	5.8%	5.8%	19.5%	2.0%

Capabilities

Djibouti's small armed forces are almost entirely dominated by the army. Their main responsibility is securing sovereignty, combating trafficking, HADR missions and international peacekeeping operations, including to AMISOM. A defence white paper was published in June 2017, which outlined the need to modernise key capabilities, including intelligence and command. However, high debt levels are likely to hamper equipment procurements. Recent ground-forces acquisitions have focused on mobility and artillery, but armoured-warfare capability remains limited. A border dispute with Eritrea continues. Djibouti's strategic position and relative stability have made it an appealing location for foreign-military basing. Training support and external security are bolstered by the presence of the US Combined Joint Task Force–Horn of Africa at Camp Lemonnier, as well as a French base with air-combat and transport assets. Some states participating in counter-piracy missions base their forces in Djibouti, including Japan. The EU and NATO have at various times also maintained a presence in Djibouti to support their counter-piracy operations. China's first overseas logistics base was officially opened in Djibouti in 2017, while Saudi Arabia has reportedly discussed establishing a base in the country. (See pp. 434–35.)

ACTIVE 10,450 (Army 8,000 Navy 200 Air 250 Gendarmerie 2,000) **Paramilitary 2,650**

ORGANISATIONS BY SERVICE

Army ε8,000
FORCES BY ROLE
4 military districts (Tadjourah, Dikhil, Ali-Sabieh and Obock)
MANOEUVRE
 Mechanised
  1 armd regt (1 recce sqn, 3 armd sqn, 1 (anti-smuggling) sy coy)
 Light
  4 inf regt (3-4 inf coy, 1 spt coy)
  1 rapid reaction regt (4 inf coy, 1 spt coy)
 Other
  1 (Republican Guard) gd regt (1 sy sqn, 1 (close protection) sy sqn, 1 cbt spt sqn (1 recce pl, 1 armd pl, 1 arty pl), 1 spt sqn)
COMBAT SUPPORT
 1 arty regt
 1 demining coy
 1 sigs regt
 1 CIS sect
COMBAT SERVICE SUPPORT
 1 log regt
 1 maint coy
EQUIPMENT BY TYPE
ARMOURED FIGHTING VEHICLES
 ASLT 1 PTL-02 *Assaulter*
 RECCE 36: 4 AML-60†; 17 AML-90; 15 VBL
 IFV 28: 8 BTR-80A; 16-20 *Ratel*
 APC 40
  APC (W) 27+: 12 BTR-60†; 4+ AT-105 *Saxon*; 11 *Puma*
  PPV 13: 3 *Casspir*; 10 RG-33L
 AUV 22: 10 *Cougar* 4×4 (one with 90mm gun); 12 PKSV
ANTI-TANK/ANTI-INFRASTRUCTURE
 RCL 106mm 16 M40A1
ARTILLERY 73
 SP 155mm 10 M109L
 TOWED 122mm 6 D-30
 MRL 12: **107mm** 2 PH-63; **122mm** 10: 6 (6-tube Toyota Land Cruiser 70 series); 2 (30-tube Iveco 110-16); 2 (30-tube)
 MOR 45: **81mm** 25; **120mm** 20 Brandt
AIR DEFENCE • GUNS 15+
 SP 20mm 5 M693
 TOWED 10: **23mm** 5 ZU-23-2; **40mm** 5 L/70

Navy ε200
EQUIPMENT BY TYPE
PATROL AND COASTAL COMBATANTS 12
 PBF 2 Battalion-17
 PB 10: 1 *Plascoa*†; 2 Sea Ark 1739; 1 *Swari*†; 6 others
AMPHIBIOUS • LCT 1 EDIC 700

Air Force 250
EQUIPMENT BY TYPE
AIRCRAFT
 TPT • Light 6: 1 Cessna U206G *Stationair*; 1 Cessna 208 *Caravan*; 2 Y-12E; 1 L-410UVP *Turbolet*; 1 MA60

HELICOPTERS
ATK (2 Mi-35 *Hind* in store)
MRH 5: 1 Mi-17 *Hip* H; 4 AS365 *Dauphin*
TPT 3: **Medium** 1 Mi-8T *Hip*; **Light** 2 AS355F *Ecureuil* II

Gendarmerie 2,000+
Ministry of Defence
FORCES BY ROLE
MANOEUVRE
  Other
  1 paramilitary bn
EQUIPMENT BY TYPE
PATROL AND COASTAL COMBATANTS 1 PB

Paramilitary ε2,650

National Police Force ε2,500
Ministry of Interior

Coast Guard 150
EQUIPMENT BY TYPE
PATROL AND COASTAL COMBATANTS 11
  PB 11: 2 *Khor Angar*; 9 other

DEPLOYMENT

SOMALIA
AU • AMISOM 1,850; 2 inf bn

WESTERN SAHARA
UN • MINURSO 2 obs

FOREIGN FORCES
China 240: 1 mne coy(-); 1 med unit; 2 ZTL-11; 8 ZBL-08; 1 LPD; 1 ESD
France 1,450: 1 (Marine) combined arms regt (2 recce sqn, 2 inf coy, 1 arty bty, 1 engr coy); 1 hel det with 2 SA330 *Puma*; 1 SA342 *Gazelle*; 1 LCM; 1 air sqn with 4 *Mirage* 2000-5/D; 1 C-160 *Transall*; 2 SA330 *Puma*
Germany Operation Atalanta 1 AP-3C *Orion*
Italy 90
Japan 170; 2 P-3C *Orion*
New Zealand 1 P-3K2 *Orion*
Spain Operation Atalanta 1 P-3A *Orion*
United States US Africa Command: 4,700; 1 tpt sqn with C-130H/J-30 *Hercules*; 1 spec ops sqn with MC-130H; PC-12 (U-28A); 1 CSAR sqn with HH-60G *Pave Hawk*; 1 CISR sqn with MQ-9A *Reaper*; 1 naval air base

Equatorial Guinea EQG

CFA Franc BEAC fr		2016	2017	2018
GDP	fr	6.04tr	5.86tr	
	US$	10.2bn	10.1bn	
per capita	US$	12,399	11,948	
Growth	%	-9.7	-7.4	
Inflation	%	1.4	1.7	
Def exp	fr	n.k	n.k	
	US$	n.k	n.k	
US$1=fr		593.01	581.54	

Population 778,358

Age	0–14	15–19	20–24	25–29	30–64	65 plus
Male	20.2%	5.2%	4.5%	3.7%	13.9%	1.6%
Female	19.9%	5.3%	4.6%	3.8%	14.8%	2.3%

Capabilities
The armed forces are dominated by the army, the principal role of which is internal security; there is only limited capability for power projection. There has been significant naval investment in recent years, including in both equipment and onshore infrastructure at Bata and Malabo, although naval capabilities still remain limited in scope. Maritime-security concerns in the Gulf of Guinea have resulted in an increased emphasis on bolstering the country's coastal-patrol capacity. France maintains a military-cooperation detachment in Malabo, advising on institutional issues such as administration and finance and providing capacity-building support through the naval-focused regional vocational school at Tica, as well as some training activities with French forces based in Gabon.

ACTIVE 1,450 (Army 1,100 Navy 250 Air 100)

ORGANISATIONS BY SERVICE

Army 1,100
FORCES BY ROLE
MANOEUVRE
  Light
  3 inf bn(-)
EQUIPMENT BY TYPE
ARMOURED FIGHTING VEHICLES
  MBT 3 T-55
  RECCE 6 BRDM-2
  IFV 20 BMP-1
  APC 35
    APC (W) 10 BTR-152
    PPV 25 *Reva* (reported)

Navy ε250
EQUIPMENT BY TYPE
PATROL AND COASTAL COMBATANTS 11
  PSO 2:
    1 *Bata* with 1 76mm gun, 1 hel landing platform

1 *Wele Nzas* with 2 AK630M CIWS, 2 76mm gun, 1 hel landing platform
PCC 2 OPV 62
PBF 2 *Shaldag* II
PB 5: 1 *Daphne*; 2 *Estuario de Muni*; 2 *Zhuk*
LOGISTICS AND SUPPORT
AKRH 1 *Capitan David Eyama Angue Osa* with 1 76mm gun

Air Force 100

EQUIPMENT BY TYPE
AIRCRAFT 4 combat capable
 ATK 4: 2 Su-25 *Frogfoot*; 2 Su-25UB *Frogfoot* B
 TPT 4: **Light** 3: 1 An-32B *Cline*; 2 An-72 *Coaler*; **PAX** 1 *Falcon* 900 (VIP)
 TRG 2 L-39C *Albatros*
HELICOPTERS
 ATK 5 Mi-24P/V *Hind*
 MRH 1 Mi-17 *Hip* H
 TPT 4: **Heavy** 1 Mi-26 *Halo*; **Medium** 1 Ka-29 *Helix*; **Light** 2 Enstrom 480

Paramilitary

Guardia Civil
FORCES BY ROLE
MANOEUVRE
 Other
  2 paramilitary coy

Coast Guard n.k.

Eritrea ERI

Eritrean Nakfa ERN		2016	2017	2018
GDP	ERN	82.3bn	93.0bn	
	US$	5.35bn	6.05bn	
per capita	US$	823	901	
Growth	%	3.7	3.3	
Inflation	%	9.0	9.0	
Def exp	ERN	n.k	n.k	
	US$	n.k	n.k	
USD1=ERN		15.37	15.37	

Population 5,869,869

Ethnic groups: Tigrinya 50%; Tigre and Kunama 40%; Afar; Saho 3%

Age	0–14	15–19	20–24	25–29	30–64	65 plus
Male	20.2%	5.4%	4.6%	3.9%	14.0%	1.6%
Female	19.5%	5.2%	4.4%	3.8%	14.7%	2.3%

Capabilities

Eritrea maintains a large, mostly conscript, standing army. Its primary task is to defend the border with Ethiopia. Eritrea also has a territorial dispute with neighbour Djibouti. Many troops are also used for civilian development and construction tasks. Significant numbers of conscripts choose to flee the country rather than serve, or evade service in other ways, which may have some effect on military cohesion and effectiveness. An ongoing UN arms embargo will have contributed to the inventory being dominated by outdated platforms, and it is likely that many will be slowly cannibalised for parts. Reported acquisitions from North Korea have also led to the US imposing sanctions on the Eritrean Navy. Air-force investments have been designed to produce a regionally capable fighter wing, though it lacks experienced trained pilots; the navy, meanwhile, remains capable of only limited coastal-patrol and interception operations. Port and airfield facilities at Assab have been refurbished under an agreement with those Gulf states participating in military operations in Yemen. This included deployments of aircraft to Eritrea, including fast jets from the UAE.

ACTIVE 201,750 (Army 200,000 Navy 1,400 Air 350)
Conscript liability 18 months (4 months mil trg) between ages 18 and 40

RESERVE 120,000 (Army ε120,000)

ORGANISATIONS BY SERVICE

Army ε200,000
Heavily cadreised
FORCES BY ROLE
COMMAND
 4 corps HQ
MANOEUVRE
 Mechanised
  1 mech bde
 Light
  19 inf div
  1 cdo div

Reserve ε120,000
FORCES BY ROLE
MANOEUVRE
 Light
  1 inf div
EQUIPMENT BY TYPE
ARMOURED FIGHTING VEHICLES
 MBT 270 T-54/T-55
 RECCE 40 BRDM-1/BRDM-2
 IFV 15 BMP-1
 APC 35
  APC (T) 10 MT-LB†
  APC (W) 25 BTR-152/BTR-60
ENGINEERING & MAINTENANCE VEHICLES
 ARV T-54/T-55 reported
 VLB MTU reported
ANTI-TANK/ANTI-INFRASTRUCTURE
 MSL • MANPATS 9K11 *Malyutka* (AT-3 *Sagger*); 9K111-1 *Konkurs* (AT-5 *Spandrel*)
 GUNS 85mm D-44
ARTILLERY 258
 SP 45: **122mm** 32 2S1 *Gvozdika*; **152mm** 13 2S5 *Giatsint*-S
 TOWED 19+: **122mm** D-30; **130mm** 19 M-46

MRL 44: **122mm** 35 BM-21 *Grad*; **220mm** 9 9P140 *Uragan*
MOR 150+: **82mm** 50+; **120mm/160mm** 100+
AIR DEFENCE
  SAM • Point-defence 9K32 *Strela-2* (SA-7 *Grail*)‡
  GUNS 70+
    SP **23mm** ZSU-23-4
    TOWED **23mm** ZU-23

Navy 1,400
EQUIPMENT BY TYPE
PATROL AND COASTAL COMBATANTS 12
  PBF 9: 5 Battalion-17; 4 *Super Dvora*
  PB 3 Swiftships
AMPHIBIOUS 3
  LS • LST 2: 1 *Chamo*† (Ministry of Transport); 1 *Ashdod*†
  LC • LCU 1 T-4† (in harbour service)

Air Force ε350
FORCES BY ROLE
FIGHTER/GROUND ATTACK
  1 sqn with MiG-29/MiG-29SE/MiG-29UB *Fulcrum*
  1 sqn with Su-27/Su-27UBK *Flanker*
TRANSPORT
  1 sqn with Y-12(II)
TRAINING
  1 sqn with L-90 *Redigo*
  1 sqn with MB-339CE*
TRANSPORT HELICOPTER
  1 sqn with Bell 412 *Twin Huey*
  1 sqn with Mi-17 *Hip H*
EQUIPMENT BY TYPE
AIRCRAFT 16 combat capable
  FTR 8: 4 MiG-29 *Fulcrum*; 2 MiG-29UB *Fulcrum*; 1 Su-27 *Flanker*; 1 Su-27UBK *Flanker*
  FGA 2 MiG-29SE *Fulcrum*
  TPT • Light 5: 1 Beech 200 *King Air*; 4 Y-12(II)
  TRG 12: 8 L-90 *Redigo*; 4 MB-339CE*
HELICOPTERS
  MRH 8: 4 Bell 412 *Twin Huey* (AB-412); 4 Mi-17 *Hip H*
AIR-LAUNCHED MISSILES
  AAM • IR R-60 (AA-8 *Aphid*); R-73 (AA-11 *Archer*); IR/SARH R-27 (AA-10 *Alamo*)

FOREIGN FORCES
United Arab Emirates *Operation Restoring Hope* 1,000; 1 armd BG; *Leclerc*; BMP-3; G-6; *Agrab* Mk2; 2 *Archangel*; 3 AH-64D *Apache*; 2 CH-47F *Chinook*; 4 UH-60M *Black Hawk*; *Wing Loong* I (GJ-1) UAV; 4 MIM-104F *Patriot* PAC-3

Ethiopia ETH

Ethiopian Birr EB		2016	2017	2018
GDP	EB	1.53tr	1.78tr	
	US$	72.5bn	79.7bn	
per capita	US$	795	861	
Growth	%	8.0	8.5	
Inflation	%	7.3	8.1	
Def bdgt	EB	9.5bn	11.0bn	12.0bn
	US$	451m	492m	
FMA (US)	US$	0.6m	0.5m	0m
US$1=EB		21.07	22.34	

Population 105,350,020

Ethnic groups: Oromo 34.4%; Amhara 27%; Somali 6.2%; Tigray 6.1%; Sidama 4%; Guragie 2.5%; other or unspecified 19.2%

Age	0–14	15–19	20–24	25–29	30–64	65 plus
Male	21.8%	5.4%	4.5%	3.8%	12.7%	1.3%
Female	21.7%	5.5%	4.6%	3.9%	13.0%	1.6%

Capabilities

Ethiopia's principal security concerns relate to Eritrea and the activities of Somalia-based group al-Shabaab. Internal security remains a focus for the armed forces, although a ten-month state of emergency was lifted in August 2017. Ethiopia maintains one of the region's most effective armed forces, battle-hardened and experienced following a history of combat operations. The country has been engaged on a ten-year (2005–15) modernisation plan, designed to create flexible armed forces able to respond to regional contingencies. It has enough deployable capability to make significant contributions to the UN missions in Darfur and South Sudan. Ethiopia is also a key contributor to UNISFA, as well as the AMISOM mission in Somalia, although this – combined with standing deployments on the Eritrean border – has meant that it has had to develop while on operations. As of August 2017, Ethiopia was also the largest overall troop contributor to UN peacekeeping missions. The country's inventory contains mostly Soviet-era equipment. There is adequate maintenance capability within the local defence industry, but only a limited capacity to support more advanced platforms.

ACTIVE 138,000 (Army 135,000 Air 3,000)

ORGANISATIONS BY SERVICE

Army 135,000
4 Mil Regional Commands (Northern, Western, Central and Eastern) each acting as corps HQ
FORCES BY ROLE
MANOEUVRE
  Light
  1 (Agazi Cdo) SF comd
  1 (Northern) corps (1 mech div, 4 inf div)
  1 (Western) corps (1 mech div, 3 inf div)
  1 (Central) corps (1 mech div, 5 inf div)
  1 (Eastern) corps (1 mech div, 5 inf div)

EQUIPMENT BY TYPE
ARMOURED FIGHTING VEHICLES
  MBT 461+: 246+ T-54/T-55/T-62; 215 T-72
  RECCE ε100 BRDM-1/BRDM-2
  IFV ε20 BMP-1
  APC 300+
    APC (T) some Type-89
    APC (W) 300+: ε300 BTR-60/BTR-152; some Type-92
  AUV some Ze'ev
ENGINEERING & MAINTENANCE VEHICLES
  ARV T-54/T-55 reported; 4 BTS-5B
  VLB MTU reported
  MW *Bozena*
ANTI-TANK/ANTI-INFRASTRUCTURE
  MSL • **MANPATS** 9K11 *Malyutka* (AT-3 *Sagger*); 9K111 *Fagot* (AT-4 *Spigot*); 9K135 *Kornet*-E (AT-14 *Spriggan*)
  RCL **82mm** B-10; **107mm** B-11
  GUNS **85mm** D-44
ARTILLERY 524+
  SP 10+: **122mm** 2S1 *Gvozdika*; **152mm** 10 2S19 *Msta-S*
  TOWED 464+: **122mm** 464 D-30/M-30 (M-1938); **130mm** M-46; **155mm** AH2
  MRL **122mm** ε50 BM-21 *Grad*
  MOR **81mm** M1/M29; **82mm** M-1937; **120mm** M-1944
AIR DEFENCE
  SAM
    Medium-range S-75 *Dvina* (SA-2 *Guideline*)
    Short-range S-125 *Pechora* (SA-3 *Goa*)
    Point-defence 9K32 *Strela-*2 (SA-7 *Grail*)‡
  GUNS
    SP **23mm** ZSU-23-4
    TOWED **23mm** ZU-23; **37mm** M-1939; **57mm** S-60

Air Force 3,000
FORCES BY ROLE
FIGHTER/GROUND ATTACK
  1 sqn with MiG-23ML *Flogger* G/MiG-23UB *Flogger* C
  1 sqn with Su-27/Su-27UB *Flanker*
TRANSPORT
  1 sqn with An-12 *Cub*; An-26 *Curl*; An-32 *Cline*; C-130B *Hercules*; DHC-6 *Twin Otter*; L-100-30; Yak-40 *Codling* (VIP)
TRAINING
  1 sqn with L-39 *Albatros*
  1 sqn with SF-260
ATTACK/TRANSPORT HELICOPTER
  2 sqn with Mi-24/Mi-35 *Hind*; Mi-8 *Hip*; Mi-17 *Hip* H; SA316 *Alouette* III
EQUIPMENT BY TYPE
  AIRCRAFT 19 combat capable
    FTR 11: 8 Su-27 *Flanker*; 3 Su-27UB *Flanker*
    FGA 8 MiG-23ML/UB *Flogger* G/C
    TPT 12: **Medium** 8: 3 An-12 *Cub*; 2 C-130B *Hercules*; 1 C-130E *Hercules*; 2 L-100-30; **Light** 4: 1 An-26 *Curl*; 1 An-32 *Cline*; 1 DHC-6 *Twin Otter*; 1 Yak-40 *Codling* (VIP)
    TRG 16: 12 L-39 *Albatros*; 4 SF-260
  HELICOPTERS
    ATK 18: 15 Mi-24 *Hind*; 3 Mi-35 *Hind*
    MRH 7: 1 AW139; 6 SA316 *Alouette* III
    MRH/TPT 12 Mi-8 *Hip*/Mi-17 *Hip* H

AIR-LAUNCHED MISSILES
  AAM • **IR** R-3 (AA-2 *Atoll*)‡; R-60 (AA-8 *Aphid*); R-73 (AA-11 *Archer*); **IR/SARH** R-23/R-24 (AA-7 *Apex*); R-27 (AA-10 *Alamo*)

DEPLOYMENT
MALI
UN • MINUSMA 1

SOMALIA
AU • AMISOM 4,395; 6 inf bn

SOUTH SUDAN
UN • UNMISS 1,261; 11 obs; 2 inf bn

SUDAN
UN • UNAMID 2,419; 11 obs; 3 inf bn
UN • UNISFA 4,366; 78 obs; 4 armd pl; 3 inf bn; 2 arty coy; 1 engr coy; 1 sigs coy; 1 fd hospital; 1 hel sqn

Gabon GAB

CFA Franc BEAC fr		2016	2017	2018
GDP	fr	8.31tr	8.41tr	
	US$	14.0bn	14.5bn	
per capita	US$	7,453	7,584	
Growth	%	2.1	1.0	
Inflation	%	2.1	2.5	
Def bdgt [a]	fr	120bn	175bn	
	US$	203m	302m	
US$1=fr		592.73	581.53	

[a] Includes funds allocated to Republican Guard

Population 1,772,255

Age	0–14	15–19	20–24	25–29	30–64	65 plus
Male	21.0%	5.5%	4.7%	4.1%	12.8%	1.6%
Female	20.8%	5.5%	4.7%	4.0%	12.9%	2.1%

Capabilities

Gabon's small armed forces retain sufficient airlift to ensure mobility within the country and even a limited capability to project power by sea and air. The country has benefited from the long-term presence of French troops acting as a security guarantor, while oil revenues have allowed the government to support, in regional terms, capable armed forces. There is regular training with international partners, as well as locally based French forces. Gabonese military medicine is well regarded. Gabonese and US medical personnel exercised together in mid-2017 during the US Army Africa-led Medical Readiness Training Exercise 17-4, in Libreville.

ACTIVE 4,700 (Army 3,200 Navy 500 Air 1,000)
Paramilitary 2,000

ORGANISATIONS BY SERVICE

Army 3,200
Republican Guard under direct presidential control

FORCES BY ROLE
MANOEUVRE
  Light
    1 (Republican Guard) gd gp (bn)
      (1 armd/recce coy, 3 inf coy, 1 arty bty, 1 ADA bty)
    8 inf coy
  Air Manoeuvre
    1 cdo/AB coy
COMBAT SUPPORT
  1 engr coy
EQUIPMENT BY TYPE
ARMOURED FIGHTING VEHICLES
  RECCE 77: 24 AML-60/AML-90; 12 EE-3 *Jararaca*; 14 EE-9 *Cascavel*; 6 ERC-90F4 *Sagaie*; 7 RAM V-2; 14 VBL
  IFV 12 EE-11 *Urutu* (with 20mm gun)
  APC 64
    APC (W) 30: 9 LAV-150 *Commando*; 5 Bastion APC; 3 WZ-523; 12 VXB-170; 1 *Pandur*
    PPV 34 Ashok Leyland MPV
  AUV 12 *Aravis*
ANTI-TANK/ANTI-INFRASTRUCTURE
  MSL • MANPATS *Milan*
  RCL 106mm M40A1
ARTILLERY 67
  TOWED 105mm 4 M101
  MRL 24: **107mm** 16 PH-63; **140mm** 8 *Teruel*
  MOR 39: **81mm** 35; **120mm** 4 Brandt
AIR DEFENCE • GUNS 41
  SP 20mm 4 ERC-20
  TOWED 37+: **14.5mm** ZPU-4; **23mm** 24 ZU-23-2; **37mm** 10 M-1939; **40mm** 3 L/70

Navy ε500
HQ located at Port Gentil
EQUIPMENT BY TYPE
PATROL AND COASTAL COMBATANTS 11
  PCC 2 *General Ba'Oumar* (FRA P-400) with 1 57mm gun
  PBG 1 *Patra* with 4 SS 12M AShM
  PB 8: 4 *Port Gentil* (FRA VCSM); 4 Rodman 66
AMPHIBIOUS 14
  LANDING SHIPS • LST 1 *President Omar Bongo* (FRA *Batral*) (capacity 1 LCVP; 7 MBT; 140 troops) with 1 hel landing platform **LANDING CRAFT** 13
    LCU 1 Mk 9 (ex-UK)
    LCVP 12

Air Force 1,000
FORCES BY ROLE
FIGHTER/GROUND ATTACK
  1 sqn with *Mirage* F-1AZ
TRANSPORT
  1 (Republican Guard) sqn with AS332 *Super Puma*; ATR-42F; *Falcon* 900; Gulfstream IV-SP/G650ER
  1 sqn with C-130H *Hercules*; CN-235M-100
ATTACK/TRANSPORT HELICOPTER
  1 sqn with Bell 412 *Twin Huey* (AB-412); SA330C/H *Puma*; SA342M *Gazelle*
EQUIPMENT BY TYPE
AIRCRAFT 8 combat capable
  FGA 6 *Mirage* F-1AZ
  ATK 2 MB-326 *Impala* I
  MP (1 EMB-111* in store)
  TPT 6: **Medium** 1 C-130H *Hercules*; (1 L-100-30 in store); **Light** 2: 1 ATR-42F; 1 CN-235M-100; **PAX** 3: 1 *Falcon* 900; 1 Gulfstream IV-SP; 1 Gulfstream G650ER
  TRG (4 CM-170 *Magister* in store)
HELICOPTERS
  MRH 2: 1 Bell 412 *Twin Huey* (AB-412); 1 SA342M *Gazelle*; (2 SA342L *Gazelle* in store)
  TPT 7: **Medium** 4: 1 AS332 *Super Puma*; 3 SA330C/H *Puma*; **Light** 3: 2 H120 *Colibri*; 1 H135
AIR-LAUNCHED MISSILES • AAM • IR *U-Darter* (reported)

Paramilitary 2,000

Gendarmerie 2,000
FORCES BY ROLE
MANOEUVRE
  Armoured
    2 armd sqn
  Other
    3 paramilitary bde
    11 paramilitary coy
  Aviation
    1 unit with AS350 *Ecureuil*; AS355 *Ecureuil* II
EQUIPMENT BY TYPE
HELICOPTERS • TPT • Light 4: 2 AS350 *Ecureuil*; 2 AS355 *Ecureuil* II

DEPLOYMENT
CENTRAL AFRICAN REPUBLIC
UN • MINUSCA 445; 1 inf bn(-)

FOREIGN FORCES
France 450; 1 AB bn

Gambia GAM

Gambian Dalasi D		2016	2017	2018
GDP	D	42.3bn	47.1bn	
	US$	1.0	1.0	
per capita	US$	469	488	
Growth	%	2.2	3.0	
Inflation	%	7.2	8.3	
Def bdgt	D	n.k	n.k	
	US$	n.k	n.k	
US$1=D		43.78	45.41	

Population 2,051,363

Age	0–14	15–19	20–24	25–29	30–64	65 plus
Male	18.8%	5.2%	4.8%	4.3%	14.5%	1.6%
Female	18.6%	5.3%	5.0%	4.5%	15.2%	1.8%

Capabilities

A political crisis in late 2016 and early 2017 led to the departure of long-serving President Jammeh; subsequently, there has been a focus on clarifying political–military relations. Several senior officers and the head of the armed forces were dismissed, while members of the former State Guard Battalion have been redeployed to other units. Defence cooperation with France will look to train the country's security forces, as part of moves to reform security structures. The ECOWAS mission, *Operation Restore Democracy*, extended its mandate for another year. Gambian forces have traditionally focused on maritime security and countering human trafficking. A National Maritime Security Committee was inaugurated in 2015. Gambia is expected to receive assistance in safeguarding its EEZ in the form of aerial surveillance and patrol boats. The country's small armed forces have deployed in support of UN missions, and in the past received training assistance from the US.

ACTIVE 800 (Army 800)

ORGANISATIONS BY SERVICE

Gambian National Army 800

FORCES BY ROLE
MANOEUVRE
  Light
  2 inf bn
COMBAT SUPPORT
  1 engr sqn

Marine Unit ε300

EQUIPMENT BY TYPE
PATROL AND COASTAL COMBATANTS 9
  PBF 4: 2 Rodman 55; 2 *Fatimah* I
  PB 5: 1 *Bolong Kanta*†; 4 *Taipei* (ROC *Hai Ou*) (of which one damaged and in reserve)

Air Wing

EQUIPMENT BY TYPE
AIRCRAFT
  TPT 5: **Light** 2 AT-802A *Air Tractor*; **PAX** 3: 1 B-727; 1 CL-601; 1 Il-62M *Classic* (VIP)

DEPLOYMENT

CENTRAL AFRICAN REPUBLIC
UN • MINUSCA 2; 2 obs

LIBERIA
UN • UNMIL 1 obs

MALI
UN • MINUSMA 3; 1 obs

SUDAN
UN • UNAMID 211; 1 inf coy

FOREIGN FORCES

Ghana ECOMIG 50
Nigeria ECOMIG 200
Senegal ECOMIG 250

Ghana GHA

Ghanaian New Cedi C		2016	2017	2018
GDP	C	167bn	202bn	
	US$	42.8bn	45.5bn	
per capita	US$	1,551	1,608	
Growth	%	3.5	5.9	
Inflation	%	17.5	11.8	
Def bdgt	C	761m	822m	925m
	US$	195m	185m	
FMA (US)	US$	0.3m	0.3m	0m
US$1=C		3.91	4.45	

Population 27,499,924

Age	0–14	15–19	20–24	25–29	30–64	65 plus
Male	19.1%	4.9%	4.3%	3.8%	15.1%	1.9%
Female	18.9%	5.0%	4.3%	4.0%	16.1%	2.3%

Capabilities

Ghana's armed forces are among the most capable in the region, with a long-term development plan covering both the current and the next decade. The ability to control its maritime EEZ is of increasing importance to Ghana because of growing piracy and resource exploitation, and this underpins the navy's expansion ambitions. Internal and maritime security are the forces' central roles, along with participation in peacekeeping missions. Ghanaian and US units conduct joint maritime-law-enforcement and interoperability activities as part of the Africa Maritime Law Enforcement Partnership, while Ghana receives US assistance as part of the African Peacekeeping Rapid Response Partnership programme. There is also significant defence engagement with the UK. Air-force training, close-air-support and airlift capabilities have developed in recent years. Ghana hosts the Kofi Annan International Peacekeeping Training Centre. The army is a regular contributor to UN peacekeeping operations. It has pledged to maintain 1,000 personnel in readiness for missions, including a mechanised infantry battalion, a level-two hospital, a signals company, an aviation unit and a riverine unit.

ACTIVE 15,500 (Army 11,500 Navy 2,000 Air 2,000)

ORGANISATIONS BY SERVICE

Army 11,500

FORCES BY ROLE
COMMAND
  2 comd HQ
MANOEUVRE
  Reconnaissance
  1 armd recce regt (3 recce sqn)
  Light
  1 (rapid reaction) mot inf bn
  6 inf bn
  Air Manoeuvre
  2 AB coy

COMBAT SUPPORT
1 arty regt (1 arty bty, 2 mor bty)
1 fd engr regt (bn)
1 sigs regt
1 sigs sqn
COMBAT SERVICE SUPPORT
1 log gp
1 tpt coy
2 maint coy
1 med coy
1 trg bn
EQUIPMENT BY TYPE
ARMOURED FIGHTING VEHICLES
  RECCE 3 EE-9 *Cascavel*
  IFV 48: 24 *Ratel*-90; 15 *Ratel*-20; 4 *Piranha* 25mm; 5+ Type-05P 25mm
  APC 105
    APC (W) 55+: 46 *Piranha*; 9+ Type-05P
    PPV 50 Streit *Typhoon*
ARTILLERY 87+
  TOWED 122mm 6 D-30
  MRL 3+: **107mm** Type-63; **122mm** 3 Type-81
  MOR 78: **81mm** 50; **120mm** 28 Tampella
ENGINEERING & MAINTENANCE VEHICLES
  AEV 1 Type-05P AEV
  ARV *Piranha* reported
ANTI-TANK/ANTI-INFRASTRUCTURE
  RCL 84mm *Carl Gustav*
AIR DEFENCE
  SAM • Point-defence 9K32 *Strela*-2 (SA-7 *Grail*)‡
  GUNS • TOWED 8+: **14.5mm** 4+: 4 ZPU-2; ZPU-4; **23mm** 4 ZU-23-2

Navy 2,000
Naval HQ located at Accra; Western HQ located at Sekondi; Eastern HQ located at Tema
EQUIPMENT BY TYPE
PATROL AND COASTAL COMBATANTS 14
  PCO 2 *Anzone* (US)
  PCC 10: 2 *Achimota* (GER Lurssen 57m) with 1 76mm gun; 2 *Dzata* (GER Lurssen 45m); 2 *Warrior* (GER Gepard); 4 *Snake* (PRC 47m)
  PBF 1 *Stephen Otu* (ROK *Sea Dolphin*)
  PB 1 *David Hansen* (US)

Air Force 2,000
FORCES BY ROLE
GROUND ATTACK
  1 sqn with K-8 *Karakorum**; L-39ZO*; MB-339A*
ISR
  1 unit with DA-42
TRANSPORT
  1 sqn with BN-2 *Defender*; C295; Cessna 172
TRANSPORT HELICOPTER
  1 sqn with AW109A; Bell 412SP *Twin Huey*; Mi-17V-5 *Hip* H; SA319 *Alouette* III; Z-9EH
EQUIPMENT BY TYPE†
AIRCRAFT 8 combat capable
  ATK (3 MB-326K in store)
  TPT 10: **Light** 10: 1 BN-2 *Defender*; 3 C295; 3 Cessna 172; 3 DA42; **(PAX** 1 F-28 *Fellowship* (VIP) in store)
  TRG 8: 4 K-8 *Karakorum**; 2 L-39ZO*; 2 MB-339A*

HELICOPTERS
  MRH 10: 1 Bell 412SP *Twin Huey*; 3 Mi-17V-5 *Hip* H; 2 SA319 *Alouette* III; 4 Z-9EH
  TPT 6: **Medium** 4 Mi-171Sh; **Light** 2 AW109A

DEPLOYMENT

CENTRAL AFRICAN REPUBLIC
UN • MINUSCA 4; 3 obs

DEMOCRATIC REPUBLIC OF THE CONGO
UN • MONUSCO 463; 21 obs; 1 inf bn(-)

GAMBIA
ECOWAS • ECOMIG 50

LEBANON
UN • UNIFIL 870; 1 mech inf bn

LIBERIA
UN • UNMIL 1; 1 obs

MALI
UN • MINUSMA 218; 3 obs; 1 engr coy; 1 avn flt

SOMALIA
UN • UNSOS 2 obs

SOUTH SUDAN
UN • UNMISS 716; 11 obs; 1 inf bn

SUDAN
UN • UNAMID 19; 4 obs
UN • UNISFA 3; 4 obs

WESTERN SAHARA
UN • MINURSO 8; 8 obs

Guinea GUI

Guinean Franc fr		2016	2017	2018
GDP	fr	75.9tr	87.4tr	
	US$	8.48bn	9.18bn	
per capita	US$	670	708	
Growth	%	6.6	6.7	
Inflation	%	8.2	8.5	
Def exp	fr	1.45tr	1.57tr	
	US$	162m	164m	
US$1=fr		8,959.81	9,512.67	

Population 12,413,867

Age	0–14	15–19	20–24	25–29	30–64	65 plus
Male	21.0%	5.4%	4.6%	3.8%	13.7%	1.6%
Female	20.5%	5.3%	4.5%	3.7%	13.8%	2.0%

Capabilities

Much of the country's military equipment is ageing and of Soviet-era vintage; serviceability will be questionable for some types. A military-programming law for 2015–20 is reportedly examining operational capacities. There is very limited fixed- and rotary-wing airlift capacity. China in the past donated a small amount of non-lethal military and civilian equipment. The EU has engaged in police training within the context of a broader SSR process.

ACTIVE 9,700 (Army 8,500 Navy 400 Air 800)
Paramilitary 2,600
Conscript liability 2 years

ORGANISATIONS BY SERVICE

Army 8,500
FORCES BY ROLE
MANOEUVRE
  Armoured
  1 armd bn
  Light
  1 SF bn
  5 inf bn
  1 ranger bn
  1 cdo bn
  Air Manoeuvre
  1 air mob bn
  Other
  1 (Presidential Guard) gd bn
COMBAT SUPPORT
  1 arty bn
  1 AD bn
  1 engr bn
EQUIPMENT BY TYPE
ARMOURED FIGHTING VEHICLES
  MBT 38: 30 T-34; 8 T-54
  LT TK 15 PT-76
  RECCE 27: 2 AML-90; 25 BRDM-1/BRDM-2
  IFV 2 BMP-1
  APC 59
    APC (T) 10 BTR-50
    APC (W) 30: 16 BTR-40; 8 BTR-60; 6 BTR-152
    PPV 19: 10 *Mamba*†; 9 *Puma* M36
ENGINEERING & MAINTENANCE VEHICLES
  ARV T-54/T-55 reported
ANTI-TANK/ANTI-INFRASTRUCTURE
  MSL • MANPATS 9K11 *Malyutka* (AT-3 *Sagger*); 9K111-1 *Konkurs* (AT-5 *Spandrel*)
  RCL 82mm B-10
  GUNS 6+: **57mm** ZIS-2 (M-1943); **85mm** 6 D-44
ARTILLERY 47+
  TOWED 24: **122mm** 12 M-1931/37; **130mm** 12 M-46
  MRL 220mm 3 9P140 *Uragan*
  MOR 20+: **82mm** M-43; **120mm** 20 M-1938/M-1943
AIR DEFENCE
  SAM • Point-defence 9K32 *Strela*-2 (SA-7 *Grail*)‡
  GUNS • TOWED 24+: **30mm** M-53 (twin); **37mm** 8 M-1939; **57mm** 12 Type-59 (S-60); **100mm** 4 KS-19

Navy ε400
EQUIPMENT BY TYPE
PATROL AND COASTAL COMBATANTS • PB 4: 1 Swiftships†; 3 RPB 20

Air Force 800
EQUIPMENT BY TYPE†
AIRCRAFT
  FGA (3 MiG-21 *Fishbed* non-op)
  TPT • Light 4: 2 An-2 *Colt*; 2 *Tetras*
HELICOPTERS
  ATK 4 Mi-24 *Hind*
  MRH 5: 2 MD-500MD; 2 Mi-17-1V *Hip* H; 1 SA342K *Gazelle*
  TPT 2: **Medium** 1 SA330 *Puma*; **Light** 1 AS350B *Ecureuil*
AIR-LAUNCHED MISSILES
  AAM • IR R-3 (AA-2 *Atoll*)‡

Paramilitary 2,600 active

Gendarmerie 1,000

Republican Guard 1,600

People's Militia 7,000 reservists

DEPLOYMENT

MALI
UN • MINUSMA 860; 3 obs; 1 inf bn

SOUTH SUDAN
UN • UNMISS 1

SUDAN
UN • UNISFA 1

WESTERN SAHARA
UN • MINURSO 5 obs

Guinea-Bissau GNB

CFA Franc BCEAO fr		2016	2017	2018
GDP	fr	683bn	753bn	
	US$	1.15bn	1.30bn	
per capita	US$	692	761	
Growth	%	5.1	5.0	
Inflation	%	1.5	2.8	
Def exp	fr	n.k	n.k	
	US$	n.k	n.k	
US$1=fr		592.81	581.40	

Population 1,792,338

Age	0–14	15–19	20–24	25–29	30–64	65 plus
Male	19.5%	5.3%	4.7%	4.1%	14.0%	1.3%
Female	19.5%	5.4%	4.8%	4.2%	15.0%	2.2%

Capabilities

ECOWAS mediation in 2016, amid domestic political strife, led to a six-point road map. Among other areas, this included SSR and the demobilisation of ECOMIB, six months after a suitable national force can take over its mandate. Political disputes, however, have restricted progress on these areas and still hinder foreign investment and economic assistance.

In 2016, UNIOGBIS updated a ten-year-old document on restructuring and modernising the security sector, but progress is dependent on local political stability. China has donated some non-lethal military and civilian equipment, but much of the country's military equipment is ageing and of Soviet-era vintage; serviceability will be questionable for some types.

ACTIVE 4,450 (Army 4,000 Navy 350 Air 100)

Conscript liability Selective conscription
Manpower and eqpt totals should be treated with caution. A number of draft laws to restructure the armed services and police have been produced

ORGANISATIONS BY SERVICE

Army ε4,000 (numbers reducing)
FORCES BY ROLE
MANOEUVRE
  Reconnaissance
    1 recce coy
  Armoured
    1 armd bn (sqn)
  Light
    5 inf bn
COMBAT SUPPORT
  1 arty bn
  1 engr coy
EQUIPMENT BY TYPE
ARMOURED FIGHTING VEHICLES
  MBT 10 T-34
  LT TK 15 PT-76
  RECCE 10 BRDM-2
  APC • APC (W) 55: 35 BTR-40/BTR-60; 20 Type-56 (BTR-152)
ANTI-TANK/ANTI-INFRASTRUCTURE
  RCL 75mm Type-52 (M20); 82mm B-10
  GUNS 85mm 8 D-44
ARTILLERY 26+
  TOWED 122mm 18 D-30/M-30 (M-1938)
  MOR 8+: 82mm M-43; 120mm 8 M-1943
AIR DEFENCE
  SAM • Point-defence 9K32 *Strela*-2 (SA-7 *Grail*)‡
  GUNS • TOWED 34: 23mm 18 ZU-23; 37mm 6 M-1939; 57mm 10 S-60

Navy ε350
EQUIPMENT BY TYPE
PATROL AND COASTAL COMBATANTS 4
  PB 4: 2 *Alfeite*†; 2 Rodman 55M

Air Force 100
EQUIPMENT BY TYPE
AIRCRAFT • TPT • Light 1 Cessna 208B

DEPLOYMENT

MALI
UN • MINUSMA 1

FOREIGN FORCES
Nigeria ECOMIB 100

Kenya KEN

Kenyan Shilling sh		2016	2017	2018
GDP	sh	7.16tr	8.14tr	
	US$	70.5bn	78.4bn	
per capita	US$	1,552	1,678	
Growth	%	5.8	5.0	
Inflation	%	6.3	8..0	
Def bdgt [a]	sh	124bn	124bn	130bn
	US$	1.22bn	1.19bn	
FMA (US)	US$	1m	1m	0m
US$1=sh		101.50	103.86	

[a] Includes national-intelligence funding

Population 47,615,739

Ethnic groups: Kikuyu ε22–32%

Age	0–14	15–19	20–24	25–29	30–64	65 plus
Male	20.1%	5.2%	4.3%	4.2%	14.8%	1.3%
Female	19.9%	5.2%	4.4%	4.2%	14.7%	1.7%

Capabilities

Kenya remains a key contributor to AMISOM in Somalia and continues to conduct key operations against al-Shabaab, as well as being a leading element in the East African Standby Force. Experience in Somalia has demonstrated some limited ability to project power outside its territory and regular deployment rotations have boosted the confidence and capability of Kenya's forces. The threat posed by al-Shabaab remains a significant security concern. The armed forces regularly train with UK troops in Kenya (a new defence-cooperation agreement was signed with the UK in September 2016) and take part in international exercises in Africa. There are also significant defence ties with the US and developing relationships with the Chinese and Jordanian armed forces. Modernisation is focused on helicopters, armoured vehicles, UAVs and border-surveillance equipment. The navy undertakes coastguard and counter-piracy roles. Kenya regularly participates in multinational and regional exercises, including the *Cutlass Express 2017* maritime-security exercise.

ACTIVE 24,100 (Army 20,000 Navy 1,600 Air 2,500)
Paramilitary 5,000

ORGANISATIONS BY SERVICE

Army 20,000
FORCES BY ROLE
MANOEUVRE
  Armoured
    1 armd bde (1 armd recce bn, 2 armd bn)
  Light
    1 spec ops bn
    1 ranger bn

1 inf bde (3 inf bn)
1 inf bde (2 inf bn)
1 indep inf bn
Air Manoeuvre
1 air cav bn
1 AB bn
COMBAT SUPPORT
1 arty bde (2 arty bn, 1 mor bty)
1 ADA bn
1 engr bde (2 engr bn)
EQUIPMENT BY TYPE
ARMOURED FIGHTING VEHICLES
MBT 78 Vickers Mk 3
RECCE 92: 72 AML-60/AML-90; 12 *Ferret*; 8 S52 *Shorland*
APC 189
  APC (W) 84: 52 UR-416; 32 Type-92; (10 M3 Panhard in store)
  PPV 105 *Puma* M26-15
ENGINEERING & MAINTENANCE VEHICLES
  ARV 7 Vickers ARV
  MW *Bozena*
ARTILLERY 112
  SP 155mm 2+ *Nora* B-52
  TOWED 105mm 48: 40 L118 Light Gun; 8 Model 56 pack howitzer
  MOR 62: 81mm 50; 120mm 12 Brandt
ANTI-TANK/ANTI-INFRASTRUCTURE
  MSL • MANPATS *Milan*
  RCL 84mm 80 *Carl Gustav*
HELICOPTERS
  MRH 37: 2 Hughes 500D†; 12 Hughes 500M†; 10 Hughes 500MD *Scout Defender*† (with TOW); 10 Hughes 500ME†; 3 Z-9W
AIR DEFENCE • GUNS • TOWED 94: 20mm 81: 11 Oerlikon; ε70 TCM-20; 40mm 13 L/70
AIR-LAUNCHED MISSILES • ASM TOW

Navy 1,600 (incl 120 marines)
EQUIPMENT BY TYPE
PATROL AND COASTAL COMBATANTS 7
  PCO 1 *Jasiri* with 1 76mm gun
  PCF 2 *Nyayo*
  PCC 3: 1 *Harambee* II (ex-FRA P400); 2 *Shujaa* with 1 76mm gun
  PBF 1 *Archangel*
AMPHIBIOUS • LCM 2 *Galana*
LOGISTICS AND SUPPORT • AP 2

Air Force 2,500
FORCES BY ROLE
FIGHTER/GROUND ATTACK
  2 sqn with F-5E/F *Tiger* II
TRANSPORT
  Some sqn with DHC-5D *Buffalo*†; DHC-8†; F-70† (VIP); Y-12(II)†
TRAINING
  Some sqn with *Bulldog* 103/*Bulldog* 127†; EMB-312 *Tucano*†*; *Hawk* Mk52†*; Hughes 500D†
TRANSPORT HELICOPTER
  1 sqn with SA330 *Puma*†
EQUIPMENT BY TYPE†
AIRCRAFT 38 combat capable
FTR 22: 18 F-5E *Tiger* II; 4 F-5F *Tiger* II
TPT 17 Light 16: 4 DHC-5D *Buffalo*†; 3 DHC-8†; 9 Y-12(II)†; (6 Do-28D-2† in store); PAX 1 F-70 (VIP)
TRG 30: 8 *Bulldog* 103/127†; 11 EMB-312 *Tucano*†*; 6 Grob 120A; 5 *Hawk* Mk52†*
HELICOPTERS
  ATK 3 AH-1F *Cobra*
  TPT 20: Medium 12: 2 Mi-171; 10 SA330 *Puma*†; Light 8 Bell 205 (UH-1H *Huey* II)
AIR-LAUNCHED MISSILES
  AAM • IR AIM-9 *Sidewinder*
  ASM AGM-65 *Maverick*

Paramilitary 5,000

Police General Service Unit 5,000
EQUIPMENT BY TYPE
PATROL AND COASTAL COMBATANTS • PB 5 (2 on Lake Victoria)

Air Wing
EQUIPMENT BY TYPE
AIRCRAFT • TPT • Light 6: 2 Cessna 208B *Grand Caravan*; 3 Cessna 310; 1 Cessna 402
HELICOPTERS
  MRH 3 Mi-17 *Hip* H
  TPT 3: Medium 1 Mi-17V-5; Light 2: 1 Bell 206L *Long Ranger*; 1 Bo-105
  TRG 1 Bell 47G

DEPLOYMENT

CENTRAL AFRICAN REPUBLIC
UN • MINUSCA 8; 6 obs

DEMOCRATIC REPUBLIC OF THE CONGO
UN • MONUSCO 13; 9 obs

LEBANON
UN • UNIFIL 1

MALI
UN • MINUSMA 7; 2 obs

SOMALIA
AU • AMISOM 3,664: 3 inf bn

SUDAN
UN • UNAMID 113; 3 obs; 1 MP coy

FOREIGN FORCES
United Kingdom Army 250; 1 trg unit

Lesotho LSO

Lesotho Loti M		2016	2017	2018
GDP	M	33.3bn	37.3bn	
	US$	2.26bn	2.72bn	
per capita	US$	1,179	1,414	
Growth	%	2.4	4.6	
Inflation	%	6.4	6.6	
Def bdgt	M	624m	723m	
	US$	42m	53m	
US$1=M		14.71	13.70	

Population 1,958,042

Age	0–14	15–19	20–24	25–29	30–64	65 plus
Male	16.1%	4.8%	4.4%	4.4%	16.8%	2.8%
Female	15.9%	5.1%	5.0%	5.2%	16.5%	2.7%

Capabilities

Lesotho's small armed forces are charged with protecting territorial integrity and sovereignty. Internal instability, however, is the country's most pressing concern. Military cohesion has suffered for a number of years after a coup attempt in 2014 and instability that continued in 2015. Hopes that the June 2017 general election would lead to greater stability have so far failed to materialise. The country contains significant water resources, which form a significant portion of its foreign trade. SADC held a summit as a result of the killing of the army chief – reportedly by officers from a rival faction – in September 2017, and a decision was taken to deploy a contingent force of military, security and intelligence personnel to Lesotho to support the government. Despite recommendations from the SADC at the end of 2015 for Lesotho to make constitutional and security reforms, these have yet to be realised. The need to implement the reforms was again highlighted at the September 2017 SADC summit.

ACTIVE 2,000 (Army 2,000)

ORGANISATIONS BY SERVICE

Army ε2,000
FORCES BY ROLE
MANOEUVRE
  Reconnaissance
    1 recce coy
  Light
    7 inf coy
  Aviation
    1 sqn
COMBAT SUPPORT
  1 arty bty(-)
  1 spt coy (with mor)
EQUIPMENT BY TYPE
ARMOURED FIGHTING VEHICLES
  MBT 1 T-55
  RECCE 30: 4 AML-90; 2 BRDM-2†; 6 RAM Mk3; 10 RBY-1; 8 S52 *Shorland*

ANTI-TANK/ANTI-INFRASTRUCTURE
  RCL 106mm 6 M40
ARTILLERY 12
  TOWED 105mm 2
  MOR 81mm 10

Air Wing 110
AIRCRAFT
  TPT • Light 3: 2 C-212-300 *Aviocar*; 1 GA-8 *Airvan*
HELICOPTERS
  MRH 3: 1 Bell 412 *Twin Huey*; 2 Bell 412EP *Twin Huey*
  TPT • Light 1 Bell 206 *Jet Ranger*

Liberia LBR

Liberian Dollar L$		2016	2017	2018
GDP	L$	2.10bn	2.14bn	
	US$	2.10bn	2.14bn	
per capita	US$	478	475	
Growth	%	-1.6	2.6	
Inflation	%	8.8	12.8	
Def bdgt	L$	13m	14m	13m
	US$	13m	14m	
FMA (US)	US$	2.5m	2.5m	0m
US$1=L$		1.00	1.00	

Population 4,689,021

Ethnic groups: Americo-Liberians 5%

Age	0–14	15–19	20–24	25–29	30–64	65 plus
Male	22.1%	5.5%	4.2%	3.6%	13.1%	1.4%
Female	21.2%	5.5%	4.3%	3.8%	13.3%	1.4%

Capabilities

The development of the Liberian armed forces has been underpinned by US support for almost the past decade. France has also provided military-training support. A new national-security strategy is under development and the UN reports that a public-expenditure review of the justice and security sectors will end in May 2018. In July 2016, the Liberian security forces took over full responsibility for security from the UN peacekeeping mission, UNMIL, after 13 years. UNMIL reverted to a support role, though the mission has been extended to March 2018. In May 2016, the UN Security Council voted to lift sanctions and the arms embargo against Liberia. There is still no indigenous airlift capacity, which hindered movements during the Ebola outbreak.

ACTIVE 2,100 (Army 2,000, Coast Guard 100)

ORGANISATIONS BY SERVICE

Army 2,000
FORCES BY ROLE
MANOEUVRE
  Light
    1 (23rd) inf bde with (2 inf bn, 1 engr coy, 1 MP coy)

COMBAT SERVICE SUPPORT
   1 trg unit (forming)

Coast Guard 100
All operational patrol vessels under 10t FLD

DEPLOYMENT

MALI
UN • MINUSMA 73; 1 inf coy(-)

FOREIGN FORCES
All under UNMIL comd unless otherwise specified
Benin 1 obs
China, People's Republic of 1
Egypt 2 obs
Gambia 1 obs
Ghana 1; 1 obs
Nepal 1 obs
Nigeria 234; 3 obs; 1 inf coy
Pakistan 71; 1 obs; 1 fd hospital
Russia 1 obs
Senegal 1
Serbia 1 obs
Togo 1
Ukraine 107; 1 hel sqn
United States 2
Zambia 1 obs

Madagascar MDG

Malagsy Ariary fr		2016	2017	2018
GDP	fr	31.8tr	35.7tr	
	US$	10.0bn	10.6bn	
per capita	US$	401	412	
Growth	%	4.2	4.3	
Inflation	%	6.7	7.8	
Def bdgt	fr	189bn	209bn	
	US$	59m	62m	
US$1=fr		3,176.60	3,384.556	

Population 25,054,161

Age	0–14	15–19	20–24	25–29	30–64	65 plus
Male	20.1%	5.4%	4.8%	4.1%	14.1%	1.5%
Female	19.7%	5.3%	4.8%	4.1%	14.2%	1.8%

Capabilities

The armed forces have played a significant role in the island's recent political instability, with some elements involved in an abortive coup attempt in 2010 and a mutiny in 2012. In mid-2016 there was a terrorist attack allegedly carried out by opponents of the current president. The army is the dominant force, but the state has no power-projection capability. As an island state, maritime security is an issue, as reflected in the country's participation in the US AFRICOM-sponsored *Cutlass Express 2017*, designed to improve regional maritime security and related cooperation. Much of its remaining air inventory is likely non-operational. Moves towards security-sector reform (SSR) have begun, with an African Union mission conducted in late 2015, designed to 'sensitise senior officials and civil society' on SSR.

ACTIVE 13,500 (Army 12,500 Navy 500 Air 500)
Paramilitary 8,100
Conscript liability 18 months (incl for civil purposes)

ORGANISATIONS BY SERVICE

Army 12,500+
FORCES BY ROLE
MANOEUVRE
   Light
      2 (intervention) inf regt
      10 (regional) inf regt
COMBAT SUPPORT
   1 arty regt
   3 engr regt
   1 sigs regt
COMBAT SERVICE SUPPORT
   1 log regt
AIR DEFENCE
   1 ADA regt
EQUIPMENT BY TYPE
ARMOURED FIGHTING VEHICLES
   LT TK 12 PT-76
   RECCE 73: ε35 BRDM-2; 10 FV701 *Ferret*; ε20 M3A1; 8 M8
   APC • APC (T) ε30 M3A1 half-track
ANTI-TANK/ANTI-INFRASTRUCTURE
   RCL 106mm M40A1
ARTILLERY 25+
   TOWED 17: 105mm 5 M101; 122mm 12 D-30
   MOR 8+: 82mm M-37; 120mm 8 M-43
AIR DEFENCE • GUNS • TOWED 70: 14.5mm 50 ZPU-4; 37mm 20 PG-55 (M-1939)

Navy 500 (incl some 100 Marines)
EQUIPMENT BY TYPE
PATROL AND COASTAL COMBATANTS 8
   PCC 1 *Trozona*
   PB 7 (ex-US CG MLB)
AMPHIBIOUS • LCT 1 (ex-FRA EDIC)

Air Force 500
FORCES BY ROLE
TRANSPORT
   1 sqn with An-26 *Curl*; Yak-40 *Codling* (VIP)
   1 (liaison) sqn with Cessna 310; Cessna 337 *Skymaster*; PA-23 *Aztec*
TRAINING
   1 sqn with Cessna 172; J.300 *Joker*; *Tetras*
TRANSPORT HELICOPTER
   1 sqn with SA318C *Alouette* II

EQUIPMENT BY TYPE
AIRCRAFT • TPT 16: **Light** 14: 1 An-26 *Curl*; 4 Cessna 172; 1 Cessna 310; 2 Cessna 337 *Skymaster*; 2 J.300 *Joker*; 1 PA-23 *Aztec*; 1 *Tetras*; 2 Yak-40 *Codling* (VIP); **PAX** 2 B-737
HELICOPTERS • MRH 4 SA318C *Alouette* II

Paramilitary 8,100

Gendarmerie 8,100

Malawi MWI

Malawian Kwacha K		2016	2017	2018
GDP	K	3.92tr	4.60tr	
	US$	5.49bn	6.26bn	
per capita	US$	295	327	
Growth	%	2.3	4.5	
Inflation	%	21.7	13.0	
Def bdgt	K	20.7bn	27.6bn	37.1bn
	US$	29m	38m	
US$1=K		714.05	734.00	

Population 19,196,246

Age	0–14	15–19	20–24	25–29	30–64	65 plus
Male	23.1%	5.6%	4.6%	3.7%	11.4%	1.2%
Female	23.3%	5.7%	4.7%	3.7%	11.7%	1.5%

Capabilities

The armed forces' role is to ensure the sovereignty and territorial integrity of the state. The army is the largest force, consisting mainly of infantry units supported by light armoured vehicles. The air wing and the naval unit are much smaller supporting services, for which counter-trafficking is one role. Army units were deployed in March 2017 to tackle cross-border smuggling. The army participates in and hosts multinational exercises, and is involved in supporting UN missions. The defence force is unable to deploy outside Malawi's borders without external assistance, although it has dispatched troops to the Democratic Republic of the Congo, among other UN operations, to take part in tasks assigned to the Force Intervention Brigade. US AFRICOM's senior-leader meeting, *Africa Endeavor 2017*, was held in Malawi, with a focus on cyber security and other ICTs.

ACTIVE 10,700 (Army 10,700) **Paramilitary 4,200**

ORGANISATIONS BY SERVICE

Army 10,700
FORCES BY ROLE
MANOEUVRE
  Mechanised
  1 mech bn
  Light
  1 inf bde (4 inf bn)
  1 inf bde (1 inf bn)
Air Manoeuvre
1 para bn
COMBAT SUPPORT
3 lt arty bty
1 engr bn
COMBAT SERVICE SUPPORT
12 log coy
EQUIPMENT BY TYPE
ARMOURED FIGHTING VEHICLES
  RECCE 66: 30 *Eland*-90; 8 FV701 *Ferret*; 20 FV721 *Fox*; 8 RAM Mk3
  APC • PPV 31: 14 *Casspir*; 9 *Marauder*; 8 *Puma* M26-15
ARTILLERY 107
  TOWED 105mm 9 L118 Light Gun
  MOR 81mm 98: 82 L16A1; 16 M3
AIR DEFENCE • GUNS • TOWED 72: **12.7mm** 32; **14.5mm** 40 ZPU-4

Navy 220
EQUIPMENT BY TYPE
PATROL AND COASTAL COMBATANTS 1
  PB 1 *Kasungu* (ex-FRA *Antares*)

Air Wing 200
EQUIPMENT BY TYPE
AIRCRAFT • TPT • Light 1 Do-228
HELICOPTERS • TPT 8: **Medium** 3: 1 AS532UL *Cougar*; 1 SA330H *Puma*; 1 H215 *Super Puma* **Light** 5: 1 AS350L *Ecureuil*; 4 SA341B *Gazelle*

Paramilitary 4,200

Police Mobile Service 4,200
EQUIPMENT BY TYPE
ARMOURED FIGHTING VEHICLES
  RECCE 8 S52 *Shorland*
AIRCRAFT
  TPT • Light 4: 3 BN-2T *Defender* (border patrol); 1 SC.7 3M *Skyvan*
HELICOPTERS • MRH 2 AS365 *Dauphin* 2

DEPLOYMENT

DEMOCRATIC REPUBLIC OF THE CONGO
UN • MONUSCO 855; 2 obs; 1 inf bn

SUDAN
UN • UNISFA 1

WESTERN SAHARA
UN • MINURSO 3 obs

Mali MLI

CFA Franc BCEAO fr		2016	2017	2018
GDP	fr	8.32tr	8.87tr	
	US$	14.0bn	15.0bn	
per capita	US$	768	794	
Growth	%	5.8	5.3	
Inflation	%	-1.8	0.2	
Def bdgt [a]	fr	324bn	381bn	403bn
	US$	546m	644m	
US$1=fr		592.72	591.28	

[a] Defence and interior-security budget

Population 17,885,245

Ethnic groups: Tuareg 6–10%

Age	0–14	15–19	20–24	25–29	30–64	65 plus
Male	24.2%	5.1%	3.8%	2.9%	11.0%	1.5%
Female	23.9%	5.3%	4.4%	3.7%	12.2%	1.5%

Capabilities

Mali's armed forces rely on France and the UN for training, logistical and aviation support. The shortcomings of the armed forces were exposed by their inability to deal with Islamist and Tuareg insurgents in 2013, with the latter leading to French military intervention. Tranches of the reconstituted armed forces have been trained by an EU Training Mission (EUTM). The mission has been extended until May 2018. To date, more than 10,000 soldiers have received training – many at the Koulikoro training centre. The EUTM has also trained the air force, with a focus on mobility. German security-sector assistance has included the construction of ammunition bunkers. France maintains bases, personnel and equipment in Mali as part of *Operation Barkhane*, which is intended to tackle Islamist radicals and terrorists in Mali and the broader Sahel region. For the first time, in 2017 the G5-Sahel force launched a military operation in Mali near the border with Niger and Burkina Faso. In September 2017, a peace and reconciliation agreement was signed between some parties to the conflict in Mali, yet several areas remain unresolved, including SSR and the DDR process.

ACTIVE 10,000 (Army 10,000) Paramilitary 7,800

ORGANISATIONS BY SERVICE

Army ε10,000
FORCES BY ROLE
The remnants of the pre-conflict Malian army are being reformed into new combined-arms battle groups, each of which comprise one lt mech coy, three mot inf coy, one arty bty and additional recce, cdo and cbt spt elms
MANOEUVRE
Light
8 mot inf BG
Air Manoeuvre
1 para bn

COMBAT SUPPORT
1 engr bn
COMBAT SERVICE SUPPORT
1 med unit
EQUIPMENT BY TYPE
ARMOURED FIGHTING VEHICLES
RECCE BRDM-2†
APC • **APC (W)** 22+: 3+ *Bastion* APC; 10+ BTR-60PB; 9 BTR-70
ARTILLERY 30+
TOWED **122mm** D-30
MRL **122mm** 30+ BM-21 *Grad*

Air Force
FORCES BY ROLE
TRANSPORT
1 sqn with BT-67; C295W; Y-12E
TRAINING
1 sqn with *Tetras*
TRANSPORT/ATTACK HELICOPTER
1 sqn with H215; Mi-24D *Hind*; Mi-35M *Hind*
EQUIPMENT BY TYPE
AIRCRAFT
TPT • **Light** 11: 1 BT-67; 1 C295W; 7 *Tetras*; 2 Y-12E (1 An-24 *Coke*; 2 An-26 *Curl*; 2 BN-2 *Islander* all in store)
TRG (6 L-29 *Delfin*; 2 SF-260WL *Warrior** all in store)
HELICOPTERS
ATK 4: 2 Mi-24D *Hind*; 2 Mi-35M *Hind*
MRH (1 Z-9 in store)
TPT • **Medium** 2 H215; (1 Mi-8 *Hip* in store); **Light** (1 AS350 *Ecureuil* in store)

Paramilitary 7,800 active

Gendarmerie 1,800
FORCES BY ROLE
MANOEUVRE
Other
8 paramilitary coy

National Guard 2,000

National Police 1,000

Militia 3,000

DEPLOYMENT

DEMOCRATIC REPUBLIC OF THE CONGO
UN • MONUSCO 1 obs

FOREIGN FORCES

All under MINUSMA comd unless otherwise specified
Albania EUTM Mali 4
Armenia 1
Austria 3 • EUTM Mali 12
Bangladesh 1,531; 2 obs; 1 inf bn; 1 engr coy; 1 sigs coy; 1 tpt coy; 1 hel sqn
Belgium 23 • EUTM Mali 171
Benin 260; 2 obs; 1 mech inf coy
Bhutan 3

Bosnia-Herzegovina 2
Bulgaria EUTM Mali 5
Burkina Faso 1,716; 2 inf bn
Cambodia 304; 1 EOD coy
Cameroon 2; 1 obs
Chad 1,398; 2 obs; 1 SF coy; 2 inf bn
China 403; 1 sy coy; 1 engr coy; 1 fd hospital
Côte d'Ivoire 150; 1 obs; 1 sy coy
Czech Republic 1 • EUTM Mali 41
Denmark 64; 1 avn unit
Egypt 74; 3 obs; 1 MP coy
El Salvador 104; 1 hel sqn
Estonia 10 • EUTM Mali 4
Ethiopia 1
Finland 6 • EUTM Mali 1
France 21 • *Operation Barkhane* 1,750; 1 mech inf BG; 1 log bn; 1 hel unit with 4 *Tiger*; 3 NH90 TTH; 6 SA330 *Puma*; 4 SA342 *Gazelle* • EUTM Mali 13
Gambia 3; 1 obs
Georgia EUTM Mali 1
Germany 610; 1 obs; 1 int coy; 1 hel bn • EUTM Mali 83
Ghana 218; 3 obs; 1 engr coy; 1 avn flt
Greece EUTM Mali 2
Guinea 860; 3 obs; 1 inf bn
Guinea-Bissau 1
Hungary EUTM Mali 3
Indonesia 7; 1 obs
Ireland EUTM Mali 20
Italy 1 • EUTM Mali 9
Jordan 4; 1 obs
Kenya 7; 2 obs
Latvia 2 • EUTM Mali 3
Liberia 73; 1 inf coy(-)
Lithuania 5; 1 obs • EUTM Mali 2
Luxembourg EUTM Mali 2
Mauritania 5
Montenegro EUTM Mali 1
Nepal 153; 2 obs; 1 EOD coy
Netherlands 258; 1 SF coy • EUTM Mali 1
Niger 859; 3 obs; 1 inf bn
Nigeria 83; 4 obs; 1 fd hospital
Norway 16
Portugal 2 • EUTM Mali 11
Romania 1 • EUTM Mali 1
Senegal 828; 1 inf bn; 1 engr coy
Serbia EUTM Mali 3
Sierra Leone 7; 2 obs
Slovenia EUTM Mali 4
Spain 1 • EUTM Mali 127
Sri Lanka 7
Sweden 212; 1 int coy • EUTM Mali 3
Switzerland 6
Togo 939; 2 obs; 1 inf bn; 1 fd hospital
United Kingdom 2 • EUTM Mali 8
United States 26
Yemen 4

Mauritius MUS

Mauritian Rupee R		2016	2017	2018
GDP	R	432bn	453bn	
	US$	12.2bn	12.3bn	
per capita	US$	9,613	9,672	
Growth	%	3.9	3.9	
Inflation	%	1.0	4.2	
Def bdgt [a]	R	7.66bn	8.06bn	8.63bn
	US$	215m	218m	
US$1=R		35.54	36.92	

[a] Police-service budget

Population 1,356,388

Age	0–14	15–19	20–24	25–29	30–64	65 plus
Male	10.3%	3.6%	3.8%	3.9%	23.5%	3.9%
Female	9.8%	3.5%	3.8%	3.7%	24.1%	5.7%

Capabilities

The country has no standing armed forces, but the Special Mobile Force (part of the police force) is tasked with providing internal and external security. The coastguard is currently in the process of increasing its ability to patrol the country's large EEZ and several orders with India resulted in the delivery of maritime-focused capabilities in 2016 and 2017, including the second of two fast patrol boats in April 2017. There are close ties with the Indian Navy, and there are plans for India to locate a coastal-surveillance radar in Mauritius. The country was one of the two host nations for the *Cutlass Express 2017* maritime-security exercise.

ACTIVE NIL Paramilitary 2,550

ORGANISATIONS BY SERVICE

Paramilitary 2,550

Special Mobile Force ε1,750
FORCES BY ROLE
MANOEUVRE
  Reconnaissance
  2 recce coy
  Light
  5 (rifle) mot inf coy
COMBAT SUPPORT
  1 engr sqn
COMBAT SERVICE SUPPORT
  1 spt pl
EQUIPMENT BY TYPE
ARMOURED FIGHTING VEHICLES
  RECCE 4 S52 *Shorland*
  IFV 2 VAB with 20mm gun
  APC • APC (W) 16: 7 *Tactica*; 9 VAB
ARTILLERY • MOR 81mm 2

Coast Guard ε800
EQUIPMENT BY TYPE
PATROL AND COASTAL COMBATANTS 17
  PCC 2 *Victory* (IND *Sarojini Naidu*)
  PCO 1 *Barracuda* with 1 hel landing platform

PB 14: 10 (IND *Fast Interceptor Boat*); 1 P-2000; 1 SDB-Mk3; 2 *Rescuer* (FSU *Zhuk*)
LOGISTICS AND SUPPORT
AGS 1 *Pathfinder*
AIRCRAFT • TPT • Light 4: 1 BN-2T *Defender*; 3 Do-228-101

Police Air Wing
EQUIPMENT BY TYPE
HELICOPTERS
MRH 9: 1 H125 (AS555) *Fennec*; 2 *Dhruv*; 1 SA315B *Lama* (*Cheetah*); 5 SA316 *Alouette* III (*Chetak*)

Mozambique MOZ

Mozambique New Metical M		2016	2017	2018
GDP	M	689bn	809bn	
	US$	11.3bn	12.3bn	
per capita	US$	392	418	
Growth	%	3.8	4.7	
Inflation	%	19.2	17.5	
Def bdgt	M	6.45bn	5.97bn	
	US$	106m	91m	
US$1=M		61.14	65.50	

Population 26,573,706

Age	0–14	15–19	20–24	25–29	30–64	65 plus
Male	22.5%	5.8%	4.8%	3.6%	10.8%	1.3%
Female	22.3%	5.8%	5.1%	4.1%	12.1%	1.7%

Capabilities

The armed forces are tasked with ensuring territorial integrity and internal security, as well as tackling piracy and human trafficking. Following a peace deal in 2014, RENAMO rebels declared an indefinite extension to the cessation of hostilities in May 2017. Senior RENAMO leaders reportedly want their personnel to be given positions in the armed forces as part of any overall peace agreement. Strong economic growth was tempered in 2016 by the discovery of previously undisclosed debt, although the exploitation of gas reserves may allow increased defence budgeting in the future. An agreement on defence cooperation with China signed in August 2016 included plans for bilateral training. Patrol craft on order from France began to be delivered in 2016. Russia and Mozambique reportedly signed a defence-cooperation agreement that came into effect in mid-2016. Equipment serviceability levels remain unclear, but cooperative anti-piracy patrols with South Africa have provided Mozambique's forces with experience, albeit in a supporting role. The armed forces have no capacity to deploy beyond Mozambique's borders without assistance.

ACTIVE 11,200 (Army 10,000 Navy 200 Air 1,000)
Conscript liability 2 years

ORGANISATIONS BY SERVICE

Army ε9,000–10,000

FORCES BY ROLE
SPECIAL FORCES
3 SF bn
MANOEUVRE
Light
7 inf bn
COMBAT SUPPORT
2-3 arty bn
2 engr bn
COMBAT SERVICE SUPPORT
1 log bn
EQUIPMENT BY TYPE†
Equipment estimated at 10% or less serviceability
ARMOURED FIGHTING VEHICLES
MBT 60+ T-54
RECCE 30 BRDM-1/BRDM-2
IFV 40 BMP-1
APC 326
APC (T) 30 FV430
APC (W) 285: 160 BTR-60; 100 BTR-152; 25 AT-105 *Saxon*
PPV 11 *Casspir*
ANTI-TANK/ANTI-INFRASTRUCTURE
MSL • MANPATS 9K11 *Malyutka* (AT-3 *Sagger*); 9K111 *Fagot* (AT-4 *Spigot*)
RCL 75mm; 82mm B-10; 107mm 24 B-12
GUNS 85mm 18: 6 D-48; 12 PT-56 (D-44)
ARTILLERY 126
TOWED 62: 100mm 20 M-1944; 105mm 12 M101; 122mm 12 D-30; 130mm 6 M-46; 152mm 12 D-1
MRL 122mm 12 BM-21 *Grad*
MOR 52: 82mm 40 M-43; 120mm 12 M-43
AIR DEFENCE • GUNS 290+
SP 57mm 20 ZSU-57-2
TOWED 270+: 20mm M-55; 23mm 120 ZU-23-2; 37mm 90 M-1939; (10 M-1939 in store); 57mm 60 S-60; (30 S-60 in store)

Navy ε200
EQUIPMENT BY TYPE
PATROL AND COASTAL COMBATANTS 6
PBF 5: 2 DV 15; 3 HSI 32
PB 1 *Pebane* (ex-ESP *Conejera*)

Air Force 1,000
FORCES BY ROLE
FIGHTER/GROUND ATTACK
1 sqn with MiG-21bis *Fishbed*; MiG-21UM *Mongol* B
TRANSPORT
1 sqn with An-26 *Curl*; FTB-337G *Milirole*; Cessna 150B; Cessna 172; PA-34 *Seneca*
ATTACK/TRANSPORT HELICOPTER
1 sqn with Mi-24 *Hind*†
EQUIPMENT BY TYPE
AIRCRAFT
FGA 8: 6 MiG-21bis *Fishbed*; 2 MiG-21UM *Mongol* B
ISR 2 FTB-337G *Milirole*
TPT 6: Light 5: 1 An-26 *Curl*; 2 Cessna 150B; 1 Cessna 172; 1 PA-34 *Seneca*; (4 PA-32 *Cherokee* non-op); PAX 1 Hawker 850XP

HELICOPTERS
ATK 2 Mi-24 *Hind*†
TPT • Medium (2 Mi-8 *Hip* non-op)
AD • SAM • TOWED: (S-75 *Dvina* (SA-2 *Guideline*) non-op‡; S-125 *Pechora* SA-3 *Goa* non-op‡)

Namibia NAM

Namibian Dollar N$		2016	2017	2018
GDP	N$	161bn	172bn	
	US$	10.9bn	12.6bn	
per capita	US$	4,709	5,358	
Growth	%	1.1	0.8	
Inflation	%	6.7	6.0	
Def bdgt	N$	5.95bn	5.68bn	
	US$	404m	415m	
US$1=N$		14.71	13.70	

Population   2,484,780

Age	0–14	15–19	20–24	25–29	30–64	65 plus
Male	18.6%	5.3%	4.9%	4.2%	14.2%	1.7%
Female	18.3%	5.3%	4.9%	4.4%	15.9%	2.3%

Capabilities

The armed forces' primary mission is territorial defence; secondary roles include assisting the AU and SADC, as well as supporting UN missions. The defence ministry is following the Namibian Defence Force Development Strategy 2012–22, which, among other points, said that army force design should be based on a conventional force with strategic force-projection capability. Surveillance tasks are among those noted for both the air force and navy. The navy augments civilian offshore-patrol forces, including on anti-piracy taskings. With an eye to naval-modernisation requirements, the government has stressed that 'scarce resources' need to be prioritised. Namibia has deployed on AU and UN missions and takes part in multinational exercises, including with regional states. In 2017, the country hosted regional forces for the *Blue Kunene* SADC Standby Force HADR exercise. The navy also exercises with the SADC as part of its Standing Maritime Committee. In recent years, the defence ministry established an Air Force Technical Training Centre and a School for Airpower Studies. China donated equipment, including two coastal patrol craft, in 2017, and the local industry has also supplied some basic equipment. The country is funding the renovation of existing and the construction of new infrastructure for the army and the air force. There is a very limited capacity for independent power projection.

ACTIVE 9,900 (Army 9,000 Navy 900) **Paramilitary 6,000**

ORGANISATIONS BY SERVICE

Army 9,000

FORCES BY ROLE
MANOEUVRE
Reconnaissance
 1 recce regt
Light
 3 inf bde (total: 6 inf bn)
Other
 1 (Presidential Guard) gd bn
COMBAT SUPPORT
 1 arty bde with (1 arty regt)
 1 AT regt
 1 engr regt
 1 sigs regt
COMBAT SERVICE SUPPORT
 1 log bn
AIR DEFENCE
 1 AD regt
EQUIPMENT BY TYPE
ARMOURED FIGHTING VEHICLES
 MBT T-54/T-55†; T-34†
 RECCE 12 BRDM-2
 IFV 7: 5 Type-05P mod (with BMP-1 turret); 2 *Wolf Turbo* 2 mod (with BMP-1 turret)
 APC 61
  APC (W) 41: 10 BTR-60; 3 Type-05P; 28 *Wolf Turbo* 2
  PPV 20 *Casspir*
ENGINEERING & MAINTENANCE VEHICLES
 ARV T-54/T-55 reported
ANTI-TANK/ANTI-INFRASTRUCTURE
 RCL 82mm B-10
 GUNS 12+: 57mm; 76mm 12 ZIS-3
ARTILLERY 72
 TOWED 140mm 24 G-2
 MRL 122mm 8: 5 BM-21 *Grad*; 3 PHL-81
 MOR 40: 81mm; 82mm
AIR DEFENCE
 SAM • Point-defence 9K32 *Strela*-2 (SA-7 *Grail*)‡
 GUNS 65
  SP 23mm 15 *Zumlac*
  TOWED 50+: 14.5mm 50 ZPU-4; 57mm S-60

Navy ε900

EQUIPMENT BY TYPE
PATROL AND COASTAL COMBATANTS 6
 PSO 1 *Elephant* with 1 hel landing platform
 PCC 2 *Daures* (ex-PRC *Haiqing* (Type-037-IS))
 PB 3: 1 *Brendan Simbwaye* (BRZ *Grajaú*); 2 *Terrace Bay* (BRZ *Marlim*)
AIRCRAFT • TPT • Light 1 F406 *Caravan II*
HELICOPTERS • TPT • Medium 1 S-61L

Marines ε700

Air Force

FORCES BY ROLE
FIGHTER/GROUND ATTACK
 1 sqn with F-7 (F-7NM); FT-7 (FT-7NG)
ISR
 1 sqn with O-2A *Skymaster*
TRANSPORT
 Some sqn with An-26 *Curl*; *Falcon* 900; *Learjet* 36; Y-12

TRAINING
 1 sqn with K-8 *Karakorum**
ATTACK/TRANSPORT HELICOPTER
 1 sqn with H425; Mi-8 *Hip*; Mi-25 *Hind* D; SA315 *Lama* (*Cheetah*); SA316B *Alouette* III (*Chetak*)
EQUIPMENT BY TYPE
AIRCRAFT 12 combat capable
 FTR 8: 6 F-7NM; 2 FT-7 (FT-7NG)
 ISR 5 Cessna O-2A *Skymaster*
 TPT 6: **Light** 5: 2 An-26 *Curl*; 1 Learjet 36; 2 Y-12; **PAX** 1 *Falcon* 900
 TRG 4+ K-8 *Karakorum**
HELICOPTERS
 ATK 2 Mi-25 *Hind* D
 MRH 5: 1 H425; 1 SA315 *Lama* (*Cheetah*); 3 SA316B *Alouette* III (*Chetak*)
 TPT • **Medium** 1 Mi-8 *Hip*

Paramilitary 6,000

Police Force • Special Field Force 6,000 (incl Border Guard and Special Reserve Force)

Ministry of Fisheries
EQUIPMENT BY TYPE
PATROL AND COASTAL COMBATANTS • PCO 3: 2 *Nathanael Maxwilili* with 1 hel landing platform; 1 *Tobias Hainyenko*
LOGISTICS AND SUPPORT 1
 AGOS 1 *Mirabilis*

DEPLOYMENT

SOUTH SUDAN
UN • UNMISS 1; 1 obs

SUDAN
UN • UNAMID 4; 2 obs
UN • UNISFA 2; 2 obs

Niger NER

CFA Franc BCEAO fr		2016	2017	2018
GDP	fr	4.44tr	4.67tr	
	US$	7.49bn	7.89bn	
per capita	US$	412	421	
Growth	%	5.0	4.2	
Inflation	%	0.3	1.0	
Def exp	fr	98.6bn	100bn	
	US$	166m	169m	
US$1=fr		592.70	591.30	

Population 19,245,344

Ethnic groups: Gourma 55.3%; Djerma Sonrai 21%; Touareg 9.3%; Peuhl 8.5%; Kanouri Manga 4.6%; other or unspecified 1.3%

Age	0–14	15–19	20–24	25–29	30–64	65 plus
Male	24.7%	5.3%	4.0%	3.2%	11.5%	1.3%
Female	24.3%	5.4%	4.2%	3.4%	11.2%	1.3%

Capabilities

Internal and border security are key roles for the armed forces, in light of the regional threat from Islamist groups. The country is a member of the G5-Sahel group aimed at improving the ability to counter AQIM and ISIS-affiliated jihadists in the region; in 2017, Boko Haram also mounted attacks in the country. However, the armed forces remain under-equipped and lack the resources to fully meet these challenges. Niger provides UAV basing for the US: the first site is at Niamey (which also has a French presence), while the second site is being built in Agadez. Both France and the US have been providing equipment for surveillance tasks, including Cessna 208Bs from the US and *Gazelle* helicopters from France. France has also conducted joint counter-terrorism operations with Niger's armed forces, while Germany has developed an air-transport base at Niamey to supply its troops in neighbouring Mali. Berlin has also supplied logistics vehicles and communications equipment to the Nigerien military and gendarmerie.

ACTIVE 5,300 (Army 5,200 Air 100) **Paramilitary 5,400**
Conscript liability Selective conscription, 2 years

ORGANISATIONS BY SERVICE

Army 5,200
3 Mil Districts
FORCES BY ROLE
MANOEUVRE
 Reconnaissance
 4 armd recce sqn
 Light
 7 inf coy
 Air Manoeuvre
 2 AB coy
COMBAT SUPPORT
 1 engr coy
COMBAT SERVICE SUPPORT
 1 log gp
AIR DEFENCE
 1 AD coy
EQUIPMENT BY TYPE
ARMOURED FIGHTING VEHICLES
 RECCE 132: 35 AML-20/AML-60; 90 AML-90; 7 VBL
 APC 45
  APC (W) 24: 22 Panhard M3; 2 WZ-523
  PPV 21 *Puma* M26-15
ANTI-TANK/ANTI-INFRASTRUCTURE
 RCL 14: **75mm** 6 M20; **106mm** 8 M40
ARTILLERY • MOR 40: **81mm** 19 Brandt; **82mm** 17; **120mm** 4 Brandt
AIR DEFENCE • GUNS 39
 SP 20mm 10 Panhard M3 VDAA
 TOWED 20mm 29

Air Force 100
EQUIPMENT BY TYPE
AIRCRAFT 2 combat capable

ATK 2 Su-25 *Frogfoot*
ISR 6: 4 Cessna 208 *Caravan*; 2 DA42 MPP *Twin Star*
TPT 7: **Medium** 1 C-130H *Hercules*; **Light** 5: 1 An-26 *Curl*; 2 Cessna 208 *Caravan*; 1 Do-28 *Skyservant*; 1 Do-228-201; **PAX** 1 B-737-700 (VIP)
HELICOPTERS
ATK 2 Mi-35P *Hind*
MRH 5: 2 Mi-17 *Hip*; 3 SA342 *Gazelle*

Paramilitary 5,400

Gendarmerie 1,400

Republican Guard 2,500

National Police 1,500

DEPLOYMENT

CENTRAL AFRICAN REPUBLIC
UN • MINUSCA 130; 4 obs; 1 sigs coy

DEMOCRATIC REPUBLIC OF THE CONGO
UN • MONUSCO 4; 12 obs

MALI
UN • MINUSMA 859; 3 obs; 1 inf bn

FOREIGN FORCES

France *Opération Barkhane* 500; 1 FGA det with 2 *Mirage* 2000C; 2 *Mirage* 2000D; 1 tkr/tpt det with 1 C-135FR; 1 C-160; 1 UAV det with 5 MQ-9A *Reaper*
United States 800

Nigeria NGA

Nigerian Naira N		2016	2017	2018
GDP	N	103tr	120tr	
	US$	405bn	395bn	
per capita	US$	2,208	2,092	
Growth	%	-1.6	0.8	
Inflation	%	15.7	16.3	
Def bdgt	N	443bn	465bn	
	US$	1.75bn	1.53bn	
FMA (US)	US$	0.6m	0.5m	0m
US$1=N		253.00	304.42	

Population 190,632,261

Ethnic groups: North (Hausa and Fulani), Southwest (Yoruba), Southeast (Ibo); these tribes make up ε65% of population

Age	0–14	15–19	20–24	25–29	30–64	65 plus
Male	21.7%	5.4%	4.5%	3.9%	13.8%	1.5%
Female	20.7%	5.2%	4.4%	3.7%	13.2%	1.6%

Capabilities

Nigeria continues to face numerous internal-security challenges, including the threat from Boko Haram and from militants in the Delta. These remain central concerns for the comparatively well-equipped and -trained armed forces, with countering piracy, and border and maritime security, also vital tasks. There have been reports that the difficulty in defeating the insurgents had been adversely affecting morale, even with training support from the US and other countries. Despite the presence of the Multi-National Joint Task Force, the Boko Haram threat continues, as evidenced by an attack in mid-2017 against an oil-exploration team. The armed forces have been attempting to adopt COIN tactics, and looking to establish forward-operating bases and quick-reaction groups. In 2017, efforts were made to improve training, notably in the air force, with the establishment of Air Training Command and Ground Training Command and new training aircraft from Pakistan. The army stood up a new division (6th) in 2017, with the aim of increasing the military presence in the Delta area and around oil infrastructure. In response to the continuing insurgency, equipment has been brought out of storage, including transport aircraft and light fighters. Maintenance and serviceability has been a long-standing issue. US support to Nigeria's armed forces has continued, such as with the move to supply A-29/EMB-314 *Super Tucano*s, while the German government also intends to bolster Nigerian capabilities to tackle Boko Haram, for instance by providing mobile ground-radar systems.

ACTIVE 118,000 (Army 100,000 Navy 8,000 Air 10,000) **Paramilitary 82,000**
Reserves planned, none org

ORGANISATIONS BY SERVICE

Army 100,000 FORCES BY ROLE
SPECIAL FORCES
 1 spec ops bn
 3 (mobile strike team) spec ops units
 1 ranger bn
MANOEUVRE
 Armoured
 1 (3rd) armd div (1 armd bde, 1 arty bde)
 Mechanised
 1 (1st) mech div (1 recce bn, 1 mech bde, 1 mot inf bde, 1 arty bde, 1 engr regt)
 1 (2nd) mech div (1 recce bn, 1 armd bde, 1 arty bde, 1 engr regt)
 1 (81st) composite div (1 recce bn, 1 mech bde, 1 arty bde, 1 engr regt)
 Light
 1 (6th) inf div (1 amph bde, 2 inf bde)
 1 (7th) inf div (1 spec ops bn, 1 recce bn(-), 1 armd bde, 7 (task force) inf bde, 1 arty bde, 1 engr regt)
 1 (8th Task Force) inf div (2 inf bde)
 1 (82nd) composite div (1 recce bn, 3 mot inf bde, 1 arty bde, 1 engr regt)
 1 (Multi-national Joint Task Force) bde (2 inf bn(-))
 Other
 1 (Presidential Guard) gd bde (4 gd bn)
AIR DEFENCE
 1 AD regt

EQUIPMENT BY TYPE
ARMOURED FIGHTING VEHICLES
MBT 319: 176 Vickers Mk 3; 100 T-55†; 12 T-72AV; 31 T-72M1
LT TK 157 FV101 *Scorpion*
RECCE 342: 90 AML-60; 40 AML-90; 70 EE-9 *Cascavel*; 50 FV721 *Fox*; 20 FV601 *Saladin* Mk2; 72 VBL
IFV 32: 10 BTR-4EN; 22 BVP-1
APC 646+
  APC (T) 317: 250 4K-7FA *Steyr*; 67 MT-LB
  APC (W) 282+: 110 *Cobra*; 10 FV603 *Saracen*; 110 AVGP *Grizzly* mod/*Piranha* I 6x6; 47 BTR-3UN; 5 BTR-80; some EE-11 *Urutu* (reported)
  PPV 47+: 16 *Caiman*; 8 *Maxxpro*; 23 REVA III 4×4; Streit *Spartan*; Streit *Cougar* (*Igirigi*); Streit *Typhoon*; *Bigfoot*
ENGINEERING & MAINTENANCE VEHICLES
ARV 17+: AVGP *Husky*; 2 *Greif*; 15 Vickers ARV
VLB MTU-20; VAB
ANTI-TANK/ANTI-INFRASTRUCTURE
RCL 84mm *Carl Gustav*; 106mm M40A1
ARTILLERY 517+
SP 155mm 39 *Palmaria*
TOWED 106: 105mm 50 M-56; 122mm 49 D-30/D-74; 130mm 7 M-46; (155mm 24 FH-77B in store)
MRL 122mm 42: 10 BM-21 *Grad*; 25 APR-21; 7 RM-70
MOR 330+: 81mm 200; 82mm 100; 120mm 30+
RADAR • LAND: some RASIT (veh, arty)
AIR DEFENCE
SAM • Point-defence 16+: 16 *Roland*; *Blowpipe*; 9K32 *Strela*-2 (SA-7 *Grail*)‡
GUNS 90+
SP 23mm 30 ZSU-23-4
TOWED 60+: 20mm 60+; 23mm ZU-23; 40mm L/70

Navy 8,000 (incl Coast Guard)
Western Comd HQ located at Apapa; Eastern Comd HQ located at Calabar; Central Comd HQ located at Brass
EQUIPMENT BY TYPE
PRINCIPAL SURFACE COMBATANTS 1
FRIGATES • FFGHM 1 *Aradu*† (GER MEKO 360) with 8 single lnchr with *Otomat* AShM, 1 octuple *Albatros* lnchr with *Aspide* SAM, 2 triple STWS 1B 324mm ASTT with A244 LWT, 1 127mm gun (capacity 1 med hel)
PATROL AND COASTAL COMBATANTS 119
CORVETTES • FSM 1 *Enymiri*† (UK Vosper Mk 9) with 1 triple lnchr with *Seacat*† SAM, 1 twin 375mm A/S mor, 1 76mm gun
PSOH 4: 2 *Centenary* with 1 76mm gun; 2 *Thunder* (ex-US *Hamilton*) with 1 76mm gun
PCFG 1 *Siprit* (FRA *Combattante*) with 2 twin lnchr with MM38 *Exocet* AShM, 1 76mm gun
PCO 4 *Kyanwa* (ex-US CG *Balsam*)
PCC 2 *Ekpe*† (GER Lurssen 57m) with 1 76mm gun
PBF 33: 21 *Manta* (Suncraft 17m); 4 *Manta* MkII; 3 *Shaldag* II; 2 *Torie* (Nautic Sentinel 17m); 3 *Wave Rider*
PB 74: 1 *Andoni*; 1 *Dorina* (FPB 98); 5 *Okpoku* (FPB 72); 1 *Karaduwa*; 1 *Sagbama*; 2 *Sea Eagle* (Suncraft 38m); 15 *Stingray* (Suncraft 16m); 40 Suncraft 12m; 4 Swiftships; 2 *Town* (of which one laid up); 2 *Yola*†

MINE WARFARE • MINE COUNTERMEASURES 2:
MCC 2 *Ohue*† (ITA *Lerici* mod)
AMPHIBIOUS 4
LC • LCVP 4 *Stingray* 20
LOGISTICS AND SUPPORT 1
AX 1 *Prosperity*

Naval Aviation
EQUIPMENT BY TYPE
HELICOPTERS
MRH 2 AW139 (AB-139)
TPT • Light 3 AW109E *Power*†

Special Forces 200
EQUIPMENT BY TYPE
FORCES BY ROLE
SPECIAL FORCES
1 SF unit

Air Force 10,000
FORCES BY ROLE
Very limited op capability
FIGHTER/GROUND ATTACK
1 sqn with F-7 (F-7NI); FT-7 (FT-7NI)
MARITIME PATROL
1 sqn with ATR-42-500 MP; Do-128D-6 *Turbo SkyServant*; Do-228-100/200
TRANSPORT
2 sqn with C-130H *Hercules*; C-130H-30 *Hercules*; G-222
1 (Presidential) gp with B-727; B-737BBJ; BAe-125-800; Beech 350 *King Air*; Do-228-200; *Falcon* 7X; *Falcon* 900; Gulfstream IV/V
TRAINING
1 unit with *Air Beetle*†
1 unit with *Alpha Jet**
1 unit with L-39 *Albatros*†*; MB-339A*
1 hel unit with Mi-34 *Hermit* (trg)
ATTACK HELICOPTER
1 sqn with Mi-24/Mi-35 *Hind*†
TRANSPORT HELICOPTER
1 sqn with H215 (AS332) *Super Puma*; (AS365N) *Dauphin*; AW109LUH; H135
EQUIPMENT BY TYPE†
AIRCRAFT 62 combat capable
FTR 14: 11 F-7 (F-7NI); 3 FT-7 (FT-7NI)
ELINT 2 ATR-42-500 MP
TPT 32: **Medium** 5: 1 C-130H *Hercules* (4 more in store†); 1 C-130H-30 *Hercules* (2 more in store); 3 G.222† (2 more in store†); **Light** 18: 3 Beech 350 *King Air*; 1 Cessna 550 *Citation*; 8 Do-128D-6 *Turbo SkyServant*; 1 Do-228-100; 5 Do-228-200 (incl 2 VIP); **PAX** 9: 1 B-727; 1 B-737BBJ; 1 BAe 125-800; 2 *Falcon* 7X; 2 *Falcon* 900; 1 Gulfstream IV; 1 Gulfstream V
TRG 113: 58 *Air Beetle*† (up to 20 awaiting repair); 3 *Alpha Jet* A*; 10 *Alpha Jet* E*; 2 DA40NG; 23 L-39ZA *Albatros*†*; 12 MB-339AN* (all being upgraded); 5 *Super Mushshak*
HELICOPTERS
ATK 13: 2 Mi-24P *Hind*; 4 Mi-24V *Hind*; 3 Mi-35 *Hind*; 2 Mi-35P *Hind*; 2 Mi-35M *Hind*
MRH 10+: 6 AW109LUH; 1 Bell 412EP; 3+ SA341 *Gazelle*

TPT 19: **Medium** 10: 2 AW101; 5 H215 (AS332) *Super Puma* (4 more in store); 3 AS365N *Dauphin*; **Light** 9: 4 H125 (AS350B) *Ecureuil*; 1 AW109; 1 Bell 205; 3 H135
UNMANNED AERIAL VEHICLES 1+
  CISR • Heavy 1+ CH-3
  ISR • Medium (9 *Aerostar* non-operational)
AIR-LAUNCHED MISSILES • AAM • IR R-3 (AA-2 *Atoll*)‡; PL-9C
BOMBS • INS/GPS guided FT-9

Paramilitary ε82,000

Nigerian Police

Port Authority Police ε2,000

Security and Civil Defence Corps • Police 80,000
EQUIPMENT BY TYPE
ARMOURED FIGHTING VEHICLES
  APC 80+
    APC (W) 74+: 70+ AT105 *Saxon*†; 4 BTR-3U; UR-416
    PPV 6 *Springbuck* 4x4
AIRCRAFT • TPT • Light 4: 1 Cessna 500 *Citation* I; 2 PA-31 *Navajo*; 1 PA-31-350 *Navajo Chieftain*
HELICOPTERS • TPT • Light 5: 2 Bell 212 (AB-212); 2 Bell 222 (AB-222); 1 Bell 429

DEPLOYMENT

CENTRAL AFRICAN REPUBLIC
UN • MINUSCA 2

DEMOCRATIC REPUBLIC OF THE CONGO
UN • MONUSCO 1; 15 obs

GAMBIA
ECOWAS • ECOMIG 200

GUINEA-BISSAU
ECOWAS • ECOMIB 100

LIBERIA
UN • UNMIL 234; 3 obs; 1 inf coy

MALI
UN • MINUSMA 83; 4 obs; 1 fd hospital

SOMALIA
UN • UNSOS 1 obs

SOUTH SUDAN
UN • UNMISS 3; 6 obs

SUDAN
UN • UNAMID 932; 5 obs; 1 inf bn; 1 fd hospital
UN • UNISFA 1; 2 obs

WESTERN SAHARA
UN • MINURSO 5 obs

FOREIGN FORCES

United Kingdom 300 (trg teams)

Rwanda RWA

Rwandan Franć fr		2016	2017	2018
GDP	fr	6.62tr	7.55tr	
	US$	8.41bn	8.92bn	
per capita	US$	729	754	
Growth	%	5.9	6.2	
Inflation	%	5.7	7.1	
Def bdgt	fr	74.5bn	90.4bn	92.3bn
	US$	95m	107m	
US$1=fr		787.29	846.35	

Population 11,901,484
Ethnic groups: Hutu 80%; Tutsi 19%

Age	0–14	15–19	20–24	25–29	30–64	65 plus
Male	20.8%	5.3%	4.3%	4.4%	13.0%	0.9%
Female	20.5%	5.3%	4.4%	4.5%	15.0%	1.5%

Capabilities

The principal missions for the armed forces are to defend territorial integrity and national sovereignty. A law on downsizing and demobilising elements of the armed forces was published in October 2015 (no. 38/2015) and there have been further official retirement ceremonies for those reaching rank-related retirement ages, indicating attention to force health. The country fields a comparatively large army, but units are lightly equipped, with little mechanisation. The army regularly takes part in multinational exercises and is a key contributor to the East Africa Standby Force (EASF). In late 2017, Rwanda deployed a contingent to the EASF FTX in Sudan. It is a significant contributor to UN missions and committed forces to the African Capacity for Immediate Response to Crises initiative. New deployments and rotations continued in 2017, with increased forces dispatched to UNMISS in South Sudan, where Rwanda also maintains a helicopter detachment. However, the lack of fixed-wing aircraft limits the armed forces' ability to deploy independently overseas. International training support comes from forces including the US, which in 2016 conducted civil–military cooperation training.

ACTIVE 33,000 (Army 32,000 Air 1,000) **Paramilitary 2,000**

ORGANISATIONS BY SERVICE

Army 32,000
FORCES BY ROLE
MANOEUVRE
  Light
    2 cdo bn
    4 inf div (3 inf bde)
COMBAT SUPPORT
  1 arty bde
EQUIPMENT BY TYPE
ARMOURED FIGHTING VEHICLES
  MBT 34: 24 T-54/T-55; 10 *Tiran*-5
  RECCE 106: ε90 AML-60/AML-90; 16 VBL
  IFV 35+: BMP; 15 *Ratel*-90; 20 *Ratel*-60
  APC 90+

APC (W) 50+: BTR; *Buffalo* (Panhard M3); 30 *Cobra*; 20 WZ-551 (reported)
PPV 40 RG-31 *Nyala*
ENGINEERING & MAINTENANCE VEHICLES
ARV T-54/T-55 reported
ARTILLERY 171+
SP 11: **122mm** 6 SH-3; **155mm** 5 ATMOS 2000
TOWED 35+: **105mm** some; **122mm** 6 D-30; **152mm** 29 Type-54 (D-1)†
MRL 10: **122mm** 5 RM-70; **160mm** 5 LAR-160
MOR 115: **81mm**; **82mm**; **120mm**
AIR DEFENCE SAM • Point-defence 9K32 *Strela*-2 (SA-7 *Grail*)‡
GUNS ε150: **14.5mm**; **23mm**; **37mm**

Air Force ε1,000

FORCES BY ROLE
ATTACK/TRANSPORT HELICOPTER
1 sqn with Mi-17/Mi-17MD/Mi-17V-5/Mi-17-1V *Hip* H; Mi-24P/V *Hind*
EQUIPMENT BY TYPE
HELICOPTERS
ATK 5: 2 Mi-24V *Hind* E; 3 Mi-24P *Hind*
MRH 12: 1 AW139; 4 Mi-17 *Hip* H; 1 Mi-17MD *Hip* H; 1 Mi-17V-5 *Hip* H; 5 Mi-17-1V *Hip* H
TPT • Light 1 AW109S

Paramilitary

District Administration Security Support Organ ε2,000

DEPLOYMENT

CENTRAL AFRICAN REPUBLIC
UN • MINUSCA 977; 11 obs; 1 inf bn; 1 fd hospital

SOUTH SUDAN
UN • UNMISS 1,973; 14 obs; 2 inf bn; 1 hel sqn

SUDAN
UN • UNAMID 2,446; 5 obs; 3 inf bn
UN • UNISFA 6; 3 obs

Senegal SEN

CFA Franc BCEAO fr		2016	2017	2018
GDP	fr	8.72tr	9.49tr	
	US$	14.7bn	16.1bn	
per capita	US$	943	998	
Growth	%	6.7	6.8	
Inflation	%	0.9	2.1	
Def bdgt	fr	151bn	179bn	193bn
	US$	254m	303m	
FMA (US)	US$	0.3m	0.3m	0m
US$1=fr		592.71	591.27	

Population 14,668,522

Ethnic groups: Wolof 36%; Fulani 17%; Serer 17%; Toucouleur 9%; Man-dingo 9%; Diola 9% (of which 30–60% in Casamance)

Age	0–14	15–19	20–24	25–29	30–64	65 plus
Male	20.8%	5.4%	4.7%	3.9%	12.1%	1.3%
Female	20.7%	5.4%	4.8%	4.2%	14.9%	1.6%

Capabilities

Senegal's armed forces deployed in neighbouring Gambia following a constitutional crisis in early 2017. Most personnel have now been withdrawn, but Senegal still leads the ECOWAS mission in Gambia. Traditionally, priorities for Senegal's armed forces are internal and border security, including countering an insurgency in the country's south and Islamist activity in neighbouring states, as well as combating narcotics trafficking. The military has developed ties with France and the US. France maintains force elements in Senegal, which train local forces. In 2017, Senegal took part in a maritime-security exercise with the US Coast Guard. The Senegalese military is engaged in an ongoing modernisation programme, including the procurement in 2017 of multiple-rocket launchers and armoured vehicles.

ACTIVE 13,600 (Army 11,900 Navy 950 Air 750)
Paramilitary 5,000
Conscript liability Selective conscription, 2 years

ORGANISATIONS BY SERVICE

Army 11,900 (incl conscripts)
7 Mil Zone HQ
FORCES BY ROLE
MANOEUVRE
  Reconnaissance
  4 armd recce bn
  Light
  1 cdo bn
  6 inf bn
  Air Manoeuvre
  1 AB bn
  Other
  1 (Presidential Guard) horse cav bn
COMBAT SUPPORT
  1 arty bn
  1 engr bn
  3 construction coy
  1 sigs bn
COMBAT SERVICE SUPPORT
  1 log bn
  1 med bn
  1 trg bn
EQUIPMENT BY TYPE
ARMOURED FIGHTING VEHICLES
  ASLT 12 PTL-02 *Assaulter*
  RECCE 145: 30 AML-60; 74 AML-90; 10 M8; 4 M20; 27 RAM Mk3
  IFV 26 *Ratel*-20
  APC 78
    APC (T) 12 M3 half-track
    APC (W) 19: 2 *Oncilla*; 16 Panhard M3; 1 WZ-551 (CP)
    PPV 47: 8 *Casspir*; 39 *Puma* M26-15
ENGINEERING & MAINTENANCE VEHICLES
  ARV 1 *Puma* M36
ANTI-TANK/ANTI-INFRASTRUCTURE
  MSL • MANPATS *Milan*

ARTILLERY 82
　TOWED 20: **105mm** 6 HM-2/M101; **155mm** 14: ε6 Model-50; 8 TR-F1
　MRL 122mm 6 BM-21 *Grad* (UKR *Bastion*-1 mod)
　MOR 56: **81mm** 24; **120mm** 32
AIR DEFENCE • GUNS • TOWED 33: **14.5mm** ZPU-4 (tch); **20mm** 21 M693; **40mm** 12 L/60

Navy (incl Coast Guard) 950
FORCES BY ROLE
SPECIAL FORCES
　1 cdo coy
EQUIPMENT BY TYPE
PATROL AND COASTAL COMBATANTS 5
　PCO 1 *Fouladou* (OPV 190 Mk II)
　PCC 1 *Njambour* (FRA SFCN 59m) with 2 76mm gun
　PBF 1 *Ferlo* (RPB 33)
　PB 2: 1 *Conejera*; 1 *Kedougou*
AMPHIBIOUS • LANDING CRAFT 2
　LCT 2 *Edic* 700
LOGISTICS AND SUPPORT 1
　AG 1

Air Force 750
FORCES BY ROLE
MARITIME PATROL/SEARCH & RESCUE
　1 sqn with C-212 *Aviocar*; CN235; Bell 205 (UH-1H *Iroquois*)
ISR
　1 unit with BN-2T *Islander* (anti-smuggling patrols)
TRANSPORT
　1 sqn with B-727-200 (VIP); F-27-400M *Troopship*
TRAINING
　1 sqn with R-235 *Guerrier**; TB-30 *Epsilon*
ATTACK/TRANSPORT HELICOPTER
　1 sqn with AS355F *Ecureuil* II; Bell 206; Mi-35P *Hind*; Mi-171Sh
EQUIPMENT BY TYPE
AIRCRAFT 1 combat capable
　TPT 10: **Light** 8: 1 BN-2T *Islander* (govt owned, mil op); 1 C-212-100 *Aviocar*; 2 CN235; 2 Beech B200 *King Air*; 2 F-27-400M *Troopship* (3 more in store); **PAX** 2: 1 A319; 1 B-727-200 (VIP)
　TRG 7: 1 R-235 *Guerrier**; 6 TB-30 *Epsilon*
HELICOPTERS
　ATK 2 Mi-35P *Hind*
　MRH 1 AW139
　TPT 8: **Medium** 2 Mi-171Sh; **Light** 6: 1 AS355F *Ecureuil* II; 1 Bell 205 (UH-1H *Iroquois*); 2 Bell 206; 2 PZL Mi-2 *Hoplite*

Paramilitary 5,000

Gendarmerie 5,000
EQUIPMENT BY TYPE
ARMOURED FIGHTING VEHICLES
　RECCE 11 RAM Mk3
　APC 29:
　　APC (W) 17: 5 EE-11 *Urutu*; 12 VXB-170
　　PPV 12 *Gila*

Customs
EQUIPMENT BY TYPE
PATROL AND COASTAL COMBATANTS • PB 2 VCSM

DEPLOYMENT
CENTRAL AFRICAN REPUBLIC
UN • MINUSCA 114; 1 atk hel sqn

DEMOCRATIC REPUBLIC OF THE CONGO
UN • MONUSCO 2; 2 obs

GAMBIA
ECOWAS • ECOMIG 250

LIBERIA
UN • UNMIL 1

MALI
UN • MINUSMA 828; 1 inf bn; 1 engr coy

SOUTH SUDAN
UN • UNMISS 2 obs

SUDAN
UN • UNAMID 798; 1 inf bn

FOREIGN FORCES
France 350; 1 *Falcon* 50MI

Seychelles SYC

Seychelles Rupee SR		2016	2017	2018
GDP	SR	19.0bn	20.2bn	
	US$	1.43bn	1.48bn	
per capita	US$	15,234	15,658	
Growth	%	4.5	4.1	
Inflation	%	-1.0	2.8	
Def exp	SR	n.k	n.k	
	US$	n.k	n.k	
US$1=SR			13.32	13.65

Population　93,920

Age	0–14	15–19	20–24	25–29	30–64	65 plus
Male	10.2%	3.2%	3.7%	3.5%	27.1%	3.0%
Female	9.6%	2.9%	3.3%	3.5%	24.4%	4.6%

Capabilities

The small Seychelles People's Defence Forces are primarily focused on maritime security and countering piracy. In 2014 the EU began basic-training activities for the air force, in a bid to bolster maritime-surveillance capabilities. The country hosts US military forces conducting maritime-patrol activities on a rotational basis, including the operation of unarmed UAVs. India maintains strong defence ties with the Seychelles, donating equipment, providing maintenance and supporting efforts to enhance maritime-patrol capability. The Seychelles continues to implement plans to activate a number of Indian-supplied coastal-surveillance radars. There are ongoing plans aimed at furthering the Seychelles' defence cooperation with China.

ACTIVE 420 (Land Forces 200; Coast Guard 200; Air Force 20)

ORGANISATIONS BY SERVICE

People's Defence Force

Land Forces 200
FORCES BY ROLE
SPECIAL FORCES
  1 SF unit
MANOEUVRE
  Light
    1 inf coy
  Other
    1 sy unit
COMBAT SUPPORT
  1 MP unit
EQUIPMENT BY TYPE
ARMOURED FIGHTING VEHICLES
  RECCE 6 BRDM-2†
ARTILLERY • MOR 82mm 6 M-43†
AIR DEFENCE • GUNS • TOWED 14.5mm ZPU-2†; ZPU-4†; **37mm** M-1939†

Coast Guard 200 (incl 80 Marines)
EQUIPMENT BY TYPE
PATROL AND COASTAL COMBATANTS 8
  PCO 3: 1 *Andromache* (ITA *Pichiotti* 42m); 2 *Topaz* (ex-IND *Trinkat*)
  PBF 1 *Hermes* (ex-IND *Coastal Interceptor Craft*)
  PB 4: 2 *Le Vigilant* (ex-UAE Rodman 101); 1 *Etoile* (*Shanghai* II mod); 1 *Fortune* (UK *Tyne*)

Air Force 20
EQUIPMENT BY TYPE
AIRCRAFT
  TPT • **Light** 4: 1 DHC-6-320 *Twin Otter*; 1 Do-228; 2 Y-12

Sierra Leone SLE

Sierra Leonean Leone L		2016	2017	2018
GDP	L	23.8tr	29.4tr	
	US$	3.72tr	3.90tr	
per capita	US$	577	594	
Growth	%	6.1	6.0	
Inflation	%	11.5	16.9	
Def bdgt	L	85.7bn	86.5bn	111bn
	US$	13m	11m	
US$1=L		6,417.57	7,554.61	
Population	6,163,195			

Age	0–14	15–19	20–24	25–29	30–64	65 plus
Male	20.8%	4.8%	4.1%	3.8%	13.3%	1.5%
Female	20.9%	5.1%	4.4%	4.0%	14.6%	2.2%

Capabilities

The armed forces' primary task is internal security and the provision of forces for continental peacekeeping missions. There has been much focus on institutional military development, with international support. Training has been provided by the UK and the US, and there are reports of interest in greater military cooperation with China, which provides scholarships for military education. The army has deployed a battalion to AMISOM in Somalia.

ACTIVE 8,500 (Joint 8,500)

ORGANISATIONS BY SERVICE

Armed Forces 8,500
FORCES BY ROLE
MANOEUVRE
  Reconnaissance
    1 recce unit
  Light
    3 inf bde (total: 12 inf bn)
COMBAT SUPPORT
  1 engr regt
  1 int unit
  1 MP unit
  1 sigs unit
COMBAT SUPPORT
  1 log unit
  1 fd hospital
EQUIPMENT BY TYPE
ARMOURED FIGHTING VEHICLES
  APC • **PPV** 4: 3 *Casspir*; 1 *Mamba* Mk5
ANTI-TANK/ANTI-INFRASTRUCTURE
  RCL **84mm** *Carl Gustav*
ARTILLERY 37
  TOWED **122mm** 6 Type-96 (D30)
  MOR 31: **81mm** ε27; **82mm** 2; **120mm** 2
HELICOPTERS • MRH/TPT 2 Mi-17 *Hip* H/Mi-8 *Hip*†
AIR DEFENCE • GUNS 7: **12.7mm** 4; **14.5mm** 3

Maritime Wing ε200
EQUIPMENT BY TYPE
PATROL AND COASTAL COMBATANTS • PB 2: 1 *Shanghai* III†; 1 *Isle of Man*

DEPLOYMENT

LEBANON
UN • UNIFIL 3

MALI
UN • MINUSMA 7; 2 obs

SOMALIA
UN • UNSOM 1 obs
UN • UNSOS 1 obs

SUDAN
UN • UNAMID 1; 5 obs
UN • UNISFA 2; 1 obs

Somalia SOM

Somali Shilling sh		2016	2017	2018
GDP	US$	6.34bn	6.52bn	
per capita	US$	n.k.	n.k.	
Growth	%	3.2	2.4	
Inflation	%	n.k.	n.k.	
Def bdgt	US$	n.k.	n.k.	
US$1=sh			1.00	1.00

*Definitive economic data unavailable

Population 11,031,386

Age	0–14	15–19	20–24	25–29	30–64	65 plus
Male	21.5%	5.4%	4.2%	4.0%	14.3%	0.8%
Female	21.6%	5.4%	4.0%	3.9%	13.4%	1.3%

Capabilities

Somalia's armed forces remain focused on internal stability. Despite progress by Somali and foreign forces – including the AMISOM deployment – al-Shabaab has demonstrated an ongoing capability to launch attacks in Somalia and in the region; the US launched airstrikes against the group with increasing regularity in 2017. The US authorised the deployment of regular forces to Somalia for the first time since 1994 to train Somali forces. Federal-government plans to professionalise and unite the loose collections of clan-based militia groups that form the Somali National Army have yet to be fully realised. The country's armed forces are still reliant on international support, with AMISOM, the EU and private-security companies providing training and other countries, including China, donating equipment. A Turkish training base that opened in Mogadishu in September 2017 is intended to provide longer-term reconstruction and capacity building for the armed forces, ahead of the scheduled 2020 withdrawal of AMISOM forces. Somaliland and Puntland have their own militias, while a privately funded Puntland Maritime Police Force operates a small number of rigid inflatable boats and small aircraft.

ACTIVE 19,800 (Army 19,800)

ORGANISATIONS BY SERVICE

Army 19,800 (plus further militias (to be integrated))

FORCES BY ROLE
COMMAND
  4 div HQ
MANOEUVRE
  Light
  Some cdo bn(+)
  12 inf bde (3 inf bn)
  2 indep inf bn
  Other
  1 gd bn

EQUIPMENT BY TYPE
ARMOURED FIGHTING VEHICLES
  APC 47+

APC (W) 38+: 25+ AT-105 *Saxon*; 13 *Bastion* APC; Fiat 6614
PPV 9+: *Casspir*; MAV-5; 9+ *Mamba* Mk5; RG-31 *Nyala*
AUV 12 *Tiger* 4×4

Paramilitary

Coast Guard
All operational patrol vessels under 10t FLD

FOREIGN FORCES

Under UNSOM command unless stated
Burundi 1 obs • AMISOM 5,432; 6 inf bn
Djibouti AMISOM 1,850; 2 inf bn
Ethiopia AMISOM 4,395; 6 inf bn
Finland EUTM Somalia 7
France EUTM Somalia 1
Germany EUTM Somalia 7
Ghana UNSOS 2 obs
Hungary EUTM Somalia 4
Italy EUTM Somalia 112
Kenya AMISOM 3,664; 3 inf bn • UNSOS 1 obs
Mauritania UNSOS 1 obs
Netherlands EUTM Somalia 11
Nigeria UNSOS 1 obs
Pakistan 1 obs • UNSOS 1 obs
Portugal EUTM Somalia 4
Romania EUTM Somalia 4
Serbia EUTM Somalia 6
Sierra Leone 1 obs • UNSOS 1 obs
Spain EUTM Somalia 16
Sweden EUTM Somalia 4
Turkey 1 obs
Uganda 530; 1 obs; 1 sy bn • AMISOM 6,223; 7 inf bn • UNSOS 1 obs
United Kingdom 4 obs • UNSOS 41 • EUTM Somalia 4
United States Africa Command 500

TERRITORY WHERE THE GOVERNMENT DOES NOT EXERCISE EFFECTIVE CONTROL

Data presented here represents the de facto situation. This does not imply international recognition as a sovereign state

Somaliland

Militia-unit strengths are not known. Equipment numbers are generalised assessments; most of this equipment is in poor repair or inoperable.

Army ε12,500

FORCES BY ROLE
MANOEUVRE
  Armoured
  2 armd bde
  Mechanised
  1 mech inf bde
  Light
  14 inf bde
COMBAT SUPPORT
  2 arty bde

COMBAT SERVICE SUPPORT
1 spt bn
EQUIPMENT BY TYPE†
ARMOURED FIGHTING VEHICLES
  MBT T-54/55
  RECCE Fiat 6616
  APC • APC(W) Fiat 6614
ARTILLERY • MRL various incl BM-21 *Grad*
AIR DEFENCE • GUNS • 23mm ZU-23

Ministry of the Interior

Coast Guard 600
All operational patrol vessels under 10t FLD

Puntland

Army ε3,000 (to be integrated into Somali National Army)

Maritime Police Force ε1,000
EQUIPMENT BY TYPE
AIRCRAFT • TPT 4: **Light** 3 Ayres S2R; **PAX** 1 DC-3
HELICOPTERS • MRH SA316 *Alouette* III
PATROL AND COASTAL COMBATANTS
All operational patrol vessels under 10t FLD

South Africa RSA

South African Rand R		2016	2017	2018
GDP	R	4.34tr	4.61tr	
	US$	295bn	344bn	
per capita	US$	5,302	6,089	
Growth	%	0.3	0.7	
Inflation	%	6.3	5.4	
Def bdgt	R	47.2bn	48.6bn	50.6bn
	US$	3.21bn	3.63bn	
FMA (US)	US$	0.3m	0.3m	0m
US$1=R		14.71	13.40	

Population   54,841,552

Age	0–14	15–19	20–24	25–29	30–64	65 plus
Male	14.1%	4.3%	4.4%	5.0%	19.2%	2.4%
Female	14.1%	4.3%	4.6%	5.0%	19.2%	3.3%

Capabilities

While the South African National Defence Force (SANDF) remains on paper the most capable force in the region, funding problems continue to erode capacity for sustained operations. The services also face an increasing challenge in replacing ageing equipment; in late 2016/early 2017 there was little airborne maritime-surveillance capability as the relevant type was temporarily grounded. South Africa contributes to UN operations and, since its inception, has been a key component of the Force Intervention Brigade in the Democratic Republic of the Congo. It is also a proponent of the African Union's Standby Force concept. The 2015 Defence Review highlighted the role that Pretoria sees itself playing in ensuring the stability of the continent.

Key recommendations included joint command and control for multi-domain and joint-service operations; investment in special forces; and boosting land forces' deployability. Meeting these objectives, however, requires adequate funding. The army's aim is to be able to field 22 companies on border-patrol tasks, but as of 2017 it was able to equip only 15. Higher personnel spending, including on pensions, has meant that maintenance and repair funds have had to be reallocated. Meanwhile, the army 'faces block obsolescence of its prime mission equipment'. The country also sustains the continent's most capable defence industry, but defence-budget cuts and reduced procurement have increasingly required that it look to the export market. Crucial SANDF procurement programmes are behind schedule, including the *Badger* armoured vehicle. The government was working on a revised defence-industrial strategy as of the fourth quarter of 2017, which is intended to improve domestic-procurement practices along with better government support. The SANDF still deploys regularly on peacekeeping missions and participates in national and multinational exercises. Historically, South African forces have also played a significant role in training and supporting other regional forces.

ACTIVE 66,350 (Army 40,200 Navy 7,550 Air 10,450 South African Military Health Service 8,150)

RESERVE 15,050 (Army 12,250 Navy 850 Air 850 South African Military Health Service Reserve 1,100)

ORGANISATIONS BY SERVICE

Space
EQUIPMENT BY TYPE
SATELLITES • ISR 1 *Kondor-E*

Army 40,200
FORCES BY ROLE
Regt are bn sized. A new army structure is planned with 3 mixed regular/reserve divisions (1 mechanised, 1 motorised and 1 contingency) comprising 12 brigades (1 armoured, 1 mechanised, 7 motorised, 1 airborne, 1 air-landed and 1 sea landed)
COMMAND
  2 bde HQ
SPECIAL FORCES
  2 SF regt(-)
MANOEUVRE
  Reconnaissance
  1 armd recce regt
  Armoured
  1 tk regt(-)
  Mechanised
  2 mech inf bn
  Light
  8 mot inf bn
  1 lt inf bn
  Air Manoeuvre
  1 AB bn
  1 air mob bn

Amphibious
1 amph bn
COMBAT SUPPORT
1 arty regt
1 engr regt
1 construction regt
3 sigs regt
COMBAT SERVICE SUPPORT
1 engr spt regt
AIR DEFENCE
1 ADA regt

Reserve 12,250 reservists (under-strength)
FORCES BY ROLE
MANOEUVRE
Reconnaissance
3 armd recce regt
Armoured
4 tk regt
Mechanised
6 mech inf bn
Light
14 mot inf bn
3 lt inf bn (converting to mot inf)
Air Manoeuvre
1 AB bn
2 air mob bn
Amphibious
1 amph bn
COMBAT SUPPORT
7 arty regt
2 engr regt
AIR DEFENCE
5 AD regt

EQUIPMENT BY TYPE
ARMOURED FIGHTING VEHICLES
MBT 24 *Olifant* 2 (133 *Olifant* 1B in store)
ASLT 50 *Rooikat-76* (126 in store)
IFV 534 *Ratel-20/Ratel-60/Ratel-90*
APC • PPV 810: 370 *Casspir*; 440 *Mamba*
ENGINEERING & MAINTENANCE VEHICLES
ARV *Gemsbok*
VLB *Leguan*
MW *Husky*
ANTI-TANK/ANTI-INFRASTRUCTURE
MSL
SP ZT-3 *Swift*
MANPATS Milan ADT/ER
RCL 106mm M40A1 (some SP)
ARTILLERY 1,240
SP 155mm 2 G-6 (41 in store)
TOWED 155mm 6 G-5 (66 in store)
MRL 127mm 6 *Valkiri* Mk II MARS *Bataleur*; (26 *Valkiri* Mk I and 19 *Valkiri* Mk II in store)
MOR 1,226: 81mm 1,190 (incl some SP on *Casspir* & *Ratel*); 120mm 36
UNMANNED AERIAL VEHICLES
ISR • Light up to 4 *Vulture*
AIR DEFENCE
SAM • Point-defence Starstreak
GUNS 76
SP 23mm (36 *Zumlac* in store)
TOWED 35mm 40 GDF-002
RADAR • AIR DEFENCE 6: 4 ESR 220 *Thutlwa*; 2 Thales *Page*

Navy 7,550
Fleet HQ and Naval base located at Simon's Town; Naval stations located at Durban and Port Elizabeth
EQUIPMENT BY TYPE
SUBMARINES • TACTICAL • SSK 3 *Heroine* (Type-209/1400 mod) with 8 533mm TT with AEG SUT 264 HWT (of which one cyclically in reserve/refit)
PRINCIPAL SURFACE COMBATANTS • FRIGATES 4:
FFGHM 4 *Valour* (MEKO A200) with 2 quad lnchr with MM40 *Exocet* Block 2 AShM (upgrade to Block 3 planned); 2 16-cell VLS with *Umkhonto*-IR SAM, 1 76mm gun (capacity 1 *Super Lynx* 300 hel)
PATROL AND COASTAL COMBATANTS 6
PCC 3: 2 *Warrior* (ISR *Reshef*) with 1 76mm gun; 1 *Warrior* (ISR *Reshef*)
PB 3 *Tobie*
MINE WARFARE • MINE COUNTERMEASURES 2
MHC 3 *River* (GER *Navors*) (Limited operational roles; training and dive support)
AMPHIBIOUS • LCU 2 *Delta* 80
LOGISTICS AND SUPPORT 2
AORH 1 *Drakensberg* (capacity 2 *Delta* 80 LCU; 2 *Oryx* hels; 100 troops)
AGHS 1 *Protea* (UK *Hecla*) with 1 hel landing platform

Maritime Reaction Squadron
FORCES BY ROLE
MANOEUVRE
Amphibious
1 mne patrol gp
1 diving gp
1 mne boarding gp
COMBAT SERVICE SUPPORT
1 spt gp

Air Force 10,450
Air Force HQ, Pretoria, and 4 op gps
Command & Control: 2 Airspace Control Sectors, 1 Mobile Deployment Wg, 1 Air Force Command Post
FORCES BY ROLE
FIGHTER/GROUND ATTACK
1 sqn with *Gripen* C/D (JAS-39C/D)
GROUND ATTACK/TRAINING
1 sqn with *Hawk* Mk120*
TRANSPORT
1 (VIP) sqn with B-737 BBJ; Cessna 550 *Citation* II; *Falcon* 50; *Falcon* 900
1 sqn with C-47TP
2 sqn with Beech 200/300 *King Air*; C-130B/BZ *Hercules*; C-212; Cessna 208 *Caravan*
ATTACK HELICOPTER
1 (cbt spt) sqn with AH-2 *Rooivalk*
TRANSPORT HELICOPTER
4 (mixed) sqn with AW109; BK-117; *Oryx*

EQUIPMENT BY TYPE
AIRCRAFT 50 combat capable
FGA 26: 17 *Gripen* C (JAS-39C); 9 *Gripen* D (JAS-39D)
TPT 24: **Medium** 7: 2 C-130B *Hercules*; 5 C-130BZ *Hercules*; **Light** 13: 3 Beech 200C *King Air*; 1 Beech 300 *King Air*; 3 C-47TP (maritime); 2 C-212-200 *Aviocar*†; 1 C-212-300 *Aviocar*†; 2 Cessna 550 *Citation* II; 1 PC-12; (9 Cessna 208 *Caravan* in store) **PAX** 4: 1 B-737BBJ; 2 *Falcon* 50; 1 *Falcon* 900
TRG 59: 24 *Hawk* Mk120*; 35 PC-7 Mk II *Astra*
HELICOPTERS
ATK 11 AH-2 *Rooivalk*
MRH 4 *Super Lynx* 300
TPT 70: **Medium** 36 *Oryx*; **Light** 34: 26 AW109; 8 BK-117
AIR-LAUNCHED MISSILES • **AAM** • **IIR** IRIS-T
BOMBS • **Laser-guided** GBU-12 *Paveway* II

Ground Defence
FORCES BY ROLE
MANOEUVRE
Other
12 sy sqn (SAAF regt)
EQUIPMENT BY TYPE
2 radar (static) located at Ellisras and Mariepskop; 2 (mobile long-range); 4 (tactical mobile). Radar air-control sectors located at Pretoria, Hoedspruit

South African Military Health Service 8,150; ε1,100 reservists (total 9,300)

Department of Agriculture, Fisheries and Forestry
EQUIPMENT BY TYPE
PATROL AND COASTAL COMBATANTS 4
PSO 1 *Sarah Baartman* with 1 hel landing platform
PCC 3 *Lilian Ngoyi*
LOGISTICS AND SUPPORT • **AGE** 2: 1 *Africana*; 1 *Ellen Khuzwayo*

Department of Environmental Affairs
EQUIPMENT BY TYPE
LOGISTICS AND SUPPORT • **AGOSH** 1 *S. A. Agulhas* II (used for Antarctic survey) (capacity 2 *Oryx* hels)

Cyber
South Africa published a National Cybersecurity Policy Framework in 2011. Since then, the defence-intelligence branch of the Department of Defence has been tasked to develop a comprehensive cyber-warfare strategy and a cyber-warfare implementation plan, as well as to establish a Cyber Command Centre Headquarters, intended to be fully operational by FY2018/19. A Cyber Security Incident Response Team (CSIRT) operates under the State Security Agency. State-owned company Denel announced in September 2016 the establishment of the Denel Tactical Cyber Command Centre (DTC³). According to Denel, 'DTC³ will also provide specialist cyber security solutions and services including a defensive and offensive cyber warfare capability.'

DEPLOYMENT

DEMOCRATIC REPUBLIC OF THE CONGO
UN • MONUSCO • Operation Mistral 1,358; 4 obs; 1 inf bn; 1 engr coy; 1 atk hel sqn; 1 hel sqn

MOZAMBIQUE CHANNEL
Navy • 1 FFGHM

SUDAN
UN • UNAMID • Operation Cordite 4; 1 obs

South Sudan SSD

South Sudanese Pound ssp		2016	2017	2018
GDP	ssp	143bn	333bn	
	US$	3.06bn	2.92bn	
per capita	US$	244	222	
Growth	%	-13.8	-6.3	
Inflation	%	380	182	
Def bdgt [a]	ssp	4.58bn	11.0bn	13.0bn
	US$	98m	97m	
US$1=ssp		46.95	114.18	

[a] Security and law-enforcement spending

Population 13,026,129

Age	0–14	15–19	20–24	25–29	30–64	65 plus
Male	22.6%	5.8%	4.8%	3.8%	12.3%	1.1%
Female	21.7%	5.5%	4.3%	3.6%	13.2%	0.9%

Capabilities

South Sudan's civil war continues with little progress towards implementing the 2015 peace agreement. The May 2017 unilateral ceasefire declared by President Kiir has not been widely respected, with clashes continuing. Future peace talks may be complicated by the emergence of additional rebel groups. Political and ethnic factionalism remains high, while there remain security concerns stemming from the relationship with Sudan. Planned disarmament and demobilisation remain on hold due to the fighting, as do longer-term aspirations for defence reform and capability development. US sanctions and an EU arms embargo remain in place, although a December 2016 vote for a wider UN arms embargo was unsuccessful. In August 2017, the UN bolstered its existing UNMISS deployment with an additional 4,000-personnel regional protection force designed, according to the UN, to allow existing UNMISS troops to be reassigned to locations outside the capital.

ACTIVE 185,000 (Army 185,000)

ORGANISATIONS BY SERVICE

Army ε185,000
FORCES BY ROLE
3 military comd

MANOEUVRE
Light
  8 inf div
COMBAT SUPPORT
  1 engr corps
EQUIPMENT BY TYPE
ARMOURED FIGHTING VEHICLES
  MBT 80+: some T-55†; 80 T-72AV†
  APC • PPV Streit *Typhoon*; Streit *Cougar*; *Mamba*
ANTI-TANK/ANTI-INFRASTRUCTURE
  MSL • MANPATS HJ-73; 9K115 *Metis* (AT-7 *Saxhorn*)
  RCL 73mm SPG-9 (with SSLA)
ARTILLERY 69+
  SP 122mm 2S1 *Gvozdika*; **152mm** 2S3 *Akatsiya*
  TOWED 130mm Some M-46
  MRL 122mm BM-21 *Grad*; **107mm** PH-63
  MOR 82mm; **120mm** Type-55 look-alike
AIR DEFENCE
  SAM
    Short-range 16 S-125 *Pechora* (SA-3 *Goa*) (reported)
    Point-defence 9K32 *Strela*-2 (SA-7 *Grail*)‡; QW-2
  GUNS 14.5mm ZPU-4; **23mm** ZU-23-2; **37mm** Type-65/74

Air Force

EQUIPMENT BY TYPE
AIRCRAFT • TPT • Light 1 Beech 1900
HELICOPTERS
  ATK 5: 2 Mi-24V *Hind*; 3 Mi-24V-SMB *Hind*
  MRH 9 Mi-17 *Hip* H
  TPT 3: **Medium** 1 Mi-172 (VIP); **Light** 2 AW109 (civ livery)

FOREIGN FORCES

All UNMISS, unless otherwise indicated
Australia 23; 1 obs
Bangladesh 1,604; 7 obs; 1 inf coy; 1 rvn coy; 2 engr coy
Benin 2; 1 obs
Bhutan 2; 2 obs
Bolivia 1; 3 obs
Brazil 6; 5 obs
Cambodia 77; 6 obs; 1 MP unit
Canada 5; 5 obs
China, People's Republic of 1,047; 4 obs; 1 inf bn; 1 engr coy; 1 fd hospital
Denmark 9
Egypt 1; 3 obs
El Salvador 1; 2 obs
Ethiopia 1,261; 11 obs; 2 inf bn
Fiji 4; 2 obs
Germany 5; 11 obs
Ghana 716; 11 obs; 1 inf bn
Guatemala 4; 3 obs
Guinea 1
India 2,373; 11 obs; 2 inf bn; 1 sigs coy; 1 fd hospital
Indonesia 1; 2 obs
Japan 4
Jordan 2
Korea, Republic of 299; 2 obs; 1 engr coy
Kyrgyzstan 2; 1 obs
Moldova 1; 3 obs
Mongolia 866; 6 obs; 1 inf bn
Myanmar 2
Namibia 1; 1 obs
Nepal 1,710; 11 obs; 2 inf bn
Netherlands 6
New Zealand 1; 3 obs
Nigeria 3; 6 obs
Norway 15
Pakistan 1; 1 obs
Paraguay 2 obs
Peru 1; 2 obs
Poland 1 obs
Romania 2; 4 obs
Russia 4; 2 obs
Rwanda 1,973; 14 obs; 2 inf bn; 1 hel sqn
Senegal 2 obs
Sri Lanka 178; 4 obs; 1 fd hospital; 1 hel sqn
Sweden 2 obs
Switzerland 2
Tanzania 4; 4 obs
Togo 1
Uganda 2
Ukraine 1; 3 obs
United Kingdom 373; 1 engr coy; 1 fd hospital
United States 7
Vietnam 2 obs
Yemen 3; 2 obs
Zambia 3; 3 obs
Zimbabwe 2 obs

Sudan SDN

Sudanese Pound sdg		2016	2017	2018
GDP	sdg	574bn	771bn	
	US$	91.2	119bn	
per capita	US$	2,304	2,917	
Growth	%	3.1	3.7	
Inflation	%	17.8	26.9	
Def exp	sdg	n.k.	n.k.	
	US$	n.k.	n.k.	
US$1=sdg		6.29	6.48	

Population 37,345,935

Ethnic and religious groups: Muslim 70% mainly in North; Christian 10% mainly in South; Arab 39% mainly in North

Age	0–14	15–19	20–24	25–29	30–64	65 plus
Male	19.6%	5.8%	4.9%	4.0%	14.0%	1.7%
Female	19.0%	5.6%	4.6%	3.9%	14.9%	1.5%

Capabilities

Sudan's armed forces remain focused on ongoing tensions with South Sudan and the challenge from insurgents in the south of the country. The government also relies on paramilitary forces for internal security. Sudan's extension of a unilateral ceasefire with rebels indicates progress on resolving ongoing conflicts, and has been a key contributing factor to the lifting of decades of US sanctions in October 2017. By regional standards, Sudan's armed forces are relatively well equipped, with significant holdings of both ageing and modern systems. These are complemented by the local Military Industry Corporation's manufacture of ammunition, small arms and armoured vehicles. The majority of the corporation's products are based on older Chinese and Russian systems. The armed forces' maintenance capability focuses on ground forces' equipment, but there is a limited aircraft-maintenance capacity. Regional power-projection capability has been demonstrated in Sudan's contribution to the Saudi-led intervention in Yemen, in which it initially deployed a small number of ground-attack aircraft, followed by a ground-forces contingent. (See pp. 435–40.)

ACTIVE 104,300 (Army 100,000 Navy 1,300 Air 3,000) Paramilitary 20,000
Conscript liability 2 years for males aged 18–30

RESERVE NIL Paramilitary 85,000

ORGANISATIONS BY SERVICE

Army 100,000+
FORCES BY ROLE
SPECIAL FORCES
  5 SF coy
MANOEUVRE
  Reconnaissance
  1 indep recce bde
  Armoured
  1 armd div
  Mechanised
  1 mech inf div
  1 indep mech inf bde
  Light
  15+ inf div
  6 indep inf bde
  Air Manoeuvre
  1 air aslt bde
  Amphibious
  1 mne div
  Other
  1 (Border Guard) sy bde
COMBAT SUPPORT
  3 indep arty bde
  1 engr div (9 engr bn)
EQUIPMENT BY TYPE
ARMOURED FIGHTING VEHICLES
  MBT 465: 20 M60A3; 60 Type-59/Type-59D; 305 T-54/T-55; 70 T-72AV; 10 *Al-Bashier* (Type-85-IIM)
  LT TK 115: 70 Type-62; 45 Type-63
  RECCE 206: 6 AML-90; 70 BRDM-1/2; 50–80 FV701 *Ferret*; 30–50 FV601 *Saladin*
  IFV 152: 135 BMP-1/2; 10 BTR-3; 7 BTR-80A
  APC 415+
    APC (T) 66: 20-30 BTR-50; 36 M113
    APC (W) 349+: 10 BTR-70M *Kobra* 2; 50–80 BTR-152; 20 OT-62; 50 OT-64; 3+ *Rakhsh*; 10 WZ-551; WZ-523; 55-80 V-150 *Commando*; 96 *Walid*
ANTI-TANK/ANTI-INFRASTRUCTURE
  MSL • MANPATS 9K11 *Malyutka* (AT-3 *Sagger*); HJ-8; 9K135 *Kornet* (AT-14 *Spriggan*)
  RCL 106mm 40 M40A1
  GUNS 40+: 40 **76mm** ZIS-3/**100mm** M-1944; **85mm** D-44
ARTILLERY 860+
  SP 66: **122mm** 56 2S1 *Gvozdika*; **155mm** 10 Mk F3
  TOWED 128+: **105mm** 20 M101; **122mm** 21+: 21 D-30; D-74; M-30; **130mm** 75 M-46/Type-59-I; **155mm** 12 M114A1
  MRL 666+: **107mm** 477 Type-63; **122mm** 188: 120 BM-21 *Grad*; 50 *Saqr*; 18 Type-81; **302mm** 1+ WS-1 **MOR 81mm**; **82mm**; **120mm** AM-49; M-43
RADAR • LAND RASIT (veh, arty)
AIR DEFENCE
  SAM • Point-defence 4+: 9K32 *Strela*-2 (SA-7 *Grail*)‡; FN-6; 4+ 9K33 *Osa* (SA-8 *Gecko*)
  GUNS 966+
    SP 20: **20mm** 8 M163 *Vulcan*; 12 M3 VDAA
    TOWED 946+: 740+ **14.5mm** ZPU-2/**14.5mm** ZPU-4/**37mm** Type-63/**57mm** S-60/**85mm** M-1944; **20mm** 16 M167 *Vulcan*; **23mm** 50 ZU-23-2; **37mm** 80 M-1939; (30 M-1939 unserviceable); **40mm** 60

Navy 1,300
EQUIPMENT BY TYPE
PATROL AND COASTAL COMBATANTS 11
  PBR 4 *Kurmuk*
  PB 7: 1 13.5m; 1 14m; 2 19m; 3 41m (PRC)
AMPHIBIOUS • LANDING CRAFT 5
  LCVP 5
LOGISTICS AND SUPPORT 3
  AG 3

Air Force 3,000
FORCES BY ROLE
FIGHTER
  2 sqn with MiG-29SE/UB *Fulcrum*
GROUND ATTACK
  1 sqn with A-5 *Fantan*
  1 sqn with Su-24M *Fencer*
  1 sqn with Su-25/Su-25UB *Frogfoot*
TRANSPORT
  Some sqn with An-30 *Clank*; An-32 *Cline*; An-72 *Coaler*; An-74TK-200/300; C-130H *Hercules*; Il-76 *Candid*; Y-8
  1 VIP unit with *Falcon* 20F; *Falcon* 50; *Falcon* 900; F-27; Il-62M *Classic*
TRAINING
  1 sqn with K-8 *Karakorum**
ATTACK HELICOPTER
  2 sqn with Mi-24/Mi-24P/Mi-24V/Mi-35P *Hind*
TRANSPORT HELICOPTER
  2 sqn with Mi-8 *Hip*; Mi-17 *Hip* H; Mi-171
AIR DEFENCE
  5 bty with S-75 *Dvina* (SA-2 *Guideline*)‡

EQUIPMENT BY TYPE

AIRCRAFT 66 combat capable
  FTR 22: 20 MiG-29SE *Fulcrum* C; 2 MiG-29UB *Fulcrum* B
  ATK 32: 15 A-5 *Fantan*; 6 Su-24/M *Fencer*; 9 Su-25 *Frogfoot*; 2 Su-25UB *Frogfoot* B
  ISR 2 An-30 *Clank*
  TPT 21: **Heavy** 1 Il-76 *Candid*; **Medium** 6: 4 C-130H *Hercules*; 2 Y-8; **Light** 10: 2 An-32 *Cline*; 2 An-72 *Coaler*; 4 An-74TK-200; 2 An-74TK-300; **PAX** 4: 1 *Falcon* 20F (VIP); 1 *Falcon* 50 (VIP); 1 *Falcon* 900; 1 Il-62M *Classic*
  TRG 15: 12 K-8 *Karakorum**; 3 UTVA-75
HELICOPTERS
  ATK 40: 25 Mi-24 *Hind*; 2 Mi-24P *Hind*; 7 Mi-24V *Hind* E; 6 Mi-35P *Hind*
  MRH ε4 Mi-17 *Hip* H
  TPT 27: **Medium** 23: 21 Mi-8 *Hip*; 2 Mi-171; **Light** 4: 1 Bell 205; 3 Bo-105
AIR DEFENCE • SAM • Medium-range: 90 S-75 *Dvina* (SA-2 *Guideline*)‡
AIR-LAUNCHED MISSILES • AAM • IR R-3 (AA-2 *Atoll*)‡; R-60 (AA-8 *Aphid*); R-73 (AA-11 *Archer*); **IR/SARH** R-23/24 (AA-7 *Apex*); **ARH** R-77 (AA-12A *Adder*)

Paramilitary 20,000

Popular Defence Force 20,000 (org in bn 1,000); 85,000 reservists (total 105,000)
mil wing of National Islamic Front

DEPLOYMENT

SAUDI ARABIA
Operation Restoring Hope 3 Su-24 *Fencer*

YEMEN
Operation Restoring Hope 950; 1 mech BG; T-72AV, BTR-70M *Kobra* 2

FOREIGN FORCES

All UNAMID, unless otherwise indicated
Bangladesh 371; 8 obs; 2 inf coy
Benin UNISFA 2 obs
Bhutan 1; 1 obs • UNISFA 1; 1 obs
Brazil 3 • UNISFA 2 obs
Burkina Faso 73; 4 obs • UNISFA 1 obs
Burundi 4; 4 obs • UNISFA 2 obs
Cambodia 2 obs • UNISFA 1; 2 obs
China, People's Republic of 370; 1 engr coy
Ecuador 1; 3 obs; • UNISFA 1; 1 obs
Egypt 847; 18 obs; 1 inf bn
Ethiopia 2,419; 11 obs; 3 inf bn • UNISFA 4,366; 78 obs; 4 armd pl; 3 inf bn; 2 arty coy; 1 engr coy; 1 sigs coy; 1 fd hospital; 1 hel sqn
Gambia 211; 1 inf coy
Germany 8
Ghana 19; 4 obs • UNISFA 3; 4 obs
Guatemala UNISFA 1; 2 obs
Guinea UNISFA 1
India UNISFA 3; 2 obs
Indonesia 810; 7 obs; 1 inf bn • UNISFA 2; 1 obs
Iran 1 obs
Jordan 17; 7 obs
Kenya 113; 3 obs; 1 MP coy
Korea, Republic of 2
Kyrgyzstan 1 obs • UNISFA 1 obs
Malawi UNISFA 1
Malaysia 11 • UNISFA 1 obs
Mongolia 70; 1 fd hospital • UNISFA 1; 2 obs
Namibia 4; 2 obs • UNISFA 2; 2 obs
Nepal 366; 10 obs; 2 inf coy • UNISFA 4; 2 obs
Nigeria 932; 5 obs; 1 inf bn; 1 fd hospital • UNISFA 2; 1 obs
Pakistan 1,412; 8 obs; 1 inf bn; 1 engr coy
Papua New Guinea 1; 1 obs
Peru 1; 1 obs • UNISFA 2 obs
Russia UNISFA 1 obs
Rwanda 2,446; 5 obs; 3 inf bn • UNISFA 6; 3 obs
Senegal 798; 1 inf bn
Sierra Leone 1; 5 obs • UNISFA 2; 1 obs
South Africa 4; 1 obs
Sri Lanka UNISFA 2; 5 obs
Tanzania 815; 11 obs; 1 inf bn • UNISFA 2 obs
Thailand 10; 4 obs
Togo 2 obs
Ukraine UNISFA 1; 3 obs
Yemen 3; 3 obs
Zambia 5; 2 obs • UNISFA 1 obs
Zimbabwe 3; 5 obs

Tanzania TZA

Tanzanian Shilling sh		2016	2017	2018
GDP	sh	104tr	116tr	
	US$	47.7bn	51.6bn	
per capita	US$	980	1,041	
Growth	%	7.0	6.5	
Inflation	%	5.2	5.4	
Def bdgt	sh	1.14tr	1.19tr	1.73tr
	US$	525m	528m	
US$1=sh		2,177.13	2,250.54	

Population 53,950,935

Age	0–14	15–19	20–24	25–29	30–64	65 plus
Male	22.1%	5.5%	4.4%	3.8%	12.7%	1.3%
Female	21.6%	5.4%	4.5%	3.8%	13.0%	1.7%

Capabilities

Non-state actors pose the principal threat to Tanzania's security, with terrorism, poaching and piracy of concern. There was additional focus on maritime security in 2017. Budget constraints have limited equipment-recapitalisation ambitions, which reflects a relatively benign security environment, although concerns remain about instability in the DRC. A developing relationship with China has led to a series of procurement programmes and training contacts. There is a limited ability to project power independently beyond its own territory. However, Tanzania has in recent years regularly taken part in multinational exercises in Africa and provided some training assistance to other African forces. Training relationships exist with other external armed forces, including the US. Tanzania also receives US support to strengthen its peacekeeping deployment capacity under the US African Rapid Response Partnership. Tanzania's contribution to the UN's Force Intervention Brigade in the eastern DRC, notably its special forces, will have provided many lessons for force development.

ACTIVE 27,000 (Army 23,000 Navy 1,000 Air 3,000)
Paramilitary 1,400
Conscript liability Three months basic military training combined with social service, ages 18–23

RESERVE 80,000 (Joint 80,000)

ORGANISATIONS BY SERVICE

Army ε23,000
FORCES BY ROLE
SPECIAL FORCES
  1 SF unit
MANOEUVRE
  Armoured
  1 tk bde
  Light
  5 inf bde
COMBAT SUPPORT
  4 arty bn
  1 mor bn
  2 AT bn
  1 engr regt (bn)
COMBAT SERVICE SUPPORT
  1 log gp
AIR DEFENCE
  2 ADA bn
EQUIPMENT BY TYPE†
ARMOURED FIGHTING VEHICLES
  MBT 45: 30 T-54/T-55; 15 Type-59G
  LT TK 57+: 30 FV101 *Scorpion*; 25 Type-62; 2+ Type-63A
  RECCE 10 BRDM-2
  APC • APC (W) 14: ε10 BTR-40/BTR-152; 4 Type-92
ANTI-TANK/ANTI-INFRASTRUCTURE
  RCL 75mm Type-52 (M20)
  GUNS 85mm 75 Type-56 (D-44)
ARTILLERY 344+
  TOWED 130: **122mm** 100: 20 D-30; 80 Type-54-1 (M-30); **130mm** 30 Type-59-I
  GUN/MOR 120mm 3+ Type-07PA
  MRL 61+: **122mm** 58 BM-21 *Grad*; **300mm** 3+ A100
  MOR 150: **82mm** 100 M-43; **120mm** 50 M-43

Navy ε1,000
EQUIPMENT BY TYPE
PATROL AND COASTAL COMBATANTS 10
  PCC 2 *Mwitongo* (ex-PRC *Haiqing*)
  PHT 2 *Huchuan* each with 2 533mm ASTT
  PB 6: 2 *Ngunguri*; 2 *Shanghai* II (PRC); 2 VT 23m
AMPHIBIOUS 3
  LCU 2 *Yuchin*
  LCT 1 *Kasa*

Air Defence Command ε3,000
FORCES BY ROLE
FIGHTER
  3 sqn with F-7/FT-7; FT-5; K-8 *Karakorum**
TRANSPORT
  1 sqn with Cessna 404 *Titan*; DHC-5D *Buffalo*; F-28 *Fellowship*; F-50; Gulfstream G550; Y-12 (II)
TRANSPORT HELICOPTER
  1 sqn with Bell 205 (AB-205); Bell 412EP *Twin Huey*
EQUIPMENT BY TYPE†
AIRCRAFT 17 combat capable
  FTR 11: 9 F-7TN; 2 FT-7TN
  ISR 1 SB7L-360 *Seeker*
  TPT 12: **Medium** 2 Y-8; **Light** 7: 2 Cessna 404 *Titan*; 3 DHC-5D *Buffalo*; 2 Y-12(II); **PAX** 3: 1 F-28 *Fellowship*; 1 F-50; 1 Gulfstream G550
  TRG 9: 3 FT-5 (JJ-5); 6 K-8 *Karakorum**
HELICOPTERS
  MRH 1 Bell 412EP *Twin Huey*
  TPT • Light 1 Bell 205 (AB-205)
AIR DEFENCE
  SAM
    Short-range 2K12 *Kub* (SA-6 *Gainful*)†; S-125 *Pechora* (SA-3 *Goa*)†
    Point-defence 9K32 *Strela*-2 (SA-7 *Grail*)‡
  GUNS 200
    TOWED 14.5mm 40 ZPU-2/ZPU-4†; **23mm** 40 ZU-23; **37mm** 120 M-1939

Paramilitary 1,400 active

Police Field Force 1,400
18 sub-units incl Police Marine Unit

Air Wing
EQUIPMENT BY TYPE
AIRCRAFT • TPT • Light 1 Cessna U206 *Stationair*
HELICOPTERS
  TPT • Light 4: 2 Bell 206A *Jet Ranger* (AB-206A); 2 Bell 206L *Long Ranger*
  TRG 2 Bell 47G (AB-47G)/Bell 47G2

Marine Unit 100
EQUIPMENT BY TYPE
PATROL AND COASTAL COMBATANTS
All operational patrol vessels under 10t FLD

DEPLOYMENT

CENTRAL AFRICAN REPUBLIC
UN • MINUSCA 201; 1 inf bn(-)

DEMOCRATIC REPUBLIC OF THE CONGO
UN • MONUSCO 1,266; 1 SF coy; 1 inf bn

LEBANON
UN • UNIFIL 157; 2 MP coy

SOUTH SUDAN
UN • UNMISS 4; 4 obs

SUDAN
UN • UNAMID 815; 11 obs; 1 inf bn
UN • UNISFA 2 obs

Togo TGO

CFA Franc BCEAO fr		2016	2017	2018
GDP	fr	2.63tr	2.79tr	
	US$	4.43bn	4.80bn	
per capita	US$	590	622	
Growth	%	5.0	5.0	
Inflation	%	0.9	0.8	
Def bdgt	fr	48.6bn	51.9bn	
	US$	82m	89m	
US$1=fr		592.69	581.56	

Population 7,965,055

Age	0–14	15–19	20–24	25–29	30–64	65 plus
Male	20.2%	5.0%	4.5%	4.2%	14.1%	1.5%
Female	20.0%	5.0%	4.5%	4.2%	14.5%	1.9%

Capabilities

The Togolese armed forces are adequate for the internal-security role, but they have limited deployment capacity. Togo is increasingly concerned by the piracy threat in the Gulf of Guinea, and other illegal maritime activities. Equipment, though limited, is generally well maintained and serviceable. There is ongoing military-training cooperation with France. In 2017, Togo's navy took part in the French-led fisheries-policing exercise *African NeMo*. The French also provide peacekeeping training for Togolese personnel participating in MINUSMA. The US Africa Contingency Operations Training and Assistance programme has also provided training to the Togolese forces. Togo is also seeking to procure former French Army *Gazelle* helicopters, which would significantly enhance the air force's capabilities.

ACTIVE 8,550 (Army 8,100 Navy 200 Air 250)
Paramilitary 750
Conscript liability Selective conscription, 2 years

ORGANISATIONS BY SERVICE

Army 8,100+
FORCES BY ROLE
MANOEUVRE
  Reconnaissance
  1 armd recce regt
  Light
  2 cbd arms regt
  2 inf regt
  1 rapid reaction force
  Air Manoeuvre
  1 cdo/para regt (3 cdo/para coy)
  Other
  1 (Presidential Guard) gd regt (1 gd bn, 1 cdo bn, 2 indep gd coy)
COMBAT SUPPORT
  1 cbt spt regt (1 fd arty bty, 2 ADA bty, 1 engr/log/tpt bn)
EQUIPMENT BY TYPE
ARMOURED FIGHTING VEHICLES
  MBT 2 T-54/T-55
  LT TK 9 FV101 *Scorpion*
  RECCE 87: 3 AML-60; 7 AML-90; 30 *Bastion Patsas*; 36 EE-9 *Cascavel*; 6 M8; 3 M20; 2 VBL
  IFV 20 BMP-2
  APC 34
    APC (T) 4 M3A1 half-track
    APC (W) 30 UR-416
ANTI-TANK/ANTI-INFRASTRUCTURE
  RCL 75mm Type-52 (M20)/Type-56; 82mm Type-65 (B-10)
  GUNS 57mm 5 ZIS-2
ARTILLERY 30+
  SP 122mm 6
  TOWED 105mm 4 HM-2
  MRL 122mm Type-81 mod (SC6 chassis)
  MOR 82mm 20 M-43
AIR DEFENCE • GUNS • TOWED 43 **14.5mm** 38 ZPU-4; **37mm** 5 M-1939

Navy ε200 (incl Marine Infantry unit)
EQUIPMENT BY TYPE
PATROL AND COASTAL COMBATANTS 3
  PBF 1 *Agou* (RPB 33)
  PB 2 *Kara* (FRA Esterel)

Air Force 250
FORCES BY ROLE
FIGHTER/GROUND ATTACK
  1 sqn with *Alpha Jet**; EMB-326G*
TRANSPORT
  1 sqn with Beech 200 *King Air*
  1 VIP unit with DC-8; F-28-1000
TRAINING
  1 sqn with TB-30 *Epsilon**
TRANSPORT HELICOPTER
  1 sqn with SA315 *Lama*; SA316 *Alouette* III; SA319 *Alouette* III
EQUIPMENT BY TYPE†
AIRCRAFT 10 combat capable
  TPT 5: Light 2 Beech 200 *King Air*; PAX 3: 1 DC-8; 2 F-28-1000 (VIP)
  TRG 10: 3 *Alpha Jet**; 4 EMB-326G *; 3 TB-30 *Epsilon**
HELICOPTERS
  MRH 4: 2 SA315 *Lama*; 1 SA316 *Alouette* III; 1 SA319 *Alouette* III
  TPT • Medium (1 SA330 *Puma* in store)

Paramilitary 750

Gendarmerie 750
Ministry of Interior

Sub-Saharan Africa

FORCES BY ROLE
2 reg sections
MANOEUVRE
  Other
    1 (mobile) paramilitary sqn

DEPLOYMENT

CENTRAL AFRICAN REPUBLIC
UN • MINUSCA 6; 4 obs

LIBERIA
UN • UNMIL 1

MALI
UN • MINUSMA 939; 2 obs; 1 inf bn; 1 fd hospital

SOUTH SUDAN
UN • UNMISS 1

SUDAN
UN • UNAMID 2 obs

WESTERN SAHARA
UN • MINURSO 1 obs

Uganda UGA

Ugandan Shilling Ush		2016	2017	2018
GDP	Ush	86.6tr	95.5tr	
	US$	25.3bn	26.4bn	
per capita	US$	692	701	
Growth	%	2.3	4.4	
Inflation	%	5.5	5.8	
Def bdgt	Ush	1.64tr	1.58tr	1.12tr
	US$	478m	436m	
FMA (US)	US$	0.2m	0m	0m
US$1=Ush		3,420.21	3,619.91	

Population 39,570,125

Age	0–14	15–19	20–24	25–29	30–64	65 plus
Male	23.9%	5.6%	4.8%	3.9%	10.5%	0.8%
Female	24.0%	5.7%	5.7%	3.9%	10.5%	1.1%

Capabilities

Uganda's armed forces are relatively large and well equipped. They have, in recent years, seen some advanced capability acquisitions, boosting military capacity, particularly in the air force. Ugandan forces remain deployed to Somalia as part of AMISOM, having deployed at the mission's inception in 2007. Some elements are combat experienced as a result. Due to operational experience and training, the force has developed in areas such as administration and planning, as well as in tactics, such as counter-IED and urban foot patrols supported by armour. A number of years spent targeting the Lord's Resistance Army has also ensured experience in more austere counter-insurgency tactics. Uganda is one of the largest contributors to the East Africa Standby Force. There is regular training, and the country has a number of training facilities that are used by international partners. US support to Uganda's forces in 2017 included the delivery of protected patrol vehicles, while Ugandan force elements gained experience at the US Joint Readiness Training Center. (See pp. 440–44.)

ACTIVE 45,000 (Ugandan People's Defence Force 45,000) Paramilitary 1,400

RESERVE 10,000

ORGANISATIONS BY SERVICE

Ugandan People's Defence Force ε40,000–45,000

FORCES BY ROLE
MANOEUVRE
  Armoured
    1 armd bde
  Light
    1 cdo bn
    5 inf div (total: 16 inf bde)
  Other
    1 (Special Forces Command) mot bde
COMBAT SUPPORT
  1 arty bde
AIR DEFENCE
  2 AD bn
EQUIPMENT BY TYPE†
ARMOURED FIGHTING VEHICLES
  MBT 239+: 185 T-54/T-55; 10 T-72; 44 T-90S; ZTZ-85-IIM
  LT TK ε20 PT-76
  RECCE 46: 40 Eland-20; 6 FV701 Ferret
  IFV 31 BMP-2
  APC 150
    APC (W) 58: 15 BTR-60; 20 Buffel; 4 OT-64; 19 Bastion APC
    PPV 92: 42 Casspir; 40 Mamba; 10 RG-33L
    AUV 15 Cougar
ENGINEERING & MAINTENANCE VEHICLES
  ARV T-54/T-55 reported
  VLB MTU reported
  MW Chubby
ARTILLERY 333+
  SP 155mm 6 ATMOS 2000
  TOWED 243+: **122mm** M-30; **130mm** 221; **155mm** 22: 4 G-5; 18 M-839
  MRL 6+: **107mm** (12-tube); **122mm** 6+: BM-21 Grad; 6 RM-70
  MOR 78+: **81mm** L16; **82mm** M-43; **120mm** 78 Soltam
AIR DEFENCE
  SAM
    Short-range 4 S-125 Pechora (SA-3 Goa)
    Point-defence 9K32 Strela-2 (SA-7 Grail)‡; 9K310 Igla-1 (SA-16 Gimlet)
  GUNS • TOWED 20+: **14.5mm** ZPU-1/ZPU-2/ZPU-4; **37mm** 20 M-1939

Marines ε400

All operational patrol vessels under 10t FLD

Air Wing

FORCES BY ROLE
FIGHTER/GROUND ATTACK
1 sqn with MiG-21bis *Fishbed*; MiG-21U/UM *Mongol* A/B; Su-30MK2
TRANSPORT
1 unit with Y-12
1 VIP unit with Gulfstream 550; L-100-30
TRAINING
1 unit with L-39 *Albatros*†*
ATTACK/TRANSPORT HELICOPTER
1 sqn with Bell 206 *Jet Ranger*; Bell 412 *Twin Huey*; Mi-17 *Hip* H; Mi-24 *Hind*; Mi-172 (VIP)

EQUIPMENT BY TYPE
AIRCRAFT 16 combat capable
  FGA 13: 5 MiG-21bis *Fishbed*; 1 MiG-21U *Mongol* A; 1 MiG-21UM *Mongol* B; 6 Su-30MK2
  TPT 6: **Medium** 1 L-100-30; **Light** 4: 2 Cessna 208B; 2 Y-12; **PAX** 1 Gulfstream 550
  TRG 3 L-39 *Albatros*†*
HELICOPTERS
  ATK 1 Mi-24 *Hind* (2 more non-op)
  MRH 5: 2 Bell 412 *Twin Huey*; 3 Mi-17 *Hip* H (1 more non-op)
  TPT 4: **Medium** 2: 1 Mi-172 (VIP), 1 Mi-171 (VIP); **Light** 2 Bell 206A *Jet Ranger*
AIR-LAUNCHED MISSILES
  AAM • IR R-73 (AA-11 *Archer*); **SARH** R-27 (AA-10 *Alamo*); **ARH** R-77 (AA-12 *Adder*) (reported)
  ARM Kh-31P (AS-17A *Krypton*) (reported)

Paramilitary ε1,400 active

Border Defence Unit ε600
Equipped with small arms only

Police Air Wing ε800
EQUIPMENT BY TYPE
HELICOPTERS • TPT • Light 1 Bell 206 *Jet Ranger*

DEPLOYMENT

SOMALIA
AU • AMISOM 6,223; 7 inf bn
UN • UNSOM 530; 1 obs; 1 sy bn
UN • UNSOS 1 obs

SOUTH SUDAN
UN • UNMISS 2

Zambia ZMB

Zambian Kwacha K		2016	2017	2018
GDP	K	217bn	243bn	
	US$	21.0bn	25.6bn	
per capita	US$	1,257	1,484	
Growth	%	3.4	4.0	
Inflation	%	17.9	6.8	
Def bdgt	K	3.15bn	3.20bn	
	US$	305m	337m	
US$1=K		10.32	9.51	

Population 15,972,000

Age	0–14	15–19	20–24	25–29	30–64	65 plus
Male	23.1%	5.4%	4.6%	3.8%	12.0%	1.0%
Female	22.9%	5.4%	4.6%	3.8%	12.0%	1.3%

Capabilities

Ensuring territorial integrity and border security, and a commitment to international peacekeeping operations, are key tasks for the armed forces. But Zambia's armed forces struggle with limited funding and the challenge of maintaining ageing weapons systems. A new naval unit was created in 2015 to patrol the country's riverine borders. The air force has limited tactical air-transport capability, although two C-27J *Spartan* are reportedly on order. As part of the country's plans to boost its air assets, deliveries of China's L-15 *Falcon* trainer aircraft were completed in 2017; the contract reportedly included weapons, training and support. However, there is currently no independent capacity for significant power projection. The country has no defence-manufacturing capacity, except limited ammunition production, though it is reported that exploratory discussions have taken place about establishing some manufacturing capacity for military trucks. The services have participated in exercises with international and regional partners, including the *Blue Kunene 2017* HADR exercise. Zambia's largest peacekeeping contribution is to the MINUSCA operation in the CAR.

ACTIVE 15,100 (Army 13,500 Air 1,600) **Paramilitary 1,400**

RESERVE 3,000 (Army 3,000)

ORGANISATIONS BY SERVICE

Army 13,500
FORCES BY ROLE
COMMAND
3 bde HQ
SPECIAL FORCES
1 cdo bn
MANOEUVRE
  Armoured
  1 armd regt (1 tk bn, 1 armd recce regt)
  Light
  6 inf bn

COMBAT SUPPORT
1 arty regt (2 fd arty bn, 1 MRL bn)
1 engr regt

EQUIPMENT BY TYPE
Some equipment†
ARMOURED FIGHTING VEHICLES
 MBT 30: 20 Type-59; 10 T-55
 LT TK 30 PT-76
 RECCE 70 BRDM-1/BRDM-2 (ε30 serviceable)
 IFV 23 *Ratel*-20
 APC • APC (W) 33: 13 BTR-60; 20 BTR-70
ENGINEERING & MAINTENANCE VEHICLES
 ARV T-54/T-55 reported
ANTI-TANK/ANTI-INFRASTRUCTURE
 MSL • MANPATS 9K11 *Malyutka* (AT-3 *Sagger*)
 RCL 12+: **57mm** 12 M18; **75mm** M20; **84mm** *Carl Gustav*
ARTILLERY 182
 TOWED 61: **105mm** 18 Model 56 pack howitzer; **122mm** 25 D-30; **130mm** 18 M-46
 MRL 122mm 30 BM-21 *Grad* (ε12 serviceable)
 MOR 91: **81mm** 55; **82mm** 24; **120mm** 12
AIR DEFENCE
 SAM • MANPAD 9K32 *Strela*-2 (SA-7 *Grail*)‡
 GUNS • TOWED 136: **20mm** 50 M-55 (triple); **37mm** 40 M-1939; **57mm** ε30 S-60; **85mm** 16 M-1939 KS-12

Reserve 3,000
FORCES BY ROLE
MANOEUVRE
 Light
  3 inf bn

Air Force 1,600
FORCES BY ROLE
FIGHTER/GROUND ATTACK
 1 sqn with K-8 *Karakorum**
 1 sqn with L-15*
TRANSPORT
 1 sqn with MA60; Y-12(II); Y-12(IV); Y-12E
 1 (VIP) unit with AW139; CL-604; HS-748
 1 (liaison) sqn with Do-28
TRAINING
 2 sqn with MB-326GB; MFI-15 *Safari*
TRANSPORT HELICOPTER
 1 sqn with Mi-17 *Hip* H
 1 (liaison) sqn with Bell 47G; Bell 205 (UH-1H *Iroquois*/AB-205)
AIR DEFENCE
 3 bty with S-125 *Pechora* (SA-3 *Goa*)

EQUIPMENT BY TYPE†
Very low serviceability
AIRCRAFT 21 combat capable
 TPT 23: **Light** 21: 5 Do-28; 2 MA60; 4 Y-12(II); 5 Y-12(IV); 5 Y-12E; **PAX** 2: 1 CL-604; 1 HS-748
 TRG 45: 15 K-8 *Karakourm**; 6 L-15*; 10 MB-326GB; 8 MFI-15 *Safari*; 6 SF-260TW
HELICOPTERS
 MRH 5: 1 AW139; 4 Mi-17 *Hip* H
 TPT • Light 12: 9 Bell 205 (UH-1H *Iroquois*/AB-205); 3 Bell 212
 TRG 5 Bell 47G

AIR DEFENCE
 SAM • Short-range S-125 *Pechora* (SA-3 *Goa*)
AIR-LAUNCHED MISSILES
 AAM • IR R-3 (AA-2 *Atoll*)‡; PL-2; *Python* 3
 ASM 9K11 *Malyutka* (AT-3 *Sagger*)

Paramilitary 1,400
Police Mobile Unit 700
FORCES BY ROLE
MANOEUVRE
 Other
  1 police bn (4 police coy)

Police Paramilitary Unit 700
FORCES BY ROLE
MANOEUVRE
 Other
  1 paramilitary bn (3 paramilitary coy)

DEPLOYMENT
CENTRAL AFRICAN REPUBLIC
UN • MINUSCA 943; 7 obs; 1 inf bn

DEMOCRATIC REPUBLIC OF THE CONGO
UN • MONUSCO 2; 17 obs

LIBERIA
UN • UNMIL 1 obs

SOUTH SUDAN
UN • UNMISS 3; 3 obs

SUDAN
UN • UNAMID 5; 2 obs
UN • UNISFA 1 obs

Zimbabwe ZWE

Zimbabwe Dollar Z$		2016	2017	2018
GDP	US$	16.1bn	17.1bn	
per capita	US$	1,112	1,150	
Growth	%	0.7	2.8	
Inflation	%	-1.6	2.5	
Def bdgt	US$	394m	341m	
US$1=Z$		1.00	1.00	

Population 13,805,084

Age	0–14	15–19	20–24	25–29	30–64	65 plus
Male	19.2%	5.5%	4.5%	4.3%	13.3%	1.8%
Female	19.6%	5.6%	4.8%	4.4%	14.0%	2.6%

Capabilities

The armed forces' role is to defend sovereignty and territorial integrity, although late 2017 saw the army take a more direct role in domestic politics than they had hitherto. In an overnight operation, the army secured key locations in Harare and placed President Mugabe under house arrest. The future political role of the military was uncertain as of late November, though key officers were given ministerial positions. High inflation and economic problems continue to be potentially destabilising, and limit the military's ability to recapitalise its equipment inventory. China has been the only source of defence equipment for the country's limited number of procurements. Zimbabwe has enjoyed a close relationship with Angola since the end of that country's civil war and is looking to foster bilateral military ties. Economic problems make investment in new equipment and facilities unlikely without novel financing options or credit provision, despite a stated interest in a number of equipment types. State-owned Zimbabwe Defence Industries manufactures a range of ammunition, however ageing machinery and non-profitability mean its future is uncertain. The armed forces have taken part intermittently in multinational training exercises with regional states, including *Amani Africa* II in 2015. Both the EU and the US have arms embargoes in place, which, the air-force commander acknowledged, have reduced air-force readiness.

ACTIVE 29,000 (Army 25,000 Air 4,000) **Paramilitary 21,800**

ORGANISATIONS BY SERVICE

Army ε25,000
FORCES BY ROLE
COMMAND
  1 SF bde HQ
  1 mech bde HQ
  5 inf bde HQ
SPECIAL FORCES
  1 SF regt
MANOEUVRE
  Armoured
  1 armd sqn
  Mechanised
  1 mech inf bn
  Light
  15 inf bn
  1 cdo bn
  Air Manoeuvre
  1 para bn
  Other
  3 gd bn
  1 (Presidential Guard) gd gp
COMBAT SUPPORT
  1 arty bde
  1 fd arty regt
  2 engr regt
AIR DEFENCE
  1 AD regt
EQUIPMENT BY TYPE
ARMOURED FIGHTING VEHICLES
  MBT 40: 30 Type-59†; 10 Type-69†
  RECCE 115: 20 *Eland*-60/90; 15 FV701 *Ferret*†; 80 EE-9 *Cascavel* (90mm)
  IFV 2+ YW307
  APC • APC (T) 30: 8 ZSD-85 (incl CP); 22 VTT-323
ENGINEERING & MAINTENANCE VEHICLES
  ARV T-54/T-55 reported; ZJX-93 ARV
  VLB MTU reported

ARTILLERY 254
  SP 122mm 12 2S1 *Gvozdika*
  TOWED 122mm 20: 4 D-30; 16 Type-60 (D-74)
  MRL 76: **107mm** 16 Type-63; **122mm** 60 RM-70
  MOR 146: **81mm/82mm** ε140; **120mm** 6 M-43
AIR DEFENCE
  SAM • Point-defence 9K32 *Strela*-2 (SA-7 *Grail*)‡
  GUNS • TOWED 116: **14.5mm** 36 ZPU-1/ZPU-2/ZPU-4; **23mm** 45 ZU-23; **37mm** 35 M-1939

Air Force 4,000
Flying hours 100 hrs/yr
FORCES BY ROLE
FIGHTER
  1 sqn with F-7 II†; FT-7†
FIGHTER/GROUND ATTACK
  1 sqn with K-8 *Karakorum**
  (1 sqn Hawker *Hunter* in store)
GROUND ATTACK/ISR
  1 sqn with Cessna 337/O-2A *Skymaster**
ISR/TRAINING
  1 sqn with SF-260F/M; SF-260TP*; SF-260W *Warrior**
TRANSPORT
  1 sqn with BN-2 *Islander*; CASA 212-200 *Aviocar* (VIP)
ATTACK/TRANSPORT HELICOPTER
  1 sqn with Mi-35 *Hind*; Mi-35P *Hind* (liaison); SA316 *Alouette* III; AS532UL *Cougar* (VIP)
  1 trg sqn with Bell 412 *Twin Huey*, SA316 *Alouette* III
AIR DEFENCE
  1 sqn

EQUIPMENT BY TYPE
AIRCRAFT 45 combat capable
  FTR 9: 7 F-7 II†; 2 FT-7†
  ISR 2 O-2A *Skymaster*
  TPT • Light 25: 5 BN-2 *Islander*; 7 C-212-200 *Aviocar*; 13 Cessna 337 *Skymaster**; (10 C-47 *Skytrain* in store)
  TRG 33: 10 K-8 *Karakorum**; 5 SF-260M; 8 SF-260TP*; 5 SF-260W *Warrior**; 5 SF-260F
HELICOPTERS
  ATK 6: 4 Mi-35 *Hind*; 2 Mi-35P *Hind*
  MRH 10: 8 Bell 412 *Twin Huey*; 2 SA316 *Alouette* III
  TPT • Medium 2 AS532UL *Cougar* (VIP)
AIR-LAUNCHED MISSILES • AAM • IR PL-2; PL-5 (reported)
AD • GUNS 100mm (not deployed); **37mm** (not deployed); **57mm** (not deployed)

Paramilitary 21,800

Zimbabwe Republic Police Force 19,500
incl air wg

Police Support Unit 2,300
PATROL AND COASTAL COMBATANTS
All operational patrol vessels under 10t FLD

DEPLOYMENT

SOUTH SUDAN
UN • UNMISS 2 obs

SUDAN
UN • UNAMID 3; 5 obs

Arms procurements and deliveries – Sub-Saharan Africa

Significant events in 2017

- Botswana is reportedly evaluating second-hand fighter-aircraft options to replace its F-5s. Delegations from the country have visited Saab in Sweden and KAI in South Korea in recent years, suggesting the *Gripen* C/D and T-50 are being considered.

- The United States government approved the sale of 12 A-29 *Super Tucano* aircraft to Nigeria. The sale has an estimated value of US$593 million.

- The Nigerian chief of naval staff announced that the navy requires US$1.3 billion of investment in new naval platforms, including a frigate, an OPV and a submarine.

- Denel Land System's CEO said the first *Badger* infantry fighting vehicles will start being delivered to the South African Army in May 2019, although the army chief also stated that the programme is experiencing serious delays.

- Denel left its joint venture with VR Laser Asia and Indian company Adani. The joint venture was formed in 2016 with the aim of breaking into the Indian market as well as those of other Asian countries.

- The US Defense Security Cooperation Agency approved the sale of 12 MD-530F armed multi-role helicopters to Kenya at an estimated total cost of US$253m.

- Denel and ThyssenKrupp Marine Systems (TKMS) signed a memorandum of understanding concerning upgrades for South Africa's *Heroine*-class submarines and *Valour*-class frigates. The vessels are planned to be modernised in South Africa, with TKMS providing technical and shipyard support.

Figure 26 **Sub-Saharan Africa: selected ongoing or completed procurement priorities in 2017**

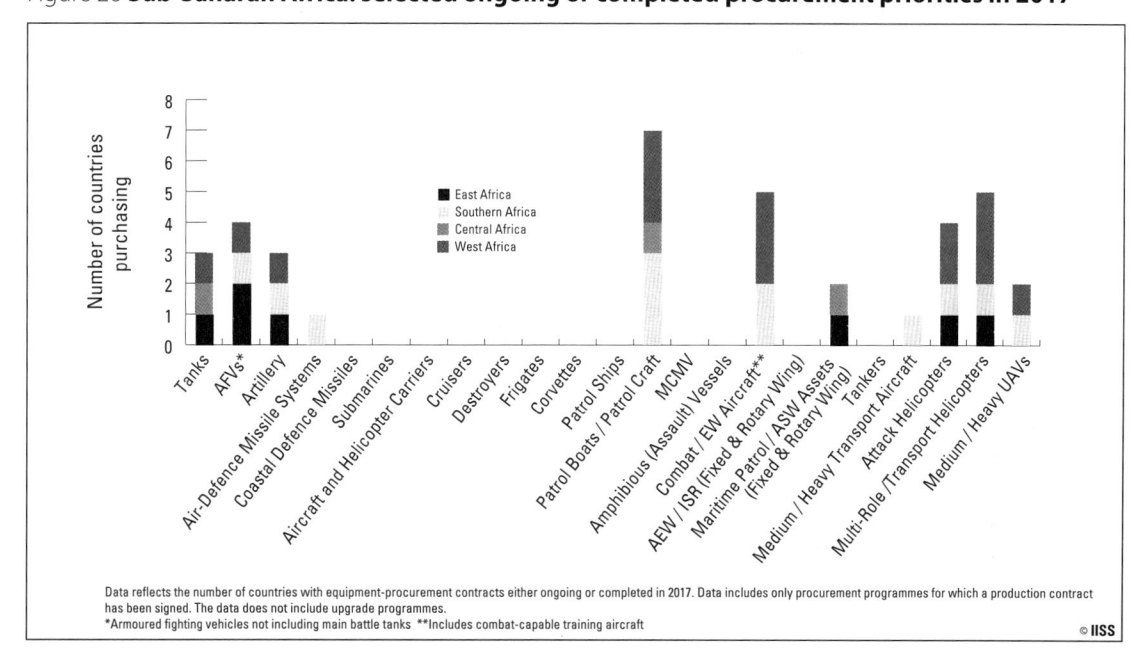

Data reflects the number of countries with equipment-procurement contracts either ongoing or completed in 2017. Data includes only procurement programmes for which a production contract has been signed. The data does not include upgrade programmes.
*Armoured fighting vehicles not including main battle tanks **Includes combat-capable training aircraft

498 THE MILITARY BALANCE 2018

Figure 27 **Ukraine: defence exports to sub-Saharan Africa, 1996–2016**

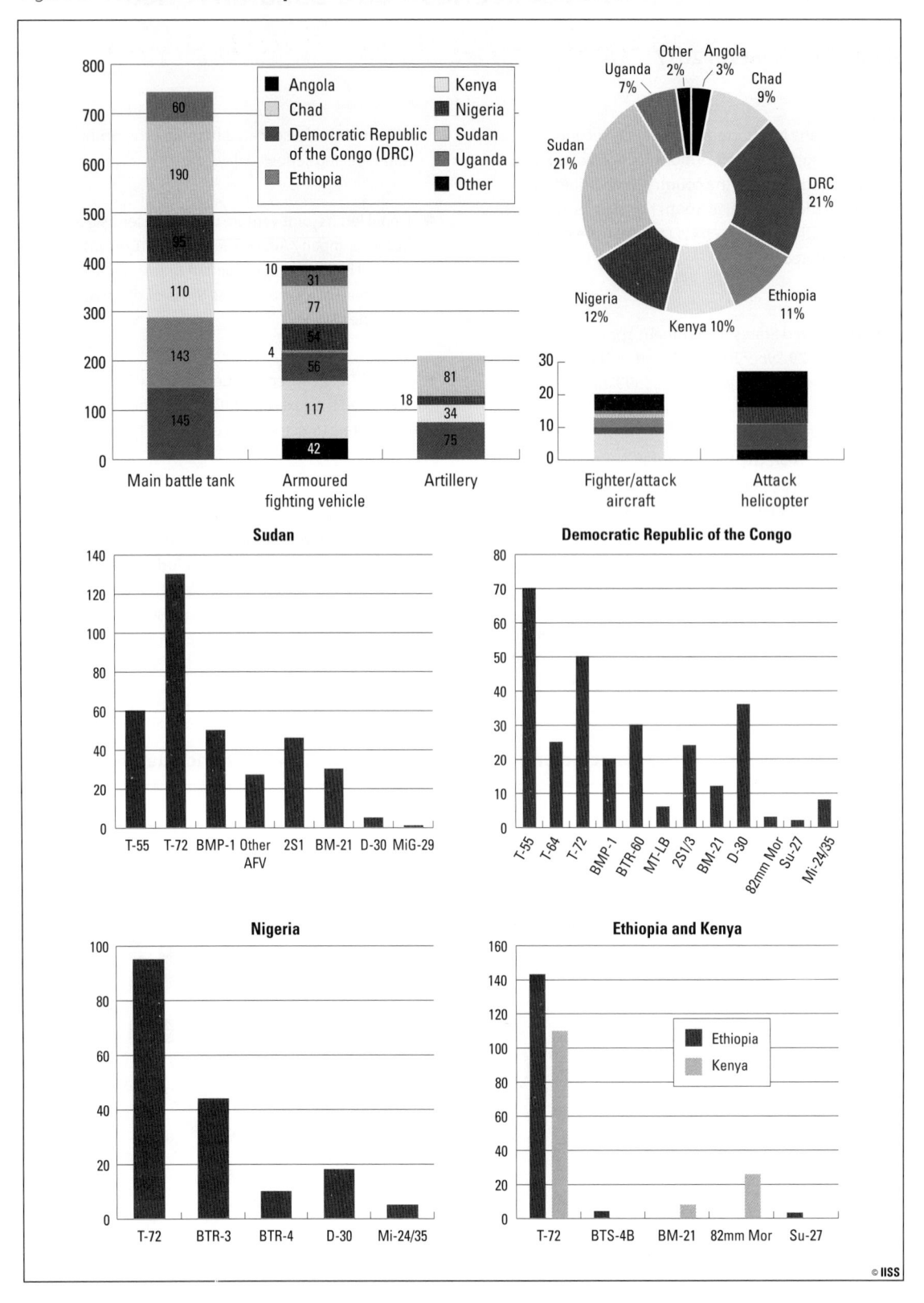

Chapter Ten
Country comparisons and defence data

Maps 14–17	**Selected training activity 2017**	500
Table 21	**International comparisons of defence expenditure and military personnel**	502

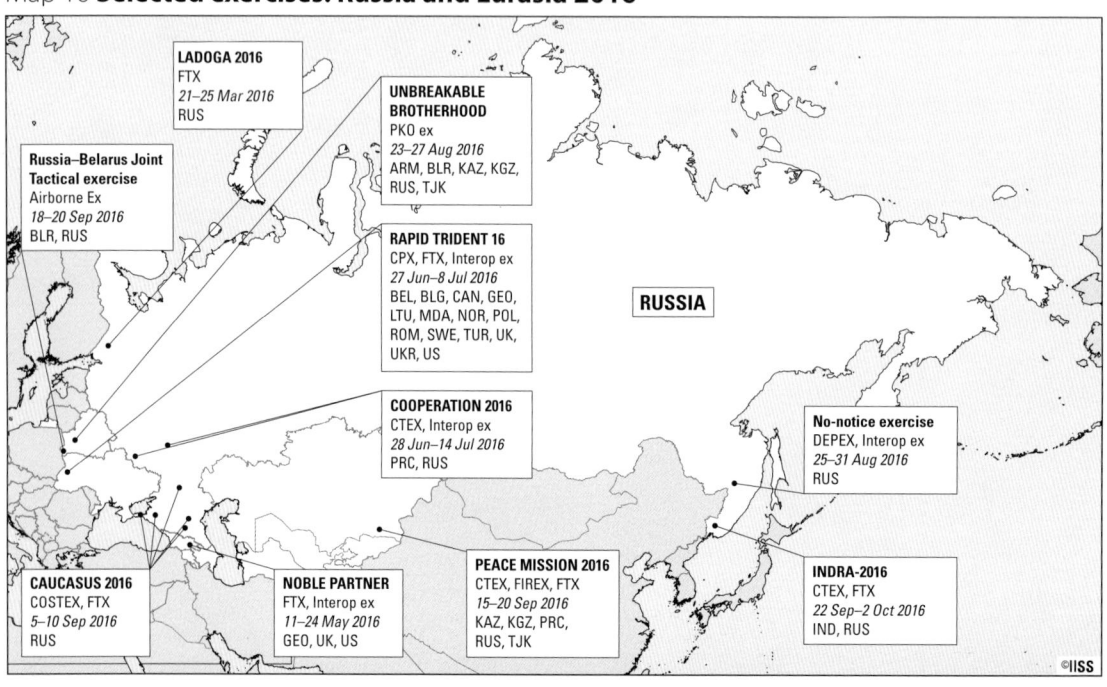

Map 14 Selected exercises: Europe 2016

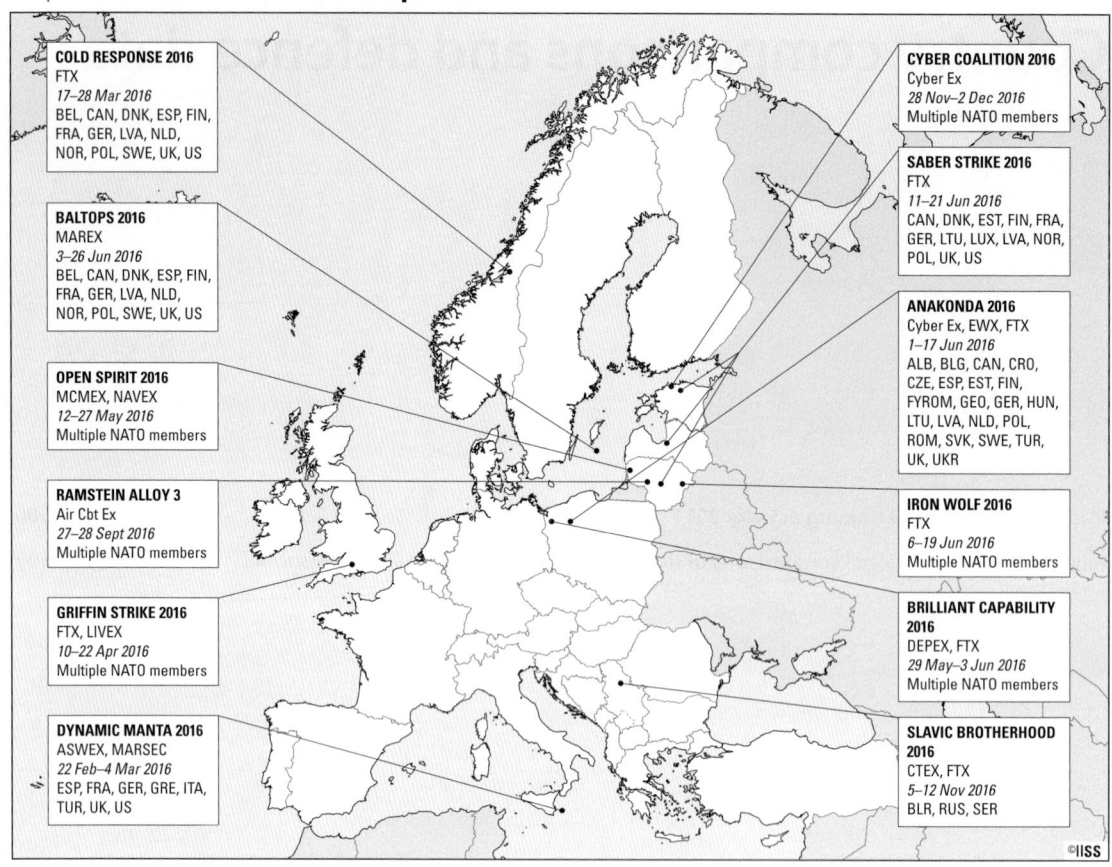

COLD RESPONSE 2016
FTX
17–28 Mar 2016
BEL, CAN, DNK, ESP, FIN, FRA, GER, LVA, NLD, NOR, POL, SWE, UK, US

BALTOPS 2016
MAREX
3–26 Jun 2016
BEL, CAN, DNK, ESP, FIN, FRA, GER, LVA, NLD, NOR, POL, SWE, UK, US

OPEN SPIRIT 2016
MCMEX, NAVEX
12–27 May 2016
Multiple NATO members

RAMSTEIN ALLOY 3
Air Cbt Ex
27–28 Sept 2016
Multiple NATO members

GRIFFIN STRIKE 2016
FTX, LIVEX
10–22 Apr 2016
Multiple NATO members

DYNAMIC MANTA 2016
ASWEX, MARSEC
22 Feb–4 Mar 2016
ESP, FRA, GER, GRE, ITA, TUR, UK, US

CYBER COALITION 2016
Cyber Ex
28 Nov–2 Dec 2016
Multiple NATO members

SABER STRIKE 2016
FTX
11–21 Jun 2016
CAN, DNK, EST, FIN, FRA, GER, LTU, LUX, LVA, NOR, POL, UK, US

ANAKONDA 2016
Cyber Ex, EWX, FTX
1–17 Jun 2016
ALB, BLG, CAN, CRO, CZE, ESP, EST, FIN, FYROM, GEO, GER, HUN, LTU, LVA, NLD, POL, ROM, SVK, SWE, TUR, UK, UKR

IRON WOLF 2016
FTX
6–19 Jun 2016
Multiple NATO members

BRILLIANT CAPABILITY 2016
DEPEX, FTX
29 May–3 Jun 2016
Multiple NATO members

SLAVIC BROTHERHOOD 2016
CTEX, FTX
5–12 Nov 2016
BLR, RUS, SER

Map 16 Selected exercises: Russia and Eurasia 2016

LADOGA 2016
FTX
21–25 Mar 2016
RUS

Russia–Belarus Joint Tactical exercise
Airborne Ex
18–20 Sep 2016
BLR, RUS

UNBREAKABLE BROTHERHOOD
PKO ex
23–27 Aug 2016
ARM, BLR, KAZ, KGZ, RUS, TJK

RAPID TRIDENT 16
CPX, FTX, Interop ex
27 Jun–8 Jul 2016
BEL, BLG, CAN, GEO, LTU, MDA, NOR, POL, ROM, SWE, TUR, UK, UKR, US

COOPERATION 2016
CTEX, Interop ex
28 Jun–14 Jul 2016
PRC, RUS

No-notice exercise
DEPEX, Interop ex
25–31 Aug 2016
RUS

CAUCASUS 2016
COSTEX, FTX
5–10 Sep 2016
RUS

NOBLE PARTNER
FTX, Interop ex
11–24 May 2016
GEO, UK, US

PEACE MISSION 2016
CTEX, FIREX, FTX
15–20 Sep 2016
KAZ, KGZ, PRC, RUS, TJK

INDRA-2016
CTEX, FTX
22 Sep–2 Oct 2016
IND, RUS

Country comparisons and defence data

Map 15 Selected exercises: Europe 2017

AURORA 2017
CBT trg ex, FTX
19–29 Sep 2017
DNK, EST, FIN, LTU, NOR, SWE, US

TRAINING BRIDGE 17
FTX
1 Jan–2 Mar 2017
CZE, EST, HUN, LTU, LVA, POL, SVK

CWIX 2017
Interop Ex
12–29 Jun 2017
Multiple NATO members

FORMIDABLE SHIELD 2017
ADEX, BMD Ex
24 Sept–18 Oct 2017
Multiple NATO members

AMPLE STRIKE 2017
Air Cbt Ex, FIREX
23 Aug–12 Sept 2017
Multiple NATO members

NOBLE JUMP 2017
DEPEX, MRX
29 May–22 Jun 2017
Multiple NATO members

DYNAMIC MANTA 17
ASWEX, MARSEC
13–25 Mar 2017
Multiple NATO members

RUSKA 2017
ADEX, JREX
9–13 Oct 2017
FIN, SWE

SABER STRIKE 2017
JTFEX, FIREX
22–24 Mar 2017
Multiple NATO members

FLAMING THUNDER 2017
ARTEX
29 May–3 Jun 2017
Multiple NATO members

BRAVE WARRIOR 2017
Air Cbt Ex, C2, MRX
26 Jun–23 Jul 2017
Multiple NATO members

SABER GUARDIAN 2017
CPX, FTX
11–20 Jul 2017
Multiple NATO members

SEA BREEZE 2017
Interop Ex
10–23 Jul 2017
Multiple NATO members

CAUCASIAN EAGLE 2017
Interop Ex, JOINTEX
5–15 Jun 2017
AZE, GEO, TUR

©IISS

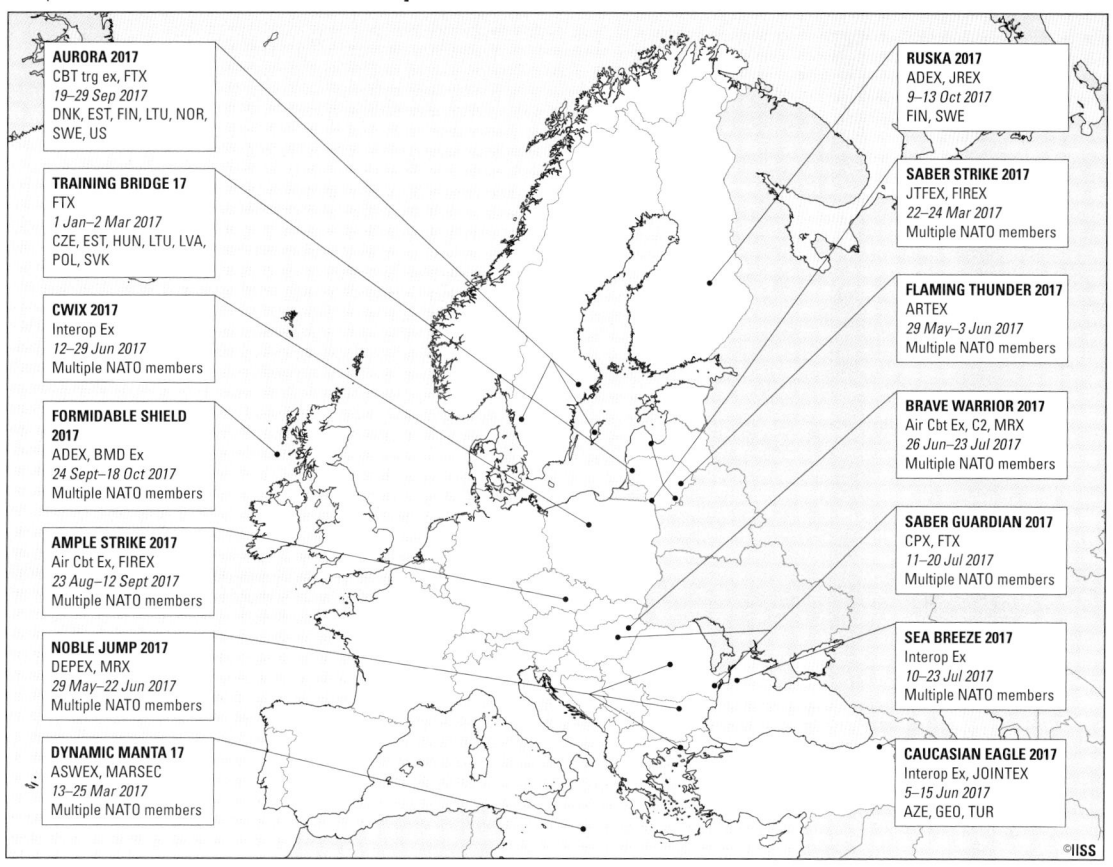

Map 17 Selected exercises: Russia and Eurasia 2017

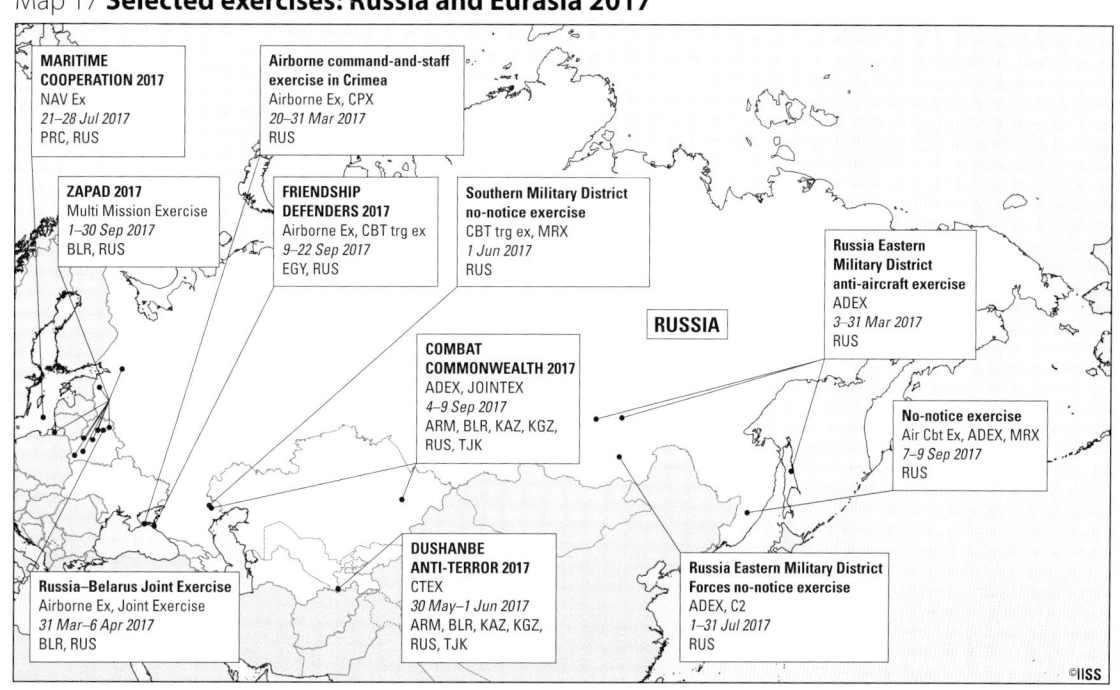

MARITIME COOPERATION 2017
NAV Ex
21–28 Jul 2017
PRC, RUS

ZAPAD 2017
Multi Mission Exercise
1–30 Sep 2017
BLR, RUS

Airborne command-and-staff exercise in Crimea
Airborne Ex, CPX
20–31 Mar 2017
RUS

FRIENDSHIP DEFENDERS 2017
Airborne Ex, CBT trg ex
9–22 Sep 2017
EGY, RUS

Southern Military District no-notice exercise
CBT trg ex, MRX
1 Jun 2017
RUS

COMBAT COMMONWEALTH 2017
ADEX, JOINTEX
4–9 Sep 2017
ARM, BLR, KAZ, KGZ, RUS, TJK

Russia Eastern Military District anti-aircraft exercise
ADEX
3–31 Mar 2017
RUS

No-notice exercise
Air Cbt Ex, ADEX, MRX
7–9 Sep 2017
RUS

Russia–Belarus Joint Exercise
Airborne Ex, Joint Exercise
31 Mar–6 Apr 2017
BLR, RUS

DUSHANBE ANTI-TERROR 2017
CTEX
30 May–1 Jun 2017
ARM, BLR, KAZ, KGZ, RUS, TJK

Russia Eastern Military District Forces no-notice exercise
ADEX, C2
1–31 Jul 2017
RUS

©IISS

Table 21 International comparisons of defence expenditure and military personnel

	Defence Spending current US$ m 2015	2016	2017	Defence Spending per capita (current US$) 2015	2016	2017	Defence Spending % of GDP 2015	2016	2017	Active Armed Forces (000) 2018	Estimated Reservists (000) 2018	Active Paramilitary (000) 2018
North America												
Canada	16,158	16,182	17,031	460	458	478	1.04	1.06	1.04	63	30	5
United States	589,564	593,371	602,783	1,834	1,831	1,845	3.25	3.19	3.11	1,348	858	0
Total	605,722	609,553	619,814	1,699	1,696	1,711	3.08	3.02	2.95	1,411	888	5
Europe												
Albania	101	114	109	33	38	36	0.89	0.96	0.84	8	0	1
Austria	2,667	2,888	2,985	308	331	341	0.71	0.75	0.73	22	152	0
Belgium	4,010	3861	4,254	354	338	370	0.88	0.83	0.87	29	0	5
Bosnia-Herzegovina	162	165	162	42	43	42	1.00	0.99	0.93	11	0	0
Bulgaria	560	671	676	78	94	95	1.12	1.28	1.21	31	3	0
Croatia	641	591	657	148	137	153	1.31	1.17	1.23	16	0	3
Cyprus	328	335	397	276	278	325	1.68	1.69	1.88	15	50	1
Czech Republic	1,780	1,955	2,205	167	183	207	0.95	1.00	1.05	23	0	0
Denmark	3,516	3,514	3,807	630	628	679	1.17	1.15	1.17	16	46	0
Estonia	467	498	543	369	396	434	2.07	2.14	2.11	6	28	0
Finland	3,074	3,100	3,191	561	564	578	1.32	1.30	1.27	22	216	3
France	46,626	46,784	48,640	701	700	725	1.92	1.90	1.89	203	32	103
Germany	36,589	37,943	41,734	453	470	518	1.08	1.09	1.14	179	28	1
Greece	4,733	4,598	4,725	439	427	439	2.43	2.36	2.31	141	221	4
Hungary	1,070	1,061	1,265	108	107	128	0.88	0.85	0.96	28	44	12
Iceland	30	46	37	91	136	110	0.18	0.23	0.15	0	0	0
Ireland	998	994	1039	204	201	207	0.34	0.33	0.32	9	2	0
Italy	21,495	22,112	22,859	348	357	368	1.18	1.19	1.19	175	18	182
Latvia	283	407	507	142	207	261	1.05	1.47	1.68	5	8	0
Lithuania	471	637	816	163	223	289	1.14	1.49	1.75	18	7	11
Luxembourg	214	235	294	375	404	494	0.37	0.39	0.46	1	0	1
Macedonia (FYROM)	102	106	112	49	50	53	1.01	0.97	0.98	8	5	8
Malta	56	58	64	135	139	154	0.54	0.53	0.54	2	0	0

Table 21 International comparisons of defence expenditure and military personnel

	Defence Spending current US$ m 2015	2016	2017	Defence Spending per capita (current US$) 2015	2016	2017	Defence Spending % of GDP 2015	2016	2017	Active Armed Forces (000) 2018	Estimated Reservists (000) 2018	Estimated Paramilitary (000) 2018	Active (000) 2018
Montenegro	67	68	74	104	106	115	1.67	1.64	1.67	2	0	10	
Netherlands	8,877	9,121	10,100	524	536	591	1.17	1.17	1.23	35	5	6	
Norway	5,815	6,000	6,078	1,117	1,140	1,143	1.50	1.62	1.55	24	39	0	
Poland	10,128	9,101	9,837	263	236	256	2.12	1.94	1.93	105	0	73	
Portugal	2,502	2,443	2,445	231	225	226	1.26	1.19	1.15	31	212	44	
Romania	2,481	2,763	4,041	115	128	188	1.40	1.47	1.97	69	50	80	
Serbia	515	501	523	72	70	74	1.39	1.33	1.33	28	50	4	
Slovakia	884	974	1,116	162	179	205	1.01	1.09	1.17	16	0	0	
Slovenia	444	446	474	224	225	240	1.03	1.00	0.99	7	2	6	
Spain	13,050	99,75	12,112	271	205	247	1.09	0.81	0.93	121	15	77	
Sweden	5,723	5738	5,962	584	581	599	1.15	1.12	1.10	30	0	1	
Switzerland	4,770	4,654	4,834	587	569	587	0.70	0.70	0.71	21	144	0	
Turkey	8,384	8,664	7,983	106	108	99	0.98	1.00	0.95	355	379	157	
United Kingdom	58,243	52,577	50,721	909	816	783	2.03	2.00	1.98	150	83	0	
Total	**251,855**	**245,698**	**257,377**	**404**	**393**	**410**	**1.37**	**1.33**	**1.34**	**1,962**	**1,838**	**791**	
Russia and Eurasia													
Armenia	416	431	429	136	141	141	3.95	4.08	3.89	45	210	4	
Azerbaijan	1,646	1,395	1,554	168	141	156	3.24	3.72	3.96	67	300	15	
Belarus	556	506	528	58	53	55	0.99	1.07	1.00	45	290	110	
Georgia	300	283	303	61	57	61	2.14	1.98	1.99	21	0	5	
Kazakhstan	1,693	1,134	1,246	93	62	67	0.92	0.85	0.80	39	0	32	
Kyrgyzstan	n.k.	n.k.	n.k.	n.k.	n.k.	n.k.	n.k.	n.k.	n.k.	11	0	10	
Moldova	24	27	29	7	8	8	0.37	0.40	0.37	5	58	2	
Russia [a]	52,201	44,470	45,600	367	312	321	3.82	3.47	3.10	900	2,000	554	
Tajikistan	225	193	192	27	23	23	2.87	2.79	2.65	9	0	8	
Turkmenistan	n.k.	n.k.	n.k.	n.k.	n.k.	n.k.	n.k.	n.k.	n.k.	37	0	5	
Ukraine	2,664	2,555	2,734	60	58	62	2.93	2.74	2.63	204	900	88	
Uzbekistan	n.k.	n.k.	n.k.	n.k.	n.k.	n.k.	n.k.	n.k.	n.k.	48	0	20	
Total**	**59,726**	**50,996**	**52,616**	**210**	**179**	**185**	**3.15**	**2.93**	**2.66**	**1,430**	**3,758**	**853**	

Table 21 International comparisons of defence expenditure and military personnel

	Defence Spending current US$ m 2015	2016	2017	Defence Spending per capita (current US$) 2015	2016	2017	Defence Spending % of GDP 2015	2016	2017	Active Armed Forces (000) 2018	Estimated Reservists (000) 2018	Active Paramilitary (000) 2018
Asia												
Afghanistan	3,142	2,593	2,166	96	78	63	15.65	13.33	10.29	174	0	149
Australia	22,034	23,617	24,963	968	1,027	1,075	1.79	1.87	1.80	58	21	0
Bangladesh	2,226	2,562	2,778	14	16	18	1.08	1.12	1.11	157	0	64
Brunei	391	409	324	910	936	731	3.02	3.59	2.71	7	1	5
Cambodia*	575	656	788	37	41	49	3.17	3.26	3.54	124	0	67
China	142,409	143,668	150,458	104	104	108	1.27	1.28	1.26	2,035	510	660
Fiji	46	52	51	51	56	55	1.06	1.10	1.00	4	6	0
India	44,843	51,453	52,494	36	41	41	2.15	2.27	2.15	1,395	1,155	1,586
Indonesia	7,909	7,380	8,981	31	29	34	0.92	0.79	0.89	396	400	280
Japan	41,143	46,456	46,004	324	367	364	0.94	0.94	0.94	247	56	14
Korea, DPR of	n.k	n.k	n.k	n.k.	n.k.	n.k.	n.k	n.k	n.k	1,280	600	189
Korea, Republic of	33,152	33,648	35,674	655	661	697	2.40	2.38	2.33	625	3,100	9
Laos	n.k	n.k	n.k	n.k.	n.k.	n.k.	n.k	n.k	n.k	29	0	100
Malaysia	4,548	4,171	3,478	149	135	111	1.53	1.41	1.12	109	52	25
Mongolia	102	100	84	34	33	27	0.87	0.91	0.77	10	137	8
Myanmar	2,135	2,282	2,095	38	40	38	3.59	3.55	3.13	406	0	107
Nepal	336	314	330	12	11	11	1.57	1.48	1.37	97	0	62
New Zealand	2,182	2,576	2,519	492	576	558	1.26	1.42	1.25	9	2	0
Pakistan	8,805	9,188	9,720	44	45	47	3.25	3.29	3.21	654	0	282
Papua New Guinea	94	83	71	14	12	10	0.45	0.40	0.32	4	0	0
Philippines	2,196	2,475	2,782	22	24	27	0.75	0.81	0.87	125	131	41
Singapore	9,544	10,017	10,221	1,682	1,733	1,736	3.22	3.37	3.34	73	313	75
Sri Lanka	2,011	1,991	1,704	91	90	76	2.53	2.47	2.04	243	6	62
Taiwan	10,007	9,902	10,429	427	422	444	1.91	1.87	1.82	215	1,657	11
Thailand	5,634	5,820	6,163	83	85	90	1.41	1.43	1.41	361	200	94
Timor-Leste	72	26	25	59	21	20	2.33	0.97	0.94	1	0	0
Vietnam*	3,829	4,073	4,319	41	43	45	2.00	2.02	2.00	482	5,000	40
Total**	349,364	365,512	378,622	88	91	94	1.45	1.46	1.43	9,319	13,346	3,928

Table 21 International comparisons of defence expenditure and military personnel

	Defence Spending current US$ m 2015	2016	2017	Defence Spending per capita (current US$) 2015	2016	2017	Defence Spending % of GDP 2015	2016	2017	Active Armed Forces (000) 2018	Estimated Reservists (000) 2018	Active Paramilitary (000) 2018
Middle East and North Africa												
Algeria	10,407	10,218	10,018	263	254	245	6.27	6.42	5.71	130	150	187
Bahrain	1,526	1,523	1,480	1,133	1,105	1,049	4.90	4.78	4.37	8	0	11
Egypt	5,335	5,300	2,669	58	56	28	1.61	1.59	1.36	439	479	397
Iran*	14,174	15,871	16,035	173	192	195	3.78	3.92	3.75	523	350	40
Iraq	21,100	16,976	19,271	569	445	492	11.73	9.89	10.00	64	0	145
Israel	15,400	19,868	18,547	1,913	2,430	2,235	5.15	6.25	5.33	177	465	8
Jordan	1,320	1,474	1,635	163	180	160	3.51	3.81	4.04	101	65	15
Kuwait	4,313	5,743	5,710	1,547	2,027	1,986	3.76	5.18	4.83	16	24	7
Lebanon*	1,495	1,740	1,867	242	279	300	3.02	3.45	3.54	60	0	20
Libya	n.k.	n.k.	n.k.	n.k.	n.k.	n.k.	n.k.	n.k.	n.k.	n.k.	n.k.	n.k.
Mauritania	137	138	142	38	37	38	2.82	2.91	2.86	16	0	5
Morocco	3,268	3,327	3,487	98	99	103	3.23	3.21	3.15	196	150	50
Oman	9,883	9,103	8,687	3,007	2,713	2,537	14.15	13.73	12.08	43	0	4
Palestinian Territories	n.k.	n.k.	n.k.	n.k.	n.k.	n.k.	n.k.	n.k.	n.k.	0	0	n.k.
Qatar	n.k.	n.k.	n.k.	n.k.	n.k.	n.k.	n.k.	n.k.	n.k.	17	0	5
Saudi Arabia	81,853	81,526	76,678	2,949	2,895	2,684	12.51	12.61	11.30	227	0	25
Syria	n.k.	n.k.	n.k.	n.k.	n.k.	n.k.	n.k.	n.k.	n.k.	158	0	150
Tunisia	979	975	826	89	88	72	2.27	2.32	2.07	36	0	12
United Arab Emirates	n.k.	n.k.	n.k.	n.k.	n.k.	n.k.	n.k.	n.k.	n.k.	63	0	0
Yemen	n.k.	n.k.	n.k.	n.k.	n.k.	n.k.	n.k.	n.k.	n.k.	20	0	0
Total**	171,190	173,782	167,051	409	408	388	5.64	5.73	5.40	2,290	1,683	1,081
Latin America and the Caribbean												
Antigua and Barbuda	27	26	27	287	279	285	1.94	1.79	1.76	0	0	0
Argentina	6,338	5,205	6,128	146	119	138	1.00	0.96	0.99	74	0	31
Bahamas	152	121	99	468	369	299	1.72	1.39	1.08	1	0	0
Barbados	36	39	38	125	135	130	0.82	0.86	0.79	1	0	0
Belize	20	21	23	56	59	63	1.12	1.21	1.26	2	1	0
Bolivia	435	442	543	40	40	49	1.31	1.30	1.44	34	0	37

Table 21 International comparisons of defence expenditure and military personnel

	Defence Spending current US$ m 2015	2016	2017	Defence Spending per capita (current US$) 2015	2016	2017	Defence Spending % of GDP 2015	2016	2017	Active Armed Forces (000) 2018	Estimated Reservists (000) 2018	Paramilitary (000) 2018
Brazil	23,659	23,551	29,408	116	114	142	1.31	1.31	1.41	335	1,340	395
Chile	3,437	3,444	3,927	196	195	221	1.42	1.39	1.49	77	40	45
Colombia	9,962	9,201	9,999	213	195	210	3.42	3.26	3.25	293	35	188
Costa Rica	450	409	389	93	84	79	0.81	0.70	0.66	0	0	10
Cuba	n.k.	n.k.	n.k.	n.k	n.k	n.k	n.k	n.k	n.k	49	39	27
Dominican Republic	444	458	496	42	43	46	0.65	0.64	0.66	56	0	15
Ecuador	1,911	1,565	1,565	120	97	96	1.91	1.60	1.59	40	118	1
El Salvador	148	146	146	24	24	24	0.57	0.55	0.53	25	10	17
Guatemala	274	283	242	18	19	16	0.43	0.42	0.34	18	64	25
Guyana	46	51	56	63	69	76	1.45	1.49	1.57	3	1	0
Haiti	n.k	7	7	n.k	1	1	n.k	0.09	0.08	0	0	0
Honduras	246	295	263	28	33	29	1.18	1.38	1.16	15	60	8
Jamaica	119	139	120	40	47	40	0.83	1.00	0.84	4	1	0
Mexico	6,015	4,917	4,532	49	40	36	0.52	0.47	0.40	277	82	59
Nicaragua	72	73	84	12	12	14	0.56	0.55	0.61	12	0	0
Panama	654	751	746	179	203	199	1.26	1.36	1.26	0	0	22
Paraguay	313	268	264	46	39	38	1.15	0.97	0.92	11	165	15
Peru	2,217	2,225	2,095	73	72	68	1.15	1.14	1.00	81	188	77
Suriname*	n.k	n.k	n.k	n.k	n.k	n.k	n.k	n.k	n.k	2	0	0
Trinidad and Tobago	394	605	596	323	496	489	1.67	2.87	2.93	4	0	0
Uruguay	514	489	513	154	146	153	0.96	0.93	0.85	25	0	1
Venezuela	2,093	1,278	1,120	69	41	36	0.86	0.54	0.52	123	8	150
Total**	**59,975**	**56,010**	**63,424**	**98**	**90**	**101**	**1.17**	**1.13**	**1.16**	**1,561**	**2,151**	**1,121**
Sub-Saharan Africa												
Angola	4,441	2,969	3,233	226	147	110	4.31	3.11	2.61	107	0	10
Benin	91	98	117	9	9	11	1.10	1.14	1.24	7	0	3
Botswana	404	561	492	185	254	222	2.80	3.60	2.94	9	0	0
Burkina Faso	148	150	189	8	8	9	1.33	1.23	1.43	11	0	0
Burundi	64	66	63	6	6	6	2.12	2.12	1.87	30	0	21

506 THE MILITARY BALANCE 2018

Table 21 **International comparisons of defence expenditure and military personnel**

	Defence Spending current US$ m 2015	2016	2017	Defence Spending per capita (current US$) 2015	2016	2017	Defence Spending % of GDP 2015	2016	2017	Active Armed Forces (000) 2018	Estimated Reservists (000) 2018	Estimated Paramilitary (000) 2018
Cameroon	354	388	404	15	16	16	1.25	1.32	1.32	14	0	9
Cape Verde	10	11	10	18	19	17	0.63	0.64	0.56	1	0	0
Central African Rep*	27	27	31	5	5	5	1.69	1.53	1.54	7	0	1
Chad*	170	160	165	15	13	14	1.56	1.58	1.70	30	0	10
Congo	590	562	481	124	116	97	6.89	7.14	6.17	10	0	2
Côte d'Ivoire	844	755	829	36	32	34	2.58	2.12	2.08	25	0	n.k.
Dem Republic of the Congo	738	762	586	9	9	7	1.92	1.94	1.45	134	0	0
Djibouti	n.k.	n.k.	n.k.	n.k.	n.k.	n.k.	n.k.	n.k.	n.k.	10	0	3
Equatorial Guinea	n.k.	n.k.	n.k.	n.k.	n.k.	n.k.	n.k.	n.k.	n.k.	1	0	0
Eritrea	n.k.	n.k.	n.k.	n.k.	n.k.	n.k.	n.k.	n.k.	n.k.	202	120	0
Ethiopia	399	451	492	4	4	5	0.62	0.62	0.62	138	0	0
Gabon	197	203	302	115	117	170	1.37	1.45	2.09	5	0	2
Gambia*	n.k.	n.k.	n.k.	n.k.	n.k.	n.k.	n.k.	n.k.	n.k.	1	0	0
Ghana	237	195	185	9	7	7	0.64	0.45	0.41	16	0	0
Guinea	221	162	164	19	13	13	2.53	1.91	1.79	10	0	3
Guinea-Bissau	n.k.	n.k.	n.k.	n.k.	n.k.	n.k.	n.k.	n.k.	n.k.	4	0	0
Kenya	927	1,222	1,194	20	26	25	1.45	1.73	1.52	24	0	5
Lesotho	44	42	53	22	22	27	1.83	1.87	1.94	2	0	0
Liberia	15	13	14	4	3	3	0.73	0.62	0.67	2	0	0
Madagascar	59	59	62	2	2	2	0.60	0.59	0.58	14	0	8
Malawi	36	29	38	2	2	2	0.56	0.53	0.60	11	0	4
Mali	467	546	644	28	31	36	3.57	3.89	4.29	10	0	8
Mauritius	240	215	218	179	160	161	2.08	1.77	1.78	0	0	3
Mozambique	132	106	91	5	4	3	0.89	0.94	0.74	11	0	0
Namibia	567	404	415	237	166	167	4.90	3.69	3.30	10	0	6
Niger*	166	166	169	9	9	9	2.30	2.22	2.15	5	0	5
Nigeria	1,948	1,751	1,529	11	9	8	0.39	0.43	0.39	118	0	82
Rwanda	89	95	107	7	7	9	1.07	1.13	1.20	33	0	2
Senegal	215	254	303	15	18	21	1.57	1.73	1.89	14	0	5

508 THE MILITARY BALANCE 2018

Table 21 **International comparisons of defence expenditure and military personnel**

	Defence Spending current US$ m 2015	2016	2017	Defence Spending per capita (current US$) 2015	2016	2017	Defence Spending % of GDP 2015	2016	2017	Active Armed Forces (000) 2018	Estimated Reservists (000) 2018	Active Paramilitary (000) 2018
Seychelles	n.k.	n.k.	n.k.	n.k.	n.k.	n.k.	n.k.	n.k.	n.k.	0	0	0
Sierra Leone	18	13	11	3	2	2	0.43	0.36	0.29	9	0	0
Somalia	n.k.	n.k.	n.k.	n.k.	n.k.	n.k.	n.k.	n.k.	n.k.	20	0	0
South Africa	3,534	3,211	3,628	66	59	66	1.11	1.09	1.05	66	0	15
South Sudan	1111	98	97	92	8	7	8.90	3.19	3.32	185	0	0
Sudan	n.k.	n.k.	n.k.	n.k.	n.k.	n.k.	n.k.	n.k.	n.k.	104	0	20
Tanzania	442	525	528	9	10	10	0.97	1.10	1.02	27	80	1
Togo	71	82	89	9	11	11	1.70	1.85	1.86	9	0	1
Uganda	358	478	436	10	12	11	1.42	1.89	1.65	45	10	1
Zambia	376	305	337	25	20	21	1.77	1.45	1.32	15	3	1
Zimbabwe	377	394	341	26	27	25	2.34	2.44	1.99	29	0	22
Total**	20,126	17,528	18,046	21	18	18	1.26	1.16	1.09	1,536	213	253
Summary												
North America	605,722	609,553	619,814	1,699	1,696	1,711	3.08	3.02	2.95	1,411	888	5
Europe	251,855	245,698	257,377	404	393	410	1.37	1.33	1.34	1,962	1,838	791
Russia and Eurasia	59,726	50,996	52,616	210	179	185	3.15	2.93	2.66	1,430	3,758	853
Asia	349,364	365,512	378,622	88	91	94	1.45	1.46	1.43	9,319	13,346	3,928
Middle East and North Africa	171,190	173,782	167,051	409	408	388	5.64	5.73	5.40	2,290	1,683	1,081
Latin America and the Caribbean	59,975	56,010	63,424	98	90	101	1.17	1.13	1.16	1,561	2,151	1,121
Sub-Saharan Africa	20,126	17,528	18,046	21	18	18	1.26	1.16	1.09	1,536	213	253
Global totals	1,517,958	1,519,079	1,556,951	210	208	211	2.06	2.03	1.99	19,510	23,875	8,033

* Estimates
** Totals exclude defence-spending estimates for states where insufficient official information is available in order to enable approximate comparisons of regional defence spending between years
[a] 'National Defence' budget chapter. Excludes other defence-related expenditures included under other budget lines (e.g. pensions) – see Table 8, p.175
All defence-spending data excludes US Foreign Military Assistance

PART TWO
Explanatory Notes

The Military Balance provides an assessment of the armed forces and defence expenditures of 171 countries and territories. Each edition contributes to the provision of a unique compilation of data and information, enabling the reader to discern trends by studying editions as far back as 1959. The data in the current edition is accurate according to IISS assessments as of November 2017, unless specified. Inclusion of a territory, country or state in *The Military Balance* does not imply legal recognition or indicate support for any government.

GENERAL ARRANGEMENT AND CONTENTS

The introduction is an assessment of global defence developments and key themes in the 2018 edition. Three analytical essays focus on Chinese and Russian air-launched weapons; big data, articifical intelligence and defence; and Russian strategic-force modernisation. A graphical section follows, analysing comparative defence statistics by domain, as well as key trends in defence economics.

Regional chapters begin with analysis of the military and security issues that drive national defence policy developments, and key trends in regional defence economics. These are followed by focused analysis, for certain countries, of defence policy and capability issues, and defence economics. Next, detailed data on regional states' military forces and equipment, and defence economics, is presented in alphabetical order. Graphics assessing important regional arms procurements and deliveries complete each region.

The book closes with comparative and reference sections containing data on military exercises and comparisons of expenditure and personnel statistics.

THE MILITARY BALANCE WALL CHART

The Military Balance 2018 wall chart assesses nuclear modernisation in China, Russia and the United States, displaying the numbers of land-, air- and sea-based nuclear-delivery systems in 1987, 2017 and 2037. It provides a breakdown of systems and associated munitions, as well as information on French and UK systems, strategic-missile defences, and a timeline showing treaties, tests and key programme developments.

USING THE MILITARY BALANCE

The country entries assess personnel strengths, organisation and equipment holdings of the world's armed forces.

Abbreviations and Definitions

Qualifier	
'At least'	Total is no less than the number given
'Up to'	Total is at most the number given, but could be lower
'About'	Total could be higher than given
'Some'	Precise inventory is unavailable at time of press
'In store'	Equipment held away from front-line units; readiness and maintenance varies
Billion (bn)	1,000 million (m)
Trillion (tr)	1,000 billion
$	US dollars unless otherwise stated
ε	Estimated
*	Aircraft counted by the IISS as combat capable
-	Part of a unit is detached/less than
+	Unit reinforced/more than
†	IISS assesses that the serviceability of equipment is in doubt[a]
‡	Equipment judged obsolete (weapons whose basic design is more than four decades old and which have not been significantly upgraded within the past decade)[a]

[a] Not to be taken to imply that such equipment cannot be used

Force-strength and equipment-inventory data is based on the most accurate data available, or on the best estimate that can be made. In estimating a country's total capabilities, old equipment may be counted where it is considered that it may still be deployable.

The data presented reflects judgements based on information available to the IISS at the time the book is compiled. Where information differs from previous editions, this is mainly because of changes in national forces, but it is sometimes because the IISS has reassessed the evidence supporting past entries. Given this, care must be taken in constructing time-series comparisons from information given in successive editions.

COUNTRY ENTRIES

Information on each country is shown in a standard format, although the differing availability of information and differences in nomenclature result in some variations. Country entries include economic, demographic and military data. Population figures are based on demographic statistics taken from the US Census Bureau. Data on ethnic and religious minorities is also provided in some country entries. Military data includes personnel numbers, length of conscript service where relevant, outline organisation, number of formations and units, and an inventory of the major equipment of each service. Details of national forces stationed abroad and of foreign forces stationed within the given country are also provided.

ARMS PROCUREMENTS AND DELIVERIES

A series of thematic tables, graphics and text follow the regional data. These are designed to illustrate key trends, principal programmes and significant events in regional defence procurements. More detailed information on defence procurements, organised by country, equipment type and manufacturing company, can be found on the IISS Military Balance+ database (*www.iiss.org/militarybalanceplus*). The information in this section meets the threshold for a *Military Balance* country entry and as such does not feature information on sales of small arms and light weapons.

DEFENCE ECONOMICS

Country entries include defence expenditures, selected economic-performance indicators and demographic aggregates. All country entries are subject to revision each year as new information, particularly regarding actual defence expenditure, becomes available. In the 'country comparisons' section on pp. 502–8, there are also international comparisons of defence expenditure and military personnel, giving expenditure figures for the past three years in per capita terms and as a % of GDP. The aim is to provide a measure of military expenditure and the allocation of economic resources to defence.

Individual country entries show economic performance over the past two years and current demographic data. Where this data is unavailable, information from the last available year is provided. Where possible, official defence budgets for the current and previous two years are shown, as well as an estimate of actual defence expenditures for those countries where true defence expenditure is thought to be higher than official budget figures suggest. Estimates of actual defence expenditure, however, are only made for those countries where there is sufficient data to justify such a measurement. Therefore, there will be several countries listed in *The Military Balance* for which only an official defence-budget figure is provided but where, in reality, true defence-related expenditure is almost certainly higher.

All financial data in the country entries is shown in both national currency and US dollars at current – not constant – prices. US-dollar conversions are calculated from the exchange rates listed in the entry.

Definitions of terms

Despite efforts by NATO and the UN to develop a standardised definition of military expenditure, many countries prefer to use their own definitions (which are often not made public). In order to present a comprehensive picture, *The Military Balance* lists three different measures of military-related spending data.

- For most countries, an official defence-budget figure is provided.
- For those countries where other military-related outlays, over and above the defence budget, are known or can be reasonably estimated, an additional measurement referred to as defence expenditure is also provided. Defence-expenditure figures will naturally be higher than official budget figures, depending on the range of additional factors included.
- For NATO countries, a defence-budget figure, as well as defence expenditure reported by NATO in local currency terms and converted using IMF exchange rates, is quoted.

NATO's military-expenditure definition (the most comprehensive) is cash outlays of central or federal governments to meet the costs of national armed forces. The term 'armed forces' includes strategic, land, naval, air, command, administration and support forces. It also includes other forces if they are trained, structured and equipped to support defence forces and are realistically deployable. Defence expenditures are reported in four categories: Operating Costs, Procurement and Construction, Research and Development (R&D) and Other Expenditure. Operating Costs include salaries and pensions for military and civilian personnel; the cost of maintaining and training units, service organisations, headquarters and support elements; and the cost of servicing and repairing military equipment and infrastructure. Procurement and Construction expenditure covers national equipment and infrastructure spending, as well as common infrastructure programmes. R&D is defence expenditure up to the point at which new equipment can be put in service, regardless of whether new equipment is actually procured. Foreign Military Aid (FMA) contributions are also noted.

For many non-NATO countries the issue of transparency in reporting military budgets is fundamental. Not every UN member state reports defence-budget data (even fewer report real defence expenditures) to their electorates, the UN, the IMF or other multinational organisations. In the case of governments with a proven record of transparency, official figures generally conform to the standardised definition of defence budgeting, as adopted by the UN, and consistency problems are not usually a major issue. The IISS cites official defence budgets as reported by either national governments, the UN, the OSCE or the IMF.

For those countries where the official defence-budget figure is considered to be an incomplete measure of total military-related spending, and appropriate additional data is available, the IISS will use data from a variety of sources to arrive at a more accurate estimate of true defence expenditure. The most frequent instances of budgetary manipulation or falsification typically involve equipment procurement, R&D, defence-industrial investment, covert weapons programmes, pensions for retired military and civilian personnel, paramilitary forces and non-budgetary sources of revenue for the military arising from ownership of industrial, property and land assets.

Percentage changes in defence spending are referred to in either nominal or real terms. Nominal terms relate to the percentage change in numerical spending figures, and do not account for the impact of price changes (i.e. inflation) on defence spending. By contrast, real terms account for inflationary effects, and may therefore be considered a more accurate representation of change over time.

The principal sources for national economic statistics cited in the country entries are the IMF, the Organisation for Economic Cooperation and Development, the World Bank and three regional banks (the Inter-American, Asian and African Development banks). For some countries, basic economic data is difficult to obtain. Gross Domestic Product (GDP) figures are nominal (current) values at market prices. GDP growth is real, not nominal growth, and inflation is the year-on-year change in consumer prices.

Calculating exchange rates

Typically, but not invariably, the exchange rates shown in the country entries are also used to calculate GDP and defence-budget and defence-expenditure dollar conversions. Where they are not used, it is because the use of exchange-rate dollar conversions can misrepresent both GDP and defence expenditure. For some countries, PPP rather than market exchange rates are sometimes used for dollar conversions of both GDP and defence expenditures. Where PPP is used, it is annotated accordingly.

The arguments for using PPP are strongest for Russia and China. Both the UN and the IMF have issued caveats concerning the reliability of official economic statistics on transitional economies, particularly those of Russia and some Eastern European and Central Asian countries. Non-reporting, lags in the publication of current statistics and frequent revisions of recent data (not always accompanied by timely revision of previously published figures in the same series) pose transparency and consistency problems. Another problem arises with certain transitional economies whose productive capabilities are similar to those of developed economies, but where cost and price structures are often much lower than world levels. No specific PPP rate exists for the military sector, and its use for this purpose should be treated with caution. Furthermore, there is no definitive guide as to which elements of military spending should be calculated using the limited PPP rates available. The figures presented here are only intended to illustrate a range of possible outcomes depending on which input variables are used.

GENERAL DEFENCE DATA

Personnel

The 'Active' total comprises all servicemen and women on full-time duty (including conscripts and long-term assignments from the Reserves). When a gendarmerie or equivalent is under control of the defence ministry, they may be included in the active total. Only the length of conscript liability is shown; where service is voluntary there is no entry. 'Reserve' describes formations and units not fully manned or operational in peacetime, but which can be mobilised by recalling reservists in an emergency. Some countries have more than one category of reserves, often kept at varying degrees of readiness. Where possible, these differences are denoted using the national descriptive title, but always under the heading of 'Reserves' to distinguish them from full-time active forces. All personnel figures are rounded to the nearest 50, except for organisations with under 500 personnel, where figures are rounded to the nearest ten.

Other forces

Many countries maintain forces whose training, organisation, equipment and control suggest that they may be used to support or replace regular military forces, or be used more broadly by states to deliver militarily relevant effect; these are called 'paramilitary'. They include some forces that may have a constabulary role. These are detailed after the military forces of each country, but their personnel numbers are not normally included in the totals at the start of each entry.

Non-state armed groups

Data on selected non-state groups that are militarily significant armed actors is now available in the IISS Military Balance+ database (*www.iiss.org/militarybalanceplus*).

Cyber

The Military Balance includes detail on selected national cyber capacities, particularly those under the control of,

Units and formation strength

Company	100–200
Battalion	500–1,000
Brigade	3,000–5,000
Division	15,000–20,000
Corps or Army	50,000–100,000

or designed to fulfil the requirements of, defence organisations. Capabilities are not assessed quantitatively. Rather, national organisations, legislation, national-security strategies, etc. are noted, where appropriate, to indicate the level of effort states are devoting to this area. Generally, civil organisations are not traced here, though in some cases these organisations could have dual civil–military roles.

Forces by role and equipment by type

Quantities are shown by function (according to each nation's employment) and type, and represent what are believed to be total holdings, including active and reserve operational and training units. Inventory totals for missile systems relate to launchers and not to missiles. Equipment held 'in store' is not counted in the main inventory totals.

Deployments

The Military Balance mainly lists permanent bases and operational deployments, including peacekeeping operations, which are often discussed in the regional text. Information in the country-data sections details, first, deployments of troops and, second, military observers and, where available, the role and equipment of deployed units. Personnel figures are not generally included for embassy staff, standing multinational headquarters, or deployments of purely maritime and aerospace assets, such as Iceland Air Policing or anti-piracy operations. Personnel deployed on OSCE missions are listed as 'personnel' rather than 'observers'.

Training activity

Selected exercises in Europe and Russia and Eurasia in 2016 and 2017 are shown on maps. They are not exhaustive. This data complements the broader range of global exercise data now available on the Military Balance+.

LAND FORCES

To make international comparison easier and more consistent, *The Military Balance* categorises forces by role and translates national military terminology for unit and formation sizes. Typical personnel strength, equipment holdings and organisation of formations such as brigades and divisions vary from country to country. In addition, some unit terms, such as 'regiment', 'squadron', 'battery' and 'troop', can refer to significantly different unit sizes in different countries. Unless otherwise stated, these terms should be assumed to reflect standard British usage where they occur.

NAVAL FORCES

Classifying naval vessels according to role is complex. A post-war consensus on primary surface combatants revolved around a distinction between independently operating cruisers, air-defence escorts (destroyers) and anti-submarine-warfare escorts (frigates). However, new ships are increasingly performing a range of roles. For this reason, *The Military Balance* has drawn up a classification system based on full-load displacement (FLD) rather than a role-classification system. These definitions will not necessarily conform to national designations.

AIR FORCES

Aircraft listed as combat capable are assessed as being equipped to deliver air-to-air or air-to-surface ordnance. The definition includes aircraft designated by type as bomber, fighter, fighter/ground attack, ground attack and anti-submarine warfare. Other aircraft considered to be combat capable are marked with an asterisk (*). Operational groupings of air forces are shown where known. Typical squadron aircraft strengths can vary both between aircraft types and from country to country. When assessing missile ranges, *The Military Balance* uses the following range indicators:

- Short-range ballistic missile (SRBM): less than 1,000km;
- Medium-range ballistic missile (MRBM): 1,000–3,000km;
- Intermediate-range ballistic missile (IRBM): 3,000–5,000km;
- Intercontinental ballistic missile (ICBM): over 5,000km.

ATTRIBUTION AND ACKNOWLEDGEMENTS

The International Institute for Strategic Studies owes no allegiance to any government, group of governments, or any political or other organisation. Its assessments are its own, based on the material available to it from a wide variety of sources. The cooperation of governments of all listed countries has been sought and, in many cases, received. However, some data in *The Military Balance* is estimated. Care is taken to ensure that this data is as accurate and free from bias as possible. The Institute owes a considerable debt to a number of its own members, consultants and all those who help compile and check material. The Director-General and Chief Executive and staff of the Institute assume full responsibility for the data and judgements in this book. Comments and suggestions on the data and textual material contained within the book, as well as on the style and presentation of data, are welcomed and should be communicated to the Editor of *The Military Balance* at: IISS, Arundel House, 6 Temple Place, London, WC2R 2PG, UK, email: *milbal@iiss.org*. Copyright on all information in *The Military Balance* belongs strictly to the IISS. Application to reproduce limited amounts of data may be made to the publisher: Taylor & Francis, 4 Park Square, Milton Park, Abingdon, Oxon, OX14 4RN. Email: *society.permissions@tandf.co.uk*. Unauthorised use of data from *The Military Balance* will be subject to legal action.

Principal land definitions

Forces by role

Command: free-standing, deployable formation headquarters (HQs).

Special Forces (SF): elite units specially trained and equipped for unconventional warfare and operations in enemy-controlled territory. Many are employed in counter-terrorist roles.

Manoeuvre: combat units and formations capable of manoeuvring. These are subdivided as follows:

Reconnaissance: combat units and formations whose primary purpose is to gain information.

Armoured: units and formations principally equipped with main battle tanks (MBTs) and infantry fighting vehicles (IFVs) to provide heavy mounted close-combat capability. Units and formations intended to provide mounted close-combat capability with lighter armoured vehicles, such as light tanks or wheeled assault guns, are classified as light armoured.

Mechanised: units and formations primarily equipped with lighter armoured vehicles such as armoured personnel carriers (APCs). They have less mounted firepower and protection than their armoured equivalents, but can usually deploy more infantry.

Light: units and formations whose principal combat capability is dismounted infantry, with few, if any, organic armoured vehicles. Some may be motorised and equipped with soft-skinned vehicles.

Air Manoeuvre: units and formations trained and equipped for delivery by transport aircraft and/or helicopters.

Amphibious: amphibious forces are trained and equipped to project force from the sea.

Other Forces: includes security units such as Presidential Guards, paramilitary units such as border guards and combat formations permanently employed in training or demonstration tasks.

Combat Support: Combat support units and formations not integral to manoeuvre formations. Includes artillery, engineers, military intelligence, nuclear, biological and chemical defence, signals and information operations.

Combat Service Support (CSS): includes logistics, maintenance, medical, supply and transport units and formations.

Equipment by type

Light Weapons: small arms, machine guns, grenades and grenade launchers and unguided man-portable anti-armour and support weapons have proliferated so much and are sufficiently easy to manufacture or copy that listing them would be impractical.

Crew-Served Weapons: crew-served recoilless rifles, man-portable ATGW, MANPADs and mortars of greater than 80mm calibre are listed, but the high degree of proliferation and local manufacture of many of these weapons means that estimates of numbers held may not be reliable.

Armoured Fighting Vehicles (AFVs): armoured combat vehicles with a combat weight of at least six metric tonnes, further subdivided as below:

Main Battle Tank (MBT): armoured, tracked combat vehicles, armed with a turret-mounted gun of at least 75mm calibre and with a combat weight of at least 25 metric tonnes.

Light Tank (LT TK): armoured, tracked combat vehicles, armed with a turret-mounted gun of at least 75mm calibre and with a combat weight of less than 25 metric tonnes.

Wheeled Assault Gun (ASLT): armoured, wheeled combat vehicles, armed with a turret-mounted gun of at least 75mm calibre and with a combat weight of at least 15 metric tonnes.

Armoured Reconnaissance (RECCE): armoured vehicles primarily designed for reconnaissance tasks with no significant transport capability and either a main gun of less than 75mm calibre or a combat weight of less than 15 metric tonnes, or both.

Infantry Fighting Vehicle (IFV): armoured combat vehicles designed and equipped to transport an infantry squad and armed with a cannon of at least 20mm calibre.

Armoured Personnel Carrier (APC): lightly armoured combat vehicles designed and equipped to transport an infantry squad but either unarmed or armed with a cannon of less than 20mm calibre.

Airborne Combat Vehicle (ABCV): armoured vehicles designed to be deployable by parachute alongside airborne forces.

Amphibious Assault Vehicle (AAV): armoured vehicles designed to have an amphibious ship-to-shore capability.

Armoured Utility Vehicle (AUV): armoured vehicles not designed to transport an infantry squad, but capable of undertaking a variety of other utility battlefield tasks, including light reconnaissance and light transport.

Specialist Variants: variants of armoured vehicles listed above that are designed to fill a specialised role, such as command posts (CP), artillery observation posts (OP), signals (sigs) and ambulances (amb), are categorised with their parent vehicles.

Engineering and Maintenance Vehicles: includes armoured engineer vehicles (AEV), armoured repair and recovery vehicles (ARV), assault bridging (VLB) and mine warfare vehicles (MW).

Nuclear, Biological and Chemical Defence Vehicles (NBC): armoured vehicles principally designed to operate in potentially contaminated terrain.

Anti-Tank/Anti-Infrastructure (AT): guns, guided weapons and recoilless rifles designed to engage armoured vehicles and battlefield hardened targets.

Surface-to-Surface Missile Launchers (SSM): launch vehicles for transporting and firing surface-to-surface ballistic and cruise missiles.

Artillery: weapons (including guns, howitzers, gun/howitzers, multiple-rocket launchers, mortars and gun/mortars) with a calibre greater than 100mm for artillery pieces and 80mm and above for mortars, capable of engaging ground targets with indirect fire.

Coastal Defence: land-based coastal artillery pieces and anti-ship-missile launchers.

Air Defence (AD): guns and surface-to-air-missile (SAM) launchers designed to engage fixed-wing, rotary-wing and unmanned aircraft. Missiles are further classified by maximum notional engagement range: point-defence (up to 10km); short-range (10–30km); medium-range (30–75km); and long-range (75km+). Systems primarily intended to intercept missiles rather than aircraft are categorised separately as Missile Defence.

Principal naval definitions

To aid comparison between fleets, the following definitions, which do not conform to national definitions, are used:

Submarines: all vessels designed to operate primarily under water. Submarines with a dived displacement below 250 tonnes are classified as midget submarines (SSW); those below 500 tonnes are coastal submarines (SSC).

Principal surface combatants: all surface ships designed for combat operations on the high seas, with an FLD above 1,500 tonnes. Aircraft carriers (CV), including helicopter carriers (CVH), are vessels with a flat deck primarily designed to carry fixed- and/or rotary-wing aircraft, without amphibious capability. Other principal surface combatants include cruisers (C) (with an FLD above 9,750 tonnes), destroyers (DD) (with an FLD above 4,500 tonnes) and frigates (FF) (with an FLD above 1,500 tonnes).

Patrol and coastal combatants: surface vessels designed for coastal or inshore operations. These include corvettes (FS), which usually have an FLD between 500 and 1,500 tonnes and are distinguished from other patrol vessels by their heavier armaments. Also included in this category are offshore-patrol ships (PSO), with an FLD greater than 1,500 tonnes; patrol craft (PC), which have an FLD between 250 and 1,500 tonnes; and patrol boats (PB) with an FLD between ten and 250 tonnes. Vessels with a top speed greater than 35 knots are designated as 'fast'.

Mine warfare vessels: all surface vessels configured primarily for mine laying (ML) or countermeasures. Countermeasures vessels are either: sweepers (MS), which are designed to locate and destroy mines in an area; hunters (MH), which are designed to locate and destroy individual mines; or countermeasures vessels (MC), which combine both roles.

Amphibious vessels: vessels designed to transport personnel and/or equipment onto shore. These include landing helicopter assault vessels (LHA), which can embark fixed- and/or rotary-wing air assets as well as landing craft; landing helicopter docks (LHD), which can embark rotary-wing or VTOL assets and have a well dock; landing platform helicopters (LPH), which have a primary role of launch and recovery platform for rotary-wing or VTOL assets with a dock to store equipment/personnel for amphibious operations; and landing platform docks (LPD), which do not have a through deck but do have a well dock. Landing ships (LS) are amphibious vessels capable of ocean passage and landing craft (LC) are smaller vessels designed to transport personnel and equipment from a larger vessel to land or across small stretches of water. Landing ships have a hold; landing craft are open vessels. Landing craft air cushioned (LCAC) are differentiated from Utility craft air cushioned (UCAC) in that the former have a bow ramp for the disembarkation of vehicles and personnel.

Auxiliary vessels: ocean-going surface vessels performing an auxiliary military role, supporting combat ships or operations. These generally fulfil five roles: replenishment (such as oilers (AO) and solid stores (AKS)); logistics (such as cargo ships (AK) and logistics ships (AFS)); maintenance (such as cable-repair ships (ARC) or buoy tenders (ABU)); research (such as survey ships (AFS)); and special purpose (such as intelligence-collection ships (AGI) and ocean-going tugs (ATF)).

Weapons systems: weapons are listed in the following order: land-attack cruise missiles (LACM), anti-ship missiles (AShM), surface-to-air missiles (SAM), heavy (HWT) and lightweight (LWT) torpedos, anti-submarine weapons (A/S), CIWS, guns and aircraft. Missiles with a range less than 5km and guns with a calibre less than 57mm are generally not included.

Organisations: naval groupings such as fleets and squadrons frequently change and are shown only where doing so would aid qualitative judgements.

Principal aviation definitions

Bomber (Bbr): comparatively large platforms intended for the delivery of air-to-surface ordnance. Bbr units are units equipped with bomber aircraft for the air-to-surface role.

Fighter (Ftr): aircraft designed primarily for air-to-air combat, which may also have a limited air-to-surface capability. Ftr units are equipped with aircraft intended to provide air superiority, which may have a secondary and limited air-to-surface capability.

Fighter/Ground Attack (FGA): multi-role fighter-size platforms with significant air-to-surface capability, potentially including maritime attack, and at least some air-to-air capacity. FGA units are multi-role units equipped with aircraft capable of air-to-air and air-to-surface attack.

Ground Attack (Atk): aircraft designed solely for the air-to-surface task, with limited or no air-to-air capability. Atk units are equipped with fixed-wing aircraft.

Attack Helicopter (Atk hel): rotary-wing platforms designed for delivery of air-to-surface weapons, and fitted with an integrated fire-control system.

Anti-Submarine Warfare (ASW): fixed- and rotary-wing platforms designed to locate and engage submarines, many with a secondary anti-surface-warfare capability. ASW units are equipped with fixed- or rotary-wing aircraft.

Anti-Surface Warfare (ASuW): ASuW units are equipped with fixed- or rotary-wing aircraft intended for anti-surface-warfare missions.

Maritime Patrol (MP): fixed-wing aircraft and unmanned aerial vehicles (UAVs) intended for maritime surface surveillance, which may possess an anti-surface-warfare capability. MP units are equipped with fixed-wing aircraft or UAVs.

Electronic Warfare (EW): fixed- and rotary-wing aircraft and UAVs intended for electronic warfare. EW units are equipped with fixed- or rotary-wing aircraft or UAVs.

Intelligence/Surveillance/Reconnaissance (ISR): fixed- and rotary-wing aircraft and UAVs intended to provide radar, visible-light or infrared imagery, or a mix thereof. ISR units are equipped with fixed- or rotary-wing aircraft or UAVs.

Combat/Intelligence/Surveillance/Reconnaissance (CISR): aircraft and UAVs that have the capability to deliver air-to-surface weapons, as well as undertake ISR tasks. CISR units are equipped with armed aircraft and/or UAVs for ISR and air-to-surface missions.

COMINT/ELINT/SIGINT: fixed- and rotary-wing platforms and UAVs capable of gathering electronic (ELINT), communications (COMINT) or signals intelligence (SIGINT). COMINT units are equipped with fixed- or rotary-wing aircraft or UAVs intended for the communications-intelligence task. ELINT units are equipped with fixed- or rotary-wing aircraft or UAVs used for gathering electronic intelligence. SIGINT units are equipped with fixed- or rotary-wing aircraft or UAVs used to collect signals intelligence.

Airborne Early Warning (& Control) (AEW (&C)): fixed- and rotary-wing platforms capable of providing airborne early warning, with a varying degree of onboard command and control depending on the platform. AEW(&C) units are equipped with fixed- or rotary-wing aircraft.

Search and Rescue (SAR): units are equipped with fixed- or rotary-wing aircraft used to recover military personnel or civilians.

Combat Search and Rescue (CSAR): units are equipped with armed fixed- or rotary-wing aircraft for recovery of personnel from hostile territory.

Tanker (Tkr): fixed- and rotary-wing aircraft designed for air-to-air refuelling. Tkr units are equipped with fixed- or rotary-wing aircraft used for air-to-air refuelling.

Tanker Transport (Tkr/Tpt): platforms capable of both air-to-air refuelling and military airlift.

Transport (Tpt): fixed- and rotary-wing aircraft intended for military airlift. Light transport aircraft are categorised as having a maximum payload of up to 11,340kg; medium up to 27,215kg; and heavy above 27,215kg. Light transport helicopters have an internal payload of up to 2,000kg; medium transport helicopters up to 4,535kg; heavy transport helicopters greater than 4,535kg. PAX aircraft are platforms generally unsuited for transporting cargo on the main deck. Tpt units are equipped with fixed- or rotary-wing platforms to transport personnel or cargo.

Trainer (Trg): a fixed- and rotary-wing aircraft designed primarily for the training role; some also have the capacity to carry light to medium ordnance. Trg units are equipped with fixed- or rotary-wing training aircraft intended for pilot or other aircrew training.

Multi-role helicopter (MRH): rotary-wing platforms designed to carry out a variety of military tasks including light transport, armed reconnaissance and battlefield support.

Unmanned Aerial Vehicles (UAVs): remotely piloted or controlled unmanned fixed- or rotary-wing systems. Light UAVs are those weighing 20–150kg; medium: 150–600kg; and large: more than 600kg.

Reference

Table 22 **List of abbreviations for data sections**

AAA anti-aircraft artillery
AAM air-to-air missile
AAR search-and-rescue vessel
AAV amphibious assault vehicle
AB airborne
ABM anti-ballistic missile
ABU/H sea-going buoy tender/with hangar
ABCV airborne combat vehicle
ac aircraft
ACV air-cushion vehicle/armoured combat vehicle
ACS crane ship
AD air defence
ADA air-defence artillery
ADEX air-defence exercise
adj adjusted
AE auxiliary, ammunition carrier
AEM missile support ship
AEV armoured engineer vehicle
AEW airborne early warning
AFD/L auxiliary floating dry dock/small
AFS/H logistics ship/with hangar
AFSB afloat forward staging base
AFV armoured fighting vehicle
AG misc auxiliary
AGB/H icebreaker/with hangar
AGE/H experimental auxiliary ship/with hangar
AGF/H command ship/with hangar
AGHS hydrographic survey vessel
AGI intelligence collection vessel
AGM space tracking vessel
AGOR oceanographic research vessel
AGOS oceanographic surveillance vessel
AGS/H survey ship/with hangar
AH hospital ship
AIP air-independent propulsion
AK/L cargo ship/light
aka also known as
AKEH dry cargo/ammunition ship
AKR/H roll-on/roll-off cargo ship/with hangar
AKS/L stores ship/light
ALCM air-launched cruise missile
amb ambulance
amph amphibious/amphibian
AO/S oiler/small
AOE fast combat support ship
AOR/L/H fleet replenishment oiler with RAS capability/light/with hangar
AOT/L oiler transport/light
AP armour-piercing/anti-personnel/transport ship
APB barracks ship
APC armoured personnel carrier
AR/C/D/L repair ship/cable/dry dock/light

ARG amphibious ready group
ARH active radar homing
ARL airborne reconnaissance low
ARM anti-radiation missile
armd armoured
ARS/H rescue and salvage ship/with hangar
arty artillery
ARV armoured recovery vehicle
AS anti-submarine/submarine tender
ASBM anti-ship ballistic missile
ASCM anti-ship cruise missile
AShM anti-ship missile
aslt assault
ASM air-to-surface missile
ASR submarine rescue craft
ASTT anti-submarine torpedo tube
ASW anti-submarine warfare
ASuW anti-surface warfare
AT tug/anti-tank
ATBM anti-tactical ballistic missile
ATF tug, ocean going
ATGW anti-tank guided weapon
Atk attack/ground attack
ATS tug, salvage and rescue ship
AUV armoured utility vehicle
AVB aviation logistic support ship
avn aviation
AWT water tanker
AX/L/S training craft/light/sail
BA Budget Authority (US)
Bbr bomber
BCT brigade combat team
bde brigade
bdgt budget
BG battle group
BMD ballistic-missile defence
BMEWS ballistic missile early warning system
bn battalion/billion
bty battery
C2 command and control
casevac casualty evacuation
cav cavalry
cbt combat
CBRN chemical, biological, radiological, nuclear, explosive
cdo commando
C/G/H/M/N cruiser/with AShM/with hangar/with SAM/nuclear-powered
CISR combat ISR
CIMIC civil–military cooperation
CIWS close-in weapons system
COIN counter-insurgency
comd command
COMINT communications intelligence
comms communications

coy company
CP command post
CPX command post exercise
CS combat support
CSAR combat search and rescue
CSS combat service support
CT counter-terrorism
CV/H/L/N/S aircraft carrier/helicopter/light/nuclear powered/VSTOL
CW chemical warfare/weapons
DD/G/H/M destroyer/with AShM/with hangar/with SAM
DDS dry deck shelter
def defence
DEPEX deployment exercise
det detachment
div division
ECM electronic countermeasures
ELINT electronic intelligence
elm element/s
engr engineer
EOD explosive ordnance disposal
EPF expeditionary fast transport vessel
eqpt equipment
ESB expeditionary mobile base
ESD expeditionary transport dock
EW electronic warfare
excl excludes/excluding
exp expenditure
FAC forward air control
fd field
FF/G/H/M fire-fighting/frigate/with AShM/with hangar/with SAM
FGA fighter ground attack
FIREX firing exercise
FLD full-load displacement
flt flight
FMA Foreign Military Assistance
FS/G/H/M corvette/with AShM/with hangar/with SAM
Ftr fighter
FTX field training exercise
FY fiscal year
GBU guided bomb unit
gd guard
GDP gross domestic product
GLCM ground-launched cruise missile
GLMS Guided Missile Launching System
gp group
HA/DR humanitarian assistance/disaster relief
hel helicopter
how howitzer
HQ headquarters
HUMINT human intelligence
HWT heavyweight torpedo

hy heavy
IBU inshore boat unit
ICBM intercontinental ballistic missile
IFV infantry fighting vehicle
IIR imaging infrared
IMINT imagery intelligence
imp improved
indep independent
inf infantry
info ops information operations
INS inertial navigation system
int intelligence
IOC Initial Operating Capability
IR infrared
IRBM intermediate-range ballistic missile
ISD in-service date
ISR intelligence, surveillance and reconnaissance
ISTAR intelligence, surveillance, target acquisition and reconnaissance
JOINTEX joint exercise
LACM land-attack cruise missile
LC/A/AC/H/M/PA/P/L/T/U/VP landing craft/assault/air cushion/heavy/medium/personnel air cushion/personnel/large/tank/utility/vehicles and personnel
LCC amphibious command ship
LGB laser-guided bomb
LHA landing ship assault
LHD amphibious assault ship
LIFT lead-in ftr trainer
LKA amphibious cargo ship
LLI long-lead items
lnchr launcher
LoA letter of acceptance
log logistic
LoI letter of intent
LP/D/H landing platform/dock/helicopter
LRIP low-rate initial production
LS/D/L/LH/M/T landing ship/dock/logistic/logistic helicopter/medium/tank
lt light
LWT lightweight torpedo
maint maintenance
MANPAD man-portable air-defence system
MANPATS man-portable anti-tank system
MAREX maritime exercise
MBT main battle tank
MC/C/CS/D/I/O mine countermeasure coastal/command and support/diving support/inshore/ocean
MCM mine countermeasures
MCMV mine countermeasures vessel
MD military district
MDT mine diving tender
mech mechanised
med medium/medical
medevac medical evacuation
MGA machine gun artillery
MH/C/D/I/O mine hunter/coastal/drone/inshore/ocean
mil military
MIRV multiple independently targetable re-entry vehicle
mk mark (model number)
ML minelayer
MLU mid-life update

mne marine
mod modified/modification
mor mortar
mot motorised/motor
MoU memorandum of understanding
MP maritime patrol/military police
MR maritime reconnaissance/motor rifle
MRBM medium-range ballistic missile
MRH multi-role helicopter
MRL multiple rocket launcher
MRX mission-rehearsal exercise
MS/A/C/D/I/O/R mine sweeper/auxiliary/coastal/drone/inshore/ocean/river
msl missile
mtn mountain
MW mine warfare
n.a. not applicable
n.k. not known
NBC nuclear, biological, chemical
NCO non-commissioned officer
nm nautical mile
nuc nuclear
O & M operations and maintenance
obs observation/observer
OCU operational conversion unit
OP observation post
op/ops operational/operations
OPFOR opposition training force
org organised/organisation
OPV offshore patrol vessel
para paratroop/parachute
PAX passenger/passenger transport aircraft
PB/C/F/G/I/M/R/T patrol boat/coastal/fast/with AShM/inshore/with SAM/riverine/with torpedo
PC/C/F/G/H/I/M/O/R/T patrol craft/coastal/fast/guided missile/with hangar/inshore/with CIWS missile or SAM/offshore/riverine/with torpedo
pdr pounder
pers personnel
PG/G/GF/H patrol gunboat/guided missile/fast attack craft/hydrofoil
PGM precision-guided munitions
PH/G/M/T patrol hydrofoil/with AShM/with SAM/with torpedo
pl platoon
PKO peacekeeping operations
PoR programme of record
PPP purchasing-power parity
PPV protected patrol vehicle
PRH passive radar-homing
prepo pre-positioned
PSO/H peace support operations or offshore patrol ship/with hangar
PTF semi-submersible vessel
ptn pontoon bridging
quad quadruple
R&D research and development
RCL recoilless launcher
recce reconnaissance
regt regiment
RFI request for information
RFP request for proposals
RIB rigid inflatable boat
RL rocket launcher
ro-ro roll-on, roll-off

RRC/F/U rapid-reaction corps/force/unit
RV re-entry vehicle
rvn riverine
SAM surface-to-air missile
SAR search and rescue
SARH semi-active radar homing
sat satellite
SDV swimmer delivery vehicles
SEAD suppression of enemy air defence
SF special forces
SHORAD short-range air defence
SIGINT signals intelligence
sigs signals
SLBM submarine-launched ballistic missile
SLCM submarine-launched cruise missile
SLEP service-life-extension programme
SP self-propelled
Spec Ops special operations
SPAAGM self-propelled anti-aircraft gun and missile system
spt support
sqn squadron
SRBM short-range ballistic missile
SS submarine
SSA submersible auxiliary support vessel
SSAN submersible auxiliary support vessel (nuclear)
SSBN nuclear-powered ballistic-missile submarine
SSC coastal submarine
SSG guided-missile submarine
SSI inshore submarine
SSGN nuclear-powered guided-missile submarine
SSK attack submarine with ASW capability (hunter-killer)
SSM surface-to-surface missile
SSN nuclear-powered attack submarine
SSW midget submarine
str strength
surv surveillance
sy security
t tonnes
tac tactical
tch technical
temp temporary
tk tank
tkr tanker
TMD theatre missile defence
torp torpedo
tpt transport
tr trillion
trg training
TRV torpedo recovery vehicle
TT torpedo tube
UAV unmanned aerial vehicle
UCAC utility craft air cushioned
UCAV unmanned combat air vehicle
utl utility
UUV unmanned undersea vehicle
veh vehicle
VLB vehicle launched bridge
VLS vertical launch system
VSHORAD very short-range air defence
WFU withdrawn from use
wg wing

Table 23 **Index of country/territory abbreviations**

AFG	Afghanistan
ALB	Albania
ALG	Algeria
ANG	Angola
ARG	Argentina
ARM	Armenia
ATG	Antigua and Barbuda
AUS	Australia
AUT	Austria
AZE	Azerbaijan
BDI	Burundi
BEL	Belgium
BEN	Benin
BFA	Burkina Faso
BGD	Bangladesh
BHR	Bahrain
BHS	Bahamas
BIH	Bosnia-Herzegovina
BIOT	British Indian Ocean Territory
BLG	Bulgaria
BLR	Belarus
BLZ	Belize
BOL	Bolivia
BRB	Barbados
BRN	Brunei
BRZ	Brazil
BWA	Botswana
CAM	Cambodia
CAN	Canada
CAR	Central African Republic
CHA	Chad
CHE	Switzerland
CHL	Chile
CIV	Côte d'Ivoire
CMR	Cameroon
COG	Republic of Congo
COL	Colombia
CPV	Cape Verde
CRI	Costa Rica
CRO	Croatia
CUB	Cuba
CYP	Cyprus
CZE	Czech Republic
DJB	Djibouti
DNK	Denmark
DOM	Dominican Republic
DPRK	Korea, Democratic People's Republic of
DRC	Democratic Republic of the Congo
ECU	Ecuador
EGY	Egypt
EQG	Equitorial Guinea
ERI	Fritrea
ESP	Spain
EST	Estonia
ETH	Ethiopia
FIN	Finland
FJI	Fiji
FLK	Falkland Islands
FRA	France
FYROM	Macedonia, Former Yugoslav Republic
GAB	Gabon
GAM	Gambia
GEO	Georgia
GER	Germany
GF	French Guiana
GHA	Ghana
GIB	Gibraltar
GNB	Guinea-Bissau
GRC	Greece
GRL	Greenland
GUA	Guatemala
GUI	Guinea
GUY	Guyana
HND	Honduras
HTI	Haiti
HUN	Hungary
IDN	Indonesia
IND	India
IRL	Ireland
IRN	Iran
IRQ	Iraq
ISL	Iceland
ISR	Israel
ITA	Italy
JAM	Jamaica
JOR	Jordan
JPN	Japan
KAZ	Kazakhstan
KEN	Kenya
KGZ	Kyrgyzstan
KWT	Kuwait
LAO	Laos
LBN	Lebanon
LBR	Liberia
LBY	Libya
LKA	Sri Lanka
LSO	Lesotho
LTU	Lithuania
LUX	Luxembourg
LVA	Latvia
MDA	Moldova
MDG	Madagascar
MEX	Mexico
MHL	Marshall Islands
MLI	Mali
MLT	Malta
MMR	Myanmar
MNE	Montenegro
MNG	Mongolia
MOR	Morocco
MOZ	Mozambique
MRT	Mauritania
MUS	Mauritius
MWI	Malawi
MYS	Malaysia
NAM	Namibia
NCL	New Caledonia
NER	Niger
NGA	Nigeria
NIC	Nicaragua
NLD	Netherlands
NOR	Norway
NPL	Nepal
NZL	New Zealand
OMN	Oman
PT	Palestinian Territories
PAN	Panama
PAK	Pakistan
PER	Peru
PHL	Philippines
POL	Poland
PNG	Papua New Guinea
PRC	China, People's Republic of
PRT	Portugal
PRY	Paraguay
PYF	French Polynesia
QTR	Qatar
ROC	Taiwan (Republic of China)
ROK	Korea, Republic of
ROM	Romania
RSA	South Africa
RUS	Russia
RWA	Rwanda
SAU	Saudi Arabia
SDN	Sudan
SEN	Senegal
SER	Serbia
SGP	Singapore
SLB	Solomon Islands
SLE	Sierra Leone
SLV	El Salvador
SOM	Somalia
SSD	South Sudan
STP	São Tomé and Príncipe
SUR	Suriname
SVK	Slovakia
SVN	Slovenia
SWE	Sweden
SYC	Seychelles
SYR	Syria
TGO	Togo
THA	Thailand
TJK	Tajikistan
TKM	Turkmenistan
TLS	Timor-Leste
TTO	Trinidad and Tobago
TUN	Tunisia
TUR	Turkey
TZA	Tanzania
UAE	United Arab Emirates
UGA	Uganda
UK	United Kingdom
UKR	Ukraine
URY	Uruguay
US	United States
UZB	Uzbekistan
VEN	Venezuela
VNM	Vietnam
YEM	Yemen, Republic of
ZMB	Zambia
ZWE	Zimbabwe

Table 24 Index of countries and territories

Country	Code	Page	Country	Code	Page	Country	Code	Page
Afghanistan	AFG	240	Georgia	GEO	186	Niger	NER	477
Albania	ALB	82	Germany	GER	107	Nigeria	NGA	478
Algeria	ALG	325	Ghana	GHA	465	Norway	NOR	132
Angola	ANG	445	Greece	GRC	111	Oman	OMN	354
Antigua and Barbuda	ATG	383	Guatemala	GUA	407	Pakistan	PAK	291
Argentina	ARG	383	Guinea	GUI	466	Palestinian Territories	PT	356
Armenia	ARM	181	Guinea-Bissau	GNB	467	Panama	PAN	415
Australia	AUS	241	Guyana	GUY	408	Papua New Guinea	PNG	294
Austria	AUT	83	Haiti	HTI	409	Paraguay	PRY	416
Azerbaijan	AZE	182	Honduras	HND	409	Peru	PER	417
Bahamas	BHS	386	Hungary	HUN	114	Philippines	PHL	295
Bahrain	BHR	327	Iceland	ISL	116	Poland	POL	135
Bangladesh	BGD	244	India	IND	260	Portugal	PRT	138
Barbados	BRB	387	Indonesia	IDN	266	Qatar	QTR	357
Belarus	BLR	185	Iran	IRN	333	Romania	ROM	140
Belgium	BEL	85	Iraq	IRQ	337	Russia	RUS	192
Belize	BLZ	387	Ireland	IRL	116	Rwanda	RWA	480
Benin	BEN	446	Israel	ISR	339	Saudi Arabia	SAU	358
Bolivia	BOL	388	Italy	ITA	118	Senegal	SEN	481
Bosnia-Herzegovina	BIH	87	Jamaica	JAM	411	Serbia	SER	143
Botswana	BWA	447	Japan	JPN	270	Seychelles	SYC	482
Brazil	BRZ	390	Jordan	JOR	343	Sierra Leone	SLE	483
Brunei	BRN	247	Kazakhstan	KAZ	188	Singapore	SGP	297
Bulgaria	BLG	88	Kenya	KEN	468	Slovakia	SVK	145
Burkina Faso	BFA	448	Korea, Democratic People's Republic of	DPRK	274	Slovenia	SVN	147
Burundi	BDI	449				Somalia	SOM	484
Cambodia	CAM	248	Korea, Republic of	ROK	277	South Africa	RSA	485
Cameroon	CMR	451	Kuwait	KWT	345	South Sudan	SSD	487
Canada	CAN	43	Kyrgyzstan	KGZ	190	Spain	ESP	148
Cape Verde	CPV	452	Laos	LAO	281	Sri Lanka	LKA	300
Central African Republic	CAR	453	Latvia	LVA	122	Sudan	SDN	488
Chad	CHA	454	Lebanon	LBN	347	Suriname	SUR	420
Chile	CHL	394	Lesotho	LSO	470	Sweden	SWE	152
China, People's Republic of	PRC	249	Liberia	LBR	470	Switzerland	CHE	154
Colombia	COL	397	Libya	LBY	349	Syria	SYR	361
Democratic Republic of the Congo	DRC	457	Lithuania	LTU	124	Taiwan (Republic of China)	ROC	302
			Luxembourg	LUX	125	Tajikistan	TJK	207
Congo, Republic of	COG	455	Macedonia, Former Yugoslav Republic	FYROM	126	Tanzania	TZA	490
Costa Rica	CRI	400				Thailand	THA	305
Côte d'Ivoire	CIV	456	Madagascar	MDG	471	Timor-Leste	TLS	308
Croatia	CRO	90	Malawi	MWI	472	Togo	TGO	492
Cuba	CUB	400	Malaysia	MYS	282	Trinidad and Tobago	TTO	421
Cyprus	CYP	92	Mali	MLI	473	Tunisia	TUN	365
Czech Republic	CZE	94	Malta	MLT	127	Turkey	TUR	156
Denmark	DNK	96	Mauritania	MRT	350	Turkmenistan	TKM	208
Djibouti	DJB	459	Mauritius	MUS	474	Uganda	UGA	493
Dominican Republic	DOM	402	Mexico	MEX	411	Ukraine	UKR	209
Ecuador	ECU	403	Moldova	MDA	191	United Arab Emirates	UAE	367
Egypt	EGY	329	Mongolia	MNG	285	United Kingdom	UK	160
El Salvador	SLV	405	Montenegro	MNE	128	United States	US	46
Equatorial Guinea	EQG	460	Morocco	MOR	351	Uruguay	URY	422
Eritrea	ERI	461	Mozambique	MOZ	475	Uzbekistan	UZB	214
Estonia	EST	98	Multinational Organisations		129	Venezuela	VEN	423
Ethiopia	ETH	462	Myanmar	MMR	286	Vietnam	VNM	309
Fiji	FJI	259	Namibia	NAM	476	Yemen, Republic of	YEM	370
Finland	FIN	99	Nepal	NPL	288	Zambia	ZMB	494
France	FRA	102	Netherlands	NLD	130	Zimbabwe	ZWE	495
Gabon	GAB	463	New Zealand	NZL	289			
Gambia	GAM	464	Nicaragua	NIC	414			